PERSPECTIVES ON THE NUREMBERG TRIAL

Perspectives on the Nuremberg Trial

Edited by
GUÉNAËL METTRAUX

UNIVERSITY PRESS

OXFORD

UNIVERSITY PRESS

Great Clarendon Street, Oxford OX2 6DP

Oxford University Press is a department of the University of Oxford.
It furthers the University's objective of excellence in research, scholarship,
and education by publishing worldwide in

Oxford New York

Auckland Cape Town Dar es Salaam Hong Kong Karachi
Kuala Lumpur Madrid Melbourne Mexico City Nairobi
New Delhi Shanghai Taipei Toronto

With offices in

Argentina Austria Brazil Chile Czech Republic France Greece
Guatemala Hungary Italy Japan Poland Portugal Singapore
South Korea Switzerland Thailand Turkey Ukraine Vietnam

Oxford is a registered trade mark of Oxford University Press
in the UK and in certain other countries

Published in the United States
by Oxford University Press Inc., New York

© Guénaël Mettraux, 2008

The moral rights of the author have been asserted

Crown copyright material is reproduced under Class Licence
Number C01P0000148 with the permission of OPSI
and the Queen's Printer for Scotland

Database right Oxford University Press (maker)

First published 2008

British Library Cataloguing in Publication Data

Data available

Library of Congress Cataloging in Publication Data

Data available

Typeset by Newgen Imaging Systems (P) Ltd., Chennai, India
Printed in Great Britain
on acid-free paper by
Antony Rowe Ltd.,
Chippenham

ISBN 978–0–19–923233–8
978–0–19–923234–5 (pbk)

1 3 5 7 9 10 8 6 4 2

Contents

I. FOREWORD

II. LEGAL PERSPECTIVES

1. Contemporary Views of the Trial and Judgment: The Charter of the International Military Tribunal

III. POLITICAL AND PHILOSOPHICAL PERSPECTIVES

IV. APPENDICES

V. BIBLIOGRAPHY

VI. INDEX

PART I
FOREWORD

Foreword

For sixty years, the Nuremberg Trial has been the subject of passionate exchanges over its legality, its legitimacy and its legacy. The emotional intensity of the debate has quieted over the course of time, but the 'Nuremberg question'[1] continues to be of relevance to legal scholarship. The questions and criticisms that haunted the Tribunal's early days have lingered and many of them remain central to any discussion of these proceedings: Were crimes against humanity and crimes against peace offences attracting individual criminal responsibility under international law at the time? Was it fair to deny defendants a defence of superior orders? Was the principle of legality fully respected? Did the defendants receive a fair trial? Were representatives of victor nations legitimate judges of their vanquished enemies?

After the Nuremberg Trial, it was professed that the value of the enterprise would be measured not against what had been achieved during the Trial, but based on what the process would be able to engender for future generations: 'History alone can judge the success or failure of this historic trial.'[2] Telford Taylor, a Nuremberg prosecutor, accurately described the long-term ambitions of the proceedings when he said:

The Nuremberg trials, of course, were not conceived as a continuing enterprise, but as an episode that would leave an enduring judicial monument, to mark a giant step in the growth of international law.[3]

For many years, it looked like the Nuremberg—and Tokyo—Trials would remain infertile, an experiment in international criminal justice that was never to be repeated. The renaissance of international criminal justice in the early 1990s has not only revived interest in the Nuremberg process, but, more importantly, it has endowed that process with a new historical resonance, as the participants in the international criminal trials of today grapple with many of the same issues that arose at Nuremberg and often turn to this process for answers and guidance. The creation in quick succession of a number of international criminal tribunals in recent time, from the *ad hoc* tribunals for the former Yugoslavia and Rwanda to the International Criminal Court, has also had the effect of shifting the focus over the meaning of the Nuremberg Trial from a discussion of the innovations

[1] T. Taylor, *Final Report to the Secretary of the Army on the Nuernberg War Crimes Trials under Control Council Law, No. 10*, (New York: William S. Hein & Co., 1997), at 236.

[2] J. Kenny, *Moral Aspects of Nuremberg* (Washington, DC: Pontifical Faculty of Theology, Dominican House of Studies, 1949), at 46.

[3] T. Taylor, *Nuremberg and Vietnam: An American Tragedy* (New York: New York Times Books, 1970), at 80.

and shortcomings of the process to a study of its contribution to the long-term development of international criminal law and international criminal justice.

With the rebirth of international criminal justice, Nuremberg's own legacy has been reshaped and its significance many times amplified by the use which modern tribunals have made of it. Nuremberg did not put an end to impunity for international crimes and its judicial successors might have fallen short of some of the most optimistic predictions that were born out of the historical trial of the Nazi leaders. The contribution of the Nuremberg Trial is no less important to international criminal justice because it did not live up to such high hopes. First, Nuremberg has contributed to eroding the idea that mass atrocities would necessarily go unpunished. The Nuremberg proceedings have also supplied many of the rules and principles that now form the core of international criminal law and it laid down the cornerstone of a still fragile construction: a system of international criminal law and international criminal justice that functions beside and complements domestic judicial systems where those are incapable of sanctioning serious violations of international humanitarian law.

It might be observed that the rebirth of international criminal justice owes more to the political forces at work in the early 1990s than it does to the ideals of Nuremberg. However, when the time came to give political and moral legitimacy to the idea of international criminal justice and to build a new house for it, Nuremberg gained renewed relevance. The political creators of the new war crimes tribunals saw fit to anchor the new courts and tribunals within the tradition of their forebear and to model those after their venerable ancestor. The spirit and the law of Nuremberg now live on in the statutes and jurisprudence of these tribunals.

Selected Essays and Articles

The present volume does not purport to provide definite and exhaustive answers about the value and the place of the Nuremberg Trial in contemporary international criminal law. More modestly, it hopes to revitalize discussion about this historical event. For those concerned with international criminal justice, an understanding of the past is crucial to addressing the challenges of today, both to learn from that past and to avoid repeating the same mistakes.

The essays and articles which have been included in this collection are among the most essential writings concerned with the Nuremberg Trial. They offer a broad and rich spectrum of views on the proceedings and the diversity of opinions should permit readers to form their own views about the value and significance of that process. Several of the articles contained in this volume are published in English for the first time.

In selecting articles for this collection, the quality of scholarship, the variety of viewpoints and the subject-matter of each paper have been the guiding criteria. The volume covers a range of issues and problems prompted by the Nuremberg Trial: the legality of the International Military Tribunal, the independence, impartiality, and legitimacy of the court, the law applicable to the proceedings and its interpretation, the accountability of individuals under international criminal law, the recognition of crimes against humanity and crimes against peace as distinct categories of international crimes, the defences available to the defendants, the fairness of the trial, the position of the Defence in the proceedings and the principle of legality. These issues are discussed often from contrasting perspectives and sometimes draw markedly different conclusions.

In selecting articles, pride of place has been given to those whose authors were personally involved in this Nuremberg Trial, whether as judges (Justice Francis Biddle, Judge Norman Birkett, Lord Lawrence, and Professor Donnedieu de Vabres), as advisors to the judges (Quincy Wright and Herbert Wechsler), as prosecutors (Robert H. Jackson, Telford Taylor, and Thomas J. Dodd), as defence counsel (Otto Kranzbuehler and Dr Hans Laternser), or as powerful political players (Henri L. Stimson). The views and positions offered in those contributions are at times critical of the process and are often reflective of the position and role of the author in this judicial enterprise. Where a prosecutor might perceive the unfortunate but unavoidable shortcomings of an *ad hoc* jurisdiction, a defence counsel might see unfairness. Where a prosecutor might see international law blooming and coming to life, counsel for a defendant may see a violation of the principle of legality. But rather than undermine these views, their *partis pris* gives the voices of these participants a contextual authenticity and authority which informs our consideration of their positions today. The collision of these opinions on some of the foundational aspects of the Trial will provide the reader with some of the keys to understanding the major controversies that have permeated the debate over international criminal justice since that time.

The majority of the papers contained in this collection are legal in character because Nuremberg was first and foremost a legal and judicial exercise. But the collection also includes important works that examine the process from a philosophical, historical, or socio-political point of view thus reflecting the fact that Nuremberg was always more than a judicial enterprise.

Legal Perspectives on the Trial—The Contemporary Views

The legal papers contained in the present volume essentially fall into two categories: those which were written shortly before, during or shortly after the Trial, and those which were written later in time with the benefit of hindsight. The papers published contemporaneously with the proceedings are perhaps most directly affected by the process itself, as they were written so close to the events that they could not escape the emotional reach of the trial. But because they are so closely related to the proceedings themselves, these essays also offer perhaps the clearest and most perceptive view of the fault lines that have characterized the Nuremberg debate since those days.

The International Military Tribunal ('IMT') was set up pursuant to a multi-national agreement between the governments of the four victorious powers: the US, the UK, the USSR, and France. Attached to that agreement was the Charter of the Tribunal, a short document made up of thirty articles which set out the main characteristics of the IMT's jurisdiction. The text of the Charter was the result of sometimes tense negotiations between the representatives of these four nations, who came to the negotiating table with different legal traditions and sometimes very different views as to the purpose of the trial. Among those who negotiated the Charter was US Supreme Court Justice Robert H. Jackson, later to become the US Chief Prosecutor at Nuremberg. Jackson is most often credited and remembered for his role as Chief Prosecutor and for the mastery of his opening and closing addresses before the Tribunal. Less well-known, but similarly important, was the role Jackson played in drafting the Charter of the Tribunal in his capacity as US representative to the International Conference on Military Trials. Jackson considered that the principles which were enshrined in the Charter constituted 'a step in the evolution of a law-governed society of nations':[4]

The charter is something of a landmark, both as a substantive code defining crimes against the international community and also as an instrument establishing a procedure for prosecution and trial of such crimes before an international court. [...] The significance of the charter's procedural provisions is emphasized by the fact that they represent the first tried and successful effort by lawyers from nations having profoundly different legal systems, philosophies, and traditions to amalgamate their ideas of fair procedure so as to permit a joint inquiry of judicial character into criminal charges.

The Charter of the Tribunal created a revolutionary framework for the trial of Nazi leaders, introducing many of the innovations that were later, and often wrongly, attributed to the Judgment of the Tribunal. In fact, as the Tribunal made clear in its Judgment, it was bound to apply the law of the Charter and did so most conscientiously, interpreting that document narrowly and sometimes quite conservatively. The majority of the legal developments that took place at Nuremberg were the result of the agreement which four nations adopted prior to the trial, rather than judicial innovations.

In an article which he wrote in 1941 as the war raged on, Jackson outlined for the first time some of the fundamental aspects and principles that he later insisted should form the basis of the Tribunal's jurisdiction and which would shape the Tribunal itself and the entire proceedings (Robert H. Jackson, 'The Challenge of International Lawlessness'). Jackson's article, which opens this collection, is an essential entry point to understanding the *philosophy* behind the trial.

---

[4] *Report of Robert H. Jackson to the International Conference on Military Trials* (London, 1945), at viii–x.

The Charter of the Tribunal also forms the core of papers written by Hersch Lauterpacht ('The Law of Nations and the Punishment of War Crimes') and Stefan Glaser ('La Charte du Tribunal de Nuremberg et les Nouveaux Principes du Droit International/The Charter of the Nuremberg Tribunal and New Principles of International Law'), two of the most distinguished scholars of their time. These articles are invaluable scholarly dissections of the IMT's Charter which set out in detail the nature, content, and purport of this document and explain its significance to the development of international law. These papers stand out as strong defences of some of the most contentious aspects of the Charter, including the recognition of certain categories of *new* criminal offences and the meaning of the principle of legality in the particular context of war crimes trials.

The general discussion of the Charter is complemented by two important papers which focus more specifically on two of the most contentious aspects of the Tribunal's jurisdiction, namely, the provision of a crime of aggressive war or crime against peace and the recognition of crimes against humanity as a distinct category of criminal offences under international law (Sheldon Glueck, 'The Nuernberg Trial and Aggressive War' and Egon Schwelb, 'Crimes Against Humanity'). At the time of the trial, the recognition that aggressive war constituted an international offence was regarded as perhaps the single most important contribution of Nuremberg to world peace and to international law generally and also as one of the most serious encroachments which the proceedings made to the principle of legality. Crimes against humanity, on the other hand, were regarded as little more than an outgrowth of war crimes and gave rise to little debate at the time. Half a century later, however, the two categories have grown in very different directions. The crime of aggressive war has never managed to transcend political deadlock and did not take firm roots in international law. In the Statute of the International Criminal Court, it remains no more than an empty shell, awaiting a definition that could render it operative. Crimes against humanity, by contrast, are now undoubtedly recognized as an independent category of international crimes and are recognized as such in the statutes of all international criminal tribunals and many domestic jurisdictions.

Looking beyond the Charter of the Tribunal, the Trial itself and the way in which it was conducted has done perhaps more than any other event to give credence to the idea that criminal justice could be delivered fairly and credibly by an international tribunal. The fairness with which the accused were dealt with at Nuremberg was evidenced by the way in which they approached the proceedings themselves. 'I am impressed', US President Harry Truman noted after the trial, 'by the change in point of view of the defendants and their lawyers from indifference and skepticism at the outset to a determination to fight for their lives.'[5] The judges of the Tribunal played a critical part in ensuring the fairness of the proceedings. They managed to do so despite the difficulty of preserving the unity

[5] Letter of US President, Harry Truman to Judge Biddle, 12 November 1946.

of the court when profound legal and cultural differences were pulling them apart. Once retired from the Nuremberg bench, several of them contributed some of the most outstanding pieces on the subject of the Nuremberg Trial. Four of those are featured in this collection (Francis Biddle, 'The Nürnberg Trial'; Henri Donnedieu de Vabres, 'Le procès de Nuremberg devant les principes modernes du Droit Pénal International/The Nuremberg Trial and the Modern Principles of International Criminal Law'; Geoffrey Lawrence (Lord Oaksey), 'The Nuernberg Trial'; Norman Birkett, 'International Legal Theories Evolved at Nuremberg').

The judges were not alone in confronting the legal and practical difficulties of this groundbreaking effort. A group of bright and committed legal assistants provided the judges with much of the legal research and with fresh ideas that would animate their debate over the interpretation of the Charter and international law. Herbert Wechsler and Quincy Wright, both of whom were assisting the American judges, played a leading, though discreet, role in the proceedings. The views and positions which these two men put forward to the judges were often bold and sometimes plainly at loggerheads, but they served to inform the views adopted by the judges themselves. In his personal notes, Justice Biddle recorded an extraordinary exchange between he, Wechsler and Wright onboard the *Queen Mary* on their way from the United States to Europe:[6]

The major split of opinion is between Wechsler and Wright, who spent most of the a.m. outlining his view on the international law problem. Wright admits that the procedure and sentence are of course ex post facto, but believes that the criticism will not be leveled at these so much as the body of international law which he claims existed when the protocol was signed and was not created but merely expressed by this instrument. Wechsler thinks not, but agrees that it is unnecessary to stress that the law is ex post facto. It seems to me that we can state that we are bound by and cannot examine into the instrument under which we are acting, particularly after we have taken an oath so to act—but that we are not thereby excluded from pointing out the large body of international law existing in 1939. Our opinion must at least have its roots in the past even if its fruits are to ripen in the future. I asked Wright to let me have, briefly, the principles of international law he would like to see established, and he has written them out as follows:

1. The definition of crimes in Article VI of the [Charter] is declaratory of preexisting international law.
2. Individuals are subjects of international law in the sense that international law confers upon them certain rights and holds them liable for certain crimes.
3. The individual cannot avoid responsibility for his acts on the ground that they were authorized by a government of the State for which the government purport[ing] to act lacked power under international law to give such an authorization.
4. States lack power under international law to authorize the exercise of rights of war except in necessary self defense or as permitted by appropriate international procedures.

---

[6] Judge Biddle's personal notes, 'Notes on Conferences', 3 October 1945.

These two lawyers contributed several academic pieces to the subject of Nuremberg and international criminal law generally. Two of their most important articles concerning the Nuremberg Trial are reprinted in this collection (Herbert Wechsler, 'The Issues of the Nuremberg Trial'; Quincy Wright, 'The Law of the Nuremberg Trial').

No less important a role was played by the prosecutors, in particular, the American-led team. Whilst the British prosecutors contributed some of the finest advocacy and cross-examination to the Trial, most of the investigation, preparation, and construction of the prosecution case were carried out by American Prosecutors. They came to Nuremberg prepared and with resources that could be matched by no other delegation. The preparation and presentation of the Prosecution case at Nuremberg was a monumental professional feat. It was often decisions of the prosecutors, rather than of the court, that shaped the Trial's course and much of its legacy. Three pieces, by Jackson ('Nuremberg in Retrospect: Legal Answer to International Lawlessness'), by his successor at Nuremberg, Telford Taylor ('The Nuremberg Trials'), and Thomas J. Dodd ('The Nurnberg Trials'), offer a masterful overview of a prosecutorial perspective onto the Trial.

From an academic perspective, three of the most respected scholars of the time contributed some vibrant and perceptive critics of the Nuremberg proceedings. The pieces by Professor Georg Schwarzenberger ('The Judgment of Nuremberg'), Professor Hans Kelsen ('Will the Judgment in the Nuremberg Trial Constitute a Precedent in International Law?') and Professor Hans-Heinrich Jescheck ('Die Entwicklung des Völkerstrafrechts nach Nürnberg/ The Development of International Criminal Law after Nuremberg') challenged and often strongly criticized what to many lesser thinkers was the fait accompli of Nuremberg. These papers remain a formidable source of inspiration for those seeking to identify and to avoid the errors and shortcomings of the Nuremberg process.

Legal Perspectives on the Trial—The Modern Views

The second group of legal papers which are included in this book were written over the course of the sixty years that followed the Trial. While these pieces may lack the dramatic tension of the earlier commentaries, they are able to bring a degree of circumspection, and emotional detachment from the Trial has served the analytical ambitions of their authors well.

This section includes two articles written by German advocates who appeared as defence counsel before the International Military Tribunal. Both contain stinging criticism of some of the shortcomings that marred the proceedings. At Nuremberg, defence counsel had to operate with very limited resources and wrestle their way against the prejudice attached to their clients. All counsel were German citizens and some of them had been Nazi supporters, but others had opposed the regime and sometimes had to represent individuals whose actions and personalities they gravely disapproved of. But they, too, contributed to making the trial a fair one. Otto Kranzbuhler was perhaps the most impressive among them. A young and dashing naval lawyer, he represented Admiral Doenitz before the Tribunal and did so with brilliance. Having been denied a defence of *tu quoque* by the Charter, Kranzbuhler ingeniously circumvented the statutory constraint by establishing that some of his client's actions had in fact ceased to be illegal, considering that the prohibitions which he was said to have breached had been disregarded by all sides during the conflict. Kranzbuhler's article, 'Nuremberg Eighteen Years Afterwards', and that of one of his colleagues, Hans Laternser ('Looking Back at the Nuremberg Trials with Special Consideration of the Processes Against Military Leaders'), offer a valuable rebuttal and counterpoint to the laudatory views of other actors in the trial.

The history of the Nuremberg Trial is often referred to in the same breath as that of the Tokyo Trial, its lesser known cousin. In marked contrast to the Nuremberg process, the Tokyo Trial is perceived by many lawyers and commentators as a judicial failure. The profoundly critical dissenting opinions of some of the judges in Tokyo and the overbearing nature of General MacArthur's involvement in the proceedings have done much to weaken the fragile sense of judicial independence that had been safeguarded at Nuremberg. The fine line that separates judicial *success* from judicial *failure* as exemplified by these two trials offers many lessons for modern war crimes tribunals. The article by Bert V. A. Röling, ('The Nuremberg and the Tokyo Trials in Retrospect'), who was a judge at Tokyo, identifies important elements and factors to understanding the differences and similarities between these two historical proceedings and why they are now discussed together more for their differences than for their similarities.

This part of the book also contains a group of important 'academic' papers which offer a panoramic view of the evolution of the Nuremberg legacy in the literature over the last forty years as seen by scholars from different legal and cultural traditions. The highly political appraisal by the Soviet scholarship (A. I. Poltorak, 'Njurnbergski Process I wopros ob otwetstwennosty za agressjo/ The Nuremberg Trials and the Question of Responsibility for Aggression'), the intensely critical and intellectual German approach (Reinhard Merkel, 'Das Recht des Nürnberger Prozesses—Gültig, Fragwürdiges, Überholtes/The Law of the Nuremberg Trial: Valid, Dubious, Outdated'), and the historical perspective of important American authors (Matthew Lippman, 'Nuremberg: Forty-Five Years Later'; M. Cherif Bassiouni, 'The "Nuremberg Legacy"') contrast to offer an intellectually challenging panorama of the academic debate surrounding the Nuremberg Trial. Another piece, by the Russian author, Larin Prigovor (Larin A. M. Prigovor, 'Nurnbergskii Process: prawo woini I fashizma/Nuremberg Trial:

The Law Against War and Fascism') focuses on an often neglected aspect of the Nuremberg Judgment: its findings of facts. For many commentators, the value of the judgment lies, not only in its legal pronouncements, but in the record of history that was written into its pages. The relative success of the Nuremberg Judgment as a historiographical record of mass atrocities has drawn modern war crimes tribunals towards the temptation of attempting to serve a similar function.

This section of the book closes with an essay that I wrote ('Judicial Inheritance: The Value and Significance of the Nuremberg Trial to Contemporary War Crimes Trials') which discusses the significance of Nuremberg to modern-day international criminal tribunals. Many of the thoughts contained in the essay were triggered by a discussion which I had in the Spring of 2006 with a client and former Bosnian Army General who had been indicted before the International Criminal Tribunal for the former Yugoslavia. General Halilović once asked me how the Yugoslav Tribunal compared with the Nuremberg Tribunal. 'It convicts more', was my first and candid answer. 'Both of them are judicial oddities which look for their place in the world order as much as they know it; both are marred by legal, political, and practical difficulties, and both are very much aware of their historical importance. They are very similar and very different at once.' 'But one of them convicts more than the other', he echoed, with an air of surprise. This paper does not attempt to measure Nuremberg against its modern equivalents, nor does it focus on the conviction rate in both institutions. Instead, it seeks to identify a number of important traits and characteristics which modern-day war crimes tribunals owe to or have borrowed from their Nuremberg forebear.

Historical, Political, and Moral Perspectives on the Trial

The third part of this collection of essays contains some of the most important, non-legal, writings on the subject of Nuremberg. These papers add much to the texture and depth of the debate over the legacy of the Nuremberg Trial. They are evidence of the fact that a discussion of the Trial cannot simply be reduced to a set of legal problems. They also provide the necessary context and perspective to engage in a proper and informed discussion of the political, historical, and moral significance of this process.

This part of the book opens with an essay by Henry L. Stimson, US Secretary of War during the Nuremberg Trial and one of its main architects. It was he, more than anyone else, who stood up against plans that suggested that war criminals should be shot summarily upon capture. It was he, also, who insisted that these men should be dealt with 'in a dignified manner consistent with the advance of civilization'.[7] Stimson's 'The Nuremberg Trial: Landmark in Law' is one of the

---

[7] R. N. Current, *Secretary Stimson—A Study in Statecraft* (New Brunswick: Rutgers University Press, 1954), at 218.

most significant moral and political defences of the Trial and of international criminal justice in general. According to Stimson, Nuremberg was both the enforcement of neglected moral values and the natural growth of international law that would set a central milestone for peace. His paper forcefully makes the case in support of this proposition.

Arthur L. Goodhart ('The Legality of the Nuremberg Trials') also takes a kindred view of the Trial and its legacy. Appraising the Nuremberg Trial from a jurisprudential point of view, Goodhart opines that the IMT was a 'legal court' and the Trial a 'legal' trial. Judges were impartial, he argues, the law sufficiently clear and fair, albeit *ex post facto* in part, and the judgment of the Tribunal was based on evidence, not prejudice. The conduct of a fair and legal process at Nuremberg, he concludes, 'helped to teach to the peoples of the world the essential lesson that "without law there cannot be peace"'.

Goodhart's optimism about the trial is not shared by all. David Luban's 'The Legacies of Nuremberg' brings out many of the ambiguities and contradictions of the Nuremberg process and offers a critical deconstruction of what has often been presented as the Trial's achievements. Nuremberg, he notices, 'perforated' the principle of state sovereignty that pervaded the entire system of international law. Paradoxically, Nuremberg might also have reinforced that principle by making it a crime to violate another state's sovereignty. Nuremberg's legacy is equally ambiguous as regards human rights. The trial was at once a 'founding moment' of the human rights movement, Luban argues, and a place where the protection of those rights was restrained by the last remnants of Eurocentric statism. In Luban's view, Nuremberg was an important moral and legal moment, but one that was compromised by the trial itself, by its refusal to shed the doctrine of state sovereignty once and for all and by the naive belief that the Tribunal could banish war and write a definite history of Nazism: 'The ambiguous legacies of Nuremberg linger at the margins of our unreliable moral memories; they inspire but also burden the conscience of our politics.'

From the days of the Nuremberg Trial up to this point, one of the most important issues of international criminal justice is the resonance which a war crime trial is capable of generating within a society that has been scarred by the commission of large-scale atrocities. Today, much thought is being given to the importance of the 'outreach' of international criminal tribunals and how their work can contribute to rebuilding the societies in which such atrocities have been committed. Perhaps the most important reflection on the matter remains Karl Jaspers' *The Question of German Guilt*, a necessary first stop in any discussion of the subject. Jaspers drew some of the fundamental lines between the various degrees, forms and types of responsibility that often shadow the commission of mass atrocities: legal, political, moral, and metaphysical. Behind the distinction between the different levels of guilt and modes of responsibility lie fundamental questions about the limits and adequacy of criminal law as a response to mass atrocities.

Jaspers' discussion of *German guilt* also gives emphasis to these grey areas where various types of responsibilities merge into one another and where the boundaries between them are uncertain and fluctuating. There lie the frontiers of international criminal law, at the touching point of law, politics, and morality.

War crimes trials such as the Nuremberg Trial have the ability to help separate and draw the lines between legal and moral or political responsibility, and are seen as powerful mechanisms for distinguishing personal responsibility from collective guilt. But their ability to draw the line between guilt and innocence should not be exaggerated. Several of the forms of liability used before these institutions attempt to reconcile the idea of individual criminal responsibility with collective types of criminality (e.g. through the concepts of 'conspiracy' and 'membership to a criminal organization' used at Nuremberg or, more recently, 'joint criminal enterprise' before the *ad hoc* Tribunals) walking a fine line between the idea of personal and group liability. Furthermore, the attribution of individual criminal responsibility to a necessarily limited group of individuals may bear the seeds of mass denial by others, allowing the vast majority of those involved in or complicit to incidents of mass atrocities to reclaim their innocence and thus to distort the nature and scope of their own responsibility in such murderous events.[8] Jaspers' writings also reveals a humbling truth; that whatever response is given to such dramatic events, judicial or otherwise, it will not in itself suffice to redress the harm done and will only sanction a narrow, and selective, type and range of responsibilities.

As the years passed by, Jackson continued to defend the decision of the victors to subject Nazi leaders to justice, a course which he said was the only acceptable policy decision that was open at the time. In his 'Introduction' to Whitney R. Harris's *Tyranny on Trial—The Evidence at Nuremberg*, Jackson explains that in the dying years of the war, others had favoured more brutal methods to dispose of these men, which would have deprived the world of the opportunity which the Tribunal seized to tell the murderous history of the Nazi regime. That history, Jackson explains, could have been presented to the court and to the world in many different ways and opinions differed within the Prosecution team as to how it should be done. Jackson favoured, and eventually opted for, a perhaps duller, but ultimately unanswerable, documentary presentation of the Prosecution case. Few witnesses were called and the case rested, for the most part, on the written records of the Nazi regime. Documents, Jackson believed, could not be accused of partiality, forgetfulness, or invention as witnesses unavoidably would. He also decided that the Prosecution would not rely on the evidence of any of the accused who would be willing to testify against his co-defendants so as to protect the integrity of the evidential basis that was to be presented to the court. These

---

[8] See, generally, J. Foschepoth, 'German Reaction to Defeat and Occupation', in R. G. Moeller (ed.), *West Germany under Construction: Politics, Society and Culture in the Adenauer Era* (Ann Arbor: University of Michigan Press, 1997), 74, at 154.

decisions, though technical in nature, have shaped the ethical quality, and eventually the legacy, of the entire process. 'The technique of trial to determine who of the enemy deserved punishment', Jackson concluded, 'is a significant development in the practice of nations.'[9]

The collection closes with an essay by Professor Mark J.Osiel ('In Defence of Liberal Show Trials—Nuremberg and Beyond'). Professor Osiel's piece is an edited and abridged version of his important book *Mass Atrocity, Collective Memory, and the Law*. In his essay, Professor Osiel explores the pedagogical aspects of war crimes trials and forcefully propounds the necessity for the *mise en scène* of such trials into 'liberal show trials'. War crimes trials, he argues, are capable of influencing collective memory of important historical events and should be organized and presented in such a way that they will foster and promote liberal virtues of toleration, moderation, and civil respect.

The articles collected in this volume represent a gateway to a vast subject-matter, which has spawned a large number of books and publications, many of which have been catalogued in the Bibliography contained in this volume. The pieces presented in this book represent some of the most essential writings on the subject. They reflect and have shaped our understanding of the Nuremberg Trial and international criminal law generally.

Acknowledgments

This volume was prepared in the middle of a very busy professional schedule and it would not have been possible to finalize it without the help and support of others who have kept it alive and spurred me forward. The author would like to express particular gratitude to Moya Magilligan who has breathed enthusiasm and much-needed good sense into organizing and editing this work.

Special thanks are owed to Brian Knowlton, Marc Cogan, and Aurélie Roche for their excellent translations of several of the articles which are contained in this collection.

I am also indebted to Professor Salvatore Zappalà for his friendship and his always precious comments. Gary Meixner has used his usual ingenuity and patience as a librarian to locate many of the documents and articles which are referred to or included in this collection.

Others have helped in various, important, ways to see this project come to fruition and deserve credit here: Marina Aksenova, Norman Farrell, Nathan Rasiah, Ida Bektas, and Professor Dermot Groome. Special gratitude is owed to

---

[9] Robert H. Jackson, 'Introduction', in Whitney R. Harris, *Tyranny on Trial—The Evidence at Nuremberg* (New York: Barnes and Nobles Books, 1954), at xxxvi.

Lina Baddour for her help in putting the manuscript together. The author is also grateful to the authors and publishing houses which have agreed to their papers being reprinted in this collection, the details of which are listed separately in the Publishing Acknowledgments. Finally, my sincere gratitude goes to John Louth and Alex Flach at Oxford University Press for their show of support and enthusiasm for this project.

Guénaël Mettraux
The Hague

9 October 2007

Publishing Acknowledgments

(In Chapter Order)

All articles are reprinted with the kind permission of the following authors, journals or publishers.

Robert H. Jackson, 'The Challenge of International Lawlessness', 374 *International Conciliation* 683–691 (1940–1941).

H. Lauterpacht, 'The Law of Nations and the Punishment of War Crimes', 21 *British Year Book of International Law* (1944).

Stefan Glaser, 'La Charte du Tribunal de Nuremberg et les Nouveaux Principes du Droit International/The Charter of the Nuremberg Tribunal and New Principles of International Law', 63 *Revue Pénale Suisse* 13–38 (1948).

Sheldon Glueck, 'The Nuernberg Trial and Aggressive War', 59 *Harvard Law Review* 396–456 (1945–1946).

Egon Schwelb, 'Crimes Against Humanity', 23 *British Year Book of International Law* 178–226 (1946).

Georg Schwarzenberger, 'The Judgment of Nuremberg', 21 *Tulane Law Review* 329–361 (1947).

Thomas J. Dodd, 'The Nuremberg Trials', 37 *Journal of Criminal Law and Criminology* 357–367 (January 1947).

Francis Biddle, 'The Nürnberg Trial', 91(3) *Proceedings of the American Philosophical Society* 294–302 (August 1947).

H. Donnedieu de Vabres, 'Le process de Nuremberg devant les principes modernes du Droit Pénal International/The Nuremberg Trial and the Modern Principles of International Criminal Law', 70 *Recueil des Cours de l'Académie de droit international de La Haye* 477–582 (1947–I).

Hans Kelsen, 'Will the Judgment in the Nuremberg Trial Constitute a Precedent in International Law?', 1(2) *International Law Quarterly* 153–171 (1947).

Geoffrey Lawrence (Lord Oaksey), 'The Nuernberg Trial', 23(2) *International Affairs* 151–159 (April 1947).

Norman Birkett, 'International Legal Theories Evolved at Nuremberg', 23 *International Affairs* 317–325 (July 1947).

Herbert Wechsler, 'The Issues of the Nuremberg Trial', 62 *Political Science Quarterly*, 11–26 (1947).

Quincy Wright, 'The Law of the Nuremberg Trial', 41 *American Journal of International Law* 38–72 (1947).

Robert H. Jackson, 'Nuremberg in Retrospect: Legal Answer to International Lawlessness', XXXC *American Bar Association Journal* 813–816 and 881–887 (October 1949).

Telford Taylor, 'The Nuremberg Trials', 450 *International Conciliation* 241–372 (1949).

Hans-Heinrich Jescheck, 'Die Entwicklung des Völkerstrafrechts nach Nürnberg/ The Development of International Criminal Law after Nuremberg', 72 *Revue Pénale Suisse* 15 (1957).

Otto Kranzbuhler, 'Nuremberg Eighteen Years Afterwards', 14 *DePaul Law Review* 333–347 (1965).

A. I. Poltorak, 'Njurnbergski Process I wopros ob otwetstwennost za agressjo/ The Nuremberg Trials and the Question of Responsibility for Aggression', 6 *Sowjetskoe gosudartswo I prawo* 58–66 (1965).

Bert V. A. Röling, 'The Nuremberg and the Tokyo Trials in Retrospect', in M. C. Bassiouni and Ved P. Nanda (eds.), *A Treatise on International Criminal Law*, Vol. I, 590–608 (Springfield, IL: Charles C. Thomas, 1973).

Hans Laternser, 'Looking Back at the Nuremberg Trials with Special Consideration of the Processes Against Military Leaders', 9 *Whittier Law Review* 557–580 (1986–1987).

Matthew Lippman, 'Nuremberg: Forty Five Years Later', 7(1) *Connecticut Journal of International Law* 1–64 (1991).

Larin A. M. Prigover MTB, 'Nurnbergskii Process: prawo woini I fashizma/ Nuremberg Trial: The Law Against War and Fascism', *Sbornik Instituta Gosudarstva I Prava RAN* (1995).

Reinhard Merkel, 'Das Recht des Nürnberger Prozesses—Gültig, Fragwürdiges, Überholtes/The Law of the Nuremberg Trial: Valid, Dubious, Outdated', in Nürnberger Menschenrechtzentrum (Hrsg.), *Von Nürnberg nach Den Haag, Menschenrechtsverbrechen vor Gericht—Zur Aktaulität des Nürnberger Prozesses* (Nuremberg: Europäische Verlagsanstalt, 1996), 68–92.

M. Cherif Bassiouni, 'The "Nuremberg Legacy"', in M. C. Bassiouni, International Criminal Law, Vol. III—Enforcement (Ardley, NY: Transnational Publishers Inc., 2nd edn, 1998), 195–213.

Henry L. Stimson, 'The Nuremberg Trial: Landmark in Law', 25(2) *International Affairs* 179–189 (January 1947).

A. L. Goodhart, 'The Legality of the Nuremberg Trials', 58 *Judicial Review* 1–19 (1946).

David Luban, 'The Legacies of Nuremberg', 54 *Social Research* 779–829 (1987).

Karl Jaspers, *The Question of German Guilt* (New York: Putnam Capricorn Book, 1961) (excerpts).

Robert H. Jackson, 'Introduction', in Whitney R. Harris, Tyranny on Trial—The Evidence at Nuremberg (New York: Barnes and Noble Books, 1954).

Mark Osiel, *Mass Atrocity, Collective Memory, and the Law* (New Brunswick/ London: Transaction Publishers, 1997) (edited and redrafted excerpts).

PART II

LEGAL PERSPECTIVES

1. Contemporary Views of the Trial and Judgment:
The Charter of the International Military Tribunal

1

The Challenge Of International Lawlessness[1]

By Robert H. Jackson

We lawyers would commit only a pardonable larceny if we should appropriate as an affirmation of the ideals of the legal profession a prayer from ancient liturgy:

...Grant us grace fearlessly to contend against evil, and to make no peace with oppression; and, that we may reverently use our freedom, help us to employ it in the maintenance of justice among men and nations....

As men experienced in the conduct of legal institutions which, among men, have largely displaced violence by adjudication, we should have some practical competence in measures to maintain justice among nations.

The Roosevelt-Churchill conference has directed discussion toward the implications of the war in terms of peace. But our people are still thinking cynically of all peace plans, for they feel frustrated and aggrieved at the interruption of a peace they had thought to be permanent. At the end of the World War our people divided into a group who were sure war was ended, because a war to end war had resulted in a fairly comprehensive organization of world powers, and an opposing group who were confident that they had assured our peace by keeping the United States out of it. Now, both awaken in disillusionment—the one to find the world not so well organized for peace as they had believed, and the other to find the United States not so well isolated from war as they had supposed.

I share the public disappointment at the renewal of war as a means of settling the problems of Europe, because I also shared some of the choice illusions of my time. But I cannot let faith be crushed, although the law of the jungle tarries long among nations and achievement of an international order based on reason and justice even now seems remote. The history of our experience with the slow but

---

[1] Delivered at the Annual Meeting of the American Bar Association, Indianapolis, Indiana, October 2, 1941.

solid evolution of domestic law[2] keeps me from expecting miracles on the one hand and from becoming cynical, on the other.

The fact is that under today's political and economic chaos there is actually functioning a relatively stable body of customary and conventional international law as a foundation on which the future may build. Lodged deeply in the culture of the world, unaffected by the transitory political structures above it, is a bedrock belief in a system of higher law. Entrenched dictators spend no end of effort to persuade their own people that they are not lawbreakers and to rationalize their policies for a law-conscious public opinion. Not one of them today would dare to boast, as did Von Bethmann-Hollweg at the opening of the World War, that he is violating international law.

Treaties, except some of the great political ones, are, contrary to a general impression, still usually applied; prisoners of war are being treated pretty generally in accordance with treaty stipulations; there are few, if any, allegations that the sick and wounded are not being treated in accordance with the Geneva Red Cross Convention. Foreign offices of all nations in protesting actions thought to be in violation of customary international law or treaty provisions, pay tacit recognition to the existence and validity of a standard of conduct higher than the transient will of officials. Various departments of the government, in addition to the Department of State, have added international law scholars to their staffs; legal arguments are steadily exchanged between foreign offices concerning international disputes, many of which are still decided on this basis.

Diplomats, together with embassies and legations, are still accorded their proper immunities, and Axis diplomats and consuls are being sent home as *personae non gratae* for overstepping the bounds of their privileges.

Our nationals abroad are still protected; aliens still generally have the benefit of the international rules respecting them; criminals are extradited pursuant to treaty; prize courts still function under international rules and in the domestic courts of the United States, as well as of the other principal powers of the world, pleas are still made to international law and decisions are rendered in accordance with its principles.

Moreover, new concepts are competing for recognition; war is being waged today, not only in self-defense but upon the ground that aggressors are

---

[2] Sir Frederick Pollock, writing of the state of English law just before the Norman conquest, says:

'But this reign of law did not come by nature; it has been slowly and laboriously won. Jurisdiction began, it seems, with being merely voluntary, derived not from the authority of the State but from the consent of the parties. People might come to the court for a decision if they agreed to do so. They were bound in honour to accept the result; they might forfeit pledges deposited with the court; but the court could not compel their obedience any more than a tribunal of arbitration appointed at this day under a treaty between sovereign States can compel the rulers of those States to fulfil its award. Anglo-Saxon courts had got beyond this most early stage, but not very far beyond it.'—

'English Law Before the Norman Conquest' in *Select Essays in Anglo-American Legal History*. Boston: Little, Brown, and Company; 1907. Vol. I, p. 95.

lawbreakers and outlaws; international sanctions are being applied; assets which would otherwise fall into the hands of aggressors are being frozen; commerce is being protected on the high seas against their paper blockades; the principle of the freedom of the seas is being actively defended; the implications of the principle of self-defense are being clarified; and an enlargement of the heretofore indefinite concept of piracy is perhaps developing.

Passing from substantive law to international institutions, we have the League of Nations, its system of mandates, the International Labour Organisation and, last but not least, the Permanent Court of International Justice. Although these do not meet the needs of the world, they have many features that represent solid progress and which I am convinced the world cannot afford to throw away.

The League of Nations, for all of its defects and in spite of all that it has left undone, has had a wholesome influence on the international thought and habit of our time. The Covenant required publicity and registration of treaties, and it authorized recommendations to reconsider treaties which became inapplicable. A more enlightened concept of trusteeship underlies the system of mandates for backward people created by the Covenant. It required mediation, arbitration, or conciliation of certain classes of controversies, and it provided for the establishment of a Permanent Court of International Justice for the adjudication of justiciable controversies. Moreover, the League Covenant, in limiting the right of war, created new obligations of good conduct. It departed sharply from the older doctrine that, in respect of their right to make war, sovereign States were above both the discipline and the judgments of any law, and that their acts of war were to be accepted as legal and just. Instead, for its members it created a category of forbidden and illegal wars—wars of aggression. It made resort to war in violation of the Covenant an act of war against all other members of the League. It provided economic sanctions to be invoked against the aggressor. Even if it was not able to end unlawful wars, it ended the concept that all wars must be accepted by the world as lawful.

The League, which we rejected, was followed by the Pact of Paris. By it the signatory nations renounced war as an instrument of national policy and agreed that the settlement of all disputes or conflicts of whatever nature or of whatever origin should be sought only by pacific means. While the United States became a party to this treaty, Secretary Kellogg said that it was out of the question to impose any obligation respecting sanctions on the United States. The Senate proceedings make clear that its ratification was due only to the assurance that it provided no specific sanction or commitment to enforce it.

This treaty, however, was not wholly sterile despite the absence of an express legal *duty* of enforcement. It had legal consequences more substantial than its political ones. It created substantive law of national conduct for its signatories and there resulted a *right* to enforce it by the general sanctions of international law. The fact that Germany went to war in breach of its treaty discharged our own country from what might otherwise have been regarded as a legal obligation of impartial treatment toward the belligerents.[3]

Regardless, however, of these juridical consequences, the disillusioning fact is that neither the League nor the Pact of Paris proved adequate to prevent war. Whether they did not actually induce a false sense of security which contributed to the undoing of those who relied on their promise is an open question. That a signatory State may lawfully support a war to punish an illegal war may mean merely bigger and better wars. It is a rough international equivalent of the ancient 'hue and cry' procedure, which involved the whole community in the troubles of an individual. What we seek is to prevent, not to intensify and spread, wars. And that tranquillity can rest only upon an order that will make justice obtainable for peoples as it is now for men.

Our institutions of international cooperation are neither time-tried nor strong, but it is hard to believe that the world would forego some organ of continuous consideration of international problems or scrap what seems to be a workable, if not perfect, pattern of international adjudicative machinery.

It is not difficult with the aid of hindsight to point out structural defects in the League or to complain of the timid use made of such powers as it had. But we can no more dismiss as a failure all international organization because the League did not prevent renewal of war between nations than we can dismiss our federal government as a failure because it did not prevent a war between its constituent States.

Intelligent opinion should not visit upon struggling international instrumentalities that condemnation which rightly may be visited upon the selfishly nationalistic policies of several nations. We must place blame only where there was power. Too many people forget that the League was merely a collective annex of foreign offices. The dependence of the League on the policy of home governments was never better stated than years ago by Sir Arthur Salter:[4]

The League is an instrument through which the real desire of the world for international cooperation can find expression and be put into effect.... But it is not, and cannot be, a short cut to supreme control. It cannot enable the best part of the world to impose its will upon a hostile, an indifferent, or an apathetic majority. It is an instrument and not an original source of power. It is a medium, but a medium only, through which the desire of the world can find expression.

Moreover, the League under the Covenant is based upon existing national authorities. The members both of the Council and of the Assembly are nominated by governments. It therefore expresses the will of the world indirectly, not directly by a parallel form of popular representation. Those who care most for the ideals on which the League was

---

[3] See address delivered by Attorney General Robert H. Jackson before the Inter-American Bar Association, Habana, Cuba, March 27, 1941. *American Bar Association Journal,* May, 1941, p. 275; 35 *American Journal of International Law,* p. 348.

[4] Salter, Sir J. A.: 'Allied Shipping Control' in *Economic and Social History of the World War.* Oxford: At the Clarendon Press; 1921. Carnegie Endowment for International Peace. pp. 264–65.

founded can indeed use the League itself in many ways to mobilize and concentrate their forces. But the route to *action* lies first through the national electorates and the various national media through which the policy of national governments can be affected.

The League's position as foreign office subsidiary was probably inevitable, but it was unfortunate for the peace of the world. A diplomat suffers less risk to his personal career if he can hush a delicate issue than if he brings it to the surface and tries to meet it with long-term remedies. The foreign office genius for suppressing issues rather than solving them was the common denominator of all nationalistic representation and became the chief, if not in fact the only, policy of the League.

Sumner Welles, in a really notable address, has aptly said:[5]

The League of Nations, as he [Wilson] conceived it, failed in part because of the blind selfishness of men here in the United States, as well as in other parts of the world; it failed because of its utilization by certain powers primarily to advance their own political and commercial ambitions; but it failed chiefly because of the fact that it was forced to operate, by those who dominated its councils, as a means of maintaining the *status quo*. It was never enabled to operate as its chief spokesman had intended, as an elastic and impartial instrument in bringing about peaceful and equitable adjustments between nations as time and circumstance proved necessary.

Some adequate instrumentality must unquestionably be found to achieve such adjustments when the nations of the earth again undertake the task of restoring law and order to a disastrously shaken world.

We now see that such an instrumentality, if it is to compose the world's discord, must have flexibility. Neither maps nor economic advantages nor political systems can be frozen in a treaty. Peace is more than the fossilized remains of an international conclave. It cannot be static in a moving world. Peace must function as a going concern, as a way of life with a dynamic of its own. Unfortunately, however, the internal structure of the League loaded the dice in favor of the perpetuation of the *status quo* which was also the policy of the dominant powers and the governing classes within them. Any peace that is indissolubly wedded to a *status quo*—any *status quo*—is doomed from the beginning. The world will not forego movement and progress and readjustments as the price of peace. Where there is no escape from the weight of the *status quo* except war, we will have war. Perhaps if that is the only escape, we should sometimes have war.

The Assembly of the League could advise 'reconsideration by members of the League of treaties which have become inapplicable and the consideration of international conditions whose continuance might endanger the peace of the world.'[6] That promise to the ear was, however, broken to the hope by the provision that action be only by unanimous consent. Any one dissenting member government could thus perpetuate the *status quo*, though all the world knew it was at the price

---

[5] Address by the Honorable Sumner Welles, Acting Secretary of State, at the laying of the cornerstone of the new wing of the Norwegian Legation in Washington, D. C., July 22, 1941.
[6] Article 19.

of eventual war. This was a fatal situation when the *status quo* in Europe was an experimental and in some respects an artificial one established by victors in an hour of heat and hate.

The world will not, I trust, be naïve enough again to believe it has so reordered its affairs as to prevent conflicts that might provoke wars. The supremacy of domestic law is not based on an absence of individual conflicts. It is predicated on a settlement of them by means that do not violate the peace of the community. The law anticipates a certain amount of wrong conduct, for which it provides damages or punishments. It does not end injustices, but it requires the victims to seek redress through the force of the law, rather than through their own strength.

In this we have to abide the imperfections of legal institutions. I am not convinced, even by my own transfiguration into a Justice of the Supreme Court, that courts have overcome the hazard of wrong decision and of occasional injustice. The triumph of the law is not in always ending conflicts *rightly*, but in ending them *peaceably*. And we may be certain that we do less injustice by the worst processes of the law than would be done by the best use of violence. We cannot await a perfect international tribunal or legislature before proscribing resort to violence even in case of legitimate grievance. We did not await the perfect court before stopping men from settling their differences with brass knuckles.

But even if we achieve a formula for order under law among all or among a considerable number of like-minded nations, we may as well recognize that its instrumentalities of justice and of adjustment will give us little security unless we give them a more real support than in the past. There is no dependence on a peace that is everybody's prayer but nobody's business. Peace declarations are no more self-enforcing than are declarations of war. Peace without burdens will no more come to a world that will not assume its risks than domestic peace would come to a community that would not assume the burdens and risks of a force of peace officers and courts for judging offenders and a form of political organization that commits the physical force of the community to support the peace officer, if necessary.

The American people seem to have believed, and some scholars have asserted, that international law can operate by the voluntary acceptance on the part of well disposed powers. But Mr. Justice Holmes pointed out that we cannot test our law by the conduct of the good men who probably behave from moral or social considerations. The test of the efficiency of the law, he said, is the bad man who cares only for material consequences to himself. Said Holmes:[7]

A man who cares nothing for an ethical rule which is believed and practiced by his neighbors is likely nevertheless to care a good deal to avoid being made to pay money, and will want to keep out of jail if he can.

---

[7] Holmes, Oliver Wendell: *Collected Legal Papers*. New York: Harcourt, Brace and Company; 1920, p. 170.

The world is in war today chiefly because its civilization had not been so organized as to impress the 'bad man' with the advisability of keeping the peace.

The German people might not have supported a war of Nazi aggression, had there been explicit understanding that it would bring against them the array of force they now face. Everything indicates that Hitler's early steps were cautious and tentative and calculated to test out the spirit and solidarity of the rest of the world. Shirer asserts, and we find little reason to doubt, that Hitler was successful in recreating the conscript army in violation of the military provisions of the Treaty of Versailles, only because of default of opposition from the former Allies.[8] He also says that when Hitler sent troops to occupy the demilitarized zone of the Rhineland, in violation of the Locarno Treaty, the troops had strict orders to retreat if the French army opposed them in any way. They were not prepared or equipped to fight a regular army.[9] Peace appears to have been lost, not for the want of a great supporting force, but for the want of only a little supporting force.

It is in the light of such facts that America will face a tough and fateful decision as to her attitude toward the peace. It is a grave thing to risk the commitments that are indispensable to a system of international justice and collective security. It is an equally grave thing to perpetuate by our inaction an anarchic international condition in which every State may go to war with impunity whenever its interests are thought to be served.

But it is a perilous thing to neglect our own defenses as if we were in a world of real security and at the same time to reject the obligations which might make real security possible. At the end of this war we must either throw the full weight of American influence to the support of an international order based on law, or we must outstrip the world in naval and air, and perhaps in military, force. No reservation to a treaty can let us have our cake and eat it too.

The tragedy and the irony of our present position is that we who would make no commitment to support world peace are making contributions a thousandfold greater to support a world war. We who would not agree to even economic sanctions to discourage infraction of the peace are now imposing those very sanctions against half the world in an effort to turn the fortunes of war.

The Roosevelt-Churchill 'Atlantic Charter' promises aid to all 'practical measures which will lighten for peace-loving peoples the crushing burden of armaments.' Certainly, the present competition, if continued, threatens the financial and social stability of free governments. Vast standing military establishments and the interests that thrive on them and the state of mind they engender are no more compatible with liberty in America than they have been in Europe. Five years of the sort of thing the world now witnesses and twenty centuries of civilization will not be worth a tinker's damn.

---

[8] Shirer, William L.: *Berlin Diary.* New York: Alfred A. Knopf; 1941. p. 30.
[9] *Id.*, p. 56.

The Roosevelt-Churchill statement affirms that all nations 'must come to the abandonment of the use of force' and it envisions the 'establishment of a wider and permanent system of general security.' Such happy days wait upon great improvement in our international law and in our organs of international legislation and adjudication. Only by well considered steps toward closer international cooperation and more certain justice can the sacrifices which we are resolved to make be justified. The conquest of lawlessness and violence among the nations is a challenge to modern legal and political organizing genius.

Men of our tradition will take up the challenge gladly. We have never been able to accept as an ultimate principle the doctrine that, in vital matters of war and peace, each sovereign power must be free of all restraint except the will and conscience of its transitory rulers. Long ago English lawyers rejected lawlessness as a prerogative of the Crown and bound their king by rules of law so that he might not invade the poorest home without a warrant. In the same high tradition our forefathers set up a sovereign nation whose legislative and executive and judicial branches are deprived of legal power to do many things that might encroach upon our freedoms. Our Anglo-American philosophy of political organization denies the concept of arbitrary and unlimited power in any governing body. Hence, we see nothing revolutionary or visionary in the concept of a reign of law, to which sovereign nations will defer, designed to protect the peace of the society of nations. We, as lawyers, hold fast to the ideal of an international order existing under law and equipped with instrumentalities able and willing to maintain its supremacy, and we renew our dedication to the task of pushing back the frontiers of anarchy and of maintaining justice under the law among men and nations.

2

The Law of Nations and the Punishment
of War Crimes[1]

By Professor Hersch Lauterpacht, M.A., LL.D.
Whewell Professor of International Law in
the University of Cambridge

I

THE question whether the punishment of war crimes committed by the enemy is desirable, expedient and practicable is a problem of politics rather than of law. It includes such questions as the relative merits and disadvantages of providing a deterrent against criminal violations of the law of war; the prospective effectiveness of such deterrent; the taking into account of a widespread and not inherently reprehensible desire for retribution; the consequences of impunity upon national and international law and morality; the desirability, partly in the interest of the culprits, of containing a hitherto ruthlessly suppressed craving for revenge within the channels of a regularized legal procedure; and the effects of a policy of punishing war crimes upon the prospects of reconciliation or, at least, of a return to a minimum degree of normalcy in international relations. It is not proposed to discuss these questions in the present article.

There is, however, one series of considerations which lies in what may be described as the realm of legal policy, but which the international lawyer and those who have at heart the future of international law may find it difficult to leave on one side. War crimes are crimes against international law. Punishment of these crimes, however distasteful it may be in its concrete application, is a by no means belated measure of enforcement of international law. The maintenance of the authority of the law of nations is inconsistent with the view that it is a system of law whose means of enforcement are confined to pressure of public opinion

---

[1] This article has grown out of a Memorandum submitted in July 1942 to the Committee concerned with Crimes against International Public Order (under the chairmanship of Sir Arnold D. McNair). The Committee was set up by the International Commission for Penal Reconstruction and Development established by the Department of Criminal Science in the University of Cambridge.

or pecuniary compensation, and that as it is a law between, but not above sovereign States, the very idea of punishment is repugnant to its fundamental notions. International law must reject the idea that it is, in this matter, doubly impotent for two contradictory reasons usually adduced in support of this view: (1) because it is legally inadmissible to punish the State as such on the ground that the corporate entity of the State cannot properly be deemed to possess a criminal intent and be the object of criminal punishment in the persons of its organs; and (2) for the alleged reason that it is legally improper to visit punishment upon individuals on the ground that the precepts and the injunctions of international law are not addressed to individuals but to the corporate entity of the State.[2] These views have been given currency with particular reference to the question of war crimes in disregard of the fact that the potentialities for irretrievable mischief inherent in the modern State call for an intensification rather than a relaxation of the repressive, deterrent and punitive consequences of criminal conduct.

Once we have dissociated ourselves from a trend of thought which is juridically unsound and retrogressive, we shall be justified in giving—and bound to give—full weight to any possible legal limitations upon the right of the victor to punish enemy nationals accused of war crimes and to any safeguards calculated to ensure the proper exercise of that right. For the cause of international law demands not only the punishment of persons guilty of war crimes. It requires that such punishment shall take place in accordance with international law. Circumstances accompanying the defeat of the enemy, the confusion surrounding the transfer of authority in territory which he had occupied, and the release of suppressed passions may result in acts of summary retribution which foresight and magnanimity may not be able to prevent. But in so far as the punishment of war crimes is intended to take place within the framework of a legal process, it will enhance both its effectiveness and the respect for international law if such limitations as the law of nations imposes are rigidly adhered to. Moreover, there must not only be in fact just punishment. That punishment must also appear to be just and in accordance with the law as the result of the effective provision of practicable measures of impartiality and mutuality.

In the existing state of international law it is probably unavoidable that the right of punishing war criminals should be unilaterally assumed by the victor. This is so in particular when, as may be the case at the close of the second World War, the victorious side represents the overwhelming majority of states and when there are few neutral states left capable of ensuring the impartial administration of justice. Circumstances such as these constitute an additional reason why the manner in which the punishment of war criminals takes place should be not a

---

[2] For a recent advocacy of this point of view see Manners in *American Journal of International Law*, 37 (1943), pp. 407–435. But see Finch, *ibid.*, pp. 81–88; Cohn in *Transactions of Grotius Society*, 26 (1940), pp. 125–51; Schwarzenberger in *Czechoslovak Year Book of International Law*, 1942, pp. 67–88; and Hyde in *Proceedings of the American Society of International Law*, 1943, pp. 39–46.

manifestation of victorious power but an act of international justice. Moreover, the very effectiveness of the attempt to punish war crimes depends to a large extent on the preservation of the essential requirements of fair and impartial judicial process inasmuch as their absence must influence the decision of neutral states to extradite or surrender persons accused of war crimes who have taken refuge in their territory. For these reasons it is proposed to examine in this article the following questions:

(1) What, if any, is the legal basis and justification of the demand, unaccompanied by a reciprocal offer, made upon the defeated State to surrender war criminals to the victor?

(2) What are the legal limitations upon the right to punish war crimes, in particular having regard to the absence or the varying degrees of criminal *mens rea* as the result:
   (i) of obedience to superior orders;
   (ii) of the uncertainties of rules of warfare;
   (iii) of the operation of reprisals?

(3) What are, in this matter, the possible safeguards of impartiality and of a requisite measure of legal equality as between the victor and the vanquished?

(4) What are the basis and the extent of the legal duty, if any, of neutral States to extradite or to surrender war criminals who have taken refuge on their territory?

It is proposed to examine these questions in a general manner, though much of what follows necessarily refers, directly or by implication, to the question of the punishment by the United Nations of war crimes committed during the second World War by Germany and her allies.

II. The Legal Basis of the Demand for Surrender of War Criminals

In the course of the second World War, the Governments of most of the United Nations gave repeated expression to their intention to demand, as one of the terms of the armistice, the surrender, for trial and punishment, of nationals of their adversaries accused of war crimes.[3] What is the legal basis of such a

---

[3] These include: the Declaration of 13 January 1942, adopted by the Governments of Belgium, Czechoslovakia, Greece, Luxemburg, the Netherlands, Norway, Poland and Yugoslavia and by the Free French National Committee (Document issued by the Inter-Allied Information Committee, London, H.M. Stationery Office, 1942); the statement by Lord Simon, Lord Chancellor, on 7 October 1942 in the House of Lords, outlining the task of the proposed United Nations Commission for the Investigation of War Crimes (*Parl. Debates*, House of Lords, vol. 124, pp. 577 *et seq.*) and endorsed on the same day by the President of the United States; the Declaration

demand? Is it the mere power of the victor to exact vindictive retribution from the defeated State and to challenge accepted notions of equality before the law by the underlying assumption that his—the victor's—forces or authorities have been free of any imputation of violating the law of war? Or is it a right, or the corollary of a right, which is firmly grounded in the principles and in the practice of international law?

There may be room for the view that the war crimes committed by Germany and her allies during the second World War were so unprecedented in their premeditation and ruthlessness as to warrant a departure from accepted forms and principles of international law. That view might be supported by the independent, and probably unimpeachable, argument that the armistice or the treaty of peace are not acts of application of international law. The law of these instruments is the will of the victor; there are, in theory, few limits to his power to change established law and precedent as between himself and the vanquished. However, the victor may justly consider it unwise to disdain the aid which existing law is in a position to offer. He may consider it unwise to do so at the close of a war the essential purpose of which is to vindicate the law of nations—a claim on the part of the United Nations which history is unlikely to stigmatize as sanctimonious and false. For a considerable period after the first World War German writers gave emphatic and repeated expression to the accusation that the provisions of the Treaty of Versailles for the surrender of German war criminals were in flagrant contradiction both with international law and with general principles of law. They were supported by writers in other countries.[4] It is possible that

on Atrocities adopted in October 1943 at Moscow by Great Britain, the United States, and Russia. The main part of the Declaration may conveniently be quoted:

'At the time of the granting of any armistice to any Government which may be set up in Germany, those German officers and men and members of the Nazi Party who have been responsible for or have taken a consenting part in the above atrocities, massacres and executions will be sent back to the countries in which their abominable deeds were done in order that they may be judged and punished according to the laws of these liberated countries and of the Free Governments which will be erected therein. Lists will be compiled in all possible detail from all these countries, having regard especially to the invaded parts of the Soviet Union, to Poland and Czechoslovakia, to Yugoslavia and Greece, including Crete and other islands, to Norway, Denmark, the Netherlands, Belgium, Luxemburg, France and Italy.

'Thus Germans who take part in wholesale shootings of Polish officers or in the execution of French, Dutch, Belgian or Norwegian hostages or of Cretan peasants, or who have shared in the slaughters inflicted on the people of Poland or in the territories of the Soviet Union which are now being swept clear of the enemy, will know that they will be brought back to the scene of their crimes and judged on the spot by the peoples whom they have outraged. Let those who have hitherto not imbrued their hands with innocent blood beware lest they join the ranks of the guilty, for most assuredly the three Allied Powers will pursue them to the uttermost ends of the earth and will deliver them to the accusers in order that justice may be done.

'The above declaration is without prejudice to the case of German criminals, whose offences have no particular geographical location and who will be punished by a joint decision of the Governments of the Allies.'

[4] It may be of interest, as showing the strength of the feelings of German jurists on the subject, to quote a passage from the Opinion of Professor Meurer, a German Privy Councillor and

that view, somewhat uncritically accepted, was not without some effect on the eventual fate of these clauses of the Treaty. It is, accordingly, of importance to scrutinize the accuracy of any similar accusation in relation to the corresponding demand of the United Nations in the second World War.

The first relevant fact in the situation is that the practice and the doctrine of international law as well as the municipal law of a considerable number of states recognize that a belligerent is entitled to punish for war crimes those members of the armed forces of the opponent who fall into his hands. There is hardly a dissenting voice in the general approval of that rule. Neither is it a new doctrine in international law. Francisco de Vitoria, writing in 1532, stated the underlying principle in *De Jure Belli*: '...etiam parta victoria, recuperatis rebus, pace etiam securitate habita, licet vindicare injuriam ab hostibus acceptam, & animadvertere in hostes, & punire illos pro injuris illatis....' He elaborated the wider reasons of the validity of this principle: '...nec pax, nec tranquillitas, quae est finis belli, aliter haberi potest, nisi hostes malis & damnis afficiantur, quibus deterreantur, ne iterum aliquid tale committant.'[5] Grotius, while pleading for prisoners of war who have surrendered or desire to do so, says: 'in order to warrant their execution it is necessary that a crime shall have been previously committed, such a crime, however, as a just judge would hold punishable by death.'[6] Christian Wolff, the German philosopher and lawyer, writing in 1764, reproduces, almost literally, the same view.[7] Johann Jakob Moser, a leading German positivist writer of the same period, is even more emphatic: 'Enemy combatants who act contrary to international law need not, when they fall into the hands of the belligerent, be treated as prisoners of war, but may be treated as robbers, murderers and so on.'[8] The Institute of International Law expressed the same view in 1882.[9] Holland, writing in 1908, was very definite on the subject: 'Individuals offending against the laws of war are liable to such punishment as is prescribed by the military code of the belligerent into whose hands they fall, or in default of such code, then to such punishment as may be ordered, in accordance with the laws and usages of war, by a military court.... When a whole corps systematically disregards the

---

an international lawyer of repute, delivered in the course of the work of the Commission on War Crimes appointed by the German *Reichstag* after the first World War. Referring to Articles 228–30 of the Treaty of Versailles, he said: 'The Allies thus imposed upon Germany a breach of most elementary legal principles and a forced departure from entire German legal history. Already in 1356 the Golden Bull prohibited "for all times" the delivery of Germans for punishment by a foreign State. It declared that this prohibition was merely a confirmation of an immemorial right and custom.... The German Government could not, it is true, prevent Articles 228–30 of the Treaty of Versailles from becoming law, but when it came to giving effect to their provisions, the torn German people rediscovered its unity and resisted like one man a demand which constituted a cultural outrage' (*Völkerrecht im Weltkrieg* (as to which see below, p. 42), vol. III (1), p. 57).

[5] V. Prop., 19.
[6] Book III, XVI. I.
[7] *Jus Gentium Methodo Scientifica Pertractatum*, § 798.
[8] *Grundsätze des Völkerrechtes in Kriegszeiten* (1752), § 18.
[9] *Annuaire*, V (1881–2), p. 174.

laws of war, e.g., by refusal of quarter, any individuals belonging to it who are taken prisoners may be treated as implicated in the offence.'[10] It is unnecessary to amplify these citations of authorities.

As will be submitted presently, this generally acknowledged right of the belligerent to punish enemies guilty of war crimes, far from being irrelevant to the question of the legal propriety of demanding the handing over of criminals to the victorious belligerent, is closely related to it. In the meantime it is sufficient to note that the general recognition of that right supplies a conclusive answer to those who regard as legally abhorrent the idea of the belligerent, favoured by the accident of being able to possess himself of the person of the enemy, acting as judge in his own cause. In default of a reasonable prospect of war crimes being punished by the offender's own State,[11] and in the absence of conditions rendering possible a truly international tribunal, there may be justification, subject to practicable judicial safeguards, for risking the taint of partiality associated with the application of the law by the injured party.

However, the generally acknowledged right of the belligerent to penalize the infractions of the law of war committed by the forces of his opponent is grounded in legal considerations more persuasive than the mere fact of the general recognition of that right. What are these considerations? In so far as war crimes have been perpetrated in the territory of the belligerent claiming the right to inflict punishment, they may be deemed to be covered by the ordinary territorial principle of criminal law. A State is entitled to punish crimes committed on its territory.[12] The application of the territorial principle covers, in the first instance, all violations of international law in the territory under military occupation of the enemy—the main source of war crimes in the second World War. For it is fundamental that the territory occupied by the enemy remains under the sovereignty of the belligerent temporarily divested of his jurisdictional rights. For this

---

[10] *The Laws of War on Land*, §§ 117, 118.

[11] See below, p. 44.

[12] The issue has been occasionally obscured in reliance on the principle of immunity of armed forces on foreign soil. The ordinary rules of extraterritoriality, based on international comity and consent implied from the mutual respect for the rights of sovereignty in time of peace, do not obtain in time of war. They cover armed forces present on foreign soil *with the permission* of the lawful sovereign—a distinction clearly laid down by Hyde, *International Law*, § 247. In time of peace the operation of the principle of extraterritoriality of foreign armed forces stops short of an immunity for acts directed against the safety of the State. In time of war even forces of an ally are not necessarily immune from local criminal jurisdiction in respect of crimes committed by the members of these forces. See, e.g., the British-Czechoslovak Treaty of 25 October 1940. The conferment of such immunity upon the forces of the United States in Great Britain in 1942 was in the nature of a concession which was not granted without serious consideration of the problems involved. See United States of America (Visiting Forces) Act, 1942, and the Schedule thereto embodying notes exchanged on the subject between the British and American Governments. In any case, the very notion of punishment of war criminals implies an obvious exception to the principle, if any, of the jurisdictional immunity of foreign armed forces. On the contrary view, the belligerent would be entitled to punish war crimes committed by the forces of the adversary in the territory of the latter, but not in his own, occupied, territory.

reason, jurisdiction thus accruing under the territorial principle covers crimes committed not only against the nationals of the State whose territory is subject to belligerent occupation, but also against the nationals of other states, including those of the occupying power—as in the case of the Jewish nationals of Germany brought by her to occupied territories during the second World War in pursuance of a proclaimed policy of racial extermination—and against stateless persons. The same territorial principle includes crimes committed in and from the air over the territory of the State assuming jurisdiction. The question of the extent to which acts committed in the course of air warfare may properly come within the purview of punishment of war criminals is discussed below,[13] but there ought to be little doubt that, in so far as they have taken place over the territory of the State which is in a position to claim jurisdiction, they are covered by the territorial principle. This is so particularly in view of the almost universal acceptance of the principle of the sovereignty of the state in the superincumbent air. The same applies, finally, to acts committed on the high seas by naval or air forces of the enemy seeing that the effect of such acts takes place on the vessels of the belligerent claiming the right to punish war crimes. This extension of the territorial principle received the approval of the Permanent Court of International Justice in *The Lotus* case; even prior to that case it had substantial authority behind it.[14] Thus interpreted, the territorial principle would cover effectively any war crimes committed against vessels—and their passengers and crews—of the United Nations by enemy ships or enemy aircraft.

The territorial principle—the principle that a State is entitled to punish unlawful acts committed within its territory—supplies a substantial, though not the only and not the most important, explanation of the existing rule authorizing a belligerent to punish war crimes committed by the enemy. In the circumstances of the second World War, in the course of which the major part of the European continent was occupied by Germany, the territorial principle thus conceived would cover most of the war crimes with which Germany has been charged. With regard to acts committed in the territory of the adversary, like maltreatment of prisoners of war, the belligerent may, in applying his municipal law to war criminals, rely on the rule, which many states have adopted and which general international law has not stigmatized as illegal, that a State may punish criminal acts committed by foreigners abroad against its own safety or against its nationals.

It has been shown that there exists a broader basis, in addition to the fact of an uncontroverted custom of warfare, for the rule of international law which concedes to belligerents the right to punish such war criminals as may fall into his hands. That basis is the generally recognized right of the State to punish crimes committed within its territory as well as the right claimed by some states and

---

[13] See below, p. 32.
[14] See below, pp. 46–47.

not denied by international law to punish crimes wherever committed against the safety of the State and its nationals. However, this explanation of the established rule, although probably satisfactory, in itself, lacks the persuasive force which is indicated in the circumstances unless we realize that the belligerent is, in essence, enforcing not only his municipal law, but also the law of nations. For acts committed by members of the armed forces of the belligerent in the course of hostilities can be treated by the municipal law of the adversary as criminal acts only if there is no justification for them in international law, that is to say, only if they are contrary to the law of war. Such taking of life as is in accordance with the law of war is not murder according to municipal law. Such taking of property as is in accordance with the law governing contributions and requisitions is not theft or robbery. War criminals are punished, fundamentally, for breaches of international law. They become criminals according to the municipal law of the belligerent only if their action finds no warrant in and is contrary to international law. When, therefore, we say that the belligerent inflicts punishment upon war criminals for the violation of his municipal law, we are making a statement which is correct only in the sense that the relevant rules of international law are being applied, by adoption or otherwise, as the municipal law of the belligerent. Intrinsically, punishment is inflicted for the violation of international law. When the British *Military Manual* authorises punishment for the violation of 'recognized rules of warfare' it is referring to violations of international law, and not of English municipal law. The rules of warfare, like any other rules of international law, are binding not upon impersonal entities, but upon human beings. The rules of war are binding not upon an abstract notion of Germany, but upon members of the German Government, upon German individuals exercising governmental functions in occupied territory, upon German officers, upon German soldiers. When we say that a belligerent has the right to punish members of the enemy forces for violations of the Hague Conventions, we do not intend to assert that he has the right to punish them for the infraction of his municipal law. The Hague Conventions have not, in the case of most states, become part of their municipal law by any express act of incorporation.[15] In no other sphere does the view that

---

[15] In Great Britain the Hague Conventions ratified by the Crown are probably binding upon courts independently of special legislation (see McNair, *The Law of Treaties* (1938), p. 17). In Germany, Convention No. IV was appended in 1911 as Annex II to the Army Regulations. This was only in a loose sense in accordance with Article I of the Convention which laid down that 'the Contracting Powers shall issue instructions to their armed forces which shall be in conformity with the Regulations respecting the Laws and Customs of War on Land, annexed to the present Convention.' In March 1914 the German military authorities issued regulations concerning collective punishment which the *Reichstag* Commission on War Crimes designated as clearly contrary to the Hague Regulations. When in 1901 Major Friederich was instructed to prepare for the use of the army a manual entitled 'Customs of War on Land' (*Kriegsbrauch im Landkriege*), he did not refer to the Hague Regulations. He testified on oath before the Commission that he had no detailed knowledge of the Hague Regulations at that time (*Völkerrecht im Weltkrieg*, I, p. 27). The comprehensive Italian Code of the Laws of War and Neutrality of 8 July 1938 does not refer to the Hague Conventions.

international law is binding only upon States and not upon individuals lead to more paradoxical consequences and nowhere has it in practice been rejected more emphatically than in the domain of the laws of war. In the course of the second World War the Supreme Court of the United States, in a case involving spying and sabotage, affirmed emphatically the direct criminal liability of individuals for violations of the laws of war.[16] The immediate subjection of individuals to the rules of warfare entails, in the very nature of things, a responsibility of a criminal character.

Some confusion has been caused, without good reason, by such provisions as Article 3 of Hague Convention No. IV, which lays down that 'a belligerent party which violates the provisions of the Regulations shall be liable to pay compensation', and Article 24 of the unratified Hague Rules of Air Warfare, according to which a belligerent State is liable to pay compensation for injuries to persons or property caused by the violation by any of its officers or forces of the provisions relating to aerial warfare.[17] From these and similar rules the conclusion has occasionally been drawn that responsibility for the violation of rules of warfare is limited to pecuniary compensation. There ought to be no doubt that these provisions refer to the responsibility of the State as a whole, and that they were not intended to exclude the responsibility of individuals or the customary right of States to punish enemy individuals for the violation of rules of war.

There is a weighty additional reason why the Hague Conventions must be considered to be binding upon individuals irrespective of the question whether they have been expressly incorporated as part of municipal law. This is so for the reason that they formulate and are largely declaratory of the fundamental rules of warfare as dictated by generally recognized principles of humanity. The same applies to the main aspects of the provisions of the Geneva Conventions of 1929 on the treatment of prisoners of war and of sick and wounded, or of the London Naval Treaty of 1930 and of the London Protocol of 1936 in respect of the elementary duty of safeguarding the lives of civilians in submarine warfare. In their broad purpose, as distinguished from their specific regulations, these international conventions are expressive, in the words of the preamble to Hague Convention No. IV, 'of the principles of the law of nations, derived from usages established among civilized peoples, from the laws of humanity, and from the dictates of public conscience'. Similarly, the relevant provisions of the London Naval Treaty of 1930 are expressly prefaced by the significant statement: 'The following are accepted as established

---

[16] *Ex parte Quirin et al.* (1942) 317 U.S. 1. And see comment thereon, from this point of view, by Hyde in *American Journal of International Law*, 37 (1943), pp. 88–91. And see Brierly in *The Norseman*, vol. 2 (1944), pp. 166–172, for a lucid exposition of the view that war crimes are violations of international law as distinguished from the municipal law of the State against which they have been committed.

[17] The Commission which drafted the Rules decided not to include a provision for the punishment of persons guilty of breaches of the crucial articles of the Rules. But, it added, 'its absence will not in any way prejudice the imposition of punishment on persons who are guilty of breaches of the laws of aerial warfare' (Cmd. 2201, p. 59).

rules of international law.' When the German *Staatsgerichtshof*, on 16 July 1921, in the case of *The Llandovery Castle*, found the accused guilty of killing defenceless persons in lifeboats, it did so on the ground that they acted against a clear and uncontested principle of international law as against which even the plea of superior orders offered some but not an absolute defence.[18]

The above considerations supply also a corrective to any undue preoccupation with the question as to what law must be applied in connection with the prosecution and punishment of war criminals. That law is, and must be, primarily, the law of nations.[19] For, it must be repeated, it is only to the extent that the acts of

---

[18] *Annual Digest of Public International Law Cases,* 1923–4, Case No. 235.

[19] With regard to the law applied by British military courts, a distinction must be made between the law applied by ordinary courts-martial in the narrower sense of the word and that applied by military courts under martial law. The first is the law mainly laid down in the Army Act, the Naval Discipline Act and the Air Force Act; it governs the conduct and the internal discipline of officers and men of the British armed forces in time of peace and war, both at home and abroad; it is administered by courts-martial—regimental, district, or general—established under these Acts. On the other hand, the law applied by military courts under martial law comes into operation: (*a*) in relation to the civilian population in connection with the suspension of the ordinary law in case of invasion, riots and insurrection, and (*b*) in connection with the application and enforcement of the laws and customs of war by the armed forces of the Crown in occupied enemy territory or in the theatre of war operations generally. We are here concerned with the latter courts only.

These courts, in addition to enforcing the laws and regulations laid down by the commanding general in charge of the occupied territory, apply the laws and customs of war as set forth in Chapter XIV of the *Manual of Military Law* (1929) (Amendment No. 12) notified by the Army Council in the Army Orders for January 1936. Although Chapter XIV of the *Military Manual* has not been given statutory force it is, in general, an exposition of the conventional and customary rules of international law as understood by Great Britain. The business of the military courts, in this particular sphere, is not to apply English criminal law either in its substantive or procedural sense. As said, they apply international law as well as the specific law prescribed by the commanding general in charge of the occupied territory. The discretion of the commanding officer and of the military courts established under his authority is circumscribed by the duty to follow the laws and usages of war. It is significant that in the 1936 edition of the *Military Manual* certain passages in the previous editions of the *Manual*, which emphasized the discretion of the occupying general, have been omitted. The law which these courts apply covers, accordingly, both civilians and members of the enemy armed forces. It is highly improbable that they are bound by the territorial principle of English criminal law. In fact, their primary purpose is to punish offences committed in occupied enemy territory or in the theatre of war operations generally.

At the same time it does not seem to be essential that military courts engaged in applying the laws and usages of war (including the prosecution of war crimes) should be established either within occupied territory or within the immediate vicinity of military operations. The view has been widely held that when Great Britain is at war any portion of its territory is, in relation to enemy aliens, within the 'zone of operations'. It would appear therefore that the operation of military courts in the wider sense (i.e. courts applying the laws and usages of war) is not necessarily confined to occupied territory or to the area of military operations. Similarly, courts-martial established under the Army Act (or the Naval Discipline Act or Air Force Act) may have conferred upon them by statute jurisdiction over persons, or in respect of acts, not otherwise subject to military law in the narrower sense. Thus in 1914 the Defence of the Realm Consolidation Act (5 Geo. V, c. 8) provided for punishment by courts-martial of certain categories of persons assisting the enemy as if they were subject to military law and had on active service committed an offence under the Army Act. The Treachery Act, 1940, which provided for the death penalty for acts 'designed or likely to give assistance to the naval, military or air operations of the enemy, to impede such operations of His Majesty's Forces, or to endanger life', laid down that an alien enemy may be prosecuted for such offences before a court-martial as if he were at the time of the commission of the offence

the offenders are prohibited by international law, that they can at all be considered as crimes according to the law of the individual states. The fact that the law of nations may be regarded as forming part of the municipal law of the belligerent in question is an important but in no way essential addition to the strength of the jurisdictional claim of the belligerent proceeding to punish persons guilty of war crimes. This being so, it is proper, in assuming jurisdiction over war criminals, to lay stress not on any exceptional or summary character of such jurisdiction, military or otherwise, but on its essential conformity with the law of nations. Once it is realized that the offenders are being prosecuted, in substance, for breaches of international law, then any doubts due to inadequacy of the municipal law of any given State determined to punish war crimes recede into the background. There is in this matter no question of any vindictive retroactivity arising out of the creation of crimes of which the accused could not possibly be cognizant. There is even no question of procedural retroactivity by subjecting him to a foreign jurisdiction in defiance of established law and principles. The law of Great Britain, of the United States, and of many other States, does not, as a rule, recognize the competence of national courts in respect of criminal acts committed by aliens abroad. But there would be no question of any retroactivity, contrary to justice and to established principles of law, if Great Britain were to alter her law so as to enable her tribunals, civil or military, whether functioning in Great Britain or abroad, to assume jurisdiction over German nationals who committed in Germany criminal offences against British prisoners of war or British civilians in circumstances not authorized by international law.

It would thus appear that there is no novelty about the principle that a belligerent is entitled to punish such perpetrators of war crimes as fall into his hands; that that principle, far from being a mere assertion of power, grudgingly assented to by international law, on the part of the fortunate belligerent is, in turn, grounded in the fact of recognition by international law of the jurisdiction of States based on the territorial and cognate principles as well as in the fact that in punishing war criminals the belligerent applies and enforces, in essence, the rules of the law of nations which are binding upon the individual members of the armed forces of all belligerents; and that there is no question of any retroactive application of the law from any material point of view.

subject to military law. According to the Naval Discipline Act there are subject to the Act spies and persons on board H.M. ships endeavouring to seduce persons subject to the Naval Discipline Act from their duty of allegiance.

With regard to ordinary criminal courts, it is clear that they cannot, according to existing law, exercise jurisdiction with regard to offences committed abroad (except in the matter of offences committed on the high seas or from the air on the high seas and affecting persons on board a British ship). There is probably no serious legal difficulty which would make it impossible for Parliament to alter the existing law in regard to specified categories of war crimes committed abroad. The fact that, as mentioned above, ordinary courts-martial in Great Britain have, by virtue of special war legislation, had conferred upon them jurisdiction over civilians with regard to a number of offences, shows that there is no particular difficulty in the way of modifying established principles, in particular those of a jurisdictional character, in order to meet situations arising out of the war.

However, granted that the belligerent is entitled to punish enemy war criminals who happen to fall into his hands, where is the warrant, apart from the undoubted right of the victor to lay down the conditions of the armistice, for the claim that the defeated State should hand over the accused to the victorious belligerent? The answer is that international law permits the punishment of war criminals by the opposing belligerent regardless of the manner in which they happen to fall into his power. The war criminal may fall into the hands of the enemy as a prisoner of war in the course of military operations. But this result may be achieved by other means. The belligerent may possess himself of the war criminals of the enemy as the result of the occupation—before or after the armistice or even after the peace treaty—of enemy territory. Such occupation may be actual or, in the case of the total defeat of the enemy, it may be constructive. After the enemy has been totally defeated, his adversary may proceed to the occupation of the entire enemy territory—a course which, with regard to German territory, was advocated by some at the end of the first World War. In that case he is legitimately in a position to lay his hands on the offenders. If, while abstaining voluntarily from occupying the territory of the defeated belligerent, he stipulates for the handing over of the criminals, what he is in fact doing is to exact from the authorities of the defeated State the performance of a task which he would be in a position to fulfil but for the self-denying decision to refrain from occupation. The entire territory of the defeated opponent is at the mercy and within the reach of the victor. The war criminals are, constructively, in his hands. The defeated and disarmed army of the opponent, as well as his government and administration, are, in a real sense, in the hands of the victorious belligerent. In the event of the second World War terminating with the occupation of the entire German (or Japanese) territory by the armed forces of the United Nations, the war criminals will be seized, either by the occupying Powers or by the German (or Japanese) authorities acting under their direction, and the conditions for the application of the established rule will be fully and literally realized. The situation is hardly different if for political reasons counselling restraint the victorious State refrains from actually occupying the territory of the defeated opponent. The rule of international law which authorises the belligerent to mete out punishment to war criminals who fall into his hands thus covers fully the case of his right to punish those who are, at his will, in his power. This is no mere juridical quibble. To quarrel with it is to quarrel with a rule which is well established as a matter of practice and which has behind it sound legal principle.

In this context it is necessary to consider the objection, on the ground of the absence of mutuality, to the exercise of the right of punishment, on the part of the victorious belligerent, of persons handed over by the enemy. For, clearly, no similar right is conceded to the defeated State.[20] It will be submitted presently[21] that

---

[20] The word 'objection' is not used here in a technical sense. In strict law, there is, as pointed out above, nothing to prevent the victorious belligerent from imposing his own conditions of the armistice.

[21] See below, p. 39.

ways may be found for securing a measure of mutuality. But, essentially, the position is not dissimilar to that which arises when the belligerent punishes a prisoner of war for a war crime committed prior to capture. He does so regardless of the ability of the adversary to exercise, effectively, the same right. The same applies to the situation in which war criminals fall, *en masse*, into the hands of the victorious belligerent as the result of an actual or what may be termed a constructive occupation of enemy territory. Undoubtedly, it may happen that the power, thus secured, to exercise the right of punishment may become the monopoly of the belligerent who, in the ultimate judgment of history, has identified himself with the cause of evil. The removal of such contingencies, resulting from the deficient organization of international society, must, like the eventual elimination of war itself, be regarded as a legitimate and desirable object of political endeavour. In the meantime, the victorious belligerent, while applying an inelegant and rough rule of law, must fortify himself by the conviction that in meting out justice he has conscientiously observed the canons of impartiality and the limitations which the existing law of war imposes upon the punishment of war crimes. These will now be considered.

III. The Limits of Punishment of War Crimes

The problem of confining the punishment of war crimes within the limits of international law can be conveniently examined under three heads:

(1) the plea of superior orders;
(2) the uncertainties of the law of war;
(3) the operation of reprisals.

(1) The Plea of Superior Orders

The limitation connected with the so-called plea of superior orders constitutes what is from the practical point of view perhaps the most important problem incidental to the punishment of war crimes. It was widely discussed during the first World War. In its report presented to the Preliminary Peace Conference at Paris in 1919 the Commission on Responsibilities stated: 'We desire to say that civil and military authorities cannot be relieved from responsibility by the mere fact that a higher authority might have been convicted of the same offence. It will be for the court to decide whether a plea of superior orders is sufficient to acquit the person charged with responsibility.'[22] Although this reference to the plea of superior orders was, in its context, limited to one particular situation, the above statement was probably intended to give a general answer to the problem raised

[22] Printed in *American Journal of International Law*, 14 (1920), p. 117.

by the plea of superior orders. It appears from the statement as quoted: (*a*) that the Commission desired to dissociate itself from the view expressed, among others, in the British *Military Manual* (as well as in the United States *Rules of Land Warfare*) that 'members of the armed forces who commit such violations of the recognized rules of warfare as are ordered by their Governments or by their commander are not war criminals and cannot therefore be punished by the enemy',[23] and (*b*) that the Commission did not consider it within its province—or within the reach of agreement among its members —to lay down detailed principles for the guidance of national courts in the matter.

It is not surprising that the Commission found it necessary to dissociate itself from the view that superior orders are a sufficient justification. A rule of this nature, unless reduced to legitimate proportions, would in most cases result in almost automatic impunity in consequence of responsibility being shifted from one organ to another in the hierarchy of the State or its armed forces. If the rule as stated in the British and American military manuals actually represented the existing position in international law, the prospect of bringing to justice any substantial portion of offenders would indeed be slender.

The activity of the German *Reichsgericht* in the course of the Leipzig trials in 1921, in connection with the charges put forward by the Allied Powers against higher German officers, illustrates in an illuminating manner the true implications of an unqualified acceptance of the doctrine of superior orders. The person first on the British list of individuals whose prosecution for war crimes was demanded was Grand Admiral Tirpitz, Secretary of State of the German Navy between August 1914 and March 1916.[24] He was charged with having ordered

---

[23] Section 443, which continues as follows: 'He may punish the officials or commanders responsible for such orders if they fall into his hands, but otherwise he may only resort to the other means of obtaining redress which are dealt with in this chapter.' This principle appears for the first time in Chapter XIV, prepared in 1914 by Professor Oppenheim and Colonel Edmonds, under the title 'The Laws and Usages of War on Land'. Article 366 of the United States *Rules of Land Warfare* repeats, almost literally, the British rule. There is no trace of it in the Instructions, drafted by Lieber in 1863, for the Government of Armies of the United States in the Field (for these Instructions see Halleck, *International Law*, vol. II, pp. 40–55). Chapter XIV of the British Manual has no statutory force. However, published as it is by the War Office and under the authority of the Army Council, it may fairly be regarded as representing, at the time, an authoritative British view. It is probable that in any case its provisions must be interpreted by reference to other parts of the Manual, in particular to those which stress the duty of obedience to lawful orders only. The view of the law as expressed in § 443, though disapproved of by the Commission on Responsibilities, which included a British representative, set up by the Peace Conference of 1919, appears, unaltered, in the 1936 edition of the Military Manual. It is at variance with the corresponding principles of English criminal and constitutional law (see below, p. 29). It is not believed to represent a sound principle of the law of war, and it is in no sense binding upon Great Britain in the international sphere. But it is clear that, unless the scope of prosecutions for war crimes is to be drastically and unduly curtailed, any British enactment relating to the prosecution of war crimes by British courts, military and other, will have to free them, by means of an express provision from the shackles of the rule as at present formulated.

[24] The list, with a summary of the decisions of the *Reichsgericht*, is compiled in *Völkerrecht im Weltkrieg* (a report of the Commission of Enquiry set up by the German National Assembly in 1919, as to which, see below, p. 42), vol. IV (1927), pp. 337 et seq.

unrestricted submarine warfare. The *Reichsgericht* quashed the proceedings on the ground that, in addition to the fact that unrestricted submarine warfare was not contrary to international law, the Grand Admiral was not responsible for the order in question. The *Reichsgericht* found also that that order was not given by Admiral von Capelle, who was Secretary of the Navy from March 1916 to July 1918; nor by Admiral Scheer, Commander of the Fleet from January 1916 to June 1918; nor by Admiral Hipper, Commander of the Fleet from August 1918 to November 1918; nor by Admiral Muller, Chief of the Naval Cabinet of the Emperor throughout the war—all of whom were on the list of accused persons. Who *did* give the order? The judgments of the *Reichsgericht* do not elucidate this point. But in the decision concerning Admiral von Hipper the *Reichsgericht* to some extent lifted the veil of discretion by stating that it was not the Chief of Fleet who was responsible for the order of unrestricted submarine warfare, but the Head of the Supreme Command of Naval Operations—presumably the Emperor himself. In view of this it is not surprising that the Supreme Court acquitted, as having acted under superior orders, individual naval commanders whom the British list charged 'with sinking ships without warning in circumstances of unusual cruelty and inhumanity'. If this interpretation of the plea of superior orders were to prevail, then it is clear that in many cases no one but the Head of the State, especially under a regime of absolutism or dictatorship, could be held responsible for decisions of major importance involving a breach of international law—a solution the futility of which is enhanced by the international irresponsibility, asserted by some, of the Head of the State.

The problem raised by the plea of superior orders is, by general admission, one of great complexity both in international and in municipal law. How intricate it is may be gauged from the fact that the solution adopted in the British and American military manuals with regard to war crimes is at variance with that in force in both countries in the domain of constitutional and criminal law. Moreover, the law on the subject in these and other countries in the field of municipal law is not free of ambiguities and apparent inconsistencies. In Great Britain and in the United States a soldier cannot validly adduce superior orders as a circumstance relieving him of liability for an illegal act. This is a rule established by a long series of decisions in both countries. On the other hand, according to English law, the soldier is bound to obey lawful orders of his superiors, and he is liable to punishment by the summary process of a court-martial in case of disobedience—though, when an order which on the face of it is lawful turns out to have been illegal, the soldier who obeyed it is answerable before ordinary courts if obedience to the order involved a crime. The difficulties resulting from the possible conflict between the duty of the soldier to obey orders[25] and his subjection

[25] For, it will be noted, according to English military law the soldier is bound to obey lawful commands only. The wording of Section 9 of the Army Act is explicit on the matter. The law on the subject has undergone significant changes. The Military Code of 1715 provided that 'any officer or soldier who should refuse to obey the military orders of his superior officer' shall be liable to

to the general law of the land are appreciated by judges and writers, and sympathy is occasionally expressed with the predicament of the soldier who is thus subject to two possibly conflicting jurisdictions. But the major rule, although qualified in some decisions and although mitigated by the admitted right of executive remedial action in the form of the right of pardon, has remained intact.

The fact is that the law—even military law—does not reduce the soldier to the status of a mere mechanism. While enjoining upon him obedience to orders, it adds the substantial qualification to the effect that obedience is due only to lawful orders. The law oscillates, with perhaps unavoidable hesitation, between the dictates of absolute discipline and efficiency in what is essentially an instrumentality of power and the equally inescapable subjection of that instrument of power to the authority of the law. The result is that in addition to the natural risks of his calling the soldier has, in theory, to face the dangers of a conflict between his duty of obedience to orders and his duty to obey the law. We say 'in theory', for in fact the law does not ignore altogether the resulting difficulty. Numerous decisions of courts in the United States recognize that while, in principle, superior orders are not a valid defence, obedience to an order which is not on the face of it illegal and is within the scope of the superior officer, relieves the soldier of liability. Some State laws go even further in that direction. In England, where the courts have been loth to depart from the logical rigour of the established rule, it is generally recognized that the exercise of the right of pardon by the Executive is in such cases a proper remedy. As Dicey says: '... a soldier runs no substantial risk of punishment for obedience to orders which a man of common sense may honestly believe to involve no breach of law.'[26] And there are judicial decisions to the effect that the soldier obeying orders which are not 'necessarily or manifestly illegal' will be protected by the courts themselves.[27]

---

capital punishment. The Code contained no qualifications as to the lawfulness of the command. But in 1749 the wording of the Military Act was changed so as to render criminal disobedience to any *lawful* command. Judicial decisions show the same tendency. In *Sutton* v. *Johnstone* (1786, 1 T.R. 493, 546) we still find Lord Mansfield saying: 'A subordinate officer must not judge of the danger, propriety, expediency, or consequence of the order he receives: he must obey; nothing can excuse him but a physical impossibility.' It will be noted that notwithstanding the apparent rigidity of this statement, there is no reference in this passage to the question of the *legality* of the order. In any case this pronouncement must now be read in the light of the express wording of statutory enactments like the Army Act and of subsequent decisions. Thus the case of *Warden* v. *Bailey* (1811, 4 Taunt. 67) is described in Chapter VIII of the Military Manual as discountenancing the duty of absolute obedience in a soldier enunciated in *Sutton* v. *Johnstone*. As pointed out, according to English military law the duty of obedience, far from being absolute, extends only to lawful orders. There is a significant passage on the subject in Stephen's *History of Criminal Law of England* (vol. I, pp. 205–6). He says: 'The doctrine that a soldier is bound under all circumstances whatever to obey his superior officer would be fatal to military discipline itself, for it would justify the private in shooting the colonel by the orders of the captain, or in deserting to the enemy on the field of battle on the order of his immediate superior.' It is probably accurate to say that no warrant can be found in British military law for the view that the existence of any duty of absolute obedience gives colour to an unqualified recognition of the plea of superior orders.

[26] *The Law of the Constitution*, 8th ed. (1927), p. 302.
[27] Mr. Justice Willes in *Keighley* v. *Bell* (1866), 4 F. & F. 763, at p. 790.

Conversely, many countries which, in the interest of the efficiency of their armed forces, have adopted the rule that obedience to superior orders excludes liability, make an exception in cases in which the orders are illegal. They, in turn, differ as to the necessary degree of the obviousness of the illegality. The German Code of Military Criminal Law, prior to the second World War, provided that the subordinate is liable to punishment as an accomplice if, when obeying an order, he knows that the act ordered involves a crime or misdemeanour.[28] According to the law of other states, the immunity of the soldier obeying orders ceases if he knows or *ought to have known* of the unlawful nature of the order.[29] There are indeed some states, in particular France, in which there is, apparently, no qualification to the rule that, in relation to the armed forces, superior orders are in all circumstances a valid excuse. Writers of authority, like Duguit, have defended that rule with vigour on the ground that it is indispensable to the cohesion and to the efficiency of the army.[30] But it has not been asserted that its effect is to relieve French nationals of responsibility when tried before foreign tribunals for violation of the municipal law of those countries or of international law even if the foreign country concerned has itself adopted an identical rule. For it is, by necessary implication, a rule applicable only to the State's own nationals and only in respect of its own municipal law. In fact, no country has more emphatically than France rejected the plea of superior orders when put forward by enemy soldiers and officers accused of war crimes.[31] It is an interesting gloss on the complexity of the problem that in Great Britain and in the United States the plea of superior orders is, on the whole, without decisive effect in internal criminal or constitutional law, although it is apparently treated as a full justification in relation to war crimes, while in France, where the plea of superior orders is an absolute defence in the municipal sphere, it is disregarded in the matter of war crimes.

There is no international judicial authority on the subject, but writers on international law have almost universally rejected the doctrine of superior orders as an absolute justification of war crimes.[32]

---

[28] S. 42 (2).   [29] E.g., Article 3 of the Polish Military Penal Code of 1932.

[30] *Traité de droit constitutionnel* (2nd ed., 1923), vol. III, pp. 289, 290—while denying that superior orders offer a valid excuse in other spheres: *ibid.*, pp. 286–9.

[31] Mérignhac in *Revue générale de droit international public*, 24 (1917), p. 53. But see Nast, *ibid.*, 26 (1919), p. 123. The crucial *sedes materiae* in French law appears to be Article 64 of the Criminal Code according to which an act committed under duress (which, apparently, includes the case of a soldier bound to obey orders) is neither a crime nor a misdemeanour. Article 327 excludes liability in case of acts 'ordonnés par la loi et commandés par l'autorité'. So does Article 190. Articles 70 and 71 of the Belgian Penal Code reproduce substantially Articles 64 and 327 of the French Penal Code. Article 43 of the Dutch Criminal Code recognizes generally the defence of superior orders, while Article 40 lays down the general exception of duress. On the other hand, the Military Criminal Code of Czechoslovakia (which is in this respect based on the Austrian Military Penal Code of 1855) lays down, in Article 8, that, subject to the exceptions provided by the law, the order of a superior does not justify a crime or a misdemeanour. The exception is that of Article 158 relating to the duty to obey orders—unless such orders clearly aim at the commission of a crime or of a misdemeanour.

[32] For the literature on the subject see Oppenheim, *International Law*, vol. II (6th ed., 1940), p. 454. n. 2. See also Sack in *Law Quarterly Review*, 60 (1944), pp 63–8.

In view of the substantial diversity, both apparent and real, in the judicial and legislative practice of various states, it is necessary to approach the subject of superior orders on the basis of general principles of criminal law, namely, as an element in ascertaining the existence of *mens rea* as a condition of account-ability. In the first instance, there can be no liability, or there must be diminished liability, if the accused acted in the legitimate belief that he was proceeding in accordance with law, both municipal and international. In his estimate of the legal position, the circumstance that he has received orders to act in a certain way must be regarded, *prima facie*, as creating in the accused the conviction of the lawfulness of the action as ordered. By the same token, the clearly illegal nature of the order—illegal by reference to generally acknowledged principles of international law so identified with cogent dictates of humanity as to be obvi-ous to any person of ordinary understanding—renders the fact of superior orders irrelevant.[33] Secondly, such a degree of compulsion as must be deemed to exist in the case of a soldier or officer exposing himself to immediate danger of death as the result of a refusal to obey an order excludes *pro tanto* the accountability of the accused—unless, indeed, we adopt the view, which cannot lightly be dismissed, that the person threatened with such summary punishment is not entitled to save his own life at the expense of the victim or, in particular, of many victims.[34] The result of the combination of these two principles will be, at the one end, that a person obeying an obviously unlawful order the refusal to obey which would not put him in immediate jeopardy, will not be able to shield himself behind the excuse of superior orders. At the other end, a person obeying, in an isolated case, an illegal order which is not on the face of it unlawful and disobedience to which would expose him to the full rigours of summary military discipline, may rely on the plea of superior orders. There will be a variety of intermediate situations between these two extremes.

There ought to be no doubt that should courts entrusted with the trial of war crimes disregard altogether the plea of superior orders, they would be adopting a course which could not be regarded as defensible. On the other hand, while the fact of superior orders sets a limit to the punishment of acts which might otherwise constitute war crimes, it need not warp the effectiveness of the law in a manner which may rightly be regarded as a perversion of justice. It will not cover crimes committed by superior authorities and officers acting under their own responsibility and initiative; it will not protect criminal acts committed by subordinates for purposes of private gain and lust; it will not shield acts com-mitted in pursuance of orders so glaringly offending against fundamental con-ceptions of law and humanity as to remove them from the orbit of any possible justification, including that of immediate danger to the person charged with

---

[33] This was clearly recognized by the German Supreme Court in 1921 in *The Llandovery Castle*, though it treated the fact of superior orders as an extenuating circumstance: *Annual Digest*, 1923–4. Case No. 232.

[34] *R. v. Dudley* (1884), 14 Q.B. 273.

the execution of the orders; it will not excuse crimes committed in obedience to unlawful orders in circumstances in which the person executing the crime was not acting under the immediate impact of fear of drastic consequences of summary martial justice following upon a refusal to act (the latter being crimes perpetrated by the vast army of officials in the occupied territories). If these limits of the doctrine of superior orders are taken into consideration, then its judicious application, far from defeating the ends of justice, may testify in a significant manner to the determination of the victorious belligerent to abide by the limitations of international law.

(2) Uncertainties of the Law of War

Similar considerations apply to the second factor which must in some ways limit both the scope of prosecutions for war crimes and their punishment. That factor results from the controversial character of some of the most important aspects of modern war. There are acts of warfare which an impartial international tribunal would hold to be contrary to international law, but the lawfulness of which has been to a sufficient degree a subject of controversy or uncertainty to preclude them from properly being the subject of a criminal prosecution before the tribunals of the victorious belligerent. Thus, for instance, it appears probable that—apart, perhaps, from the doubtful operation of the law of reprisals—an international tribunal would hold that the methods adopted by Germany in both World Wars in the matter of mine-laying or general devastation were contrary to international law. Yet, because of the controversial state of international law on those matters, there may be lacking in respect of such acts that degree of *mens rea* which, in matters of this kind, constitutes an essential condition of criminality. Such acts as general devastation or indiscriminate mine-laying may supply ample reason for condemnation and protest; they may afford ground for retaliatory action of a most sweeping and comprehensive nature like the British Retaliatory Orders in Council of November 1939 and July 1940; they may, at the end of the war, justify the imposition of collective sanctions by way of compensation or otherwise as distinguished from individual penalties of a criminal nature. But criminal proceedings before the municipal courts of the victor may seem to many a questionable method of removing outstanding doubts and laying down authoritatively the existing law on subjects of controversy.

Total war has altered the complexion of many a rule. At a time when the 'scorched earth' policy, with regard to the belligerent's own territory, has become part of a widespread practice, general destruction of property ordered as an incident of broad military strategy will not properly form the subject-matter of a criminal indictment. Modern warfare has raised, and, in some respects, left unsolved the problem of reconciling the fundamental distinction between combatants and non-combatants with the advent of new weapons and with the increase of the numbers of both combatants and non-combatants engaged in work of vital importance for the war effort. This applies in particular to the question of aerial bombardment of centres of population. The ubiquity and indefiniteness, enhanced by elaborate camouflage and by the dangers of vastly improved methods of defence, of legitimate objectives; the difficulty of localizing the effects of bombardment; and bombing by way of retaliation—all these factors may make it difficult to answer the question of the legitimacy of aerial bombardment by way of criminal prosecutions against individuals. It is doubtful whether, in this and similar matters, tribunals entrusted with the task of punishing war criminals are a proper agency for solving controversial and difficult problems of the law of war. For this reason it is probable that retribution for much of the ravages of war, of loss of life, and of destruction of property perpetrated with a criminal intent may have to remain outside the scope of prosecution of individuals for war crimes before the courts of the former enemy. This does not mean that the guilty State will escape all the consequences of such actions committed on its behalf. There remains, in particular, the duty of compensation such as is envisaged in Article 3 of Hague Convention No. IV or in Article 25 of the so-called Hague Air Warfare Rules of 1923. Neither will any uncertainty of the law shield persons accused of clearly criminal acts unrelated to the major aspects of disputed rules, such as deliberate machine-gunning of civilian refugees or, possibly, such acts of mere terrorism and frightfulness as the bombardment of Rotterdam in April 1940.

Moreover, it does not appear that the difficulties arising out of any uncertainty as to the existing law have a direct bearing upon those violations of the rules of war which have provided the impetus for the almost universal insistence on the punishment of war crimes. Acts with regard to which prosecution of individuals for war crimes may appear improper owing to the disputed nature of the rules in question arise largely in connection with military, naval and air operations proper. No such reasonable degree of uncertainty exists as a rule in the matter of misdeeds committed in the course of military occupation of enemy territory. Here the unchallenged authority of a ruthless invader offers opportunities for crimes the heinousness of which is not attenuated by any possible appeal to military necessity, to the uncertainty of the law, or to the operation of reprisals.

The fact of the controversial character of some of the rules of war tends not only to impose a limitation upon the scope of offences which may properly be prosecuted as war crimes. It has a direct bearing on the question of the plea of superior orders. If it is true that, as pointed out above, the obviousness and the indisputability of the crime tend to eliminate one of the possible justifications of the plea of superior orders, then the controversial character of a particular rule of war adds weight to any appeal to superior orders. An international tribunal may find that the order was illegal. But any justifiable element of doubt, however ill-founded, preliminary to such a finding must weigh with particular force in the decision of the court to dismiss the plea of superior orders.

(3) The Effect of the Operation of Reprisals

The same considerations apply, with even greater force, to the effect of the operation of reprisals—both in general and in relation to the plea of superior orders. In the first and in the second World War reprisals have been the legal cloak for the departure, some of which was unavoidable, from many of the accepted rules of warfare. In the sphere of maritime war the operation of reprisals in both World Wars has, in practice, replaced most of the traditional rules. In a sense, reprisals have often fulfilled the function which would normally have been left to agreement between States, namely, that of the adaptation of the law to the changed conditions of modern warfare. For this reason it is not always profitable to enquire whose original illegality opened wide the flood gates of retaliation. It is sufficient to note that the torrent swept away with devastating thoroughness many of the elaborate, though often controversial, rules.

A war crime does not necessarily cease to be such for the reason that it is committed under the guise of reprisals. But, as a rule, an act committed in pursuance of reprisals, as limited by international law, cannot properly be treated as a war crime. A tribunal confronted with the plea of reprisals as a justification of the offence will be faced with a task of considerable difficulty. International law regulates, in a necessarily rough and indeterminate manner, the occasions for and the use of reprisals both in peace and in war. It postulates the requirements of a prior attempt at redress by negotiation, of proportionality, of reasonableness, of compliance with fundamental principles of war such as respect for the lives of non-combatants, and of due consideration for the legitimate interests of neutrals. But the law on the subject is necessarily elastic.

The element of reprisals may have a significant and perplexing bearing upon the plea of superior orders. It has been shown that the strength of the plea of superior orders is conditioned by the degree of heinousness of the offence and its approximation to a common crime apparently divorced both from belligerent necessity and from elementary considerations of humanity. But the force of this latter consideration may become considerably impaired—though never totally eliminated—when the act has been ordered, or represented to the subordinate as having been ordered, in pursuance of reprisals against a similar or identical crime committed by the adversary. The subordinate may be expected, when confronted with an order utterly and palpably contemptuous of law and humanity alike, to assert, at the risk of his own life, his own standard of law and morality. This is an exacting though unavoidable test. But no such independence of conviction and action may invariably be expected in cases where the soldier or officer is confronted with a command ordering an act admittedly illegal and cruel but issued as a reprisal against the similarly reprehensible conduct of the adversary. We may attribute to the accused a rudimentary knowledge of the law and an elementary standard of morality, but it may be more difficult to expect him to be in possession of the necessary information to enable him to judge the lawfulness of the retaliatory measures in question in relation to the circumstances alleged to have given rise to them. An example will illustrate the position: No person can be allowed to plead that he was unaware of the prohibition of killing prisoners of war who have surrendered at discretion. No person can be permitted to assert that, while persuaded of the utter illegality of killing prisoners of war, he had no option but to obey an order. But the situation is more complicated when the accused pleads not only an order, but the fact that the order was represented as a reprisal for the killing by the adversary of the prisoners of his own State. When the German Supreme Court in the case of *The Dover Castle* acquitted in 1921 the accused who pleaded guilty of torpedoing a British hospital ship, the Court expressed the view that the accused were entitled to hold, on the information supplied to them by their superiors, that the sinking of enemy hospital ships was a legitimate reprisal against the abuse of hospital ships by the enemy in violation of Hague Convention No. X.[35] Moreover, there is room for the view that if the victorious belligerent has himself, in pursuance of reprisals, set aside international law in a particular sphere, he cannot properly make such acts on the part of his opponent the subject of prosecution for a war crime.

On the other hand, as in the matter of the uncertainty of the law of warfare, the impact of the operation of reprisals is not as considerable as would appear at first sight. In particular, it does not seriously affect that most potent source of war crimes which originates in the lawlessness and the brutality of the occupying State.

While it is imperative that we should bear in mind the limitations upon the prosecution and punishment of war criminals—limitations such as those following from the plea of superior orders, from the controversial character of some of the laws of war, and from the application of reprisals—it is of equal importance that we should not in this matter lose sight of the wood for the trees. These exceptions may make the work of the tribunals more intricate and more responsible, but there is no reason to assume that they will invariably affect the issue. Superior orders may be invoked, uncertainties of the law of war may be relied upon, and reprisals may be cited as an excuse—but that does not mean that when thus appealed to they will confound the ends of justice. They will be subjected to judicial scrutiny. They may be found sufficiently weighty to warrant acquittal; they may be considered in the light of and as having the effect of extenuating circumstances; or they may, upon careful investigation, be brushed aside as a flimsy device to cover the horrors of a war crime. At the same time, it is clear that all these three factors imply a limitation upon the punishment of war crimes which cannot be disregarded consistently with the determination to conduct the trials of war criminals within the limits which law and justice impose.

In addition to the limitations which the absence of *mens rea* imposes, in various degrees, upon the right of punishing war crimes there must be considered the question as to what can properly be regarded as a war crime such as to warrant

---

[35] *Annual Digest*, 1923–4, Case No. 231.

the demand for extradition or surrender to and punishment by the victorious belligerent. In particular, does every violation of a rule of warfare constitute a war
crime? It appears that, in this matter, textbook writers and, occasionally, military
manuals and official pronouncements have erred on the side of comprehensiveness. They make no attempt to distinguish between violations of rules of warfare and war crimes. The Commission on Responsibilities set up by the Paris
Conference in 1919 included under the list of charges of war crimes such acts as
'usurpation of sovereignty during military occupation', 'attempts to denation-
alize the inhabitants of occupied territory', 'confiscation of property', 'exaction
of illegitimate or exorbitant contributions and requisitions', 'debasement of the
currency and issue of spurious currency', 'imposition of collective penalties', and
'wanton destruction of religious, charitable, educational and historic buildings
and monuments'. In view of the comprehensiveness of this list it is in the nature
of an anti-climax to note that the number of persons whose delivery the Allied
States eventually demanded was inconsiderable.[36] It is possible that one of the
reasons for the failure to give effect to the decision to prosecute war criminals
after the first World War was the extent of the list of offences as adopted by the
Conference and the absence of a distinction between violations of international
law and war crimes in the more restricted sense of the term.

In drawing up, in an exhaustive fashion, the list of war crimes the Paris
Commission followed the somewhat academic treatment of the subject found in
some of the manuals of military law. Thus the British *Manual*[37] adopts a vague
and somewhat tautologous definition of 'war crimes' as 'the technical expression
for such an act of enemy soldiers and enemy civilians as may be visited by punishment or capture [*sic*] of the offenders'.[38] These war crimes, according to the
Manual, include, in particular, 'violations of the recognized rules of warfare by
members of the armed forces'. Within that category the *Manual* enumerates the
following as 'the more important violations': making use of poisoned and otherwise forbidden arms and ammunition; killing of wounded; refusal of quarter;
treacherous request of quarter; maltreatment of dead bodies on the battlefield;
ill-treatment of prisoners of war; firing on undefended localities; abuse of the flag
of truce; firing on the flag of truce; abuse of Red Cross flag and badge, and other
violations of the Geneva Conventions; use of cvilian clothing by troops to conceal their military character during battle; bombardment of hospitals and other
privileged buildings; improper use of privileged buildings for military purposes;
poisoning of wells and streams; pillage and purposeless destruction; ill-treatment
of inhabitants of occupied territory.

The above enumeration is admittedly by way of example. In that order of
thought, a more detailed list might include such violations of the rules of warfare

---

[36] The list comprised eight hundred and ninety-seven persons.
[37] Following closely the section on 'Punishment of War Crimes' in Oppenheim's *International
Law*, vol. II, §§ 251 and 252.
[38] Chapter XIV, s. 441.

as capturing enemy vessels employed in coast fisheries, or vessels charged with scientific or philanthropic missions; interference with mail boats or mailbags in breach of Hague Convention No. XI; unjustified destruction of enemy prizes; laying mines in breach of Hague Convention No. VIII; violation of such accepted rules of international law as exist in the matter of contraband and blockade; or the breach of any of the numerous and detailed provisions of the Geneva Convention of 1929 on the treatment of the sick and wounded and of prisoners of war.

It must be a matter for serious consideration to what extent an attempt to penalise by criminal prosecution at the hand of the victorious belligerent all and sundry breaches of the law of war may tend to blur the emphasis which must be placed on the punishment of war crimes proper in the limited sense of the term. These may be defined as such offences against the law of war as are criminal in the ordinary and accepted sense of fundamental rules of warfare and of general principles of criminal law by reason of their heinousness, their brutality, their ruthless disregard of the sanctity of human life and personality, or their wanton interference with rights of property unrelated to reasonably conceived requirements of military necessity. There is room for the view that the punishment of war crimes by the victorious belligerent ought to be limited to offences of this nature—offences which, on any reasonable assumption, must be regarded as condemned by the common conscience of mankind. Suggestions for some such limitation will occasionally be found in textbooks. Hall, in his weighty and precise manner, expressed an opinion to this effect. Referring to the right of the belligerent of 'punishing persons who have violated the laws of war, if they afterwards fall into his hands', he points out that no objection can be felt to the exercise of this right 'so long as the belligerent confines himself to punishing breaches of universally acknowledged laws'.[39] More recently, an able Italian writer, in a careful examination of the question, has suggested some such limitation.[40]

The task of defining, from this point of view, the scope of violations of the laws of war which ought to fall within the purview of punishment by the victorious belligerent is one of considerable difficulty. A seemingly administrative act of a political nature, like deportation or segregation of large sections of the population of the occupied territory, may, in its effects upon human life and in the cruelty of its execution, be indistinguishable from the common crime of deliberate murder. But it is a task which ought to be attempted. The result of the differentiation thus established between the two categories of violations of the law of war would not necessarily be to render immune from punishment or from the duty of compensation the less heinous manifestations of lawlessness. But these would be governed by a different procedure; in particular they would not fall within the purview of any demand for surrender as part of the armistice stipulations. On the other hand, it is probably unprofitable to attempt a distinction between the acts

---

[39] *International Law*, 3rd ed. (1883), s. 135.
[40] Balladore Pallieri, *La Guerra* (1935), p. 385.

of the defeated State as such and acts attributable directly to individuals. All acts of the State are attributable to individual persons. There are none which cannot be traced to a decision of an individual or of a plurality of individuals. Neither is it helpful to establish a rigid distinction between offences against life and limb and those against property. Pillage, plunder and arbitrary destruction of private and public property may, in their effects, be no less cruel and deserving of punishment than acts of personal violence. There may, in effect, be little difference between executing a person and condemning him to a slow death of starvation and exposure by depriving him of shelter and means of sustenance. Finally, no just or working differential test can be found in the possibility of establishing a direct connection between the criminal act and any individual victim or victims. The person who issues general orders for the killing of hostages is no less guilty than the person to whom we may be able to bring home a specific order for shooting a particular hostage or group of hostages. A commander who issues a general order calculated to prevent the saving of life after the sinking of merchant vessels is no less guilty than an officer or soldier who is found to have committed on his own initiative a crime of this kind. Assuming that indiscriminate bombardment of towns for the purpose of terrorizing the civilian population and the deliberate machine-gunning of civilian refugees are to be treated as war crimes irrespective of the plea of superior orders, the mere fact that an individual formed part of a bombing squadron responsible for such acts may be sufficient to stamp him as a war criminal although it is impossible to prove a direct connection between his conduct and the death of any individual person. Some legal systems recognize that when a group of persons, such as a gang of robbers, commit a crime, each and every member of the group may be convicted without proving that any particular member committed the criminal act.

IV. Safeguards of Impartiality and of Legal Equality in the Trial of War Criminals

It is incumbent upon the victorious belligerent intent upon the maintenance and the restoration of international law, to make it abundantly clear by his actions that his claim to inflict punishment on war criminals is in accordance with established rules and principles of the law of nations and that it does not represent a vindictive measure of the victor resolved to apply retroactively to the defeated enemy the rigours of a newly created rule. The persuasive force of any such professions must be impaired unless it is accompanied by the provision of safeguards of impartiality and by a measure of equality in the application of the law. The preservation both of the substance and of the appearance of impartiality is of particular importance in view of the fact that, in the circumstances of the situation, there cannot be any question of formal equality by a concession to the defeated belligerent of the identical right to punish any war criminals of the victor. Under existing international law this is in no way a condition of the valid exercise of that right by the victorious belligerent. Even in this respect, there may be means for mitigating the inequality fully authorized by the existing law.[41]

However, the most important aspect of the problem is that of guarantees of impartiality in the punishment of war crimes. These guarantees may, in theory, be achieved in three ways: I. By means of an International Criminal Court; II. By way of appropriate modifications of the organization of the municipal courts of the victorious belligerents adjudicating upon war crimes; III. By a system of quasi-international courts conceived as municipal courts of the belligerent the composition of which is not confined to its own nationals.[42]

I. *The International Criminal Court.* The problem of an International Criminal Court, in particular with reference to the punishment of war crimes, has been an almost continuous subject of discussion since the first World War. Not all of the reasons which have been adduced against the establishment of a court of this nature can be described as sound. This applies in particular to the objection based on the difficulty of reaching an agreement as to the law to be applied by it. In principle, there appear to be compelling reasons for the establishment in the future of an International Criminal Court having jurisdiction to try the crime of war (i.e. resort to war in violation of international law[43]) as well as certain categories of war crimes arising out of the conduct of hostilities proper and not involving common crimes against life and property. The jurisdiction over the latter, especially when committed in occupied territory, would seem more properly to lie within the province of local tribunals suitably reinforced by an international and neutral element acting expeditiously and having direct access to available evidence. However, regardless of the feasibility of establishing an International Criminal Court in the future, weight must be given to the following considerations of a practical nature:

(i) The establishment of an international institution of a novel character and of the scope and significance of an International Criminal Court is not a task which can be accomplished within a short period. At the same time there are compelling reasons which make it undesirable and impracticable to

---

[41] See below, p. 39.

[42] For a detailed discussion of the various types of court to try war criminals sea Glueck in *Harvard Law Review*, 56 (1942–3), pp. 1059–89. See also the judicious suggestions by Professor Hyde in *Proceedings of the American Society of International Law*, 1943, pp. 43–6.

[43] In this matter the position is now different from that which obtained in 1914 and which prompted the Commission on Responsibilities set up in 1919 by the Paris Conference to declare that 'by reason of the purely optional character of the institutions at The Hague for the maintenance of peace (International Commissions of Enquiry, Mediation and Arbitration) a war of aggression may not be considered as an act directly contrary to positive law'. The law of any international society worthy of the name must reject with reprobation the view that between nations there can be no aggression calling for punishment. It must consider the responsibility for the premeditated violation of the General Treaty for the Renunciation of War as lying within the sphere of criminal law.

postpone the punishment of war crimes for any prolonged period of years. It follows that, unless an International Criminal Court is already in existence at the time of the cessation of hostilities, those who link up the punishment of all war crimes with the establishment of such a court run the danger of sacrificing the substance of an urgent task for what may well prove to be the shadow of its intricate machinery.

(ii) In so far as the primary purpose of the establishment of an International Criminal Court is to secure an unimpeachable measure of impartiality, that purpose must be viewed in the light of the contingency, such as will arise at the termination of the second World War, that the world may be divided, with insignificant exceptions, into two opposing camps of belligerents. In such circumstances an International Criminal Court would hardly partake of the character of an impartial and detached judicial body. This is also a contingency which must be taken into consideration in connection with any war involving the great majority of states. No 'international' court in any true sense of the word is possible in such cases.

(iii) For the same reasons no adequate solution can be found in the establishment of an international tribunal composed of neutral judges or, generally, in giving neutral States a major share in the proceedings. There may be only a very few neutral states left. Some of them may be only nominally neutral. They may have identified themselves for many purposes with the cause or the outlook of one side. In a general war in which the overwhelming majority of States is animated by the consciousness that their cause is one of vindication and of survival of law and civilization, there will be a tendency to view at least some of the remaining neutral States as having shown themselves deficient in their sense of international solidarity at a supreme period of trial.

II. *Means for Securing Impartiality within the Framework of Municipal Tribunals.* If the establishment of an International Criminal Court is not an adequate instrument for securing the requisite degree of impartiality in the trial of war criminals, there arises the further question as to the possible safeguards on that behalf within the framework of the municipal courts of the victorious belligerent. The following are believed to deserve consideration:

(i) *Jurisdiction of Special Courts Composed of Professional Judges with the Participation of Military Assessors or Judges.* Some such composition of tribunals for the trial of war criminals, while not interfering seriously with their efficiency, would add to their authority and remove from them the reproach of a purely summary procedure. Exclusively military jurisdiction is fully justified during the actual hostilities. The justification is less obvious after the cessation of hostilities in respect of persons not captured in the course of military operations but surrendered by the enemy or neutral States after the conclusion of the armistice.

(ii) *The Expansion of Military Tribunals by the Inclusion of Lay Judges.* There is no compelling reason to assume that the result of some such expedient would be a serious impairment of the speed of the trials. There are weighty reasons for disposing of the trials of war criminals in the period between the armistice and the peace treaty, but it is doubtful whether this implies the necessity for anything in the nature of a summary procedure. The state of popular feeling in the period immediately following the armistice and the legal difficulties likely to be involved in some of the prosecutions may require that purely military courts should be reinforced by the inclusion of persons of judicial experience and possessing a wider knowledge of the law.

(iii) *Participation of Neutral Assessors.* Subject to what has been said above concerning the position of neutral States at the end of hostilities, there is a strong case for associating neutral assessors with the trial of war criminals. Neutral assessors might be given the right to participate actively in the trial by addressing questions to witnesses and to the accused, by being present at the deliberations of the court, and by being entitled to express concurrence with or dissent from its decision. It might be found possible to attach practical consequences to any dissent on their part, for instance, by way of granting to the accused a right of appeal in such cases.

(iv) *Participation of Enemy Assessors.* The attempt to secure not only the substance but also the forms of impartiality and of equality before the law need not stop at this point. There is force in the view that the defeated enemy should be given the opportunity, by providing assessors of his own, of participating in the work of the courts of his adversary engaged in trying war criminals. In particular, it must be considered whether, in the case of the participation of both neutral and enemy assessors, a judgment from which they have both dissented should not automatically be liable to review by a superior court regardless of any appeal by the accused.

III. *Quasi-international Courts of Appeal and Courts of First Instance.* Quasi-international tribunals are, in this connection, municipal tribunals of the victorious belligerent enlarged by the inclusion of judges from other countries, co-belligerent and neutral. This is a machinery particularly suitable for any appellate jurisdiction which may be set up. There may be obvious advantages from the point of view of justice and expediency in providing appellate courts which, while acting with all requisite expedition, would be in a position to bring to bear upon the cases before them a higher degree of detachment and a wider range of legal knowledge. Quasi-international courts thus set up might prove to a large extent a substitute for an International Criminal Court adjudicating upon war crimes. The presence of judges of foreign nationality, while not calculated decisively to influence the issue and while in no way derogating from the authority or reputation for impartiality of the national courts, would add to their proceedings the indispensable elements of publicity and detachment.

In considering these and similar safeguards it is necessary to bear in mind the fact that the due punishment of war criminals, unless it is accompanied by all practicable safeguards of impartiality and, to some extent, of mutuality, may be deficient both in effectiveness and in the part which it might otherwise play in the re-establishment of international law. Such proposals may be severely criticized by those who may see in them legalistic attempts to interfere with the just rigour of retribution; they may be adversely commented upon by others as not going far enough in preventing the punishment of war crimes from becoming a one-sided weapon of revenge wielded by the victors. In any case they must be studied in the light of the situation brought about by the victory of one of the belligerents able to impose upon the defeated enemy the surrender of war criminals. In a situation like this there can be no such degree of mutuality as alone would satisfy the purist, namely, the delivery to the defeated States of nationals of the victorious belligerents accused of having perpetrated war crimes. But even here there is room for a consideration of measures likely to ensure some approximation to equality. The victorious belligerent may openly proclaim his determination to investigate and to bring to trial any charges of violations of the law of war committed by his armed forces; he may give full publicity to the resulting judicial proceedings; he may offer to invite neutral or enemy participation in any procedure that may be adopted. Thus while taking steps towards ensuring an impartial trial of enemy nationals accused of war crimes, the victorious belligerents would at the same time do much to meet the reproach that justice has overtaken only the criminals among the defeated and not those among the victors. True statesmanship ought not to give any justifiable and avoidable excuse for any such reproach. Strengthened by the consciousness that he has gone to the extreme practicable limit of securing impartiality and equality before the law, the victorious belligerent will be in a position to disregard the charge that, amidst a sanctimonious claim to virtue, he has combined the roles of party and judge. In addition, he will be entitled to insist that, as a matter both of probability and of experience, the impartiality of the courts of the defeated State cannot be assumed. This is so not because the courts of the victorious belligerent are intrinsically entitled to a higher claim to excellence and impartiality. The reason is that the courts of the defeated State must, in the circumstances, act under the impact of bitter national resentment and hostility unredeemed by such magnanimity and foresight as the victor may be able to afford.

This latter consideration merits special emphasis. It may be usefully illustrated by reference to the activity of German courts which, in 1923 and 1924, were called upon to conduct the trial of German nationals accused of war crimes. German writers have repeatedly asserted that the German Supreme Court which tried the accused persons displayed a high degree of conscientiousness and impartiality. It is doubtful in the extreme whether that claim can be substantiated. Of the 901 cases which came before the Supreme Court, only thirteen ended in the condemnation and conviction of the accused. In those few cases the Supreme Court found the accused guilty of such crimes as maltreatment of prisoners of war[44]

---

[44] The *Muller* and *Neumann* cases, Cmd. 1422, pp. 26, 36.

and firing on the boats of survivors from hospital ships sunk by a submarine.[45] The Court inflicted relatively mild sentences of imprisonment. In 692 cases the Court came to the conclusion that there were no legal grounds justifying the continuation of proceedings. In a considerable number of cases relating to mal-treatment of prisoners of war the Court found that the accused, far from having been guilty of the charges, had gone out of their way to treat the prisoners with special consideration. The doctrine of superior orders and the plea of military necessity were elevated to paramount legal principles—a line of conduct which the Supreme Court pursued in subsequent years in connection with the interpre-tation of the Hague Regulations[46] and with attempts to punish for high treason German nationals accused of denouncing to the Allied Powers the violations by Germany of her obligations in the matter of disarmament under the clauses of the Treaty of Versailles.[47]

Neither, in the light of experience, are we in a position to place reliance upon the findings of any special commission of investigation instituted by a legislative body of the defeated State, however democratically constituted. In August 1919 there was set up, as part of a general committee on war responsibilities appointed by the German *Reichstag*, a sub-committee to investigate the charges of violations of the laws of war committed by both Germany and her allies. The Commission, whose work was largely under the direction of Professor Schücking, a distinguished international lawyer and subsequently one of the Judges of the Permanent Court of International Justice, produced a series of reports published in 1927 in five vol-umes under the title *Völkerrecht im Weltkrieg*. A study of these volumes permits the conclusion that the Commission did not exhibit a degree of detachment higher than that displayed by the Supreme Court. It exonerated Germany from the major charges of lawlessness and levelled grave accusations against the Allied Powers.

In the matter of charges of ruthlessness and terrorism in the course of the occu-pation of Belgium, the Commission accepted as proven the fact that there was waged a popular war (*Volkskrieg*) against the German forces and that there existed, accordingly, full justification for the resulting acts of suppression. In this connec-tion Professor Meurer, the principal *rapporteur* of the Commission, justified the indiscriminate killing of hostages. He said: 'In war every one is a sacrificial lamb. What appears to be humane is, from a higher standpoint, often the most inhu-mane. Is it not the innocent soldier who falls victim to the war crime on the part

---

[45]   *The Llandovery Castle, ibid.*, p. 45.

[46]   Thus in a case decided in November 1924, the German *Reichsgericht* held that the requisition by Germany of machines in occupied Belgium and their subsequent sale to private manufacturers was legitimate although contrary to the Hague Regulations. For these, in the view of the Court, left intact the principle that a State's right of self-preservation has precedence over international treaties (*Annual Digest*, 1923–4, Case No. 230).

[47]   The *Reichsgericht* rejected the view that the conviction of the accused would violate the rule of international law which prescribes that treaties must be fulfilled in good faith. For that principle, in the view of the Court, binds only the contracting party and not individuals (March 14, 1939: *Annual Digest*, 1927–8, Case No. 5).

of the inhabitant, and is not the killing of hostages meant to prevent this?... The commander who wishes to be humane may in fact prove very inhumane in relation to the soldiers entrusted to him and thus incur a grave responsibility.'[48] The Commission had no difficulty in holding that the 'dragging' (*Verschleppung*) by the French authorities of the inhabitants of the occupied parts of Alsace and Lorraine to France at the outbreak of war was contrary to international law.[49] But it expressed the considered view that the German decree of October 28, 1916, by virtue of which 'unemployed Belgian workmen who, after they had refused to accept work offered to them in Germany and, as the result, had become a charge upon public resources, were compulsorily transported to Germany in order to be provided with employment, was in accordance with Article 43 of the Hague Regulations and with international law at a time where there was not sufficient employment in Belgium and when that measure seemed to be urgently required for the restoration and maintenance of public order and public life.' The Commission had no doubt that these measures were not inconsistent with Articles 46 and 52 of the Hague Regulations which guarantee the rights of inhabitants, seeing that military requirements are paramount and that the maintenance of public order and public life are a military necessity.[50] The *Reichsgericht* had previously decided, in the course of criminal proceedings against Field-Marshal Hindenburg in respect of this charge, that his action was lawful.

With respect to the use of poison gas by the German armies, the Commission agreed that artillery projectiles containing such gases were first used by the German armies. But it declined to see in that practice a violation of the prohibition, contained in the Hague Declaration of 1899, 'of the use of projectiles the sole object of which is the diffusion of asphyxiating and deleterious gases' on the ground that this was not the 'sole object' of the explosives launched by the German artillery.[51] Neither, in the view of the Commission, was the use of these projectiles contrary to the prohibition, laid down in Article 23 (*a*) and (*e*) of the Hague Regulations, of the use of poison and poisoned weapons on the ground that these did not include poison gas. At the same time the Commission found that the French army was equipped with and first used weapons clearly prohibited by the Hague Declaration and the Hague Regulations, and that the subsequent use of the gas weapon by Germany was justified as a measure of reprisals. In the matter of air warfare, and in particular of air bombardment, the conclusion of the Commission was that the rules of international law on the subject had been violated not by Germany but by the Allied Powers.[52] The conduct of unrestricted submarine warfare by Germany was declared to have been in accordance with international law as a legitimate measure of reprisals against the unlawful blockade proclaimed by the Allies.[53]

[48] *Das Völkerrecht im Weltkrieg*, vol. II, p. 221.
[49] *Ibid.*, vol. I, pp. 167–85.   [50] *Ibid.*, vol. I, p. 193.
[51] *Ibid.*, vol. IV, pp. 7–9, 39–42.
[52] *Ibid.*, vol. IV, p. 53.   [53] *Ibid.*, vol. IV, p. 113.

Occasionally, it was only after a circuitous legal argument that the Commission arrived at a conclusion favourable to Germany. Thus with regard to Article 23 (*g*) of the Hague Regulations which prohibited 'belligerents to destroy or seize enemy property unless such destruction or seizure be imperatively demanded by the necessities of the war', the Commission agreed that that article lent itself both to a restricted and to a wide interpretation. 'Necessities of war' could mean either imperative military necessity directly connected with offensive or defensive action, or, generally, any military advantage accruing from devastation. The Commission expressed the view that the restricted interpretation was to be preferred. However, in a curious *non sequitur*, it proceeded to state that for the purposes of the investigation it was sufficient if it was satisfied that the military authorities in question considered in good faith military necessity to be involved: 'The Commission could not safely undertake a technical review of military necessity.' Having gone thus far, it had no difficulty in considering as legitimate the general devastation effected by the German army at the time of the retreat in 1917 to the so-called Siegfried line; the devastation during the retreat in 1918; and the destruction of the mines in Northern France and Belgium.[54] As a rule, however, the Commission avoided the appearance of undue restraint. With regard to the action of the Allied Powers in Greece it put on record its conclusion that 'there was hardly a rule of neutrality which had not been flagrantly violated by the Entente'.[55] The Commission entertained no doubts as to its own impartiality. It described its work as an 'historic innovation, seeing that never before had a parliamentary organ undertaken the task of pronouncing, exclusively by reference to international law, legal judgment on events and measures'.[56]

The above record of the German Supreme Court and of the Commission on Violations of the Laws of War throws light on the prospects of impartial application of international law by the courts and other agencies of a defeated State. It is a much-needed reminder of the fact that the cause of impartial justice may be served in ways other than a mechanical equality in procedure. It cannot in any way be interpreted as justifying the victorious belligerent in adopting methods summary in their nature and deficient in the essential safeguards of orderly judicial process and, within the limits dictated by circumstances, of a minimum measure of reciprocity.

V. Surrender from Neutral States

The provision of safeguards of impartiality and of other essential requirements of judicial procedure in the prosecution and trial of war criminals is directly relevant

---

[54] *Ibid.*, vol. I, pp. 61–4.
[55] *Ibid.*, vol. II, p. 16.
[56] *Ibid.*, vol. I, p. 6.

to the question of any duty of neutral States to refuse admission to or to surrender to the victorious belligerent persons accused of war crimes. For should the neutral State have reasonable ground to assume that a prosecution in respect of which surrender is requested is of a political character by virtue either of the nature of the alleged offence or of the absence of normal judicial safeguards of fair trial,[57] then in granting asylum and in insisting on maintaining it it may, it is submitted, be deemed to rely on the established principle of asylum for political offences. That principle, whatever may be its legal nature or extent, cannot accurately be denied a place in existing international law. This is one of the reasons why the question of admission of war criminals to and their surrender from neutral states cannot be exhaustively answered by the proposition that such persons have no right to asylum.[58] The implications of that proposition seem to be of some difficulty and must be considered in relation to admission, to extradition and to other forms of surrender.

The statement that there is no individual right of asylum is probably unimpeachable when viewed as a matter of admission of persons to the territory in which they claim asylum. It requires further consideration when looked at from the point of view of extradition. In this respect we must distinguish between any right of the individual under municipal and under international law. In some countries, like Great Britain and the United States, a person, once admitted, may be said, in respect of extradition, to have an individual right of asylum in two senses: in the first instance, in the absence of an extradition treaty he cannot be extradited. It is a rule of the common law that the Executive cannot hand over a person to a foreign jurisdiction unless in pursuance of a statute.[59] In these countries, statutory law makes extradition dependent upon the existence of a treaty of extradition with the foreign Power concerned. Secondly, by statute, a fugitive who is charged with a political offence or whose extradition has in fact been

---

[57] The close connection between non-extradition for political offences and the proper trial of the accused may be gauged from the fact that some States decline extradition if it is proved that it is intended to try the accused before an extraordinary tribunal: see, e.g., Article 9 of the Swiss Extradition Law.

[58] A proposition cogently expressed by Lord Simon, the Lord Chancellor, in his speech on 7 October 1942. He said: 'There is not, as many people suppose, any private right, recognized in International Law, called the right of asylum. That is to say, the fugitive—the criminal—who manages to get over the border into some other country, is not thereby by International Law entitled to claim to stay there.... It is perfectly competent for the country which receives the criminal, whether there is an extradition treaty or not, if that country thinks that it will be fulfilling its duty to the world, or if its conception of public policy requires or justifies it, to hand the criminal over': *Parl. Debates*, House of Lords, vol. 124, p. 582. For a qualification of the latter statement see below, p. 88. See also Moore, *Digest of International Law*, vol. II, § 291, on the laxity in the use of the term 'right of asylum'. And see Resolution of the Swiss Federal Council of 23 March 1921 (cited by Schlesinger in *Columbia Law Review*, 43 (1943), p. 964): 'L'étranger n'a pas droit à l'asile. L'Etat a simplement la faculté, en vertu de sa souveraineté, d'admettre sur son territoire un étranger, et il prononce en toute liberté.'

[59] For an emphatic affirmation of this rule see *Valentine* v. *United States* (1936) 299 U.S. 5.

requested with the intention of trying him for a political offence,[60] cannot be extradited. In other countries—like Sweden, Switzerland, and Turkey[61]—a person can be extradited regardless of the existence of an extradition treaty, but not in respect of political offences. In these countries the fugitive may still be said to possess, under municipal law, a right of asylum so far as political offences are concerned.

To what extent can it be said that there is a right of asylum under international law? It is difficult to reject with emphasis the view that there is such a right in respect of political offences—though, having regard to the procedural incapacity of the individual in the international sphere, it is even more difficult to assert its existence. However, apart from the latter limitation, we are confronted with the impressive fact that in the legislation of modern states there are few principles so universally adopted as that of non-extradition of political offenders. This being so, can we not maintain that the principle has become one of those 'general principles of law recognized by civilized states' which Article 38 of the Statute of the Permanent Court of International Justice has elevated to the authority of a source of international law?[62] The question may properly be raised although, in the context, it is largely theoretical for the reason that, as will be pointed out presently, war criminals are not, as a rule, political offenders.

Once we have reduced to its true proportions the question of the individual right to asylum, we may inquire into the legal grounds on which the victorious[63] belligerent can base his claim for the surrender of enemy war criminals who have taken refuge in neutral territory. That legal basis is provided, in the first instance, by the existing extradition treaties between the neutral State and the belligerent. These cover primarily, though not exclusively, offences committed in such parts of the territory of the requesting State as were occupied by the enemy. Thus, for instance, war crimes committed during the second World War in Russia by members of the German army of occupation and German officials who have taken refuge in Sweden will be covered by any extradition treaty in force between Russia and Sweden. Probably, if we take into account the locality of the causation (or of the origin) of the injurious action as distinguished from the locality of its effect,

---

[60] See s. 3 (1) of the Extradition Act, 1870.

[61] See below, n. 67.

[62] Suppose State A surrenders to State B a national of State C on a charge of having committed a political offence. The alleged offender clearly has no enforceable right under international law. But can his State complain that State A has violated an established principle of international law? Has the principle of non-extradition of political offenders crystallized into a customary rule of international law? In *Fiscal* v. *Samper*, decided in 1934, the Spanish Supreme Court held that 'delinquents who take refuge in a foreign country relying on legislation which promises them protection have acquired a true right, disregard of which would tend to weaken the law of nations and to introduce lack of confidence into international relations': *Annual Digest*, 1938–40, Case No. 152.

[63] The problem, it will be noted, does not arise as between the defeated belligerent and neutral states. The former, even if it were not prevented from doing so by the terms of the peace treaty, will have no occasion for requesting the surrender of the war criminals of the victorious belligerent. These will not find it necessary to take refuge in neutral territory.

the treaty will cover orders issued in Germany and taking effect in Russia. There are impressive judicial authoritative pronouncements in the national and international sphere asserting some such extension of the territorial principle.[64] Thus, while the provisions of the extradition treaties in existence between neutral states and the belligerent must be studied in detail in relation to any concrete situation, it is clear that they are likely to cover most of the possible war crimes both *ratione loci* and *ratione materiae*. They will cover, *ratione loci*, acts committed in such parts of the territory of the requesting State as were under enemy occupation; acts in or from the air over the territory of the requesting State and having effect in its territory; acts, wherever committed, having effect on what is constructively State territory, namely, vessels flying the flag of the belligerent;[65] and, probably, acts ordered by persons present in enemy territory but having effect in the territory of the belligerent requesting extradition. They will include, *ratione materiae*, the common crimes usually enumerated in extradition treaties like murder, assassination, manslaughter, wilful assault resulting in death or permanent disablement, rape, false imprisonment, crimes against personal liberty, robbery, and so on. Most of the illegalities perpetrated in occupied territory can be reduced to crimes such as those enumerated above.

Moreover, the limitation of extraditable offences to those committed within the territory of the requesting State is not an invariable feature of extradition treaties.[66] It is therefore possible that the extradition treaty between the belligerent and the neutral may cover offences committed in the territory of the defeated belligerent.

Although it is only the existence of an extradition treaty which entitles the victorious belligerent to insist on extradition as a matter of strict legal right, the municipal law of most states permits the granting of extradition irrespective of treaty—usually on the assurance of reciprocity or, occasionally, as a matter of international solidarity in the suppression of crime.[67] In so far as it is permissible to

---

[64]　See the authorities surveyed in the Dissenting Opinion of Judge Moore in *The Lotus* case, Permanent Court of International Justice, Series A, No. 10, pp. 73–83.

[65]　See, for a clear statement of the underlying principle, Moore, *Extradition* (1891), § 104.

[66]　For numerous examples of treaties in which this is not the case see *Harvard Research in International Law, Extradition* (1935), pp. 92, 93. See also *In re Amper*, decided by the Italian Court of Cassation, for an emphatic refusal to admit the relevance of 'questions of territorial jurisdiction if its own jurisdiction is not involved': *Annual Digest*, 1933–4, Case No. 149.

[67]　Article 1 of the Swiss Law on Extradition of 22 January 1892 provides for extradition 'on the condition of reciprocity [not necessarily through an extradition treaty], or, as an exception, even without that condition.' The same article lays down that extradition may be granted for an offence not envisaged in the treaty (*Harvard Research, Extradition*, p. 420). Similarly, the Swedish Extradition Law of 4 June 1913 provides, in Arcicle I, that extradition may be granted in the absence of an extradition treaty if the requesting State promises reciprocity (*ibid.*, p. 414). The position in Turkey is similar (*ibid.*, p. 428). The German Extradition Law of 23 December 1929 merely requires reciprocity (*ibid.*, p. 385). So does the Argentinian Extradition Law of 25 August, 1885 (*ibid.*, p. 356). The French Extradition Law of 10 March 1927 is to the same effect: see *Decerf's Case, Annual Digest*, 1935–7, Case No. 164. In *In re Vilca* the Supreme Court of Chile decided, notwithstanding the absence of an extradition treaty, to ask for the extradition of the accused from

speak of principles of international law in the matter of extradition, there is therefore no principle which requires the existence of a treaty as a condition of extradition or which prevents a State whose municipal law has hitherto been based on that requirement from abandoning it when necessary. If it attaches importance to its maintenance and if no valid extradition treaty exists between the neutral State and the victorious belligerent, it may still be open to and proper for the former to conclude an extradition treaty on traditional lines and subject to the accepted safeguards in the matter of political offences. A treaty so concluded and covering acts committed prior to its conclusion would in no way amount to an introduction of the reprehensible principle of retroactivity in the sphere of criminal law. There is high authority in support of that view.[68] A treaty thus concluded would not convert into a crime acts which hitherto had been blameless. It would not constitute an abandonment of the principle of political asylum properly conceived. It would testify to the recognition on the part of the neutral State of its moral duty to co-operate in the maintenance of international law and in the international suppression of crime whether committed under the guise of war or otherwise.

Assuming that the offence is otherwise covered by a treaty of extradition or that extradition can be effected without an extradition treaty, to what extent does the principle of non-extradition of political offenders—a venerable principle of impressive universality—exclude the duty of surrender of persons accused of war crimes? This question is of paramount importance, for no demand for extradition from neutral states is likely—or ought—to succeed if it is contrary to the principle of non-extradition of political offenders. On the other hand, the very sanctity of that principle requires that it should not be abused for sheltering persons who, behind the screen of war, have been responsible for common crimes which have outraged civilized mankind.

The law of extradition as applied by municipal courts provides a useful and necessary corrective to the view that any act having a political complexion is a

---

Peru on the ground that the crime (homicide) with which he was charged was 'in the nature of a serious crime against humanity' and that 'these are circumstances in which extradition of fugitives is proper, according to rules of public international law uniformly accepted by both States': *ibid.*, 1931–2, Case No. 136. In *In re Fernando Benet* the Federal Court of Venezuela, while denying, in the absence of a treaty, extradition on the charge of embezzlement, admitted that 'it was a generally admitted doctrine of Public International Law that crimes for which extradition must be granted [in the absence of a treaty] are crimes of a serious character and grave consequences constituting an equal danger to all nations': *ibid.*, 1925–6, Case No. 225. Soc also, to the same effect, *In re Diogenes Gonzalez, ibid.*, Case No. 226. For other examples of extradition notwithstanding the absence of a treaty see *In re Doelitzsch* (decision of the Italian Court of Cassation), *ibid.*, 1923–4, Case No. 156, and *In re Tsiaras* (a decision of the Roumanian Court of Cassation), *ibid.*, 1929–30, Case No. 173.

[68] See, for instance, *United States v. Hecht*, decided in 1927 by the United States Circuit Court of Appeals, where the court held not only that extradition treaties cover offences committed prior to their conclusion, but also that there is nothing to prevent a contracting party from recognizing 'somewhat belatedly...as criminal a well-known fact of commercial immorality': *Annual Digest*, 1927–8, Case No. 234. And see Hackworth, *Digest of International Law*, vol. IV (1942), p. 36. See also to the same effect the Swiss Law of Extradition referred to above, n. 67, and Articles 5 of the Japanese Extradition Law of 1895 (*Harvard Research, Extradition*, p. 411).

political act for the purposes of extradition. The conception of a political crime has a definite meaning in the law of extradition. A political crime is, in the first instance, one committed in the attempt to substitute one government for another or one form of government for another. Courts, including German courts, have attached decisive importance to that distinguishing feature of political crimes. Crimes committed by anarchists opposing all government;[69] crimes perpetrated as an act of political revenge;[70] crimes committed for motives of patriotism but unrelated to any attempt to change the government or the form thereof[71]—all these have been held by the highest municipal tribunals not to come within the category of political crimes protected from extradition. Municipal courts have long discarded the idea that the mere absence of a motive of personal gain is sufficient to impart to an offence the character of a political crime.[72] In the legislation of some countries, as, for instance, in the Belgian *attentat* clause, the predominance of particularly objectionable features of a common crime has sufficed to divest the offence of the otherwise clearly discernible complexion of a political offence.

It is probable that the conception of a political crime as limited to acts aiming at a change in the government or in the form thereof, does not exhaust all possible connotations of a political offence—although this is the usual meaning of political crimes as interpreted by courts in connection with extradition treaties.[73] In particular, it is clear that political offences must be deemed to cover all acts of treason in its wider sense, including treason committed during war by joining or assisting the enemy.[74] In connection with war crimes it is submitted that the notion of a political offence must be deemed to cover, in particular, the following three categories: (1) persons upon whom the victorious belligerent intends to wreak his vengeance for the sole reason that they participated in a war waged against him; (2) persons accused of such violations of the law of war as do not on the face of it amount to a common crime against individuals or property; (3) persons accused of acts whose criminality is subject to legitimate dispute for the reason either of the controversial nature of the rules of war in question or of their having been committed by one or both sides in the course of reprisals. Thus, for instance, if extradition were asked for in respect of the crime of initiating the

---

[69]   *In re Meunier* [1894] 2 Q.B. 415; *In re Kaphengst,* decided in 1930 by the Swiss Federal Court, *Annual Digest,* 1929–30, Case No. 189.

[70]   *Pavan Case,* decided in 1928 by the Swiss Federal Court, *ibid.,* 1927–8, Case No. 239; *In re Richard Eckerman,* decided in 1929 by the Supreme Court of Guatemala, *ibid.,* Case No. 189.

[71]   *Noblot Case,* decided in 1928 by the Swiss Federal Court, *ibid.,* Case No. 240.

[72]   There is an interesting analogy between this development and the more recent practice of states which refuses to treat *animus furandi* as the decisive characteristic of piracy.

[73]   A person who, during war, has committed treason by having joined the enemy of his country is a political offender—although his act does not aim at a change in the government or of its form.

[74]   The Supreme Federal Court of Brazil has described as political the offence of trading with the enemy: *In re Dr. Paulo Deleuze, Annual Digest,* 1919–22, Case No. 187. It will also be noted that the legislation of most States excludes from extradition purely military offences, (i.e. desertion and offences against discipline) as well as fiscal offences.

war in violation of the General Treaty for the Renunciation of War; if it were requested in connection with the charge of commencing the war in disregard of Hague Convention No. III providing for a declaration of war; if it were insisted on in respect of a decision on military policy in the conduct of war like the ordering of general devastation, or the abuse of a flag of truce; if it were demanded on account of requisitions and contributions contrary to the Hague Convention; or even, to adduce an extreme and controversial example, if extradition were requested of persons accused of sinking merchant vessels without warning—in all these cases there is room for asserting that they come within the general notion of political crime.

On the other hand, acts which *per se* constitute common crimes and which are contrary to rules of war cannot legitimately be assimilated to political offences. The fact that certain acts, otherwise criminal, like taking of life or causing bodily injury, are committed in pursuance of lawful warfare, deprives them of the stigma of criminality according to common law and renders them, in a certain sense, political. But once it has been established that such acts have been perpetrated in violation of the rules of lawful warfare, there vanishes the decisive factor which lifts them above the reprobation of common criminality.

Undoubtedly the border-line between lawful and unlawful acts of war is often a shadowy one, and to that extent the neutral State may deem itself entitled to considerable latitude in granting or refusing extradition. But the discretion wielded by the executive and judicial authorities of the neutral State must be exercised in good faith. Should the neutral State or its courts adopt a general policy of non-extradition in the matter of war crimes on the ground that they are political, the belligerent asking for extradition would, it is believed, be confronted *prima facie* with a breach of any existing extradition treaty. Should that happen, a remedy for the breach of the treaty might be found in some cases in any surviving obligation of compulsory judicial settlement. Thus, at the end of the second World War, as between Switzerland, for instance, and Poland, or Belgium, or Holland, the provisions of the Optional Clause might be found sufficient for the purpose. A decision of the Permanent Court of International Justice on the matter would, in substance, not be without effect as between states in whose relations the Optional Clause never was or has ceased to be operative, as, for instance, may be the case of Great Britain as the result of the British declaration of September 1939 suspending the operation of the Optional Clause with regard to disputes arising out of events occurring during the hostilities. A neutral State refusing to comply with its treaty obligations or to submit their disputed interpretation for international judicial decision would not only expose itself to a denunciation of the existing extradition treaties. The consequences of a breach of a treaty of this kind, in defiance of the public opinion of the world and in a misplaced insistence on the principle of asylum, may justifiably cover acts of reprisals and self-help appropriate to the occasion, especially if the neutral State can adduce no justifiable doubts as to the prospects of a fair and impartial trial.

It is now necessary to consider the question of surrender from neutral countries apart from the existence or the applicability of extradition treaties. What, in such cases, are the means by which neutral states may pursue a policy of abstaining from granting asylum to persons accused or likely to be accused of war crimes which cannot justifiably be treated as being of a political character? Assuming prudence and good faith on the part of the neutral State, the abuse of the right of asylum may be considerably reduced by its refusal to admit indiscriminately such persons to its territory. Their exclusion would be an administrative measure unlikely to raise problems of grave difficulty in the field of the municipal law of the neutral State. The belligerent may be in a position—and it will as a rule be wise for him to do so—to supply the neutral State with lists of persons accused of war crimes, with an indication of the nature and the circumstances of such crimes, so as to enable the neutral State to exercise discretion in the admission of enemy persons in case it does not wish to adopt a policy of general exclusion, a measure which it may deem incompatible with the principle of political asylum.

However, to consider this matter merely from the point of view of the admission of war criminals to neutral territory is to simplify the problem. The neutral State may not be able to prevent the illegal entry of such persons by land, by sea and, especially, by air. In that case, if it is unable or unwilling to surrender them to the *belligerent* owing to the absence or the inapplicability of an extradition treaty, it may still *depart* to their *home State* persons accused of war crimes who have entered its territory and with regard to whom no obvious considerations of political asylum prevent their deportation. The victorious belligerent will find means for bringing the deported individuals to justice in the same way as other enemy nationals accused of war crimes. Any previous warning by the neutral State against entering its territory will strengthen its position in the matter—just as any previous warning addressed by the belligerent to the neutral State[75] will put the latter on its guard against indiscriminate admission of fugitives fleeing from justice. Deportation is in most countries within the province of the executive authorities and although the law often limits their discretion in the matter, the antecedents of the persons concerned and the fact of their illegal entry are, generally, substantial factors in determining the discretion of the Executive. In proceeding to such measures of deportation, the neutral State will be legitimately guided by the respect due to the principle of political asylum conceived in the broad sense as indicated above. It will refrain, and legitimately and properly refrain, from a course of action which, in the natural course of events, might result in the delivery to the victorious belligerent of persons who, while having been guilty of violations of rules of warfare, are not accused of common crimes against life and, for reasons of private gain, against property. It will be entitled to take into consideration the prospects of a fair trial.

---

[75] Such as that addressed by Great Britain and the United States in July 1943 to Switzerland, Sweden, Spain, Portugal, Liechtenstein, Turkey, the Vatican City and Argentina.

We may now examine the legal implications of the situation arising from any obstructive attitude of a neutral State which, in acting out of a misplaced attachment to the humanitarian principle of asylum or out of ideological affinity with the defeated State, insists on offering the shelter of impunity to persons accused of war crimes of a non-political character and on refusing to surrender them either by way of extradition or by way of deportation. If that attitude is in violation of a valid treaty of extradition, the legal position does not give rise to difficulty.[76] In strict law the position would also seem to be clear when there is no applicable extradition treaty; there is in such cases no legal duty to extradite or to surrender the fugitive. It is generally maintained that in such cases the duty, if any, is a moral one. However, this is a view which is too rigid to be fully acceptable. Undoubtedly, in any specific case a State is under no legal duty to extradite unless it is bound to do so by treaty. But if a State were to decide to refrain altogether from concluding extradition treaties and to open its doors to criminal fugitives to the detriment of the peace and safety of its neighbours, would its action be legally unobjectionable? Ought we not to distinguish between the refusal to conclude any particular extradition treaty and a general licence to fugitives from justice? Do extradition treaties merely prescribe the conditions on which States agree to limit their sovereign discretion or do they give expression to an underlying general duty of extradition? Moore, who speaks with authority in his own right and as the author of a leading treatise on extradition, says: 'The right [to grant or to refuse asylum], therefore, is coupled with the duty, amply acknowledged by the multiplication of extradition treaties, to abstain from asserting the sovereign power for the purpose of shielding individuals charged with the crime from trial by competent judicial authorities. The right of sovereignty is conserved in determining the conditions and limitations under which the fugitive is to be delivered up.'[77] On the other hand, Hall, in a weighty exposition, gives expression to the predominant view in maintaining that 'positive international law . . . does not recognize the duty of extradition'.[78]

It is probable that a correct legal appreciation of the position must be sought by reference not to the limited subject of extradition but to the operation of the prohibition of an abuse of rights in relation to the territory of the State. The State's right of sovereignty over its territory, including its right to grant asylum to fugitives, is, in the absence of treaty obligations, exclusive and absolute. But if that right is used in a way prejudicial to the legitimate interests and claims of other States then it degenerates into an abuse of right which international law will not countenance. International law prohibits injurious use of territory not only in such matters as nuisance caused by uncontrolled emission of noxious fumes[79] or toleration of preparations for hostile expeditions into neighbouring territory.

---

[76] See above, p. 46.   [77] *Digest of International Law*, vol. III (1906), p. 757.
[78] *International Law*, § 13 (3rd ed., 1890, p. 61).
[79] See the Award in the *Trail Smelter Arbitration* (*United States* v. *Canada*), *Annual Digest*, 1938–40, Case No. 104.

The privilege and the moral duty of granting asylum to the persecuted ought not rashly to be interfered with. But the respect due to that privilege must, in turn, be conditioned by the manner in which it is exercised. The principle of asylum is put in jeopardy when it is used in a way amounting to a denial of justice to States which, in their collective capacity and in the persons of their citizens, deem themselves to have been victims of cruel and systematic crimes. An abuse of a right is not lightly to be presumed. The doctrine of abuse of rights is an innovation in international law. But, although an innovation, it has received endorsement by the Permanent Court of International Justice and, in obvious cases, it provides a legitimate starting point for remedial action.[80] The circumstance that extradition or surrender is refused in respect of crimes condemned by international law and international conventions to which the neutral State in question is a party, would be particularly relevant. The situation, in that case, would be totally different from that which arose as the result of the refusal of Holland to deliver William II of Hohenzollern whom the Allied and Associated Powers arraigned, in Article 227 of the Treaty of Versailles, 'for a supreme offence against international morality and the sanctity of treaties'. Neither the accusation of the Treaty of Versailles nor the request subsequently made in pursuance thereof was primarily based on law. As M. Clemenceau put it in his Note of January 11, 1920, this 'was not a case of a public accusation fundamentally of a legal character, but of an act of high international policy demanded by the conscience of mankind'. The situation is different when the insistence on extradition or surrender is based on charges of violation of the law and when the victorious belligerent is in a position to assert that the crimes perpetrated by the enemy were unprecedented both in their extent and in their studied disregard of legal restraints. Any dogmatic and obstructive attitude of the neutral in defiance of the sentiment of the overwhelming majority of States and in disregard of the moral obligation to co-operate in the enforcement of international law may create a situation in which the belligerent concerned may, in the interests of justice, feel called upon to enforce the law by self-help and by acts of retaliation—not to mention such measures of retorsion as every State is entitled to adopt in face of an unneighbourly and unfriendly attitude. Such measures, when prompted by the righteous indignation of powerful and numerous States and their peoples resisting what they deem to be a parochial and short-sighted generosity displayed in aloof disregard of the outraged sentiment of the vast majority of mankind may, in their effect, be indistinguishable from many a drastic sanction normally reserved for glaring breaches of the law of nations.

Undoubtedly, neutral States are entitled to ask for an assurance that the intended prosecution for war crimes will not be used as an instrument of revenge. They are entitled to claim the right to refuse extradition or deportation in cases in which, in their view, the alleged offence partakes of the character of an offence

---

[80] See Oppenheim, *International Law*, vol. 1 (5th ed., 1927), § 155*aa*.

against the rules of warfare in its wider sense rather than of a common law crime and in which they are prepared to submit that preliminary question to judicial determination. They may avail themselves of any offer, and insist on making it as effective as possible, to associate neutral assessors with the work of the courts charged with the trial of war criminals. But once such guarantees may be reasonably held to exist, any insistence by neutral states on sheltering war criminals constitutes not only an unfriendly act but also an assertion of formal rights of sovereignty in denial of that community of law which alone, in the long run, renders possible the normal observance of accepted rules of international law.

3

The Charter of the Nuremberg Tribunal and New Principles of International Law[1]

By Professor Stefan Glaser
Brussels

As I begin my presentation, I must make a remark right at the outset which will simultaneously be a clarification and an excuse. As you know, the issue of the legal nature of war crimes is so vast and complex that in a one-hour presentation, I will only be able to touch upon a few questions, and those only in a most superficial manner. And so, pardon me in advance if, in this brief exploration, you hear nothing revealing or new. This whole issue has been, especially in these recent days, considered under all of its aspects.

I propose to take as my point of departure the Charter of the International Military Tribunal that was a product of the Agreement of 8 August 1945, and was ultimately approved by 23 States.[2] Putting aside the Nuremberg trial and judgment which followed from this Charter, I would like to bring out several principles which, it seems to me, are of fundamental importance for public international law in general, and for international criminal law in particular.

Let us begin by noting that the Charter has pierced through the principle, or even the idea, of state sovereignty. Two facts lead us to this conclusion: first of all, the Charter recognized *individuals as subjects of international law*—that is, as subjects of international rights and obligations; second, the Charter broke with the doctrine of *immunity for what is called an 'act of State'*.

---

[1] Conference held at the Faculty of Law, University of Bâle, May 8, 1947.

[2] As is known, the Agreement of 8 August 1945, was concluded between the provisional government of the Republic of France and the governments of the United States of America, the United Kingdom of Great Britain and Northern Ireland, and the Union of Soviet Socialist Republics. The governments of the following countries subsequently indicated their adherence to the Agreement: Greece, Denmark, Yugoslavia, Holland, Czechoslovakia, Poland, Belgium, Ethiopia, Australia, Honduras, Norway, Panama, Luxembourg, Haiti, New Zealand, India, Venezuela, Uruguay, and Paraguay.

Considering the first of these issues, we see that the principle of individual responsibility, especially of those who acted in the name of and in the interests of their State, was established in similar ways by both the Agreement (Article 1) and the Charter (Article 6, Section 1) of 8 August 1945.[3]

It seems to me that this aspect of the Charter is entirely consistent with the modern tendency in public international law.

The theory which holds that international law is a law binding upon States only owes its origin, or at least its consolidation within international law, primarily to the idea of state sovereignty, an idea long pre-eminent in the doctrine of the State as well as in the law of nations. As the notion of absolute and discretionary sovereignty developed, it led to the doctrine that considered nothing but States in international relations. And thus, subjected to the States' supremacy, individuals were completely eclipsed from the realm of international law.

However, this concept was, as Politis rightly stated,[4] too much in conflict with reality to remain unchallenged for long. As we know, the most remarkable trend in human history has been the one leading the collective to the individual, the individual to the man. This evolution marked, at the same time, the progressive route taken by both human civilization and Christian culture. And it is thanks to it that, over the course of time, the very notion of the State has changed, along with its legal nature, its social role, and above all, its mission in regard to individual rights.

This is the reason why the concept of state sovereignty—which in the past regarded the State as a sort of supernatural creature, omnipotent and irresponsible, a fetish that swallowed men up—seems archaic to us today. An understanding that the State is only one mechanism among others which organizes relations among men, progressively gained ground in all civilized countries and shaped their respective doctrines of the State. As Dabin remarks,[5] the state exists only through individuals and for individuals; it proceeds from them, from the combination of their efforts and sacrifices, and it is destined to flow back to them in the form of all those advantages which result from participation in the public sphere. In fact, the sole creature which is a value in itself—and an infinite value—is the individual human. That is why Hauriou has maintained that individual rights form the basis of any form of social organization, which is, indeed, anterior and superior to any political constitution.[6]

---

[3] The first Article of the Agreement reads as follows: 'There shall be established after consultation with the Control Council for Germany an International Military Tribunal for the trial of war criminals whose offenses have no particular geographical location whether they be accused *individually* or in their capacity as members of the organizations or groups or in both capacities.' Article 6, Section 1 of the Charter, for its part, says: 'The Tribunal established by the Agreement referred to in Article 1 hereof for the trial and punishment of the major war criminals of the European Axis countries shall have the power to try and punish persons who, acting in the interests of the European Axis countries, whether *as individuals* or as members of organizations, committed any of the following crimes.'

[4] Politis, N., *Les Nouvelles Tendances du Droit International*, 1927, at 58.

[5] Dabin, J., *Doctrine Générale de l'Etat*, 1939, at 344.

[6] Hauriou, M., *Précis de Droit Constitutionnel*, 1929, at 611 and following.

Turning to international law, we must first of all recognize the fact that the community of nations must have human structures, which are similar in kind to those of our internal societies. It is, quite simply, composed of individuals grouped into nations. This explains, moreover, Bossuet's well-known saying that 'it is not on the nation, but on humanity in general, that the union of men must be founded'.

Nor, by the way, is the doctrine that provides that international law—like internal law—relates to individuals a recent one. On the contrary, it was already recognized and expressed by Grotius. He not only maintained that such law governed the relations of a State to its individual citizens and even to the subjects of other States, but also that international law allowed for capital punishment in regard to an individual who violated its precepts.[7]

From the middle of the nineteenth century, this doctrine began to gain more and more adherents. One of the first, Heffter, taught that a man per se—regardless of his nationality—had international rights and duties.[8] Later, these ideas were adopted and developed by Fiore in Italy, Westlake in England, Bonfils in France, Kaufmann and Rehm in Germany. And recently, to the extent that international law has become more democratic, this trend has taken even more radical forms. When one holds that the individual is the true end of all laws, one places the individual as the core subject of international law; further, one makes the individual the sole subject of this law. Thus, according to La Pradelle, 'the State is nothing by itself; the State is not an end in itself; ... the State is an instrument for an end'; and, when he poses the question, 'What is this end?' his answer is: 'Man.'[9] The same thought has most recently been reiterated by an eminent jurist in the following terms: 'The State—the person in international law—is at the service of man, the person of the law of nations.'[10]

In fact, the doctrine that recognizes the individual as an international persona, and therefore as a subject endowed with international rights and duties, is not only dominant in the science of public law, but, more importantly, it has increasingly penetrated into international practice. Limiting this to the field in which we are interested—that is, international criminal law—it should be enough to cite the 1864 Geneva Convention, revised in 1906 and 1929, or the Paris Agreement of 4 May 1910 on the white slavery trafficking, or, finally, the Treaty of Washington of 6 February 1922 on submarines and poison gas—all of which recognize the criminal responsibility of individuals for breaches of international law.

That is the principle which has finally been given formal recognition in the Agreement and the Charter of 8 August 1945.

---

[7] Grotius, *De Jure belli Ac Pacis*, III, c. XI § 16, Cl. 1. We can read there, among other things: 'There is no danger from prisoners and those who have capitulated or have wanted to do so. Hence, to justify their execution, it is necessary that a crime have been committed, and further, that it be such a crime as a fair judge would have considered meriting the death penalty.'

[8] Heffter, A. G., *Le Droit international de l'Europe*, 4th French ed., par Geffcken, 1883.

[9] De La Pradelle, A., *Les Principes Généraux du Droit International*, 1930, 2nd lesson, at 20.

[10] De La Pradelle, A., *La Paix Moderne*, 1947, at 88.

Turning to the 'act of State' doctrine, which still has its adherents today (suffice it to name Funck-Brentano and Albert Sorel)[11]—according to which no State can hold the citizen of another State responsible for acts which a person committed on the orders of, or with the approval of and in the name of his State, even if such an act constitutes a flagrant violation of international law—this doctrine, too, is based on the dogma of state sovereignty. I do not want to insist any more on the modern conception of this idea, but would merely like to emphasize that sovereignty in the external expression in reality signifies nothing more than the right of independence, the right to self-preservation, and the protection of the State's own interests. A well-known American internationalist, Coker, expressed himself recently in this manner:

International law...using the most general terms...recognizes that each State, as a sovereign community, has the legal right to choose its own form of government and to regulate its domestic affairs and the personal and financial relations of its citizens as it wills—*as long as it does not exercise this right in a manner which could endanger the peace and security of other States.*[12]

Thus are expressed the real limits of what is called the independence of the State: these limits result from the equal independence and autonomy of other States. This is why the views that the concept of sovereignty in reality no longer exists at the international level, has spread ever more widely. Karl Strupp expresses himself in the same manner, saying that 'the notion of sovereignty must be eliminated from international public law'.[13] We see the same kind of ideas in Garner's observations that 'the powers of the State come to an end at its borders',[14] and in Dabin's that 'the notion of external sovereignty is self-contradictory' and that 'no sovereignty is possible for one State in relation to another'.[15] Moreover, the same thought was expressed by Professor O. A. Germann in 1927 in the following terms: 'the rigid concept of state sovereignty in the international context contradicts not only the concept of a true international law but also, in reality, the sociological basis of modern international development'.[16]

[11] Here is what they say in their *Précis* of the law of nations at 224, 225: 'In principle, States are responsible only to themselves. The idea of a reciprocal responsibility between States contradicts the idea of sovereignty...'; and, later, 'If States took these principles literally, they would be perpetually at war. When...States believe that they must, in certain cases, consider themselves responsible, it is not a right they concede one to another, because then their sovereignty would be altered. It is a duty some impose on others, in the interests of general peace.'

[12] [My italics.] See Coker, 'Sovereignty', in 14 *Encycl. Soc. Sci.*, 1937, at 266.

[13] Strupp, K., *Eléments du Droit International Public, Universel, Européen, et Américain*, 2nd ed., 1930, at 40.

[14] Garner, J.-W., 'Des Limitations à La Souveraineté Nationale dans les Relations Extérieures', *Revue de Droit international et de Législation Comparée*, VI, 1925, at 37 and following, in particular page 41.

[15] Ibid. at 457.

[16] Germann, O. A., *Imperative und Autonome Rechtsauffassung*, 1927; reprinted in 1946 in *Methodische Grundfragen* (Problèmes de Méthode), at 31.

These observations make clear that the essential foundation of the old doctrine of an 'act of State' no longer applies in modern international law. Further, in the community of nations that we see in our time, the very idea of the independence of States has itself been effectively transformed into something different, namely, into the idea of interdependence. As the most recent events in the international arena have demonstrated—and as has always been the case—all States, big or small, are in reality reciprocally dependent, as much from the political point of view as from the economic point of view.

The entire doctrine of 'act of State' appears today to be a mere anachronism. All the more so since, according to modern doctrines of constitutional law, the State is responsible, not only for the actions it takes both in the administration of its assets and in the management of its public services, but also for its executive actions, that is, wherever the State invokes its imperium.[17] It would be completely contrary to modern principles of international law, as well as the contemporary ideas which underlie international relations between states, to recognize as a justification executive actions of states. Le Fur is certainly right in saying that: 'the State's competence is fixed by international law; if it goes beyond this competence, it violates international law, and must make reparation for the irregular act it committed'.[18] Clyde Eagleton expresses the same idea when he says that: 'there is no argument whether a State must submit to ever greater responsibility in matters of international law—that is inevitable. The only question that remains is to know what mechanism is the most effective for interpreting, applying, and imposing this responsibility.'[19]

And, in fact, international law has on several occasions recognized the principle of individual criminal responsibility for acts committed in the name of, or with the approval of, the State. We should recall the disposition of Article 3 of the Washington Treaty of 1922, in which the individual responsibility of an agent 'of any power whatever' is explicitly recognized, whether or not he acts 'on the orders of a hierarchical superior'. And then the dispositions of the Treaty of Versailles should be recalled, especially Article 227, which dealt with the indictment of the former German emperor. This example merits particular attention, since it clearly concerns responsibility for the actions of a State. For it is evident that an offence against 'the sacred authority of treaties'—which the article in question refers to—can only be committed by someone acting in the name of and in the interests of the State.[20]

Thus, in recognizing the responsibility of those who acted 'in the interests' of their states (Article 6), as well as the responsibility of heads of state (Article 7), the

---

[17] See on this issue Michoud, L., *La Théorie de la Personnalité Morale et son Application au Droit Français*, 3rd ed., 1932, v. II, 257 and following.

[18] Le Fur, 'Règles Générales du Droit de la Paix', in the *Recueil des Cours*, vol. LIV, 1935–IV, at 11.

[19] Clyde Eagleton, *The Responsibility of States in International Law*, 1928, at 229.

[20] The entire falsehood of the theory of 'Acts of State', according to which all responsibility is made to disappear, has recently been demonstrated by Professor Sheldon Glueck, of Harvard University, in his book, *The Nuremberg Trial and Aggressive War*, 1946, at 46 and following.

IMT Charter has done nothing more than to consecrate a principle previously recognized by public international law.

In recognizing the criminal responsibility of the State in the person of its agents, the IMT Charter at the same time *rejected the idea of the state being responsible as a legal entity.*

It is true that the old axiom: *Universitas delinquere non potest* (A corporation can do no wrong), is no longer a commonplace of legal doctrine. On the contrary, it is often contested in doctrine and jurisprudence. Its opponents base their position on the idea that legal persons are capable of having a will distinct from that of the physical persons of which they are composed. Whether one speaks here of the 'separate will of a federation' (Hafter),[21] or of 'a collective will' which is 'greater in intensity, and consequentially different from the sum of its individual wills' (Mestre),[22] or of 'a real and proper will which can exert itself for ends condemned in criminal law' (Valeur),[23] or finally of 'a concentration of criminal responsibility which is produced in the underlying artificial person' (Hauriou)[24]—all these arguments lead to the same idea, expressed by Sighele: that an action resulting from the cooperation of several individuals will never be a mere addition, but a product.[25]

All of these notions may have some relevance from a psychological or philosophical point of view, but they are devoid of any legal value, especially in the context of criminal law. Besides, their proponents recognize that their applicability depends on the actual circumstances of each case. Thus, Hauriou requires—in order that such responsibility be admitted—that criminal intent be found, not only in the executive bodies, but also that it be shared by all the members of the group (or, at least, by the great majority of them), and that it has been developed in the context of the concept of the State or that of the community.[26] However, this condition—which would, in any case, be difficult to establish—is certainly not often satisfied. If we take a war of aggression as an example, something which would be recognized today as an international crime, we will recall Bismark's words that 'it is never the nations which want war; it is always only small minorities [which do]'. The events of the war from which we have just emerged simultaneously test and demonstrate the profound significance of these words. How well we still remember the words of Winston Churchill's broadcast not long ago, about his country's entrance into the war: 'This is a war of one man, and of one

---

[21] Hafter, E., *Die Delikts- und Straffähigkeit der Personenverbände*, 1902, at 19. As far as I know, the distinguished author no longer maintains this opinion of the criminal responsibility of artificial entities.

[22] Mestre, *Les Personnes Morales et le Problème de leur Responsabilité Pénale*, 1899, at 20.

[23] Valeur, R., *La Responsabilité Pénale des Personnes Morales dans le Droit Français et Anglo-Américains avec les Principaux Arrêts Faisant Jurisprudence en la Matière*, 1931, at 21.

[24] Ibid. at 207, footnote 42.

[25] Sighele, 'Le crime collectif', in *le Compte Rendu du 5e Congrès d'anthropologie criminelle*, Amsterdam, 1901, at 74.

[26] Op. cit. at 207, footnote 42.

man alone.' We find the same idea elsewhere, in Politis, when he says: 'The true, the only responsible parties in wars are the governments which choose or tolerate the recourse to force.'[27]

From the standpoint of contemporary criminal law, we must reject this doctrine for several reasons. It is well known that criminal law has evolved from what was called objective responsibility—that is, responsibility for the consequences produced—toward subjective responsibility—that is, responsibility for fault. This evolution has culminated in two incontestable facts: first, that modern criminal law is, solely and exclusively, applicable to or interested in individuals—that is, a living human being—as the possible subject of a criminal prosecution. Second, that it makes liability dependent upon the culpable state of mind of the agent. Now, it is certain that the concept of criminal responsibility for legal persons is in flagrant contradiction with these facts.

First of all, say what you like, nothing could change the fact that a legal person is not a living human being. No matter which attitude one takes—that is, which standpoint one chooses, or what theory is advanced—we must always recognize that such entities are actually merely legal creatures, a product of a legal artifice. The legal person is a creation, invented by jurists and justified by the needs of social, economic, or political life. It is not a being which 'can laugh or cry', as Kohler says.[28] It follows that such a being manifestly does not have a proper biological or psychic life, and, as a consequence, as far as it is concerned, is not affected by all issues regarding conditions or factors relevant to responsibility or culpability.

The Swiss Criminal Code, similarly, only recognizes the individual responsibility of the representatives or agents of legal entities (Articles 172 and 326).

Next, does the Charter which is our subject *reject the principle of legality of crimes and punishments* that is expressed in the adage: '*nullum crimen, nulla poena sine lege*'? That is the fundamental issue, so controversial and contested at present. Our response is the following: in effect, the Charter rejects the literal application of this principle, but it does not reject the spirit or the idea conveyed by it.

First of all, it must be noted that this principle is not mandatory in public international law. As is well known, the principle first appeared and later developed on the basis of written law, as its very content makes clear. It is evident that it cannot be applied to customary rules, given that it requires that an action, to be punishable, be first recognized in legislation. From which it follows that wherever the law does not have a written, legal foundation (that is, is not codified)—as, for example, in England where, we know, the law is formed by judicial rulings, as well as by means of analogy—the principle is in fact unknown. The *ex post facto* application, even of a statutory provision, is recognized in judicial practice. Thus, retroactivity in law is not, as is stressed in the literature, 'hostile to the spirit of English law'.

---

[27] Ibid., at 129.
[28] Kohler, J., in 'Kritische Vierteljahrsschrift', v. XXXVI, at 518–19.

Now, with regard to international law, we know very well that thus far, despite all the efforts expended and all attempts made, especially in America, this law has still not been codified, but remains based on custom or usage. One could claim, perhaps, that the first success in these codifying efforts in the field of criminal law is precisely the Charter, inasmuch as Article 6 defines those crimes that are within the Tribunal's jurisdiction. But even in those cases where regulations do have a written basis, as in the case of treaties or conventions, the source of the law may still be found in custom. It would be difficult, in fact, to grant to conventions the same status we attach to a codification, given that they merely consolidate a prior state of affairs: they specify and perhaps complete a pre-existing international custom. In this regard, the London Naval Treaty of 1930 is very instructive. The declaration which precedes its provisions affirms in clear terms: 'The following are accepted as established rules of international law.' A contrary theory would be inadmissible, since it would lead to the conclusion that there could be a divergence between the state of affairs established by a convention and that established by international custom.

We therefore conclude that in current international law there is no place for the principle *nullum crimen sine lege*. As with other matters which comprise the subject of international law, here, too, one must trace the source of its regulations back to customs. It would therefore be untenable to claim, based on that principle, that only those acts which violate rules that have been written down into conventions could be regarded as criminal offences or crimes of war. No distinction can be made in this matter between rules stipulated by conventions and other rules of international law.

The best evidence of what is the proper point of view on this subject is furnished by the Fourth Hague Convention, regarding the laws and customs of war on land. As is clear from the Preamble of that Convention, its authors were well aware that the rules embodied in the Convention do not exhaust the recognized principles applicable to this subject. In the Preamble—after having declared that: 'It has not, however, been found possible at present to concert regulations covering all the circumstances which arise in practice'—the authors conclude:

Until a more complete code of the laws of war has been issued, the High Contracting Parties deem it expedient to declare that, in cases not included in the Regulations adopted by them, the inhabitants and the belligerents remain under the protection and the rule of the principles of the law of nations, as they result from the usages established among civilized peoples, from the laws of humanity, and the dictates of the public conscience.

This statement in the Preamble is also of great practical importance. It not only provides precious interpretive guidelines whilst also acknowledging that the lacunae of the Convention could always be filled by those principles specific to international law. Even though this declaration is to be found in the preamble of a specific convention—the Hague Convention—we must, nonetheless, take notice that it is certain that the principle which it formally recognizes also affects other conventions which have followed it. For example, we must admit that the dispositions of the 1949 Geneva Conventions on the treatment of prisoners of war or of the sick and wounded, or the London Naval Treaty of 1930, or the 1936 London Protocol (as to the fundamental obligations for saving the lives of civilians in submarine warfare) should also be interpreted on the basis of the principle that is stated in this Preamble.

However, to such an argument one could respond with the following: the relevance of that principle is limited to the situation where it is an international jurisdiction that is called upon to apply it. But, what is the situation in cases where national tribunals—in States where the principle of legality of crimes and punishments holds sway—are involved in judging war criminals?

In such cases, let us note from the start that the legal basis for the identification and punishment of acts considered as war crimes *has always been international law, and not internal law.* Today, it is common knowledge that war criminals may be prosecuted and punished only for violations of international law, whether the proceedings take place before an international or a national tribunal. It would be incorrect, then, to claim that a belligerent applies its own laws when prosecuting a war criminal within its own jurisdiction. Such a view would be correct only insofar as the internal law merely represents a confirmation by a state of existing rules of international law. Nowadays, it is a universally admitted principle that states which recognize public international law are thereby subject to it, and are obligated to adapt their internal legislation to its rules. In some countries, moreover, such as the United States and Great Britain, international law is even considered to be part of their national law. Whence it is, for example, that the 'British Military Manual', in authorizing punishment for violations of the 'recognized rules of war-fare', refers to violations of international law, and not of British law.

In light of this state of affairs, we could conclude that in those cases, too, where national courts administer justice for such violations, the rule, *nullum crimen sine lege,* cannot be validly invoked.

Nonetheless, were we to set aside this line of reasoning, would it then in effect be true that national tribunals, when judging war crimes which are not clearly specified in their national law, do so in contradiction of the principle of legality of crimes and punishments?

To answer this question, we must take into account the significance of this principle and its role in criminal law generally. As we know, the principle appears in the legislation of continental countries in reaction to the arbitrariness that had earlier prevailed in the realm of law and jurisprudence. It owes its existence to political circumstances above all; in its evolution, it is the operation of constitutional law that certainly plays the most important role. It was first regarded as a most effective guarantor of individual liberty and of the security of law. Only later was it developed and expanded from the standpoint of criminal law. And here, too, its role was to insure the protection of the innocent and to prevent abuses in the administration of justice. It aimed especially at ensuring that an act which was permitted, and was therefore legal, at the moment when it was done, could not later be punished. This is the essential point and the reason for the existence of this principle. And we must admit that, from this point of view, its value is incontestable.

But, if its essential role lies in such an idea, does it actually stand in the way of the prosecution and punishment of war crimes when these crimes were not explicitly defined in criminal law, even though the authors of these crimes violated fundamental principles of international law?

It seems to me that in regard to such offences, the principle is in fact not violated. It is not that the acts in question have only recently come to be stigmatized as illegal by the decisions of tribunals or by a new law. Quite the contrary, they have possessed that character for a long time. At the time when they were committed, they were considered illegal, not only in the public conscience of the civilized world, but also in the legislation of civilized countries. If these crimes had not yet been explicitly dealt with in a given criminal code, it is only because the author of the code had a less inventive mind than the perpetrators of these crimes. It was always duly recognized that criminal law would protect certain values and interests: human life, liberty, honor, etc. But what had not been foreseen were the new *forms*, generally more inhumane, by which these interests could be violated. It had not been foreseen, for instance, that recourse could be made to all the scientific methods of psychological and moral torture to which we have, unfortunately, been witnesses during this war. One could not foresee all the modern means of humiliation. The legislator wanted to protect life, but he had not considered that there were indirect means which could deprive a man of his life, as for example by forbidding him to consult a doctor or to obtain necessary medication. One could not imagine that a woman could be forced to become pregnant, that men could be buried alive, etc. In a word, one could not imagine or foresee when writing the law that criminals could become so barbarous, that the civilization of a nation could descend to such a level. But *who* could maintain that such acts are not, and were not already, stigmatized as illegal by all civilized nations when they were committed? *Who* could claim that a law which declared that these were punishable acts would have surprised the perpetrators?

As noted above, the principle (*nullum crimen*) has as its guiding idea that an act which was legal at the time when it was committed cannot be punished *ex post facto*; but this idea was never—never—to be that the most abominable of crimes could go unpunished simply because a lawmaker had not foreseen all the forms or methods possible to accomplish them! As Graven has said recently, to apply this principle blindly to international subjects would signify, in effect, 'the complete reversal of the meaning of the maxim; it would no longer assure the rule of law and the protection of the innocent from unjust condemnation; on the contrary, it would block the law and shield the guilty from justified punishment'.[29]

---

[29] Graven, J., 'En Assistant au Procès des Criminels de Guerre', *Les enseignements de Nuremberg*, 1946, at 21.

The IMT Charter of 8 August 1945, *rejects in principle a defence drawn from orders given by a hierarchy or by a superior officer*, what is called in Anglo-Saxon doctrine, 'the plea of superior orders'.

It rules in Article 8, in fact, that: 'The fact that the Defendant acted pursuant to order of his Government or of a superior shall not free him from responsibility, but may be considered in mitigation of punishment if the Tribunal determines that justice so requires.'

This is an issue that occupies a respectable place in criminal law and has long been discussed in the literature. The modern tendency is, as we know, rather reluctant if not plainly opposed, to recognize such a circumstance as a legal justification. Domestic criminal laws, the French and Belgian codes, for instance, regard this fact as a justification but limit it in such a way as to reduce its practical effect, whilst other laws, such as the Swiss criminal code (Article 64), regard it as a mitigating factor; yet other laws may well be silent on the whole question, which means that such circumstances could be taken into consideration only from the perspective of a mistake [on the part of the accused] or a state of necessity—this is the position of the Polish Code of 1932.

The same tendency appears in military criminal codes, with the exception of Anglo-Saxon law. The 'British Military Manual', along with the 'United States Rules of Warfare', clearly provides a valid legal justification in such cases. It is interesting to learn, however, that the principle adopted in the military manuals is completely opposed to the position of prevailing criminal and constitutional law in both countries. In Great Britain (as well as in the United States), a soldier can never invoke the order of a superior order as a valid defence, and such an excuse will never absolve him of the responsibility for an illegal act. This is a principle that has long been established in the jurisprudence of that country, and we recognize in it an effective guarantee of democracy itself.

In international law, similarly, the trend is manifestly one of clear rejection of the defence of superior order. The Commission on Responsibilities, instituted by the 1919 Peace Conference, expressed itself in that sense;[30] the expression of similar views may be found in the commentaries on Article 3 of the 1922 Washington Convention, where it is provided that one cannot invoke such a defence in the case of unlimited submarine warfare; finally, the same approach is manifested in a German judgment concerning the case known as 'The Llandovery Castle', in which a Leipzig court ruled that: 'an order does not absolve the accused of his crime...if such an order is universally known to be contrary to the law'. However, as we know, this observation did not prevent the same Court from acquitting defendants on the basis that they acted 'under orders', as was the case in the notorious case of Karl Neumann, the commander of a submarine which sank the English hospital ship, *Dover Castle* without prior warning.[31]

[30] The Commission on the Responsibility of the Authors of the War and Sanctions. See *La Documentation Internationale*. La Paix de Versailles, III, 1930, at 475.

[31] Dumas, J., *Responsabilité Internationale des Etats à Raison de Crimes ou de Délits Commis sur leur Territoire au Préjudice d'Etrangers*, 1930, at 391.

It seems that under international law this issue may be resolved on the basis of general principles recognized by criminal law. It is certain that a rule establishing the receipt of an order as a basis for acquittal would be incompatible with modern principles of individual criminal responsibility. On the other hand, it does not follow that such circumstances—an offence committed under orders—*never* could or should provide a justification for its author, that is, absolve him of responsibility. What we argue is that the perpetrator's liability for a crime should be examined in each particular case, according to the general rules of criminal responsibility. It could turn out, in fact, that the perpetrator of a war crime acted without culpability because he was ignorant of the illegality of his act, or because he was acting in a situation that would amount to a state of necessity. It would be useful, however, to establish in such cases (that is, where an act constitutes a violation of international law, but can be justified in the specific circumstances by reason of ignorance of its illegality) a presumption of wrongdoing. This, in effect, would amount to an exception to the general principle in criminal matters that the accused should be presumed innocent.

Such are the admissible limits of exoneration for war crimes. To go beyond them would, in practice, render justice powerless. In this domain especially (that is, in matters of war crimes), to admit the principle of a perpetrator justifying himself as acting under orders would, in effect, mean that these crimes could be committed with impunity. In an absolutist or dictatorial regime, notably, it would irresistibly lead to the responsibility—however illusory—of a single individual!

Does the Charter adopt *the principle of collective responsibility*, as it seems it might according to certain of its provisions? It does, in fact, establish in Article 9, paragraph 1, that: 'At the trial of any individual member of any group or organization the Tribunal may declare (in connection with any act of which the individual may be convicted) that the group or organization of which the individual was a member was a criminal organization.' And Article 10 continues,

In cases where a group or organization is declared criminal by the Tribunal, the competent national authority of any Signatory shall have the right to bring individuals to trial for membership therein before national, military or occupation courts. In any such case the criminal nature of the group or organization is considered proved and shall not be questioned.

However, such a conception is not in fact synonymous with the idea of collective responsibility as generally understood. The idea behind such forms of responsibility is understood as responsibility *for another*, or *for someone else's act*: responsibility, therefore, *for wrongdoing committed by a third person*—while in the case dealt with in the Charter, everyone must answer for his own conduct, that is, *his own participation* in one of these organizations. Such an interpretation is not, in fact, contrary to the principle of subjective responsibility which, we know, forms the foundation of modern criminal law.

Moreover, such an interpretation is not without precedent in the history of criminal law. A very interesting precedent on this subject is provided by the British India Act, No. 30, 15 November 1836, published in the *British India Statute Book* of 1836. This Act concerns a very dangerous Indian criminal organization known by the name 'The Thugs'. This was a powerful fraternity of assassins who killed under cover of a religious idea. The Act provides that 'whoever shall be proved to have belonged either before or after the passing of this Act to any gang of thugs either within or without the territories of the East India Company shall be punished with imprisonment for life with hard labour'.

However, it is not necessary to go all the way to India to find a similar conception of criminal responsibility. It is well known that in France as in Belgium, the Criminal Codes recognize the notion of 'criminal conspiracies' (*societas scelerum*), whose members may be held responsible by the sole fact of their membership to such an organization, regardless of crimes committed subsequently. Membership in itself is considered a crime against public order and the security of the state. Likewise, a similar concept has been adopted by the new Swiss Criminal Code which provides for the concept of 'unlawful associations' in its Article 275.

The Charter recognizes *initiating a war of aggression as a crime 'against peace'*. In doing this, has the Charter established a new principle in international law?

We do not think so. In fact, from medieval canon lawyers, up to Grotius and Vattel, international law has strived to distinguish between cases where the use of force was legal and those where it was not. Credence began to be given to the rule that a war was legitimate only if it was undertaken to restore a law that had been violated; in all other cases, it would be held to be an abuse of force. Unfortunately, this doctrine was lost with the triumph of the concept of absolute power. The idea of sovereignty, as Politis remarked, killed the theory of the *jus ad bellum* (just war).[32]

But the necessities of life never ceased to react against such abuses of force. In the final decades of the nineteenth century, they succeeded in reawakening the conscience of mankind to the earlier idea that unjust war should be forbidden. That is the spirit which brought about the Hague Conferences, whose mission it was to 'call for the reign of peace throughout the world'.[33] If, as M. de Beaufort says, these Conferences marked a decisive moment in history, it is because, for the first time, they brought forth—above the sovereignties of States—a human creation, a superior sovereignty, instituted directly by the universal Creator.

Several years later, in the preamble of the 1924 Geneva Protocol, wars of aggression were explicitly stigmatized as an international crime, as it had been, moreover, a year earlier in the project for a treaty of mutual assistance. Since that time, the idea that such war would constitute an international crime has reappeared continually in international acts and in the doctrine of the law of nations.

---

[32] Ibid., at 100 and 101.
[33] De La Pradelle, A., *La Paix Moderne*, 1947, at 18.

One could say, without exaggeration, that it has been adopted by the universal conscience of civilized nations.

We know that the Pact of Paris has placed wars of aggression formally outside law, and that in the 1933 London Conventions, the notion of the aggressor found a precise definition.[34] One knows as well that the Treaty of Versailles not only characterized such wars as an international crime, but, even more, recognized and held to be criminally accountable the individual responsible for starting the First World War.

The same trend appeared in the other hemisphere, too. Let us recall that in 1928, during the course of the sixth Pan-American Conference in Havana, twenty-one American republics unanimously adopted a resolution which declared that: a 'war of aggression constitutes an international crime against the human species'. The same idea reappeared in the treaty of 'Non-Agression [*sic*] and Conciliation', signed in Rio de Janeiro in 1933, and ratified by twenty-five nations, including the United States.[35]

Finally, let us recall that the same idea—that considers wars of aggression an international crime—was adopted by other international Congresses and by unofficial international institutions. It should be enough to mention resolutions adopted at the Universal Peace Conference in Athens in 1929, at the conferences of the Inter-Parliamentary Union, of the 'International Law Association', and of the International Association of Criminal Law.[36]

All of which proves sufficiently that well before the outbreak of the Second World War, the consideration that a war of aggression constitutes a crime against the law of nations had developed in the conscience of peoples and in international relations to such an extent that one must recognize that an international custom had been formed in this regard, and in consequence that this consideration had already acquired the significance of a principle of international law. It is therefore not astonishing that in front of the General Assembly of the League of Nations, M. Politis, one of the reporters of the 1924 Geneva Protocol, could maintain on this subject that: 'War of aggression is not only condemned, not only considered an international crime, but is also hemmed round with sanctions, and accompanied by the punishment needed to prevent it and if need be to repress it.'[37]

---

[34] Quincy Wright, 'The Concept of Aggression in International Law', in *The American Journal of International Law*, v. 29 n. 13, July 1935, at 373 and following.

[35] Sheldon Glueck, quoted above, at 31 and following.

[36] See on this whole issue the report by V.-V. Pella, *La Guerre-Crime et les Criminels de Guerre, Réflexions sur la Justice Pénale Internationale, Ce qu'elle Est et Ce qu'Elle Devrait Etre*, 1946, at 31 and following. See also: Sottile, A., 'Les Criminels de Guerre et le Nouveau Droit Pénal International Seul Moyen Efficace pour Assurer la Paix du Monde', in the *Revue de Droit International* 4, 1945.

[37] Kelsen, formerly of the University of Vienna and at present at the University of California, in an article which appeared in the *California Law Review* of December 1943, expressed himself on this subject in the following manner: 'Any inquiry into authorship of the Second World War does not raise problems of extraordinary complexity. Neither the *questio juris* nor the *questio facti* offers any serious difficulty to a tribunal. Hence there is no reason to renounce a criminal charge made against the persons morally responsible for the outbreak of World War II', (546). Finally, it

Thus, the Charter has, on this subject, done nothing more than confirm a principle that had already been well established in public international law.

Finally, the Charter invokes, when defining criminal acts, *the laws of humanity*. It establishes, in effect, a category of offences under the name of 'crimes against humanity'.

That is one of the Charter's most characteristic features, one which is, moreover, entirely consonant with the guiding principle of the evolution of international law. Have not laws of humanity in fact always been a source from which international law drew its precepts and commandments? Grotius and Vattel had long ago taught—well before humanity intervened so dramatically on the scene of the nineteenth century[38]—that a Sovereign had the right to take up arms in order to punish nations which committed grievous wrongs against the law of humanity (natural law). In 1876, Professor Arntz very precisely set out the principle that humanity is justified in intervening 'whenever a government, though acting within the limits of its right of sovereignty, violates the rights of humanity'.[39] Professor Antoine Rougier, in 1910 dedicated a fine and masterful study to these multiple instances of humanity's appearance. In fact, how often in recent times has international law not made a clear appeal to the principles of humanity? We have already cited the famous imperative of the Preamble to the Fourth Hague Convention of 1907, which invokes 'the laws of humanity and the dictates of the public conscience'. And we know, in accordance with the regulations concerning the laws and customs of war, that prisoners of war (as is said in Article 4) 'must be humanely treated', and that (as is said in Article 22) 'the right of belligerents to adopt means of injuring the enemy is not unlimited', but that those alone are permitted which are consonant with principles of humanity. Moreover, the very prohibition of the war of aggression, the placing of such wars outside the law, and its condemnation by international law as a crime against the law of nations: this fact, formally recognized at last by this Charter, wasn't it also dictated by reason of humanity? In effect, as Politis had emphasized, there is nothing more inhumane than war itself; and it is surely for this reason that the Nuremberg Tribunal stigmatized the initiation of a war of aggression as 'a supreme international crime'.

Nonetheless, we must emphasize that the Charter, in admitting the notion of 'crimes against humanity' as such, made an important step forward: in effect, it consecrated the idea that a universal principle of humanity forms part of the contemporary law of nations; even more, it established, at the same time, that humanity would be protected by the imposition of criminal sanctions.

---

is interesting to learn what Professor Lauterpacht of Cambridge University said on this subject in a talk he presented to the 'International Commission for Penal Reconstruction and Development' in Cambridge: 'The law of any international society worthy of that name must reject with reprobation the view that between nations there can be non aggression calling for punishment, and it must consider the responsibility for the premeditated [*sic*] violation of the General Treaty for the Renunciation of War as lying within the sphere of criminal law.'

[38] See on this issue Dumas, J., cited above, at 303 and following.

[39] See Arntz, in the *Revue de Droit International et de Législation Comparée*, 1876, at 675.

It is to this special feature of the law of nations that, if you will permit me, I would like to address one final remark.

We know how ancient the controversy is—and it is still vibrant with us— concerning the idea of natural law and its relation to positive law. We know, as well, that Catholic authors have shown unwavering fidelity to natural law, most often taking St Thomas Aquinas' classic conception and dressing it up (as Claude Du Pasquier has said most recently)[40] in modern clothes. Clearly, this is not the moment for me to dive into this study. But, if I might be permitted to say this: international law provides us with an eloquent testimony—while at the same time demonstrating the fact—that the real source of the idea which forms the essence of the law—the idea of justice—*is natural law*: that law is made of eternal moral truths which are born with mankind, which each of us has in his conscience, and which are immutable. As we have seen, every time there has been a search for fundamental principles of conduct to impose upon States and individuals as the ruling concepts in international relations and the mutual relations of States, nothing has been found better or more certain than to refer to those moral ideas which are the foundation of natural law—to that idea of international morality to which Politis consecrated his fine posthumous study.[41] We are familiar with the famous imperative in the preamble to the Fourth Hague Convention which invokes 'the laws of humanity'; we also know that, when the former German emperor, Wilhelm II of Hohenzollern, was placed under public indictment, it was done 'for supreme offense against international morality'. The British manual of military law, too, lays down that the source of the laws of war has been sought in the commandments 'of religion, of morality, of civilization, and of knightly honor'. Plato, too, expressed the same ideas in the fifth book of his 'Republic', more than two thousand years ago. Most recently, in the Statute of the International Court of Justice, we find—amongst those sources of international law which the Court should apply—'the general principles of law recognized by civilized nations', the rules of natural law, that is, which coincide with those rules admitted by the generality of civilized states. Finally, what other than natural law could the authors of this Statute have had in mind when they authorized the Court to render its judgments *ex aequo et bono* (according to equity and the good)—when they invoked, that is, this idea of 'equity' which even today remains so characteristic and so dear to the English juridical spirit?

Positive or juridical law is, it is true, the instrument of the State in its policies. But whatever these may be, the supreme—and, at the same time, essential—goal of juridical law must be to serve justice, defend it and safeguard it. This is also the mission of international law, as far as war crimes are concerned: every time someone violates 'the commandments of religion, of morality, of civilization, and

---

[40] Du Pasquier, Cl., *Introduction à la Théorie Générale et à la Philosophie du Droit*, 2nd ed., 1942, at 297.
[41] Politis, N., *La Morale Internationale*, Editions de la Baconnière, Neuchâtel, 1943.

of knightly honor', it is the role of international law to re-establish these ideals, to re-establish the reign of justice. It is its role to give satisfaction to the conscience of the peoples, to the demand for retribution which the illustrious Cardinal Mercier affirmed in his unforgettable words: 'Public retribution is a virtue. Crime— justice's despoiler—whether committed by an individual or a collectivity, must be repressed. Our consciences are stirred, are anxious, are tortured, as long as the guilty have not been put in their place.'

4

The Nuernberg Trial and Aggressive War

By Sheldon Glueck
Harvard Law School

I

On August 8, 1945, the four major Powers entered into an executive agreement,[1] in which they provided for the establishment of an *ad hoc* International Military Tribunal for the trial of war criminals whose offenses 'have no particular geographical location,' and, in an Annex to the agreement, set forth a Charter for the 'Constitution of the International Military Tribunal.'

Article 6, clause (b) of the Charter includes, among the acts to 'be considered criminal violations of International Law' and 'within the jurisdiction of the Tribunal,' the act of *'Launching a war of aggression.'* And the indictment which is the basis for the historic prosecution of the Nazi ringleaders at Nuernberg implements this in 'Count Two: Crimes Against Peace,' the opening paragraph of that charge being as follows:

All the defendants, with divers other persons, during a period of years preceding 8th May 1945, participated in the planning, preparation, initiation and waging of wars of aggression, which were also wars in violation of international treaties, agreements and assurances.[2]

Is there a rational and just basis for regarding a war of aggression (*i.e.*, one not clearly justifiable on the grounds of self-defense or as an executive act of punishment by the community of law-abiding States against a law-violating member) as an international crime? And if the launching of an aggressive war is to be deemed a criminal offense, who is the criminal? The aggressive State? Its responsible

---

[1] *Agreement by the Government of the United States of America, the Provisional Government of the French Republic, the Government of the United Kingdom of Great Britain and Northern Ireland and the Government of The Union of Soviet Socialist Republics for the Prosecution and Punishment of the Major War Criminals of the European Axis* (1945) 13 U. S. Dept. of State Bull. 222; Trial of War Criminals (Dept. of State Publication 2420, Washington, 1945) 13 [hereinafter cited as Trial of War Criminals].

[2] Trial of War Criminals 39.

(*i.e.*, policy-making) statesmen? Its responsible military leaders, such as members of its General Staff?

Judging from available published data, this idea of including the launching of an aggressive war—a 'crime against peace'—among the offenses for which the Axis Powers were to be held liable had its origin,[3] so far as American policy is concerned, in a report to the President made on June 7, 1945 by the American Chief of Counsel for the prosecution of major war criminals. Justice Robert H. Jackson there said:

It is high time that we act on the juridical principle that aggressive war-making is illegal and criminal.[4]

Speaking of the alleged 'retroactive' nature of a trial and punishment for the launching of legally prohibited (*i.e.*, aggressive) warfare, Justice Jackson argued:

International Law is more than a scholarly collection of abstract and immutable principles. It is an outgrowth of treaties or agreements between nations and of accepted customs.[5] But every custom has its origin in some single act, and every agreement has to be initiated by the action of some state. Unless we are prepared to abandon every principle of growth for International Law, we cannot deny that our own day has its right to institute

---

[3] During the preparation of the author's book, WAR CRIMINALS: THEIR PROSECUTION AND PUNISHMENT (1944) (hereinafter cited as GLUECK) he was not at all certain that the acts of launching and conducting an aggressive war could be regarded as 'international crimes.' He finally decided against such a view, largely on the basis of a strict interpretation of the Treaty for the Renunciation of War (Briand-Kellogg Pact), signed in Paris in 1928. He was influenced, also, by the practical question of policy. Since liability of the leading Nazi malefactors under familiar principles of the laws and customs of war and the Hague and Geneva Conventions was clear, it seemed to be an unnecessary and dangerous complication to resort to prosecution for the 'crime' of aggressive war, involving a doctrine open to debate and one which might require long and questionable historical inquiries not suited to judicial proceedings. *Id.* at 37–38. Further reflection upon the problem has led the writer to the conclusion that for the purpose of conceiving aggressive war to be an international crime, the Pact of Paris may, together with other treaties and resolutions, be regarded as evidence of a sufficiently developed *custom* to be acceptable as international law.

[4] Report of June 7, 1945, from Justice Robert H. Jackson, Chief of Counsel for the United States in the prosecution of Axis War Criminals reprinted in (1945) 39 AM. J. INT. L. (Supp.) 178, 187; (1945) 12 U. S. DEPT. OF STATE BULL. 1071, 1077; TRIAL OF WAR CRIMINALS 9. But see Bernays, *Legal Basis of the Nuremberg Trials* (1946) 35 SURVEY GRAPHIC 5–9; Levy, *The Law and Procedure of War Crime Trials* (1943) 37 AM. POL. SCI. REV. 1052, 1077.

[5] Compare the following: 'A major fallacy of the American representatives on the Commission of Responsibilities, as of the German delegates to the Versailles peace conference, was to take it for granted that the characteristics of a fully developed system of law are indispensable to all "Justice according to law." Lansing and Scott wanted a world legislature and world criminal *legislation* to exist before establishment of a world criminal court. But a court can also enforce the common or unwritten law….As Sir James Stephen points out, "It is not till a very late stage in its history that law is regarded as a series of commands issued by the sovereign power of the state. Indeed, even in our own time and country that conception of it is gaining ground very slowly. An earlier, and to some extent a still prevailing, view of it is that it is more like an art or science, the principles of which are at first enunciated vaguely, and are gradually reduced to precision by their application to particular circumstances. Somehow, no one can say precisely how…certain principles came to be accepted as the law of the land." That branch of the law of nations which deals with prohibited acts of warfare is as yet as undeveloped as was the early English common law.' GLUECK 97–98.

customs[6] and to conclude agreements that will themselves become sources of a newer and strengthened International Law. International Law is not capable of development by legislation, for there is no continuously sitting international legislature. Innovations and revisions in International Law are brought about by the action of governments designed to meet a change in circumstances. It grows, as did the Common-law, through decisions reached from time to time in adapting settled principles to new situations.[7] Hence I am not disturbed by the lack of precedent for the inquiry we propose to conduct.[8]

Nevertheless, the case for prosecuting individuals and States for the 'crime' of launching an aggressive war is not as strong as the case for holding them responsible for violations of the recognized laws and customs of legitimate warfare.

　　Is it strong enough to support the relevant count in the Nuernberg indictment?

II

At the outset it is not amiss to refer to the fact that the United Nations could have executed the Nuernberg defendants without any judicial procedure whatsoever. The 'law' of an armistice or a treaty is, in the final analysis, the will of the victor. Although duress may be a good ground for repudiation of an international contract entered into during a period of peaceful relationships between law-observing States, compulsion is to be expected and is an historic fact in the case of international agreements imposed by a victorious belligerent State upon the vanquished. It is frequently claimed that all agreements between States must be in conformity with international law; but it must not be forgotten that such inter-State 'agreements' as armistices and treaties of peace also *make* international law. In the final analysis, the main considerations which limit the action of a victorious belligerent in imposing an armistice or a treaty of peace are a decent respect for the judgment of history, and the fear of later reprisal. One can only recall, in passing, to what extent these considerations played a part in the agreements imposed by the Germans upon the States they vanquished.

　　The United Nations could, then, have disposed of the Nazi ringleaders summarily by 'executive' or 'political' action, without any trial at all and without any consideration whatsoever of whether the acts with which the accused were charged had or had not previously been prohibited by some specific provision of international penal law. The exile of Napoleon to St. Helena is frequently cited as an example of such executive action.[9] And a political disposal of the case

---

　　[6] 'Much of the law of nations has its roots in custom. Custom must have a beginning; and customary usages of States in the matter of national and personal liability for resort to prohibited methods of warfare and to wholesale criminalism have not been petrified for all time. "International Law was not crystallized in the seventeenth century, but is a living and expanding code." ' *Id.* at 14.

　　[7] See note 5.

　　[8] Report of Chief of Counsel, *supra* note 4 at 187; TRIAL OF WAR CRIMINALS 9.

　　[9] Napoleon's first exile—to Elba—is also an illustration. By the Convention of April 11, 1814, entered into between Austria, Prussia, Russia and Napoleon, the latter agreed to retire to Elba.

presented by notorious enemies of international law need not be limited to mere imprisonment. If ever there was a gang of malefactors who deserved extermination without the privilege of legal defense, it is the Nazi ringleaders. Assuredly, enough reliable information of their deliberate mass-murders was at hand to have amply justified their execution without a formal trial. In his historic address after the sinking of the *Greer*, President Roosevelt correctly called the Nazi ringleaders 'international outlaws,'[10] just as Napoleon, before his banishment to St. Helena, had been formally declared to be an international outlaw. It would have been poetic justice of the most appropriate kind to have dealt with the Nazi-Fascist ringleaders summarily.

But the United Nations wished to proceed in a more civilized way. So the victors provided for indictment and trial. They wished to give the accused every reasonable opportunity to disprove, by documents and witnesses,[11] the charges as formally drawn and as supported by an overwhelming mass of evidence. 'The victor may justly consider it unwise to disdain the aid which existing law is in a position to offer...at the close of a war the essential purpose of which is to vindicate the law of nations.'[12] Even notorious criminals caught red-handed ought, in a civilized polity, to be given an opportunity to explain and defend. And, even pirates, who under the law of nations may be punished by any State capturing

---

After his escape and re-entry into France with an armed force, the Congress of Vienna on March 13, 1815, issued a Declaration that by having violated his agreement Napoleon had 'destroyed the sole legal title upon which his existence depended...placed himself outside the protection of the law, and manifested to the world that it can have neither peace nor truce with him.' The Powers declared that Napoleon had put himself outside 'civil and social relations, and that, as Enemy and Perturbator of the World, he has incurred liability to public vengeance.' Had the Powers followed the recommendation of Field Marshal Blücher, Napoleon would then have been shot on sight as one who, under the above Declaration, was an 'outlaw.' But after Napoleon's surrender to the British, a Convention was entered into on August 2, 1815 by which Napoleon was 'considered by the Powers...as their Prisoner,' his custody to be 'specially entrusted to the British government,' the 'choice of the Place and of the measures which can best secure the object of the present stipulation' being 'reserved to His Britannic Majesty.' BRITISH AND FOREIGN PAPERS (1814–15) 665; see also 727 *et seq.*; *id.* (1815–16) 200 *et seq.*; 56 GEO. III, cc. 22, 23 (1816). Statesmen of the United Nations have at various times solemnly declared the Nazi leaders to be subject to punishment for their war crimes. See note 75 *infra.*

[10] *Address by the President, September 11, 1941* (1941) 5 U. S. DEPT. OF STATE BULL. 193, 196.

[11] Section IV (Art. 16) of the Charter of the International Military Tribunal is entitled, 'Fair Trial for Defendants,' and provides for the giving of detailed particulars in the indictment; the furnishing of the indictment and all appurtenant documents, in appropriate translation, to the accused; the permitting of the defendant, during preliminary examination or trial, to give any relevant explanation of the charges; the translation of the examination and trial proceedings into a language understandable by the accused; the granting to him of the right to conduct his own defense or have the assistance of counsel; and the granting to him of the right to present any evidence in support of his defense and to cross-examine the prosecution's witnesses. TRIAL OF WAR CRIMINALS 19. When it is remembered that the victors could have shot the Nazi leaders with no trial at all without violating international customary law, it must be conceded that the United Nations are treating the Nazi leaders with high consideration. One recoils from the thought of what the Nuernberg defendants would have done to our leaders had they won the war.

[12] Lauterpacht, *The Law of Nations and the Punishment of War Crimes* (1944) BRIT. Y. B. INT. L. 58.

them, should, according to modern international law, be given the benefit of a trial if that be feasible.[13]

There are, of course, dangers in the subjection of such international outlaws as the Nazi ringleaders to a formal trial; and many publicists and lawyers would have preferred the summary execution of the Nuernberg defendants. In fact the most authoritative statement on the fate awaiting war criminals—the Moscow Declaration of October 30, 1943, which was made by the foreign secretaries of the United States, the United Kingdom and the Soviet Union, 'in the interests of the thirty-two United Nations'—hinted that disposition of the Nazi ringleaders might be by executive action; for, after promising to return the ordinary offenders to the scenes of their crimes for trial by local courts, it provided that that decision was 'without prejudice to the case of German criminals whose offenses have no particular geographical localization, and who will be *punished by joint decision* of the Governments of the Allies.'[14] However, it was finally decided to subject them to trial;[15] and this involves the application of international law.

Before considering the question whether the waging of an aggressive war may legitimately be regarded as an international crime, it will be helpful to review certain of the proceedings at the close of the first World War.

III

The Commission of Fifteen appointed by the Preliminary Peace Conference at the end of World War I to examine the responsibility for starting that war and for atrocities committed during its conduct went into the question whether 'acts which provoked the World War and accompanied its inception,'[16] such as the invasion of Luxemburg by the Germans in violation of the Treaty of London of 1867 and their invasion of Belgium in violation of the Treaties of 1839, were criminal. It pointed out that the deliberate breaches of these 'contracts made between the high contracting parties to them,'[17] which involved 'an obligation which is recognized in international law,'[18] were the cynical work not of 'some outside Power, but by one of the very Powers which had undertaken not merely

---

[13] 'In former times it was said to be a customary rule of International Law that pirates could at once after seizure be hanged or drowned by the captor. But this cannot now be upheld, although some writers assert that it is still the law. It would seem that the captor may execute pirates on the spot only when he is not able to bring them safely into a port for trial....' I OPPENHEIM, INTERNATIONAL LAW (5th ed., Lauterpacht, 1937) 492.

[14] 'It should not be assumed that the procedure of trial will be necessarily adopted.' Winston Churchill, Statement of October 4, 1944, N. Y. Times, Oct. 5, 1944, p. 4 col. 4. But see note 75.

[15] TRIAL OF WAR CRIMINALS 13.

[16] *Commission on the Responsibility of the Authors of the War and on Enforcement of Penalties* (1920) 14 AM. J. INT. L. 95, 118.

[17] *Id.* at 119.

[18] *Ibid.*

to respect [Luxemburg's and Belgium's] neutrality, but to compel its observance by any Power which might attack it.'[19] But despite these 'culpable acts,' despite this 'high-handed outrage . . . committed upon international engagements, deliberately, and for a purpose which cannot justify the conduct of those who were responsible,'[20] the Commission was 'of opinion that no criminal charge can be made against the responsible authorities or individuals [and notably the ex-Kaiser] on the special head of these breaches of neutrality.'[21] Nevertheless, concluded the Commission, 'the gravity of these gross outrages upon the law of nations and international good faith is such that the Commission thinks they should be the subject of a formal condemnation by the Conference.'[22] The Commission gave two reasons for not regarding as *crimes* the treaty-violating acts of aggression, 'which the public conscience reproves and which history will condemn':[23]

First, 'by reason of the purely optional character of the institutions at The Hague for the maintenance of peace [International Commission of Inquiry, Mediation and Arbitration] a war of aggression may not be considered as an act directly contrary to positive law, or one which can be successfully brought before a tribunal such as the Commission is authorized to consider under its terms of reference;'[24] second, it was felt that thorough inquiry into the authorship of the war would entail many handicaps of proof, involving 'difficult and complex problems which might be more fitly investigated'[25] by the more leisurely methods of historians and statesmen than by a court. The latter must obviously depend upon recollections of witnesses and must insist upon reasonable celerity of trial and punishment.

But while recoiling from the charge of *crime* and from trial before a court, the Commission nevertheless recommended that 'it would be right for the Peace Conference, in a matter so unprecedented, to adopt special measures, and even to create a special organ in order to deal as they deserve with the authors of such acts,'[26] and declared it to be 'desirable that, *for the future, penal sanctions* should be provided for such grave outrages against the elementary principles of international law.'[27]

However, throughout the quarter-century between the two world wars nothing so specific was done by the nations of the world to implement the Commission's recommendation. The treaty for the Renunciation of War (Briand-Kellogg Pact or 'Pact of Paris'), signed in Paris on August 27, 1928, to which Germany was a party (and, ironically, the first signatory), condemned recourse to war for the solution of international controversies, renounced it as an instrument of national policy, and bound the signatories to seek the settlement of all disputes by pacific means only. But that historic Pact, too, failed to make violation of its terms an

---

[19] *Ibid.*   [20] *Id.* at 120.
[21] *Ibid.*   [22] *Ibid.*
[23] *Ibid.*   [24] *Id.* at 118.
[25] *Ibid.*   [26] *Id.* at 120.
[27] *Ibid* (italics supplied).

international crime punishable either by an international tribunal or by national courts.[28] Therefore, the technical legal basis for prosecution for violations of the Pact of Paris as international crimes may be said to be still open to some question, though the moral grounds are crystal clear.[29]

However, a few authorities have insisted that the Pact of Paris did establish aggressive warfare as an international crime. Thus Frangulis takes it for granted that 'the ratification of the Briand-Kellogg Pact has proclaimed war to be a crime and it has been recognized as such by a large number of States. Hence, in our time penal sanctions are possible, although this was not the case in respect to the war of 1914 and its authors.'[30] And George Scelle claims that

La doctrine est généralement d'accord pour admettre que le recours à la guerre d'aggression constitue un crime international.[31]

But even the framers of the Pact of Paris did not believe its violation to be criminal as well as illegal; and Mr. Kellogg, in the following passage, implies that the

---

[28] The treaty entered into force on July 24, 1929, with 46 States depositing ratifications or instruments of adhesion and 16 more then signifying their intention to adhere to the treaty. For an illuminating debate on the meaning of the Briand-Kellogg Pact, especially with reference to sanctions, see INTERNATIONAL LAW ASSOCIATION, REPORT OF THE THIRTY-EIGHTH CONFERENCE HELD AT BUDAPEST, SEPT. 6 TO 10, 1934 (1935) 1–70. Fred H. Aldrich, on page 43, referred to an address by Secretary of State Henry L. Stimson in New York in which he said: 'The Briand-Kellogg Pact provides for no sanction of force. It does not require any signatory to intervene with measures of force in case the Pact is violated. Instead, it rests upon the sanction of public opinion, which can be made one of the most potent sanctions of the world.' STIMSON, THE PACT OF PARIS THREE YEARS OF DEVELOPMENT (Dept. of State Publication 357, 1932) 7. See also *id.* at 10, 11. The contrast in points of view was most sharply brought out at the discussions in Budapest, in the following statements by Mr. Reut-Nicolussi and Dr. Jaroslav Žourek, respectively: '...when we were in Oxford I pointed out that we have no criminal law in International Law; therefore we cannot adopt the analogy of criminal law by interpreting the Briand-Kellogg Pact, saying that if an action is forbidden by criminal law everybody else has to abstain from aiding the criminal. The contents of the Briand-Kellogg Pact are but a renouncement of war,' etc. On the other hand it was argued: *'Le premier membre de la phrase constituant l'article I comprend la* condemnation *du recours à la guerre. Le verbe 'condamner,' aussi bien dans l'acception française de ce mot que dans l'acception anglaise, comprend un jugement moral de désapprobation fort accentué. On voit par là que le premier membre de phrase de l'article I comprend une* norme du droit international pénal, *protégeant l'ordre public et l'intérêt général. La violation de cette norme doit être considérée comme un* délit international.' REPORT OF THE THIRTY-EIGHTH CONFERENCE, *op. cit. supra* at 54. It should be pointed out that the Budapest Articles of Interpretation do not specifically state that the violation of the Briand-Kellogg Pact is a crime, although article (6) provides that 'A violating State is liable to pay compensation for all damage caused by a violation of the Pact to any signatory State or to its nationals.' *Id.* at 68. For the expressions of contemporary public opinion on the significance of the Pact of Paris, see GEROULD, SELECTED ARTICLES ON THE PACT OF PARIS (1929); Dewey, *Outlawry of War* in 11 ENCYC. SOC. SCI. 508–510 (and bibliography therein cited); MANDELSTAM, L'INTERPRÉTATION DU PACTE BRIAND-KELLOGG (1934) 108–13, 122–23, 137, 146–47, 156.

[29] GLUECK 37–38.

[30] *Responsables de la Guerre* in 2 DICTIONNAIRE DIPLOMATIQUE (1933) 581, 585 (author's translation). See also *Levy, supra* note 4, at 1052, 1077.

[31] SCELLE, PRÉCIS DE DROIT DES GENS, DEUXIÈME PARTIE (1934) 47. See also *id.* PREMIÈRE PARTIE (1932) at 65–66. *Cf.* HASSMANN, DER KELLOGG-PAKT (1932) 52; Borah, Interview, N. Y. Times Mar. 25, 1928, § 3, p. 1, col. 6.

historic treaty which bears his name leaves to a State the determination of its own guilt or innocence when charged with a violation of that treaty:

There is nothing in the American draft of an antiwar treaty which restricts or impairs in any way the right of self-defense. That right is inherent in every sovereign state and is implicit in every treaty. Every nation is free at all times and regardless of treaty provisions to defend its territory from attack or invasion and *it alone is competent to decide* whether circumstances require recourse to war in self-defense. If it has a good case, the world will applaud and not condemn its action.[32]

Mr. Henry L. Stimson, a statesman and lawyer whose opinion is deserving of the highest respect, in 1932 voiced the American conception of the legal effect of the Briand-Kellogg Treaty in these words:

War between nations was renounced by the signatories of the Briand-Kellogg Treaty. This means that it has become *illegal* throughout practically the entire world. It is no longer to be the source and subject of rights. It is no longer to be the principle around which the duties, the conduct, and the rights of nations revolve. It is an *illegal thing*. Hereafter when two nations engage in armed conflict either one or both of them must be wrongdoers— violators of this general treaty law. We no longer draw a circle about them and treat them with the punctilios of the duelist's code. Instead, we denounce them as law-breakers. By that very act, we have made obsolete many legal precedents and have given the legal profession the task of reexamining many of its codes and treatises.[33]

But the fact that the contracting Parties to a treaty have agreed to render aggressive war illegal does not necessarily mean that they have decided to make its violation an international crime.[34] Even an international contract and one dealing with a subject so vital to the survival of nations as the Briand-Kellogg Pact is not a penal statute;[35] and the remedy for breach of contract does not consist of prosecution and punishment of the guilty party, but rather of obtaining

---

[32] TREATY FOR THE RENUNCIATION OF WAR [Dept. of State Publication 468 (1933)] 57 (italics supplied). It will be noticed that the analogy to the law of self-defense in criminal cases, which has frequently been said to exist, is not sound; for in that field it is the jury and the tribunal, not the accused, which determine whether or not there was legitimate self-defense, while the provision in the Briand-Kellogg Pact left it to the implicated State itself to decide whether or not it had legitimate grounds for a self-defensive resort to war. See Borchard, *The Multilateral Treaty for the Renunciation of War* (1929) 23 AM. J. INT. L. 116.

[33] STIMSON, *op. cit. supra* note 28, at 4–5. Quoted by Jackson in TRIAL OF WAR CRIMINALS 9–10. *Cf.* Kunz, *Der Kellogg-Pakt* (1929) 9 MIT. DER D. G. FÜR VÖLKERRECHT 75, 83.

[34] See note 28; and compare the following statement by Mr. Justice Jackson, upon the signing of the Agreement referred to in note 1: 'Repeatedly, nations have united in abstract declarations that the launching of aggressive war is illegal. They have condemned it by treaty. But now we have the concrete application of these abstractions in a way which ought to make clear to the world that those who lead their nations into aggressive war face individual accountability for such acts' (1945) 13 U. S. DEPT. OF STATE BULL. 227. *Cf.* Bullard, *Europe and the Kellogg Treaty* in GEROULD, SELECTED ARTICLES ON THE PACT OF PARIS (1929) 268, 274: 'Calling a criminal an "outlaw" does not do much good unless you have some machinery for arresting him and locking him up.'

[35] The *illegality* of aggressive war under the Briand-Kellogg Pact can, however, be used in connection with the defenses of 'justification and excuse,' in prosecutions under *municipal* criminal law. Perhaps, through recognition of the uniform provisions found in the domestic-law penal codes

compensation for its breach. In addition to the sanction of a so-called punitive war, and to the economic sanctions provided in the famous Article 16 of the Covenant of the League of Nations, the remedies available under international law for violations of treaties are: publication of the facts with the aim of influencing public opinion against the offending belligerent; protest and demand for punishment of individual offenders, sent to the offending belligerent through neutral diplomatic channels; reprisals; post-war recompense. It is a notorious fact, however, that both during the first World War and the second, such means have proved ineffective in dealing with a militaristic and arrogant Power such as Germany has shown itself to be.

The most effective recourse is, indeed, not at all to be found against recalcitrant States, but rather in the prosecution and punishment of individuals—that is, members of the Government and armed forces who have caused their States ruthlessly to trample upon all law in their orgy of aggression and conquest.

Thus we are back to the major question—whether aggressive war can be denominated an international crime—with the additional question, whether individuals comprising the Government and General Staff of an aggressor State may be prosecuted as liable for such crime.

IV

The Charter under which the International Military Tribunal at Nuernberg is supposed to operate gives dogmatically affirmative answers to both these questions. Article 6 provides as follows:

The Tribunal established by the agreement referred to in Article 1 hereof for the trial and punishment of the major war criminals of the European Axis countries shall have the power to try and punish persons who, acting in the interests of the European Axis countries, whether as individuals or as members of organizations, committed any of the following crimes . . . for which there shall be individual responsibility:

(a) Crimes against peace: Namely, planning, preparation, initiation or waging of a war of aggression, or a war in violation of international treaties, agreements or assurances, or participation in a common plan or conspiracy for the accomplishment of any of the foregoing.[36]

And Article 7 of the Charter of the Tribunal provides as follows:

The official position of defendants, whether as heads of state or responsible officials in government departments, shall not be considered as freeing them from responsibility or mitigating punishment.[37]

---

of most civilized States as evidence of a general custom (a common denominator) accepted as law, it could also be used in prosecutions in a tribunal applying international law. See Appendix.

[36] TRIAL OF WAR CRIMINALS 16.
[37] *Id.* at 17.

There is no question but that, as an act of the will of the conqueror, the United Nations had the authority to frame and adopt such a Charter. And it may well be that the Tribunal at Nuernberg will deem itself completely bound by the restrictions above quoted. It is nevertheless valuable to examine the issues involved, for the sake of those lawyers who insist that it is 'illegal' and '*ex post facto*' to regard aggressive war as a crime and to hold individual members of a Government responsible for such a crime. Perhaps, also, despite the restrictions of its organic act, the International Military Tribunal will deem itself competent to hear argument on these basic questions and to dispose of them in a written decision for the sake of legal doctrine and precedent.[38]

As to the first question, when one passes in review the numerous expressions of multinational agreement and opinion—to many of which Germany herself was a Party—solemnly promising non-aggression toward neighboring States, condemning aggressive war as an instrument of national policy, and, in several instances, specifically declaring it to be an international crime, one may reasonably conclude that the time has arrived in the life of civilized nations when an international custom has developed to hold aggressive war to be an international crime.

It is familiar law in the international field that custom may, in the words of Article 38 of the Statute of the Permanent Court of International Justice, be considered 'as evidence of a general practice accepted as law.' If, therefore, a reasonable amount of proof can be adduced of a customary recognition among nations in the modern era that aggressive war is a crime, it need not at all be claimed that the violations of the Briand-Kellogg Pact or of any of the other treaties which Germany has chronically treated as 'scraps of paper' in themselves constitute international crimes, in order to hold Germany, Japan and other Axis nations liable for crimes against the Community of States as protected by international law. All that is necessary is to show that during the present century a widespread custom has developed among civilized States to enter into agreements expressive of their solemn conviction that unjustified war is so dangerous a threat to the survival of mankind that it must be branded and treated as criminal.

What is the evidence of this custom and of this conviction? In addition to the Pact of Paris, the following solemn international pronouncements may be mentioned:

(1) The agreements limiting the nature of the deeds permissible in the extreme event of war, that is, the Hague Conventions of 1899[39] and 1907[40] and the Geneva Conventions of 1929 regulating the treatment of prisoners of war[41] and

---

[38] See note 142.
[39] 2 MALLOY, TREATIES (1910) 2042; 32 STAT. 1803. This was superseded by the Hague Convention (IV) of 1907 as between those nations that are Parties to the 1907 agreement, but remained in force as between other States.
[40] U. S. TREATY SER. (1910) No. 539; 36 STAT. 2277 (1910).
[41] U. S. TREATY SER. (1932) No. 846; 47 STAT. 2021 (1932).

ameliorating the condition of wounded and ill soldiers.[42] Germany and Japan had ratified (with reservations) the 1907 Hague Convention; Italy, the 1899 one. Germany and Italy had ratified the Geneva Convention respecting Prisoners of War. Upon the Government of the United States expressing its intention to observe that convention as to both prisoners of war and civilian internees during the recent war, Japan agreed to do likewise.[43] The Hague and Geneva Conventions, to be sure, took for granted the legality of war; but, from motives both of humanitarianism[44] and mutual prudence, they went so far in the direction of limiting the methods of opening hostilities [Hague Convention (III), 1907] and conducting war, as to be signposts on the road toward a growing conviction that aggressive war must somehow be abolished.[45]

(2) The draft of a treaty of mutual assistance sponsored by the League of Nations in 1923, solemnly declared (Article 1) 'that aggressive war is an *international crime*,' and that the Parties would 'undertake that no one of them will be guilty of its commission.'[46] About half of the 29 States who replied to a submission of the draft treaty wrote in favor of accepting the text. A major objection was that it would be difficult to define what act would comprise 'aggression,'[47] rather than doubt as to the criminalism of aggressive war. The United States was unable to adhere because it was not a member of the League.

(3) The preamble to the League of Nations' 1924 Protocol for the Pacific Settlement of International Disputes ('Geneva Protocol'), after 'recognising the solidarity of the members of the international community,' solemnly asserted that 'a war of aggression constitutes a violation of this solidarity and an *international crime*.' It went on to say that the contracting parties were 'desirous of facilitating the complete application of the system provided in the Covenant of the League of Nations for the pacific settlement of disputes between the States and of ensuring the repression of *international crimes*.'[48] The meticulously-drafted Geneva Protocol was prepared after years of labor by some of the most distinguished and

---

[42] U. S. TREATY SER. (1932) No. 847; 47 STAT. 2074 (1932).

[43] (1944) 10 U. S. DEPT. OF STATE BULL. 78.

[44] Care was taken in Hague Convention (IV) to provide that 'Until a more complete code of laws of war has been issued, the high contracting Parties deem it expedient to declare that, in cases not included in the Regulations adopted by them, the inhabitants and the belligerents remain under the protection and the rule of the principles of the law of nations, as they result from the usages established among civilized peoples, from the laws of humanity, and the dictates of the public conscience.'

[45] It should be pointed out that the provision of rules of humane warfare and treatment of civilians in wartime is not necessarily inconsistent with a belief that aggressive war ought to be altogether abolished; since even if all the nations of the world solemnly agreed never to resort to aggressive war, there would still be the chance of violation of that agreement, in which event the offending nation might or might not aggravate its original criminalism by acts of gratuitous cruelty in the conduct of an illicit war.

[46] *Records of the Fourth Assembly, Plenary Meetings*, LEAGUE OF NATIONS OFFICIAL JOURNAL (Special Supp. No. 13, 1923) 403 (italics supplied).

[47] MYERS, ORIGIN AND CONCLUSION OF THE PARIS PACT (1929) 13.

[48] RECORDS OF THE FIFTH ASSEMBLY, LEAGUE OF NATIONS OFFICIAL JOURNAL (Special Supp. No. 23, 1924) 498 (italics supplied).

learned jurists and statesmen. It was warmly welcomed and earnestly recommended to the Members of the League of Nations by a resolution unanimously passed in the Assembly by the vote of 48 Members of the League (including Italy and Japan—Germany was not as yet a Member), and signed by the representatives of many countries.[49] Not only did it definitely declare aggressive war to be an international crime, but by Article 6 it provided that the sanctions of Article 16 of the Covenant of the League should be applicable to a State resorting to war in disregard of its undertakings under the Protocol. Although it never legally came into force (since the plan of disarmament called for in Article 17 had first to be accepted and since Great Britain, in 1925, found herself unable to accept compulsory arbitration and had doubts as to just how such a treaty could be effectively implemented[50]) the historic Protocol of Geneva did express the strong attitude of leading jurists and statesmen of most of the nations of the world regarding both the illegality and the criminalism of aggressive war.[51]

(4) The Convention on Conciliation and Arbitration, signed at Helsingfors, January 17, 1925, which was an outgrowth of the Geneva Protocol, was entered into between Estonia, Finland, Latvia and Poland. It declared, in its preamble, that the Parties desired 'to give in their mutual relations the widest possible application to the principle of the settlement of international disputes by pacific means.'[52]

(5) At the eighteenth plenary meeting of the Assembly of the League of Nations, September 24, 1927, all the delegations (including the German, Italian and Japanese) having pronounced in favor of a Resolution of the Third Committee comprising a Declaration Concerning Wars of Aggression, the Declaration was declared to be unanimously adopted.[53] Both the eloquent addresses in support of this Declaration,[54] and the preamble to the Declaration, show how strong was the conviction that the time had arrived, in the affairs of States and their peoples, to call a spade a spade:

The Assembly,
  Recognising the solidarity which unites the community of nations;
  Being inspired by a firm desire for the maintenance of general peace;

---

[49] *Id.* at 497. Although the Protocol was not ratified, this fact does not destroy the validity of the argument in the text. The signature of the Protocol by the leading statesmen of the world, representing the vast majority of civilized States and peoples, is itself evidence of a strongly entrenched custom to regard aggressive war as an international crime.

[50] Letter of J. Ramsay MacDonald to Secretary-General, League of Nations, in CORRESPONDENCE BETWEEN HIS MAJESTY'S GOVERNMENT AND THE LEAGUE OF NATIONS RESPECTING THE PROPOSED TREATY OF MUTUAL ASSISTANCE (1924) 10–14.

[51] See the debates, LEAGUE OF NATIONS OFFICIAL JOURNAL (Special Supp. No. 23, 1924) 192 *et seq.*; the *Report of the First and Third Committees, id.* at 479–97; MILLER, THE GENEVA PROTOCOL (1925) 112; SCHÜCKING, DAS GENFER PROTOKOLL (1924) 5.

[52] LEAGUE OF NATIONS TREATY SER. (1925) 359; 3 HUDSON, INTERNATIONAL LEGISLATION (1931) 1571.

[53] *Records of the Eighth Ordinary Session of the Assembly,* LEAGUE OF NATIONS OFFICIAL JOURNAL (Special Supp. No. 54, 1927) 155–56.

[54] *Id.* at 82 *et seq.*

Being convinced that a war of aggression can never serve as a means of settling international disputes and is, in consequence, an *international crime....*[55]

(6) The unanimous Resolution (February 18, 1928) of the twenty-one American Republics at the Sixth (Havana) Pan-American Conference, declared that 'war of aggression constitutes an *international crime against the human species.*'[56]

(7) At the International Conference of American States on Conciliation and Arbitration, assembled in Washington in December, 1928, representatives of all twenty republics at the Conference signed a General Convention of Inter-American Conciliation. The preamble contains the statement, 'Desiring to demonstrate that the condemnation of war as an instrument of national policy in their mutual relations [set forth in the Havana Resolution] ... constitutes one of the fundamental bases of inter-American relations....'[57]

(8) The Anti-War Treaty of Non-Aggression and Conciliation signed at Rio de Janeiro October 10, 1933, was ratified by 25 States, including the United States of America. The preamble to that treaty states that the Parties were entering into the agreement 'to the end of condemning wars of aggression and territorial acquisitions that may be obtained by armed conquest, making them impossible and establishing their invalidity.'[58]

(9) Finally, the authoritative expression of American opinion on aggressive war was made on December 12, 1927, when Senator William E. Borah introduced in the Senate a resolution, the last in a long series since 1922, of which a pertinent provision was 'That it is the view of the Senate of the United States that war between nations should be outlawed as an institution or means of the settlement of international controversies by making it *a public crime under the law of nations.*'[59]

All these solemn expressions of the conviction of civilized States regarding the need for conciliation, for the settlement of international disputes by pacific means only, for the renunciation of war as an instrument of national policy, and, logically, for the recognition that aggressive war is an international crime,[60] greatly

---

[55] *Id.* at 155 (italics supplied).
[56] Quoted in Papers Relating to Foreign Relations of the United States [Dept. of State Publication 1839 (1928)] 13 (italics supplied).
[57] (1929) 63 Bull. of the Pan American Union 114.
[58] 4 Treaties, Conventions, International Acts, Protocols, and Agreements Between the United States and Other Powers 4793 [Sen. Doc. No. 134, 75th Cong., 3d Sess. (1938)].
[59] Sen. Res. No. 45, 70th Cong., 1st Sess. (1927) (italics supplied).
[60] I have not included the various treaties of 'mutual guarantee,' such as The Treaty of Locarno of October 16, 1925, and the many treaties entered into by Germany with her neighbors shortly preceding her planned attack on them. See note 126 *infra.* These treaties, also, speak of the determination of the Parties to submit their international disputes to conciliation or judicial decision, and thereby, at least inferentially, condemn resort to aggressive war. I have not included the views of many distinguished statesmen in support or interpretation of some of the foregoing international pronouncements which regard aggressive war as a crime. To cite one, however, that of Senator Arthur Capper (especially significant since it came from a statesman from the Middle West) in

re-enforce whatever inference to that effect is derivable from the Briand-Kellogg Pact itself. They may be regarded as powerful evidence of the existence of a widely prevalent juristic climate which has energized a spreading *custom* among civilized peoples to regard a war of aggression as not simply 'unjust' or 'illegal' but downright *criminal*.

Prevalent custom may legitimately be regarded as a source of international law. As Sir Frederick Pollock long ago pointed out:

... where an agreement or declaration is made not by two or three states as a matter of private business between themselves, but by a considerable proportion, in number and power, of civilized states at large, for the regulation of matters of general and permanent interest... there is no doubt that, when all or most of the great Powers have deliberately agreed to certain rules of general application, the rules approved by them have very great weight in practice even among states which have never expressly consented to them. It is hardly too much to say that declarations of this kind may be expected, in the absence of prompt and effective dissent by some Power of the first rank, to become part of the universally received law of nations within a moderate time. As among men, so among nations, the opinions and usage of the leading members in a community tend to form an authoritative example for the whole.... It is quite possible that some of the recommendations recorded at the Peace Conference at the Hague in 1899 [and in 1907] may sooner or later... be adopted as part of the public law of civilized nations by general recognition *without any formal ratification*.

On the whole, then, the law of nations rests on a general consent which, though it may be supplemented, influenced, and to some extent defined, by express convention, can never be completely formulated under existing conditions. This is as much as to say that the law of nations must be classed with *customary law*.[61]

The validity of custom as a source of international law is a matter not new to the Germans. German authorities have gone so far as to say that the 'customs of war [part of international law] are substantive penal law as good as the State's penal legislation';[62] and that the fact that a State has not previously enacted a penal code setting forth detailed definitions and prescribing various punishments is

commenting upon his resolution in favor of the efforts of Briand which led to the Pact of Paris: 'There is every reason to consider this proposal for civilized nations to renounce war as an instrument of public policy, a logical and necessary step toward peace. It goes farther, it seems to me, than merely declaring war criminal.' SHOTWELL, WAR AS AN INSTRUMENT OF NATIONAL POLICY (1929) 97. I have also not included the notable Draft Treaty of Disarmament and Security Prepared by an American Group and carefully considered by the Third Committee (on disarmament) of the Assembly of the League of Nations, 1924, Article 1 of which provides that 'The High Contracting Parties solemnly declare that aggressive war is an *international crime*,' and 'severally undertake not to be *guilty* of its commission,' while Article 2 provides that 'A State engaging in war for other than purposes of defence commits the *international crime* described in Article 1.' *Records of the Fifth Assembly, Meetings of the Committees, Minutes of the Third Committee*, LEAGUE OF NATIONS OFFICIAL JOURNAL (Special Supp. No. 26, 1924) Annex 4, p. 169 (italics supplied). This draft also made a notable contribution to the definition of acts of aggression. See also TRAININ, HITLERITE RESPONSIBILITY UNDER CRIMINAL LAW (trans. Rothstein, 1945) 30–31.

61 Pollock, *The Sources of International Law* (1902) 2 COL. L. REV. 511, 512 (italics supplied).
62 8 Schätzel, *Bestrafungen nach Kriegsbrauch*, ARCHIV FÜR MILITÄRRECHT (1920) 13–24.

irrelevant, since it can legitimately resort to enforcement of the customs of war as part of the common law of nations.[63]

The prosecution at Nuernberg under Count Two of the historic indictment, 'Crimes Against Peace,' for the crimes of 'planning, preparation, initiation and waging wars of aggression, which were also in violation of international treaties, agreements and assurances,'[64] is, then, strictly speaking, not based upon proof of the breach of any specific provision of any particular one or more of the above-mentioned international treaties or conventions. It is rather based upon violation of customary international law—a system of law that is as obviously subject to growth as has been the law of any other developing legal order, by the crystallization of generally prevailing opinion and practice into law under the impact of common consent and the demands of general world security. Acquiescence of all members of the Family of Nations is not necessary for this purpose.[65] All that is needed is reasonable proof of the existence of a widespread custom; and the numerous multilateral anti-war treaties, agreements and resolutions, as well as the statements and writings of experts in connection with such international pronouncements, comprise such proof. Obviously, a requirement of unanimity would permit the most lawless State to prevent the recognition of the custom as evidence of the existence of the principle of law.

It is true that among the tests of legally acceptable custom usual in English courts has been the requirement of very long if not 'immemorial' usage.[66] But such a requirement developed during a period in world history when the tempo of life was very slow. It is no exaggeration to say that more relevant opinion and custom recognizing the dangers of aggressive war and the need of its suppression by all means have been crowded into the short compass of the first half of the twentieth century than in the entire preceding period of recorded history. One has only to think of the tremendous technologic development of the present epoch, with its immense multiplication of dangers to the very survival of mankind, to recognize that for the legal recognition of custom the content of the years, rather than their mere duration, is of prime importance. Moreover, the

[63] VERDROSS, DIE VÖLKERRECHTSWIDRIGE KRIEGSHANDLUNG UND DER STRAFANSPRUCH DER STAATEN (1920) 30–32.

[64] TRIAL OF WAR CRIMINALS 37. TRAININ, *op. cit. supra* note 60, at 33 aptly defines international crime as 'an infringement of the foundations of international communion.'

[65] 'Rules of customary law have had their origin in the practice of a single state or of a group of states; then in time other states have been led from various motives to adopt the same practice until a well-defined usage has grown up, which in its turn has slowly hardened into fixed custom carrying with it a recognition that the practice is no longer voluntary but of obligation. In a broad view, customary law may be regarded as embracing the evolution of general principles as well as the growth of detailed rules from the common practice of states.' FENWICK, INTERNATIONAL LAW (2d ed. 1934) 62–63. 'A custom, in the intendment of law, is such a usage as hath obtained the force of law, and is in truth a binding law to such particular places, persons and things which it concerns. . . . But it is *ius non scriptum*. . . . Viner, *Abr.* vii, 164, citing *Tanistry Case,* Dav. 31 b.' Cited by ALLEN, LAW IN THE MAKING (1927) 28 n.1.

[66] *Id.* at 89; see also *id.*, Appendix B, 'Reasonableness of Custom' 359–77.

English test for the acceptability of custom as law developed in areas of private rights and duties which, being in the domain of municipal law, had slowly grown over a long period of time. But systematic international law pertaining to war, its conduct, obligations, rights, and abolition is of relatively recent development; and the time-requirement for the legal validity of custom in that field must, correspondingly, be telescoped.

The claim that in the absence of a specific, detailed, pre-existing *code* of international penal law to which all States have previously subscribed, prosecution for the international crime of aggressive war is necessarily *ex post facto* because no world legislature has previously spoken is specious. At the close of the first World War, in arguing against the application of the common law of nations to individuals, the American representatives on the Versailles Commission (Robert Lansing and James Brown Scott) insisted upon the applicability to the present problem of the reasoning in 'the leading case of *United States v. Hudson* (7 Cranch, 32), decided by the Supreme Court of the United States in 1812, that "the legislative authority of the Union must first make an act a crime, affix a punishment to it, and declare the court that shall have jurisdiction of the offense." '[67] The American commissioners argued that 'what is true of the American States must be true of this looser union which we call the Society of Nations.'[68] But this is a *non sequitur*. In the *Hudson* case a tribunal of a special federation of states was interpreting a specific written constitution in which powers are distributed between the United States of America and the individual states of the Union. But for an historic accident, the case might well have been decided the other way.[69] It is highly questionable whether the *Hudson* case—confined to a local eighteenth-century constitutional arrangement within a single nation, and involving the Supreme Court's failure to consult the Senate files for the original draft of the Federal Judiciary Act of 1789—is at all relevant to the issue whether an International Criminal Court established by the majority of civilized States in 1919 or 1945 could or could not

[67] *Commission on the Responsibility of the Authors of the War and on Enforcement of Penalties* (1920) 14 Am. J. Int. L. 145–46.

[68] *Id.* at 146.

[69] The case arose under the Federal Judiciary Act of 1789, c. 20, §§ 9, 11, giving the federal courts jurisdiction of all 'crimes and offences... cognizable under the authority of the United States.' The original draft of this Act which was submitted to Congress gave those courts jurisdiction of all 'crimes and offences cognizable under the authority of the United States *and defined by the laws of the same* [italics supplied],' but the last eight words of the draft were not approved by Congress and did not therefore appear in the statute. The implication is that by striking them Congress did not intend to limit the jurisdiction of the federal courts to offenses defined by act of Congress. This significant change in the draft of the bill was not known until Charles Warren discovered the original draft in the archives of the United States some twenty years ago. 'Had the Supreme Court consulted these Senate Files, it is probable that the decisions in *United States v. Hudson*, in 1812, and *United States v. Coolidge*, in 1816, might have been otherwise than they were.' Warren, *New Light on the History of the Federal Judiciary Act of 1789* (1923) 37 Harv. L. Rev. 49, 51, 73. It should also be borne in mind that Madison was President of the United States from 1809 to 1817 and the Jeffersonian party to which he belonged did not wish to enlarge the powers of the Federal Government more than was necessary. See also 1 Bishop, Criminal Law (9th ed. 1923) 129–32.

legitimately apply the common law of nations to individuals without some world 'legislative authority' having first enacted an international penal statute, made its violations crimes, and affixed a specific punishment to each crime.

In the international field, then, as in the domestic, part of the system of prohibitions implemented by penal sanctions consists of customary or common law. In assuming that an act of aggressive war is not merely lawless but also criminal, the Nuernberg court would merely be following the age-old precedent of courts which enforce not only the specific published provisions of a systematic code enacted by a legislature, but also 'unwritten' law. During the early stage (or a particularly disturbed stage) of any system of law—and international law is still in a relatively undeveloped state—the courts must rely a great deal upon non-legislative law,[70] and thereby run the risk of an accusation that they are indulging in legislation under the guise of decision, and are doing so *ex post facto*.[71] Whenever an English common-law court for the first time, held that some act not previously declared by Parliament to be a crime was a punishable offense for which the doer of that act was now prosecuted and held liable,[72] or whenever a court, for the first time, more

---

[70] '*Legislative power comparatively late:* In that centralization of different powers included in the modern idea of Sovereignty, the most important, according to general opinion, of the functions referred to—the Legislative—is, in all probability one of the latest.... The Judge and the law may follow the Chief, but certainly come before the King: the Lawgiver comes last of all.' CLARK, HISTORY OF ROMAN PRIVATE LAW (1919) (Part III Regal Period) 388–89. 'Particularly the very notion itself of an oral, unwritten law, delivered down from age to age by custom and tradition merely, seems derived from the practice of the Druids, who never committed any of their instructions to writing, possibly for want of letters....' 4 BLACKSTONE, COMMENTARIES *408. See also 2 MONTESQUIEU, THE SPIRIT OF THE LAWS (3d ed. 1758, trans. by Nugent) 251–52; MAINE, ANCIENT LAW (1st ed. 1861) 8, 13, 370–74; HUEBNER, A HISTORY OF GERMANIC PRIVATE LAW (1918) 5–6.

[71] There is indeed, a school of juristic thought which perhaps lets too much of the cat out of the bag, in insisting that courts *usually* indulge in *ex post facto* reasoning and decision: 'And this brings us to the reason why courts and jurists have so struggled to maintain the preexistence of the Law, why the common run of writers speak of the judges as merely stating the Law, and why Mr. Carter, in an advance towards the truth, says of the judges that they are discoverers of the Law. That reason is the unwillingness to recognize the fact that the courts, with the consent of the State, have been constantly in the practice of applying in the decision of controversies, rules which were not in existence and were, therefore, not knowable by the parties when the causes of controversy occurred. It is the unwillingness to face the certain fact that courts are constantly making *ex-post facto* Law.' GRAY, THE NATURE AND SOURCES OF THE LAW (2d ed. 1921) 99–100; see also *id.* at 231–32. 'It is just by the proper use of elasticity in the authorities that the law is advanced. If that were not so, the law could never have changed. How otherwise explain the difference between the law of tort, or of trusts, or of the sale of goods as it was a hundred years ago and as it is now? In these matters statutory changes have on the whole been of minor importance, yet the law might almost be regarded as a new and different law, were it not that we can trace the development from point to point, as the judges found the requirements of justice compelled them to modify or vary or innovate on the law, creating new or partially new principles, but keeping, actually or ostensibly, within or close to the decided cases. This, apart from the decision of matters of fact, is the great work of the English judges. There was reposed on them the great responsibility of making the law, which on the whole they have worthily fulfilled.' Lord Wright, *The Common Law in its Old Home*, in THE FUTURE OF THE COMMON LAW (1937) 79.

[72] In England, even the most serious offenses (*e.g.*, murder, manslaughter, robbery, rape, arson) originated as crimes by way of usage. From the earliest times of legal development, both before and after prosecution in the royal courts for violation of the 'King's peace' had taken the place of the

specifically than theretofore defined the constituents of a crime and applied that definition to a new case,[73] the court in one sense 'made law.' Yet, fundamentally, it thereby did no violence to the technique of law-enforcement or the requirements of man-made justice, unless it acted most unreasonably and arbitrarily. Even the legal 'command' which, since Austin's time is deemed by many to be the indispensable and distinctive hallmark of law, was essentially present. It is true that the command which the accused was held to have violated did not come directly and specifically from the legislature or sovereign; but since the prohibition represented the consensus of the people as reflected in customary usage, it contained enough of the imperative element to warn its prospective violators, to impel judges to recognize it as an existing part of the law of the land, and to hold its violators guilty of a crime.

So is it with modern international common law, in prohibiting aggressive war on pain of punishment. Every recognition of custom as evidence of law must have a beginning some time; and there has never been a more justifiable stage in the history of international law than the present, to recognize that by the common consent of civilized nations as expressed in numerous solemn agreements and public pronouncements the instituting or waging of an aggressive war is an international crime.

V

Assuming modern aggressive war to be a crime, *i.e.*, an offense against the Family of Nations and its international law, then the defendant must normally be the

ancient practices of private vengeance, the *Wergild*, and trial by ordeal, such customary crimes were recognized; and when the King's courts took over, they accepted common-law crimes without specific prior statute or royal decree. Even later '... from 1660 to 1860, the [English] courts, without any specific precedent, frequently punished conduct which was *contra bonos mores*, or which openly outraged public decency, or which was subsumable under some similar generalization; and there are scattered instances of the courts having continued this practice after 1860.' Hall, *Nulla Poena Sine Lege* (1937) 47 YALE L. J. 165, 179. It should be pointed out that the consequences of conviction for these common-law offenses were serious in a period of severe penalties during which the magistrates might 'punish the offenders by fine, imprisonment, and such other corporal punishment as the circumstances may require,' for such offenses as 'contempt of the established religion' or 'open breaches of morality exhibited in the face of the people,' which offenses tend to breaches of the peace or 'sap public morals.' 1 EAST, PLEAS OF THE CROWN (2d ed. 1803) c. 1, § 1. See also *id.* c. 4, § 10 (counterfeiting foreign coin). Evidently, also, the non-statutory offense of 'delay in discovering high treason, whatever excuses the party might have for it, was deemed an assent to it, and consequently high treason,' and therefore punishable capitally. HAWKINS, PLEAS OF THE CROWN (8th ed. 1824) c. 5, § 2.

73 'So far as I have been able to discover, there are hardly any definitions of crimes in the early [Anglo-Saxon] laws.... Of offenses against property, theft is the one most commonly referred to. I have found no definition of it in any of the laws, though I think it may be said to be the subject to which they refer most frequently.... Robbery, *roberia*, is frequently mentioned; but I think no definition of it is given.... Of mischievous offences against property *bernet* or arson is several times mentioned, but with no detail.' 1 STEPHEN, A HISTORY OF THE CRIMINAL LAW OF ENGLAND (1883) 53, 56–57.

implicated State. A familiar analogy is the prosecution of a business corporation. In both cases, of course, the punishment upon conviction can only be in terms of a fine or deprivation of certain rights or privileges. But, as experience has shown, action against a State must necessarily be ineffective in reducing international criminalism, compared to the imposition of penal sanctions upon members of a cabinet, heads of a general staff, or other persons in authority in a Government who have led a State into aggressive war and the breach of basic treaties designed for the security of all States.

As indicated, Article 6 of the Charter of the International Military Tribunal recognizes this fact. By implication, also, Article 1 of the Agreement for the Establishment of an International Military Tribunal, of which the Charter is an integral part, provides for personal rather than State liability:

There shall be established after consultation with the Control Council for Germany an International Military Tribunal for the trial of war criminals whose offenses have no particular geographical location whether they be accused *individually* or in their capacity as members of organizations or groups or in both capacities.[74]

So also the numerous solemn warnings to the Axis leaders by statesmen of the chief Member-States of the United Nations during the conduct of the war implied a plan to hold them personally responsible for their crimes.[75]

---

[74] TRIAL OF WAR CRIMINALS 14 (italics supplied). This followed the formula of the Moscow Declaration of November 1, 1943.

[75] On October 25, 1941, Roosevelt and Churchill made simultaneous statements in respect to the acts of barbarity committed by the Germans. Roosevelt said: 'Frightfulness can never bring peace to Europe. It only sows the seeds of hatred which will one day bring fearful retribution.' (1941) 5 U. S. DEPT. OF STATE BULL. 317. Churchill declared: 'Retribution for these crimes must henceforward take its place among the major purposes of the war.' The Molotov Note of November 27, 1941 (and one of January 6, 1942) warned that the German crimes were being noted and registered, and would be punished. At an historic conference in London, the nine European governments directly participating (the major powers and certain others of the United Nations sent Observers) adopted the Declaration of St. James's Palace on January 13, 1942, of which the following clauses are relevant: 'Whereas Germany, since the beginning of the present conflict which arose out of her policy of aggression, has instituted in the occupied countries a regime of terror characterised in particular by imprisonments, mass expulsions, the execution of hostages and massacres,' etc., 'The undersigned Representatives of: the Government of Belgium, the Government of Czechoslovakia, the Free French National Committee, the Government of Greece, the Government of Luxembourg, the Government of the Netherlands, the Government of Norway, the Government of Poland and the Government of Yugoslavia: (1) affirm that acts of violence thus perpetrated against the civilian populations are at variance with accepted ideas concerning acts of war and political offences, as these are understood by civilised nations, (2) take note of the declaration made in this respect on 25th October, 1941, by the President of the United States of America and by the British Prime Minister, (3) place among their principal war aims the punishment, through the channel of *organised justice*, of those *guilty* and responsible for these *crimes*, whether they have ordered them, perpetrated them or in any way participated in them, (4) determine in a spirit of international solidarity to see to it that (a) those guilty and responsible, whatever their nationality, are sought for, handed over to justice and *judged*, (b) that the *sentences* pronounced are carried out.' (Italics supplied. Note that this is a promise of judicial, not political, treatment.) The principles of the Declaration were accepted (January 9, 1942) by the Chinese Government, and subscribed to also (October 14, 1942) by the Government of Soviet Russia. On August 21, 1942, Roosevelt referred to the Declaration

These were all manifestations of the power of the victor, which could be the sole 'law' to govern the treatment of the Nazi ringleaders. But assuming the application of normal legal principles, conservative international lawyers and publicists have pointed to two fundamental obstacles to the prosecution and punishment of the Nazi leaders for the crime of waging a war of aggression; namely, the doctrine

of St. James's Palace, and in condemning the crimes committed against the civil population in occupied lands, solemnly announced that 'the time will come when' the *criminals* 'will have to stand in *courts of law* in the very countries which they are now oppressing, and to answer for their acts.' (1942) 7 U. S. DEPT. OF STATE BULL. 709, 710 (italics supplied). On September 8, 1942, Mr. Churchill promised that 'those who are *guilty* of Nazi *crimes* will have to stand up before *tribunals* in every land where the atrocities have been committed, in order that an indelible warning may be given to future ages and that successive generations of men may say "So perish all who do the like again."' N. Y. Times, Sept. 9, 1942, p. 4, col. 8 (italics supplied).

On October 7, 1942, a decision was made public by Washington and London to establish a United Nations' Commission for the Investigation of War Crimes. It provided that named *criminals* wanted for war crimes should be arrested and handed over at the time of the armistice and as one of the conditions in the armistice, with surrender of others deemed implicated after investigation. (1942) 7 U. S. DEPT. OF STATE BULL. 797. On July 30, 1943, Roosevelt addressed a Note of warning to neutral countries: '... There are now rumors that Mussolini and members of his Fascist gang may attempt to take refuge in neutral territory. One day Hitler and his gang and Tojo and his gang will be trying to escape from their countries. I find it difficult to believe that any neutral country would give asylum to or extend protection to any of them. I can only say that the Government of the United States would regard the action by a neutral government in affording asylum to Axis leaders or their tools as inconsistent with the principles for which the United Nations are fighting and that the United States Government hopes that no neutral government will permit its territory to be used as a place of refuge or otherwise assist such persons in any effort to escape their just deserts.' (1943) 9 U. S. DEPT. OF STATE BULL. 62. On April 9, 1943, a similar warning was sent the Japanese Government. (1944) 10 U. S. DEPT. OF STATE BULL. 145–46. A concurrent resolution regarding Nazi atrocities declared in 1943 'that it is the sense of this Congress that those guilty, directly or indirectly, of these *criminal* acts, shall be held accountable and punished in a manner commensurate with the offenses for which they are responsible.' CONCURRENT RES. OF MARCH 18, 1943 (57 STAT. 721, 722) (italics supplied). The Moscow Declaration previously mentioned sternly warned that 'at the time of the granting of any armistice to any government which may be set up in Germany, those German officers and men and members of the Nazi party who have been responsible for, or have taken a consenting part [in the various] atrocities, massacres and executions, will be sent back to the countries in which their abominable deeds were done in order that they may be *judged and punished according to the laws* of these liberated countries and of the free governments which will be erected therein,' and that the 'Allied Powers will pursue them to the uttermost ends of the earth and will deliver them to the accusers in order that justice may be done.' (1943) 9 U. S. DEPT. OF STATE BULL. 310–11 (italics supplied). In reply to a question in the House of Commons, Churchill said (September 26, 1944): 'The governments are resolved to do their utmost to prevent Nazi criminals finding a refuge in neutral territory from the consequences of their crimes.... It is not our intention to allow the escape of these men to be effected without exerting almost every resource which a civilized power can contemplate.' The American-British-Russian Declaration of Potsdam, published July 26, 1945, announced (par. 10): '...stern *justice* shall be meted out to all war *criminals*, including those who have visited cruelties upon our prisoners.' (1945) 13 U. S. DEPT. OF STATE BULL. 137–38 (italics supplied). Arts. III A 5 and VII of the Report on the Tripartite Conference in Berlin (Potsdam) also provide for the arrest and *bringing to judgment of war criminals*, and affirms the intention of the three major Governments to bring 'those major war *criminals* whose *crimes* under the Moscow Declaration of October 1943 have no particular geographic location... to swift and sure justice.' (1945) 13 U. S. DEPT. OF STATE BULL. 155, 158 (italics supplied). By the instruments of unconditional surrender, Germany and Japan accepted the terms. (1945) 13 U. S. DEPT. OF STATE BULL. 105 *et seq.*; *id.* at 205; *id.* at 362 *et seq.*

of 'acts of State,' and the related principle that international law obligates and binds only States, not individual human beings.

Taking up the first objection, it is argued that international law forbids a State to make a subject of another State responsible for an act committed by him upon direction or with approval and ratification of his State,[76] even if that act is a flagrant war crime and as such clearly contrary to international law itself. Responsibility for such a breach, it is claimed, rests not on the individual, who acted as a mere instrument or 'organ' of his State, but only upon the 'collectivity of individuals,' the corporate entity; which comprises the State. The reason assigned for this principle is that since the act of the individual must be 'imputed' to the State, 'prosecution of an individual by courts of the injured State for an act which, according to international law, is the act of another State, amounts to exercising jurisdiction over another State; and this is a violation of the rule of general international law that no State is subject to the jurisdiction of another State.'[77] It is, moreover, claimed that 'there is no sufficient reason to assume that the rule of general customary law under which no State can claim jurisdiction over the acts of another State is suspended by the outbreak of war, and consequently that it is not applicable to the relationship between belligerents.'[78]

This argument must be met if the act-of-State doctrine is not, in the minds of certain lawyers, to render all prosecution of the Nazi ringleaders 'illegal' and in the nature of 'lynch law.'

It may be admitted that there are sound reasons for the familiar application of the act-of-State doctrine to the normal, peaceful intercourse of nations,[79] without it necessarily following that it is also to be applied to the situation presented by the acts of the Nazi ringleaders in instituting a criminal war and conducting it barbarously. However, the American members of the Commission on Responsibility which was set up by the Peace Conference at Versailles in 1919, in their Memorandum of Reservations (April 4, 1919), insisted upon the applicability of the act-of-State argument to the plan to try the former German Kaiser. They relied upon 'the masterly and hitherto unanswered opinion of Chief Justice Marshall, in the case of the *Schooner Exchange v. McFaddon and Others* [7 Cranch 116], decided by the Supreme Court of the United States in 1812, in which the reasons are given for the exemption of the sovereign and of the *sovereign agent of a*

---

[76] Kelsen, *Collective and Individual Responsibility in International Law with Particular Regard to the Punishment of War Criminals* (1943) 31 Calif. L. Rev. 530, 539–41. See also Professor Kelsen's Peace Through Law (1944).

[77] Kelsen, *supra* note 76, at 540.

[78] *Id.* at 542.

[79] *E.g.*, to prevent interference by the domestic courts of one State with the conduct of the affairs of a friendly foreign State within that State's own borders, thus imperilling friendly relations: 'To permit the validity of the acts of one sovereign State to be reëxamined and perhaps condemned by the courts of another would very certainly "imperil the amicable relations between governments and vex the peace of nations."' Oetjen v. Central Leather Co., 246 U. S. 297, 304 (1918); see also Underhill v. Hernandez, 168 U. S. 250, 252 (1897); 2 Montesquieu, The Spirit of the Laws, (3d ed. 1758, trans by Nugent) c. 21.

state from judicial process.'[80] But that classic decision (as Chief Justice Marshall was careful to point out) dealt with the normal, peacetime relations of friendly sovereigns. The immunity which a sovereign and his agents enjoy by virtue of the privilege granted him and them by other sovereigns is based upon international comity and courtesy;[81] and its recognition is dependent upon an important condition precedent: that the sovereign in question, or his agent, be conducting himself in conformity with international law. The host sovereign can otherwise refuse to grant immunity. Starting with the proposition that 'all sovereigns have consented to a relaxation, in practice, in cases under certain peculiar circumstances, of that absolute and complete jurisdiction within their respective territories which sovereignty confers,'[82] Marshall recognized a class of cases 'in which every sovereign is understood to waive the exercise of a part of that complete exclusive territorial jurisdiction, which has been stated to be the attribute of every nation.... One of these is admitted to be the exemption of the person of the sovereign [or his agent] from arrest or detention within a foreign territory.'[83] But he went on to say that:

...all exemptions from territorial jurisdiction, must be derived from the consent of the sovereign of the territory... this consent may be implied or expressed; and... when implied, its extent must be regulated by the nature of the case, and the views under which the parties requiring and conceding it must be supposed to act.[84]

Thus, while holding it to be 'a principle of public law, that national ships of war, entering the port of a friendly power, open for their reception, are to be considered as exempted by the consent of that power from its jurisdiction,'[85] the court

---

[80] (1920) 14 Am. J. Int. L. 135 (italics supplied).

[81] 'International law... speaking very generally... recognizes that every state has, as a sovereign community, the legal right to select its own form of government and to regulate as it chooses its own territory and the personal and property relations of its citizens and subjects—*in so far as it does not exercise this right in such ways as to endanger the peace and safety of other states.*' Coker, *Sovereignty* in 14 Encyc. Soc. Sci. (1937) 266 (italics supplied).

[82] 7 Cranch 116, 136 (1812).

[83] *Id.* at 137.

[84] *Id.* at 143.

[85] *Id.* at 145. The ship in question, a public armed vessel of France, commissioned by and in the service of Napoleon, came into Philadelphia after rough weather, to make necessary repairs and lay in supplies. She conducted herself in accordance with both municipal and international law. The United States was then at peace with France. As the schooner was about to depart, she was seized on process issued under a libel filed in a U. S. District Court, which alleged that her libellants had been the sole owners when, previously, she had sailed from Baltimore bound for a Spanish port; that while en route she had been seized by persons acting under decrees of the French Emperor and disposed of in violation of the libellant's rights; that a sentence of condemnation had never been pronounced against her by a court of competent jurisdiction; and that she was still the property of libellants. The United States attorney informed the court that the schooner was a public armed vessel of a friendly power; told of the circumstances under which she had involuntarily had to enter the port of Philadelphia; pointed out that if she had been the property of libellants such property was divested and became vested in Napoleon within a port of his Empire or a country occupied by his arms, outside the jurisdiction of the United States, under the laws of France; and therefore moved dismissal of proceedings and release of the vessel. The District Court sustained the motion; the

was careful to point out that 'without doubt, the sovereign of the place is capable of destroying this implication.'[86]

Surely, it cannot reasonably be argued that the license in question, which is dependent upon the consent of sovereigns and therefore upon the existence of friendly relations between the States involved and upon the lawful behavior of the sovereign who seeks immunity from extraterritorial jurisdiction for himself or his agents, is applicable to the situation of the Nazi ringleaders. Surely, it is more reasonable to assume that by invading neighboring countries in flagrant violation of treaty obligations and for purposes of aggression, conquest and the mass-extermination of the subjects of neighboring States, an offending sovereign destroys any implied consent that he be exempt from the jurisdiction of others, and strips himself and his agents of any mantle of immunity he may have claimed by virtue of international comity.

An issue of this kind ought not to be disposed of on the basis of blind legalistic conceptualism; it should be dealt with realistically in the light of the practical as well as logical results to which one or the other solution will lead. An examination of the act-of-State doctrine from such a point of view shows it to be so unreasonable and dangerous to law-abiding peoples as to cast grave doubt on the question whether it ever was sound law.

Wharton, commenting on *People v. McLeod*,[87] and the historic debate between Webster and Calhoun on the question of the liability of a foreign national for

---

Circuit Court reversed; the Supreme Court reversed the judgment of the Circuit Court and held that the libel must be dismissed and the schooner released.

[86] *Id.* at 145, 146.

[87] 25 Wend. 481 (N. Y. 1841); 26 Wend. 663 (N. Y. 1841). The case arose early in American history and brought about a great deal of discussion among statesmen and jurisconsults. During an insurrection in Canada in 1837 against the British Government, members of the colonial authorities' military force invaded the American steamer *Caroline* while she was moored on the American side of the Niagara River, attacked passengers believed to be insurgents, burned the steamer and set her adrift over Niagara Falls. An American citizen was killed. In 1840 McLeod, a British subject, was arrested by the New York authorities and held for trial in a state court on arson and murder charges in connection with the attack on the *Caroline*. The British minister at Washington demanded McLeod's immediate release on the ground that the destruction of the *Caroline* was a 'public act of persons in Her Majesty's service, obeying the order of their superior authorities'; that therefore it could 'only be the subject of discussion between the two national Governments,' and could 'not justly be made the ground of legal proceedings in the United States against the persons concerned.' Secretary of State Webster, while declaring that the Federal Government was then unable to comply with the demand, acknowledged the validity of the British argument: 'That an individual, forming part of a public force, and acting under the authority of his Government, is not to be held answerable as a private trespasser or malefactor, is a principle of public law sanctioned by the usages of all civilized nations, and which the Government of the United States has no inclination to dispute.' The New York court refused to release McLeod at the intervention of the Federal Government, and he was tried but acquitted on proof of an alibi. The episode was followed by enactment by Congress in 1842 (5 Stat. 538, c. 257, § 1) of the provision authorizing courts of the United States to issue a writ of *habeas corpus* where a subject of a foreign State is in custody for an act done or omitted under an alleged right or privilege claimed under the sanction of a foreign State, 'the validity and effect whereof depend upon the law of nations.' *Cf.* Underhill v. Hernandez, 65 Fed. 577 (C. C. A. 2d, 1895).

crimes committed by order of his State on American soil, pointed out that: 'To admit to its full extent the principle that we cannot subject to our municipal laws aliens who violate such laws under direction of their sovereigns, would be to give such sovereigns jurisdiction over our soil.'[88] From this it must follow that a sovereign's agent will *not* be exempt from liability, if his act is not justifiable under international law.

Moreover, as Marshall implied, even in an age when the doctrine of sovereignty had a strong hold,[89] the non-liability of agents of a State for 'acts of State' must rationally be based upon an assumption that no member of the Family of Nations will order its agents to commit flagrant violations of international and criminal law. It must rest upon an assumption that a State will prohibit its own subjects from committing acts of defiance of law so grave as to endanger the peace and security of other States, as well as its own, and, far from condoning such acts, will punish them. As Blackstone long ago pointed out:

...where the individuals of any state violate this general [*i.e.*, international] law, it is then the interest as well as duty of the government under which they live to animadvert upon them with a becoming severity that the peace of the world may be maintained. For in vain would nations in their collective capacity observe these universal rules, if private

Calhoun, in the Senate, contraverted the position of the British 'that where a government authorizes or approves of the act of an individual, it makes it the act of the government, and thereby exempts the individual from all responsibility to the injured country.' He argued that 'the laws of nations are but the laws of morals, as applicable to individuals, so far modified, and no further, as reason may make necessary in their application to nations. Now, there can be no doubt that the analogous rule, when applied to individuals, is, that both principal and agents, or...instruments, are responsible in criminal cases; directly the reverse of the rule on which the demand for the release of McLeod is made....Suppose, then, that the British, or any other government, in contemplation of war, should send out emissaries to blow up the fortifications erected, at such vast expense, for the defense of our great commercial marts...would the production of the most authentic papers, signed by all the authorities of the British Government, make it a public transaction, and exempt the villains from all responsibility to our laws and tribunals?' 2 Moore, A Digest of International Law (1906) 23–30, 409–14.

It will be noted that the above transaction involved the action of a Government on *neutral* territory in *peacetime*; and the British and Webster's views of the act-of-State exemption are at all events therefore not applicable to the relations of belligerents in wartime.

[88] 1 Wharton, A Digest of the International Law of the United States (1886) 67. See Glueck 230–32.

[89] Those statesmen and lawyers who have raised the concept of 'Sovereignty' to the status of some holy fetish have ignored historical facts. The more rigid, legalistic notions of sovereignty are of comparatively late (nineteenth-century) origin or rebirth. 'As in the sixteenth century, so again in the nineteenth century practical political consideratons influenced the precise formulation of a theory that attributed to a definite sovereign an authority unrestrained by law.' Coker, *supra* note 81, at 265, 267 (and authorities therein cited). Practical considerations in our time, such as the fact that sovereigns of certain nations have several times clearly demonstrated their self-appointed divine right to trample over the territory and lives of neighboring peoples in violation of solemn treaty obligations, and particularly the sobering fact of the advent of the atomic bomb, should bring about a reformulation of the theory of national sovereignty. It is to be noted that the basis of sovereign immunity in the field of civil liability has, partly under the impact of the facts of modern technology and the modifications in culture thereby brought about, been breaking down. See Angell, *Sovereign Immunity—The Modern Trend* (1925) 35 Yale L. J. 150.

subjects were at liberty to break them at their own discretion, and involve the two states in a war. It is therefore incumbent upon the nation injured, first, to demand satisfaction and justice to be done on the offender by the state to which he belongs; and, if that be refused or neglected, *the sovereign then avows himself an accomplice or abettor of his subject's crime, and draws upon his community the calamities of foreign war.*[90]

Blackstone assumed that a sovereign would not willingly ally himself with the criminal acts of his agents. But where a State clearly sets out to put into effect its own calculated plan of criminally aggressive warfare, mass-murder, and mass-pillage it is absurd to believe that it will disclaim the crimes of its agents in carrying out its plan, or will punish them if left to its own devices.[91]

It could very reasonably be argued, moreover, that in modern times a State is—*ex hypothesi*—incapable of ordering or ratifying acts which are not only criminal according to generally accepted principles of domestic penal law but also contrary to that international law to which all States are perforce subject. Its agents, in performing such acts, are therefore acting outside their legitimate scope; and must, in consequence, be held personally liable for their wrongful conduct. It is interesting to note that a similar view on the part of the German Supreme Court may be deduced from its judgment in the case of General Stenger, tried in 1920 for the slaying of wounded French soldiers during the first world war:

The lawfulness or unlawfulness of an act of war is determined by the rules of international law. The killing of enemies in war *is in accordance with the will of the State* which wages the war and whose laws are decisive for the question of legality or illegality *only to the extent that it is done under the conditions and within the limits which international law establishes.*[92]

---

[90] Blackstone, Commentaries *68 (italics supplied). How much more civilized it is if, instead of the sovereign accomplice drawing 'upon his community the calamities of foreign war,' he and the other planners and executors of a war in violation of solemn treaty obligations are subjected to the civilized methods of prosecution and trial and, if convicted, to individual punishment.

[91] The whole sorry mess of the trial of German war criminals after the first World War in the German Supreme Court at Leipzig tends to demonstrate this. The 896 serious offenders submitted for prosecution on the Allied list were soon cut down to a 'test' list of only 45. The number actually tried was only 12; the number convicted, 6. The sentences were for imprisonment only, and that usually for absurdly brief periods of months; and the two convicts sentenced for U-boat atrocities soon escaped, with what appears to have been official connivance. A German general, clearly guilty of ordering the massacre of wounded prisoners of war, was found not guilty despite abundant proof; and his acquittal was greeted with applause and flowers by the Germans attending the trial. Glueck 31–32. Even the most distinguished German legal scholars applied a perverted, justifying rationalization to the war crimes problem, which clearly demonstrates that the peculiar and dangerous chauvinistic 'reasoning' that the world attributes to Nazi-Germany's leaders had its origin much earlier. See Professor Lauterpacht's references to the Opinion of Professor Meurer as reflecting the reasoning of German jurists on the Commission on War Crimes appointed by the German *Reichstag* after the first World War. Lauterpacht, *The Law and the Punishment of War Crimes* (1944) 21 Brit. Y. B. Int. L. 58, 61 n.1. But see Schücking, *Die deutschen Professoren und der Weltkrieg*, in 5 Flugschriften des Bundes 'Neues Vaterland' (1915).

[92] Drucksachen des Reichstags, Wahlperiode (1920) Aktenstück Nr. 2584, I, 2542, 2568 (author's translation; italics supplied).

It is perfectly obvious that the application of a universal principle of non-responsibility of a State's agents could easily render the entire body of international law a dead letter. For any group of criminally minded persons comprising the temporary Government that has seized power in a State could readily arrange to declare all of its violations of the law of nations—either in initiating an illegal war or in conducting it contrary to the laws and customs of recognizedly legitimate warfare—to be 'acts of State.' Thus all its treaty obligations and international law generally could be rendered nugatory; and thus the least law-abiding member of the Family of Nations could always have a weapon with which to emasculate the very law of nations itself. The result would be that the most lawless and unscrupulous leaders and agents of a State could never be brought to account. If such a State won an aggressive war, the politicians, militarists and industrialists who had planned, ordered or executed even the most flagrant atrocities and cynical breaches of international and municipal law, would of course not subject themselves to prosecution in their own courts. And if they happened to lose—as Germany and its chronic militarists have in our day happened twice to do—they would again be assured of personal immunity through application of an irrational technicality. Only the State would have to pay reparations; and that would mean that either the war-impoverished losing State would gradually wriggle out of its obligation, and even transform it into a loss to the people of the victor State (as was true of Germany *vis à vis* the United States after the first World War); or many ordinary citizens of the losing State, who had had nothing to do with initiating or conducting an unjust and ruthless war, would be penalized through heavy taxation to meet the fine imposed upon their nation. The scoundrels at the top, who had actually plotted and carried out the breaches of international and municipal law, would conveniently escape with their lives and fortunes and conserve their strength for still another try at world domination—a process in which they have nothing to lose and everything to gain.

If a doctrine so contrary to reason and justice has indeed been accepted as unconditionally valid international law, it is high time the error were remedied.[93] 'It is an universal principle of jurisprudence that in cases otherwise doubtful the rule or interpretation which gives the most reasonable results [is] to be applied; and the law of nations is as much entitled to the benefit of that principle as any other kind of law.'[94] Since law is supposed to embody the rule of reason in the

[93] Article 3 of the Washington treaty of February 6, 1922, dealing with the use of submarines and noxious gases in warfare (ratified by the United States of America, the British Empire, Italy and Japan) specifically provided that for determination of the guilt of the attacking *individual*, it shall be immaterial whether or not the attacker 'is under orders of a governmental superior,' the offender being 'deemed to have violated the laws of war and...liable to trial and punishment as if for an act of piracy...before the civil or military authorities of any Power within the jurisdiction of which he may be found.' France's failure to ratify rendered the treaty abortive, but her action was not based upon a lack of sympathy with the provision regarding personal liability for acts of State.

[94] Pollock, *The Sources of International Law* (1902) 2 COL. L. REV. 511, 514.

interests of justice, and the unqualified act-of-State doctrine emasculates both reason and justice, it cannot be regarded as sound law.[95]

There was therefore ample justification for the disavowal of the act-of-State doctrine in both the report to the President (June 7, 1945) by the American Chief of Counsel and the Charter of the International Military Tribunal.[96] The idea that the act-of-State doctrine is universally and unconditionally operative is simply bad law; and bad law should be replaced with good law. 'Where error has been detected as society has advanced, the customary law has been gently modified; it has been modified by the same power to which it owed its existence, and by which alone it can be modified—the expressed or tacit consent of nations; and by this it may still further be altered, when improvements shall be suggested by the greater progress of human society.'[97]

VI

It has also been objected that, even assuming aggressive war to be a crime, and assuming the invalidity of the act-of-State doctrine for the issue before the Nuernberg tribunal, the law of nations cannot be applied directly to individuals.[98] This is true, it is argued, because in the first place international law is a body of norms applicable only to the actions of sovereign States and, in the second place, it provides no sanctions applicable to individuals, no punishments for natural persons.

[95] It is the above basis, and not the one stated in the following quotation, that justifies the prosecution of individuals for the planning and execution of an aggressive war: 'One difficulty with that reply is that the body of growing custom to which reference is made is custom directed at sovereign states, not at individuals. Aside from the abortive submarine convention of 1922, where is the convention or treaty which places obligations upon the individual not to aid in waging an aggressive war?' WYZANSKI, THE NUREMBERG WAR CRIMINALS TRIAL (a communication to the Academy of Arts and Sciences, Dec. 12, 1945) 3. [Hereinafter cited as WYZANSKI.]

[96] TRIAL OF WAR CRIMINALS 3–4, 8, 17.

[97] MANNING, COMMENTARIES ON THE LAWS OF NATIONS (Amos ed., 1875) 82.

[98] It is an 'orthodox principle that individuals are not subjects of the law of nations'; there is an absence '... of international war crimes chargeable either to the collectivity of persons forming a nation or to its members individually...In the absence of international authority, international conventions on the conduct of warfare as a rule make it the duty of States to transform or incorporate their provisions into national regulations and to enforce the latter against the persons subject to their control.' Manner, *The Legal Nature and Punishment of Criminal Acts of Violence Contrary to the Laws of War* (1943) 37 AM. J. INT. L. 407–10. A convincing series of studies in opposition to the traditional view has in recent years grown up. See POLITIS, THE NEW ASPECTS OF INTERNATIONAL LAW (1928) (and references therein); VERDROSS, DIE VÖLKERRECHTSWIDRIGE KRIEGSHANDLUNG UND DER STRAFANSPRUCH DER STAATEN (1920) 33 *et seq.*; Schwarzenberger, *War Crimes and the Problem of an International Criminal Court* in CZECHOSLOVAK YEARBOOK OF INTERNATIONAL LAW (1942) 67–69; Aufricht, *Personality in International Law* (1943) 37 AM. POL. SCI. REV. 217, 235–43; Kelsen, *Collective and Individual Responsibility in International Law with Particular Regard to the Punishment of War Criminals* (1943) 31 CALIF. L. REV. 531, 534–38. And compare *Ex parte* Quirin, 317 U. S. 1, 27–28 (1942).

Historically, and in a practical sense, this traditional view is also open to question. To cite a familiar case, violation of the rule that prohibits piracy—regardless of whether or not that offense has also been previously constituted a crime by the statutory law of the State which happens to have seized the pirate—is clearly a violation of a norm of the law of nations. On the one hand, no prior international legislative enactment making a piratical act a crime was necessary to the criminalization of piracy; on the other hand, no prior enactment of municipal law was necessary to make the act also a local crime. Yet individuals are prosecuted as pirates.

So, also, those American States which administer the common law of crimes have from the beginning punished violations of the law of nations by individuals, without prior legislative prohibition of them as crimes. Thus in Pennsylvania a defendant was convicted and sentenced to imprisonment and fine for insulting and threatening bodily harm to the Secretary of the French Legation.[99] The indictment set forth that the victim was then 'under the protection of the law of nations and this Commonwealth.'[100] The prosecution argued 'the necessity of sustaining the law of nations... the connection between the law of nations and the municipal law, and the effect which the decision of this case must have upon the honor of Pennsylvania, and the safety of her citizens abroad.... Upon the same principle that the infringement of a statute is an indictable offense, though the mode of punishment is not pointed out in the act itself, an offense against the laws of nations, while they compose a part of the law of the land, must necessarily be indictable.'[101] It rejected the defendant's contention that 'the reparation sought, and the remedy offered, are confined to the *municipal law of Pennsylvania*, where the offense was committed; and [that] in all cases of menaces, the law of Pennsylvania yields no further relief than the imposition of a legal restraint on the execution of those menaces.'[102] The court expressed the opinion that the case 'must be determined on the principles of the law of nations, which form a part of the municipal law of Pennsylvania; and, if the offenses charged in the indictment have been committed, there can be no doubt, that those laws have been violated.'[103] In imposing sentence of a large fine, two years' imprisonment and the furnishing of heavy 'security to keep the peace, and be of good behavior to all public Ministers, Secretaries to Embassies and Consuls... for seven years....' the court said:

The first crime in the indictment is an infraction of the law of nations. This law, in its full extent, is part of the law of this State, and is to be collected from the practice of different nations and the authority of writers. The person of a public minister is sacred and inviolable. Whoever offers any violence to him, *not only affronts the Sovereign he represents, but also hurts the common safety and well-being of nations—he is guilty of a crime against the whole world.*[104]

---

[99] Respublica v. De Longchamps, 1 Dall. 11 (Pa. 1784).
[100] *Ibid.*   [101] *Ibid.*
[102] *Id.* at 113 (italics supplied).
[103] *Id.* at 114.   [104] *Id.* at 116 (italics supplied).

The Supreme Court of the United States, in the *Saboteurs' Case*,[105] has more recently held, in effect, that individual offenders against the laws and customs of warfare can be punished under the law of warfare branch of the common law of nations, without prior intervention of specific domestic legislation. Careful examination of that decision will show it to be very probably correct to say, with Professor Hyde, that it 'is impressive judicial testimony to the effect not only that'[106] the 'law of nations may, and oftentimes does, address its injunctions to *individuals* by attaching an *internationally* illegal quality to particular acts,'[107] but that 'the law of war as a part of the law of nations is a part of the local law,'[108] and 'also that its applicability by the courts in reference to penal matters need not await precise legislative appraisal or definition.'[109]

During the trial of German war criminals after the close of the first World War by the German Supreme Court at Leipzig, that tribunal, also, was impelled to acknowledge the direct obligatoriness of the law of nations upon individuals. In the decision of the case involving the torpedoing of the British hospital ship *Llandovery Castle* and the machine-gunning of survivors in lifeboats, the German court said:

The firing on the boats was an offense against the *law of nations.... Any violation of the law of nations in warfare is... a punishable offense,* so far as in general a penalty is attached to the deed.... The rule of *international law*, which is here involved, is simple and is universally known.... The court must in this instance affirm Patzig's guilt of killing contrary to *international* law.[110]

It might be pointed out, moreover, that at the time the accused committed the offense, the Weimar Constitution, with its specific embodiment of the law of nations into the law of the German Republic, was not yet in force.

The authorities cited and others[111] amply support the conclusion that the relevant principles of the law of nations may and do obligate individuals; and that there is nothing in the law of nations itself that necessarily prohibits the direct application of its relevant prohibitions to natural persons, if a State chooses to do

---

[105] *Ex parte* Quirin, 317 U. S. 1 (1942). And see Matter of Yamashita, 14 U. S. L. WEEK 414 (Feb. 4, 1946).

[106] Hyde, *Aspects of the Saboteur Cases* (1943) 37 AM. J. INT. L. 88 (italics supplied). One of the arguments of the defense was that there is a 'serious question as to whether there was any such offense as the violation of the law of war.' This was probably based on the theory that inasmuch as Congress has been given specific power by the Constitution (Art. I, Sec. 8) to define offenses against the law of nations, there can be no offense of this kind in the absence of a specific statute, in accordance with the doctrine in *United States v. Hudson*, 7 Cranch 32 (U. S. 1812). See also Matter of Yamashita, 14 U. S. L. WEEK 414 (Feb. 4, 1946).

[107] Hyde, *supra* note 106, at 91 (italics supplied).

[108] *Id.* at 88. [109] *Ibid.*

[110] (1922) 16 AM. J. INT. L. 721 (italics supplied). So, also, on other occasions some of the decisions of German courts 'seem to indicate a willingness on the part of some German judges, at least, to apply customary international law directly.' MASTERS, INTERNATIONAL LAW IN NATIONAL COURTS (1932) 46.

[111] See 2 HALLECK, INTERNATIONAL LAW (4th ed. 1908) 351 n.1. See also 75 BRITISH AND FOREIGN STATE PAPERS (1883–84) 672–75; 74 *id.* (1882–83) 591.

so. The duty of a State as a member of the Family of Nations to punish violations of the prohibitions imposed by international law is a matter of the law of nations; but whether any particular local sovereignty requires prior specific 'implementation' of international law by 'conversion' of its prohibitions into those of municipal criminal or military law, or prefers to punish them directly without such intercession of domestic legislation, is a matter of each State's own constitution—an arrangement of municipal law. No State whose national is being proceeded against in a foreign State's criminal or military court has any right to insist that before the defendant can be prosecuted for acts obnoxious to international law the prohibitions of that system of law must first have been 'transformed' into the prosecuting State's statutory criminal law. All it can claim is the same treatment of its nationals as is afforded the prosecuting State's own subjects.

Consequently, when the great majority of civilized States, after due warning to the Axis leaders, united in prosecuting individuals for violating the tenets of international law they were doing no more than could have been done had each of them proceeded individually. Indeed, they are doing a service to the Family of Nations and its international law, in combining their individual jurisdictions into a single agency speaking on behalf of world law and order. The same considerations that led to the universal recognition that pirates were violators of the law common to all States and could therefore be prosecuted by any, apply, only with much more force, to the kind of acts committed by the Nazi leaders, especially the planning, launching, and conducting of a series of aggressive wars in violation of the most solemn treaty obligations and of international law generally. In the absence of a world authority and an international criminal tribunal, the prosecutions had perforce in the past to be conducted in the courts of the State which seized the pirate, and the punishment to be meted out by that State; but the violation of the law involved always was one which concerned the entire Community of Nations, and the prosecuting State was acting, in effect, as agent of all civilized States in vindicating the law common to them all. However, given an international court such as the International Military Tribunal at Nuernberg, the task of trying and sentencing individuals accused of violating international law can more appropriately be performed by such a court as agent of the entire Family of Nations.

But it is also objected that international law provides no sanctions applicable to individuals.

This claim, too, is open to question. Grotius, the father of modern international law, clearly implies that the law of nations provides for the death penalty in case of its violation by individuals:

There is no danger from prisoners and those who have surrendered or desire to do so; therefore in order to warrant their execution it is necessary that a crime shall have been previously committed, such a crime, moreover, as a just judge would hold punishable by death.[112]

---

[112] GROTIUS, DE JURE BELLI AC PACIS. bk. III, c. XI § 16, cl. 1. Compare Respublica v. De Longchamps, 1 Dall. 111, 117 (Pa. 1784).

Any lesser punishment is merely a matter of grace to the offender; and a State (or a group of States acting jointly as agent of the Family of Nations) is free under international law to impose the penalties it deems appropriate to the particular offense.[113]

Holland, a distinguished twentieth-century authority, after an exhaustive study of the most reliable sources of customary international law, also concludes that:

Individuals offending against the laws of war are liable to such punishment as is prescribed by the military code of the belligerent into whose hands they may fall, or, in default of such code, then to such punishment as may be ordered in accordance with the laws and usages of war, by a military court.[114]

Furthermore, most States, including Germany, have long provided for various appropriate punishments of individual violators of the laws and customs of war.

These authorities speak, to be sure, of breaches of the 'laws of war'; but the same principle would apply to breaches of any other prohibition of international law capable of being violated by individuals, including a breach of the peace of the world by the initiation and conduct of an illegal and criminal war.

Moreover, the situation with reference to the execution of sentence and the imposition of punishment on those of the accused at Nuernberg who will be found guilty is much more favorable than that which is usual with international courts. 'The imperfect state of the law of nations, in respect that it lacks a cosmopolitan judicial court with power to execute its decrees, is a well-worn topic.... it seems fit to be considered that in the early history of all jurisdictions the executive power at the disposal of the courts has been rudimentary, if indeed they had such power at all.'[115] The International Criminal Court sitting at Nuernberg, on the other hand, has, at its disposal, the United Nations Control Council. Article 29 of the Charter, which is part of the Four-Power Agreement of August 8, 1945, to which many States have since acceded, provides that:

In case of guilt, sentences shall be carried out in accordance with the orders of the Control Council and the Control Council may at any time reduce or otherwise alter the sentences but may not increase the severity thereof.[116]

---

[113] Elsewhere I have gone into some of the complex political, ethical and penologic issues involved in the determination of appropriate punishment for those Nazi leaders who will be convicted. GLUECK 171–77.

[114] HOLLAND, THE LAWS AND CUSTOMS OF WAR ON LAND AS DEFINED BY THE HAGUE CONVENTION OF 1899 (1904) 45. See also Bartlett, *Liability for Official War Crimes* (1919) 35 L. Q. REV. 177, 186. 'A military commission may impose any lawful and appropriate sentence, including death or life imprisonment.' MILITARY GOVERNMENT (U. S. War Dept., Basic Field Manual, FM 27–5, 1940) 15.

[115] Pollock, *supra* note 61, at 514.

[116] TRIAL OF WAR CRIMINALS 21.

VII

It will be seen from the foregoing that it is not doing unpardonable violence to the law to exclude both the act-of-State argument and that which insists that international law is not and cannot ever be applicable to individual offenders. However, in the statement of November 21, 1945, made by counsel for the defense at the opening of the Nuernberg trial, the claim was insistently urged that to hold the accused, as individuals, for acts of State was *ex post facto* and unjust. It was argued that until that trial, jurists and nations had:

...never even thought of incriminating statesmen, generals and economic leaders of a state using force, and still less bringing these men before an international criminal court....As far as crimes against peace are concerned, the present trial has, therefore, no legal basis in international law but is a procedure based on a new penal law; a penal law created only after the act. This is in contradiction to a legal principle that is cherished in the world. It has been violated partly in Hitler Germany. This violation has been emphatically disapproved within and without the Reich. This principle is the maxim: punishment is possible only if a law has been violated that was in existence at the time the act was committed and that provided punishment....This principle is not a matter of opportunism but based on the knowledge that every defendant must feel treated unjustly if he is punished under a murder law created *ex post facto*.[117]

---

[117] N. Y. Times, Nov. 22, 1945, p. 3, col. 1. (The official transcript was not available). One may perhaps be pardoned for viewing with some skepticism this sudden Wagnerian trumpet-call against the terrible legal sin of 'a murder law created *ex post facto*.' The Nazis, who through their lawyers now nobly enter the lists to slay the fire-breathing dragon of retroactive liability, were not particularly famous for their interest in such a holy crusade when they were in power and dealt with their numerous victims. Indeed, to justify most of their tortures, mass-murders and mass-lootings, the Nazis were not greatly troubled about the existence of *any* law—retroactive or other. Since the administration of justice does not operate in a vacuum it is perhaps not altogether irrelevant, in judging the theory and proceedings of the Nuernberg trial, to advert to the fact that the defendants there, who evidently insist upon a strictly technical interpretation of law only when such an interpretation will redound to their benefit, do not come into court with clean hands. Nor were many members of the German bar and bench altogether unsympathetic with the Nazi lawlessness. It is notorious that a great deal of clear and serious *ex post facto* legislation was enacted or decreed in Nazi Germany. For example: 'Whoever commits an act which...deserves punishment according to the principles of criminal law and to the *sound feelings of the people*, [*i.e.*, the Nazis] will be punished.' Section 2 of the law concerning alteration of the criminal code, June 28, 1935 REICHSGESETZBLATT I, 839 (italics supplied). The Nazis also prosecuted and punished many nationals of the countries they overran, for alleged crimes committed before 1939, the acts of which, by the laws of those countries, were not crimes at that time. Although the German constitution of 1919 contained a clause prohibiting *ex post facto* laws, this did not prevent the Nazi government from retroactively changing arson from a non-capital to a capital crime in the Van der Lubbe *Reichstag* fire case in 1933. So, also, following the murderous 'purge' of Roehm and his companions during the falling-out of the Nazi gangsters, Hitler later 'legalized' the 'execution.' The claim (in the quotation in the text) of counsel for the Nuernberg defendants that violation of the principle *'Nulla poena sine lege'* was *'emphatically disapproved* within the Reich [italics supplied]' is something that will call for a great deal of proof before it is acceptable.

The indignant protest against alleged retroactive liability made by the Germans at Nuernberg may be taken with a rather large grain of salt. Not so the support of their position by certain American lawyers, as to whose sincerity there can be no doubt.[118]

It is therefore necessary to examine the supposed 'retrospective'[119] nature and consequent injustice allegedly involved in the Nuernberg trial and particularly in holding individual members of a lawless Government criminally responsible for their deeds.

The doctrine, 'no crime and no punishment without pre-existing law,' has a long and honorable pedigree;[120] but there has been a tendency to insist upon its literal observance regardless of the factual question whether its non-application formally in the given set of circumstances will or will not actually work an injustice. One can understand the spirit with which, in domestic constitutional law, the application of the *ex post facto* test to legislation is jealously insisted upon. For it is rightly concluded that 'the antagonism to *ex post facto* laws rests upon this sound principle: if the law can be created after the offense then power is absolute and arbitrary... (the very notion which is most repugnant to constitutionalism).'[121] But the essence of the doctrine in question as applied to a novel situation can only be grasped when one views its actual effects upon the person accused of crime.

The reason, the humanity, and consequently the social policy, behind the doctrine *nulla poena sine lege* are based upon an avoidance of unfairness to the accused which, when analyzed, is shown to involve the following elements:

(1) It is unjust to punish for an act which prior to its commission was not officially prohibited, because to do so would be to change, arbitrarily, the legal consequences of an act.

(2) The failure to prohibit the act until after it was done is particularly obnoxious to justice, because, inasmuch as the prohibition of retroactive penal legislation involves the principle that all conduct *not* legally prohibited is *permissible*,

---

[118] See, *e.g.*, these thought-provoking articles: Radin, *War Crimes and the Crime of War* (1945) 21 VA. L. Q. 497–516; Vambery, *Law and Legalism* (1945) 161 THE NATION 573; *The Nürnberg Novelty* (1945) 32 FORTUNE 140–41; WYZANSKI; KONVITZ, *Will Nuremberg Serve Justice?* (1946) 1 COMMENTARY (American Jewish Committee) 9–15.

[119] While it is true that 'retrospective' or 'retroactive' laws must for certain purposes be distinguished from constitutionally prohibited *ex post facto* criminal statutes [see Calder v. Bull, 3 Dall. 386 (U. S. 1798)], the terms are used interchangeably in the text, since no ambiguity can result, and Continental lawyers most frequently speak of 'retroactive' or 'retrospective' legislation.

[120] See authorities cited by Shulman, *Retroactive Legislation* in 13 ENCYC. SOC. SCI. (1937) 355; Smead, *The Rule Against Retroactive Legislation: A Basic Principle of Jurisprudence* (1936) 20 MINN. L. REV. 775; Hall, *Nulla Poena Sine Lege* (1937) 47 YALE L. J. 165; WYZANSKI. Some American sources for the constitutional prohibition of *ex post facto* laws (Art. 1 § 9, cl. 3; § 10, cl. 1) are the Maryland and North Carolina Declarations of Rights of 1776, the Massachusetts Constitution of 1780, and the New Hampshire Constitution of 1784. FISHER, THE EVOLUTION OF THE CONSTITUTION OF THE UNITED STATES (1897) 210–11.

[121] WYZANSKI 3. See STORY, A FAMILIAR EXPOSITION OF THE CONSTITUTION OF THE UNITED STATES (1883) 144.

the act in question is typically one which, according to prevailing popular opinion and legislative belief at the time it was done, was deemed harmless or at least relatively venial.[122]

(3) It is unjust to punish for such an act, because the prospective malefactor had received no prior notice that his deed would be punished.

(4) The law supposedly violated, notice of the existence of which had not been given, must at all events have been enacted by a sovereign to which the accused is subject, and one vested with authority and power to prohibit and punish acts deemed harmful to the general welfare.

The analyzing of the issue and its ramifications thus tangibly, in terms of what *ex post facto* application of law means to the accused, ought to disclose whether or not, in *substance* if not in literal form, any real retroactivity or true injustice is involved in prosecuting the Nazi leaders as personally responsible for planning and executing aggressive wars.

(1) Is it changing the legal consequences of the aggressive acts of warfare and their instrumental mass-murders and mass-thefts to hold the Nazi leaders personally responsible? It has been argued, above, that because of the status of custom among the vast majority of peoples in our day, aggressive warfare may legitimately be regarded as an international crime. It has further been argued that it is very doubtful if the act-of-State doctrine, by which the accused seek immunity, ever was sound law so far as concerns its applicability to the kind of deeds done by the Nazi leaders. If the International Military Tribunal, representing many of the States of the Family of Nations and the great majority of civilized peoples, should decide that as a matter of reasonable law the act-of-State principle is not applicable to the Nazi leaders, there could be no sound reason for the claim that they were being held liable retrospectively; for the court would then be merely settling an unsettled state of the law by a reasonable construction of the law.[123]

(2) Are the acts involved in the waging of an aggressive war such as, were it not for the supposed holding of them to be criminal only after they were committed,

---

[122] Historically, *ex post facto* penalization for *serious* acts has been very rare. For a few illustrations, see King v. Thurston, 1 Lev. 91, 83 Eng. Rep. 312 (1663); Calder v. Bull, 3 Dall. 386, 389 (U. S. 1798).

[123] Compare a similar argument by Wyzanski, speaking of the unsettled state of the law of 'superior orders': 'If the International Military Tribunal in connection with a charge of a war crime, *strictu sensu*, refuses to recognize superior orders as a defense it will not be making a retroactive determination or applying an *ex post facto* law. Proof of that assertion is this: suppose tomorrow the grand jury for the District of Massachusetts should indict Private Jones for whipping a German prisoner of war at Fort Devens, and the private defended himself on the ground that he was obeying the order of the commanding officer at Devens,—would not the District Judge face the precise problem the Nuremberg tribunal now faces? And if the District Judge should decide adversely to Jones would any reasonable person say that construction of the law was a violation of the *ex post facto* clause of the United States Constitution, Article I, s. 9?' WYZANSKI 2. (Incidentally, both the United States and the British Rules of Warfare greatly weakened the superior orders defense during the war).

would generally be regarded as quite harmless? It was pointed out in the argument of counsel in the Nuernberg trial that the *nulla poena sine lege* principle is 'based on the knowledge that every defendant must feel treated unjustly if he is punished under a murder law created *ex post facto.*' This very quotation gives their whole case away: for it speaks of a '*murder* law created *ex post facto.*' In other words, it is brazenly claimed that because the civilized world cannot put its finger on some specific section in an international penal code which prohibits the slaughter of millions in an aggressive, unlawful and unnecessary war, such acts were *permissible* since, technically, they were not labeled 'murder' by world law at the time the killings occurred, even though by the laws of all civilized States unjustified killings are stigmatized as murders.[124] Even to state the German lawyers' proposition is to demonstrate its mélange of impudence, cynicism, and absurdity.

(3) But in addition to the argument that those acts which are not specifically prohibited by some international penal code are permissible—however terrible and dangerous to the rest of humanity they may be, and however universally they are deemed crimes—there is the further argument that to hold men retroactively responsible is bad because the accused had no advance notice that the acts they were about to do were to be punished as crimes; otherwise, presumably, they would not have done them. Now what are the facts with respect to the defendants at Nuernberg? Can they seriously claim injured innocence because of lack of advance notice that their acts would be regarded as crimes? Surely, Hitler, Goebbels, Himmler, Goering, Frank, Doenitz, Keitel, Ribbentrop, Schacht, and the rest of those in the inner political, military and economic circle of the Nazi Government knew that Germany had signed and ratified a solemn treaty which outlawed war and in which it agreed to resort only to peaceful methods of settling international disagreements.[125] Surely they knew that Germany had again and again entered into treaties with its neighbors in which it solemnly assured them of peaceful and friendly intentions.[126] Surely, also, the leading Nazis on trial at Nuernberg knew of the international pronouncements to which Germany was a Party, which conceived of a war of aggression as an international crime. And surely they knew that a State could not unilaterally make a mere 'scrap of paper' of such basic security treaties as the Briand-Kellogg pact.[127]

---

[124] See Appendix.

[125] In the German reply to the letter of the American Ambassador proposing the Treaty for the Renunciation of War (April 27, 1928), the German Government (by Stresemann) had welcomed '... most warmly the opening of negotiations for the conclusion of an international pact for the outlawry of war.' TREATY FOR THE RENUNCIATION OF WAR [Dept. of State Publication 468 (1933)] 40.

[126] For details of the numerous treaties entered into and violated by Germany during her orgy of aggression, see Appendix C to Indictment Number I, 'Charges and Particulars of Violations of International Treaties, Agreements and Assurances Caused by the Defendants in the Course of Planning, Preparing and Initiating the Wars,' TRIAL OF WAR CRIMINALS 82–89.

[127] 'A signatory State cannot by denunciation or nonobservance of the Pact release itself from its obligations thereunder.' *Articles of Interpretation Proposed by the Committee on Conciliation Between*

Not only did they know all this, but they had had notice from Versailles of the strong view expressed by all but the American and Japanese members of the Commission on Responsibility at the close of World War I that 'all persons belonging to enemy countries, however high their position may have been, without distinction of rank, including Chiefs of States, who have been guilty of offences against the laws and customs of war or the laws of humanity, are liable to criminal prosecution.'[128] Certainly it may be said that the waging of an aggressive, unnecessary and particularly brutal war is a crime against 'the laws of humanity.' And, again, the Germans were warned at Versailles that, '... in the hierarchy of persons in authority, there is no reason why rank, however exalted, should in any circumstances protect the holder of it from responsibility when that responsibility has been established before a properly constituted tribunal.'[129]

Furthermore, they had notice again and again, from Roosevelt, Churchill and Stalin, as well as from groups of statesmen of the lesser Powers—all on behalf of the united front of peace-loving nations—that they would be held responsible personally and individually for their crimes.[130] While some of these pronouncements emphasized barbarities committed against civilians, hostages, and prisoners of war, others spoke in general terms of the Nazi crimes, without specifically excluding the parent crime of a war of aggression which made possible the numerous murders, rapes, thefts and other derivative crimes; and one at least, Stalin's speech of November 6, 1943, specifically announced the necessity of the Allies sternly punishing 'Fascist criminals, guilty instigators of the present war....'[131]

Not only has the evidence introduced at the Nuernberg trial shown that Hitler and his clique well knew they were trampling international law under foot, but also that they deliberately planned to use and did use assurances of adherence to their international obligations as political soporifics to lull the law-abiding nations into a false sense of security and to conceal an elaborate and ruthless program of universal lawlessness, murder, rapine and plunder. At the same time they threatened, to a world at once amazingly gullible and hopefully unbelieving, that they would trample all law under foot. 'I shall shrink from nothing,'

Nations of The International Law Association, REPORT OF THE THIRTY-EIGHTH CONFERENCE, BUDAPEST, 1934 (1935) p. 4, Art. 3.

[128] *Commission on the Responsibility of the Authors of the War and on Enforcement of Penalties* (1920) 14 AM. J. INT. L. 95, 117.

[129] *Id.* at 116.

[130] The United States Commission for the investigation of War Crime, established in October, 1942, after referring to the different classes of atrocities of which it would take cognizance, stated as among its functions, 'to investigate, consider and report upon *any other instances or classes of war crimes* referred to them by the general consent of the Governments of the United Nations.' The Declaration of St. James's Palace begins with the words: 'Whereas Germany, since the beginning of the present conflict *which arose out of her policy of aggression*, has instituted in the occupied countries a regime of terror characterized among other things by imprisonments, mass expulsions, the execution of hostages and massacres,' etc. PUNISHMENT FOR WAR CRIMES (The Inter-Allied Information Committee, 1942) 3 (italics supplied). See also note 67.

[131] N. Y. Times, Nov. 7, 1943, p. 45, col. 7.

shouted Hitler. 'No so-called international law, no agreements will prevent me from making use of any advantage that offers.'[132] And again, 'These so-called atrocities spare me a hundred thousand individual actions against disobedience and discontent.'[133]

Surely, also, Hitler, Himmler, Goering, Ribbentrop, Frank, Keitel, Doenitz and the rest of the unholy alliance in supreme authority in Nazi Germany knew full well that murder is murder, whether wholesale or retail, whether committed in pursuance of a gigantic conspiracy to disregard all treaties and to wage lawless wars or of a smaller conspiracy evolved by a group of domestic murderers.

Surely, also, the accused knew that they could be executed for their deeds without being granted the privilege of any trial at all. Can they now be heard to complain that they had no notice that they would have to stand trial under an interpretation of international law which they do not like because they deem it to involve retroactivity?

That which Hitler and his clique did *not* know was that while they would be given every reasonable facility for defense, they would not be permitted to escape personal liability by hiding their flagrant deeds behind the protective mantle of the convenient 'State.' Is their ignorance of that suddenly to transform them into innocents whose prosecution is frightfully unjust, and fatally 'illegal,' and obnoxiously '*ex post facto*' because it involves something of which they had had no prior notice?

Reviewing the historic facts, it becomes abundantly clear, then, that the Nazi leaders knew that Germany's numerous unlawful and unprovoked assaults upon her peaceable neighbors constituted wars of aggression; that wars of aggression had been outlawed by the action of the great majority of civilized States including Germany, Italy and Japan; that several international pronouncements had declared such deeds to constitute, specifically, international crimes; and that the United Nations were in no way limiting themselves with reference to the type of acts they would regard as war crimes but, on the contrary, were not unlikely to include the planning and waging of aggressive war among the criminal acts for which individuals would be held responsible.

(4) Were the accused subject to a competent sovereign who could lawfully prohibit aggressive wars and declare them to be criminal? If the pre-existence of a single 'World State' under a written World Constitution be deemed indispensable, then it must be admitted there was no such sovereign. If, however, the solidarity of opinion of practically the entire membership of the Community of Nations and its peoples (excepting only those nations and peoples charged with the commission of the crimes in question) may be regarded as expressing the juridical consensus of civilized States, then the sovereign power emerges as an international force; for the peoples of the world have with sufficient clarity

---

[132] RAUSCHNING, HITLER SPEAKS (1939) 21.
[133] *Id.* at 90.

made plain their conviction that aggressive warfare is and should be punished as a crime against international peace and order. The right of law-abiding States to punish, in the name of the entire civilized Community of Nations, acts which by their nature threaten the very existence of international law itself must be regarded as inherent, by the nature of modern technologic development; for this has twice in a quarter-century enabled a single, highly industrialized nation to come close to the enslavement of the entire world. Until that elemental right was invoked at Nuernberg, it was latent, although it had been clearly foreshadowed in the Report of the Allied Committee on Responsibilities at Versailles after defeat of the Central Powers in the first World War;[134] but events of our century have demonstrated the indispensability of recognizing such an international jurisdiction and have also demonstrated that its emergence into the field of action cannot depend upon complete unanimity of agreement among members of the Family of Nations, since certain States have clearly proved their preference for international violence rather than international law.

On this question of sovereignty in its relation to the growth of law two points of view are possible:

In the one, the essence of law is that it is imposed upon society by a sovereign will. In the other, the essence of law is that it develops within society of its own vitality. In the one case, law is artificial: the picture is that of an omnipotent authority standing high above society, and issuing *downwards* its behests. In the other case, law is spontaneous, growing *upwards*, independently of any dominant will. The second view does not exclude the notion of sanction or enforcement by a supreme established authority. This, in most societies, becomes necessary at some stage in the ordinary course of social growth. But authority so set up and obeyed by agreement is not the sole and indispensable source of all law. It is itself a creation of law.[135]

History is on the side of the second view. For history has afforded numerous examples of varying degrees of crystallization of that power disciplined by concepts of law which lies behind 'sovereignty' and 'jurisdiction'; and there have heretofore been periods in history when law was enforced, to the extent that it could be, by a 'sovereign' whose power was as yet incompletely developed and who had to compete with other authorities in claiming jurisdiction over subjects.[136]

---

[134] See *Report of Commission on the Responsibility of the Authors of the War and on Enforcement of Penalties* (1924) 14 AM. J. INT. L. 95 *et seq.*; *Treaty of Peace with Germany, Articles 228–230* (1919) 13 AM. J. INT. L. (Supp.) 151, 250.

[135] ALLEN, LAW IN THE MAKING (1927) 2. See also SCHRIVER, *Holmes, Austin, and the Nature of Law* in JUSTICE OLIVER WENDELL HOLMES (1936) 21–29; *Holmes on Austin's Theory of Law, id.* at 36.

[136] For example, it was not until the reign of Henry II (1154–1189) in England that national courts were developed, administering law for the entire realm in vindication of the 'King's Peace' through the King's judges (*cf.* Constitutions of Clarendon, 1164). 4 BLACKSTONE, COMMENTARIES *422. Consider, also, the jurisdictional conflicts at various stages during the vicissitudes of the Holy Roman Empire, especially periods of decay (*e.g.*, the fifteenth to seventeenth centuries), when the authority of the emperor was successfully challenged by that of the local princelings. As to

Summarizing the historic evidence, an authority correctly concludes: 'In early forms of society the conduct of men in forming legal relationships is governed by customary rules. These are recognized and followed as *law* independently of any "sovereign" injunction or enforcement.'[137] Internationally organized society is still in such 'early form' today. In acting jointly and as agents of all civilized States in the vindication of international law through the prosecution of individuals who brought about its wholesale violation, the United Nations needed no pre-existent World State or World Legislature to justify their jurisdiction. Their agreement during both the first and the second World Wars to pool their rights

Roman antiquity, Clark points out that 'as a general proposition Sovereignty is not necessarily *sole.*...The original constitution, or pre-constitutional condition, of Rome was probably a loose kind of federation, which might be called an aristocratic democracy. The sole Sovereignty, which undoubtedly preceded the Republic, was...a comparatively late development, compounded of earlier offices which did not amount to Sovereignty proper. These inchoate Headships I propose to identify with the names of *tribunus* and *pontifex:* the ultimate development with that of *rex.*...Sole Sovereignty...even when attained, has not been historically by any means a permanent institution but has sometimes had to give way to the plural, but minor, authorities which preceded it, revived under slightly different forms; sometimes, though nominally retained, [it] had to share its powers with other officials in such a manner as to reduce it to a government nominally "limited" but constituting in fact a "Corporate" Sovereignty. The history of Rome, after the fall of the Tarquinian dynasty, is, I believe, an example of the first case. On the other hand, in the Teutonic settlers in Britain, as in some Continental associations of the same and kindred stocks, an originally sole military leadership has been developed into something more nearly resembling true Sovereignty.' CLARK, HISTORY OF ROMAN PRIVATE LAW, PART III REGAL PERIOD (1919) 398, 401, 386–87. See also *id.* at 455; ALLEN, *op. cit. supra* note 135, at 5, 28 *et seq.* It may be pointed out that if the founding fathers had implemented the Articles of Confederation with a court, serious conflicts of sovereignty and jurisdiction between the Confederation and the separate sovereign States might therein have been aired. For though the new Congress was given only weak powers, the Confederation would have had to try, sooner or later, to enforce such powers. 'The Congress itself, under the Articles of Confederation, had, within two months before the sitting of the Federal Convention, adopted resolutions, drafted by John Jay, in which it was declared that when a treaty was made and ratified by authority of those Articles, it became "part of the law of the land, and not only independent of the will and power of the [State] Legislatures, but also binding and obligatory on them"; that all existing State laws repugnant to the treaty ought to be forthwith repealed "to avoid the disagreeable necessity there might otherwise be of raising and discussing questions touching their validity and obligation"; and further that the States ought to provide that their Courts should decide all cases according to the intent of the treaty "anything in the Acts...to the contrary notwithstanding." These resolutions were not explicit in their recognition of the right of the State Courts to disregard State statutes without express authority from the States; but they contained a clear intimation that the Congress expected that the State Courts would take such action; and it is to be noted that arguments in behalf of such action were at once made in cases in such Courts...*Secret Journals of Congress, Foreign Affairs*, March 21, 1787; see also letters of Congress to the States, April 13, 1787. While the Federal Convention was still sitting, a case was argued in the Supreme Court of Pennsylvania at the September term of 1787, *Doane's Adm'rs v. Penhallow*, 1 Dallas 218, in which counsel argued that a law enacted by the Continental Congress, prior to the Articles of Confederation was without authority, and that actions taken under such law were null and void. The President of the Court stated that the point involved in it, "the sovereignty of the separate States on the one hand and the supreme power of the United States in Congress assembled on the other,...is indeed, a momentous question"; but the case was decided on another point; see also *Respublica v. Gordon* (1788), 1 Dallas 233.' WARREN, CONGRESS, THE CONSTITUTION, AND THE SUPREME COURT (1925) 48–49.

137 ALLEN, *op. cit. supra* note 135, at 102.

and duties in enforcement of international law as agents for the entire Family of Nations was in itself an exercise of world sovereignty in behalf of world law. Any formal charter of united action could only have been declaratory of an existent situation.

VIII

It is true that the agencies sitting in judgment upon the acts of the Nuernberg defendants are those set up by former enemies of Germany. But although it would have been preferable to establish a truly international tribunal—one containing representatives of the former Axis nations and neutrals as well as of the United Nations[138]—it by no means follows that painstakingly fair and careful administration of justice is otherwise not possible. The actions of the International Military Tribunal at Nuernberg so far have demonstrated the earnest desire of the judges to do justice fairly and according to generally accepted standards—something acknowledged by defense counsel themselves.

Surely, it will not be seriously contended that the trial of the Nazi and Japanese war criminals should have been postponed until such time as the successor governments to the Axis misrulers had clearly demonstrated to the world their sincere desire and capacity to administer justice according to civilized standards, so that they might participate in the membership of the International Criminal Court. By the time that situation could be reached, the evidence would be 'cold,' most of the accused and witnesses would be dead, the public would have lost all interest, the punishments all deterrent value. Justice would thereby be completely outwitted. Nor could the few neutrals of the recent war have been entrusted with the difficult and dangerous task of prosecuting the Nazi war leaders. For example, it is extremely questionable whether Fascist Spain could have been relied upon to undertake such an enterprise and to carry it out impartially; and small Switzerland, in the shadow of a Germany that might some day again develop into a military colossus, might well have shied away from the task.

It was practical necessity, then, and not some deep-dyed plot, that compelled a prosecution before a court in which the country of the accused is unrepresented except by counsel of the defendants' own choosing and by a panel of fair-minded, legally-trained judges.

Here, again, therefore, in examining the proceedings at Nuernberg, it is the law in action rather than the law in books that should be scrutinized. It is not amiss to recall, in this connection, the Allies' reply to the same argument of 'one-sided

---

[138] See GLUECK 114, 180. It should be pointed out that if an American subject were in the toils for a crime allegedly committed against German law, he would not be heard to complain in a German court that no judge of his own nationality sat on the tribunal trying him, or that German law, which he had had no hand in framing, did not apply to him.

justice' raised in 1919 when it was proposed to try the former German Emperor in a special Allied tribunal:

As regards the German contention that a trial of the accused by tribunals appointed by the Allied and Associated Powers would be a one-sided and inequitable proceeding, the Allied and Associated Powers consider that it is impossible to entrust the trial of those directly responsible for offenses against humanity and international right to their accomplices in their crimes. Almost the whole world has banded itself together in order to bring to naught the German plan of conquest and dominion. The tribunals they will establish will therefore represent the deliberate judgment of the greater part of the civilised world. The Allied and Associated Powers are prepared to stand by the verdict of history as to the impartiality and justice with which the accused will be tried.[139]

But it has been objected that if wars of aggression are to be deemed international crimes, then some of the United Nations who are acting as prosecutors, especially Russia in respect to the attacks on Poland and Finland, ought to be willing to subject their actions to the scrutiny of the International Criminal Court.[140] Without knowing the inside facts more thoroughly than have thus far been disclosed, it is impossible to pass judgment.[141] The case of Germany's

---

[139] *Notes of a meeting held at President Wilson's House, Paris, June 13, 1919*, in 16 MILLER, MY DIARY AT THE CONFERENCE OF PARIS (1924) 400–01. *Cf.*, JACKSON, THE CASE AGAINST THE NAZI WAR CRIMINALS (1946) 71: 'The agreement which sets up the standards by which these prisoners are to be judged does not express the views of the signatory nations alone. Other nations with diverse but highly respected systems of jurisprudence also have signified adherence to it.... You judge, therefore, under an organic act which represents the wisdom, the sense of justice, and the will of nineteen governments, representing an overwhelming majority of all civilized people.'

[140] WYZANSKI 3: 'And what is most serious is that there is doubt as to the sincerity of our belief that all wars of aggression are crimes. A question may be raised whether the United Nations are prepared to submit to scrutiny the attack of Russia on Poland, or on Finland, or the American encouragement to the Russians to break their treaty with Japan, or the American transfer to England of 50 destroyers in what to many seems a disregard of the principles of the *Alabama* case.' See note 141.

[141] Without attempting to go into any technical definition of 'aggression,' something that greatly troubled the experts on the various committees of the League of Nations, it would seem not to be giving proper weight to differences in kind as well as degree to place the numerous carefully planned and brutal invasions of neighboring lands by Germany on the same plane with the acts of the United States or even those of Soviet Russia, as is done in the statement in note 140. The 'inside facts' about the Russian actions are not completely available, although some respectable proof has already been introduced at the Nuernberg trial that Finnish Government leaders were implicated in German plans of aggression against Russia. See N. Y. Times, Feb. 9, 1946, p. 7, col. 4; *id.*, Feb. 13, 1946, p. 15, col. 4. Japan, as a member of the Axis, was in fact an enemy of Russia, though technically at peace. So far as the 'destroyer deal' is concerned, the Opinion of the Attorney General in favor thereof was based on Oppenheim's international law distinction between the *building of ships to the order of a belligerent* with intent or reasonable cause to believe they would enter the service of a belligerent, and the selling of existing armed vessels to a belligerent as contraband. 39 Ops. ATT'Y GEN. (1941), 494–96 (italics supplied). And see Briggs, *Neglected Aspects of tlte Destroyer Deal* (1940) 34 AM. J. INT. L. 569. But apart from such a technical argument, the act of the British during the American Civil War in permitting the outfitting of the *Alabama* for use of the Confederacy [*The Alabama Claims*, United States-Great Britain, Claims Arbitration, 4 PAPERS RELATING TO THE TREATY OF WASHINGTON (1872) 49], is hardly comparable to the action of the United States in 1940, in exchanging destroyers for air bases. Before the destroyer deal was entered into, Hitler had ruthlessly trampled upon all rights of neutrals, as Belgium, Denmark, Holland,

wholesale aggressions is in the meantime crystal clear. Unquestionably, where 'probable cause' exists that a State has conducted a war of aggression that State ought, ideally, to be haled before the International Tribunal. But it should be pointed out that in the meantime the question whether Russia is or is not guilty of a war of aggression is not relevant to the present issue before the court at Nuernberg. There the question is whether or not Germany and her agents are guilty of such a war. The fact that a government—whether a domestic or an international one—is not at some particular time in a position of power and authority sufficient to prosecute certain individuals whom it suspects of violating the law is no reason why it should not proceed with the prosecution of those who are within its power. If the law has indeed been violated by a party temporarily outside the power of the sovereign authority, the offense still remains; there is no statute of limitations involved. In the meantime, it cannot reasonably be argued that the prosecution of so patent and chronic an aggressor nation as Germany should be indefinitely postponed until such time as all alleged malefactors can be haled before an international court.

IX

The foregoing discussion justifies the conclusion, it is believed, that the waging of an aggressive war is not only unlawful but also criminal, and that there is nothing fundamentally 'retrospective' or unjust either in recognizing this fact or in holding individual members of a Government personally liable for criminal acts committed in the name of the State. At the very worst, there is only formal

---

Norway, Yugoslavia and other countries learned only too sorrowfully. Therefore, Germany could not at that time legitimately claim the observation by neutrals of their duties as neutrals. This is especially true in view of the fact that the neutral in question, the United States of America, was at that time (1940) clearly in imminent and serious danger, by virtue of Hitler's publicized program of world aggression. The instinct of self-preservation, itself, called for the American recourse to the elementary right of anticipatory self-defense in a situation in which belated defense, according to the textbook rules of the strictest technical neutrality, would very probably have proved fatal both to England and the United States and therefore to the cause of international law itself. (On the policy of 'fool-proof neutrality,' see Coudert, *International Law and American Policy During the Last Thirty-Five Years* (1941) 35 Am. J. Int. L. 429.) One has only to go back to Grotius, in 1625, to see clearly the legality of the action of the United States in 1940: 'It is the duty of those who stand apart from a war to do nothing which may strengthen the side whose cause is unjust, or which may hinder the movements of him who is carrying on a just war, and, in a doubtful case, to act alike to both sides....' GROTIVS, DE JURE BELLI AC PACIS, bk. III, c, XVII, § III, cl I. Incidentally, 'it has been noted that during the war between Russia and Japan in 1904 and 1905, the German Government permitted the sale to Russia of torpedo boats and also of ocean liners belonging to its auxiliary navy. See Wheaton's International Law, 6th ed. (Keith), Vol. 2, p. 977.' 39 Ops. Att'y Gen. (1940) 484, 496. Finally, there is no valid reason to believe that the United States of America would not be willing to submit the question of the alleged violation of neutrality by the destroyer deal (which, incidentally, cannot reasonably be denominated 'aggressive war') to an international tribunal for adjudication.

retroactivity.[142] The term '*ex post facto*' is not a legal shibboleth; it ought not to be applied blindly and mechanically, but with reason and discretion, in the light both of its historic significance and of the realities of the modern situation.

As has been shown, the progress of international custom has given recognition to and has supplied ample evidence of the fact that a war of aggression is not only a lawless war but a criminal one. But to limit liability and punishability to guilty States is to emasculate this tremendously important principle of international law. It is not the punishment of the corporate entities called States that has done or will do any good in the way of deterrence. It is rather the prosecution and castigation of power-drunk heads of State and members of Governments that give promise of whatever deterrence there may be in condign punishment. As was said in 1918 by Lord Birkenhead, then Attorney General of England, with reference to the former German Kaiser:

It is necessary for all time to teach the lesson that failure is not the only risk which a man possessing at the moment in any country despotic powers and taking the awful decision between Peace and War, has to fear. If ever again that decision should be suspended in nicely balanced equipoise, at the disposition of an individual, let the ruler who decides upon war know that he is gambling, amongst other hazards, with his own personal safety.[143]

This view was echoed by England's redoubtable war leader, Winston Churchill, on September 8, 1942, when he assured the House of Commons that:

those who are guilty of Nazi crimes will have to stand up before tribunals in every land where their atrocities have been committed, in order that an indelible warning may be given to future ages and that successive generations of men may say 'So perish all who do the like again.'[144]

Lord Digby's famous statement regarding the Strafford Bill of Attainder has been cited[145] as a warning against the United Nations' policy of subjecting the

---

[142] If the Court at Nuernberg will decide it has jurisdiction to examine into the alleged *ex post facto* nature of the count charging individual Nazi leaders with the crime of aggressive war (something that may be doubtful in view of the fact that the organic Charter of the Court, its constitution, includes, among crimes 'coming within the jurisdiction of the Tribunal for which there shall be individual responsibility,' the crime in question), it could legitimately be argued that not even *formal* retroactivity is involved. It was shown above that the rule of universal nonliability of members of a Government invested with absolute powers, for plotting and executing wholesale violations of both international law and the principles of criminal law common to all civilized peoples is so contrary to reason and justice, and so dangerous to the security of law-abiding peoples and to the very existence of law itself, that it must be regarded as extremely doubtful whether it ever was true law. If, now, the Nuernberg Tribunal should find it to have been bad law, not even a formal retrospective liability would be involved; for the Court, after hearing argument, would declare that the law was in fact not what the accused had assumed it to be; and a defendant's mistake as to the true status of the law, even though that mistake be inevitable, cannot, under a familiar principle of penal law, be the basis of justification or excuse. KENNY, OUTLINES OF CRIMINAL LAW (1907) 62.

[143] LLOYD GEORGE, MEMOIRS OF THE PEACE CONFERENCE (1939) 60; see also *id.* at 63–64.

[144] N. Y. Times, Sept. 9, 1942, p. 4, col. 8.

[145] WYZANSKI 4.

Nazi leaders to trial instead of disposing of them by summary execution as a frankly political act:

… There is in Parliament a double Power of Life and Death by Bill, a Judicial Power, and a Legislative; the measure of the one, is what's legally just; of the other, what is Prudentially and Politickly fit for the good and preservation of the whole. But these two, under favour, are not to be confounded in Judgment: We must not piece up want of legality with matter of convenience, not the defailance of prudential fitness with a pretence of legal Justice.[146]

But examination of the policy being carried out at Nuernberg will show that the caveat in the quotation is not altogether relevant. At Nuernberg it is not 'defailance of prudential fitness' that is being pieced out 'with a pretence of legal Justice.' There was ample prudential and political fitness, and precedent, for the execution or imprisonment of the defendants at Nuernberg (with, possibly, one or two exceptions), without any trial at all; and the proceedings at Nuernberg are not a mere 'pretence of legal Justice.' At Nuernberg, prudential fitness is being implemented by the reality of legal justice. The provision of an opportunity to be heard, of counsel for the defense, of witnesses for the defense, of translations of all proof into German, of an impartial, judicially-trained tribunal is not a matter of hypocrisy, but a genuine desire to provide those accused of crime with an opportunity for explanation, justification, or excuse. To test the matter, one should lay aside the books and ask the defendants at Nuernberg whether they would have preferred summary execution or imprisonment, without formal proof of their guilt, without any chance to prepare and present a defense, without any chance to cross-examine the witnesses for the prosecution, and without careful and fair judicial oversight of the proceedings.

The fear has been expressed that the Nuernberg case might become a precedent in domestic law.[147] But the likelihood of that is extremely remote. The flow of precedent has been in the opposite direction: from the developed legal systems of municipal law to the less developed system of international law. The Nuernberg trial *will* become a precedent in international law. And what kind of precedent? One which establishes that members of governments, military cliques, industrialists or others actually in power in a State, who deliberately lead their country into an unjustified, inexcusable, aggressive and therefore criminal war may be held personally liable; and that, instead of their being disposed of politically and arbitrarily, with little or no chance to be heard in defense, the accused will be afforded every reasonable opportunity to present their case before as neutral a tribunal as the progress of world organization and world law will permit. It is difficult to see in such a precedent anything but a gain for international law, for the

---

[146] Quoted by McIlwain, High Court of Parliament (1910) 153 from Rushworth, The Tryal of Thomas Earl of Strafford (1700) 53.

[147] See Wyzanski, urging that the accused should have been disposed of, as were Napoleon and the Boxer rebels, by executive or political, rather than judicial ('quasi-judicial'), action.

cause of justice, and for the goal of world security, when the alternative action of one-sided, summary execution is contemplated. Most administration of justice, in the early stages, contained some element of force which may be deemed arbitrary. The Nuernberg trial is being conducted under a system of law that is still in an early stage of evolution. The proceedings at Nuernberg can most fairly be judged not by the fact that at the present stage of world jurisdiction perfect justice cannot be had; but rather by the degree of fairness actually shown by the court. Thus far it has demonstrably acted in harmony with the highest traditions of judicial dignity and impartiality.

Finally, it may be asked, since there is less doubt about the culpability of the Nazi leaders so far as violations of the familiar laws and customs of war are concerned than there is about whether they can be convicted of the crime of launching and conducting an aggressive war, why complicate the issues before the Nuernberg court by including the latter in the bill of indictment? That is a question of policy beyond the ken of the writer. But it should be pointed out that the reason for prosecuting the Nazi leaders for the crime of aggressive war is not merely or chiefly the fact that if the launching of such a war is found to be criminal then *all* acts in pursuance of such a master-crime are criminal—whether they be within or without the laws and customs of warfare, whether they be classifiable as ordinary soldierly deeds or atrocities. That is important, but not too important; for there was ample proof to bring against the Nuernberg defendants on the ordinary counts in the indictment, without resort to the aggressive-war-is-a-crime formula. They could have been (and, judging solely from the case presented by the prosecution, they have been) shown to have violated, wholesale, practically every prohibition of either customary or conventional international law dealing with the conduct of war.

The value of establishing aggressive war as a crime and the Nuernberg defendants as master criminals in the planning, launching, and conducting of such a war is rather a moral one. If the law behind this count in the historic indictment is finally accepted by the Nuernberg tribunal,[148] and if, after the defense has been given ample opportunity to be heard, the charge is proved down to the hilt, the Nazi leaders will be shown to all the world and inscribed in the book of history in their true light: as not merely ordinary criminals, whose crimes differ from others only because there are more of them, but as national leaders who, for the first time in history, have been tried, convicted and punished for having brought upon the world the scourge of illicit war and having thereby attacked all law and all humanity. Perhaps this is what Professor Lauterpacht had in mind when he wrote:

The law of any international society worthy of that name must reject with reprobation the view that between nations there can be no aggression calling for punishment, and it must

---

[148] See note 142.

consider the responsibility for the premeditated violation of the General Treaty for the Renunciation of War as lying within the sphere of criminal law.[149]

It would be a social value of supreme significance if, out of the courthouse at Nuernberg, the dreams of the designers of the Covenant of the League of Nations, the Geneva Protocol, the Briand-Kellogg Pact, and the Charter of the United Nations Organization sprang to life in the form of deterrent sanctions for the assassins of world peace. It would be a heartening demonstration of a long overdue international firmness of purpose to maintain the people's peace through living law, if once and for all there were cast into the teeth of war-worshippers and war-mongers the cynical words of Field-Marshal-General von Moltke: 'Perpetual peace is a dream, and it is not even a beautiful dream.'[150]

Appendix

Even if it be granted that violations of the Briand-Kellogg Pact and other international agreements do not in themselves constitute crimes—only acts of illegality—there is another valid basis for employing the Pact of Paris in connection with the prosecution of the Nazi leaders. Since the initiation and conduct of such a war of aggression is at least unlawful, all acts of warfare in pursuance thereof, whether they violate the laws and customs of war or do not do so, are illegal. They also become criminal in considering the effect of illegality upon the defense of 'justification' in criminal law. Although a soldier, in killing an enemy soldier, is for obvious reasons usually exempt from responsibility for murder,[151] this rule of exemption nevertheless requires that the killing, even if done in warfare, be lawful. Soldiers, like civilians, are bound to act within the confines of the prevailing law. As in the case of any other type of justification which cancels liability for acts otherwise criminal (*e.g.*, execution of a felon by the proper officer, in the prescribed manner, under a valid warrant, following lawful conviction and sentence for a capital crime), the indispensable prerequisites for exemption from liability must exist. And where an act normally prohibited (*e.g.*, killing) is committed by

---

[149] MEMORANDUM TO CAMBRIDGE COMMITTEE ON WAR CRIMES (1942).

[150] HOLLAND, LETTERS TO 'THE TIMES' UPON WAR AND NEUTRALITY (1881–1909) (1914) 25. Some of the rest of this famous letter of von Moltke's is: 'War is an element in the order of the world ordained by God. In it the noblest virtues of mankind are developed... Without war the world would stagnate, and lose itself in materialism... Every law presupposes an authority to superintend and direct its execution, and international conventions are supported by no such authority. What neutral States would ever take up arms for the sole reason that, two Powers being at war, the "laws of war" had been violated by one or both of the belligerents? For offences of that sort there is no earthly judge.' *Id.* at 25. See also the persuasive reply by Professor Bluntschli, *id.* at 27–29.

[151] See State v. Gut, 13 Minn. 341, 357 (1868); Commonwealth v. Holland, 62 Ky. 182, 183 (1864): 'The act being belligerent in the legal import of that comprehensive term, it was not robbery in the technical sense'; 1 HALE, PLEAS OF THE CROWN (1st Am. ed. 1847) 59, 433; BISHOP, CRIMINAL LAW (9th ed. 1923) § 131, p. 86; 2 *id.* at § 631, pp. 477–78.

a soldier, even in the course of warfare, an indispensable condition for its justification is the lawfulness of the act of warfare involved. Were *all* acts of warfare lawful, mere proof that a killing was done by a soldier would be enough to exempt him from liability; but if, for example, the killing occurred after the victim, a surrendered enemy soldier, had laid down his arms, or after an armistice had been declared and the accused had been given notice thereof, the killing would be unlawful and therefore unjustifiable.

Now lawfulness, as was correctly held by the German Supreme Court in the Leipzig trials,[152] requires the acts of the soldier to be legitimate not only under domestic criminal law, but also under the law of nations, which all States and their subjects are bound to obey. Stripped of the mantle of such legality, the act in question stands out starkly as an unjustifiable and inexcusable killing of a human being—something which, by all civilized military and civil penal codes, constitutes plain murder. Herein lies the true significance of Mr. Stimson's interpretation of the effect of the Briand-Kellogg Treaty, quoted above.[153] Aggressive war having been rendered illegal, said Mr. Stimson, 'it is no longer to be the principle around which the duties, the conduct, and the rights of nations revolve.' As applied to acts chargeable as crimes, aggressive war can therefore no longer be a legal justification and shield.

It is, moreover, possible to proceed from this to the internationalization of domestic criminal law. The universal condemnation of murder, rape and theft in all civilized penal codes may legitimately be received by an international tribunal (in the words of Article 38 of the Statute of the Permanent Court of International Justice[154]) to demonstrate both 'international custom, as evidence of a general practice accepted as law,' and one of 'the general principles of law recognized by civilized nations.'

Such a procedure would involve no retroactivity: For if it were decided that the law to be applied by the international tribunal were the pre-existent penal law of the country in which the particular crime had been committed, there could not be the slightest argument that the procedure was *ex post facto*. And since the various injured States all provide in their common law and codes for the punishment of murders, rapes, and thefts, their decision to combine their forces in an international criminal court for the purposes of such a prosecution could also not be objected to as involving substantive retroactivity. For the definitions of such crimes, the defenses of justification or excuse, and even the punishments are all

---

[152] 'The Court must in this instance affirm Patzig's guilt of killing contrary to *international law*.' *Judgment in case of Lieutenants Dithmar and Boldt* (1922) 16 Am. J. Int. L. 674, 721 (italics supplied).

[153] See p. 79 *supra*.

[154] Publications of the Permanent Court of International Justice, Series D. No. 1 (3d ed.) The Permanent Court of International Justice, Statute and Rules (1922) 58. For an instructive account of the application of this Article by the Permanent Court, see Pfankuchen, *Article 38 of the Statute of the Permanent Court of International Justice and International Law* (unpublished thesis in the Harvard Law School Library, 1931).

founded on essentially the same *common denominator* of legal and moral principle. And, since the accused, if the specific acts with which they were charged
were established beyond a reasonable doubt, would unquestionably be guilty of
the crimes in question under domestic penal law, no practical injury of the kind
involved in true *ex post facto* legislation would be done them in proceeding, by
the method suggested, under *international* law deriving therefrom through the
channel of customary usage.

5

Crimes Against Humanity[1]

By Egon Schwelb, Dr.Jur. (Prague), LL.B. (London)

I. Introductory

ARTICLE 6 of the Charter of the International Military Tribunal, annexed to the Four-Power Agreement of 8 August 1945,[2] provides that the Tribunal established by the Agreement for the Prosecution and Punishment of the Major War Criminals of the European Axis

'shall have the power to try and punish persons who, acting in the interests of the European Axis countries, whether as individuals or as members of organisations, committed any of the following crimes:

(a) Crimes against peace: namely, planning, preparation, initiation or waging of a war of aggression, or a war in violation of international treaties, agreements or assurances, or participation in a common plan or conspiracy for the accomplishment of any of the foregoing;

(b) War Crimes: namely, violations of the laws of customs of war. Such violations shall include, but not be limited to, murder, ill-treatment or deportation to slave labour or for any other purpose of civilian population of or in occupied territory, murder or ill-treatment of prisoners of war or persons on the seas, killing of hostages, plunder of public or private property, wanton destruction of cities, towns or villages, or devastation not justified by military necessity;

(c) Crimes against humanity: namely, murder, extermination, enslavement, deportation, and other inhumane acts committed against any civilian population, before or during the war;[3] or persecutions on political, racial, or religious grounds in execution of or in connection with any crime within the jurisdiction of the Tribunal, whether or not in violation of the domestic law of the country where perpetrated.'

---

[1] The Editor proposes to include in the next issue of this *Year Book* an article devoted to a discussion of the place of the Nuremberg trial, as a whole, in the field of international law.

[2] Misc. No. 10 (1945), Cmd. 6668; Treaty Series No. 27 (1946), Cmd. 6903.

[3] As to the replacement of this semi-colon in the English text by a comma and the alteration of the French text of Article 6 (*c*), see the Protocol signed at Berlin on 6 October 1945, U.S. Department of State Publication 2461, Executive Agreement Series 472, U.S. Government Printing Office, Washington: 1946, pp. 45 ff.; and see below, p. 130.

The provision of sub-paragraph (*c*), referring to crimes against humanity, has, from the very beginning, caught the imagination of international lawyers as laying down, prima facie, a set of novel principles of law. The provisions relating to crimes against humanity have been acclaimed as 'a revolution in international criminal law'.[4] Others have described it as an innovation inconsistent with international law.

The following three phrases appear to embody these startling and controversial changes: (1) 'before and during the war'; (2) 'against any civilian population'; (3) 'whether or not in violation of the domestic law of the country where perpetrated'. Ignoring for a moment the other parts of Article 6 (*c*), which, as will be explained in due course, contain quite considerable qualifications of the rules apparently expressed by the three phrases quoted, the following principles seem to have been laid down in the Charter:

The first, indicated by the words 'before or during the war', apparently implies that international law contains penal sanctions against individuals, applicable not only in time of war, but also in time of peace; this, in other words, means that there is in existence a system of international criminal law under which individuals are responsible to the community of nations for violations of rules of international criminal law, and that—in certain circumstances—inhumane acts constitute international crimes. The second principle, which appears to be deducible from the words 'against any civilian population', is to the effect that 'any civilian population' is under the protection of this system of international law, and this implies that civilian populations are protected against violations of international criminal law also in cases where the alleged crimes have been committed by sovereign states against their own subjects. The third principle expressed by the words 'whether or not in violation of the domestic law of the country where perpetrated', appears to establish the absolute supremacy of international law over municipal law.

If this prima facie impression, created by Article 6 (*c*) of the Charter, is correct, if the community of nations is entitled to intervene judicially against crimes committed against any civilian population, before or during the war, and if for this purpose it is irrelevant whether or not such crimes were committed in violation of the domestic law of the country where perpetrated, then certainly a radical inroad has been made into the sphere of the domestic jurisdiction of sovereign states. It is the purpose of this article to examine the question, in the light of the historical events preceding the Charter of 8 August 1945, of the proceedings and the judgment of the International Military Tribunal at Nuremberg and of state practice, centring on the problem of 'crimes against humanity'.

---

[4] Albert de la Pradelle, *Nouvelle revue de droit international privé*, no. 2, 1946: 'Une Révolution dans le Droit Pénal International'.

II. The History of the Concept of Crimes Against Humanity

1. The Fourth Hague Convention of 1907

In the London Charter of 8 August 1945, the term 'crimes against humanity' has a specific meaning. It connotes one of the three types of crimes over which the International Military Tribunal has jurisdiction and is in this way juxtaposed to 'crimes against peace' and to 'war crimes'. We shall see that under the Charter the notions of 'war crimes' and 'crimes against humanity' overlap and that most war crimes are also crimes against humanity, while many crimes against humanity are simultaneously war crimes. In spite of this overlapping, the term 'crime against humanity', as used in the Charter, is a technical term, and as such distinguished from the term of art 'war crime'. In older international documents, however, the expressions 'humanity', 'laws of humanity', 'dictates of humanity' were used in a non-technical sense and certainly not with the intention of indicating a set of norms different from 'the laws and customs of war', the violations of which constitute war crimes within the meaning of Article 6 (*b*) of the Charter.

The Fourth Hague Convention of 1907 concerning the Laws and Customs of War on Land,[5] which is an instrument concerned with war crimes in the technical and narrower sense, recalls in paragraph 2 of the Preamble that the Contracting Parties are 'animated by the desire to serve', even in the case of war, 'the *interests of humanity* and the ever-progressive needs of civilization'. In the often-quoted eighth paragraph of the Preamble the Contracting Parties declare, *inter alia*, that 'the inhabitants and belligerents remain under the protection and governance of the principles of the law of nations, derived from the usages established among civilized peoples, from the *laws of humanity*, and from the dictates of the public conscience'. Here the 'interests of humanity' are conceived as the purpose which the laws and customs of war serve, and the 'laws of humanity' as one of the sources of the law of nations.

2. The First World War

In January 1919 the Preliminary Peace Conference decided to create a Commission of Fifteen Members for the purpose of inquiring into the responsibilities relating to the war. The Commission was instructed, *inter alia*, to inquire into and to report upon 'the facts as to breaches of the laws and customs of war committed by the forces of the German Empire and their Allies, on land, on sea, and in the air during the present [*sc.* 1914–1919] war'.[6]

---

[5] Miscellaneous, No. 6 (1908), Cmd. 4175, p. 46.
[6] *Violation of the Laws and Customs of War*. Report of Majority and Dissenting Reports of American and Japanese Members of the Commission on Responsibilities, Conference of Paris, 1919. Carnegie Endowment for International Peace, Division of International Law, Pamphlet No. 32.

The report, dated 29 March 1919, stated, in Chapter II, that 'in spite of the explicit regulations, of established customs, and of the clear *dictates of humanity*, Germany and her allies have piled outrage upon outrage'. The majority of the Commission came to the conclusions that the First World War 'was carried on by the Central Empires together with their allies, Turkey and Bulgaria, by barbarous or illegitimate methods in violation of the established laws and customs of war and the elementary *laws of humanity*', and that 'all persons belonging to enemy countries... who have been guilty of offences against the laws and customs of war or the *laws of humanity*, are liable to criminal prosecution'.

It is submitted that the distinction which was made in 1919 between violations of the laws and customs of war on the one hand and offences against the laws of humanity on the other corresponds roughly to the two categories of 'war crimes' and 'crimes against humanity' as they are now distinguished in Article 6 (*b*) and (*c*) of the London Charter. The report of the 1919 Commission contained an Annex I, 'Tableau sommaire des infractions commises par les autorités et les troupes des empires centraux et de leurs alliés en violation des lois et coutumes de la guerre et des lois de l'humanité'.[7] It is referred to in the Report as containing, by way of illustration, a certain number of examples which have been collected. This Annex I consists of a list of charges submitted by different Allied Governments, the overwhelming majority of which can be classified as charges of war crimes in the narrower sense. There appear, however, in the list also such crimes as were committed on the territory of Germany and her allies against nationals of, e.g., Turkey and Austria. We find there charges of murder and massacre, systematic terrorism, putting hostages to death, torture of civilians, rape, abduction of girls and women for the purpose of enforced prostitution, deportation of civilians, and pillage, committed by Turkish and German authorities against Turkish subjects. These charges refer mainly to the massacres of Armenians by the Turks and the massacres, persecutions, and expulsions of the Greek-speaking population of Turkey, both European and Asiatic. The Annex also contains a charge of pillage allegedly committed in 1915 by Austrian troops against the population of Gorizia, which, at the time, was an Austrian town. It may be added, in this connexion, that already on 28 May 1915 the Governments of France, Great Britain, and Russia made a declaration regarding the massacres of the Armenian population in Turkey, denouncing them as '*crimes against humanity and civilization* for which all the members of the Turkish Government will be held responsible together with its agents implicated in the massacres'.[8]

The Dissenting (Minority) Report of the American members (Mr. Robert Lansing and Mr. James Brown Scott) took objection to the use of the term 'laws

---

[7] Not reproduced in the publication mentioned in note 6.

[8] The Note is quoted in the Armenian Memorandum presented by the Greek delegation to the Commission of Fifteen on 14 March 1919.

of humanity', and their opposition was mainly directed against the majority report having 'improperly added' the words 'and the laws of humanity'.

'War was and is', the American Representatives pointed out, 'by its very nature inhuman, but acts consistent with the laws and customs of war, although these acts are inhuman, are nevertheless not the object of punishment by a court of justice. A judicial tribunal only deals with existing law and only administers existing law, leaving to another forum infractions of the moral law and actions contrary to the laws and principles of humanity.' A further objection was based on the fact that there was no fixed and universal standard of humanity, and that it varied with time, place, and circumstance and, it may be, even according to the conscience of the individual judge.

The outcome was as follows: In the texts of the Peace Treaties of Versailles (Arts. 228–30), Saint-Germain-en-Laye (Arts. 173–6), Trianon (Arts. 157–9), and Neuilly-sur-Seine (Arts. 118–20) the phrase 'laws of humanity' does not appear; those Treaties dealt only with acts committed in violation of the laws and customs of war. The Treaty of Sèvres,[9] however, signed on 10 August 1920, contained in addition to the provisions of its Articles 226–8, which correspond to Articles 228–30 of the Treaty of Versailles, and to Article 229, which regulates the position in such territories as ceased to be parts of the Turkish Empire, a further provision (Art. 230), the relevant parts of which read as follows:

'The Turkish Government undertakes to hand over to the Allied Powers the persons whose surrender may be required by the latter as being responsible for the massacres committed during the continuance of the state of war on territory which formed part of the Turkish Empire on the 1st August, 1914.

'The Allied Powers reserve to themselves the right to designate the Tribunal which shall try the persons so accused, and the Turkish Government undertakes to recognise such Tribunal.

'In the event of the League of Nations having created in sufficient time a Tribunal competent to deal with the said massacres, the Allied Powers reserve to themselves the right to bring the accused persons mentioned above before such Tribunal, and the Turkish Government undertakes equally to recognise such Tribunal.'

Here, in conformity with the Allied note of 1915, it was intended to bring to justice persons who, during the war, had committed on Turkish territory crimes against persons of Turkish citizenship though of Armenian or Greek race, a clear example of 'crimes against humanity' as understood in the 1945 Charter. The Treaty of Sèvres was, however, not ratified and did not come into force. It was replaced by the Treaty of Lausanne,[10] which not only did not contain provisions respecting the punishment of war crimes, but was accompanied by a 'Declaration of Amnesty' for all offences committed between 1914 and 1922 which were evidently connected with the political events; this covered any military or political action taken.

---

[9] Treaty Series No. 11 (1920).   [10] Treaty Series No. 16 (1923), Cmd. 1929.

The provision of Article 227 of the Treaty of Versailles, under which the German Emperor was arraigned 'for a supreme offence against international morality and the sanctity of treaties', is the predecessor of Article 6 (*a*) of the London Charter, with the important distinction that the crimes against peace under Article 6 (*a*) are not considered to be merely contraventions of a moral code, but violations of legal provisions. The problem of crimes against peace is, however, outside the scope of this article.[11]

3. The Developments During the Second World War

It is not difficult to show that the insertion in the Charter of the International Military Tribunal of the provisions regarding 'crimes against humanity' was due to the desire expressed over and over again during the Second World War, in discussions, in semi-official and official statements and proclamations, that the retributive action of the Allies should not be restricted to bringing to justice those who had committed war crimes in the narrower sense, i.e. violations of the laws and customs of war, perpetrated on Allied territory, or against Allied citizens, but that also such atrocities should be investigated, tried, and punished as have been committed on Axis territory against persons of other than Allied nationality. The writers, politicians, statesmen and organizations who advocated this had in mind the atrocities committed, e.g., by Germans in Italy and against Italians, both before and after the Italian surrender, the persecutions by the Nazi Government of its political opponents inside Germany (trade unions, Social-Democrats, Communists, the Churches), and, of course, the persecution of the Jews, irrespective of their citizenship—cases which were not covered by the traditional notion of war crimes.

The declarations referring to this problem, made between 1942 and 1945, are legion. The following examples have been selected to illustrate the gradual development:[12]

On 17 December 1942 a declaration regarding the barbarous and inhuman treatment to which Jews were being subjected in German-occupied Europe was made on behalf of the Governments of Belgium, Czechoslovakia, Greece, Luxembourg, the Netherlands, Norway, Poland, the United States of America, the United Kingdom, the Union of Soviet Socialist Republics, Yugoslavia, and the French National Committee. It referred to numerous reports from Europe

---

[11] An example of the use between the two wars of the expression 'dictates of humanity' in a non-technical sense is the Preamble of the Nyon Agreement for Collective Measures against Piratical Attacks in the Mediterranean by Submarines (Treaty Series No. 38 (1937), Cmd. 5568), where it is said of attacks committed by submarines against merchant ships, arising out of the Spanish conflict, that they are violations of the rules of international law *and* constitute acts contrary to the most elementary *dictates of humanity*, which should be justly treated as acts of piracy.

[12] For an analysis of some of the relevant statements see Eugène Aroneanu, 'Le Crime contre l'Humanité', *Nouvelle revue de droit international privé*, no. 2 (1946).

'that the German authorities, not content with denying to persons of Jewish race in all the territories over which their barbarous rule has been extended, the most elementary human rights, are now carrying into effect Hitler's oft repeated intention to exterminate the Jewish people in Europe'. The statement continued: 'From all the occupied countries Jews are being transported, in conditions of appalling horror and brutality, to Eastern Europe.... The above mentioned Governments and the French National Committee condemn in the strongest possible terms this bestial policy of cold-blooded extermination. They declare that such events can only strengthen the resolve of all freedom loving peoples to overthrow the barbarous Hitlerite tyranny. They reaffirm their solemn resolution that those responsible for these crimes shall not escape retribution and to press on with the necessary practical measures to this end.'[13]

It will be seen that this statement, in its careful wording, is restricted to crimes committed against persons of Jewish race in the territories over which the barbarous rule of Nazi Germany 'has been extended'. It speaks of Jews 'from all the occupied countries' and of crimes committed in Poland, i.e. on Allied territory. There is nothing in the declaration indicating that crimes committed against Jews of Axis nationality on Axis territory should be included in the retribution which the Allied Governments pledged themselves to ensure.

In 1943–4 the London International Assembly recommended that in defining the scope of the retributive action of the Allies, 'a comprehensive view should be taken, including not only the customary violations of the laws of war...but any other serious crime against the local law, committed in time of war, the perpetrator of which has not been visited by appropriate punishment'.[14] In respect of the extermination of Jews, it was recommended 'that punishment should be imposed not only when the victims were Allied Jews, but even when the crimes had been committed against stateless Jews or any other Jews in Germany or elsewhere'. This formulation indicated that the London International Assembly still felt some reluctance in committing itself to a proposition expressly applying the retribution to crimes against Jews of German nationality, although these are, no doubt, included in the term 'any other Jews'.

The United Nations War Crimes Commission, an inter-governmental agency established in 1943, at an early date recommended to the Allied Governments that the retributive action of the United Nations should not be restricted to what was traditionally considered a war crime in the technical sense, namely, a violation of the laws and customs of war. The unprecedented record of crimes committed by the Nazi régime and the other Axis Powers, not only against Allied combatants but also against the civilian populations of the occupied countries

---

[13] *Hansard, House of Commons*, vol. 385, col. 2083, 17 December 1942; see also the *United Nations Review* 3 (1943), no. i, p. 1; Raphael Lemkin, *Axis Rule in Occupied Europe* (1944), p. 89, note 45.

[14] *The Punishment of War Criminals. Recommendations of the L.I.A.* (London International Assembly). Report of Commission I, p. 7.

and of the Axis countries themselves, made it necessary to provide that these crimes also should not go unpunished.[15]

The Instrument of Surrender of Italy (Additional Conditions signed on 29 September 1943 at Malta),[16] in Article 29, foreshadows an extension of the retributive action of the Allies beyond the perpetrators of war crimes in the traditional sense. It imposes on Italy the obligation to apprehend and surrender into the hands of the United Nations not only 'Benito Mussolini, his Chief Fascist Associates and all persons suspected of having committed war crimes', but also persons suspected of 'analogous offences', the latter expression roughly indicating what eventually has become known as crimes against humanity.

The expression 'war crimes or analogous offences' also occurs in Article 11 of the Berlin Declaration regarding the defeat of Germany dated 5 June 1945,[17] which was drawn up nearly two years later, and repeated in the Proclamation No. 2 to the people of Germany, respecting 'certain additional requirements imposed on Germany', dated 20 October 1945.[18] The armistices with Roumania,[19] Finland,[20] Bulgaria,[21] and Hungary,[22] on the other hand, speak only of persons accused of war crimes without expressly mentioning an extension to 'analogous offences'.[23] With regard to Austria, Article 11 of the Berlin Declaration of 5 June 1945 is applicable by virtue of Article 8 of the Four-Power Agreement on Control Machinery in Austria of 4 July 1945.[24] The later Agreement on the Machinery of Control in Austria, dated Vienna, 28 June 1946,[25] speaks, in Article 5, of persons wanted for war crimes and crimes against humanity. The Proclamation to the Japanese people made on 26 July 1945 at Potsdam,[26] and accepted by Japan,[27] mentioned among the Allied terms that 'stern justice will be meted out to war criminals, including those who have visited cruelties upon our prisoners'.[28]

---

[15] *The Times* newspaper, 18 December 1946.

[16] Italy No. 1 (1945). *Documents relating to the Conditions of an Armistice with Italy*, Cmd. 6693, p. 8.

[17] Germany No. 1 (1945), Cmd. 6648, p. 5.

[18] *Official Gazette of the Control Council for Germany*, no. 1, p. 8; *Military Government Gazette, Germany, British Zone of Control*, no. 5, p. 27; Section x, paragraph 36.

[19] Miscellaneous No. 1 (1945), Cmd. 6585, Art. 14.

[20] Miscellaneous No. 2 (1945), Cmd. 6586, Art. 13.

[21] Miscellaneous No. 3 (1945), Cmd. 6587, Art. 6.

[22] *American Journal of International Law*, 39 (1945), Supplement, p. 97, Art. XIV.

[23] As to the provisions of the Draft Peace Treaties, see below, p. 153.

[24] Treaty Series No. 49 (1946), Cmd. 6958, p. 4.

[25] Ibid., p. 21.

[26] *U.S. Department of State Bulletin*, vol. xiii, no. 318 (29 July 1945), p. 137.

[27] Instrument of Surrender, dated 1 September 1945 (*American Journal of International Law*, 39 (1945), Supplement, p. 264).

[28] In the trial of the persons accused as the major Japanese war criminals, it was submitted by the defence that the term 'war criminals' used in the Potsdam Declaration did not comprise 'crimes against peace' and 'crimes against humanity' and that the International Military Tribunal for the Far East lacked jurisdiction to try the latter crimes. The Tokyo trial was not concluded when the present paper was sent to press.

The United States Under-Secretary of State, Mr. Grew, said on 1 February 1945 that the State Department plan calls 'for the punishment... for the whole broad criminal enterprise, including offences wherever committed against... minority elements, Jewish and other groups, and individuals'.[29] In the House of Commons on 4 October 1944, in reply to a question asking that the names of those responsible for crimes against German democrats and anti-Nazis, such as the murder of 7,000 internees of Buchenwald Concentration Camp, should be added to the list of war criminals, the then Foreign Secretary stated: 'Crimes committed by Germans against Germans, however reprehensible, are in a different category from war crimes and cannot be dealt with under the same procedure. His Majesty's Government have this matter under consideration, but I am not in a position to make any further statement at present.'[30] In reply to a further question as to whether the murder of anti-Nazi Germans in Germany was not just as criminal as the murder of other anti-Nazis elsewhere, Mr. Ederi said: 'I was not trying to measure the degree of the reprehensible in any of these deeds; all I was saying was that it was not a war crime in the sense of other crimes that are being committed, and other means would have to be found for dealing with it.'

In the House of Commons on 31 January 1945,[31] the then Minister of State, Mr. Richard Law, said in reply to a question:

'Crimes committed by Germans against Germans are in a different category from war crimes and cannot be dealt with under the same procedure. But in spite of this, I can assure my hon. Friend that His Majesty's Government will do their utmost to ensure that these crimes do not go unpunished. It is the desire of His Majesty's Government that the authorities in post-war Germany shall mete out to the perpetrators of these crimes the punishments which they deserve.

'The authorities to which I refer are the authorities who will be in control in Germany when the war comes to an end. I think I can leave it to my hon and learned Friend to imagine who those authorities will be.'

On 2 May 1945 the President of the United States made an Executive Order,[32] providing for representation of the United States in preparing and prosecuting charges of atrocities and war crimes against the leaders of the European Axis Powers and their principal agents and accessories. In this document the terms 'atrocities' and 'war crimes' are used, the former obviously comprising what later were called 'crimes against humanity'. In his report to the President dated 7 June 1945,[33] Justice Robert H. Jackson, Chief of Counsel for the United States in the Prosecution of Axis War Criminals, outlined the legal charges against the top Nazi leaders and those voluntary associations such as the S.S. and the Gestapo,

---

[29] Quoted by Judex (M. de Baer); *The Treatment of War Crimes and Crimes incidental to the War*, p. 12.

[30] *Hansard, House of Commons*, 4 October 1944, col. 906.

[31] *Hansard, House of Commons*, 31 January 1945.

[32] Executive Order 9547, later amended by Executive Order of 16 January 1946.

[33] *American Journal of International Law*, 39 (1945), Supplement, p. 178.

which he intended to make the subject of the proposed trial. In addition to 'atrocities and offences against persons or property, constituting violations of International Law, including the laws, rules, and customs of land warfare', which were eventually embodied as war crimes in the narrower sense in Article 6 (*b*) of the Charter, and 'invasions of other countries and initiation of war aggression in violation of International Law or treaties', which were eventually called 'crimes against peace' and dealt with in Article 6 (*a*) of the Charter, he characterized what has eventually been given the name of crimes against humanity in the following words:

'(*b*) Atrocities and offences, including atrocities and persecutions on racial or religious grounds, committed since 1933. This is only to recognize the principles of criminal law as they are generally observed in civilized states. These principles have been assimilated as a part of International Law at least since 1907. The Fourth Hague Convention provided that inhabitants and belligerents shall remain under the protection and the rule of "the principles of the law of nations, as they result from the usage established among civilized peoples, from the laws of humanity and the dictates of the public conscience".'

The Potsdam Conference of July–August 1945, which was held while negotiations on the American proposals outlined in the Jackson report were already in progress, and which took note of these discussions, dealt with war crimes and related subjects in the agreement regarding 'The Political and Economic Principles to Govern the Treatment of Germany in the Initial Control Period', paragraph 5. It was provided there that 'war criminals and those who have participated in planning or carrying out Nazi enterprises involving or resulting in atrocities or war crimes shall be arrested and brought to judgment'.[34] 'Nazi enterprises involving or resulting in atrocities' as distinguished from those involving or resulting in war crimes correspond to crimes against humanity as distinguished from violations of the laws and customs of war.

4. The Berlin Protocol of 6 October 1945

Before embarking upon an analysis of the London Charter of 8 August 1945 it is necessary to mention a document which, in point of time, is of more recent date than the Charter, but which is relevant to the interpretation of those of its provisions which form the main subject of this article. The four Governments who had concluded the Agreement of 8 August 1945 drew up in Berlin on 6 October 1945 a Protocol[35] in the Preamble of which it was stated that a discrepancy had been found to exist between the originals of Article 6, paragraph (*c*) of the Charter of 8 August 1945, in the Russian language on the one hand, and the originals in the English and French languages on the other. It should be mentioned that the

[34] *The Times* newspaper, 3 August 1945.
[35] Not published in this country. U.S. Department of State Publication 2461, Executive Agreement Series No. 472, p. 45.

London Agreement was executed in triplicate, in English, French, and Russian, each text to have equal authenticity (Art. 7). The discrepancy which was found to exist was this: in the English and French texts, Article 6 (*c*) was divided into two parts by a semicolon between the words 'war' and 'or persecutions'. In the Russian text, however, which was equally authentic, there was no semicolon dividing the paragraph, but a comma had been placed between what corresponds to the words 'war' and 'or persecutions' in Russian.

In the Berlin Protocol, the Contracting Parties declared that the meaning and intention of the Agreement and Charter required that the semicolon in the English and French texts should be changed into a comma. In the French text some additional alterations have been made which will be discussed in greater detail later. The correction made by the Berlin Protocol is, as will be seen, of considerable importance, *inter alia*, because it entails that the qualification contained in the second part of the paragraph, and expressed by the words 'in execution of or in connection with any crime within the jurisdiction of the tribunal', refers to the whole text of Article 6 (*c*).

III. Analysis of the Text of Article 6 (c) of the Charter

(*a*) From the words 'against *any* civilian population', it follows that a crime against humanity can be committed both against the civilian population of territory which is under belligerent occupation and against the civilian population of other territories, irrespective of whether they are under some other type of occupation or whether they are under no occupation at all. The civilian population protected by the provision may therefore also include the civilian population of a country which was occupied without resort to war, e.g. Austria and parts of Czechoslovakia in 1938–9. It may be the civilian population of territories where armed forces of one belligerent were stationed without effecting an occupation, which was the case, e.g., with German forces in Italy at some stages of the Second World War. The civilian population protected by the provision may also be the civilian population of countries neighbouring on a certain belligerent, e.g. Germany, without German armed forces being permanently stationed there. The population protected may finally be the civilian population of the respective belligerent itself, e.g. the German civilian population in its relations with the German authorities and military and para-military organizations, or the Italian population either of Italian or, e.g., Slovene racial origin, which may have become the victim of outrages by Italian military and fascist formations.

(*b*) Crimes against humanity can be committed against a civilian population both of territories to which the provisions of Section 3 of The Hague Regulations annexed to the Fourth Hague Convention of 1907 respecting military authority over the territory of the hostile state apply, and of such territories to which they do not apply. This means that a crime against humanity under Article 6 (*c*) of the Charter may or may not simultaneously be a violation of the laws and customs of war and therefore a war crime in the narrower sense, coming under Article 6 (*b*) of the Charter. It follows that the terms 'crimes against humanity' on the one hand, and 'war crimes' or 'violations of the laws and customs of war' on the other, overlap. Many crimes against humanity are also violations of the laws and customs of war; many, though not all, war crimes are simultaneously crimes against humanity. 'In so far as these crimes (viz. crimes against humanity) constitute violations of the laws of war there is no juristic problem because they are merely the same crimes as those set forth in Count Three[36] under a different name, but novel considerations arise when the acts charged cannot be brought within this category.'[37]

The Indictment against the Major German War Criminals[38] presented to the International Military Tribunal, in stating the offences coming under Count Four,[39] accordingly submits that 'the prosecution will rely upon the facts pleaded under Count Three as also constituting crimes against humanity'.[40] The Judgment of the International Military Tribunal delivered at Nuremberg on 30 September and 1 October 1946,[41] which will be analysed in greater detail below, also proceeded on the assumption that the terms 'war crime' and 'crimes against humanity' overlap, but that, as Professor Goodhart has stated, where they overlap, no independent legal problems arise. It is natural that the notion of crimes against humanity had to be examined by the International Military Tribunal particularly in such cases where it was alleged that facts which did not simultaneously constitute violations of the laws of war constituted crimes against humanity.[42]

(*c*) The Charter speaks of 'any *civilian* population'. This appears to indicate that the term 'crime against humanity' is restricted to inhumane acts committed against civilian populations as distinguished from members of the armed forces. This restriction applies at least to those acts constituting crimes against humanity which are enumerated in the passage of Article 6 (*c*) preceding the words 'against any civilian population', i.e. to murder, extermination, enslavement, deportation, and other inhumane acts. In interpreting the text, doubts may arise as to whether this restriction to the civilian population applies also to such acts constituting crimes against humanity as do not fall under any of these enumerated categories of

---

[36] Violations of the laws and customs of war.

[37] Goodhart, 'The Legality of the Nuremberg Trials', *The Juridical Review*, 85 (April 1946), at p. 15.

[38] Indictment presented to the International Military Tribunal on 18 October 1945, Cmd. 6696. The Indictment is also reproduced in *The Trial of German Major War Criminals. Proceedings.* Published under the authority of H.M. Attorney-General by H.M. Stationery Office, Part I, pp. 2 ff.

[39] Crimes against humanity.

[40] P. 30.

[41] The Judgment will be quoted throughout this article on the basis of the United Kingdom White Paper, Misc. No. 12 (1946), Cmd. 6964.

[42] See particularly p. 65 of the Judgment.

the murder type. On the face of it, it would appear that 'persecutions on political, racial, or religious grounds' are such acts. It could therefore be maintained that persecutions, as distinguished from crimes of the murder type, may be committed by acts directed against members of the armed forces. It is, however, doubtful whether this division of crimes against humanity into crimes of the murder type on the one hand, and mere persecutions on political, racial, or religious grounds on the other, can be maintained in view of the Berlin Protocol of 6 October 1945.

An interpretation distinguishing between crimes of the murder type and persecutions would in respect of this particular phrase not lead to satisfactory results for the following reasons: Crimes of the murder type, to which the words 'any *civilian* population' undoubtedly pertain, are certainly graver offences than 'persecutions on political, racial, or religious grounds', if we restrict the latter to persecutions which do not go as far as murder, extermination, enslavement, and deportation. It would be difficult to understand the *rationale* of a provision under which the number of persons afforded protection against a less serious crime (persecution) would be larger than that of potential victims protected against the graver offences of the murder type.

In respect of the armed forces of those countries with which Germany was at war, the question is academic because persecutions of their members by the German authorities on political, racial, or religious grounds obviously constitute also violations of the laws and customs of war, particularly of the conventional provisions respecting the treatment of prisoners of war. The practical problem of interpretation would, therefore, boil down to the question whether persecutions of Axis soldiers by the Axis authorities or by Axis nationals in general on political, racial, or religious grounds constitute crimes against humanity. It is not suggested that acts which could be viewed from this angle have not been committed. There is, however, little probability that persons accused of such conduct have been or will be tried under the law laid down by the Charter. Acts possibly coming under such a heading would be persecutions of, say, Italian soldiers of Jewish or Slovene origin, by the authorities of the Italian army, or of anti-Nazi members of the German armed forces.

(*d*) The Charter speaks of 'any civilian *population*'. This indicates that a larger body of victims is visualized and that single or isolated acts committed against individuals are outside its scope.

(*e*) The bearing which the words 'in execution of or in connection with any crime within the jurisdiction of the Tribunal' have on the interpretation of the expression '*any* civilian population' will be discussed presently.

(*f*) The acts enumerated in Article 6 (*c*) as crimes against humanity are similar to, but not identical with, those which are mentioned as war crimes in Article 6 (*b*).

The provision dealing with war crimes expressly states that its enumeration is not exhaustive: 'Such violations shall include, but not be limited to....' No such statement expressly pointing out the exemplative character of the list is to be found in Article 6 (*c*). The wide scope of the term 'other inhumane acts' indicates, however, that the enumeration of Article 6 (*c*) is exhaustive in form only, but not in substance.

If the English rule of interpretation, known as the *eiusdem generis* rule, could be applied to Article 6 (*c*) the words 'other inhumane acts' would cover only serious crimes of a character similar to murder, extermination, enslavement, and deportation. Then, offences against property would be outside the scope of the notion of crimes against humanity. But even quite apart from the *eiusdem generis* rule, this view appears to be supported by the fact that, while the exemplative enumeration of Article 6 (*b*) contains such items as 'plunder of public or private property', 'wanton destruction of cities, towns, or villages, or devastation not justified by military necessity', there is no indication in the text that similar offences against property were in the minds of the Powers when agreeing on Article 6 (*c*).

It is, however, doubtful whether this is a sound interpretation. As Professor Lauterpacht has said, 'it is not helpful to establish a rigid distinction between offences against life and limb, and those against property. Pillage, plunder, and arbitrary destruction of public and private property may, in their effects, be no less cruel and deserving of punishment than acts of personal violence. There may, in effect, be little difference between executing a person and condemning him to a slow death of starvation and exposure by depriving him of shelter and means of sustenance.'[43]

(*g*) Murder is included both in the list contained in Article 6 (*b*) and in the list contained in Article 6 (*c*). Extermination, mentioned in Article 6 (*c*) only, is apparently to be interpreted as murder on a large scale.

The inclusion of 'extermination', in addition to 'murder', may be taken to indicate that it was intended to bring the earlier stages in the organization of a policy of extermination under the action of the law, and that steps which are too remote from an individual act of homicide to constitute complicity in that act may be punishable as complicity in the crime of extermination.

(*h*) Whether there is a difference between 'deportation to slave labour or for any other purpose', as mentioned under (*b*), and the two separate items 'enslavement' and 'deportation', contained in paragraph (*c*), it is difficult to decide. It might be held that 'deportation to slave labour' (*la déportation pour des travaux forcés*) is a less grave offence than 'enslavement' (*la réduction en esclavage*), the criminality of the former consisting, apart from the element of a forced change of residence, mainly in the fact that men are compelled to do certain work under bad conditions and for inadequate remuneration, though otherwise remaining free, while in the case of the latter a *capitis deminutio* takes place, the victim's status in its entirety is affected, a free man is transformed into an outlawed inmate of a concentration camp. If this assumption is correct, deportation is a crime only

---

[43] This *Year Book*, 21 (1944), p. 79.

if inflicted upon the civilian population of, or in, occupied territory; a belligerent Power is, however, not prevented from deporting its own nationals to forced
labour; under this interpretation, only reducing them to the actual state of slavery
is a crime against humanity.

(*i*) That there was a tendency to make the list of war crimes proper more comprehensive than the list of crimes against humanity is further shown by the omission, in paragraph (*c*), of the word 'ill-treatment', which is contained under (*b*).
Whether or not ill-treatment falls under 'other inhumane acts' depends on the
general interpretation of the latter expression, particularly in connexion with the
four grave offences the enumeration of which precedes it.

(*j*) The Charter provides that it is irrelevant whether an offence alleged to be
a crime against humanity was or was not committed in violation of the domestic
law of the country where perpetrated.

Under the original English and French texts, which contained the division of
paragraph 6 (*c*) by a semicolon, it could be said that this provision applied only
to the words following the semicolon, i.e. to persecutions on political, racial, or
religious grounds. This interpretation would have led to somewhat absurd results.
Through the Berlin Protocol of 6 October 1945, and its replacement of the semi-
colon by a comma, it seems to be quite clear that the principle of the irrelevancy
of the *lex loci* applies to both kinds of crimes against humanity and that it is no
defence that the act alleged to be a crime against humanity was lawful under the
domestic law of the country where it was perpetrated. This is made particularly
clear by the new French text of Article 6 (*c*), which expressly says 'if such *acts or
persecutions*, whether they have or have not constituted a violation of the internal
law of the country where they were perpetrated, were committed . . .' ('lorsque ces
actes ou persécutions, qu'ils aient constitué ou non une violation du droit interne du
pays où ils ont été perpétrés'). The exclusion of this plea is closely connected with
the provisions of the Charter (Art. 8) regarding the defence of superior orders.
Just as a defendant cannot free himself from responsibility because he acted pursuant to order of his government or of a superior, in the same way it avails him
nothing that the inhumane act was lawful under municipal law. The close connexion between these two provisions emerges particularly clearly if one realizes
that the persons to be tried under the Charter were members of a very small circle
in whom legislative powers were vested under the Nazi régime.

(*k*) The words 'in connection with or in execution of any crime within the
jurisdiction of the Tribunal' are of particular importance for the problem here
discussed. In the first instance it is necessary to determine whether these words
relate only to the second part of paragraph (*c*) or to the whole of it, in other words,
whether they qualify only 'persecutions' or both 'persecutions' and what has been
called in this Article 'crimes of the murder type'. The first interpretation would
mean that crimes of the murder type, committed against any civilian population
at any time, are crimes against humanity subject to the Tribunal's jurisdiction,

irrespective of whether or not they are connected with the crime against peace or a war crime proper, while persecutions on political, racial, or religious grounds come within the definition only if they are so connected. Under this interpretation, 'any crime within the jurisdiction of the Tribunal' would mean either a crime against peace, a war crime, or a crime against humanity of the murder type. The second interpretation would amount to the proposition that not only persecutions, but also crimes of the murder type, are outside the notion of crimes against humanity, unless it is established that they were connected with a crime against peace or a war crime. In order to arrive at an opinion on this vital question, it will be useful to recall the wording of the original English text of Article 6 (*c*), as it was quoted *supra*,[44] and to add the original French text which, in the Agreement dated 8 August 1945, read as follows:

'(*c*) LES CRIMES CONTRE L'HUMANITÉ: c'est-à-dire l'assassinat, l'extermination, la réduction en esclavage, la déportation, et tout autre acte inhumain commis contre toutes populations civiles, avant ou pendant la guerre; ou bien les persécutions pour des motifs politiques, raciaux ou religieux, commises à la suite de tout crime rentrant dans la compétence du Tribunal International ou s'y rattachant, que ces persécutions aient constitué ou non une violation du droit interne du pays où elles ont été perpétrées.'

The reader of the English text will, by simple grammatical interpretation, arrive at the conclusion that 'in execution of or in connection with any crime within the jurisdiction of the Tribunal' refers to 'persecutions' and to 'persecutions' only, and if the English text left any doubt, recourse to the equally authentic French text would show that 'commises à la suite de tout crime rentrant dans la compétence du Tribunal International ou s'y rattachant' determines 'les persécutions' and that, being the feminine form, it does not refer to the words from 'l'assassinat' to 'autre acte inhumain'.

By the Berlin Protocol of 6 October 1945 the semicolon dividing Article 6 (*c*) has been replaced by a comma in both the English and French texts. It is submitted that the change of punctuation marks in itself would not bring about a fundamental alteration in the law if regard were not had to the circumstances attending this alteration. If we consider, however, that the four Great Powers went out of their way to negotiate an international protocol and to have it drawn up and signed on behalf of their respective governments, it is quite clear that the intention must have been to alter the law such as it appeared to be laid down in the English and French texts of the Charter in a significant manner. Even quite apart from the obvious grammatical conclusions arising from the original French text, the comma, followed by 'or', would, in normal circumstances, have sufficed to divide the paragraph of the English text into two parts with the consequence that the words 'in execution of or in connection with any crime within the jurisdiction of the Tribunal' would have related only to persecutions and not to crimes of

---

[44] p. 120.

the murder type. In view of the Preamble and the operative text of the Protocol, however, it is obvious that it has been the intention of the Contracting Parties to remove a certain barrier which, in the original texts, appeared to exist between the first and second parts of the paragraph. Any possible doubt about the conse-quence of the Berlin Protocol has, however, been removed by the alteration made in the French text, which, by virtue of the Berlin Protocol, now reads as follows:

'(*c*) LES CRIMES CONTRE L'HUMANITÉ: c'est-à-dire l'assassinat, l'extermination, la réduc-tion en esclavage, la déportation, et tout autre acte inhumain commis contre toutes pop-ulations civiles, avant ou pendant la guerre, ou bien les persécutions pour des motifs politiques, raciaux ou religieux, lorsque *ces actes ou persécutions*, qu'ils aient constitué ou non une violation du droit interne du pays où ils ont été perpétrés, ont été commis à la suite de tout crime rentrant dans la compétence du Tribunal, ou en liaison avec ce crime.'

Instead of containing the words 'commises à la suite de tout crime rentrant dans la compétence du Tribunal International ou s'y rattachant', determining 'les persécutions' and severed from the preceding part of the paragraph by a semico-lon, the new text, in addition to abolishing the semicolon, expressly speaks of 'ces actes ou persécutions', 'ces actes' being 'l'assassinat, l'extermination, la réduction en esclavage, la déportation, et tout autre acte inhumain', or, in other words, the crimes against humanity of the murder type. The new French wording of Article 6 (*c*) is the more important and decisive in view of the fact that it is contained not only in the French, but also in the English and Russian, texts of the Berlin Protocol, so that it is clear that all four Contracting Parties have agreed that the text, as it is declared in the amended French wording, correctly reproduces the meaning of the Agreement and the intention of all four Parties.

Having regard to the English and French texts as they now stand, and to the Russian text as it has read from the beginning, it is now beyond doubt that the qualification 'in execution of or in connection with any crime within the jurisdic-tion of the Tribunal' undoubtedly applies to the whole context of the paragraph and constitutes a very important restriction on the scope of the concept of crimes against humanity. This is the opinion which was hinted at in the Indictment,[45] which was extensively elaborated in the speeches of the Chief Prosecutors at the close of the case against the individual defendants,[46] and which was finally adopted by the Judgment of the International Military Tribunal.[47]

(*l*) The word 'humanity' (*l'humanité*) has at least two different meanings, the one connoting the human race or mankind as a whole, and the other, humane-ness, i.e. a certain quality of behaviour. It is submitted that in the Charter, and in the other basic documents which will be discussed in this article, the word 'humanity' is used in the latter sense. It is, therefore, not necessary for a certain

---

[45] Cmd. 6696, p. 30.
[46] Published under the authority of H.M. Attorney-General by H.M. Stationery Office, London, 1946, p. 4 (Mr. Justice Jackson) and p. 63 (Sir Hartley Shawcross).
[47] Cmd. 6964, p. 65.

act, in order to come within the notion of crimes against humanity, to affect mankind as a whole. A crime against humanity is an offence against certain general principles of law which, in certain circumstances, become the concern of the international community, namely, if it has repercussions reaching across international frontiers, or if it passes 'in magnitude or savagery any limits of what is tolerable by modern civilisations'.[48]

The French text of the Briand–Kellogg Pact[49] provides an example of the use, in an international instrument, of the word *l'humanité* as meaning the human race as a whole. In its Preamble the signatories declare themselves as 'ayant le sentiment profond du devoir solennel qui leur incombe de développer le *bien-être de l'humanité*', which in the equally authentic (Art. 3) English text is rendered: 'Deeply sensible of their solemn duty to promote *the welfare of mankind*.'

In his Report to the President of the United States on the Nuremberg trial, Mr. Francis Biddle, the American member of the International Military Tribunal, advocates the affirmation by the United Nations of the principles of the Nuremberg Charter 'in the context of a general codification of offences against *the peace and security of mankind*'.[50] The latter phrase has also been adopted in the Resolution of the United Nations Assembly of December 1946, directing the Committee on the Codification of International Law 'to treat as a matter of primary importance plans for the formulation, in the context of a general codification of offences *against the peace and security of mankind*, or of an International Criminal Code, of the principles recognized in the Charter of the Nuremberg Tribunal and in the judgment of the Tribunal'.[51]

(*m*) Apart from the task of distinguishing crimes against humanity from acts which are legitimate and therefore do not come within the notion, it is also necessary to distinguish them from (1) crimes against peace, (2) war crimes in the narrower sense, and (3) simple or common crimes punishable under municipal criminal law.

In a certain general sense, nearly every crime is inhumane and therefore a crime against humanity. The planning, preparation, initiation, and waging of a war of aggression, if a crime, is also a crime against humanity in this non-technical sense. Moreover, what could be considered more inhumane than most violations of the laws and customs of war and particularly the type of violations enumerated in Article 6 (*b*) of the London Charter?

Reference has already been made to the Preamble of the Fourth Hague Convention, where it has been stated that the laws of humanity are the basis and source of the laws and customs of land warfare. The text of Article 6 (*c*) ('any

[48] Mr. Justice Jackson in his opening speech at Nuremberg; *Opening Speeches of the Chief Prosecutors*, published under the authority of H.M. Attorney-General by H.M. Stationery Office, p. 25.
[49] Treaty Series No. 29 (1929), Cmd. 3410.
[50] *U.S. Department of State Bulletin* (24 November 1946), p. 957.
[51] Doc. A/236.

civilian population') leaves no room for doubt that crimes committed against the civilian population of occupied territory are both violations of the laws and customs of war (Art. 6 (*b*)) and crimes against humanity (Art. 6 (*c*)). Where enemy combatants are the victims of a crime—irrespective of whether or no such crime is an inhumane act—we are faced with a war crime in the narrower sense not coming under the notion of a crime against humanity.

Most of the common crimes of the municipal law of civilized nations are in some sense or other offences against 'humanity'. There can be no doubt that homicide (murder, manslaughter) is an offence against humanity in its non-technical meaning. The same applies to the causing of grievous bodily harm, assault, sexual offences, and the like. Also, among the common crimes against property there are such as may be considered inhuman, e.g. robbery, arson. More often than not, a crime against humanity is also a crime under municipal law, and, in many cases, also a war crime in the narrower sense. Only in exceptional cases is the position such that an inhuman act which is visited by punishment in civilized systems of law has been made expressly or impliedly 'legal' under provisions which have been enacted under such régimes as the German Nazi régime. In such cases the municipal enactment is to be disregarded under Article 6 (*c*).

(*n*) Lord Wright, writing in 1946,[52] dealt with the objection of the American members of the 1919 Commission[53] against the use of the term 'laws of humanity' and their implied allegation that, like equity in the Anglo-American system, 'the laws of humanity' were a roguish thing; equity, he replied, has established itself as a regular branch of the Anglo-American legal system. Taking another parallel from Anglo-American law, he added that it might equally be said that 'negligence is too indeterminate a concept as to constitute a legal head of liability, but we all know that in the Anglo-American law of tort it has become one of the widest and most comprehensive and most important categories of liability'. Under the 1945 Charter 'crime against humanity' is clearly a legal term. To come under the notion, a certain act must be universally recognized as a crime under the penal law of civilized nations. The Nuremberg Tribunal had, therefore, a more objective yardstick to use than the medieval Chancellor; the rules that the International Military Tribunal had to apply may be criticized from different angles; they certainly did not vary, however, as 'the length of the Chancellor's foot'.

IV. Crimes Against Humanity in the Nuremberg Indictment

The Tribunal in its decision[54] referred to the Indictment in laying down which inhumane acts, committed after the beginning of the war, constitute crimes

---

[52] *Law Quarterly Review*, 62 (1946), p. 9.
[53] See *supra*, p. 123.   [54] Cmd. 6964, p. 65.

against humanity. For this reason, and also because the Indictment throws considerable light on the way in which the Charter was interpreted by the Prosecution, it will be appropriate to deal at some length with the Nuremberg Indictment, although in assessing its relevance for the problems under consideration it must be kept in mind that its pronouncements were not made by the Committee of Prosecutors in any legislative capacity.

The general theory on which the Indictment was based in respect of the charge of crimes against humanity was lucidly put forward by the British Chief Prosecutor, Sir Hartley Shawcross, in his closing speech delivered on 26 and 27 July 1946:[55]

'So the crime against the Jews, insofar as it is a Crime against Humanity and not a War Crime, is one which we indict because of its association with the Crime Against the Peace. That is, of course, a very important qualification, and is not always appreciated by those who have questioned the exercise of this jurisdiction. But, subject to that qualification, we have thought it right to deal with matters which the Criminal Law of all countries would normally stigmatise as crimes: murder, extermination, enslavement, persecution on political, racial or economic grounds. These things done against belligerent nationals, or, for that matter, done against German nationals in belligerent occupied territory, would be ordinary War Crimes, the prosecution of which would form no novelty. Done against others they would be crimes against Municipal Law except in so far as German law, departing from all the canons of civilised procedure, may have authorised them to be done by the State or by persons acting on behalf of the State. Although so to do does not in any way place those defendants in greater jeopardy than they would otherwise be, the nations adhering to the Charter of this Tribunal have felt it proper and necessary in the interest of civilisation to say that these things, even if done in accordance with the laws of the German State, as created and ruled by these men and their ringleader, were, when committed with the intention of affecting the international community—that is in connection with the other crimes charged—not mere matters of domestic concern but crimes against the Laws of Nations. I do not minimise the significance for the future of the political and jurisprudential doctrine which is here implied. Normally International Law concedes that it is for the State to decide how it shall treat its own nationals; it is a matter of domestic jurisdiction. And although the Social and Economic Council of the United Nations Organisation is seeking to formulate a Charter of the Rights of Man, the Covenant of the League of Nations and the Charter of the United Nations Organisation does recognise that general position. Yet International Law has in the past made some claim that there is a limit to the omnipotence of the State and that the individual human being, the ultimate unit of all law, is not disentitled to the protection of mankind when the State tramples upon his rights in a manner which outrages the conscience of mankind.'

After quoting Grotius, who affirmed, with reference to atrocities committed by tyrants against their subjects, that intervention is justified for 'the right of

---

[55] *Speeches of the Chief Prosecutors at the close of the case against the individual defendants.* Published under the authority of H.M. Attorney-General by H.M. Stationery Office (Cmd. 6964), p. 63.

social connection is not cut off in such a case', and the expression of the same idea by John Westlake, Sir Hartley Shawcross went on to say:

'The same view was acted upon by the European Powers which in time past intervened in order to protect the Christian subjects of Turkey against cruel persecution. The fact is that the right of humanitarian intervention by war is not a novelty in International Law—can intervention by judicial process then be illegal? The Charter of this Tribunal embodies a beneficent principle—much more limited than some would like it to be—and it gives warning for the future—I say, and repeat again, gives warning for the future, to dictators and tyrants masquerading as a State that if, in order to strengthen or further their crimes against the community of nations they debase the sanctity of man in their own countries, they act at their peril, for they affront the International Law of mankind.'[56]

V. The Nuremberg Judgment on Crimes Against Humanity

(a) The General Attitude of the Tribunal to the Law of the Charter

The manner in which the Tribunal interpreted its function in relation to the provisions of the Charter is illustrated by the following two passages in its judgment:

'The law of the Charter is decisive and binding upon the Tribunal. The making of the Charter was the exercise of the sovereign legislative power by the countries to which the German Reich unconditionally surrendered; and the undoubted right of these countries to legislate for the occupied territories has been recognised by the civilised world. The Charter is not an arbitrary exercise of power on the part of the victorious nations, but in the view of the Tribunal, as will be shown, it is the expression of international law existing at the time of its creation; and to that extent is itself a contribution to international law.'[57]

'The Tribunal is, of course, bound by the Charter in the definition which it gives both of "war crimes" and "crimes against humanity".'[58]

The Tribunal conceived its task to be one of interpretation and application of the law as laid down in the Charter. It did not consider itself to be called upon to make new law on the one hand or to examine the legality or otherwise of its constituting Charter on the other, although it did express the opinion—respecting crimes against humanity, not with too much emphasis—that the law as laid down by the Charter was in accordance with the existing international law and in conformity with the law of all nations.

---

[56] Ibid., p. 64.
[57] Ibid., p. 38.
[58] Ibid., p. 64.

(b) The Crime Against Peace as the Supreme War Crime

In dealing with Count 1 of the Indictment (Common Plan or Conspiracy) and Count 2 (Aggressive War; Crimes against Peace), the Tribunal stated:

'To initiate a war of aggression, therefore, is not only an international crime; it is the supreme international crime differing only from other war crimes in that it contains within itself the accumulated evil of the whole. The first acts of aggression referred to in the Indictment are the seizure of Austria and Czechoslovakia; and the first war of aggression charged in the Indictment is the war against Poland begun on 1st September 1939.'[59]

The Tribunal further stated with regard to the aggression against Austria that: 'The facts plainly prove that the methods employed to achieve the object were those of an aggressor.'[60] The Tribunal also accepted the proposition of the Prosecution as to the aggressive character of the seizure of Czechoslovakia.[61] And it stated: 'The Tribunal is fully satisfied by the evidence that the war initiated by Germany against Poland on 1st September 1939 was most plainly an aggressive war, which was to develop in due course into a war which embraced almost the whole world, and resulted in the commission of countless crimes, both against the laws and customs of war, and against humanity.'[62]

The passage of the Judgment quoted here is interesting also from a terminological point of view. In describing the crime against peace as the supreme international crime, and saying that it differs from *other* war crimes in that it contains within itself the accumulated evil of the whole, the Tribunal uses the expression 'war crime' in a wider sense, comprising also the crime of aggression and, for that matter, also crimes against humanity. In doing so the Tribunal does not deviate from the terminology used in relevant international documents. The Four-Power Agreement of 8 August 1945 is called an 'Agreement for the Prosecution and Punishment of the Major War Criminals of the European Axis' and under its Article 1 there shall be established an International Military Tribunal for their trial. Throughout (in the Preamble and in Arts. 3, 4, and 6), the Agreement speaks of 'war criminals'. The same applies to Articles 1, 6 (para. 1), and 14 of the Charter annexed to the Agreement. In all these places the term is used in the wider sense and comprises not only violations of the laws and customs of war, but also crimes against peace and crimes against humanity. In Article 6 (*b*), however, the expression 'war crime' is used in a narrower sense.

The Italian and German Armistice Documents which were quoted above[63] use the term 'war crime' in the narrower sense; crimes against peace are covered by the reference to Mussolini's 'chief Fascist associates' and to the 'principal Nazi leaders'; crimes against humanity by the term 'analogous offences'. The Potsdam

---

[59] Ibid., p. 13.
[60] Cmd. 6964, p. 19.
[61] Ibid., pp. 19–22.
[62] Ibid., p. 27.
[63] See p. 127, nn. 16, 17.

Declaration on Germany, too, distinguishes between war crimes in the narrower sense and 'atrocities'. The Armistices with Romania, Finland, Bulgaria, and Hungary[64] speak only of the apprehension and trial of persons accused of war crimes, and the Potsdam Declaration to the Japanese people[65] of 'war criminals'.

(c) Rejection of the Charges of Conspiracy to Commit War Crimes and Crimes Against Humanity

In the statement of the law as to the common plan or conspiracy, the Tribunal said:

'Count One, however, charges not only the conspiracy to commit aggressive war, but also to commit war crimes and crimes against humanity. But the Charter does not define as a separate crime any conspiracy except the one to commit acts of aggressive war. Art. 6 of the Charter provides: "Leaders, organizers, instigators and accomplices participating in the formulation or execution of a common plan or conspiracy to commit any of the fore-going crimes are responsible for all acts performed by any persons in execution of such plan." In the opinion of the Tribunal these words do not add a new and separate crime to those already listed. The words are designed to establish the responsibility of persons participating in a common plan. The Tribunal will therefore disregard the charges in Count One that the defendants conspired to commit war crimes and crimes against humanity, and will consider only the common plan to prepare, initiate and wage aggressive war.'[66]

The Tribunal, therefore, dismissed the indictment as far as it charged the defendants with having conspired to commit war crimes and crimes against humanity.

(d) Killing of 'Useless Eaters' as a Crime Against Humanity

In the part of the Judgment which deals with war crimes and crimes against humanity generally, the Tribunal referred to the killing of insane and incurable people as follows:

'Reference should also be made to the policy which was in existence in Germany by the summer of 1940, under which all aged, insane, and incurable people, "useless eaters", were transferred to special institutions where they were killed, and their relatives informed that they had died from natural causes. The victims were not confined to German citizens, but included foreign labourers who were no longer able to work and were therefore useless to the German war machine. It has been estimated that at least some 275,000 people were killed in this manner in nursing homes, hospitals and asylums, which were under the jurisdiction of the defendant Frick, in his capacity as Minister of the Interior. How many foreign workers were included in this total it has been quite impossible to determine.'[67]

---

[64] See p. 127, nn. 19, 20, 21, 22. [65] See p. 127, n. 27.
[66] Cmd. 6964, p. 44. [67] p. 60.

It will be noted that the Tribunal is careful to point out that the victims were not confined to German citizens, but included foreign labourers, and that it was quite impossible to determine how many foreign workers were included in the estimated total of people killed.

(e) The Persecution of Jews as a Crime Against Humanity

The Judgment states that the persecution of the Jews at the hands of the Nazi Government was proved in the greatest detail before the Tribunal. It was a record of consistent and systematic inhumanity on the greatest scale.[68] The Tribunal recalled the anti-Jewish policy as formulated in Point 4 of the Programme of the Nazi Party of 24 February 1920,[69] and examined, in great detail, acts committed long before 1939:

'The Nazi Party preached these doctrines throughout its history. "Der Stürmer" and other publications were allowed to disseminate hatred of the Jews, and in the speeches and public declarations of the Nazi leaders, the Jews were held up to public ridicule and contempt.

'With the seizure of power, the persecution of the Jews was intensified. A series of discriminatory laws were passed, which limited the offices and professions permitted to Jews; and restrictions were placed on their family life and their rights to citizenship. By the autumn of 1938, the Nazi policy towards the Jews had reached the stage where it was directed towards the complete exclusion of Jews from German life. Pogroms were organised, which included the burning and demolishing of synagogues, the looting of Jewish businesses, and the arrest of prominent Jewish business men. A collective fine of one billion marks was imposed on the Jews, the seizure of Jewish assets was authorized and the movement of Jews was restricted by regulations to certain specified districts and hours. The creation of ghettoes was carried out on an extensive scale, and by an order of the Security Police, Jews were compelled to wear a yellow star to be worn on the breast and back.

'It was contended for the Prosecution that certain aspects of this anti-Semitic policy were connected with the plans for aggressive war. The violent measures taken against the Jews in November 1938 were nominally in retaliation for the killing of an official of the German Embassy in Paris. But the decision to seize Austria and Czechoslovakia had been made a year before. The imposition of a fine of one billion marks was made, and the confiscation of the financial holdings of the Jews was decreed, at a time when German armament expenditure had put the German treasury in difficulties and when the reduction of expenditure on armaments was being considered. These steps were taken, moreover, with the approval of the defendant Goering, who had been given responsibility for economic matters of this kind, and who was the strongest advocate of an extensive rearmament programme notwithstanding the financial difficulties.

'It was further said that the connection of the anti-Semitic policy with aggressive war was not limited to economic matters.'[70]

---

[68] p. 60.
[69] pp. 60 and 64.
[70] Cmd. 6964, p. 61.

The Court then referred to a German Foreign Office circular of 25 January 1939, entitled: 'The Jewish Question as a Factor in German Foreign Policy in the year 1938', and stated:

'The Nazi persecution of Jews in Germany before the war, severe and repressive as it was, cannot compare, however, with the policy pursued during the war in the occupied territories. Originally the policy was similar to that which had been in force inside Germany. Jews were required to register, were forced to live in ghettoes, to wear the yellow star, and were used as slave labourers. In the summer of 1941, however, plans were made for the "final solution" of the Jewish question in all of Europe. This "final solution" meant the extermination of the Jews, which early in 1939 Hitler had threatened would be one of the consequences of an outbreak of war, and a special section of the Gestapo under Adolf Eichmann, as head of Section B₄ of the Gestapo, was formed to carry out the policy.'[71]

After describing the atrocities against Jews committed in occupied territories the Court stated the following:

'Special groups travelled through Europe to find Jews and subject them to the "final solution". German missions were sent to such satellite countries as Hungary and Bulgaria, to arrange for the shipment of Jews to extermination camps, and it is known that by the end of 1944, 400,000 Jews from Hungary had been murdered at Auschwitz. Evidence has also been given of the evacuation of 110,000 Jews from part of Roumania for "liquidation".'[72]

(f) War Crimes and Crimes Against Humanity in 'Subjugated' Territories

In the chapter dealing with the law relating to war crimes and crimes against humanity, the Tribunal quoted the wording of Article 6 (*b*) and (*c*) of its Charter, and repeated that the Charter does not define as a separate crime any conspiracy except the one set out in Article 6 (*c*) dealing with crimes against peace.[73] The Tribunal further dealt with the plea based on the alleged complete subjugation of some of the occupied countries in the following way:

'A further submission was made that Germany was no longer bound by the rules of land warfare in many of the territories occupied during the war, because Germany had completely subjugated these countries and incorporated them into the German Reich, a fact which gave Germany authority to deal with the occupied countries as though they were part of Germany. In the view of the Tribunal it is unnecessary in this case to decide whether this doctrine of subjugation is the result of the crime of aggressive war. The doctrine was never considered to be applicable so long as there was an army in the field attempting to restore the occupied countries to their true owners, and in this case, therefore, the doctrine could not apply to any territories occupied after the 1st September 1939.

---

[71] Ibid., p. 62.
[72] Ibid., p. 64.
[73] Ibid.

As to the war crimes committed in Bohemia and Moravia, it is a sufficient answer that these territories were never added to the Reich, but a mere protectorate was established over them.'[74]

(g) General Statement by the Court on the Law as to Crimes Against Humanity

The Court gave its general opinion on the notion of crimes against humanity in the following words:

'With regard to crimes against humanity, there is no doubt whatever that political opponents were murdered in Germany before the war and that many of them were kept in concentration camps in circumstances of great horror and cruelty. The policy of terror was certainly carried out on a vast scale; and in many cases was organized and systematic. The policy of persecution, repression and murder of civilians in Germany before the war of 1939, who were likely to be hostile to the Government, was most ruthlessly carried out. The persecution of Jews during the same period is established beyond all doubt. To constitute crimes against humanity, the acts relied on before the outbreak of war must have been in execution of, or in connection with, any crime within the jurisdiction of the Tribunal. The Tribunal is of the opinion that revolting and horrible as many of these crimes were, it has not been satisfactorily proved that they were done in execution of, or in connection with, any such crime. The Tribunal cannot, therefore, make a general declaration that the acts before 1939 were crimes against humanity within the meaning of the Charter, but from the beginning of the war in 1939 war crimes were committed on a vast scale, which were also crimes against humanity; and in so far as the inhumane acts charged in the Indictment, and committed after the beginning of the war did not constitute war crimes, they were all committed in execution of, or in connection with, the aggressive war, and therefore constituted crimes against humanity.'[75]

(h) The General Statement Analysed

From the statement, quoted verbatim, in the preceding paragraph the following can be seen:

(1) The International Military Tribunal, proceeding on the basis of the Berlin Protocol, which, however, is not quoted in the Judgment,[76] considers paragraph (c) of Article 6 of the Charter as one whole and, in accordance with the submission in the closing speeches of the prosecution, particularly in the closing speech of Sir Hartley Shawcross, applies the qualification 'in execution of or in connection with any crime within the jurisdiction of the Tribunal' to the whole provision, i.e. both to crimes of the murder type and to persecutions: in other

---

[74] Ibid., p. 65.
[75] Ibid.
[76] The English text of the Judgment reproduces Article 6 (c) of the Charter on p. 64 with, and on p. 3 without, the semicolon.

words, the Tribunal does not distinguish between the two types of crimes against humanity. In the opinion of the Tribunal, all the crimes formulated in Article 6 (*c*) are crimes against humanity only if they were committed in execution of or in connexion with a crime against peace or a war crime.

(2) The scope of the phrase 'before or during the war' is therefore considerably narrowed as a consequence of the view that, although the time when a crime was committed is not alone decisive, the connexion with the war must be established in order to bring a certain set of facts under the notion of a crime against humanity within the meaning of Article 6 (*c*). As will be seen later, this statement does not imply that no crime committed before 1 September 1939 can be a crime against humanity. The Tribunal recognized some crimes committed prior to 1 September 1939 as crimes against humanity in cases where their connexion with the crime against peace was established. Although in theory it remains irrelevant whether a crime against humanity was committed before or during the war, in practice it is difficult to establish a connexion between what is alleged to be a crime against humanity and a crime within the jurisdiction of the Tribunal, if the act was committed before the war.

(3) On the other hand, if the commission of an inhumane act charged in the Indictment took place during the war, its connexion with the war was presumed by the Tribunal. Inhumane acts committed in Austria after the occupation by Germany are to be considered crimes against humanity because of their connexion with the occupation of Austria, which was an act of aggression and therefore a crime against peace. Inhumane acts committed on Czechoslovak territory after the occupation of the so-called Sudeten territory are, in the light of the Nuremberg Judgment, either crimes against humanity or war crimes in the narrower sense.

VI. General Observations on Crimes Against Humanity in the Nuremberg Judgment

(1) As pointed out, the International Military Tribunal, in interpreting the notion of crimes against humanity, lays particular stress on that provision of its Charter according to which an act, in order to come within the notion of a crime against humanity, must have been committed in execution of or in connexion with any crime within the jurisdiction of the Tribunal, which means that it must be closely connected either with a crime against peace or a war crime in the narrower sense. Therefore the Tribunal declined to make a general declaration that acts committed before 1939 were crimes against humanity within the meaning of the Charter. This represents, however, only the general view of the Tribunal and did not prevent it from treating as crimes against humanity acts committed by individual defendants against German nationals before 1 September 1939 if

the particular circumstances of the case appeared to warrant this attitude. The verdict against the defendant Streicher is a case in point, but even in his case the *causal nexus* has been pointed out between his activities and the crimes committed on occupied Allied territory and against non-German nationals, and the most that can be said is that he was also found guilty of crimes against humanity committed before 1 September 1939 in Germany against German nationals. It cannot be said in the case of any of the defendants that he was convicted only of crimes committed in Germany against Germans before 1 September 1939.

The restrictive interpretation placed on the term 'crimes against humanity' was not so strictly applied by the Tribunal in the case of victims of other than German nationality. With respect to crimes committed before 1 September 1939 against Austrian nationals, the Tribunal established their connexion with the annexation of Austria, which is a crime against peace, and came, therefore, to the conclusion that they were within the terms of Article 6 (*c*) of the Charter. This consideration is particularly evident in the reasons concerning the case of Baldur von Schirach and, though expressed less precisely, in the case of the defendant Seyss-Inquart. The same applies *mutatis mutandis* to crimes committed in Czechoslovakia before 1 September 1939, as illustrated in the verdicts on the defendants Frick and von Neurath. With regard to the inhumane acts charged in the Indictment and committed after 1 September 1939, the Tribunal made the far-reaching statement that in so far as they did not constitute war crimes they were all committed in execution of, or in connexion with, aggressive war and therefore constituted crimes against humanity. The case of Ribbentrop and his activities with respect to Axis satellites is particularly illustrative of this view.

(2) It will be seen that the Tribunal treats the notion of crimes against humanity as a kind of subsidiary provision to be applied whenever any particular area where a crime was committed is not governed by The Hague Rules of Land Warfare. Germanization is, therefore, considered as criminal under Article 6 (*b*) in the areas governed by The Hague Regulations and as a crime under Article 6 (*c*) as to all others. The crime against humanity, as defined in the London Charter, is not, therefore, the cornerstone of a system of international criminal law equally applicable in times of war and of peace, protecting the human rights of inhabitants of all countries, 'of any civilian population', against anybody, including their own states and governments. As interpreted in the Nuremberg Judgment, the term has a considerably narrower connotation. It is, as it were, a kind of by-product of war, applicable only in time of war or in connexion with war and destined primarily, if not exclusively, to protect the inhabitants of foreign countries against crimes committed, in connexion with an aggressive war, by the authorities and organs of the aggressor state. It serves to cover cases not covered by norms forming part of the traditional 'laws and customs of war'. It denotes a particular type of war crime, and is a kind of *clausula generalis*, the purpose of which is to make sure that inhumane acts violating general principles of the laws of all civilized

nations committed in connexion with war should not go unpunished. As defined in the Nuremberg Judgment, the crime against humanity is an 'accompanying' or an 'accessory' crime to either crimes against peace or violations of the laws and customs of war.[77]

(3) Before the Nuremberg proceedings and the Judgment were made accessible, it was assumed by many that for the purpose of deciding whether a crime against humanity has been committed, not only the time (peace or war) was irrelevant, but also the territory and the nationality of the victims. Here, again, the proposition remains true in theory, but must, according to the view of the Nuremberg Tribunal, be considerably qualified with regard to acts committed by the German major war criminals before the war in Germany against German nationals. Even with regard to revolting and horrible crimes the connexion with aggression or with war crimes in the narrower sense must be proved, and where the proof is not satisfactory they are not considered by the International Military Tribunal as crimes against humanity within the meaning of the Charter.

(4) The present article is devoted to the examination of the question whether the propositions set forth in the introductory chapter, which assert a far-reaching and revolutionary nature of the notion of crimes against humanity, as embodied in the Charter, are borne out by the proceedings and by the result of the trial. Our conclusion, in the light of the analysis given above, is that all such far-reaching assumptions are subject to very considerable qualifications. Concerning the first principle, assumed to be implied in the Charter, according to which international law contains penal sanctions against individuals guilty of inhumane acts, which are applicable not only in time of war but also in time of peace, it is clear that what has been introduced by the Charter are not international criminal provisions of universal application, but provisions concerning a crime which may be described as subsidiary or accessory to the traditional types of war crimes. Nor can the second principle, according to which it should not make any difference where the crimes are committed and what the nationality of the victim is, be said to be part of the law laid down in the London Agreement and applied at Nuremberg. It is, on the contrary, subject to fundamental reservations.

The third principle ascribed to the Charter, namely, the sweeping away of national sovereignty as an obstacle to bringing to justice perpetrators of crimes against humanity, can hardly be deduced from the terms of that document. The one state sovereignty involved, namely, the sovereignty of the German Reich, has been swept away not by the Charter of the International Military Tribunal nor by the Nuremberg proceedings and Judgment, but by the temporary disappearance of Germany as a sovereign state.[78] As far as state sovereignty was concerned, both the draftsmen of the Charter and the Court were operating in a vacuum, as it

---

[77] Jacob Robinson, 'The Nuremberg Judgment', *Congress Weekly*, vol. 13, no. 25, p. 6.

[78] The Berlin Declaration of 5 June 1945, Cmd. 6648; cf. Kelsen, 'The Legal Status of Germany according to the Declaration of Berlin', *American Journal of International Law*, 39 (1945), p. 518,

were, the sovereignty of the German state as the obstacle barring the enforcement of justice having been destroyed by the historic events of May and June 1945. In view of this fact, it is doubly significant that the Charter and the Tribunal respected German sovereignty to the extent of subjecting to the Court's jurisdiction only such criminal activities as were connected with either crimes against peace or with violations of the laws and customs of war, i.e. only such acts as directly affected the interests of other states. It is by no means a novel principle in international law that the sovereignty of one state does not prevent the punishment of crimes committed against other states and their nationals. The laws and customs of war are not a restriction on state sovereignty. They regulate the relationship between one state and persons who are not subject to its sovereignty. The Hague Regulations, e.g., set the limits of what an occupant is permitted to do, and what is forbidden to him; the question of sovereignty is not involved. The Hague Regulations state, as it were, what is *intra vires* and what is *ultra vires* of an occupant *qua* occupant as distinguished from the sovereign. The Nuremberg Tribunal showed itself willing to extend the protection which the laws and customs of war on land afford to the population of territory under belligerent occupation to foreign territory other than under *occupatio bellica* (Austria, parts of Czechoslovakia in 1938), and, in time of war, to any population. As for the consistent extension of this principle so as to safeguard human rights also in time of peace against the victims' own national authorities, the Charter and the Tribunal proceeded with great caution and reserve.

This becomes still more apparent if we consider the views expressed by the International Tribunal as to its own status.

(5) To assess properly the importance of the Nuremberg Proceedings for the development of international law, it is necessary to examine in more detail the exact status of the International Military Tribunal. If the International Military Tribunal were an organ of the community of nations, then the fact that it was seised of a case and exercised jurisdiction against defendants accused, among other things, also of crimes committed against their own nationals, would in spite of all qualifications and restrictions amount to the establishment of a principle asserting the supremacy of international law over municipal law, and the overriding of national sovereignty by this organ of the international community.

An examination of the Charter of 8 August 1945 shows that it contains both such features as make the court established by it a judicial organ of the international community, and such as make it appear a tribunal of considerably lesser standing, hierarchically subject to the Control Council for Germany and therefore being, in substance, an occupation court for Germany.

The features which give to the International Military Tribunal the stature of a court of the international community of nations, such as, e.g., the Permanent

---

R. v. Bottrill, ex parte Küchenmeister, [1946] 1 All E.R., p. 635, and note in *American Journal of International Law*, 40 (1946), p. 811.

Court of Arbitration or the International Court of Justice, or at least the character of a quasi-international court,[79] are:

(a) the name given to the court, The International Military Tribunal;

(b) the reference in the Preamble to the fact that the four Signatories are 'acting in the interests of all the United Nations';

(c) the provision of Article 5 of the Agreement giving any Government of the United Nations the right to adhere to the Agreement, a right of which the following 19 states have availed themselves: Greece, Denmark, Yugoslavia, the Netherlands, Czechoslovakia, Poland, Belgium, Ethiopia, Australia, Honduras, Norway, Panama, Luxemburg, Haiti, New Zealand, India, Venezuela, Uruguay, and Paraguay;[80]

(d) the provision of Article 6 of the Charter, according to which the jurisdiction of the Tribunal is not restricted to German major war criminals, but, in theory at least, comprises also the right to try and punish the major war criminals of all other European Axis countries;

(e) the provision of Article 10 of the Charter providing for the binding character, in proceedings before courts of the signatory States, of a declaration by the Tribunal that a group or organization is criminal.

The following provisions of the Four-Power Agreement and the Charter may be adduced in support of the opposite opinion, namely, that the International Military Tribunal is a local occupation court for Germany:

(a) Article 1 of the Agreement provides for the establishment of an International Military Tribunal 'after consultation with the Control Council for Germany'.

This provision might, of course, also be explained by saying that such consultation with the Control Council for Germany has not been provided for because of the fact that the Tribunal will be an organ of the allied *condominium* of Germany, but that consultation with the Control Council is necessary because of the latter's capacity as the local sovereign of Germany, in the same way as, e.g., consultation with the Netherlands Government was necessary to establish on Dutch territory the Permanent Court of International Justice.

(b) Article 22 of the Charter provides, *inter alia,* that the first meetings of the members of the Tribunal and of the Chief Prosecutors shall be held at Berlin in a place to be designated by the Control Council for Germany.

Here a similar explanation as in the case of Article 1 is not possible because if the Control Council for Germany were nothing but the organ of the host country of the court, it could certainly not unilaterally designate a place for the court's meeting.

(c) Article 28 of the Charter lays down that the Tribunal shall have the right to deprive the convicted person of any stolen property and order its delivery to the Control Council for Germany.

---

[79] Cf. Lauterpacht, op. cit., p. 82.   [80] Cmd. 6964, p. 1.

(d) Article 29 of the Charter provides for the sentences to be carried out in accordance with the orders of the Control Council for Germany, which may at any time reduce or otherwise alter the sentences, but may not increase the severity thereof. Under Article 29, the Control Council for Germany is also bound to report to the Committee of Prosecutors with a view to a re-trial of defendants on the discovery of fresh evidence.

This provision obviously vests in the Control Council part of such jurisdiction with regard to decisions of criminal courts as is very often reserved to the sovereign. Here the subordination of the International Military Tribunal to the Control Council is expressed in rather clear terms.

(e) Under Article 30 of the Charter, the expenses of the Tribunal and of the trials shall be charged by the Signatories against the funds allotted for maintenance of the Control Council for Germany.

(6) The Tribunal itself adhered to the second of the two possible opinions. It has expressed the opinion that the making of the Charter was the exercise of the sovereign legislative power by the countries to which the German Reich unconditionally surrendered; and the undoubted right of these countries to legislate for the occupied territories has been recognized by the civilized world.[81]

The Tribunal further stated: 'The Signatory Powers created this Tribunal, defined the law it was to administer, and made regulations for the proper conduct of the Trial. In doing so, they have done together what any one of them might have done singly; for it is not to be doubted that any nation has the right thus to set up special courts to administer law.'[82]

The Tribunal therefore allots to itself the standing of an occupation court having jurisdiction over Germany and German nationals. It is certainly a novel and revolutionary step to subject to international jurisdiction matters 'which are essentially within the domestic jurisdiction' of the state concerned (Art. 2, para. 7 of the San Francisco Charter). It is by no means so, if the court in which this jurisdiction is vested is considered to be not a court of the international community, but a court to the jurisdiction of which the defendants are subject *ratione loci* and *ratione personae*, if the court is a court which, as a consequence of military events, has simply taken the place of the local courts to the jurisdiction of which the defendants would otherwise be subject.

(7) It is, however, submitted that a classification of the Tribunal as a local occupation court pure and simple does not sufficiently take into account those features which were indicated under (5) (*supra*), and which tend to give to the Tribunal the character of an international judicial body, exercising jurisdiction, not only on behalf of the local sovereign of Germany, but also on behalf of the international community, which at the relevant time was, and is now, represented

---

[81] p. 38.
[82] Ibid.

for all practical purposes by the United Nations. If the Tribunal based the legislative powers of the signatories of the Charter on the unconditional surrender of Germany and the right to legislate for occupied territory, it did not exclude the construction that the Nuremberg proceedings had, in addition to this territorial basis, also a wider foundation in the provisions of international law and the Court the standing of an international judicial body.

The London Charter of 8 August 1945 has been classified by American writers as an Executive Agreement.[83] It is, however, submitted that the description as an Executive Agreement refers to its classification in United States constitutional law and does not affect its character as an international legislative instrument. It is not relevant in this connexion whether and to what extent the London Agreement codified existing international law and to what extent it has created new law. That the London Agreement is more than a local enactment for Germany is also borne out by the Control Council Law No. 10,[84] which was issued for the purpose, *inter alia*, of embodying the London Charter in the local law applicable in Germany.

(8) The problem arises whether the attitude of the International Military Tribunal with regard to the notion of crimes against humanity (and for that matter its interpretation of the law in general) is binding for the decision in other cases to be tried either before the International Military Tribunal itself (if such trials should take place, which seems hardly probable at present), or by other courts, be it the International Military Tribunal for the Far East, or any municipal, occupation, or military tribunals of other United Nations or Axis Powers.

This question is closely connected with the problem dealt with, in the preceding paragraph of this article. If it emanates from an occupation Tribunal for the territory of Germany, the judgment of the Tribunal certainly does not constitute a binding precedent in the technical sense for other countries and other courts, irrespective of whether or not the laws of the countries in question are based on the system of *stare decisis*. For other courts the decision is therefore only of persuasive authority, which means that any other court may follow the Nuremberg interpretation, if it considers it correct, and may disagree with it, if it considers it incorrect. The position is not different if the Tribunal is considered a court of the international community, as, e.g., the International Court of Justice under its San Francisco Statute. In Article 59 of the Statute of the International Court of Justice it is laid down (as it was in Art. 59 of the Statute of the Permanent Court of International Justice) that the decision of the Court has no binding force except between the parties in respect of that particular case. This general rule applies, of course, only to the extent to which there is no express provision to the contrary in the Charter. The latter is the case with respect to decisions of the Tribunal concerning criminal organizations; in such cases the criminal nature of the group

---

[83] Professor Sheldon Glueck, 'The Nuernberg Trial and Aggressive War', *Harvard Law Review*, 59 (1946), no. 3, p. 396.
[84] See below, p. 157.

or organization is, under Article 10 of the Charter, considered proved and shall not be questioned in national, military, or occupation courts of any Signatory (Great Britain, France, the United States of America, and the U.S.S.R.). Apart from this particular aspect, the decision of the International Military Tribunal *ius facit inter partes* only. This is not to say that the decision of the Tribunal is not bound to influence any court throughout the world, which will be faced with similar facts. He would be a bold judge of any national, occupation, or military court who would decline to be guided by the reasoned judgment of a court composed of four eminent members of the legal profession of the four Great Powers, arrived at after a trial, unique in history, backed by the authority not only of the four Signatories, but also of nineteen 'adherent' states, always provided that the facts—and the law to be applied—are the same.

VII. Crimes Against Humanity in the Draft Peace Treaties of 1946. Endorsement by the United Nations

The Draft Peace Treaties, prepared by the Council of Foreign Ministers for consideration by the Peace Conference of Twenty-one Nations, which began in Paris on 29 July 1946, contain provisions regarding war criminals in the wider sense, including not only persons accused of war crimes and crimes against peace or humanity, but also traitors and collaborators. The Draft Peace Treaty with Italy[85] provides that Italy shall take the necessary steps to ensure the apprehension and surrender for trial of:

(a) Persons accused of having committed, ordered, or abetted war crimes and crimes against peace or humanity;
(b) Nationals of the Allied and Associated Powers accused of having violated their national law by treason or collaboration with the enemy during the war.

At the request of the United Nations Government concerned, Italy will likewise make available as witnesses persons within its jurisdiction whose evidence is required for the persons referred to under (*a*) and (*b*).

Similar provisions are also contained in the Draft Peace Treaties with Romania,[86] Hungary,[87] Bulgaria,[88] and Finland.[89] None of these Draft Peace Treaties contains a definition of the term 'crime against humanity' or, for that matter, of 'crime against peace' or 'war crime'. It is highly probable that the three

---

[85] Italy, No. 1 (1946), Cmd. 6892, Part III: War Criminals, Art. 38.
[86] Romania, No. 1 (1946), Cmd. 6896, Art. 6.
[87] Hungary, No. 1 (1946), Cmd. 6894, Art. 5.
[88] Bulgaria, No. 1 (1946), Cmd. 6895, Art. 5.
[89] Finland, No. 1 (1946), Cmd. 6897, Art. 9.

expressions used in the Draft Peace Treaties have, in these Treaties, the same connotation as in the Four-Power Agreement of 8 August 1945.

The United Kingdom, the United States of America, the U.S.S.R., and France
were Signatories of the Four-Power Agreement. The same four Powers were the
members of the Council of Foreign Ministers which prepared the five Draft Peace
Treaties. In interpreting the terms of Article 38 of the Italian Treaty (and the corresponding provisions of the four other Treaties) recourse may, therefore, be had
to the explanation of the terms 'crimes against peace', 'war crimes', and 'crimes
against humanity' contained in the London Charter.

The five Draft Treaties are a further step in making the notion of 'crime
against humanity' (and 'crime against peace') part of the common law of nations.
Originally, the law regarding these two types of crimes had been stated by the
four Great Powers only. Eventually, the provisions of the London Agreement were
endorsed by nineteen Allied states which adhered to it under its Article 5. On 13
February 1946 the General Assembly of the United Nations passed a Resolution
regarding the surrender of war criminals,[90] in the Preamble of which it took
note of the definition of war crimes, crimes against peace, and crimes against
humanity contained in the Charter of the International Military Tribunal dated
8 August 1945. In December 1946, at a time when three states which had been
neutral during the Second World War had joined the ranks of the United Nations
(Sweden, Iceland, and Afghanistan), the General Assembly again took note 'of
the Agreement for the establishment of an International Military Tribunal for
the prosecution and punishment of the major war criminals of the European
Axis signed in London on 8 August 1945, and of the Charter annexed thereto,
and of the fact that similar principles have been adopted in the Charter of the
International Military Tribunal for the trial of the major war criminals in the Far
East, proclaimed at Tokyo on 19 January 1946', and affirmed 'the principles of
international law recognized by the Charter of the Nuremberg Tribunal and the
Judgment of the Tribunal'.[91]

Once the five Peace Treaties are signed and ratified and come into force, the
notion of crimes against peace and crimes against humanity will also have been
accepted by five former Axis and satellite countries.[92]

Further developments of the law, particularly concerning the concept of 'genocide' which, to a certain extent, covers the same ground as the notion of crimes
against humanity,[93] are outside the scope of this article.

---

[90] Resolutions adopted by the General Assembly during the first part of its first session from 10
January to 14 February 1946 (Doc. A/64), p. 9.

[91] Resolution (9) passed in the 55th plenary meeting, 11 December 1946. *General Assembly
Journal*, no. 75: Supplement A–64, Add. 1, p. 945.

[92] After this article had gone to press the final text of the Peace Treaties was published as Cmd.
7022 and the Treaties were subsequently signed on 10 February 1947. The provisions quoted in the
text have undergone verbal amendments only. Art. 45 of the Italian Treaty corresponds to Art. 38
of the Draft.

[93] Resolution (10), ibid.

VIII. Crimes Against Humanity in Other Documents

It is useful to compare the law as laid down by the London Charter of 8 August 1945, and applied by the Nuremberg Judgment, with the law on which decisions of other courts, international, national, and occupation, will have to be based in similar circumstances, and an attempt will be made here to examine to what extent the conclusions reached by the Nuremberg Tribunal apply also under the provisions under which other courts than the Nuremberg Tribunal are called upon to interpret and to apply the concept of crimes against humanity.

1. Crimes Against Humanity in the Charter of the International Military Tribunal for the Far East

The International Military Tribunal for the Far East was established by Special Proclamation of the Supreme Commander for the Allied Powers (General Douglas McArthur) on 19 January 1946.[94] This Special Proclamation, to which the Charter of the International Military Tribunal for the Far East is annexed, is, as a matter of form, not based on an international agreement like the Charter of 8 August 1945, but emanates from the Allied Commander-in-Chief, who recalls in the Preamble that he has been designated by the Allied Powers as Supreme Commander to carry into effect the general surrender of the Japanese armed forces. The Preamble also recalls that by the Instrument of Surrender of Japan, executed on 2 September 1945, the terms set forth in the Declaration of Potsdam[95] were accepted by Japan, and that at the Moscow Conference held on 26 December 1945 the Governments of the United States, Great Britain, and Russia, with the concurrence of China, agreed that the Supreme Commander should issue all orders for the implementation of the terms of surrender. The legal basis of the International Military Tribunal for the Far East differs therefore from that of the Nuremberg Tribunal in that it is primarily a United States Military Tribunal, which, however, also includes among its members persons appointed by the Supreme Commander from the names submitted by the signatories of the Japanese terms of surrender (United States of America, China, United Kingdom, U.S.S.R., Australia, Canada, France, the Netherlands, New Zealand), and by India and the Philippines.

The provisions corresponding to Article 6 of the Charter of the (European) Tribunal are contained in Article 5 of the Charter of the International Military

---

[94] The Charter of the International Military Tribunal for the Far East, issued by General McArthur on 19 January 1946 (General Orders No. 1), as amended by General Orders of the same Supreme Commander, No. 20, dated 26 April 1946.

[95] See *supra*, p. 127, n. 126.

Tribunal for the Far East, which reads as follows:

ARTICLE 5. Jurisdiction over Persons and Offences. The Tribunal shall have the power to try and punish Far Eastern War Criminals who as individuals or as members of organisations are charged with offences which include crimes against peace. The following acts, or any of them, are crimes coming within the jurisdiction of the Tribunal for which there shall be individual responsibility:

a. Crimes against Peace: namely, the planning, preparation, initiation or waging of a declared or undeclared war of aggression, or a war in violation of international law, treaties, agreements or assurances, or participation in a common plan or conspiracy for the accomplishment of any of the foregoing;

b. Conventional War Crimes: namely, violations of the laws or customs of war;

c. Crimes against Humanity: namely, murder, extermination, enslavement, deportation, and other inhumane acts committed before or during the war, or persecutions on political or racial grounds in execution of or in connection with any crime within the jurisdiction of the Tribunal, whether or not in violation of the domestic law of the country where perpetrated. Leaders, organizers, instigators and accomplices participating in the formulation or execution of a common plan or conspiracy to commit any of the foregoing crimes are responsible for all acts performed by any person in execution of such plan.[96]

If we compare the position according to the Far Eastern Charter with that under the Charter of the Nuremberg Tribunal, the following differences become apparent:

(a) The difference in the status of the Court. In one case there is the Four-Power Agreement, adhered to by nineteen other states in Europe; in the other the proclamations by the United States Commander-in-Chief in Japan. In one case the judges were appointed by the four Signatories; in the other by the Supreme Commander in Japan.

(b) No government of Germany existed either at the time of the London Agreement of 8 August 1945 or at the time of the Nuremberg Trial (November 1945–October 1946); there have been a Japanese Government and a Japanese state throughout.

(c) In theory, the inroad into the principle of sovereignty effected by subjecting to outside jurisdiction relations between the authorities of one state and its subjects is therefore much more pronounced in the Far Eastern case because, as has been submitted earlier in this article, the main obstacle to subjecting the internal affairs of the German state to international jurisdiction had been removed by the at least temporary abolition of a German Government. This difference is, however, only a theoretical one because the Indictment presented to the International Military Tribunal for the Far East on 29 April 1946 does not charge the major Japanese war criminals with crimes against humanity committed against

---

[96] See *supra*, p. 155, n. 94.

Japanese subjects on Japanese territory, but is restricted to offences against foreign states and citizens. In the Japanese trial it is still more true to say that the term 'crimes against humanity' is merely another description of war crimes. Where the persons arraigned as the major Japanese war criminals have been charged with crimes against humanity, the alleged crimes were always committed against persons other than Japanese nationals.

(*d*) The Far Eastern Charter, having been drafted and promulgated after the Berlin Protocol, which removed the discrepancy existing between the English and French and the Russian texts of the London Agreement of 8 August 1945, contains a text which is based on the London Charter as amended in Berlin and has therefore the comma in place of the original semicolon.

(*e*) The provision that the accused person must have been 'acting in the interests of the European Axis countries' is, of course, not included in the Far Eastern Charter. The latter speaks of 'Far Eastern war criminals'.

(*f*) The definition of crimes against peace differs in so far as the Far Eastern Charter speaks of the 'waging of declared or undeclared war of aggression', and adds international law, obviously international customary law, to international treaties, agreements, or assurances.

(*g*) War Crimes in the narrower sense are in the Far Eastern Charter called 'conventional war crimes', namely, violations of the laws and customs of war. The illustrations contained in Article 6 (*b*) of the European Charter are omitted.

(*h*) The definition in the Far Eastern Charter of crimes against humanity differs only in that religious grounds of persecution are omitted. Persecutions on political and racial grounds are crimes against humanity both under the London Charter and under its Far Eastern counterpart. Persecutions on religious grounds are punishable only under the European Charter. The latter is probably due to the fact that the draftsmen assumed that persecutions on religious grounds had actually not been committed on a larger scale in connexion with Japanese aggression and warfare.

2. Crimes Against Humanity in the Control Council Law No. 10

On 20 December 1945 the Control Council for Germany enacted a law regarding the punishment of persons guilty of war crimes, crimes against peace and against humanity which is generally known as 'Control Council Law No. 10'.[97] This law was passed 'in order to give effect to the terms of the Moscow Declaration of 30 October 1943 and the London Agreement of 8 August 1945 and the

---

[97] *Official Gazette of the Control Council for Germany*, no. 3, p. 22; *Military Government Gazette, Germany, British Zone of Control*, no. 5, p. 46; *Journal Officiel du Commandement en Chef Français en Allemagne*, no. 12 of 11 January 1946.

Charter issued pursuant thereto, and in order to establish a uniform legal basis in Germany for the prosecution of war criminals and other similar offenders, other than those dealt with by the International Military Tribunal'.

Article I of Law No. 10 provides, *inter alia*, that the London Agreement is made an integral part of the law. Article II provides that each of the following acts is recognized as a crime and enumerates under (*a*) crimes against peace, under (*b*) war crimes, under (*c*) crimes against humanity, and under (*d*) membership in a category of criminal groups or organizations declared criminal by the International Military Tribunal. The provision concerning crimes against humanity reads as follows:

'(*c*) Crimes against Humanity: Atrocities and offences, including but not limited to murder, extermination, enslavement, deportation, imprisonment, torture, rape, or other inhumane acts committed against any civilian population, or persecutions on political, racial or religious grounds, whether or not in violation of the domestic laws of the country where perpetrated.'

If we compare the definition of crimes against humanity under Law No. 10 with the definition of crimes against humanity in the Charter of the International Military Tribunal, we find the following differences:

(1) The definition of Law No. 10 begins with the words 'Atrocities and offences, including but not limited to...'. These words are not contained in the Charter. This means that the enumeration in the Charter is exhaustive, in Law No. 10 exemplative. This difference, however, is not important, because the words used in the Charter, 'or other inhumane acts', are so wide that the enumeration is, in practice, also merely exemplative.

(2) Law No. 10 enumerates the following acts which are not contained in the Charter, namely, 'imprisonment, torture and rape'.

(3) The word 'and' before 'other inhumane acts' is replaced in Law No. 10 by the word 'or'. This again indicates that it was the intention of the makers of Law No. 10 to give it a wider scope, although the practical effect of this alteration should not be too great.

(4) The words 'before or during the war' are omitted in Law No. 10. It is submitted that this alteration has no practical importance because from other provisions of Law No. 10 it is quite clear that Law No. 10, too, applies to crimes committed both before and during the war. One of the provisions bearing this out is Article II (5) of Law No. 10 regarding the Statutes of Limitation. It provides: 'In any trial or prosecution for a crime herein referred to, the accused shall not be entitled to the benefits of any statute of limitation in respect of the period from 30 January 1933 to 1 July 1945, nor shall any immunity, pardon or amnesty granted under the Nazi régime be admitted as a bar to trial or punishment.'

The implication of this provision is, of course, that crimes committed before 30 January 1933 can be made the subject of criminal prosecution. In other words, even crimes committed during Hitler's 'struggle for power', i.e. before 1933, can be investigated and prosecuted. The words 'before or during the war' may have been omitted because the legislators intended the provisions to cover not only acts committed before and during the war, but also acts committed after the war.

(5) Law No. 10 does not contain the words 'in execution of or in connection with any crime within the jurisdiction of the Tribunal'. This, of course, is the most fundamental and most striking difference between the Charter and Law No. 10, particularly in view of the great importance attributed by the Nuremberg Prosecution and by the International Military Tribunal to these very words. From this difference between the text of the Charter and the text of Law No. 10 it follows that this qualification of the term 'crime against humanity', as understood by the International Military Tribunal, is entirely inapplicable in proceedings under Law No. 10. Contrary to what was said by the International Military Tribunal with regard to the law to be applied by it, it is not necessary for an act to come under the notion of crime against humanity within the meaning of Law No. 10 to prove that it was committed in execution of, or in connexion with, a crime against peace or a war crime.

Owing to this difference between the Charter on the one hand and Law No. 10 on the other, the whole jurisprudence evolved in the Nuremberg proceedings with a view to restricting crimes against humanity to those closely connected with the war becomes irrelevant for the courts which are dealing or will be dealing with crimes against humanity under Law No. 10. At first sight it seems rather startling that the law applied to the major war criminals who were tried under the Charter should be less comprehensive and therefore less severe than the law applied to not-so-high-ranking perpetrators. In reply to this objection it may be said: (*a*) that the objection is a theoretical and doctrinal one only, because the major war criminals were certain to be caught in the net of the law in spite of the qualification contained in Article 6 (*c*) of the Charter; (*b*) that the striking difference in the texts of the Charter on the one hand, and of Law No. 10 on the other, does not permit of any other interpretation; (*c*) that the difference between the Charter and Law No. 10 probably reflects the difference both in the constitutional nature of the two documents and in the standing of the tribunals called upon to administer the law. As we have attempted to show, the International Military Tribunal is, in addition to being an occupation court for Germany, also—to a certain extent—an international judicial organ administering international law, and therefore its jurisdiction in domestic matters of Germany is cautiously circumscribed. The Allied and German courts, applying Law No. 10, are local courts, administering primarily local (municipal) law, which, of course, includes provisions emanating from the occupation authorities.

There remains one difficulty in the interpretation of Law No. 10. Article I makes the London Charter an integral part of that Law. Article II contains, as

shown, provisions respecting, *inter alia*, crimes against humanity which differ
from the London Charter. Which provision is to prevail? It is submitted that
Article II is the operative provision, the quoted part of Article I only incorporat-
ing the provisions regarding major war criminals in the local law of Germany.
The question of the guilt or innocence of persons other than the major war criminals is, then, governed by Article II.

   In the British Zone of Control in Germany, a special Ordinance concerning
crimes against humanity has been made in accordance with Control Council
Law No. 10,[98] which authorizes German ordinary courts to exercise jurisdiction in all cases of crimes against humanity committed by persons of German
nationality against persons of German nationality or stateless persons. This
Ordinance contains a provision pertaining to the relationship between the
concept of crimes against humanity and offences under ordinary German law.
Article II of the Ordinance provides that if in a given case the facts alleged,
in addition to constituting a crime against humanity, also constitute offences
under ordinary German law, the charge against the accused may be framed in
the alternative and that the above-quoted provision of Law No. 10 regarding
the statutes of limitation and the irrelevance of Hitler's amnesties apply *mutatis
mutandis* to the offences under ordinary German law. In the United States Zone
of Occupation, the Control Council Law No. 10 has been carried out by the
Military Government Ordinance No. 7, which became effective on 18 October
1946.[99] In the French Zone of Occupation, Ordinances of 25 November
1945 and 8 March 1946 have been promulgated by the French Commander-
in-Chief.[100] In the Instructions issued by the French Supreme Command in
Germany, General Directorate of Justice, for the investigation, prosecution,
and trial of war crimes, the term 'crime against humanity' is defined as follows:
'Crimes against humanity are crimes committed against any civilian population
of whatever nationality including persecutions on political, racial or religious
grounds.' It is added in the Instructions that where such crimes have been committed against nationals of Axis countries the prosecution and punishment of the
offenders may involve considerations affecting the general policy of the Allies;
investigations in regard to such matters should therefore only be undertaken in
pursuance of instructions from higher quarters.[101]

---

[98] Ordinance No. 47, published in *Military Government Gazette, Germany, British Zone of
Control*, no. 13. p. 306.
   [99] Military Government, Germany, Ordinance No. 7.
   [100] *Journal Officiel du Commandement en Chef français en Allemagne. Ordonnance No. 20
du Commandant en Chef, relative à la répression des crimes de guerre* of 25 November 1945, and
*Ordonnance No. 36 relative à la répression des crimes de guerre, contre la paix et l'humanité et de
l'affiliation à des associations criminelles* of 25 February 1946.
   [101] Commandement en Chef Français en Allemagne. Direction Générale de la Justice. Crimes
de Guerre. Instructions sur la recherche, la poursuite et le jugement des crimes de guerre. 28
August 1946.

3. Crimes Against Humanity in Trials Before American Military Commissions in the Far East

The United States military authorities have issued different sets of Regulations for the United States Military Commissions in the Far Eastern and China Theatres of War, which also contain provisions regarding crimes against humanity, and which, in general, are based on the definition contained in the London Charter of 8 August 1945.[102] Under the Regulations which were issued by General Headquarters of the United States Armed Forces, Pacific, on 24 September 1945, the Military Commissions have jurisdiction to try all three types of crimes defined in Article 6 of the London Charter, namely, war crimes, crimes against peace, and crimes against humanity. Crimes against humanity are, though this term is not actually used, defined as follows: 'Murder, extermination, enslavement, deportation or other inhumane acts committed against any civilian population, or persecution on political, racial, national or religious grounds, in execution of or connection with any offence within the jurisdiction of the Commission, whether or not in violation of the domestic law of the country where perpetrated.'

It will be seen that while the Regulations are, in general, based on Article 6 (*c*) of the London Charter, the following differences occur:

(a) While the London Charter speaks of persecutions on political, racial, or religious grounds, the Pacific Regulations add the concept of 'national grounds'. This is the more remarkable because, as was already stated, the Charter of the International Military Tribunal for the Far East speaks only of political or racial grounds, omitting one of the grounds contained in the European Charter, namely, religious grounds.

(b) The words 'before or during the war' are omitted in the Pacific Regulations of 24 September 1945.

Both these differences between the Pacific Regulations and the London Charter were removed when the Regulations of 24 September 1945 were replaced by similar Regulations of 5 December 1945, in which the definition of crimes against humanity is as follows: 'Murder, extermination, enslavement, deportation and other inhumane acts, committed against any civilian population before or during the war, or persecutions on political racial or religious grounds, in execution of, or in connection with, any crime defined herein, whether or not in violation of the domestic laws of the country where perpetrated.' The 'national' grounds have been omitted, and the expression 'before or during the war' has been added. The latter phrase has been extended by a further provision, which reads as follows: 'The offences need not have been committed after a particular date to render the responsible party or parties subject to arrest, but in general should have been

---

[102] See *Law Reports of Trials of War Criminals*, selected and prepared by the United Nations War Crimes Commission, English ed., vol. i, Annex II, p. 111.

committed since or in the period immediately preceding the Mukden incident of September 18, 1931.'

Provisions on the same lines as those contained in the Regulations for the Pacific Theatre, dated 24 September 1945, were made for the China Theatre on 21 January 1946. Under the Regulations issued for United States Military Commissions in Europe, their jurisdiction is restricted to war crimes in the narrower sense and does not include crimes against humanity.

4. Regulations for British Military Courts

The instrument under which the trials of persons charged with war crimes by British Military Courts are conducted is the Royal Warrant of 14 June 1945.[103] This instrument restricts the jurisdiction of the Military Courts to the trial of 'war crimes', and 'war crime' is defined as 'violation of the laws and usages of war committed during any war in which His Majesty has been or may be engaged at any time since the 2nd September 1939'. Acts committed before the war, and acts which are not violations of the rules of warfare, are, therefore, outside the jurisdiction of British War Crimes Courts. They cannot, therefore, try crimes against humanity, unless they are simultaneously violations of the laws and customs of war and have been committed after 2 September 1939. The Canadian Order in Council, the 'War Crimes Regulations (Canada)',[104] which came into force on 30 August 1945, and which has been re-enacted in statutory form with effect from 30 August 1945 by the War Crimes Act of 1946,[105] contains a definition based on the same principle:[106] ' "War crime" means a violation of the laws or usages of war committed during any war in which Canada has been or may be engaged at any time after the ninth day of September, 1939.' The Commonwealth of Australia War Crimes Act, 1945,[107] defines 'war crime' as meaning: (*a*) a violation of the laws and usages of war; (*b*) any war crime within the meaning of a previous instrument of appointment of a Board of Inquiry, committed in any place whatsoever, whether within or beyond Australia, during any war. The Instrument of Appointment referred to in the Act[108] explains the term 'war crime' by adopting the list of thirty-two items drawn up in 1919, by the Commission of Fifteen, with a few modifications and additions, the most important among the latter being the crime against peace as defined in Article 6 (*a*) of the London Charter.

---

[103] Army Order 81/1945; amended by Royal Warrants A.O. 127/1945, 8/1946, and 24/1946. Cf. *Law Reports of Trials of War Criminals*, selected and prepared by the United Nations War Crimes Commission, English ed., vol. i, Annex I, p. 105.

[104] P.C. 5831 of 30 August 1945, made by the Governor-General in Council under the authority of the War Measures Act of Canada.

[105] An Act, respecting War Crimes: 10 George VI, c. 73, assented to 31 August 1946.

[106] Regulation 2 (*f*).

[107] No. 48 of 1945, assented to 11 October 1945.

[108] Instrument of Appointment of the Board of Inquiry of 3 September 1945, under the National Security (Inquiries) Regulations, Statutory Rules 1941, No. 35, as amended.

There is, however, no item in the enlarged list corresponding to Article 6 (*c*) of the London Charter.

5. Crimes Against Humanity in Municipal Legislation

The legislative instruments so far discussed afford the basis for proceedings against alleged perpetrators of crimes against humanity, in military and occupation courts and in courts, such as the German courts, which derive their jurisdiction in this respect from Allied legislation. Where the ordinary municipal courts of a territory, be it Allied or former enemy, are trying similar offences, they do so, as a rule, under pre-existing positive penal law; it is therefore neither necessary nor has it happened frequently that the concept of crimes against humanity has expressly been made part of codified municipal criminal law. The French Ordinance of 28 August 1944,[109] which was passed at Algiers and forms the basis of the prosecution of war criminals by French courts, is a good illustration of the general attitude of the laws of continental countries to the problem of war crimes in the wider sense. The French Ordinance provides, *inter alia*, that enemy nationals or agents of other than French nationality who are, or have been, serving enemy administration or interests, and who are guilty of crimes or offences committed since the beginning of hostilities either in France or in territories under the authority of France, or against a French national, or a person under French protection, or a person serving or having served in the French armed forces, or a stateless person resident in French territory before 17 June 1940, or a refugee residing in French territory, or against the property of any natural person enumerated above, or against any French corporate bodies, shall be prosecuted by French Military Tribunals and shall be judged in accordance with the French laws in force and according to the provisions set out in the Ordinance, *where such offences*, even if committed at the time or under the pretext of an existing state of war, *are not justified by the laws and customs of war*. This French provision subjects perpetrators of war crimes (in the wider sense) to the provisions of internal penal law and exempts from their operation acts of legitimate warfare. Similarly, the Netherlands Royal Decree establishing a Commission for the Investigation of War Crimes[110] defines war crimes as 'facts which constitute crimes considered as such according to Dutch law and *which are forbidden by the laws and usages of war*'.

What, in the London Charter, are called war crimes and crimes against humanity are treated as violations of the pre-1938 provisions of municipal penal law in the Retribution Decree of Czechoslovakia.[111] This contains, *inter alia*, provisions relating to membership in criminal organizations (Sections 2

---

[109] *Codes français et lois usuelles*, (53rd ed., 1946), p. 1195. Cf. Professor Michel de Juglart, *Répertoire méthodique de la jurisprudence militaire* (1946), pp. 232 ff.

[110] Decree of 29 May 1946, no. F 85, Art. I.

[111] Decree of 19 June 1945, Collection of Laws and Decrees, no. 16.

and 3 (2)), deportations for forced labour (Section 6), unjustified imprisonment (Section 7), and also refers to 'national, political or racial persecution' (Section 10). The following are examples of enactments in the passing of which the legislature has either referred, in a general way, to such conceptions as 'laws of humanity' or 'obligations of humanity' or has positively embodied the notion of 'crimes against humanity' in the respective system of internal penal law.

(*a*) In Belgium the Decree (*Arrêté*) of 13 December 1944, regarding the establishment of a Commission charged with the investigation of violations of international law and of the laws and customs of war,[112] in its Preamble recalls that 'numerous violations of the rules of International Law and of the obligations of humanity (*des devoirs d'humanité*) have been committed by the invaders'. The Commission is described as a commission of inquiry into the violations of the laws and customs of war and the obligations of humanity (Art. 1).

(*b*) Similarly, in Luxemburg the Grand Ducal Decree of 3 July 1945, establishing a National Office for the Investigation of War Crimes,[113] in its Preamble refers 'to the numerous violations of international law and of the obligations of humanity (*des devoirs de l'humanité*) which have been committed by the invader', and the National Office is charged, in particular, to collect evidence concerning violations of the rules of international law, of the laws and customs of war, of the obligations of humanity, and of all crimes and offences committed by the invader.

In both the Belgian and Luxemburg statutes the term 'obligations of humanity' (*des devoirs de l'humanité*) is hardly used in the technical sense in which the expression 'crimes against humanity' has been adopted in the (subsequent) London Charter to which both Belgium and Luxemburg eventually adhered.

(*c*) Vespasien V. Pella draws attention to the Romanian Decree-Law of April 1945, regarding the prosecution of war criminals and those responsible for the national disaster.[114] According to Pella, this law seems to anticipate the Charter annexed to the Four-Power Agreement of 8 August 1945. It subjects to punishment, in addition to violators of the rules of warfare, *inter alia*, persons 'who have ordered or have committed acts of suppression either collective or individual, in accordance with a political or racial plan', or 'the removal and transportation of persons in order to exterminate them', or 'have imposed inhumane treatment upon those who were in their power', all of which are facts either covered by, or very akin to, crimes against humanity as defined in Article 6 (*c*) of the London Charter.

(*d*) The Austrian Constitutional Law of 26 July 1945, concerning war crimes and other National-Socialist misdeeds,[115] also enacted before the London

---

[112] Arrêté du 13 décembre 1944. Commission d'enquête sur les violations des règles du droit des gens, des lois et des coutumes de la guerre.
[113] *Mémorial du Grand-Duché de Luxembourg*, no. 33, of 7 July 1945. p. 373.
[114] Vespasien V. Pella, *La Guerre-crime et les criminels de guerre* (1946), p. 71.
[115] Staatsgesetzblatt No. 32, amended 18 October 1945, Staatsgesetzblatt No. 199.

Four-Power Agreement, distinctly juxtaposes war crimes and crimes against humanity in providing[116] that:

'Any person who, in the course of the war launched by the National Socialists, has intentionally committed or instigated an act repugnant to the natural principles of humanity or to the generally accepted rules of International Law or to the laws of war, against the members of the armed forces of an enemy or the civilian population of a state or country at war with the German Reich or occupied by German forces shall be punished as a war criminal.

'Any person who, in the course of this war, acting in the real or assumed interest of the German armed forces or of the National Socialist tyranny, has committed or instigated an act repugnant to the natural principles of humanity against any persons, whether in connection with warlike or military actions or the actions of militarily organised groups, shall be considered guilty of the same crime.'

(*e*) The Danish Act concerning the punishment of war crimes,[117] after stating that a foreigner who has infringed the rules or customs of international law regulating occupation and war and has performed, in Denmark or to the detriment of Danish interests, any deed punishable *per se* in Danish law, can be prosecuted in a Danish court, goes on to provide as follows:

'In addition to the instances cited in paragraph I, persons having committed the following crimes shall be liable to prosecution under this Act: war crimes or crimes against humanity such as murder, ill-treatment of civilians, prisoners or seamen, the killing of hostages, looting of public or private property, requisitioning of money or other valuables, violation of the Constitution, imposition of collective punishments, destruction by explosives or otherwise, in so far as such actions were performed in violation of the rules of International Law governing Occupation and War. This Act shall further apply to deportation or other political, racial or religious persecution contrary to the principles of Danish law, and further to all actions which, though not specifically cited above, are covered by Article 6 of the Charter of the International Military Tribunal.'

Here Article 6 of the London Charter, including its provision concerning crimes against humanity, is expressly embodied in Danish domestic law.

IX. Conclusions

'An undisputed gain coming out of Nürnberg is the formal recognition that there are crimes against humanity' said President Truman in his letter to the American member of the International Military Tribunal.[118]

---

[116] Section I (1) and (2).
[117] Of 12 July 1946, ch. i (1) and (2).
[118] 12 November 1946, *U.S. Department of State Bulletin* (24 November 1946), p. 954.

While not dissenting from this view in principle, the international lawyer cannot but bear in mind the many restrictions, laid down in the Charter and the Berlin Protocol and adopted at Nuremberg, which qualify its scope and application. The idea of external judicial interference within the area of exclusive domestic jurisdiction has certainly made some progress, if we compare the position after World War II with that on the conclusion of its 1914–19 predecessor. Whereas, a quarter of a century ago, the subjection to outside jurisdiction of the internal matters of a state, even though the state was a vanquished state and the matters concerned war-time occurrences, had not proceeded beyond inclusion in a Treaty of Peace which was not ratified and has never come into force, in 1945/6 matters of domestic jurisdiction, provided only they were connected with the war, have been made the subject of criminal proceedings in a court which, in addition to being a local court, also functioned as an organ of the international community. A connexion with the war, moreover, has been presumed in respect of actions committed during the war. And where inhumane and criminal conduct had occurred in territories occupied before the outbreak of war in the traditional and technical sense of the word (i.e. before 1 September 1939), it was subjected to international jurisdiction because of its connexion with the aggression.

The notion of crimes against humanity, freed, moreover, from the fetters of the Charter and Berlin Protocol, has entered the sphere of many municipal legal orders. This, too, is certainly a gain, though it must be said that the jurisdiction over crimes against humanity of occupation and municipal courts in Germany and elsewhere has little bearing on the great principle which it is the desire of many to see embodied in the law of crimes against humanity, namely, the principle that the protection of a minimum standard of human rights should be guaranteed anywhere, at any time, and against anybody. The international aspect of such protection disappears in trials before courts which are unambiguously local courts. Interference in internal German affairs, e.g. under the Control Council Law No. 10, is not founded on the intention of protecting human rights from outside, but it is a hardly avoidable corollary to the disappearance of German sovereignty and to the temporary abolition of judicial and humanitarian standards in that country. The International Military Tribunal was established for the trial and punishment of the major war criminals of the European Axis. It was, therefore, an *ad hoc* Tribunal. Article 5 of the Charter provided for the setting up of other tribunals, the establishment, functions, and procedure of which should have been identical and governed by the Charter. Only German accused, however, were tried under the Agreement and no second International Military Tribunal has been set up under it. 'The conclusions of Nuremberg may be ephemeral or may be significant.'[119] The task of making the protection of human rights general, permanent, and effective still lies ahead.

---

[119] Justice Francis Biddle, *U.S. Department of State Bulletin* (24 November 1946), p. 956.

6

The Judgment of Nuremberg

By Georg Schwarzenberger[†]

'We must never forget that the record on which we judge these defendants to-day is the record on which history will judge us to-morrow.' [*]

The International Military Tribunal for the Trial of German Major War Criminals has been described as a tribunal of a totally unprecedented character. It has been held that there is no precedent for this Tribunal,[1] and that there is *no need* for any precedent.[2] The first proposition seems hardly tenable, while the second is based on rather questionable assumptions.

The trial of real and alleged war criminals by victorious opponents can be traced back to the dawn of modern international law. In the year 1268 the sovereign prince Conraddin was executed, after mock proceedings by Charles of Anjou, for having illegally waged war as a rebel. The abuse of judicial proceedings by Charles of Anjou, and the execution of Conraddin, may even be said to have given rise to the first monograph on international law. To its author Succaria, a civilian, goes the credit for having critically examined the more than dubious basis of the trial.[3]

[†] Ph. D., Dr. Jur.; Reader in International Law in the University of London; Sub-Dean, Faculty of Laws, University College, London.

The writer wishes to acknowledge his indebtedness to Dr. E. Schwelb, Legal Officer of the United Nations War Crimes Commission, for his unfailing courtesy in dealing with numerous requests for information, and for valuable criticism. The responsibility, however, for any views expressed in this article rests exclusively with the writer.

[*] Mr. Justice Jackson in his Opening Speech at Nuremberg.

[1] Opening statement by the President of the Nuremberg Tribunal (November 20, 1945), Proceedings of the International Military Tribunal at Nuremberg (London 1946) Part 1, p. 1; and the Speaker of the House of Commons (November 22, 1945), Hansard, Parliamentary Debates, House of Commons, Vol. 416, col. 598.

[2] Sir Hartley Shawcross, Speech at the Close of the Case against the Individual Defendants (London 1946) 57; Lord Wright in a Broadcast, The Meaning of Nuremberg (November 22, 1946).

[3] 2 de Burigny, Histoire de Sicile (The Hague 1745) 173, 174.

The first trial of war crimes in the technical sense of the term, that is to say, of violations of the laws or customs of war,[4] appears to be the trial in 1305 of Sir William Wallace by an English court. The charge against Wallace of having waged war against his liege lord was as little justified as that laid against Conraddin by Charles of Anjou. Wallace never had taken an oath to Edward I.[5] Whatever ground there was for Wallace's trial and condemnation rests on the charge of his conduct of the war. Even judged by the rather low standards which, in fourteenth century warfare, were observed towards non-combatants, Wallace appears to have gone far beyond ordinary license and to have engaged in a war of extermination against the English population, 'sparing neither age nor sex, monk nor nun.'[6]

On an international scale, the trial of Sir Peter of Hagenbach, henchman of the Duke of Burgundy, at Breisach in 1474 by a tribunal which was composed of judges delegated by the Allies in the war against Burgundy, may claim to be a forerunner of the proceedings at Nuremberg.[7] There is, therefore, no need to do more than refer, in passing, to the trial during the English Civil War of Le Strange before the Commissioners for Martial Law in 1644,[8] or to the trials of Boer War criminals which were reserved by the Peace Treaty of Vereeniging of May 31st, 1902.[9] Thus, the trial at Nuremberg is far from being the first of its kind.

Could it not, however, be argued that there is no need for any precedent in order to justify the Nuremberg proceedings,[10] just as there was no need to justify

---

[4] Article 6 (b), Charter of the International Military Tribunal, annexed to the Agreement of August 8, 1945, between France, the United Kingdom of Great Britain and Northern Ireland, the United States of America, and the U. S. S. R.; Cmd. 6668. See further Schwarzenberger, International Law and Totalitarian Lawlessness (London 1943) 57 *et seq.*; and Mr. McNeil in the House of Commons (February 4, 1946), Hansard, Parliamentary Debates, House of Commons, Vol. 418, col. 1355.

[5] With regard to those who had not made their submission to Edward I, the situation was very much as described in a subsequent treaty of 1381 between England and Scotland: '*ex quo Reges Angliae et Scotiae non habent ipsis superiorem, qui possit quaestionem hujusmodi terminare, justum est et aequum quod in alium compromittant.*' 3 Rymer, Foedera (The Hague 1740) Part III, p. 122.

[6] The commission and the record of the Trial are to be found in 1 Stubbs, Chronicles of the Reigns of Edward I and Edward II (Rolls Series, London 1882) 137 *et seq.* The relevant passage reads as follows: '*nemini qui lingua Anglicana utebatur pepercit, sed omnes senes an juvenibus, sponsas cum viduis et virginibus, infantes cum lactanibus, graviore morte quam excogitare sciverat afficiebat.*' *Id.*, at p. 141. *Cf.* also 2 Hume, The History of England (London 1810) 556; D. Carrick, The Life of Wallace (London 1840); C. W. C. Oman, The Art of War in the Middle Ages (Oxford 1885) 96 *et seq.*; T. F. Tout, Edward the First (London 1893). On the conception of treason in English law during the reign of Edward I, see 2 Holdsworth, A History of English Law (London 1923) 359, 360.

[7] *Cf.* Melanchton, Chronica Carionis (Wittemberg 1588) 1037–1042; 9 de Barante, Histoire des Ducs de Bourgogne de la Maison de Valois 1364–1477 (Paris 1827–1839) 405 *et seq.*; 10 *id.* at pp. 1–21; Schwarzenberger, The Breisach War Crime Trial of 1474, in The Manchester Guardian (September 28, 1946), or 20 War Crimes News Digest (United Nations War Crimes Commission 1946) Supplement.

[8] Rushworth, Historical Collections (London 1692) 804 *et seq.*

[9] Parliamentary Papers, 1902 (LXIX–Cd. 1096).

[10] *Supra* note 2. *Cf.* also Lord Wright, War Crimes Under International Law, 62 L. Quar. Rev. 40 *et seq.* (1946).

by precedent the first trial for murder? It is not to be contested that the parties to the agreement of August 8th, 1945 are entitled by right of *debellatio* to do in Germany what they like.[11] Yet, there is a minor difficulty in likening the Second World War to the first murder. Unfortunately, the history of international relations prior to 1939 does not easily lend itself to description in terms of an international Garden of Eden in which the original sin has still to be committed. Nevertheless, it may be held that international law is a growing and dynamic body; that, in the course of this evolution, acts which have been tolerated before may come to be considered in a different light, and that at last, international society has evolved institutions which permit such acts not only to be stigmatized as crimes but also, irrespective of the transgressor, to be punished as such. In order to judge whether such significance may justly be attributed to the Judgment of Nuremberg, it appears essential to discuss the organization and jurisdiction of the International Military Tribunal before proceeding to an analysis of the law applied by the Tribunal.[12]

I. Organization

The four Powers who are parties to the agreement of August 8th, 1945, established by this Treaty what they called an International Military Tribunal. Each of the three characteristics indicated by the official title of the Tribunal requires attention.

(a) The Military Character of the Tribunal. Under international customary law, persons accused of war crimes are entitled to trial by a military court of the enemy.[13] To this extent, the Charter of the Nuremberg Tribunal is merely declaratory of international customary law. By appointing a 'Major-General Jurisprudence' as a member of the Tribunal and a Lieutenant-Colonel as his alternate, the U.S.S.R. has emphasized the traditional character of such proceedings. The preponderance, however, of civilians amongst the members of a Tribunal is not decisive for attributing a non-military character to a tribunal. The essential feature of a military court is emphasis on expedition of proceedings rather than on maximum protection of the accused. Even in countries which, in the ordinary course of the administration of criminal justice, insist on the observance of high standards of a fair trial, a certain relaxation in the requirements of due process of law in the case of proceedings before courts-martial is considered compatible

---

[11] See II., Jurisdiction, *infra*.

[12] See III., The Law Applied by the Tribunal, *infra*.

[13] *Cf. Ex parte* Quirin, 317 U. S. 1, 63 Sup. Ct. 1, 87 L. Ed. 3 (1942); Application of Yamashita, 66 Sup. Ct. 340 (U. S. 1946), noted in 40 Am. Jour. Int. Law 432 (1946); United States War Department, Basic Field Manual on Rules of Land Warfare (Washington 1940) Article 356; British Regulations for the Trial of War Criminals, Special Army Order of June 18, 1945; Schwarzenberger, *op. cit. supra* note 4, at pp. 60, 61.

with the rule of law. For this reason, however, the sentences of courts-martial are not necessarily *res judicata* with regard to ordinary courts and still less do they rank as precedents. To judge from information divulged by Mr. Justice Jackson in the course of the Nuremberg Trials, this aspect of the matter was a decisive reason why the Nuremberg Tribunal was established as a military tribunal. 'One of the reasons this [Tribunal] was constituted as a military tribunal, instead of an ordinary Court of Law, was to avoid the precedent-creating effect of what is done here on our own law and the precedent control which would exist if this were an ordinary judicial body.'[14]

(b) The International Character of the Tribunal. The Moscow Declaration of 1943 provided for the punishment by a joint decision of the Allies of Germans who might be accused of having committed war crimes without particular geographical location.[15] In such cases, the Peace Treaty of Versailles of 1919 had already envisaged joint military tribunals.[16] Like these tribunals, which were never actually put into operation,[17] the Nuremberg Tribunal may claim to be international in the formal sense of the word. It derives its existence and jurisdiction from an international treaty like any other international court or tribunal. It appears, however, to have been the intention of the parties to establish in substance joint military tribunals under municipal law rather than a truly international tribunal. This view of the intentions of the contracting parties is compatible with the fact that, in the Agreement of 1945, the Tribunal is described as an international tribunal. In a formal sense, this is in any case a correct classification and, furthermore, *falsa demonstratio non nocet.* Such a construction of the Treaty of 1945 may draw support from the fact that whether the Allies wanted it or not, by *debellatio*, they became the joint sovereigns of Germany.[18] Little importance need, therefore, be attached to the circumstance that the joint sovereigns exercised their jurisdiction as the fountain of law and justice in Germany by an international treaty; for this mode of co-ordinating their sovereign wills is not so much determined by the object of their joint deliberations as by the character of the joint sovereigns as four distinct subjects of international law. As the Tribunal stated in its Judgment, there would have been little doubt regarding the municipal character of the Tribunal if one State alone had overrun Germany and established such a tribunal, instead of four victorious Powers combining their efforts towards the same end: 'The Signatory Powers created this Tribunal, defined the law it was to administer, and made regulations for the proper conduct of the Trial. In doing so,

---

[14] Proceedings of the International Military Tribunal at Nuremberg (London 1946) Part 2, p. 307. See also Mr. Justice Jackson, Speech at the Close of the Case against the Individual Defendants (London 1946) 4.

[15] Royal Institute of International Affairs, United Nations Documents (London 1946) 15, 16.

[16] Treaty of Versailles (1919), Article 229.

[17] See Schwarzenberger, *op. cit. supra* note 4, at pp. 74, 75.

[18] See II., Jurisdiction, *infra.*

they have done together what any of them might have done singly.'[19] The passage quoted above[20] from a speech of Mr. Justice Jackson, who was one of the signatories of the Agreement of 1945, corroborates the classification of the Nuremberg Tribunal as—in substance—a joint municipal tribunal. If the Tribunal had been conceived by the Powers as an international tribunal, there was no need to guard either against precedent control or against the precedent-creating effect of the Judgment on the municipal law of the four Powers. If, however, the Tribunal was a joint tribunal under municipal law and had not been given the status of an extraordinary tribunal by being labelled a military tribunal, it could at least have been argued that the Judgment of the Tribunal had such effects. Furthermore, in accordance with Article 29 of the Tribunal's Charter, the right of pardon rests with the Control Council for Germany.[21] In substance, therefore, the Tribunal is a municipal tribunal of extraordinary jurisdiction which the four Contracting Powers share in common.

(c) The Judicial Character of the Tribunal. The procedure laid down in the Charter of the Tribunal and in the Rules of Procedure which were adopted by the Tribunal in acccordance with Article 13 of the Charter, is intended to secure 'just and prompt trial and punishment of the major war criminals of the European Axis.'[22] In view of the expected length of the trial the provision for alternate judges was only reasonable and certainly preferable to the possibilities of starting the trial all over again in the case of prolonged illness or death of one of the judges, of introducing a new member in the course of the trial, or of continuing the trial with a gradually dwindling bench. This device does not adversely affect the judicial character of the Tribunal. Equally, the provision in the Charter that neither the Tribunal nor its members can be challenged[23] is compatible with the minimum standards which, under international customary law, persons accused of war crimes in the technical sense can expect to be observed towards them. Nor have persons accused of war crimes any claim to be judged by nationals of neutral countries or to have one of their co-nationals on the bench, though much is

---

[19] Cmd. 6964, p. 38.

[20] *Supra* note 14.

[21] On December 20, 1945, the Control Council for Germany, which is composed of representatives of the Parties to the Agreement of August 8, 1945, passed Law No. 10 on Punishment of Persons Guilty of War Crimes, Crimes against Peace and against Humanity. See 5 Military Government Gazette (British ed.) 46. The Law was intended, *inter alia*, 'to give effect to...the London Agreement of 8 August, 1945, and the Charter issued pursuant thereto,' and in Article I made the Agreement of August 8, 1945, an integral part of this Law. In a formal sense, the transformation of the Agreement into German municipal law can be adduced as evidence of the international basis of the Tribunal. However, in substance it appears that the dual international and municipal basis of important acts of inter-Allied legislation in Germany is typical for the exercise of *condominium* by sovereign States.

[22] Agreement of August 8, 1945 (Cmd. 6903); Article 1, Charter of the International Military Tribunal.

[23] Article 3, Charter of the International Military Tribunal.

to be said in favour of such additional guarantees of judicial impartiality.[24] The question whether the law to be applied by the Tribunal and the exclusion of certain defences amounted to subjecting the accused to an *ex post facto* law, and for this reason impaired the judicial standing of the Tribunal, can be raised but not answered at this stage.[25] Yet a point which must be discussed in this connection is the absence in the Charter of provisions regarding the minimum qualifications of the members of the Tribunal. In retrospect, the actual choice made by the signatory Powers was amply justified by the dignified manner in which the President, and the Tribunal as a whole, conducted the trial. The governments of the four Powers appear, however, to have fallen victim to the widespread illusion that any lawyer of distinction in the legal hierarchy of his own country may be deemed to be conversant with international law. The collective slip of the Tribunal over the *Caroline* cases[26] shows that such an assumption ignores a simple truth. Like most branches of municipal law, international law has become a technical subject. In his time, Coke was right when he maintained that an English judge required more than natural reason in order to discharge adequately his function. A twentieth century tribunal, which is charged with the application of international law must apply—as much as any English court of the seventeenth century—'artifical reason and judgment of law, which law is an act which requires long study and experience, before that a man can attain to the cognizance of it.'[27]

---

[24] The Allied and Associated Powers refused to associate neutral States with the contemplated war crime trials, on the ground that almost the whole world had 'banded itself together in order to bring to nought the German plan of conquest and dominion. The tribunals they will establish will therefore represent the deliberate judgment of the greater part of the civilized world.' See Reply of the Allied and Associated Powers to Germany (June 16, 1919); Cmd., Miscellaneous, No. 4 (1919). *Cf.* also Lauterpacht, The Law of Nations and the Punishment of War Crimes, 21 British Year Book of International Law 82 (1944); III. (e), Declaration of Groups and Organizations to be of a Criminal Character, *infra*.

[25] See III., The Law Applied by the Tribunal, *infra*.

[26] See III. (d), Defences, *infra*; Proceedings of the International Military Tribunal at Nuremberg (London 1946) Part 3, p. 40.

[27] See Prohibition del Roy, 12 Co. Rep. 63, 65, 77 Eng. Rep. 1342, 1343 (1607).

A more detailed examination of the procedure applied by the Tribunal will have to wait until the whole of the transcripts of the proceedings have been published. From what can be seen so far, it appears that the Tribunal has attempted to hold a fair balance between the prosecution and the defence. However, it must be remembered that the Agreement of August 8, 1945, and the Charter annexed to it which had been drafted by one prospective chief of counsel for the prosecution and two future members of the Tribunal, weighed the scales heavily in favor of the prosecution; and that the prosecution had all the advantages which resulted from the then existing state of affairs in Germany. To judge by the attitude of the defence during the period for which full transcripts have been published, it does not appear as if the prosecution had abused this near-monopoly of material and communications.

The fact that the Tribunal made full use of the power granted in Article 19 of the Charter to ignore technical evidence, and evolved a procedure *sui generis*, consisting of a mixture of Anglo-Saxon and Continental criminal procedures, seems to have been as much in the interest of the administration of justice as of expediting proceedings. The tactics of the prosecution which, wherever possible, relied on documents issued under the responsibility of, or by, the accused, were unimpeachable and provided very much better evidence than the necessarily more unreliable memory of any witness. The dangers resulting from a too selective use of documents were clearly realized

(d) *The ad hoc Character of the Tribunal.* In accordance with the Charter, the Tribunal was established for the trial of the major war criminals of the European Axis. The enormity of the deeds which had been committed by the Nazi leaders was in itself more than sufficient justification for any retribution which was to be meted out to these international gangsters. Once, however, it was decided to let the law take its course, an issue—the dignity of the law—transcending in significance the fate of these individuals was at stake. If a permanent court had been established under the auspices of the United Nations for the purpose of applying in the future the law of the Nuremberg Charter to any transgressor, something would have been done to safeguard the principles of the generality of the law and of equality before the law.[28] As it was, the drafters of the Charter of the United Nations carefully refrained from any initiative in this direction. Thus the law of the Nuremberg Charter did not appear so much as a pointer to the future than as a law laid down by the victors for the defeated and as a law from the operation of which, on the grounds of being victorious, some of the victors had been able to exempt themselves.[29] The weight of this objection to the *ad hoc* character of the Tribunal would be diminished if it could be shown that, after all, the Tribunal, though an *ad hoc* institution, strictly limited itself to the application of the rules of existing international customary law and at least did not attempt to apply an *ad hoc* law in *ad hoc* proceedings.

The conclusions reached so far may be summarized as follows:

Firstly, the Nuremberg Tribunal is international more in form than in substance. It is more akin to a joint tribunal under municipal law than to an international tribunal in the normal sense of the word.

Secondly, the status of the Tribunal within the judicial hierarchy of municipal courts and tribunals of the States which share it is that of a military *ad hoc* tribunal.

Thirdly, the status of the Tribunal as an agency which applies international law is similar to that of other courts which are composed of eminent exponents of municipal law, and the freedom of the Tribunal to apply international customary law is limited by its overriding duty to apply the law of its Charter whether or not such law is declaratory of existing international law.[30]

---

by the Tribunal and countered right from the start. The Tribunal also encouraged prosecution and defense to come to an understanding on the documents which should form part of the record. See Proceedings of the International Military Tribunal at Nuremberg (London 1946) Part 1, p. 152; *id.*, Part 2, p. 441; *id.*, Part 4, pp. 220, 221; *id.*, Part 5, pp. 97–99.

[28] *Cf.* 13 Smith, The Nuremberg Trials, Free Europe (1946) 203. See also the Attorney-General's reply in the House of Commons on February 6, 1946. Hansard, Parliamentary Debates, House of Commons, Vol. 418, cols. 414–415.

[29] See the Nuremberg Judgment (Cmd. 6964) at p. 109, on offences by Great Britain and the United States of America which had been alleged by the defence; also III., The Law Applied by the Tribunal, *infra*.

[30] *Ibid.*

II. Jurisdiction

The international basis of the Nuremberg Tribunal is provided by the Agreement of August 8th, 1945, as modified by the Protocol of October 6th, 1945.[31] The adhesion to the Agreement of nineteen members of the United Nations before delivery of the Judgment further strengthened this source of the Tribunal's jurisdiction.[32]

There is, however, another source of the Tribunal's jurisdiction: the exercise by the occupying Powers of *condominium* over Germany. As becomes evident from the Declaration and Statements of the Four Powers issued on June 5th, 1945[33] and other subsequent acts and pronouncements,[34] the situation arising out of Germany's unconditional surrender is very different from Japan's position in international law. In the case of Japan, the State machinery has survived under the terms of the Potsdam Proclamation. All acts, therefore, of the occupying Powers in Japan which go beyond the limits of Hague Convention IV of 1907 derive their validity from the consent on the part of the defeated enemy which is inherent in a practically unconditional surrender. In the case of Germany, however, there did not remain any 'central Government or authority... capable of accepting responsibility for the maintenance of order, the administration of the country and compliance with the requirements of the victorious Powers.'[35] In view of Germany's complete breakdown owing to *debellatio*, the four Powers very logically declared that they assumed 'supreme authority' over Germany. The joint sovereignty of the four Powers over Germany is not affected by the reservation that the assumption of supreme authority did not 'effect the annexation of Germany.' This merely means that the joint sovereigns administer Germany as a separate international entity. In the words of a certificate, recently issued by the British Foreign Secretary, 'the Allied Control Commission are the agency through which the Government of Germany is carried on.'[36]

In its Judgment, the Tribunal leaned heavily on this second source of its jurisdiction: 'The jurisdiction of the Tribunal is defined in the Agreement and

---

[31] See United States Department of State Publication No. 2461, Executive Agreement Series 472, pp. 45–48.

The date of the Protocol which alters the law applied by the Tribunal is significant. It is the date on which the Indictment was signed by the four chief prosecutors. See III. (c), Crimes against Humanity, *infra*; Cmd. 6696, p. 32.

[32] See also II., Jurisdiction, and III., The Law Applied by the Tribunal, *infra*.

[33] Cmd. 6648.

[34] *Cf. supra* note 21; Agreement of May 25, 1946, between the Allied Delegations and Switzerland concerning the Liquidation of German Property in Switzerland (Cmd. 6884); see Kelsen, The Legal Status of Germany according to the Declaration of Berlin, 39 Am. Jour. Int. Law 518 *et seq.* (1945).

[35] *Supra* note 33.

[36] R. v. Bottrill. *Ex parte* Kuechenmeister [1946] 1 All E. R. 635, 636; see also the decision of the Court of Appeal, confirming the judgment of the Divisional Court, [1946] 2 All E. R. 435.

Charter... The making of the Charter was the exercise of the sovereign legislative power by the countries to which the German Reich unconditionally surrendered.'[37]

The duality of the sources of the Tribunal's jurisdiction is legally significant from the point of view of the Judgment as *res judicata*. The treaty basis of the Judgment is valuable in that it gives the character of *res judicata*[38] to the Judgment not only with regard to the original signatories of the Agreement of 1945, but also with regard to each of the nineteen States which adhered to the Treaty. Conversely, the character of the Judgment as a decision under German (Allied-decreed) municipal law makes the Judgment *res judicata* with effect against any court in Germany which has to administer Law No. 10.[39]

In so far as the effect of the Judgment as a precedent in international law is concerned, it matters little whether emphasis is put on the international or municipal character of the Judgment. In the former case, the Judgment is merely a precedent in a non-technical sense; for international law has not accepted the principle of *stare decisis*.[40] In the latter, the Powers have made sure to avoid any such consequences, with regard to their own systems of municipal law, by giving to the Tribunal the character of a military tribunal.[41] From the point of view of international law the Judgment then may claim at most the standing of twenty-three identical judgments of municipal courts. The significance, therefore, of the Judgment for the development of international law depends entirely on its persuasive authority, that is to say, on the question whether, and to what extent, the Tribunal has done more than merely apply its Charter: whether it has convincingly declared international customary law.

III. The Law Applied by the Tribunal

The Parties to the Agreement of August 8th, 1945 laid down in Article 6 of the Charter the law which the Tribunal was to apply. In the words of the Judgment, 'these provisions are binding upon the Tribunal as the law to be applied to the case.'[42] In another passage of the Judgment, the Tribunal reiterated that 'the law

[37] Cmd. 6964, p. 38.

[38] On the meaning and scope of *res judicata*, see further 1 Schwarzenberger, International Law (London 1945) 418 *et seq.*; see also III. (e), Declaration of Groups and Organizations to be of a Criminal Character, *infra*.

[39] *Supra* note 21; Article 11, Charter of the International Military Tribunal, which appears to envisage the possibility of subsequent trials in any of the zones for crimes of a localized character. This construction of Article 11 does not conflict with treating the Judgment of the International Military Tribunal as *res judicata*, and leaves its proper scope to Article 4 of the Agreement of August 8, 1945. *Cf.* also Article III (6) of Law No. 10.

[40] *Cf.* Schwarzenberger, *op. cit. supra* note 38, at p. 420 *et seq.*

[41] See I. (a), The Military Character of the Tribunal, *supra*.

[42] Cmd. 6964, p. 3. See Wright, War Criminals, 89 Am. Jour. Int. Law 257 *et seq.* (1945).

of the Charter is decisive, and binding upon the Tribunal.'[43] The Tribunal could have lived up even to the standards of international courts or tribunals if it had contented itself with the application of the Charter. It would thus have implied that, in accordance with Article 38 of the Statute of the International Court of Justice, international conventional law had precedence over international customary law. It is to the credit of the Tribunal that it did not evade in this manner the issue whether the Charter is derogatory from, or declaratory of, international customary law. On the contrary, the position taken by the Tribunal is stated with commendable clarity: 'The Charter is not an arbitrary exercise of power on the part of the victorious nations, but in the view of the Tribunal . . . it is the expression of international law existing at the time of its creation; and to that extent is itself a contribution to international law.'[44] In the last phrase, the Tribunal expressed a profound truth. The Judgment is a contribution to international law to the extent to which it is declaratory of international law, and to which the Tribunal has made itself an instrument for declaring pre-existing law. Like other courts—municipal and international—the Tribunal was entitled to consider international law as a growing and dynamic body and was not limited to leaving the law exactly where it found it. Such law-making in disguise must, however, be organically connected with what has happened before in order to be accepted as a declaration of existing law.

In order to test the Tribunal's assertion that the Charter is merely declaratory of international law as it existed at the time of the Tribunal's creation, it is proposed to examine separately the three groups of offences which have been declared criminal by the Charter. In the Tribunal's view, the crime against peace is 'not only an international crime; it is the supreme international crime differing only from other war crimes in that it contains within itself the accumulated evil of the whole.'[45] In spite of the central position allocated to crimes against peace by the Tribunal, it appears advisable to introduce this survey with war crimes in the technical sense; for in this sphere there is least controversy regarding the declaratory character of the Tribunal's Judgment.

(a) War Crimes. 'Violations of the laws or customs of war' (as war crimes in the narrower sense are defined in the Charter) have been treated of old[46] as criminal

---

[43] Cmd. 6964, p. 38.

[44] *Ibid.* See also Mr. Justice Jackson's opening speech on the evolution of international law by the case method. Proceedings of the International Military Tribunal at Nuremberg (London 1946) Part 1, p. 81.

[45] Cmd. 6964, p. 13.

[46] Apart from the instances mentioned in the Introduction, it may be of interest to record that a Declaration, issued by the Commissioners of Parliament in Scotland in 1652, exempted from confiscation certain classes of merchants, apart from, *inter alios*, 'such as have killed or committed outrages against the English soldiers contrary to the laws and customs of war.' The Memoirs of Edmund Ludlow (1698), edited by C. H. Firth (Oxford 1894) vol. 1, p. 309. See also Harris, An Historical and Critical Account of the Life of Oliver Cromwell (London 1762) 285.

acts for which members of the armed forces or civilians engaged in illegitimate warfare are held individually responsible by the enemy. In this regard, and
especially in so far as violations of Hague Convention IV of 1907 are concerned,
there is no doubt that such crimes are war crimes under international customary
law.[47] It may be controversial whether all rules of warfare which had been generally recognized by civilized nations in the pre-1914 period, have survived the
impact on warfare of modern technological developments. Yet even allowing for
an unprecedented and unavoidable measure of ruthlessness which follows from
the use of the most up-to-date forms of mechanized mass-killing, there remain
too many deeds for which even the conception of total war does not provide any
cover. On this point, the Judgment of Nuremberg is on strong ground and may
justly claim to be a fair exposition of international customary law. Whatever misgivings remain are connected with the *ad hoc* character of the Tribunal and the
impossibility of referring to a tribunal similar to that set up at Nuremberg those
who allege war crimes on the part of the United Nations and who especially point
to the use of the atomic bomb on the eve of Japan's surrender.[48]

An omission in the Indictment must be mentioned in this connection. In
accordance with the established principles of land warfare, it might have been
held that there was never a more indiscriminate weapon than the flying bombs
and rockets which were used by Germany against Great Britain. Yet there was no
attempt to stigmatize the use of such weapons as war crimes. On the contrary,
the competition of the United Nations in securing the services of the German
technicians who had been engaged in the production of these weapons appears to
amount to a recognition by implication of the legality of such weapons or at least
to the practically undisguised admission of an intention to use such weapons in
any war of the future.

(b) Crimes against Peace. This category of crime is defined in the Charter as
'planning, preparation, initiation or waging of a war of aggression, or a war in
violation of international treaties, agreements or assurances, or participation in
a common plan or conspiracy for the accomplishment of any of the foregoing.'[49]
As such acts had been made crimes by the Charter, the Tribunal did not think
it 'strictly necessary to consider whether, and to what extent, aggressive war was
a crime before the execution of the London Agreement.'[50] Thus, in spite of the
fact that the subject was fully argued before the Tribunal by the Prosecution and
the Defence, the views expressed by the Tribunal on the criminal responsibility

---

[47] Cmd. 6964, p. 64.
[48] See I. (d), The *ad hoc* Character of the Tribunal, *supra.* Such misgivings might at least be
expected from any one who does not accept the view of the totalitarian aggressors having become
international outlaws. See note 62 *infra* and text thereof.
[49] Article 6 (a), Charter of the International Military Tribunal.
[50] Cmd. 6964, p. 38.

under international customary law of offences against peace are merely *obiter dicta*.[51]

Rightly, the Tribunal drew attention to Hague Convention IV of 1907 in order to show that the violation of an international treaty may amount to a war crime in the technical sense. Less convincing is the Tribunal's argument *a minore ad majorem* from the Hague Convention to the Kellogg Pact, the violation of which was held to be 'equally illegal, and of much greater moment than a breach of one of the rules of the Hague Convention.'[52] The Hague Conventions were based on the assumption of the legality of even aggressive war and on the absence of any test in international law regarding the legality or illegality of war between sovereign States.[53] If, however, the analogy is derived from the illegality of a breach of treaty in both cases, such argument begs the question when the breach of a treaty also involves the commission of an international tort or of a crime analogous to war crimes in the technical sense. If the evil character of war and its disastrous effects on international society as a whole are adduced to give further support to the thesis of the criminal character of aggressive war in international customary law,[54] such judgment involves a well-deserved condemnation of power politics. However, it ignores the functions of war in a system of power politics and the legality of all forms of war under international customary law since at least the nineteenth century.

The Judgment's references to the Draft Treaty of Mutual Assistance of 1923, to the unratified Geneva Protocol of 1924 and to the League Resolution of 1927 on aggressive war rather tend to weaken the conclusion at which the Tribunal arrived. Draft treaties and unratified conventions are legally nonexistent and resolutions of the Assembly of the League of Nations—even if unanimously adopted—were widely held not to be legally binding on the members of the League of Nations.[55] Similarly the arraignment of ex-Emperor William II in 1919 for 'a supreme offense against international morality and the sanctity of treaties'[56] tends to show the true position in the then existing international law rather than to make the case which it was desired to make.

Thus, the view expressed by the Tribunal on the character of aggressive war as a crime under international customary law in the inter-war period stands and falls with the criminal character of any breach of the Kellogg Pact: 'In the opinion of

---

[51] The distinction between the operative parts of a judgment and mere *obiter dicta* is not only relevant for legal systems which have accepted the principle of *stare decisis*, but also in order to determine the scope of *res judicata*. See further Schwarzenberger, *op. cit. supra* note 38, at p. 408 *et seq.*

[52] Cmd. 6964, p. 40.

[53] In the absence of specific treaty obligations to the contrary. *Cf.* Mr. Justice Jackson's Opening Speech, Proceedings of the International Military Tribunal at Nuremberg (London 1946) Part 1, pp. 79, 80; Schwarzenberger, Jus Pacis ac Belli?, 37 Am. Jour. Int. Law 465 *et seq.* (1943).

[54] Cmd. 6964, p. 13.

[55] *Cf.* Smith, The Binding Force of League Resolutions, 16 British Year Book of International Law (1935) 157 *et seq.*

[56] Treaty of Versailles (1919), Article 227. *Cf.* Cmd. 6964, p. 39.

the Tribunal, the solemn renunciation of war as an instrument of national policy necessarily involves the proposition that such a war is illegal in international law; and that those who plan and wage such a war, with its inevitable and terrible consequences, are committing a crime in so doing.'[57] It will be observed that again the Tribunal describes justly any breach of the Kellogg Pact as illegal, but, without further ado jumps to the conclusion that such an illegal act must be a crime. It is true that the stigmatization of war as a crime corresponds to a change in public opinion which has its roots in the experiences of the First World War. The Tribunal, however, chose to ignore the discrepancies between the standards which the man-in-the-street applied to the conduct of international affairs and those standards which governments applied to themselves and each other. It might not be irrelevant to quote the restrained opinions which, during the inter-war period, some distinguished international lawyers expressed on the legal significance of the Kellogg Pact.[58] It may suffice, however, to let State practice since the conclusion of the Kellogg Pact speak for itself.

In 1929 the Soviet Union seized forcibly two places in Manchuria, which were garrisoned by Chinese troops, and agreement with China was achieved only on the basis of a Russian ultimatum. Then came the Japanese invasion of Manchuria, repeated large-scale battles between Soviet and Japanese forces on the Soviet-Manchurian frontier at a time when both countries were formally not at war with each other; the Italian aggression against Abyssinia and the express recognition of the King of Italy as Emperor of Italian East Africa by France and Great Britain; the practically undisguised intervention of first Italy and Germany, and then France and the U.S.S.R., in the Spanish War; the German invasion of Austria and Czechoslovakia—the latter with Hungarian and Polish participation; Italy's occupation of Albania; the secret German-Soviet Protocols of August 23rd and September 28th, 1939; the Soviet occupation of the Eastern parts of Poland; the incorporation into the U.S.S.R. of the Baltic States and the preventive Soviet War against Finland. Even if judgment is suspended on the wars in disguise which are taking place at present in Greece, Persia and China—on the surface between partisans of one or the other faction in these

[57] Cmd. 6964, p. 39. In view of the central position given by the Tribunal to the Kellogg Pact, it is worth mentioning that the President of the Tribunal did not apply to it the maxim *iura novit curia*, but asked the British Chief Prosecutor: 'Shall we find it among the documents?' Sir Hartley Shawcross replied: 'It will be put in. I do not think you have it at the moment.' See Proceedings of the International Military Tribunal at Nuremberg (London 1946) Part 2, p. 51.

[58] See Lauterpacht, The Pact of Paris and the Budapest Articles of Interpretation, 20 Transactions of the Grotius Society (London 1935) 178 *et seq.*, 184, 190; 2 Oppenheim, International Law (Lauterpacht ed., London 1935) 160–162, and 162 n. 1: 'In so far as the science of International Law can legitimately assist the cause of the effectiveness of the Paris Pact, it can do so by showing that the Pact has paved the way to parallel changes in the law. The actual incorporation of these changes as part of International Law is a matter for Governments.' *Cf.* also Wright, The Meaning of the Pact of Paris, 27 Am. Jour. Int. Law 39 *et seq.* (1933); Harvard Research Draft Convention on Rights and Duties of States in Case of Aggression, 33 *id.* 823 *et seq.* (Supplement 1939); 3 Hyde, International Law (Boston 1945) 1679–1685; Schwarzenberger, *op. cit. supra* note 4, at p. 45 *et seq.*

countries—can it really be said that the governments of the world in the period since 1928 regarded the parties who were guilty of flagrant aggressions in most of these cases as criminals?

In Mr. Justice Jackson's words, 'the world's statesmen again went only as far as they were forced to go. Their efforts were timid and cautious and often less explicit than we might have hoped.'[59] Yet not even by implication did the governments of the nations, which during the inter-war period permitted the aggressors to receive from their own countries indispensable raw and war materials, indicate that they considered such policies more than as breaches of treaties. The actions—as distinct from words—of these governments failed to conform with the standards of international morality which were postulated by wide sections of public opinion in the Western democracies.

An instance from another field may illustrate the significance of a distinction between action which public opinion considers reprehensible (but which, in law, does not amount to crime) and a crime in a strictly legal sense. It was suggested by the Chairman of the British Delegation to the Preparatory Commission of the Food and Agriculture Organization that the destruction of surplus basic foodstuffs which had been practiced in the inter-war period as a measure of price control should be recognized 'as an international crime and banned from use by civilized nations.'[60] Would it be considered as an expression of existing international customary law if, under a Freedom from Want Charter, the persons who were responsible for the destruction of the stocks of food in question were tried on a charge of having committed crimes in the meaning of this Charter during the inter-war period?

Thus we are brought up against the question whether crimes against peace are merely *ex post facto* crimes and are so treated in the Charter contrary to the principle of *nullum crimen, nulla poena sine lege*. The Tribunal admitted the relevance of this maxim as a 'principle of justice,' but held that it did not apply to the present case; for 'the attacker must know that he is doing wrong,' and at least some of the accused 'must have known that they were acting in defiance of all international law when in complete deliberation they carried out their designs of invasion and aggression.'[61]

In order to answer the question whether an act which has been made criminal under the Charter is only retrospectively of a criminal character, as distinct from an immoral or possibly tortious character, it is important to understand the meaning of the term 'crime' in the Charter. An international crime presupposes the existence of an international criminal law. Such a branch of international law does not exist. If the evolution of criminal law within the State offers any

---

[59] Proceedings of the International Military Tribunal at Nuremberg (London 1946) Part 1, p. 80.

[60] The Times (London), November 23, 1946. See also the Nuremberg Judgment (Cmd. 6964), p. 120.

[61] Cmd. 6964, p. 39. However, see Professor Smith, Speech at the Belsen Trial of J. Kramer and 44 Others, Official Transcript, No. 45, p. 34 *et seq.*

guidance, the reason for the absence so far of international criminal law is not far to seek. Criminal law postulates the existence of a strong government which is capable of enforcing order against even the mightiest transgressors. On the plane of inter-State relations, such central government is sadly lacking. Optimists may hold that the United Nations represents the transition from international anarchy to world order. Yet all that has happened so far is that the number of actually sovereign States has dwindled to two or possibly five world powers. The veto is the visible expression of this new hierarchy in world affairs.

In the absence, therefore, of a world authority which, in case of need, could confidently apply justice to such world powers as the United States and the U.S.S.R., it appears premature to speak of international criminal law. It may, however, be objected that this argument proves too much. Are not piracy and war crimes in the technical sense evidence of the reality of international criminal law? Actually, this is far from being the truth. In time of peace, any State may exercise jurisdiction only over ships sailing the high seas under its own flag. A pirate vessel, however, is not under the protection of any subject of international law. Thus, international law merely authorizes any State to exercise in such cases its criminal jurisdiction right to the limit, that is to say, including the application of the death penalty.

Equally, in the case of war crimes in the technical sense, belligerents are authorized to exercise over members of the enemy's armed forces and enemy civilians a jurisdiction which is granted to them only in time of war.[62] It, therefore, was for the Tribunal to show that at least since the conclusion of the Kellogg Pact, a rule of international customary law had grown up, in accordance with which in the case of crimes against peace, belligerents acquired a similar right to exercise criminal jurisdiction over enemy nationals whom they wished to indict of such crimes. If this cannot be shown—and the effort made by the Tribunal in this regard can hardly be said to have been convincing—this merely means that such extension of domestic jurisdiction cannot rely on international customary law, but must be based on the Charter of the Tribunal and on the rights of criminal jurisdiction which flow from the exercise of sovereignty over Germany.

Does this argument imply that international customary law is absolutely helpless if faced with the phenomenon of totalitarian aggression? The answer is emphatically in the negative. Even in a system of power politics, there is a difference between a State which slides into war and international gangsters which

---

[62] It was held by the Tribunal that 'international law imposes duties and liabilities upon individuals as well as upon States.' Cmd. 6964, p. 41. Yet it is submitted that the case referred to, and the instance mentioned, can only very artificially be explained by elevating spies, war criminals and pirates into subjects of international law or by presuming that, in such cases, international law addresses prohibitive norms directly to what, otherwise and normally, are mere objects of international law. *Cf.* Schwarzenberger, *op. cit. supra* note 4, at p. 60 *et seq.*, p. 89 *et seq.* See also Brierly, The Nature of War Crimes Jurisdiction, 2 The Norseman 169 (1944) ; Mr. Justice Jackson, Speech at the Sitting of the Nuremberg Tribunal of November 21, 1945, Proceedings (London 1946) Part 1, p. 82. However, see Lemkin, Axis Rule in Occupied Europe (Washington 1944); Trainin, Hitlerite Responsibility under Criminal Law (London 1945).

(like the totalitarian States) deliberately plan wholesale aggression and indiscriminately flout every rule of international law as well as all standards of civilization or humanity. Such States forfeit their international personality and put themselves beyond the pale of international law. In short, they become outlaws, and subjects of international law may treat them as their own standards and conscience permit. It is submitted that, in the present state of international society, such treatment of international gangsterism is less artificial than the assertion that aggressive war is already a crime under international customary law.[63]

(c) Crimes against Humanity. In Article 6 (c) of the Charter as modified by the Protocol of October 6th, 1945,[64] crimes against humanity are defined as 'murder, extermination, enslavement, deportation, and other inhumane acts committed against any civilian population, before or during the war, or persecutions on political, racial or religious grounds in execution of or in connection with any crime within the jurisdiction of the Tribunal, whether or not in violation of the domestic law of the country where perpetrated.'

In the original versions of the English and French texts of Article 6 (c), the two phrases had been separated by a semi-colon. It was thus possible to maintain that any inhumane acts (*semble*: of a criminal character in the light of the general principles of criminal law as recognized by civilized nations)[65] against any civilian population and not limited to mere persecution, amounted to a crime under the Charter whether the act had been committed before or after the outbreak of war. To judge by the Protocol of October 6th, 1945, the Russian version read differently and declared criminal only such inhuman acts as had been committed in execution of, or in connection with, war crimes or crimes against peace. According to Article 7 of the Agreement of August 8th, 1945, each of the four texts was to have equal authority, and it was a question of three texts against one. The fact that, in the American and English texts, the semi-colon was replaced by a comma, and the French text still further modified—and all with the solemnity of a Protocol—suggests that at least one of the signatories to the original Agreement felt strongly about having admitted, perhaps unwittingly, the existence of a

---

[63] On the conception of outlawry in international law, see further Schwarzenberger, *op. cit. supra* note 4, at p. 82 *et seq. Cf.* also Mr. Justice Jackson, Report to the President of the United States, June 7, 1945, 39 Am. Jour. Int. Law 184 (Supplement 1945).

It may be mentioned expressly that, as the Tribunal held that certain of the accused had planned and waged aggressive wars against twelve nations, it did not consider in detail the extent to which these aggressive wars were also 'wars in violation of international treaties, agreements or assurances' within the meaning of the Charter. Cmd. 6964, p. 36.

In accordance with an interpretation of the Charter which was more restrictive—and more in accord with the text of the Charter—than that adopted in the Indictment, the Tribunal further held that, under the Charter, only conspiracy to commit acts of aggressive war, but not conspiracies to commit war crimes or crimes against humanity, were separate crimes. *Id.*, at pp. 43–44; *cf.* the Tribunal's construction of the last paragraph of Article 6 of the Charter. *Id.*, at p. 44.

[64] *Cf.* note 31 *supra*, and the texts as printed in Cmd. 6668 and Cmd. 6903.

[65] *Cf.* the Indictment. Cmd. 6696, p. 30.

crime against humanity which consists in the violation of minimum standards regarding the treatment of human beings anywhere.

The interpretation of crimes against humanity in the Judgment of the Nuremberg Tribunal conforms with the restrictive construction of Article 6 (c), as required by the Protocol of October, 1945. The existence of the Protocol is, however, nowhere mentioned in the Judgment, and both in the original transcript and in the official British text of the Judgment the old and new versions of Article 6 (c) are to be found side by side.[66]

As interpreted by the Tribunal, crimes against humanity are of a merely subsidiary character and cover acts as enumerated in Article 6 (c) if a connection can be shown between such acts and crimes within the Tribunal's jurisdiction, that is to say, war crimes and crimes against peace. In accordance with the Charter, it is then irrelevant whether crimes against humanity have been committed before or during the war and whether they have been committed in violation of the domestic law of the country where perpetrated. The significance of this auxiliary crime consists in the fact that, within the limits laid down by the Tribunal, it includes acts by civilians against civilians which either would be covered by the conception of exclusively domestic jurisdiction if committed before the war or, if committed during the war, would not amount to war crimes in the technical sense of the word.

In one place, it is asserted in the Judgment that the Charter merely gives expression to international customary law as applied at the time of the creation of the Tribunal.[67] A subsequent passage of the same Judgment, however, appears to give vent to a different opinion of the Tribunal regarding crimes against humanity: 'The Tribunal is of course bound by the Charter, in the definition which it gives both of war crimes and crimes against humanity. With respect to war crimes, however, as has already been pointed out, the crimes defined by Article 6, section (b), of the Charter were already recognized as war crimes under international law.'[68] It is hard to overlook the argument *a contrario* which is implied in this statement.

In any case, the rather artificial limitation in the Charter of crimes against humanity to those connected with crimes against peace and war crimes hardly recommends itself as declaratory of international customary law. Under international customary law there is no room for such subtle qualifications. Either criminal responsibility exists for all forms of the abuse of national sovereignty with regard to individuals, such as extermination, enslavement or deportation of civilian populations, or such behaviour is covered in peacetime by the conception of exclusively domestic jurisdiction. Then such deeds involve international responsibility only if practised against populations of occupied territories in time of war and then amounting to war crimes in the technical sense. By their Protocol of October 6th, 1945 the signatories apparently wished to guard themselves against a possible interpretation of the Charter in the former sense. By doing so, they made it impossible to argue that the emasculated type of crime against

---

[66] *Cf.* Cmd. 6964, pp. 3, 45.   [67] See text to note 44 *supra*.
[68] Cmd. 6964, p. 64.

humanity which survived their joint efforts was anything but the creation of the Charter. This view of the Protocol is confirmed by the attitude taken before 1939 in civilized countries towards acts such as those described in Article 6 (c) and then—and now—continuously committed as part of administrative routine in most authoritarian States and by any totalitarian regime.[69]

(d) Defences. The Charter of the Tribunal excludes the defences of superior orders and action in the capacity of State organs as grounds of justification or excuse, but admits the former as a circumstance that may be considered in mitigation of punishment. In so far as the defence of superior orders is concerned, the Charter extends to crimes under the Charter rules which, since the Breisach War Crime Trial of 1474, had become generally accepted with regard to war crimes in the technical sense.[70] The test which the Tribunal actually applied and which it derived from the general practice of nations is 'whether moral choice was in fact possible.'[71] It would, however, be a mistake to assume that the exclusion by the Charter of these two defences in law forced the accused to fall back on merely factual defences. It has already been mentioned that the Defence made, and the Tribunal considered, submissions such as the effect of modern war on existing rules of warfare[72] and the applicability of the maxim *Nullum crimen, nulla poena sine lege* to crimes against peace.[73] Other defences of a legal nature which are considered in the Judgment are those of the effects of the annexation of a territory in time of war on the character of acts indicted as crimes under the Charter[74] and the justification of acts as reprisals[75] and measures taken in self-defence.[76]

---

[69] See, for instance, Papers Concerning the Treatment of German Nationals in Germany 1938–1939, Cmd. 6120. In the words of the official Introduction, 'these documents [describing the treatment of inmates of German concentration camps] were not written for publication, and, indeed, so long as there was the slightest prospect of reaching any settlement with the German Government it would have been wrong to do anything to embitter relations between the two countries.' *Id.*, at p. 4. In the light of the selective attitude taken by practically all States towards offences against minimum humanitarian standards, it appears hypocritical to deduce from a few instances of humanitarian intervention a supposed rule of international customary law.

See also Mr. Justice Jackson, Opening 'Speech, Proceedings (London 1946) Part 1, p. 68; Sir Hartley Shawcross, Speech at the Close of the Case against the Individual Defendants (London 1946) 62. Even in so far as relations between members of the United Nations are concerned, the hierarchy between Article 1, Paragraph 3, and Article 2, Paragraph 7 still remains to be determined.

[70] *Cf.* note 7 *supra*; Schwarzenberger, *op. cit. supra* note 4, at p. 62 *et seq.*

[71] Cmd. 6964, p. 42. For a critical view regarding this test, see Smith, *op. cit. supra* note 28, at p. 204; Glueck, War Criminals. Their Prosecution and Punishment (New York 1944) 140 *et seq.* On the Tribunal's attitude to the argument that conspiracy in the meaning of Article 6 (a) of the Charter (see note 63 *supra*) was not possible in a totalitarian State, *cf.* Cmd. 6964, pp. 43, 44.

[72] See text to notes 47, 48 *supra*.

[73] See III. (b), Crimes against Peace, *supra*.

[74] Cmd. 6964, pp. 65, 125.

[75] *Id.*, at pp. 108, 109.

[76] *Id.*, at p. 27 *et seq.*

In discussing the last-mentioned justification which had been put forward by the Defence with special reference to the German invasion of Norway, the Tribunal quoted with approval the principle that preventive action in foreign territory was justified only in case of 'an instant and overwhelming necessity for self-defence, leaving no choice of means, and no moment of deliberation.'[77] According to the reference in the Judgment, this principle had been applied by Sir William Scott in the case of *The Caroline*.[78] Actually, the sentence is taken from a Note which, in another *Caroline* case, the United States Secretary of State addressed in 1841 to the British Minister in Washington.[79] In addition, this latter case was never decided on a judicial level, but was settled by diplomatic means.[80]

(e) Declaration of Groups and Organizations to be of a Criminal Character. The Charter authorizes the Tribunal to declare at the trial of any individual member of any group or organization 'that the group or organization of which the individual was a member was a criminal organization.' The Charter further contains a procedural rule which defines the legal effects of such a declaratory judgment of the Tribunal. In the words of the Judgment, the meaning of Article 10 of the Charter is that 'the declaration of criminality against an accused organization is final, and cannot be challenged in any subsequent criminal proceedings against a member of that organization.'[81]

Thus, Article 10 of the Charter defines the scope of *res judicata* of the declaratory part of the Judgment for any subsequent trials of individuals for membership in such organizations.[82] In the Tribunal's view, a declaration of criminality with regard to organizations and groups determines the criminality of the members, as membership in such organizations or groups is likened to participation in a criminal conspiracy.[83] In the circumstances, the Tribunal attempted at least to circumscribe such declarations so as to insure as much as possible the exclusion of innocent persons from the circle of those comprehended in the definition of criminal organizations and groups: 'since the declaration with respect

[77] *Id.*, at p. 28.
[78] The Caroline Case, (1808) 6 C. Rob. 461. This quotation is to be found both in the official transcript of the Judgment and in the official British version. An *erratum* subsequently published by H. M. Stationery Office contains the following correction: 'For "The Caroline Case, (1808) 6 Rob. 461" read "The Caroline Case, Moore's Digest of International Law, II. 412."'
[79] The actual passage in the Note from Mr. D. Webster to Mr. H. S. Fox, dated April 24, 1841, reads as follows: A Government alleging self-defence must show a 'necessity of self-defense, instant, overwhelming, leaving no choice of means, and no moment for deliberation.' 29 British and Foreign State Papers (1840–1841) 1129, at p. 1138. See also Lord Ashburton's Note to Mr. Webster, dated July 28, 1842. 30 *id.* (1841–1842) 195, at p. 196.
[80] Parliamentary Papers 1843, vol. LXI, p. 46 *et seq.* See also Jennings, The Caroline and McLeod Cases, 32 Am. Jour. Int. Law 82 *et seq.* (1938).
[81] Cmd. 6964, p. 66.
[82] See, for instance, Article 2 of Law No. 10 enacted by the Control Council for Germany. 5 Military Government Gazette (British ed.) 46, 47.
[83] Cmd. 6964, p. 67.

to the organizations and groups will...fix the criminality of its members, that definition should exclude persons who had no knowledge of the criminal purposes or acts of the organization and those who were drafted by the State for membership, unless they were personally implicated in the commission of acts declared criminal by Article 6 of the Charter as members of the organization.'[84] In dealing with the individual organizations and groups,[85] the Tribunal was anxious not to cast its net too widely. In contrast to the views expressed by the Soviet member of the Tribunal,[86] the majority was very much alive to the danger that the application of this procedure, 'unless properly safeguarded,' was likely to 'produce great injustice.'[87]

The Tribunal twice emphasized the novelty of the doctrine of group criminality, and made it clear that it was going to exercise the discretion granted to it by the Charter in keeping with its status as a judicial body and 'in accordance with well settled legal principles.'[88] From this starting point, the Tribunal proceeded to lay down tests on which the criminal character of a group or organization depends. The group or organization must have an individuality of its own and have acted as such.[89] It must be connected with the commission of crimes within the meaning of Article 6 of the Charter.[90] Such connection must not be too remote.[91] Finally, the whole procedure being justified only by the mass character of the crimes which had been committed by the totalitarian aggressors, the organization or group must be big enough to justify resort to a procedure of such an unorthodox character.[92]

Conclusions

The Judgment of the Nuremberg Tribunal is not unprecedented. It focuses attention, however, on sanctions of the rules of warfare which, throughout the centuries, have been known and applied. Its treatment of crimes against peace and humanity makes the world conscious of issues which, if settled at all, are settled so far only on paper.

The organization of the Court as a joint *ad hoc* tribunal of the victorious Powers and its military character should serve as warnings against attributing undue

---

[84] *Ibid.*

[85] *Id.*, at pp. 71, 75, 79.

[86] *Id.*, at p. 142 *et seq.*

[87] *Id.*, at p. 64. In the same spirit, the Tribunal made recommendations for further legislation by the Control Council on the subject. See *id.*, at p. 67.

[88] *Id.*, at pp. 66, 67. See also I. (c), The Judicial Character of the Tribunal, *supra.*

[89] *Id.*, at pp. 81, 82.

[90] *Id.*, at pp. 67, 75.

[91] *Id.*, at p. 80.

[92] *Id.*, at p. 81. On the history of Articles 9 and 10 of the Charter, see Mr. Justice Jackson's speech at the sitting of the Tribunal on December 14, 1945. Proceedings (London 1946) Part 2, p. 440.

significance to the Judgment. If, in this respect, caution may be counselled, this is certainly not due to any lack in judicial bearing on the part of the members of the Tribunal or to any shortcomings in the actual conduct of the trial. Such reserve follows from the incongruity between parts of the Tribunal's Charter and the present state of world organization. The Charter did not overstep these bounds in its definition of war crimes in the technical sense of the word. It appears, however, that the signatories took a too narrow view of the phenomenon of totalitarian aggression when they attempted to include it within the categories of war crimes and crimes against peace and humanity. The leaders of the aggressor nations did not merely violate this or that rule of international law: they challenged world civilization as such and, therefore, necessarily came in conflict with all the basic principles of religion, morality and law. To attempt to deal with international gangsterism of this sort as a criminal phenomenon amounts to making a very large assumption. It means asserting that international society has exchanged the state of hue and cry for that of world order.

It was said before by the victors in another world war that 'the trial and punishment of those proved most responsible for the crimes and inhuman acts committed in connection with a war of aggression, is inseparable from the establishment of that reign of law among nations which it was the agreed object of the peace to set up.'[93] The idealism of a credulous world has been disappointed once and given way to an air of sceptical detachment. In such an atmosphere, the outlawry of the chief totalitarian gangsters and even judicial proceedings against them on such a basis would have offered tangible advantages as compared with the procedure that was actually adopted. It would have made it clear that the totalitarian aggressors were different in kind from the rest of the world. It is true that in a world in which tribalism, race antagonism, emotional nationalism, imperialist greed, half-baked ideologies and the blind mechanics of power politics are rampant, Nazism, Fascism and Japanese militarism may be seen merely as the extremes of forces which are at work everywhere. Yet there comes a point where, in Hegel's language, quantity changes into quality. When this point is reached, a subject of international law becomes an outlaw and can no longer claim the protection of international law. He can merely rely on the limitations which civilized nations set themselves.

The four Powers aimed at a more ambitious goal. They have not merely tried to safeguard existing international society against its wholesale assailants, but they gave it to be understood—and the Tribunal supported this claim—that the law of the Charter was substantially declaratory of existing international law and thus applicable to any future transgressor. In the words of Mr. Justice Jackson, these principles applied as much to the nations 'which sit here now in judgment' as to any other nation, and the trial had to be understood as 'part of

---

[93] See note 24 *supra*.

the great effort to make peace more secure.'[94] Assuming that the Charter and the Tribunal's Judgment could be interpreted in such a way, future transgressors are warned that:

Firstly, aggressive war involves personal responsibility of the leaders of aggressor States akin to responsibility for war crimes in the technical sense of the word.

Secondly, the same responsibility applies in the case of crimes against civilian populations if such offences against humanity are committed in preparation of, or in connection with, crimes against peace and war crimes.

In the age of atomic warfare a premium is put on preventive war, and the origin of atomic bombs which have been deposited in enemy capitals beforehand, or are contained in directed missiles, may be hard to determine. Therefore, the unreality of the first rule only indicates the self-contradictions which are involved in the attempt to maintain a system of power politics and to establish the rule of international law.

The odd limitations of the second rule are again an uncomfortable reminder of the real crux of the matter: the sacrosanctity of the sphere of exclusively domestic jurisdiction.

What is certain, however, is that even the Judgment of Nuremberg has not led to the creation of an international criminal law. Within the framework of its Charter, the Nuremberg Tribunal has extended the normal range of municipal jurisdiction in the field of criminal justice and, in this respect, assimilated jurisdiction in crimes under the Charter to jurisdiction in war crimes under international customary law.

The successful combination of the accusatory and inquisitorial systems, and of Anglo-Saxon with Continental rules of criminal procedure in the Charter and during the trial are pointers to the more constructive aspects of the matter. The results achieved within the framework of this *ad hoc* international institution indicate that when there is a will amongst the world powers to co-operate, a common denominator for such joint effort can be found. If in the future the Powers should be able to make such an effort not only *against* a common foe, but also *for* the common and over-riding purpose of establishing world order under law, those who consider Nuremberg a landmark and not merely an episode, as the expression of the moral conscience of organized mankind and not as a symptom of the hypocrisy of their leaders, may still be justified. Whether the 'idealists' or 'realists' are right can only be determined in retrospect. Both camps, however, may find common ground in the proposition that the Judgment of Nuremberg should not primarily be thought of as a matter of the past. It presents a challenge which has to be accepted in its full magnitude. The evil has been

---

[94] Proceedings of the International Military Tribunal at Nuremberg (London 1946) Part 1, p. 85. See also Sottile, Les Criminels de Guerre et le Nouveau Droit Pénal International (Geneva 1945) 15 *et seq.*; Honig, Nuremberg—Justice or Vengeance?, 1 World Affairs 79 *et seq.* (1947).

diagnosed so often that a repetition of the diagnosis and of available cures must appear equally redundant. If the present cosmic rearmament race that is the most obvious and disturbing symptom of the real situation is permitted to reach its wont culmination, it will matter little whether the victor—if any—in a third world war will consider the Judgment of Nuremberg as a valuable precedent. The constructive task ahead consists in making a Judgment of Washington or Moscow unnecessary.

7

The Nurnberg Trials

By Thomas J. Dodd

The author, a resident of Lebanon, Conn., is special assistant to the Attorney General of the U. S. and has been Chief Trial Counsel for the U. S. in many important prosecutions. During the war years he prosecuted espionage in war fraud cases. He is Vice-President of the International Penal Law Society and was Executive Trial Counsel to Mr. Justice Robert H. Jackson, the Chief American prosecutor at the Nurnberg trial.—EDITOR.

Before writing here of the problems of a working lawyer in the International Military Tribunal at Nurnberg, Germany I want to set down a statement of the magnitude of the case of the *United States et al. v. Herman Goering et al.*

As Mr. Justice Robert H. Jackson has well said:

Never before in legal history has an effort been made to bring within the scope of a single litigation the developments of a decade, covering a third of a continent and involving a score of nations, countless individuals, and innumerable events.

The Nurnberg Trial was all of that and more. It was a detailed and exhaustive analysis, under judicial authority and through adversary proceedings, of the historical facts and forces, before and during the worst war in history. It was one of the most shocking conspiracy cases of all time. It was the greatest murder trial of record, covering, in a conservative estimate, six or seven million homicides, not including, of course, those killed in the armed services. Of course, the case involved many months of preliminary work, more than ten months of continuous trial, five and a half days a week, six hours per day. The translations, the examination and study of thousands of documents, the hearing of hundreds of witnesses, and the handling of hundreds of thousands of affidavits. Lawyers experienced at the criminal bar will understand, therefore, that in the space available, I can do no more than briefly touch upon some features of the trial which I hope will be of interest.

A great amount of physical evidence was offered. In addition, many visual aids, consisting of charts and graphs covering nearly all of the activities of the

Nazi State and of its functions. Thousands of captured still photographs were studied, thousands of feet of captured Nazi film were reviewed, and at least three full length films, consuming hours of time in their showing, were presented for the Tribunal's consideration.

The record itself, when completed, will exceed by considerable margin much more than fifteen thousand printed pages. In it will be found the substance for ten thousand discussions, for innumerable analytical reviews, and, I expect, for hundreds of volumes. It is a vast reservoir of information, bearing the stamp of hard judicial examination. But it is more than a record; it is more than a reservoir of information; it is more than a library. It is the written history of the first post-mortem on a catastrophy that cost millions upon millions of lives. The sweep of the proof is so enormous as to stagger even those who lived with it for many months. It is, consequently, impossible of description or of adequate discussion in its entirety at any one place or in any one time.

The working prosecuting staff would fill a large room. The files would fill a warehouse. The story of the physical problems connected with the conduct of this case would make a fascinating account in itself. And that story would start with the reconstruction of a court house before we could begin to talk about the problems of the trial. For penologists and those interested in detention and security problems, there is the engaging story of security at Nurnberg, maximum security for twenty-one important defendants in an enemy country mostly in ruins and without ordinary facilities or conveniences of any kind.

The statistical story of Nurnberg would warm the heart of the coolest accountant. The story of International cooperation between the lawyers of the four great powers, at a time when international affairs were not at their very best, contains, we hope, a lesson and a moral and some direction for our own generation and those who are to follow. At Nurnberg we were lawyers representing these four powers, trained in the procedures and fundamentals of our own jurisprudence, but we discovered that basically our systems were more alike than different. For we were all concerned about having a fair trial, and we were all concerned about ultimate justice. Thus, with a knowledge of the responsibility we carried, we found that in this common concern we met on a common ground. Now, let me make it clear that I do not intend to defend the Nurnberg Trial. It needs no defense. Nor do I intend to apologize for what may have been imperfections. I shall not discuss the *ex post facto* question; the matter of immunity for officials of state; the doctrine of 'let's shoot them out of hand and be done with it'; the charge that the case is weak because the victors judged the vanquished, or the more remarkable proposition lately advanced in a high place that, although the trial was illegal *ab initio*, the court should have sentenced all the defendants to a maximum of life imprisonment. I am sorely tempted by these questions but they have been thoroughly discussed already and will be discussed in the future. There are now available some considerable thousands of printed words on these subjects.

I discuss here some of the practical problems of this trial with lawyers who tussle with criminal cases in our own country. Let me say that every big case is bigger than the lawyers who are in it. The Nurnberg Trial was no exception to this rule.

First of all, this case was not tried to satisfy the newspaper reading public or to convince only the Nurnberg judges of the guilt of these particular defendants. Likewise, it was tried with more than the usual careful concern for the record. It was prepared and tried in great detail. It was tried without regard to high-spots or 'pin-up' evidence. It was tried with great pains because it was tried for more than twenty-one convictions. It was tried so as to include every last bit of obtainable evidence, with the object not of overwhelming *alone* those in the dock, but as well to establish the fact of the crimes beyond the slightest question of doubt—now and forever.

Not only was there no court house in a proper condition in which to hold this trial until one had been reconstructed, but, in addition, there was not even a court. There had never been an international military criminal court. But long before the trial started—as far back as October 30, 1943, in what is now known as the Moscow Declaration, the Allied Powers laid the groundwork for the proceedings. After the surrender, the representatives of these four Allied Powers negotiated the London Agreement in June and July of 1945, and signed it on the 8th of August of that year. In that London Agreement it was established that the promise of prosecution made in the midst of war in Moscow in 1943 would become a practice in the days of peace after the war. Then was written the Charter of the International Military Tribunal, a document which will take its place among the great monuments marking the progress of man. The Charter was not born easily. But it was born well. And it is significant that its most severe critics have yet to make a suggestion that would have brought to it more clarity, more preciseness of language, or added strength to its basic character.

It established the Tribunal, the number of its members and alternates, gave it powers, granted it jurisdiction, and provided general workable rules for its operation. It set up safeguards and standards to assure a fair trial. And in language that all men can understand it stated the specific crimes falling within the Tribunal's jurisdictional sphere—crimes against the peace, war crimes, and crimes against humanity.

But the Charter did more. It charged each signatory with the responsibility for investigation and prosecution of all persons acting in the interest of the European Axis countries, whether as individuals or as members of organizations who committed any of the crimes defined in the Charter. This responsibility included the searching out of organizations as well as individuals. In due course the four prosecutors, after careful consideration, charged twenty-four individuals and six organizations in a four-count indictment. The first count charged a conspiracy, and the second, third, and fourth counts were substantive. This indictment was filed on October 20, 1945. It is not altogether unlike those in use in the United States—certainly as to form and, to a considerable extent, as to substance. It is a detailed indictment. It had to be. It pleads evidence when necessary, and it states conclusions where required. No doubt it will allow of more artful drafting. But under all the circumstances, under the difficulties of language and of custom and tradition, it was completely adequate for the court, prosecution, and the defense. Certainly the defendants knew the nature of the charges, the court was well able to control the proof, and the prosecution was in no doubt as to its burden.

The division of the case in chief for the prosecution among the four participating delegations was not settled in the Charter. Article 23 of the Charter merely provided that: 'One or more of the Chief Prosecutors may take part in the prosecution at each trial.'

After the indictment was drawn up, a decision was made by the four Chief Prosecutors under which each undertook to present a separate portion of the proof. The United States undertook to present the evidence relating to Count One which charged the defendants with conspiracy to commit crimes against the peace; war crimes, and crimes against humanity. The British were assigned the proof of crimes against the peace under Count Two. The Soviet and French prosecutors assumed responsibility for both Counts Three and Four which charged war crimes and crimes against humanity, dividing the field between them on a geographical basis. The French were responsible for proof relating to crimes which took place in the West and the USSR for crimes committed in the East. The line of demarcation was drawn through Germany, running approximately north and south through Berlin.

It was contemplated under the Charter that members of the United Nations would investigate and report on crimes committed against their nationals by the Germans. Article 21 of the Charter specifically directed the Tribunal to take judicial notice of findings of fact incorporated in such reports. Delegations from some fifteen of the United Nations came to Nurnberg as official observers, and in the course of their duties supplied such material to the prosecution. Under the division of responsibility established by the Prosecutors, evidence relating to Counts Three and Four on behalf of the western European countries was presented by the French prosecution, and that on behalf of the eastern European countries was presented by the USSR.

That the Moscow Declaration was something more than an instrument of psychological warfare and was understood as something more by the Allied armies is clearly evident from the fact of the establishment of special army units with the mission of capturing Nazi files and documents intact. So it was that long before the surrender of the Nazi armies tons of documents were lodged in army document centers. And immediately after the surrender new masses of written records were located, catalogued, and filed in these centers. All of these were placed at the disposal of the prosecuting powers in Nurnberg. Never before did the files of an enemy government fall so completely into the hands of the victor. The Teutonic passion for making every last detail a matter of written record provided us with our greatest trial weapon. At least 90 percent of the proof offered in Nurnberg consisted of the Nazis' own written records, in the form of orders, directives, diaries, journals, memoranda, and correspondence. And much of it bore the actual signature of the defendants in the dock. Of all the thousands of documents offered in evidence, only two items were questioned by the defense on the grounds of authenticity. Both of these items were withdrawn by the prosecution in order to make sure that our evidence was foolproof. This, in itself, is something of a record for litigation.

The fact that the case was mainly a documentary one was not just happenstance. On the contrary, the possession of this great mass of written evidence presented one of the first major questions on overall trial strategy and technique. Should we rest our case on these written records, on these captured documents, or should we make use of the very great number of Germans, Nazis, half-Nazis, and anti-Nazis who could and would make dramatic appearances on the witness stand under direct and cross examination? We were not all of one mind. The documents at this stage of the case were, of course, all in German. The translation problem was very great and it held some real dangers. Besides, the documents, or some of them, might be forgeries. On the other hand, there was considerable hazard in adopting the plan calling for live witnesses. So soon after the cessation of hostilities it was almost impossible to be dead certain about anyone living in Germany. We were very reluctant to assume any responsibility for living German witnesses. Passions were running high. All kinds of selfish motives were at play. The American staff split into two schools of thought and both pressed for the adoption of their own reasoning. Compelling arguments were offered on both sides, and our Chief Counsel, Mr. Justice Jackson, heard them out. He made his decision. It was to be principally a documentary case. That decision, never regretted by any member of his staff, was, I believe, one of great strategical and tactical importance. It was, however, more than a decision of trial strategy or of trial tactics, for it made secure the complete truth of the trial, as a landmark in the progress of man. It was a decision that went to the very heart of our philosophy of the case. It demonstrated in a practical way the application of our resolution to try this case on the highest moral level and thus to write a record without stain or blot upon it. And thus it was that the American prosecution presented only a handful of witnesses, carefully selected on the basis of competency and credibility. So it was that we presented a great mass of Nazi documents. It was not, however, as simple to do as it is to relate. There was the translation problem. The document had to be in language that the Judges could understand, and we had to give the defense counsel an opportunity to study the document in order to be able to challenge its authenticity or its relevancy. In addition, there was the matter of the proper method of offering documents. Obviously we could not hold up the proceedings by the traditional use of the competent witness. It was decided to use affidavits and so avoid the burdensome and time-consuming technique ordinarily used to introduce written proof. But this was the least of our problems. Soon enough we found it was a physical impossibility to translate and mimeograph in sufficient numbers for either the Tribunal or the defense counsel and our colleagues or, indeed, for ourselves. As a consequence, the Tribunal ruled that only that portion of a document which was actually read into the record would be deemed in evidence. In this way, through the simultaneous translating system in use in the courtroom, any document would be automatically transmitted in all four languages as it was read into the microphone. Necessarily, this cut down drastically on the evidence to be offered as the submission of a document meant the expenditure of time in reading it. And many of the documents were more than fifteen or twenty pages in length.

From the point of view of the lawyer, this ruling, although obviously required, proved extremely difficult. An argument or presentation appeared disjointed and lost effect when it was punctuated with long recitals of documents which covered more points than the one under discussion. Mechanically it was not feasible to refer back and forth to several documents as the argument logically required. As the result, I repeat, the ruling excluded a large body of evidence and made it difficult to point out at the time the full significance of some of the documents which were put into evidence.

The Tribunal did relax the rule in exceptional cases to permit documents in German to be placed in evidence without being read when translations into French, English, and Russian were prepared for the use of the Tribunal. To enable defense counsel to examine a document in advance of its presentation, the Tribunal required the prosecution to furnish to the defense counsel two photostatic copies of the original document and, in addition, a number of copies in English, French, and Russian translation so that the defense counsel could maintain a reference file as well as compare the translation with the original text to check its accuracy.

Due to the mechanical problems involved, the Tribunal allowed defense counsel to object to a document at the time it was offered into evidence, or, if they chose, the document could be received into evidence without prejudice to their right later to move to strike it for cause. Thus, excerpts from speeches of defendants, Gestapo arrest reports, and directives, minutes of meetings, and the like were offered into evidence without objections. And in the great majority of instances defense counsel after ample time for careful consideration failed to make any objection at all.

The rule requiring the submission of our proof to the defense well in advance of the offer worked something like the Rules of Discovery in civil cases which Federal Court practitioners are familiar with. The philosophy underlying the Rule of Discovery as we know it was the philosophy of the Nurnberg Trial procedure. The facts of the case were wide open and known to both sides before the proof was submitted to the Tribunal. It was serious business and not a game. On cross examination, the rule was limited, and both prosecution and defense were free to use new documentary evidence provided that it was, at the time of its use, ready in the German, French, Russian, and English languages. The reason for this modification is too clear to all trial lawyers to need amplification here.

I wish it were possible in the space available to describe some of the documents that were offered in evidence. The Hossbach minutes—the Schmundt notes—all on-the-spot records of conspirators' actual conversations well in advance of the start of the war. Through these papers I suppose we came close to the proverbial conspiratorial setting in the dark room, so often referred to in criminal courts and so seldom proved at trial. Many of the documents were offered as physical evidence. For example, the death rolls of the Mauthausen Concentration Camp—consisting of several volumes and containing some seventy thousand names—were offered as a whole. In these books the German passion for the written record took on a grisly form. Here were listed the names and some identifying data on those who had been murdered. In one volume, entries covering page after page listed deaths for March of 1945—only a few weeks before the war ended. In the space of twelve and three-quarter hours, for example, two hundred and three persons were recorded as having died. The deceased all died of the same ailment—heart trouble. They died a few minutes apart—they died in alphabetical order. The first who died, as listed for that day in the record, was named Ackerman. He died at 1:15 a.m. The last, named Zynger, died about midnight.

Very early in the proceedings it became clear that it would be necessary to use affidavits in order to conclude the trial in anything like a reasonable time. Indeed, the Charter specifically provided for the use of affidavits. But the Tribunal adopted a rule which allowed the use of affidavits with a safeguard. Either side could offer an affidavit in proper form, but if the opposing side made the request, the offering side was required to place the affiant on the witness stand for cross examination. Perhaps this procedure can best be explained by describing a concrete situation in the course of the trial. A witness offered by the United States prosecution with respect to concentration camps was a Czech physician named Dr. Blaha, who was arrested as a hostage in March of 1939 and after a long imprisonment without trial was shipped off with other similar victims to Dachau Concentration Camp, where he remained for four years. Dr. Blaha, a noted physician in Prague, was assigned to work in the morgue in the concentration camp where there were a variety of duties, including extraction of gold teeth from the dead victims for the SS, tanning of human skins for lampshades and ornaments, and establishment of the causes of death of the inmates who were subjected to medical experiments by SS doctors. The evidence on this subject matter was reduced to an affidavit which ran to considerable length in pages. The defense requested that Dr. Blaha appear for cross examination so the witness was placed on the stand and the affidavit was read into evidence after he was properly sworn. He was then asked if this was the affidavit that he had executed, and he affirmed that it was. He was then briefly interrogated on a few matters not covered in the affidavit. As a matter of interest, he specifically testified that five of the defendants—Rosenberg, Frick, Kaltenbrunner, Funk, and Sauckel—had visited the Dachau Concentration Camp while he was an inmate. He was then examined to some extent by both the French and the Soviet prosecutors, by the members of the Tribunal, and was turned over for cross examination to the defense counsel. Now the importance of the testimony of the witness Blaha was one of the most dramatic moments of the trial. But an interesting comparison from the point of view of the mechanics of presenting proof is offered by the fact that the witness Blaha was on the stand for approximately three hours, a longer period of time than was required by the United States to present the entire documentary case dealing with concentration camps, but not nearly as long as would have been required had Blaha's testimony been adduced by direct examination. It is significant, I believe, that this case was prosecuted without the use of any defendants as a prosecution witness. In most criminal prosecutions involving many defendants, the State is happy to have one or more of those on trial 'turn State's evidence.' Some overtures, always vague and carefully veiled, were made at Nurnberg before the trial started and after it was well under way. Mr. Justice Jackson made clear that we were not interested in any deal or understanding of any kind in exchange for any help from the dock. We had the proof, and we were content to rest on it. The intermediaries were told that the defendants could tell their stories from the witness stand and so help themselves if they so desire, but not under the sponsorship of the American prosecution.

Defense Counsel

Readers will be interested, perhaps, in some comment on the attitude and the demeanor of defense counsel. First of all, they were in the main selected by the defendants themselves. Some of them were outstanding lawyers at the German Bar—long before the advent of Nazism. One of them, indeed, was a pro-Nazi president of the German Bar. Some were Nazi Party members. As a whole, I think it is fair to say they were competent and, as a general group, despite the terrible years under Nazi lawlessness, they conducted their defenses according to the best traditions of the profession. To be sure, some of the techniques were new to them—as some were new to us. But they made their adjustments as we made ours. It is my own observation that out of the experience at Nurnberg we have reason to hope that the Germany of tomorrow will be a better nation because, in part at least, of the members of the legal profession who participated in the trial. Stated simply, it was high class and convincing denazification, although on a small scale.

Those of us who were privileged to serve at the Nurnberg Trial are proud of the fairness of the entire proceeding. Whatever else may be said about the case, no man can charge that it was tried unfairly. Every right of the defendants was scrupulously observed. They were given opportunity to make every possible explanation and every possible defense. Witnesses were obtained for them merely at their request. Documents were made available, library facilities were at their disposal, and throughout every hour of the trial they were afforded every opportunity to answer every charge. German secretarial and legal assistance was placed at the disposal of defense counsel, and military officials were assigned solely and entirely to assist them in preparing and conducting the defense. The defense itself, I am sure, would be the first to express appreciation for the way it was treated, for the manner in which the trial was conducted, by counsel and by the Court. And this leads me to observe that not the least of the benefits of Nurnberg was the moral victory that was won over the defendants and over their counsel and over thinking German people by the demonstration of judicial process honestly at work. I saw it take place—this moral victory—from day to day, slowly but surely in the dock and at the defense tables.

As a matter of interest, I would like to make reference to the manner in which the Tribunal handled matters of judicial notice. Article 21 of the Charter directed the Tribunal to take judicial notice of official documents, and under this provision it accepted not only comprehensive reports on concentration camps and on other matters as well as the findings, and the sentences of the United States Military Courts and the Courts of other powers, and the Tribunal took notice as well of official German laws and decrees, an example being the Nazi suspending the right of Habeas Corpus and vesting in the Nazi State the power to take persons into so-called protective custody. With respect to all documents which were subject to judicial notice, the Tribunal did not require that they be read into the record in order to be received into evidence. As a practical matter, this rule was not of very great value to the prosecution because unless such documents were read into the record it was difficult, if not impossible, for the judges who did not understand the language in which the document was written to utilize it for a basis of decision.

These are but a few of the problems that confronted us as matters of procedure and operation in the course of the Nurnberg Trial. No discussion of the Nurnberg Trial can be had without reference to the United States Chief of Counsel, Mr. Justice Robert H. Jackson. More than that of any other man, the Nurnberg Trial was his case. For the lawyers of his staff he was a sustaining inspiration. For our colleagues he was a tower of strength. For the bench he was a great intellectual aide. He was the architect of this great proceeding. He was the conscience of the case. His was the vision, the patience, the character, and the strength that made it possible. The imprint of his character and of his intellect is on every page of the record. Those of us who served under him for these many long and difficult months know best what he gave for this cause of peace by law in which he so passionately believes. We are all in his debt, and some day men will thank him for what he did in Nurnberg.

The operation of the International Military Tribunal at Nurnberg indicates that an International Criminal Court can function successfully. The procedures worked out at the trial I feel sure will make it easier for similar courts to operate in the future. Much of the success of the trial has been due to the ingenuity and the work of administrative and technical personnel, without whom the lawyers would have found their problems insoluble.

It is expected that as the world recovers from the ravages of the war, the mechanical aspects of this form of trial will assume less and less importance. But the present trial, which has been organized under the most unfavorable physical conditions, establishes conclusively, we think, that a trial of this character is feasible. A vital code of International Law with sanctions and an effective enforcement machinery is an essential element in the maintenance of peace. The practical solution of the problems of procedure before an International Tribunal which has been accomplished in Nurnberg represents an important contribution to this goal.

8

The Nürnberg Trial

R. A. F. Penrose, Jr., Memorial Lecture
By Francis Biddle
U. S. Member of the International Military Tribunal
(April 24, 1947)

MORE than six months have now elapsed since the International Military Tribunal rendered its judgment in Nürnberg. It has been widely discussed, and although public opinion is by no means unanimous, approval, with some reservations, is general; much of the early criticism, necessarily theoretical since the trial had not yet taken place, has disappeared; and some of the most sincere and intelligent critics have, with unusual courage and honesty, taken the trouble to state their change in point of view, giving their reasons. I refer particularly to Mr. Sheldon Glueck, professor of criminal law at Harvard, who, in his book *The Nuremberg Trial and Aggressive War*,[1] explains why he now believes that the trial of these war criminals on the charges brought against them was clearly justified; and to Judge Charles E. Wyzanski's article, in the *Atlantic Monthly* for December, 1946.

I think that this gradual change in public opinion comes from a better understanding of the facts and of the historical and legal circumstances culminating in the trial. Misunderstandings, however, still prevail. And in this paper I shall try to deal with a few of the most common misconceptions, and summarize, in conclusion, what seem to me to be the significant results of a trial which Mr. Henry L. Stimson has called a 'landmark in the history of international law.'[2]

A frequent misunderstanding is as to the nature of the trial itself. This was in an exact sense, as the name of the Tribunal indicates, a military proceeding, established by four of the victorious powers, to try Germans in a Germany occupied by those powers as the result of their victory. That the powers were represented in the Nürnberg Tribunal chiefly by civilians (the Russian member and alternate were officers) does not of course alter the nature of the trial. It is accepted law everywhere that victorious powers may set up tribunals, with defined law, jurisdiction, and procedure, in the territories they have conquered and occupied. Realization

[1] Alfred A. Knopf, 1946.
[2] *Foreign Affairs* 25 (2): 179, 1947.

of this simple fact as to the status of the Tribunal, cuts away the ground for the rather superficial suggestion that the trial could not have been fair because the Tribunal was composed of individuals chosen from the conquering countries. So might it have been said that in 1942 the German saboteurs, landing in this country in submarines, were unfairly tried because the special military commission appointed by President Roosevelt consisted only of American officers.

The proof of the pudding was the eating. Mr. Harold Nicolson, who came to Nürnberg to have a look at the proceeding, wrote in the *Spectator*:[3] 'But in the court room at Nuremberg something more important is happening than the trial of a few captured prisoners. The inhuman is being confronted with the humane, ruthlessness with equity, lawlessness with patient justice, and barbarism with civilization.' After the trial got under way and as it continued for ten months, the conception that the whole procedure was but an act of elaborately disguised vengeance gradually disappeared. In accordance with a provision of the Charter the individual defendants were allowed to choose their own lawyers, and in the few cases where they did not exercise this privilege the Tribunal appointed counsel to represent them. At first the defendants and their counsel were skeptical and even hostile. But gradually as they grew to realize that the rulings of the Tribunal were objective, often against the contentions of the Prosecution, this attitude changed. There was no longer any indication that the trial was to be regarded as an opportunity for propaganda. The defendants were fighting for their lives. To them that was more important than the creation of a myth of martyrdom. This was true of all the defendants, all, that is, except Goering. One had the sense that he was acting a part, addressed perhaps as much to future generations as to the living audience in his own country. Captain G. M. Gilbert, the prison psychologist at Nürnberg, reports that in February, 1946, Goering told Funk that he should be prepared to 'die a martyr's death—and he needn't worry, because some day—even if it takes fifty years—the German people would rise again and recognize them as heroes, and even move their bones to marble caskets in a national shrine.'[4]

In the *Saboteur* case as Attorney General I was assigned to take charge of the prosecution. My mail was filled with hundreds of indignant letters suggesting that the saboteurs should be immediately shot and not tried. So too in the Nürnberg case it was urged that what is loosely termed 'political' treatment would have been appropriate—i.e. execution or expulsion to some convenient Elba, without trial; but that punishment after trial was illegal, unfair, and unjust. Yet all standards of justice required some measure of trial even where 'political' methods are used. The defendants must be identified, their guilt to some extent established. Under the Geneva Convention, and in the domestic statutes of many countries, as for instance in our own Articles of War, prisoners of war are entitled to trial. And the

---

[3] May 10, 1946.
[4] *Nuremberg diary*, Farrar, Straus and Co., New York, 1947.

German war leaders, the great powers had repeatedly said during the war, would be tried. Shooting them without reference to the extent of their guilt or the nature of their crimes, would doubtless have satisfied the natural impulse for prompt revenge. But, to quote Mr. Nicolson again, the Allies did 'not desire to imitate Nazi methods or to murder people without defense.' 'We gave to the Nazis,' wrote Mr. Stimson, 'what they had denied their own opponents—the protection of the Law.'[5] The Nürnberg Tribunal was thus in no sense an instrument of vengeance but the reverse. In his opening statement at the trial Mr. Justice Jackson said: 'That four great nations, flushed with victory and stung with injury stay the hand of vengeance and voluntarily submit their captive enemies to the judgment of the law is one of the most significant tributes that Power ever has paid to Reason.'[6]

In the midst of the shattered city of Nürnberg the American army rebuilt the 'Palace of Justice' and transported, housed, and fed the members of the Tribunal, the large staffs of the Prosecution, the defendants' lawyers, the witnesses. The Tribunal arranged that the defendants should apply for witnesses and documents months in advance of the time when their cases would be called, and authorized the use of any witnesses and documents which might be considered even remotely relevant. Almost all this evidence was obtained, in spite of the unsettled state of the country. The trial was conducted in four languages—English, Russian, French, and German. The system of 'instantaneous translation' through earphones was a device that saved an enormous consumption of time. Counsel for defendants were furnished with copies of the German documents introduced by the Prosecution, and German translations of documents in other languages. The trial began on November 20, 1945, and judgment was rendered on September 30 and October 1, 1946.[7]

Before the trial began the Tribunal adopted general rules of procedure. As the trial proceeded it became necessary, however, to rule almost daily on questions regarding the admissibility of evidence and the construction of the Charter. Rulings were often given from the bench after brief consultation. Where there was no immediate agreement among the members, the Tribunal adjourned to settle the question in chambers. Two or three times a week the Tribunal held regular 'executive' sessions, after the public hearings, to consider motions and applications for witnesses.

The procedure followed, and, to some extent, the construction of law defined by the Charter, were necessarily subject to compromise. The Charter, wisely in my opinion, left the procedure almost entirely in the discretion of the Tribunal, providing in Article 19: 'The Tribunal shall not be bound by technical rules of evidence. It shall adopt and apply to the greatest possible extent expeditious and non-technical procedure, and shall admit any evidence which it deems to have

---

[5] *Op. cit.*, 180.
[6] *The case against the war criminals*, Alfred A. Knopf, 1946.
[7] For a full report of the Judgment see 6 Federal Rules Decisions, 69.

probative value.' Crimes against peace, war crimes, and crimes against humanity, were defined in general terms. The result was a combination of some features
of both Anglo-American and Continental law. Evidence because it was hearsay
was not excluded, yet the test that it must to some extent be relevant was applied.
All the defendants present (Bormann was tried *in absentia*) except two testified,
and were allowed the 'final word,' after completion of all arguments, in order to
satisfy the European conception. Technical rules were discarded in the interest of
justice. Cumulative evidence was excluded in the interest of a prompt trial.

The actual production of evidence and arguments covered about eight months.
There were continual suggestions, particularly in the American press, that the
proceeding was dragging out at inordinate length. In retrospect, however, it
does not seem, considering the difficulties involved and the importance of giving the defendants ample time to present their cases, that the trial should have
been shortened. The Prosecution took pains not only to prove the particular facts
implicating the individuals concerned, but indeed to present for the world to
read the terrible account of the rise and fall of the Nazi rule from the inception
of the party to the final bloody conquest of the nation of Germany. History and
the needs of the human race demanded that this record should be made of the
mass murders and tortures, the killing of prisoners, the hideous concentration
camps, systematically developed and minutely planned. Words lose their sting
and edge in trying to describe them. I remember the remark of the wife of one
of the French officials. All day we had heard the terrible evidence: at night we
listened to a local German quartet play Brahms and Beethoven and Bach. 'Queer
people,' I said. 'Yes,' she answered, 'and they tell me that they make excellent hus-
bands and fathers. But they are not good neighbors.'

Of course only the victors could bring to trial and punish the aggressors. There
are those whose moral scruples would have inhibited any punishment because
the Allies in some degree were not blameless. Yet a beginning had to be made.
The obligation assumed at Nürnberg was an obligation to brand aggressive war
as a crime. As Mr. Stimson said, 'the central moral problem is war and not its
methods.'[8] This obligation has now been accepted by those nations which have
created peaceful mechanisms for the solution of international disputes.

The Charter, which was executed on August 8, 1945, was the act of four powers. Subsequently nineteen others adhered. And the approval of the General
Assembly of the United Nations finally made the principles expressed in the
Charter and adopted by the Judgment of substantially universal application.
Article 13 of the United Nations Charter provides that the General Assembly
should initiate studies and make general recommendations, to encourage 'the
progressive development of international law and its codification.' At its meeting on October 31, 1946, the General Assembly referred this obligation to its
Legal Committee. On November 9, in a report to the President, I recommended

[8] *Op. cit.*, 189.

that immediate attention be given to drafting a code of international criminal law embodying the principles of the Nürnberg judgment, after the most careful study and consideration by the members of the United Nations. The President, in acknowledging the report, expressed his hope that the United Nations in line with this proposal would 'reaffirm the principles of the Nürnberg Charter in the context of a general codification of offenses against the peace and security of mankind.'[9] On November 15 the United States delegation to the United Nations proposed a resolution relating to the principles of international law recognized at Nürnberg, which was referred to the Legal Committee. On December 11, 1946, the General Assembly, adopting the report of this Committee, affirmed 'the principles of international law recognized by the Charter of the Nürnberg Tribunal and the judgment of the Tribunal,' and directed its Committee on the Codification of International Law to 'treat as a matter of primary importance plans for the formulation, in the text of a general codification of offenses against the peace and security of mankind, or of an International Criminal Code, of the principles recognized in the Charter of the Nürnberg Tribunal and in the Judgment of the Tribunal.'[10]

Indications are that the Committee will proceed with caution, recognizing the great difficulties involved, such as defining aggressive war, which in 1923 prevented the adoption of the Treaty of Mutual Assistance sponsored by the League of Nations declaring in Article 1 'that aggressive war is an international crime.' It has been suggested that a set-back might follow the failure of the nations to agree on a codification to the principles of international law established at Nürnberg. But those principles have now been formally approved for the entire civilized world by the representatives of fifty-four nations, and it is hard to believe that inability to agree on more specific definition would seriously weaken their authority. To what extent these principles were law before Nürnberg has been vigorously debated. That they now are part of the fabric of international law cannot be doubted. The Tribunal found it unnecessary to define aggressive war, but had not the slightest hesitation in recognizing its existence in this case. So it may be that the Committee will not attempt to define aggression more exactly, realizing that to do so would necessarily involve the consideration of many hypothetical cases not susceptible to concise definition. Moreover, under the Charter of the United Nations, the signatory powers have accepted specified responsibilities for solution of their disputes by enquiry, mediation, and judicial settlement. Where a breach would afford the basis of reprisive action, it would presumably also constitute aggression.

But the definition of aggressive war is less important, if indeed desirable at all, than is a restatement of the theory of individual responsibility recognized in the Judgment. When does it arise and how far does it extend? If 'waging' aggressive

[9] The Department of State bulletin, XV No. 386: 954.
[10] *Journal of the United Nations*, No. 58. Supp. A–A/P.V./55: 485.

war is a crime—as stated by the Charter—how direct is the responsibility required to involve a particular individual? How about the common soldier? In most circumstances, as to him, superior orders must constitute a defense. Can the significance of the part played be defined or even suggested in general terms?

There are many other problems of international law in this field which need clarification. Has a neutral the same duties to an aggressor as to the nation attacked? Should the rules of naval warfare, disregarded by the powers on both sides during the last war, be amended or repealed, or should a further attempt be made to abolish the use of the submarine, an attempt which failed after World War I? For there is force in the argument that a law which is generally disobeyed brings the enforcement of other laws into contempt, and thus injures the cause of peace. Should not the rules of land warfare of the Hague Convention, or some of them, be made expressly applicable to an army of occupation *after* conquest has terminated war?

What then were the principles of international law recognized and affirmed at Nürnberg?

I do not propose to discuss in any detail the question as to whether or not the Nürnberg trial was *ex post facto* and thus violated the principle of *nullum crimen sine lege, nulla poena sine lege*; in other words whether the crimes with which they were charged existed when the prisoners were brought, as Mr. Justice Jackson has phrased it, to the first international criminal assize. First it should be remembered, as the Tribunal pointed out, that the maxim *nullum crimen sine lege* is not a limitation of sovereignty but a general principle of justice. By that is meant that there is no international law which forces a nation to recognize the doctrine. Most nations have recognized it in their basic law, the United States, for instance, in its Constitution. The question then was not whether it was lawful but whether it was just to try Goering and his associates for letting loose, without the slightest justification, the brutally aggressive war which engulfed and almost destroyed Europe. Put thus the answer is obvious.

It has been said, however, that there was no objection to trying the Nazi leaders for war crimes, but aggressive war was a new and unknown conception, unrecognized by law.

'The Charter,' reads the Judgment, 'is not an arbitrary exercise of power on the part of victorious nations, but . . . is the expression of international law existing at the time of its creation; and to that extent is itself a contribution to international law.' The Judgment points out that in 1928 the General Treaty for the Renunciation of War, more generally known as the Kellogg-Briand Pact, or the Pact of Paris, ratified by sixty-three nations, including Germany, Italy, and Japan, condemned resource to war as an instrument of national policy and expressly renounced it. In 1932 Mr. Henry L. Stimson, then Secretary of State of the United States, referring to the Pact, said: 'War between nations was renounced by the signatories of the Kellogg-Briand Treaty. This means that it has become throughout practically the entire world . . . an illegal thing.' This treaty did not expressly state in so many words that aggressive war was a crime. When the Hague Convention in 1907 prohibited resort to certain methods of waging war, they were not stated to be criminal, nor were any penalties imposed, or mention made of a court to punish offenders. Yet since then individuals guilty of violating the rules of land warfare laid down by the Convention have been tried frequently and punished as criminals by military tribunals. The Tribunal cited several instances of international action tending to show that during the years immediately before the execution of the Pact aggressive war had come to be considered criminal.

Those not familiar with its development are often apt to consider international law in the mirror of municipal, or national law. But the reflection is inexact. Municipal law has gradually developed into a compact and comparatively exact body of defined statutory pronouncement. But in its early stage of development, a stage far more accurately comparable to the present status of international law, criminal law grew case by case. As Mr. Stimson puts it: 'There was, somewhere in our distant past, a first case of murder, a first case where the tribe replaced the victim's family as judge of the offender.... The analogy is exact ... new decisions ... do not become *ex post facto* law merely because until the first decision and punishment comes, a man's only warning that he offends is in the general sense and feeling of his fellow men.'[11] 'International law,' said the Judgment, 'is not the product of an international legislature, and ... such international agreements as the Pact of Paris have to deal with general principles of law, and not with administrative matters of procedure. The law of war is to be found not only in treaties, but in the customs and practices of states which gradually obtained universal recognition, and from the general principles of justice applied by jurists and practiced by military courts. This law is not static, but by continual adaptation follows the needs of a changing world. Indeed, in many cases treaties do no more than express and define for more accurate reference the principles of law already existing.'

Another principle of international law, expressed in the Charter and recognized by the Judgment, has been passed over almost without comment. I refer to the application of international law to fix individual guilt. The Tribunal dismissed the argument, vigorously pressed by defendants, that international law should not be invoked against individuals, that they have always been protected when they carry out state orders by the doctrine of the sovereignty of the state. But this often repeated generality is inexact. Our own Supreme Court has recently held in the *Saboteur* case[12] that international law does impose duties and liabilities upon individuals as well as upon States. The saboteurs landed on our shores in two German submarines in order to commit espionage and sabotage in violation of the law of war. They were tried by a special military commission and found guilty. On appeal. Chief Justice Stone, speaking for the Court, said: 'From the

---

[11] *Op. cit.*, 185.
[12] Ex parte Quirin, 1942, 317 U.S. 1.

very beginning of its history this Court has applied the law of war as including that part of the law of nations which prescribes for the conduct of war, the status, rights and duties of enemy nations as well as enemy individuals.'

There is moral value in fixing responsibility in a field of anonymous irresponsibility. A state, after all, like a corporation, is a fictitious body. To quote again from the Judgment: 'Crimes against international law are committed by men, not by abstract entities, and only by punishing individuals who commit such crimes can the provisions of international law he enforced.' Of course the representatives of a state under certain circumstances are protected under the doctrine of international comity. But authors of acts criminal under international law cannot shelter themselves behind their official positions. If the state moves outside of its competence under international law the authority to act cannot create immunity. As the Tribunal said: 'On the other hand the very essence of the Charter is that individuals have international duties which transcend the national obligations of obedience imposed by the individual state.' This is the very essence of a positive and moral international law.

The defense that these officials were taking orders from the Führer, put forward by most of them, was shortly dismissed. As I have already suggested it poses, perhaps, a problem which, under different circumstances, might present difficulties of justice and of law. Must a soldier, ordered to act, balance the nice intricacies of international law against the plain probability that he will be shot if he disobeys? But here that was not the issue. As the Tribunal pointed out, that a soldier was ordered to kill or torture prisoners, obviously in violation of the law of war, has never been recognized as an absolute defense. Moreover these men were the leaders of Nazi Germany, putting into effect by responsible personal orders the ruthless and barbarous program of their leader. Others had demurred and were permitted to retire. The proof did not establish that moral choice was impossible; nor was there any honest or convincing evidence of the kind of resistance that might have been expected from decent men.

I have discussed aggressive war in general terms. The Charter defines as a crime against peace the 'planning, preparation, initiation or *waging* |italics mine| of a war of aggression, or a war in violation of international treaties....' Those who framed it, I believe, had in mind the punishment of the politicians, military leaders, and industrialists who were responsible for unleashing war against a world at peace. They did not propose to authorize the indictment of every soldier or civilian who had taken part in the war. Such a construction would have been absurd, and would have led to a gravely unjust result. And yet, the words 'waging of a war of aggression,' taken literally, would have authorized the trial of any soldier, who, under the compulsion of patriotism and of German law, drafted for service, fought in the army. The significance of the role played in any given case, of the extent of the authority, of the nature and time of the participation—all these might have to be considered in determining guilt. But the Tribunal did not have to weigh such considerations, for, as I have suggested, the men convicted were guilty of the essential crime that the framers of the Charter had in mind—that of starting and, as leaders, carrying on a war of aggression.

Yet, it may be argued, the act of beginning a war of aggression is very different, morally speaking, from the act of carrying it on after it has been started. Is not the 'waging' of aggressive war a mistaken standard of culpability? Once a country is at war does it not become the duty of its soldiers to fight?

No light is thrown on this difficulty in the Judgment. Doubtless if the Tribunal had adopted the Prosecution's theory of an all embracing conspiracy the problem, in this case at least, would not have been present. For under the American and English conception of conspiracy those taking part in a conspiracy after it has been put into execution themselves become conspirators if they are aware of its criminal purposes. But the Tribunal did not accept this conception, and four of the defendants,[13] who were indicted on both counts one and two, that is on the conspiracy to wage war and on the actual waging of war, were held not guilty on the conspiracy charge yet guilty on the substantive offense charged in count two, 'planning, preparation, initiation or waging' aggressive war. Funk, said the Tribunal, although 'not one of the leading figures in originating the Nazi plans for aggressive war... did, however, participate in the economic preparation for certain of the aggressive wars....'

But there is no such finding with respect to the other three—Frick, Seyss-Inquart, and Doenitz—whose guilt under count two was not 'originating' the war, but carrying it on. 'Doenitz,' said the Tribunal, 'was active in waging aggressive war.' They were also, however, condemned for their participation in war crimes. It may be concluded that although 'waging' a war of aggression was held to be a crime under international law the standards for more precisely fixing and applying this conception were not formulated in the Judgment.

A word as to the Tribunal's construction of conspiracy. Only eight of the twenty-two defendants were found guilty of conspiracy. Eleven were acquitted on this charge. Mr. Stimson thought the Tribunal would have been justified in making a 'broader construction of the law of conspiracy'; but added: 'In this first great international trial, however, it is perhaps as well that the Tribunal has very rigidly interpreted both the law and the evidence.'[14]

The doctrine of conspiracy known to Anglo-Saxon law is not accepted in its breadth and application in continental jurisprudence. The Tribunal's approach to its scope under the Charter, which made no attempt to define it, may be considered a compromise between the two systems. The Prosecution under the concept of conspiracy as including everything that the Nazis did from their first party organization to the surrender of Germany, claimed that the seizure of power, the destruction of trade unions, the attack on Christianity and the churches, the persecution

---

[13] Frick, Funk, Seyss-Inquart, and Doenitz. The first three were indicted under all four counts; Doenitz under the first three.

[14] *Op. cit.*, 187–188.

of Jews, the regimentation of youth were steps deliberately taken (to use the language of the Judgment) 'to carry out the common plan' to overthrow the Treaty of Versailles and acquire territory, by the use of aggressive war if necessary. The Tribunal refused to accept such a theory for application in a criminal case, holding that the conspiracy 'must be clearly outlined in its criminal purpose...must not be too far removed from the time of decision and action.' and must consist of 'a concrete plan to wage war.' Narrowed to this extent the Tribunal naturally concluded that the guilt of fewer defendants was established than would have been involved in the broader construction. Those held guilty of conspiracy constituted the group who, with Hitler, made and carried specific plans to wage aggressive wars.

There has been almost no discussion of the Tribunal's treatment of the so-called 'Criminal Organizations.' The Charter provides in Article 9: 'At the trial of any individual member of any group or organization the Tribunal may declare (in connection with any act of which the individual may be convicted) that the group or organization of which the individual was a member was a criminal organization.' Article 10 provides further that where an organization had been declared criminal its members might in subsequent proceedings be tried for membership, and that in such cases the criminal nature of the organization could not be questioned. Less than a month after the trial had begun the Control Council of Germany passed a law[15] recognizing as a crime, without further showing, membership in an organization which had been declared criminal by the Tribunal, punishable, in the complete discretion of the body trying the member, by sentences ranging from deprivation of civil rights to death. The Tribunal, referring to these provisions, showed its concern by saying: 'In effect, therefore, a member of an organization which the Tribunal has declared to be criminal may be subsequently convicted of the crime of membership and be punished for that crime by death.... This is a far-reaching and novel procedure. Its application, unless properly safeguarded, may produce great injustice.'

This was, indeed, a novel procedure. I know of no other instance, with one recent possible exception, where an individual could be convicted and sentenced for *mere membership* in a group which had been declared criminal in proceedings to which he had not been a party. I am informed that a similar procedure was adopted in France, shortly after the end of this war, in connection with those who had belonged to the Vichy government.[16] The analogies in our law suggested in the Prosecution's argument do not hold an analysis. Conviction of a corporation does not taint its stockholders with its guilt. And the so-called Smith Sedition Act of 1940, which made membership in certain organizations in itself criminal, while possibly objectionable on other grounds of American constitutional law, did not attempt to eliminate the necessity of individual trials to determine the essential fact of membership.

[15] Law Number 10, Dec. 20, 1945.
[16] Ordonnance du 26 Décembre, 1944; Loi No. 45–0146 du 27 Décembre, 1945.

Article 9, it is true, gives the Tribunal discretion to exercise this power. But the discretion, as the Judgment points out, was a judicial one and was not intended to permit arbitrary action. 'If satisfied of the criminal guilt of any organization or group, this Tribunal should not hesitate to declare it to be criminal because the theory of "group criminality" is new, or because it might be unjustly applied by some subsequent tribunals.'

The Tribunal declared criminal the Leadership Corps of the Nazi Party, the Gestapo and S. D. (intelligence agency), which had been treated together by the Prosecution, and the S.S. For various reasons the Tribunal refused to declare that the S.A. ('the strong-arm of the Party'), the Reich Cabinet, and the General Staff and High Command were criminal organizations. The S.A. after 1934—a date remote from the crimes charged—ceased to exist as an effective organization. After 1937 the Cabinet never met or functioned as a group. The declaration as to the Cabinet would have applied at most to only twenty-three persons (the other members were either dead or defendants in this trial). The Tribunal thought that they should be tried individually. The General Staff, the Tribunal concluded, never constituted an organization; and its members, only 130 in all, many of whom had died, could, as in the case of the Cabinet, be prosecuted through the ordinary procedure of individual trials. The reasons for these provisions of the Charter, which were intended to permit the guilt of the organizations to be settled once for all in a single trial rather than to have to meet the issue many thousands of times in connection with organizations whose total memberships ran into several millions, did not here apply, as to the Reich Cabinet and General Staff.

Even as to the organizations that were declared criminal the Tribunal employed criteria that limited strictly the scope of its findings and substantially eliminated the possibility of their misuse in subsequent proceedings. The organizations were defined in terms to include in their membership only persons who voluntarily became or remained members with knowledge that the organizations were being used for the commission of acts declared criminal by the Charter. In net result therefore it will be necessary to establish individual guilt in subsequent proceedings. The declarations are thus deprived of all but psychological significance, and there is no shadow of precedent to encourage the practice of mass prosecution.

The Charter defined crimes against humanity as 'murder, extermination, enslavement, deportation, and other inhumane acts committed against any civilian population, before or during the war... in execution of or in connection with any crime within the jurisdiction of the Tribunal.' The authors of the Charter evidently realized that the crimes enumerated were essentially domestic, and hardly subject to the incidence of international law, unless partaking of the nature of war crimes. Their purpose was evidently to reach the terrible persecution of the Jews and liberals within Germany before the war. But the Tribunal held that 'revolting and horrible as many of these crimes were,' it had not been established that they were done 'in execution of or in connection with' any crime within its jurisdiction. After the beginning of the war, however, these inhumane acts were held to have been committed in execution of the war, and were therefore crimes against humanity.

Of the nineteen defendants convicted, fourteen were found guilty of both war crimes and crimes against humanity. Doenitz and Raeder were indicted for war crimes, but not for crimes against humanity, and both were found guilty on this count. Hess, who was indicted on all four counts, was held guilty of the two crimes against peace, but not guilty on the two other counts. Streicher and Schirach were indicted on counts one (conspiracy) and four (crimes against humanity), but not on war crimes. They were found not guilty under count one, and guilty under count four. The incidents on which von Schirach was convicted all occurred after July 1, 1940, when he was appointed Gauleiter of Vienna, a part of the Austrian territory, 'occupied,' in the words of the Tribunal, 'pursuant to a common plan of aggression,' and therefore constituted a crime against humanity. Streicher was publishing articles in *Der Stürmer* after the war had begun, inciting murder and extermination of the Jews, while, to his knowledge, they were being murdered in vast numbers in Poland and other occupied countries. This evidence was apparently secured after the Indictment was filed, and undoubtedly would have justified a finding of guilt on a charge of war crimes.

Crimes against humanity constitute a somewhat nebulous conception, although the expression is not unknown to the language of international law. I have made this analysis to show that, with one possible exception, von Schirach, crimes against humanity were held to have been committed only where the proof also fully established the commission of war crimes. Mr. Stimson suggested in his article that 'the Tribunal eliminated from its jurisdiction the question of the criminal accountability of those responsible for wholesale persecution before the outbreak of the war in 1939,' which involved 'a reduction of the meaning of crimes against humanity to a point where they become practically synonymous with war crimes.'[17] I agree. And I believe that this inelastic construction is justified by the language of the Charter, and by the consideration that such a rigid interpretation is highly desirable in this stage of the development of international law.

The Soviet member dissented with respect to Schacht, Von Papen, Fritzsche, and Hess. In Schacht's case the majority judgment reviewed in detail the evidence, concluding that although he was 'a central figure in Germany's rearmament program... the inference that Schacht did in fact know of the Nazi aggressive plans... has not been established beyond a reasonable doubt.' It is interesting to note that the Tribunal used the 'reasonable doubt' formula in weighing the evidence of guilt. Schacht had not been charged with war crimes or crimes against humanity. As to Von Papen, the Tribunal said, substantially the only evidence was that he had aided the acquisition of Austria in the Anschluss; and Anschluss was not charged as an aggressive war. Von Papen was not shown to have been an accomplice to the conspiracy that launched the aggressive wars. He was not

---

[17] *Op. cit.*, 187.

charged with war crimes or crimes against humanity. Fritzsche was a subordinate of one Dietrich, who was in turn a subordinate of Goebbels, the Minister of Popular Enlightenment and Propaganda. Fritzsche was never informed of the decisions taken by the leaders, and 'his activities cannot be said to be those which fall within the definition of the common plan to wage aggressive war....' Although he was indicted on war crimes and crimes against humanity, the evidence did not convince the Tribunal that his broadcasts 'were intended to incite the German people to commit atrocities on conquered peoples....'

The dissent involved no disagreement with the majority Judgment on the fundamental principles of international law, but only over the inferences that should be drawn from conflicting evidence. Schacht, Von Papen, and Fritzsche, said General Nikitchenko, should not have been acquitted on the evidence against them, which he detailed at length. He expressed his belief that the only justified sentence in the case of Hess, who was sentenced to life imprisonment, was death. He thought that the Reich Cabinet and the General Staff should have been declared criminal organizations.

The Charter provides that three votes out of four were necessary to convict. In the case of these three defendants the acquittal meant only that three members had not voted for their conviction. The inference that the Soviet Member was alone in his views, because he alone filed a dissent, was not therefore justified. Other members of the Tribunal felt that whatever their individual views, a dissent was not warranted.

'We have now seen again,' wrote Mr. Stimson, 'in hard and deadly terms, what had been proved in 1917—that peace is indivisible. The man who makes aggressive war at all makes war against mankind.'[18] This is, above all, the lesson of Nürnberg. The trial was a step in international cooperation. War is now no longer seen as a romantic adventure, but as a degrading crime, a crime which cannot be permitted if life itself is to continue. And the only alternative to war is the acceptance and development of a universal law based on the necessity of living together in peace.

[18] *Op. cit.*, 184.

9

The Nuremberg Trial and the Modern Principles of International Criminal Law

By Henri Donnedieu de Vabres

Introduction

On 8 August 1945—barely two years ago—an agreement was reached on the constitution of the International Military Tribunal for Major War Criminals. A few months earlier, the United Nations Charter, devised by the representatives of the nations that emerged victorious from the Second World War, had established the principles of a new society of states. Appended to the Agreement was a Charter governing the structure and functioning of the International Military Tribunal.[1]

Thus it was that a design conceived by canonists in the Middle Ages and by Grotius, the founder of international public law,[2] and which had begun taking shape in the aftermath of the First World War and that had been reaffirmed in response to German atrocities by the governments in exile in London and in the Moscow Declaration of 3 October 1943,[3] was realized.[4] It was standard practice

---

[1] We will quote the official text, as well as the indictment and the judgment from the following source: *Trial of the Major War Criminals before the International Military Tribunals, published in 1947, Nuremberg: vols. 1–3.* [Page references correspond to the French version of the judgment, as cited by the author—Editor's note.]

[2] *Les Fondateurs de Droit International*, preface by M. Pillet, Giard, 1904: *Grotius*, by J. Basdevant.

[3] In this solemn declaration, F. Roosevelt, W. S. Churchill and Stalin, in the names of their respective governments stated: 'Au moment d'accorder un armistice quelconque à un pays quelconque qui aurait pu se créer en Allemagne, les officiers, sous officiers et soldats allemands ou membres du parti nazi responsables ou coupables d'avoir pris une part consentante aux atrocités, massacres et exécutions mentionnées, seront renvoyés dans les pays où leurs actes abominables auront été commis, de telle sorte qu'ils puissent être jugés et punis suivant les lois des pays libérés et des gouvernements libres qui y seront institués. Quant aux individus dont la responsabilité est générale sans que les crimes puissent être localisés (notamment les chefs politiques et militaires nazis), ils seront châtiés suivant des règles et une procédure qui restent encore à définir.' (F. Rey, *Violations du Droit International Commises par les Allemands en France dans la Guerre de 1939*, in Revue Générale de Droit International Public, 1941–45, p. 95 and following.)

[4] H. Donnedieu de Vabres, *Les Principes Modernes du Droit Pénal International*, Paris, Sirey, 1928, p. 403 and following.

that the common perpetrators of war crimes—that is, those who have committed acts in violation of international conventions, notably The Hague Conventions of 1899 and 1907—should be tried, by virtue of the principle of jurisdiction *ratione loci* and *ratione materiae*, by the military tribunals of the States which these acts had injured. However, those statesmen, administrators, financiers, propagandists and military chiefs from whom the criminal impetus and its direction had originated, these 'major war criminals' whose offences under the terms of the agreement of 8 August 1945 had 'no particular geographic localization'[5] because they stretched across all theatres of war, remained criminally immune for lack of an available jurisdiction.

For the first time, their responsibility was invoked before an international criminal tribunal. For the first time, the pretext that the public character of their acts, and the responsibility of the state as a 'legal person' that—so people claimed—immunised their actions, was set aside. For the first time, they were held personally accountable for their misconduct.

That this innovation of 1945 responded to a common understanding of justice, even to a demand of universal conscience, was made clear by the welcome generally extended to the judgment of Nuremberg. Still, no one could ignore the reservations and objections which, in certain philosophical and literary circles, this judgment aroused. The Nuremberg Tribunal, it was said, presents itself under the false pretence of an international jurisdiction, an expression of a universal conscience. It is, as the letter of the Agreement and the Charter testifies, a jurisdiction of the Allies, a jurisdiction of victors who stand as judges of the vanquished.[6] The ancient Hebrews, Greeks and Romans offer plenty of examples of this practice, in which a collective vengeance takes the appearance of a sanctions-based justice system.[7] Are these victors who fashion themselves as judges in their own cause so alien to the crimes they pretend to punish? Did they not, to a degree, make them possible by their negligence, even through their cowardice? Had the stigmatizing label of aggressor not once been used by the League of Nations against a government whose action later became the decisive factor in victory? Does the present state of the city of Nuremberg not attest to the ferocity of the bombardments that were to be followed by the unprecedented explosion of the atomic bomb? Let us beware of not creating martyrs. Let us fear the twists and turns of fortune that can make the vanquished of today the victors of tomorrow and, in turn, our judges!

---

[5] See Article 1 of the agreement (*Trial of Major War Criminals*, vol. I, p. 8).

[6] Léo Massenon, *Après Nuremberg* (Questions Actuelles, November, 1946).

[7] On the 'trial' by Nebucadnetsar, King of Babylon, against Sedecias, King of Juda, Kings II, XXV, 6; Diodore of Sicilia talks about a trial of Athenian generals who were defeated in Sicily during the 5th Century BC. According to Tite-Live, after the defeat of the Samnites, Brutulus Papius was recognized as the main culprit for the breach of a treaty; his extradition was requested at the same time as reparation for the harm; he killed himself to avoid extradition and punishment (Bauer, *Die Kriegsverbrecher von Gericht*, Zurich–New York, 1945, p. 28; Graven, *Revue du Droit International*, 1946, p. 195).

We shall not dally on the historical, philosophical and moral terrain where these objections are to be found. They contain an evident truth and even form a truism, inasmuch as they reflect the infirmity of human justice, and in particular of political justice, of which the Nuremberg Trial is one manifestation. But in the end, the grievances which they imply are ineffective, because their rational scope goes beyond the intentions of their authors. If these criticisms have any validity, they are valid not only against the justice rendered in Nuremberg, but against any sort of criminal justice rendered anywhere. There is no criminal justice that is not conditioned by a preliminary recourse to force. There is no criminal justice that is administered by men who are above all reproach. There is no criminal justice that does not have vengeance as its origin, whether individual or collective, as reflected by the popular expression 'vindicte sociale' (social vengeance). Once the technical and social transformations of the war made intolerable the state-based anarchy that characterized earlier times, once the necessity of a 'society of nations'—an 'organization of united nations'—became clear, then a sanctioning regime became necessary as well, for it is an essential element of any society. The flaw in the thesis that we criticize is that it offers no alternative to human punishment, which is fallible and imperfect, other than the abandonment of such punishment altogether.

Once the principle of punishment had been accepted, a series of organizational problems arose. After the opening session of the Tribunal, held in Berlin on 18 October 1945,[8] the hearings began on 20 November 1945 in the Palace of Justice of Nuremberg—a citadel of Nazism. The trial continued under the conditions set by the Charter. It closed on 1 October 1946, with a judgment condemning to death 12 of the 22 accused, sentencing 7 others to various terms of imprisonment, and ruling that three Nazi 'groups' or 'organizations' were criminal. We do not intend to analyse the composition of the Tribunal, on which were represented four judges and four alternates from England, the United States, France and the Soviet Union, nor do we intend to delve into the procedure that generally governed the accusatorial system, which was linked to the Anglo-American legal tradition.[9] Rather, we wish exclusively to examine the judgment of Nuremberg in light of the principles of international criminal law, or 'droit pénal interétatique' (inter-state penal law).[10]

---

[8] It was during this meeting that the indictment was solemnly delivered by the public prosecution before the tribunal; it was preceded by the elaboration of 'The Rules of Procedure'. See *Trial of Major War Criminals*, vol. I, p. 21 and following.

[9] On these issues, see J. Descheemaecker, *Le Tribunal Militaire International des Grands Criminels de Guerre*, Paris, Pedone, 1947, p. 11 and following. On the differences between the French system of procedure and the British system of procedure, see the study of David Maxwell Fyfe in *La Revue Internationale de Droit Pénal*, 1947, p. 1 and following.

[10] International criminal law governs the offences committed by individuals. Here is the definition we have suggested: International criminal law is the science which decides upon the competence of criminal jurisdictions of the State or of foreign jurisdictions, the application of these criminal laws in relation to the location and persons and upon the authority of the sanctions decided by foreign jurisdictions in their territory (H. Donnedieu de Vabres, *Introduction à l'Etude*

This type of law has evolved under the pressure of two features of modern times: the development of international criminality and the creation of great powers. As its name indicates, it borrows from the principles of two branches of the law: criminal law and public international law. Notably, it draws from the first the principle of legality of crimes and punishment, thus safeguarding the fundamental rights of the accused; it draws from the second the rule that the relationships that arise from the society of nations essentially pull these great political units together, and affect only indirectly the condition of the individual. Yet, it is undeniable that these principles have been shattered by the judgment of the International Military Tribunal. It is the double violation of these traditional rules by the jurisprudence of Nuremberg that creates discomfort in the minds of many jurists.

The reasons of justice and social utility from which the principle of legality emanates have both general and permanent value. But the lack of foresight of the founders of the League of Nations, who neither created an international criminal jurisdiction nor spelled out those obligations that arise from the types of relationships found in international public law and which are of crucial importance, thus forced the authors of the Agreement and Charter of 8 August 1945 to break new grounds.

The International Military Tribunal is an *ad hoc* jurisdiction, set up only after the commission of the crimes which it is charged to sanction. The offences are vague, whilst the punishments are left almost entirely to the discretion of the judges.

In the international political arena, the status of subject of law is linked to the concept of sovereignty, which is an attribute of the state. Natural persons are in no way—regardless of their interests and responsibilities—parties to the sort of relations recognized by public international law. Yet, the absence of a German state, following its unconditional surrender on 5 June 1945, and the suspension of German sovereignty, placed the occupying powers in necessary and direct contact with the individuals who were to blame for initiating criminal actions. Their personal responsibility is recognized by the terms of the Charter.

While there did not exist, in our sense, between the International Military Tribunal and the Charter the sort of subordination as would normally subject the people to the law, the will of the Charter's authors was generally binding upon the judges of Nuremberg. And it has sometimes been suggested that this obligation—to obey the drafters' will—provided sufficient justification for the innovations contained in the judgment; nevertheless, the Tribunal did not think

du Droit Pénal International, Sirey, 1922, p. 6). Inter-state criminal law governs offences committed by individuals acting in an official capacity on behalf of the state, and is thus a matter among states. Some scholars have suggested calling it 'the new international criminal law'. But this name is inexact because it puts back into the past a science that still has today all its relevance. International criminal law is in the same position vis-à-vis inter-state criminal law, as international private law is vis-à-vis public international law. See on that matter, V. V. Pella, *La Guerre Crime et les Criminels de Guerre*, Genève-Paris, 1946, p. 19 and following.

so. It believed that an exact interpretation of the Charter and the necessity to fill its inevitable lacunae required that the Charter be connected with existing principles, or at least that the Charter be measured against those. It took the view that it would not be responding adequately to the aspirations of the universal conscience if it were to base consequential findings on the sole basis of partly improvised provisions. That is the reason why, in many parts of the judgment, one may find views expressed in light of the traditional rules of international law that were mentioned above: 'The Charter,' says the Tribunal, 'does not constitute an arbitrary exercise, by victorious nations, of their supremacy. It expresses the international law in force at the moment of its creation; it contributes, in that very way, to the further development of this law.'

It is this development that the Tribunal seeks to pursue in a traditional though innovative spirit, respectful of truths consecrated by experience, mistrustful of certain impudence, ever sensitive to the growing demands of a 'changing world'. It endeavoured to consider successively the crimes charged in indictment, to address preliminary exceptions relevant to those charges and to consider defences as arose from general rules of responsibility. This work will follow this path, in the hope of drawing out certain lessons for the future of an endeavour that has its roots in the past but which will manifest its full *raison d'être* and will be justified in the eyes of the general public only if it lives on.

Chapter I
Crimes Against Peace

Crimes against peace were the *second* category of charges. We shall not feel obliged to attempt, in the following discussion, to reproduce the order of charges from the indictment as set out before the opening of the trial by the commission of the four Chief Prosecutors any more than we would feel obliged to follow the order laid out in the judgment itself. Crimes against peace, or wars of aggression, are the initial and fundamental charge from which all others spring. If the Prosecution assigned it the second position, this is because, taking into account the chronology of events, he placed another charge first, that of 'conspiracy', something the Tribunal was to handle, justifiably in our view, with the greatest of prudence.

The succession of wars of aggression determined by Hitler's policies began on 1 September 1939, with the armed invasion of Poland. A series of acts of aggression, committed in violation of treaties, had preceded it, from the remilitarization of the Rhineland (7 March 1936) to the occupation of Bohemia and Moravia, in the spring of 1939.[11]

---

[11] These operations are described in the indictment under the heading 'Use of the Nazi control for purposes of aggression against foreign countries', see *Trial of Major War Criminals*, p. 37 and following.

The war of aggression constitutes the core element of crimes against peace, the very object of the charges. In the terminology used in the indictment and in the judgment, the concept of an *act of aggression*, which must be distinguished from a war in that it does not necessarily involve the use of armed force, constitutes a simple preparatory act.

The premeditated character of Hitler's actions is revealed, first, by his manifesto, *Mein Kampf*, written in 1924 in the Landsberg prison. Monsieur de Menthon, the French Senior Prosecutor, in his opening statement before the Nuremberg tribunal, summed up as follows the views expressed by this book, which received extraordinary publicity:[12] 'War to reconquer the territories lost in 1919, war to annihilate French power, war to acquire vital space in Eastern Europe, war, finally, against any state that would be, or could become, a counterweight to the hegemony of the Reich—that is the plan of *Mein Kampf*.'

The execution of the plan is laid out in a series of speeches delivered by Hitler in the course of meetings with various statesmen and military leaders, his confidants and his accomplices. The main parts of those were preserved in the minutes that were kept with German precision, by staff officers. These were introduced into evidence at the Nuremberg trial under the names of those officers. We will limit ourselves to singling out three among them, which mark decisive moments in the aggression.

The *Hossbach* document (386 PS)[13] describes the meeting held on 5 November 1937, in the Reich's Chancellery. In attendance were: Goering, Raeder, von Neurath, von Blomberg, von Fritsch...Hitler declared the necessity, in order to guarantee the security of the German people and with a view to maintain its standard of living, of conquering 'living space' (Lebensraum). He was to occupy Austria and Czechoslovakia, at the latest in the 1943–1945 period. The possibility of a revolution in France, of a French–Italian conflict in the Mediterranean basin sparked by the Spanish Civil War, would provide a pretext. The annexation of Austria and Czechoslovakia not only procured human and material resources but it also shortened the borders of the Reich. It also offered a clear strategic value with a view to future operations either to the west or to the east.

The *Schmundt* document (L.79)[14] concerns a conference held at the new Chancellery of the Reich on 23 May 1939. Goering, Raeder, Brauchitsch, Keitel, Milch, Halder, Warlimont and von Below were present. The objectives set in 1937 had been achieved. The Reich had concluded a non-aggression pact with Poland on 26 January 1934, and Hitler himself had earlier offered assurances of friendship. But now the attack on Poland was in sight. 'Dantzig,' said Hitler, 'is in no way the subject of the quarrel.' It was necessary to beat Poland 'with a view to extending our living space to the east, conquering an agro-production base, and

---

[12] *Documents de la Guerre*, Mr de Menthon, Opening Statement, p. 20.
[13] *Trial of Major War Criminals*, vol. I, Judgment, p. 199 and following; R. Cartier, *Les Secrets de la Guerre dvoilés par Nuremberg*, Fayard, 1947, p. 63 and following.
[14] *Trial of Major War Criminals*, vol. I, Judgment, p. 209; R. Cartier, p. 101.

solving the Baltic problem.' Without flinching before the risk of a global conflict, it was necessary to isolate Poland by persuading England, and perhaps Russia, to lose interest in the fate of the Polish state.[15]

On 23 November 1939, Hitler achieved this new goal. Since he had taken power, the attitude of the great powers, most recently that of the Soviet Union, had nearly always acted as he expected, in contradiction to the pessimistic views of his subordinates. The Polish campaign demonstrated to the General Staff his strategic superiority. The war against France and England is in a stage of stagnation. The instant is propitious for a recapitulation of past successes before his military chiefs. Hitler concludes: 'The destiny of the Reich depends on me, and me alone' (789 PS).[16]

It is on the basis of these facts that the Prosecution built up its case as regards crimes against peace. In law, the Prosecution relied upon numerous treaties or pacts of non-aggression concluded by Germany both before and since the rise of Hitlerism, with various European powers, including England, France, Belgium, Czechoslovakia, Poland...; the collective security regime initiated with The Hague Conventions of 1899 and 1907, institutionalized by the Pact of the League of Nations, and expanded by the Peace Pact of Paris or the Kellogg–Briand Pact of 27 August 1928, which counted Germany, France, England, the United States, Poland, and others among its signatories.

It is true that the violation of contractual obligations does not in itself constitute a penal offence. It is also true that, once Hitler came to power in October 1933, Germany withdrew from the League of Nations. But it remained linked to The Hague Conventions and the other treaties it had ratified. A resolution by the Assembly of the League of Nations, before Germany's withdrawal—dating back to 1927—included this solemn affirmation: 'A war of aggression is an international crime.' This affirmation was also included in a resolution voted in 1928 by the 21 republics represented at the sixth Pan-American Conference. 'A war of aggression is a crime against humanity.' In 1929, the Congress held in Bucharest by the International Association of Penal Law called for the establishment of an

[15] This conference was followed, on 22 August 1939, a few days after the signature of the agreement between the USSR and Germany made public in Moscow on the 21st, by a meeting where Hitler told the high commanders: 'It was clear to me that a conflict with Poland had to come sooner or later. I had already made this decision in the Spring, but I thought that I would first turn against the West in a few years, and only afterwards against the East...I wanted to establish an acceptable relationship with Poland in order to fight against the West. But this plan, which was agreeable to me, could not be executed since essential points have changed. It became clear to me that Poland would attack us in case of a conflict with the West.' And further on: 'Now...Poland is in the position in which I wanted her...I am only afraid that at the last moment some "Schweinehund" will make a proposal for mediation...A beginning has been made for the destruction of England's hegemony.' (*Trial of Major War Criminals*, vol. I, Judgment, p. 212 and following of the French version. R. Cartier, p. 109 and following); the document PS 708 bears the official version; an even more comprehensive version can be found in *Trial of Major War Criminals*, p. 212 and R. Cartier, p. 109 and following.

[16] *Trial of Major War Criminals*, vol. I, Judgment, p. 199 and following. R. Cartier, p. 37 and following.

international criminal jurisdiction and the recognition of the criminal responsibility of states and natural persons in case of aggression.

In the face of these multiple expressions of universal public opinion, Hitler's Germany cannot argue that its break with the Geneva entity relieves it of responsibility—even less so since, on 27 August 1928, it became a party to the Peace Pact of Paris, whose language is still binding on it. The Pact of Paris imposes upon its signatories, which in number and political importance exceeds even the members of the League of Nations, the solemn renunciation of war 'as an instrument of national policy'. This is interpreted as implying an implicit condemnation of all wars that are neither defensive nor undertaken through a collective procedure, such as that provided for in the Covenant of the League of Nations. From this stems the prohibition on third-party states to come to the aid of an aggressor state and perhaps even an obligation to maintain a position of neutrality in a conflict between an aggressor state and its victim.[17]

Finally, how could we overlook the fact that various states, and notably Germany, incorporated these new prescriptions of international law into their national practices and in their domestic law? The clause on the renunciation of war was written into bilateral treaties, including the German–Polish non-aggression treaty of 26 January 1934, and the German–Soviet non-aggression treaty of 23 August 1939. Article 4 of the Constitution of Weimar stipulates that the rules of international law are to be regarded as a binding part of German Reich law. New penal codes, notably those of Poland and Romania, punish (as a crime of propaganda for war of aggression) any incitement to war.

Thus, the doctrinal, contractual and legislative movement that stripped war of its legitimacy was taking shape. On the subject of the Kellogg–Briand Pact, Briand said: 'Once considered as divine law and entrenched in the international ethic as a prerogative of sovereignty, such a war has finally been juridically stripped of that which constituted its gravest danger: its legitimacy. Marked henceforth with illegality, it is subjected to the conventional regime, genuinely placed outside the law . . .';[18] and what could this mean, if not that the substitution of a new public international law for the traditional public international law made wars of aggression a crime? This change calls for criminal punishment. But this is ineffective if the prohibition seeks to target only states as legal entities, which is to say, abstractions. It must strike at individual people, who alone are capable of conceiving and executing an aggressive design. This was well understood by the authors of the Versailles Treaty (Article 227, etc.). Its semi-failure can only be imputed to the imperfections of the international community, and to the survival of national prejudices and self-interest.

[17] A. Mandelstam, 'L'Interprétation du Pacte Briand-Kellog par les Gouvernements et les Parlements des Etats Signataires' (*Revue Générale du Droit International Public*, p. 537 and following).

[18] United States Department of State, General Treaty for the Renouncement to War, Descheermaeker, p. 7.

The application of these methods, of course, requires a test for what may constitute a war of aggression. This could be derived, almost automatically, from a closed system of collective security, such as that constituted by the Covenant of the League of Nations as completed by the Geneva Protocol[19] or in parallel with the Kellogg–Briand Pact—and, at the regional level—the Locarno Treaties or the conventions of London, of 3 July 1933, and the Litvinov–Titulesco accords reached between the USSR and its neighbours.[20] But the different texts which sought to fill the gaps of the Covenant have remained at the drafting stage. Hitler's Germany repudiated and violated the Locarno Treaties. In this situation, the determination of the aggressor is, just as in the determination of self-defence, a pure question of facts.

Although there may be ambiguous cases where the absence of a legal criterion might be regretted, such doubt can be eliminated when, in addition to the facts of an armed attack, there is proof of a mature and settled plan. [21]

It would be pointless to develop further the well-known thesis of the Prosecution. More interesting is the argument of the Defence, which was presented in the opening address by one of the masters of German public international law, Professor Hermann Jahreiss.[22]

He did not deny the existence of the facts that we have just noted. He abstained from repeating the pretext of 'encirclement' so dear to the diplomats of the Second Reich, or its successor, that of 'vital space' (Lebensraum), the leitmotiv found in *Mein Kampf.* What he does contest is the existence, among the accused, of the relevant *mens rea*, that is, a criminal intent, which is the moral and subjective element of crimes against peace.

He argues that even if one were to admit that the 'old' public international law has been replaced over time with a 'new' public international law that condemns

---

[19] The Geneva Protocol would hold as aggressor—unless otherwise decided by unanimity by the Council—any State refusing to submit its dispute to arbitration or refusing to comply with the decision of the arbitrator. P. De Lapradelle, 'Le procès des Grands Criminels de Guerre et le Développement du Droit International' (*Nouvelle Revue de droit International Privé*, 1947, p. 12).

[20] The analytic method, consisting of laying down a limitative list of acts constituting aggression, is recommended by the Committee of Arbitration and the League of Nations (see the Politis report; see Bruns, *Traités Politiques*, vol. II, Part II, p. 537 and following, notably for the texts at pp. 563–569). The conclusions of the committee directly influenced the London Convention of 3 July 1933. P. De Lapradelle, p. 12. See also the project of a universal repressive code written by Prof. V. V. Pella, *La Guerre Crime*, p. 145 and following.

[21] This criterion of a psychological nature is, according to P. De Lapradelle (p. 13), the one from the Charter of 8 August 1945. It lists as crimes against peace the planning, preparation, initiation or the waging of wars of aggression... or the participation in a common plan or in a conspiracy aimed at accomplishing any of the foregoing acts. Article 6 (a): 'C'est en fonction d'un plan d'agression que, rapproché de la direction et préparation, le déclenchement d'une guerre recevait sa qualification criminelle. Aux lieux et place d'une détermination automatique, tirée de la seule évidence momentanée de l'acte , l'incrimination de l'agression par le Statut supposait une recherche d'intention, d'évidence prolongée, de durée que l'accusation de complot, plus expressément, rendait indispensable.'

[22] The argument presented by Prof. Jahreiss had not yet been published at the time this article was written.

the war of aggression as a crime, and further admit that this change represents a progress, it is still necessary, in order for an accusation to be well-based, that the accused be shown to have been aware of that fact. Proof of this fact must be established by the Prosecutor, and any doubt must be resolved in favour of the accused. If we are in a transitional phase in which the abandonment of old principles in favour of new ones remains uncertain, or where the clarity of the new principle is still fluctuating, the rule of restrictive interpretation of criminal law demands an acquittal.

The sensational declarations that stigmatize wars of aggression—war as 'an instrument of national policy' and as a crime—do not provide for any sanction. They are *leges imperfectae*. In any case, a conviction would undermine the principle of *nulla poena sine lege*. In addition, is it certain that the term 'crime', as it figures in these resolutions, must be understood in a technical sense? Certain remarks by the rapporteur of the Polish proposition from which the League of Nations text emerged point to the opposite conclusion. The epithet 'criminal', when applied to a war of aggression, can imply a kind of moral stigmatization, as well as a crime. Where doubt exists, the meaning that favours the defence must prevail.

The collective security regime provided in the Covenant of the League of Nations had its deficiencies. It was dominated by the rule of unanimity which the Charter of the United Nations—with stringent reservations—was later to repudiate. When, in a particular case, the report presented by the Council failed to obtain the unanimous approval of the members of the Assembly, each state remained free to act according to its own notion of justice, that is to say, to adopt the remedy it saw fit (Article 15 S 7). It was a return to the old regime, that of the jungle. And yet every effort to fill the gaps of the Covenant was in vain.

The Kellogg–Briand Pact renounced war 'as an instrument of national policy'. It provided no explanation for this formula; and its concision, its ambiguity, alien to the Covenant of the League of Nations, opened the door to all sorts of tendentious interpretations. Testifying to that were both the discordant comments to which the Covenant gave rise during its ratification by the United States Congress and the restrictions that the signatory governments imposed on it from the moment of its adoption: the Americans made a reservation as concerns the application of the Monroe Doctrine; the English reserved their entitlement to act in certain unspecified 'zones of special interests' and those two, as well as all others, reserved for themselves the freedom to decide on cases in which they could be said to be acting in self-defence.

In addition to this imprecision and these exceptions dictated by nationalist policies contrary to its objective, we must draw attention to a surprising lacuna. The Covenant of the League of Nations foresaw a procedure allowing for the revision of treaties whose stipulations could in some instances endanger world peace. There thus existed, at the disposal of governments in difficulty, an exit, an escape route, a peaceful means to resolve differences, which would render inexcusable any resort to arms. Yet, the Kellogg–Briand Pact contains no clause on the revision of treaties.[23]

For it to be regarded as more than a mere moral pronouncement, the Kellogg–Briand Pact would have had to provide for sanctions. But not only—following the example of the Covenant of the League of Nations—did it not provide criminal sanctions, but, unlike the Covenant, it did not provide for sanctions of any sort: it embodied, to an even higher degree than its predecessor, the character of a *lex imperfecta*. In particular, although it declares unjust a war undertaken as an instrument of national policy, it fails to explain what consequences this would have for the belligerents. Are the ordinary laws of war inapplicable to wars of aggression? Is the state that is the victim of an aggression exempt from obeying the prohibitions contained in The Hague Regulations? Inversely, do the agents of an aggressor state such as its officers and soldiers cease benefiting from these provisions of The Hague Regulations that would normally legalize the conduct, so that they are to be treated as mere assassins if they kill an enemy?... Such decisions, which conform to logic, are rejected by good sense and equity.[24] The contradiction still had to be resolved. The Kellogg–Briand Pact is as poorly coordinated with The Hague agreements as with its immediate successor, the Covenant of the League of Nations.[25] Having no roots in the past, it will remain ineffective in the future.

The position of third states with regard to war 'as an instrument of national policy' is as poorly defined as that of the belligerents. Other than the affirmation of the legality of defensive war—which is a truism—the only effect one could attach to the letter of the Kellogg–Briand Pact is a sort of 'permit to wage war' (by argument *a contrario*) granted to states that, out of goodwill, would take it upon themselves to punish the aggressor. And yet, it seemed to have been agreed to go further than this and to find in the Pact of Paris a condemnation—at least on moral and political grounds—of the position of neutrality. During the debates in the US Senate concerning the ratification of the Pact, Senator Borah declared that one could not conceive that the United States could remain a spectator in the event of a conflict. The repeated warnings addressed by President Roosevelt to the Führer and Il Duce, before and after Munich, all pointed to a coming action. From that point, the declaration of neutrality of the United States of 5 September

[23] On the necessity of such a clause, see J. Politis, *L'Avenir de l'Europe*, Neuchâtel, 1947, p. 89.

[24] 'Il ne viendrait à l'idée de personne,' wrote M. Paoli (Contribution à l'Etude des Crimes de Guerre et des Crimes contre l'Humanité en Droit Pénal International in *La Revue générale de Droit International Public*, 1941645, vol. II, p. 133); 'de soutenir que le soldat de l'Etat agresseur commet un crime en se battant contre celui de l'Etat attaqué. Les lois de la guerre autorisent cet acte; En sens contraire, le soldat de l'Etat victime de l'agression commettrait indiscutablement un crime, s'il achevait un blessé ennemi. Il existe donc des lois et coutumes de la guerre distinctes de celles dont la violation constitue le crime contre la paix. Mais comment comprendre le fait lui-même de cette existence indépendante? Comment expliquer logiquement et juridiquement que l'on puisse se retrouver en possession de lois écrites ou coutumières même pour la guerre illégale?'

[25] A. Mandelstam, 'L'Interprétation du Pacte Briand-Kellog par les Organes de la Société des Nations' (*Revue Générale du Droit International Public*, 1935, p. 214 and following).

1939 had only one meaning. The United States, following England and the USSR, announced the coming demise of the idea of collective security!

Indeed, cracks had begun to appear for some time in the edifice built upon the Covenant of the League of Nations. The repeated declarations by British, Russian, and American statesmen testified to its failure, notably that of Neville Chamberlain to the House of Commons, on 22 February 1938, on the eve of the *Anschluss*. So did the abstention of the League of Nations following the Sino-Japanese conflict. And so did the comedy of economic sanctions put in place against Italy over the Italo-Abyssinian conflict, and the final withdrawal of sanctions once the goal of the aggression had been achieved. And so it was, finally, when, in 1939, in the face of an imminent attack by the Reich on Poland, and under cover of a pact of non-aggression, the USSR concluded a secret treaty providing that it would divide up Poland with the government of the Reich!

Faced with such a spectacle, how can we criticize the defendants for believing that they were acting in accordance with the rules of classical public international law, when all the facts pointed to the current reality? How can we subject them to the prescriptions of a new public international law, the superiority of which is not in question, but which was only in a stage of gestation? Doing so would amount to judging them *ex post facto*, inflicting upon them the effects of an unjust retroactivity. That applies to the indictment. As for the penalties, not only did no criminal sanctions exist, but none of the remedies provided for in international texts effectively targeted natural persons. The responsibility which they triggered was that of the states, which alone are parties to those categories of relationships recognized under public international law.[26]

The argumentation of Professor Jahreiss is striking in the picture he paints of the failures suffered by the system of collective security, as it was conceived by the authors of the Treaty of Versailles. We must admit that this picture is accurate. We must also admit that these shortcomings cannot be blamed entirely on the imperfections of the Pact, the most serious of which was the absence of any coercive mechanism and of any pre-constituted judicial or military apparatus. They stem from the realism of the governments which fought against a policy demanded by the solidarity of the peoples, as well as from the short-sightedness of those who deserted it and the weakness of those who, at critical moments— such as the remilitarization of the Rhineland—sacrificed to their blind love for peace, or to their fear of defeat, the demands of the new law. But to conclude from these repeated failures, from this division of responsibilities, that the most guilty—the very perpetrators of the aggression—should enjoy impunity, is to reason strangely. The very tightly argued case offered by Professor Jahreiss has a weak point, which is to rely upon the thesis of his predecessors, Hegel, Laband,

---

[26] The only sanction provided by the Kellogg–Briand pact was of a political and collective nature: 'Toute puissance signataire qui chercherait désormais à développer ses intérêts nationaux en recourant à la guerre devra être privée du bénéfice du présent Traité.'

Jellinek, for whom facts alone can create law, and thus law is ultimately dependent on the availability of force: this thesis has contributed largely to the misfortunes of our time. To admit that repeated infractions of criminal law would lead to the tacit abrogation of this law amounts to ruling out all organized punishment and, in the absence of punishment, any viable form of society. This is no less true of the international society.

The establishment of a new regime will, no doubt, meet with incomprehension, and with conflicting interests and feelings. It is no less true that a return to the ancient anarchy of states—given the means of destruction that now exist—is not acceptable. It would offend the collective conscience whose demands seem to grow in proportion to the disappointments which it encounters. There truly did exist, at the time of the commission of the crimes, a new public international law which made war a crime, whose regulations were tied to criminal sanctions, and which applied to both, as will be seen, states (legal persons) and individuals (natural persons).

Professor Jahreiss objects that these provisions are not, or were not, at the time of the acts charged, spelled out in binding legislation. But this objection sets the *nullum crimen, nulla poena sine lege* principle out of the historical context in which the principle was born and which limits the scope of its actual relevance. This principle was not known to Roman law, nor to the law of ancient France. It appeared in our country only as the crowning point of a well-developed, codified and relatively fixed body of law. It is for a legal system of this sort that the principle subordinates criminal repression to adequate notification of the charges, and sanctions as regard both their nature and scale.[27] It is not necessary to recall that this principle was transgressed countless times by National-Socialist law, that it is unknown to Soviet law, and that it is alien to British law, with its liberal tradition.[28] Even in France, the principle of the legality of crime and punishment is truncated, as regards political crimes, by the sovereign power recognized to the High Court.[29] The reason for this lies in the fact that the forms of political delinquency are less constant and less predictable than those of common criminality.

---

[27] If the *nullum crimen sine lege* principle may be justified based on critical reasons in the rational and legislative sphere, it is more difficult to do so in relation to the *nulla poena sine lege* principle. It is true that French positive law only accepts the retroactivity of criminal law with regard to relatively minor criminal laws. But the extension of the retroactive application to more severe laws may not systematically offend justice; it could also be commanded by imperious reasons of social interest. See on the issue the observations made by J. A. Roux, 'A Propos de la Non-Rétroactivité de la Loi Pénale', abstract from *La Revue de Droit International, de Sciences Diplomatiques et Politiques*, No 3, 1947.

[28] M. Ancel, *La Règle 'Nulla poena sine lege' dans les Législations Modernes* (Annales de l'Institut de Droit Comparé, 1936, II, p. 245). Dr. J. Schem, *Die Analogie im Strafrecht*, Breslau, 1936, notably on English law, p. 154 and following.

[29] 'Ajoutons,' M. Malézieux wrote ('Le Statut International des Criminels de Guerre', in *La Revue Générale de Droit International Public*, 1941–45, p. 174), 'que la non observation de la règle *nullum crimen sine lege* semble inhérente à l'absence d'un système de sanctions organisées. Ainsi en était-il, et pour la même raison, en droit constitutionnel français sous les régimes parlementaires: la chambre haute, érigée en cour de justice, définissait elle-même les éléments constitutifs de la haute

Because of the official position of its authors, the motives that inspire such an offence and in light of the interests that it directly violates, a crime of peace may be said to constitute a political crime. Inter-state criminal law does not only consist of the laws of these states, but also of the particular conventions entered into by certain states, of the decisions of national or international tribunals which, influenced by the doctrine, ultimately create a customary practice. Inter-state criminal law is part of customary law; and it is not suggested that this character is limited to the formative phase in which the law finds itself. But this character explains that when applied in the context of this body of law, the *nullum crimen, nulla poena sine lege* principle must be interpreted in a rather supple manner.

Besides its technical advantages, the principle of the legality of crime and punishment flows from a conception of justice whose value is absolute. It would be unfair for an individual to be penalized for acts whose illegality was unknown to him at the moment of their commission. And that is why we repudiate as simplistic and arbitrary the proposition that this principle is a rule of domestic law that does not apply in the context of international relations. But as to the criminal character of wars of aggression, of the nature and degree of the punishment incurred for such crimes, it would be paradoxical to assert, as Professor Jahreiss does, that the accused of Nuremberg were uninformed criminals. What guided Hitler and his henchmen, what explains their criminal perseverance, is not the hope that, even if conquered and arrested, they would be forgiven; it is the conviction that they were the strongest. In the absence of a formal definition of wars of aggression, the International Military Tribunal has considered the state of mind and the premeditation of the accused. It is after a *psychological* analysis of these elements that they were condemned as aggressors:[30]

'One must remember,' says the Tribunal,[31] 'that the maxim *nullum crimen sine lege* does not limit the sovereignty of states; it merely formulates a generally followed rule. It is wrong to present as unjust the punishment inflicted on those who, in contempt for solemn commitments and treaties have, without prior

---

trahison, et la sanction pénale applicable à ceux qui en étaient convaincus. Le tribunal militaire international, institué par la Charte du 8 Août 1945, est de même compétent pour déterminer les peines applicables aux grands criminels de guerre.'

[30] 'Préméditation et préparation, est-il dit dans le jugement (*Trial of Major War Criminals*, vol. I, Judgment, p. 236), voilà les éléments essentiels de la guerre. Suivant l'avis du tribunal, la guerre d'agression est un crime international... Le premier chef d'accusation vise le plan concerté ou complot. Le second chef d'accusation vise la préparation et la conduite de la guerre. A l'appui de ces deux chefs d'accusation les mêmes documents ont été produits. Nous traiterons simultanément de l'un et de l'autre.' This psychological point of view has inspired the tribunal regarding its opinion on the preventive war. The latter can only be justified in the absence of premeditation and preparation. Concerning the German attack on Denmark and Norway, opening to a potential occupation of the UK, the Tribunal holds the following: 'Il y a lieu de rappeler qu'une action preventive en territoire étranger ne se justifie que dans le cas "d'une nécessité pressante et urgente" de défense, qui ne permet ni de choisir les moyens, ni de délibérer.' (Caroline Case, *Moore's Digest of International Law*, II, 412); *Trial of Major War Criminals*, Judgment, p. 217.

[31] *Trial of Major War Criminals*, vol. I, Judgment, p. 231.

warning, assaulted a neighbouring state. In such cases, the aggressor knows the odious character of his action. The conscience of the world, quite far from being offended if he is punished, would be shocked if he was not. Considering the positions that they occupied in the government of the Reich, the accused (or at least some of them) were familiar with the treaties, signed by Germany, which prohibited the resort to war to settle international disputes. They knew that wars of aggression were outlawed by most of the states of the world, including Germany itself; it was in full awareness of the situation that they violated international law when they deliberately followed their aggressive intentions with their plans for invasion.'

And, further on:[32]

'In interpreting the Pact, one must consider that, at the present time, international law is not the work of a legislative body common to the states. Its principles, such as the Pact of Paris, result from agreements that deal with things other than administrative or procedural matters. Independently of the treaties, the laws of war flow from ways and customs progressively and universally recognized, from the doctrine of jurists, from the jurisprudence of military tribunals. This law is not immutable; it is constantly adapted to the needs of a changing world. Often, treaties merely express and specify the principles of law already in force.'

This reasoning applies to 'crimes against peace'. Does it also apply to the charges relating to war crimes and crimes against humanity? This we must now examine.

Chapter II
War Crimes and Crimes Against Humanity

The indictment deals with war crimes and crimes against humanity under two different counts (the third and fourth).

The charge of 'war crimes' is a traditional one. It was quite common, even before the conclusion of The Hague agreements, that officers or soldiers from the enemy side who would transgress the rules of war could be brought before the military jurisdiction of the state that has captured them. This practice was based on both formal instructions laid out by some governments for their armed forces and codes of military justice.

By contrast, the concept of 'crimes against humanity' is a new one. It had probably been conceptualized by some authors for a certain time; but only with the Nuremberg trial did this notion enter into judicial practice.

There is no hermetic barrier between the two categories. Their interrelationship is the result of the provisions of the Charter. This is not difficult to explain.

---

[32] *Trial of Major War Criminals*, vol. I, Judgment, p. 233.

Most war crimes, such as the murder of hostages or prisoners, or mutilations, etc., hurts human sensitivity. In addition, up to now, it is only in the context of an armed conflict or in relation to some hostilities that crimes have been regarded as crimes against humanity.

That is why the distinction between crimes against humanity and war crimes, as well as the respective scope of the two notions are very difficult to delineate or differentiate. This question may have been the one that has embarrassed the International Military Tribunal the most, and without much benefit to be drawn from it, we believe.

We can only achieve some degree of clarity as regard these two concepts by studying them consecutively in their genesis and legal foundation. From this analysis, we will be able to identify the particular issue—*de lege ferenda*—which is raised by the concept of crimes against humanity.

I

The first category of crimes is historically linked to the full development of traditional public international laws. It existed before the creation of a system of collective security; it actually dates back to the time when war was perceived as a necessary and legitimate means of settling international disputes. Confronted with the technical changes that improved means of warfare, the idea was to try to limit the consequences of hostilities for civilians. From there ensued a series of texts among which the most famous are The Rules of Laws and Customs of Land Warfare annexed to the two Hague Conventions of 1899 and 1907. This series of texts contained an older text in which medical issues were dealt with (Geneva Convention of 22 August 1864 for the improvement of the protection of wounded and the sick in the armies in campaign, first amended in 1906 and then in 1929), and was later developed in the context of conventions applicable to prisoners of wars (27 July 1929) and conventions related to the war at sea (Washington Treaty, 6 February 1922; London Treaty, 22 April 1930).[33] It is also important to mention, because of its doctrinal authority, the Oxford Manual written in 1880 by the Institute of International Law. The obligations emerging from these agreements would be illusory if their violations were to go unpunished.[34]

---

[33] A comprehensive list of texts governing the rules of land warfare may be found in the article by M. Rey, 'Violations du Droit International' (*Revue Générale du Droit International Public*, 1941–45, vol. II, p. 5). See also Paoli, previously cited, p. 142 and following, for rules on sea warfare and the drafts on the codification of the laws and customs of war.

[34] Several governments have decided to establish sanctions. The 1863 Instructions for the Governments of Armies of the United States in the Field anounced during the war of secession lay down the duty to sanction pillage committed by troops (Art. 47). Article 71 reads as follows: 'Whoever intentionally inflicts additional wounds on an enemy already wholly disabled, or kills such an enemy, or who orders or encourages soldiers to do so, shall suffer death, if duly convicted, whether he belongs to the Army of the United States, or is an enemy captured after having committed his misdeed.' The German Manual on warfare published by the staff of the German army in

The Statute of the International Military Tribunal provides the following list of war crimes:

Art 6b—War Crimes: namely, violations of the laws or customs of war. Such violations shall include, but not be limited to, murder, ill-treatment or deportation to slave labour or for any other purpose of civilian population of or in occupied territory, murder or ill-treatment of prisoners of war or persons on the seas, killing of hostages, plunder of public or private property, wanton destruction of cities, towns, or villages, or devastation not justified by military necessity.[35]

This list is purely enunciative, as the wording of the article makes clear. Other lists—both at the international and national levels—have been more comprehensive in that the conventional provisions, notably those of The Hague agreements, have been coordinated with the relevant provisions of criminal codes and codes of military justice.[36] Several definitions of war crimes have been suggested.[37] Ultimately, it would seem that the following is agreed upon:

War crimes may be committed by civilians or combatants; but to qualify they must be related to the hostilities and must contain an international element. Thus, physical abuses committed by a government against its own citizens even in time of a conflict

1902 and translated in French under the title *Les Lois de la Guerre Continentale* by Carpentier, contains similar prohibitions and sanctions. In 1906, during the revision of the Geneva Convention (1864), a 28th Article was added (which became Article 29 in the 27 July 1929 Convention) by which signatory governments committed themselves to adopting criminal provisions punishing violations of the Geneva Convention in their national legislation. This provision was the result of a resolution adopted in Cambridge on 12 August 1895 by the Institute of International Law. Article 3 of the 6 February 1922 Washington Treaty related to submarine warfare provides that every individual, working for any power, acting or not under the order of a superior officer, who violates the rules would be treated as having violated the rules of war and could be judged and punished as if he had committed an act of piracy: 'Il pourra être mis en jugement devant les autorités civiles et militaries de toute puissance dans le resort de l'autorité de laquelle il sera trouvé.' (Rey, p. 94.)

[35] See IMT Statute, 8 August 1945.
[36] This work was prepared by a commission nominated by the Conference on the preliminaries of peace on 25 January 1919 in order to study responsibilities in time of warfare. The work of this commission, published in 1930, has facilitated the work of the UN Commission for War Crimes (headquarters in London). This Commission was publicly nominated by the English Chancellor and M. Roosevelt on 7 October 1942. It established a table on the offences committed by the authorities and troops of the central empires and their allies in violation of the laws and customs of war and the laws of humanity. An enumeration of the war crimes and crimes against humanity compared with Article 6 of the Statute is presented by M. Paoli (p. 144 and following).
[37] These definitions are reported by Rey (p. 89 and following). The narrowest seems to be the one presented by Sir Cecil Hurst, former vice-president of the Permanent Court of International Justice: 'un acte commis en temps de guerre en violation des règles de la guerre, écrites ou universellement admises'; the broadest and the most recent is the one by the UN Commission for War Crimes, according to which the charges for war crimes can correspond to three categories of offences: (1) Atrocities or crimes against persons or properties which constitute violations of international law, including the laws, rules and customs of war on land and on sea. (2) Atrocities and aggressions committed since 1933, including racial or religious atrocities and persecutions. (3) The invasion of other countries and the initiation of aggressive wars in violation of international law or treaties. This definition would include the concept of war crimes, crimes against humanity, and crimes against peace.

do not amount to war crimes. The breach of certain duties incumbent upon individuals towards their state such as acts of treason and other offences against the external security (Article 75 and following of the penal code) are not considered as war crimes either. The international responsibility of the *Quislings*, i.e. nationals who were accomplices of war crimes attributable to foreign leaders present particular problems that will not be discussed here.'[38]

The legal foundation of war crimes was at the heart of a long discussion at the *Société Générale des Prisons* in 1915.[39] In the midst of the silence left by The Hague agreements (they only provide for civil damages by the state itself), the rapporteurs Mr Renault and Mr Garçon argued that this foundation laid in the criminal law common to all States. It is indeed easy to notice that most violations of the laws and customs of war are also violations of applicable criminal law or codes of military justice. In several instances, tables have been drawn up to underline the parallel. If the similarity is not complete, it is possible to ensure their coherence as was done in the French law of 28 August 1944 on the repression of war crimes. Forced labour and civilian deportation, for instance, are associated with the crime of sequestration (Article 341 and following of the criminal code); the imposition of collective fines is associated with pillage (Article 221 and following). Criminal law, indeed positive criminal law, thus lays down the basis for repression; international law being used only to delineate its reach.

This explanation, whose origin goes back to Mr Garçon and Mr Renault, is generally accepted;[40] and we believe it to be exact. It is true that a new theory has criticized it for misrepresenting the autonomy and primacy of public international law. According to this theory, public international law contains its own jurisdictional and substantive rules, its own regime of sanctions, and it is only in its name that war crimes are being punished.[41] But this theory, as the thesis

---

[38] See the British response to the 13 January 1942 St. James Declaration, 6 August 1942.

[39] *Revue Pénitentiaire et de Droit Pénal*, 1915, p. 448 and following; 1916, p. 13, 107 et al. See also Renault, 'De l'Application du Droit Pénal aux Faits de Guerre' (*Journal du Droit International Privé*, 1915, p. 316).

[40] See notably Herzog, 'Les Principes Juridiques de la Répression des Crimes de Guerre' (*Revue Pénale Suisse*, 1946, p. 284): 'Dans l'ordre juridique interne et pour le temps de paix, écrit Paoli (p. 135), ces droits (les droits fondamentaux de l'homme) ont tous été sanctionnés depuis longtemps, sans distinction entre belligérants et non-belligérants, par la loi pénale, et cette protection nous paraît tellement naturelle que nous voyons en elle une sorte de principe supra-constitutionnel. Mais en temps de guerre, certains de ces droits, ceux à la vie et à la liberté, subissent dans la personne du belligérant une éclipse partielle ou temporaire. Il en subsiste cependant toujours un minimum inviolable, et ils tendent à se reconstituer intégralement dès que prennent fin certaines circonstances. Le non-belligérant a seulement droit à une protection plus complète que le belligérant. La loi de la guerre vient donc limiter les droits de l'un et de l'autre, ne leur en laissant qu'un minimum, qui n'est pas le même chez tous les deux et ne conservant, par conséquent, comme intangible qu'une partie de l'ordre juridique interne.' This is what M.Paoli calls 'le minimum d'ordre juridique international local.'

[41] P. De Lapradelle, cited earlier. For this author, presenting war crimes as common crimes amounts to disregarding the inherent nature of the laws of war. 'Loin de constituer des règles permissives, justificatives de l'infraction de droit commun, celles-ci forment autant de règles prohibitives, constitutives d'infractions de droit international, sauf exceptions expréssement prévues

that international relations are unrelated to the principle of legality of crimes and punishments, seems to be disconnected from reality.[42]

In the eyes of the supporters of the 'monist' theory of international law, asserting the primacy of international law over constitutional laws,[43] the competence of local judges and the applicability of domestic criminal law may be interpreted as a delegation of *jus gentium* as may be exemplified in a number of conventions. For instance, Article 21 of The Hague Convention X (10 October 1907) refers to the principles of domestic law for the punishment of individual acts of pillage or ill-treatment towards the wounded or sick at sea, in order to adapt the principle of the Geneva Convention to maritime warfare. But the Tribunal rather relied upon the 'dualist' theory—putting international and national law on equal footing[44] when it asserted its jurisdiction by reference to the principle of territoriality:

The state signatories have created this Tribunal, determined what law is applicable and adopted adequate rules of procedure. By doing so the signatories have done collectively what they could have done individually. The ability to apply the law through the establishment of special tribunals is a prerogative that is common to all states.[45]

par les conventions.' See also Malézieux on that theory, 'Le Statut International des Criminels de Guerre' (*Revue Générale de Droit International Public*, 1941–45, vol. II, p. 170 et al.)

[42] It is contrary to positive law. Notably the French Ordinance of 28 August 1944 curbs 'conformément aux lois françaises en vigueur…les nationaux ennemis ou agents non français au service de l'administration ou des intérêts ennemis coupables de crimes ou de délits…' An enumeration of offences set out by the French penal code, and an assimilation of certain facts to offences follow (Art. 2); see for the application: Permanent Military Cassation Tribunal of Paris, 13 September 1945, Szabados, JCP 1945, II, 2880 and the note signed PEC; 21 September 1945, Pousel, *Gazette du Palais*, 2 November 1945. According to the report related to this ordinance, 'un crime de guerre est un crime de droit commun qui tombera sous le coup des lois pénales françaises, soit qu'il ait été commis en Allemagne ou ailleurs contre des ressortissants français ou des apatrides résident en France dès 1940'. (Rey, p. 98) We saw before and we will see later that different agreements give national criminal law the power to punish violations of the laws and customs of war. Article 84 of the 1880 Oxford Manual provides that the 'Offenders against the laws of war are liable to the punishments specified in the penal law…' The 1 November 1943 Moscow Declaration referred to earlier provides that the '[war criminals] will be sent back to the countries in which their abominable deeds were done in order that they may be judged and punished according to the Laws of these liberated countries […]'.

[43] Kelsen, 'Les rapports de Système entre le Droit Interne et et Droit International Public' (*Recueil de Cours de l'Académie de Droit International de la Haye*, vol. 14, 1926, pp. 279–80). A. Verdross, Le Fondement de Droit International (same *Recueil*, vol. 16, 1927, p. 287 and following).

[44] See Triepel, 'Les Rapports entre le Droit Interne et le Droit International' (*Recueil de Cours*, vol. 1, 1923, p. 84); H. Donnedieu de Vabres, 'La Cour Pénale Internationale pour la Répression du Terrorisme devant la Constitution Belge', abstract from *La Revue de Droit Pénal et de Criminologie* (October 1938, p. 11).

[45] *Trial of Major War Criminals*, vol. 1, Judgment, p. 230. There is, nevertheless, a confusion regarding the legal basis of the parallel which the Tribunal later draws between the criminal sanction set out in the Briand–Kellog Pact and the criminal sanction laid out in The Hague Agreements (*Trial of Major War Criminals*, p. 232): 'The Hague Convention of 1907 prohibited resort to certain methods of waging war. These included the inhumane treatment of prisoners, the employment of poisoned weapons, the improper use of flags of truce, and similar matters. Many of these prohibitions had been enforced long before the date of the Convention; but since 1907 they have certainly been crimes, punishable as offences against the laws of war; yet The Hague Convention nowhere designates such practices as criminal, nor is any sentence prescribed, nor any mention made of a court to try and punish offenders. For many years past, however, military tribunals

The Tribunal, without renouncing the universalist nature of its mission, has carefully avoided breaking away completely with the firm grounds of positive law. When sanctioning war crimes, it thus adopts solutions which are consonant with the individual rights of the accused:

a) It admits that the jurisdiction of the tribunals of the territorial State or that of the injured state is concurrent with the jurisdiction of military tribunals which are competent to judge the criminals. The competence of the first is at least, equal to the second;[46]

b) It notes that the list of war crimes shall go neither beyond the prohibitive provisions of customary international law and international law, nor beyond the provisions of the applicable criminal codes: *nullum crimen, nulla poena sine lege*;

c) It finally underlines that the only applicable sanctions are those provided by the applicable criminal codes, penal codes and codes of military law.

It is true however, that these principles only apply with some important restrictions to those known as 'war criminals':

1. In addition to the territorial jurisdiction of the International Military Tribunal, it has a universal competence: the States which set up the tribunal did not only represent the interest of the victorious nations but also those of the international community at large. In a way, those States are custodians acting on behalf of the international community.

2. The accused have not personally committed the underlying conduct constitutive of war crimes. They are the instigators and promoters of those crimes understood in a broad sense. The notion of 'moral author' ('auteur moral') which is not unknown to the new criminal law[47] here takes all its meaning.

3. It follows from the above that the principle of legality of crimes and punishments is to be interpreted with some flexibility as regards the perpetrator of such crimes. The sanction is left to a large extent to the discretion of the Tribunal.

have tried and punished individuals guilty of violating the rules of land warfare laid down by this Convention. In the opinion of the Tribunal, those who wage aggressive war are doing that which is equally illegal, and of much greater moment than a breach of one of the rules of The Hague Convention.' The analogy is wrong, and the reasoning a fortiori without value because the basis for the punishment of war crimes—already existing before 1907—lies in common criminal law, while this is not the case for the crime against peace (see, for instance, Rouen, 16 June 1871; Crim, 15 December 1871, S 72.1.44).

[46] Rey, p. 101: 'Il faut poser en principe que la compétence des tribunaux du pays occupé est la règle, et la compétence des tribunaux de l'armée d'occupation l'exception. Ces derniers ne doivent exercer leur juridiction que dans la limite où son application est nécessaire, c'est-à-dire pour garantir la discipline et la sécurité de l'armée : hors de ces limites, la règle reprend ses droits, ce qui est le cas pour les crimes de droit commun commis par des membres de l'armée d'occupation, et que celle-ci n'a pas poursuivis.'

[47] H. Donnedieu de Vabres, *Traité de Droit Criminel et de Législation Pénale Comparée*, 3rd edn, Sirye, 1947, vol. 438, p. 254; vol. 452, p. 263; vol. 481, p. 283.

It would, nevertheless, be dangerous to completely disregard the principles of which the above are derogations. The exceptional nature of these derogations is to be kept in mind when examining the work of the tribunal, in particular the following three delicate issues:

A. The first issue, which is of general importance, concerns the applicability of the above-mentioned Hague Regulations to Germany following the war.

Article 2 of the 1907 Convention contains a 'general participation' clause: 'The provisions contained in the Regulations referred to in Article 1, as well as in the present Convention, do not apply except between Contracting powers, and then only if all the belligerents are parties to the Convention.'[48] This requirement would not be satisfied. For instance, Italy signed the 1907 Convention but never ratified it. This exigency would not be satisfied also in relation to the USSR.[49]

Several responses were put forward to answer this objection.

The rules provided by the 1899 Convention, later replaced by the 1907 Convention and to which the current belligerents are parties, remain applicable.[50] And there are only minor differences between the text of the regulations annexed to the 1899 Convention and the text of the 1907 Rules.[51]

We have already pointed to a common provision in the preambles of the 1899 and 1907 Conventions. It follows from it that, in cases not covered by the Convention until a more comprehensive Convention on the laws of war is adopted, 'the inhabitants and the belligerents remain under the protection and the rule of the principles of the law of nations, as they result from the usages established among civilized peoples, from the laws of humanity, and the dictates of the public conscience'.

The idea contained in this provision is applied in the judgment. It reinforces the idea closely related to the customary formation of the *jus gentium* that the precepts of this body of law, in including its penal consequences, are binding on

---

[48] 1907 Hague Convention

[49] R. Cartier, *Les Secrets de La Guerre Dévoilés par Nuremberg*, p. 280. In May 1941, according to Marshal Halder, Hitler told the generals: 'L'URSS n'a pas ratifié la Convention de La Haye. En conséquence, les violations du droit international par nos troupes doivent être excusées, à l'exception de celles qui constitueraient des atteintes aux lois civiles, comme le meurtre ou le viol.'

[50] Some authors claimed that the 1907 Convention abrogated the 1899 Convention, and thus that one could not rely upon the latter in case the former was inapplicable. Article 89 of the 27 July 1929 Convention on prisoners of war shows that this view is false: 'In the relations between Powers bound by the Hague Convention respecting the Laws and Customs of War on Land, whether it is a question of that of July 29, 1899, or that of October 18, 1907, and who participate in the present Convention, this latter shall complete Chapter 11 of the Regulations annexed to the said Hague Conventions.' (Rey, p. 8.)

[51] On the other hand, the 1868 Declaration of St Petersburg is confirmed by Article 23 of The Hague Rules; Article 21 of the same Rules refer to the Geneva Convention for the Wounded and Sick; the 1929 Convention on prisoners of war is meant to supplement chapter II of the Rules on the issue. In sum, it is The Hague Convention that sets out the applicable rules for land warfare. (Rey, p. 9.)

a state, regardless of the fact that this state is a party to the treaty from which that rule has grown.

'The rules of land warfare expressed in the Convention undoubtedly represented an advance over existing international law at the time of their adoption. But the convention expressly stated that it was an attempt "to revise the general laws and customs of war", which it thus recognized to be then existing, but by 1939 these rules laid down in the Convention were recognized by all civilized nations, and were regarded as being declaratory of the laws and customs of war which are referred to in Article 6 (b) of the Charter.'[52]

Regarding the war of aggression, the Tribunal had already stated that: 'Ordinarily, the treaties do no more than to specify the principles of laws that are already in force.'[53]

B. The second issue was about submarine warfare. Admiral Doenitz was found to have ordered—by Order 154 of November 1939 and the Laconia Order of 17 September 1942—the commanders of submarines not to assist the crews of torpedoed ships, and maybe even in a silent way to destroy them.[54] These orders were in violation of the provisions related to the torpedoing of merchant ships of the Washington Treaty of 6 February 1922 and the London Treaty of 22 April 1930. Because this amounted to a case of homicide (whether it was committed by an act or an omission), a criminal punishment should not have raised any doubt.[55]

The defence of Admiral Doenitz argued that the progress in air warfare since the above provisions had been adopted exposed submarine crews assisting the shipwrecked to an almost certain death. This argument seems close to the reality. Many provisions of the 1922, 1930 and even 1936 agreements have proved inadequate in the present state of aerial and naval warfare and, in a sense, call for a revision of the texts in question. The argument presented by the defence of Admiral Doenitz relied upon the *pacta sunt servanda, rebus sic stantibus* principle.

We have already stated that the violations of an international agreement, even if repeated, shall not lead to the tacit abrogation of its prohibitions. The issue is different here. The question is whether or not the abrogation can follow technical changes that modify the conditions of application of a rule to a significant

---

[52] *Trial of Major War Criminals*, vol. I, Judgment, p. 267.

[53] Ibid., p. 233.

[54] 'L'amiral Doenitz, par un ordre du 1er janvier 1940, prescrivit aux commandants de sous-marins d'attaquer les navires sans avertissement, de ne pas recueillir les naufragés, mais de tirer sur eux. Cet ordre portait notamment: (Ne vous préoccupez pas des rescapés. Peu importent le temps et l'éloignement de la côte. Ne songez qu'à votre prochain succès. Il faut être durs dans cette guerre.) Un autre ordre, du 7 octobre 1943, enjoignait de couler les navires de sauvetage attachés aux convois.' (Rey, p. 27.)

[55] See p. 20 (French version); *American Journal of International Law*, 1922, Supplement p. 57. It is true that the 22 April 1930 London Treaty for the Limitation and Reduction of Naval Armaments took up the provisions of the Washington treaty related to submarines in its Article 22. The sanctions were removed from this article, likely due to the impossibility of their enforcement.

extent. We would be tempted to agree with this view, at least as far as criminal sanctions are concerned, taking into account the constant evolution of public international law. Facts, as much as laws, treaties, judgments, doctrines are among the factors that propel this evolution.[56] It is evidently a consideration which the International Military Tribunal took into account when mitigating the sentence imposed on Admiral Doenitz, referring in particular to certain practices of the British marines and the submarine war operations conducted by the US in the Pacific Ocean (testimony of the American Admiral Nimitz).

C. The third question is one that the Military Tribunal did not have to resolve, but which is likely to arise in the future and may offer certain practical insights concerning the judicial nature of the war crimes attributed to the accused in Nuremberg. Are these crimes political crimes or common crimes? The interest of this matter resides in the nature of the possible sanctions, as well as in the possibility or otherwise of extraditing the perpetrator of such a crime. The question is discussed in the well-known opinion delivered by Mr Larnaude and Mr de Lapradelle after the First World War concerning William II.[57]

There is no doubt that war crimes, considered from the perspective of their direct perpetrators, are common crimes. They are the expression of basic instincts, they are committed against ordinary criminal laws, and they cause prejudice to private interests. The same reasoning would prevail in relation to those accused if they could be seen as the accomplices of the former in the sense of having incited or ordered these crimes. But the charge of complicity had to be set aside here for the same reasons dismissed as when it was against William II in the context of the request for his extradition. The elements of liability for complicity, notably under Article 60 of the criminal code, are lacking. The accused in question had no knowledge of the nature of the crimes committed, no knowledge of the circumstances in which they were committed, nor of the identity of the victims. The criminal responsibility or liability of such participants points rather to the idea of mental perpetrators ('auteur moral') or even more appropriately to the idea of a separate offence.

This in turn raises issues about the official position of the agent, his motives, the protected interest... These elements led us to regard wars of aggression as a political offence. But this qualification could be dismissed in the case of major war

[56] See notably the observations of M. Paoli regarding changes in the laws of war on aerial bombings (p. 143): 'Ils apparaissaient à l'époque du traité de Versailles, écrit cet auteur, comme un crime de guerre, et en 1923, encore à la Haye, un projet unanimement accepté interdisait de recourir à eux comme moyens d'épouvante destines à contraindre un people à demander la paix. Peut-on méconnaître aujourd'hui, au seuil surtout de ce qu'on appelle l'âge atomique et au lendemain des premiers essais qui furent faits dans la guerre du Pacifique de la bombe du même nom, que les lois de la guerre qui les prohibaient semblent avoir été emportées par les faits? Sans doute ceux-ci sont-il s si gros de menace pour le monde qu'il devra revenir en arrière dans la voie de l'interdiction. Mais une réglementation nouvelle s'impose.' Such a new regulation is equally justified as regard submarine warfare. See article by M. P. de Leyrat in Cahiers du Monde Nouveau, vol. II, No 5.

[57] *Journal du Droit International Privé*, 1919, p. 137 and following.

criminals where the specific elements of complicity would be established. It could also be set aside where there is proof of knowledge of and acquiescence to odious practices which would suggest a state of mind that is incompatible with the relative indulgence that political offenders enjoy. Under both customary and domestic law, the qualification and the regime applicable to 'complex' crimes depends on this factor. This goes a long way to explain the heavy sentences imposed upon defendants at Nuremberg. The same considerations will arise, with even greater force, in relation to crimes against humanity.

II

Crimes against humanity are very different from war crimes, if not by reason of their substance, at least by reason of their origin and the legal basis that underlies the charge.

This crime stems from the general indignation aroused by the excesses of racism. We realized that the brutalities perpetrated by the SA and SS, the tortures of the Gestapo, the horrors of the concentration camps discovered after the entrance of the Allied armies into Germany[58] were the mere continuation of a policy against the German opponents of the Nazi regime, which held sway since the rise to power of the Nazi Party. Was not the elimination of the Jews, communists and socio-democrats a way to shatter the potential partisans of a peace policy? Was not it a prelude to the war of aggression? Did not this community of goals justify an extension of the prosecution to acts revolting humanity, even if these were anterior to the war, even if, committed later among Germans and within Germany, they took place outside of the hostilities? Thus understood, the repression of such crimes, beyond the framework of states' interests, would aim at protecting human values; and it would become universal, not simply international.

There were precedents which went in the same direction. Grotius,[59] after Vitoria and Suarez, declared a war against a monarch whose subjects ate human flesh or openly practised impiety as just. Modern times provide a series of diplomatic or military interventions, so called 'humanitarian' interventions that are intended to protect persecuted groups such as, for instance, the Armenian people.[60] The

---

[58] See notably on the issue the discussion initiated by M. Aldermann, Prosecutor for the US, *Trials of Great War Criminals*, vol. III, Debates, p. 471 and following.

[59] Grotius wrote (*De Jure Belli ac Pacis*, vol. II, ch. XX,XI,1): 'Il faut savoir encore que les Rois et en général tous les Souverains ont le droit de punir, non seulement les injures faites à eux et à leurs sujets, mais encore celles qui ne les regardent point en particulier, lorsqu'elles renferment une violation énorme du droit de la nature ou celui des gens, envers qui que ce soit.'

[60] These interventions are not solely governmental. Indeed after a series of executions of Russian partisans of the previous regime, the president of the International Committee of the Red Cross, Gustave Ador, addressed a declaration to the USSR (27 June 1927): 'C'est avec une profonde émotion que le Comité international de la Croix Rouge a pris connaissance des nouvelles venues de Russie et relatives à des executions en masses. Le Comité se réfère aux décisions des conférences internationales de la Croix Rouge, qui condamnent les représailles et réclament la protection des prisonniers et otages, et il fait appel au sentiment de la responsabilité morale des autorités

protection of minorities, as provided by the Treaty of Versailles, is motivated by similar concerns.[61] An International Declaration of the Rights of the Man and of Citizen was formulated in 1929 by the Institute of International Law. A similar declaration was made in San Francisco on 26 June 1945. Signatories stated that they were 'determined to reaffirm their faith in fundamental rights' of human beings; and that natural law should thus be the subject of international criminal sanctions.

This view is not unfamiliar to the authors of the Charter, as they included in the jurisdiction of the International Military Tribunal crimes against humanity, which consist of: (Article 6c) 'murder, extermination, enslavement, deportation, and other inhumane acts committed against any civilian population, before or during the war,[62] or persecutions on political, racial, or religious grounds in execution of or in connection with any crime within the jurisdiction of the Tribunal, whether or not in violation of domestic law of the country where perpetrated.'

If some elements of this enumeration are similar to the list of war crimes, it in fact goes beyond it. One distinguishing factor concerns the elasticity of certain expressions such as *enslavement* and *persecution*. It also expressly encompasses acts that are not punishable under ordinary criminal law. As for the acts which would qualify as both war crimes and crimes against humanity, the latter is designed to prevail when the acts were committed before the war or during the war, if they were committed within the jurisdiction of German sovereignty.

It is noteworthy that when drawing up the jurisdiction of the International Military Tribunal for these crimes, the authors of the Charter demonstrated the same sort of timidity that the representatives of the US government in 1919, Mr Lansing and Mr Brown Scott, had shown in 1919.[63] The jurisdiction of the Tribunal over crimes against humanity is not introduced in full independence;

soviétiques à l'égard de toute l'humanité. Le Comité prie instamment les autorités soviétiques de renoncer à des mesures qui constituent une offense à la raison.' This text comes from a note by the Telegraphic Office of the Wolf Agency. H. Kraus, 'La Morale Internationale' (*Recueil de Cours de l'Académie internationale de La Haye*, 1927, vol. 16, p. 483).

[61] The Treaty on the Protection of Minorities signed with Poland, which became a prototype text for this kind of agreement, contains a provision ensuring the equal protection of inhabitants. Article 2 reads 'le Gouvernement Polonais s'engage à accorder à tous les habitants pleine et entière protection de leur vie et de leur liberté sans distinction de naissance, de nationalité, de langage, de race, de religion'.

[62] An agreement concluded on 6 October 1945, has substituted a comma to a semi-colon firstly chosen in the French and English versions of the text. The comma appeared to be limiting the scope of the requirement of a link with 'any crime within the jurisdiction of the Tribunal' to 'persecutions' and the other prohibitions that followed in the text.

[63] In 1919, Mr Robert Lansing and Mr James Brown Scott blamed the Commission nominated by the Preliminary Peace Conference to study the responsibilities of the war for having exceeded its mandate in founding its responsibilities not only on the laws and customs of war but also on the laws of humanity. 'Les lois et les coutumes de guerre, écrivaient-ils sont un critérium certain que l'on peut trouver dans les livres qui font autorité et dans l'expérience pratique des Nations. Les lois et principes d'humanité varient avec les individus.' (*La Documentation Internationale... Responsabilités*, p. 538).

it is recognized only insofar as it is sufficiently connected with those crimes and the violations which come under the *normal* jurisdiction of the tribunal; and this connectivity in fact conditions the punishment.

And yet, the law of crimes against humanity has developed since the time of the Nuremberg trial to an extent that could hardly have been foreseen in view of its modest beginnings. The writings of two distinguished criminal lawyers, Mr Aroneanu[64] and Mr Lemkin,[65] the debates initiated within the French national movement for the Judiciary in Paris in October 1946, and then at the international Conference for the unification of criminal law in July 1947, and the votes at the end of the Conference gave a boost to this theory by reinvigorating it through the sort of universalism that animated its founders: Vitoria, Suarez, and Grotius. Though more of the new conceptions[66] may seem somewhat woolly, it is necessary to deal with them quite carefully to underline the scope of the problem which the judges at Nuremberg had to solve, and also to explain the solution they opted for.

The recent doctrine takes the opposite view of what is said in the Charter. According to that view, crimes against humanity constitute a genre, of which war crimes only represent one sort. The leitmotiv of such a charge—crimes against humanity—is to punish those who, by fanaticism, oppress a national, racial, religious or political minority. It is important to curb this oppression and guarantee respect for fundamental human rights; and it is up to the international community, which in a way stands outside and above local interests and passions, to undertake such a task. The international community will fulfil this mission in time of peace and in time of war; and war crimes are nothing other than crimes against humanity adapted to the circumstances particular to hostilities. Taking into account the various suggested definitions which are being considered here, the theory of crimes against humanity allows for the following conclusions:

1. A crime against humanity is a common crime, not only because of the motives underlying the crime and the injured interests but also because of the odious means (murder, homicide, torture) used to carry them out. From these, two consequences ensue, namely, that the perpetrators of crimes against humanity are subject to extradition and are susceptible to be subject to ordinary sentences;[67]

---

[64] Aroneanu, 'Le Crime Contre l'Humanité' (*Nouvelle Revue de Droit International Privé*, 1946, vol. 26).

[65] Lemkin, 'Le Crime de Génocide' (*Revue de Droit International*, 1946, p. 213 and following).

[66] This obscurity is apparent in the terminology itself. The word 'humanity' has a double meaning. Crimes against humanity can mean crimes against humankind or crimes committed in violation of human sentiments (benevolence, charity). The first meaning is the most appropriate, putting crimes against humanity among the violations of international law. The second meaning comes from the German language: 'humanity' in German corresponds to 'Menschlichkeit' (human sentiment), not 'Menschheit' (humankind). The term 'genocide' is a neologism formed of a Greek word and a Latin word.

[67] A. Boissarie, 'La Répression des Crimes Nazis Contre l'Humanité...Rapport Général au congrès international du Mouvement National Judiciaire' (*Revue Internationale de Droit Pénal*, Sirey, 1947, p. 11).

2. Crimes against humanity reach beyond the national framework, damage interests common to the whole of humanity, outside statist forms, and constitute a crime under *jus gentium* just like the slave-trade of women and children, drug trafficking, forgery, and terrorism. This explains that the perpetrator of such a crime would be subject to the principal jurisdiction of the judge of the location of the arrest (*judex deprehensionis*).

3. However, because the punishment of such crimes necessitate a concerted effort of states; it is preferable that the perpetrators of such offences be handed over to an international criminal jurisdiction.

The fundamental characteristics are thus identified, but many other aspects remain open to debate:

1. Are *racial groups* identified by the precedents of the 1939–45 war the only groups criminally protected, as appear to be concerned by the notion of 'genocide'?[68] Or is the protection also applicable to social, political, ethnic, and linguistic minorities?

2. Is the material element of the offence an attack against the life, the health, or the physical integrity of the person (*génocide physique*)?[69] Would it be sufficient to adopt measures intended to hinder the development of the group through incitement to abortions, sterilizations... (*génocide biologique*) or to impoverish the group by the forced removal of its leaders, the prohibition of their national language (*génocide culturel*)?

3. Is liability for such a crime to be limited to the leaders who initiated the collective measures, or tolerated them,[70] or will it be extended to ordinary individuals who have committed the crimes charged with or without the connivance of the government?[71]

---

[68] R. Borel, 'Le Crime de Génocide, Principe Nouveau de Droit International' (*Le Monde*, 5 December 1945). According to M. Paoli (p. 152 and following), 'la doctrine du génocide permet de corriger, au moins dans une certaine mesure, l'iniquité à laquelle conduit la stricte application du Règlement de La Haye aux francs tireurs et aux faits de résistance à l'occupant... Elle met tout citoyen des pays occupés en état de légitime défense en face des groupes ou organisations de caractère criminel et répute délictueux tous les actes accomplis par les membres de ces groupements.'

[69] The temporary limitation of the physical 'genocide' charge is taken into consideration in the following definition endorsed by the 8th International Conference for the Unification of Criminal Law (Brussels, July 1947): 'Constitue un crime contre l'humanité et doit être réprimé en tant qu'assassinat tout homicide ou acte de nature à entrainer la mort, commis en temps de guerre comme en temps de paix à l'encontre d'individus ou de groupes humains, en raison de leur race, de leur nationalité, de leur religion ou de leurs opinions.'

[70] The limitation of the crime to those in a position of leadership comes from the definition advocated by M. Aroneanu: 'Le crime contre l'humanité est un crime international de droit commun par lequel un Etat se rend coupable d'atteinte à titre racial, national, politique ou religieux, à la liberté, aux droits ou à la vie d'une personne ou d'un groupe de personnes innocents à toute infraction ou, en cas d'infraction, d'atteinte dépassant la peine prévue.'

[71] The broader definition, which would include the acts committed by ordinary individuals, was adopted by the French National Movement for the Judiciary (Paris, 24–27 October 1946): 'Sont coupables de crimes contre l'humanité et sont punissables comme tells ceux qui exterminent

We will particularly try to avoid these controversies because the purpose of the perpetrator and his motives, are—unusually—elements of the crime, it is thus unavoidable that racial, national and social prejudices come to the fore. In a way, the theory of crimes against humanity leaves the door wide open to subjectivism.

Turning to practical considerations, one distinction must be made:

a) The idea that such a crime should apply to any individual in the criminal code of a state seems dangerous and a bit premature. Would it also constitute the crime of homicide or aggravated assault? The crime of genocide would be redundant with the crimes recognized under domestic law, and would have an unfortunate restricting effect on its scope.[72] Does it amount to varying expressions of racist or social fanaticism that the provisions of ordinary law could not cover? The danger is to open the door to prosecutions that will give rise to hatred, resentment, and blackmailing and would thus stir up, through the stains of a choice that will not convey unanimity, the passions we are trying to extinguish.

b) The fact that the implication of governments responsible for criminal activity or inertia gives rise to some discomfort should not be concealed. It is to be feared that the threat against great powers remains a matter of pure form, while 'crimes against humanity' serve as a pretext to interfere with the national affairs of small states—a kind of interference which the United Nations Charter has prohibited. Such a proposition—if it were to be accepted—would be contrary to any kind of development in the field of inter-state criminal law. The prosecution of leaders responsible for grave violations of fundamental human rights fills a gap in existing law. It also responds to a feeling that is as strong and as widespread as the feeling against wars of aggression. They also accord with the factual circumstances and the logical necessities that, going back to the time of Grotius, link together the two sets of charges.[73]

We wanted to specify, by limiting them, the perspectives open—*de lege ferenda*—to the theory of crimes against humanity. It is clear that judges at Nuremberg had to take into account an additional consideration concerning the application of the theory, namely, the principle of legality of crime and punishment. The link between the relevant underlying conduct with other crimes falling under the jurisdiction of the tribunal is not enough to justify the prosecution of such conduct when it does not violate 'the laws applicable in the state where they were committed'. Doing so would banish from the realm of international relations,

ou persécutent un individu ou un groupe d'individus en raison de leur nationalité, de leur race, de leur religion ou de leurs opinions. Ces crimes seront punis même lorsqu'ils seront commis par des individus ou organisations agissant comme organes de l'Etat, ou avec l'encouragement ou la tolérance de l'Etat.'

[72] See Herzog, 'Les Principes de la Répression...' (*Revue Pénale Suisse*, 1946, p. 302: 'Ce n'est pas parce que des millions d'hommes sont morts dans les camps de concentration que leurs assassins cessent d'être des criminels de droit commun.'

[73] See above reference to Grotius and quotation earlier in this article.

both the spirit and the letter of the principle *nulla crimen, nulla poena sine lege*. In accordance with Article 6 of the Statute, the tribunal did not exclude the notion of 'crimes against humanity'; but it is instructive to explain the effort it made to minimize its consequences.

When it applied Article 6 of the Charter in relation to these crimes, which are linked from a jurisdictional point of view to crimes against peace and war crimes, the Tribunal took the view that such a link did not exist in relation to crimes committed before the war:

'To constitute crimes against humanity, the acts relied on before the outbreak of war must have been in execution of, or in connection with, any crime within the jurisdiction of the Tribunal. The Tribunal is of the opinion that revolting and horrible as many of these crimes were, it has not been satisfactorily proved that they were done in execution of, or in connection with, any such crime. The Tribunal therefore cannot make a general declaration that the acts before 1939 were crimes against humanity within the meaning of the Charter.'

As for the wartime period, the Tribunal gathered 'war crimes' and 'crimes against humanity' under the same heading for most of the accused, thus side-stepping a problematic distinction and, practically merging, the crimes against humanity into the 'war crimes' category. That is how, for instance, the Tribunal dealt with the criminal responsibility of von Neurath as regard the ill-treatments committed in Bohemia-Moravia where he had acted as Protector and where the law of war remained applicable since the Protectorate had been incorporated into the Reich.

It is only in relation to two of the accused that the category of 'crimes against humanity' was isolated, Streicher and Baldur, because the Prosecution had not charged either of them with war crimes. The Tribunal has, nevertheless, pointed out that the war crimes charge would have been justified for Streicher, who during the hostilities continued to call for the extermination of the Jews. 'Because Streicher was calling for the murder and extermination of the Jews in the East at the time when they were being massacred, his actions qualify as persecutions on political or racial grounds which constitute both a war crime under the Charter and a crime against humanity.'[74] As for Baldur von Schirach's criminal

[74] M. P. de Lapradelle, (p. 24 n. 1) observes that there is a material inaccuracy, and that if racial persecutions fall under the category of 'crimes against humanity', they are not considered as war crimes *under the Statute*. In making this comment, he forgets that the list of Article 6(b), as it is expressly stated, is not exhaustive. Nothing forbids to consider persecutions as a war crime as long as the circumstances of time and location are met and that criminal law provisions cover these facts. M. Paoli thus admits a similarity in nature between 'war crimes' and 'crimes against humanity' (p. 131): 'Il n'est pas douteux écrit-il que tous les crimes contre l'humanité constituent des crimes de guerre, lorsqu'ils ontété perpétrés pendant la guerre par l'occupant contre des populations civiles des territoires occupés, car tous sont compris parmi les violations des lois et coutumes de la guerre.' The author refers to murder and deportation as examples (Article 6(b) and 6(c)), and adds : 'Rien que ce texte ne fasse mention des persécutions pour des motifs politiques, raciaux ou religieux qu'à propos des crimes contre l'humanité, on peut en dire autant d'elles.' The wording of the judgment—correct or not—once again underlines the intention of the Tribunal to limit its competence to war crimes.

responsibility as the Gauleiter of Austria for the acts committed during the war, it was justified because the occupation of Austria had been carried out in conformity with a concerted plan of aggression, which constitutes a crime falling under the jurisdiction of the Tribunal pursuant to Article 6(c) of the Statute.

The category of crimes against humanity which had entered the Tribunal's jurisdiction through a small statutory door, evaporated in the judgment. Nowhere in the judgment can findings of inhumane acts be found which would be independent of the circumstances of the war. It is noteworthy that, in his opening statement, the French Prosecutor expressed the same reservation. The crimes 'against human condition' to which he referred and which included all violations of The Hague Regulations may not be equated with crimes against humanity. [75]

The charge of conspiracy will give rise to similar observations as pertains to the approach taken by the Tribunal.

Chapter III
The Issue of Conspiracy

Conspiracy is the subject of the first count of the indictment. This position reflects the prevailing importance given by the Prosecution to this crime. The Prosecution was attracted to the idea of presenting the nationalist-socialist epic as an enterprise whose primary goal was to engineer wars of aggression which led, indirectly, to the commission of war crimes and crimes against humanity. The indictment and the statements of the Prosecutors are built on this hypothesis.

This conception is noticeable not only in the Prosecution's arguments, but also through some telling details of form. The indictment, for example, does not endorse the common opinion and the popular view which insists on the overwhelming responsibility of one man of great power, Hitler, whilst others are relegated to the background; instead, it lays out a collective formula which is from the outset relatively surprising: 'They (the conspirators) led Germany to leave the League of Nations...; they told the world that they would respect the treaty of Versailles...; they caused a treaty to be entered into between Germany and Austria.'[76] Some critics argue that because the real culprits, Hitler, Himmler, and Goebbels, chose to take their own lives, the role of their accomplices and that of lesser players had to be overblown. Rudolf Hess was one of Hitler's 'ersatz', Kaltenbrunner one of Himmler's, and Fritzche one of Goebbel's. Similarly, when the trial of Krupp von Bohlen turned out to be impossible because of health issues, wasn't the appearance of his son suggested?

---

[75] The expression 'crimes against the human condition', in M. de Menthon's mind and according to the views later adopted by other members of the French Prosecution, refers less to offences against fundamental human rights [a view supported by M. Deschee-Maeker, p. 35] than to the encroachment of the sovereign rights of an occupied state, a violation of Article 43 of the 1907 Hague Convention IV (M. Paoli, p. 155 and following).

[76] *Trial of Major War Criminals*, vol. I, Indictment, p. 34 and following.

The legal roots of the charge of conspiracy (the 'complot' in French text) is to be found in British law. While in French law, the charge of conspiracy has a relatively narrow scope, being focused on the internal security of the state (Article 89 of the Penal Code), the English conspiracy has a broader scope of application. Any agreement aimed at committing an illegal act would be punishable as conspiracy, whether that act constitutes a crime, a misdemeanor or even an act which is contrary to the law and moral principles, though not necessarily sanctioned by a punishment.

According to the doctrine,[77] conspiracy is made of two elements: a meeting of minds (an agreement) and an accord as regard the means to achieve the common goal (common plan). It seems that in practice, however, the first element is sufficient to support criminal charges. The charge of conspiracy as a crime distinct from the one it intended to commit comes from the observation that the criminal enterprise is particularly dangerous when it is the result of the common efforts of several individuals. Such a charge then presents two aggravating circumstances: premeditation and collaboration. It thus calls for particular measures. The prosecution of that charge is a social necessity from which both the laws of continental Europe and of the United Kingdom have been inspired. But the technical means are different in those systems. Continental law, for example French law, captures the acts of a multitude of individuals under the label of complicity or accessory participation in relation to the crime they intend to commit. The notion of complicity does not require an active participation in the commission of the crimes; it can result from preparatory acts such as a provocation, orders or the supply of means (Article 60 of the Penal Code). In addition, 'collaboration' plays a role in certain crimes: it constitutes an aggravating factor, notably in case of theft (Article 381 of the Penal Code), rebellion (Article 210 and following of the Penal Code), mendacity (Article 276 and following), pillage (Article 440) and offence against public decency (Article 333). The English notion of conspiracy is narrower. In short, the British point of view is an *objective* one; it focuses upon the external indications of a concerted criminal resolution, and which, by reason of this concertation, disrupts the public order. The French point of view is a *subjective* one: a psychological or moral element connects separate conducts which aim at the same result, namely to the commission of a common crime.

The French conception is more consistent with modern doctrines which insist on the idea of individualized punishment. Admittedly, though, the British system has been gaining ground even in continental Europe. Legislation is ever more often adopted that criminalizes as a separate crime preparatory actions which take place before an irreparable injury has been committed.

The charge of conspiracy gives to the Hitlerian enterprise the cover of a romantic prestige that is not without seductive appeal. Indeed, it brings a pleasing intellectual coherence to successive episodes. It would be bold to assert that it is absolutely necessary to ensure justice. We already said that, if we accept the broad

---

[77] Kenny, *Esquisse du Droit Criminel Anglais*, Paris, 1921, p. 364 and following.

notion of complicity from French law, all of the aspects of such a criminal enterprise are broached. The classical aspect in support of this charge is the case where justice demands punishment although the 'common plan' has not yet been put in motion. But this consideration cannot be applied in the case of national-socialism, as their guilty aims actually reached the peak of their realization. We have, nevertheless, identified two examples where the consequences of the notion of conspiracy go beyond the legal effects of complicity. The charge of conspiracy would cover criminal acts committed prior to the accused joining the conspiracy, as well as those crimes committed after this time. It holds all the conspirators criminally responsible for the consequences of the conspiracy, including those which were not intended or foreseen. From this double point of view, it creates among the conspirators a solidarity broader than the one existing among accomplices. Men such as von Papen and Schacht, who have greatly facilitated Hitler's accession to power, were certainly included in the conspiracy. They created the scourge, whether or not they had anticipated its devastating effects. It is, nevertheless, difficult to say that they were accomplices of the crime against peace, war crimes, and crimes against humanity because, as they were not core members of the national-socialism enterprise, it remained unproven that they intended or fomented these offences.[78] Similarly, the activities of the SA, as a criminal organization and as the main channel of the extermination of the opponents to the emerging national-socialism, cannot avoid the charge of conspiracy. But because this group was regarded as suspect by the Reichswehr, it fell into sharp decline just after Hitler's execution of Roehm and his companions and thus before the beginning of the war, it appears to have taken no part in the crime against peace or in the crimes later committed.

Legally, the charge of conspiracy in the Nuremberg trial met with a preliminary exception: one based on the *principle of legality of crime and punishment*. We have seen that under international law, this principle must be subject to a broad interpretation, and that the literal application of the *nullum crimen, nulla poena sine lege* principle, corresponding to the final phase of a developed body of law, is unacceptable. However, these reservations are not meant to forgo the elementary idea of justice: an individual must not be punished for a conduct that he could not suspect to be criminal when committed.

The charge of conspiracy is specific to British law. It is unknown to both German law and the French penal code. Its originality is that it creates a crime distinct from the crime against peace, the war crimes and crimes against humanity. The practical interest of such a charge is that it covers acts not included in the crimes referred to above because they are preparatory acts. How then can it be justified in such conditions that its *ex post facto* application respects the principle or even the spirit of the legality of crimes and punishments?[79]

---

[78] See Reuter, *Le Jugement du Tribunal Militaire International de Nuremberg* (Dalloz, 7 and 14 November 1946, *chronique XX*).

[79] In their consultations of January 1919, Mr Larnaude and Mr Lapradelle wrote on the extradition of William II: 'Il est anti-juridique de vouloir assimiler la guerre à un complot, à une conspiration accompagnée de crimes et délits.' (*Journal de Droit International Privé*, 1919, p. 157.)

There is thus no surprise that in such conditions, the main argument presented by counsel for the defendants is the negation of a conspiracy. This denial has roots in a number of factual considerations.

The first one deals with the alleged incompatibility of the concept of conspiracy with that of the *Führerprinzip*. The existence of a conspiracy surely does not involve equality among all conspirators. There may exist differences of motive, conduct, prestige, or influence among them. That is why when it comes to armed bands, a crime similar to the *'association de malfaiteurs'* or criminal conspiracy, the French Penal Code (Articles 96 to 99) distinguishes, for both the findings and the sentence, those who in the group exercised a position of command or staff and the others. But can we talk about a meeting of wills when one rules over all the others? Can we really talk of a common plan when all details of the common plan were set out by one individual?

In national-socialist Germany, Hitler held all powers: legislative, executive, and even judiciary towards the end of his reign. Legal provisions and regulations were the expression of the will of one man, and not, as in democratic countries, the expression of a collective will established after consultation. Hitler's laws— ordinances or orders—whether they came from the Reich Cabinet, from a minister, a high-ranking civil servant, or a commander of the armies and bearing the famous 'the Führer recommends...the Führer orders...' were all and only Hitler's laws. This includes the decisions and decrees of the Reich Cabinet, such as the decree on the creation of the Bohemia-Moravia Protectorate (16 March 1919); ordinances, such as the one on the enforcement of the Four-Year Plan (19 October 1936); or military orders, such as the decree of *Nacht und Nebel* (7 December 1941),[80] the directive related to the *Barbarossa* plan aiming at the removal of the Soviet representatives (18 December 1940),[81] the order on commandos (18 October 1942),[82] the *Krugel* decree of March 1944 on the treatment of prisoners[83] and the orders of 6 May 1944 that require German armed forces to take collective measures against inhabitants of entire villages.[84]

The documents studied in M. Cartier's book, *Les Secrets de la Guerre Révélés par le Procès de Nuremberg*,[85] show that Hitler, relying upon his experience as a lance corporal in the First World War, imposed his views on matters of strategy

[80] The 'Nacht und Nebel' decree, signed by Keitel recommended the handing over of individuals guilty of crimes against the Reich or of members of armed forces from occupied territories to the SD (security police), except in cases where the death penalty was certain. These civilians were to be secretly transferred to Germany where they could not contact their families.

[81] Special plans concerning Soviet commissars were set up more than a month before the invasion of the USSR territory on 22 June 1941. One of the plans provided that political 'commissars' of the army should not be recognized as prisoners of war and should be executed at the latest in transit camps. (*Trial of Major War Criminals*, vol. I, Judgment, p. 241.)

[82] This order recommended the extermination of members of special units (even the ones wearing uniforms) after their capture. They used the excuse of retaliation. (Rey, p. 26.)

[83] The Kugel decree or 'Ballo' recommended the transfer of prisoners captured after an attempt to escape to the SD (for execution). See *Trial of Major War Criminals*, vol. I Judgment, p. 240.

[84] Rey, p. 61.

[85] Librairie Arthème Fayard editions, 1947.

on Reichwehr generals. It is against their will that on 11 March 1935, he rein-
stated mandatory national service and increased the number of divisions in time
of peace to thirty-six; and that in February 1936, he decided to remilitarize the
Rhineland.[86] It is against their will that on 11 March 1938, he entered Vienna
and triggered the Czechoslovak crisis.[87] As for the invasion of Poland, he substituted the campaign plan prepared by the staff headquarters for his plan which
was to come out from the eastern side of Prussia and attack the Polish troops from
the rear.[88] In October 1939, the Western offensive was undertaken, despite von
Brauchitsch's disapproval, who was apparently scared of the lack of preparation
of the people and the army and who were in favour of a diplomatic settlement of
the dispute.[89] During the attack on the West, the Sedan manoeuvre, consisting
in breaking off the centre of Allied forces, replaced the encirclement of Belgium,
the Schlieffen classical plan conceptualized by the staff... [90]

    This domination of one man over military chiefs, diplomats, administra-
tors, financiers, all men whose arrogance and professional pride are well known,
testifies to the rise of the genius. An exceptional will power, both magnetic and
morbid, imposes itself on others armed with normal will-powers. On the passive
side, one must take into account the docility and suggestibility of the German
mindset; this led the masses to Hitler, the orator, and subjugated the initiative and
independence of his subordinates, even the most talented among them, including
Goering. These various factors have contributed to the establishment of perhaps
the most absolute dictatorship in history.

    One may point to the role played by consultative bodies, such as the Reich
Cabinet, the secret Council, or the Reich Defence Council.[91] But the documents
presented during the Nuremberg trial show that, since 1934, the existence of
such bodies was, in fact, purely formal. The ministers stopped meeting to adopt
governmental decisions: instead, a mere rotation of documents was instituted so
that every member could put his signature on it.[92] The secret Council was created
in 1938 only to hide von Neurath's dismissal from the public and to give him an

---

[86] See Aldermann on the circumstances of this remilitarization, *Trial of Major War Criminals*,
vol. II, Debate, p. 344 and following. See also Cartier, p. 57 and following.

[87] *Trial of Major War Criminals*, vol. II, Debate, p. 351 and following; vol. III, Debate, p. 44 and
following; R. Cartier, p. 81 and following.

[88] R. Cartier, p. 108 and following.

[89] R. Cartier, p. 130.

[90] R. Cartier, p. 123 and following.

[91] This is against these bodies gathered under the generic name of 'Reich Cabinet'
(*Reichsregierung*) that a declaration of criminality was sought by the Prosecution. As we will see
further on, the Tribunal refused such a qualification because these groups of people did not fall
under the Charter's criteria of a 'group' or of an 'organization'.

[92] 'As to the first reason for our decision, it is to be observed that from the time that it can be said
that a conspiracy to make aggressive war existed, the Reich Cabinet did not constitute a governing
body, but was merely an aggregation of administrative officers subject to the absolute control of
Hitler. Not a single meeting of the Reich Cabinet was held after 1937, but laws were promulgated in
the name of one or more of the cabinet members.' (*Trial of Major War Criminals*, vol. I, Judgment,
p. 291).

official position. The aforesaid meetings of 5 November 1937, 23 May, 22 August and 23 November 1939, are meetings of people selected according to the mood of the moment. During these conferences, one voice can be heard, that of Hitler. He does not consult with his colleagues; he informs them of the decisions when those are about to be enforced or the day before their entry into force. Timorous objections against these decisions may have been voiced at the outset, but they never prevailed and were quickly withdrawn. After the speech of 5 November 1937, when Hitler announced the simultaneous conquest of Austria and Czechoslovakia (an opening to a potential conflict with France and Italy (386 PS)), field-marshal von Blomberg, general-colonel von Fritsch and the Minister of Foreign Affairs von Neurath dared questioning the imminence of the conflict.[93] Having followed at the beginning of 1938, the dismissals of von Blomberg and von Fritsch, and the disgrace of von Neurath,[94] Fritsch was replaced by Brauchitsch, and von Blomberg by Hitler himself.[95] In June 1938, a memorandum in which General Beck criticized the plans of attack on Czechoslovakia triggered his resignation and his replacement by Halder.[96] When on 23 May 1939, at the new Chancellery, Hitler announced the invasion of Poland and endorsed the idea of a war on two fronts, which is an idea he strongly hinted at in *Mein Kampf*, the great Admiral Raeder and all the others remained silent.[97]

Hitler's constant tactic vis-à-vis his colleagues was to lock them in their respective assignments. The similarity and the number of statements supporting this conclusion put this view beyond challenge. Hitler imposed a hermetic secrecy among his associates. Each of them knew about one aspect of the programme; he was the only one to know all about it. How can we talk about a concerted plan? Of course, among the colleagues themselves there were disagreements mainly resulting from conflicts of ambitions and powers. For instance, Schacht was jealous of Goering because the latter was in charge of the Four-Year Plan; Rosenberg, who was the appointed diplomat of the Nazi regime, was coveting the Ministry of Foreign Affairs attributed to Ribbentrop, after the departure of von Neurath. There were also serious problems between, on the one hand, the *statthalters* von Neuraht, Frank, Seyss-Inquart, and, on the other hand, Himmler and Heydrich regarding

[93] R. Cartier, p. 71 and following.
[94] Von Blomberg had to resign after a scandal apparently stirred up by Himmler and the Gestapo: an affair with a prostitute; von Fritsch was accused of being a homosexual. This accusation also fomented by the Gestapo was said to be incorrect by a Tribunal presided by Goering. This, nevertheless, led to the disappearance of von Fritsch. (R. Cartier, p. 73 and following); it is at the same time that von Neurath left the Ministry of Foreign Affairs to become the 'President' of the secret council.
[95] R. Cartier, p. 78. (it is during the same period of time that the OKW (*Oberkommando der Wehrmacht*) was created; which brought together the command of the army, the marine, the air force; the heads of this organization in times of war were Hitler and Keitel, its Chief-of-Staff.
[96] R. Cartier, p. 86. At the same time, the Minister of Finance, Scherin-Krosigk, was addressing prophetic warnings to Hitler which resulted in similar consequences. Halder—as well as Beck—who plotted against Hitler, was killed by the Gestapo on 20 July 1944 (R. Cartier, p. 88).
[97] R. Cartier, p. 104.

the competence and authority over the police forces. In a way, these disagreements have been another impediment in the way of the charge of conspiracy.

Finally, the idea of a concerted plan presupposes some degree of unity and continuity in the execution of the plan. And yet, if one follows the theory presented by the Prosecution in which crimes against peace, war crimes, and crimes against humanity were part of the plan, it is difficult or indeed impossible to exclude or ignore that sudden and unforeseeable necessities have influenced the events in such a way that most of those could not have been foreseen in the initial plan.

Before they came to power, a common resolution to cast off the chains of the Treaty of Versailles and to create the 'vital space' might have been reached. But without an agreement on the means, this resolution could not be regarded as a conspiracy or concerted plan. At that point, the sole real purpose of the enterprise was the seizure of power, which does not constitute a crime in itself.

After the coming to power, Hitler's strategy was altered on many occasions by the course of events. There never was any precise and fixed decision regarding the date or the order of the aggression. We know from instructions given by Hitler to the army during the autumn of 1938, that an international conflict had not been foreseen until 1944–45. The haste seemed to have resulted from Hitler's impatience and his firm belief that he would die quickly.[98] He then planned an attack on France to be followed by an attack on Poland; because, according to *Mein Kampf*,[99] if the expansion was to take place towards the East, the decision was to be found in the West. In *Mein Kampf*, Hitler contemplates wiping out France, but he has no war designs against England; in practice, he stuck to these opinions until the last months of 1939. The unofficial negotiations through Dahlerus, an industrialist, delayed the invasion of Poland for a few days and allowed the British Empire to remain outside of the dispute.[100] That is probably for the same reason that, the day before the attack on the USSR, Rudolf Hess secretly flew to London.[101] Similarly, the invasion of Norway that took place during the spring of 1940 was not part of Hitler's earlier intentions; it happened unexpectedly, to everybody's surprise, except for Raeder and Rosenberg who had provoked it.[102] The invasion of Yugoslavia was suddenly decided by Hitler alone, and against Ribbentrop and Jodl's advice first to give an ultimatum to the Yugoslav government.[103] The attack against the USSR was decided only after the failed project of landing in England and the failure to take Gibraltar and drive away the

---

[98] R. Cartier, p. 100.

[99] See on that matter, Hitler's speech of 23 April 1939 (798 PS); R. Cartier, p. 100.

[100] *Trial of Major War Criminals*, vol. I, Judgment, p. 214; R. Cartier, p. 117 and following.

[101] It seems that prior to June 1940, Hitler had not contemplated the invasion of England. He believed the defeat of France would push England to negotiate. R. Cartier, p. 168; see on R. Hess' flight, *Trial of Major War Criminals*, vol. I, Judgment, p. 301; R. Cartier, p. 203 and following.

[102] *Trial of Major War Criminals*, vol. I, Judgment, p. 215 and following; R. Cartier, p. 145 and following.

[103] *Trial of Major War Criminals*, vol. I, Judgment, p. 222 and following; R. Cartier, p. 187. See the report on the conference held by Hitler on 27 March 1941 with his staff (1746 PS).

British from the Western Mediterranean Sea (Spain refused to cooperate in that endeavour).[104] The aggression towards the East, decided by Hitler in February 1941, was feared and disapproved of by Hitler's main associates, Goering, Ribbentrop, Keitel, Raeder... [105] The actual attack was, in fact, delayed by the Balkans campaign after Mussolini suddenly and imprudently attacked Greece. This delay marked a failure of the Reich before Moscow.

How could we, in those circumstances, talk about a conspiracy or a concerted plan to commit 'crimes against peace', especially considering the difficulties to locate this conspiracy in both time and place?

As for war crimes—murders of hostages, shootings of captured airmen, pillage of public and private properties—and crimes against humanity—racial persecution, deportation of civilians—they are acts of either individual or collective nature which are linked to modern warfare and its constant changes and the temptations which this brings. As shown by a memorandum of Rosenberg dated 2 April 1941, it is beyond doubt that the cynical exploitation of the Soviet territory, including the displacement of starving populations had been planned.[106] It is equally clear that partisan warfare which started behind the Eastern front also created the opportunity for the appalling treatment of prisoners, massacres of hostages, and numerous killings by the Einsatz-Kommandos.[107] It has not been proven—and, in fact, appears to contradict the evidence—that the aggressive intentions of Hitler included the commission of these crimes.

These facts, which are a refutation of the general conspiracy theory, may have been overlooked by the four prosecution teams as they were laying out the seductive, yet somewhat fictionalized, theory of the indictment. The Prosecution may also incur criticism concerning its conception of the Tribunal's jurisdiction: it went beyond the limits of Article 6 of the Charter when it decided to present the crime of conspiracy as a distinct count in the indictment.

The Charter provides for three alternative crimes falling within the Tribunal's jurisdiction: crimes against peace, war crimes, and crimes against humanity.

It defines the crime against peace as follows: planning, preparation, initiation or waging of a war of aggression, or a war in violation of international treaties, agreements or assurances; similarly, it provides for *participation in a common plan or conspiracy for the accomplishment of any of the foregoing*. Conspiracy is designed only as a form of participation in crime against peace.

Reference to conspiracy is not contained in the definitions of 'war crimes' or 'crimes against humanity'.

[104] R. Cartier, p. 177 and following.
[105] See Goering's testimony during the trial; R. Cartier, p. 246. See also the transcripts of the War Council held on 3 February 1941 (872 PS).
[106] *Trial of Major War Criminals*, vol. I, Judgment, p. 314. See also on this memorandum the commentary of the prosecutor for the US, Aldermann, *Trial of Major War Criminals*, vol. III, Debates, p. 361.
[107] See on these abuses the testimony of witness Lahousen in *Trial of Major War Criminals*, vol. II, Debates, p. 437 and following.

Only Article 6 of the Charter provides, *in fine*, that:

'Leaders, organizers, instigators, and accomplices participating in the formulation or execution of a common plan or conspiracy to commit any of the foregoing crimes are responsible for all acts performed by any persons in execution of such plan.'[108]

This provision is not intended to provide for a distinct crime, which would be in contradiction with the aforesaid list. Its sole purpose is to identify the categories of the persons responsible, as principals or accessory, for any of the above-mentioned crimes. By focusing on the leaders, organizers, instigators, or accomplices, it endorses the principles of ordinary criminal law. Leaders and organizers are either moral authors or accomplices who supplied means, depending on the extent of their participation. Instigators or agitators are regarded, under French law, as accomplices,[109] and under other continental legal systems, they form a distinct category of participants.[110] The only particularity of the text is that it links participation to a conspiracy directly, instead of linking it with the criminal acts which the concerted plan is intended to see committed. But this particularity is purely formal, as in ordinary criminal law, participation in preparatory acts would be regarded as a type of complicity. The final formula involves a meeting of intentions between the participant in question and the actual perpetrator. In effect, it is the French notion of complicity that the final provision of Article 6 adopts.

It is also the interpretation which has been adopted in the Nuremberg judgment:[111]

'In the opinion of the Tribunal these words do not add a new and separate crime to those already listed. The words are designed to establish the responsibility of persons participating in a common plan. The Tribunal will therefore disregard the charges in Count One that the defendants conspired to commit war crimes and crimes against humanity, and will consider only the common plan to prepare, initiate and wage aggressive war.'

Even regarding the crime against peace, the Tribunal refrained from asserting the existence of a general conspiracy. Punishment is dependent on proof having been made of participation in a plan to commit a particular act of aggression:[112]

'In the opinion of the Tribunal, the evidence establishes the common planning to prepare and wage war by certain of the defendants. It is immaterial to consider whether a single conspiracy to the extent and over the time set out in the Indictment has been conclusively proved. Continued planning, with aggressive war as the objective, has been established beyond doubt. The truth of the situation was well stated by Paul Schmidt, official

---

[108] Article 6, IMT Charter.
[109] H. Donnedieu de Vabres, *Traité du Droit Criminel et de Législation Pénale Comparée*, 3rd edn, 1947, No 438, p. 254.
[110] H. Donnedieu de Vabres, No 452, p. 262 and following.
[111] *Trial of Major War Criminals*, Judgment, p. 238.
[112] Ibid., p. 237.

interpreter of the German Foreign Office, as follows:

"The general objectives of the Nazi leadership were apparent from the start, namely the domination of the European Continent to be achieved first by the incorporation of all German speaking groups in the Reich, and secondly, by territorial expansion under the slogan 'Lebensraum.' The execution of these basic objectives, however, seemed to be characterised by improvisation. Each succeeding step was apparently carried out as each new situation arose, but all consistent with the ultimate objectives mentioned above." '

The Tribunal, nevertheless, denied the objection taken from the *Führerprinzip*:[113]

'The argument that such common planning cannot exist where there is complete dictatorship is unsound. A plan in the execution of which a number of persons participate is still a plan, even though conceived by only one of them; and those who execute the plan do not avoid responsibility by showing that they acted under the direction of the man who conceived it. Hitler could not make aggressive war by himself. He had to have the co-operation of statesmen, military leaders, diplomats, and business men. When they, with knowledge of his aims, gave him their co-operation, they made themselves parties to the plan he had initiated. They are not to be deemed innocent because Hitler made use of them, if they knew what they were doing. That they were assigned to their tasks by a dictator does not absolve them from responsibility for their acts. The relation of leader and follower does not preclude responsibility here any more than it does in the comparable tyranny of organised domestic crime.'

As a result, whilst the charge of conspiracy extended to all of the accused in the indictment, the judgment only admitted such a charge against those who worked towards a particular war of aggression: Goering, Hess, Ribbentrop, Keitel, Rosenberg, Raeder, and von Neurath. As may be seen from this list, the main criterion to establish participation remained, in the eyes of the Tribunal, the presence at meetings during which Hitler revealed his criminal plans.

The same notion of conspiracy was to influence the declarations of criminality for groups and organizations.

Chapter IV
Criminal Responsibility of Groups and Organizations

In the judgment,[114] the criminal organization is defined as a 'conspiracy in action'. The common feature to criminal organization and conspiracy is indeed that both involve a plurality of agents who associate and coordinate their efforts with a view to achieve the purposes of a criminal enterprise. The collective nature of the criminal activity is in conformity with a mindset of meticulous preparation, discipline, and conscientiousness so peculiar to the Germans. It actually represents

---

[113] Ibid., p. 237.
[114] *Trial of Major War Criminals*, vol. I, Judgment, p. 270: 'A criminal organization is analogous to a criminal conspiracy in that the essence of both is cooperation for criminal purposes.'

the bad, dangerous, and indeed satanic aspect of that collective feature. Some figures clearly highlight the role of these organizations in the accomplishment of Hitler's goals. According to the judgment,[115] the number of SA at the end of 1933 is 4.5 million; at the same date, the *Allgemiene* SS force is composed of 240,000 men who are organized militarily in divisions and regiments; the *Waffen* SS is a force of 500,000 men and 40 divisions at the end of the war. As for the number of political leaders (including the *Zellenleiter* and the *Blockleiter*), estimates are between 600,000 and 650,000 men. The number of employees of the Gestapo is 20,000 in 1940.

The groups and organizations are the German people itself, the entire German population mobilized for the execution of the Nazi agenda. The above-mentioned statement in the judgment underlining the executive role of Hitler's individual collaborators in his work requires that the following qualification be made: any Hitler in any country would have been able to recruit a horde of ambitious men and henchmen similar to a Ribbentrop, a Keitel, a Sauckel. Nowhere, or almost nowhere, could he have procured collective forces with the cruel sophistication and baleful power as that of the Gestapo.

The issue which this collective feature of the criminality brings is one of balance between individual responsibility based on the principles of justice and the necessity of a wide punishment. Articles 9 and 10 of the Charter outline more than they define a solution:

Article 9—'At the trial of any individual member of any group or organization the Tribunal may declare (in connection with any act of which the individual may be convicted) that the group or organization of which the individual was a member was a criminal organization. After receipt of the Indictment the Tribunal shall give such notice as it thinks fit that the Prosecution intends to ask the Tribunal to make such declaration and any member of the organization will be entitled to apply to the Tribunal for leave to be heard by the Tribunal upon the question of the criminal character of the organization. The Tribunal shall have power to allow or reject the application. If the application is allowed, the Tribunal may direct in what manner the applicants shall be represented and heard.'

Article 10—'In cases where a group or organization is declared criminal by the Tribunal, the competent national authority of any Signatory shall have the right to bring individuals to trial for membership therein before national, military, or occupation courts. In any such case the criminal nature of the group or organization is considered proved and shall not be questioned.'

The wording of the Charter implicitly resolves in the affirmative a problem with which its authors had had some hesitation with, namely, the criminal responsibility of legal entities. Although the Charter does not provide for the possibility of criminal sanctions being imposed on groups which belong to the past (they were dissolved as soon as the Allies entered the German territory), it requires the

---

[115] *Trial of Major War Criminals*, vol. I, Judgment, p. 290.

Tribunal to make a determination as to their criminal nature. The critical issue at the heart of the problem of the criminal responsibility of legal entities does not lie in the sanctions one could impose upon such entities (one can think of financial sanctions or sanctions which deprive it of rights[116]) but in the conditions that must be satisfied by the activities of members of this group to trigger or generate the criminal responsibility of the group.

The doubts of the authors of the Charter can be felt in the fact that they considered the criminality of the group as accessory in character. They only allowed the Tribunal to make a finding of criminality in the context and as part of its considerations as pertain to the actions of members of such groups. For example, the Gestapo was found to be a criminal organization in the context of the conviction entered against Kaltenbrunner who was a member of that group. It is in a way similar to the previous example: the jurisdiction of the Tribunal over crimes against humanity—a somewhat confusing notion—was justified by the linking of such crimes with a crime against peace or a war crime. We do not think that another meaning or a broader scope should be attached to such a link, a link which the Defence has widely relied upon and benefited from in its submissions.

A declaration of the criminality of a group by the International Military Tribunal has the definitive authority of *res judicata*. It cannot be questioned in any individual proceeding against members of these groups, either before military tribunals of different occupation zones or before the national jurisdictions of the states in question. In a way, the Tribunal was called upon to resolve a preliminary question relevant to these subsequent proceedings.

Beyond that, the Charter is silent. It lays out the principle of these individual proceedings whose exercise is optional—the discretionary power of the prosecuting authorities prevails in this matter; but it does not set up the elements, or the conditions that would render a member guilty of a crime, nor does it specify the intentional or objective nature of the crime or the sentences incurred for it. The International Military Tribunal is in a position that is similar to that of a French criminal jury when the latter has to decide on the guilt of an accused without being aware of the criminal consequences that could ensue from such a verdict. The situation here is even more disturbing because the jury is, or should be, confident in the Court's judgment, whereas the application of the declaration of criminality by the IMT will be left to the discretion of tribunals in various states which might be animated by all kinds of interests, prejudices and conflicting passions and which could bring a diversity of verdicts harmful to the prestige of international justice.

Was it the Tribunal's responsibility to prevent this, by specifying in one way or another the legal effects to be attached to its declaration? This question, it seems, was a preliminary matter which for the practical reasons just outlined had to

---

[116] H. Donnedieu de Vabres, *Traité du Droit Criminel et de Législation Pénale Comparée*, No 263, p. 149.

be answered in the affirmative. We will see that, in fact, it is the approach that prevailed. The remarkable lacuna of the Charter, nevertheless, resulted in a state of experimentation: the criminal responsibility of groups and organizations was discussed before the Tribunal without anybody knowing the effect it would later have. We will follow this process in our analysis: first, the *elements* and then the *effects* of the criminal responsibility of groups and organizations.

I

The criminal responsibility of groups and organizations was to be defined before the judgment. Pursuant to Article 9, this determination had to be made at the opening of the large investigation carried out in the camps where most SA, SS, and members of the charged organizations were being detained. It was then that the 'applicants' were to be questioned, under the authority of a representative of the Tribunal, by counsel for the Defence of the organizations in question, before a hundred or so of them—acting as sort of 'legitimate opponents'—were to be heard at Nuremberg before the special Commission which the Tribunal was empowered to set up pursuant to Article 17 of the Charter. A smaller number of people—about twenty of them—would be heard in public sessions before the Tribunal.

These consultations could only occur if the Tribunal specified this notion of criminal responsibility of groups and organizations in a preliminary ruling. It did so and laid out the following three conditions:[117]

1. The actions of the group involved the commission of one of the crimes falling under Article 6 of the Charter and thus within the jurisdiction of the Tribunal: crimes against peace, war crimes, and crimes against humanity.
2. The majority of members of the group were volunteers.
3. The majority of members of the group were aware of the criminal activity of the group.

Out of these three conditions, the first two can be ascertained relatively easily; on the other hand, it is a difficult and uncertain question—although an often discussed one—to determine how far or how deep the knowledge of crimes committed in concentration camps had penetrated into the German population and how far it had reached among the leaders being prosecuted at Nuremberg. The

---

[117] *Trial of Major War Criminals*, Judgment, p. 270:
  'The group must be formed or used in connection with the commission of crimes denounced by the Charter. Since the declaration with respect to the organizations and groups will, as has been pointed out, fix the criminality of its members, that definition should exclude persons who had no knowledge of the criminal purposes or acts of the organization and those who were drafted by the State for membership, unless they were personally implicated in the commission of acts declared criminal by Article 6 of the Charter as members of the organization. Membership alone is not enough to come within the scope of these declarations.'

testimony of witnesses such as Hoess, the commander of the Auschwitz Camp where more than 3 million Jews were gassed and cremated over four years following Himmler's orders, showed the fog of secrecy that surrounded the extermination. The silence of the few who had been freed was guaranteed by threats and terror. On the other hand, the fact that a number of detainees were in contact through their work with the population in factories or building sites excludes the hypothesis of complete secrecy. The atmosphere of terror hanging over the camps dates back to the outset of Nazism.[118] The horror of what was happening was probably suspected, although its actual scope was most likely unknown because many of those who could have known did not want to know.

It has been suggested that the investigation instigated by the Tribunal was incapable of revealing the truth, as the 'applicants' themselves could be later convicted if the group to which they had belonged was declared criminal. Like many witnesses who appeared at Nuremberg, they were motivated by self-interest. Naturally, in such circumstances, they talked more about the compulsory nature of their membership and their own ignorance of the crimes committed than of the collective aspects of the group. Despite these imperfections which were hard to avoid, the Tribunal was able to collect from the large amount of material which was the technical information required for its findings. It was able to identify distinguishing factors between the accused organizations and, within each organization, between its various components, taking into account different timeframes.

A declaration of criminality was entered in relation to three out of the six accused organizations.

– The SS (*Schutzstaffeln der National-Sozialistischen Deutschen Arbeiterpartei*)[119]— the protection unit of the National Socialist German Workers' Party—was created in 1925 to maintain order and keep an eye on the public when mass demonstrations were organized by the party. It included the *Allgemeine SS*, who were often responsible for the guarding and administration of concentration camps, and later, the *Waffen* SS (German for 'Armed SS'), who constituted the military branch of the organization. Some central service departments (*Ahnenerbe*) were in charge of cultural and scientific research. Membership, which was first voluntary, often became mandatory after the formation of the *Waffen* SS in 1940: high-ranking officials from the order police and from the security police ('*Ordnungspolizei*' and '*Sicherheitspolizei*') were then automatically enrolled. The SS is partly responsible for aggressive acts in the Sudetenland and in Memel, for executions of prisoners and hostages, for crimes at Oradour-sur-Glane and Lidice (Waffen SS division *Das Reich*), for forced labour, deportation of Jews, and pseudo-scientific experiments. The Tribunal's declaration of criminality does not apply to the *Reiterkorps* (SS cavalry division).

---

[118] *Trial of Major War Criminals*, Judgment, p. 188 and following.
[119] *Trial of Major War Criminals*, Judgment, p. 283 and following.

– The Gestapo and the SD (*Geheime Staatspolizei* and *Sicherheitsdienst des Reichsführers* SS, the Secret State Police and Security Service of the SS Reichsführer),[120] the former was a political police of the Reich, (established by Goering and headed by Heydrich), and the latter the Party's intelligence service, which from 1936 onwards was linked to the Kripo (*Kriminalpolizei*), also headed by Heydrich.

In 1939, Heydrich brought all the services that were under his supervision into a unique body, the RSHA (*Reichssicherheits-Hauptamt*). It was made up of seven divisions (*Ämter*) and combined the Gestapo (Amt 4) and the SD (divisions 3, 6, and 7), whose actions spread both inside and outside Germany.

While the call-up was at first voluntary, administration officials were then automatically assigned to the Gestapo. Resigning from this new position was not an option as it simply meant losing one's job.

The following charges are imputable to the Gestapo: administrative confinements, extermination of certain categories of prisoners, torture inflicted on members of the Resistance (method of third-degree interrogation), and the *Einsatzkommandos'* actions behind the troops in the Eastern territories (the *Einsatzkommandos* combined Gestapo, Kripo and SD members, and sometimes also Waffen SS and Reichswehr's soldiers).

The judgment states that the declaration of criminality does not apply to some technical services, such as Customs border guards, the services for the safety of the Army, administrative officials, shorthand typists, etc....

– The Nazi Party Leadership Corps[121] was the official body of the Nazi Party, with the Chief of the Party Chancellery at its head (Hess, succeeded by Bormann).

Under the Chief of the Party Chancellery were the *Gauleiter*, the *Kreisleiter*, the *Ortsgruppenleiter*, the *Zellenleiter*, and then the *Blockleiter*, all assisted by a directorate, and with territorial jurisdiction over more or less wide administrative regions.

The lower positions (*Zellenleiter* and *Blockleiter*), as opposed to the others, acted under definite verbal instructions, with no discretion in interpreting orders. Membership in these two positions may have been compulsory.

The Leadership Corps controlled the conduct and activities of the Party's members through propaganda and card indexing. Its authority extended to the occupied territories, where it directed *Germanization* and coordinated the persecution of Jews along with the Gestapo and the SD. In 1942, it issued the 'confidential information bulletins on the final solution' and sent them to the *Gauleiter* and the *Kreisleiter*. The Leadership Corps also participated in instances of forced labour, inhuman treatment of foreign labourers and of

---

[120] *Trial of Major War Criminals*, vol. I, Judgment, p. 283 and following.
[121] *Trial of Major War Criminals*, vol. I, p. 271 and following. See also on the organization of the political leaders, the opening statement by the Prosecutor from the US, Albrecht, in *Trial of Major War Criminals*, vol. II, p. 106 and following.

certain categories of prisoners, as well as the lynching of airmen. The judgment states that the declaration of criminality only applies to the upper echelons of the organization. Thus, the declaration of criminality does not apply to the staff of the *Ortsgruppenleiter, Zellenleiter, Blockleiter*, and to the *Zellenleiter* and *Blockleiter* themselves.

Due to various reasons, the declaration of criminality does not apply to three groups or organizations accused by the Prosecution: the SA, the Headquarters Staff and the Reich Cabinet.

- The SA (*Sturmabteilungen der National-Sozialistischen Deutschen Arbeiterpartei*), was the elite unit of the National Socialist German Worker's Party, and was created in 1921 to protect the political activity of the party. In April 1933, a likely forced call-up of a group of war veterans—the *Stahlhelm* ('Steel Helmet')—added 1.5 million members to the SA.

  They were the party's henchmen. They took part in Austria's occupation, in the recruiting and equipping of the forces in the Sudetenland, and in the violence against the Jews. Yet, their political role kept decreasing after the successive liquidations that followed the Roehm putsch (30 June, 1 and 2 July 1934).

- The group composed of the Headquarters Staff and the High Command consisted of 130 officers (alive or missing), who had leadership positions in the three branches of the army during the period 1938–1945: OKH (*Oberkommando des Heeres*, the Army), OKM (*Oberkommando der Marine*, the Navy), OKL (*Oberkommando der Luftwaffe*, the Air Force). Above them, the supreme authority (OKW *Oberkommando der Wehrmacht*) was in Hitler's hands. Keitel was only the chief of staff. The judgment condemns those officers who participated in the crimes of the *Einsatzgruppen*, in the execution of orders like the *Nacht und Nebel* decree, and in the extermination of Soviet commissars.

  Yet they can hardly be presented as a group. They never held meetings and Hitler only had direct and personal contacts with the commanders of the armies.

The Cabinet of the Reich (*Reichsregierung*)[122] was not regarded as a criminal organization for the same reason. The Cabinet of the Reich consisted of the Cabinet as it was set up on 30 January 1933, the Council for Defence of the Reich, and the Secret Cabinet Council. The first two bodies did not meet after 1937. The Secret Cabinet Council also never met. It was founded to maintain von Neurath's position when Ribbentrop was put in charge of foreign affairs.

The reason for the non-application of the declaration of criminality to the SA is known: their political activities took place prior to the start of the war. The finding is related to the rejection of the theory of an all-encompassing conspiracy.[123]

---

[122] *Trial of Major War Criminals*, vol. I, Judgment, p. 291.

[123] *Trial of Major War Criminals*, vol. I, Judgment, p. 291: 'After the purge, the S.A. was reduced to the status of a group of unimportant Nazi hangers-on. Although in specific instances some units

It is for the same reason that when it declared the SS, the Gestapo, and the leadership of the Nazi Party to be criminal, the Tribunal was careful to exclude from this finding, 'the persons who have ceased to fill the functions that are enumerated in the above paragraph before September 1, 1939'.[124]

Moreover, the Tribunal also excluded from the 'declared criminal group' the persons whose recruitment was forced and who did not know that 'the organisation was used to commit acts declared criminal by Article 6 of the Charter'. The composition of the 'declared criminal group' is thus not similar to the official composition of the accused organisation.[125] By this roundabout means, the Tribunal expresses its will that the crime of membership to a criminal organization not be seen as a purely objective crime but also as an intentional offence. It imposes this view to the judges who will later on be in charge of individual proceedings; but it cannot be accused of going beyond its authority by regulating the effects of its declaration. Indeed, all persons forced into membership or unaware of the criminal activity of the organization are excluded from the composition of the group declared criminal.

It is true, however, that the delicate issue related to the powers of the Tribunal arose in the context of the issue of sentencing.

II

We have already said that the Charter does not contain any provision or indication as to the nature and level of sentences that could be incurred by individual members of the organizations which have been declared criminal.

One can imagine that laws similar to the provisions of the French law of 28 August 1944 fill this gap in the legislation of interested states. In the various zones of occupied Germany, a law (No. 10) enacted by the Control Council on 20 December 1945 provides that:[126]

'Each of the following acts is recognized as a crime:
   (d) Membership in categories of a criminal group or organization declared criminal by the International Military Tribunal.
3. Any persons found guilty of any of the crimes above mentioned may upon conviction be punished as shall be determined by the tribunal to be just. Such punishment may consist of one or more of the following:
   (a) Death.
   (b) Imprisonment for life or a term of years, with or without hard labour.
   (c) Fine, and imprisonment with or without hard labour, in lieu thereof.
   (d) Forfeiture of property.

of the S.A. were used for the commission of war crimes and crimes against humanity, it cannot be said that its members generally participated in or even knew of the criminal acts.'

[124] *Trial of Major War Criminals*, Judgment, pp. 289, 283, 276.
[125] See the reasoning of the judgment in this article, mentioned above.
[126] *Trial of Major War Criminals*, Judgment, p. 269 and following.

(e) Restitution of property wrongfully acquired.
(f) Deprivation of some or all civil rights.'

Resulting from this text is the fact that a member of an organization that has been declared criminal incurs a punishment at the discretion of the judge on a scale going from a mere deprivation of his civil rights to capital punishment.

The mere possibility of a punishment may give rise to some discomfort in light of the *nullum crimen, nulla poena sine lege* principle. Was the accused member of the criminal organization aware at the time of his affiliation of the punishment, which he could be subjected to?

The objection could not be answered if the Tribunal had regarded the crime of membership as an objective crime, as is the case in our legal system, for instance, with the offence of 'indignité nationale' ('national indignity'). But the Tribunal, by limiting the composition of the criminal group to members who joined freely and in full awareness of its activities, established a necessary relationship between the conviction and a psychological element (consciousness and free will) giving that offence an element of intent. The principle of legality is thus respected because the member of the group in reality became an accomplice of the crimes—crime against peace, war crimes, crimes against humanity—which constitute the basis of the declaration of criminality. When narrowing the crime of membership in such a way, the Tribunal has prevented the objection which Article 10 of the Charter could have raised. Furthermore, the burden to prove the volitional and intentional nature of the membership, which forms the moral element of that offence, is upon the Prosecution.

The objection concerning the discretionary power given to the judges to decide upon the nature and level of the sanction is a more serious one. It is clear that there may exist substantial differences between the states represented in the military tribunals of the zones or in the national jurisdictions as regard the assessment of the gravity of German crimes. Even among judges from one state, there can be differences of temper, background, and political opinions. Do we really realize the effect which differing sanctions applied to similar factual circumstances might have on the public opinion of Germany or that of the Allied countries? This inequality is the result of Control Council Law 10 and of the inadequacies of national legislations. The prestige of international justice is here at stake since the declarations of criminality are at the roots of the problem.

But shouldn't such harm have been prevented by the International Military Tribunal itself which could have filled the gap left in the Statute by outlining the potential sanctions for members of the organizations or, even better, by setting out sensible limitations to the powers of the local tribunals? Such an approach would be all the more useful since it would go beyond the territorial limitations of all judges responsible for applying the declarations of criminality.

We are in full support of such an option. It may involve going beyond the powers which on a literal reading were conferred by Article 9 to the international jurisdiction; but, as we underlined earlier, the complete division of power between the authority to make a determination of criminality and the power to impose sanctions is irrational and rather regrettable. We also underlined both the progressive and customary nature of international criminal law. The International Military Tribunal was not in the position of an ordinary criminal judge applying the laws and statute that are binding upon him. Ordinary criminal law is the result of experiences accumulated over many years. The Charter is an improvisation which responds to an unprecedented situation. If the Charter is, in theory, meant to express the will of the signatory states, it is, in reality, the work of a handful of technicians among which a few later became members of the International Military Tribunal.[127] Should they have been prevented from using the additional experience offered by the Tribunal and limit the scope of the declaration to the limits set by the Charter?

The strength of these considerations finally prevailed despite the fact that the IMT in a preliminary ruling had denied itself any legislative powers. It is indeed a legislative, or quasi-legislative, power which it eventually assumed, when it required, after recommendations whose authority cannot easily be detached from the authority of the disposition of the judgment, that Control Council Law 10 should be modified and corrected in relation to the Bavarian law on de-Nazification, and in which it also set out rules relevant to both of these laws.

The law of 5 March 1946 for the *Liberation from Nazism and Militarism* was put into effect under the auspices of the Control Council in the American Zone. Its object was the punishment by an administrative body of individuals whose connection to Nazi groupings was regarded as dangerous. The distinction between groupings related to the party or to the state is further complicated by the question of the scope or degree of participation to the activities of any such groupings. Therefore, the law distinguishes between the *Hauptschuldige*, the *Belastete*, the *Minderbelastete*, and the *Mitlaufer*. Sentences of imprisonment do not exceed ten years. Impunity is granted to members who did what they could to oppose the Nazi regime, although they might have joined the organization voluntarily.

The recommendations included in the Nuremberg judgment thus read as follows:[128]

'1. That so far as possible throughout the four zones of occupation in Germany the classifications, sanctions and penalties be standardised. Uniformity of treatment so far as practical should be a basic principle. This does not, of course, mean that discretion in sentencing should not be vested in the court; but the discretion should be within fixed limits appropriate to the nature of the crime.

2. Law No. 10, to which reference has already been made, leaves punishment entirely in the discretion of the trial court even to the extent of inflicting the death penalty.

---

[127] The London Agreement, 8 August 1945, notably bears the signatures of M. M. Nikitchenko, R. Falco, and R. H. Jackson. The first one held the position of associate judge for the USSR; the second was the alternate judge for France; the third was the head of the Prosecution team for the United States.

[128] *Trial of Major War Criminals*, vol. I, Judgment, p. 271.

The De-Nazification Law of 5th March, 1946, however, passed for Bavaria, Greater-Hesse and Wuerttemberg-Baden, provides definite sentences for punishment in each type of offence. The Tribunal recommends that in no case should punishment imposed under Law No. 10 upon any members of an organisation or group declared by the Tribunal to be criminal exceed the punishment fixed by the De-Nazification Law. No person should be punished under both laws.

3. The Tribunal recommends to the Control Council that Law No. 10 be amended to proscribe limitations on the punishment which may be imposed for membership in a criminal group or organisation so that such punishment shall not exceed the punishment prescribed by the De-Nazifiction Law.'

There is currently no superior authority in charge of verifying the conformity of the decisions that follow the declarations of criminality. That is why we have pointed out that there are no meaningful differences in terms of the effectiveness between the findings made in the judgment and the recommendations attached to it. The value of those, in both cases, is primarily moral.

It would, nevertheless, be a welcome development if an international judicial organ were set up to extend the work of the IMT and supervise the effort made in the above-mentioned recommendations to guarantee coherence and unification. There is today a real tendency emerging in favour of the creation of a permanent international criminal jurisdiction. This jurisdiction would certainly have a role to play as a trier of fact. But its legal responsibility in settling conflicts of jurisdiction, in resolving or forestalling the contradictions in the jurisprudence and guaranteeing the coherent interpretation of treaties, though perhaps less sensational might be no less favourable to the development of an international public order. And the limited task which we suggest should be attributed to this jurisdiction would set a precedent.

Chapter V
General Means of Defence and the Issue of Responsibility

The earlier chapters focused on the examination of the charges raised by the Prosecution, and the evaluation of exceptions and defences raised on behalf of the accused. A problem of general nature arises from the status of those whose responsibility is at stake here.

As the declaration of criminality of certain groups and organizations demonstrates, the authors of the Charter and the judges took the view that the responsibility of certain individuals is not the only type of liability engaged by the drama of the Second World War. Organizations form an active part of German society. In his opening statement at the Nuremberg trial,[129] the representative of the

---

[129] *Documents*, Opening Statement by F. de Menthon, p. 7 and following.

French Prosecution, M. Francois de Menthon said the following:

'In order to progressively establish an international society based on morals, international law and the free cooperation of peoples, it is necessary that Nazi Germany be declared guilty and that its leaders and main responsible individuals be punished as such after premeditating, preparing and triggering a war of aggression that provoked the death of millions of people as well as the ruin of a great number of nations, and after accumulating the most horrible crimes during the time of the hostilities. This work of justice is also mandatory for the future of the German population. The latter has been indoctrinated for years by the Nazi regime; some of its deepest eternal aspirations were given monstrous expression by this regime; the people took on total responsibility not only through general acceptance of the regime, but also through active participation in a large number of its crimes. The people must be re-educated...Your Tribunal's condemnation of Nazi Germany will be a first and necessary lesson for the people and will constitute the best point of departure for the work on the revision of values and the re-education of the people, which should be the Tribunal's greatest concern in the years to come.'

It is relatively common today to separate Germany from national-socialism so that the heaviest charges weigh upon the latter. This choice, which can be explained by foreign policy considerations, has been enshrined in the indictment[130] which links the Hitlerian aggressions with the alleged 'conspiracy' whilst refraining from scrutinizing its deeper causes, unlike Mr De Menthon. The term 'conspiracy' suggests the occurrence of an isolated accidental incident, and provides the key to the following shortcomings. It is a simplistic explanation, too comprehensive in one sense and insufficient in other regards. In reality, the war of aggression of 1939 cannot be well understood if it is isolated from the two previous wars where the same goal and the same methods are apparent, albeit with some differences in time and techniques.

The statist and realist doctrine goes back, beyond Treitschke and Nietzsche, to Fichte and Hegel, and without a doubt, further back through the past. In the terrifying work of criminal organizations, we find, marked by a man and by a party, a population whose passivity, plasticity and gregarious instinct are allied with a certain ancestral brutality, with a taste for the 'colossal' and for excesses. These observations are useful for regulating certain modalities and perspectives of the re-educative effort envisaged by Mr de Menthon. They may also be used to establish a hierarchy of responsibilities in which the German people occupy the first row, Hitler's strange personality the second, and the personalities of the accused—which are quite insignificant, except for Goering—occupy the third.

---

[130] *Trial of Major War Criminals*, vol. I, Indictment, p. 30 and next. 'Nous considérons le peuple allemand tout entier', wrote Mr Rey, 'de l'intellectuel à l'ouvrier, du bourgeois au paysan, comme responsable des atrocities commises, la plupart du temps de sang-froid, par les membres de l'armée et de la police allemande.' It was a German, the historian Mommsen, who wrote: 'Un peuple qui tolère trop longtemps les mauvaises actions est le complice de tous les crimes. Cette guerre ne l'a que prouvé!' (Rey, 'Violations du Droit International' in *Revue Générale de Droit International Public*, 1941–1945, vol. II, p. 91).

The observations made above are sociological in nature. But they have their necessary corollaries in the legal and criminal spheres. The involvement of criminal organizations, fathered by national-socialism or impregnated with national-socialism, underscores, as already pointed out earlier, the criminal responsibility of these legal persons. It is only because they were dissolved before the trial that there is an obstacle to the infliction of collective sanctions. Also, the personality of the German state had disappeared, because of the unconditional surrender of 5 June 1945. The instruments of surrender implied, in addition to the recognition of Germany's defeat, that supreme authority over the German territory was taken over by France, Great Britain, the United States, and the USSR.[131] This state of affair excluded the possibility for the Charter to provide for the responsibility of the state which was the only type of responsibility provided for in times of war in the various agreements, drafts and declarations adopted in the context of the League of Nations: notably the project for a treaty of mutual assistance, the Geneva Protocol of 1924 and Stimson's declaration of 1932.[132]

Theorists vainly oppose the fictional character of legal persons, from which the irresponsibility of the state would logically result. The status of legal subject, whether as a natural person or as a legal person is always a legal creation, based on motives of utility. It has been denied to certain categories of human beings in the past, the slaves. A growing jurisprudential and legislative movement, notably in France, is pushing for the recognition of groups as legal subjects.[133] The legal entities with which public international law is concerned are principally, if not exclusively, the states. So that it would seem normal that the criminal as well as civil responsibility lay on states for the damage which they cause.[134]

Such is the classical theory of public international law. Nothing in the recent events disproves these arguments; and we believe that they will remain valid for the future.[135] However, that is the negative aspect of this thesis, the interpretation of it, which Professor Jahreiss put forth in his argument mentioned earlier. He relies upon it to exclude the idea of individual responsibilities. The acts reproached being public in character, done in the name of the state, responsibility should fall upon the state. The agent cannot be substituted as far as legal sanctions are concerned for the entity on whose behalf he is acting without distorting judicial truth. Individual justice does not suffer from this exclusion,

---

[131] Mr de Menthon, *Documents*, Opening statement says, p. 55: 'in these conditions we cannot consider that a German state order subsists, that is capable of drawing consequences from the recognition of the Reich's responsibility in the violation of the Briand-Kellogg Pact in terms of individuals who are, in fact, the authors, as organs of the Reich, of this violation'.

[132] P. de Lapradelle, p. 8 and following.

[133] H. Donnedieu de Vabres, *Traité de Droit Criminel et de Législation Pénale Comparée*, Nos. 264 and 264*bis*, pp. 150 and following.

[134] Malézieux, pp. 172 and following.

[135] See, in favour of this thesis: H. Donnedieu de Vabres, *Principes Modernes de Droit Pénal International*, Sirey, 1928, pp. 418 and following. The thesis of 'The criminal state' was defended during the Nuremberg debates, by the British attorney-general, Sir Hartley Shawcross, *Trial of Major War Criminals*, vol. III, p. 115.

because secondary action of the state exists against the physical perpetrators of the acts which form the basis of the liability. Those perpetrators will be judged by a German tribunal, following German law which is doubly competent—as territorial law and national law of the accused. Professor Jahreiss puts forward the precedents of 1919 to support his view.

We have already mentioned the reasons which stand in the way of such a system. German law cannot apply as territorial law since the crimes are without geographical location. German law as nationalist-socialist law could no more apply to the accused as personal law since this law itself stands accused in the trial. The German state sovereignty has been suspended, if not abolished, and therefore is no longer qualified to take responsibility for its acts or to prosecute its people. The Allied states which have replaced it and which exercised its competencies were faced with guilty individuals who were directly responsible to them. This is the *positivist* terrain on which the Tribunal stands when justifying its competence *ratione loci* and *ratione materiae* over war criminals in the following terms:[136]

'The Signatory Powers created this Tribunal, defined the law it was to administer, and made regulations for the proper conduct of the Trial. In doing so, they have done together what any one of them might have done singly; for it is not to be doubted that any nation has the right thus to set up special courts to administer law.'

There is also a broader and more permanent basis on which the enforcement of individual responsibilities by an international judge may be justified. It is the basis recognized by the new public international law. Here, the criminal responsibility of the state as a legal entity is not excluded. In fact, only extremists deny the reality of the personality of this intermediary which has been imposed by history and sociology in the relations between the universal community and the individual, but it coexists with the responsibility of natural persons. In his classical book *Les Tendances Modernes du Droit International*,[137] Mr. Nicolas Politis highlights changes in the law that, since the war of 1914–1918, have recognized the individual to be a party before international authorities, mixed tribunals of arbitration, international prize courts and made him, concurrently with the state, a subject, active and passive, of public international law: 'the war that has just ended', writes Mr Paoli,[138] 'has accelerated the drive towards the recognition of individual responsibilities, which is consistent with the trend towards the creation of a common international law whose principles are directly addressed to human beings'.[139]

This double terrain—both positivist and doctrinal—*lex lata* and *lex ferenda*—is the one that shall be held up in order to appreciate the means of defence drawn from certain personal attributes or personal circumstances of the accused.

---

[136] *Trial of Major War Criminals*, vol. I, Judgment, p. 230.
[137] N. Politis, *Les Nouvelles Tendances du Droit International*, Paris, 1927 pp. 13 and following, 45 and following, 129 and following.
[138] Paoli, p. 132.
[139] G. Scelle, *Manuel Elémentaire de Droit International Public*, 1943, p. 432.

We plead, in their favour, the immunity of heads of state and the immunities of diplomatic agents is brandished in their favour. The charges are detrimental to the prestige which is necessary to the conservation and the dignity of each State. This was the position that benefited William II in 1919 when his extradition, requested *pro forma* it seems, was denied by the Netherlands. It is this position that benefited the emperor of Japan not long ago.

However, under positive law, the immunity of a head of state and that of diplomatic agents is not synonymous with criminal irresponsibility. Such immunity only provides for a particular allocation of competences. The responsibility of the leaders of a State for ordinary crimes falls under ordinary jurisdictions (Articles 114 and 115 of the French penal code), with some rare exceptions (the British Empire).[140] In France, for instance, the doctrine based on the principle of equality for all under the law (1789 Declaration of Rights, Article 6) admits that, for common crimes, the President of the Republic is subject to criminal law and must face the same tribunal as any other citizen.[141] Special rules govern the responsibility of the head of state and that of ministers only when political offences are concerned (Constitution of 27 October 1946, Articles 42, 56, and 57). Diplomats are exempt from the jurisdiction—both criminal and civil—of the state in which they are accredited; but a complaint suffices to force them to answer to their national jurisdiction for crimes committed on the territory of the state to which they have been accredited. These provisions form the law of peacetime: they cease to apply in times of war because they have then lost their *raison d'être*, which is to maintain relations of courtesy. A monarch fallen in the hands of an enemy is treated by them just as any other prisoner would be. Moreover, with the death of Mussolini and the presumed death of Hitler, this theory has lost the greatest part of its relevance; it is, in fact, only applied to Admiral Doenitz who carried out the function of German Head of State for a few weeks (May 1945).

We have just said that international courtesy is the basis for the recognition of immunities of leaders and diplomats. To this, allowance must be made for a desire to stay clear of all interference in a state's internal affairs, thereby respecting its independence. However, when values that are guarded by the universal community are at stake, not only are the rules of courtesy relegated to the background, but public order which is characterized by the reciprocal respect of each state's independence vanishes in favour of the idea of a superior public order.

This reasoning explains Article 7 of the Charter: 'The official position of defendants, whether as Heads of State or responsible officials in Government departments, shall not be considered as freeing them from responsibility or mitigating punishment.'

---

[140] In England, the immunity which the monarch enjoys is a reflection of the idea that 'the King can do no wrong' and that 'the King cannot be accused for he is himself the accuser' (Descheemaeker, *cited above*, p. 58).

[141] H. Donnedieu de Vabres, *Traité*, No 1664, p. 940.

This inspired the following finding in the judgment:[142]

'The principle of international law, which under certain circumstances, protects the representatives of a state, cannot be applied to acts which are condemned as criminal by international law. The authors of these acts cannot shelter themselves behind their official position in order to be freed from punishment in appropriate proceedings.'

The state of necessity raises a more delicate problem.

The abuse of this justifying factor by the aggressive policies of the Reich took different forms.

The pretext of 'encirclement' served as the *leitmotiv* for the outburst of the war of 1914–1918. After the demand of 'national minorities' in Austria and Czechoslovakia, the pretext of a 'vital space' accompanied the thirst for conquests in the East. At Nuremberg, the defence pointed to the 'injustice of the Versailles Treaty' to legitimize a policy said to have been intended to 'shake off the chains of this treaty' or, at least, to attenuate the responsibility of its promoters. Finally, the formula 'Not kennt kein Gebot', 'Necessity has no law', has long been brandished as an excuse for war crimes and crimes against humanity. According to that view, the laws of war, *Kriegsbrauch*, would contain the normal laws of war and the derogations to this law, which are justified by the circumstances or realities of the war, *Kriegsrason*, thus authorizing the recourse to procedures that would otherwise be forbidden by the regular laws. This is formulated in the German Rules of War Manual of 1902 which says that 'any and all means of war may be used, without which the goal of war would not be reached'.[143]

These arguments have gone on for long enough. The justifications based on the 'encirclement' and the 'vital space' had expired by the time the debates opened in Nuremberg: they were not presented in the pleadings. The International Military Tribunal regarded as 'irrelevant' the argument drawn from the alleged injustice of the Treaty of Versailles. Irrespective of the extent of the Tribunal's usual permissiveness, it is clear that evoking very distant historical precedents would have opened a discussion without any possible outcome, and that a limit needed to be imposed to narrow the scope of the debate. It is no less certain that the exception drawn from the state of necessity, if it were admissible and if it were to be determined by each belligerent, that is by the interested parties themselves, it would render the laws and customs of war worthless. This exception is also contrary to both the letter and the spirit of The Hague Conventions. It has been pointed out that by expressly admitting the necessities of the war as a justifying fact for the cases covered by Articles 15 and 23g, The Hague Regulations have implicitly excluded this justification in all other cases.[144]

---

[142] *Trial of Major War Criminals*, Judgment, p. 235.

[143] See, on this right and necessity, Ch. De Vischer, 'Les Lois de La Guerre et la Théorie de la Nécessité' (*Revue Générale de Droit International Public*, 1916, p. 74 and following); Rey, p. 9.

[144] See also Articles 49 and 52: 'Là où les deux conférences de la Haye ont subordonné la force obligatoire de telle ou telle disposition à la condition que les nécessités du succès des opérations militaires n'exigent point une rérogation aux règles tracées par elles, elles l'ont dit.' (Paoli, p. 160.)

On the other hand, the defence of 'superior order' holds, within the means of defence, an even more notable position because it can be backed up by a fundamental principle of the national-socialist organization, the principle of the Führer.

In domestic law, the existence of a justifying factor supposes the reunion of the following elements: the order of the law and a command by a legitimate authority.[145] Thus, it follows from this that if the order from a superior is to commit an act regarded as a crime by the law, the subordinate who followed that order has no justification to excuse his conduct. In some specific cases (Articles 114, 184, 188 to 190 of the penal code), he may benefit from a complete defence ('excuse absolutoire'). Outside of these cases, this fact could only be considered as a mitigating factor relevant to sentencing. Such are the provisions of the French penal code (Articles 327, 114, 184). They can be found with small variations in most other legislations.[146]

The above-mentioned ordinance of 28 August 1944, generally applies the same rules to international relations. Article 3 provides that laws, decrees, or regulations emanating from the enemy's authority, but also orders or authorizations given by this authority or by authorities depending on the former, or having depended upon the former, cannot be invoked as justifiable factors, but only as mitigating circumstances or absolving excuses. The only existing innovation consists of the extension of the domain of the absolving excuse.

The London Charter takes the opposite view on this last point. Article 8 is thus phrased: 'The fact that the Defendant acted pursuant to order of his Government or of a superior shall not free him from responsibility, but may be considered in mitigation of punishment if the Tribunal determines that justice so requires.' Thus, the benefit of a justifying factor ('l'excuse absolutoire') is excluded.[147] It must be noted, however, that on this point, as on others, the terms of the Charter is relaxed by the judgment, in a spirit that is favourable to the defence. The Charter takes the view that the relevance of discipline, which would command impunity in this matter, should give way to considerations inherent to the international public order and which demand repression. The Tribunal does not contradict that point; but it does envisage the situation where the authority of the superior was such as to negate all freedom of appreciation or action on the part of

---

[145] H. Donnedieu de Vabres, *Traité*, No 490, p. 236.

[146] See, notably, on Anglo-Saxon law, meaning English and US law: Paul Coste-Floret, *La Répression des Crimes de Guerre et le fait Justificatif Tiré de l'Ordre Supérieur* (Dalloz, 12 and 18 July 1945, Chronicle V). Cf. Joseph-Barthélemy, 'L'Influence de l'Ordre Hiérarchique sur la Responsabilité des Agents' (*Revue de Droit Public*, 1914, p. 491 and following).

[147] Article 3 of the Belgian law related to the competence of military jurisdictions on war crimes is conceived in that manner and contrary to the French Ordinance of 28 August 1944: (Moniteur Belge) 'Le fait que l'inculpé a agi conformément aux prescriptions de lois ou règlements ennemis et aux ordres d'un supérieur hiérarchique ne peut être considéré comme cause de justification, au sens de l'article 70 du Code Pénal, lorsque l'acte reproché constituerait une violation flagrante des lois et coutumes de la guerre ou des lois de l'humanité. Il pourra éventuellement être considéré comme circonstances atténuantes.'

subordinates. It is, therefore, general principles of law that impunity should prevail in such a case. This solution is not the consequence of a justifiable factor, but the result of the non-imputability of the act, or *duress* ('contrainte morale'). The basis for the discussion is changed, but the result is the same: neither the crime nor the punishment subsists.

Article 8 of the Charter is in fact commented upon in the following manner:[148]

'The provisions of this Article are in conformity with the law of all nations. That a soldier was ordered to kill or torture in violation of the international law of war has never been recognised as a defence to such acts of brutality, though, as the Charter here provides, the order may be urged in mitigation of the punishment. The true test, which is found in varying degrees in the criminal law of most nations, is not the existence of the order, but whether moral choice was in fact possible...'[149]

But how do we measure the liberty of this choice? The practice in most countries brings into play a traditional distinction between civilian functionaries and military servicemen.

With civilians, in a free country, the hierarchical structure is not strong enough to prevail upon the imperative character of criminal law. In this case, ordinary law applies, which has inspired the text of Article 8. Apart from those cases where it constitutes *l'excuse absolutoire*, which is admitted to various degrees in domestic laws, a superior order would only be regarded as a mitigating factor for sentencing.

The military situation is more complex. The idea that 'discipline is the primary force of the army', and thus that a subordinate is covered by the injunction of his superior, is nowhere admitted without limitations. It is there that new distinctions intervene and are uneasily expressed in a simple formula.

The simplest case is the one involving officers and soldiers who, during a war of aggression waged by their state, commit acts that in and of themselves constitute crimes or offences, but which are authorized by the laws of war. Mr de Menthon has argued with perfect logic that because of the criminal nature of the war of aggression, the laws of war do not protect the agents of the aggressor:[150]

'The acts committed in the pursuit of war are attacks on goods, which are themselves prohibited and sanctioned by all the legislatures. A state of war will not render them legal. Indeed, since the Briand–Kellogg Pact, it is no longer the case; and these acts have become purely and simply crimes of ordinary law. As has been demonstrated with irrefutable logic by Judge Jackson all recourse to war requires recourse to means which are, by their nature, criminal.'

---

[148] *Trial of Major Criminals*, vol. I, Judgment, p. 235.

[149] P. de Lapradelle, p. 14. Article 47 of the German Code of Military Justice provides 'la responsabilité de l'auteur de l'acte criminel si celui-ci est allé au delà des ordres reçus, ou bien a agi en connaissance du caractère criminel de l'acte ordonné': see P. Coste-Floret; Descheemaeker, p. 30.

[150] *Documents*. The Nuremberg Trial—French Public Prosecution—Opening Statement, p. 28.

The application of these ideas to all those who partook in the war is inadmissible. Mr de Menthon notes:

'It is clear that in a modern State, responsibility is limited to those who are acting directly for the state, they being the only ones in a position to appreciate the regularity of orders given. All the others, who have not taken part in the decisions and have not distinguished the criminal character are covered by the *force majeure* principle.'

Finally, contrary to his initial formula, Mr de Menthon comes to the conclusion that, in conformity with good sense and equity, the laws of war are applicable to all belligerents, independently of the justice or injustice of their cause.

The question remains open for acts which are contrary to the laws of war and which a serviceman, an officer or a soldier has committed in pursuance of orders from his superior. Multiple factors have to be taken into consideration. The more or less strict relationship of hierarchical subordination between the superior and the subordinate, the presence or absence of the superior at the time when the order was executed, the despicable nature of the prescribed acts, or, inversely, the possible doubt in terms of their illegality, are among the circumstances upon which the assessment could depend. A squad of soldiers who under the authority are ordered to shoot a Soviet 'commissar' or a detained pilot are not criminally responsible for their actions. By contrast, an officer who after receiving an order such as the Kommandos order or the *Kugel* decree, orders a mass execution, would incur the full extent of the criminal law.

'There is nothing in mitigation. Superior orders, even to a soldier, cannot be considered in mitigation where crimes so shocking and extensive have been committed consciously, ruthlessly, and without military excuse or justification.'[151]

In the relationship between Hitler and his immediate subordinates, the ascendancy that the Führer held, both in law and in fact, over them, should not be disregarded. In a dictatorship, we can admit that all responsibilities—including those of civilian bureaucrats—must be appreciated in terms of rules similar to those governing the military in a free country.

But should we go further than that? Should we agree with Professor Jahreiss and say that the regime generated by Hitler's irresistible will, the *Führer* who quickly became the *Herrscher*, liberates from all responsibility all those who were only obeying his orders? Those who obeyed his commands, he adds, could not have had the feeling of committing an injustice, because for them, his Will was synonymous with Law. The feeling of an injustice would, in fact, emerge if they were to be punished on this count. The intentional element was lacking in their actions.

Such reasoning goes beyond the requirements of individual injustice. It deliberately sacrifices the legitimate interest of victims, as well as the necessities of the international order. Despite Hitler's absolutism, there have been, under his regime, infractions to common discipline and resounding resignations that

---

[151] *Trial of Major War Criminals*, vol. I, Judgment, p. 309.

received no sanctions. In 1941, Brauschitsch and von Leeb were able to show their intention to sabotage the Führer's instructions concerning the treatment of Soviet commissars. Jodl brags that he was in conflict with him on more than one occasion, in 1942 concerning his conduct with the generals, in 1943 concerning the operations in the Caucasus, in 1944 concerning the measures to be taken in the face of the landing of the allies.[152] At no time were those challenges sanctioned.[153] It would be misleading, however, to cite these as examples of a systematic pattern. Hitler's fits of weakness were followed by grim acts of vengeance; in a similar way, the singular audacity of his politics of aggression is mixed with a strange shyness.[154] Inconsistencies are abundant. But looking at the whole picture, no one would admit that the men who were deeply involved or associated— and sometimes very complacent—with Hitler's actions, could invoke their lack of moral freedom to escape the consequences of his defeat.

Concerning the inherent responsibility of the general staff, the judgment contains the following finding:[155]

'Many of these men have made a mockery of the soldier's oath of obedience to military orders. When it suits their defense they say they had to obey; when confronted with Hitler's brutal crimes, which are shown to have been within their general knowledge, they say they disobeyed. The truth is they actively participated in all these crimes, or sat silent and acquiescent, witnessing the commission of crimes on a scale larger and more shocking than the world ever had the misfortune to know. This must be said.'

The harshness with which the repressive consequences imputed to these facts is imposed is not only, in the mind of the Tribunal, a tribute to the supremacy of conscience; it is also a tribute to the sovereignty of international law.

'The very essence of the Charter is that individuals have international duties which transcend the national obligations of obedience imposed by the individual State. He who violates the laws of war cannot obtain immunity while acting in pursuance of the authority of the State if the State in authorising action moves outside its competence under international law.'

Conclusion

After the above observations, there remains the need to characterize the position of the International Military Tribunal regarding two objections that were raised concerning its competence: one derives from the principle of legality; the other

[152] R. Cartier, pp. 280, 282, 284, 288.
[153] See Jodl's speech on 7 January 1943 in Munich, *Trial of Major War Criminals*, vol. II, Debates, p. 309.
[154] This is how the wait or search for 'pretexts' ended up in delaying the attack against Czechoslovakia (*Trial of Major War Criminals*, vol. III, Debates, p. 135 and following), Poland (*Trial of Major War Criminals*, vol. III, p. 68 and following) and Norway. R. Cartier, p. 83, 148.
[155] *Trial of Major War Criminals*, vol. I, Judgment, p. 295.

from the individual character of liability. This summary might bring out conclusions that are of interest to the future.

I. The Tribunal does not exclude the *nullem crimen, nulla poena sine lege* principle from international law; but it renders it more flexible in order to take into account the various social, technical and other factors which are peculiar to interstate relations. Thus understood, the principle requires knowledge of the criminal nature of the impugned conduct. It does not, however, require a rigorous definition of the offence, nor does it entail a detailed specification of the possible punishments. Those who engineered wars of aggression received sufficient notice to be held criminally responsible. But the interpretation of that principle adopted by the Tribunal has led the Tribunal to narrow down, if not completely to reject, two particular counts: that relating to conspiracy and the one relating to crimes against humanity.

Some authors have agreed that, in the future, a stricter application of the principle of legality would more effectively guarantee individual rights. During the Nuremberg Trial, the general and permanent value to be given to the Charter's principles was asserted by the Prosecution.[156] 'Unless we are prepared to abandon every principle of growth for international law, we cannot deny that our own day has the right to institute customs and to conclude agreements that will themselves become sources of a newer and strengthened international law.' The British representative of the Prosecution, Sir Hartley Shawcross stated:[157] 'insofar [...] as this Charter has put on record the principle of the criminal responsibility of the state, it must be applauded as a wise and far-seeing measure of international legislation'. A UN Commission for the 'progressive development and codification of international law' has recommended to the General Assembly the establishment of a 'plan for the general codification of crimes against peace and human security'. This plan contains the Nuremberg principles and will be followed by the drafting of an international criminal code.[158]

Does it mean that the crimes and sanctions contained in such a code would take on the precision and the fixity of a national legislation? We do not think so.

---

[156] *Trial of Major War Criminals*, vol. II, Debates; *Documents*, Opening Statement by Jackson, p. 36. See also P. De Lapradelle, p. 25.

[157] *Documents*, Opening Statement, p. 57; *Trial of Major War Criminals*, vol. III, p. 115; P. de Lapradelle, p. 25.

[158] The text of the recommendation made by the UN Commission for the progressive development and codification of international law reads as follows: 'La Commission recommande à l'unanimité d'inviter la Commission de droit international (dont elle propose la creation) à preparer:

a) Un projet de convention contenant les principes de droit international reconnus par le Statut de la Cour de Nuremberg et sanctionnés par l'arrêt de cette Cour et,

b) Un projet détaillé de plan de codification générale des crimes contre la paix et la sécurité de l'humanité, établi de telle façon que le plan indique clairement la place qu'on doit accorder aux principes mentionnés à l'alinéa a du présent paragraphe.

La Commission tient, en outre, à signaler qu'à son avis cette tâche ne doit pas empêcher la commission de droit international de rédiger en temps voulu un Code de droit pénal international.'

The factors that have explained the mobility and the instability of the community of States and the changing forms of international criminality have not ceased to operate since the Nuremberg judgment. It is part of the essence of international law to be, in part, a customary law.

II. The International Military Tribunal was accused of being an improvised tribunal that was set up for the needs of a particular case, an *ad hoc* tribunal constituted after the crimes it is tasked to judge. As a consequence, the bias of the tribunal and its lack of competence to judge *individuals* were put forward, since under the classical conception, states are the sole—active or passive—subjects of public international law.

The Tribunal, in line with the positive law approach, underlined the fact that if the principle of legality applies to material law, procedural law, i.e. laws on the judicial organisation and procedure, is, as in domestic systems, subject to immediate application. It added that the allied governments, by joining forces to judge the perpetrators of crimes that challenged their common interests, have, in fact, exercised their jurisdiction *ratione loci* and *ratione materiae*. They have undertaken together what each of them could have done separately.

This reasoning clearly does not represent the entirety of the Tribunal's reasoning; the latter does not present itself as a mere proxy for the four signatory states, the nineteen states which became party to the 8 August 1945 Agreement. The Tribunal adopts a universal mandate to judge the major war criminals who have violated fundamental human rights. In that sense, it openly sides with the new public international law where subjects are not only states but also individuals.

These considerations have the same permanent and general value as the Nuremberg principles that have previously been mentioned. They have value for the future. But if the rules governing the competence of the International Military Tribunal can be seen as justified and certain, it is different for the rules governing the organization of the Tribunal. Only factual circumstances explain and excuse the composition of this Tribunal where only judges nominated by victorious states were appointed. This was one of the critical shortcomings of the Covenant of the League of Nations, which failed to provide for a permanent international criminal jurisdiction or to attribute repressive powers to the Permanent International Court of Justice. It would be strange if, after the recent events and the partly justified criticisms that have arisen, this gap would not be filled. It would be strange if an *ad hoc* tribunal had to be set up after every manifestation of international criminality. The affirmation of the Nuremberg principles are an illusion if there is no permanent and pre-existing organ capable of sanctioning them. It seems that within the United Nations itself there are some worrying hesitations in that regard.[159]

---

[159] The UN Commission for the Progressive Development and Codification of International Law made the following statement on the issue:

'La Commission a décidé à la majorité d'attirer l'attention de l'Assemblée générale sur le fait que, pour metre en oeuvre les principes contenus dans le statut de la Cour de Nuremberg et l'arrêt de

The years to come will certainly be a turning point in History which has witnessed the intermingling of bursts of violence with the triumphs of the law. If violence prevails, the Nuremberg judgment will remain a historic fact unique to a trend that existed at some point in time, and nothing more; otherwise, it will set a precedent of an incomparable importance. Only a sound understanding of human interests and the rise of a universal conscience can avert the dangers involved in the opposition of two sprawling states and, in the atomic era, the risks which the dizzying progress of science is bringing about.

cette Cour, et pour garantir la châtiment d'autres crimes internationaux qui pourraient être reconnus comme tels par des conventions multipartites internationales, il peut être désirable d'instituer une autorité judiciaire internationale pour connaître ce ces crimes. Les représentants de l'Egypte, de la Pologne, du Royaume Uni, de l'URSS et de la Yougoslavie ont tenu à faire inscrire dans le présent rapport leur désapprobation au sujet de cette décision. D'après eux, la question de création d'une Cour internationale dépasse le mandat que l'Assemblée générale a confié à la présente commission.'

10

Will the Judgment in the Nuremberg Trial Constitute a Precedent in International Law?

By Professor Hans Kelsen,
University of California

1. In his report to the President of the U.S. of October 15, 1946, on the Nuremberg Trial, Mr. Justice Jackson said that the rules of law applied by the International Military Tribunal in the trial of the German war criminals have been 'incorporated' into a 'judicial precedent'. 'A judgment such as has been rendered shifts the power of the precedent to the support of these rules of law. No one can hereafter deny or fail to know that the principles on which the Nazi leaders are adjudged to forfeit their lives constitute law—law with a sanction'.[1] The correctness of this statement is doubtful.

A precedent is a judicial decision which serves as a model for subsequent decisions of similar cases. In order to be a precedent, the decision of a tribunal must conform with certain formal and material conditions which the judgment of Nuremberg does not fulfil.

The first condition is that the judicial decision must establish a new rule of law. This rule of law must be created by the judicial decision, not by the act of a legislative organ, or by custom, or by an international treaty (which is equivalent to legislation). It is generally recognised that precedents are, beside legislation and custom, a source of law, and as such law-making acts. It is the essential function of a precedent to establish principles[2] and that means general rules of law. It is only because of the general rule of law established by a judicial decision that other judicial decisions can follow the first one, that similar cases can be decided in the same way as the first case has been decided by the precedent. It is only on the basis of a general rule that two cases can be recognised as being 'similar'. If a precedent has binding force, it is the general rule of law established by it which is binding upon the tribunals in deciding similar cases. Hence a judicial decision

---

[1] New York Times, October 16, 1946, p. 23.
[2] Carleton Kemp Allen, *Law in the Making*, 3rd ed., 1939, p. 302.

that merely applies a pre-existent rule of substantive law, that is to say, a judicial decision by which no new rule of law is created, cannot have the character of a precedent. If the general rule applied by a judicial decision to an individual case is identical with a general rule of pre-existent statutory or customary law, and if subsequent similar cases are decided in the same way, it is not the authority of the first decision, but the authority of the statutory or customary law, pre-existent to and applied by the first judicial decision, which directs the decisions of the subsequent cases. The most characteristic element of a precedent is its law-creating function. In so far as the law is already created by legislation, custom, or international treaty, there is no room for a precedent. It is true that judicial decisions which are considered to be precedents, frequently pretend to apply pre-existing substantive law; but, in fact, they create new law under the disguise of interpreting existing law. Only in so far as they create new law, are they true precedents.[3]

2. The judgment rendered by the International Military Tribunal in the Nuremberg Trial cannot constitute a true precedent because it did not establish a new rule of law, but merely applied pre-existing rules of law laid down by the International Agreement concluded on August 8, 1945, in London, for the Prosecution of European Axis War Criminals, by the Governments of Great Britain, the United States of America, France, and the Soviet Union. The rules created by this Treaty and applied by the Nuremberg Tribunal, but not created by it, represent certainly a new law, especially by establishing individual criminal responsibility for violations of rules of international law prohibiting resort to war. These violations are called in the Agreement 'crimes against peace' and defined as 'planning, preparation, initiation or waging of a war of aggression, or a war in violation of international treaties, agreements or assurances, or participation in a common plan or conspiracy for the accomplishment of any of the foregoing'. The London Agreement establishes individual criminal responsibility also for other crimes, defined by the Agreement, such as 'war crimes' and 'crimes against humanity'; but the precedentary character of the Nuremberg judgment will be discussed here only with respect to the 'crimes against peace', because it is in this respect that the problem is of foremost importance.

The treaties for whose violation the London Agreement establishes individual criminal responsibility are in the first place the Briand-Kellogg Pact of 1928, and

---

[3] Some writers maintain that a tribunal in rendering a precedent does not really create a new rule of law but only gives evidence of an already existing rule of law. This doctrine is applied also to the other law-creating acts, such as custom and legislation. At the basis of this doctrine is the idea that positive law as established by custom, precedent, or legislation, is not the result of an original production, but of a more or less imperfect re-production of a perfect but invisible law, the archetype of positive law; the natural or objective law. This is the typical approach of the natural-law-doctrine to the problem of the sources of law, however, from a positivistic point of view, legislation, custom and precedent must be considered as true law-creating acts. Cf. my *General Theory of Law and State* (20th Century Legal Philosophy Series, Vol. I), Cambridge, Mass. (1945), pp. 126 ff. and, A. L. Goodhart, 'Precedent in English and Continental Law' (reprinted from the *Law Quarterly Review*, January, 1934) (1934), p. 14.

certain non-aggression pacts concluded by Germany with States against which Germany, in spite of these treaties, resorted to war. All these treaties forbade only resort to war, and not planning, preparation, initiation of war or conspiracy for the accomplishment of such actions. None of these treaties stipulated individual criminal responsibility. For their violation the sanctions provided by general international law applied, that is to say, the State whose right was violated was authorised to resort to reprisals or counter-war against the violator. The Briand-Kellogg Pact, it is true, does provide in its preamble a special sanction for its violation; but this sanction constitutes no individual criminal responsibility. The Pact stipulates 'that any signatory power which shall hereafter seek to promote its national interests by resort to war should be denied the benefits furnished by this Treaty'. That means that all states parties to the Pact, and not only the immediate victim of an illegal war, are authorised to resort to war against a State which in violation of the Pact has resorted to war. Reprisals and war as sanctions are directed against a State as such, and not against the individuals, forming its government. These sanctions constitute collective responsibility, not criminal responsibility of definite individuals performing the acts by which international law is violated. A war waged in violation of treaties prohibiting resort to war, especially in violation of the Briand-Kellogg Pact, is certainly illegal. It is not necessarily a 'war of aggression', as the London Agreement assumes. A war of aggression is a war on the part of the State which is the first to enter hostilities against its opponent. Such action may be legal as well as illegal. When France and Great Britain, in 1989, resorted to war against Germany without being attacked by her, their war was technically a war of aggression but in complete conformity with the Briand-Kellogg Pact, and, hence, legal. An illegal war may be called an 'international crime', and has been so called in the Geneva Protocol of 1924 for the Pacific Settlement of International Disputes, and in a Resolution of the Eighth Assembly of the League of Nations (but not in the Briand-Kellogg Pact). This term, however, does not mean—as the International Military Tribunal erroneously declares in its judgment—'that those who plan and wage such a war, with its inevitable and terrible consequences, are committing a crime in so doing'.[4] This statement implies that the Briand-Kellogg Pact, according to the interpretation of the tribunal, established individual criminal responsibility for its violation. But such responsibility can be established only by a rule of international or national law providing punishments to be inflicted upon definite individuals. To deduce individual criminal responsibility for a certain act from the mere fact that this act constitutes a violation of international law, to identify the international illegality of an act by which vital human interests are violated with its criminality, meaning individual criminal responsibility for it, is in contradiction with positive law and generally accepted principles of international jurisprudence.

[4] Judgment of the International Military Tribunal, etc., Presented by the Secretary of State for Foreign Affairs to Parliament by Command of His Majesty Cmd. 6964, London, 1946, p. 39.

3. In his opening address, Mr. Justice Jackson declared: 'Any resort to war—to any kind of war—is a resort to means that are inherently criminal. War inevitably is a course of killings, assaults, deprivation of liberty and destruction of property. An honestly defensive war is, of course, legal and saves those lawfully conducting it from criminality. But inherently criminal acts cannot be defended by showing that those who committed them were engaged in war, when war itself is illegal. The very minimum legal consequence of the treaties making aggressive wars illegal is to strip those who incite or wage them of every defence the law ever gave, and to leave war-makers subject to judgment by usually accepted principles of the law of crime'.[5] It is especially the defence of the act of State which, according to this doctrine, does not apply if the war, waged as an act of State, is illegal.

This doctrine implies some fundamental errors. The first is the assumption that an act loses its character as a crime under national law if it is legal under international law. That an act is 'legal' under a certain law means that no sanction is attached to it by that law. That no sanction is attached to an act and that, consequently, this act is legal under one legal system, does not prevent a sanction from being attached to this very act and that act from being illegal under another legal system; and vice versa. That international law attaches a sanction to an act and thus makes the act internationally illegal, does not preclude national law from omitting to attach a sanction to this act, so that the act remains legal under national law. That an act is illegal under international law does not necessarily imply that the act is also illegal under national law, especially under national criminal law. Breach of blockade is illegal under international law, being the condition of a sanction provided by this law; but it may be not illegal at all under the national law of the State to which the individual belongs who committed the breach of blockade. Killings, assaults, deprivation of liberty, destruction of property performed in war are no crimes under national law, not because—and only if—the war is legal under international law, that is to say, because international law does not attach to these acts, which form in their totality the action called war, one of its specific sanctions. These acts are not punishable under national law for the same reason that killing in the execution of capital punishment is not punishable under national law: because national law does not provide punishment for these acts. Acts are punishable, and that means, criminal, only under a definite—national or international—legal order. Nobody is 'subject to judgment by usually accepted principles of the law of crime', as Mr. Justice Jackson says. One is subject only to a judgment rendered by a competent court on the basis of positive criminal law. And criminal law is either the national law of a definite state, or rules of international law providing individual punishment. Whether an act which is illegal under international law is also illegal and especially criminal,

---

[5] This doctrine has been presented by J. W. Garner, *International Law and the World War* (1920), Vol. II, p. 472. Garner followed Renault, 'De l'application du droit penal aux faits de guerre'. *Revue Generale de Droit International Public* (1918), Vol. 25, p. 10. Cf. my *Peace Through Law*, Chapel Hill (1944), pp. 91 ff.

under national law, and that means, under the law of a definite State, depends upon whether also the national law provides a sanction, especially a punishment for this act.

It can hardly be denied that international law prior to the London Agreement, did not provide punishment of those individuals who performed the acts of an illegal war. It is likewise undeniable that the national laws of the States which waged a war, illegal under international law, but carried out in conformity with the law of the State concerned, do not provide punishment for those who perform the acts of such war. Only under the law of the State against which an internationally illegal war is waged could the individuals, who perform the acts of the illegal war as acts of their State, be treated as criminals, if the law of the State against which the illegal war was waged provided punishment for such acts. Since no criminal law of an existent State expressly refers to killing, assault, deprivation of liberty, destruction of property performed in an illegal war, except as acts of legitimate warfare, the punishment of these acts under national law is possible only in the way of interpretation. It stands to reason that an interpretation is excluded according to which the definitions of these crimes include acts performed in a war, which is internationally illegal but constitutionally waged by the State whose criminal law is in question. Nobody will be tried by a court of his own State for murder on the ground that he, as a soldier, has killed in warfare an enemy soldier, even if the war has been declared illegal by an international tribunal. If the criminal law of a State is interpreted as not referring to acts committed by members of the State's own army in an internationally legal or illegal war, then it is hardly possible to interpret the same law to mean that killings, assaults, deprivation of liberty, destruction of property performed in an illegal war as acts of the enemy State, are crimes. The criminal laws of all States have been established at a time when it was generally taken for granted that no State could violate international law by resorting to war, when no treaty existed outlawing war, and when the doctrine of bellum justum was almost generally rejected, so that the distinction between legal and illegal war did not play any role at all. Even after the Briand-Kellogg Pact, it is necessary to distinguish between acts of legitimate and of illegitimate warfare, and this distinction applies as well to legal as illegal wars. If the 'crimes against peace' as defined by the London Agreement and interpreted by the International Military Tribunal imply killings, assaults, deprivation of liberty and destruction of property performed in an illegal war, they refer to acts of legitimate warfare; for the acts of illegitimate warfare are covered by the concept of 'war crimes'. There is no national criminal law that refers to acts of legitimate warfare, whether performed in a legal or illegal war. Hence there is no national criminal law under which the 'crimes against peace' are punishable.

4. Even if it were possible to interpret the criminal law of a State to mean that killings, assaults, deprivation of liberty and destruction of property performed as acts of legitimate warfare in an illegal war waged by the enemy State are crimes punishable under this law, the latter would not be applicable. For there is a rule

of positive international law that excludes the application of such national law to acts of another State. It is the rule that no State can claim jurisdiction over another State, meaning jurisdiction exercised by courts of one State over acts of another State. Since a State manifests its existence only in acts of individuals performed as acts of State, jurisdiction over a State means jurisdiction of one State exercised over acts of another State. The jurisdiction excluded by this rule cannot be the jurisdiction a State exercises in reacting against the violation of its right by resorting to sanctions provided by general international law: reprisals and war, against the violator of its right; nor jurisdiction exercised by an international tribunal established with the consent of the State whose acts are subjected to the jurisdiction of this tribunal. It means only the jurisdiction exercised unilaterally by the courts of one State over acts of another State, without the latter's consent. This is the rule of positive international law which prevents that an individual be tried by a court of one State or by the common court of two or more States for having committed a delict performed as an act of another State (except with the consent of the latter).

This rule, it is true, has some exceptions. Thus, international law authorises the States to punish, through their courts, espionage committed against them (but does not oblige the States to punish espionage performed in their own interest), even if the act has been performed at the command or with the authorisation of a government, that is to say, as an act of State. But such exceptions must be established by special rules of customary or contractual international law.

5. The International Military Tribunal in its judgment, did not follow the doctrine advocated by Mr. Justice Jackson in his inaugural address. The tribunal used a somewhat different doctrine to prove that the Briand-Kellogg Pact had already established individual criminal responsibility for resorting to war in violation of the Pact. The judgment contains the following statement:

... it is argued that the Pact does not expressly enact that such wars are crimes, or set up courts to try those who make such wars. To that extent the same is true with regard to the laws of war contained in the Hague Convention. The Hague Convention of 1907 prohibited resort to certain methods of waging war. These included the inhumane treatment of prisoners, the employment of poisoned weapons, the improper use of flags of truce, and similar matters. Many of these prohibitions had been enforced long before the date of the Convention; but since 1907 they have certainly been crimes, punishable as offences against the laws of war; yet the Hague Convention nowhere designates such practices as criminal, nor is any sentence prescribed, nor any mention made of a court to try and punish offenders. For many years past, however, military tribunals have tried and punished individuals guilty of violating the rules of land warfare laid down by this Convention. In the opinion of the tribunal, those who wage aggressive war are doing that which is equally illegal, and of much greater moment than a breach of one of the rules of the Hague Convention.[6]

[6] Judgment, p. 40.

The jurisdiction of the military tribunals which for many years past have tried and punished individuals guilty of violating the rules of land warfare laid down by the Hague Convention of 1907 is totally different from the jurisdiction conferred upon the International Military Tribunal by the London Agreement. The military tribunals referred to in the judgment applied positive national criminal law, the law of the State which had transformed the rules of the Hague Convention—rules regulating the conduct of war—into its own criminal law. No State has, so far, transformed the rules of international law prohibiting resort to war—different from the rules of warfare—into national criminal law; and no military tribunal has, so far, tried and punished individuals for having resorted to an internationally illegal war. The military tribunals to whose practice the judgment refers, tried and punished individuals for acts of illegitimate warfare performed by them as private persons, not as act of State. The acts forbidden by the Hague Convention, it is true, may be acts of State, as well as acts of private persons performed on their own initiative, not at the command or with the authorisation of their government. However, as to its violation by acts of State, the Hague Convention constitutes only collective responsibility of the States as such.[7] Because the Convention forbids also violation of the rules of warfare by acts of private persons one may assume that general international law obliges the States to punish, in application of their own law, their own subjects, and authorises belligerents to punish subjects of the opponent, if they fall into their hands as prisoners of war, for having violated the rules of warfare, and for this purpose to adapt their own law to the Hague Convention.[8] A typical example of such national law is the Basic Field Manual: Rules of Land Warfare (FM 27/10), issued by the Department of War of the United States in 1940. Article 347, after enumerating the possible offences, stipulates:

Individuals of the armed forces will not be punished for these offences in case they are committed under the orders or sanction of their government or commanders. The commanders ordering the commission of such acts, or under whose authority they are committed by their troops, may be punished by the belligerent into whose hands they may fall.

Acts committed under the order or sanction of government—that is acts of State, are not punishable. Only commanders of troops, not members of the government, are punishable and only for offences not committed under the orders or sanction of their government, that is to say, as acts of State.

---

[7] Article 3 of the Convention stipulates only that a belligerent party which violates the provisions of the regulations respecting the laws and customs of war on land 'shall, if the case demands, be liable to pay compensation. It shall be responsible for all acts committed by persons forming part of its armed forces'. Hence also for acts not performed at the command or with the authorisation of the government. Under general international law, a belligerent party may resort to reprisals against the enemy which has violated the Convention.

[8] Article 1 of the Convention only stipulates that 'the contracting Powers shall issue instructions for their armed land forces which shall be in conformity with the regulations respecting the laws and customs of war on land...'.

The differences between the Hague Convention on the rules of warfare and the Briand-Kellogg Pact is that the former can be violated by acts of State as well as by acts of private persons, whereas the latter can be violated only by acts of State. The Briand-Kellogg Pact does not—as does the Hague Convention—forbid acts of private persons. Consequently it cannot be assumed that general international law obliges or authorises the States, contracting parties to the Pact, to punish under their own law the individuals who, in their capacity as organs of a State, violated the Pact. In establishing such individual criminal responsibility the London Agreement created law not yet established by the Briand-Kellogg Pact, or valid as a rule of general international law.

It seems that the International Military Tribunal did not have great confidence in the doctrine that to punish individuals for private acts of illegitimate warfare is the same as to punish officials of States for resorting to an illegal war. For it states that the law of war

is not static, but by continual adaptation follows the needs of a changing world. Indeed, in many cases treaties do no more than express and define for more accurate reference the principles of law already existing.

This is not an appeal to the law that has existed 'for many years past', but to a new law adapted to a changing world. That the London Agreement is only the expression, not the creation, of this new law, is the typical fiction of the problematical doctrine whose purpose is to veil the arbitrary character of the acts of a sovereign law-maker.[9]

Neither by the doctrine of the American prosecutor nor by the doctrine of the tribunal is it possible to prove that existing international law, especially the Briand-Kellogg Pact, has already established individual criminal responsibility for acts by which a State resorts to an internationally illegal war. Nor was there any national criminal law applicable to those accused of having committed the crimes against peace determined in the London Agreement. The International Military Tribunal was authorised to apply, and did apply, only the rules of law laid down in the Agreement of London. This Agreement, and no national criminal law, provided the punishment inflicted by the tribunal upon the accused persons for having committed the acts determined by the Agreement. Hence, there was no question as to whether the acts for which these persons were tried were criminal under any national law. For the tribunal they were criminal, and that means punishable, only under the law created by the London Agreement, which is the only legal basis of the judgment.

In creating the law to be applied by the tribunal, in providing for individual criminal responsibility not only for waging war in violation of existing treaties but also for planning, preparation or initiation of such war and participation in

---

[9] Cf. note 3 above. The Judgment (p. 38) expressly states: 'The Charter [as part of the London Agreement] is not an arbitrary exercise of power on the part of the victorious nations, but in the view of the Tribunal, ... it is the expression of international law existing at the time of its creation'.

a conspiracy for accomplishment of these actions, the London Agreement has certainly created new law. But the International Military Tribunal established by this Agreement had no part in the creation of this law. Its function was limited to the strict application of the rules laid down in the Agreement to concrete cases. Apart from the individualisation of the general rules of the Agreement, which necessarily is implied in any judicial decision applying a general rule to a concrete case, there was no creative function in the judgment of the tribunal. This judgment is not a source of law in the sense a true precedent is. The source of law is the London Agreement; and it is a source of law only and exclusively for the International Military Tribunal established by this Agreement.

6. A true precedent must have binding force. That means that the general rule established by the precedent must be legally binding upon the tribunal which rendered the precedent, and upon other tribunals, inferior to it, in the decision of similar cases. There is no rule of general international law conferring upon the decision of any international tribunal the power to render binding precedents. It is highly significant that the Statute of the Permanent Court of International Justice as well as the Statute of the International Court of Justice provide in Article 59 (identical in both Statutes):

The decision of the Court has no binding force except between the parties and in respect to that particular case.

The decision of a court by which a new rule of law is established can be actually followed by other decisions of similar cases only if the court itself is competent to decide not only the case in which the precedent has been rendered, but also other similar cases, and if there exist other inferior tribunals having the same competence. The judgment of the International Military Tribunal does not fulfil these requirements. For this tribunal is not a permanent court and there exist no other international tribunals competent to decide similar cases. According to its Article 7 the London Agreement 'shall remain in force for the period of one year and shall continue hereafter, subject to the right of any signatory to give through the diplomatic channel one month's notice of intention to terminate it'. Even if the tribunal should be in a position to decide other cases than those decided in its judgment delivered on September 80, 1946, it could apply only the rules established by the Agreement, and not follow any rule established by its first judgment. Still more important is the fact that there exists no international tribunal competent to try individuals for having violated rules of international law prohibiting resort to war. Such tribunals may come into existence only by special treaties conferring upon them the power to inflict punishments upon definite individuals for having committed crimes as determined in these treaties. If such international tribunals should be established and inflict punishments upon definite individuals for having planned, prepared, initiated or waged an illegal war, they would and could do so only in application of the rules laid down in the basic treaties. The judgment of the Nuremberg trial would and could not be of any legal importance to their decisions. It is not superfluous to note that the only permanent international court that actually exists, the International Court of Justice, the principal judicial organ of the United Nations, is not competent at all to try individuals, since Article 84, paragraph 1 of its Statute expressly stipulates that 'only States may be parties before the Court'.

If, as within the system of international law, there is no legal rule conferring upon certain tribunals the power to establish by their decisions general rules legally binding upon this and other tribunals, if there is no possibility of a legally binding precedent, then it is not possible to answer the question as to whether the decision of a tribunal has the character of a precedent, immediately after the decision has been rendered. The answer depends on whether or not this tribunal and other tribunals will actually decide other cases in the same way. The statement of Mr. Justice Jackson that the judgment of Nuremberg constitutes a judicial precedent, is at least premature.

7. If there is no legal rule conferring upon a judicial decision the character of a legally binding precedent, this decision has a certain chance of being followed by other decisions on condition that it is recognised as a worthy example for the decision of subsequent similar cases. This condition is usually formulated by the statement that a judicial decision will become a precedent only if the new rule embodied in it is generally considered to be just. The judgment of Nuremberg, even if it complied with all the formal requirements of a true precedent, will hardly be considered as worthy to be followed. For there are some serious objections against the appropriateness of the adjective as well as the substantive law applied by it.

The objection most frequently put forward—although not the weightiest one—is that the law applied by the judgment of Nuremberg is an ex post facto law. There can be little doubt that the London Agreement provides individual punishment for acts which, at the time they were performed were not punishable, either under international or under any national law. The rule against retroactive legislation has certainly not been respected by the London Agreement. However, this rule is not valid at all within international law, and is valid within national law only with important exceptions.[10] The rule excluding retroactive legislation is based on the more general principle that no law should be applied to a person who did not know the law at the moment he behaved contrarily to it. But there is another generally accepted principle, opposite to the former, that ignorance of the law is no excuse. If knowledge of a non-retroactive law is actually impossible—which is sometimes the case since the assumption that everybody knows the existing law is a fiction—then there is, psychologically, no difference between the application of this non-retroactive law and the application of a retroactive law which is considered to be objectionable because it applies to persons

---

[10] Cf. my article: 'The rule against ex post facto laws and the Prosecution of the Axis War Criminals' in *The Judge Advocate Journal*, 1945, Vol. II, No. 3, p. 8 ff. and 46.

who did not and could not know it. In such a case the law applied to the delin-
quent has actually retroactive effect although it was legally in force at the time the
delict has been committed.

The rule excluding retroactive legislation is restricted to penal law and does
not apply if the new law is in favour of the accused person. It does not apply to
customary law and to law created by a precedent, for such law is necessarily retroactive in respect to the first case to which it is applied.

A retroactive law providing individual punishment for acts which were illegal though not criminal at the time they were committed, seems also to be an
exception to the rule against ex post facto laws. The London Agreement is such
a law. It is retroactive only in so far as it established individual criminal responsibility for acts which at the time they were committed constituted violations of
existing international law, but for which this law has provided only collective
responsibility. The rule against retroactive legislation is a principle of justice.
Individual criminal responsibility represents certainly a higher degree of justice
than collective responsibility, the typical technique of primitive law. Since the
internationally illegal acts for which the London Agreement established individual criminal responsibility were certainly also morally most objectionable,
and the persons who committed these acts were certainly aware of their immoral
character, the retroactivity of the law applied to them can hardly be considered
as absolutely incompatible with justice. Justice required the punishment of these
men, in spite of the fact that under positive law they were not punishable at the
time they performed the acts made punishable with retroactive force. In case
two postulates of justice are in conflict with each other, the higher one prevails;
and to punish those who were morally responsible for the international crime of
the second World War may certainly be considered as more important than to
comply with the rather relative rule against ex post facto laws, open to so many
exceptions.

8. Unfortunately the London Agreement is not consistent in this respect. Its
greatest merit is that it puts into force the idea of individual criminal responsibility for violations of international law and thus improves—though not in
general but for some particular cases—the primitive technique of general international law with its collective responsibility. But, at the same time, the London
Agreement authorises the International Military Tribunal to declare 'groups or
organisations' as criminal, and confers upon the competent national authorities
of any signatory 'the right to bring individuals to trial for membership therein
before national, military or occupation courts'. That means that an individual
may be subjected to a criminal sanction not because he, by his own behaviour, committed a crime, but because he belonged to an association declared as
criminal. That means collective criminal responsibility. The Nuremberg judgment, it is true, tries to restrict as far as possible the scope of this collective
responsibility. The judgment states that punishing individuals for the crime of

membership in certain organisations 'is a far-reaching and novel procedure'.[11] It states further:

... the tribunal is vested with discretion as to whether it will declare any organisation criminal. This discretion is a judicial one and does not permit arbitrary action, but should be exercised in accordance with well settled legal principles, one of the most important of which is that criminal guilt is personal, and that mass punishments should be avoided. If satisfied of the criminal guilt of any organisation or group, this tribunal should not hesitate to declare it to be criminal because the theory of 'group criminality' is new, or because it might be unjustly applied by some subsequent tribunals.

If 'criminal guilt is personal', how is 'group criminality' possible at all? The judgment says:

On the other hand, the tribunal should make such declaration of criminality so far as possible in a manner to insure that innocent persons will not be punished.

Consequently, the judgment states that the definition of the criminality of individuals, members of an organisation declared criminal by the tribunal

should exclude persons who had no knowledge of the criminal purposes or acts of the organisation and those who were drafted by the State for membership, unless they were personally implicated in the commission of acts declared criminal by Article 6 of the Charter as members of the organisation. Membership alone is not enough to come within the scope of these declarations.

However, all these principles are not laid down in the London Agreement. They are not legally binding upon the tribunals in trying individuals for the crime of membership in a criminal organisation. And the restrictions suggested by the International Military Tribunal, even if accepted by the competent tribunals, would not have the effect of substituting for the collective responsibility established by the London Agreement, the principle that members of a criminal organisation are to be punished only for actual participation in the performance of crimes determined in the Agreement. Only the provisions laid down in this Agreement concerning criminal organisations count; and these provisions constitute a regrettable regress to the backward technique of collective criminal responsibility, in open contradiction to the progress made by the Agreement in establishing the opposite principle in its provisions concerning crimes against peace.

9. This progress is impaired not only by the inconsistency just shown, but also by the way in which the principle of individual criminal responsibility for violations of international law has been realised. This principle, applied to acts of State, is, as pointed out, a restriction of the rule that no State has jurisdiction over the acts of another State. Consequently, it can be put into force in conformity with existing international law only with the consent of the State whose acts are placed

[11] Judgment, pp. 66 f.

under the jurisdiction of a national court of another State, or of an international
tribunal. When the victors in the first World War intended to bring William II
to trial—not for a crime against peace—but 'for a supreme offence against international morality and the sanctity of treaties', they thought it necessary to insert
the provisions establishing, with retroactive force, his individual criminal responsibility for acts he performed in his capacity as organ of the German Reich into
the peace treaty, signed and ratified by this State. This is the only correct way to
bring into effect the principle in question on the basis of international law. Since
the purpose of this principle is to guarantee the observance of international law,
it should not be put into force in a way which is not in complete conformity with
the very law. As to Germany the situation was rather difficult if, for some reason
or another, it was not possible to obtain the consent of a German national government to the treaty establishing individual criminal responsibility for acts of
the German Reich, the criminal prosecution of Germans for illegal acts of their
State could have been based on national law, enacted for this purpose by the competent authorities. These authorities were the four occupant powers exercising
their joint sovereignty in a condominium over the territory and the population
of subjugated Germany through the Control Council as the legitimate successor
of the last German Government.[12] The Control Council could have appointed
a tribunal composed of Germans or neutrals, or organised in the same way as
the International Military Tribunal established by the London Agreement. The
Control Council could also have enacted the law to be applied by the tribunal.
But, in spite of the fact that actually only German war criminals were intended to
be brought to justice, another way has been chosen. The trial has not been placed
on a national or quasinational (condominium), but on an international legal basis.
An international agreement was concluded—not for the prosecution of German
war criminals only but 'for the Prosecution of European Axis War Criminals'.
The Agreement makes no difference between Germany, whose national government had been abolished and replaced by a condominium government of the four
occupant Powers, and the other European Axis States over which the Signatories
had not assumed sovereign legislative power. The Agreement is an international
treaty concluded not only by the four occupant Powers, but also by many other
United Nations, invited in Article 5 of the Agreement to adhere to it. The tribunal is expressly designated an 'International' Military Tribunal, and its members
were not appointed by the Control Council for Germany but by the governments
of the United States, Great Britain, France and the Soviet Union, with the consent, subsequently given, of the States which adhered to the Agreement. The four
Signatories declared in the Preamble of the Agreement that they were acting—
not as the sovereigns over the former German territory but—'in the interest of
all the United Nations'. The intention to place the trial of the war criminals on
an international legal basis and to create for this purpose new international law,

---

[12] Cf. my above-quoted article on the Legal Status of Germany.

results clearly from Mr. Justice Jackson's Report to the President of June 7, 1945,[13] as well as from his Report to the President of October 15, 1946.[14] In the latter he says of the Agreement: 'It is a basic charter in the international law of the future'. The creation of a new international law—at least with respect to the individual responsibility for crimes against peace—was legally possible only with the consent of the European Axis Powers. Although it is not of legal, but only of political, importance, it should not be overlooked that in order to ascertain that crimes against peace have been committed, the International Military Tribunal had first to ascertain that the European Axis Power concerned had violated certain treaties in resorting to war. Under general international law it is upon each contracting State to decide for itself whether a violation of the treaty has occurred, if agreement as to this fact (for instance by a peace treaty) cannot be brought about. If, however, a tribunal is instituted to make individuals criminally responsible for their State's violation of a treaty, it is not exactly an improvement of general international law to establish this tribunal without the consent of the State accused of the treaty violation.

On December 20, 1945, the Control Council for Germany enacted a law concerning 'punishment of persons guilty of war crimes, crimes against peace and against humanity'. (Control Council Law No. 10.) Article 1 declares the London Agreement of August 8, 1945 an integral part of this law. It is, however, not this law of the Control Council; it is the international agreement signed at London which is the legal basis of the Nuremberg trial. It is to this agreement that the judgment refers as to the legal basis of its jurisdiction,[15] not to the law of the Control Council. The judgment refers to this law only in so far as the latter contains provisions concerning the punishment for membership of organisations declared criminal by the International Military Tribunal.[16] The law was enacted (1) 'to give effect to the terms of the Moscow Declaration of October 80, 1948, and the London Agreement of August 8, 1945, and the Charter issued pursuant thereto' and (2) 'in order to establish a uniform legal basis in Germany for the prosecution of war criminals and other similar offenders, *other* than those dealt with by the International Military Tribunal' (Preamble). As to the first mentioned purpose the law was necessary since the Agreement conferred certain functions on the Control Council (in spite of the fact that its text referred not only to German war criminals). The law of the Control Council was certainly not enacted to furnish the legal basis for the Nuremberg trial.

However, in the judgment of Nuremberg the tribunal declares that 'the making of the Charter' [an intrinsic part of the London Agreement containing the rules of law to be applied by the tribunal] was 'the exercise of the sovereign legislative power by the countries to which the German Reich unconditionally

---

[13] New York Times, June 8, 1945, p. 4.
[14] New York Times, October 16, 1946, p. 23.
[15] Judgment, p. 38.
[16] Judgment, p. 66.

surrendered'.[17] In view of the above-mentioned facts the correctness of this statement seems to be problematical. Besides, by the Act of Military Surrender signed
by the representatives of the German High Command at Berlin on May 8, 1945,
no legislative power has been conferred upon the States to which the German
army surrendered. It was by the Declaration made at Berlin on June 5, 1945,
that the four occupant Powers—not all the States to which the German army
surrendered—assumed sovereign legislative power over the former German territory and its population.

10. It must be admitted that in relation to the German delinquents the difference between a legislative act of the four occupant powers in their capacity
as legitimate successors of the German Government, and a treaty concluded by
them and adhered to by other States belonging to the United Nations, is rather
formal than substantial. And, though in the realm of law the formal aspect is
essential, the objection against the Nuremberg trial arising out of this deficiency
is not the most serious one. What really impairs the authority of the judgment is
that the principle of individual criminal responsibility for the violation of rules of
international law prohibiting war has not been established as a general principle
of law, but as a rule applicable only to vanquished States by the victors. This is specially manifest by the fact that the principle laid down in the London Agreement
for the punishment of European Axis war criminals has not been inserted into
the Charter of the United Nations which, although supposed to be the basis of
the international law of the future, still stipulates only collective responsibility of
the States as such for violations of the Charter, imputable to the responsible State,
not to the acting individuals.[18] And even more objectionable than the fact that
the London Agreement has the character of a privilegium odiosum imposed upon

[17] Judgment, p. 38.
[18] To insert into the Charter the principles laid down in the London Agreement an amendment
to the Charter is necessary. The resolution adopted by the General Assembly on December 11,
1946, is not equivalent to such amendment. It runs as follows:

The General Assembly,

Recognises the obligation laid down by Article 13, paragraph 1, subparagraph a. of the Charter,
to initiate studies and make recommendations for the purpose of encouraging the progressive
development of international law and its codification; and

Takes note of the Agreement for the establishment of an International Military Tribunal for the
prosecution and punishment of the major war criminals of the European Axis signed in London
on August 8, 1945, and of the Charter annexed thereto, and of the fact that similar principles had
been adopted in the Charter of the International Military Tribunal for the trial of the major war
criminals in the Far East, proclaimed at Tokyo on January 19, 1946.

Therefore

Affirms the principles of international law recognised by the Charter of the Nuremberg Tribunal
and the judgment of the Tribunal;

Directs the Committee on the codification of international law established by the resolution of
the General Assembly of December, 1946, to treat as a matter of primary importance plans for the
formulation, in the context of a general codification of offences against the peace and security of
mankind, or of an International Criminal Code, of the principles recognised in the Charter of the
Nuremberg Tribunal and in the judgment of the Tribunal (*Journal of the General Assembly*, No. 75,
p. 945).

vanquished States by the victors is that the tribunal established by the Agreement was composed exclusively of representatives of victorious States directly affected by the crimes over which this tribunal had jurisdiction. Not only representatives of the vanquished States, but also—what is more important—representatives of neutral States were excluded from the bench. One of the fundamental questions to be decided by the tribunal was the question as to whether Germany, in resorting to war against Poland and the Soviet Union, violated international treaties concluded with the States whose representatives formed the court. Thus these States made themselves not only legislators but also judges in their own cause. Among the States whose representatives were the judges and prosecutors in the Nuremberg trial was one which had shared with Germany the booty of the war waged against Poland, a war declared by the tribunal, in conformity with the London Agreement, as a crime against peace because waged in violation of a non-aggression pact. It was the State which, in addition to this, committed exactly the same 'crime' in resorting to war against Japan in violation of a still existing non-aggression pact. If the principles applied in the Nuremberg trial were to become a precedent—a legislative rather than a judicial precedent—then, after the next war, the governments of the victorious States would try the members of the governments of the vanquished States for having committed crimes determined unilaterally and with retroactive force by the former. Let us hope that there is no such precedent.

11

The Nuremberg Trial[1]

By The Rt. Hon. Lord Justice Lawrence
(The Lord Oaksey)

The Prime Minister, THE RT. HON. CLEMENT R. ATTLEE:

Ladies and Gentlemen: It is a great privilege to me tonight to introduce to you an old schoolfellow who has done, I think, a very great work. We have seen in the past decade all kinds of standards of civilization swept away. At the Nuremberg Trial it fell to Lord Justice Lawrence to show the whole world what British justice means, and I hold that in that he did a high honour to himself, a high honour to this country and a great service to the world.

LORD JUSTICE LAWRENCE:

It is very kind of the Prime Minister, with all his burdens, to have come here to take the chair for an old schoolfellow.

When I was first asked to speak about the Nuremberg Trial, I was inclined to think that the subject had been worn threadbare after a ten months' trial and the great publicity which it had been given in the press of all countries. But on reflection it seems to me that there are matters which you may find it interesting for me to discuss.

This house, Chatham House, being an Institute of International Affairs, a trial such as the international Trial at Nuremberg does seem a subject of special interest to its members, for every aspect of the Trial was international: the judges, the law, the languages—one may call them international—and the scientific devices which made it practicable.

The subjects which I propose to discuss this evening are: whether a trial was necessary at all; whether the jurisdiction conferred upon the Tribunal by the Charter was valid according to international law; the results of such an assertion of jurisdiction by the four Great Powers; and the technical system which was employed.

I will speak first about the technical system and the organization of the Trial and the Court. The world, I think, is generally impatient and it seemed apparently

---

[1] An address given at Chatham House on December 5, 1946. The Rt. Hon. Clement R. Attlee, C.H., M.P. in the Chair.

to the man in the street a very long time between the end of the war and August 8, 1945 when the Charter was agreed upon.[2] The Tribunal was anxious therefore not to allow the Trial to be delayed any longer than was absolutely necessary. It was accordingly begun on the day fixed, November 20, 1945, exactly thirty days after the Indictment, which specified the alleged crimes in detail, had been served upon the defendants.

On the same day that the Indictment was served, a British officer, Lieutenant-Colonel Neave, who did most distinguished work throughout the Trial, as he had indeed done throughout the war, explained to the defendants, personally, their rights under the Charter and helped them in the selection of their counsel. They all selected German counsel.

An enormous number of German orders and documents of all sorts had been discovered hidden away in salt mines, behind brick walls and in other places, and the task of selection from among these documents naturally took the prosecution many months and continued long after the case had begun. Mr. Justice Jackson, who had given up his work on the Bench of the Supreme Court of the United States to conduct the prosecution for the United States, took the principal part in the organization of the Court and it was due to his energy and optimism and to the energy and optimism of his principal officer, General Gill, that the Trial became practicable at all. The Court House and the Court had to be to a large extent rebuilt because it suffered from bombing; the ear-phone system was installed; a number of photographic galleries were built; an elaborate lighting system was put in; a vast translating, interpreting and shorthand-typist division was engaged from all over the world and trained; and an electrical sound recording system was installed. The result was that on November 20, 1945, the Court was ready to hold nearly 600 people including 250 members of the press of the world, all supplied with earphones and able, by merely turning the pointer on a small metal disc attached to their earphones to the appropriate figure, to hear the words spoken in Court in English, Russian, French or German, and by just flicking this pointer over they could hear first one and then the other. So efficient was this system—although it sometimes broke down—and so expert were the interpreters that cross-examination, where speed is of considerable importance was frequently carried on as fast, or nearly as fast, as in an English Court, and it will be readily understood that to undertake such a trial in four languages without some such system would have been almost interminable. Great care was taken to get an accurate record by checking back from the shorthand notes against the electrical sound recording of the words spoken.

So much for the technical system and the organization of the Court. I will now turn to the question of the necessity of a trial at all.

---

[2] *Agreement for the Prosecution and Punishment of Major War Criminals of European Axis*, London, 8th August, 1945, Cord 6668, (H. M. Stationery Office).

I, of course, had nothing to do with the political decisions which led to the Trial, but it is impossible for me to discuss such subjects without trenching upon world politics.

After the surrender of Germany, the discovery of the conditions in the concentration camps and in the occupied territories was so appalling that the civilized world stood aghast. There were also many other dreadful crimes known to the Allied Governments and to some individuals, but not by any means to the majority. Incidentally, the United States, the Soviet Union and Great Britain had already declared their intention of punishing the crimes that Germany had committed. There were, I suppose, three possible courses: to let the atrocities which had been committed go unpunished; to put the perpetrators to death or punish them by executive action; or to try them. Which was it to be? Was it possible to let such atrocities go unpunished? Could France, could Russia, could Holland, Belgium, Norway, Czechoslovakia, Poland or Yugoslavia be expected to consent to such a course? We, in England, I think must remember that though we suffered, we have not suffered as they did. We were not neutrals. We had no pact with the Germans. We were not bombed without a declaration of war. We were not invaded. Our people were not deported to work as slaves. Few, if any, of our nationals were shot as hostages and few were, I think, in concentration camps. The question one must remember was a practical international one. What would have happened if Great Britain and the United States had refused to participate in any form of punishment? Would they have done any good by refusing to act with their Allies? It was inevitable then, it seems to me, that punishment should be meted out and, if so, it surely was right that it should be after a trial which was intended at any rate to be fair. In all probability, if there had been no trial, all the major war criminals who were tried at Nuremberg would have been executed and the Tribunal at least did not think that that was just.

It will be remembered that after the first world war alleged criminals were handed over to be tried by Germany, and what a farce that was! The majority got off and such sentences as were inflicted were derisory and were soon remitted. It is said that there should have been neutral judges, but it must be remembered that agreement had to be obtained to such a proposal: that it would probably have involved a further language difficulty; and lastly that war crimes frequently, if not always, have been tried by the judges of the country aggrieved.

But the fundamental purpose of the Trial was not only the punishment of those who were guilty but the establishment of the supremacy of international law over national law and the proof of the actual facts, in order to bring home to the German people and to the peoples of the world, the depths of infamy to which the pursuit of total warfare had brought Germany. Had it not been for the long drawn out and elaborate Trial, the production of German documents, the authenticity of which could not be and was not denied, and the actual evidence of several of the worst criminals themselves, no one would have believed what the Germans did. It would all have been ascribed to Allied propaganda.

Would anyone have believed, had it not been proved by the evidence and the documents, that the Germans ordered the Polish intelligentsia, the Polish nobility and the Polish clergy to be killed out of hand; that actually before making war on the Soviet Union they ordered all commissars to be killed on capture; that they ordered that the Jews and other prisoners should be gassed if unable to work; and that in accordance with these inhuman orders many millions of human beings had been butchered? One frequently meets ignorant or prejudiced people who do not believe it still. But the major war criminals tried at Nuremberg did not deny it and one would think that no German in the future will have the face to deny it. It was suggested by some of the defendants that they were ignorant of the conditions in the concentration camps and of the most brutal atrocities, and it is possible that some of them were, but it seemed to the Tribunal incredible that the substance of these conditions was unknown to many of the defendants, and as for the orders to which I have referred there was and can be no dispute that the principal defendants were parties to them.

I have not time to deal with details or particular incidents but I will read you a few extracts from one witness named Hoess:

I was ordered to establish extermination facilities in Auschwitz in June 1941. At that time there was already in the General Government three other extermination camps, Belzek, Treblinka and Walzek...I visited Treblinka to find out how they carried out their exterminations. The Camp Commandant at Treblinka told me that he had liquidated eighty thousand in the course of one half-year. He was principally concerned with the liquidation of the Jews from the Warsaw ghetto.

Hoess described the improvements that he made at Auschwitz. He introduced the new gas, Cyclone B, which:

took from three to fifteen minutes to kill the people in the death chamber, dependent upon climatic conditions. We knew when the people were dead because their screaming stopped...Another improvement we made over Treblinka was that we built our gas chambers to accommodate two thousand people at a time, whereas at Treblinka their ten gas chambers only accommodated two hundred people each.

And he described the selection of the victims from the daily transports that arrived:

Those who were fit for work were sent into the camp. Others were sent immediately to the extermination plant. Children of tender years were invariably exterminated since, by reason of their youth, they were unable to work. Still another improvement we made over Treblinka was that at Treblinka the victims almost always knew they were to be exterminated, and at Auschwitz we endeavoured to fool the victims into thinking that they were going through a delousing process. Of course frequently they realized our true intentions. Very frequently the women would hide their children under their clothes, but of course when we found them we would send the children in to be exterminated. We were required to carry out these exterminations in great secrecy, but of course the foul and nauseating stench from the continuous burning of bodies permeated the entire area and all the people living in the surrounding communities knew that exterminations were going on at Auschwitz.

That was the evidence of Hoess, Commandant of Auschwitz.

One would almost have thought that these were the exaggerations of a megalomaniac had they not been fully corroborated by other evidence and by what was found in the camps and photographed.

The other principal object of the Trial as it appears to me was to bring home to Germany and the world that a nation cannot with impunity resort to total warfare in defiance of international law and laws of war which have been recognized as a part of international law since the Middle Ages.

The Trial was held under the Charter agreed upon on August 8, 1945, and it seems to me, who had nothing to do with it, that it was a great achievement of legal diplomacy to have secured agreement to that Charter. I go further and submit to you that it was a matter of the highest international importance that such an assertion of international jurisdiction should have been made by the four Great Powers with the adherence of so many States and with the silent acquiescence and recognition of the rest of the civilized world. One must remember that international law grows by custom, agreement and precedent and not by the action of an international legislature, and no greater international step has been taken in the history of the world than was taken on August 8, 1945. The Charter provided for a fair but expeditious trial, but it also provided that no technical rules of procedure should be observed, but that any evidence which appeared to have any probative value should be admitted. As there were twenty-two defendants and all were charged with conspiracy over a period of ten to twenty years, it will perhaps be realized that to hold a fair trial expeditiously was not altogether an easy task. There were great difficulties, too, arising from the differences in the systems of law which the judges had practised. For instance, the very existence of the crime of conspiracy is foreign to the laws of France and Germany, a fact which introduced great difficulties into our deliberations. But the Charter agreed on by the four Powers in August 1945 stood the test of the Trial and will I hope stand the test of time. It laid down that aggressive war was a crime, that breaches of the laws of war were crimes and that crimes against humanity committed in connection with an aggressive war were crimes. It was argued on behalf of the defendants, and has been argued by many lawyers; that aggressive war was not a crime in 1939 when the war began and that the Charter was therefore retroactive and offended against the maxim *nullum crimen sine lege.* But the Tribunal was of opinion first that it (the Tribunal) was bound by the Charter; secondly, that the Charter was a valid exercise of sovereign legislative authority by the only sovereign authority for Germany and the occupied territories which had power *de facto* by virtue of occupation and *de jure* by virtue of the surrender of Germany's constitutional sovereign and the recognition of the civilized States of the world; thirdly, that the maxim *nullum crimen* is not a limitation of sovereignty but merely a general rule of justice to which there may be exceptions of which the present was in any event one; and, lastly, that in view of the declarations, resolutions and agreements of the civilized States of the world from 1923 to 1928 which led up to the Kellogg-Briand Pact, to which Germany was a party, aggressive war was an international crime in 1939. It will be remembered that in the Kellogg-Briand Pact, signed by sixty-two nations, war was expressly condemned and solemnly renounced as an instrument of policy. It seems difficult to hold in face of these words that the sixty-two States who signed the Pact intended that an aggressive war should be legal and it was not so contended by Counsel for the Defence, but what they did contend was that, although it was illegal, yet it did not constitute crime. But if illegal must it not, with its inevitable consequence of the death of thousands or in the present case of millions, be criminal?

It may be that the words of the Charter might have been interpreted in such a wide sense as to include everyone who fought in an aggressive war, but the acquittal of Fritsche, who was regarded as an underling of Goebbels, and the refusal to declare the Reich Cabinet or the General Staff and High Command criminal organisations show that the Tribunal did not put any such wide interpretation on the words. The judgement of the Tribunal deals with all these matters in detail but it is, I think, necessary for me to restate them shortly.

It is, I believe, argued by critics of the Trial that in future no statesman or general will be safe, and that the result will be that all States will rearm so as to make certain of victory. But is that the natural or probable result? It is not easy to be certain of victory, and, if the war is truly aggressive, is it not more probable that the world will see that the aggressor is not victorious? Germany has at any rate tried twice at least and not succeeded. On each of the last two occasions her obvious aggression roused the civilized world against her. But the fact that international law may limit the free action of States is no more an objection than that national laws may limit the freedom of individuals. The world can no more tolerate another aggressive war than a State can tolerate anarchy. Must not nations be compelled to observe rules of good faith and conduct which for centuries have been imposed by national laws upon and observed by individuals? The arguments of these critics are really arguments against any punishment at all, but, whether a trial is held or not, a victorious nation will always be able justly or unjustly to punish the vanquished either with or without trial. The fact that it may be difficult to decide when a war is aggressive is no argument against setting up some legal standard. The only question is whether you want the matter to be decided by law or by power. The dictatorship of Hitler was of course pleaded as a defence to every atrocity, but such a plea is simply a denial of the existence of international law. It makes no difference whether sovereign power is vested in a dictator or in a parliament; unless the orders of either are to be controlled by the law of nations there is no security for the nations of the world. It is true that a German faced by the orders of Hitler may have been in a position of personal danger, but in matters of life and death anyone can be placed in such positions. Moreover the Charter provided that the defence of superior orders might be considered in mitigation. But it was not for a single lapse that the criminals at Nuremberg were condemned, but for acquiescing year after year in the brutal and obviously criminal orders of Hitler. The German generals who were tried at Nuremberg acquiesced in orders to kill all Russian commissars who surrendered, to kill all the Polish intelligentsia, nobility and clergy, to kill Commando troops who had surrendered, although in uniform, to gas prisoners who were unfit for work; they did not even contend that they thought these orders were lawful, but still they continued year after year right up to the end to wage a war they had been themselves planning for years without any regard for the admitted laws of war.

The generals and admirals who were charged as major war criminals were not men who had merely carried out the duties of staff officers; they were close associates of Hitler for years. Their plans were not mere staff appreciations of military problems which had not been decided on, such as are made by the staffs of every country. They were political in their nature, made with the full knowledge that they were aggressive and secret. Keitel and Raeder were present at the conference of November 5, 1937 when Hitler announced his intention of attacking Czechoslovakia; Keitel was present when Schussnigg and again when President Hacha were put under political pressure. You will have observed that neither the Reich Cabinet nor the General Staff and High Command were declared criminal by the Tribunal. They were composed to a large extent of ordinary political departmental chiefs and of commanding generals and of their staff officers. But Keitel, Jodl, Raeder and Donitz were, the Tribunal thought, something very different. Hitler with his cunning and ruthless outlook foresaw that the German Army and Navy would take some time to be converted to his ideas of relentless ferocity and he accordingly set up the para-military organizations of the S.S., S.A., and Gestapo, which he could trust to do the work which might prove too dirty for the Army and Navy. In order to co-ordinate the military activities of these para-military organizations with those of the Army and Navy he needed soldiers and sailors who were not too scrupulous about international law, the laws of war or the honour of their professions, and he found them in the soldiers and sailors tried at Nuremberg. To have ordered such men, if found to be fully guilty, to be shot would in the opinion of the Tribunal have given the impression that they were merely professional men who had mistakenly carried out superior orders. But the Tribunal felt forced to a very different conclusion in the cases of Keitel and Jodl.

It must also be remembered in connection with crimes so devastating that one cannot arrange sentences in a progression descending from the death sentence, or many who deserve death would escape because their crimes were less appalling than those of the worst criminal tried.

So far as the charge of planning aggressive war was concerned, there was no defendant who was condemned to death or even to imprisonment for this crime alone, and if the Tribunal was wrong in its interpretation of the Kellogg-Briand Pact and aggressive war is not an international crime for which those responsible are punishable, it is open to the civilized States of the world, or some of them, to declare that they deny the validity of any such proposition.

Now I think you may wish to hear something of my impressions of the persons involved in the Trial, prisoners, counsel and judges. It interested me very much to compare the difference of approach of the four teams of prosecution. The English Bar is accustomed to argue the case orally in Court and is therefore prepared to be interrupted by the judge at any time for the purpose of elucidating the argument. American lawyers, and I think the French too, rely more upon written arguments; their case is most carefully prepared but they are not as a rule as resilient in argument as our Bar. Mr. Justice Jackson left much of the work to Mr. Dodd in the latter stages of the case, and Mr. Dodd greatly distinguished himself. General Rudenko, the leader of the Soviet team, was a most popular advocate who worked, I believe, most harmoniously with the other prosecutors. He was ably assisted by his associates and particularly by Colonel Smirnoff. The French were led by M. Champetier de Ribes, but unhappily his health prevented him from taking a very active part. M. Dubost and M. Faure, who made a particularly able speech in the early stages, bore the brunt of the French prosecution. You will doubtless have read or heard with what ability and distinction Sir David Maxwell Fyfe led the members of the British prosecution in the absence of the Attorney General, whose duties in England only allowed him to make the opening and closing speeches. The most important British cross-examination and the leading part in the prosecution generally fell upon Sir David's shoulders and, by common consent of everyone at Nuremberg, he achieved a position of pre-eminence and popularity in which he was implicitly trusted not only by all members of the various prosecution delegations, but also by the defence counsel as well. The other members of the British prosecution all took part with credit both in cross-examination and speeches. The defence counsel acquitted themselves with great credit, particularly in view of the fact that the procedure of the Charter was not their own and I do not think that any one of them wilfully took up any time unnecessarily.

As to the prisoners, they all bore themselves with dignity and discipline. Goering, Speer and Schacht appeared to be probably the ablest. Ribbentrop did not appear to advantage, but all showed ability with the exception of Hess, Kaltenbrunner, Frick and Streicher.

From the first the Tribunal sat in Court and out of Court with their alternate members, who, although they did not vote, took part in all our discussions and were of the greatest assistance. All decisions were by a majority, though I had a casting vote, except in the matter of conviction and sentence, where there had to be a three to one majority. All the seven other members of the Tribunal gave me throughout the most loyal support and, though of course we differed upon some points which arose in the course of the Trial, in spite of our different systems and our different languages, we remained, I think, up to the very end a singularly united and happy body. Sir Norman Birkett, who is probably well known to many of you, was of the greatest assistance to me and to the whole Tribunal. I do not think that he and I ever differed in opinion. He is that rare man who writes as well as he speaks; an idea has only to be suggested and his pen is immediately at work putting it in appropriate words out of the storehouse of his great literary memory. If his lot had been cast in Lincoln's Inn he would, I am sure, have been as successful as an Equity draftsman as he has been in the King's Bench and Assizes. His intimate knowledge of the evidence and his drafting skill were invaluable in the preparation of the judgement. I had the assistance not only of Sir Norman Birkett but also of a most able and devoted marshal in Major John Phipps. Mr. Francis Biddle and Judge Parker, our American colleagues, saw eye to eye with us on most questions. Mr. Biddle's experience of the great department of the United States Attorney General and Judge Parker's long service on the Bench were of the greatest assistance. M. Donnedieu de Vabres and M. Falco of the Cour de Cassation, who had assisted in drafting the Charter, added much strength to the Tribunal. The Soviet judges were throughout most reasonable and fair-minded, and General Nikichenko's views in conference were expressed with an ability, a clarity and a detachment which were of real assistance.

You will realize that there were some difficulties of communication when I tell you that neither M. Donnedieu de Vabres nor General Nikichenko understood English and interpreters therefore had to be employed at every closed session of the Tribunal. At these sessions, often after the Tribunal had risen for the day, all questions of admissibility of evidence, of law, of procedure and of administration, often involving questions of difficulty and of fine shades of meaning, had to be debated and decided. The Tribunal was naturally anxious not only that justice should be done but that it should also appear to be done, and I may give as instances the issue of interrogatories and answers of the United States Admiral Nimitz on the unrestricted warfare carried on by the United States in the Pacific and also the fact that the German counsel were permitted to inspect the archives of the British Admiralty in their search for evidence for the defence. Moreover it should be emphasized that every witness for the defence had to be found and brought to Nuremberg by the Allied authorities, and when the case was heard for and against the organizations indicted, namely the Gestapo, S.S., S.A., High Command, Reich Cabinet and Leadership Corps, an elaborate system of commissions was instituted to take evidence, which enabled the evidence of many thousands of witnesses to be brought before the Tribunal on the constitution and activities of the accused organizations.

The Trial has of course been one of more than usual anxiety. All capital charges are, but a trial of twenty-one men who face you on such charges for ten months is an ordeal for the Tribunal as well as for them. Familiarity breeds sympathy and it is more difficult to sentence those one knows so well. There was always the urge to get on, to be expeditious and to finish it, but I have always been convinced that the length of the Trial if not forgotten may be forgiven, but that any unfairness would never be forgotten or forgiven.

12

International Legal Theories Evolved at Nuremberg*

By *Norman Birkett*

THE final verdict upon Nuremberg will no doubt be passed in the distant future; it will be the verdict of history. What we can do at the present time is, in quietude, to discuss some of the important matters upon which the verdict of history may finally rest. I say 'in quietude' for at Nuremberg we had movie cameras, and brilliant lighting, and 250 press representatives from one country alone; and in all those circumstances it was a little difficult to realize that it was a trial at all comparable with the kind of trial with which we are familiar in Great Britain.

In estimating the legal theories evolved at Nuremberg, it is perhaps important to realize the nature of the International Military Tribunal; for at that point, when the verdict of history comes to be recorded, very much will be said upon one side or upon the other.

Apart from a most interesting international trial in the fifteenth century, the trial at Bresach of a war criminal for, curiously enough, what we in our day would call 'crimes against humanity,' because it was said of him that he had trampled underfoot the laws of God and Man, the proceedings at Nuremberg were unique. It was the first time that an international criminal court had been set up to try alleged criminals. Strangely enough, at the fifteenth century trial only one defence was put forward by the counsel, whose speeches have been preserved; that defence was also raised at Nuremberg—the defence of 'superior orders.' Just as at Nuremberg it was said, 'We did this because Hitler commanded it,' so in the fifteenth century trial a similar defence was claimed: and the Court of the fifteenth century, in the same way as the Court of the twentieth century, rejected that contention. The principal matters upon which I think criticism has already centred and will possibly centre more and more may be summarized in a sentence or two.

* An address given at Chatham House on March 27, 1947.

First, the Court was composed entirely of representatives of the victorious belligerents: Great Britain, the United States of America, France and the Soviet Union; and of course it was said then, and no doubt will be said with greater force in the future, that, with a Court so constituted, with no neutral sitting upon it, and no enemy either, a fair trial, a judicial trial, could not be held.

Secondly, the defendants were entirely in the power of the victorious belligerents. I used to look at them, as I did over twelve months—Goering and Hess and Ribbentrop and Keitel and Jodl and Saukel and the rest—all shadows of their former selves, but men who had once been powerful enough to inspire fear in all the countries of the world, including their own; but now their every waking moment, indeed their every sleeping moment, was under the supervision of those Powers who had appointed the very judges of the Court.

Thirdly, the law which the Court was to administer was the law which, by the London Charter of August 8, 1945, had been laid down by the selfsame Powers who now nominated the judges to administer it. In that body of law it was stated (Article 6 of the Charter) that the defendants could be tried for the following crimes:

(a) *Crimes against peace:* namely, planning, preparation, initiation or waging of a war of aggression, or a war in violation of international treaties, agreements or assurances, or participation in a common plan or conspiracy for the accomplishment of any of the foregoing;

The count of 'conspiracy' was entirely new in international law. No charge of conspiracy had ever been made before, and it became a matter of great contention.

(b) *War crimes:* namely, violations of the laws or customs of war. Such violations shall include, but not be limited to, murder, ill-treatment or deportation to slave labour or for any other purpose of civilian population of or in occupied territory, murder or ill-treatment of prisoners of war or persons on the seas, killing of hostages, plunder of public or private property, wanton destruction of cities, towns or villages, or devastation not justified by military necessity;

These were offences against the Geneva and the Hague Conventions, which had been designed not to outlaw war so much as to mitigate its hardships and severities. All the defendants were indicted for war crimes.

(c) *Crimes against humanity:* namely, murder, extermination, enslavement, deportation, and other inhuman acts committed against any civilian population, before or during the war; or persecutions on political, racial or religious grounds in execution of or in connection with any crime within the jurisdiction of the Tribunal, whether or not in violation of the domestic law of the country where perpetrated.

This was a new section and created some difficulty. The Charter provided that the crimes against humanity must have been carried out in connection with the war. Therefore some of the earlier atrocities in Germany, notably against the Jews, could not be included.

Leaders, organizers, instigators and accomplices participating in the formulation or execution of a common plan or conspiracy to commit any of the foregoing crimes are responsible for all acts performed by any persons in execution of such plan.

This section was also entirely new, and under it were indicted the named organizations, the Leadership Corps of the Nazi Party, the Reich Cabinet, the S.A., the S.S., the Gestapo and the S.D., the General Staff and High Command of the German Armed Forces.

The fourth principal point on which criticism has centred is that the political element would keep creeping in. In our Courts in England the political element is most rigorously excluded, and it is very wise that it should be so. But in this Trial it was impossible to do it. On the Bench, sitting in judgment upon the German Nazi defendants, so it was urged from time to time by the defending counsel, were the representatives of one Power which, at one time during the war, had been in alliance with the Nazis and had entered into secret treaties which were given in evidence at the Trial for the disposition of certain territory which formed the subject matter of some of the charges in the indictment.

Those elements in themselves naturally created this body of opinion upon the one side or the other upon which history ultimately will have to judge. I will try to state the two main positions that were taken up in view of them.

There was a great body of opinion which said it was a mistake to have the Trial at all. Nobody appears to doubt the power and the right of victorious belligerents to set up a Court, because that would be easily demonstrated. For example, in the Treaty of Versailles, the famous article 227 was inserted providing that the Kaiser should be brought to trial. Although it was never put into effect, the provision was there, and it was put into the Treaty expressly on the ground that international morality should be vindicated. It would be easy to prove from the jurisprudence of almost every country that the right of the victorious belligerent to set up a Court, to try the defeated enemy, could not be challenged. But people said: 'We doubt its wisdom,' and those who took that view suggested that the crimes charged against the defendants were so notorious, had been so openly and publicly committed, that to hold a trial was a farce. As day succeeded day during that long-drawn-out twelve months, that feeling grew in power and intensity, and its protagonists said: 'The proper way to deal with these men is by executive action' which, in plain terms, means that they should have been shot out of hand.

The opposing view was: 'It is a wise and prudent and necessary thing to hold this trial. It may vindicate international law and may possibly, if it is done wisely and properly, ultimately be the cornerstone in the house of peace.'

My own view is that it was wise and right and expedient and indeed essential that that Trial should be held. History would have passed a very adverse verdict upon any country that had taken people and shot them without trial. After all, the principle of the law of England is that a man is presumed to be innocent until he is found guilty; and the view that men could be shot without trial, whatever their alleged crimes might have been, would, in my opinion, savour far too much of the Nazi doctrine itself to have any wide commendation to reasonable people.

Again, during the war years, credible information reached the Allied Governments of barbarities and atrocities, particularly in the occupied countries, about which at that time the Allied Powers could do nothing. When the Trial was held, I think it sober language to say that there never was such a record in the history of the world of inhumanity and cruelty and barbarity. Never. I can certainly say that, speaking for myself, and having listened to every word of the evidence and heard it delivered. I can recall in the witness box at Nuremberg a man in an ordinary civilian suit, who looked a very ordinary sort of man—he did not look a villain at all; if you had met him in the street you would have thought him a decent, ordinary citizen—who admitted with his own lips that he had been responsible, in one of the concentration camps, for the death of over two million people. Two million people! And the description of the way the poor people met their deaths, and the horrible barbarities practised upon them was appalling. And there upon the screen in the Court were shown the films of the concentration camps, with the bones of the victims piled so high that it took American bulldozers to make a way through them. Those things were proved; in accordance with the decisions at the Moscow and Yalta Conferences, those who had been found guilty of these atrocities and these horrors should stand up in a Court to answer the charges to be made against them. There was no going back from that.

Moreover, the feeling which was evoked in the occupied countries is something of which we in Britain have really no adequate conception. In the occupied countries, where they knew of women and children hounded into a church which was then burnt over their heads, and horrors of that kind, there was such a wave of feeling, such a call and a cry for retribution, that it was essential, unless worse should befall, that it should be guided into proper channels. It was by this Trial that that harmonizing influence was brought about; otherwise there would, in my judgment, have been a perfect bloodbath throughout Europe.

Finally, it was important for international law that the Trial should be held to vindicate the law and to make it known now and hereafter that for crime in the international sphere there shall ultimately be punishment.

As to the fact that the Court was composed entirely of the victorious belligerents, I think it would have been quite impracticable for neutrals to have sat upon the Court. It was difficult enough with the languages we had to deal with, but what it would have been if we had had very many more I really do not know. The system installed in the Court was a really marvellous one. The German prosecutor would be speaking from his place in the Court; the German witness or defendant would be in the box; the question would be asked in German and, by the head-phones which were attached to every seat in the building, including the Bench, immediately, without waiting, the German question to the witness came through upon the Russian *et seq* 'phones in Russian, upon the French 'phones in French, upon the English and American 'phones in English. And by the manipulation of a switch attached to each 'phone it was possible to listen to the German, the Russian, the French or the English. But if there had been many more, Czech and Norwegian and Swedish and Abyssinian, I do not know what we should have done. At any rate it was difficult to find many neutrals at that time. There were not very many left.

With regard to the victorious belligerents having Germans sitting on the Court, the experience of the first world war was not a very happy one. Provision was made then for the trial but finally the Allies agreed to allow the German Supreme Court at Leipzig to act itself, and in 1921 the Court opened at Leipzig. The Allies had produced originally nine hundred names of alleged war criminals. They had to reduce their list to forty-five. Of these only six were tried. Of those six only four were convicted, and the highest sentence imposed, for a most dreadful case of shooting unarmed survivors on rafts after a submarine had sunk the ship, was four years imprisonment, and the two officers sentenced to that imprisonment escaped—no doubt by connivance—in a very short time, and that was the end of the war trials. So it was not an experience to encourage the Allies to try it again.

The main point on which true criticism will fasten will be this: was it a fair trial? That is the only thing defendants are really entitled to ask. That is the only thing they can ask in Britain. They cannot ask to have particular judges on the Bench; all they are entitled to ask is that they shall be tried in accordance with justice. I will not develop the theme that this was a fair trial. It certainly was. The indictment, which was a long indictment, was translated into German and served upon each one of the defendants thirty days before the Trial. They had thirty days to ponder the indictment. The Tribunal arranged for the best German counsel to defend them. The defendants selected their own counsel and they said 'I would like Mr. So-and-so from Hamburg; I would like Mr. So-and-so from Berlin,' and wherever he could be found he was assigned, and paid and housed and looked after by the Tribunal, because the defendants had nothing. With regard to their documents, the Tribunal made it a rule that no document should be used in the whole of those twelve months' proceedings which was not first translated into the German language and of which copies were not supplied to the defendants. So nothing was done in the Trial without their full knowledge. The defendants said: 'We would like to call witnesses.' 'Very well, call your witnesses. Where are they? Give us their names, tell us where they are to be found, and we will bring them here.' And at great cost and infinite trouble witnesses were brought from all over Europe in order that they might speak and testify for the defence. In the cases where a man could not be brought, they were permitted to send a list of interrogatories, or questions, to which answer was made. So the whole Trial proceeded upon that footing, that they should have the fullest opportunity of making their defence—and, indeed, they did.

I mentioned earlier that Goering and Hess and Keitel were shadows of their former selves, but there were occasions, as I thought, when they rose to very great heights of dignity. The Charter provided that when the Trial was done, when the German counsel had made their final speeches, when the prosecution had finished all their speeches, the prisoners, the defendants, might make their own statements; and on two days, which I myself will never forget, the defendants spoke in that Court—some of them, I think, with the knowledge that it was the very last time that they would ever speak on this earth—and with dignity. The defendants spoke in their own defence. Keitel, the soldier; Jodl, the soldier; Speer, the Armaments Minister, entirely forgetful of himself and speaking only in that last solemn moment of what it meant to the world to be rid of the curse of war. And so on. It was a part of the administration of the Court, so that history would ultimately say it was a fair trial.

Those who have read the judgment would probably criticize it upon a good many grounds. It is, I think, a judgment not so much declaring guilt as a judgment of limitation. Von Papen was acquitted: and Von Papen was, ordinarily speaking, the last kind of man whom you would like to acquit. He was disliked in almost every nation of the world. But Von Papen was acquitted because it was said: 'You charge him under this count of conspiracy; you seek to make it a ground of conspiracy that he was instrumental in putting Hitler into power'—as, indeed, he was. Without Von Papen, Hitler would very probably never have achieved power. 'But was it proved,' said the Tribunal, 'that Von Papen, when he put Hitler into power, knew that Hitler's purpose from the first to the last was to be what was subsequently proved?' Indeed, in the defence of Von Papen, evidence was given of two very brave speeches made when the Hitler régime was exercising its most villainous power, and he denounced it. In consequence, his secretaries were killed in the blood purge, when Roehm died, and it was only by the last minute personal intervention of Hitler that Von Papen himself was saved.

I have set out these facts at some length because they are the foundation of everything. If the foundation is wrong, nothing that comes from it can be right. And the case which I venture to submit, and which I think ultimately history will consider, is that this great proceeding at Nuremberg, upon which the attention of the world was centred for twelve months, whatever its shortcomings, and there were many, whatever the imperfections, and they were obvious, was conducted in accordance with the highest standards of international law, and was, in its essence, fair.

The first international theory of supreme importance, which evolved from the Trial is that the waging, initiation and preparation of aggressive war is declared to be a crime. I will not go into great technical detail about it. These things will be debated by the international lawyers for generations, and every society and every organ that deals with law will continue to write about it. The waging, the preparation, the taking part in aggressive war is an international crime. There are many people who say: 'Yes, but you have no power to call it a crime. No sovereign body has ever described it to be a crime. No statute has ever laid it down to be a crime. There has been no provision for the setting up of any Court to give it power to call it a crime.' And yet the International Military Tribunal said it is a crime. In international law it is not essential that there shall be a sovereign body to create a law. The rules of the Geneva Conventions and the Hague Conventions, with which we are all familiar, that you must not shoot upon the white flag, that you must not poison wells, and other rules for ameliorating the hardships and horrors of war, have not been enacted by any sovereign body. They were merely conventions. No penalty is laid down in the Hague Convention; no Court is specified or described. But yet the conventions regarding war crimes have been binding upon every people the world over. So it does not matter very much that there is no sovereign body. International law is not created by a sovereign body. It is not laid down in statutes. It is not a static thing. It grows and develops as the consciousness of nations grows and widens and deepens. That is how international law becomes law, and there must come a point when some authority, for the first time, says: 'This is now the law.' Aggressive war, therefore, has been characterized for the first time as an international crime.

I advise everyone to read the four documents, one of November 1937 and the other three of May, August and November 1939, when Hitler called his chiefs together to tell them at length what he was going to do. They were 'Top Secret'; but there they all are now, public. They were so secret that Hitler said in one document 'I cannot even discuss this in the Cabinet. I have called you here,' and a Lieutenant-Colonel Hosbach took careful notes. Why they were ever preserved has been a mystery to me. One of the interesting features of this Trial is why the Germans persisted in saving all their documents. They went to incredible lengths to do it. They hid them in salt mines, where they were discovered by the invading armies; they hid them in every conceivable place where they thought they could never be detected; but one thing they could not bring themselves to do was to burn them. I must not exaggerate this but I think Jodl had a diary of daily events of considerable length. Frank, the Governor-General of Poland, kept a diary in which he recorded important events in the frankest possible detail. One sentence in his diary addressed to his colleagues which was quoted against him was: 'Gentlemen, you realize that we are all on President Roosevelt's list of war criminals and I have the honour to be war criminal Number One.' Nobody thought of destroying the diary.

When the legal theory evolved at Nuremberg that aggressive war is a crime is discussed, the fact should always be kept in mind that there never was any doubt on the evidence that all the acts of Germany, from the invasion of Austria onwards, were aggressive war. None whatever. All will remember our feelings in Britain when Mr. Chamberlain flew to Munich, when the threat of war lay over the world. Austria had gone: Czechoslovakia was now going. The documents that I have referred to set the whole plan out with a time-table. Austria first; then, after an interval, Czechoslovakia; then, after an interval, Poland. It is all written there in 1937. So never doubt that it was aggressive. In 1938 Czechoslovakia, according to the plan, was to be taken. Mr. Chamberlain flew to Germany to try to make a settlement, and the Pact of Munich was entered into. The exact date of the Pact of Munich was September 29, 1938, and that date is really rather important. Mr. Chamberlain came back—I am not criticizing Mr. Chamberlain, I am merely recording history—and brought the decisive piece of paper, and said: 'We have plucked freedom out of the nettle, danger,' and spoke to the crowds in Downing Street from the window, believing it all. Hitler had said—and there was the piece of paper—'We are never going to war any more.' A very few days later—Hitler sent a message to Keitel, the defendant Keitel who sat there in the dock, and said: 'I want to know what forces I will require for the complete subjugation of Bohemia and Moravia, the part of Czechoslovakia into which we have not entered,' and on October 11, 1938, about twelve days after Mr. Chamberlain came home, Keitel sent the answer, stating the forces needed, and on October 21, there is the German directive. Those four documents deal at great length with the position of England, the position of the United States, the position of France, the position of all the other countries; the aggression was planned from the beginning, from 1937.

A criticism is levelled that this was a good illustration of what is called *ex post facto* legislation. It says 'What you did by the Charter was to make aggressive war a crime when it was not a crime at the moment it was committed.' It is rather an involved argument. The great maxim is *Nullum crimen sine lege: nulla poena sine lege:* No crime without a law: no punishment without a law; and it is, of course, repugnant to all mankind that one should condemn people afterwards for something that was not a crime at the time it was committed. But the principle of *Nullum crimen sine lege* is not a rigid thing. It is a principle of justice, that is all. It is unjust that one should make people responsible for a crime which was not a crime when they committed the act complained of. But one must be sensible about it. The Kellogg-Briand Pact of Paris of 1928, upon which the Tribunal founded its judgment, was signed by sixty-three nations, including Germany and Japan, and they were all agreed in outlawing war, on the ground that it was no solution of international difficulties. The League of Nations and international committees have been branding aggressive war as a crime for years and years, and after 1928 every leader in Germany knew that if Germany attacked a defenceless neighbour without warning, that was aggressive war. And how can it be said to be unjust? Is anybody going to say that Ribbentrop did not know that the Pact of Paris had outlawed war? Of course he did; Goering did. There are plenty of German documents which bear this out. The view the Tribunal took was that sixty-three nations in 1928 had said that aggressive war was illegal, and if, in view of that, the illegality were committed, then the Tribunal said it was a crime. I have no doubt that the verdict of history will be that the Tribunal was wise and right to say so. If they had not, international law was really not worth the paper it was written on. It was time that the nations of this world, instead of always indulging in pious hopes and pious resolutions, said: 'Since 1928, sixty-three nations of this world have agreed that war, as an aggressive thing, not as a defensive thing, is outside the pale of international relations. People embark upon it at their peril.'

The second legal theory evolved at Nuremberg was that international law affects sovereign States but it also affects individuals, and the individual cannot claim immunity for acts he himself has committed. It was elaborated in some detail in the judgment. Aggressive war is a crime: those who take part in its waging or its initiation are personally responsible. There is nothing new about that; it has been the practice. A very great case was in the United States Supreme Court, *ex parte* Quirin, where the Chief Justice reviewed the whole of the American law making it absolutely plain that they have always, in their military courts, adopted the view of individual responsibility.

The third point was the defence that the individual was acting under superior orders—'I was ordered to do this and I had no opportunity but to obey.' The Court said that may be a mitigation but is never a defence.

Those were the three main theories evolved at Nuremberg. In what was called the Group Criminality—the political leaders—the Tribunal limited its judgment, because it was repugnant to convict as members of a criminal group two million people whom they had never seen, or of whom they had only seen a representative or two, or to invoke criminal legislation and criminal sanctions against them.

In conclusion, the Charter was, of course, the law which governed the Tribunal. Whatever the private theories of the judges may have been, they were compelled to follow the Charter. But the submission was, and I think it is right, that the Charter did not contain an arbitrary selection of law, but it was merely law that had been scheduled there because it was existing international law. But, as it stands, it applies only to the enemy. One could not, for example, bring before that Court, say, the Soviet Union because of what they did in Finland, or because of what they did in Poland. You could not bring the United States of America, or indeed Britain to judgment for dropping the atomic bomb on Japan. It does not apply. If it continues to apply only to the enemy, then I think the verdict of history may be against Nuremberg. What is really needed is that, after this start—if I may say it with great respect and modesty, this very fine start—the United Nations should build upon it a code that is applied not merely to the enemy but to all. And if that is done, then I believe that Nuremberg will stand the test of history and may indeed be the corner-stone in that House of Peace to which every loyal and true citizen aspires.

13

The Issues of the Nuremberg Trial*

By Herbert Wechsler
Columbia University

ONE may say without impertinence to historians that the judgment that history will render upon a legal proceeding is not usually a matter of acute concern either to counsel or to the court. In this respect, at least, the Nuremberg trial was a highly exceptional affair; for the perspective of most of the participants, and even that of the defendants, was focused very much on the future, distant and problematical as it is. The dominant mood was put in words by Justice Jackson, in opening the case for the prosecution: 'We must never forget that the record on which we judge these defendants to-day is the record on which history will judge us to-morrow.'[1]

The verdict of history will not be rendered for a long time, but we may be certain that the process of deliberation will be active and that the debate has already begun. The trial is extolled as a crucial achievement in the development of international law, a triumph of reason and justice in the bitter wake of the war. But voices have been raised from the beginning to proclaim the battle cry of the attack: novelty and confusion, error and pretense, a peril to essential liberties safeguarded by domestic law. What are the issues that challenge examination as this active critique unfolds? What are the factors to be weighed in the balance by those who will record for the judgment of posterity the history of our turbulent time?

I

It is a lawyer's habit, that I would not resist if I could, to begin with a statement of the case.

Credible information received in the course of the war reported cruelties and atrocities perpetrated by the Germans, especially in the occupied countries, that

---

* This paper, with some omission of detail, was read at the Annual Meeting of the American Historical Association, December 30, 1946.

[1] See the mimeographed daily transcript in English (hereafter cited as Transcript), 21 November, 1945, p. 11.

no conception of military necessity could sustain. Impotent to render physical assistance, the heads of state of the principal Allies responded with warnings, jointly and severally repeated, that the guilty would be apprehended and punished. The triumph of arms brought with it the physical custody of thousands of persons suspected of complicity in the conduct to which these warnings had been addressed. It brought the custody of the survivors among the principal enemy personalities believed, upon probable cause, to be responsible for the initiation of the war. Most of these persons had, indeed, made frantic efforts to surrender to the forces advancing from the west; and by far the largest number when the firing ceased were in American hands. Within Germany no governmental authority survived the unconditional surrender, save that which the Potsdam Powers themselves exercised by the military occupation. It took no great foresight in the last days to anticipate that these conditions would obtain. It was essential that a policy be formulated for dealing with the individuals in question when the fighting should finally come to an end.

The problem thus presented was answered by the principal Allies in the Agreement executed in London on August 8, 1945, to which nineteen other nations thereafter adhered. It is no secret that this protocol represented, in its major content, the proposals put forward by Justice Jackson on behalf of the United States. It provided for the creation of a Tribunal, deemed to exercise military powers and therefore entitled the 'International Military Tribunal'; each of the four signatories was to designate one member and an alternate. The Tribunal was accorded jurisdiction 'to try and punish persons who, acting in the interests of the European Axis countries,' might be charged and convicted of any of the conduct which the Charter defined as a crime. The crimes thus defined were called 'crimes against peace', 'war crimes' and 'crimes against humanity'. Crimes against peace comprehended in substance the 'planning, preparation, initiation or waging of a war of aggression, or a war in violation of international treaties ... or assurances' or conspiring so to do. War crimes comprehended generally 'violations of the laws or customs of war' with some specification of the behavior, such as the murder or ill-treatment of prisoners of war, deemed to constitute such violations. The definition of crimes against humanity supplemented that of crimes of war—but the concept was accorded very little scope because of the requirement that the acts of inhumanity included be committed 'in execution of or in connection with' some other crime within the jurisdiction of the Tribunal, that is, a crime against peace or a war crime.

For such conduct the Charter declared that 'there shall be individual responsibility'; that 'leaders, organizers, instigators and accomplices' conspiring to commit such offenses shall be mutually responsible for the actions perpetrated in the execution of their common plan; that official position shall be neither an excuse nor a mitigation; and that superior orders may be a mitigation if justice so requires, but not a defense.

In addition, the Charter provided that in the trial of any individual and in connection with any act of which he might be convicted, the Tribunal might declare that 'the group or organization of which the individual was a member was a criminal organization.' The point of such a declaration was that thereafter the members of the organization might be prosecuted for their membership in 'national, military or occupation courts' of the signatories—in which event the Charter provided that 'the criminal nature of the group or organization is considered proved and shall not be questioned.'

These are the substantive provisions of the Charter and they are the only ones which give rise to any significant problems; for the procedural portion, designed to safeguard the rights of individual defendants and to protect the fairness of the trial, embodies, with small exceptions, the major lessons of civilization in relation to criminal procedure. Representing as they do a combination of the inquisitorial and the accusatorial systems, I put them aside with the assertion that, as implemented by the Nuremberg Tribunal, they include most of the salutary features of each. I wish, indeed, that the average impecunious defendant in an American court could count on assistance as extensive in the preparation and presentation of his defense.

The issues that are important are those presented by the Charter in its substantive aspects, as interpreted and applied by the Nuremberg Court. The Charter was, of course, binding upon the Tribunal in the same way that a constitutional statute would bind a domestic court. But the generalizations set forth in the Agreement demanded, as legislation always does, creative interpretation in its application to the challenging facts of a particular case.

On October 18, 1945, in a reconstruction of the chamber in Berlin where Nazi justice had its last major exhibition, the Tribunal constituted under the Charter held its first public session. Prosecutors representing the United States, the United Kingdom, the Soviet Union and France filed a joint indictment against Goering and twenty-three others, charging crimes against peace, war crimes and crimes against humanity, committed pursuant to a conspiracy alleged to be criminal in itself, in the sense that it had or grew to have these criminal ends. The indictment recited in great detail the particulars of the conduct which the defendants were charged with planning and carrying out: the long course of bellicose aggression, the acts of systematic inhumanity—of which simple murder was far from the worst—committed in the preparation and conduct of the war. It specified the alleged complicity of each of the defendants. In addition, it prayed for a declaration that six organizations, the Reich Cabinet, the Leadership Corps of the Nazi Party, the Gestapo (including the S.D.), the S.A., the S.S., and the General Staff and High Command, constituted 'criminal organizations'.

Twenty-two of the twenty-four individual defendants were brought to trial, one of them, Martin Bormann, *in absentia*. After a trial lasting the better part of a year, on a record exceeding 17,000 pages depicting horrors never before recorded in a court, Schacht, Von Papen and Fritsche were acquitted; the declaration of

criminality was denied in the case of the Cabinet, the General Staff and the
S.A., and granted, but in highly qualified and limiting terms, with respect to
the Leadership Corps, the Gestapo and the S.S. Nineteen individuals were convicted, of whom eleven, including Bormann, were sentenced to death, the others
to imprisonment for terms ranging from ten years to life. All of those sentenced
to death were convicted of war crimes or crimes against humanity; all but four,
Kaltenbrunner, Frank, Sauckel and Bormann, were also convicted of crimes
against peace.

History will ask whether these men and these organizations were justly condemned or acquitted. The inquiry will involve many phases not all of which can
be examined here. I shall attempt no more than to direct attention to the general
issues.

II

Should the United States—and the question may be put with equal validity for
each of the victors—have cast its influence against any punitive proceedings,
declining to participate and refusing to surrender the persons of its prisoners
to other countries clamoring to proceed? Such a course would have forsaken
the pledges and the warnings issued as an instrument of war and would have
responded with a blanket *nolumus* to the demand for retribution that rose like a
plaintive chant from all the desolated lands. Certainly only the firmest conviction that punishment in this situation could serve no adequate temporal purpose would have sanctioned dismissal of the millions of complainants with the
admonition that 'vengeance belongs to God.' In truth, the volume of accumulated passion sufficed in itself to establish such a temporal purpose—for who
can doubt that indiscriminate violence, a blood bath beyond power of control,
would have followed an announcement by the responsible governments that
they were unwilling to proceed? If nothing else was to be accomplished, it was
essential that some institutional mechanism be provided that would reserve the
application of violence to the public force, to cases in which punishment might
serve a constructive purpose and in which reason would conclude that it was
deserved.

It is not to be conceded, however, that this negative function, whatever its
importance, is the only purpose that was to be served. The assumption of domestic society that punishment is a preventive weapon is not as irrelevant to international behavior as some persons seem disposed to affirm. In so far as the penalty
eliminates a danger presented by the particular individual—hardly an objective
of indifference, to a military occupation—the function is no less plain in this
situation than it is in municipal affairs. But the dominant justification of punishment, especially of the punishment of death, is usually felt to be the deterrence
of others; and here it has been asserted that the justification must fail because

victory carries immunity whether or not the victor was the aggressor and whatever the measures by which victory was attained.

The argument has a degree of validity but it does not prove enough to prevail. Treason, too, is punishable only when it is abortive; when 'it prospers,' as
the old verse goes, 'none dare call it treason'; it is the traitors who call the turn.
With respect to war and the manner in which it is conducted, as with respect to
treason, there are men who, valuing personal survival, will take account of the
contingency of failure. It is to them that the threats are addressed. Moreover, the
threat of punishment is not limited in the mode of its operation to the weight that
it carries as a factor in decision at the climactic moment of choice. It also operates,
and perhaps more significantly, at anterior stages in the patterns of conduct, the
dark shadow of organized disapproval eliminating from the ambit of consideration alternatives that might otherwise present themselves in the final competition
of choice. These considerations point to some deterrent efficacy; that, and not the
assurance of prevention, is all that we can claim for punishment as an instrument
of domestic law. It is deemed to be sufficient in municipal affairs, not because of
a mathematical calculation of its efficiency, but rather because society, so des-
perately in need of instrumentalities of prevention, cannot dispense with such
potency as condemnation and punishment have.

III

If punishment cannot be dismissed as intrinsically ineffective in the situation
with which we are dealing, we must consider whether it was in fact conditioned
upon proper grounds.

Putting aside for the moment any special conception of legality, who will
assert that the conditions of punishability prescribed by the London Charter are
not accurately addressed to the evils incident to war that international society
should seek to prevent? The greatest evil is, of course, the initiation of war itself.
Once the evil of war has been precipitated, nothing remains but the fragile effort,
embodied for the most part in the conventions, to limit the cruelty by which it
is conducted. These are the two major branches of the Charter: crimes against
peace and violations of the laws and customs of war. Of these two challenges to
life and to all that makes life worth living, who will deny that the larger offense is
the unjustified initiation of a war?

Goering, having admitted organizing the Nazi program of slave labor—a plain
violation of the conventions and a traditional war crime—defended himself, in
effect, by attacking the Hague Conventions as inapplicable to modern war.[2] It
would be a mistake to suppose that his point is entirely without substance—
though no conception of modern military necessity could have justified what the

---

[2] Transcript, p. 5982.

evidence showed. But is it not clear that the attention that would be accorded to a complaint of this order fails when it is remembered that the military necessity asserted was at best that of his own creation? One who viewed as the basic question for Germany—and I quote Hitler's words—'where the greatest possible conquest could be made at the lowest cost',[3] had hardly the same position to justify extremes in the use of force as his victims might have, acting in an honest estimate of what was necessary in their own defense. But this is only to demonstrate that the Tribunal was right in declaring that the initiation of a war of aggression 'is the supreme international crime'.[4]

There are, of course, problems, and difficult ones indeed, in the ultimate definition of aggression—at least under conditions of world organization as they have obtained in the last years. There may be difficult issues in defining the scope of national authority to act in what it conceives to be necessary self-defense—one of the points of our reservation on the Kellogg-Briand Pact. But those issues were not involved in Nuremberg—for not even Hitler, had he stood in the dock, could have asserted against the verified minutes of his own meetings that when he gave the marching orders against Poland he was acting in self-defense. Measured by the Nuremberg evidence the problem of the conditions of punishment did not inhere in the general character of the rules laid down in the London Charter, but rather in the extent of the liability of individuals that those rules undertook to prescribe.

IV

We cannot canvass all the problems of this order, but they can be illustrated by references to the case.

1. Article 6 (a) of the Charter defines as a crime against peace not only the preparation and initiation of a war of aggression but also the 'waging' of such a war. Does this mean that, once it is established that the German war was, in fact, one of aggression, everyone who participated in waging it has committed an international crime? If so, every soldier who fought in the Wehrmacht in the field, everyone who participated in war production would, at the least, be brought within the rule. To be sure, the prosecution disclaimed any such sweeping contention, insisting, especially in the case of the military men, that it was for their part in fomenting and initiating the war and in the perpetration of war crimes that the charges against them had been filed. Common sense would, indeed, rebel at any conception of liability that failed to take adequate account of the actual choice open to particular individuals living within a national state

---

[3] *Ibid.*, p. 16825.
[4] *Ibid.*, p. 16819.

or, to state the same point in a different way, of the compulsions to support a national policy that they may be wholly unable to influence or to change. The point would perhaps be best met if it were recognized that there are cases in which, so far as international sanctions are concerned, justice may require that superior orders be recognized as a complete defense. Whether such orders should constitute a defense or only a mitigation or neither would, in this view, depend on the actual freedom of choice open to individuals in the society of nations as it exists at the particular time. Since the Charter provision barred such orders as a defense in any case, the Tribunal was forced to deal with the issue in other terms. The conviction of Doenitz of waging a war of aggression, compared with the acquittal of Fritsche, who functioned as a propagandist during the war, suggests that the Tribunal, extremely sensitive to problems of this kind, actually drew the line in terms of the significance of the rôle played by the particular individual and the extent of his opportunity for ascertaining the underlying facts about the character of the war.

2. A similar problem is posed by the affirmation, under the Charter, of liability for conspiracy to wage aggressive war—both as a crime in itself and as a basis of responsibility for substantive offenses committed pursuant to the common plan.

It was, in effect, the submission of the prosecution that the Nazi leaders and their associates were engaged from the start in the furtherance of a program having for its specific objective the attainment of large territorial gains at least in Europe; that from the beginning they were committed to the attainment of those ends by any necessary means—including aggressive wars; that the development of the Nazi Party, the seizure of power, the suppression of free labor, the attack on the Church, the regimentation of youth, the persecution of the Jews and other minorities, the reorganization of the state, rearmament, reoccupation of the Rhineland, Austria, Czechoslovakia and ultimately Poland, and the general war were all contemplated steps in the unfolding of the conspiratorial plan; that after the war began, the plan developed to embrace, as systematic objectives, deportation, pillage and extermination in general disregard of the laws of war; and, finally, that these objectives were so widely publicized and otherwise generally understood that anyone who occupied an important position in party or government or otherwise rendered significant aid to the Nazi cause would necessarily be guilty of criminal participation.

This position, however valid it might be as to Hitler or Goering or even others, was rejected by the Tribunal in so far as it swept everyone into the net. For conspiracy to be criminal under the Charter, 'it must not be too far removed from the time of decision and action'; the Tribunal must find evidence of a specific 'concrete plan' and 'determine the participants in that concrete plan'.[5] Everyone who supports a political program is not to be labeled a criminal conspirator merely because, in the perspective of history, the program seems a coherent unity leading

[5] Transcript, p. 16882.

to criminal ends. It is for this reason that eleven of the defendants were acquitted on the charge of conspiracy, leading to the total acquittal of Fritsche, Von Papen and Schacht. Shocking it was to give support to Hitler's regime, and repulsive to men of our persuasion, but measured, as it should be, by the standards we would apply to ourselves, more was required to establish complicity in the criminal conspiracy alleged.

It was not enough that Von Papen supported the Nazi accession to power, that he aided the Austrian venture (which, being before Munich, was not charged as an aggressive war) or that he served during the war at Ankara—for it was not shown that he was privy to any of the planning that launched the series of aggressive wars. Schacht was in charge of rearmament until 1937, of the Reichsbank until 1939, and not finally dismissed from the government until 1943—but a majority of the Tribunal was not satisfied that he was privy to the specific purpose of utilizing those armaments for aggressive war. These conclusions involved, of course, the inferences to be drawn from the evidence, and anyone who knows the record will attest the vitality in the judgment of the Tribunal of the principle of reasonable doubt. The point would be indicated less controversially by suggesting a clear case: a welfare officer who concluded that social service was a good even in a Nazi environment, and who did not delude himself as to what Hitler was about, could not have been convicted of criminal participation merely by proving that welfare services contributed to the maintenance of the Nazi hold.

The necessity of such limiting principles is particularly apparent when a charge of criminality pierces the insulation of the national state and the defendants rely heavily on national patriotism to justify their participation in government affairs. It is apparent also for another reason. If liability were asserted in such broad terms that practically everyone within the offending state would sense himself as subject to it, once the die were cast by the initiation of war, the sanctions of the laws of war would have no field of operation. There would, in short, be no incentive for anyone within the country to mitigate the rigors of the conflict or, indeed, to help bring it to an end.

3. Points such as these apply with special force to the charges leveled against the six organizations. The extraordinary provisions of the Charter on which these charges were based were formulated in the view that it would be practically impossible to enforce responsibility under generally accepted theories of accessorial liability if it were necessary to repeat in every individual case the necessarily elaborate proof of the criminal character of particular organizations and groups. It was concluded, accordingly, that a procedure should be employed to permit the issue of the culpability of organizations to be determined in a single trial in which their leaders would be individual defendants, reserving to particular members the opportunity, should they be prosecuted for their membership, of adducing any evidence that might free them from personal culpability despite their membership in the criminal group. The justification for the device was that it could work no essential injustice since, on the assumptions made, if the evidence in the major trial had

been repeated in any of the individual proceedings, the state of the evidence would be such that the defendant would, in any event, be put to his proof.

However plausible in conception, this aspect of the Nuremberg proceeding proved to be a doubtful element. Two million persons at least were included within the scope of the charges and, as the organizations were defined by the indictment, there were inescapable ambiguities in the measure of their actual scope. More than this, the underlying theory faced procedural difficulties of major moment as thousands of members of the challenged organizations offered to testify that they were unaware of the criminal purposes alleged and innocent of any criminal acts. Was the Tribunal to try the issues thus presented, and could it undertake to do so without protracting the main proceeding to wholly impossible lengths?

The problem was resolved, in substance, by the criteria employed by the Tribunal to determine criminality.[6] In the first place, it was held to be essential that the organization charged have actual existence as a group entity, so that individuals when they became members understood that they were identifying themselves with a collective purpose. In the second place, it was required that criminal objectives be shown to be the pervasive purpose of the group as a whole and not merely the secret intentions of its leaders or of some isolated portion of the whole. In the third place, in estimating the criminality of group objectives, the Tribunal employed the same limiting conceptions that were addressed to the conspiracy charge as a whole.[7]

The consequence was not only denial of the declaration of criminality as to three of the accused organizations but rigorous limitations of the declarations made with respect to the Gestapo, the S.S. and the Leadership Corps. Some categories of membership were excluded entirely, notably those which terminated prior to 1939. Even more significantly, the membership to be included was re-defined in the declaration to comprise only those persons who became or remained members voluntarily with knowledge of the criminal objectives, or who themselves participated in the formulation or execution of criminal plans. In the final result, therefore, the declaration of criminality is all but deprived of significance, for in any subsequent proceeding against individual members it will be necessary for the prosecution to establish guilty knowledge or participation; and the proof that will suffice for this purpose would, under ordinary circumstances, suffice to make out an individual case. And this, I submit, is as it should be, for in actual fact, in the present state of knowledge in Germany, there is little excuse for prosecuting anyone if the evidence will not establish an individual case. The denazification program applies, of course, to all Germans and is more than sufficient for other situations—but its justification inheres less in punitive considerations than in the simple premise that the Nazis are least eligible to participate

---

[6] See Transcript, pp. 16929–16931.
[7] See p. 315, *supra*.

in the reconstruction of Germany and most eligible to perform the disagreeable labor involved in cleaning up the debris of the war. Indeed, the Tribunal recommended, in terms that the Control Council will undoubtedly accept, that anyone convicted only of membership in an organization declared criminal should, in any event, be treated no more severely than the denazification law would allow.

I have said enough, I trust, to indicate the type of problem involved in the application of the Charter that seems to me to warrant the closest attention as the process of historical inquiry proceeds. Issues of this kind are inherent in any effort to apply international sanctions to individuals; they find their parallel within the nations in the surprisingly universal conceptions of culpability embodied in municipal penal law.

V

It will be said that I have spoken of the Nuremberg trial in terms that ignore the entire controversy and, in a genuine sense, my critic will be right. I have not addressed myself to whether a tribunal of the victors could be impartial, to whether the law of the Charter is *ex post facto* or whether it is 'law' at all. These are, indeed, the issues that are currently mooted. But there are elements in the debate that should lead us to be suspicious of the issues as they are drawn in these terms. For, most of those who mount the attack on one or another of these contentions hasten to assure us that their plea is not one of immunity for the defendants; they argue only that they should have been disposed of politically, that is, dispatched out of hand. This is a curious position indeed. A punitive enterprise launched on the basis of general rules, administered in an adversary proceeding under a separation of prosecutive and adjudicative powers is, in the name of law and justice, asserted to be less desirable than an *ex parte* execution list or a drumhead court-martial constituted in the immediate aftermath of the war. I state my view reservedly when I say that history will accept no conception of law, politics or justice that supports a submission in these terms. Those who choose to do so may view the Nuremberg proceeding as 'political' rather than 'legal'—a program calling for the judicial application of principles of liability politically defined. They cannot view it as less civilized an institution than a program of organized violence against prisoners, whether directed from the respective capitals or by military commanders in the field.

I will go further, however, and assert that history would have granted short shrift to a program of summary execution, for such a program is intrinsically unreasonable and could not have been carried out without mistake. Moreover, despite the controversy as to whether the Geneva Convention survives unconditional surrender, when no army remains in the field, I cannot conceive for myself that such a program comports with the Convention's demands. If the execution of prisoners without trial is a war crime while hostilities are in progress, I do not see why it is in any better position when hostilities have come to an end. In my view, Justice Jackson was wrong in arguing that the defendants could point to no other law than the London Charter to assure them any hearing at all.[8] They could point to the Geneva Convention. But the substance of his argument was right. Those who relied upon a treaty for their protection could not argue that treaties were without significance as a basis of liability, if their punishment was otherwise just.

No one who examines the record and the judgment, as most of the commentators have not, will question the disinterestedness of the Tribunal; and those who argue that disinterestedness is inherently impossible in this situation may ask themselves why nations that can produce such impartial critics should be intrinsically incapable of producing equally impartial judges. The fact is that the judgment of the Tribunal was mainly a judgment of limitation, its principal operation more significantly that of protecting innocence than that of declaring and punishing guilt. When I speak of 'innocence' I mean not only a technical freedom from responsibility under the rules laid down; I mean, more deeply, the exculpation of those who could not justly be declared to be guilty under rules of liability that we would be prepared to apply to ourselves.

No one who is satisfied that the conditions of punishment laid down by the Charter and the Tribunal are essentially just and constructive, in the terms I have previously advanced, will in the end deny them his endorsement on the ground that they are retroactively defined. There is, indeed, too large a disposition among the defenders of Nuremberg to look for stray tags of international pronouncements and reason therefrom that the law of Nuremberg was previously fully laid down. If the Kellogg-Briand Pact or a general conception of international obligation sufficed to authorize England, and would have authorized us, to declare war on Germany in defense of Poland —and in this enterprise to kill countless thousands of German soldiers and civilians—can it be possible that it failed to authorize punitive action against individual Germans judicially determined to be responsible for the Polish attack? To be sure, we would demand a more explicit authorization for punishment in domestic law, for we have adopted for the protection of individuals a prophylactic principle absolutely forbidding retroactivity that we can afford to carry to that extreme. International society, being less stable, can afford less luxury. We admit that in other respects. Why should we deny it here?

VI

There is, however, one point in the current debate that we cannot summarily dismiss. It is the point that the punitive enterprise we have undertaken applies only

---

[8] See especially Transcript, p. 14332, also Transcript, 21 November, 1945, pp. 12, 36.

to the enemy. My concern on this score is not with the contention that sanctions must for this reason be ineffective, a point that I have previously met. Nor is it with the argument that we have established a precedent that some future victor may invoke against us. If we are guilty of aggression we shall merit its invocation; if we are not, we can ask for no more—not alone for ourselves but for our cause— than the opportunity to establish our innocence that the Nuremberg defendants received. My concern is with the point of equality itself, so important an element of justice—equality in the sense that the sanctions do not apply either to our allies or to ourselves. The Russians cannot be put to their defense in relation to Finland or to Poland. We are obliged to present to no Tribunal the considerations we would advance to justify the manner in which we exhibited to Japan the power of the atom bomb. This is a genuine difficulty—to which the Tribunal indicated its sensitivity in various ways, such as refusing to assess a penalty against Doenitz for submarine violations that did not differ significantly from our own practice in the Pacific, as attested by Admiral Nimitz. To be sure, the depravity of our enemies and the fact that theirs was the aggression accord us such large leeway in this connection that our relative moral position is secure. But this is a mitigation rather than a defense to the inequality that Nuremberg involves.

I do not think that the difficulty argues that we should have abstained from the Nuremberg venture and accorded immunity to the guilty defendants, the only terms on which abstinence would have been real. It argues rather that Nuremberg, far more than San Francisco, was the assumption of an irrevocable obligation—to build a world of just law that shall apply to all, with institutions strong enough to carry it into effect. It is, moreover, as Justice Jackson has so properly reiterated, an obligation assumed as well by those of our allies who participated in the trial or gave it their sanction by adhering to the Charter. If we succeed in that great venture—and no nation can succeed alone—Nuremberg will stand as a cornerstone in the house of peace. If we fail, we shall hear from the German ruins an attack on the Nuremberg judgment as the second 'diktat' of Versailles; and, notwithstanding the goodness of our intentions, we may have no sufficient answer.

14

The Law of the Nuremberg Trial

By Quincy Wright*

On the afternoon of October 1, 1946, the International Military Tribunal at Nuremberg sentenced twelve of the twenty-two Nazi defendants to death by hanging and seven to imprisonment for terms ranging from ten years to life. Three were acquitted. Three of the six accused organizations were found to be criminal. The reading of these sentences was preceded by the reading, through the whole of September 30, of the general opinion of the Tribunal on the four counts of the indictment and, on the morning of October 1, of the opinion on the charges against each defendant.[1] The Control Council for Germany considered applications for clemency for most of those convicted but did not grant them and carried out the executions of those sentenced to death on October 16 with the exception of Martin Bormann who had not been found and Hermann Goering who had succeeded in committing suicide a few hours earlier. Thus came to an end what President Truman described as 'the first international criminal assize in history.' 'I have no hesitancy in declaring,' continued the President, 'that the historic precedent set at Nuremberg abundantly justifies the expenditure of effort, prodigious though it was. This precedent becomes basic in the international law of the future. The principles established and the results achieved place International Law on the side of peace as against aggressive warfare.'[2]

A similar thought was expressed by Warren R. Austin, Chief Delegate of the United States, in his opening address to the General Assembly of the United Nations on October 30:

Besides being bound by the law of the United Nations Charter, twenty-three nations, members of this Assembly, including the United States, Soviet Russia, the United Kingdom and France, are also bound by the law of the Charter of the Nuremberg

---

* Of the Board of Editors [AJIL].

[1] The judgment was mimeographed on 283 pages of legal size paper with a table of contents and also appeared, followed by the sentences, on pp. 16794 to 17077 of the daily record of the trial. The former is here referred to as 'Judgment' and the latter as 'Record.' The judgment is reproduced below, pp. 172–331, and citations to it in these notes refer to that text.

[2] *Department of State Bulletin*, Vol. 15, p. 776 (Oct. 27, 1946).

Tribunal. That makes planning or waging a war of aggression a crime against humanity for which individuals as well as nations can be brought before the bar of international justice, tried and punished.[3]

Origin of the Trial

The trial originated in the declaration of German atrocities by Roosevelt, Churchill, and Stalin 'speaking in the interest of the thirty-two United Nations' and released at the Moscow Conference on November 1, 1943. This declaration provided that:

Those German officers and men and members of the Nazi party who have been responsible for, or have taken a consenting part in the above atrocities, massacres and executions, will be sent back to the countries in which their abominable deeds were done in order that they may be judged and punished according to the laws of these liberated countries and of the free governments which will be created therein...without prejudice to the case of the major criminals, whose offenses have no particular geographical localization and who will be punished by the joint decision of the Governments of the Allies.[4]

Trials in accord with the first part of this declaration have been carried on in Allied military commissions and criminal courts and hundreds of war criminals have been dealt with.[5] A plan for carrying out the second part concerning major criminals was proposed in his report to the President on June 7, 1945, by Justice Robert H. Jackson who had been appointed Chief of Counsel for the United States in prosecuting the principal Axis war criminals.[6] In accordance with this plan Justice Jackson negotiated for the United States with representatives of Great Britain, France, and the Soviet Union with the result that an agreement for the

---

[3] *The New York Times*, Oct. 31, 1946. President Truman had made a similar statement in his address to the General Assembly on October 23, 1946: *Department of State Bulletin*, Vol. 15, p. 809 (Nov. 3, 1946).

[4] Same, Vol. 9, p. 311 (Nov. 6, 1943). See declaration by nine governments in exile on 'Punishment of War Crimes,' Jan. 13, 1942, in United Nations Information Office, *War and Peace Aims*, January 30, 1943, p. 116. In the Yalta Conference of February 11, 1945, Messrs. Roosevelt, Churchill, and Stalin declared their 'inflexible purpose to... bring all war criminals to just and swift punishment' and this purpose was affirmed in the Berlin Conference of August 2, 1945, by Stalin, Truman and Attlee who 'regarded it as a matter of great importance that the trial of those major criminals should begin at the earliest possible date.' United States Department of State, *The Axis in Defeat, a Collection of Documents on American Policy toward Germany and Japan*, 1945, pp. 7, 9, 12, 17; see also pp. 3, 46.

[5] The United Nations War Crimes Commission reported on Nov. 16, 1946, that up to Oct. 31 of that year 1108 war criminals had been tried in Europe, 413 sentenced to death, 485 imprisoned, and 210 acquitted. In the Far East 1350 had been tried, 384 sentenced to death, 704 imprisoned and 262 acquitted. In the cases of *Ex parte* Quirin, 1942, 317 U. S. 1, and *In re* Yamashita, 1946, 66 Sup. Ct. 340, the Supreme Court of the United States sustained the jurisdiction of United States Military Commissions in such cases.

[6] *Department of State Bulletin*, Vol. 12, 1071 (June 10, 1945).

establishment of an International Military Tribunal was signed in London on August 8, 1946.[7]

The Charter and the Trial

Attached to this agreement was 'The Charter of the International Military Tribunal.' This document provided for a tribunal composed of one judge and one alternate from each of the four powers; for a procedure designed to assure the defendants a fair trial; and for jurisdiction 'to try and punish persons who, acting in the interests of the European Axis countries, whether as individuals or as members of organizations,' committed any of the crimes defined in the Charter. The Charter authorized a committee consisting of the chief prosecutors of each country to prepare the indictment and present the evidence on the basis of the law set forth in the Charter.[*]

The Tribunal was promptly established, consisting of Lord Justice Geoffrey Lawrence of the British Court of Appeals as President; Francis Biddle, former Attorney General of the United States; Major General I. T. Nikitchenko, Vice-Chairman of the Soviet Supreme Court; and Donnedieu de Vabres, Professor of Law at the University of Paris. The alternates were Sir Norman Birkett, Judge of the High Court of England; John J. Parker, Judge of the United States Circuit Court of Appeals; Lt.-Col. A. F. Volchkov, Judge of the Moscow District Court; and Robert Falco, Judge of the Court of Cassation of France. The Tribunal held its first public meeting in Berlin on October 18, 1945, and received the indictment from the Committee of the Chief Prosecutors consisting of Justice Robert H. Jackson for the United States, Sir Hartley Shawcross for Great Britain, Francois de Menthon for France, and General R. A. Rudenko for the Soviet Union.[8] Twenty-four Nazi leaders were indicted each on two or more counts.

The Tribunal then established itself in the Palace of Justice at Nuremberg where it decided upon its rules and assisted the defendants, who had been brought there, to find the counsel of their choice and to obtain the witnesses necessary for their defense. It also decided that Gustav Krupp von Bohlen, who had been indicted, was too sick to be tried; that Martin Bormann, who had not been found, should be tried *in absentia*; that Rudolph Hess, who was alleged to be suffering from loss of memory, was not in such a condition as to prevent his trial and that Julius Streicher was not in such a mental condition as to prevent

---

[7] U. S. *Executive Agreement Series* No. 472. This and other documents connected with the trial were printed by the Department of State in *Trial of War Criminals, Documents*, Washington, 1945. See also similar publication *Trial of Japanese War Criminals, Documents*, Washington, 1946.

[*] Arts. 6–10; this JOURNAL, Vol. 39 (1945), Supplement, pp. 259–260.

[8] Department of State, *Trial of War Criminals*, pp. 23–89. Sir Hartley Shawcross succeeded Sir David Maxwell Fyfe as Chief British Prosecutor though the latter continued to serve in Nuremberg during the trial. M. Champetier de Ribes succeeded M. de Menthon as Chief French Prosecutor.

his trial. One defendant, Robert Ley, committed suicide while in custody.[9] Thus only twenty-one defendants were present in person during the trial.

The trial was begun on November 20, 1945, and continued until October 1, 1946. It was conducted in four languages facilitated by a simultaneous interpretation device. The case of the prosecution was opened by the Americans who dealt with the first count, conspiracy to commit war crimes, on which all defendants had been indicted. The British prosecution followed with the second count, planning, preparing, initiating or waging aggressive war on which sixteen defendants had been indicted. The French prosecution then dealt with counts 3 and 4, as applied to the West, and the Soviet prosecution followed with the same counts in the East. Count 3 charged violation of the laws and customs of war, and count 4 crimes against humanity. Nineteen defendants were indicted under each of these counts. The prosecution consumed three months. The defense, represented by able German lawyers,[10] then presented its case with many witnesses during five months, concluding with legal arguments in behalf of each defendant. The prosecution made its final arguments during the last days of July, 1946. The case of the accused organizations was then heard. On the last day of August the defendants each made final statements.[11] After a few weeks' adjournment the Court read its opinion and sentenced the defendants on the first of October. Three of the defendants (Schacht, von Papen, and Fritzsche) were found not guilty on any counts. Seven (Hess, Funk, Doenitz, Raeder, von Schirach, Speer, and von Neurath) were sentenced to prison terms varying from ten years to life. The remaining twelve (Goering, von Ribbentrop, Keitel, Kaltenbrunner, Rosenberg, Frank, Frick, Streicher, Saukel, Jodl, Bormann and Seyss-Inquart) were sentenced to hang. The Soviet judge dissented from the acquittals and thought Hess should have been sentenced to death.

Of the seventy-six counts on the indictment against the twenty-two defendants the Court sustained fifty-two. All those sentenced to hang were found guilty of crimes against humanity and in most cases of other crimes also. Four defendants,—Funk, Neurath, Schirach, and Speer,—though found guilty of crimes against humanity, were given prison sentences because of mitigating circumstances. Defendants found guilty of aggressive war or conspiracy to commit that crime were given life sentences (Hess, Raeder, and Funk) unless there were mitigating circumstances as in the case of Neurath and Doenitz.

---

[9] Judgment, p. 173.

[10] They are listed on p. 4 of the original text.

[11] The Tribunal held 403 open sessions and listened to evidence from 33 witnesses for the prosecution and 80 witnesses for the individual defendants including 19 defendants themselves. One hundred and forty-three witnesses for the individual defendants gave evidence by written answers to interrogations and 1809 submitted affidavits. The Tribunal heard 22 witnesses for accused organizations and appointed a commission to hear 100 witnesses for such organizations. One thousand eight hundred and nine affidavits were submitted in behalf of accused organizations. In addition several thousand documents were received in evidence, the essential portion being, in most cases read into the record. Judgment, p. 173.

The Tribunal also declared that the SS (Black Shirts) and its subsidiary the SD, the Gestapo, and the Leadership Corps of the Nazi Party were criminal. The SA (Brown Shirts), the Reich Cabinet and the General Staff and High Command were acquitted without prejudice to the individual liability of members. The Soviet judge dissented from the acquittal of the two latter organizations.

The trial has had both champions and critics. The former point out that it gave publicity to thousands of documents discovered by the prosecution and over 17,000 pages of oral evidence and argument of great historic and educational value in establishing the activities of the Nazis and the origins of the war.[12] It manifested the practicability of a fair trial of war crimes in an international tribunal, and may encourage the establishment of a permanent tribunal with a wider jurisdiction for the trial of such crimes and other offenses against the law of nations not dealt with by national tribunals.[13] It established important precedents for the development of international law concerning the definition of certain crimes, particularly that of aggressive war, and concerning the criminal liability of individuals acting in the name of a state, under official orders, or as members of criminal conspiracies or organizations. These principles, if established, will add important sanctions to the numerous international agreements, including the Briand-Kellogg Pact and the Charter of the United Nations, outlawing war as an instrument of national policy.[14]

---

[12] Many of the Documents will appear in a publication in eight volumes entitled *Nazi Conspiracy and Aggression* prepared by the American Prosecution and published by the United States Government.

[13] For past proposals of this type see Manley O. Hudson, *International Tribunals, Past and Future*, Washington, 1944, pp. 180 ff. and for the text of *Convention for Creation of an International Criminal Court* signed by thirteen states at Geneva in 1937, Hudson, *International Legislation*, Washington, 1946, Vol. 7, p. 878.

[14] A number of jurists have considered the extent to which 'war crimes' were crimes under international law before 1939. There seems to have been an almost unanimous opinion that war crimes in the narrow sense were, but with respect to the initiation of aggressive war there has been some dissent. The following support the criminality of 'aggressive war' with arguments drawn from international custom, the Briand-Kellogg Pact, or other treaties: Lord Wright, 'War Crimes Under International Law,' in *Law Quarterly Review*, Vol. 62 (1946), pp. 40–52; Sheldon Glueck, 'The Nuremberg Trial and Aggressive War,' in *Harvard Law Review*, Vol. 59 (1946), pp. 396–456, reprinted by Knopf, New York, 1946 (differing on this point from the author's earlier volume, *War Criminals, Their Prosecution and Punishment*, New York, 1944, p. 37); Murray C. Bernays, 'Legal Basis of Nuremberg Trials,' in *Survey Graphic*, January, 1945, p. 5; A. N. Trainin, *Hitlerite Responsibility Under Criminal Law, New York*, 1945; Hans Kelsen, 'Collective and Individual Responsibility in International Law, With Particular Regard to the Punishment of War Criminals,' in *California Law Review*, Vol. 31 (1943), p. 530; the same, 'The Rule Against *Ex Post Facto* Laws and the Prosecution of the Axis War Criminals,' in *Judge Advocate Journal*, Vol. 2 (1945), p. 8; Willard B. Cowles, 'Universality of Jurisdiction Over War Crimes,' in *California Law Review*, Vol. 33 (1945), pp. 177–218; the same, 'High Government Officials as War Criminals,' in American Society of International Law, *Proceedings, 1945*, p. 54; the same, 'Trial of War Criminals by Military Tribunals,' in *American Bar Association Journal*, June, 1944; Albert G. D. Levy, 'The Law and Procedure of War Crime Trials,' in *American Political Science Review*, Vol. 37 (1943), pp. 1052–1081; the same, 'Criminal Responsibility of Individuals and International Law,' in *University of Chicago Law Review*, Vol. 12 (1945), pp. 313–332; A. N. Sack, 'War Criminals and the Defense of Superior Orders in International Law,' in *Lawyers Guild Review*, Vol. 5 (1945); H. Lauterpacht,

Criticisms of the Trial

Critics of the trial fall into two classes, those who object to the decisions and sentences and those who object to the law. Critics of the first class question the judgment of the Tribunal in weighing the evidence and appraising the magnitude of offenses. No attempt can be made here to examine the careful weighing of evidence applicable to each individual defendant and each accused organization in the judgment. The Tribunal's theory in sentencing may, however, be considered. The Charter authorized death sentences or less, thus confirming the usual practice of military commissions. Some critics, including the Soviet judge, have expressed dissatisfaction that some of those found guilty on counts 1 and 2 (conspiracy and aggressive war), like Hess, were not given death sentences. The Tribunal declared that 'to initiate a war of aggression is the supreme international crime, differing only from other war crimes in that it contains within itself the accumulated evil of the whole.'[15] It gave no reason for deciding that this crime deserved a less severe punishment than crimes against humanity. The following explanation may be suggested. Though aggressive war may result in larger losses of life, property and social values than any other crime, yet the relationship of the acts constituting the crime to such losses is less close than in the case of crime against humanity. The latter implies acts indicating a direct responsibility for large-scale homicide, enslavement or deportation of innocent civilians. The initiation of aggressive war, on the other hand, implies only declarations or other acts of political or group leadership, the consequences of which depend upon the

---

'The Law of Nations and the Punishment of War Crimes,' in *British Year Book of International Law*, 1944, pp. 58–95; Nicholas Doman, 'Political Consequences of the Nuremberg Trial,' in American Academy of Political and Social Sciences, *Annals*, Vol. 246 (July, 1946), pp. 81–90; Q. Wright, 'War Criminals,' in this JOURNAL, Vol. 39 (1945), pp. 257–285; the same, 'Due Process and International Law,' in this JOURNAL, Vol. 40 (1946), pp. 398–406; the same, 'The Nuremberg Trial,' in *Chicago Bar Record*, Vol. 27 (1946), pp. 201–219; the same, 'The Nuremberg Trial,' in American Academy of Political and Social Science, *Annals*, Vol. 246 (July, 1946), pp. 72–80. The following are doubtful on this point: Charles E. Wyzanski, Jr., 'The Nuremberg War Criminal Trial,' a communication to the American Academy of Arts and Sciences, December 12, 1945; Max Radin, 'War Crimes and the Crime of War,' in *Virginia Law Review*, Vol. 21 (1945), p. 497; the same, 'Justice at Nuremberg,' in *Foreign Affairs*, Vol. 24 (1946), pp. 369–404; Georg Schwarzenberger, 'War Crimes and the Problem of an International Criminal Court,' in *Czechoslovak Year Book of International Law*, London, 1942, pp. 67–88; George Finch, 'Retribution for War Crimes,' in this JOURNAL, Vol. 37 (1943), pp. 81–88; Erich Hula, 'Punishment for War Crimes,' in *Social Research*, Vol. 13 (1946), p. 1; the same, 'The Revival of the Idea of Punitive War,' in *Thought*, Vol. 21 (1946), pp. 405–434. Reports of the Section on International and Comparative Law of the American Bar Association, July, 1945, and of the National Lawyers Guild, December, 1944 (*Lawyers Guild Review*, Vol. 4, p. 18), were inconclusive on this point. See also discussions in American Society of International Law participated in by C. C. Hyde, E. D. Dickinson, Charles Warren, Edward Hambro, Quincy Wright, George A. Finch, and others (*Proceedings*, 1943, pp. 39–58), and by Willard B. Cowles, Edward Dumbault, Alwyn V. Freeman, Charles Prince, John B. Whitton, Elbert Thomas, George A. Finch, Frederick R. Coudert and others (same, 1945, pp. 68–76).

[15] Judgment, p. 186.

circumstances and the mode in which they are carried out, although to be called aggressive war there must be some hostilities.[16] Some of the aggressions before the Tribunal resulted in the loss of millions of lives but others, such as the invasions of Austria and Czechoslovakia, resulted immediately in little loss of life because the victims submitted without resistance. The crime of aggressive war resembles those of piracy and filibustering. They may lead to large-scale hostilities and serious losses but they may, on the other hand, succeed or be suppressed without serious damage. A pirate, a filibusterer or an aggressor may be a gentleman or he may be a brute. Only those defendants in the Nuremberg trial who added brutality, manifested by other crimes, to aggression were sentenced to hang. The others were given life imprisonment or even less if there were special mitigating circumstances. It is interesting to notice that in 1794 when the Congress of the United States defined the setting on foot of a military expedition from American territory against a friendly country (filibustering) as an offense against the law of nations, it considered fine and imprisonment adequate punishment.[17] Piracy as defined by the law of nations is now punishable under United States Statutes only by life imprisonment.[18] Napoleon, who was sentenced by a political declaration of the allied powers, was not executed but condemned to life imprisonment.[19]

Critics from a legal point of view have contended that the Tribunal had no jurisdiction in international law and that it applied *ex post facto* law.[20] Related to these criticisms have been the contention that morally the trial was unfair because constituted by one side in a war[21] or because some of the prosecuting

[16] The judgment followed the indictment in distinguishing 'acts of aggression,' such as the seizures of Austria and Czechoslovakia, and 'wars of aggression,' including the operations against Poland, Denmark, Norway, The Netherlands, Belgium, Luxembourg, Jugoslavia, Greece, Soviet Union and the United States. Same, p. 186.

[17] U. S. Code, Tit. 18, sec. 25.

[18] U. S. Code, Tit. 18, sec. 481. Piracy was originally a capital offense.

[19] Q. Wright, 'The Legal Liability of the Kaiser,' in *American Political Science Review*, Vol. 13 (1919), pp. 127 ff.

[20] These arguments were included in a motion by Goering's counsel at the opening of the trial. The Tribunal gave it consideration and declared on November 21, 1945: 'Insofar as it may be a plea to the jurisdiction of the Tribunal, it conflicts with Article 3 of the Charter and will not be entertained. Insofar as it may contain other arguments, which may be open to the defendants, they may be heard at a later stage.' (Record, p. 94.) Unable to attack the jurisdiction of the Tribunal or the validity of the Charter, subsequent arguments of defendant's counsel urged a restrictive, in some cases nullifying, interpretation of the law set forth in the Charter or confined themselves to evidence to sustain the 'not guilty' pleas. Those in the first category sought to eliminate the aggressive war charge altogether by insisting that it was based on *ex post facto* law (Goering), or to restrict its interpretation by consideration of the practical necessities of diplomacy (Ribbentrop, p. 13058), and war (Goering thought the Hague Conventions were not applicable to total war) under existing conditions of international relations, technology and moral opinion in Germany (especially because of the 'iniquities' of the Treaty of Versailles and the natural aspirations of a defeated people to rehabilitate themselves) (Hess). Others, relying mainly on evidence, did not deny that crimes had taken place but sought to escape liability by pleading Hitler's orders, unawareness of the crimes at the time, lack of criminal intent in issuing orders, or lack of participation in any action which was criminal under the terms of the Charter (Schacht, Von Papen, Fritsche).

[21] This argument also appears in Goering's motion. It has been suggested that the Tribunal administered 'political justice' based on the desire for 'vengeance' sacrificing 'democratic' for

states had been guilty of the same offenses for which they were trying their enemies;[22] and that politically the trial was inexpedient because it may make conciliation between victor and vanquished more difficult,[23] because it may make heroes and martyrs of the defendants, or because its principles if generally accepted may reduce the unity of the state, increase the difficulties of maintaining domestic order, and deter statesmen from pursuing vigorous foreign policies when necessary in the national interests.[24] These moral and political arguments depend upon ethical, psychological, and sociological assumptions which are controversial. They should be distinguished from the legal arguments which alone are under consideration here.

Legally belligerent states have habitually assumed jurisdiction to try in their own military commissions captured enemy persons accused of war crimes and to try in their own prize courts captured enemy and neutral vessels. All states in time of peace have assumed jurisdiction to try captured pirates in their own criminal courts and some states have extended the jurisdiction of such courts to other offenses against the law of nations committed by aliens abroad.[25] The Hague Conference of 1907 adopted a convention for an international prize court to which cases could be appealed from national prize courts, and a conference held at Geneva in 1937 adopted a convention for an international criminal court to try persons accused of 'terrorism' in certain circumstances but these conventions never came into force. In practice the legal competence of national criminal, military, and prize courts to try aliens for certain offenses against the law of nations committed outside the state's territory has not been questioned.

Sovereign states, it is true, cannot be subjected to a foreign jurisdiction without their consent[26] but no such principle applies to individuals. The Nuremberg Tribunal did not exercise jurisdiction over Germany but over certain German individuals accused of crimes.

'totalitarian' concepts. See Barron's *National Business and Financial Weekly*, October 7, 1946. Senator Robert Taft mingled this argument with the suggestion that the defendants should not have been found liable because the law was *ex post facto* and, rather inconsistently, that those sentenced to death should have been sentenced only to life imprisonment. See press reports of address at Kenyon College, October 5, 1946.

[22] Under the head 'Aggressor Nations' *The Chicago Tribune*'s leading editorial for October 2, 1946, writes: 'The truth of the matter is that no one of the victors was free of the guilt which its judges attributed to the vanquished.'

[23] C. Arnold Anderson, 'The Utility of the Proposed Trial and Punishment of Enemy Leaders,' in *American Political Science Review*, Vol. 37 (1943), pp. 1081 ff.; Erich Hula, 'The Revival of the Idea of Punitive War,' in *Thought*, Vol. 21 (1946), pp. 405 ff.

[24] See *Chicago Tribune*, cartoon and editorial, Oct. 2, 1946. Some of these arguments are discussed by the present writer: 'War Criminals,' in this JOURNAL, Vol. 39 (1945), pp. 259, 263.

[25] Below, notes 36–39.

[26] Eastern Carelia Case, *Publications*, PCI, Ser. B, 5; 1 *World Court Reports*, 190; *Harvard Research in International Law*, Competence of Courts in Regard to Foreign States, in this JOURNAL, Supplement, Vol. 26 (1932), pp. 455 ff.

Furthermore, the equitable principle of 'clean hands' is not recognized as a defense in criminal trials.[26a] Whether or not statesmen or individuals of the United Nations have been guilty of any of the offenses for which the defendants were tried was not a question legally relevant to this trial, nor is it legally relevant to consider whether other persons who have not been indicted or who were not within the jurisdiction of the Tribunal may have been guilty of the same offenses. Unreasonable discrimination in initiating prosecution of persons probably liable under law would certainly not appear to be just and when the law applied is international law justice seems to call for a tribunal with jurisdiction over all persons subject to that law.[27] Such justice, however, has never been realized. Courts applying international law have always had a more limited jurisdiction. It has not been considered unreasonable for the jurisdiction of national tribunals applying international criminal law to be limited to those whose acts were injurious to the state establishing the tribunal.[28]

The object of legal procedure is to segregate issues sufficiently narrowly to permit of a thorough examination of the factual evidence and the legal sources bearing upon those issues. Criminal courts have not considered it appropriate to inquire during a trial whether their jurisdiction ought to be wider, whether others ought to have been indicted, whether punishment for the crime charged or for any crime is expedient, but have concerned themselves only with the questions: Does the Court have jurisdiction? How should it proceed to assure a fair trial? Does the evidence support the charges? Do the charges if proved render the accused liable under the law? Whether some statesman of the United Nations should be accused of aggressive war or of crimes against humanity, whether some soldiers or sailors of the United Nations should be accused of war crimes, whether the court should have been differently constituted with a different jurisdiction, whether Goering and the other defendants will become heroes and martyrs, whether it is desirable that aggressive war be a crime or that national sovereignty be unable to throw a cloak of immunity around persons accused of crimes—all these are important questions, but not legal questions which the Tribunal could deal with. They were doubtless considered by the four powers that made the agreement and Charter of August 8, 1945 and criticisms based on these questions are criticisms of these powers or of international law not of the Tribunal.

[26a] Even an infamous person is protected by criminal law (Wharton, *Criminal Law*, pp. 138, 139). Grotius, quoting the *Bible* (John VIII, 7), thought that under natural law 'a guilty person ought not to be punished by an equally guilty' (*De Jure Belli ac Pacis*, II, cxx, 3, 2), but recognized that this had no application to punishment by a superior authority established by positive law (*De Jure Belli ac Pacis*, II, cxx, 40, 1). Judge Hudson in a concurring opinion in the Permanent Court of International Justice suggested that international law permitted a 'sparing application' of equitable principles such as 'He who seeks equity must do equity' (Case of Water Diversion from the Meuse, 1937, 4 *World Court Reports* 232–3) but this had no reference to criminal liability.

[27] Quiney Wright, *War Criminals*, note 4.

[28] Harvard Research, Jurisdiction with Respect to Crime, Arts. 7, 9, in this JOURNAL, *Supplement*, Vol. 29 (1935), p. 543.

Some of the critics who have emphasized these points appear to dislike the trend of international law recognized in the Charter. Opinion is coming to realize that international law cannot survive in the shrinking world, threatened by military instruments of increasing destructiveness, if sanctioned only by the good faith and self-help of governments. Sanctions to be effective must operate on individuals rather than on states. But regularly enforced world criminal law applicable to individuals necessarily makes inroads upon national sovereignty and tends to change the foundation of the international community from a balance of power among sovereign states to a universal federation directly controlling individuals in all countries on matters covered by international law. In such a regime of law, aggressive war is necessarily outlawed and with it the right of states to decide when forceable self-help is permissible. Many, doubtless, look upon this reduction of national sovereignty with apprehension. Some may even be concerned lest the free decision of their government to make a 'preventive war' be impaired. The Charter of the Tribunal recognized principles generally believed to be essential for a law governed world under present conditions, and naturally those who are afraid of the restrictions of a law governed world upon the nation or who think world opinion has not developed to a point that would make such a world possible, view these principles with apprehension. The United Nations in the Charter of the International Military Tribunal, as in the Charter of the United Nations, performed an act of faith in, and commitment to, a law governed world and the principles which must be accepted and applied if there is to be such a world.[29] The Tribunal did not hesitate to accept these principles as established in developing international law at the time the acts for which the defendants were being tried were committed.

The present article will not attempt to analyze or weigh the evidence. Few, if any, of the critics have questioned that if the law is accepted, the evidence justified the convictions.[30] The Tribunal recognized that it was bound by the Charter and that its jurisdiction established by the Charter could not be challenged.[31] Nevertheless, it listened to arguments and expressed an opinion upon the principles of general international law which might effect the interpretation, if not the validity, of that instrument.

[29] The nature, extent, and reason for these commitments are discussed in a Symposium on World Organization, in *Yale Law Journal*, August, 1946. The general concern is suggested by Justice Wm. O. Douglas in his introduction: 'The use of force by any nation may now destroy it as well as those against whom it is used. Internally and externally we must untie our Gordian knots; we cannot cut them except at our peril. The instruments with which we must contrive that men live peacefully together are more intricate and difficult ones. They are the instruments for peaceful adjustment of conflicts between groups and nations. Those instruments are law—law administered in accordance with civilized traditions, law conceived and administered by politically competent people.' Same, p. 868.

[30] Some, including the Soviet judge and the Prosecution, have thought that it would have justified further convictions. If the court erred it was in too liberal an application of the principle that the defendants should have the benefit of the doubt.

[31] Answer to Goering's motion, above, note 20. See also Judgment, p. 216.

The defense contested the validity of the Charter if it were construed in a way to transgress fundamental principles of justice and argued that to apply *ex post facto* laws in a criminal trial and to judge one's own case would transgress such principles.[32] It is a commonly asserted principle of international law that international agreements bind only the parties and cannot adversely modify the legal position of non-parties.[33] The Tribunal did not deny this principle but it failed to find that any rights of third parties, either Germany or the individual defendants, had been violated by the terms of the Charter establishing its jurisdiction, procedure, and law.

The Tribunal's Jurisdiction

The making of the Charter (said the Tribunal) was the exercise of the sovereign legislative power by the countries to which the German Reich unconditionally surrendered; and the undoubted right of these countries to legislate for the occupied territories had been recognized by the civilized world. The Charter is not an arbitrary exercise of power on the part of the victorious nations, but in the view of the Tribunal, as will be shown, it is the expression of international law existing at the time of its creation; and to that extent is itself a contribution to international law.

The Signatory Powers created this Tribunal, defined the law it was to administer, and made regulations for the proper conduct of the Trial. In doing so, they have done together what any one of them might have done singly; for it is not to be doubted that any nation has the right thus to set up special courts to administer law. With regard to the constitution of the court, all that the defendants are entitled to ask is to receive a fair trial on the facts and law.[34]

This statement suggests two distinct grounds of jurisdiction—that enjoyed by the four powers as the government of Germany and that enjoyed by any state to administer law. The latter statement is far from complete. International law does not permit states to administer criminal law over any defendant for any act. There are limits to the criminal jurisdiction of a state.[35] Every state does, however, have authority to set up special courts to try any person within its custody who commits war crimes, at least if such offenses threaten its security. It is believed that this jurisdiction is broad enough to cover the jurisdiction given by the Charter.[36] If each party to the Charter could exercise such jurisdiction individually, they

---

[32] See especially Goering's motion of Nov. 20, 1945; argument by Jodl's counsel, Dr. Jahrreiss, July 4, 1946; argument by Goering's counsel, Dr. Otto Stahmer, July 4, 1946; and final word by Goering, Aug. 31, 1946, Record, pp. 12906, 12959, 16729.

[33] This principle is subject to qualifications, see R. F. Boxburgh, *International Conventions and Third States*, London, 1917.

[34] Judgment, p. 216.

[35] Harvard Research, Jurisdiction with Respect to Crime, this JOURNAL, Vol. 29 (1925), Supplement, p. 439.

[36] See Cowles, 'Universality of Jurisdiction over War Crimes,' as cited, and below, notes 38, 39.

can agree to set up an international tribunal to exercise the jurisdiction jointly. The context of the Court's statement suggests that the Tribunal intended this limitation.

As already noted, states have habitually authorized military commissions, prize courts and criminal courts to exercise jurisdiction over many offenses against international law committed by aliens abroad.[37] While many states apply the universality principle of criminal jurisdiction only in the case of piracy,[38] some states have applied it to all offenses against the law of nations especially if dangerous to their security.[39] In principle international law imposes few limitations upon the competence of states to try individuals for such acts. In the case of the steamship *Lotus,* the Permanent Court of International Justice held that a state can extend its criminal jurisdiction to any case whatever unless a rule or principle of international law forbids.[40] There appears to be no rule or principle of international law which forbids the parties to the Charter from exercising jurisdiction over the defendants for the offenses alleged in the Charter, provided they threatened the security of those states, a condition which can hardly be doubted, and that they were crimes under international law, a matter to be considered later.

The derivation of the Tribunal's jurisdiction from the sovereignty of Germany also appears to be well grounded. The Nazi government of Germany disappeared with the unconditional surrender of Germany in May, 1945, and on June 5, 1945, the four Allied powers, then in complete control of Germany by public declaration at Berlin, assumed 'supreme authority with respect to Germany, including all the powers possessed by the German Government, the High Command, and any state, municipal, or local government or authority' in order 'to make provision for the cessation of any further hostilities on the part of the German armed forces, for the maintenance of order in Germany, and for the administration of the country,' but without intention to 'effect the annexation of Germany.'[41] Under international law a state may acquire sovereignty of territory by declaration of annexation after subjugation of the territory if that declaration is generally recognized by the other states of the world. The Declaration of Berlin was generally recognized, not only by the United Nations but also by neutral states. This Declaration, however, differed from the usual declaration of annexation in that it was by several states, its purposes were stated, and it was declared not to effect the annexation of Germany.

There is no doubt but that sovereignty may be held jointly by several states as has been the case in a number of *condominia.* There also have been instances

[37] See above, pp. 326–27.
[38] Harvard Research, Piracy, this JOURNAL, Vol. 26 (1932), Supplement, p. 743; and same, Jurisdiction with Respect to Crime, Art. 9, at p. 563.
[39] Harvard Research, Jurisdiction with Respect to Crime, Arts. 7–10, pp. 440, 569–73, 579.
[40] The Lotus (France and Turkey), P. C. I. J., *Publications,* Ser. A., No. 10, 2 *World Court Reports* 34–35; Cowles, p. 178.
[41] Department of State, *The Axis in Defeat,* p. 63.

of temporary exercise of sovereignty for purposes more limited than permanent annexation. The American position in Cuba from 1899 to 1903 was of this type and so also are Mandates under the League of Nations and Trusteeships under the United Nations.[41a] In principle it would appear that if a state or states are in a position to annex a territory they have the right to declare the lesser policy of exercising sovereignty temporarily for specified purposes with the intention of eventually transferring the sovereignty to someone else. This appears to be the proper construction of the Declaration of Berlin. The four Allied powers assumed the sovereignty of Germany in order, among other purposes, to administer the country until such time as they thought fit to recognize an independent German government. Their exercise of powers of legislation, adjudication, and administration in Germany during this period is permissible under international law, limited only by the rules of international law applicable to sovereign states in territory they have subjugated. Their powers go beyond those of a military occupant.[42] It would appear, therefore, that the four states who proclaimed the Charter of August 8, 1945, had the power to enact that Charter as a legislative act for Germany provided they did not transgress fundamental principles of justice which even a conqueror ought to observe toward the inhabitants of annexed territory.[43]

The idea that the four powers acting in the interest of the United Nations had the right to legislate for the entire community of nations, though given some support by Art. 5 of the Moscow Declaration of November 1, 1943, and by Art. 2 (6) of the Charter of the United Nations was not referred to by the Tribunal. The preamble of the agreement of August 8, 1945, however, declares that the four powers in making the agreement 'act in the interests of all the United Nations' and invited any government of the United Nations to adhere, and nineteen of them did so. Since the Charter of the United Nations assumed that that organization could declare principles binding on non-members, it may be that the United Nations in making the agreement for the Nuremberg Tribunal intended to act for the community of nations as a whole, thus making universal international law. While such an assumption of competence would theoretically be a novelty in international law, it would accord with the practice established during the nineteenth century under which leading powers exercised a predominant influence in initiating new rules of international law.[44] It is not, however, necessary to make

[41a] Q. Wright, *Mandates under the League of Nations*, Chicago, 1930, pp. 13, 306–9, 315–39, 530–37.

[42] Hans Kelsen, 'The Legal Status of Germany According to the Declaration of Berlin,' this JOURNAL, Vol. 39 (1945), p. 518.

[43] C. C. Hyde, *International Law*, Boston, 1945, 2nd ed., Vol. I, pp. 397–8.

[44] As in declaring rules of diplomatic precedence at Vienna, in 1815, rules of treaty validity at London, 1871, and rules of maritime international law at Paris, 1856, and London, 1909. *The International Law of the Future*, published by a group of American jurists in 1944, includes the statement: 'It is assumed that at the conclusion of the present war the lodgment of power will be such that the states which desire an effective organization will have dominant voice, and that other

any such assumption in order to support the right of the parties to the Charter to give the Tribunal the jurisdiction it asserted. That right can be amply supported by the position of these powers as the Government of Germany or from the sovereign right of each to exercise universal jurisdiction over the offenses stated.

Procedure of the Trial

'With regard to the constitution of the court,' said the Tribunal, 'all that the defendants are entitled to ask is to receive a fair trial on the facts and law.'[45] International law requires that any state or group of states in exercising criminal jurisdiction over aliens shall not 'deny justice.'[46] The Charter provided suitable procedure with this in view.[46a]

The rules adapted by the Tribunal in pursuance of Art. 13 of the Charter elaborated these provisions by assuring each individual defendant a period at least thirty days before his trial began to study the indictment and prepare his case, and ample opportunity to obtain the counsel of his choice, to obtain witnesses and documents, to examine all documents submitted by the prosecution, and to address motions, applications, and other requests to the Tribunal, and by assuring members of accused organizations opportunity to apply to be heard. At the first public session of the Tribunal, held in Berlin on October 18, 1945, the Presiding Judge, General Nikitchenko, called attention to these rules and said a 'special clerk of the Tribunal has been appointed to advise the defendants of their right and to take instructions from them personally as to their choice of counsel, and generally to see that their rights of defense are made known to them.'

In addition to requiring that the trial be 'fair,' the Charter required that it be 'expeditious' and that the Tribunal 'take strict measures' to prevent 'unreasonable delay' and rule out 'irrelevant issues and statements.' Some critics have deplored the length of the trial but few have suggested any unfairness in the procedure. The Counsel of some of the defendants mildly objected to some rulings on the relevance of evidence or argument, to some limitation on the length of speeches, and to some admissions of affidavit evidence presented by the prosecution.[47] The

states will be willing, or will feel themselves constrained, to follow the lead. If one or more states should hold aloof, competence might none the less be vested in the organization to act on behalf of the whole Community of States': p. 81.

[45] Judgment, pp. 216–217.

[46] Harvard Research, Responsibility of States for Damage done in their Territory to the Person and Property of Aliens, Art. 9, this JOURNAL, Vol. 23 (1929), Supplement, p. 173; Jurisdiction with Respect to Crime, Arts. 12, 13; Q. Wright, 'Due Process and International Law,' this JOURNAL, Vol. 40 (1946), pp. 398 ff.; A. V. Freeman, *The International Responsibility of States for Denial of Justice.* New York, 1938, pp. 262 ff., 547 ff.

[46a] Art. 16; this JOURNAL, Vol. 39 (1945), Supplement, p. 260.

[47] The Tribunal curbed the disposition of some defendants' counsel to expand on what they considered the iniquities of the Versailles Treaty and to submit evidence concerning the policies or

Tribunal, if anything leaned over backwards to assure the defendants an opportunity to find and present all relevant evidence, to argue all legal problems related
to the case and to present motions concerning the mental and physical competence of defendants which might bear upon their triability.[48]

The Supreme Court of the United States held that General Yamashita was
given due process of law in his trial by a United States Military Commission in
the Philippines, but two dissenting Justices thought the admission of hearsay and
opinion evidence and the haste of the proceedings giving the defense insufficient
opportunity to present its case denied 'due process of law.'[49] The latter charge has
not been made against the Nuremberg Tribunal. Like other international tribunals, like military commissions, and like continental European criminal courts,
it did not apply common law rules of evidence, but it has never been contended
that those rules of evidence are required by international law.[50]

It seems to be generally recognized that the application of *ex post facto*
laws in criminal cases constitutes a denial of justice under international law.
Constitutional guarantees and proposed bills of human rights have usually forbidden the application of *ex post facto* criminal law.[51] Though few international
claims have turned on this issue that may be because modern states have rarely
applied such laws.[52] The Supreme Court of the United States in the Yamashita
case[53] and the Nuremberg Tribunal seem to have assumed that the application

acts of members of the United Nations unless in support of a contention that the defendants initiated wars in necessary self defence or that war measures were justifiable reprisals.

[48] The Tribunal appointed expert commissions to examine Krupp von Bohlen, Hess, and
Streicher and, after listening to argument, found Krupp too sick to be tried and the other two in a
mental condition permitting trial.

[49] *In re* Yamashita, 1946, 66 Sup. Ct. 340 and comment, this JOURNAL, Vol. 40 (1946), p. 398.

[50] The Tribunal received affidavits if circumstances prevented personal attendance of witnesses
whose evidence appeared to be relevant and important. It refused to receive documents or to summon witnesses if it considered the subject matter of their evidence irrelevant or merely cumulative
(Charter, Arts. 17–21; Rules 4, 7). The task of considering applications consumed a great deal of
the Tribunal's time in private sessions. To assure availability of all evidence in all the languages it
required that the important part of all documents offered in evidence be read into the record unless
copies were provided in advance in all four languages (Charter, Art. 25).

[51] See Statement of Essential Human Rights by a Committee appointed by the American Law
Institute, Art. 9; American Academy of Political and Social Science, *Annals*, Vol. 243 (Jan., 1946),
p. 22; H. Lauterpacht, *An International Bill of the Rights of Man*, New York, 1945, pp. 93, 99.

[52] In the Van Bokkelen Case (U. S. and Hayti, 1888) the United States contended 'that continuous imprisonment for debt, when there is no criminal offense imputed, is contrary to what
are now generally recognized principles of international law' but this aspect of the matter was not
discussed in the arbitration: (J. B. Moore, *Digest of International Law*, Vol. 6, pp. 699, 772). See
E. M. Borchard, *Diplomatio Protection of Citizens Abroad*, New York, 1919, p. 99; A. V. Freeman,
The International Responsibility of States for Denial of Justice, New York, 1938, pp. 522, 550. The
Harvard Research did not include the application of *ex post facto* laws among prohibited procedures
in its draft convention in jurisdiction with respect to crime (Arts. 12, 13) but did so in its draft
convention on extradition (Arts. 2 (a), 12 (3) b): this JOURNAL, Vol. 29 (1935), Supplement, pp. 77,
163, 596 ff.

[53] Q. Wright, 'Due Process and International Law,' as cited. The dissenting justices thought the
offense charged was inadequately defined in pre-existing international law and cited this among
other reasons for believing that 'due process' had been denied the defendant.

of *ex post facto* laws would be a denial of justice because both took pains to show that the rules of international law which they applied were not *ex post facto*. They treated the issue as one of substantive law and not of procedure or jurisdiction.[54]

The Law Applied

The law, defining the crimes and the conditions of liability to be applied in the trial, was set forth in the Charter[55] and the Tribunal recognized that the law 'is decisive and binding upon the Tribunal.'[56] Was this law declaratory of pre-existing international law binding the defendants at the time they committed the acts charged? The issue has been discussed particularly in regard to the crime of 'aggressive war.'

The Tribunal listened to argument on the question[57] and concluded that a rule of international law, resting upon 'general principles of justice,' affirmed in this respect by several recent international declarations that aggressive war is an international crime,[58] had been formally accepted by all the states concerned when they ratified the Pact of Paris which condemned recourse to war for the solution of international controversies and renounced it as an instrument of national policy. This rule had made 'resort to a war of aggression not merely illegal but criminal.'[59]

The Tribunal therefore considered that the well-known legal maxim *nullum crimen sine lege* had been duly observed in the case.[60]

It quoted the text of the Pact of Paris of August 27, 1928, binding sixty-three nations, including Germany, Italy, and Japan at the outbreak of the war in 1939, referred to the analogous situation of the Hague Convention, violation of which created individual criminal liability, and held that the result was to make the waging of aggressive war illegal and those committing the act criminally liable.[61] The Tribunal then cited various draft treaties, and resolutions of the League of Nations and the Pan American Organization declaring aggressive war a crime and added:

All these expressions of opinion, and others that could be cited, so solemnly made, reinforce the construction which the Tribunal places upon the Pact of Paris, that resort to a

[54] 'It is to be observed,' says the Nuremberg judgment, 'that the maxim *nullum crimen sine lege* is not a limitation of sovereignty but is in general a principle of justice': Judgment, p. 217.

[55] Arts. 6–9, quoted above.

[56] Judgment, p. 216.

[57] See note 32, above.

[58] These include the Draft Treaty of Mutual Assistance, 1923; the Geneva Protocol, 1924; the League of Nations Assembly Resolution on Aggressive War of September 24, 1927; the Resolution of the Pan-American Conference of Havana, Feb. 18, 1928.

[59] Judgment, p. 220.

[60] Judgment, p. 217.

[61] Same, pp. 218–219.

war of aggression is not merely illegal, but is criminal. The prohibition of aggressive war demanded by the conscience of the world, finds its expression in the series of Pacts and Treaties to which the Tribunal has just referred.[62]

Turning to the status of the individual in international law the Tribunal said:

It was submitted that international law is concerned with the actions of sovereign states, and provides for no punishment for individuals; and further, that where the action in question is an act of state, those who carry it out are not personally responsible, but are protected by the doctrine of the sovereignty of the State. In the opinion of the Tribunal both these submissions must be rejected. That international law imposes duties and liabilities upon individuals as well as upon states has long been recognized.[63]

After referring to the United States Supreme Court decision in *Ex parte* Quirin[64] and the practice cited in that case, the Tribunal said that individuals could be held responsible for criminal acts even if committed on behalf of their states 'if the state in authorizing action moves outside its competence under international law.' Furthermore they could not shelter themselves behind the plea of superior orders if 'moral choice was in fact possible.'[65]

These statements of the Tribunal will be commented on by examining the concept of offenses against the law of nations as it has developed in international practice and custom, the applicability of the *ex post facto* rule in a legal system which develops by practice, the extent to which the specific offenses laid down in the charter had been recognized in customary international law with especial reference to aggressive war and criminal conspiracy and organization, and the extent to which international law recognized 'act of state' as a defense against criminal charges.

Offenses Against the Law of Nations

The concept of offenses against the law of nations (*delicti juris gentium*) was recognized by the classical text writers on international law[66] and has been employed

---

[62] Same p. 220. The Tribunal also referred to Arts. 227 and 228 of the Treaty of Versailles for the trial of the Kaiser and German war criminals of World War I.

[63] Judgment, p. 220.

[64] *Ex parte* Quirin, 1942, 317 U. S. 1.

[65] Judgment, p. 221.

[66] 'The fact must also be recognized that kings, and those who possess rights equal to those of kings, have the right of demanding punishments not only on account of injuries committed against themselves or their subjects but also on account of injuries which do not directly affect them but excessively violate the law of nature or of nations in regard to any persons whatsoever. For liberty to serve the interests of human society through punishments, which originally, as we have said, rested with individuals, now after the organization of states and courts of law is in the hands of the highest authorities, not, properly speaking, in so far as they rule over others but in so far as they are themselves subject to no one. For subjection has taken this right away from others': *De Jure Belli ac Pacis*, Bk. II, c. 20, sec. 40, Carnegie ed., p. 504. See Hackworth, *Digest of International*

in national constitutions and statutes.[66a] It was regarded as sufficiently tangible in the eighteenth century so that United States Federal Courts sustained indictments charging acts as an offense against the law of nations, even if there were no statutes defining the offense.[67] Early in the nineteenth century it was held that the criminal jurisdiction of federal courts rested only on statutes[68] though the definition of crimes denounced by statutes might be left largely to international law. Thus 'piracy as defined by the law of nations' is an indictable offense in federal courts[69] and all offenses against the law of nations are indictable at common law in state courts.[70]

In the nineteenth century the development of the positivist doctrine that only states are subject to international law and that individuals are bound only by the municipal law of states with jurisdiction over them led to a decline in the application of the concept of offenses against the law of nations. This idea, however, has acquired renewed vigor in the twentieth century and has been discussed by numerous text writers[71] and in many international conferences.[72] There is, however, still disagreement as to the scope of the concept.[73] An analysis of general principles of international law and of criminal law suggests the following definition: A crime against international law is an act committed with intent to violate a fundamental interest protected by international law or with knowledge that

Law, Vol. 2, p. 687. According to B. W. Lee, 'Since the First World War, and more than ever today, the Grotian conception of international law has reemerged into the light. The Nuremberg trial is a testimony to its cogency': *Law Quarterly Review*, Vol. 62 (1946), p. 56.

[66a] A Dutch act of 1651 penalized persons who committed certain offensives against foreign diplomats as 'violators of the law of nations' and the same term was used in the Statute of Anne which arose out of an assault upon the Czar's Ambassador (Harvard Research, Draft Convention on Diplomatic Privileges and Immunities, in this JOURNAL, Vol. 26 (1932), Supplement, p. 94; Feller and Hudson, *Diplomatic and Consular Laws and Regulations*, Washington, 1933, Vol. I, p. 211). The Continental Congress of the United States, in several resolutions adopted from 1779 to 1781, called upon the States to provide for punishment of 'offenses against the law of nations.' The Constitution gives Congress power 'to define and punish piracies and felonies committed on the high seas and offenses against the law of nations': Art. 1, sec. 8, cl. 10. See Q. Wright, *The Enforcement of International Law Through Municipal Law in the United States*, Urbana, 1916, p. 221.

[67] *In re* Henfield, 1793. Fed. Cas. 6360; Moore, Digest, Vol. 7, p. 880; U. S. vs. Ravara, 1793, 2 Dall. 297, Moore, *Digest*, Vol. 5, p. 65; Q. Wright, *Control of American Foreign Relations*, New York, 1922, pp. 196–7.

[68] U. S. vs. Hudson, 7 Cranch 32; U. S. vs. Coolidge, 1 Wheat. 415; Wharton, *Criminal Law*, Vol. 1, sec. 254; Q. Wright, *Control of American Foreign Relations*, pp. 197–8.

[69] U. S. Criminal Code, 1909, sec. 290; U. S. vs. Smith, 1820, 5 Wheat. 153, 161–2, Hackworth, *Digest*, Vol. 2, p. 685.

[70] Res Publica vs. Delongchamps, 1 Dall. 111, Moore, *Digest*, Vol. 4, p. 622; Sec. of State Bayard to Mr. Harris, April 2, 1885, Moore, *Digest*, Vol. 2, p. 432; Q. Wright, *Control of American Foreign Relations*, pp. 177–9.

[71] Maurice Travers, *Le droit penal international*, Paris, 1920–4, 6 vols., Donnedieu de Vabres, *Les principes modernes du droit penal international*, Paris, 1928; Trainin, *Hitlerite Responsibility under Criminal Law*, New York, 1945; Cowles, 'Universality of Jurisdiction over War Crimes,' as cited; Harvard Research, Piracy, this JOURNAL, Vol. 26 (1932), Supplement, pp. 752–3.

[72] For texts of resolutions, see this JOURNAL, Vol. 29 (1935), Supplement, pp. 641–5.

[73] Same, pp. 476–7, 569–72.

the act will probably violate such an interest, and which may not be adequately punished by the exercise of the normal criminal jurisdiction of any state.[74]

States ordinarily punish crime in the interest of their own peace and security and those interests are often parallel to the general interests of the community of nations, defined by international law. Consequently the latter interests are in considerable measure protected by the normal exercise of criminal jurisdiction by states. There are, however, circumstances when this exercise of normal criminal jurisdiction is not adequate. To protect itself in such circumstances international law has recognized four methods of supplementing the normal criminal jurisdiction of states.

International law has imposed obligations on states to punish certain acts committed in their territory, punishment of which is primarily an interest of other states or of the community of nations and which therefore might be neglected in the absence of such a rule. Offenses against foreign diplomatic officers, against foreign currencies, or against the security of foreign states fall in this category.[75]

International law has permitted a state to exercise jurisdiction over acts committed by aliens abroad either on the ground that such acts endanger the prosecuting state's security or on the ground that they endanger all states or their nationals. The jurisdiction of military commissions over offenses against the law of war, of prize courts against contraband carriers and blockade runners, of admiralty courts against pirates, and of criminal courts against offenses defined in general international conventions or customary international law are of this character.[76]

International law has recognized the competence of states to establish international tribunals for the trial of grave offenses not dealt with by national tribunals such as terrorism and aggression.[77]

International law has favored or, in the opinion of some writers, required, the cooperation of states in the apprehension and punishment of fugitive criminals through extradition or other treaties.[78] This cooperation concerns particularly persons accused of universally recognized crimes such as murder, rape, mayhem, arson, piracy, robbery, burglary, forgery, counterfeiting, embezzlement, and theft.[79] Political and military offenses are normally excluded.[80] Consequently

---

[74] If an interest is 'protected by international law' every state is obliged by international law not to authorize, and to take due diligence within its jurisdiction to prevent, acts which would violate that interest. Consequently the individual who commits such an act enjoys no general immunity on the ground that he acted in pursuance of a lawful act of state. See U. S. vs. Arjona, 1887, 120 U. S. 479, Moore, *Digest*, Vol. 1, p. 61; Donnedieu de Vabres, pp. 143–4; Trainin, pp. 26, 32, 41; Q. Wright, *Study of War*, Chicago, 1942, pp. 912, 1345; and 'War Criminals,' this JOURNAL, Vol. 39 (1945), pp. 279–84.

[75] Same, pp. 280 ff.   [76] Same, pp. 274 ff, 282 ff.

[77] See discussion on *The Tribunal's Jurisdiction*, above; on the Geneva Conventions on Terrorism and an International Criminal Court, 1937, see Hudson, *International Legislation*, Vol. 7, pp. 862, 878, and *International Tribunals*, Washington, 1944, p. 183.

[78] Harvard Research, Extradition, this JOURNAL, Vol. 29 (1935), Supplement, pp. 32 ff.

[79] For list of offenses mentioned in extradition treaties see same, pp. 244 ff.

[80] Same, Arts. 5, 6, pp. 107–122.

many of the offenses dealt with in the preceding categories have escaped this procedure.

From a consideration of the obligation arising from these principles of international law, of the fundamental interests of states and of the community of nations protected by international law, of the acts which violate these obligations and threaten these interests, and of the circumstances which are likely to prevent punishment of such acts by the exercise of the normal jurisdiction of states, it is possible to determine whether a given act is a crime against the law of nations.

The *Ex Post Facto* Principle

The sources of general international law are general conventions, general customs, general principles, judicial precedents and juristic analysis.[81] International law, therefore, resembles the common law in its developing character. According to Sir James Stephen the common law is less like a series of commands than 'like an art or a science, the principles of which are first enunciated vaguely, and are gradually reduced to precision by their application to particular circumstances.'[82]

Wharton discusses the meaning of the rule against *ex post facto* criminal law in the common law system as follows:

A crime can only be regarded as a violation of a law in existence at the time of its perpetration. When a punishment is inflicted at common law, then the case is brought within the principles just stated by the assumption that the case obviously falls within a general category to which the law attaches indictability. It may be said, for instance,—'all malicious mischief is indictable. This offense (although enumerated in no statute, and never in the concrete the subject of prior adjudication) is malicious mischief. Therefore this offense is indictable.' Strike out 'malicious mischief' and insert 'nuisance,' and the same conclusion is reached. It is no reply to this reasoning that we have, by this process, judge made law, which is *ex post facto*. Supposing the minor premise be correct, the objection just stated could not prevail without being equally destructive to most prosecutions for offenses prohibited by statute under a *nomen generalissimum*. In many of our States, for instance, neither murder, burglary, nor assault is so described as to leave nothing remaining to the court by way of explanation or application.[83]

---

81 Statute, International Court of Justice, Art. 38.

82 J. F. Stephen, *Digest of Criminal Law*, 1877, Sec. 160, quoted by Francis Wharton. *A Treatise on Criminal Law*, Philadelphia, 1880 (8th ed.), Sec. 14, Vol. 1, p. 19; Stephen, *General View of the Criminal Law of England*, London, 1863, pp. 32 ff.; T. E. Holland, *Jurisprudence*, Oxford, 1910 (11th ed.), p. 66, quoting Willes, J., in Millar vs. Taylor, 4 Burr. 2312: 'Justice, moral fitness, and public convenience, when applied to a new subject, make common law without a precedent.' For meaning of the proposition that international law is part of the common law see Cyril M. Picciotto, *The Relation of International Law to the Law of England and of the United States*, London, 1915, pp. 75 ff.; Q. Wright, *Control of American Foreign Relation*, pp. 171, 196.

83 Wharton, Sec. 29, Vol. I, pp. 41–2.

That such a conception of the *ex post facto* principle must apply in international law was recognized by the Tribunal when it said: 'This law is not static, but by continual adaptation follows the needs of a changing world.'[84] Baron Wright, Lord of Appeal in Ordinary and Chairman of the United Nations War Crimes Commission, has recently developed this thought:

The common lawyer is familiar with the idea of customs which developed into law and may eventually receive recognition from competent Courts and authorities. But the Court does not make the law, it merely declares it or decides that it exists, after hearing the rival contentions of those who assert and those who deny the law....

International Law is progressive. The period of growth generally coincides with the period of world upheavals. The pressure of necessity stimulates the impact of natural law and of moral ideas and converts them into rules of law deliberately and overtly recognized by the consensus of civilized mankind. The experience of two great world wars within a quarter of a century cannot fail to have deep repercussions on the senses of the peoples and their demand for an International Law which reflects international justice. I am convinced that International Law has progressed, as it is bound to progress if it is to be a living and operative force in these days of widening sense of humanity. An International Court, faced with the duty of deciding if the bringing of aggressive war is an international crime, is, I think, entitled and bound to hold that it is.[85]

Considering international law as a progressive system, the rules and principles of which are to be determined at any moment by examining all its sources, 'general principles of law,' 'international custom,' and the 'teachings of the most highly qualified publicists' no less than 'international conventions' and 'judicial decisions,' there can be little doubt that international law had designated as crimes the acts so specified in the Charter long before the acts charged against the defendants were committed.

War Crimes and Crimes Against Humanity

No one has questioned this conclusion as regards the 'war crimes' in the narrow sense. Military commissions in wars of the past have habitually tried and punished enemy persons captured and found to have been guilty of acts in violation of the customary and conventional law of war.[86] The Tribunal considered that the Hague Convention on land warfare was declaratory of customary international

---

[84] Judgment, p. 219.

[85] 'War Crimes under International Law,' in *Law Quarterly Review*, Vol. 62 (1946), pp. 40, 51. To similar effect Mr. Justice Jackson said, in his opening address at Nuremberg: 'The fact is that when the law evolves by the case method, as did the Common Law and as international law must do if it is to advance at all, it advances at the expense of those who wrongly guessed the law and learned too late their error. The law, so far as international law can be decreed, had been clearly pronounced when these acts took place': *Record*, p. 166.

[86] *Ex parte* Quirin, 1942, 317 U. S. 1; *In re* Yamashita, 1946, 66 Sup. Ct. 340; Q. Wright, *War Criminals*, this JOURNAL, Vol. 39 (1945), pp. 274 ff.

law binding all the belligerents,[87] and that it bound Germany in all the territories it had occupied,[88] but that the defendants were entitled to the benefit of the principle of reprisals recognized in the customary law of war.[89]

The 'crimes against humanity' were considered with the 'war crimes' from which they differed only in being directed against German nationals rather than against enemies. The Tribunal had no doubt that the acts in pursuance of policies of 'genocide' and clearing land by extermination of its population, if carried on in occupied territories or against enemy persons, constituted 'war crimes.'[90] Acts of that type, when carried on in a state's own territory against its own nationals have in the past often occasioned 'humanitarian intervention' by other states.[91] The preamble of the Hague Convention on laws and customs of war on land refers to the 'laws of humanity' and the 'dictates of the public conscience' which would apply to atrocities against nationals as well as against aliens. International conferences have proposed action when faced by brutalities within a particular country 'in violation of the most elementary dictates of humanity' and 'repugnant to the conscience of civilized nations.'[92] An international standard of justice has long been recognized as binding states in their treatment of resident aliens[93] and many conventions bind states to respect certain fundamental rights of minorities, backward peoples, workers, and other persons within their jurisdiction. The idea that the individual is entitled to respect for fundamental rights, accepted by the earlier writers on international law, has come under extensive consideration recently and has been accepted in the United Nations Charter, one of whose purposes is 'to achieve international cooperation in promoting and encouraging respect

[87] Some belligerents in the war were not parties to the Hague Convention on Land Warfare but the Tribunal considered it unnecessary to consider the effect of the 'general participation clause' in this convention because 'by 1939 these rules laid down in the Convention were recognized by all civilized nations, and were regarded as being declaratory of the laws and customs of war': Judgment, p. 248.

[88] The defendants argued that Germany was not bound by the law of war in certain territories because they had been completely subjugated. The Tribunal suggested a doubt whether 'subjugation' resulting from the crime of aggressive war could give any rights to the aggressor but rejected the argument on the ground that subjugation could never apply so long as 'there was an army in the field attempting to restore the occupied countries to their true owners.' The doctrine could not, therefore, apply to countries occupied after September, 1939, and as to countries occupied earlier the Tribunal pointed out that Bohemia and Moravia had not been annexed but merely made protectorates; consequently, after the war began in September, 1939, Germany was at war with these countries. The Tribunal did not make clear the position of Austria.

[89] Doenitz and Raeder were not held liable for unlimited submarine warfare against British vessels, which were under order to attack, nor for any submarine activity after the United States began to engage in unlimited submarine warfare in the Pacific as testified by Admiral Nimitz: Judgment, pp. 304, 305, 308. None of the defendants had been indicted for terror bombing of cities, a practice indulged in by all belligerents.

[90] Judgment, p. 248.

[91] E. C. Stowell, *Intervention in International Law*, Washington, 1921, pp. 51 ff.

[92] Resolution of the Council of the League of Nations, 1937, concerning conditions in Spain.

[93] E. M. Borchard, 'The Minimum Standard in the Treatment of Aliens,' in American Society of International Law, *Proceedings*, 1939, p. 61; Harvard Research, Responsibility of States, Arts. 7–13, this JOURNAL, Vol. 23 (1929), Supplement, pp. 133–5.

for human rights and for fundamental freedoms for all without distinction as to race, sex, language or religion.'[94]

It is also to be noted that the acts which constitute 'crimes against humanity' have habitually been the subject of extradition treaties. States have recognized the duty of cooperating in bringing persons guilty of such crimes to justice. As Wharton points out:

The presumption of knowledge of the unlawfulness of crimes *mala in se* is not limited by state boundaries. The unlawfulness of such crimes is assumed wherever civilization exists.[95]

The Tribunal pointed out that, according to the Charter, 'to constitute crimes against humanity the acts relied on before the outbreak of war must have been in execution of, or in connection with, any crime within the jurisdiction of the Tribunal.'[96] It therefore declined to make a general declaration that acts of the character described committed before September 1, 1939, when the first war of aggression began, were crimes against humanity within the meaning of the Charter.[97] In general, liability for both war crimes and crimes against humanity was confined to acts committed after that date.[98]

It is to be observed that a concrete plan for aggressive war was found to have been made at least as early as November, 1937. Furthermore the law of war has been held to apply to interventions, invasions, aggressions, and other uses of armed force in foreign territory even when there is no state of war.[99] Consequently the Tribunal might have found that some of the acts before that date were war crimes or crimes against humanity in the sense of the Charter. Its refusal to do so seems to have manifested its prevailing disposition to give the defendants the benefit of any doubt.

The Tribunal had no difficulty in assuming that war crimes and crimes against humanity in the narrow sense of the Charter were crimes under customary international at the time the acts were committed and felt it unnecessary to give

---

[94] *International Law of the Future*, 1944, Principle 2, pp. 44–48; Q. Wright, 'Human Rights and the World Order,' in *International Conciliation*, No. 389 (April, 1943), pp. 238 ff.; H. Lauterpacht, *An International Bill of the Rights of Man*, New York, 1945.

[95] Work cited, Sec. 285.

[96] This was made clear by a supplementary agreement of the Powers on Oct. 6, 1945, conforming the English and French to the Russian text of the Charter by substituting a comma for the semi-colon which originally appeared after the word 'war' in Art. 6: U. S. *Executive Agreement Series* No. 472, pp. 4, 25, 45. See also Jacob Robinson, 'The Nuremberg Judgment, Crimes against Humanity,' in Institute of Jewish Affairs, *Congress Weekly*, Oct. 25, 1946.

[97] Judgment, p. 248.

[98] Thus persons who, before Sept. 1, 1939, ceased to be members of organizations found to be criminal because of participation in war crimes or crimes against humanity, were excluded from the group declared criminal: Judgment, pp. 256, 262, 266–267.

[99] G. G. Wilson, *International Law*, St. Paul, 1939 (3rd ed.), p. 41; Q. Wright, 'The Bombardment of Damascus,' this JOURNAL, Vol. 20 (1926), p. 270; Harvard Research, Aggression, Art. 14, this JOURNAL, Vol. 33 (1939), Supplement, p. 905.

to this question the elaborate discussion which it devoted to the 'crimes against peace.' It merely said:

In so far as the inhumane acts charged in the Indictment, and committed after the beginning of the war, did not constitute war crimes, they were all committed in execution of, or in connection with, the aggressive war, and therefore constituted crimes against humanity.[100]

Crimes Against Peace

The argument has already been set forth by which the Tribunal reached the conclusion that the Charter declared pre-existing international law when it provided that individuals were liable for 'crimes against peace.'[101] This argument emphasized the development of an international custom which regarded the initiation of aggressive war as illegal and which had been given formal sanction by substantially all states in the Pact of Paris of 1928. The nexus between the obligation of states not to resort to aggressive war and the criminal liability of individuals who contribute to the violation of this obligation was illustrated by analogy to the generally recognized individual liability for committing acts forbidden by

[100] Judgment, p. 249.

[101] It dealt with the arguments which had been presented by defendants' counsel, emphasizing the sovereignty of states under international law, the right to resort to war traditionally deduced from that sovereignty, and the immunity of individuals acting in pursuance of an 'act of state.' It was contended that these principles had not been modified by the Pact of Paris or any other instrument because these agreements had become obsolete through non-observance in practice. International law, therefore, did not make resort to aggressive war illegal, much less an individual crime when the acts charged were committed. In view of this the Charter should be interpreted so as to give effect to the principle of justice, *nullum crimen sine lege* (argument by Jahrreiss, Counsel for Jodl, July 4, 1946, *Record*, pp. 12903–50). It was argued that the Tribunal was free to make such a construction and in fact was obliged to judge according to law rather than expediency (argument by Stahmer, Counsel for Goering, July 4, 1946, *Record*, pp. 12954–68). See also argument by Horn, Counsel for Ribbentrop, who contended that there was no generally accepted definition of 'aggressive war' nor an institution for determining it and that the Soviet-Finnish hostilities of 1939 indicated that the effort to outlaw aggressive war had been abandoned (*Record*, July 5, 1946, pp. 13046–67). These arguments were answered in general by Mr. Justice Jackson who, in his concluding argument, emphasized the clear evidence of planning aggressive war by the defendants, the absence of any justification of necessary self defence, the absence of justification in superior orders of Hitler, and the propriety of assuming knowledge of the plan from the defendant's position and acts (*Record*, July 26, 1946, p. 14371). Sir Hartley Shawcross in his final address answered the defendants arguments in detail insisting that the Pact of Paris made aggressive war a crime, that this Pact continued valid in spite of some violations because the success of crime does not change the law, that the Pact was not invalidated by the reservations of self defense because self judgment on the necessity of self defense was permissible only in first instance and ultimate judgment must always be by an international procedure, that sovereignty did not imply superiority to international law, that international law imposes certain duties on individuals, that 'acts of state do not confer immunities to commit crime, and that superior orders could give no immunity for acts which every one knew were contrary to the law of nature of which the law of nations was a part': *Record*, July 26, 1946, pp. 14442–51.

the Hague Convention on land warfare. The argument holds that if an individual act is of a criminal character, that is *mala in se*, and is in violation of the state's international obligation, it is a crime against the law of nations. This conception conforms closely to that adopted by the Supreme Court of the United States in deciding whether criminal legislation of Congress can be justified by the constitutional power of Congress to define and punish offenses against the law of nations.[102] The same argument was developed by Lord Wright who pointed out that the Pact of Paris converted the principle that aggressive war is illegal from a rule of 'natural law' to a rule of 'positive law,' which like the rules of war is binding on individuals as well as states. He emphasized the multiple character of international crimes.

The nation is liable as a treaty-breaker, the statesmen are liable as violating a rule of International Law, namely, the rule that unjust or aggressive war is an international crime. The Pact of Paris is not a scrap of paper. This, in my opinion, is the position when the Pact of Paris is violated. It is on this principle, as I apprehend, that crimes against peace may be charged personally against the leading members of the Nazi government.[103]

This exposition differs somewhat in emphasis from that presented to the Tribunal by counsel for the prosecution. Thus Mr. Justice Jackson, Chief of the American Prosecution, said:

Any resort to war—to any kind of a war—is a resort to means that are inherently criminal. War inevitably is a course of killings, assaults, deprivations of liberty, and destruction of property. An honestly defensive war is, of course, legal and saves those lawfully conducting it from criminality. But inherently criminal acts cannot be defended by showing that those who committed them were engaged in a war, when war itself is illegal. The very minimum legal consequence of the treaties making aggressive wars illegal is to strip those who incite or wage them of every defense the law ever gave, and to leave war-makers subject to judgment by the usually accepted principles of the law of crime....

The principle of individual responsibility for piracy and brigandage, which have long been recognized as crimes punishable under International Law, is old and well

---

[102] U. S. vs. Arjona, 1887, 120 U. S. 479, Moore, *Digest*, Vol. 1, p. 61; U. S. vs. White, 1886, 27 Fed. 200. In the following cases chiefs, or other high officers, of state were tried by judicial or political procedures for initiating or contributing to the initiation of aggressive war: in antiquity, Aristonicus, Jugurtha, Artabasdus (Grotius, work cited, Bk. II, c. xxi, Sec. 4; Bk. III, c. xi, Secs. 7, 3, Carnegie ed., pp. 527, 733); in the middle ages, Henry the Lion, 1180; John Lackland, 1202; Otto von Wittelsbach, 1208; Conradin of Suabia, 1268; Robert of Anjou, King of Naples, 1313 (Albert Levy, 'Criminal Responsibility of Individuals and International Law,' in *University of Chicago Law Review*, Vol. 12 (1945), p. 319); Sir Peter of Hagenbach, 1474 (Georg Schwarzenberger, in *Manchester Guardian*, Sept. 28, 1946); in modern times, Mary Queen of Scots, 1568; Charles I of England, 1649; Lords Portland, Sommers, Orford, and Halifax, 1700; Napoleon Bonaparte, 1815; Kaiser Wilhelm II, 1919 (indicted but not tried) (see Levy, as cited, and Q. Wright, 'Legal Liability of the Kaiser,' pp. 120 ff.). On distinction between international responsibility of individuals for starting wars, responsibility of states for failure to punish acts productive of wars, and responsibility of states for initiating aggressive wars, see Q. Wright, 'The Outlawry of War,' in this JOURNAL, Vol. 19 (1925), pp. 78 ff.

[103] *Law Quarterly Review*, Vol. 62 (1946), pp. 50–51.

established. That is what illegal warfare is. This principle of personal liability is a necessary as well as a logical one if International Law is to render real help to the maintenance of peace.... Only sanctions which reach individuals can peacefully and effectively be enforced. Hence the principle of the criminality of aggressive war is implemented by the charter with the principle of personal responsibility. Of course the idea that a state, any more than a corporation, commits crime, is a fiction. Crimes always are commited only by persons.[104]

Mr. Jackson's theory seems to have been that aggressive war in the sense of the Charter is an individual offense differing from piracy, brigandage, and filibustering only in that it is done in the name of the state by persons in temporary control of the state. The significance of the Pact of Paris and of other anti-war treaties in which states themselves renounced war was to withdraw the 'act of state' defense from those who initiate aggressive war.[105]

Sir Hartley Shawcross, Chief of Counsel for Great Britain, argued:

International law, it may be said, does not attribute criminality to states and still less to individuals. But can it really be said on behalf of these Defendants that the offense of these aggressive wars, which plunged millions of people to their deaths,... is only an offense, only an illegality, only a matter of condemnation perhaps sounding in damages, but not a crime justicable by any tribunal.... They (the powers responsible for the Charter) refused to reduce justice to impotence by subscribing to the out-worn doctrines that a sovereign state can commit no crime and that no crime can be committed on behalf of the sovereign state by individuals acting in its behalf.[106]

Sir Hartley then adverted to the difficulties of collective punishment which fall upon the guilty and innocent alike and pointed out that the Charter imposes individual responsibility.

It is a salutary principle, a principle of law, that politicians who embark upon a particular policy of aggressive war should not be able to seek immunity behind the intangible personality of the State. It is a salutary legal rule that persons who, in violation of the law, plunge their own and other countries into an aggressive war should do so with a halter round their necks.

To say that those who aid and abet, who counsel and procure a crime are themselves criminals is a commonplace in our municipal law. Nor is the principle of individual international responsibility for offense against the law of nations altogether new. It has been applied not only to pirates. The entire law relating to war crimes, as distinct from the crime of war, is based upon the principle of individual responsibility. The future of international law, and indeed, of the world itself, depends on its application in a much wider sphere, in particular, in that of safeguarding the peace of the world. There must be acknowledged not only, as in the Charter of the United Nations, fundamental human

---

[104] *Record*, pp. 70–71.
[105] Such an argument was deduced by S. O. Levinson, the originator of the 'outlawry of war' movement from the Pact. See John E. Stoner, *S. O. Levinson and the Pact of Paris*, Chicago, 1943, pp. 196, 209; Q. Wright, 'War Criminals,' in this JOURNAL, Vol. 39 (1945), p. 282.
[106] *Record*, Dec. 4, 1945, p. 832.

rights, but also, as in the Charter of this Tribunal, fundamental human duties, and of those none is more vital, none is more fundamental, than the duty not to vex the peace of nations in violation of the clearest legal prohibitions and undertakings. If this be an innovation, it is an innovation which we are prepared to defend and to justify, but it is not an innovation which creates a new crime. International law had already, before the Charter was adopted, constituted aggressive war a criminal act.[107]

Sir Hartley emphasized the criminality of the aggressive state and deduced the criminality of individuals from a theory of accessoryship and procurement. This emphasis which rests on the doubtful ground that a state can commit a crime, a position generally denied by arbitral tribunals in refusing punitive damages,[108] seems unnecessary.

The Tribunal's theory does not rest upon this assumption but rather upon the inherently criminal character of intentional initiation of aggressive war because of the probable consequence of such act in mass homicide and the inability to justify such action as an 'act of state' when it is contrary to the state's specific international obligations.

The individual crime of aggressive war, therefore, differs from the international delinquency of aggressive war though both are involved in determining the criminal liability of a defendant.[109] Aggressive war as an international delinquency means any resort to hostilities by the government or from the state's territory in violation of the state's international obligations. Since these obligations are usually stated broadly, they ordinarily require interpretation by reference to the general rights of states under international law. With such interpretation a state is guilty of the international delinquency of aggressive war if it authorizes or toler-

---

[107] Same, pp. 834–5.

[108] Sir Hartley stated that Tribunals 'have held that a state may be bound to pay what is in effect penal demands' referring to the *I'm Alone* case between the United States and Canada in 1935 in which damages which may have been punitive were awarded against the United States with concurrence of the American member of the Tribunal (Marjorie M. Whiteman, *Damages in International Law*, Washington, 1937, Vol. 1, p. 154). He also referred to the 'sanctions' article of the League of Nations Covenant and to a statement by Dr. Lushington, an English admiralty judge of the mid-nineteenth century, that a state might be a pirate (*Record*, Dec. 4, 1945, p. 833). Other instances might be cited and certainly early writers on international law developed the concept of the 'criminal state' (Grotius, Bk. II, c. xx, Sec. 38; c. xxi; Carnegie ed., pp. 502, 522 ff.; C. Van Volenhoven, *The Three Stages in the Evolution of the Law of Nations*, The Hague, 1919, pp. 8 ff.), but the prevailing view has been that state responsibility is exclusively civil in character (Case of the Lusitania, U. S.-German mixed Commission, pp. 25, 27; Whiteman, Vol. 1, pp. 710 ff., Vol. 3, p. 1874; Clyde Eagleton, *The Responsibility of States in International Law*, New York, 1928, pp. 189–90; Oppenheim, *International Law*, Vol. I, Sec. 151; L. Reitzer, *Réparation comme conséquence de l'acte illicite en Droit international*, Paris, 1938, pp. 209 ff.). 'At no time,' writes Judge Manley O. Hudson, 'has any authoritative formulation of international law been adopted which would brand specific state conduct as criminal, and no international tribunal has ever been given jurisdiction to find a state guilty of a crime' (*International Tribunals*, p. 180). On reluctance to ascribe criminal liability to corporate bodies see Wharton, *Criminal Law*, Sec. 91; Wright, *A Study of War*, pp. 911–15.

[109] Lord Wright emphasized the different liability of the state and the individual for aggressive war; above, note 103.

ates hostilities proceeding from its territory, with or without declaration of war against another state, without consent of the state attacked, without a necessity for individual or collective defense, or without authorization by a competent international organ.[110] The fact that operations against a peaceful state were planned long in advance and that they were stated to be for the advancement of expansive or predatory purposes creates a presumption that no justifying circumstances existed.[111] The international delinquency arises from an act or omission of the state, and the element of individual intention is not involved.

On the other hand, in the individual crime of aggression, the element of individual intention is of major importance. This crime as stated in the Charter consists in 'planning, preparation, initiation or waging of a war of aggression, or a war in violation of international treaties, agreements or assurances, or participation in a common plan or conspiracy for the accomplishment of any of the foregoing.' To determine whether an individual is guilty of this crime it is necessary to examine the extent of his authority over the armed forces involved or his importance as an advisor of, or collaborator with, the person exercising such authority, and his intention in authorizing, or in advising or collaborating in authorizing, the use of such forces.

The Tribunal made it clear that an individual's activity or authority in the Nazi conspiracy was not conclusive evidence that he was guilty of aggressive war, if that activity or authority ended before concrete plans to make aggressive war had been arrived at or if it began at a time after the aggressive war had begun and the German position had become defensive.[112] Thus Schacht's financial and armament building activity which he terminated in November, 1937, as soon as he had discovered Hitler's intention to resort to aggressive war, was not considered 'preparation' of aggressive war[113] and Fritzsche's propaganda activity to sustain morale after Germany was involved in war was not considered 'waging' of aggressive war.[114] These activities were not considered inconsistent with the defensive intent which these defendants claimed to have.

---

[110] This resembles the definition proposed in the Soviet treaties of 1933, referred to by Mr. Justice Jackson with approval (*Record*, p. 168). See also Q. Wright, 'The Meaning of the Pact of Paris,' this JOURNAL, Vol. 27 (1933), p. 39; 'The Concept of Aggression in International Law,' in same, Vol. 29 (1935), p. 373; Harvard Research, Aggression, in same, Vol. 33 (1939), Supplement, pp. 847, 871. The defense attempted to prove that Austria had consented to the Nazi occupation in 1938 (Judgment, p. 194) and that the attack on Norway in 1940 was justified in defense against a planned British attack, and that on the Soviet Union in 1941 by danger that that country would attack Germany. But the Tribunal found that the evidence did not support these contentions. Since the wars began with Nazi aggression it was assumed that the United Nations were all justified in resorting to hostilities in individual or collective defense. It would, therefore, seem that the Soviet Government would have been justified in initiating hostilities against Germany if it did so as a measure of 'collective defense,' that is in aid of the states already the victims of Nazi aggression.

[111] Judgment, pp. 189–213.

[112] Judgment, p. 222 and interrogation by Judge Biddle, *Record*, p. 5266.

[113] Judgment, pp. 300–301.

[114] Same, pp. 327–328.

This interpretation narrows the meaning of the words 'planning' and 'preparation' to activities intended by the individual to contribute to the 'initiation' of a war which he knows will be 'aggressive,' and it narrows the word 'waging' to activities intended by the individual to win such a war. The soldier who wages war which he thinks is defensive, the factory worker who makes weapons with no knowledge of the nature of the war in which they will be or are being used, the cabinet member who advises defensive armament building are not presumed to be guilty of 'aggressive war.' The planning, preparation, initiation and waging must be related to an actual or concretely planned war which the individual believes has been, or is about to be, initiated for aggressive purposes in the sense that the hostilities do, or would, constitute the international delinquency of aggressive war. Proof that the individual intended his acts for necessary defense or other object consistent with the international obligations of the state in whose name or from whose territory the attack has been or is to be launched will demonstrate that his intent was not aggressive. Even if his intent was aggressive, he would still be immune from liability if he acted in pursuance of a lawful act of state, that is if in fact the war was not aggressive. He is not guilty unless both in his intention and in international law the war was, or would be, aggressive.

Criminal Conspiracy and Criminal Organization

The Tribunal found that the conspiracy charge could apply only to the crime of aggressive war, although in the indictment it had been applied to all the offenses named in the Charter. The prosecution had treated the final paragraph of Article 6 as an independent crime but the Tribunal held that this paragraph was 'designed to establish the responsibility of persons participating in a common plan,'[115] that is, it was intended to include accomplices as well as principals in each crime, not to add a crime of conspiracy. Consequently, the Tribunal considered the conspiracy charge on the basis of Article 6, paragraph (a), which makes 'participation in a common plan or conspiracy for the accomplishment' of aggressive war a crime. This crime, however, differs little from 'planning and preparation' of aggressive war. The evidence showed that concrete plans to make aggressive war were made as early as November 5, 1937.[116] Consequently persons aware of and aiding in these plans after that date were guilty of the conspiracy charge. The prosecution's theory that 'any significant participation in the affairs of the Nazi party or government is evidence of a participation in a conspiracy that is in itself criminal' was rejected.[117]

---

[115] Same, p. 224.
[116] Same, pp. 189, 222.
[117] Same, p. 222.

In the opinion of the Tribunal the conspiracy must be clearly outlined in its criminal purpose. It must not be too far removed from the time of decision and of action. The planning, to be criminal, must not rest merely on the declarations of a party program, such as are found in the twenty-five points of the Nazi party, announced in 1920, or the political affirmations expressed in 'Mein Kampf' in later years. The Tribunal must examine whether a concrete plan to wage war existed, and determine the participants in that concrete plan.[118]

In this sense the Tribunal found that the evidence 'establishes the permanent planning to prepare and wage war by certain of the defendants' and considered it immaterial whether there were several plans or a single conspiracy. Furthermore, they were not impressed by the idea of the defense that a dictatorship was incompatible with 'common planning.'

A plan in the execution of which a number of persons participate is still a plan, even though conceived by only one of them; and those who execute the plan do not avoid responsibility by showing that they acted under the direction of the man who conceived it. Hitler could not make aggressive war by himself. He had to have the cooperation of statesmen, military leaders, diplomats and business men. When they, with knowledge of his aims, gave him their cooperation, they made themselves part to the plan he had initiated. They are not to be deemed innocent because Hitler made use of them, but they knew what they were doing. That they were assigned to their tasks by a dictator does not absolve them from responsibility for their acts. The relation of leader and follower does not preclude responsibility here any more than it does in the comparable tyranny of organized domestic crime.[119]

With this interpretation, the court found only twelve of the twenty-two defendants indicted on the conspiracy charge guilty, that is, those whom the evidence showed were significantly engaged in the inner Nazi circle after November, 1937 and who participated in the planning of aggressive war. The Austrian and Czech occupations, though aggressive acts, were not aggressive wars.[120] Consequently, activities intended to bring about these occupations such as those of von Papen who was German ambassador to Austria, did not in themselves prove guilt on this charge unless there was specific evidence that the defendant was aware of the plan to resort to aggressive war in these cases if it had proved necessary. In its treatment of the conspiracy charge the Tribunal applied the rule of strict construction of criminal statutes and gave the defendants the benefit of the doubt when the evidence of criminal intent was not clear.[121]

In exercising its power to declare organizations criminal, the Tribunal limited its declarations by definitions and recommendations so that in practice members of the organization could not be found liable unless guilty of conspiracy in the

---

[118] Same, p. 222.
[119] Same, p. 223.
[120] Same, p. 186.
[121] Same, pp. 302, 318.

sense in which that term was used by the Tribunal. The Tribunal recognized that under the Charter and the laws passed by the Control Council of Germany in pursuance thereof

A member of an organization which the Tribunal has declared to be criminal may be subsequently convicted of the crime of membership and be punished for that crime by death. This is not to assume that international or military courts which will try these individuals will not exercise appropriate standards of justice. This is a far-reaching and novel procedure. Its application, unless properly safeguarded, may produce great injustice.[122]

Emphasizing that the Charter gave it discretion whether to declare any organization criminal, the Tribunal stated that it would exercise its discretion in accord with 'well settled legal principles, one of the most important of which is that criminal guilt is personal and that mass punishments should be avoided.' While the Tribunal would not hesitate to declare an organization or group criminal because 'the theory of group criminality is new' or 'because it might be unjustly applied by some subsequent tribunals,' the Tribunal 'should make such declaration of criminality so far as possible in a manner to insure that innocent persons will not be punished.'[123] It, therefore, applied the following definition:

A criminal organization is analogous to a criminal conspiracy in that the essence of both is cooperation for criminal purposes. There must be a group bound together and organized for a common purpose. The group must be formed or used in connection with the commission of crimes denounced by the Charter. Since the declaration with respect to the organizations and groups will, as has been pointed out, fix the criminality of its members, that definition should exclude persons who had no knowledge of the criminal purposes or acts of the organization and those who were drafted by the State for membership, unless they were personally implicated in the commission of acts declared criminal by Article 6 of the Charter as members of the organization. Membership alone is not enough to come within the scope of these declarations.[124]

Furthermore the Tribunal recommended that classifications, sanctions, and penalties applied by other tribunals dealing with members of criminal organizations be standardized, that the penalties under Law No. 10 passed by the Control Council for Germany should not exceed those under the de-Nazification laws, and that the Control Council amend Law No. 10 to this effect.[125]

In its declarations finding three of the accused organizations to be criminal the Tribunal in each case limited its declaration to those

who became or remained members of the organization with knowledge that it was being used for the commission of acts declared criminal by Article 6 of the Charter, or who were personally implicated as members of the organizations in the commission of such crimes.[126]

---

[122] Same, p. 250.   [123] Same, p. 251.
[124] Same, p. 251.   [125] Same, p. 251.
[126] Same, pp. 256, 262, 266.

Since in each case the finding of criminality resulted because the organization participated in war crimes and crimes against humanity connected with the war, the group declared criminal did not include persons who ceased to be members prior to September 1, 1939.[127] In the case of the SS persons drafted into membership who had committed no individual crimes were also excluded.[128]

It is clear that in dealing with the problem of conspiracy and criminal organization the Tribunal took great care to observe the principles of criminal justice which interpret criminal statutes restrictively, which consider criminal responsibility an individual matter, and which give the benefit of the doubt to the accused. Under its rules no person could be convicted unless as an individual he had conspired in criminal activities or purposes.

'Acts of State'

The notion that a government or officer acting in the name of a sovereign state enjoys an unlimited power to shield individuals from liability for acts otherwise criminal developed as a deduction from absolute sovereignty. The state, it was said, is the only subject of international law and if it adopts the act of an individual as its own the individual is immune and reclamations can be made only against the state. The doctrine was applied not only to give wide immunity to heads of state and diplomatic officers, where it had some justification because such officials must be personally immune if they are to represent states properly, but also to consuls performing official functions, and to soldiers and seamen acting under superior orders. In accordance with this doctrine, Secretary of State Webster wrote the British Minister in the McLeod case:

That an individual forming part of a public force, and acting under the authority of his Government, is not to be held answerable as a private trespasser or malefactor, is a principle of public law sanctioned by the usages of all civilized nations, and which the Government of the United States has no inclination to dispute.[129]

This position was disputed by many at the time on the ground that the government's authority could not confer immunity upon its agents for acts beyond its powers under international law.[130] The latter position has been sustained in the numerous trials of soldiers for breaches of the law of war even when acting in pursuance of the authority of their government.[131]

---

[127] Same.

[128] Same, p. 266.

[129] Moore, *Digest*, Vol. 2, p. 25; Q. Wright, 'War Criminals,' this JOURNAL, Vol. 39 (1945), p. 271; Wharton, Criminal Law, Sec. 284.

[130] Wright, 'War Criminals,' p. 266; Wharton, *Digest of International Law*, Vol. 1, p. 67.

[131] *Ex parte* Quirin, 1942, 317 U. S. 1.

The limits of the immunity of individuals for acts otherwise criminal committed in pursuance of official functions or under official orders is well stated by Sir James Stephen.

In all cases in which force is used against the person of another, both the person who orders such force to be used and the person using that force is responsible for its use, and neither of them is justified by the circumstance that he acts in obedience to orders given him by a civil or military superior; but the fact that he did so act, and the fact that the order was apparently lawful, are in all cases relevant to the question whether he believed, in good faith and on reasonable grounds, in the existence of a state of facts which would have justified what he did apart from such orders.[132]

The foregoing discussions suggest that the law stated in Articles 7 and 8 of the Charter and supported by the Tribunal[133] was amply supported by general principles of law which constitute a source of international law.

* * *

The opinion of the Nuremberg Tribunal marks an important step in the development of international criminal law. This law will be further developed in the trial of major Japanese war criminals proceeding at this writing in Tokyo[134] and by the trial of numerous lesser war criminals in national military commissions.[135] Especially significant is the clear pronouncement that aggressive war is an individual crime, and the development of the conception of that crime.

War (said Judge Biddle in his report of the results of the trial to President Truman) is not outlawed by such pronouncements, but men learn a little better to detest it when as here, its horrors are told day after day, and its aggressive savagery is thus branded as criminal. Aggressive war was once romantic; now it is criminal. For nations have come to realize that it means the death not only of individual human beings, but of whole nations, not only with defeat, but in the slow degradation and decay of civilized life that follows that defeat.[136]

The world shattered by two world wars needs to have its confidence in law restored. Such confidence can only develop if people believe that formal law embodies justice and that it will be enforced. The Nuremberg trial is likely to contribute to both of these ends. The general opinion that aggressive war and mass massacre are crimes has been recognized in formal international law and that law has been sanctioned by trial and punishment of many of the guilty. Much remains to be done but opinion will be reassured that international law is neither esoteric

---

[132] Stephen, *Digest of Criminal Law*, Art. 202, quoted in Wharton, *Criminal Law*, Sec. 94, Vol. 1, p. 130. See also case of Dithmar and Boldt, German Reichsgericht, 1921, this JOURNAL, Vol. 16 (1925), p. 708.
[133] Judgment, p. 221.
[134] State Department, *Trial of Japanese War Criminals*, 1946.
[135] Above, note 5.
[136] *Department of State Bulletin*, Vol. 15, No. 6 (Nov. 24, 1946), p. 956.

nor helpless. The time may be ripe for further development by the establishment of a permanent international criminal court as drafted in the Geneva Convention of 1937 and the codification of international criminal law as suggested by Judge Biddle with President Truman's approval,[137] and recommended by the General Assembly of the United Nations on December 11, 1946.

[137] Same, pp. 954, 957.

15

Nuremberg in Retrospect: Legal Answer to International Lawlessness

By Robert H. Jackson
Associate Justice of the Supreme Court
of the United States

This is an authoritative account of the legal bases of the trials of the major Nazi war criminals before the International Military Tribunal at Nuremberg written by the American Chief Prosecutor. Taken from an address delivered before the Canadian Bar Association meeting at Banff, Alberta, on September 1, Justice Jackson reviews in detail the legal foundations on which the trial rested and explains how the procedure used was determined.

The Nuremberg Trial of the major Nazi war criminals was an attempt to answer in terms of the law the most serious challenge that faces modern civilization—war and international lawlessness.

The legal profession, by most countries, has been conceded leadership in working out rules of law which will keep their peace, security and liberty. As the lawyer is the most frequently chosen legislator, diplomat, executive and political leader, the intellectual discipline which we call 'the law' saturates Western World statesmanship and diplomacy.

Judged by its fruits, there must have been serious shortcomings in our practice, and perhaps in our teachings, of international law. Our own times may easily rate as the most bloody and cruel in recorded history. Our record includes two world wars, millions of human beings put to death for no cause other than their race, other millions seized and transported to forced labor, and a whole continent gripped by terror of the concentration camp. The worst perhaps is that these things still go on. Civilization seems to have lost control of itself. What a record for an age governed more than any other by men of our profession! Certainly here is lawlessness which challenges not only the lawyer but the law itself.

At the opening of this tortured and bloody century, law-trained men dominated the councils of most Western nations. They were thinking about problems of state in relation to certain assumptions supplied by their legal discipline. Four of these, at risk of oversimplification, may be thus condensed:

First, each state is sovereign, its right absolute, its will unrestrained, and free to resort to war at any time, for any purpose. Second, courts, therefore, must everywhere regard any war as legal, and engagement in warfare must be accepted as a good defense to what otherwise would be crime. Third, measures by high officials such as planning, instigating and waging war constitute 'acts of state', in performance of which they owe no legal duty to international society and for which there is no accountability to international law. Fourth, for obedience to superior orders an individual incurs no personal liability.

It would be hard to devise an intellectual discipline that would do more to encourage international lawlessness and aggression. German leaders who precipitated World War II were ardent disciples of these teachings. When they led to catastrophe, they all invoked the shelter of one or more of these four doctrines as a defense. They pleaded that their acts, however shocking, could not be criminal because these doctrines of the nineteenth century still stood as the law in the third and fourth decades of the twentieth century.

The Nuremberg prosecutions constitute this century's most definite challenge to this anarchic concept of the law of nations. Save the Nuremberg proceedings, too little has come out of the war to challenge the catastrophic doctrines invoked to excuse starting it. If those guilty of inciting World War II had been held immune from prosecution; any who might tomorrow plot a third one would be equally immune. Furthermore, machinery to make new international law is so inadequate, inertia is so great, conflict and suspicion are today so paralyzing, that we can foresee no time when aggressive wars will be outlawed or their perpetrators legally punishable if the Nuremberg basis for doing so was not valid.

If mankind were still helpless and hopeless in the throes of antiquated teachings it would be disheartening, for those who insist that there was no such law as Nuremberg applied generally agree that there should be such law.

Critics Deny Validity of Trials, but Admit their Value

At the opening of the international trial, Dr. Otto Stahmer, on behalf of all defendants, asserted to the court that 'a real order among the states is impossible as long as every state has the sovereign right to wage war at any time and for any purpose.' He acknowledged that public opinion already distinguished between just and unjust wars and demanded that the men guilty of launching unjust war be punished. He said, 'Humanity wishes that in the future this idea will be more than a postulate, that it will become valid international law. But today it is not yet existing international law.' And later he declared, 'In fact, this [indictment] is far ahead of its time, as is the whole way of argumentation by Justice Jackson.' A German critic, Dr. Hans Ehard, Minister-President of Bavaria, recently argued strongly that Nuremberg did not apply existing law, but nevertheless said, 'We must salute the Nuremberg trial as a guide-post for the further development of the law of nations.'

It is illuminating that these interested and learned opponents of the Nuremberg proceedings find it impossible to condemn the trial by standards of the past without also commending it by standards of the future. Their contention is that the trial has fallen, in a legal sense, 'between two worlds—one dead, the other powerless to be born.'

Of course a first attempt to conduct an international criminal trial against the highest surviving officials of a once powerful state for crimes against the peace of the world and the dignity of mankind was bound to cause lasting controversy. As contemporaries we all lack the perspective to anticipate the verdict of history on this effort. Those whose energies were engaged in the struggle lack objectivity most of all. But I recognize that there is room for honest and intelligent difference of opinion as to many aspects of the enterprise. Whatever view one takes, Nuremberg witnessed a legal event of importance. So, with such detachment as I can summon, I shall try to tell something of the origin of the trial and some of its more interesting problems, and of the use we made of the lawyers' hearing procedures and trial technique in this novel situation.

As, one after another, a dozen unprepared countries, with each of which Germany had a treaty of friendship and nonaggression, were overrun by undeclared wars, the opinion was almost universal that the hostilities had no cause except Germany's ambition for conquest. As it went on, the world was also shocked and horrified by Germany's wantonly brutal and savage conduct. Appeals and protests alike were scorned. Then came a series of unequivocal warnings that the course of its leaders was regarded as outside the bounds of modern warfare and criminal. In 1942 representatives of nine occupied countries met in London and issued the 'St. James Declaration', that the war criminals would be 'sought out, handed over to justice and judged'. This brought replies from President Roosevelt that 'they shall have to stand in courts of law . . . and answer for their acts', and from Mr. Churchill that they would 'have to stand up before tribunals', and a Soviet declaration that they must be 'arrested and tried under criminal law'. As the terrorism grew, seventeen nations formed the 'United Nations War Crimes Commission', headed first by Sir Cecil Hurst and later by Lord Wright. It did valiant service in gathering information as to war crimes and suspects. As the horrors did not abate, Churchill, Stalin and Roosevelt, by the Moscow Declaration of November, 1943, pledged the Allies to return accused Germans for trial by the country in which atrocities were committed, but declared that those whose offenses had no particular geographical location 'will be punished by a joint decision of the Governments of the Allies'.

Wartime accusations, of course, rested upon information that appeared credible, but in large part did not measure up to the standard of legal evidence, and could not then be verified. But the Allies were forced to decide whether to investigate these charges or to abandon them when they found the survivors of the accused among Allied prisoners. Shortly before the German surrender, I was appointed to represent the United States in negotiating the joint decision promised in the Moscow Declaration and, as Chief of Counsel, to conduct in its behalf such trial as might be decided upon.

Trial of War Criminals was Only Course

Only three dispositions have ever been suggested as possible for these accused captives. One was to free them and abandon the accusations. That course, at that time, had almost no responsible advocates. The second possible method was a political decision to execute, exile or otherwise punish them. Some favored doing this by simple fiat of the Allied powers, but others would have camouflaged it with some kind of farcical trial. For example, one periodical editorialized, 'In our opinion the proper procedure for this body would have been to identify the prisoners, read off their crimes with as much supporting data as seemed useful, pass judgment upon them quickly, and carry out the judgment without any delay whatever.' And a professor of political science was widely quoted in the press to this effect: 'What, in my opinion, they should have done is to set up summary courts martial. Then they should have placed these criminals on trial before them within twenty-four hours after they were caught, sentenced them to death, and shot them in the morning.' Such insistent and popular, but stultifying, counsel was rejected.

The only course remaining was to hold a good-faith trial for specific offenses, to be proved by evidence, with full opportunity to the accused to offer evidence or argument in defense or mitigation. How else than by our traditional hearing process could it be determined who was and who was not really responsible for particular reprehensible acts? How else would we discriminate among those who should be executed, who imprisoned and who exculpated? And how could anything we did be justified before the future if we did not make and act upon a record? On June 7, 1945, I reported to President Truman, recommending against 'undiscriminating executions or punishments without definite findings of guilt, fairly arrived at' and in favor of trying the accused not only for the planned campaign of atrocities but for the instigation and waging of wars of aggression as well. This report, approved by the President, was published and became an integral part of the foreign policy and occupation program of the United States.

However, the decision to hold a trial was made in the face of obstacles so formidable that many well-wishers thought it a quixotic undertaking beyond our power to accomplish. There was no beaten path to follow, no precedents to teach former successes or failures. No court was in existence to hear such a case. The prosecution must be conducted in four languages by lawyers trained in four different legal systems, two being of the common law tradition and two of the civil or Roman law school. The defense would be made by counsel whose practice, especially under the Nazis, was in many respects different from all the others. Many differences in their customs and practice in criminal cases must be reconciled in some yet undrafted code of procedure. While substantive law could be gleaned from scattered sources, there was no codification of applicable law. Moreover, very little real evidence was in our possession, the overwhelming mass of documents being still undiscovered and their existence largely unsuspected. We did not even know whether a courthouse that could house such a trial was still standing in Germany, or if so, where it was to be found. Most of our preparation and all of the trial must be carried on where we would be surrounded by enemies, and where transport and communication were at a standstill and the ordinary facilities for living, as well as for work, had been destroyed.

To try to bring some order out of this chaos, representatives of the four powers met in London in June of 1945. The published minutes of this conference record the discussions and conflicts, concessions and compromises which produced the Charter of the Nuremberg International Military Tribunal. I doubt whether a more novel or challenging task ever was set before members of the legal profession. All countries chose delegates who were pre-eminently lawyers rather than diplomats or politicians, although not strangers to these activities. All had long practical trial experience and approached the negotiations as a technical professional task, with the utmost good will toward each other and a determination to succeed. All agreed in principle that no country reasonably could insist that an international trial should be conducted under its own system and that we must borrow from all and devise an amalgamated procedure that would be workable, expeditious and fair. The conference resulted in an agreement, signed for the four powers by delegates high in their respective judicial systems, who had shared responsibility for negotiating it. These were Jowitt, Lord Chancellor, for the United Kingdom; Falco, Judge of the *Cour de Cassation*, for France; Nikitchenko, Vice President of the Soviet Supreme Court, for the Soviet Union; and myself, for the United States.

Differences Between Soviet and Allies Faced at London

It is not easy to explain fairly and accurately all the ideological conflicts that perplexed the London Conference. The chief differences, however, had their roots in two conflicting fundamental concepts—one as to the relation between a court and the government which establishes it; the other as to the nature of the criminal process.

A hasty general glance at the Soviet legal tradition will make the Soviet doctrine easier to understand, but not easier to accept. As you know, the Russian people received their philosophy of law and government from the ancient Mediterranean world through the same geographical route by which they received their religion—Byzantium and the East. Also, modern Russia remained largely insulated from the intellectual forces which liberalized Western Europe and shaped the institutions of both Canada and the United States. The English conception, expressed by Coke, that 'the King is under God and the law', would have been regarded by Russian jurists as treason, and French liberalism, expressed by such writers as Montesquieu, never effectively persuaded them. The authoritarianism of Russia's venerable institutions has had no amelioration over the centuries. The Bolshevist Revolution appropriated, rather than reformed, the instruments of despotic power. Prime Minister Atlee recently described the Soviet Union as merely an 'inverted czarism'. Soviet jurists teach that this union of Marxism with czarism, through a dictatorship of the proletariat, is enough to make the Soviet Union 'democratic'. Hence, the Soviet revolution has done very little to bring Russian legal thinking any closer to our Western tradition.

The able Soviet representative brought to London from this background his conception of a court and of the law. An earlier revolutionary writer expressed it in these terms: 'The court has always been and still remains, as it ought to be according to its nature—namely, one of the organs of governmental power, a weapon in the hands of the ruling class for the purpose of safeguarding its interests.' Vyshinsky's more recent book, *The Law of the Soviet State*, reiterates that a court is merely another implement of a dominant class in advancing its interests. He pronounces the idea of 'bourgeois theorists' that courts are organs 'above classes and apart from politics' to be radically false.

In accord with this philosophy, the Soviet representative took the position that any tribunal we set up must be bound by the Moscow Declaration of Roosevelt, Churchill and Stalin that our Nazi captives were criminals and hence would consider the personal guilt of each only as a basis for sentencing him. All other delegations, of course, rejected this idea and insisted that the tribunal independently determine the whole question of each defendant's guilt or innocence upon the evidence and the law. The Soviet yielded and this Western concept of the court was finally adopted and governed the trial.

Continental Concept of Criminal Trial Versus Common-Law Concept

The other fundamental difference concerned the nature of a criminal proceeding and consequently the manner in which it should be conducted. Our common-law criminal trial is an adversary proceeding before a jury, in which the judge is a moderator or arbitrator between combatant counsel. The Continental countries generally, including the Soviet Union, regard the criminal trial as an inquest to solve the crime, conducted on behalf of society by the court, not as a moderator, but as an active inquisitor. The Soviet delegates, with particular reference to the

United States, expressed dislike for the extremes to which we carry the adversary theory, and suggested that some of our methods are unfair to defendants, tend to promote contests, and permit trials to drag out into endurance tests, like sporting events. I could not deny that these criticisms have some truth as to criminal trials in the United States, some of which have degenerated close to the limits of toleration.

These differences of fundamental theory manifested themselves in several procedural disagreements. One concerned the contents of an indictment. Soviet and also Continental jurists consider that our method of providing the accused with only a skeleton statement of charges, withholding the evidence until he is in court, does not give an innocent man fair opportunity to prepare for trial, and leads a guilty one to contest charges to which he might plead guilty if he knew the government's evidence. There is much to be said in support of these criticisms. The Russians proposed that this indictment should furnish to the court and to defendants a dossier of the evidence, including statements of all witnesses, and all documents relied upon. Our compromise was that the indictment should contain much more than would be customary in the United States, while giving the defendant much less information than would be given in France, Germany or Russia.

Another manifestation of the difference in systems concerned the relative functions of the court *vis-à vis* the prosecution. We believed that the tribunal should have no responsibility for preparation or conduct of the prosecution, but should receive the indictment, hear the evidence offered by the parties, and render judgment. The Soviet idea was that the case would actively be conducted by the tribunal, with the prosecutors as subordinates. The tribunal, they thought, should decide what witnesses to call, what documents to put in evidence, and should examine the witnesses and interrogate the accused.

The Soviet finally acceded, in general, to common-law methods of trial, saying that it was contrary to their procedural legislation, but was more widely known because it was used in the English-speaking countries.

Solution Adopted for Problem of Testimony of Accused

Another conflict between Continental and common-law practice arose over allowing a defendant to testify under oath in his own behalf. Soviet, like Continental law generally, does not permit him to do so. At one time this was the rule at common law also and it still prevails in at least one of our states. Continental and Soviet practice, however, gives the accused what is regarded as an equivalent. At the end of all proceedings except judgment, he is entitled to make an unsworn statement in which he may deny guilt, plead for mercy, attack the prosecution, or advance any arguments he chooses, and it does not subject him to cross-examination. We felt that English-speaking countries would not regard a procedure as fair which refused defendants the right to testify. Our Continental associates felt that no process which denied the defendant his traditional final statement would be regarded as fair in France, Germany or the Soviet Union. Our solution was to allow the Germans both privileges, and nearly all of the defendants testified for themselves under oath, subject to cross-examination, and also made final statements.

The rules of evidence that should govern the tribunal might have caused serious disagreement if we had insisted on our own. Continental lawyers regard our common-law rules of evidence with abhorrence. Since they were evolved in response to the peculiarities of trial by jury, we saw no reason to urge their use in an international trial before professional judges. They have not generally been followed by international tribunals. We settled, therefore, upon one simple rule: that the tribunal 'shall admit any evidence which it deems to have probative value'. While this vested considerable discretion in the tribunal, it had the merit of making admission of evidence turn on the value of what was preferred rather than upon compliance with some formal rule of evidence.

This compromise criminal procedure which we adopted was put to a hard test by experience. The trial extended through more than 400 sessions of court, covering ten months. Prosecutors for the four nations called thirty-three witnesses and put in evidence over 4000 documents. In addition to the defendants themselves sixty-one witnesses testified in their behalf, 143 more gave evidence for them by written answers to interrogatories, and they offered a large number of defense documents. Yet less time was devoted to disputes over procedure and admissibility of evidence than would be so consumed in a criminal trial of any comparable magnitude in the United States. It was the demonstrated success of our procedure which led Dr. Ehard, while voicing German criticism of the legal basis of the trial, to declare that, 'From a technical point of view, the trial was an important accomplishment.'

Counsel representing all of the governments associated in the prosecution, as well as the judges, spared no effort to assure the fundamental integrity of the process. The charter allowed each defendant counsel of his choice, and if he had none, a German advocate was appointed for him by the tribunal. Defense counsel included leaders of the practicing and academic profession in Germany. Many were Nazis, but defendants were permitted to have their cases presented by sympathetic advocates. All such counsel were paid, fed and housed by Military Government. They were furnished office space, stenographers and supplies. Copies of documents presented as a part of the prosecution's case were given to them at least twenty-four hours in advance of presentation in court. They were given access to captured documents that were not used by the prosecution. They were allowed, so far as physical conditions permitted, to have the deposition or presence at the trial of any witness they could convince the tribunal had information relevant to their defense. How far they were allowed to go will appear from the record showing depositions from Nimitz, an admiral of the United States Navy, and Halifax, former Foreign Secretary of Great Britain. We sent airplanes to Sweden and to Switzerland to bring defense witnesses from neutral territory to testify. A transcript of proceedings, in his own language, was furnished daily to each counsel. The prosecution made its case in three months, while the defendants offered evidence for nearly five months. Our closing speeches occupied three days, while defendants used twenty days to complete their argument. The trial record will stand the most severe scrutiny of history, for we knew that as we judged, so would the future judge us.

Why Judges Were Not Chosen from Neutral Countries

In prescribing the structure of the tribunal we had to consider whether to draw the judges from the prosecuting countries or to attempt to enlist some or all of them from neutral nations. The scope of the war, however, left few neutrals, and formal neutrality of a government did not mean disinterestedness on the part of all its citizens. There was no escape from selection of the judges by the victorious powers and it seems naïve to believe that they would have chosen more dispassionate or just jurists from other lands than from England, France and the United States. Those countries which enjoy the blessing of an independent judicial tradition rely upon the individual integrity, detachment and learning of the judge to shape his decisions rather than upon the source of his commission, his nationality or his class. In making these defendants stand trial before a court of the aggrieved countries we followed an almost universal criminal law. If an offender escapes into jurisdiction of an indifferent society, he is extradited and the fugitive brought back to trial in the territory interested in his prosecution. In your courts and mine, the Government constantly litigates before the judges it appoints and maintains and it frequently meets with defeat. That indeed happened at Nuremberg. No men did we plead more earnestly to convict than Schacht and Von Papen, both of whom the tribunal acquitted. Indeed, all but six of the defendants were acquitted on one or more of the counts. These defendants were before judges who, with their alternates, attended every session of the trial, except one alternate who suffered an illness of two or three days. Their undivided attention to the evidence, their impartial rulings and judicial bearing and their dispassionate and discriminating written judgment won for the tribunal the commendation of all disinterested observers. It set a high standard of judicial conduct for all future international tribunals.

However, participation of a Soviet judge is a grievance much exploited by Germans. It is urged that since the Soviet Union joined with Hitler in the aggression against Poland, it was an accomplice and should not have had a seat in judgment. Regardless of the merits I do not doubt that German pride and nationalism found judgment by Russians especially objectionable and that it will always injure the repute of the trial with the German people. But I think the grievance is more symbolic than substantial.

The charter provided that convictions and sentences should require affirmative votes of at least three members of the tribunal. Hence a Soviet vote to convict or sentence could be effective only if two, constituting a majority of the remaining three judges, concurred, so the same result would be reached as if the Soviet seat had been left vacant. No defendant, therefore, was found guilty or punished because of Soviet participation. At all events, it was hardly to be expected that, within two months of the German surrender we would refuse the Soviet a seat on the Bench and thus initiate a break in an alliance that had just won the war. Perhaps it would have been better for Germany and the rest of the world if other efforts to retain Soviet cooperation had been as successful as ours.

But however one looks at the propriety of Soviet participation, a righteous judgment is not impeached by the unworthiness of a judge, just as our clerical brethren hold that the effectiveness of the Sacraments is not diminished even when they be 'ministered by evil men'. The ultimate question with which history will be concerned is whether the end of this process was a right judgment.

Validity of Judgment Rests upon Record

No one can intelligently decide whether the legal foundation for this judgment is valid, so that it amounts to a judicial conviction and not a mere political condemnation, without consideration of the record on which it is based. The judgment, unlike the wartime accusations, rests on proved facts. Of course I can not adequately review these, but neither can I adequately discuss the law until we know just what kind of acts our opponents say are beyond the law and which we say the law may punish.

At about the time that Mr. Roosevelt was elected President of the United States, Adolf Hitler engineered what his partisans aptly called 'the seizure of power'. The Nazi party overthrew the parliamentary institutions of the Weimar Republic and set up a strong dictatorship admittedly as a step towards re-establishing Germany's predominance in Central Europe—by war if need be. To this end, two great policies were embarked upon: one was to prepare for war; the other was to crush all internal opposition to the regime.

All constitutional liberties were suspended, courts were purged of independent judges, special 'people's courts' of partisans were set up, and concentration camps were established for dissenters. Trade unions were seized and brought under the regime and Jews were excluded from all civil rights. Goering testified that 'If for any cause someone was taken into custody for political reasons, this could not be reviewed in any court'. He gave this summation of the ultimate achievement: 'So far as opposition is concerned in any form, the opposition of each individual person was not tolerated unless it is a matter of no importance.'

Meanwhile, as early as 1935, Schacht was secretly appointed to prepare the economy for war, and within a year Goering, Co-ordinator of the Economy, brought the departments of government together and informed them that 'all measures are to be considered from the standpoint of an assured waging of war'. A gigantic armament program was commenced, compulsory military service was re-established, and a military air force and a submarine navy were planned superior to any in the world. Remilitarized Germany tested its strength in several instances without encountering opposition enough to cause a war. The German Army re-entered the Rhineland, an *Anschluss* was forced upon Austria and Czechoslovakia was taken over. Not satisfied with this, Hitler then threw his armed forces against Poland, which constituted the aggression that plunged the world into war. It is fortunate that the first occasion on which military aggression was sought to be punished as a crime was also an occasion on which the aggression was so clear and its proof so indisputable that there was no choice except to convict or to abandon the principle that military aggression is a crime.

In November, 1937, nearly two years before the war, Hitler called a meeting of his High Command at the Reichschancellery in Berlin. The captured minutes, kept by Colonel Hoszbach, were admitted to be authentic by defendants who attended the conference. Hitler said, 'It is not a case of conquering people, but of conquering agriculturally useful space.' And after reviewing Germany's needs, he concluded with this observation: 'The question for Germany is where the greatest possible conquest could be made at the lowest cost.' At this time he only disclosed an aim to conquer Czechoslovakia and Austria. He had them both in his possession within about a year, and without a war.

These acquisitions did not satisfy his ambitions and on May 28, 1939, he held another meeting at which he announced his intention to attack Poland—which attack was carried out four months later. Captured minutes, kept by Lieutenant Colonel Schmundt, record Hitler as saying, 'There is no question of sparing Poland and we are left with the decision to attack Poland at the first suitable opportunity. We cannot expect a repetition of the Czech affair. There will be war.' He anticipated that England and France would enter a life-and-death struggle that might last a long time, and ordered preparations made accordingly.

A final meeting was held at Obersalzburg on August 22, 1939, and again we captured minutes of Hitler's speech. He announced the decision to invade at once, and said: 'I shall give a propagandist cause for starting the war, never mind whether it be plausible or not. The victor shall not be asked later on whether we told the truth or not. In starting and making a war, not the truth is what matters, but victory.' His attitude is shown by his further statement: 'I am only afraid that at the last moment some *Schweinehund* will make a proposal for mediation.' Appeals from President Roosevelt, from His Holiness the Pope, and from Daladier, Prime Minister of France, to refrain from war were scorned. On the 1st of September, the German forces invaded Poland, and for the second time in a generation a world war was begun.

Defendants had Violated International Agreements

The tribunal found that Hitler, aided and abetted by certain of the defendants on trial, planned and waged aggressive wars against twelve nations. Invasion of similarly aggressive character of Denmark and Norway, Belgium, Netherlands and Luxembourg, Yugoslavia and Greece, in rapid succession, followed that of Poland, and *every one was in violation of repeated assurances and nonaggression treaties.* I shall not detail the story of the secret and undeclared attack in June of 1941 on the Soviet Union, to whom she was then bound by treaties of friendship and nonaggression—an attack that was pursuant to a plan issued by Hitler and initialed by his High Command more than six months before. Nor shall I recite the somewhat tentative plans which were considered for the prosecution of a war against the United States at a later date, or the plotting which ultimately induced Japan to attack us.

As the *Wehrmacht* expanded the area of Nazi conquest, the terrors of the Nazi regime were spread over Europe with increasing efficiency and ferocity. We paid no attention at Nuremberg to such atrocities as were spontaneous outbursts of passion. We charged systematic and planned organization to subdue populations by terror and to get rid of races the Nazis disliked and of peoples who lived on lands they wanted for themselves.

In announcing to his High Command at Obersalzburg the purpose of invading Poland, Hitler twice commanded a war of cruelty. He told his generals, 'Our strength is in our quickness and brutality. Ghengis Khan had millions of women and children killed with a gay heart. History sees in him only a great state builder.... Thus, for the time being, I have sent to the East only my "Death's Head Units" with the order to kill without pity or mercy all men, women and children of Polish race or language. Only in such a way will we win the vital space that we need.' Again, the notes show, him commanding, 'Have no pity. Brutal attitude.' And, 'The aim is the elimination of living forces.'

The two outstanding applications of this Hitler policy were the slave labor program and persecution of the Jews. In all occupied territories, compulsory labor service was instituted. A vast labor supply was recruited for shipment to labor in Germany. Defendant Sauckel, who had charge of the program, was shown by captured documents to have reported, 'Out of the five million workers who arrived in Germany, not even two hundred thousand came voluntarily.' The largest slaving operation in history, this was also one of the most cruel. The tribunal summarizes the recruitment in occupied countries: 'Manhunts took place in the streets, at motion picture houses, even at churches, and at night in private houses. Houses were sometimes burnt down and the families taken as hostages.' These persons were transported under the most inhuman conditions and turned over to employers for use in agriculture and industry. Sauckel's instructions of April 20, 1942, read: 'All the men must be fed, sheltered and treated in such a way as to exploit them to the highest possible extent, at the lowest conceivable degree of expenditure.' It takes little imagination to picture how German employers would behave when self-interest was added to such official commands. The slaves were treated with great cruelty and died in vast numbers. The remnants of this labor horde constitute 'displaced persons' in Germany today.

The persecution of the Jews began in Germany with discriminatory laws and soon descended to pogroms organized with police approval, burning and demolishing of synagogues, looting of Jewish businesses, violence to Jewish people, and their confinement in ghettos. But anti-Semitism was a foreign as well as a domestic policy. Hitler declared that his war would bring about extermination of the Jews of Europe. As fast as his power spread, Jews were compelled to register and wear the yellow star, and were forced into ghettos where they were required to work on war material. It was in the summer of 1941 that plans were made for what was called 'the final solution of the Jewish problem'— extermination. A special section of the Gestapo was set up under Eichmann to carry out this program of extinction. Our evidence was gruesome, ghoulish and indisputable that it was carried out with relentless efficiency. I can only indicate its character. We captured General Stroop's report of the burning of the Warsaw ghetto, in which he reported to Berlin that he had cleaned out the ghetto 'with utter ruthlessness and merciless tenacity' and caused the death of a proved total of 56,005 Jews. He said: 'Jews usually left their hideouts but frequently remained in the burning buildings and jumped out of the windows only when the heat became unbearable. Then they tried to crawl with broken bones across the street into buildings which were not afire.... Countless numbers of Jews were liquidated in sewers and bunkers with blasting.'

We also had captured reports of the operators of the gas wagons, detailing how they herded the people into closed trucks and suffocated them with the motor exhaust. Extermination squads even prepared a map, which fell into our hands, of the eastern territories with the symbol of a coffin in each province on which a figure represented the Jews exterminated and outside of the coffin another figure representing the Jews yet to be killed.

Another phase of the program was to gather Jews from all occupied Europe in concentration camps, where those fit to work were used as slaves and those not fit to work were destroyed in gas chambers and their bodies burned. Hoess, commandant of the Auschwitz extermination camp, called as a defense witness, testified that in his administration alone two and a half million persons were thus done away with, and he gave lurid and technical details of the process. One extermination institution kept a death register which showed that all inmates died of 'heart failure', and that each day they invariably died in alphabetical order.

These were not merely sadistic deeds of unimportant people. In the vaults of the great Reichsbank, the central financial institution of Germany, we found stored great quantities of gold fillings taken from the teeth and rings taken from the fingers of concentration camp victims, which were turned over to the financiers who supplied credit to help carry on the program.

The evidence showed that at least six million Jews were killed, of which four million were killed in the extermination institutions. These are the things which caused Hans Frank, Nazi Governor-General of Poland, to cry out from the witness stand: 'We have fought against Jewry. We have fought against it for years. And we have allowed ourselves to make utterances and my own diary has become a witness against me in this connection. Utterances which are terrible....A thousand years will pass and this guilt of Germany will still not be erased.'

All Defendants Admitted Facts

Such were the courses of conduct that the German documents revealed and that all defendants admitted had occurred. The only issue of fact left was the degree of personal responsibility of those indicted for having so written German history in blood. The last stand of those implicated was not that the evidence failed to convict of the acts, but that the law had failed to make the acts crimes. Admitting that they were moral wrongs of the first magnitude, it was contended that they fell within that realm that the law leaves to the free choice of the individual and for which he must answer to no forum except his own conscience. In short, their position was that there are no binding standards of conduct for states or statesmen that they disregard at risk of answering to international law. If that is so, it is a sad conclusion for the world, for it reduces the whole body of what we have called international law to 'such stuff as dreams are made on'. If courses of conduct that rise so far beyond injury to mere individuals, and destroy the peace of the world and subvert civilization itself are not international crimes, then law has terrors only for little men and takes note only of little wrongs.

To laymen it is incomprehensible that lawyers should be in doubt as to what law is and how it gets to be law. But that fundamental enigma is the root of the controversy as to the legal validity of the Nuremberg trial. That controversy, I think, is more interesting than important, for no matter what conclusion it reaches the result of the Nuremberg process, the execution and imprisonment of the Nazis, is valid and legitimate by the very tenets that its opponents invoke. Even by conventional international law it can not be denied that the victors could properly impose punishments on the vanquished by political decision. Certainly what they legally could do summarily would not be less valid because they paused to hear the explanations of the accused and to make certain that they punished only the right men and for right reasons. And, of course, if the opponents of the trial could establish that there was no law which required German statesmen to respect the lives and liberties of other peoples, it follows that no law compelled the Allies to respect the lives or liberties of Germans. In this connection, it must not be forgotten that the Allies had succeeded to the German state's own sovereignty over these defendants by the unconditional surrender. The argument of the defendants does not affect the legitimacy of the punishment; it only goes to the question whether the trial must be looked upon as a political and military measure incident to victory, or as an exercise of judicial power in applying a law binding upon victor and vanquished alike.

If no moral principle is entitled to application as law until it is first embodied in a text and promulgated as a command by some superior effective authority, then it must be admitted the world was without such a text at the time the acts I have recited took place. No sovereign legislative act to which the Germans must bow had defined international crimes, fixed penalties and set up courts to adjudge them. From the premise that nothing is law if not embraced in a sovereign command, it is easy to argue that the Nuremberg trial applied retroactive, or *ex post facto*, law. European lawyers generally, and particularly those of the German school, think of the command as making the law, and of the law as only the command. And with the increasing reliance of all society upon the legislative process there is a growing tendency of common-law peoples to think of law in terms of a specific sovereign enactment.

Common Law Disproves Point that
Legislation is Source of Law

The fallacy of the idea that law is found only in such a source appears from the fact that crimes were punished by courts under our common-law philosophy long before there were legislatures. The modern law of crimes may largely be traced to judicial decision of particular cases earlier than it appeared in statute. While of late years legislation is more frequent, in England today no statute defines murder or fixes its penalty, and the same is true of many crimes. Some states of our Union still recognize common-law crimes, and those which do not, have codes which, in the main, only declare what before was common law. The early English judge was confronted with an evil act. He dealt with it, unaided by statute, as reasonably and justly as he could; what he did made a precedent. A series of leading cases, each adding something in response to its particular facts, made a body of law. This slow and inductive process of developing general rules from particular decisions is quite opposite that of the Continental jurist, who starts with the general command and reasons somewhat deductively to the specific case. The common-law judge is less text-bound. Common law depends less on what is commanded by authority and more on what is indicated by reason. The judge reaches a decision more largely upon consideration of the inherent quality and natural effect of the act in question. He applies what has sometimes been called a natural law that binds each man to refrain from acts so inherently wrong and injurious to others that he must know they will be treated as criminal.

Unless international law is to be deprived of this common-law method of birth and growth, and confined wholly to progression by authoritarian command, then the judges at Nuremberg were fully warranted in reaching a judicial judgment of criminal guilt. The common-law authorship of the tribunal's judgment was betrayed by the fact that while it does not deny the authority of the London charter, it did not rest upon it, but explored its antecedents after the common-law method and rested, in part at least, upon common-law justifications as well as upon the charter.

Under this philosophy of law, it is clear that by 1939 the world had come to regard aggressive war as so morally wrong and illegal that it should be treated as criminal if occasion arose. The change in world opinion probably dates from Germany's launching of World War I, at which moment Chancellor von Bethmann-Hollweg was cynically telling the Reichstag 'this violates the rules of international law', and added, 'The wrong—I speak openly—the wrong that we now do we will try to make good again, as soon as our military ends have been reached.' Men everywhere saw that civilization could not abide such irresponsible nationalism. When that war ended, the Treaty of Versailles provided for a special tribunal to try the former Kaiser for offenses not vitally different from certain of the crimes defined by the London Agreement, a fate from which he was saved by sanctuary in a country neutral in that war. Moreover, that treaty recognized the right of the allied power to try persons accused of violating the laws and customs of war, although the Hague Conventions, which forbid such conduct, do not expressly name such conduct criminal, nor set up courts to try such offenses nor fix any penalties.

In 1923 a draft treaty sponsored by the League of Nations flatly declared that 'aggressive war is an international crime' and that the parties 'undertake that no one of them will be guilty of its commission'. That treaty was not consummated because of disagreement over what would constitute aggression rather than because of doubt as to the criminality of aggressive war. The next year, the so-called Geneva Protocol, by unanimous resolution of the forty-eight members of the League of Nations Assembly, which at that time included Italy and Japan but not Germany, declared that a war of aggression 'is an international crime'. In 1927 all the delegations, which then included the German, Italian and Japanese, unanimously adopted a declaration that 'a war of aggression can never serve as a means of settling international disputes and is in consequence an international crime.' In 1928 twenty-one American Republics at the Sixth Pan-American Conference, united in a declaration that 'war of aggression constitutes an international crime against the human species'.

Most important of all, of course, was the General Treaty for the Renunciation of War of August 28, 1928, known as the Pact of Paris or the Kellogg-Briand

Pact, which became binding on sixty-three nations including Germany, Italy and Japan, 'uniting civilized nations of the world in a common renunciation of war as an instrument of their national policy' and agreeing that all disputes or conflicts, of whatever nature or origin, shall be solved only by pacific means.

These solemn acts in which statesmen held out their promises, and in which peoples put their hopes, can not be brushed aside as mere extravagant expressions of disapproval of war and pious avowals of a will to peace. And unless these repeated declarations are regarded as legally meaningless and the statesmen of the world have been lulling people into complacency with a gigantic hoax, the charter and judgment of Nuremberg apply law that responsible representatives of all nations had proclaimed as such before the acts prosecuted took place.

Long-Term Results of Nuremberg Cannot Now be Determined

We must not forget that we did not invoke the outlawry of war as a sword to punish acts that were otherwise innocent and harmless. On the contrary, it was the accused who had to establish the lawfulness of their belligerency to excuse a course of murders, enslavements, arsons and violence which, except in war, is criminal by every civilized concept. They were like pirates or buccaneers who are punishable wherever, whenever and by whomever caught unless they can show that their acts fall within the protection the law always has afforded those who commit acts of violence in prosecuting war. The very least legal consequences that follow outlawing wars of aggression is to withdraw from one knowingly and voluntarily causing or promoting such aggression the defense of lawful warfare. Thus if the treaties outlawing this war did not expressly create a new crime, they took away the immunity of war makers from prosecution for old crimes.

It is much too early to appraise the influence of Nuremberg. But I would disclaim any expectation that it alone is enough to prevent future wars. When stakes are high enough, and chances of success look good enough, I suppose reckless leaders may again plunge their people into war, just as men still resort to murder, notwithstanding the law's penalty. But I do think that we have forever laid to rest in the minds of statesmen the vicious assumptions that all war must be regarded as legal and just, and that while the law imposes personal responsibility for starting a street riot, it imposes none for inciting and launching a world war.

Dr. Philip Jessup, writing of a *Modern Law of Nations*, has set out the two 'keystones of a revised international legal order'. He describes the old idea of absolute sovereignty as 'the quicksand upon which the foundations of traditional international law are built', and he says that 'international law, like national law, must be directly applicable to the individual'.

It may, too, be significant of a more promising intellectual attitude that the new organic law adopted by the Germans provides that the general rules of international law shall take precedence over German federal law and shall create rights and duties directly for the inhabitants of German territory. It also provides 'activities tending to disturb, or undertaken with the intention of disturbing, peaceful relations between nations, and especially preparing for aggressive war shall be unconstitutional. They shall be made subject to punishment.'

Thus 'the old order changeth, yielding place to new.' Like much legal work ours at Nuremberg has far-reaching implications rarely apparent to laymen and often missed by lawyers. Its value to the world will depend less on how faithfully it interpreted the past than on how accurately it forecasts the future. It is possible that strife and suspicion will lead to new aggressions and that the nations are not yet ready to receive and abide by the Nuremberg law. But those who gave some of the best effort of their lives to this trial are sustained by a confidence that in place of what might have been mere acts of vengeance we wrote a civilized legal precedent and one that will lie close to the foundations of that body of international law that will prevail when the world becomes sufficiently civilized.

16

The Nuremberg Trials

By Telford Taylor*

In Justice Jackson's own estimation, his service at Nuremberg was 'the most important, enduring, and constructive work of my life.'[1] The man who wrote these words was looking back on twenty-one fruitful years at the bar in western New York State, seven phenomenally successful years as legal spokesman of the Executive branch, culminating in his achievements as Solicitor General and Attorney General, and twelve years of outstanding service on the nation's supreme bench. Yet in final retrospect, the Justice saw as the climax of this richly varied and distinguished career of forty-odd years, his eighteen months as Representative and Chief of Counsel of the United States 'in preparing and prosecuting charges of atrocities and war crimes against the Leaders of the European Axis Powers and their Principal Agents and Accessories.'[2]

If the Justice's character was such as to choke any challenge to the sincerity of this, his own judgment on his works, that quality equally calls for acknowledgment that there is sharp division of opinion about the soundness of his verdict. The record and memory of Nuremberg still bristle with issues political, legal, and jurisprudential. His participation therein, both as architect and protagonist, made of the Jamestown lawyer a world figure. But he would be the first to repel as meretricious blandness any disposition, even *in memoriam*, to blink at the certain prospect that Nuremberg will be denounced as well as acclaimed for many years to come. Justice Jackson deeply believed that controversy shapes truth, and he faced these issues with abundant faith that from time's chisel the Nuremberg monument will emerge, not as the tombstone of a black era, but as a cornerstone of 'justice under the law among men and nations.'[3]

---

* Member, New York and District of Columbia Bars; former Administrator, Small Defense Plants Administration, U.S. Chief of Counsel for war crimes, General Counsel of FCC.

[1] Jackson, Introduction to Harris, Tyranny on Trial xxxvii (1954).

[2] Exec. Order No. 9547, 10 Fed. Reg. 4961 (1945). Justice Jackson's resignation as Chief of Counsel took effect October 17, 1946.

[3] Jackson, *The Challenge of International Lawlessness*, 374 International Conciliation 683, 691 (1941).

I

Justice Jackson's Nuremberg concepts were begotten of problems he had faced when Attorney General. He held that office from January, 1940 to July, 1941; these months comprised most of the uneasy period—for America a time almost of cold war, though the phrase was then unknown—between the outbreak of World War II and Pearl Harbor. As the Axis conquests mounted toward their zenith, the United States veered rapidly from orthodox neutrality to non-belligerency. The Department of Justice was faced with new and searching problems of law and policy, abundantly reflected in Jackson's opinions as Attorney General.[4]

In August, 1940, upholding the President's authority to exchange overage naval craft for bases variously located in the British Empire, Jackson still recognized a 'duty of impartiality' between the belligerents owed by the neutral states.[5] But in May, 1941, approving the training of British aviators in the United States by members of the Army Air Corps, he spoke a very different language.[6] By enactment of the Lend-Lease Act,[7] Congress had 'explicitly enunciated the policy that defense of certain countries now at war, including Great Britain, is vital to our own defense and that the furnishing of aid to such countries is essential to the security of the United States.'[8] Bluntly Jackson admitted that his opinion did not consider 'whether there is involved any question of international law,' inasmuch as 'the question has been resolved for present purposes, by the settled national policy of aid to other countries whose defense is vital to our own, and is not deemed to be opened for further consideration by the [President's] memorandum of reference to me.'[9]

In fact, however, Jackson had already and publicly considered the implications of non-belligerency and 'all aid short of war' in terms of international law. Addressing the Inter-American Bar Association at Havana, shortly after passage of the Lend-Lease Act,[10] he flatly rejected the view that all wars are legally alike and that neutrals invariably owe a duty of impartiality as between the participants: 'To the mind untutored in such sophisticated thought it seems to be characterized by more of learning than of wisdom. It does not appear to be necessary to treat all wars as legal and just simply because we have no court to try the accused.'[11]

---

[4] See 39 Ops. Att'y Gen. 411 (1940); 40 Ops. Att'y Gen. 1 (1941).

[5] 39 Ops. Att'y Gen. 411, 484 (1940). For that reason, supported by a long quotation from 2 Oppenheimer, International Law § 334 at 574 (5th ed. 1937), Jackson ruled that 'mosquito boats' then under construction could not be turned over to the British. 39 Ops. Att'y Gen. 411, 494–96.

[6] See 40 Ops. Att'y Gen. 58 (1941).   [7] 55 Stat. 31 (1941).

[8] 40 Ops. Att'y Gen. 58, 62 (1941).   [9] Id. at 63.

[10] Jackson's speech was read by Ambassador George L. Messersmith on March 27, 1941, as bad weather had prevented Jackson's flight to Havana. This address is printed in 35 Am. J. Int'l L. 348 (1941).

[11] Id. at 350.

Boldly Jackson advanced the proposition that 'aggressive wars are civil wars against the international community.'[12] The Axis powers were plainly the aggressors, and the nations of the Western Hemisphere, though neutral, need not be impartial; on the contrary, aid to Britain was imperative if international law and order were to be restored. Had not Grotius himself distinguished the 'just' from the 'unjust' war? To be sure, the distinction had frequently been rejected, especially during the nineteenth century, but since the First World War belligerent aggression had been condemned as unlawful, not only by famous lawyer-statesmen such as Elihu Root and Henry L. Stimson, but by numerous international agreements and declarations—the Covenant of the League of Nations, the Kellogg-Briand pact and the Argentine Anti-War Treaty of 1933. Germany, Japan and Italy had all renounced war as an instrument of national policy; now they had shamelessly broken their pledge. International law would indeed be a broken reed were it to be construed so as to require neutrals to treat aggressor and victim alike:

[W]e may not stymie international law and allow these great treaties to become dead letters. . . . A system of international law which can impose no penalty on a law-breaker and also forbids other states to aid the victim would be self-defeating and would not help . . . to realize mankind's hope for enduring peace.

The principle that war as an instrument of national policy is outlawed must be the starting point in any plan of international reconstruction.

It is upon these considerations that I have advised my government in the hope that its course may strengthen the sanction against aggression and contribute to the realization of our aspiration for an international order under law.[13]

A few days before he took his seat on the Supreme Court, Jackson returned to the same theme in an address at Indianapolis before the American Bar Association.[14] The American lawyer has always worked in a legal world of constitutions, statutes, and constitutional tribunals; he is usually trained in the positivist spirit of Austin, Holland, and Gray.[15] Accordingly, Jackson was at pains to point out to his audience the difficulties that attend a rigorously analytical-positivist approach to international law. To survive, mankind must find a means of settling international disputes without war; international law must grow to meet this moral and practical necessity; lacking international legislatures and courts, that growth must be fed by other means:

The world will not, I trust, be naive enough to believe it has so reordered its affairs as to prevent conflicts that might provoke wars. The supremacy of domestic law is not based on an absence of individual conflicts. It is predicated on a settlement of them by means that

---

[12] *Id.* at 353.

[13] *Id.* at 356–59.

[14] Jackson, *The Challenge of International Lawlessness*, 374 INTERNATIONAL CONCILIATION 683 (1941). The speech was delivered at the Association's annual meeting, held in Indianapolis on October 2, 1941. Jackson (who had taken the oath as a Justice in July) took his seat four days later.

[15] See POUND, LAW AND MORALS 1–2, 24–25, 43–52 (1926).

do not violate the peace of the community. The law anticipates a certain amount of wrong conduct, for which it provides damages or punishments. It does not end injustices, but it requires the victims to seek redress through the force of the law, rather than through their own strength.

In this we have to abide the imperfections of legal institutions. I am not convinced, even by my own transfiguration into a Justice of the Supreme Court, that courts have overcome the hazard of wrong decision and of occasional injustice. The triumph of the law is not in always ending conflicts *rightly*, but in ending them *peaceably*. And we may be certain that we do less injustice by the worst processes of the law than would be done by the best use of violence. We cannot await a perfect international tribunal or legislature before proscribing resort to violence even in case of legitimate grievance. We did not await the perfect court before stopping men from settling their differences with brass knuckles.[16]

Once the aggressor nations were put down by 'a rough international equivalent of the ancient "hue and cry" procedure,'[17] the United States would 'face a tough and fateful decision as to her attitude toward the peace.'[18] In making this decision, the legal profession had a proud and serious responsibility:

It is a grave thing to risk the commitments that are indispensable to a system of international justice and collective security. It is an equally grave thing to perpetuate by our inaction an anarchic international condition in which every State may go to war with impunity whenever its interests are thought to be served.…

Men of our tradition will take up the challenge gladly.… Long ago English lawyers rejected lawlessness as a prerogative of the Crown and bound their king by rules of law so that he might not invade the poorest home without a warrant. In the same high tradition our forefathers set up a sovereign nation whose legislative and executive and judicial branches are deprived of legal power to do many things that might encroach upon our freedoms. Our Anglo-American philosophy of political organization denies the concept of arbitrary and unlimited power in any governing body. Hence, we see nothing revolutionary or visionary in the concept of a reign of law, to which sovereign nations will defer, designed to protect the peace of the society of nations. We, as lawyers, hold fast to the ideal of an international order existing under law and equipped with instrumentalities able and willing to maintain its supremacy, and we renew our dedication to the task of pushing back the frontiers of anarchy and of maintaining justice under the law among men and nations.[19]

Weeks later, Pearl Harbor brought the United States into the war. On the bench, Jackson had little occasion to pursue the problems of war and peace in which he had been so deeply immersed. No doubt his mind turned again in this direction in the case of the German saboteurs,[20] but he did not write; like the other associate justices, he simply concurred in Chief Justice Stone's opinion

---

[16] Jackson, *The Challenge of International Lawlessness*, 374 INTERNATIONAL CONCILIATION 683, 688–89 (1941).

[17] *Id.* at 686.

[18] *Id.* at 690.

[19] *Id.* at 690–91.

[20] *Ex parte* Quirin, 317 U.S. 1 (1942).

upholding the trial of the saboteurs by a military commission as in accordance with 'the common law of war.'[21]

Elsewhere, however, the basic ideas of Jackson's Havana and Indianapolis speeches—that aggressive war is a crime against international law, and that its perpetrators should be condemned by international adjudication—were the subject of eager consideration and development. The focus of this activity was in London, where the governments-in-exile of countries overrun by the Wehrmacht were established. Naturally, the attention of these governments was initially concentrated on the atrocities and outrages, in violation of the laws of war relating to belligerent occupation, committed in the lands from which they had fled. In January, 1942, the London representatives of nine German-occupied countries[22] promulgated the St. James Declaration, calling attention to these crimes and stating as a principal war aim 'the punishment, through the channels of organized justice, of those guilty of or responsible for these crimes....'[23]

Thereafter the United Nations War Crimes Commission was established by the joint action of seventeen Allied governments,[24] and, from the beginning of 1944, the Commission and its constituent committees gave intense and continuing study to such questions as the tribunals—national or international, military or civilian—by which those accused of war crimes would be tried and the scope and nature of the international penal law that would be invoked and applied.[25] A draft convention for the establishment of an international war crimes tribunal was approved (despite British opposition) by the Commission. On the question whether aggressive war should be regarded as a 'crime against peace' under international law, however, the members were divided and came to no conclusion before the end of the war.[26]

In the United States, the formulation of a national war crimes policy became the subject of serious consideration by the interested executive departments (chiefly State, War, Treasury and Justice) in the fall of 1944.[27] In some circles there was a strong disposition simply to list the Nazi leaders generally regarded as villains and shoot them without benefit of trial.[28] But this course was vigorously opposed

[21] *Id.* at 30, 34.

[22] Belgium, Czechoslovakia, France, Greece, Luxembourg, Norway, The Netherlands, Poland and Yugoslavia.

[23] See HISTORY OF THE UNITED NATIONS WAR CRIMES COMMISSION 90 (1948); Taylor, *The Nuremberg War Crimes Trials*, 450 INTERNATIONAL CONCILIATION 243, 245–46 (1949).

[24] Including the United States, the United Kingdom and all of the major Allied countries except the Soviet Union.

[25] See HISTORY OF THE UNITED NATIONS WAR CRIMES COMMISSION 169–87 (1948); Taylor, *supra* note 23, at 336–48.

[26] See HISTORY OF THE UNITED NATIONS WAR CRIMES COMMISSION 180–87 (1948).

[27] See STIMSON & BUNDY, ON ACTIVE SERVICE IN PEACE AND WAR 584–90 (1947); TAYLOR, FINAL REPORT TO THE SECRETARY OF THE ARMY 1–3, 130–31 (1949); U.S. DEP'T OF STATE, INTERNATIONAL CONFERENCE ON MILITARY TRIALS 3–20, 22–27 (1949) (hereinafter cited as INT'L CONFERENCE).

[28] See STIMSON & BUNDY, *op. cit. supra* note 27, at 584–85.

by Secretary of War Stimson, within whose department were being evolved concepts of international criminality reminiscent of Jackson's 1941 speeches and at least as broad as those then under discussion at London.[29] An interdepartmental memorandum was handed to President Roosevelt on the eve of his departure for Yalta, in which it was proposed that an international tribunal be established by agreement among the United Nations, to try the 'German leaders and the organizations employed by them... such as SA, SS, Gestapo' for 'joint participation in a broad criminal enterprise' tantamount to a conspiracy, comprehending 'the prewar atrocities... as well as the waging of an illegal war of aggression with ruthless disregard for international law and the rules of war.'[30]

Apparently President Roosevelt approved these recommendations.[31] At all events, he designated Judge Samuel Rosenman as his personal representative on war crimes matters, and sent the Judge to England to present the American plan. Churchill, Eden, and the Lord Chancellor (Lord Simon) were all 'determinedly opposed,' and favored the political execution without trial of six or more top Nazis.[32] A talk with Churchill at Chequers on April 9, 1945, failed to break the impasse, and the matter was laid over for further discussion at the coming United Nations conference at San Francisco.[33] Three days later President Roosevelt died, and Judge Rosenman immediately returned to Washington.

The day after the President's death Jackson addressed the American Society of International Law in Washington on 'The Rule of Law among Nations.'[34] The holocaust was nearing an end; its lesson was plain. Future international issues must be settled peaceably, and to this end international law must be brought 'out of the closet' and put to work. Even 'the worst settlement of international disputes by adjudication or arbitration is likely to be less disastrous to the loser and certainly less destructive to the world than no way of settlement except war.'

---

[29] As Chief Legal Officer of the Allied Military Government of Italy in 1943 at the time of Mussolini's incarceration by the Badoglio government, Colonel William C. Chanler (with Colonel Robert D. Gorman) proposed that the fallen dictator be tried for waging aggressive war. Mussolini's spectacular rescue from the Gran Sasso by Otto Skorzeny soon rendered this plan academic, but Colonel Chanler renewed his proposal, for application to Hitler and the other Nazi leaders, when he returned to the Pentagon in 1944 as Deputy Director of Military Government. At about the same time Colonel Murray Bernays of the War Department general staff (G-1) made recommendations which furnished the basis for the subsequent interdepartmental report to the President. See Bernays, *Legal Basis of the Nuremberg Trials*, 35 SURVEY GRAPHIC 5 (1946); Stimson & Bundy, *op. cit. supra* note 27, at 587 n.3.

[30] The memorandum, initialled by Secretaries Stettinius and Stimson and Attorney General Biddle, is printed in full in INTERNATIONAL CONFERENCE ON MILITARY TRIALS 3–17 (1949).

[31] See ROSENMAN, WORKING WITH ROOSEVELT 518–19, 542 (1952); STIMSON & BUNDY, *op. cit. supra* note 27, at 586–87.

[32] See ROSENMAN, *op. cit. supra* note 31, at 542–45. The British named Hitler, Goering, Ribbentrop, Goebbels, Himmler, Streicher and one or two others.

[33] See *id.* at 543, 545.

[34] See 39 AM. SOC'Y INT'L L. PROC. 10 (1945); the speech is also printed in 19 TEMP. L.Q. 135 (1946).

But steps in this direction, to be successful, must be grounded on judicial independence and the reality of law as something other and higher than power or policy. A true international court must rise above 'obligation to any nation or interest.' Unfortunately, 'there are some who candidly would use courts as an instrument of power and many more who favor all of the premises of that philosophy without recognizing the conclusion.' Indeed, 'this philosophy is strikingly demonstrated by the attitude of many people toward the trial of war criminals.' And thus Jackson's thought drew him into the subject that was under such intense scrutiny in Washington and London:

I have no purpose to enter into any controversy as to what shall be done with war criminals, either high or humble. If it is considered good policy for the future peace of the world, if it is believed that the example will outweigh the tendency to create among their own countrymen a myth of martyrdom, then let them be executed. But in that case let the decision to execute them be made as a military or political decision. We must not use the forms of judicial proceedings to carry out or rationalize previously settled political or military policy. Farcical judicial trials conducted by us will destroy confidence in the judicial process as quickly as those conducted by any other people.

Of course, if good faith trials are sought, that is another matter. I am not so troubled as some seem to be over problems of jurisdiction of war criminals or of finding existing and recognized law by which standards of guilt may be determined. But all experience teaches that there are certain things you cannot do under the guise of judicial trial. Courts try cases, but cases also try courts.

You must put no man on trial before anything that is called a court ... under the forms of judicial proceedings if you are not willing to see him freed if not proven guilty. If you are determined to execute a man in any case, there is no occasion for a trial; the world yields no respect to courts that are merely organized to convict. I am not arguing against bringing those accused of war crimes to trial. I am pointing out hazards that attend such use of the judicial process—risk on the one hand that the decision which most of the world thinks should be made may not be justified as a judicial finding, even if perfectly justified as a political policy; and the alternative risk of damage to the future credit of judicial proceedings by manipulations of trial personnel or procedure temporarily to invest with judicial character what is in fact a political decision ... any trials to which lawyers worthy of their calling lend themselves will be trials in fact, not merely trials in name, to ratify a predetermined result.[35]

Jackson's tolerance for summary political execution of the Nazi leaders did not survive the Nuremberg experience.[36] His insistence that war crimes tribunals should be *bona fide* courts independent of political dictation, and that punishment should be contingent upon proven criminal guilt, remained throughout the touchstone of his thinking.

---

[35] 39 Am. Soc'y Int'l L. Proc. 15–17 (1945). There is no available evidence that Jackson had participated in any way in the State-War-Justice discussions, but it is quite possible that he had heard about them through normal social and professional contacts.

[36] See his almost surgical handling of the issue in Harris, *op. cit. supra* note 1, at xxxi–xxxiv.

Perhaps as a consequence of this speech,[37] President Truman decided to ask Jackson to take leave from the Court and represent the United States in formulating the Allied war crimes program and conducting the prosecution. Informed by Judge Rosenman of the President's desire, Jackson reflected for several days before accepting.[38] He was fully aware that his undertaking such an assignment while holding supreme judicial office would be critized. Indeed, as a general proposition he himself believed that members of the Court should not undertake nonjudicial official assignments.[39] Nevertheless, within a few days Jackson accepted the designation, and his decision was so unclouded by doubt that he quite deliberately refrained from consulting Chief Justice Stone and other justices who, he knew, would have counselled refusal.[40] What governed his judgment?

In part, his reasons were negative. Generally speaking, the work of the Court during the war did not embrace such throbbing political and profound constitutional problems as had been its portion during the Thirties. The nation's absorption in the war effort made the quiet bench seem a backwater and Jackson, fresh from the tensions and pressures of executive responsibility, chafed audibly. Personal relations within the Court also left much to be desired. When Jackson took leave from the bench, he was by no means sure that it would be temporary.

Such factors surely made it easier for Jackson to follow his inclination and yield to the strong attraction of the proffered assignment. After all, he had spent the greater part of his professional life as an advocate, and the leadership of the prosecution in a great international trial was an alluring challenge. Far more important, however, was the opportunity to give substance to the ideal of 'international order under law' which he had first evoked at Havana. If ever the vision were to be turned into reality, the time was at hand. As he had told the international lawyers a few weeks earlier:

[W]e are at one of the infrequent moments in history when convulsions have uprooted habit and tradition in a large part of the world and there exists not only opportunity, but necessity as well, to reshape some institutions and practices which sheer inertia would otherwise make invulnerable. Because such occasions rarely come and quickly pass, our times are put under a heavy responsibility. It is not enough that we restore peace....

It seems to me that we now have an opportunity, not likely soon to recur, to bring international law out of the closet where President Wilson found it and impress it upon the consciousness of the people. At no time have the materials of persuasion been more

[37] According to Judge Rosenman's recollection, President Truman's attention had been called to Jackson's address, and it was a major factor in guiding the President's choice.

[38] According to the Justice's personal records, Judge Rosenman came to his chambers on Thursday, April 26, 1945. The exchange of letters and press release announcing the appointment were prepared by the two at the Justice's home the following Sunday, April 29.

[39] See Mason, *Extra-Judicial Work for Judges: The Views of Chief Justice Stone*, 67 HARV. L. REV. 193, 211 n.54 (1953).

[40] *Id.* at 209–10. Justice Jackson's personal records and subsequent statements to Justice Frankfurter indicate that, for this reason, he spoke to neither Chief Justice Stone nor Justice Frankfurter before accepting the appointment.

abundant or more compelling. I should not be greatly surprised if today the people are not actually less timid on the subject than those who should lead in this field.[41]

Given the chance to lead in pursuit of so high and vital a goal, Jackson grasped it, and embarked with what Justice Holmes called 'fire in the belly' upon what was for him, in every sense, a legal and moral crusade.

II

The first test of Jackson's dedication to the ideal was not long delayed. He took office as Representative of and Chief of Counsel for the United States on May 2, 1945,[42] and within ten days, without stirring foot beyond Washington, found himself embroiled in a sharp intra-governmental issue. Officials of the Treasury and other departments proposed to announce that members of Nazi organizations (including the SA and SS) to be charged with criminality at the coming international trial should immediately be allocated to penal labor repairing the Wehrmacht-ravaged areas of liberated Europe.

To Jackson, it was plain that any such step would impugn the integrity of the trial in precisely the respect he had condemned in his speech to the international lawyers. If the members of these organizations were to be tried, their guilt could not be taken for granted before the trial began. He objected immediately, firmly, and successfully; the Treasury proposal was abandoned.[43]

In the meantime, at the United Nations Conference in San Francisco, the British (abandoning their earlier opposition), French and Soviet representatives informally agreed in principle to the American proposals envisaging trial of the accused Axis leaders by an international tribunal and prosecution by a quadri-national committee of counsel.[44] On May 22, Jackson briefly visited Europe to open discussions with the other Allied governments and lay plans for the administrative and evidentiary conduct of the trial. Upon his return to Washington he submitted a public Report to the President in which, for the first time, Jackson outlined his conception of the task he had undertaken.[45] It was, as Walter Lippmann described it,[46] 'an historic state paper,' and it set the tone for the entire future course of events at Nuremberg.

[41] 39 Am. Soc'y Int'l L. Proc. 11, 13; 19 Temp. L.Q. 135, 136, 138 (1946).

[42] See note 2 *supra*. The order is reprinted in Int'l Conference 21.

[43] Justice Jackson's personal records contain his undated memorandum of May, 1945, and notes of the conference thereafter in which the proposal was considered and ultimately rejected. See also Harris, *op. cit. supra* note 1, at xxxii–xxxiii.

[44] See Int'l Conference 22.

[45] Report to the President, June 6, 1945, printed in *id.* at 42–54 and in Jackson, The Nuremberg Case 3–18 (1947).

[46] N.Y. Herald-Tribune, June 9, 1945, p. 13, col. 1; 19 Temp. L.Q. 157 (1946).

Already voices had been lifted in opposition to an international trial, whether as more than the Nazi leaders deserved or more than positive law warranted. But Jackson saw no other fit and worthy way to deal with these men:

To free them without a trial would mock the dead and make cynics of the living.... But undiscriminating executions or punishments without definite findings of guilt, fairly arrived at, would violate pledges repeatedly given, and would not sit easily on the American conscience or be remembered by our children with pride. The only other course is to determine the innocence or guilt of the accused after a hearing as dispassionate as the times and horrors we deal with will permit, and upon a record that will leave our reasons and motives clear.[47]

The record, indeed, was all-important:

... The groundwork of our case must be factually authentic and constitute a well-documented history of what we are convinced was a grand, concerted pattern to incite and commit the aggressions and barbarities which have shocked the world. We must not forget that when the Nazi plans were boldly proclaimed they were so extravagant that the world refused to take them seriously. Unless we write the record of this movement with clarity and precision, we cannot blame the future if in days of peace it finds incredible the accusatory generalities uttered during the war. We must establish incredible events by credible evidence.[48]

After outlining the major legal concepts, procedural and substantive, upon which the trial would be based, Jackson recurred to what for him remained, from the Havana speech of 1941 until his death, the dominant theme. For all 'men of good will and common sense ... the crime which comprehends all lesser crimes, is the crime of making unjustifiable war.' He was not disturbed by the lack of precedent: 'International law is not [presently] capable of development by legislation.... Innovations and revisions in International Law are brought about by the action of governments designed to meet a change in the circumstances. It grows, as did the Common-law, through decisions reached from time to time in adapting settled principles to new situations.'[49] Once again, Jackson's words breathed an almost desperate anxiety lest the 'rare moment' pass and the opportunity perish:

... In untroubled times, progress toward an effective rule of law in the international community is slow indeed. Inertia rests more heavily upon the society of nations than upon any other society. Now we stand at one of those rare moments when the thought and institutions and habits of the world have been shaken by the impact of world war on the lives of countless millions. Such occasions rarely come and quickly pass. We are put under a heavy responsibility to see that our behavior during this unsettled period will direct the world's thought toward a firmer enforcement of the laws of international conduct, so as to make war less attractive to those who have governments and the destinies of peoples in their power.[50]

---

[47] INT'L CONFERENCE 46.   [48] *Id.* at 48.
[49] *Id.* at 52.   [50] *Id.* at 53.

Formal discussions among the representatives of the four major Allied powers, looking toward a quadripartite agreement for the international trial, were opened in London on June 26, 1945.[51] They lasted for six wearing and contentious weeks. Jackson was lucid and impressive, but he was not the cosmopolitan sort and was often ill at ease with foreigners. Had he been a finished diplomat, the difficulties were formidable enough.

Not surprisingly, the Soviet preconceptions were extremely troublesome, though the personal demeanor of the Russian delegate, General I. T. Nikitchenko, was unexceptionable. At the very outset,[52] a problem by then already too familiar to Jackson was encountered: the Russians, like some of Jackson's compatriots, thought the Nazi leaders were already guilty. As Nikitchenko put it:

We are dealing here with the chief war criminals who have already been convicted and whose conviction has been already announced by both the Moscow and Crimea declarations by the heads of the governments.... The fact that the Nazi leaders are criminals has already been established. The task of the Tribunal is only to determine the measure of guilt of each particular person and mete out the necessary punishment—the sentences.[53]

To which Jackson replied that, in the American conception, the Moscow and Yalta declarations 'are an accusation and not a conviction.' He could not be a party 'to setting up a mere formal judicial body to ratify a political decision to convict.' The United States had decided against 'political executions,' and 'if we are going to have a trial, then it must be an actual trial.' It may be doubted that these observations worked much change in the Soviet attitude,[54] but the result of the deliberations—the London Agreement and Charter of August 8, 1945 constituting the International Military Tribunal—embodied Jackson's rather than Nikitchenko's conception.[55]

Even more disturbing to Jackson was Soviet insistence that the Charter describe the crime of aggressive war (in the final version denominated 'crimes against peace') in terms restricted to acts of the European Axis powers.[56] As late as July 25, Nikitchenko inquired whether it was proposed 'to condemn aggression or initiation of war in general or to condemn specifically aggressions started by the Nazis in this war,' and declared that if 'the attempt is to have a general

[51] Documents embodying the course of these talks comprise the bulk of *International Conference on Military Trials* (1949). See also Alderman, *Negotiating the Nuremberg Trial Agreements* in NEGOTIATING WITH THE RUSSIANS 49 (1951).

[52] See INT'L CONFERENCE 72.

[53] *Id.* at 104–05, 303; see *id.* at 107.

[54] Three weeks later Nikitchenko reiterated the same attitude. See *id.* at 303. Subsequently, sitting as the Soviet member of the International Military Tribunal, he dissented from all judgments of acquittal.

[55] The Agreement and Charter are printed in *id.* at 420–29 and in many other official publications. Arts. 4(c), 16, 24 and 26 plainly envisage acquittals, and the defendants Schacht, von Papen and Fritzsche were in fact acquitted.

[56] See *id.* at 42–54, 327, 373. The French representatives also manifested a tendency in this direction. See *id.* at 293.

definition, that would not be agreeable.'[57] Whether this was the reflection of bad conscience (Finland) or of a doctrinaire Communist distinction between 'imperialist' and 'peoples' wars, Nikitchenko was adamant until the final meeting, when he accepted[58] Jackson's objections and counter-proposal that the crimes be defined generally but the Tribunal's jurisdiction be limited to crimes 'of the European Axis':

If certain acts in violation of treaties are crimes, they are crimes whether the United States does them or whether Germany does them, and we are not prepared to lay down a rule of criminal conduct against others which we would not be willing to have invoked against us. Therefore, we think the clause 'carried out by the European Axis' so qualifies the statement that it deprives it of all standing and fairness as a juridical principle....

....I don't think we can define crimes to be such because of the particular parties who committed the acts, but for the purpose of meeting General Nikitchenko's suggestion that we are only supposed to deal with the Axis powers, we could in the opening paragraph state that this Tribunal has jurisdiction only over those who carried out these crimes on behalf of the Axis powers....[59]

Neither the Russians nor the French took kindly to declaring aggressive war *per se* a crime under international law. The latter were disturbed by *ex post facto* worries,[60] and Professor Gros pithily observed that 'the Americans want to win the trial on the ground that the Nazi war was illegal, and the French people and other people of the occupied countries just want to show that the Nazis were bandits.'[61] Jackson's fervent and intransigent reply carried back to events and problems four years earlier:

It is probably very difficult for those of you who have lived under the immediate attack of the Nazis to appreciate the different public psychology that those of us who are in the American Government dealt with. Our American population is at least 3,000 miles from the scene. Germany did not attack or invade the United States in violation of any treaty with us. The thing that led us to take sides in this war was that we regarded Germany's resort to war as illegal from its outset, as an illegitimate attack on the international peace and order. And throughout the efforts to extend aid to the peoples that were under attack, the justification was made by the Secretary of State, by the Secretary of War, Mr. Stimson, by myself as Attorney General, that this war was illegal from the outset and hence we were not doing an illegal thing in extending aid to peoples who were unjustly and unlawfully attacked. Now we believed, and the American people believed, just the doctrine that I have put into this definition.... I am not here to confess... error nor to confess that the United States was wrong in regarding this as an illegal war from the beginning and in believing that the great crime of crimes of our century was the launching of a needless war in Europe....

[57] *Id.* at 387; see *id.* at 392.
[58] See *id.* at 419.
[59] *Id.* at 330, 361.
[60] See *id.* at 295–97.
[61] *Id.* at 381–82.

... it may become necessary to abandon the effort to try these people on that basis, but there are some things worse for me than failing to reach an agreement, and one of them is reaching an agreement which would stultify the position which the United States has taken throughout. I can realize that our position may seem academic and theoretical to those who have been subject to more direct attack, but it was not too theoretical a basis for our help in action. I do not consider that I would be authorized to abandon the American position, and, if I were so authorized and it were left to my discretion, I would not be willing to do it.[62]

This was not the only occasion when Jackson's patience wore thin. On July 23, understandably irked by disagreements that were delaying preparations for the trial, he was 'very discouraged about the possibility of conducting an international trial' in view of the divergent national viewpoints, and warned the conferees that 'the United States might well withdraw from this matter and turn our prisoners over to the European powers to try, or else agree on separate trials, or something of that sort.' Three days later, after Nikitchenko had again rejected a general proscription of aggressive war,[63] Jackson interrupted the discussions by flying to the Potsdam conference to report to Secretary of State Byrnes.[64] It was an effective maneuver; the Potsdam Agreement, promulgated as Jackson returned to London, urged that 'the negotiations in London ... result in speedy agreement' and that 'the trial ... should begin at the earliest possible date.'[65]

Spurred by this admonition, the London conferees resolved their remaining differences at their next and last meeting,[66] and the London agreement 'for the Prosecution and Punishment of the Major War Criminals of the European Axis' was promulgated on August 8, 1945. It had been an arduous and at times painful experience for Jackson, who had little experience in or disposition for such quasi-diplomatic undertakings. So much the greater was his achievement in preserving the essential principles of the original American proposals in the Charter under which the trial was to be held.

When the indictment came to be drawn, the procedural differences between the common-law and continental systems were highlighted. The French and Russians, accustomed to intensive investigation and preparation of a full dossier of evidence in advance of the trial, thought that the indictment should embody the evidence to be submitted. The common-law method of submitting the evidence for the first time at the trial struck them as very unfair to the defense;[67] the French representatives, indeed, were openly 'shocked' at the notion of surprising the defendants with evidence of which they had not been apprised prior to the trial.

---

[62] *Id.* at 383–85; see *id.* at 126–27.
[63] See *id.* at 387, 392.
[64] See *id.* at 390.
[65] Quoted in HARRIS, *op. cit. supra* note 1, at 21–22.
[66] See INT'L CONFERENCE 390.
[67] See *id.* at 153–54, 270 and 319. See JACKSON, THE NURNBERG CASE vi (1947): 'It was something of a shock to me to hear the Russian delegation object to our Anglo-American practice as not fair to the defendant.'

Whatever the relative merits of the two systems under normal circumstances, rigid adherence to the continental practice was quite impossible under the prevailing conditions. Jackson, whose staff was already at work collecting the documentary evidence, was acutely aware of its enormous mass and scattered and disorganized state. Europe was a shambles, the whereabouts of many key witnesses was unknown, and new caches of stored or secreted documents were being uncovered almost daily. Obviously, fresh and highly pertinent evidence of war crimes was bound to be turned up throughout the trial and long thereafter.

On this matter Jackson's common sense prevailed and the indictment did not purport to recite the proof, which was to be introduced in the course of trial. So far as circumstances permitted, however, documentary evidence was made available to the defense in advance of its introduction.[68] The indictment itself emerged as a truly international document; the counts relating to aggressive war (drafted principally by Jackson's staff) are in a narrative style rather like an American anti-trust indictment, while those charging war crimes and persecutions (in which the French and Russians were principally interested) include many detailed recitals of particular atrocities.

Charters and indictments were by no means Jackson's only worries during these months. The American prosecution staff had to be recruited and organized; good relations had to be established and maintained with the American occupation forces in Europe and with other governmental agencies that would support the trial in various ways; a site for the trial had to be selected and adequately equipped; preparations for trial had to be commenced; the trial itself presented staggering physical, linguistic, and administrative problems; numerous and usually unexpected difficulties of the most diverse description were constantly precipitated by this extraordinary and far-flung inquest, pursued under unprecedented circumstances of physical devastation and emotional tension.

Many of these matters were no more congenial to Jackson than the conflicts encountered in framing the Charter. He was not a born administrator. He did not relish controversy with or among his subordinates, and tended to withdraw from administrative and executive difficulties. He delegated his authority extensively and sometimes mistakenly. The staff at Nuremberg was plagued with irritations and misunderstandings that a firmer administration might at least have mitigated, and some of Jackson's ablest assistants soon departed because of policy disagreements or because their tasks and responsibilities were not sufficiently defined.

For all these shortcomings, Jackson rarely overlooked a major policy problem, and he had a sure eye for the grand design of the enterprise. One such problem arose soon after the defendants and many other war crimes suspects had been brought to Nuremberg. Far from being immune to the internecine conflicts that

---

[68] That is, documents other than those reserved for use in cross-examination of the defendants and their witnesses.

beset most governments, the Third Reich was a hotbed of jealousies and murderous enmities. Several members of the prosecution staff proposed to exploit this situation by inducing some defendants, present or potential, to 'turn state's evidence.'

In routine law enforcement it is, of course, sometimes necessary for the district attorney to bargain with criminals in order, say, to smash a dope ring and convict the smugglers. But Jackson saw immediately that such a method was altogether out of place in a great international trial involving profound legal and moral issues. If the Tribunal's judgment was to give voice to the outraged conscience of humanity, that judgment must not be based on testimony extracted from criminals by promise of leniency or immunity.[69]

The launching of the Nuremberg trials was an incredibly complicated and difficult undertaking. It was accomplished with manifest imperfections, but with dignity and integrity. For this achievement Jackson, far more than any other individual, was responsible. As he himself, in a lighter vein, once described his burden:

This is the first case I have ever tried when I had first to persuade others that a court should be established, help negotiate its establishment, and when that was done, not only prepare my case but find myself a courtroom in which to try it.[70]

III

After several preliminary sessions, the trial before the International Military Tribunal began on November 20, 1945. By agreement among the four Chief Prosecutors, Jackson made (on the following day) the opening statement for the prosecution. Of his many talents, certainly his greatest was for the written word. What he wrote that month and spoke that day rang in men's minds like a great bell.

'I don't know what the war's about' sang the dough-boy in 1917, and was little the wiser twenty years later. The Second World War was easier to understand, after Manchuria, Ethiopia, Spain, and the long sequence of Axis conquests and Nazi atrocities. To this understanding, pervasive but for the most part inarticulate, Jackson gave eloquent and enduring expression:

The privilege of opening the first trial in history for crimes against the peace of the world imposes a grave responsibility. The wrongs which we seek to condemn and punish have been so calculated, so malignant and so devastating, that civilization cannot tolerate their being ignored because it cannot survive their being repeated. That four great nations,

---

[69] See Justice Jackson's own account of this episode in HARRIS, *op. cit. supra* note 1, at xxxvi; JACKSON, THE NURNBERG CASE ix (1947).

[70] Gordon Dean's preface to JACKSON, THE CASE AGAINST THE NAZI WAR CRIMINALS xiii (1946).

flushed with victory and stung with injury stay the hand of vengeance and voluntarily submit their captive enemies to the judgment of the law is one of the most significant tributes that Power ever has paid to Reason.

This... inquest represents the practical effort of four of the most mighty of nations, with the support of seventeen more, to utilize international law to meet the greatest menace of our times— aggressive war. The common sense of mankind demands that law shall not stop with the punishment of petty crimes by little people. It must also reach men who possess themselves of great power and make deliberate and concerted use of it to set in motion evils which leave no home in the world untouched....

In the prisoners' dock sit twenty-odd broken men. Reproached by the humiliation of those they have led almost as bitterly as by the desolation of those they have attacked, their personal capacity for evil is forever past.... Merely as individuals, their fate is of little consequence to the world.

What makes this inquest significant is that these prisoners represent sinister influences that will lurk in the world long after their bodies have returned to dust. [They are] living symbols of racial hatreds, of terrorism and violence, and of the arrogance and cruelty of power. They are symbols of fierce nationalisms and of militarism, of intrigue and warmaking which have embroiled Europe generation after generation, crushing its manhood, destroying its homes, and impoverishing its life. They have so identified themselves with the philosophies they conceived and with the forces they directed that any tenderness to them is a victory and an encouragement to all the evils which are attached to their names. Civilization can afford no compromise with the social forces which would gain renewed strength if we deal ambiguously or indecisively with the men in whom those forces now precariously survive.[71]

Victors were about to judge vanquished. There was no alternative: 'The worldwide scope of the aggressions carried out by these men has left but few real neutrals.' Therefore, the 'dramatic disparity between the circumstances of the accusers and of the accused' underlined the victors' responsibility for a 'fair and dispassionate' trial and judgment:

The former high station of these defendants, the notoriety of their acts, and the adaptability of their conduct to provoke retaliation make it hard to distinguish between the demand for a just and measured retribution, and the unthinking cry for vengeance which arises from the anguish of war. It is our task, so far as humanly possible, to draw the line between the two. We must never forget that the record on which we judge these defendants today is the record on which history will judge us tomorrow. To pass these defendants a poisoned chalice is to put it to our own lips as well. We must summon such detachment and intellectual integrity to our task that this trial will commend itself to posterity as fulfilling humanity's aspirations to do justice.[72]

---

[71] 2 International Military Tribunal, Trial of the Major War Criminals 98–99 (1947) (hereinafter cited as Trial of the Major War Criminals); Jackson's opening statement is also contained in *The Case Against the Nazi War Criminals, supra* note 70, at 3–91 (1946); Jackson, The Nurnberg Case 30–90 (1947); 1 Office of U.S. Chief of Counsel for Prosecution of Axis Criminality, Nazi Conspiracy and Aggression 114–73 (1946) (hereinafter cited as Nazi Conspiracy).

[72] 2 Trial of the Major War Criminals 101.

The defendants, therefore, would be dealt with justly and according to law:

These defendants may be hard pressed but they are not ill-used. . . . If these men are the first war leaders of a defeated nation to be prosecuted in the name of the law, they are also the first to be given a chance to plead for their lives in the name of the law. Realistically, the Charter of this Tribunal, which gives them a hearing, is also the source of their only hope. It may be that these men of troubled conscience, whose only wish is that the world forget them, do not regard a trial as a favor. But they do have a fair opportunity to defend themselves—a favor which these men, when in power, rarely extended to their fellow countrymen. Despite the fact that public opinion already condemns their acts, we agree that here they must be given a presumption of innocence, and we accept the burden of proving criminal acts and the responsibility of these defendants for their commission.[73]

As for the conquered nation, 'we have no purpose to incriminate the whole German people.'[74] Hitler had not achieved power by majority vote, but had seized it by means of 'an evil alliance' of revolutionists, reactionaries, and militarists.[75] Jackson traced the 'lawless road to power'[76] and its consequent repression of organized labor, harassment of the church and persecution of Jewry,[77] the terror that settled over Germany,[78] the long series of German aggressions and conquests,[79] and the havoc wrought in the occupied territories[80]—a concise and searing synthesis of the mountain of incriminating German documents that had already been brought to light.

In conclusion, Jackson faced the argument that the Charter, especially the concept of crimes against peace, was 'new law.' Such a challenge was not for these defendants to make:

I cannot, of course, deny that these men are surprised that this is the law; they really are surprised that there is any such thing as law. These defendants did not rely on law at all. . . . That men may be protected in relying upon law at the time they act is the reason we find laws of retrospective operation unjust. But these men cannot bring themselves within the reason of the rule which . . . prohibits *ex post facto* laws. They can not show that they ever relied upon international law in any state or paid it the slightest regard.[81]

Furthermore, since the first World War there had been numerous international treaties and declarations, more than enough to put the defendants on notice that civilized men and nations regard aggressive war as a crime.[82] But there were far more important reasons for holding the defendants to that standard. To be sure,

---

[73] 2 *id.* at 101–02.
[74] 2 *id.* at 102.
[75] 2 *id.* at 102–03.
[76] 2 *id.* at 105.
[77] See 2 *id.* at 106–27.
[78] See 2 *id.* at 127–31.
[79] See 2 *id.* at 131–36.
[80] See 2 *id.* at 136–42.
[81] 2 *id.* at 144.
[82] See 2 *id.* at 145–49.

judicial action could not ensure the future peace of the world; 'wars are started only on the theory and in the confidence that they can be won.'[83] Nevertheless,

...the ultimate step in avoiding periodic wars, which are inevitable in a system of international lawlessness, is to make statesmen responsible to law. And let me make clear that while this law is first applied against German aggressors, the law includes, and if it is to serve a useful purpose it must condemn aggression by any other nations, including those which sit here now in judgment. We are able to do away with domestic tyranny and violence and aggression by those in power against the rights of their own people only when we make all men answerable to the law. This trial represents mankind's desperate effort to apply the discipline of the law to statesmen who have used their powers of state to attack the foundations of the world's peace and to commit aggressions against the rights of their neighbors.[84]

Therefore,

The real complaining party at your bar is Civilization. In all our countries it is still a struggling and imperfect thing. It does not plead that the United States, or any other country, has been blameless of the conditions which made the German people easy victims to the blandishments and intimidations of the Nazi conspirators.

But it points to the dreadful sequence of aggressions and crimes I have recited, it points to the weariness of flesh, the exhaustion of resources, and the destruction of all that was beautiful or useful in so much of the world, and to greater potentialities for destruction in the days to come. It is not necessary among the ruins of this ancient and beautiful city with untold members of its civilian inhabitants still buried in its rubble, to argue the proposition that to start or wage an aggressive war has the moral qualities of the worst of crimes. The refuge of the defendants can be only their hope that international law will lag so far behind the moral sense of mankind that conduct which is crime in the moral sense must be regarded as innocent in law.

Civilization asks whether law is so laggard as to be utterly helpless to deal with crimes of this magnitude by criminals of this order of importance. It does not expect that you can make war impossible. It does expect that your juridical action will put the forces of international law, its precepts, its prohibitions and, most of all, its sanctions, on the side of peace, so that men and women of good will in all countries may have 'leave to live by no man's leave, underneath the law.'[85]

After this magnificent prologue, Jackson left the presentation of the prosecution's evidence to his staff and to counsel for the other three nations. His next major appearance before the Tribunal was in order to expound the theory and purpose of indicting the Nazi organizations—the SS, SA, Reich Cabinet, General Staff, and Party leadership.[86] It was a confusing subject, and Jackson acknowledged that no one had 'yet evolved any satisfactory technique for handling a great number of common charges against a great multitude of accused persons.'[87]

---

[83] 2 *id.* at 153.   [84] 2 *id.* at 154.   [85] 2 *id.* at 155.

[86] See 8 *id.* at 353–77, 438–55. Jackson's statement on the Nazi organizations is also printed in JACKSON, THE NURNBERG CASE 95–119 (1947).

[87] 8 TRIAL OF THE MAJOR WAR CRIMINALS 357.

Under the Charter, he declared, the purpose was to determine conclusively the criminality of the organization as a whole, so that subsequent prosecutions of individual members would not have to relitigate that basic issue, but only the culpability of the individual.[88] In its judgment, the Tribunal followed this general viewpoint,[89] but the declarations of organizational criminality never assumed the importance that originally attached to this matter.[90]

When the defendants and their witnesses took the stand, Jackson undertook the leading responsibility for cross-examining Goering,[91] Schacht, and Speer. His questioning of Goering was not an unqualified success.[92] Prison deprivation of the opportunity for self-indulgence had reawakened something of Goering's formidable mental powers; he was, naturally enough, better informed about the events under consideration than anyone else in the courtroom, and he testified with the brisk audacity of a man who had nothing to lose but his pride in a career that had run its course. Replying to questions about military and diplomatic matters, he scored off his interrogator repeatedly. Nevertheless, Jackson achieved the essential purpose of showing Goering in his true colors and drawing from the witness a picture of the Third Reich that abundantly supported the charges in the indictment.

With Schacht, the prosecution's problem was altogether different. The wily financier did not undertake to defend the Nazi regime, but to separate himself from it. On cross-examination,[93] Jackson underlined Schacht's retention of official position until 1943, and public appearances in support of Hitler as late as June, 1940. The sincerity of Schacht's professed opposition to the regime was heavily clouded, but the Tribunal was unable to find that his guilt had been established 'beyond a reasonable doubt,'[94] and he was acquitted.[95]

---

[88] See *ibid.*

[89] The Tribunal observed 'that criminal guilt is personal, and that mass punishments should be avoided,' and accordingly limited its findings of organizational criminality against the SS, Gestapo and SD, and Nazi Party leaders (the only accused organizations convicted) to those categories of members who knew of or participated in the organizations' criminal acts. 1 TRIAL OF THE MAJOR WAR CRIMINALS 255–57, 262, 268, 273.

[90] The deep involvement of these organizations, especially the SS, in the Nazi atrocities had aroused such repugnant horror in the course of the war that severe punishment of most members as criminals was widely anticipated. There was also some thought that guilty members might be used as penal labor to repair war damage. In the upshot, the Tribunal's declarations of organizational criminality were of some importance in the later de-Nazification proceedings, but otherwise of small significance. In retrospect, Jackson acknowledged that 'the procedure to declare organizations criminal was one of the most troublesome and least useful features of the Nurnberg Trial.' See Jackson, *Some Problems in Developing an International Legal System*, 22 TEMP. L.Q. 147, 149 (1948).

[91] As well as Goering's witnesses, to wit: Field Marshals Kesselring and Milch, General Bodenschatz, Colonel Bernd von Brauchitsch, and Paul Koerner.

[92] See 9 TRIAL OF THE MAJOR WAR CRIMINALS 417–56, 499–571; WEST, A TRAIN OF POWDER 17 (1955).

[93] See 12 *id.* at 562–602; 13 *id.* at 1–35.

[94] 1 *id.* at 310. Schacht had been indicted only upon the counts of the indictment relating to aggressive war.

[95] Among the American participants in the Nuremberg trials, opinion has remained divided on the issue of Schacht's guilt. Jackson was disappointed by his acquittal, and nine years later wrote:

With Speer, the most reflective and contrite of the defendants, Jackson's passage was not so much cross-examination as exploratory dialogue.[96] The witness made no effort to deny his responsibility, as Reich Minister for Armaments and Munitions, for the larger outlines of the Nazi forced labor program that uprooted millions of European workers and dragged them to German factories and mines and, all too often, to misery and death. He seemed genuinely interested in exploring the nature and consequences of totalitarianism, and Jackson gently drew him into a practical *critique* of dictatorship[97] and racism. Soon he was acknowledging that the Nazi anti-Semitic program had seriously interfered with German war production,[98] and that atomic research had been disastrously crippled 'because the finest experts we had . . . had emigrated to America'; driving dissenters out of Germany had proved 'a great disadvantage to us.'[99] By the end of the trial, Speer had arrived at a conception of its meaning that paralleled Jackson's own:

After this Trial, the German people will despise and condemn Hitler as the proven author of its misfortune. But the world will learn from these happenings not only to hate dictatorship as a form of government, but to fear it. . . .

Today the danger of being terrorized by technocracy threatens every country in the world. In modern dictatorship this appears to me inevitable. Therefore, the more technical the world becomes, the more necessary is the promotion of individual freedom and the individual's awareness of himself as a counterbalance. . . .

A new large-scale war will end with the destruction of human culture and civilization. Nothing can prevent unconfined engineering and science from completing the work of destroying human beings, which it has begun in so dreadful a way in this war.

Therefore this Trial must contribute towards preventing such degenerate wars in the future, and towards establishing rules whereby human beings can live together.[100]

In his closing summation, Jackson undertook to 'outline with bold strokes the vitals of this Trial's mad and melancholy record,'[101] observing that the 'future will never have to ask, with misgiving, what could the Nazis have said in their favor,' because 'whatever could be said, they were allowed to say.'[102] Now the time had come for final judgment, 'and if the case I present seems hard and uncompromising, it is because the evidence makes it so.'[103] Hard it was, as Jackson fitted it to the dock: Goering ('half militarist and half gangster' who 'stuck his pudgy finger

---

'We decided it would be better to lose our case against some defendants than to win by a deal that would discredit the judgment. We did lose our case against Schacht, against whom testimony might have been obtained by concession; but still I think we made the better choice.' See HARRIS, *op. cit. supra* note 1, at xxxvi.

[96] See 16 TRIAL OF THE MAJOR WAR CRIMINALS 514–63.
[97] See *id.* at 533.
[98] See *id.* at 520.
[99] *Id.* at 529.
[100] 22 *id.* at 405–7.
[101] 19 *id.* at 397–432.
[102] *Id.* at 399.
[103] *Id.* at 400.

in every pie'); Ribbentrop ('salesman of deception, who was detailed to pour wine on the troubled waters of suspicion by preaching the gospel of limited and peaceful intentions'); Keitel ('weak and willing tool'); Kaltenbrunner ('the grand inquisitor'); Rosenberg ('intellectual high priest of the "master race,"' whose 'woolly philosophy added boredom to the long list of Nazi atrocities'); Streicher ('the venomous vulgarian'); and Sauckel ('the greatest and cruelest slaver since the Pharaohs of Egypt').[104] Especially blameworthy were the more 'respectable' and educated defendants—Schacht, von Neurath, Speer, von Papen, Raeder, Doenitz, Keitel, and Jodl:

It is doubtful whether the Nazi master plan could have succeeded without their special-ized intelligence which they so willingly put at its command.... Their superiority to the average run of Nazi mediocrity is not their excuse. It is their condemnation.[105]

And what was their defense? Crimes there were, but they were the crimes of other men—Hitler, Himmler, Heydrich, Goebbels, and Bormann—all dead: 'It is a temptation to ponder the wondrous workings of a fate which has left only the guilty dead and only the innocent alive.'[106] But the defense that 'the world is enti-tled to retribution only from cadavers' was ghoulish and mendacious:

It is against such a background that these defendants now ask this Tribunal to say that they are not guilty of planning, executing, or conspiring to commit this long list of crimes and wrongs. They stand before the record of this Trial as blood-stained Gloucester stood by the body of his slain King. He begged of the widow, as they beg of you: 'Say I slew them not.' And the Queen replied, 'Then say they were not slain. But dead they are....' If you were to say of these men that they are not guilty, it would be as true to say that there has been no war, there are no slain, there has been no crime.[107]

IV

The Tribunal pronounced judgment on October 1, 1946, just short of a year after it had first convened in Berlin to receive the indictment,[108] and after 216 days of actual trial. If the opinion was marred here and there by internal inconsistencies—hardly surprising in view of the Tribunal's multinational composition and the scope and gravity of the issues—it was undeniably an able document and its tone, like that of the courtroom proceedings, was dispassion-ate and dignified.[109] Twelve of the defendants were sentenced to death and seven

---

[104] *Id.* at 415–17.
[105] *Id.* at 417–18.
[106] *Id.* at 429.
[107] *Id.* at 432.
[108] The minutes of the Tribunal's opening session of October 18, 1945, in Berlin are printed in 1 *id.* at 24–26.
[109] See *id.* at 171–341.

to imprisonment for terms from ten years to life; three (Schacht, von Papen, and Fritzsche) were acquitted.[110] A week later Jackson submitted his final report and resignation to President Truman, and shortly thereafter resumed his place on the Supreme Court. As major accomplishments, he pointed to the recognition of aggressive war as a crime under international law, the development of judicial procedures for multinational use, and the historical documentation of the development of totalitarian dictatorship in the Nazi era.

The Tribunal's judgment and Jackson's report alike were widely acclaimed at the time. In December, 1946, the General Assembly of the United Nations affirmed 'the principles of international law recognised by the Charter of the Nuremberg Tribunal and the Judgment of the Tribunal,' and declared that the codification of those principles was 'a matter of primary importance.'[111] And yet today, eight years later, efforts to achieve such a codification are at an impasse, and it is common report at the United Nations that the United States—of all countries the most responsible for and most deeply committed to the Nuremberg principles—is no longer favorably disposed to their development and perpetuation.[112] Far from fading away with the passage of time, controversy has continued to surround the trials and has even sharpened in recent years. Why?

Paradoxically, it was the very intensity of feeling against the Nazi leaders that first aroused serious objection to trying them. They appeared so hideously culpable that their execution was regarded as a foregone conclusion, and to try them under such circumstances would be farcical.[113] In syllogistic form: Hitler and his gang must be executed, for their innocence is unthinkable; a trial with a predetermined outcome would be a travesty of the judicial process; therefore they should be executed without trial by virtue of a 'political decision.'

This notion of 'political' execution as a means of disposing of Hitler and his cohorts arose at the April, 1945, meeting of the American Society of International Law, immediately after Jackson finished his speech to that body.[114] During the ensuing discussion, several members spoke in favor of the 'political way,' and Vice President Finch declared bluntly that no court would acquit Hitler, and consequently any trial 'would simply be a farce and ridiculous.'[115]

---

[110] See *id.* at 365–66. The Soviet member (General Nikitchenko) dissented from the acquittals and the sentencing of Rudolf Hess to a life term instead of death. See *id.* at 342–64.

[111] By resolution of December 11, 1946. See HISTORY OF THE UNITED NATIONS WAR CRIMES COMMISSION 187, 211–12, 259–60 (1948).

[112] See Norman Cousins' editorial, *Are We Men or Murderers*, Sat. Rev. of Lit., Feb. 19, 1955, p. 22.

[113] This is the basic reasoning of the United Kingdom *aide-memoire* of April 23, 1945, opposing a trial, while assuming 'that it is beyond question that Hitler and a number of arch-criminals associated with him…must…suffer the penalty of death for their conduct....' See INT'L CONFERENCE 18–20.

[114] See text at note 34 *supra*.

[115] See 39 AM. SOC'Y INT'L L. PROC. 72–76 (1945), containing the remarks of Messrs. Finch, Coudert, and Dennis.

At various times the same point of view was espoused by such a varied assortment of advocates as Josef Stalin, Cordell Hull, Professor Hans Morgenthau, *The Nation*, and Chief Justice Stone.[116] Its most considered expression is to be found in an article published during the course of the trial by Judge Charles E. Wyzanski:[117] 'No one anticipates that the defense...will be given as long a time to present its evidence as the prosecution takes,' he wrote, adding that there would be no presumption of innocence, as 'The basic approach is that these men should not have a chance to go free.' Much better would be an 'executive determination' which by its 'naked and unassumed character...confesses itself to be not legal justice but political.' Whereas Nuremberg, by purporting to be a trial, presented a 'deceptive appearance, big with evil consequences for law everywhere....'

But Jackson was determined that the trial should not be a parody.[118] 'To pass these defendants a poisoned chalice is to put it to our own lips as well,' he had said in opening the case, and the proceedings remained suffused with that spirit. The defense was given much more time than the prosecution; the presumption of innocence was respected; the defendants were given every opportunity to show that they deserved to go free, and three of them succeeded. Chief Justice Stone did not survive to reconsider his privately-expressed denunciations of Nuremberg[119] in the light of actuality. Judge Wyzanski, upon further inquiry, retracted his earlier criticism; Nuremberg was no farce but a real trial, and the world had 'every reason to be profoundly grateful to Mr. Justice Jackson.'[120]

But for every one who, like Judge Wyzanski, is painstaking enough to learn the truth and large-minded enough to confess error, there are more who, having made up their minds, prefer not to be confused by the facts. Indeed, Nuremberg sometimes seems to have a traumatic effect on some of even the most powerful minds. Winston Churchill, as we have seen, opposed a trial and favored the 'political' solution when Judge Rosenman approached him on the matter in April, 1945.[121] A month later, however, on being shown a photograph of Mussolini and Clara Petacci strung up by their heels in Milan, Churchill was 'profoundly shocked' and wrote to Field Marshal Alexander:

The man who murdered Mussolini made a confession...gloating over the treacherous and cowardly method of his action. In particular he said he shot Mussolini's mistress. Was she on the list of war criminals? Had he any authority from anybody to shoot this woman? It seems to me the cleansing hand of British military power should make inquiries on these points.[122]

---

[116] See HARRIS, *op. cit. supra* note 1, at xxxii–xxxiv; Mason, *supra* note 39, at 209–14.

[117] See Wyzanski, *Nuremberg—A Fair Trial? Dangerous Precedent*, Atlantic Monthly, April 1946, p. 66.

[118] See text at notes 43, 53–55, 72, and 73 *supra*.

[119] See Mason, *supra* note 39, at 209–11; Solow, *The Integrity of the Supreme Court*, Fortune, Feb. 1954, p. 101. Chief Justice Stone died on April 22, 1946.

[120] Wyzanski, *Nuremberg in Retrospect*, Atlantic Monthly, Dec. 1946, p. 56.

[121] See text at note 32 *supra*.

[122] CHURCHILL, THE SECOND WORLD WAR: TRIUMPH AND TRAGEDY 528–29 (1953).

Recalling these events in 1953, Sir Winston commented, with magnificent inconsistency, 'at least the world was spared an Italian Nuremberg.'[123] But it is precisely because there *was* a Nuremberg (and other war crimes authorities and proceedings) that the Milan scene which so shocked Churchill was not repeated many fold all over Germany, Austria, and Italy. As Justice Jackson trenchantly observed in his last word on the point:

What we should have done with these men is a question always evaded by those who find fault with what we did do.... To have turned the men over to the anti-Nazi factions in Germany would have been a doubtful benevolence. Even a year and a half later, when Schacht, von Papen, and Fritzsche were acquitted by the Tribunal, they begged to remain within the protection of the American jail lest they be mobbed by the angry and disillusioned elements of the German population. They knew the fate of Mussolini.[124]

As for execution of the Nazi leaders by political decision, that proposal was defective for the very practical reasons embodied in the single word 'who.' Chief Justice Stone, for example, had spoken of punishing them as 'a bad lot,' but—

When did it become a crime to be one of a 'bad lot?'... what individuals were included in the bad lot?... If it would have been right to punish the vanquished out-of-hand for being a bad lot, what made it wrong to have first a safeguarded hearing to make sure who was bad, and how bad, and of what his badness consisted?[125]

Hitler's liquidation of Ernst Roehm and a few hundred others during the bloody 'Night of the Long Knives' in June, 1934, might aptly be described as a 'political' or 'executive' disposition of a vexing question. Neither the morality nor the legality of this purge was widely acclaimed. In domestic law such affairs, like lynchings or Soviet mock trials, are simply a species of murder, because the law prescribes a way by which guilt is determined and punishment measured out, and not even the Chief of State can take the law into his own hands; it is not his law to take.

---

[123] *Id.* at 529. The comment is not only extraordinary for the reason given in the text, but is also inconsistent with Churchill's admission to Rosenman in 1947 that President Roosevelt 'was right' in insisting on a trial and 'I was wrong.' See ROSENMAN, WORKING WITH ROOSEVELT 545 (1952).

[124] HARRIS, *op. cit. supra* note 1, at xxxi–xxxii.

[125] *Id.* at xxxiii–xxxiv; see Jackson, *Justice Jackson Weighs Nuremberg's Lessons*, N.Y. Times, June 16, 1946, Magazine, p. 12.

In a critical book review of Mr. Harris' work, Mr. Morton Kaplan favors 'political killings... after proper identification of the culprits.' See *The Unanswered Question of Nuremberg*, The New Leader, Nov. 1, 1954, p. 25 at 26. Unhappily for his thesis, in modern legal systems there is no way to identify a 'culprit' other than by trial and conviction on charges. Mr. Kaplan's further comment that political executions would have been 'within our legal rights,' in a review intended to show that our great mistake was to invoke law at all, indicates how deep the confusion of thought on this subject can be. Nobody else has ever suggested that there is a *legal* right to liquidate the vanquished summarily, whether they are nefarious or estimable; the argument (analyzed in the text) is rather that law does not cover the relations between victor and vanquished nations, and therefore the victor can prescribe the vanquished's fate, for in the absence of law might is the only remaining standard of conduct.

If a contrary conclusion is to be reached after a war between nations, it can only be on the theory that there is no applicable law whatsoever—that a condition of *lawlessness* prevails as between victor and vanquished. Advocates of 'political' execution of the Nazi leaders often cite Napoleon's extra-judicial sequestration at St. Helena as a precedent.[126] It is not a very good one,[127] but that is of small importance. From the sack of Troy down through the Old Testament and Roman and medieval times there is no lack of precedent for putting the vanquished to the sword, slavery, or durance vile. Had the Allies put Goering, Hess, and Schacht to death as a 'bad lot,' there surely would have been ample precedent over many centuries, but that would not have made it any less lawless.[128] After trial, the Tribunal judged that, on the charges and the evidence, Hess' life should be spared and Schacht acquitted. Was not such a procedure more lawful than summary political execution? I do not believe the Justice's spirit will be much troubled by doubts on this score.

At the very time that their countries lay prostrate under the German boot, there were no such doubts among the representatives of the European nations that suffered most at the hands of the Nazis. The St. James Declaration of 1942 warned against 'acts of vengeance on the part of the general public'—just such acts as the Mussolini-Petacci killings—and called for retribution 'through the channels of organised justice.'[129] The entire subsequent course of war crimes planning in both London and the United States envisaged trials to determine individual

---

[126] See, *e.g.*, Justice Douglas, concurring, in Hirota v. MacArthur, 338 U.S. 197, 209 (1949); see Wyzanski, *supra* note 117, at 70.

[127] Napoleon went on board the British ship Bellerophon on July 15, 1815, asking the Prince Regent for protection against 'the factions which distract my country' and 'the enmity of the greatest powers of Europe.' He had by no means lost all support in France and the British, fearing another 'return from Elba,' took him to St. Helena. No theory of punishment seems to have prompted this step, but only the removal from the European scene of a potentially disruptive influence. See, *e.g.*, Ropes, The First Napoleon 295 (12th ed. 1895). Interestingly enough, however, the German General von Gneisenau (Bluecher's chief of staff and one of the great names in German military history) considered trying Napoleon before an international court. See Goerlitz, History of the German General Staff 46 (1953).

[128] Judge Wyzanski in his original criticism of Nuremberg frankly acknowledged the extralegal character of political execution: 'To be sure, such an executive determination is *ex post facto*. Indeed, it is a bill of attainder.... But its very merit is its naked and unassumed character. It confesses itself to be not legal justice but political.' Wyzanski, *supra* note 117, at 70. And in the discussions of the American Society of International Law, Mr. Dennis, supporting political execution, quoted Attorney General Knox's remark to President Theodore Roosevelt on the Canal Zone episode. 'Mr. President I think it would be better not to have any taint of legality about this matter.' 39 Am. Soc'y Int'l L. Proc. 76 (1945). Mr. Churchill in his letter to Field Marshal Alexander described the political execution of Mussolini as murder. See text at note 122 *supra*. It is also noteworthy that the protagonists of political execution of Hitler *et al.* often fall into the language of law in justifying the idea. Mr. Coudert, of the American Society of International Law, referred to 'crimes against the human race,' 'atrocities against all the laws that are common to mankind' and 'the men who committed those hideous crimes.' *Id.* at 74–76. Yet he boggled at the idea of a trial to determine who was guilty of these crimes.

[129] See note 23 *supra*.

guilt or innocence.[130] When the American Army entered Germany, General Eisenhower's first proclamation as Military Governor ordered that: 'Military and Party leaders, the Gestapo, and others suspected of crimes and atrocities will be tried and, if guilty, punished as they deserve.'[131]

Indeed, the idea of executing the Nazi leaders out of hand, as Octavian and Mark Antony pricked a list after the defeat of Brutus, was not seriously proposed until nearly the end of the war. Its acceptance then by many who should have known better must be accounted an aberration born of the flush of victory and the release of long-pent indignation.[132] Its survival even today as a basis for criticism of the war crimes trials[133] reflects chiefly, I believe, misunderstandings generated by the cold war which are even more closely related to another aspect of Nuremberg that Jackson regarded as fundamental—the condemnation of aggressive war as a crime against international law.

Put forth by lawyers such as Stimson, Jackson, McCloy, Chanler and Bernays, it was likewise among lawyers, in the first instance, that this concept aroused articulate opposition,[134] for reasons we have already touched upon.[135] Whether the laying of this charge against the Nazi leaders violated the principle against *ex post facto* law is, at bottom, a question of jurisprudence. As Dean Pound has put it, '... the analytical jurist thinks of an authoritative precept as established and enforced by some agency of politically organized society' and 'conceives that the sanction of law is enforcement by the judicial and administrative organs of the state and that nothing which lacks that direct and immediate backing of organized force is law.'[136] This is a legal philosophy especially congenial in a constitutional republic embodying a separation of legislative, executive, and judicial powers. It was certainly the dominant legal philosophy in our universities at

[130] *Ibid.* Even Churchill's acknowledgment of the St. James Declaration stated that the accused would 'have to stand up before tribunals,' and the Lord Chancellor (Simon), speaking in the House of Lords in 1943, warned against forgetting 'that war criminals shall be dealt with because they are proved to be criminals.' 2 WAR AND PEACE AIMS OF THE UNITED NATIONS 449–50 (Holborn ed. 1948).

[131] This Proclamation was read, immediately after Jackson's address to the American Society of International Law, by the next speaker, the Hon. Julius Holmes, Assistant Secretary of State. See 39 AM. SOC'Y INT'L L. PROC. 26–27 (1945). Mr. Holmes then remarked 'yesterday this was posted on the walls in Nuremberg...,' a comment more remarkable for its accidental prevision than its accuracy, inasmuch as the Army (XV Corps) did not reach Nuremberg until three or four days later. See EISENHOWER, CRUSADE IN EUROPE 412 (1948), and the official communiques for April 13–17, 1945.

[132] I well remember returning to the United States from Europe late in 1944 and again in May, 1945, and finding myself labelled 'soft' and 'unsound' on the peace because I observed that some of the German troops had behaved correctly in occupied France, and argued against the summary execution of all members of the SS.

[133] See, *e.g.*, Kaplan, *supra* note 125.

[134] The reactions of Chief Justice Stone, as described in Mason, *supra* note 39 at 211–12, and Judge Wyzanski, *supra* note 117, are typical.

[135] See text at notes 15 and 60 *supra*.

[136] POUND, LAW AND MORALS 22, 23 (1926).

the turn of the century,[137] and it still commands wide adherence, both here and in Europe.

Dyed-in-the-wool positivists instinctively balked at Nuremberg, for reasons that are easy to apprehend. Even the Hague and Geneva Conventions, which, among the principles invoked at the war crimes trials, most closely resemble statutory or codified law, prescribe no specific penalties for their violation. Much less did the Kellogg-Briand pact and other post-World War I treaties and international declarations against war resemble 'law' of the kind with which American judges and professors are familiar. Indeed how could they be similar, when there was no international legislature or court of criminal jurisdiction? But it was for precisely this reason, as Jackson pointed out in his Havana speech, that a slavish positivism would emasculate international law:

In the evolution of law we advance more rapidly with our concepts of substantive rights than with our machinery for their determination. Rough justice is done by communities long before they are able to set up formal governments. And where there is a legal obligation not to resort to armed force it can be effectuated as legal obligations have always been effectuated on the frontiers of civilization before courts and machinery of enforcement became established... we may not stymie international law and allow these great treaties to become dead letters.[138]

International law, in short, must grow as did the common law in the days of its rude origins, before there were statutes, judicial opinions, and legal definitions. It is a theme to which he often recurred,[139] as in his opening statement before the International Military Tribunal:

International law is not capable of development by the normal processes of legislation, for there is no continuing international legislative authority.... It grows, as did the common law, through decisions reached from time to time in adapting settled principles to new situations.[140]

---

[137] See *id.* at 2; CARDOZO, THE GROWTH OF THE LAW 34, 35 (1924).

[138] 35 AM. J. INT'L L. 348, 355–56 (1941).

[139] In his speech to the American Bar Association in October, 1941, *supra* note 14, at p. 683 Jackson referred to the 'history of our experience with the slow but solid evolution of domestic law,' and quoted Sir Frederick Pollock, *English Law Before the Norman Conquest*, in I SELECT ESSAYS IN ANGLO-AMERICAN LEGAL HISTORY 95 (1907):

But this reign of law did not come by nature; it has been slowly and laboriously won. Jurisdiction began, it seems, with being merely voluntary, derived not from the authority of the State but from the consent of the parties. People might come to the court for a decision if they agreed to do so. They were bound in honour to accept the result; they might forfeit pledges deposited with the court; but the court could not compel their obedience any more than a tribunal of arbitration appointed at this day under a treaty between sovereign States can compel the rulers of those States to fulfil its award. Anglo-Saxon courts had got beyond this most early state, but not very far beyond it.

[140] 2 TRIAL OF THE MAJOR WAR CRIMINALS 147. In its judgment, the Tribunal followed the same reasoning: 'it must be remembered that international law is not the product of an international legislature.... The law of war is to be found not only in treaties, but in the customs and practices of states... and from the general principles of justice applied by jurists and practised by military courts. This law is not static, but by continual adaptation follows the needs of a changing world.' 1 *id.* at 221.

International jurisprudence must, therefore, by its very nature lie closer to the historical than the analytical school, and international law is generally customary rather than positive.[141] This viewpoint is in tune both with that of the libertarian, utilitarian and often free-thinking Founding Fathers[142] and that of Roman Catholic theological jurisprudence.[143] The theory and practice of the international law of war abundantly manifest its customary basis,[144] as was fully recognized by Chief Justice Stone when he was confronted with the responsibility of decision justifying men's execution,[145] rather than privately venting his understandable annoyance at Jackson's long absence from the Court.[146] Justice Cardozo, in a case wherein property rather than life was at stake, described 'the capacity of the law to develop and apply a formula consonant with justice and with the political and social needs of the international legal system,' and observed that

International law, or the law that governs between states, has at times, like the common law within states, a twilight existence during which it is hardly distinguishable from morality or justice, till at length the *imprimatur* of a court attests its jural quality.... 'The gradual consolidation of opinions and habits'... has been doing its quiet work.[147]

To be sure, much of this is anathema to the positivist disciples of Austin and Gray, and their refusal to recognize aggressive war as a crime is understandable in

[141] *Cf.* POUND, LAW AND MORALS 26 (1924).

[142] See, *e.g.*, a lecture delivered in 1790–91 by James Wilson, a Justice of the Supreme Court and one of the framers of the Constitution, on 'the universal moral principles of which positive laws are but declaratory,' quoted in Pound, *op. cit. supra* note 141, at 1–2. In a later lecture, Justice Wilson declared that the purpose of law is 'that justice may be done and war may be prevented,' and inquired: 'Are states too wise or too proud to receive a lesson from individuals? Is the idea of a common judge between nations less admissible than that of a common judge between men?' See I THE WORKS OF JAMES WILSON 338–39 (Andrews ed. 1896).

[143] See EPPSTEIN, THE CATHOLIC TRADITION OF THE LAW OF NATIONS (London 1935) *passim*, and especially Chapter X (pp. 247–275), entitled The Natural Society of Nations, and the quotation at 262 from Suarez, *De Legibus ac de Deo Legislatore*, Lib. II, Cap. XIX, ¶ 6: 'The Precepts of the Law of Nations differ in this from those of civil law, that they are not in writing, but in customs not of any one city or province, but of all or almost all nations. For human law is twofold, written and unwritten.... But unwritten law is deduced from customs:... if it is introduced by the customs of all nations and binds all, we believe this to be the Law of Nations properly speaking,' citing Justinian, Isidore, and St. Thomas. In his Foreword, Robert Wilberforce describes 'the Church's unbroken tradition of international justice running through the ages.' *Id.* at xiv.

[144] Thus the eighth paragraph of the Preamble to the Hague Conventions of 1907 speaks of 'the principles of the law of nations, derived from the usages established among civilized peoples...' See also the interesting account of the international war crimes trial at Breisach in 1474, in Schwarzenberger, *A Forerunner of Nuremberg*, The Manchester Guardian, 28 Sept., 1946.

[145] See *Ex parte* Quirin, 317 U.S. 1 (1942), in which Stone, upholding the trial of the Nazi saboteurs by a Military Commission, refers (at p. 30) to 'the system of common law applied by military tribunals' and declares (at p. 34) that the written Rules of Land Warfare are partial and only 'illustrative of the applicable principles of the common law of war.' See also *In re* Yamashita, 327 U.S. 1 (1946); Mason, *supra* note 39, at 213–14.

[146] See *id.* at 209–14.

[147] *See* New Jersey v. Delaware, 291 U.S. 352, 383–84 (1934). *See* also *Paquete Habana*, 175 U.S. 677, 700, 708 (1900); *The Antelope*, 23 U.S. (10 Wheat.) 66, 120–22 (1825); United States v. Smith, 18 U.S. (5 Wheat.) 153, 160–61 (1820); United States v. White, 27 Fed. 200, 201–03 (C.C.E.D. Mo. 1888).

the light of their conception of 'law.' Less defensible, however, are the strictures of those who, whether from malice or misinformation, spread the utterly erroneous impression that the aggressive war charge was the entire basis of the Nuremberg trials, and that the defendants therefore went to the gallows or to prison for conduct that was not in fact criminal.[148] Of the 209 defendants indicted in the thirteen Nuremberg trials, two—Schacht and von Papen—were charged only with the crime of aggressive war, and both were acquitted. Of the 161 defendants convicted, exactly one—Rudolf Hess—was found guilty on the aggressive war counts alone; all the others were convicted of complicity in murders, atrocities, and violations of the rules of warfare. The impact of the aggressive war condemnation on the Nuremberg defendants, therefore, was almost entirely *in principium* rather than *in poenam*.

Indeed, the *ex post facto* issue raised by the aggressive war charge, like the relative merits of trial and political execution, would probably have remained chiefly a lawyers' debate—grave and important as are the implications—had the world settled back from the war into an era of peace and good feeling. Instead, the cold war has kept these issues alive and hotly controversial, though it can hardly be said to have clarified them in the public mind. Thus it has come about that Nuremberg is now attacked as Communist-inspired,[149] even though it was precisely Jackson's insistence on a *bona fide* trial rather than a political determination, and on a general condemnation of aggressive war no matter by whom committed, that led to his sharpest differences with the Soviet representative at the London conference.[150]

In aftermath, it is the bare fact of Soviet participation in the London Charter and the first trial that has most damaged Nuremberg in American eyes. Put to the test in terms of Jackson's discharge of his responsibilities, this criticism rests on the contention that he should have insisted on Russia's exclusion from the international proceeding. The impossibility and irresponsibility of such a course of action in 1945 needs no elaboration.

---

[148] Douglas, An Almanac of Liberty 96 (1954) states 'Hitler and his colleagues were guilty of murder over and again and deserved the death penalty under the common law of those crimes.... But they were not tried for murder.... The defendants were tried for the crime of waging an aggressive war.' With all respect to the distinguished author and to the general utility of almanacs, they are a sadly inadequate vehicle for the rendition of measured judgments on profound legal and moral issues. See also Kaplan, *supra* note 123: 'In fact, the Nazis were not tried at Nuremberg for their most horrendous activity, the attempt to exterminate the Jews, except to the extent that it was connected with Hitler's war effort.' As indicated in the text, the statements that the Nuremberg defendants (other than von Papen and Schacht) were not tried for murders and other atrocities (including extermination of the Jews, and quite independent of the aggressive war charge) are wholly wrong.

[149] See, *e.g.*, Utley, The High Cost of Vengeance 169 (1949); Veale, Advance to Barbarism 141 (1953): 'At Nurnberg, the proceedings were outwardly European, but throughout the driving force behind them was Russian.' We have noted (see text at notes 52–64 *supra*) how far this charge is wide of the mark; see also the review of Veale by Drexel A. Sprecher in 14 La. L. Rev. 447, 460–61 (1954).

[150] See text at notes 52–64 *supra*.

Russian participation did not, to be sure, conform to the domestic judicial standards of a highly-developed political democracy such as our own. But insistence upon the observance of such standards in the constitution of a court of the international community is utterly unrealistic.[151] In terms of jurisdiction and participation (as distinguished from procedure, wherein modern standards may more readily be transplanted from domestic to international usage), the international community is not far beyond the time of the Norman Conquest when 'the great struggle was really to replace primitive methods of self-help by individuals one against the other' and 'to enforce obedience to any law' whatsoever. Those days knew no professional judges above and aloof from crimes and quarrels. The 'law'—consisting principally of 'old customary rules' evolved for 'the prevention of bloodshed by the recognition of certain elementary rights of property and personal freedom and the substitution of compensation for the prosecution of a blood feud'—was administered by the manorial lords, bishops and ealdormen.[152] Often these were men with black and bloody records, and many a defendant might have challenged his judges for guilt of far worse crimes than those of which he stood accused.

And yet, as Jackson succinctly put it, men 'did not await the perfect court before stopping men from settling their differences with brass knuckles.'[153] We may well be thankful that they did not, for in the growth of law lay mankind's hope of advancing civilization, and it lies there still. Crude and violent as were the judges and governors of past centuries, continued practical application of the law constantly refined the judicial process as men became ever more deeply committed to its use to resolve their disputes and keep the peace.

Russian participation at Nuremberg has committed the Soviet government to the legal propositions that national leaders who unleash their country's military forces to wage aggressive war are criminals; that they are also criminals if they use their official power for extermination, enslavement, or other atrocious ends; that sanctions for these crimes may be judicially imposed if the accused has had fair opportunity to defend himself at a trial.[154] Sadly true it is that many of these

---

[151] If Russian participation at Nuremberg had resulted, or had seriously threatened to result, in unjust and vengeful judgments and punishments, the objections that have since been raised to their presence would be disturbing, despite the considerations set forth above. In fact, however, there were no such unhappy consequences. At the first Nuremberg trial, the Soviet judge voted to convict all the defendants, but his views did not prevail with his colleagues. Nor were the trial procedures adversely affected by Soviet participation, thanks to the wisdom and firmness of the other judges and the skill of Lord Lawrence in presiding. After the first trial, there was no further Soviet participation in the Nuremberg proceedings.

[152] POTTER, AN HISTORICAL INTRODUCTION TO ENGLISH LAW AND ITS INSTITUTIONS 6–15 (2d ed. 1943).

[153] See text at note 16 *supra*.

[154] Nevertheless, critics of Nuremberg persist in declaring that it has established 'a dangerous precedent under which our victorious enemy could put us on trial.' As we have seen, prior to Nuremberg there was abundant precedent for the lawless execution of a defeated nation's leaders without any trial at all. See text at note 129. The precedent of Nuremberg is that punishment of

crimes still go unpunished. But the Soviet Union has joined with other governments in acknowledging this to be the law, and it was Jackson's wise intransigence at London that forced the Russians to that acknowledgment.

Nevertheless in the world of today, dominated as it is by the cold war, logic is not all that matters, and there can be no gainsaying the psychological inroads on Nuremberg's reputation that have resulted from Soviet participation.[155] The same is true of the circumstance that the International Military Tribunal was entirely composed of representatives of the victorious powers; the lack of any feasible alternative[156] has not assuaged the discomfort and repugnance with which many have viewed a 'trial of the vanquished by the victors.'[157]

The lesson of these things should not be forgotten in the future development and application of international penal law. But whether these defects are real or fancied, Nuremberg is not to be judged exclusively in terms of its shortcomings, nor are defensive words apt for Jackson's epitaph.

---

vanquished national leaders depends upon criminal guilt determined at a trial. As Jackson once stated in answer to this question:

If the United States should lose a war to any potential enemy that is now in sight, it is not likely that they would even wait to give most of us a trial. American military men might be begging for the privilege of defending themselves in the same way that the German officers were allowed to defend themselves. This is not the first time that losers of a war have been put to death or imprisoned for long periods. At Nurnberg was the first time that they ever were allowed a hearing before being punished. Even Napoleon was imprisoned for life on St. Helena, but he was never given a trial at which he could confront his accusers and tell his side of the story. The accused Germans, however, were allowed these rights; and the Tribunal acquitted three of those who were accused. If an enemy were honestly to apply the Nurnberg precedent, it could not punish any officer without a trial and it could not convict an officer unless it could show beyond reasonable doubt that he had participated in the crimes of which he was accused. If an enemy were so unscrupulous as to misapply the precedent, it is not likely that he would engage in any trial at all. The purpose of those who conducted the Nurnberg trials was to distinguish between those who were guilty and those who were innocent, and to protect the innocent as well as to convict the guilty, and there is no reason known to me why we as Americans should fear an honest application of this principle.

Jackson, *War and War Crimes Trials*, mimeographed transcript of his remarks to naval reserve officers in judge advocate training, November 2, 1948.

[155] Jackson was well aware of this: 'Regardless of the merits I do not doubt that German pride and nationalism found judgment by the Russians especially objectionable and that it will always injure the repute of the trial with the German people.' Jackson, *Nuremberg in Retrospect: Legal Answer to International Lawlessness*, taken from an address before the Canadian Bar Association, September 1, 1949, reported in 35 A.B.A.J. 813, 882 (1949).

[156] See Jackson's Introduction to Harris, *op. cit. supra* note 1, at xxxii: 'Where in the world were neutrals to take up the task of investigating and judging? Does one suggest Spain? Sweden? Switzerland? True, these states as such were not engaged in the war, but powerful elements of their society and most leading individuals were reputed not to be impartial but to be either for or against the Nazi order. Only the naive or those forgetful of conditions in 1945 would contend that we could have induced "neutral" states to assume the duty of doing justice to the Nazis.'

[157] In this respect, Nuremberg followed the precedent of previous war crimes trials. By unfortunate necessity, such trials have always found judges and defendants on opposite sides of the conflict. This is likely to remain the practice until we have an international court of general penal jurisdiction. The United Nations now offers the possibility of constituting a tribunal the jurisdiction of which would not be limited to the nationals of defeated powers, but this avenue was not available when Jackson assumed his war crimes responsibilities.

V

'The major primary sources of materials for this study are located in the documentation of the so-called Ministries Trial...held at Nürnberg...'—so begins the bibliographical note to a recently-published study of the German Foreign Office under the Nazi regime.[158] A monumental treatise on the Third Reich and *Festung Europa*, edited by the Toynbees and recently published by the Royal Institute of International Affairs, manifests throughout a reliance on the Nuremberg documents as the most important single source.[159] These are but two of a long succession of historical and narrative works of the last decade for which the record made at Nuremberg has furnished the foundation.[160] Surely there could be no more compelling demonstration than these works afford of the truth of Jackson's retrospective observation that: 'Never have the archives of a belligerent nation been so completely exposed as were those of Nazi Germany at the Nuremberg trial.... The result is a documentation unprecedented in history as to any major war.'[161]

Even before he became aware of the documentary wealth that preparations for the trial were bringing to light, Jackson had stressed the importance of 'a well-documented history... of this movement' which would 'establish incredible events by credible evidence.'[162] When the enormous historical significance of this avalanche of records became apparent, Jackson promptly acted to make them publicly available in a systematic way. The financial support of the State and War Departments was obtained, and a selection of the most important documents was published in official form beginning early in 1946.[163] No substantial study of European affairs since the First World War can now be undertaken without the benefit of the Nuremberg record.

As the trials ran their course, and different aspects of the Third Reich one after another were brought into focus—diplomacy, the civil bureaucracy, medicine, the legal profession and the courts, military leadership, industry and labor, the church, the press and radio—Nuremberg became, in Jackson's phrase, 'the world's first post mortem examination of a totalitarian regime.'[164] It was an indelible experience for the participants, and it might have been made the vehicle of

---

[158] SEABURY, THE WILHELMSTRASSE 203 (1954).

[159] HITLER'S EUROPE (Arnold & Veronica M. Toynbee ed. 1954).

[160] See, *e.g.*, BLOND, THE DEATH OF HITLER'S GERMANY vi (1954); FORESTER, THE NIGHTMARE viii (1954); GATZKE, STRESEMANN AND THE REARMAMENT OF GERMANY 119 (1954); GOERLITZ, DER DEUTSCHE GENERALSTAB 705–08 (1950); HINSLEY, HITLER'S STRATEGY xi–xii (1951); MARTIENSSEN, HITLER AND HIS ADMIRALS viii–x (1949); WHEELER-BENNETT, THE NEMESIS OF POWER 767–68 (1953); WILMOT, THE STRUGGLE FOR EUROPE 719–20 (1952).

[161] See HARRIS, *op. cit. supra* note 1, at xxix.

[162] In his interim report of June 6, 1945, to President Truman, *supra* note 45.

[163] NAZI CONSPIRACY, published by the United States Government Printing Office, volumes I–VIII (1946), and Supplements A (1947) and B (1948):

[164] In his final report to President Truman, October 7, 1946. See INT'L CONFERENCE 438.

salubrious enlightenment in Germany had the occupation authorities exploited the results more intensively and imaginatively. For, as Jackson brought out during his cross-examination of Speer,[165] the Nuremberg record provides, above all, an eloquent demonstration of the terrible handicaps under which any nation labors when burdened by dictatorship.[166] Never have there been more powerful witnesses than those who spoke at Nuremberg—whether from the witness box or by the written word, from the grave or in the flesh—to expose the disaster and disgrace of a citizenry that abjures its civic responsibilities,[167] or to extol the democratic way.

As the years pass, the Nuremberg documentation will be merged with other sources and will lose its unique historical value. The guilt of the criminals and the abomination that was the Third Reich afford no sufficient gauge of Nuremberg's or Jackson's stature in the course of human events. That is best measured, I believe, by those dimensions of Nuremberg that its denigrators most persistently seek to distort or minimize. For it is Nuremberg's continuing function to prick the memory and conscience of governments and peoples, and it is precisely where the pain is sharpest that the loudest protests are evoked.

The vigor and endurance of this conscience-pricking power spring principally from the integrity and dignity of the Nuremberg proceedings. Many individuals contributed notably to these attainments, but none so much as Jackson. His limitations as diplomat and administrator seemed almost to strengthen his leadership in launching and maintaining the trials as the embodiment of high principles. The standards he set became the architecture of the Nuremberg process.

It was a marvellous and memorable achievement. There were so many obstacles, doubts and pitfalls—so many occasions when a weaker or cruder man must have stumbled or succumbed to pressure, ambition or a vulgar exploitation of popular sentiments. But the man whose first use of his power was to prevent the eye-for-an-eye impressment of vanquished Germans into forced labor to repair the Wehrmacht's havoc,[168] and who insisted in the face of widespread cynicism, impatience and blindness that the accused Nazi leaders must be given fair opportunity for defense—that man was untouched by vengeful motives.[169] The man who rejected, and so decisively as to drive from his side eminent colleagues, pro-

---

[165] See text at notes 97–99 *supra*.

[166] See Taylor, *The Nuremberg War Crimes Trials: An Appraisal*, 23 ACAD. POL. SCI. PROC. 239, 250–52 (1949).

[167] The distinction between the German people's guilt and responsibility for the crimes of the Nazi era is penetratingly analyzed in MUHLEN, THE RETURN OF GERMANY (1953) *passim*.

[168] See text at note 43 *supra*.

[169] Nevertheless, efforts to picture Nuremberg as an act of vengeance are by no means lacking. See, *e.g.*, BARDÈCHE, NUREMBERG OU LA TERRE PROMISE (1948); BELGION, VICTORS JUSTICE (1949); DOUGLAS, AN ALMANAC OF LIBERTY 96 (1954); GRENFELL, UNCONDITIONAL HATRED 135, 256–57 (1953); UTLEY, THE HIGH COST OF VENGEANCE 162–81 (1949); VEALE, ADVANCE TO BARBARISM (1953). Thirty-six death sentences were pronounced at Nuremberg, and twenty-one executions were carried out (Goering committed suicide, Bormann was never apprehended, and there were thirteen commutations). Four years, millions of dollars, and the energies of thousands

posals to obtain convictions by playing the accused against each other knew that it was not enough for him to be a zealous advocate. He was impervious to the blandishments of a cheap theatricalism, and his pen took fire and brought to the proceedings an unmatched clarity and eloquence. He sought no reward other than the satisfaction of giving body to the principles he had espoused, a satisfaction expressed in his final report to the President:

The nations have given the example of leaving punishment of individuals to the determination of independent judges, guided by principles of law, after hearing all of the evidence for the defense as well as the prosecution. It is not too much to hope that this example of full and fair hearing,[170] and tranquil and discriminating judgment will do something toward strengthening the processes of justice in many countries....

In the present depressing world outlook it is possible that the Nurnberg trial may constitute the most important moral advance to grow out of this war. The trial and decision by which the four nations have forfeited the lives of [some] ... leaders of Germany because they have violated fundamental International Law does more than anything in our time to give to International Law what Woodrow Wilson described as 'the kind of vitality it can have only if it is a real expression of our moral judgment.'[171]

The 'depressing world outlook' that Jackson deplored in 1946 is still with us and is, I believe, the primary source of most of the doubts and fears about Nuremberg that find expression today. The emergence of Communism in succession to the Axis as the *bete noir* of our outlook abroad has revived attitudes that were prevalent from Munich to Pearl Harbor, and were only temporarily submerged by the latter. It has become official policy to rebuild German military power as a counterpoise to Russia's, and unpleasant memories of the Third Reich sit uneasily on these efforts.

But the long-continued cold war has corroded American public opinion in a much more fundamental way—it has badly shaken our faith in the value of international organization and endeavor of all sorts. Our Allies of long standing are mistrusted, and the United Nations has fallen short of the bright hopes that attended its birth. At least, that is how things appear to many Americans, and the memory of Nuremberg—the most intense and meaningful application of international law in recorded history—has suffered accordingly. For in the last analysis, the 'Nuremberg question' is whether international law has intrinsic validity or practical efficacy in this day and age.

Psychologically, it is easy to understand the desperation and cynicism evoked by these murky horizons. Logically, however, the course of events has confirmed

---

were invested in the trial of some 200 accused. If this was vengeance, it was the slowest, costliest, and most meticulously inefficient that human ingenuity has yet devised.

[170] The procedural rules and practices developed at the Nuremberg trials are systematically presented in 15 TRIALS OF WAR CRIMINALS BEFORE THE NUREMBERG MILITARY TRIBUNALS (U.S. Gov't P.O. 1953).

[171] See INT'L CONFERENCE 438–39.

the validity and magnified the necessity of the Nuremberg concepts. 'If mankind really is to master its destiny or control its way of life, it must first find means to prevent war,' Jackson reiterated shortly before his death.[172] If any doubts about this apothegm might once have been entertained, they have been eliminated by the atom and its progeny.

Men are often slow to recognize the principles that govern their actions. And so it is that today Nuremberg, disparaged by some and forgotten by many, is the true source and justification of our conduct in the community of nations. To what end do we build huge fleets of intercontinental bombers and store the most terrible explosives that our ingenuity can devise? To what end do we deploy our military power in all quarters of the globe? To what end did we drive out of South Korea the invaders that would have taken those lands by conquest?

It is not enough to answer that the national security requires all this, true as that may be. Time and again our leaders, regardless of political persuasion, have declared that the purpose of these acts is to keep the peace by making aggression an unpromising adventure.[173] For all the lawyers' debates about *ex post facto* laws, no voice is raised today to defend the legality of aggressive war, or to say that those who launch it are not criminals. Enduring peace cannot rest upon a 'balance of power' that now means merely a nice distribution of man's capacity for self-destruction.[174] The great question today is not whether the Nuremberg

---

[172] See HARRIS, *op. cit. supra* note 1, at xxix. Jackson's other post-Nuremberg writings on the subject include: '*The Significance of the Nuremberg Trials to the Armed Forces*,' address before the National War College on December 6, 1946, in Military Affairs, Winter 1946, p. 3; '*Some Problems in Developing an International Legal System*,' address at The School of Advanced International Studies on August 25, 1948, in 22 TEMP. L.Q. 147 (1948); '*Nuremberg in Retrospect: Legal Answer to International Lawlessness*,' taken from an address at the Canadian Bar Association, on September 1, 1949, in 35 A.B.A.J. 813 (1949); '*The United Nations Organizations and War Crimes*,' address at the American Society of International Law on April 26, 1952, in 46 AM. SOC'Y INT'L L. PROC. 196–204 (1952), commenting on the critical book by Viscount Maugham, U.N.O. AND WAR CRIMES (1951).

[173] See the remarks of H. Struve Hensel, Assistant Secretary of Defense for International Affairs, N.Y. Times, Jan. 18, 1955, p. 12, col. 3: 'Our aim is to make it clear that aggression can be and will be severely punished.' At his press conference on March 2, 1955, when asked whether the United States is committed to assist the Chinese Nationalists to return to the Mainland, President Eisenhower replied: 'The United States is not going to be a party to an aggressive war. That is the best answer I can make.' See the New York Times, Mar. 3, 1955, p. 1, col. 8.

[174] Compare the remarks of Henry R. Luce, whose publications (especially *Fortune* Magazine) have been among the most vehement critics of Nuremberg, speaking at the fortieth Anniversary Dinner of the *New Republic* Magazine on November 17, 1954, quoted in 2 *The Federalist Newsletter* (Jan. 1955):

But how much have intellectuals concerned themselves with this matter of Law in the world? What explorations have our Advance Guard made into questions of Law as governing the relations of nations and all people within all nations? . . . It is a deep and prickly subject. Easier to ignore it. But like the Hound of Heaven, this question will pursue you—for the fact is: there can be no peace without law. Nor freedom either.

Personally, I wish that right now the United States would be putting herself in the forefront of the great worldwide concern for Law and the rule of Law. But she cannot be expected to do this unless from the Advance Guard we get vivid suggestions as to how this ideal can be progressively incarnated. Meanwhile, mankind lives on the brink of anarchy. The United States cannot

principles are valid, but whether mankind can live up to them, and whether it can live at all if it fails.[175]

Jackson brought one of the brightest legal and literary talents of our time to bear on the great subject of war and peace. The quality of a man's endeavor is not to be measured by its immediate success. Jackson sought to speak man's hope, and he never lost faith that Nuremberg would contribute to its fulfillment:

Like much legal work ours at Nürnberg has far-reaching implications rarely apparent to laymen and often missed by lawyers. Its value to the world will depend less on how faithfully it interpreted the past than on how accurately it forecasts the future. It is possible that strife and suspicion will lead to new aggressions and that the nations are not yet ready to receive and abide by the Nürnberg law. But those who gave some of the best effort of their lives to this trial are sustained by a confidence that in place of what might have been mere acts of vengeance we wrote a civilized legal precedent and one that will lie close to the foundations of that body of international law that will prevail when the world becomes sufficiently civilized.[176]

move forward in this, its historic mission to promote the rule of Law, unless the intellectuals have schooled themselves—and us—to know and to speak of the great concepts of Law as the necessary counterpart of Liberty and the actual basis of peace between men and nations.

[175] See, *e.g.*, the address by Pope Pius XII to the Sixth International Congress of Penal Law on October 3, 1953, printed in 28 St. John's L. Rev. 1, calling for the codification of international penal law with specified sanctions, in which His Holiness declared: 'The Community of nations must reckon with unprincipled criminals who, in order to realize their ambitious plans, are not afraid to unleash total war. This is the reason why other countries, if they wish to preserve their very existence and their most precious possessions, and unless they are prepared to accord free action to international criminals, have no alternative but to get ready for the day when they must defend themselves. This right to be prepared for self-defense cannot be denied, even in these days, to any state. That, however, does not in any way alter the fact that unjust war is to be accounted as one of the very gravest crimes which international penal law must proscribe, must punish with the heaviest penalties, and the authors of which are in every case guilty and liable to the punishment that has been agreed upon.' *Id.* at 5.

[176] See Jackson, *Nuremberg in Retrospect: Legal Answer to International Lawlessness*, in 35 A.B.A.J. 813, 886–87 (1949).

17

The Development of International Criminal Law after Nuremberg*

By Professor Hans-Heinrich Jescheck
Freiberg im Breisgau; Director of the Institute of
Foreign and International Criminal Law

Ten years have passed since the judgment of the International Military Tribunal (IMT) in Nuremberg. The twelve findings of the American military tribunals that were announced after the main trial and on the basis of the legal principles developed during the trial belong to history. Only a few of the defendants sentenced to imprisonment are still behind bars; some have had to serve their sentence up to the last day; most were released from incarceration before time. The world has all but forgotten the arguments of the Nuremberg judgments. They could be summarized as follows: under international law, the individual has direct responsibility in criminal law; criminal acts under international law are, in particular, a war of aggression, war crimes and crimes against humanity; the duties of the individual under international law have precedence over those established in national law.

While for us Germans, the trials may be mixed with a feeling of bitterness, I, nonetheless, feel sufficiently free at heart to ask myself without prejudice what in the meantime has become of the international law that had been created with so much hope and confidence. A lawyer who wishes not to betray the mission of his calling, to act without bias for justice, must repeatedly ask this question simply because a final assessment of the problem as a whole depends particularly on what the international law community was or will be able to make in due course of the legal principles applied in Nuremberg.

Yet, what does the attitude of the post-war world have to do with the legitimation of judgments delivered a decade ago? Even the most hidebound proponents of the legal principles developed in Nuremberg have agreed from the start that the application of this criminal law should not remain restricted to members of the

---

* A presentation given by the author on 28 February 1957 at the invitation of the Law Faculty of the University of Berne.

populations conquered in 1945 but should have future use. In 1945, the Western Powers decidedly opposed the Russian attempt to regard the London Agreement of 8 August from the start only as exceptional law against the defeated.[1] The prosecutors of the Western Powers, Jackson,[2] Shawcross[3] and de Menthon[4] advocated 'the same measure', by which all should be judged in the future. We find the same attitude amongst the judges, Donnedieu de Vabres[5] and Francis Biddle,[6] and no lesser a person than Truman postulated in October 1946 for the United Nations courts (UN) that statesmen who might be found guilty in the future of one of the criminal acts condemned in Nuremberg should be hauled before an international court to be held accountable.[7] In the instance of the American delegation, the UN General Assembly confirmed the Nuremberg Principles on 11 December 1946, and initiated preliminary work towards co-defining them. The desire for the general application and for the positive implementation of Nuremberg law was therefore alive from the start, especially amongst its adherents, although they regarded it as an expression of international law applying *in any event*. This objective had also, of course, to be brought home to those who were disinclined to recognize full reconciliation of the Nuremberg legal principles with current international law and regarded Nuremberg, in brief, as a 'revolution' in the legal system. Counsel for Karl Dönitz, Otto Kranzbühler, wrote 'Nuremberg is a revolution . . . its value or lack of value depends on what the future has in store for it.'[8] However, there is no lack of voices abroad that have reached the same conclusion.[9] I agree with this view,[10] because in London and Nuremberg, new law could not be created from scratch. The verdict of the IMT was based on the London

---

[1] See on this point Jescheck, *Die Verantwortlichkeit, der Staatsorgane nach Völkerstrafrecht*, Bonn 1952, 143 *et seq.*

[2] Proceedings against the main war criminals before the International Military Tribunal in Nuremberg (German version), Nuremberg 1947, II, 118.

[3] Nuremberg III, 107 *et seq.*

[4] Nuremberg V, 480.

[5] 'Le procès de Nuremberg devant les principes modernes du droit pènal international', *Recueil des Cours*, 1947, I, 487.

[6] 'Report to President Truman', printed in *Revue de science criminelle et de droit penal comparé*, 1947, 141.

[7] United Nations, Public Document for the Second Part of the First Session of the General Assembly, 684.

[8] *Nürnberg als Rechtsproblem, Festive Gift for Erich Kaufmann*, Stuttgart and Cologne, 1950, 219.

[9] Thus de Lapradelle, 'Une révolution dans le droit pénal international': *Nouvelle revue de droit international privé* 1946 (5); Röling, 'Duitsland en het vonnis van Neurenberg', *International Spectator*, VIII (1954), 307, and 'The United Nations and the Development of International Criminal Law' in *The United Nations Ten Years' Legal Progress*, 1995 (65); C. A. Pompe, *Aggressive War an International Crime*, The Hague, 1953, 277; Reut-Nicolussi, *Zum Problem der Friedenssicherung durch Strafgerichtsbarkeit*, Festschrift für Rudolf Laun, Hamburg 1953, 372; Eustathiades, *Recueil des Cours*, 1953, III, 520; Donnedieu de Vabres, op. cit. 486, 574; Schwarzenberger, *Current Legal Problems*, 1950, 290.

[10] See also Jescheck, 'Verbrechen gegen das Völkerrecht', *German National Reports to the IV International Congress on Comparison Laws*, Dusseldorf, 1956, 364.

Agreement[11] of the four major Powers, which were subsequently joined by nine-teen additional states, but certainly not by all participants in the war, especially not by Germany. These successive American trials were based on German domes-tic occupation law, the Control Council Act No. 10,[12] which is largely in line with the London Agreement. Both are legal sources, whereby no general inter-national law could be created with regard to Germany, but only occupation law, and this, too, only within the limits to which occupation law is permissible at all.[13] The Nuremberg courts knew this and therefore made every effort to prove the internal cohesion of the principles applied by them with current international law.[14] However, many have come to the conclusion in international philosophy of law that this harmony does *not* exist on all points and that the Nuremberg stand-ards were *new* in Western relations.[15] They must therefore first prove their value as *legal* rules by their application in due course.[16]

I should like to present to you how these attempts at proving their value have turned out so far. In doing so, I shall limit myself strictly to legal considera-tions and leave the question of why the Nuremberg Law has not been applied to the various wars and armed conflicts since 1945 untouched, although this political consideration, of course, might also have something to tell us as lawyers.

I

We must consider whether the Nuremberg legal principles, which I shall discuss individually in a moment, have already become a 'solid' component of general international law, and were confirmed by the UN General Assembly in two resolutions of 1946 and 1947. Such a state of affairs has often been assumed[17] and, if correct, it would transform future efforts to establish and generally intro-duce this law as a simple problem of formulation. Let us see whether this is indeed the case.

1. The first resolution of 11 December 1946 says: 'The General Assembly affirms the principles of international law recognized by the Charter of the

---

[11] Printed in Nuremberg, I, 7.

[12] *Control Council Bulletin*, 1945, 50.

[13] Cf. on this point Hague National War Rules, Article 43 and now Geneva Convention to Protect the Civilian Population, Article 64.

[14] Nuremberg, I, 244, and in Heinze-Schilling, 'Die Rechtsprechung der Nürnberger Militärtribunale', Bonn, 1952, nos. 229 *et seq.*, combined judgment quotations.

[15] Cf. the authors quoted in notes 1–3 on p. 3, also Wegner, 'Der strafrechtliche Schutz des Völkerrechts', *Materials for the Reform of Criminal Law*, Bonn, 1954, I, 357.

[16] W. Sauer, *System des Völkerrechts*, Bonn, 1952, 449–50.

[17] See, e.g., Scelle, 'Summary Records of Discussions in the International Law Commission', 1949 (A/CN 4/SR 26), 4; Glaser, *Indroduction à l'étude du droit international pénal*, Brussels–Paris, 1954, 3–4; Graven, 'Les crimes contre l'humanité', *Recueil des Cours*, 1950, I, 462.

Nuremberg Tribunal and the judgment of the Tribunal.' In addition, the codification committee was instructed 'to treat as a matter of primary importance plans for the formulation, the context of a general codification of offences against the peace and security of mankind, or of an International Crime Code, of the principles recognized in the Charter of the Nuremberg Tribunal and the judgment of the Tribunal'.[18] Should this resolution now be regarded as the decisive turning point in the whole history of international law? Should the assumption of the entirety of Nuremberg law into general international law now be inferred from this?[19] That would be difficult! The General Assembly in its resolution, as the wording clearly indicates, proceeded on the assumption that the Nuremberg Legal Principles already belong to general international law and were simply acknowledged by the Statute of the Court of Justice and by the IMT judgment. The General Assembly confirmed only this position and only if we assume this to be correct does this confirmation make sense. However, research into the science of law has shown in the meantime that substantial parts of the Nuremberg law were *new* and could *not* be reconciled with general international law. However, if this is true, the General Assembly's Resolution loses its *legal* significance, because there was in no way any intention to initiate the creation of new international law and to subject the government and other bodies of all of the world's states to a different law than existed before. While this does not render the resolution unimportant, its significance is not legal but *political* and consists in the declaration that the desire was in principle to acknowledge the procedures of the four Powers in Nuremberg and to apply this law generally in the future. That the General Assembly did not interpret the matter differently is clear from the fact that, in the same Resolution, the codification committee was instructed to formulate the Nuremberg Principles once only. Since then, the General Assembly has never again reached such unanimity in legal conviction, which even then could be explained only through the tremendous impression left by the announcement of the great Nuremberg Judgment just then.

2. What has now become of the General Assembly's admission of 1946? The resolution of 21 November 1947[20] does not even contain a renewed confirmation, but merely entrusts the formulation of a Code concerning offences against peace and the security of mankind (Draft Code of Offences Against the Peace and Security of Mankind; hereinafter called the 'Draft Code') to the newly created International Law Commission. Initially, this code formulated the Nuremberg law in seven principles[21] and submitted the result of its discussions to the UN for

---

[18] UN Doc. A/CN 4/5, pp. 14–15, printed also in *History of the United Nations War Crimes Commission*, London, 1948, 260.

[19] Cf. on this point Röling, *The United Nations and the Development of International Criminal Law*, op. cit. 70; Dahm, *Zur Problematik des Völkerstrafrechts* Göttingen, 1956, 66.

[20] Printed in the *American Journal of International Law*, Supplement 44 (1950), 8.

[21] Printed similarly, 125, *et seq.*

a resolution in 1950. In the face of much criticism in the Sixth Committee,[22] the General Assembly did *not* approve the Principles but simply sent them to Member States for comment. The International Law Commission was instructed at the same time to take account of the opinions of the Governments and UN delegates when drawing up the Draft Code. The draft of the Nuremberg Principles was never developed further in the UN. Similarly desolate was the fate of the Draft Code. The draft of this basic statute in international criminal law was adopted by the International Law Commission at its second reading in 1954,[23] but so far a sober and objective discussion in the General Assembly has not taken place. The question was deferred initially to 1956 so that first of all a special committee, which was to develop a definition of the concept of aggressor,[24] could have an opportunity to undertake this task. In 1956, the General Assembly once again deferred the questions of our concern to autumn 1957, because the report of the special committee mentioned above could not be submitted in good time[25] and every effort had to be made to prevent a new major war.

3. Overall, it can be said with good reason that the General Assembly has been dilatory in considering the problems of substantive international criminal law ever since 1950 and a general debate never followed, and perhaps was not wanted, either. What decision will eventually be taken is difficult to foretell and as I do not have to make political prophecies here, I shall leave the question unanswered in order to come back to it briefly only at the end of my comments. On the other hand, there can be no doubt that the victor, if every similar situation should arise as it did in 1945, will hark back to the leading case of the Nuremberg judgments in order to apply the same principles against the defeated.[26] While, depending on the nature of the situation, such a procedure will perhaps be no more unjust than the application of the Nuremberg law ten years ago, one must, nonetheless, regret that despite frequent efforts no one has so far succeeded in obtaining clear recognition of the major principles of international criminal law from the peoples of the world.[27]

---

[22] UN Doc. General Assembly, Off. Rec. 5th Session, Sixth Committee, 1950, 131–98, New York, 1950.

[23] UN Doc. General Assembly, Off. Rec. 9th Session, Supplement, no. 9 (A/2693), New York, 1954.

[24] Cf. on this point Röling', 'On Aggression, on International Criminal Law, on International Criminal Jurisdiction', *Nederlands Tijdschrift voor Internationall Recht*, 1955, 167 *et seq.* and 279 *et seq.* In addition, Quincy Wright, 'The Prevention of Aggression', *American Journal of International Law* 50 (1956), 514 *et seq.*

[25] UN Doc. A/Bur/143 of 9 November 1956, 2 (4).

[26] Cf. the clear reference by the Russian author L. A. Modsshoryan in the paper 'Zur Frage der Völkerrechtssubjekte', *Science of Law Information Service*, 1956, 685 (translated from Sovyetskoye Gossudarstvo Pravo, 1956, issue 6, 92–101).

[27] Röling, op. cit., 185, has formulated these principles as I have myself (1 above):

'1. The principle of the individual criminal responsibility for the violation of the law of nations, including the responsibility for acts of state;

II

Fortunately, the present position of the problem of international criminal law has not been exhausted with the fate that the drafts underwent in the UN. There are many other questions that still require essential legal thought and occasionally allow us a prospect for practical success for our efforts.

1. One of the main points in dispute under the Nuremberg judgments has been *criminal liability for a war of aggression* under international law. In international philosophy, a view has certainly gained ground by now which one of the best observers of the history of international law, Hans Wehberg of Geneva, has formulated as follows: 'from the previous comments the conclusion may be drawn in full safety that in 1939 no principle of international law existed that individuals could be prosecuted in criminal law for an offence against peace.'[28] While individual liability for a war of aggression was therefore not yet recognized in international law at the time of the Nuremberg judgments, it must nonetheless be admitted on the other hand that the penalties as such fully corresponded to the general desire for justice. The legal problem lies not so much in the nations of the world recognizing the principle of criminal liability, as in defining the group of persons who can be held generally liable for such an event in world history. The principle of criminal liability for a war of aggression has in the meantime found some kind of international recognition through the International Refugees Convention of 1951,[29] which Germany has also signed, which withholds protection from refugees against whom a strong suspicion of an offence against peace (war crimes or crimes against humanity) exists. But the concept of the war of aggression has also been further developed significantly in material terms. While the principle No. VIa formulated by the International Law Commission still adopted the old version of the London Statute (war of aggression or war in violation of international treaties) verbatim, the wording of the Draft Code of 1954

---

   2. the principle of the threefold individual responsibility, for crimes against peace, war crimes and crimes against humanity;

   3. the principle that individuals have international duties which transcend the national obligations of obedience imposed by the individual state.'

[28] Wehberg, *Die völkerrechtliche Verantwortlichkeit von Individuen wegen Friedensbruchs im Zeitalter des Völkerbundes*, Festschrift for Rudolf Laun, Hamburg 1953, 395; similarly,C. A. Pompe, *Aggressive War an International Crime*, The Hague, 1953, 175; Heinitz, *Journal for the General Science of Criminal Law* 66 (1954) 267, 268; Dahm, op. cit. 48, with further details in note 123. The contrary view is represented especially by Glaser, op. cit., 38 *et seq.* and 'La guerre d'agression à la lumière des sources du droit international', *Revue Générale de Droit International Public*, 1953, no. 3, 1 *et seq.*; Oppenheim–Lauterpacht, *International Law*, 7th ed., London/New York/Toronto, 1952, II, 192; Quintano Ripolles, *Tratado de derecho penal internacional e internacional penal*, Madrid, 1955, I, 486.

[29] Agreement on the Legal Position of Refugees of 28 July 1951 (BGBl 1953, II, 560); see on this point Röling, op. cit., 189.

now includes 'any active aggression' including the application of armed force,[30] so that an international conflict settled through military force without overt hostilities, such as the Austrian *Anschluss* in 1938 or the occupation of Czechoslovakia in 1939, could therefore simply be regarded as criminal aggression, not to mention the military incidents that we have experienced more recently. However, the International Law Commission went a good deal further: according to the Draft, a threat with aggressive action against another state, the preparation of military violent measures against another state for purposes not existing in one's own or collective self-defence or in furtherance of UN resolutions, the maintaining of armed gangs for the purpose of attacking an area in a foreign state, the incitement of civil unrest in another state, support for terrorism, the breach of disarmament obligations, the annexation of foreign territory in violation of international law, and even intervention in the internal or external affairs of another state through political or economic enforcement measures (newly introduced in 1954) are criminal acts.[31] That the General Assembly has time and again deferred a resolution on this wide-ranging programme is understandable, but still regrettable, since we have seen in contrast that the principle of criminal liability for a war of aggression can be established only by a legal principle of *international law* and can be achieved only through *international* bodies. There is no place here for a state's criminal law. A telling example of this is the fate of the parliamentary experiments in Germany. Article 26 of the Federal Republic's Constitutional Act bans preparations for a war of aggression as an unconstitutional enterprise. However, the legislator's instructions to sanction a war of aggression by Federal law have so far remained a dead letter because people have recognized that the task of monitoring the peacefulness of one's own government's foreign policy cannot be undertaken by the courts but is a matter of political control of the government by Parliament. It makes even less sense, of course, in legal terms, to state already in the preamble that only the opponent can ever be regarded as an aggressor, as happened in the Act for the Protection of Peace[32] of the Soviet occupied zone of Germany of 1950. In such a case, the law is no longer an instrument of justice but becomes a weapon in the ideological struggle between the major parties in the world's political debate.

2. The position in the area of *war crimes* in the stricter sense is different and more likely to allow for the creation of a truly international criminal law.

a) The Nuremberg judgments, in punishing war crimes, went well beyond the limits of what this concept used to entail.[33] This phenomenon can be explained by the fact that the Second World War was in fact conducted in

---

[30] Quincy Wright, op. cit., 526, stresses that this is something quite different from the concept of 'act of aggression' in Article 39 of the UN Charter.

[31] Dahm, op. cit., 37, note 92 also considers the latter provision as going too far.

[32] *Gesetzblatt der Deutschen Demokratischen Republik*, 1950, 1199.

[33] The classic term of war crime can still be found at the end of the Second World War in Oppenheim-Lauterpacht, *International Law*, 6th Edition, London/New York/Toronto,

forms, and elicited fearful events, of a kind never hitherto known in a war in modern times. However, other factors also had a bearing. *Delimiting the—relevant—facts* must therefore be seen as the legal task for the future, which is of special concern to continental jurists who are used to a clear legal description of a punishable misdeed.[34] Unfortunately, the work of the International Law Commission has contributed nothing whatever towards such clarification,[35] since both Principle VIb and Article 2 (12) of the Draft Code with the formula: 'Acts and violation of the laws or customs of war' simply repeats the London Statute where the expression 'Acts' in the heading is too narrow because it appears to exclude the not insubstantial offences of omission that accompany war crimes.

b) The decisive progress in this area results from the activities of the *International Committee of the Red Cross* since 1948. On the basis of a draft that the expert committee had drawn up under the chairmanship of Max Huber,[36] punitive provisions were included in each of the four new Geneva Conventions of 12 August 1949.[37] Particularly significant is that the newly created articles of the Conventions concerning 'grave breaches' lay down *which* offences would in the future be regarded as punishable war crimes under international law. True, the Conventions contain no specific criminal acts as would be familiar in a Continental European codification, but merely instruct the high contracting states to penalize serious offences regarded as punishable; but they are more strictly defined than in the London Charter. In line with practical requirements, the Geneva Conventions have placed the emphasis on indirect protection for international law on domestic law. However, this does not really remove the old principle of direct criminal liability for war crimes under international law. A country that may not have introduced criminal provisions in its domestic law or has not done so adequately could have its courts punish serious violations within the terms of the Conventions through its own courts

---

1944, II, 451. As to the judgments themselves, see, M. W. Mouton, *War Crimes and International Law*, The Hague, 1947.

[34] As to the structure of the concept of an offence in the case of war crimes, see Würtenberger, *Zur Rechtswidrigkeit der Kriegsverbrechen*, Festschrift für Mezger, Munich-Berlin, 1954, 193 *et seq.* Wegner, op. cit., 365, also expressly demands clarity as to the facts. The facts certainly cannot be 'valueless', 'simply material' (370, 373). My own work on a draft of German criminal circumstances for the protection of international law of war has again confirmed this.

[35] Donnedieu de Vabres, op. cit., 575, correctly pointed out that it is very difficult to achieve 'precision and fixity' in domestic law in this area.

[36] Cf. Pictet, *La Convention de Genève relative à la protection des personnes civiles en temps de guerre*, Geneva, 1956, 627 *et seq.* and *Remarques et propositions du Comité International de la Croix-Rouge*, Geneva, 1949, 18 *et seq.*

[37] Cf. Further Strebel, 'Die strafrechtliche Sicherung humanitärer Abkommen', *Zeitschrift für ausl. öff. Recht u. Völkerrecht* 15 (1953), 31 *et seq.*; Pilloud, 'La protection pènale des Conventions humanitaires internationals', *Revue internationale de droit pénal* 24 (1953), 661 *et seq.*, and Jescheck, 'Der strafrechtliche Schutz der internationalen humanitären Abkommen', *Zeitschrift für die gesamte Strafrechtswissenschaft* 65 (1953), 458 *et seq.* (French version in *Revue internationale de droit pénal* 24 (1953), 13 *et seq.*)

under international law, provided the domestic constitution does not link the offence and punishment to the existence of a formal law, as is the case both in Switzerland and Germany.[38] The high contracting states saw fit to reach for the necessary statutory measures to punish all serious offences characterized as 'grave breaches'.[39] This ensures that all offences about which there can be no doubt as to their meriting punishment are in fact also punishable in every member state.

c) The way in which *individual states* have discharged their obligations under the Geneva Conventions is significant with respect to the approach of the various legal systems.[40] The United States directly applies international law as the punitive standard, at least against foreigners, while the concept of general assumption of international law into domestic law undoubtedly has a bearing. Article 505e of the *New Field Manual* states:

'As the international law of war is part of the law of the land in the United States, enemy personnel charged with war crimes are tried directly under international law without recourse to the statutes of the United States.'[41]

The Netherlands[42] introduced a general clause in Article 8 of the War Crimes Act of 1952 that also includes less serious offences against the Geneva Convention and, in my view, goes too far on these points, because quite minor offences are also indifferently covered and are criminalized just like the serious ones. Following the additions to the Military Criminal Code of 1950, *Swiss criminal law*[43] covers a series of special criminal circumstances in this area, but in addition also adds a subsidiary provision that makes all offences against international law of warfare punishable as dereliction of duty under Article 72 of the Military Criminal Code and consequently comes close to the Dutch general clause. *Yugoslavia*, on the other hand, has taken up all 'grave breaches' of the Geneva Conventions, partly verbatim, into the new Criminal Code of 1950. The new Ethiopian Criminal Code of 1957 prepared by Jean Graven[44]

---

[38] Similarly, Dahm, op. cit., 70.

[39] Discussions in Germany on this point are at present in progress in a sub-committee of the Major Criminal Law Committee on the basis of a formulated preliminary draft.

[40] Regarding the status of German law, see Jescheck, op. cit., 464 *et seq.* (in French version, op. cit., 21 *et seq.*).

[41] *Field Manual*, no. 27–10 'The Law of Land Warfare', Department of the Army of 18 July 1956. The text was kindly sent to me by Mr Monroe Leigh, Assistant General Counsel in the Department of Defence, Washington.

[42] Cf. Mouton, 'La protection pénale des conventions internationales humanitaires', *Revue internationale de droit pénal* 24 (1953), 845 *et seq.*

[43] On this point Eugster, 'La protection pénale des conventions internationales humanitaires', *Revue internationale de droit pénal* 24 (1953), 55 *et seq.*, especially 61.

[44] The text of Articles 293–307 was submitted by Professor Graven to the Second Geneva Expert Committee in 1956 (see note 45 below on this). Cf. for the system of these provisions Graven, 'La répression pénale des infractions aux Conventions de Genéve', *Revue internationale de criminologie et de police technique* 1956, 251.

contains under the title of 'Criminal Acts Against International Law' a whole list of circumstances, some of them independently formulated, of war crimes and crimes against humanity. At the Second Expert Committee, convened by the International Committee of the Red Cross in 1956, representatives of Switzerland (Graven), France (Paucot) and the Federal Republic of Germany (Jescheck) advocated a further factual definition of war crimes.[45] The most important working result of this committee has now been the general recognition of the constructive offence of omission in the area of war crimes, following the model of a draft of a Belgian government committee drawn up by the Belgian Committee member Dautricourt.[46] Altogether, the general recognition of criminal liability for serious offences against the international law of warfare and the obligation on states[47] to prosecute them, irrespective of the place where the crime was committed, the nationality of the perpetrator and own participation in the war,[48] will now be regarded as one of the most important and most beneficial effects of the Nuremberg judgments.

3. In the area of *crimes against humanity*, the state of affairs is similar to that of war crimes, if altogether less promising for the development of a powerful international criminal law that also has practical effect. The Nuremberg principles and the Draft Code here, too, closely follow the IMT Statute, while it must be stressed that Article 2(11) of the Draft Code has removed the customary linkage with offences against peace and war crimes, which Principle No. VIc had still adopted from Nuremberg law. It is therefore now clear that crimes against humanity, even if committed against one's own population and in peacetime, should be punishable under international law. The parallels with the positive approach to war crimes are formed by the international convention from 9 December 1948 to prevent and punish genocide,[49] which has been ratified by more than forty states,

---

[45] Cf. on the work of the Committee Graven, op. cit., 1956, 254 *et seq.* The Commission was chaired by Messrs Siordet and Pilloud of the ICRC and consisted in addition to the members mentioned in the text of Messrs Dautricourt (Belgium), Draper (UK), Leigh (USA) and Mouton (the Netherlands).

[46] Cf. Royaume de Belgique, Permanent Commission for the Examination of Questions of Criminal Law in International Relations. Notice Regarding the Geneva Conventions, Nivelles 1956, Article 1, Article 4 (4) and p. 28. On this, Dautricourt, 'La protection pénale des Conventions internationales humanitaires', *Revue de droit pénal et de criminologie*, 1954/55, 745.

[47] This obligation, that arises clearly from the new Geneva Conventions, has been endorsed by the International Law Commission insofar as criminal acts under international law 'shall be punished', according to the second version of the Draft Code of 1954 (no longer, as in the first Draft, 'shall be punishable').

[48] Neutral states are also obliged to bring criminal prosecutions.

[49] The drawing up of the Convention goes back to a decision of the UN General Assembly on the same day, 11 December 1946, as that on which the Nuremberg Principles were confirmed (UN Doc. A/231 p. 1134/35, also printed in History of the United Nations War Crimes Commission, p. 200). Cf. further on the Convention, Graven, 'Les crimes contre l'humanité', *Recueil des Cours* 1950, I, 462 *et seq.* Quintano Ripollés, *Tratado de derecho penal internacionale internacional penal*, Madrid, 1955, I, 625 *et seq.*; Jescheck, 'Das internationale Genocidium-Abkommen

although in fact not by the United States, the United Kingdom or the Soviet Union. The Federal Republic of Germany has also endorsed the Convention and discharged its parliamentary duty by including Article 2 of the Convention as s. 220a in the Criminal Code. The concept of crimes against humanity, established at Nuremberg, is intended when the Convention declares certain violent acts against national, ethnic, racial or religious groups to constitute crimes under international law. However, the Convention at the same time points beyond Nuremberg by also including crimes committed in peacetime. Despite its good intentions, the Genocide Convention would not be entirely satisfactory from the point of view of international criminal law. The formula contained in the preamble 'Crime Under International Law' may well be sufficient to identify criminal liability under international law now that this expression is also used in Article 1 of the Draft Code.[50] However, an unfortunate defect is that the Convention has retreated to the principle of territoriality, unlike the first draft that was prepared by Donnedieu de Vabres, Pella and Lemkin and which was intended to lay down the principle of universality in accordance with the Geneva Conventions.[51] Since the offence of genocide is hardly conceivable without at least indirect government participation,[52] the Convention is hardly to gain practical importance—simply because of this essential error, since states will not of their own accord submit atrocities committed by them to the criminal courts, unless the political situation is turned completely upside down, as in Germany after 1945. In addition, the definition of genocide does not extend to the political and cultural groups,[53] which we consider no less worthy of protection than the others. If, however, we compare the circumstance of genocide under the Convention with the Draft

vom 9 Dezember 1948 und die Lehre vom Völkerstrafrecht, *Zeitschrift für die gesamte Strafrechtswissenschaft* 66 (1954), 193 *et seq.*

[50] I would consequently no longer maintain my criticism expressed in the past, loc. cit., 209.

[51] One could even infer from the negotiations, that were simply discouraging in terms of international criminal law, of the *ad hoc* committee on genocide, which produced the second draft in 1948 on a remit by the UN Economic and Social Council, that the principle of universality is no longer recommended, or should even be rejected as contrary to international law, because it might lead to 'evaluation of the acts of foreign governments' and would consequently 'infringe sovereignty' (cf. Annex to UN Doc. E/794 'Rejected Proposal, the Principle of Universal Repression'). The Committee's attitude also throws the customary light on the question discussed in Section III (3) below of jurisdiction over foreign sovereign acts. Dahm. op. cit., 36, also raises objection to the principle of universality in the case of offences against humanity. On the application of the principle of universality under all circumstances of international criminal law, Glaser, ZStrR 68 (1953), 356.

[52] This is also assumed by the Draft Code, since Article 2 (11) of the 1954 version refers to offences against humanity under international criminal law only as 'acts committed by the authorities of a State or by private individuals acting at the instigation or with the toleration of such authorities'.

[53] The original resolution of the UN General Assembly of 11 December 1946 (cf. 14 n. 3) moreover declares genocide punishable 'on political or other grounds'. This, in turn, clearly shows that resolutions of this kind should not implicitly be regarded as sources of general international law, since the Genocide Convention clearly restricts the groups—excluding political and cultural—after the majority of Western states had bitterly fought for its extension, but in vain.

Code, we immediately notice a peculiar inconsistency. While Article 2 (10) of the Draft Code takes over the Convention content verbatim, a definition of an offence against humanity follows in paragraph 11, based on the example of the London Charter. This definition also declares all inhuman acts on political and cultural grounds as punishable, so that something is implicitly added here that had to be left out of the Genocide Convention on account of opposition from the Soviet Union (political groups) and the US (cultural groups). Despite these inadequacies and objections, we can regard one thing as a result of developments in the years following Nuremberg and express it in the words of the International Courts of Justice from a legal opinion concerning reservations made with regard to the Genocide Convention, namely, 'that the principles underlying the convention are principles which are recognized by civilized nations as binding on States even without any conventional obligation'.[54]

III

From the three traditional Nuremberg statutory criminal offences, I shall now turn to questions from the *General Part of International Criminal Law*.

1. In doing so, I shall deal quickly with the formerly much discussed topic of *individual responsibility* under international law,[55] since there can be no further doubt today that responsibility in criminal law, according to international law, can only be individual, if it exists at all. The idea of criminal law against states seems to have been superseded,[56] and the view has altogether taken the place of the traditional conception of international law as purely a law governing states that there are at least certain areas where a system of law above the state can penetrate directly to the individual with rights and obligations, breaking the veil of sovereignty.[57] The Nuremberg Principles and the Draft Code consequently begin quite understandably with the principle of individual responsibility in criminal law under international law. The same emerges from a principle that the Geneva Expert Committee in 1948 drew up and made the basis of the criminal provisions in the Geneva Conventions. These certainly transfer criminal sanctions to

---

[54] International Court of Justice, Reports, 1951, 15.

[55] Cf. The good overview by Korowicz, 'The Problem of the International Personality of Individuals', *American Journal of International Law* 60 (1956), 533 *et seq.*

[56] See the Decision of the International Law Commission following discussions in 1950, cf. UN Doc. Suppl. No. 12 (1316) s. 151, and on the basis of the discussions in 1954, cf. UN Doc. Suppl. No. 9 (A/25 93) s. 50. Similarly, Article 25 of the Draft Statute for an International Criminal Court. Cf. further on the whole subject Eustathiades, 'Les sujets du droit international et la responsabilité internationale', *Recueil des Cours* 1953, III, 434 *et seq.*

[57] Cf. Eustathiades, op. cit., 397, *et seq.*; Wegner, 'Die Stellung der Einzelperson im gegenwärtigen Völkerrecht', Festschrift für Rudolf Laun, 341 *et seq.* and 'Der strafrechtliche Schutz des Völkerrechts', in: *Materialien zur Strafrechtsreform*, Bonn 1954, I, 357 *et seq.* Dahm, op. cit., 14, *et seq.*

the States but Article 99 of the Prisoner of War Convention clearly shows that, as the creator of the Convention sees it, apart from criminal liability under domestic law, such a liability also exists in international law.[58] As evidence, reference may further be made to Article 7 (1) of the European Human Rights Convention of 1950,[59] Article 11 (2) of the General Declaration of Human Rights of 1948 and Article 2 of the Draft Statute for an International Criminal Court of 1953. Today, the principle of individual criminal liability under international law can no longer be doubted.[60]

2. The second question that we shall consider, namely, whether the principle *nullum crimen, nulla poena sine lege* can claim validity in international criminal law as to its effect of excluding *retroactive effect* of the rules of criminal law, was already ambiguous during the Nuremberg Trials with regard to what was new and could not be clearly proved in traditional international law.[61] In the future, this problem will continue to be a test question for the systematic positing of international criminal law, since the issue is whether this law is criminal law or not.[62] Should it be possible, we have to ask, to declare the breach of a formal provision concerning the treatment of prisoners of war retrospectively to be a punishable crime, although the offence at the time it was committed was only a less serious infringement and thus not threatened with punishment? In addition, should the decision on whether to punish the breach of the provisions of international law be left to the appropriate bodies of the international law community, to which the future defeated nation also belongs, or should it be placed in the hands of the victor or the courts whom the latter may appoint? Both questions are of course closely interrelated, since one would more willingly entrust a decision on the criminal nature of conduct to a court possessing the wisdom and impartiality for which the English judges, for example, are famous, than to a special political court. I wish to believe that the Nuremberg Tribunal, although a special court, was a model of impartiality.[63] Nonetheless, the fact remains that a power was represented on the judges' bench that participated in the war of aggression

---

[58] Correctly so, Strebel, op. cit., 46, 56. Characteristically, it is communist authors who passionately question direct criminal liability for war crimes under international law; the natural law element of international criminal law is feared here as is international criminal liability. Cf. Graefrath, 'Die Strafsanktionen in den Genfer Abkommen', *Staat und Recht* 5 (1956), 849 *et seq.*, 853. Similarly Modshorjan, op. cit., 684, and Koretsky (the latter quoted after Korowicz, op. cit., 543).

[59] On this v. Weber, 'Die Strafrechtliche Bedeutung der europäischenMenschenrechtskonvention', *Strafrechtswissenschaft* 65 (1953), 347, and Jescheck, 'Die europäische Konvention zum Schutze der Menschenrechte und Grundfreiheiten', *Neue Juristische Wochenschrift* 1954, 785.

[60] Eustathiades, op. cit., 460.

[61] Cf. on this Jescheck, Völkerstrafrecht 370 *et seq.*, and the excerpts from judgments summarized under the key words *nullum crimen sine lege* in Heinz-Schilling, op. cit.

[62] A similar problem arises in tax law, where an attempt is similarly made to draw consequences from tax law that conflict with criminal law and can never be recognized in the latter; cf. on this point Hartung, *Neue Juristische Wochenschrift* 1956, 41 *et seq.*

[63] Thus, Leon Cornil, 'Les possibilités du droit international pénal', *Revue internationale de droit pénal* 26 (1956), 19.

against Poland with remarkable and lasting benefit and that this power, also, further instructed its representatives on the IMT to blame the Germans for the murder of 4,143 Polish prisoner of war officers at Katyn,[64] although they must have known better than anyone else that it was their own people who committed this crime against the flower of the Polish nation.[65] I therefore remain sceptical with regard to objectivity in such situations and would leave the question as to what is worthy of punishment and what is not, in international law, rather to the appropriate bodies of the international law community for a preliminary decision than to those who have decisive power later at the critical moment. I am therefore worried that the validity of the retroactive effect prohibition will be disputed time and again by outstanding scholars of international criminal law.[66] Their arguments, however, are difficult to refute. The ban on retroactivity is not only applicable to written law but also to customary law. Whether an act should be punished must in this case be inferred from the legal usage existing at the time: *'nullum crimen sine jure'*.[67] The opponent's reference to English common law fails, since while the ban on retroactive effect is weakened in it, this weakening is also assumed for statute law.[68] The relativity of the application of the ban on retroactive effect is therefore not at all a consequence of the unwritten nature of English common law but affects common law and statute law in general. There are, in my opinion, two reasons for the difference that exists on this important point compared with the Continental legal approach. For the British, the ban on retroactive effect is only a question of justice, while we, as co-heirs of the declaration of Human and Citizen Rights of 1789, regard this principle above all as an unconditional postulate of legal *certainty*. Secondly, the division of authority under the English constitutional system does not entirely exclude law-making by the courts, while we entrust the position of law-maker only to the *supreme* body of the general will, Parliament.[69] It is very characteristic that the ban on retroactive effect is adhered to just as strictly in American criminal law as in Continental law, despite the application of numerous Common Law principles, because the United States has followed the Continental European tradition on this point.[70] Furthermore,

---

[64] Cf. on this point Nuremberg, XVII, 301 *et seq.*

[65] On this point, Thieme, 'Katyn—ein Geheimnis?', *Vierteljahreshfte für Zeitgeschichte* 1955, 409; General Anders, *Katyn*, Paris and London 1949; Mackewicz, *Katyn—ungesühntes Verbrechen*, 1949.

[66] Thus, Glaser, *Introduction à l'étude du droit international pénal*, 77 *et seq.*; Graven, Les principes de la légalité, de l'analogie et de l'interprétation et leur application en droit pénal suisse', *ZStrR* 66 (1941) 387; Mouton, *Oorlogs misdrijven* 418; recently, also, Dahm, op. cit., 64.

[67] Thus, rightly, Germann, *Kommentar zum Schweizerischen Strafgesetz I*, note on Article 1 N 2 ² (31).

[68] Graveson, 'Der Grundsatz "nulla poena sine lege" und Kontrollratsgesetz Nr. 10', *Monatsschrift für deutsches Recht* 1947, 278; Schönke, 'Materialien zum englisch-amerikanischen Strafrecht', *Deutsche Rechts-Zeitschrift* 1948, 4th edn., pp. 4 and 5; Ancel, *Annales de l'Institut de droit comparé de l'Université de Paris*, II (1936), 251 *et seq.*

[69] On this, very convincingly, Germann, op. cit., No. 1 (p. 30) and No. 2 ² (p. 31).

[70] Cf. Hall, *General Principles of Criminal Law*, Indianapolis 1947, 27 *et seq.*; Jescheck, Völkerstrafrecht, 240.

English law cannot be decisive for the application or non-application of the ban on retroactive effect in international criminal law, because this question has been clearly decided in the Continental sense in the latest international documents, which clearly takes into consideration that the punishability of an offence may result both from domestic law (generally written) and from international law (generally unwritten).

Article 99 (1) of the Geneva Prisoners of War Convention of 1949 requires the offence to be expressly punishable under domestic law or international law at the time it is committed. The same emerges from Article 11 (2) of the General Declaration on Human Rights of 1948. Article 7 of the European Human Rights Convention of 1950 is not so unambiguous, since here the ban on retroactive effect is weakened insofar as it is sufficient if punishability at the time of the offence existed under the general legal principle recognized by civilized peoples.[71] The same provision appears in Article 12 (2) of the draft drawn by the UN of a Convention on civil and political rights. However, this weakening concerns only the *degree* of the positivity of the legal source, since generally recognized legal principles are also a component of international law and of the *punishability* of the offence at the time it is committed but arise clearly from it. Ultimately, Reut-Nicolussi's statement from a Vienna rector's speech on this question applies: 'If retroactive acts already present a risk to legal certainty, a retroactive criminal law contradicts the essence of orderly conduct of the criminal law.'[72]

3. Of essential importance to the spirit and application of international criminal law is, furthermore, the question of whether *precedence of international law* over contradictory domestic law must be recognized.[73] The Nuremberg Courts have emphatically advocated this.[74] However, it must be noted that the IMT judgment refers at the decisive part of the text[75] only to the London Statute and does not attempt to derive the precedence theory from the state of current international law. This attempt would also have had to fail, since domestic practice at the time was then, no more than now, willing to accept such a far-reaching surrender of sovereignty. Even as decisive a proponent of the precedence theory as Lauterpacht, who transformed the leading textbook from the dualistic theory of Triepel and Oppenheim to the monistic doctrine of Kelsen and Verdross, still examines the question in the latest edition of the work of 1955 in terms of domestic practice and, with regard to English and American law, for example, comes

---

[71] Cf. on this and on the reservation of the Federal Government, v. Weber, op. cit., 348, and Echterhölter, 'Die Europäische Menschenrechtskonvention in der juristischen Praxis', *Juristenzeitung* 1956, 146, and Wegner, op. cit., 373.

[72] Op. cit., 374; also, Rittler, 'Der Kampf gegen das politische Verbrechen seit dem zweiten Weltkrieg ', *ZStrR* 64 (1949), 146 *et seq.*, and evidently also Germann, op. cit., N 2 ⁵ (32/33).

[73] This is supported in particular by Glaser, op. cit., 86, but a contrary view Verdross, *Völkerrecht*, 2nd edn., Vienna, 1950, 61, 62, with predominant international law doctrine. Cf. on this, also, Jescheck, *Völkerstrafrecht*, 212 *et seq.*

[74] Cf. on this Jescheck op. cit., 322 *et seq.*; Heinze-Schilling, op. cit., nos. 197–201.

[75] Nuremberg, I, 249.

to the conclusion that the precedence of international law is in no way acknowledged in all circumstances.[76] The work of the International Law Commission is not productive on these points either. The Draft Code contains indeed nothing on the question of precedence and Principle No. II states only that criminal liability also exists under international law if domestic law contains no appropriate threat of sanctions. To establish this principle, the Report of the International Law Commission refers to the 'supremacy of international law over national law', but essentially the text says nothing further than that there are independent circumstances under international criminal law which no one doubts who recognizes international criminal law.[77] The solution of conflict proves difficult and here it remains, in fact, doubtful whether it is permissible to expose the individual to the conflict of two legal systems, of which the second is always able to attract attention, even if it is not legally entitled to recognition. A weak form of protection would then exist only in the emergency rule. German constitutional law has taken this step from domestic law: Article 25 of the Constitutional Act states that the general rules of international law are not only a component of Federal law, which they were already under Article 4 of the Weimar Constitution, but *take precedence* over the laws. However, this statement does not at all lay down generally recognized rules of international law, but is a decision of a parliament that had reason to draw very far-reaching conclusions from the history of its people. Today, only the 'restricted dualism' or 'moderated monism' based on the *natural law* that concedes to the weight of the rules for international law will be recognized as *general*,[78] and in each case the domestic rule conflicting with international law will be regarded only as provisional, having no relevance before a true court of international law.[79]

4. Furthermore, in order to be able to assess the question of *penalizing of sovereign acts*, above all, the problem must be correctly classified.[80] It is a matter of the power of the courts (jurisdiction), not substantive criminal law, and of the material quality of the offence as a sovereign act of the state, not the personal exemption of the body of state (immunity). The powers of jurisdiction concerning sovereign acts undoubtedly exist for an international legal body if the State concerned has recognized these legal powers.[81] The question becomes difficult only when no recognition exists and the power of criminal law is exercised by an ordinary foreign court or occupation court. On these points, a remarkable development seems

---

[76] *International Law*, 8th Edition 1955, I, 41 *et seq.*

[77] This can be said against Glaser, op. cit., 94.

[78] Thus, Jescheck, Völkerstrafrecht, 217 *et seq.* The criticism by Dahm, op. cit., 68, n. 166, is incorrect, as my comments do not refer to Article 25 of the Constitutional Act but to the position of the question in international practice.

[79] On this, Verdross, op. cit., 61 with references in note 1.

[80] On this, very pertinently, Dahm, op. cit., 40/41.

[81] Here lies the legal importance of Article 227 *et seq.* of the Versailles Peace Treaty. Sovereign acts are consequently also included in Article 25 of the Draft Statute for an International Court, but the application of the Statute in fact presupposes recognition by the State concerned.

to be under way. That the powers of the courts are not excluded by the character of the offence, as a sovereign act of State was one of the basic principles of
Nuremberg law.[82] However, this principle certainly does *not* go without saying,
since the equality of sovereign States has also remained intact as a structural principle of the international law community since the Second World War, and when
we see how vehemently numerous states under the leadership of the Soviet Union,
but not only communist ones, have reacted to the formation of an International
Criminal Court incompatible with Article 2 (7) of the UN Charter, the end of
the age of sovereignty does not yet appear nigh.[83] The statement that only legitimate sovereign acts of foreign legal authority are excluded goes to the heart of
the problem, since the consideration of *whether* something is lawful or unlawful
necessarily presupposes recourse to legal authority.[84] The view adopted also by
Dahm[85] that legal authority may always be exercised over and above a sovereign act if the state concerned has exceeded its own sovereign limits seems to
fall short in my opinion, since legal authority is, as we know, claimed precisely
for cases of crimes against humanity against citizens on a state's own territory.
If this principle of Nuremberg law is not therefore implicitly compatible with
general international law, we have to ask ourselves once again what attitude has
subsequently been taken. The answer is that developments appear to be proceeding in the direction of recognition of jurisdiction over foreign sovereign acts. We
find a principle of this kind as point III amongst the Nuremberg Principles and
as Article 3 in the Draft Code, both of which, of course, take account, not only
of international, but also of domestic, jurisdiction. Article 25 of the Statute for
an International Criminal Court cannot be put up against this as further proof,
because an international law judicial body is presupposed here with jurisdiction
recognized by the states. However, the Geneva Conventions of 1949 are neither
probatory, as they have included without exception the *ordering* of grave breaches
to the universal principle,[86] so that each member state will be able to pass sentence on sovereign acts by another state, insofar as these constitute war crimes.
However, the Genocide Convention has also here receded behind the Nuremberg
judgments. The second draft already considered the principle of universality too
dangerous for sovereignty, because every member state would thereby be granted
jurisdiction over acts committed abroad, especially sovereign acts. Article IV,
which expressly lays down the principle of criminal liability of government members and state institutions, therefore, proves meaningless, since it has never been

---

[82] Nuremberg I 249/250.

[83] What Glaser has commented against this, *ZStrR* 68 (1953), 325 *et seq.* does not correspond to
the reality of state practice.

[84] Consequently rightly Dahm, op. cit., 42.

[85] Dahm, op. cit., 43.

[86] However, the arrangement for which the Geneva Expert Committee of 1948 provided in
paragraph 2 of its Principle III was clear and not exposed to any misconceptions.

doubted that a state's own sovereign acts are subject to its own jurisdiction. The picture is therefore not entirely uniform and you may well still be confronted with an open question. I will not try to decide, but only ask for an explanation for why the abandonment of the old acts of state doctrine is so frequently advocated. It would seem that in view of the existential threat to the international community from forces that are capable of any breach of the law and in view of the absence of international criminal jurisdiction, states no longer feel that the formal principle of equality prevents them from punishing themselves where safeguarding the essential assets of human culture is concerned.

5. I will not end the General Part of international criminal law without addressing the problem that is dear to everyone who has ever borne military responsibility: the *order*.[87] The London Charter, through Article 8 which permitted acting under orders only as a ground for mitigation and not as an excuse,[88] has also substantially tightened up the strictest national laws. However, the Nuremberg courts took a more lenient view and consequently reduced the Charter back to the more or less common position under national laws. The IMT judgment referred to the aspect of necessity (problem of 'moral choice');[89] amongst the other verdicts, several have recognized that an order is a special case of misconception regarding the prohibition of the act in conjunction with the particularly compelling situation of military subordination.[90] A soldier may assume without further thought that the orders of his superiors are lawful. Loyalty to the superior, the habit of obedience and the unconditional nature of military discipline complicate a decision to refuse to obey. Hence, it all comes down to whether the subordinate was aware of the criminal nature of the order or whether the latter was so obvious that lack of knowledge could not serve as an excuse.[91] This was also the starting point for subsequent development.[92] Point IV of the Nuremberg Principles initially still reflects the IMT view and consequently goes by the possibility of 'moral choice'. The International Law Commission modified the originally identically worded Article 4 of the Draft Code in the 1954 version, so that the subordinate is responsible in criminal law 'if, in the circumstances at the time, it was possible

---

[87] On this Eustathiades, 'Quelques aspects de la jurisprudence concernants les criminels de guerre: l'exception des ordres reçus et autres moyens de défense similaires', Festschrift for Rudolf Laun, Hamburg, 1953, 395 *et seq*.; Mouton, *Orlogsmisdrijven*, 369 *et seq*., with an overview of comparative law; v. Weber, 'Die strafrechtliche Verantwortlichkeit für Handeln auf Befehl', *Monatsschrift für deutsches Recht*, 1948, 34 *et seq*., comparing the Continental and Common Law approaches.

[88] That is how I understood the provision in *Völkerstrafrecht* 385 in the light of the sources. Similarly also Eustathiades, op. cit., 399, note 15a, and Dahm, op. cit., 74. The different view, Glaser, *ZStrR* 68 (1953), 345 and 'L'Ordre hiérarchique en Droit pénal international', *Revue de droit pénal et de criminologie*, 1953, 325 *et seq*.

[89] Nuremberg, I, 250.

[90] Cf. Jescheck, *Völkerstrafrecht* 388/389.

[91] Cf. Eustathiades, op. cit., 405, 411.

[92] Cf. On the question of obviousness of breach of the law, Würtenberger, 'Der Irrtum über die Völkerrechtmässigkeit des höheren Befehls im Strafrecht', *Monatsschrift für deutsches Recht*, 1948, 271.

for him not to comply with that order'. This provision certainly avoids the over-narrow reference to an emergency situation, but the new formulation is so vague that the decision is practically left to the judgment of the court without any legal guidance. By contrast, the principle assumed by the Geneva Expert Committee of 1948 is essentially correct, which held 'that, according to the circumstances, the accused could reasonably be aware that he was participating in breach of the present Convention'. Unfortunately, the acting under orders rule was not taken up in the Geneva Convention itself, a mistake whose source can no longer be traced and explained with the available material.[93] My impression is that states no longer wished to come to a conclusive agreement about the point just a few years after 1945, since this was in any event the reason why the problem of acting under orders was similarly avoided under the Genocide Convention.

An answer to the question in light of more recent doctrine on error is now offered by the two most recent provisions applying to acting under superior orders under military law. The possibility of an emergency is not mentioned in either case but always has a bearing, of course, as an independent reason for exculpation *after* the question of errors. Article 11 (2) 2 of the *German Soldiers Act* of 1956,[94] initially, like item 50 of the Swiss Service Rules of 1954, stated that an order to obey which would result in a crime or offence is not binding.[95] Under the present German rules, a subordinate is criminally liable for an order carried out 'if he recognizes or when it was *obvious* in the light of the circumstances, of which he was aware, that an offence or crime would thereby be perpetrated'.[96][97] Incidentally, a formula to the same effect was adopted by the Criminal Law Committee of the six participating Powers during preparation of the joint Military Criminal Law for the European Defence Community. Item 500 of the *American Field Manual* of 1956 that has basically the same meaning forbids a subordinate from relying on an order given 'unless he did not know and could not reasonably have been expected to know that the act ordered was unlawful'. This statement, I feel, deals squarely with the problem of orders received. It comes down to whether the subordinate recognizes the criminal nature of the order or whether his lack of knowledge should be held against him, whereupon the habit of obedience and trust in the superior may be assumed in his favour so that only *apparent* unlawfulness

---

[93] Cf. on this Maunoir, *La répression des crimes de guerre devant les tribunaux français et alliés*, Thesis Geneva, 1956, 233.

[94] Act concerning the Legal Position of Soldiers of 19 March 1956 (BGBl I 114). Cf. on this Brandstetter, *Freiwilligengesetz*, Cologne-Berlin, 1955, 97 *et seq.*

[95] Consequently, the binding nature of an order conflicting with criminal law, which is still accepted by v. Knierim, Nürnberg, Stuttgart, 1953, 260/261, no longer exists under German law.

[96] The Swiss military criminal code, also in Article 18, deals with an order as a problem of guilt, but like Article 47 of the old German military criminal code demands *full* awareness on the part of the subordinate; cf. Comtesse, *Das Schweizerische Militärstrafgesetzbuch*, Zurich, 1946, Article 18, Notes 5–7. The change from German Law to the Common Law formula is remarkable.

[97] The same arrangement appears in s. 5 (1) of the new German Wehrstrafgesetzes Cf. Arndt, *Goltdammers Archiv* 1957, 46 *et seq.*

can be argued. Essentially, therefore, the doctrine of 'legal blindness' (Mezger) has been applied here, with particular regard to the military circumstances. The aspect of emergency is considered separately if it is clear that the soldier cannot be exculpated on grounds of error. If the soldier is guilty under military law, the requirement to obey orders still applies as an extraordinary but optional ground for mitigation of punishment.[98]

IV

The Nuremberg Trials stirred up the demand for *international criminal jurisdiction* repeatedly made since the First World War.[99]

1. The Nuremberg International Military Court was indeed only an inter-allied *ad hoc* occupation court and not an organ of international law, since Germany did not recognize this jurisdiction;[100] but the moral obligation to create a true international criminal jurisdiction that would propagate the substantive international criminal law as it is created, has been felt ever more strongly abroad. Already during the first consultations on the Nuremberg Principles in 1947, Donnedieu de Vabres raised again the question in a monograph[101] and it has been present on the UN agenda since then. While the response of states was initially not unfriendly, being still under the influence of the Nuremberg Trials, attitudes cooled down ever more strongly in the course of time. Above all, growing opposition was evident from the start amongst the communist states, which regarded international jurisdictions as an encroachment on their sovereignty, a breach of Article 2 (7) of the principle of non-interference guaranteed by the UN Constitution and, as a result, a threat to peace.[102] They therefore no longer participated in the preparatory work as from 1950 onwards and appeared only to cast negative votes in the Sixth Committee and the General Assembly. A large group of states headed by the United Kingdom considers the setting up of an international Criminal court as premature, because it is practically

---

[98] Thus s. 5(2) of the German Wehrstrafgesetzes of 30 March 1957 (BGBl I 298).

[99] Cf. 'Historical Survey of the Question of International Criminal Jurisdiction', UN Doc.A/CN 4/7/Rev. 1; v. Weber, *Internationale Strafgerichtsbarkeit*, Berlin and Bonn, 1934; Glaser, *Droit international pénal,* 145 *et seq.*; Carjeu, *Projet d'une juridiction pénale internationale*, Paris, 1953; Jescheck, op. cit., 41 *et seq.*

[100] Glaser, *ZStrR* 68 (1953), 336; Donnedieu de Vabres, *Recueil des Cours*, 1947, I, 482; Dahm, op. cit., 18; E. Sauer, *Grundlehre des Völkerrechts*, Cologne-Berlin 1955, 276; Reut-Nicolussi, Laun *Festschrift* 372; Heinitz, *Zeitschrift für die gesamte Strafrechtswissenschaft* 66 (1954), 266; Jescheck, op. cit. 283 *et seq.*; similarly, also various members of the International Law Commission, cf. UN Doc. A/CN. 4/SR 43, p. 5.

[101] UN Doc. A/CN 10/21.

[102] Cf. the opinion of the Soviet Union, White Russia, Poland, and Czechoslovakia in the 6th Commission for Discussion of the Report of the International Law Commission, end-1950; cf. General Assembly, Fifth Session Off. Rec., Sixth Committee, 1950, 223 *et seq.*

pointless at the present time, and has therefore continued to work towards this goal with minor efforts. The only proponents of the idea who have remained true and unconditional are France and the Netherlands.

2. In view of this political position, developments in thinking on international criminal jurisdiction have simply been disappointing since 1946. While the principles of the Geneva Expert Committee of 1948 still mention an international criminal jurisdiction together with the national one, the Geneva Conventions of 1949 make no mention of this point. The Genocide Convention of 1948 still mentions an international criminal jurisdiction as a possibility, but opposition in the Sixth Committee was so forceful that even this really mild reference was nearly discarded. After the International Law Commission essentially came out in favour of this concept,[103] two of the special committees set up by the General Assembly in 1951 and 1953 have drawn up a Statute for an International Criminal Court,[104] significantly contemplating the road of a Convention of participating states, because in view of the unambiguous attitude of the Soviet Union, the constitutional changes required to set up a UN body appeared unachievable from the start. However, the results of the work of the special committee have been really disappointing. So many obstacles were built into the Statute for the International Criminal Court that one really wonders what purpose a court set up with such distrust can really serve and what it should do.[105] The transfer of jurisdiction by member states presupposes an agreement or unilateral declaration by the states concerned. An accused can never be summoned before the court unless both the home state and also the state of the place of performance have transferred jurisdiction for *this* case to the international criminal court. Any state may also revoke transfer of jurisdiction and such a declaration will already be effective within one year after the UN Secretary-General has been notified. In the interests of maintaining peace, a competent body of the UN can intervene and prevent a case from being brought before the court or remove further consideration of the matter from the court. Altogether, the attitude of states is that they will on no account accept a 'de facto international jurisdiction',[106] as called for in 1945. The General Assembly is in no particular hurry to examine the drafts.[107] Discussion was postponed from one year to the next, in the autumn of 1956 again to 1957, based on the already familiar grounds that the special committee's draft defining an aggressor was not yet available and international criminal jurisdiction was materially closely tied to this question.

---

[103] UN Doc. A/CN 4/34, Part IV s. 140.

[104] UN Doc. A/2136 Suppl. No. 11 and A/2645 Suppl. No. 12. On this see Quincy Wright, *American Journal of International Law* 46 (1952), 60 *et seq.*; Yuen-Li Liang, ibid., 73 *et seq.*; Finch, ibid., 89 *et seq.*; Yuen-Li Liang, ibid. 47 (1953), 638 and *Yearbook of the United Nations*, 1953, 683 *et seq.*

[105] Ibid., Glaser, *Droit international pénal* 155, *et seq.*

[106] Donnedieu de Vabres, *Recueil des Cours*, 1957, I, 576.

[107] Cf. on this Quintano Ripollés, 'Dix ans après Nuremberg', *Revue internationale de droit pénal* 26 (1956), 45 *et seq.*

If we consider developments since 1946 in their entirety, we find no reason for more than sober scepticism. Or should we entirely reject the whole direction and rejoice that so little has emerged? That is not my view, but I follow the gains and reversals in international criminal law with the interest of a person for whom the matter has become important. The two objections in principle against the existence of true international criminal law are well known: they are directed against a Utopian pre-assumption of a world-state order and against an impermissible shift in the legitimation of law-making from the traditional law-maker to a nebulous international community. Both objections must be taken seriously but are not ultimately decisive. Common organization and an interlinking of interests is gathering force in the mutual relationship amongst Western states, which is beginning to show all-embrasive elements of the federal state.[108] The Mining Union, for example, acknowledges a jurisdiction of the senior authorities, and developments are bound to proceed further with the formation of a common market. As far as legitimation for law-making is concerned, I do not consider it wrong, after all that has happened in the past, for a super-national criminal-law-maker to exist *over* the states. As we know, criminal law not only threatens the malefactor with sanctions, but above all, protects the weak against violence and arbitrariness, and in this respect, the states have by no means always taken the necessary steps in the past, as otherwise the call for international criminal law would never have been heard to start with. I therefore consider it a blessing for law-making powers in criminal law that this does not end with the states. International law will thereby become a comprehensive system of natural law, which in an extreme emergency can assume the defence of the supreme assets of mankind. The legal philosophy of Switzerland that accommodates so many international bodies on its soil, is familiar with this view. However, it also corresponds to the law as the common man understands it. It was the leader of the peasants from Schwyz in whose mouths a German poet placed the undying words:

> When the oppressed can find justice nowhere,
> When intolerable becomes the burden—he reaches
> To heaven for hope and encouragement
> And pulls down his eternal rights,
> That float up high, as unalienable
> And unchanging, as the stars themselves—
> The original state of nature returns again.

---

[108] Jescheck, 'Die Strafgewalt übernationaler Gemeinschaften', *Zeitschrift für die gesamte Strafrechtswissenschaft* 65 (1953), 502 *et seq.*

2. Historical Perspectives—The Nuremberg Legacy

18

Nuremberg Eighteen Years Afterwards

By Otto Kranzbuhler*

AFTER my learned friends, Professor Herbert Krauss and Professor Carl Haensel, have presented their thoughts on the Nuremberg trials in the previous issue of this Review, it will be difficult for me to be heard on the same topic without boring or shocking my readers. In order to avoid both, I should like to begin by saying that my approach is different in several respects, maybe because my personal position was, and is, completely different.

Until the end of the war, I was a naval career officer in the Judge Advocate's branch and, as Fleet Judge-Advocate, was vested with a rather high rank. Through the agency of the British Royal Navy, I was called to Nuremberg in October, 1945, to act as defense counsel for the last German head of state, Grand-Admiral Dönitz. After having defended Dönitz before the International Military Tribunal, which lasted until November, 1946, I acted as defense counsel in the trials of the big industrialists, *i.e.* Friedrich Flick and Alfried Krupp, before the American courts in Nuremberg, and defended the Saar industrialist, Hermann Röchling, before a similarly constituted French court in Rastatt. After that period, which lasted until 1949, I was concerned as a corporation lawyer with the consequences of these penal proceedings on the German enterprises affected thereby, particularly with problems of confiscation of private property and of decartellization. The tasks connected therewith were, and continue to be even today, of a political rather than a legal character.

If today, twenty years after the war, I am to express my opinion about the merits, or lack of merit, of the Nuremberg trials, I do so at a time when the effects of Nuremberg are still felt, in spite of the time which has elapsed.

By Nuremberg trials, I mean the big, so-called international trial, from 1945 to 1946 before the International Military Tribunal, of leading political and military men of the National Socialist regime, proceedings where the four Occupying Powers participated both on the bench and in the prosecution. Furthermore, I mean by this term the twelve subsequent purely American trials.

* MR. KRANZBUHLER *was Chief Counsel for Grand Admiral Karl Dönitz, Commander-in-Chief of the German Navy and last Führer of Germany, at the Nuremberg International War Crimes Trial, and is currently a practicing attorney of Dusseldorf, Germany.*

Of these trials, three were directed against the sphere of activities of the SS—the cases of the 'Special Commandos' (*Einsatzgruppen*), the Chief Office for Racial and Settlement Policies (*Rasse- und Siedlungspolitisches Hauptamt*), and the *Pohl* case which dealt with the administration of concentration camps—three were concerned with the military sphere, which included the cases of Field-Marshal Milch, the South-Eastern Generals, and the German Supreme Command of the Armed Forces (OKW)—and three were concerned with the industrial sphere, Flick, I. G. Farben, and Krupp. In addition, there was one trial of jurists, one trial of medical doctors and the last trial, referred to in the jargon of Nuremberg as the 'omnibus case,' against all those whom the prosecution had been unable to accommodate before—the most important group being six diplomats headed by State Secretary von Weizsäcker.

I think it is necessary to consider these trials together because they are based on a common idea of the American prosecution. As may be seen from the way the groups of the accused are combined, the idea was not to try criminals for crimes allegedly committed by them, but to prove by means of judicial proceedings that members of all the higher strata, regardless of whether they had directly participated or not, were responsible for everything which Hitler and his aiders and abettors had thought up and carried out. Thus they were political trials, or one might use the term 'historical trials,' in which one political system, namely the democratic one, held court over another system, that is, the dictatorial one. That the delegates of Stalin sat on the democratic bench of the International Military Tribunal was just one of its defects which prompted criticism. The trials being organized in this manner, any consideration analyzing their substance cannot be limited to the legal aspect, it must include the political aspect.

The question may be raised as to whether a period immediately following an embittered war could contain the necessary conditions for the spiritual controversy which any historical trial constitutes. This question I wish to answer in the affirmative with due regard to the situation as it existed in Germany at the time. The conviction that a wrong committed required some sort of expiation, some sort of analysis and discussion, existed not only on the side of the victors or on the part of the neutrals, but also in, or at least gradually began to dawn upon, the German nation. Thus I believe that the conditions for discussion, argument and analysis, and thus for a historical trial, were most favorable during the years 1945 to 1948 and that, consequently, if a trial of such a nature can make sense at all and be justified, optimum results ought to have been achieved.

In assessing the merits of the Nuremberg trials, I should like to combine juridical analysis with consideration of legal policy. It may appear somewhat peculiar to submit a trial to the requirements of legal policy and to a test according to the criterion of legal policy; but the judges at the Nuremberg trials never left any doubt, and it clearly appears from the history of the origins of the Nuremberg trials that they did not intend to administer existing law in the sense we are used to it, or as we would expect from our national administration of criminal justice.

This was expressed very clearly by the judges in the Weizsäcker case. They stated in their judgment that they considered it to be the task of the court to find standards of conduct for the citizens, officials and civil servants of a state which they would have to comply with in the future, in all situations where the law of nations was applicable and in a position to lay down rules of conduct for an individual. Thus, it was their intention to lay down a sort of categorical imperative for the political conduct of the individual in international affairs. This intention has not remained unopposed. In the same Weizsäcker case, Judge Powers wrote a dissenting opinion protesting violently against this usurpation of functions. But the discussion that took place during that trial, and that has come to the notice of the public, shows that the judges were clearly aware of the importance of the proceedings and of their decisions.

For yet another reason, one should combine the juridical with the legal policy consideration; Nuremberg was conceived, and can only be understood as, a revolutionary event in the development of international law. If one were to tackle the criticism of the venture with the idea that no ex post facto laws may be applied, or similar conservative conceptions, one need not speak about Nuremberg at all. Law in the conventional sense of the term had been knowingly disregarded at Nuremberg. One was fully aware that a step forward was being ventured. Mr. Robert Jackson, the American chief prosecutor, stated repeatedly, and in a very dramatic way, particularly in connection with the greatly contested concept of a Crime against Peace, that a beginning must be made at some time and peace-breakers must be punished in order to free humanity from the scourge of war. This step was thus taken consciously, and it would be senseless to apply tests and standards other than those which may be applied to revolutionary events. Such events are always connected with a certain measure of injustice and a certain measure of force, and thus they have to be judged by their results for humanity. Accordingly, if I go back to the rules, doctrines or practices of international law that exist—or rather existed up to Nuremberg—my intention is not to brand as an injustice everything that is not in accordance therewith, but merely to clarify the direction and aim of the development initiated at Nuremberg and to raise a question as to whether the development has actually proceeded in the desired direction. The value or lack of value of those trials must in my opinion be judged as to whether the findings of these courts are suitable to constitute effective precedents in the future, whether they are suitable to be generally accepted as binding and whether, in actual fact, they have been or will be so accepted.

From the outset the trials were burdened by the manner in which they came into existence. It might be imagined that an independent tribunal composed of well-known members of the legal profession and experts in international law would have developed with greater success and with greater authority new principles of international law, including even revolutionary principles, than was possible at Nuremberg in view of the history of its origin.

I would consider the Anglo-American procedure as such, particularly suitable for a political criminal trial, subject to one requirement—equality of arms between the two parties. That was not the case at Nuremberg. The prosecution, through a multitude of investigators, had searched all the German archives, which had been confiscated, in order to find material in support of the prosecution's case. And the defense counsel had to live on what was left over, so to speak, from the documents which the prosecutor had introduced into evidence against the defendants. For the defense counsel, access to the archives was barred. Thus, they were unable to make the investigations, always necessary for the defense, but particularly necessary in an historical trial. It is easily recognized what this means whenever judging particular sets of facts in the fields of foreign policy or strategy. A further deficiency was that the defense was restricted to using purely German material; and this was a matter of grave importance in an historical trial. It was the ambition of the prosecution to dispose of the Nazi war criminals on the basis of their own documents, and that meant that foreign archives remained strictly barred. The picture unfolded to the court was thus one-sided and incomplete. As an example, I merely wish to refer to the German-Soviet Treaty of August 23, 1939, the political basis of the occupation of Poland, which was not submitted to the court. Its existence was proved to the court by many detours through affidavits, subject to continued objections on the part of the Russian prosecution. This is one small instance, indicating the historical imperfection and thus the deficiency in fact-finding which appears in a trial of this kind.

The rules that were applied in this trial were not, as is generally assumed, rules of international law. The law of nations, at Nuremberg, was applicable only secondarily. This the judges knew very well, and it appeared to restrict some of them. Primarily, the laws created for the purpose of the Nuremberg Trial were as follows: the London Charter, which was based on discussions between the four occupying powers in July and August, 1945, and which was applicable to the International Military Tribunal; and Law No. 10 of the Control Council which reshaped the rules of the London Charter into German occupation law, with some changes, and which applied to the succeeding American war crime trials. The London Charter was created in a manner which was not calculated to increase the authority of the legislator or the judge. We know about it from the very extensive report submitted by American Chief Prosecutor Jackson to the President of the United States.

No attempt was made to come to a really thorough understanding of what was defensible under international law. The Charter obviously was merely intended to bring certain defendants to prosecution and conviction. As an instance I refer to the discussion aimed at introducing the American concept of conspiracy, *i.e.* a common plan or design to commit criminal acts. The Continental participants at the conference had considerable doubts about including this concept, which was unknown to them, in the rules of the London Charter. But when the argument was brought forward that without this concept a man such as Schacht could not be convicted, this was accepted as a sufficient basis for including conspiracy in the London Charter.

In connection with the origin of the Charter, another phenomenon must be considered that greatly weakens the authority of this administration of justice. Since the French Revolution it has been considered a basic requirement of true administration of justice that the separation of powers is strictly observed in legal proceedings. In Nuremberg, in the International Military Tribunal, it appeared that two of the legislators of the London Charter, that is the American, Jackson, and a Britisher, Sir David Maxwell Fyffe, acted as chief prosecutors, thus as part of the executive power, while two other legislators of the London Charter, a Frenchman, Falco, and a Russian, Nikichenkow, reappeared at Nuremberg in the capacity of judges. By this personal overlapping, the doctrine of separation of powers was grossly neglected and thus the authority of the administration of justice greatly impaired from the very outset.

Dealing with the contribution of the Nuremberg trials to substantive law, I should like to start with the classic concept of a war crime in order to emphasize the tribunal's revolutionary aspect. As a basis, I refer to a definition which will be found in all textbooks on international law. I proceed on the definition from *Oppenheim-Lauterpacht, International Law* (1944), which distinguishes the following types of war crimes, that is crimes that may be the subject of criminal prosecution by the opposing belligerent. The elements of these crimes are very simple: (1) violations of the rules of war by members of the armed forces, or (2) armed hostilities by non-members of the armed forces. These two points are essential. There are two further grounds, war-treason and marauding, which are of no importance in connection with our discussion. Thus, I repeat, violation of the rules of war by the members of the armed forces and armed hostilities by non-members of the armed forces are the two elements of war crimes.

This conservative definition of a war crime certainly would not provide a sufficient basis for the prosecution of statesmen or public officers for a policy leading to war, or the prosecution of generals on account of the military preparation for war, or the prosecution of members of the legal profession on account of their participation in certain legislation, or, even less, the prosecution of industrialists on account of their participation in the war economy of their country. As I said, I mention these two matters, the classic war crime and the Nuremberg practice, in juxtaposition in order to demonstrate the enormous step that was taken at Nuremberg, which I do not wish to criticize as it was a step forward. I merely examine whether this step forward continues to have authority as a precedent for the future.

The supposition underlying this step was the recognition of a completely new doctrine; the doctrine that international law is binding upon the individual citizen. One can read in any textbook on international law that the law of nations is the law regulating the relations between sovereign states. The binding character of this law on individuals is a novum that was introduced at Nuremberg, and had to be introduced there in order to make the individual punishable. This step results in really tragic consequences if a conflict between international law and national law ensues. Until the trials, it was generally accepted that in the case of conflict, national law would prevail over international law. The citizen, the argument stated, owes primarily allegiance to the state to whose legislation he is subject. Thus, the law of nations merely had a subsidiary validity as to individuals and never had a direct effect on them; in the case of a conflict of laws, the national law prevailed. The Nuremberg courts took the opposite point of view and submitted the individual citizen to the obligation of acting in accordance with the rules of international law in the event of an incompatibility, that is, to resist national law. This duty to resist is a postulate which makes its way as a ghost-like apparition through the judgments of Nuremberg; a postulate that cannot be reconciled to the actual facts of life, and that has never been recognized by jurisprudence or by the legal practice of states. The Roman Catholic Church, which often enough had to struggle to resist state power, made a very impressive statement in this respect, in connection with the attempt made in 1948 to create a court with power to hear appeals from the Nuremberg judgments. At that time Cardinal Frings, at the request of the Bishops' Conference in Fulda, wrote to General Clay. In his letter there is the following passage: 'It may be a complex question of conscience whether one is to follow one's own judgment or supra-national rules against the order of one's legal superior, state authority. No state has ventured until now to lay down rules on this question for its own citizens, much less to provide a sanction in criminal law for such rules.' This is as true now as it was then. The duty under international law to act in resistance, a duty construed by the Nuremberg courts at the time, and a necessary construction in the light of their *raison d'etre*, cannot be and is not being required of the citizen. The purpose of creating a precedent on this point, has certainly not been of any lasting import.

The second big step taken at Nuremberg was to set up a very simple equation, an equation that until that time had never been mentioned at all, viz., a violation of international law equals punishability. In national law, which uses definite, published, generally known rules, a prescription of this type would be received with indignation. No one would think of equating illegality and punishability in national law, but rather would hold that punishability requires a specific law be in existence, which provides that a given unlawful act shall be subject to punishment. From this it will be clear, to what degree of legal uncertainty the individual is subjected by such a doctrine. International law, with its vague and fluctuating rules, its many undecided questions and the widely shared doubt whether, in an individual case, a certain action is unlawful or not, cannot attach punishability to unlawfulness. As an example of how impossible the results of such adjudication are, I might mention that in the case against Grand Admiral Raeder at the International Military Tribunal, hours and hours were spent discussing violations of the Versailles Treaty committed before the war, from the point of view that, as violations of international law, they were material as punishable acts. The idea that the violation of international treaties, as such, would have penal consequences is absurd in present-day international relationships. In another case, the Flick judgment, the court arrived at the conclusion that the employment of prisoners of war in a factory making railroad cars is not in conformity with the Hague Regulations Respecting the Laws and Customs of War on Land and the Geneva Convention, and convicted an industrialist on account of this 'war crime,' a matter which speaks for itself. The step from unlawfulness to punishability certainly is among those taken at Nuremberg most subject to criticism. One can only hope that it will not be recognized as a precedent.

This step was accompanied by the third great innovation, which became most evident to the outside world, that is, the extension of the scope of punishable acts. I should like to take up the acts which have been treated as offenses under international law in the sequence in which they become more distant from the classic concept of war crime, *i.e.*, first of all the extension of the concept of war crime as such, then the Crime against Humanity and, finally, the Crime against Peace.

With respect to actual war crimes, it appears very significant that the rules of war applied by the Nuremberg judges, as distinguished from their revolutionary attitude in other respects, are more than conservative. The Hague Regulations on land warfare were applied according to the standards of the year 1907 and without regard to the technological development which war had seen, namely in the effect of weapons of air warfare upon the country behind the fighting lines, economic warfare, propaganda warfare, radio, in short, total warfare. Total war for some of the Nuremberg judges was a diabolical invention of the Nazis, and they ignored it as a necessary consequence of the development of warfare itself. This has a regrettable effect. I believe all experts agree that the rules of warfare, the laws of war, will have to be rewritten. The Nuremberg courts would have been a good place and a good body to have rewritten these rules of war to bring them up to date with the actual developments that have taken place. In this connection, I proceed on the assumption that historical experience has shown how wrong it was to rely on the prohibition of war as such, and thereby forget to regulate and secure the humanizing of war to the extent this is feasible, considering the frightful set of facts which war constitutes. The most urgent task, in my opinion, would have been to fix those rules of humanity that can still be observed and secured even in total war. Simply to deny total war as such and to retain the position of the year 1907 is such a misjudgment of reality that it cannot be expected to find the least consideration in any future conflict.

In connection with war crimes, I should like to take up another subject which is of special importance in this respect and also in reference to the crime against humanity: the appreciation of the military order. Controversy about this problem has come to fill libraries. Until 1945, it appears to have been generally recognized that the military order constituted justification for the subordinate unless—as expressed in the German Military Penal Code—he realized the intention to commit a felony or other crime by means of such an such order.

The Anglo-American military penal law, until 1944, treated the military order in the same way. Then it was suddenly changed, as is openly admitted, with a view to the intended punishment of German war criminals. After this change of the English and American rules, a superior order only constituted a ground of extenuation. The Nuremberg judges took firmly the position that superior orders could never constitute justification and at most could amount to a mitigating factor in assessing punishment, and they maintained this view to the extent of undermining the very foundation of military discipline, on which the striking force and the very right to existence of armies rests. The courts rendering decisions in this field were submitted to repeated criticism after the war by national courts, even in Allied countries. By such decisions, the subordinate was burdened with a responsibility which he cannot bear and which, in an institution such as the armed services, by its very nature, he is not even allowed to bear. I admit that circumstances may differ in the top ranks of the armed services. I admit that there is a difference as to whether an order is received by a field marshal or by an officer of lower rank or a non-commissioned officer or a private. However, the principle that the order is binding upon the subordinate, who is not justified in examining the order, appears to me to be definitely recognized. As an example, the 'Commando Order,' rightly considered to be in violation of international law (which provided that commando troops were to be killed before or after having been taken prisoner even if they wore uniforms) was given on the purported grounds that it constituted a reprisal under international law. It is impossible to expect from a subordinate that he should examine whether the requirements of a reprisal existed or not. Thus, I believe that the Nuremberg jurisprudence on this point also has failed completely.

Where conscientious judges dealt with the cases, they tried to free themselves from the predicament of their own decisions through the defense of duress. To a large extent, they found the somewhat constructive formula, that nonobservance of an order that was illegal under international law, would have submitted anyone who refused to comply with that order to a state of duress. We as defense counsel of course supported and promoted this doctrine, but if critically examined as to its substance, one must say that in many cases it is not true. With this point I leave the criticism concerning the treatment of the war crime in the sense of a violation of the rules applicable to the armed forces, and conclude that this adjudication cannot claim the effect of having created real precedents.

I now refer to the other great new complex: the Crime against Humanity. The Crime against Humanity has become a slogan nowadays to such an extent that many do not know any longer what its actual substance was. It was the intention of the Nuremberg courts to punish the abuse of legal forms and devices by the government in the commission of acts, apparently carried out in legal form, or in the form of orders appearing to be lawful, but which in substance constituted the gravest crimes against humanitarian principles, against humanity itself. Against the creation of such elements of a punishable offense, one might raise the objection that the sovereignty of the state is negatived and thereby disregarded. This objection carries some weight because it is in conformity with the entire system of international law as we know it. Nevertheless I believe that in this case, the Nuremberg jurisprudence has taken a step which corresponds to a necessary development and which should be accepted; not in the multitude of instances in which this has subsequently been improperly employed but in its basic concept.

In its basic concept, a Crime against Humanity is a crime of the government, and thus a prosecution should only be levelled against the government, that is, against the policy-making level. It is not a crime which, as such, should involve subordinates who merely carried matters into effect and who should and can only be judged according to the principles of their own national criminal law, not according to the principles of super-national law created in order to prevent the abuse of governmental power, in the past as well as in the future. In the Convention against Genocide, the family of nations has taken up at least the grossest example of a Crime against Humanity. In the political circumstances in which we live, with the danger of states abusing their powers in a grave manner in violation of all rules of humanity, I consider such a step to be justified and believe that in this case the effect of a precedent can be created, and I hope that it has been created.

The International Military Tribunal tried to find the legal basis for the Crime against Peace in the Briand-Kellogg Pact in the sense that this offense had already found the sanction of international law. This attempt was extremely weak and it is more honest to say in this respect, as Jackson did, 'Once there must be a beginning.' But here the precise question must be raised as to whether it really was a beginning or whether it was not at the same time the end of a legal concept that was applied only on one occasion and that has no chance of being applied repeatedly. To begin with, the War of Aggression is a concept which was not defined at Nuremberg and which, despite all efforts, it has not been possible to define. Great conflicts of interest exist and the peculiar situation nowadays is that the Eastern part of the world insists that the war of aggression should be defined, while the Western world shows considerable reserve, which is understandable because the West is afraid that any definition might leave loopholes of which advantage could be taken. Thus we have a criminal offense, subject to the severest penalties, that cannot be defined.

The other problem, no doubt, is that a finding of a war of aggression is a political problem of the first order. War guilt, in modern days, is regarded as the very basis for the claim against the vanquished to repair the damages of the war and to submit to other sacrifices of territory and economic power. One cannot very well imagine that any court—and I am referring not only to a national court, or a court of the victorious powers, but to any court in the present organization of the world—would be in the position to render such a judgment without bias and with historical truth. If a court existed that was in a position to deprive the victor of the fruits of victory by declaring him to be the aggressor this would presuppose an organization capable of preventing war from the outset. Such an organization, as may be stated without detailed argument, is lacking now, as it was lacking nineteen years ago. This appears to be the decisive issue in considering the crime of war of aggression: can a war be prevented by means of the judiciary? Is the prevention of war not an aim that surpasses by far the deterrent power of a judicial decision?

One cannot very well imagine that those who in our day have to decide about war and peace could be influenced in their decision by the idea that they would be held personally responsible if things went wrong. It would seem to amount to an underestimation of those who are burdened with the weight of such a decision, if one believed personal fear to be a substantial element of their considerations. The responsibility which they bear, and which may rest upon them perhaps for much more than for their nation alone, is so immense that their own personal risk can, in my opinion, be of no importance to them.

The problems of preventing war, I think, cannot be achieved with the instruments of justice in our present world organization. We have merely to review the events that have taken place since 1945 in order to see that such prevention has not been achieved. Historians will be able to say more precisely than I how many wars have been conducted in the meantime. I merely mention Korea, Laos and Vietnam, which were, no doubt, wars according to the criteria of Nuremberg, or Egypt, Cuba or, what might be particularly interesting, Israel. In Israel, even now, there is a state of war. No one so far has had the courage to state who is the aggressor in that war, much less to attempt to call that aggressor to account. Why is that so? Because the family of nations is not in a position to solve the conflict existing in that part of the world by its own force. For that reason, the ancient instrument of war cannot be outlawed, as there is no other or better means available. This is a regrettable realization which, however, in my opinion must be faced in order to protect oneself from illusions. The judgments at Nuremberg have not increased the security of the world against wars by one jot.

If I now refer to political, especially foreign policy, considerations, this may need an additional word of justification. May these judgments be evaluated in terms of foreign policy at all? My answer is that this is permissible because those who organized the trials provoked such a judgment. At the very beginning of the Nuremberg trials, in my capacity as one of the two spokesmen for the defense, I had the opportunity for a very interesting discussion. In Nuremberg many very important matters occurred behind locked doors, different from German criminal procedure which as a rule is dominated by the principle of public proceedings. Matters of great weight, such as the access of defense counsel to the seized German archives had to be discussed by defense counsel, judges and prosecutors *in camera* and do not appear in any record of the court. At the very beginning of the Nuremberg trials there was a big problem, namely that the defense was flooded with doucuments issued in English, the existence of which was unknown to the defense before they were presented by the prosecution. Therefore, we demanded that these documents be made available to the defense in the German original before being submitted to the court. A meeting was held about this matter, at which the only participants were the judges, the chief prosecutors of the four nations and two spokesmen for the defense, attorney Dr. Dix and myself. In the course of the discussion, the American chief prosecutor refused to submit the documents, stating as the reason that such a time consuming procedure would be completely contrary to the purpose of the Nuremberg trials. Thereupon, he was asked by British Lord Justice Lawrence, what that purpose was? Mr. Jackson answered without hesitation, and disregarding the presence of the two German defense counsel, not, as might have been imagined, that the purpose of the trials was to bring criminals to conviction, but that it had two purposes: one, to prove to the world that the German conduct of war had been illegal and unjustified just as the United States had alleged throughout the world by her propaganda before her entry into the war; and the other, to make it clear to the German people that it deserved severe punishment, and to prepare them for such punishment. These were purely political purposes, objects of foreign policy, as we expressed at the time. In the meantime, and unknown to me then, confirmation of the objects of foreign policy behind the Nuremberg trials existed in Mr. Jackson's report, mentioned earlier. In that report the chief prosecutor elucidates the special interest of the United States in a finding that Germany conducted an illegal war, on the grounds that some of the measures taken by the President of the United States before the United States entered the war—such as the well-known delivery of fifty destroyers to the British—could be legally justified only if there were a finding of the unlawfulness of German warfare as a whole.

Has this aim of foreign policy been achieved? With respect to the pinning down of war guilt, one of the essential points, a peculiar result has been obtained, showing that political trials can have a boomerang effect on their promoters. It is widely unknown that in Nuremberg neither the German conflict with France, nor that with Great Britain, nor that with the United States was found to constitute a German war of aggression. Of the four principal Allied powers represented on the Nuremberg bench, only the Russians had the satisfaction of hearing the war against them characterized as a German war of aggression. The tribunal was very careful to refrain from finding who had been the aggressor in the other three cases.

Another aim in the field of foreign policy was the re-education and democratization of the German people. No one familiar with present day Germany will doubt that this process was largely successful. Whether the Nuremberg trials contributed to that result, or whether in view of their many faults they have rather impeded this development, is a difficult question, which I am unable to answer. Doubtless, the reaction of the general public in Germany to the Allied war crimes trials initially was that one had had enough of it; and the German legal administration for all practical purposes did not bother for years with the prosecution of real crimes committed in wartime, even after it became legally possible to do so. Only gradually, after the creation of a central prosecuting authority for all offenses of this nature, did investigations and new indictments again begin. What had been left undone for years was now done with 'German thoroughness.' As a consequence, hundreds, if not thousands, of trials are still to be expected, many against people of lesser account who acted within the scope of their mission or orders. In considering these unfortunate prospects I share the opinion of Sir Hartley Shawcross, the British Attorney General during the International Military Tribunal, who recently stated in a German periodical that he felt the time had come to put an end to these proceedings.

In spite of all of the criticism of the Nuremberg trials, I should like to stress one effect of the International Military Tribunal. It was clear that after the obvious crimes committed under Hitler's leadership, particularly the annihilation process against the Jews, something had to happen to discharge the tension between victors and vanquished. The British would have preferred at the time to shoot summarily some of the principal leaders of the Third Reich. The Soviets would certainly have liked to adhere to this procedure, multiplying the victims. It was the United States who insisted that expiation must be sought and found by way of a judicial trial. The International Military Tribunal proceedings did, in my opinion, perform this function. It was the painful starting point for building the relations that exist today between Germany and her Western Allies.

19

The Nuremberg Trials and the Question of Responsibility for Aggression

By A. I. Poltorak

The entire world is troubled by the aggressive actions of the US against the Vietnamese people. During this war, unleashed by the United States, the American warmongers have started to use barbaric means of warfare, such as napalm bombs and poisonous gases which are prohibited under the Geneva Protocol of 1925. The policy being implemented by the US towards the Vietnamese people is a brutal infringement of the UN Charter and the Geneva Agreements of 1954 and it is, in essence, an open and blatant act of aggression, i.e., a crime according to Article 6(a) of the Charter of the International Military Tribunal.

The chief prosecutor for the US at the Nuremberg Trials, R. Jackson, stated in his opening address: 'And let me make clear that while this law [Charter of the International Military Tribunal—A.P.] is being applied for the first time against German aggressors, it must condemn aggression by any other nations, including those that have been presented today at the Tribunal, provided it is to serve a useful purpose.' R. Jackson emphasized that the Nuremberg Trials represented humanity's desperate attempt to apply the disciplining influence of the law to identify those who used their power to undermine the foundations of universal peace.[1]

Yesterday, these words of the Nuremberg prosecutor were launched at Hitler's clique; today, they are addressed to the American aggressors who have set out on the very same road of aggression and unparalleled crimes, a road which has been stigmatized and condemned by the International Military Tribunal.

It is no coincidence therefore that the verdict by the International Tribunal, read out almost twenty years ago, continues to be the subject of attacks from the pages of the reactionary American press. The American reaction as early as in the last months of the Second World War opposed the creation of an international tribunal and the condemnation of Hitler's clique for the aggression. The warmongers were fearful of setting a precedent of responsibility for aggression.

---

[1] See M. Gosyurizdat, *Nuremberg Trial Against the Main German War Criminals: Collection of Materials in Seven Volumes*, vol. 1, 1957, p. 338.

History has condemned the aggression as an international crime. The Nuremberg Tribunal stigmatized Hitler's aggression in its verdict. However, the ink had barely dried on the signatures of the judges from the International Tribunal before the Americans and other reactionaries in the West spoke out against the recognition of aggression as an international crime. G. Finch, Editor-in-Chief of the *American Journal of International Law*, for example, sharply criticized the Nuremberg verdict in January 1947, claiming that it was based not on law but on the arbitrary behaviour of the victors against the vanquished.[2] In essence, he was continuing the attempts of the official defence team at the Nuremberg Trials whose position could be basically summarized that the history of international law had not known any agreements or accords which would establish with fundamental clarity the illegality and criminality of aggression. Consequently, applying the provisions of the Charter of the International Tribunal on responsibility for the aggression (passed only in 1945) to the accused at Nuremberg is a blatant infringement of the generally acknowledged principles *nullum crimen sine lege* and *ex post facto*. As is already known, the meaning of these principles is that an action cannot be declared punishable if it has not been recognized as criminal at the time it is committed and that criminal law does not apply retrospectively in respect of actions not considered criminal at the time they are committed.

The defence took this position at the International Tribunals in Nuremberg and Tokyo during the judicial trials of the leaders of the German dictatorships. As has already been indicated, the very same position was taken by a significant group of Western lawyers such as G. Dahm, A. Knierim, H. Echard, V. Grewe, M. Radin and others.[3]

It is possible to draw the conclusion from this that the International Tribunal unlawfully convicted the accused of aggression at the Nuremberg Trials. In his book, *UNO and War Crimes*, Maugham writes that the world was astonished when it read in the Nuremberg verdict that the Charter of the International Tribunal was 'an expression of existing international law', and how at that time not one state had claimed earlier that aggression was a crime.[4] Based on the work of Western lawyers, West German propaganda, in its attempts to rehabilitate Nazism, goes as far as calling the Nuremberg Trials 'not a court but judicial murder' of the vanquished by the victors.

Critics of the Nuremberg principles try to create the impression that the International Tribunal, in convicting Hitler's clique for the aggression, relied entirely and exclusively on the Briand–Kellogg Pact which was so legally flawed that it cannot be taken seriously as a basis for criminal responsibility for

---

[2] G. Finch, 'The Nuremberg Trial and International Law', *American Journal of International Law* (1947), p. 26.

[3] G. Dahm, *Zur Problematik des Volkerstrafrechts*, Göttingen, 1956, p. 179; A. Von Knieriem, *The Nuremberg Trials and International Law*, W., 1959, p. 79; H. Echard, 'The Nuremberg Trial Against the Major War Criminals and International Law', (*American Journal of International Law* 2 (1949), p. 364; W. Grewe, *Nurnberg als Rechtsfrage: Eine Diskussion*, Stutgart, 1947; *Foreign Affairs*, April, 1946, 24, p. 370.

[4] See Maugham, *UNO and War Crimes*, London, 1951, p. 18.

aggression. Some opponents of the Nuremberg principles are still prepared to admit that this pact establishes the illegality of the aggression but in no way its criminality. However, it is also claimed here that the pact lost its meaning after the League of Nations ignored a series of aggressive acts (against Abyssinia, Manchuria, Austria, Czechoslovakia) whilst the pact was in force.

'The complete discreditation of the League of Nations and the Briand–Kellogg Pact in the Abyssinian conflict brought classic international law back to its old position', said the lawyer, H. Jahreiss, at the Nuremberg Trials. Jahreiss did not hide the fact that the 'old position' is the right to war, the situation when, as he states, 'each state is the only judge whether in each separate case it wages a defensive war or not'.[5]

And so the position is clear. As claimed by the Nuremberg critics, prior to 1928, international law had not been faced with one act which would have qualified an aggressive war as illegal and moreover criminal. In 1928, when the Briand–Kellogg Pact was signed, it was the only document which dealt with the matter under consideration. However, based on its contents, this pact gives no basis for the claim that criminal responsibility for aggression is established once the pact has been passed. This is the reason for the claim that the International Tribunal was in a position to pass judgment on the main Nazi war criminals only by blatantly infringing the principle *nullum crimen sine lege*.

When viewed simply, the question is as follows—either the verdict of the International Tribunal, having condemned aggression and aggressors, has a solid legal basis, or its basis is unlawful because in establishing the guilt of the accused for aggression it cannot cite any norms of international law. This question is not only of theoretical importance in the circumstances of a revanchist loss and the increasingly strong revisionist tendencies in the politics of the Federal Republic of Germany. Undermining the Nuremberg verdict in full is one of the aims of revanchist propaganda from Bonn. The Bonn revanchists in these efforts find allies in the camp of American reactionaries.

The reactionary character of the US government, having taken an aggressive path in their policies after the Second World War, also regard the Nuremberg verdict as an ideological obstacle to the implementation of this policy. This is where the attempt to tarnish the verdict comes from, a verdict which declared the aggressive war an international crime and for the first time in history severely punished the aggressors. This is also where the attempt comes from to return to previous times where aggressors were not punished, after overturning the conclusions of the Nuremberg Tribunal. This is why the defence of the principles of the Nuremberg Trials is one of the forms taken in the battle against aggression and the fight for peace.

* * *

It is well known that the principles *nullum crimen sine lege* and *ex post facto* were promoted by the young *bourgeoisie* in the fight against the arbitrary rule of

---

[5] 'Stenograficheski otchot Nyurembergskovo procesa' [Stenographic Report of the Nuremberg Trial], vol. 31, p. 14972.

royal power and against judicial tyranny. Ideologues of the *bourgeoisie* demanded an end to the tyranny of the monarchy and to a state of affairs where judges, acting in the name of the monarch and not strictly tied to the standards of law, could legislate by themselves and in essence create abuses of power. Without doubt, *nullum crimen sine lege* was and remains a progressive principle of criminal law. The same should be said of the principle *ex post facto*, meaning the inadmissibility of enforcing criminal law retrospectively in those cases when it establishes the punishability of one or another action which at the time it is committed was indifferent from the point of view of the law.

This was always the case and it is why it is necessary to establish that the International Tribunals in Nuremberg and Tokyo did not infringe on these principles in their verdicts. They did not infringe and could not infringe by their very idea because these principles are not applicable, either legally or morally, to the nature of the matters being considered there. N. N. Polyanski was correct when he wrote: 'Referring to the slogans of democracy for the defence of the aggressor means distorting these slogans, means using their letters whilst ignoring their meaning and genuine intention. In their time, they were born in the battle with the past tyranny of absolutism and now they wish to make them the mainstay for tyrants and usurpers within states, for rapists in international relations.'[6]

It should also be remembered that the principles referred to were developed as principles of national criminal law, i.e., a system of law which has a codified legislation, where law and only law is the source of justice. It is not clear whether the mechanical transfer of these principles from national to international law, which has been formulated to a significant degree as standard law and whose source until now, together with agreements and conventions, has been custom, would be totally incorrect. And how to treat those countries whose legislation and judicial practice are governed by judicial precedent? Is it possible to talk about the application of these principles in such cases?

The International Tribunal in Nuremberg rejected any reference to these principles with complete justification.[7]

* * *

Opponents of the Nuremberg principles, recognizing only the Briand–Kellogg Pact as a source of international law (applied to the problem of aggression), hereby reducing its international legal importance to zero, firmly deny the

---

[6] *Sovyetskoye gosudarstvo i pravo* [Soviet State and Law], No. 1, 1946, p. 46.

[7] In response to the critics of the Charter, the International Tribunal indicated in its verdict: 'Above all, it is necessary to note that the principles of *nullum crimen sine lege* and *ex post facto* do not signify a restriction on sovereignty but are just a general principle of justice. It is entirely obvious that the claim of injustice of the punishment of those who attacked neighbouring states without warning despite agreements and guarantees is incorrect. In such circumstances, the attacker should know that he is committing an illegal act and not only is it not unjust to not punish him but, on the contrary, it is unjust for the evil committed by him to remain unpunished' (M. Gosyurizdat, *Nyurnbergski protses* [Nuremberg Trial], vol. 7, 1961, p. 364).

importance of any other international legal acts in the period from 1919 to 1939, i.e., resolutions, protocols, and agreements which were passed in the framework of the League of Nations and outside it and which declared aggressive war to be criminal.

It is correct that the acts referred to often did not arise from the very essence of the policy of the state which passed them. In fact, the largest imperialist states of the world were involved in their preparation and approval. The aggressive policy was not only alien to them but over the course of many decades formed the basis of their behaviour on the international stage. It can even seem paradoxical at first glance that the efforts to prohibit aggressive war, to criminalize it, actively began not in the period of relative stabilization of capitalism but in the period of active escalation of the inter-imperialist conflicts, the period of general crisis in capitalism. The policy of the countries of the Entente, of course, had a certain importance in this regard, imposing on Germany the Versailles Treaty and trying to maintain the status quo for a period of time. However, this importance was only of a certain degree. The main reason defining the activity of the League of Nations in passing the acts set out above had reasons of an entirely different nature. The victory of the Great October Socialist Revolution, the universal strengthening of the revolutionary and democratic movement caused by this revolution, one of the most important slogans of which became the fight for peace against aggression—this is the main factor affecting the appearance of various acts which declared aggression to be illegal and criminal. The enormous influence of the principles of peaceful Soviet foreign policy and the pressure of people on their *bourgeoisie* governments—these are what forced these governments in each individual case to pass these or other peace-making acts.

Critics of the Nuremberg verdict do not attribute any legal significance to these acts. Some acts are declared legally baseless on account of the fact that, although they were signed by the relevant governments, they did not receive a sufficient number of ratifications—others because they proclaimed the illegality of aggression but they did not establish its criminality.[8]

These critics analyze all the acts referred to only from the position of whether they meet the requirements of an agreement or convention. In the meantime, the very nature of these acts and the degree to which they were prepared in an international legal context give sufficient grounds for concluding that over the course of many years, a process of crystallization of international legal norms has taken place, a gradual change in international law.

With each year, public consciousness of the need to disallow war from happening again and to achieve a prohibition of aggression has become increasingly clear, firm and determined. And, insofar as the danger of war has been exposed,

---

[8] See G. Finch, op. cit. p. 26; Maugham, op. cit., 64; L. Gross, 'The Criminality of Agressive War', *American Political Science Review* (1947), pp. 2005–225); C. Wisansky, 'The Dangerous Precedent', *Atlantic* 4 (1946), pp. 69–70).

modern and destructive war, which contradicts the interests of all mankind, the idea of its criminal and legal prohibition has become a national idea, expressing legal awareness of all mankind.

The striving of the masses towards peace and their determined fight against war in the most immediate of ways have influenced the activity of various international organizations, in particular the League of Nations, as well as the process of change of international law in terms of the gradual creation of an international legal standard for prohibiting aggressive war in the period between the World Wars.

The greatest importance to the formation of the principle of prohibition of aggressive wars was in the manifesto of the first socialist state in the world, the Decree on Peace. It was this very decree, with its authority and the support given to it by peoples of the entire world, which brought about to a significant degree the appearance in the following years of a number of acts of the League of Nations and other acts dedicated to the prohibition of war. The most direct repercussion of the Decree on Peace, declaring aggressive war as the greatest crime against humanity, was the provision of the Versailles Treaty on the criminal responsibility of Wilhelm II.

A further development in the process to establish the unlawfulness and punishability of aggression could be found in the Covenant of the League of Nations. Not overestimating its importance, it should be said that it was a step forward in the battle against aggression. In fact, together with some articles which created loopholes to legalize war, the Covenant contained Article 16 which dealt with the use of sanctions against the aggressor. The League of Nations received considerable means for armament to bring about real pressure against the aggressor.[9]

Included in the documents which provide evidence of the gradual formation of a standard in international law which put aggression outside the law and declare it an international crime, the draft Treaty of Mutual Assistance dated 28 September 1923 should be mentioned. It was developed by the Temporary Mixed Commission of the League of Nations to reduce armaments and it contained direct recognition of the fact that 'aggressive war is an international crime'. In order to assess the legal importance of this document, which was of course only a draft, it is necessary to consider that it was submitted by 29 states and around half of them spoke out in favour of passing this draft.[10]

On 2 October 1924, 51 states, represented at the Assembly of the League of Nations, passed the Geneva Protocol on the Peaceful Settlement of International

---

[9] M. M. Litvinov, speaking in 1936 at the Assembly of the League of Nations, announced: 'I maintain that Article 17 has provided the League of Nations with a powerful weapon which in the event of its release can smash any aggression. What is more, singular belief in the possibility of releasing it could discourage the aggressor from carrying out its criminal plans' (*Pravda*, 21 July 1936).

[10] G. I. Tunkin is right in noting that in the 'draft agreement on mutual assistance... the motives of the Soviet Decree on Peace sounded already more precise' (G. I. Tunkin, *Questions on the Theory of International Law*, M. Gosyurizdat, 1962, p. 28).

Disputes. 'The states who signed—referred to in Article 2 of the Protocol—agree that under no circumstances should they wage war amongst themselves or against another state....' The Protocol solemnly declared that 'aggressive war is an international crime'. It is telling that this Protocol has been passed unanimously at the Assembly of the League of Nations. It did not come into effect due to the opposition of the Conservative Government of England, which had replaced at that time the Labour Government, to ratify the Geneva Protocol. Nevertheless, the Geneva Protocol is further proof that the process of creating a traditional international legal standard for the criminal prohibition of aggression was continuing successfully under the beneficial influence of Soviet foreign policy and under pressure from the peoples.

In describing the legal importance of the Geneva Protocol, the International Tribunal indicated in its verdict: 'Although this Protocol has never been ratified, it was signed by the leading politicians of the world who represented the overwhelming majority of civilized states and peoples and can be seen as convincing proof of the intention to stigmatize aggressive war as an international crime.'[11]

On 24 September 1927, at the Thirteenth Session of the Assembly of the League of Nations, the Declaration on Aggressive Wars was passed unanimously and contained, as with the Geneva Protocol, the recognition that aggressive wars 'constitute international crime'.[12]

This action by the League of Nations, as already shown, was stimulated in every way by the active fight of different international and national organizations for peace and against aggression. Thus, the General Congress of Peace in Athens in 1927, indicated in its resolution that the 'incitement to war...is an international crime'. The Congress directed the attention 'of governments to the need to introduce into the criminal code of each country a decree on criminal responsibility for a crime against peace'. At the same time, the Inter-Parliamentary Union raised the question of establishing criminal responsibility for aggression. The International Association of Criminal Law at its Brussels Congress in 1925, posed the question of organizing an international tribunal on criminal matters. In addition, the draft statute of this tribunal included a provision that the tribunal's jurisdictions would include 'crimes and offences carried out in times of peace and peaceful relations between states which can fluctuate'.[13] The draft Universal Criminal Code and International Criminal Code published at the time contained special articles on criminal responsibility for aggression. This idea found its way into the criminal codes of several European countries.

All this is proof that the idea of establishing criminal responsibility for aggression has taken deep root in the legal awareness of peoples and this has allowed the

---

[11] *Nyuremberg process* [Nuremberg Trial], vol. 7, p. 367.

[12] *Garantii bezopasnosti po Statuti Liga Natsii* (Guarantee of Security According to the Statute of the League of Nations), ed. NKID, M., 1937, p. 213.

[13] See A. Traynin, *Zashita mira i ugolovni zakon* (Defence of Peace and Criminal Law), M., 1937, pp. 54, 130.

development of a process of creating an international legal norm for the criminal and legal prohibition of aggression.

In this atmosphere, different inter-state bodies have also believed it impossible to remain impartial. Thus, the Sixth Havana Conference on 18 February 1928, passed the Declaration of 21 American Republics which stated that, 'aggressive war is an international crime against the human species'. At the International Conference of American States for the Peaceful Resolution of Disputes and Arbitration in December 1928, representatives from twenty states signed the General Convention on the Peaceful Settlement of Disputes, which contained the condemnation of war as an instrument of national policy.

The Briand–Kellogg Pact was of great importance in the general chain of international legal acts designed to prohibit and condemn aggressive wars. The signatories to the pact indicated in it that they 'condemn the use of war as a means to resolve international disputes and refuse to use it as an instrument of national policy in relations with each other'.

On the issue of the legal importance of the pact in defining the illegality and criminality of aggressive war, the most divergent opinions and evaluations appear even until now. In some cases, the pact qualifies as the first and only pre-war act which provides the basis for considering aggressive war not only as illegal but also criminal. In other cases, the legal importance of the pact when applied to the problem of the criminalization of aggressive war can be reduced to zero on the basis that there is no categoricalness in the formulations and, in particular, the words 'illegality' and 'criminality' are missing.

The over-evaluation and under-evaluation of the Briand–Kellogg Pact can be explained by the fact that it is evaluated in isolation from all international legal acts that preceded it and is devoted to the problem of condemning aggressive wars.

One should not underestimate the pact because it was the most significant multilateral international legal act where its participants solemnly renounced war. There is no dispute that the language of the pact is not considered above reproach from the perspective of the requirements of criminal law. The text does not refer directly to the criminality of aggression and criminal responsibility for unleashing and waging aggressive wars. On this basis, one can often conclude that only the illegality of aggression can be deduced from the pact but not criminality which, of course, is not the case. This is incorrect because one should not compare directly the infringement of a common international treaty (economic, trade, navigation of the seas, etc.) to the infringement of an agreement which is based on the protection of international law. Modern war, with its ever-developing destructive technology threatens the life of all peoples. Under these conditions, there is no basis for creating a distinction between illegality and criminality for such an infringement of an agreement which leads to war. This is why the Decree on Peace was entirely correct and unambiguous in qualifying aggressive war, calling it the greatest crime against humanity. This is why the language in the above-mentioned Acts of 1923, 1924, and 1927 is preferable compared to the Briand–Kellogg Pact, as they directly defined aggressive war as an international crime.

This situation was also taken into account by the International Tribunal, giving a high legal appraisal of the Briand–Kellogg Pact in its verdict and indicating that 'that point of view which the tribunal has in relation to the correct interpretation of the Pact is strengthened by the history of international relations which preceded this pact'. And here the tribunal reveals what it means by 'history of international relations which preceded this Pact',[14] referring to the draft agreement of the League of Nations on Mutual Assistance of 1923, the Geneva Protocol of 1924, the resolution of the League of Nations of 1927 and others. Listing these acts, the International Tribunal indicates in its verdict that they 'strengthen the significance which the tribunal gives to the Paris Pact'.[15] Thus, the International Tribunal creates a direct link and a particular continuity between the resolutions reviewed above and other acts of the League of Nations and the Briand–Kellogg Pact, emphasizing by this the development of the process of the gradual 'crystallization' of an international legal standard on the criminality of aggression.

The Briand–Kellogg Pact summarized a certain period in the development of the idea of the international illegality and criminality of aggression but did not exhaust efforts in this area. In the period that followed the pact's entry into force, acts were signed on international illegality and criminality of aggression. Above all, these were the London Conventions on the definition of aggression of 1933, signed on the initiative of the Soviet Government. The conventions contained a definition of aggression, developed by the Soviet Union, covering the most typical types of aggression. The prosecutors at the Nuremberg Trials referred broadly to it and the chief prosecutor from the United States, Mr. Jackson, called it 'one of the most authoritative sources of international law on this matter'.[16] In the same year, 1933, international law was enriched by new evidence of the further development of the idea of the criminalization of aggressive war. On 10 October 1933, the Treaty on Non-Aggression and Conciliatory Procedure was signed in Rio de Janeiro. As indicated in this agreement, it was signed 'with the aim of condemning aggressive wars'. Of exceptional importance in the creation of a standard on the international illegality and criminality of aggression are the Soviet bilateral agreements on non-aggression.

Thus, even before 1939, that is, prior to the start of the Second World War, an international legal standard had formed in international law which put aggressive war beyond [*sic*] the law and declared it an international crime.

---

[14] *Nyuremberg process* (Nuremberg Trial), vol. 7, p. 366.

[15] Ibid. at p. 367.

[16] *Nyuremberg process* (Nuremberg Trial), vol. 1, p. 331. With regard the definition of aggression see, P. S. Romashkin, 'Aggresiya—tyagchayshi prestupleniye protiv mia i chelovechestva' (Aggression—the Gravest Crime Against Peace and Humanity' (*Sovyetskoye gosudarstvo i pravo* [Soviet State and Law], 1963, no. 1).

It is generally known that the standard norms of international law evolve on the basis of international practice. In the theory of international law, it is considered indisputable that the usual norm appears as a result of the repeated actions of states. 'The element of repetition'—writes G. I. Tunin—'is the point of departure when rules of behaviour are formed.'

In the majority of cases, it is the repetition of certain actions in similar situations which can lead to a crystallization of this practice as a rule of conduct.[17]

The practice of passing numerous acts, mentioned above, meets precisely these criteria. This practice also meets another requirement—the requirement for generality. It is known that many of the acts listed above were passed and declared on behalf of a majority of states. With regards to the Briand–Kellogg Pact, it is second only to the Universal Postal Union in terms of participants (sixty-three countries). The acts referred to above are proof that they express the agreed will of a significant number of states which have agreed to declare aggressive war illegal and criminal. Since the passing of such resolutions, in particular, arose from the general aims of the Charter of League of Nations, these resolutions in reality represent stages in the development of the corresponding standard of international law. It is typical that, although documents of the League of Nations (1923, 1924, 1927) did not receive the required ratifications, none of those who joined in their condemnation spoke out against them from a position of their non-compliance with international law.

Thus, the attempts of the critics of the Nuremberg verdict to prove that before 1939 in international law there were no foundations for criminal responsibility on the part of aggressors are without legal persuasiveness.

A further strengthening of the effectiveness of international law in the fight for peace requires a precise definition of aggression which would have facilitated the interests of restraining the aggressor and supporting peace and security. This is why the Soviet Union, continuing its attempts over many years in this field and overcoming resistance of the aggressive groups of the US and their allies, is currently investing its energies in trying to pass a definition of aggression at the United Nations and thus make more effective the standards of international law that are based on the preservation of peace.

[17] Tinkin, op. cit., p. 85.

20

The Nuremberg and the Tokyo Trials in Retrospect

By Bert V. A. Röling*

To see things and their real significance one needs the correct distance. Too close, and one is struck only by the details, one does not see the forest for the trees. Too far away, and one may have a good view on the whole, but one misses the particulars and their impact on the direct surroundings; that impact has often more to do with details than with the general structure.

Do we already have enough distance to evaluate the Tokyo Trial, in which after World War II Japanese statesmen and military leaders were sentenced? To give a balanced judgment directly after the war is almost impossible, beyond human capacity. War propaganda—one of the unavoidable tools of warfare—has brought about hatred and anger. This propaganda may have been somewhat careless of the truth—but people are too angry and too indignant to care. In war it is only a question of black and white, and nowadays every one is involved. War does not stop with the ending of hostilities. It rages on in the minds of men. A young Dutch author wrote in a remarkable war novel: 'War ceases only when the last one who participated in it has died.'[1]

Still we need an evaluation of the Nuremberg and Tokyo trials now that almost twenty-five years have passed. We need an evaluation, because they stand in history as a fact. On the facts of the past, starting from history, we have to build the future.

At the time, participating in the Tokyo trial as one of the judges, the words of Macbeth alarmed me:

'that he but teach Bloody instructions, which being taught, return
To plague the inventors' (*Macbeth*, Act I, Sc. 7)

Are the 'bloody instructions,' as formulated in the charters and executed in the judgments to plague us? Or to guide us? Will they be an asset, or a liability in the

---

* Ed.: Judge, International Military Tribunal for the Far East (Tokyo trial).
[1] Harry Mulish, HET STENEN BRUIDSBED 95 (1959).

shaping of the future? Reappraisal of what happened in the postwar trials may contribute to the answers on that question.

The essence of the postwar judgments was not that war criminals were tried and sentenced. War criminals were tried also during and after World War I. If nothing but conventional war crimes had been brought before tribunals, the mass scale of it would have been remembered, and perhaps the fact that only the vanquished was brought to account for his criminal behavior. That one-sidedness indeed annoys the lawyer and is repulsive to the defeated. Every army commits war crimes. On the allied side one needs only to remember the mass bombings (Dresden, Tokyo). As a matter of fact, from World War II above all two things are remembered: the German gas chambers and the American atomic bombings.

Still one might say that one-sided prosecution of war criminals is better than no prosecution at all. Provided, of course, that the victor does not claim as a right, what is charged against the vanquished as a crime. *Quod licet Jovi non licet bovi* has factual, not normative, validity. The principle of *tu quoque* was introduced by the defendants, in Nuremberg as well as in Tokyo. It was partly recognized in this way, that from the list of war crimes, drawn up by the Commission on Responsibilities of the Paris Peace Conference in 1919, some were deleted by the U. N. War Crimes Commission 'as these refer to acts which, in the present war, the forces of the United Nations have themselves been obliged to commit.'[2]

Moreover, some crimes, *e.g.* mass bombing of civilian population, were not inserted in the indictment. Lastly, it occurred that the Tribunal, after having heard the Allied practice, refused to base its judgment on similar acts, charged as crimes.[3]

More important was the introduction of the concept of the crime against humanity, formulated in view of German behavior toward German Jews. Persecution of a group of people, on the basis of race or religion, in occupied territory would already have been covered by the concept of the conventional war crimes. Consequently, in most cases the indictment for crimes against humanity amounted only to a charge of qualified war crimes, committed on a large scale, on the ground of a specific policy. German atrocities against German Jews compelled the Allies to prosecute for a specific internal policy. This amounted to a new concept of the place of the national state, of the individual within his national state, and of the role of humanity as a guardian of a minimum standard of state decency. The Genocide Convention, 1948, has consolidated this new concept, and has recognized its validity, in peace and in war. For the Pacific theatre this new concept of the crime against humanity has had less importance

---

[2] Report of the Subcommittee, consisting of Sir Cecil Hurst, de Baer, Eoer, de Moor and Glaser.

[3] The Nuremberg Tribunal, having heard of the Allied submarine warfare, declared: '[T]he sentence of Doenitz is not assessed on the ground of his breaches of the international law of submarine warfare' (JUDGMENT NUREMBERG 109 (Brit ed. 1946)).

than it had in Europe. In the Tokyo indictment the defendants were accused of a mass-annihilation policy toward China (opium policy) and the white population of Asia. It seems to me that this charge was not proved, notwithstanding the fact that out of anger and hate many crimes against the Chinese and Europeans were committed. From shortsightedness, incompetence, and greed, many grave faults were committed in the opium policy. The effort to dethrone European authority easily led to the impression that Japan aimed at the annihilation of the European population.

More important still was the new concept of the crime against peace. This concept of the crime of aggressive war slowly developed out of the European-American world. Until recently traditional international law had regarded the *jus ad bellum* as one of the prerogatives of the sovereign state.[4] The development of the techniques of war gradually caused war to be considered an unbearable institution. Hence the quest for peace, the more desirable since in centuries of fighting gradually states had settled, borders were fixed, aspirations had become conservative. The same applied for the United States of America. In the imperialist period of the Theodore Roosevelt era, the United States succeeded in rounding off its territory and in securing its strategic position. Joseph C. Grew, the former U.S. Ambassador to Japan, could write: 'We have now attained the desired maximum of our national entity as well as adequate national strength. International morality, including, respect for legal commitments and permanent abandonment of force as an instrument of national policy, has become for us at once a watchword and a religion.'[5] The latecomers—Germany, Russia, and Japan—consequently were to be kept in check. The strivings, as formulated in the 1928 Pact of Paris, were not at all adequate to the uncertain relations in the Asian world, in which the instability of nations and power concentrations, and the newly awaked self-confidence, hardly provided a theater for the application of European peace principles. As it was clearly formulated by Stimson: 'The peace treaties of modern Europe made out by the Western nations of the world no more fit the three great races of Russia, Japan, and China, who are meeting in Manchuria, than...a stovepipe hat would fit an African savage.'[6]

The European quest for peace, combined with the deeply felt indignation about Nazi-German criminality led to the Nuremberg Trial, one great indictment of the Nazi regime, not only related to the waging of the war but also comprising the Nazi-methods of warfare. The combination of the two charges made it possible to bring about the prosecution of individuals for the crime against peace. The conscience of the world was at rest because both charges were made.

---

[4] *Cf.* Oppenheim INTERNATIONAL LAW, vol. II DISPUTES, WAR AND NEUTRALITY 145 (6th ed. Lauterpacht 1944); C. FENWICK, INTERNATIONAL LAW 441 (2d ed. 1943): 'This right was, indeed, so well established that it was used as a sort of final test of a "sovereign" as distinguished from a semisovereign or dependant state.'

[5] J. GREW, TEN YEARS IN JAPAN 300 (1944).

[6] H. STIMSON: I ON ACTIVE SERVICE IN PEACE AND WAR 233 (1947).

It is an open question if public opinion would have easily approved of a trial only related to the crime of aggression. A confusion did exist in the public mind between the violations of the *jus ad bellum* and the *jus in bello*. Max Radin justly remarked:

It is impossible to determine with certainty whether public opinion at the present time supports the doctrine of individual guilt for crimes against peace. The impossibility is due to the fact that the three types of crimes are inevitably fused in the public mind by being combined in a single trial. To regret any one of the three creates the impression of defending men whose vicious actions seem to place their guilt beyond the reach of any sort of clemency.[7]

The unheard-of Nazi atrocities have been one of the reasons that individuals were indicted for the crime of aggression. Looking back at the postwar trials it becomes more and more clear that the German issue played the central role. The German situation was decisive, and in its wake followed the Japanese solution. The Nuremberg trial is the central problem, if one tries to explain what happened after World War II. It is for that very reason that something more should be said about it.

Public opinion approved of the triple charges made against the German defendants. But why was it that the 'crime of aggressive war' was created and the indictment of the German major war criminals concentrated on aggressive war? We know that England did not want a criminal prosecution for the crime against peace. In an aide memoire of April 23, 1945, the British Government expressed that it was not at all clear that unprovoked attacks could properly be described as crimes under international law.[8] The French Government expressly declared that it did not consider aggressive war to be a crime,[9] and that it wished to prosecute the Nazi leaders for the cruelties committed during their illegal war. Russia, though Marshall Stalin himself had introduced the concept of the crime of aggressive war in his speech of November 6, 1943,[10] followed the French line. The Russian representatives feared endless discussions on the causes

---

[7] Max Radin, *Justice at Nuremberg*, 24 FOREIGN AFFAIRS 381 (1946).

[8] *Cf. Report of Robert H. Jackson, U.S. Representative to the International Conference on Military Trials, London 1945*, Dep't of State Publication 3080, at 19 (1949). The British intended to kill the major war criminals without trial. The same opinion was shared by influential statesmen in the U.S., *e.g.*, Cordell Hull—THE MEMOIRS OF CORDELL HULL, vol. II, at 1289 (1948). Against these opinions Justice Jackson reacted in his famous 'Report to the President,' June 7, 1945, in justification of the Nuremberg Trial: 'To free them without a trial would mock the dead and make cynics of the living. But undiscriminating executions or punishments without definite findings of guilt, fairly arrived at, would violate pledges repeatedly given, and would not set easily on the American conscience or be remembered by our children with pride' [hereinafter cited as Report of Robert H. Jackson].

[9] Report of Robert H. Jackson, at 293, 334, 385.

[10] 'In conjunction with our Allies we shall have to take measures to ensure that all the fascist criminals who are responsible for this war and the suffering the peoples have endured shall meet with stern punishment and retribution for all the crimes they have committed, no matter in what country they may hide,' J. STALIN, ON THE GREAT PATRIOTIC WAR OF THE SOVIET UNION (1946).

of the war,[11] and probably disliked the chance that Soviet-Russian policy as to Finland and Poland and the role of its neutrality pacts with Germany and Japan would be dealt with in court. That the Nuremberg trial took place and that the Charter of Nuremberg contained the 'crimes against peace' are due to the attitude of the United States, so ably defended and brought to victory by Justice Jackson. Jackson was disarmingly honest on this point: the United States entering the war, had violated the existing laws of neutrality on the ground that the German aggression was criminal. A public trial should prove that the American attitude had been correct and justified. To quote his own words:

Our attitude as a nation, in a number of transactions, was based on the proposition that this was an illegal war from the moment that it was started, and that therefore, without losing our rights as neutrals and nonbelligerents, it was our right to extend aid to the nations under illegal attack, and the lend-lease program, the exchange of bases for destroyers, and much of American policy was based squarely on the proposition that a war of aggression is outlawed.... Therefore, our view is that this is not merely a case of showing that these Nazi-Hitlerite people failed to be gentlemen in war; it is a matter of their having designed an illegal attack on the international peace, which to our mind is a criminal offense by common-law tests, at least, and the other atrocities were all preparatory to it or done in execution of it.... [12] Now we come to the end and have crushed her aggression, and we do want to show that this war was an illegal plan of aggression. We want this group of nations to stand up and say, as we have said to our people, as President Roosevelt said to the people, as members of the Cabinet said to the people, that launching a war of aggression is a crime and that no political or economic situation can justify it. If that is wrong, then we have been wrong in a good many things in the policy of the United States which helped the countries under attack before we entered the war.

The United States wanted the Germans and anybody else to know that as far as the United States is concerned it regards any attack on the peace of the world as an international crime. It may become necessary to abandon the effort to try these people on that basis, but there are some things worse for me than failing to reach an agreement, and one of these is reaching an agreement which would stultify the position which the United States has taken throughout.[13]

The political reasons for having a trial in which Germans would be tried for the crime against peace are very clear. The U.S. Government had acted on the assumption that launching any attack on the peace was an international crime, and it wanted to prove by charter and judgment that launching a war of aggression constituted a criminal violation of the law of nations. It is beyond doubt that before World War II there had been no question of individual criminal responsibility for a violation of the Kellogg-Briand pact. Neither this treaty nor the resolutions of the League of Nations or the abortive treaties in which it was stated that

---

[11] Report of Robert H. Jackson, at 298.
[12] Report of Robert H. Jackson, at 299.
[13] Report of Robert H. Jackson, at 384.

aggressive war was an international crime had the effect of creating international criminal law.

It is at this moment a practically undisputed thesis that before World War II positive international law did not recognize the crime of aggressive war for which individuals could be punished.[14] No wonder that the U.N. War Crimes Commission did not consider aggressive war an international crime. A minority opinion to the contrary (Dr. Ecer) did not find support, until after the Charter of Nuremberg had been formulated. The UNWCC was unanimous in its opinion that aggressive war should be made a crime in the future. This opinion was communicated to the San Francisco Conference. Only in its Resolution of January 30, 1946, did it recognize the 'crime against peace.'[15]

The initiative to punish the individuals responsible for the aggressive war was taken by Marshall Stalin in his speech of November 6, 1943. Some authors had suggested similar ideas.[16] Benes proposed in 1941 'political punishment of those who are responsible for this war,'[17] and Dr. Ecer defended the same opinion in the UNWCC. But these suggestions had not met with any response. After Stalin's statement, the London International Assembly changed its former opinion and inserted in its December, 1943, report the 'crime of war,' 'in accordance with Stalin's views as expressed on November 6, 1943.'[18] The suggestion of Stalin was elaborated in the book of Professor A.N. Trainin: 'The criminal responsibility of the Hitlerites' (Moscow, 1944).[19] Against the doubts and misgivings of international lawyers and many statesmen—Stimson considered the concept 'a little in advance of international thought'[20]—the new idea gradually won acceptance. Growing indignation about ever more gruesome atrocities prevented the sharp distinction between the law as it stood and the law as it should be in view of the factual development of warfare. Mass bombing and atomic warfare made war into something that should be prevented by all means, including the attribution of criminal responsibility for launching it.

Even before the atomic bombs fell on Hiroshima and Nagasaki, the United Nations had come to the conclusion that war should be outlawed in the future. The Covenant of the League of Nations had not forbidden waging war. The Pact

[14] *Cf.* Q. WRIGHT, A STUDY OF WAR 893 (1944); Hans Wehberg: Die völkerrechtliche Verantwortlichkeit von Individuen wegen Friedensbruchs im Zeitalter des Volkenbundes, Festschrift für Rudolf Laun, 379–394 (1952); C.A. POMPE, AGGRESSIVE WAR AN INTERNATIONAL CRIME 277 (1953).

[15] *Cf.* HISTORY OF THE UNWCC AND THE DEVELOPMENT OF THE LAW 187 (1948).

[16] H. MANNHEIM, WAR AND CRIME 171 (1941) G. SCHWARZENBERGER, LAW AND TOTALITARIAN LAWLESSNESS, (1943) p. 65.

[17] THE PUNISHMENT OF WAR CRIMINALS: RECOMMENDATIONS OF THE LONDON INTERNATIONAL ASSEMBLY 7.

[18] *See* Q. Wright, *War Criminals*, 39 A.J.I.L. 260 (1945).

[19] Trainin was one of the Soviet-Russian delegates to the London Conference which formulated the Charter of Nuremberg.

[20] *Supra* note 6, vol. II, at 587.

of Paris had maintained the freedom to start war in self-defense, and from its *travaux préparatoires* it appears that it left to every state the right to determine whether a case of self-defense existed. In the Charter of the United Nations the parties renounced the right to use armed force (art. 2 (4)), except in case of an armed attack (art. 51).

The Tokyo Trial was a natural and unavoidable consequence of the Nuremberg Trial. As a matter of fact, in many quarters there was little inclination to apply 'the advanced thought' to the Asian world. In the past, Europe had conquered Asia in forceful actions that hardly could be called defensive wars. Japan, a century ago compelled to enter into the family of nations, rising as a big power, was out to gain the position of world supremacy. It wished to expel Europe from Asia, to liberate the colonies, and to gain with the realization of the principle of 'Asia for the Asians' undisputed might in the Far East. If it had been able to continue the policy, outlined by Hirota and pursued by Konoye, to stir up independence movements, to conclude pacts of mutual assistance with every Asian people which had declared itself independent—in the meantime making itself so strong militarily that no European nation would dare to start fighting—it would have developed into the most powerful nation in the world. But it needed a strong army, and when the strong army was built, the government was unable to keep it under control. Hence the Manchurian Incident and the Marco Polo Bridge Incident, which led inevitably to the Pacific War. The Japanese military, especially the army, has indeed an enormous responsibility. They set the conditions for the fateful development. But to approach Japan's 'war of liberation' with the concept of the crime of aggression was for Europe not self-evident at all.

As a matter of fact only little inclination existed in high American circles to bring Japanese leaders before a Court charging them with the crime against peace. One wish did exist in American military and political circles, and that was to revenge the attack on Pearl Harbor, the surprise attack which had crippled the American Pacific Fleet, taking 4000 American lives. For the United States, Pearl Harbor was the symbol of Japanese guile, if not of Japanese criminality. For this attack without declaration of war the responsible leaders should be punished exemplarily. That was the opinion of General Douglas MacArthur, as he told me personally.

Political reasons for such a charge and such a punishment were many. In the United States, heated debate was going on about the question of who was responsible for the catastrophe of Pearl Harbor—one of the most disgraceful episodes in the history of the United States, as it was called—the local commanders or the central Government in Washington? The commanding officers had obeyed the order 'to take appropriate measures against sabotage,' and rumor circulated that in Washington the attack had been less unexpected than in Pearl Harbor itself. Military investigating committees were set up, but they did not advise to court-martial Admiral Kimmel and General Short. Neither did the Congressional investigation, begun November 15, 1945, clear the air. In view of mutual accusation, accusations with strong political implications, it is easily understood that prosecution of the Japanese for this 'treacherous attack'[21] in violation of the laws of war was a relief for every one. The more it would appear that this undeclared attack amounted to a criminal outrage, the more American negligence or even guilt might diminish. How much Washington, in November and December, 1941, knew of the imminent danger is not known at this moment,[22] but it was more than the government later was inclined to admit. One cannot escape the impression that the urge to punish the Japanese for the unexpected attack on Pearl Harbor, was nourished by the wish to show Japan's action as perfidious and treacherous to such an extent that scarcely anybody had the duty to reckon with such unheard-of knavery.

The Tokyo indictment has extensively dealt with the attack on Pearl Harbor in an undeclared war. This part of the indictment was not very strong from the legal point of view. For, a Convention on the declaration of war did exist,[23] but it did not ask for a specific period between the declaration of war and the opening of hostilities. The Netherlands' proposal in 1907 to insert a time limit of twenty-four hours was rejected because the powers were not prepared to sign away the possibility of a surprise attack. According to the treaty provision, it was permitted to declare war at Washington at 12:00 and to start hostilities at Pearl Harbor at 12:01. It is a fact that a Japanese declaration of war was not delivered in clear terms and in due time. Formally, the attack on Pearl Harbor was in violation of the provisions of international law. But for the very reason that it had not been the intention of the Hague Convention to eliminate the possibility of a surprise attack, this violation cannot be compared in viciousness with other acts committed by the Axis Powers as well as by the Allied armies.

The American urge to organize a big trial against Japan was intrinsically based on Pearl Harbor. Since, however, the precedent of Nuremberg was set, it was hardly possible to avoid prosecuting Japanese leaders for the crime against peace. Restricting the Japanese indictment to the undeclared attack on Pearl Harbor would have amounted to the repudiation of the Nuremberg principles. Thus

[21] As President Roosevelt had called it in his special message to Congress, Dec. 15, 1941; Secretary Hull's statement of Dec. 7, 1941 read: 'Japan has made a treacherous and utterly unprovoked attack on the United States.'

[22] With the Nov. 26 Memorandum, Hull was aware of having ended the negotiations with Japan. 'I have washed my hands of it and it is now in the hands of you and Knox—the Army and the Navy,' he remarked Nov. 27 to Secretary Stimson. At the Nov. 25 White House Conference, Roosevelt had brought up the event that the U.S. was likely to be attacked by the Japanese perhaps as soon as next Monday. 'The question was how we should maneuver them into the position of firing the first shot without allowing too much danger to ourselves' (Diary of Stimson for Nov. 25, 1941). The actual attack brought a feeling of relief, to Stimson, according to his Diary for Dec. 7. The moral conflict had come to an end.

[23] Hague Convention, 1907, on the opening of hostilities.

developed from different roots the Tokyo Trial, 'the biggest trial in recorded history.'

The Tokyo Charter, drawn up by General MacArthur, and except for some deviations of little significance, similar to the Charter of Nuremberg, demanded a fair trial for the accused. Has there been a fair trial? Is a fair trial conceivable, humanly possible, just after a cruel war? An American newspaper wrote: 'We'll give them a fair trial and then hang them.' During the years that the trial lasted, the American occupation policy was based on the assumption that Japan had started an aggressive war. In the directive prepared by the Department of State, containing the basic post-surrender policy for Japan, 'the aggressions of past decades' were mentioned, and it states: 'Every effort shall be made to bring home to the Japanese people that part played by those who have deceived and misled them into embarking on world conquest, and those who collaborated in so doing.'[24]

The main issue before the International Military Tribunal for the Far East was the external policy of Japan, from 1929 up till 1945. What were the causes of the Pacific War? And who were the principal actors in this tragedy? An American historian wrote in 1946[25]:

Should the thesis of responsibility for World War II be so formulated as to lay a share of blame on other nations or on the three aggressors, an examination of its validity would assume Herculean proportions. It would involve, first of all, an informed judgment on the most perplexing questions of historical interpretation, including the issues connected with 'causation' and 'free will' in the making of history, national and universal. It would also raise special questions of challenging intricacy, *e.g.*, at what point in time should history of the 'blameworthy' nations be taken up in search for the characteristics to which war guilt is to be ascribed? Or again, for instance, how did Japan, after clinging to a hermitlike foreign policy for more than two hundred years, rather suddenly acquire, near the end of the nineteenth century, the propensities of a rabid imperialism and crusade against 'white' supremacy in the Far East? Moreover, an inquiry so broad in scope would call for a mastery of languages, documentation, and philosophic thinking which few, if any, students of history or political science command.

It is very difficult indeed in such a case of world history to determine individual guilt of one nation, and the guilt of individuals within that nation. Do individuals shape history, or are they merely 'les étiquettes de l'histoire' as Tolstoi so forcefully argued?[26] There is another question: are perhaps the events too big, too colossal, to bring individuals to account for them? In Roman times the rule

---

[24] Text in E.G. LEWE VAN ADUARD, JAPAN, FROM SURRENDER TO PEACE 317 (1953).
[25] C. BEARD, AMERICAN FOREIGN POLICY IN THE MAKING, 1932–1940, A STUDY IN RESPONSIBILITIES 42 (1946).
[26] LEO TOLSTOI, II LA GUERRE ET LA PAIX, ch. IV.: 'Les pretendus grands hommes ne sont que les étiquettes de l'Histoire: ils donnent leurs noms aux évenements, sans même avoir, comme les étiquettes, le moindre lien avec le fait lui-même'. Decisive is, according to Tolstoi, 'la marche générale de l'histoire et de l'humanité'.

existed: *de minimis non curat praetor.* Has the present time room for a similar kind of principle *de maximis non curat lex?*[27] The adoption of such a principle might be defended with the argument that it is an almost superhuman task to decide, just after the war, about individual war guilt, and that applies to guilt of individual nations as well as to guilt of individual persons.

Has there been a fair trial? Only the victor nations were represented in the Court, including Soviet Russia, which had concluded a neutrality pact with Japan. That neutrality pact was one of the reasons that Japan at the time dared to start the war. There were no neutrals or Japanese on the bench. This was a grave error. Neutrals and even the vanquished should have been represented. It would have prevented in the verdict the generalities which the tribunal too easily adopted. Neutrals and Japanese judges might have formed a counterpoint against the prevailing, and at the time almost undisputed, official attitudes of the victors.

How is the situation? War propaganda is used by both sides. Exaggerations, distortions, and one-sidedness are needed to make the people and the army morally capable of using the means of destruction available in warfare. The masses need to be made fanatical, to make them willing to use and to tolerate the modern weapons of destruction. No one can escape the influence of such systematic war propaganda and everyone gets used to living in a world of black and white. Trials after the war are the unavoidable consequence of the scientifically cultivated moral indignation of the victor.[28] As such, postwar trials are the by-product of total war in which the masses of the contesting nations are involved. It is easily understood that the chance is tempting to use the trials for making good the war propaganda, for obscuring the misbehavior of the victor, for enlarging on the crimes of the vanquished. It is certainly incorrect to hold that the trials were organized only to distort history.[29] But it cannot be denied that distortions of history did take place in the postwar trials. Neither Nuremberg nor Tokyo needed very much such distortion. But where it suited the victors, it took place. That it happened only on such a small scale is easily explained from the circumstance that the victors begrudged one another some distortions.

One example of the one-sidedness of the Tribunal may suffice. The defendants claimed to have acted in China against the menace of communism. The majority of the Tribunal ruled 'that no evidence of the existence or spread of communism or of any other ideology in China or elsewhere is relevant in the general phases.'[30] Later development in China and elsewhere shows that this exclusion was incorrect.

---

[27] *Cf.* E. Cohn, *The Problems of War Crimes Today* 26 Trans. Gro. Soc'y, 141 (1940).

[28] This postwar attitude may explain that in the Tokyo judgment all the accused were found guilty. In my Dissenting Opinion, I showed that Shigemitsu, Togo, Hirota, Kido, and Hata should have been acquitted.

[29] This was the main thesis of M. Belgion's Epitaph on Nuremberg (1947). *See also* his very critical Victors' Justice.

[30] *See* Transcript of Proceeding 21081; *compare also* 22451.

From the majority judgment and the dissenting opinions it appears that considerable difference of opinion existed among the Tokyo judges. The dissenting opinion of the French judge Bernard partly discloses the consequences these conflicting opinions had with regard to the cooperation of the judges in chambers.

As to the law of the case, one need only compare the majority judgment and the dissenting opinion of the Indian judge R.B. Pal[31] to note the wide difference on fundamental points. The majority judgment holds that 'the law of the Charter is decisive and binding on the Tribunal.' It observes that victorious powers, creating tribunals and formulating a law to be applied by these tribunals, may act only within the limits of international law. But, expressing its unqualified adherence to the relevant opinions of the Nuremberg Tribunal, it mentioned especially from the Nuremberg Judgment the phrase 'The Charter is not an arbitrary exercise of power on the part of the victorious nations but is the expression of international law existing at the time of its creation,' and 'In the opinion of the Tribunal, the solemn renunciation of war as an instrument of national policy necessarily involves the proposition that such a war is illegal in international law; and that those who plan and wage such a war, with its inevitable and terrible consequences, are committing a crime in so doing.' Further on, the majority judgment states: 'Aggressive war was a crime at international law long prior to the date of the Declaration of Potsdam.' It does not specifically repeat the sentence from the Nuremberg Judgment: 'To initiate a war of aggression, therefore, is not only an international crime; it is the supreme international crime differing only from other war crimes in that it contains within itself the accumulated evil of the whole.' But this strong statement in the Nuremberg Judgment is covered too by the 'unqualified adherence.'

In his elaborate 'Dissentient Judgment,' Judge Pal discusses the several opinions about the criminality of aggressive war, and comes to the conclusion 'no category of war became a crime in international life up to the date of commencement of the world war under our considerations.'[32] The general conclusion of Pal's Judgment reads: 'For the reasons given in the foregoing pages, I would hold that each and everyone of the accused must be found not guilty of each and every one of the charges in the indictment and should be acquitted of all those charges.'[33]

It is indeed a real contrast: the supreme international crime, in the opinion of Nuremberg and the majority Tokyo judgment—no crime at all according to the dissenting opinion of Judge Pal.

However, this opinion of the majority about the supreme international crime is not borne out by the verdicts. In the Nuremberg Judgment, those defendants

---

[31] The DISSENTIENT JUDGMENT OF JUSTICE PAL is the only part of the judgment that appeared in print (1953).
[32] *Id.* at 70.
[33] *Supra* note 31, at 697.

found guilty of the crime against peace, who were not, or only to a limited degree, found guilty of conventional war crimes, were given only prison sentences (Hess, Doenitz, Raeder, Funk, von Neurath). The same we find in the Tokyo verdict. Nobody is sentenced to death for having committed the crime against peace only. The death sentences are pronounced against the accused found guilty of considerable war crimes. For Tokyo is valid what Stimson observed with regard to the Nuremberg verdicts: 'Certainly, then, the charge of aggressive war has not been established in international law at the expense of any innocent lives.'[34] This leniency with regard to the 'supreme crime,' *e.g.*, Shigemitsu was found guilty of the crime against peace and sentenced to seven years imprisonment, has been explained by the newness of the crime. But it might also be that a difference existed between the verdict and its reasoning.

The very mild verdicts pronounced for the 'supreme crime' are remarkable. Remarkable, too, is the fact that so very few people were accused of and sentenced for the crime against peace. In the Pacific theater only the Tokyo trial dealt with the charge of aggressive war. In Europe[35] tribunals were very reluctant to declare individuals guilty of the crime of aggressive war. Minor figures, such as Fritsche, were found too small for so great a crime. Industrialists and military people were considered not to belong to the group who 'waged' aggressive war, unless they contributed to shaping the aggressive policy.[36] In the I.G. Farben trial this thought is further elaborated: 'To depart from the concept that only major war criminals—*i.e.*, those persons in the political, military, and industrial fields, for example, who were responsible for the formulation and execution of politics—may be held liable for waging wars of aggression would lead far afield. Under such circumstances there could be no practical limitation on criminal responsibility....'[37] In the Krupp trial all accused were acquitted from the charge of having committed crimes against peace.[38]

As already indicated above, aggression was not considered a true 'crime' before and during a good part of the last war. The dreadfulness of World War II made us realize the necessity of preventing wars in the future. It was the irony of history that the horror of the atomic bombings contributed to the recognition of

---

[34] H. Stimson, *The Nuremberg Trial, Landmark in Law*, 25 Foreign Aff. 188 (1947).

[35] I leave aside the Helsinki-trial, in which Finnish statesmen were punished for having waged an aggressive war against Soviet Russia; in this trial the punishments amounted to prison terms of some years.

[36] In the High Command Case all accused were acquitted from the charge of 'aggressive war.' The sentence reads: 'If and as long as a member of the armed forces does not participate in the preparation, planning, initiating, or waging of aggressive war on a policy level, his war activities do not fall under the definition of Crimes Against Peace. It is not a person's rank of status, but his power to shape or influence the policy of his state, which is the relevant issue for determining his criminality under the charge of Crimes Against Peace.' The German High Command Trial, XII Law Reports of Trials of War Criminals 69 (1949).

[37] *I.G. Farben Trial*, 10 L.R. 38.

[38] *Krupp-Trial*, 10 L.R. 103.

the criminality of Japanese aggression. On the wave of indignation, mixed with a conscious or unconscious feeling of guilt about Allied behavior, the conviction was carried that to plan and initiate aggressive war was a crime. This conviction signified a revolution in legal thought. It introduced in international law the concept of individual criminal responsibility for the maintenance of a minimum standard of human behavior, as formulated in some essential rules of the law of nations.

In this respect Nuremberg and Tokyo were a turning point, or—to use the words of the French judge Donnedieu de Vabres—'un oeuvre révolutionaire,'[39] a revolution in law. In the words of the judgment in the Justice Trial[40] 'the force of circumstances, the grim fact of worldwide interdependence, and the moral pressure of public opinion' resulted in international recognition that certain activities constituted criminal violations of common international law.

The factors brought about the emotional and revolutionary considerations and declarations about the 'supreme crime.' If we are compelled to make a distinction between postwar sentences and their reasoning, it will be easily understood that the moral indignation, together with 'the felt necessities of the time,' led to the expression that the crime against peace was the supreme crime comprising all the lesser evils.

However, with this moral indignation the real punishments meted out are hardly compatible. These punishments, not giving death sentences for the supreme crime, need a separate explanation.

There is no doubt that powers victorious in a *bellum justum*, and as such responsible for the frail peace, have, according to international law, the right to counteract elements consitituting a threat to the newly established order, and that they are entitled, as a means of preventing the recurrence of gravely offensive conduct, to seek and retain the custody of the pertinent persons. Napoleon's elimination offers a precedent. The responsible powers felt entitled to take, in political action, 'les mesures de précaution, que le repos et le salut public peuvent exiger à son égard.'[41] Napoleon was eliminated from the European scene 'comme ennemi et perturbateur du repos du monde,' as the Vienna Congress had called him.

After World War I the responsible powers tried to achieve the same against the German emperor in judicial action. The Treaty of Versailles (art. 227) provided for an international tribunal of five members to try the Emperor 'for a supreme offense against international morality and the sanctity of treaties.' Not stern justice in a criminal trial would be meted out, but the tribunal would be guided 'by

---

[39] Donnedieu de Vabres, *La procès de Nuremberg devant les principes modernes du droit pénal internation*, Recueil des Course de l'Académie de Droit International de l'Hague 481 (1947).

[40] 6 L.R. 43.

[41] Decision of the Congress of Aix la Chapelle, 1810. *Cf.* H. Hale Bellot, *The Detention of Napoleon Bonaparte*, 39 L.Q. Rev. 170 (1923).

the highest motives of international policy.' The Allied Powers, requesting from the Netherlands Government the Emperor's extradition, emphasized 'the special character of their demands, which contemplate, not a juridical accusation, but an act of high international policy.'[42] It need not cause surprise that lawyers did not consider the contemplated trial as a criminal trial. Garner wrote (*op cit.* II at 494): 'Since he was not charged with a crime, he would hardly seem liable to the penalties prescribed for the violations of the criminal law....' The refusal to extradite William II prevented the realization of the trial. As contemplated, the trial would have amounted to the taking of political measures of security, after judicial inquiry and judgment about the politic dangerousness of the accused and the adequate sanctions.

The duty of the victors to take adequate measures of security was, after World War II, emphasized in the Potsdam Declaration:

There must be eliminated for all time the authority and influence of those who have deceived and misled the people of Japan into embarking on world conquest, for we insist that a new order of peace, security and justice will be impossible until irresponsible militarism is driven from the world.

In his opening statement, the Chief Prosecutor in the Tokyo Trial stressed this point of danger:

For the accused in the dock are no contrite penitents. If we are to believe their claims as already asserted in this trial, they acknowledge no wrong and imply that if they were set free they would repeat their aggression again and again. So that from the sheer necessity for security they should be forever restrained.[43]

The same thought was expressed by the Russian prosecutor:

The accused have not laid down arms.... they continue actively advocating their criminal aggressive policy which brought innumerable calamities and suffering to millions of people. The conspirators now in the dock are also dangerous because around them rally the most reactionary elements in Japan represented by former generals, intelligence agents and diplomats who appearing in this court as witnesses are doing their best to shield their former bosses.[44]

Mere political action could have achieved the same goal for protection. That the judicial way was chosen to select those who had been and who were the driving forces of aggression is a novelty that marks a difference with the past.

The concept of crime in international law is applied to different phenomena. It ranges from the really immoral act, such as the wanton killing of prisoners of war, to the merely hostile action, like the 'illegal action' of the 'freie Heldentum' which was denied protection by the Hague Conventions. The crime against

---

[42] *Cf.* J.W. GARNER, II INTERNATIONAL LAW AND THE WORLD WAR 493 (1920).
[43] Official Transcript of the Tokyo Trial, at 469.
[44] *Id.* at 39738.

peace—described in the *reasonings* of the postwar judgments as the 'supreme crime,' as the utmost immorality—might also be conceived as indicating an act comparable to merely political crimes in domestic law. The *punishments* delivered in the post war judgments indicate that they were based on this concept of the political crime, where the decisive element is the political danger rather than the criminal guilt, where the 'criminal' is considered an enemy rather than a villain, and where the sanction emphasizes the *mesure de sureté* rather than the judicial retribution. In this sense the crime against peace, as formulated in the Charters, was in perfect accordance with existing international law. Consequently, there seems to be a divergence between the verdicts of the judgments, and their reasoning. Where the judgment of Nuremberg stresses the point that the Charter is 'the expression of international law existing at the time of its creation'[45]—a pronunciation reiterated in the Tokyo verdict[46]—it might be suggested that such opinion holds good only with regard to the concept of international crime handled in the verdicts.[47]

Different motives brought about the postwar trials and the indictment for the crime of aggressive war. Different lines of thought were followed by the victorious powers, which at the same time organized trials to decide whether the wars waged were aggressive, and based their postwar policies on the assumption that the vanquished nations had been out for military conquest of the world. Different opinions were held by the individuals who sat in judgment. Different concepts were at the basis of the reasonings of the judgments and of the verdicts pronounced and the sanctions applied. Anger and hate played their role, as did sincere moral indignation and practical policy. The multitude of motives and intricacy of their interplay are apt to confuse the mind. Elements of foul play are easily exaggerated, dishonesty in official statements easily too much stressed. Altogether Nuremberg and Tokyo amounted to a revolution in law, and revolutions are usually the outcome of many factors, in which good and bad are intermingled. As in every revolution the new concepts were based on the conscience of the people. The world conscience was aroused by the horrors of the war and by the experience of the new weapons. In an emotional outburst the world demanded that war should be outlawed to the extent that individual warmakers should be made criminally responsible. This world sentiment was carried in the general *considerations and reasonings* of the judgments. The Charter was, according to the Nuremberg Judgment, at the same time 'the expression of international law existing at the time of its creation' and 'itself a contribution to international law.'[48] One might say that the Charters were not decisive. It was the judgments that made the crime against peace enter into positive law.[49] The

---

[45] Judgment Nuremberg 88 (Brit. ed. 1946).
[46] Judgment Tokyo 27.
[47] The 'Dissenting Opinion' I delivered is based on this concept of the crime of aggression.
[48] *Supra* note 45.
[49] *Cf.* C.A. Pompe, Aggressive War an International Crime 281 (1954).

judgments stand in history as indelible facts. They form a precedent. They have the power of the beaten path.

It need not cause surprise that the revolutionary character of Nuremberg and Tokyo is emphasized by German and Japanese scholars. It should not be denied. But there is no sense in measuring the significance of a revolution with the standards it intended to destroy. It is nonsense to judge a revolution by the laws it abolished. Its worth is determined by its value for the future.[50]

It need also not cause surprise that German and Japanese scholars enlarge on the negative aspects of Nuremberg and Tokyo. These aspects too should not be denied. But one should never forget that new law often is created with mixed motives and out of mixed reasons. It holds good for the growth of law, in the national as well as in the international field, that sometimes the birth of law appears as the consequence of rape. New legal thoughts often find strange ways to realization, good ideas often take advantage of bad intentions. As Whitehead put it: 'Great ideas often enter into reality with evil associates and with disgusting alliances.'[51] That criticism on Nuremberg and Tokyo is warranted does not imply that the principal idea materialized in these trials would necessarily be wrong.

Stimson, in 1944, considered the concept of individual criminal responsibility for the crime against peace 'a little in advance of international thought.'[52] Later he called the Nuremberg Trial 'Landmark in Law.'[53] It is a landmark that indicates the beginning of international law of the atomic era. One might say that, after World War II, in a hurricane of emotion the world swept aside obsolete conceptions of national sovereignty and established new law. As such the law of Nuremberg and Tokyo signifies an outpost of legal development. It is law 'in advance' of actual legal concepts and juridical situations. But this new law on the maintenance of peace is not at all in advance of the facts of international relations. The world needs new law, to prevent universal catastrophe. The natural law of the atomic age includes as a matter of course the criminal responsibility of the individual bent on aggressive war. It is therefore the task of the United Nations to implement the revolution of Nuremberg and Tokyo, and one may doubt whether the United Nations is living up to that responsibility.[54] That many other legal

---

[50] In this sense Otto Kranzbühler, *Nürnberg als Rechtsproblem*, *in* Festgabe für Erich Kaufmann 219 (1950).

[51] A.N. Whitehead, Adventures of Ideas 28 (1948).

[52] *Supra* note 6, vol. II, at 587.

[53] *Supra* note 34.

[54] Compare the present writer's: *The United Nations and the Development of International Criminal Law*, *in* The United Nations, Ten Years' Legal Progress (1956). At its XIIth Session (1954) the General Assembly adopted Res. 1187 (XII) shelving for the time being the agenda item 'Code of Offences against the Peace and Security of Mankind.' As the Netherlands representative, I voted, as a token of protest, against this Resolution, which was adopted with 74 votes in favor and 1 against.

developments belong to 'the necessities of the time' is beyond question. It is also beyond question that on many other points the law of international relations has to change if criminal individual responsibility is to become the keystone of an effective law on peace. To maintain the outpost, the legal forces of the rear will have to advance.

Lawyers know that law is not logic. Some parts occasionally may leap forward pushed by special emotions and by special interest. Often it takes a long time to arrive at a closed system of legal provisions. However, *to arrive at a stage of legal development in which this individual criminal responsibility is but the logical consequence of the international juridical situation may be the precondition of the survival of civilization.*

For our time some principles applied in the Nuremberg and Tokyo trials are of paramount importance. The first is *that aggressive war is illegal and criminal.* It seems to me that the post war world has not lived up to this principle. If one looks at the postwar legal development, it might seem that more and more exceptions are recognized.[55]

A second principle should be mentioned: *that individuals are criminally responsible for the crime against peace.* It means that the individual is called upon to disobey his national government in case this government is out on aggression. According to the judgments some rules of world law, expressing the loyalty that everyone should have to humanity as a whole, prevail upon national obligations. The Nuremberg Judgment expressed this fundamental idea when it explained the intrinsic significance of its Charter: '[T]he very essence of the Charter is that individuals have international duties which transcend the national obligations of obedience imposed by the individual state.'[56] This principle is also relevant in connection with conventional war crimes.

With respect to the violation of the laws and customs of war, the conventional war crimes, the Tokyo Judgment made an essential contribution. In the Judgment of Nuremberg punishments were only meted out to those who themselves had committed war crimes or had ordered them to be committed.[57] In Japan the main question was in how far the accused were responsible for the crimes which were committed in the field—regularly and on a mass scale—but which had not been ordered by them. The Tokyo Judgment acknowledged this responsibility for not having acted, for not having prevented the violation of the laws of war, in case the accused knew of the crimes, and were in a command position which made it

---

[55] An enumeration of these exceptions is given in B. Roling, *Hat das Kriegsverbot noch einen Sinn?* in JAHRBUCH FÜR INTERNATIONALES RECHT 74 (1969).

[56] *Supra* note 45, at 42.

[57] *See, e.g.,* the discussions with respect to the responsibility of Admiral Donitz in relation to his Laconia-order. The question of his responsibility for not having prevented the practice of the killing of survivors was not even mentioned (*Supra* note 45, at 109).

possible for them to stop the criminal practice.[58] This responsibility for omission
to act seems at present to be totally disregarded.

[58] Count 55 of the Tokyo Indictment charged the accused that they 'being by virtue of their
respective offices responsible for securing the observance of...the Laws and Customs of War in
respect of the armed forces...and in respect of many thousands of prisoners of war and civilians
then in the power of Japan..., deliberately and recklessly disregarded their legal duty to take adequate steps to secure the observance and prevent breaches thereof.' In the Judgment this question of negligence in the duty to enforce the rules of war is discussed with regard to each of the
defendants. With respect to the scope of this responsibility differences may exist. According to the
Majority Judgment in Tokyo, Hata, Hirota, and Shigemitsu were guilty of negligence (pp. 1155,
1160, 1195). In my Dissenting Opinion, I discussed the guiding principles concerning 'responsibility for omission' (pp. 54–61) and came to the conclusion that Hata, Hirota, and Shigemitsu were
to be acquitted on this score (pp. 189, 203–210, 238–242), applying the legal principles adopted
by the Supreme Court of the United States *in re* Yamashita, 327 U.S.1 (1946) also Reel, the case
of General Yamashita (1949). For a more contemporary appraisal see Taylor, Nuremberg and
Vietnam: An American Tragedy 1970 and Bassiouni, The War Power and the Laws of War: Theory
and realism, 18 DePaul L. Rev. 188 (1968).

21

Looking Back at the Nuremberg Trials with Special Consideration of the Processes Against Military Leaders

By Dr. Hans Laternser
Attorney at Law, Frankfurt am Main

Almost four decades ago on October 1, 1946, the International Military Tribunal in Nuremberg pronounced its verdict in the so-called great process against Goering *et al.* and especially against the indicted organizations. Shortly thereafter, twelve further processes were carried out in Nuremberg. All these trials belong to history. Yet we are approaching a time which is ripe for a valid appraisal of this significant segment of the development of international law.

The hope was that these processes would usher in a new era in international relations in which the principle of might would be replaced by that of right. From this hope it follows that right (*i.e.* law) is the *sole* standard by which they can be assessed. Because a violation of fundamental principles of law would be a very dubious foundation and a poor beginning for a future safeguarding of international relations, the jurist is bound to examine precisely these Nuremberg trials according to a strict standard of law.

The topic of the Nuremberg trials is virtually inexhaustible; a work of many volumes could be written on it. The difficulty in preparing these articles was that of limiting oneself. First of all, I will give a brief survey. Then I will consider several important legal questions of formal and material nature in order to give the reader the possibility of judging these Nuremberg trials for himself.

I

In the so-called Nuremberg trials, Germans were called to account for the charge of having committed: (1) crimes against the peace; (2) war crimes; and, (3) crimes against humanity.

The first of the Nuremberg trials, the so-called great process, began toward the end of 1945. It lasted from October 1945 to October 1946. The judges were provided by the United States of America, Great Britain, France, and the Soviet Union.

Political and military leaders, groups and organizations were indicted. The collective indictments against the groups and organizations—unknown at any rate to German law—involved the government of the Reich, political leaders, SS, SD, Gestapo, SA, the General Staff, and the High Command of the German Armed Forces. This last group included the commanders-in-chief of the branches of the armed forces, the chiefs of the General Staff, the chief of the High Command, the chief-of-staff of the High command and his deputy, as well as all commanders-in-chief of the army groups and armies. The indictments charged that these groups and organizations were to be declared criminal with the effect that any member, solely because of his membership, could be punished with any penalty, including the death penalty, by any zonal court of the respective occupying power. (*Cf.* Control Council Law No. 10 of December 20, 1945.)

As to the individual defendants, the International Military Tribunal pronounced eleven death sentences and seven sentences of long imprisonment. Three defendants, Papen, Schacht and Fritzsche who, as substituted for the deceased Goebbels, had to take his place in the prisoners' dock, were acquitted. Of the accused organizations, the International Military Tribunal's judgment declared several, under certain modifications, as criminal. These were the Gestapo, SD, political directors, and SS. The judgment also acquitted several organizations. These were the SA, the government of the Reich, and the so-called 'General Staff and High Command' group comprised of about 129 generals.

This so-called great process was followed by twelve more processes against 170 to 180 accused persons. These twelve processes were tried before the International Military Tribunal but without the participation of Great Britain, France and the Soviet Union. These were the following twelve processes. One was against physicians, and one was against jurists. Three were against the most influential industrial firms of Flick, Krupp, and members of the board of directors of the IG-Farben-Industrie. Three more were against military leaders. These leaders were Field Marshal Milch, the generals who were deployed in the Southeast, and twelve other generals (summarized in the so-called High Command process). Still, three more were against SS leaders. These were the operational groups (Ohlendorf and others), the SS leaders who were engaged in the administration of the concentration camps (Pohl and others), and the High Office of Racial Policy. The last of these twelve processes was directed against a number of persons thrown together from various groups. Among the accused in the twelfth process were several diplomats. This group gave this twelfth process the name 'Wilhelmstrasse' process. Because of the heterogeneous composition of the accused persons, the twelfth process was also called the 'omnibus' process.

I know from statements by attorneys of the American prosecuting authority that, for example, the question of how many persons were charged in a planned process depended in actuality, for example, on what courtroom would be available in the Nuremberg court house for holding the trial. The number of seats for defendants in the available courtroom was, therefore, in one case or another, determinative in fixing the number of defendants. This certainly is a very curious method to prepare a process held necessary.

Another example of the selection of defendants is found in the first session of the so-called High Command (OKW) process. It was delayed in its start even though all the participants in the process were present in the courtroom—with the exception of the defendants. The writer inquired of an American prosecutor what was the reason for the delay, apparently just then communicated to him. The latter told him that in the transfer of the defendants to the courtroom, Generaloberst Blaskowitz had fallen several stories on the staircase of the prison and had died. The prosecutor then stated, further, that Blaskowitz did not need to do that as he would certainly have been acquitted. The counter-question of why had he then been indicted remained unanswered. Blaskowitz was an army commander who had submitted a memorandum to Hitler just after the Polish campaign. The memorandum discussed the excesses of the Gestapo and the SD in Poland.

For months and, in part, for years the Nuremberg trials were prepared for by the prosecuting authority. The prosecuting authority had at its disposal an unlimited number of persons and an unlimited number of technical aids. In the High Command process, for example, eighty volumes of documents with an estimated 12,000 to 15,000 pages were submitted by the prosecuting authority.

In the Nuremberg processes, the principles of Anglo-American criminal procedure were used. According to these principles, each party submits to the court only the evidence supporting its own case. The court itself does not participate in the investigation of the truth. The prosecuting authority must only prove its own thesis of the case; it is not, for example, interested in determining and arguing circumstances exonerating the accused. This contradicts, for example, the principles of the German code of criminal procedure (§ 160 StPO). In the great process before the International Military Tribunal, the defense had objected to this one-sided position. None of the participants in the process from the Anglo-American legal circuit showed any kind of understanding for this demand by the defense. Jackson, the chief American prosecutor, declared rather that he could not serve two masters. A modification of this position by the prosecuting authority was not to be achieved, even up to the conclusion of the Nuremberg trials.

The result of the Anglo-American procedure was that the prosecuting authority, better familiar with this procedure, withheld such evidence as could not be brought in line with its theory of its case. The evidence was withheld, not only from the court, but in particular from the defense. Such conduct does, indeed, lie within the rules of this procedure. But when the defense does not have the same opportunities as the prosecuting authority to ascertain or to confiscate evidence, the presuppositions for the correct functioning of this Anglo-American criminal process are missing. The possibilities were and remained unequal. The respective results from the hearing of evidence, therefore, can be appraised only with the reservations which arise from the inequality of the weapons.

The German defense counsel began their activity in October 1945 in the severely bombed city of Nuremberg. They stood there with literally empty hands. To perform their jobs they had, for the time being, a small library room in which not even every defense counsel had his own working place. Later a large library room was placed at the disposal of all of the defenders. There they each had a working table. At that time, however, they did not yet have a single telephone. In the course of the later procedures, every chief defense attorney received a room for himself. But even then the *entire* defense of the processes running in part simultaneously had only a single telephone connection from which they could make long distance calls. The situation of the prosecuting authority stood in no expressible proportion to this.

At the beginning of the court proceedings in Nuremberg, the prosecuting authority already possessed an extremely extensive mass of evidence. The evidence had been seized in the advance of the Allied Forces and examined by suitable German-speaking officials for the possibility of its utilization in the planned processes. The defenders could utilize this entire confiscated material only so far as the prosecuting authority decided, in the course of the processes, to submit it to the court as evidence. The defenders themselves had no possibility whatsoever to look through the archives in Washington and London for exonerating evidence. Because of these facts, valuable material for the defense has most certainly not been used.

In all of the Nuremberg processes, German documentary material was almost exclusively presented just as German witnesses were principally examined. There were a few exceptions such as in the process against the Southeast generals. Foreign documentary material was not submitted in the processes. From this, it follows that the history of the origin of the war could not be judged according to the world-wide political situation and the intentions of the individual nation-states. The archives in London, Paris, or Moscow are surely very interesting in this respect, but they were left out of the account of the war in the process.

I cannot within the scope of this essay discuss the contents of the sentences that were imposed in Nuremberg. However, I can within this framework point out two important circumstances. In judging the organizations which, according to the petition of the prosecuting authority, were to be declared criminal with the possible consequence of the death penalty for the members, a problem arose. This was whether the mass annihilations of human beings had become generally known, so that one could conclude from them a collective guilt on the part of the German people. The International Military Tribunal did not assume the existence of such a collective guilt. Although the Tribunal did not explicitly express this, the Tribunal stated that to punish the members of the organizations declared criminal, evidence that the accused individual became or remained a member with the knowledge of the criminal activity of the organization was necessary. If the International Military Tribunal had, as petitioned, declared all organizations to be criminal, the effects would have become incalculable. A very large part of the German population would have been affected by such a declaration, without the possibility of exculpation before the zonal courts. The importance of the complex of organizations stood in no proportion to the fate of the small number of individual defendants in the first process.

Strong reproaches have been made against the manner of the German warfare. With regard to land war, for example, two orders have been assessed, probably justly, as severe offenses against the laws and customs of war. These are the detachment order to 'cut down' hostile sabotage troops, also in uniform, 'down to the last man,' and the commissar order to shoot all Soviet commissars after their capture. I must remark that these commands, however, were personal orders of Hitler. In the area of the prisoner of war system, highly dubious orders had been issued by the High Command, and these orders played a considerable role in the later processes against military leaders. However, the accusations brought against the German waging of sea warfare in the U-boat war have been judged by the International Military Tribunal as not justified. Accusations against the German air force, brought forward in the course of the first process because of, *inter alia*, attacks on nonmilitary targets in Poland and Rotterdam at the beginning of the West offensive, were not discussed in the Tribunal's grounds of judgment against Goring for very obvious reasons.

II

In respect to legal considerations, I would like first of all to deal with some procedural regulations.

A

Before the beginning of the first process, the entire defense had already, in a joint petition addressed to the International Military Tribunal, pointed out their strong formal objections against the process. Among other things, it had stated— and I quote verbatim:

Finally the defense is obliged now to point out another peculiarity of this process by which it departs from generally recognized principles of modern criminal law administration: The judges are only appointed by states which have been the one party in this war. This one disputing party is all in one: Creator of the court constitution and of the criminal law norms, prosecutor and judge. Up to now it was common legal conviction that this should not be the case, just as the United States of America, as champion for the establishing of an international court of arbitration and jurisdiction, has always required that the judges' bench be occupied by neutrals under consultation of representatives of all the disputing parties. In the Permanent International Court of Justice in the Hague this has been realized in an exemplary manner.

In view of the multiplicity and the difficulty of these issues of law, the defense applies for the following: The court should obtain expert opinion of internationally recognized international law scholars about the legal foundations of this process based on the statute of the court.

The legally well-founded petition was turned down by the International Military Tribunal. If the court had entered into this search for legal foundations, the process would have been settled before it had begun.

B

This above quoted petition of the entire defense was based on the dubious legal foundations for the Nuremberg processes. The basis was formed by the London agreement of August 8, 1945. It had been entered into by Great Britain, the United States of America, France, and the Soviet Union. The nations, in this agreement, decided to form the International Military Tribunal for the purpose of trying war criminals whose crimes had no geographically defined *locus delicti*. Simultaneously, a statute for this International Military Tribunal was issued which, as laid down in article 2, was supposed to be an essential part of this London agreement.

The following is extremely interesting in regard to the London agreement and the statute for the International Military Tribunal. The agreement was signed by Jowitt for Great Britain, Jackson for the United States of America, Falco for France, and Nikichenko for the Soviet Union. Of the signers, three participated directly in the later process before the International Military Tribunal. Jackson was the chief American prosecutor. Perhaps this does not have to be so very dubious. It is at least a legal blemish. But Falco was the second French judge, and Nikichenko was even the chief Soviet judge!

Consequently, one half of the authors of such an extraordinary special law were judges in the subsequent trial. There can be no doubt that under normal legal circumstances, a decisive reason for rejecting the judges would have been given here. But a provision had already been made for this, too. Article 3 of the statute for the International Military Tribunal which was, after all, part of the London agreement, provided that neither the court nor its members or representatives could be rejected by the prosecuting authority or the defendant or his advocate. The statute with this provision also originated from the same persons who signed the London agreement. Two of the judges, therefore, had ruled for themselves that they could not be turned down as prejudiced. They thereby came to decide a question in which the judge, rejected as biased, is normally not allowed to participate in the answer.

C

With regard to the statute which laid down the procedural law for the International Military Tribunal, I want likewise to restrict myself to the discussion of two provisions, article 18 and article 24.

Article 18 states:

The court shall

a) confine the process strictly to an accelerated treatment of the points made by the prosecution,

b) take strict measures to avoid any action that could cause an unnecessary delay and to turn down irrelevant questions and explanations of any kind whatsoever,

c) punish unseemly conduct by imposing suitable penalties, including the exclusion of the defendant or his defense attorney from any or all of the further process actions; the relevant discussion of the accused must not be impaired hereby.

The provision contained in c), for example, led to the temporary arrest of several defense attorneys in the Krupp process. Some of them had been absent from a session and this incident, on grounds of insult to the court—a so-called contempt of court—led to their temporary arrest. In this connection I may also point out that the bar association of Cologne had proposed at that time to take measures against the German defense attorneys from the sole fact that they had taken the job of defense counsel in Nuremberg.

Article 24 was supposed to set the course of the proceedings. It stated:

The proceedings shall take the following course:

a) The charge is read out.

b) The court asks each defendant whether he pleads guilty or not guilty.

c) The prosecuting authority makes an introductory statement.

d) The court asks the prosecuting authority and the defense if and what evidence they desire to offer the court and decides upon the admissibility of every piece of evidence.

e) The witnesses of the prosecuting authority are heard. After them the witnesses of the defense. Thereafter, the counterevidence deemed admissible by the court is put forward on the part of the prosecuting authority or defense.

f) The court may at any time address questions to witnesses or defendants.

g) Prosecuting authority and defense attorneys are to hear every witness and defendant who gives testimony and are authorized to cross-examine them.

h) The defense then has the floor.

i) After the defense, the prosecuting authority is given the floor.

j) The defendant has the last word.

k) The court pronounces the sentence and penalty.

This regulation supplied the framework for the course of the trial. I would like to call attention to the following points relating to the course of the trial.

First, the prosecuting authority had the right to make an introductory statement. The prosecuting authority made use of the right in the first process with special copiousness—each of the four Allied chief prosecutors spoke for several hours. By so doing, the prosecuting authority was able to set forth to the court its aims in the future hearing of evidence. Thus, the judges were able to perceive in what context, for example, the depositions of witnesses were to be appraised. This surely was an important procedural tactic. The defense did not have this right.

Second, I would like to refer to c) of article 24, according to which the court was to decide on the admissibility of evidence offered by both the prosecuting authority and the defense. This regulation was only unilaterally handled. Without any resistance by the court, the prosecuting authority produced the evidence which it desired to have admitted. The evidence of the defense, however, and particularly the hearing of witnesses, had to be explicitly approved beforehand by the court.

Third, a considerable legal offense had been committed in the first process in connection with the hearings of witnesses. The prosecuting authority's witnesses through whom the criminal character of the organizations, for example, was to be proved were heard directly by the International Military Tribunal. The witnesses of the defense, however, who were supposed to refute this ostensible criminal character were heard only before a commission to which no judge of the International Military Tribunal belonged. The chairman of this commission, a British lieutenant colonel, made a report on the entire interrogations; the report was presented to the International Military Tribunal. The examinations themselves, therefore, were never seen by the deciding judges. Thus, the court that was deciding the fate of millions only heard directly the witnesses for the prosecution. The court neither saw nor heard the witnesses for the defense. Detailed written references to this unequal treatment for the prosecuting authority and the defense could not eliminate this regulation which the court had exclusively ordered to shorten the duration of the process. The intended shortening of the process could in no case justify such a breach of law.

Fourth, the following is also extraordinary. The prosecuting authority in its pleadings before the court was not restricted with regard to time. The defense had to restrict itself to a space of time determined by the court. This led to the result that parts of the pleadings of the defense could not be presented!

I have already pointed out that the weapons of the prosecuting authority and defense were extremely unequal at the beginning of the process. Even though this inequality was later modified somewhat, the inequalities could not be compensated, even approximately, at any phase of the processes. I would like to quote verbatim my protest in the High Command process, the last of the twelve processes, as it was set forth to the court before the defense began producing its evidence. It runs as follows:

However, before I begin with the presentation of the evidence, I would like to show the court the extraordinary difficulties under which the evidence of the defense has come about.

I am doing it for the reason that from them it follows that the prorogation of four weeks granted to the defense has not permitted a preparation appropriate to the importance of the case. I also deem it important that these difficulties be shown by the protocol.

In a recital of less than five weeks in duration, the prosecution, after years of preparation employing an unlimited number of persons and technical resources, has submitted over 1500 documents to the court without having them read out, i.e., without trying them.

The volume of this evidentiary material which the prosecution—again by the aid of numerous means—has selected from the huge mass of the confiscated and captured documentary material located in Washington becomes evident if one considers that it fills eighty volumes with approximately 12,000 to 15,000 pages.

The content of these eighty documentary volumes holds as process material set forth.

This presentation of the prosecuting authority, immense in volume, was not possible to process completely within the preparation time.

This yielded from the following:

1) The working possibilities of the defense are limited. Theoretically, each defendant may have only one chief defense attorney and the latter only one assistant and one or two secretaries. Exceptions require in each case substantiation and express approval. Even in cases in which the chief defense attorney is allowed to employ two assistants, this enlargement of the defense staff does not carry weight in a decisive manner in view of the volume of the process material.

2) In spite of the abundant resources, the prosecution has not adequately substantiated its presentation.
   a) Already the bill of indictment was drawn up summarily; consequently a preparation of the defense after its presentation was not possible.
   b) In the evidence process itself, the prosecution has not specified against whom the respective evidence is submitted. This lacking of substantiation rendered the defense extremely difficult.
   c) To this date, the defense has not yet a sure foundation as to what the scope is of the evidence. Document books in the German language handed over to the defense do not correspond in their content with the document books in English submitted to the court. Only the English documentary books, however, are valid as evidence. Spot checks have already shown that the English documentary books contain passages that are not in the German documentary books. In order to enable the defense to find out what is offered as evidence so far, 80 documentary books have to be compared with one another.

   For this purpose up to now only one licensed interpretress is at the disposal of the defense.
   d) The translation of the German language documents has to be subjected to a thorough re-examination. Quite a large number of errors in translation have already been found. This comparing of activity, likewise, has to be executed by the above-mentioned interpretress of the defense.

3) The defendants have neither seen nor heard the evidence submitted against them in the course of the trial. An orderly process (due process of law), however, requires this. They were, therefore, as has to be explicitly stated anew, unable to follow the contents of the trial.

4) In order to bring the evidence to the cognizance of the defendants—at least outside of the trial—the prosecution had been ordered to place photostats of the documents at the disposal of the defense. This has been largely done partially only during the prorogation period.

Only after the defense had the photostats of the evidence at its disposal could a conference of the defense attorney with the defendant take place on a secure foundation. Only then was it possible for the defense attorneys to procure counterevidence in substantiated form. In view of the traffic conditions, the running time for the procurement of witness and of the evidence is by no means normal. Depositions and documents already requested have so far only in part arrived.

5) Time-consuming trips, for example abroad, to produce evidence could not be undertaken before the beginning of the defense presentation.

6) It is of special importance, however, that the defenders have so far had no access to the documentary material located in Washington.

Petition was made for this access already in the first session of the court. The motion for prorogation for the duration of three weeks for this was turned down on the ground that the defense would be given sufficient time for preparation.

I notice that the defense has to begin with the submission of its evidence before it has been able to use the most important source of evidence according to the same principles as the prosecuting authority.

Thus, the defense at the beginning of its performance, in a process of such historic significance, faces the fact of being unable fully to meet its assignment. It doubts if a fair chance is left for it.

This protest was accepted without any contradiction.

D

I would like to deal with one last point which relates to the procedure. This is the question of the competence of the Nuremberg courts over the accused generals. This question is certainly very problematic.

In the first trial before the International Military Tribunal, the indicted generals Keitel and Jodl and the admirals Raeder and Donitz had been lifted up to the level of the politicians indicted and sentenced together with them. According to general principles, this International Military Tribunal was certainly not competent for the generals in highest ranks. But the competence of the International Military Tribunal could not be successfully attacked. Article 3 of the statute prohibited this.

In the other two military processes against the generals deployed in the Southeast and the generals indicted in the High Command process, the competence of the court was contested respectively in the first session and in the closing pleading. The court's competence was contested with reference to article 63 of the Geneva Convention of July 27, 1929. The defense took the position that the indicted generals were entitled to be recognized as prisoners of war. From this it followed that, according to article 63 of the Geneva Convention, the indicted generals should be juged only by the same courts and according to the same procedures which were competent for members of the armed forces of the custody state.

The Nuremberg courts rejected the objections to their incompetence by appropriating to themselves the standpoint used by the American Supreme Court in

Washington in the case of the Japanese general Yamashita. Allegedly, article 63 of the Geneva Convention was supposed to be valid only for the judging of acts committed during captivity. This argument is undoubtedly too narrow. It does not take into consideration even one word of article 8 of the appendix of the Hague Rules of Land Warfare. Article 8 explicitly places prisoners of war under the laws, regulations and orders which are valid for the soldiers of the custody state. The systematic position of this article does not permit a conclusion as had been drawn by the Supreme Court.

Moreover, the Allies were not all in agreement over the question of how to staff the courts for the process against generals. Great Britain had indicted the Field Marshals Kesselring, von Manstein, Generalobstere Stumpff, and v. Falkenhorst in courts staffed by officers. Likewise, in a criminal case against the German general Wagener which took place in Rome, Italy had staffed the military court with five Italian generals. The American courts in Nuremberg, however, before which the military cases were tried were staffed with civil judges. These courts did not at all fulfill the characteristics of a military court. A court does not become a *military* court by being so called; a court becomes a military court only by its staffing with officers whose ranks correspond to that of the defendants.

Evidently, objections of this kind had been considered. In any case, the indicted generals were abruptly discharged from captivity with simultaneous orders for their further internment as civilian internees. The writer had also submitted a sharp protest against this to the commander-in-chief of the American Third Army, but an answer to this protest was never received. This so-called release from the status of prisoner of war—without any corresponding changes in imprisonment itself, but with the continued deprivation of privileges granted prisoners of war—was an obvious offence against the Geneva Convention. After all, article 83 of this Convention explicitly provided that until the execution of their home-transportation, prisoners of war must have the enjoyment of these privileges.

These viewpoints presented to the court all remained unsuccessful. International jurisprudence, however, will have no choice but to find that the German generals indicted in Nuremberg have been sentenced by incompetent courts.

The British position which placed Field Marshals Kesselring and v. Manstein before military courts staffed with officers (one general and five field officers in the case of Kesselring and three generals and four field officers in the case of v. Manstein) was not carried through consistently. The rank of the generals as judges should have corresponded to the rank of the accused. This is what the laws of the custody-states meant at that time; this is what should have been done in the cases tried via the Geneva Convention.

E

The Geneva Convention had been violated in other respects during the processes at Nuremberg. The Geneva Convention prescribes that officers held as prisoners of war were, inter alia, to remain entitled to retain their insignia of rank. In England this regulation had been observed. When the defense called for several generals from England, among them Field Marshal v. Rundstedt, as witnesses for the great process, they came to Nuremberg wearing their insignia of rank. The remanding prison was under the supervision of an American colonel, Andrus, who viewed every imprisoned German as a criminal. On the very day of Rundstedt's arrival, he had to remove his insignia and red stripes from his uniform. Shortly before examining Rundstedt in front of the International Military Tribunal, I spoke with him and noticed that—in contrast to the day before when he had arrived in Nuremberg from England—he no longer wore any insignia whatsoever. One could even see the traces of the hasty ripping-off of the insignia and red stripes. I told him that I would question him before the public at the International Military Tribunal how the insignia came to be removed from his uniform. Rundstedt urged me not to ask this question. Unfortunately, I did not disregard his request at that time. Perhaps Rundstedt was right, though, for at the time when probably all Germans were hungry, insignia of rank played no special role. But for me, it was a question of the observance of the Geneva Convention.

III

In material-legal respect, I am restricting myself to a few questions. I shall deal with three topics. First, whether wars of aggression, the so-called crimes against peace as article 6 of the International Military Tribunal and the Control Council Law No. 10 standardized them, are punishable. Second, whether the Control Council Law No. 10 was a valid law according to general principles. (It formed the basis for 12 processes.) Finally, I am going to deal with the very interesting question of whether article 8 in the statute for the International Military Tribunal and the corresponding provision in the Control Council Law No. 10, according to which the command of a government or of a superior could not be assessed as grounds for exclusion from penalty but at best as grounds for mitigation of penalty, presents a valid regulation.

A

Of all the objections which exist, from the standpoint of law and particularly from abroad, against the statute of the International Military Tribunal, its judgment, and the Control Council Law No. 10, those which relate to the culpability of aggressive war are the weightiest. That the war brought about by Hitler was a crime cannot be seriously doubted. This, however, is not the question at issue here. What matters here is only whether this war was a crime in the sense of the criminal law from which criminal responsibility can be derived. The parties which matter are those who, on the strength of the one man's orders, became active as politicians, diplomats, military commanders, and industrialists in relation to this war. The doubts that exist in response to this question do not reflect so much the fact that one of the nation-states represented at the London agreement provided a judge for the International Military Tribunal, took part as an accomplice in the war against Poland, and shortly thereafter carried on independently an aggressive war against Finland. Neither is it crucial that the so-called crime against peace was drafted into the London agreement and the Control Council Law at the insistence of this same state, namely the Soviet Union. This was pointed out by the American international law scholar Finch.

The doubts are of a far more fundamental nature. They arise primarily from the principle that nobody may be punished for an act which was not already a punishable crime at the time of its committing. This prohibition of punishment by an ex post facto law is one of the fundamental principles of criminal law and is recognized by all civilized nations. In the United States of America, it stands under the express protection of the Constitution. The principle was likewise already guaranteed in the constitution of the German empire of 1919 and is guaranteed in the constitution now in force for the Western German Federal Republic. The prohibition has proved for a long time to be one of those generally valid principles which serves as a source for international law, and international law does not govern the application of the prohibition any less than the domestic legal systems in which the prohibition was first developed.

In examining the culpability of aggressive war, the International Military Tribunal has not taken a clear position. It stated that since the London agreement declares the planning or waging of an aggressive war to be a crime, the examination of what degree an aggressive war was a crime before the London agreement was not absolutely necessary even though the London agreement supplies the norm of applicable punishment. The International Military Tribunal's judgment, nevertheless, later enters into this question of degree and answers it in the affirmative, referring to the Briand-Kellogg pact of August 27, 1928. It should be observed that in article 1 of this pact, the thirty-six contracting nation-states made a solemn declaration to condemn war as a means of solving international quarrels and to renounce war as an instrument of national policy. However, threat of punishment against nation-states or individual persons for contravening the declaration was not included in this pact, even though a contravention constitutes an essential part of the crime of the planning or waging of an aggressive war.

If one proceeds from this fundamental legal proposition, the planning and waging of aggressive war could only be punished by statute or the Control Council Law No. 10 *if* the acts were punishable under international law *before* the enactment of the London agreement and the Control Council Law No. 10.

This question has, for manifold reasons, to be answered in the negative. First of all, a wide gap exists between the political act of the renunciation of war as pronounced in the Briand-Kellogg pact and the introduction of a crime against peace, a new concept in international criminal law, pronounced in the London agreement and the Control Council Law No. 10. What is missing between the two points becomes evident if one recalls the declaration of the government of the Netherlands in its note of January 21, 1920. The government refused the extradition of the former German emperor. At that time it stated:

If in the future the League of Nations should create an international jurisdiction which would be authorized to administer justice in the event of a war about facts which are stamped crimes and sanctioned as such by a previously worked-out statute, then the Netherlands will follow the new order of things.

One seeks in vain for such a previously worked-out statute which would have declared aggressive war to be a crime in the sense of criminal law, a crime from which criminal responsibility ensues.

It is not to be denied that a war waged under a breach of the Briand-Kellogg pact represents a violation of international law. One cannot, however, waive the proof found in the Briand-Kellogg pact's introduction of a crime, traditionally within the criminal law, into the international law as a reaction to the violation of the law's principles. This proof has not been seen in either the judgment of the International Military Tribunal or anywhere else. On the contrary, the opinions of American professors of international law, such as Kelsen and Radin, do not impute such a meaning to the Briand-Kellogg pact. In the past, the same opinion has ben expressed by authoritative statesmen of the formerly hostile side. An example is seen in the American Secretary of State Stimson's statement on August 8, 1932, before the Committee for Foreign Affairs in New York.

But above all, after the Briand-Kellogg pact was signed, several wars have been fought without raising the question of criminal responsibility on the part of participating statesmen. Recall the wars of Italy against Abyssinia, Japan against China, Russia against Finland, and in particular the participation of Russia in the war against Poland in 1939. In all of these quarrels, one side or the other conceded a violation of the Briand-Kellogg pact without questioning whether the responsible persons should be punished, criminally.

The interpretation and administration of the Briand-Kellogg pact leads, therefore, to the conclusion that a violation of this pact did not equate to criminal responsibility. By declaring the planning and waging of aggressive wars to be punishable, the London agreement and the Control Council Law No. 10 go beyond the hitherto valid international law. In this respect, the London agreement and the Control Council Law No. 10 are penal laws with retroactive force, and their application is forbidden according to general legal principles.

I have encountered this legal question of an individual's culpability for crimes against peace twice during the Nuremberg trials. One time occurred in the great process before the International Military Tribunal. This criminal charge was raised against the High Command and the General Staff and rejected. However, generals Keitel and Jodl as well as admirals Donitz and Raeder were sentenced because of such a crime. The second time I encountered this legal question was in the High Command process in which Field Marshal v. Leeb was charged with, inter alia, this criminal act. He was not sentenced for it.

How far Field Marshal v. Leeb was from such an accusation can be shown by a letter he addressed on October 31, 1939, to the commander-in-chief of the army, Field Marshal von Brauchitsch. I am also quoting this letter for historical reasons. Written after the Polish campaign, it runs as follows:

Dear Mr. v. Brauchitsch:

....

I have the urge in this fateful time to tell you once more how I feel with you the responsibility that weighs upon you. Perhaps the destiny of the entire German people will depend upon you in the next few days. For in the given situation, the commander-in-chief of the army is probably above all called upon to bring to bear in due form his conception which is supported by the entire general staff and all thinking parts of the army. I would like to hope that the commander-in-chief of the other two parts of the armed forces do not shut their eyes to this difficult fateful hour.

The military arguments that speak against the Fuhrer's intention are obvious.

....

The entire people is filled with a deep longing for peace. It does not warrant the threatening war and faces it without any inner participation. If the Party agencies report something different, they are withholding the truth. At this time the people expect the policy of its Fuhrer to give them peace, because probably they sense quite instinctively that annihilation of France and England is not possible and that further-flung plans, therefore, must be deferred. As a soldier, one has to say the same thing.

....

I am ready to stand with my person behind you completely in the days to come and to draw any conclusions desired and becoming necessary.

Always, your devoted Leeb.

This is the letter of a great officer.

B

I would like to deal with the question of the validity of the Control Council Law No. 10 only for the reason that it constituted the material-legal foundation for all twelve of the processes in Nuremberg that followed the great process. For this reason, the result of this examination is especially interesting.

The Control Council Law No. 10 had been enacted on December 20, 1945, at a time when all of the acts covered in the process were completed. Two months earlier, on October 20, 1945, the Control Council had promulgated its proclamation No. 3. In this proclamation and specifically in article II, No. 2, the Control Council stated that culpable responsibility existed only for acts which the law had declared punishable prior to the perpetration of the acts. Consequently, by knowing the contents of this proclamation, it is simply impossible to understand the statements issued two months later. The Control Council Law No. 10, just as in the statute for the International Military Tribunal, declared a crime against peace and other circumstances punishable as a violation of general principles.

At that time, the defense expressly stated that a subsequently passed penal law with retroactive force would arouse a storm of protest in the U.S.A. by its own citizens and the United States would never consent to the passing of such a law for its own country. The statements by the American Military Tribunal in the process against the Southeast generals in Nuremberg with regard to this question are remarkable. This American court expressly stated that it is the use of might and not of right (law) if as in Control Council Law No. 10, acts are to be punishable even though the culpability does not follow from the international law in effect at the time of the acts. The American Military Tribunal made this general statement and, however, then applied the Control Council Law. The other Nuremberg tribunals also applied the Control Council Law in every process even though it is, in fact, an invalid law.

C

According to article 8 of the Statute, the fact that a defendant acted by order of his government or superior could not be used as a reason to exclude him from punishment. In the court's judgment, however, such conduct could serve as a ground for mitigation of the punishment if this seemed justified. The American and British sides had prepared and brought this regulation about. In the middle of the year 1944, shortly before the end of the war, several advocates of international law tried to influence and change punishments given under this provision. Until 1944, the British Manual of Military Laws (§ 443) as well as the American Rules of Land Warfare (Article 347) granted defendants acting under a higher command complete exoneration. In the last stage of the war, however, these regulations were cancelled in both manuals. What an accident of simultaneous action by two states. Furthermore, the statute for the International Military Tribunal as well as the Control Council Law No. 10 expressly prohibited the exonerating consideration given to defendants acting under a higher order.

How did this change of conceptions happen? The cause is obvious. Two authors gave the impetus for this incisive change. These are Professor Gluck of Harvard University and Professor Lauterpacht of Cambridge University. These two scholars caused the existing regulations to be dropped and thus rendered the defense of all future defendants more difficult to an intolerable degree. If the law allowing exoneration should remain standing, they argue, it would be possible for too many to slip through the meshes of the law. This must not be and, therefore, they say, the law must be changed in all haste even though they had previously agreed with the law.

In the British Yearbook of 1944, Lauterpacht had written:

It is a very interesting gloss with regard to the intricacy of the problem that in Great Britain and in the United States the objection of the higher command is, as a whole without decisive effect in the internal criminal law or constitutional law although evidently with regard to war crimes it is treated as complete justification.

If one examines the reasons which have been cited for this transition to a more realistic regulation, one finds only pure grounds of expediency. Professor Smith of London University remarked with regard to this legislation: 'It has a striking resemblance to Hitler's doctrine on acts which contradict the sound instincts of the people.'

Professor Gluck and Professor Lauterpacht have not only fixed the course of the legislation with regard to this question; they are probably also to be addressed as the spiritual fathers of the attempt to rope the events of the past war, so far as they were set on the German side of the ledger, into a war criminal process. In his essay, Professor Smith stated that the thought of bringing Napoleon to trial for unleashing a war of aggression existed in London in 1815 but—and now I am quoting Smith verbatim: '[T]he British government preferred rather to follow the opinion of the jurists than the shouting of the crowd.' With regard to the abolition of an appeal to higher command, Professor Smith stated: 'It is completely incompatible with the traditions of our conception of justice to deprive the defense of the main ground in this matter.'

There is no doubt that article 8 and the corresponding provision in the Control Council Law No. 10 certainly cannot be applied to such acts as were terminated before the enactment of the Control Council Law. On the contrary, the opinion hitherto existing and correct is that expressed in the former regulations of the British Manual of Military Law and in the American Rules of Land Warfare. Actions taken because of an order by the higher command are excused under international law.

VI

If the question is asked whether the processes in Nuremberg were fair, then from the standpoint of the defendants—even considering the procedural regulations only—one must arrive at a negative answer. The already quoted notable British teacher of international law, Professor Smith of London University, has openly stated in an essay on the Nuremberg process procedures, 'The unfairness does not lie in the court chamber, but outside.' He was referring to the legal foundations created for the processes. What he says, however, is not enough. The unfairness had already begun outside the court chamber and therefore had to continue in it!

I must, however, be complete on this point. The defense had the liberty of speech. The liberty was not interrupted even when referring to opponents' violations of the rules of war. An American judge, namely the president of the tribunal before which the case against the Southeast generals was tried, expressed himself with unusually sharp words after the close of the process about the methods applied in part by the prosecuting authority. He stated, inter alia, that this was not justice as he knew it from the States.

It is in this very context of the processes against generals that I would like to mention again the case of the Japanese general Yamashita. He was the Japanese commander in the Philippines who, after surrendering, was brought to trial by the Americans. On July 12, 1945 he was sentenced to death by hanging.

One of the outvoted American judges in this process, Jack Murphy, made statements in a dissenting opinion on the sentence which, in my opinion, are exemplary and convincingly expose the weaknesses of the processes brought against the military leaders. Thus, inter alia, he stated:

The immutable rights of the individual are reserved not only to the members of that nation which distinguishes itself on the battlefield or who made the democratic ideology their own, no, on the contrary, they belong to every human being in the world, to the victors or the vanquished, no matter of what race, of what color, of what faith. These rights stand above any stage of warfare or of outlawry. They outlast any public feeling or enthusiasm of the moment, not even the strongest army of the world can ever destroy them.

. . . .

The petitioner was the commander of an army which was completely destroyed by the superior power of our nation. His troops committed innumerable brutal atrocities and other grave crimes when they were exposed to the heavy and destroying attack by our forces. Hostilities then ceased, and he surrendered voluntarily. At this moment he was, as an individual, entitled to chivalrous and just treatment according to the generally recognized rules of law and procedure. He was also entitled to a fair trial for any alleged criminal matter of fact and to being exempted from accusations because of legally unfounded crimes . . . .

. . . .

No military necessities or other emergencies conditioned a nonobservance of the safety precautions for a valid process. In spite of this, the applicant was rushed to trial on the strength of an improper accusation, the defense was granted only insufficient time for preparation, he was deprived of the prerogative for the most elementary rules on the hearing of the evidence, and he was summarily sentenced to death by hanging. With all this unnecessary and unsuitable rush, no serious attempt was made to charge him with the fact or to prove to him that he had committed a recognized violation of the laws of war. He was not accused of personal participation in acts of atrocity or of having ordered or forgiven their commission. Not even the charge of knowledge of these crimes was laid at his door. It was merely brought forward that he disregarded his duty unlawfully and neglected to control, as commander, the acts of his subordinates by permitting them to commit atrocities. The recorded annals of warfare and the principles of international law do not give the least precedent for such an accusation . . . .

. . . .

In my opinion, such a procedure is unworthy of the tradition of our people as well as of the endless sacrifices which were made in order to advance the common ideals of humanity. The feelings of the present time will doubtless be satisfied. But in the sober afterview the consequences of the process sanctioned today, not to be foreseen and dangerous, will be recognized . . . .

. . . .

It is also above any discussion that just punishments should befall those who are responsible for such criminal acts. But these factors do not hit the essential point of this case. They do not in any way justify the problem of our obligation to justice in the process against an overthrown enemy commander. To arrive at such a result means admitting that the enemy has lost the battle, but has destroyed our ideals....

Already a few years after the close of the Nuremberg trials I chanced to meet an American professor who had been active in two Nuremberg processes. He told me quite frankly that, in his opinion, it would probably have been better if the processes against the generals and the industrialists had never been held!

It will remain, to be sure, a historical fact that the idea for the Nuremberg processes originated essentially from the American side. The American specialist in international law, Gluck, was one of its fathers. One will, with good reasons, assail the legal foundations. One will also have to assess negatively the execution of these processes—at least some of them—because of the manner of the accusations and the circle of defendants.

22

Nuremberg: Forty Five Years Later

*By Matthew Lippman**

The year 1991 marks the forty-fifth anniversary of the verdict in the International Military Tribunal's trial at Nuremberg of leading officials of the Third Reich. This anniversary provides an opportunity to reflect on the trial and to reassess its justification and significance. This may appear to involve a retracing of well-worn ground. However, the trial has received relatively limited attention from international law scholars over the last several decades.[1] This article sketches the events leading up to the trial. The judgment is then outlined and considered, and the importance of the trial is evaluated. This article concludes that the Nuremberg Principles should be revitalized and that defendants in American courts should be permitted to rely upon the 'Nuremberg defense.'

I. War Crimes and the First World War

A. Conventions and Traditions Relating to War Crimes Before World War I

The debate over the prosecution of alleged German war criminals following World War I anticipated the controversies which plagued the Nuremberg trial. In the early twentieth century, the law of war was codified in the Hague Convention of 1907.[2] The regulations annexed to the Convention regulated areas such as the

---

* Associate Professor, University of Illinois at Chicago; Ph.D., Northwestern University; J.D., American University; LL.M., Harvard University. This article is dedicated with love to Lidia Janus. May she continue to inspire us to overcome our self-imposed limitations. Dreams can become reality.

[1] The Nuremberg Trial's fortieth anniversary passed with little comment or discussion. For a rather perfunctory discussion, see M. Cherif Bassiouni, Nuremberg Forty Years After: An Introduction, 18 CASE W.RES.J.INT'L L. 261 (1986).

[2] Hague Convention (IV) Respecting The Laws And Customs Of War On Land, Oct. 18, 1907, 36 Stat. 2277, T.S. No. 539, 1 Bevans 631 [hereinafter Hague Convention (IV)].

treatment of prisoners of war,[3] military tactics and strategies,[4] and belligerent occupation of enemy territory.[5] These provisions subsequently were incorporated into states' pre-existing military codes and distributed to each nation's armed forces.[6] Article 3 of the Convention provided that a belligerent party which violated the provisions of the regulations was liable to pay compensation to the aggrieved party.[7] Negotiations over the appropriate compensation often were long and complex, and the payment of compensation was criticized as having little deterrent effect on individual combatants.[8]

The other traditional mechanisms for punishing violations of the law and customs of war were the trial of those accused of war crimes by their state of nationality[9] and military reprisals against the offending state.[10] However, prosecutions were rarely pursued, and the appropriate scope, nature, and justification for reprisals were subject to debate. Further, reprisals were criticized for simply escalating hostilities.[11] Therefore, following the end of hostilities, it was customary for an amnesty to be extended to all combatants accused of war crimes.[12] The amnesty was granted in the interests of comity. However, even if a state desired to prosecute an enemy soldier, such may not have been legally permissible. It was uncertain whether a belligerent state could extend its jurisdiction over enemy combatants, particularly in the case of extra-territorial offenses.[13] In addition, states differed on how to treat issues such as the status of the superior orders defense or command responsibility.[14] Heads of state were traditionally immune from trial or punishment before a foreign court under the act of state defense.[15]

---

[3] Annex To The Hague Convention (IV) Respecting The Laws And Customs Of War On Land, Oct. 18, 1907, arts. 4–20, 36 Stat. 2277, T.S. No. 539, 1 Bevans 643, 644–47 [hereinafter Annex to Hague Convention (IV)].

[4] Annex to Hague Convention (IV), supra note 3, arts. 22–28, 1 Bevans at 647–49.

[5] Annex to Hague Convention (IV), supra note 3, arts. 42–56, 1 Bevans at 651–53.

[6] See Hague Convention (IV), supra note 2, art. 1, 1 Bevans at 639.

[7] See Hague Convention (IV), supra note 2, art. 3, 1 Bevans at 640.

[8] See Hugh H.L. Bellot, War Crimes: Their Prevention And Punishment, 2 TRANSACTIONS OF THE GROTIUS SOCIETY 31, 37–38 (1917).

[9] See generally James W. Garner, Punishment Of Offenders Against The Laws And Customs Of War, 14 AM.J.INT'L L. 70, 73–76 (1920).

[10] Bellot, supra note 8, at 34–35. A reprisal is an act of violence intended to deter a belligerent State from continuing in its alleged violation of the laws and customs of war. Id. at 34.

[11] Id. at 35.

[12] JAMES F. WILLIS, PROLOGUE TO NUREMBURG: THE POLITICS AND DIPLOMACY OF PUNISHING WAR CRIMINALS OF THE FIRST WORLD WAR 13, 19 (1982).

[13] See generally Garner, supra note 9, at 70–87.

[14] Id. at 83–88. Superior orders permits a combatant to raise the fact the criminal act with which they are charged was committed pursuant to the orders of a military superior. States disagree whether superior orders should be treated as a defense or in mitigation of punishment. G. VON GLAHN, LAW AMONG NATIONS: AN INTRODUCTION TO PUBLIC INTERNATIONAL LAW 775–76 (5th ed. 1986).

[15] But see Quincy Wright, The Legal Liability of the Kaiser, 13 AM.POL.SCI.REV. 120 (1919). The act of state doctrine requires every sovereign State to respect the independence of other

B. War Crimes in World War I

German strategies and tactics in World War I were a source of constant outrage.[16] The execution of Captain Fryatt particularly inflamed British opinion. Fryatt was the English commander of the civilian ship Brussels. He refused to permit a visitation and search by a German U-boat. Instead, he unsuccessfully attempted to ram the German vessel. Fryatt was captured, tried, and executed by the Germans as a war criminal.[17] A 1916 analysis of the Fryatt case in the American Journal of International Law concluded that

there is nothing in the law nor in the practice of nations which prevents a belligerent merchant vessel from defending itself from attack and capture, [and therefore] the execution of Captain Fryatt appears to have been without warrant in international law and illegal, whatever it may have been according to the municipal ordinances of Germany.[18] Hugh H.L. Bellot, in a paper read in 1916 before the Grotius Society in London, vowed that 'the public opinion of the civilised world will not rest satisfied unless, upon the termination of the conflict, not only the instigators but also the actual perpetrators of the more heinous offences against the usages of war are brought to trial before some impartial tribunal.'[19] He warned that the Allies possessed a 'grim determination that in war even as in peace justice shall prevail and the reign of law...shall be maintained.'[20]

C. Efforts of the Commission on the Responsibility of the War and Enforcement of Penalties

In January, 1919, the Paris Peace Conference appointed a multinational Commission on the Responsibility of the War and Enforcement of Penalties.[21] The Commission placed primary responsibility for the war on Germany and Austria-Hungary and also criticized Turkey and Bulgaria for their support of German and Austrian aggression.[22] As for the perpetration of war crimes, the commission determined that there was 'abundant evidence of outrages of every description.'[23] It concluded that the Central Empires and their allies, Turkey

---

sovereign States. Under this doctrine, the courts of one sovereign State refuse to review the legality of the acts of a foreign State. This insulates government officials from criminal prosecution in a foreign or international court. G. VON GLAHN, supra note 14, at 133.

[16] WILLIS, supra note 12, at 3–64.
[17] Id. at 30.
[18] James Brown Scott, The Execution Of Captain Fryatt, 10 AM.J.INT'L L. 865, 877 (1916).
[19] Bellot, supra note 8, at 54.
[20] Id. at 54–55.
[21] Commission On The Responsibility Of The Authors Of The War And On The Enforcement of Penalties, Mar. 29, 1919, reprinted in 14 AM.J.INT'L L. 95 (1920).
[22] Id. at 98, 107. Germany and Austria-Hungary were subject to particular criticism for their violation of the neutrality of Belgium and Luxemburg. Id. at 107–12.
[23] Id. at 113.

In spite of the explicit regulations, of established customs, and of the clear dictates of humanity, Germany and her allies have piled outrage upon outrage. Additions are daily and continually being

and Bulgaria, practiced 'barbarous or illegitimate methods in violation of the established laws and customs of war and the elementary laws of humanity.'[24] It recommended the appointment of a commission to systematically compile a comprehensive list of facts concerning violations of the laws and customs of war.[25]

In an unprecedented recommendation, the Commission proposed that criminal liability should be extended to all individuals responsible for war crimes, including heads of state. The Commission contended that international law did not recognize the principle of sovereign immunity.[26] It argued that it would 'shock the conscience of civilized mankind' to conclude that 'the greatest outrages against the laws and customs of war and the laws of humanity, if proved, ... could in no circumstances be punished.'[27] The Commission also noted that it would frustrate the enforcement of the laws of war if high-level officials were able to plead either act of state or superior orders as a defense to criminal liability. This would mean that heads of state would be immune from criminal liability under the act of state defense while their advisors and subordinates would be able to plead superior orders.[28]

As for the acts for which criminal liability should be imposed, the Commission stated that 'premeditation of a war of aggression' did not violate positive law and thus did not constitute a war crime cognizable before a judicial forum.[29] An inquiry into the responsibility for authorship of the war would also involve a lengthy and complex factual analysis and delay the adjudication.[30] However, the Commission rather ambiguously recommended that this outrage against the

---

made. ... It is impossible to imagine a list of cases so diverse and so painful. Violations of the rights of combatants, of the rights of civilians, and of the rights of both, are multiplied in this list of the most cruel practices which primitive barbarism, aided by all the resources of modern science, could devise for the execution of a system of terrorism carefully planned and carried out to the end. Not even prisoners or wounded, or women, or children have been respected by belligerents who deliberately sought to strike terror into every heart for the purpose of repressing all resistance. Murders and massacres, tortures, shields formed of living human beings, collective penalties, the arrest and execution of hostages, the requisitioning of services for military purposes, the arbitrary destruction of public and private property, the aerial bombardment of open towns without there being any regular siege, the destruction of merchant ships without previous visit and without any precautions for the safety of passengers and crew, the massacre of prisoners, attacks on hospital ships, the poisoning of springs and wells, outrages and profanations without regard for religion or the honor of individuals, the issue of counterfeit money reported by the Polish Government, the methodical and deliberate destruction of industries with no other object than to promote German economic supremacy after the war, constitute the most striking list of crimes that has ever been drawn up to the eternal shame of those who committed them.

Id. at 113–14.

[24] Id. at 114–15.
[25] Id. at 115.
[26] Id. at 116.
[27] Id.
[28] See id. at 117. The Commission noted that the ex-Kaiser and others in positions of authority were cognizant of and could have mitigated the barbarities committed during the war. Id.
[29] Id. at 118.
[30] Id. at 118–19.

law of nations and international comity should be the 'subject of a formal condemnation by the conference.'[31] In addition, it urged the community of nations to take steps to insure that future acts of aggression would be subject to penal sanction.[32]

The Commission recognized that the belligerent nations were empowered to prosecute captured enemy civilians and militia responsible for the violation of the laws and customs governing the conduct of war.[33] It noted that complication and delay could be avoided if many of these trials were consolidated before a single tribunal. Individuals subject to liability before a multinational tribunal should include those who committed outrages against civilians or soldiers of several Allied nations, such as at a prison camp or forced labor site, those who directed operations against several Allied armies, those who ordered or failed to intervene to prevent, terminate or repress violations of the laws or customs of war, and those whom it was considered advisable to prosecute before a multinational tribunal.[34]

The Commission further recommended the appointment of a tribunal composed of three judges from the United States as well as three judges from Great Britain, France, Italy, and Japan. Belgium, Greece, Poland, Portugal, Rumania, Serbia, and Czecho-Slovakia were each invited to appoint a single judge.[35] It was proposed that the tribunal should apply 'the principles of the law of nations as they result from the usages established among civilized peoples, from the laws of humanity and from the dictates of public conscience.'[36] The Commission suggested that the tribunal should be empowered to sentence an individual to such punishment as might be imposed for such an offense by any court in any country represented on the tribunal or in the country of the convicted person.[37] The selection of cases and conduct of prosecutions were to be the responsibility of a Prosecuting Commission composed of representatives from the five major Allied Powers. All the other governments were to be invited to delegate a representative to assist the Prosecuting Commission.[38] The multinational tribunal was envisioned as possessing exclusive and primary jurisdiction over any case. A trial or sentence before a court of an enemy country was not meant to bar prosecution before either an Allied court or another multinational tribunal.[39]

1. The U.S. Response

The United States dissented from the recommendation that persons in high authority, particularly heads of enemy states, be subject to criminal prosecution

---

[31] Id. at 120.   [32] Id.
[33] Id. at 121.   [34] Id. at 121–22.
[35] Id. at 122.   [36] Id.
[37] Id.   [38] Id. at 122–23.
[39] Id. at 123.

and punishment.[40] The American representatives pointed out that under international law 'heads of state were not hitherto legally responsible for the atrocious acts committed by subordinate authorities.'[41] They argued that heads of state were responsible to the populace of their country, and that such leaders are only subject to domestic political and legal sanctions.[42] Extending international liability to heads of states, in the view of the American representatives, was a denial of the 'very conception of sovereignty.'[43]

The United States also opposed the creation of an international military tribunal.[44] According to the Americans, such an international tribunal 'appeared to be unknown in the practice of nations.'[45] In addition, they observed that no international statute or convention made a violation of the laws or customs of war an international crime.[46] An international tribunal applying a new law, which carried a newly agreed upon penalty, would constitute an ex post facto law in violation of the United States Constitution and would therefore be unenforceable in the United States.[47] The Americans pointed out that each of the Allied Powers had domestic statutory provisions punishing violations of the laws and customs of war. Jurisdiction over such crimes resided in these states' existing domestic and military tribunals. The Americans advocated permitting each state to exercise jurisdiction over acts contrary to the law of war which affected the persons or property of their subjects or citizens.[48] Prosecution for acts which affected more than one country, such as mistreatment of prisoners of war, could be undertaken by amalgamating various national tribunals or by a joint commission.[49]

The United States also objected to holding the Germans liable under the doctrine of 'negative criminality.' Under this doctrine, German officals who failed to take affirmative acts to prevent criminal offenses would be held criminally liable.[50] The American members of the commission emphasized that the imposition of 'negative criminal liability' could only be justified if the accused had

[40] Memorandum Of Reservations Presented By The Representatives of The United States To The Report Of The Commission On Responsibilities, Apr. 4, 1919, Annex II, reprinted in 14 AM.J.INT'L L. 127 (1920).

[41] Id. at 128.

[42] Id. at 147–48.

[43] Id. at 136. The American representatives then somewhat ambiguously stated that their observations pertained to a head of state actually in office and engaged in the performance of his duties. Proceedings initiated against a head of state who had abdicated or who had been repudiated would be an action against 'an individual out of office and not against an individual in office and thus in effect against the state.' Id.

[44] Id. at 129.

[45] Id. at 145.

[46] Id. at 146.

[47] Id. at 147.

[48] Id. at 146.

[49] Id. at 146–47.

[50] Id. at 129.

knowledge of the criminal activity together with the ability to prevent its initiation or continuance and also had a duty or obligation to act.[51]

In addition, the United States criticized the Commission's finding that enemy leaders and officials had violated the 'laws [and] principles of humanity.'[52] The laws and customs of war are a 'standard certain, to be found in books of authority and in the practice of nations.'[53] In contrast, the novel concept of 'laws and principles of humanity' vary with 'time, place, and circumstance, and according... to the conscience of the individual judge. There is no fixed and universal standard of humanity.'[54] Thus, the standard of 'laws and principles of humanity' was not sufficiently precise and definite either to guide the conduct of combatants or to form the basis of prosecution before a criminal tribunal.[55]

2. *The Allied Compromise*

The Allied leaders were able to reach a compromise. Great Britain was intent on prosecuting ex-Kaiser Wilhelm in order to deter future aggression. The United States, on the other hand, held the view that heads of state should not be exposed to criminal liability.[56] Article 227 of the Treaty of Versailles provided that the Allied and Associated Powers 'publicly arraign William II of Hohenzollern, formerly German Emperor, for a supreme offence against international morality and the sanctity of treaties.'[57] The article went on to provide for the creation of a 'special tribunal' composed of representatives from the United States, Great Britain, France, Italy, and Japan.[58] In reaching its decision, the tribunal was to be 'guided by the highest motives of international policy, with a view to vindicating the solemn obligations of international undertakings and the validity of international morality. It will be its duty to fix the punishment which it considers should be imposed.'[59] Article 227 also stated that the Allied and Associated Powers intended to address a request to the Government of the Netherlands to surrender the ex-Emperor so that he could be put on trial.[60] Prosecuting the ex-Kaiser for 'a supreme offence against international morality' technically preserved the legal immunity of the Kaiser from prosecution and liability under international

---

[51] Id. at 143. It appears that the Commission did not incorporate the requirement that an individual have a duty to intervene. It provided for the punishment of those who 'ordered, or with knowledge thereof and with power to intervene, abstained from preventing or taking measures to prevent, putting an end to or repressing violations of the laws or customs of war.' Id. at 121.

[52] Id. at 133.

[53] Id. at 134. See id. at 113, 117, 122.

[54] Id. at 144.

[55] Id. The Japanese generally endorsed the American position. See Reservations By The Japanese Delegation, Apr. 4, 1919, Appendix III, reprinted in 14 AM.J.INT'L L. 151 (1920).

[56] WILLIS, supra note 12, at 80–81.

[57] Treaty of Peace with Germany (Treaty of Versailles), signed at Versailles, June 28, 1919, art. 227, 2 Bevans 43, 136 [hereinafter Versailles Treaty].

[58] See Versailles Treaty, supra note 57, art. 227, 2 Bevans at 136.

[59] See Versailles Treaty, supra note 57, art. 227, 2 Bevans at 137.

[60] Id.

law.[61] However, it also 'opened the trial of the Kaiser to charges of victor's justice to an even greater degree than a prosecution resting upon, at least, some principles of law, to which the Kaiser might also appeal in his defense.'[62]

Other German officials were to be subjected to formal legal prosecution. Article 228 provided that the German Government recognized the right of the Allied and Associated Powers to bring before military tribunals persons accused of acts in violation of the laws and customs of war.[63] If found guilty, such persons were to be sentenced to punishments 'laid down by law.'[64] This provision was to apply 'notwithstanding any proceedings or prosecution before a tribunal in Germany or in the territory of her allies.'[65] The German Government was required to hand over to the Allied or Associated Powers, or to any one of them that so requested, all persons accused of an act in violation of the laws or customs of war.[66] Article 229 adopted the American formula and provided that those accused of criminal acts against the nationals of any one of the Allied and Associated Powers was to be prosecuted before the military tribunal of that power.[67] An individual accused of acts against the nationals of more than one power was to be tried before a military tribunal comprised of members of the military tribunals of the 'powers concerned.'[68] Article 230 required the German Government to furnish all documents and information considered necessary to 'ensure the full knowledge of the incriminating acts, the discovery of offenders and the just appreciation of responsibility.'[69]

3. *The German Response*

These so-called Schmachparagraphen (shame paragraphs) met with virtual unanimous opposition in Germany.[70] The Dutch, encouraged by European royalty and moderate opinion, refused to extradite the Kaiser to stand trial.[71] The Dutch argued they 'had not signed and were not bound by the Treaty of Versailles.'[72] The Allied leaders, frustrated in their attempt to prosecute the Kaiser, also quickly abandoned the idea of forcing Germany to surrender those accused of war crimes for trial.[73] The Allies became convinced the prosecution of Germans either would provoke a civil war between right and left wing factions or lead to a renewal of the war with Germany. Their worst fear was the

---

[61] WILLIS, supra note 12, at 80. The term 'crime' specifically was not used in the paragraph.
[62] Id. at 80–81.
[63] Versailles Treaty, supra note 57, art. 228, 2 Bevans at 137.
[64] Id.
[65] Id.
[66] Id.
[67] Versailles Treaty, supra note 57, art. 229, 2 Bevans at 137.
[68] Id.
[69] Versailles Treaty, supra note 57, art. 230, 2 Bevans at 137.
[70] WILLIS, supra note 12, at 82. For a fuller discussion, see id. at 82–85.
[71] See id. at 98–112.
[72] Id. at 107–08.
[73] See id. at 113–25.

Bolsheviks would exploit German unrest and seize power.[74] Initially, the Allies determined that they would request the Germans to surrender 854 individuals.[75] However, faced with continued German opposition, the Allies agreed that the Germans should prosecute only forty-five individuals.[76] This list was arrived at after eliminating those cases which might cause political controversy or create a precedent which could later be applied against members of the Allied military.[77] The German war crimes trials were conducted at Leipzig before the Penal Senate of the Reichsgericht.[78]

The German court, as might have been expected, went to great lengths to minimize the defendants' culpability or to exonerate them from liability. First Lieutenant Karl Neumann was exonerated from liability for sinking the English hospital ship Dover Castle.[79] The court determined that he had followed superior orders and justifiably believed his conduct constituted a valid reprisal against the British for allegedly using such ships to transport soldiers and supplies.[80] In those cases in which defendants were determined to be guilty, the German court meted out relatively lenient punishments. In the trial of Emil Müller, a commander of a camp for British prisoners of war, the tribunal conceded that the accused was 'almost habitually harsh and contemptuous' and exhibited 'a frankly brutal treatment of prisoners entrusted to his care.'[81] His conduct was described as 'unworthy of a human being,' and the tribunal concluded that his conduct 'dishonors our army.'[82] Yet, he was sentenced to a total of six months imprisonment.[83]

By 1922, the Allies had concluded that the Leipzig trials had been unsatisfactory and decided to cease cooperating with the German authorities.[84] Over the next three years, the Reichsgericht proceeded to drop 861 out of the remaining 901 cases. Some of the convictions were annulled.[85] The most scandalous annullment occurred in the case of two submarine officers who directed the sinking of the lifeboats carrying the survivors of an illegal attack on the hospital ship Llandovery Castle.[86] Only 24 of over 200 individuals on board survived the attack.[87] On June 7, 1933, a few months after Adolf Hitler and the Nazis came to

---

[74] See id. at 116–19.

[75] Id. at 113, 120.

[76] Id. at 128.

[77] Id.

[78] Id. at 131.

[79] Judgment in Case of Karl Neumann (RGSt June 4, 1921) (Germany), reprinted in 16 AM.J.INT'L L. 704 (1922).

[80] Id. at 706–07.

[81] Judgment in the Case of Emil Müller (RGSt May 30, 1921) (Germany), reprinted in 16 AM.J.INT'L L. 684, 695 (1922).

[82] Id.

[83] Id. at 696.

[84] WILLIS, supra note 12, at 140.

[85] Id. at 146.

[86] Case of Lieutenants Dithmar and Boldt (RGSt July 16, 1921) (Germany), reprinted in 16 AM.J.INT'L L. 708 (1922).

[87] Id. at 710.

power, the Leipzig prosecutor formally quashed all war crimes proceedings arising from the sinking.[88]

D. The Versailles Treaty and Prosecution of World War I War Crimes in Retrospect

The Versailles Treaty signified the resolve of the international community to hold those accused of violations of the laws and customs of war personally liable. The 'public arraignment' of the Kaiser for offenses against morality and the sanctity of treaties was particularly significant. It was a step towards the abrogation of sovereign immunity and the imposition of international criminal liability upon governmental leaders. In the end, however, the effort to prosecute Germans accused of war crimes was frustrated by the continuing hold of sovereign immunity and nationalistic sentiments. In addition, the Allies' resolve to vindicate the rule of the international law of war was tainted by their decision to focus exclusively on offenses committed by enemy forces. The Versailles Treaty, by providing that jurisdiction over low-level war criminals should be based upon the nationality of the victims, also failed to fully establish that such offenses were directed against the international community rather than against individual countries.

The failed effort to prosecute German war criminals in World War I bolstered the argument of those who argued there was a need to establish institutional mechanisms for enforcing international law.[89] In 1922, Professor James W. Garner urged the community of nations to firmly warn government officials:

[H]e who provokes an unjust war, who wages it according to cruel and barbarous methods, who permits and sanctions atrocities by his troops, who approves and even encourages shocking violations of the most elementary and long-established laws and usages of war, and who rewards by decorations and promotions their authors, does so with full knowledge that if he is defeated he will be brought to the bar of justice and punished equally with the humblest soldier who has been compelled to violate the law, and who, for this and other reasons, may be a thousand times less responsible.[90]

II. The Inter-War Period

In the immediate post-World War I era, the academic international law literature was dominated by proposals for an international criminal code and an

---

[88] WILLIS, supra note 12, at 146. On the Leipzig trials generally, see G. Gordon Battle, The Trials Before the Leipsic Supreme Court of Germans Accused of War Crimes, 8 VA.L.REV. 1 (1921–22).

[89] See Willis, supra note 12, at 164.

[90] Garner, supra note 9, at 93–4.

international court for the prosecution of war criminals.[91] Lord Cave, speaking before the British Grotius Society in 1922, pointed out that, of the sixteen cases prosecuted by the Germans for crimes against Britain, France, and Belgium, only six had resulted in convictions, and that the offenders had been sentenced to prison for periods which 'anyone who reads the evidence must consider to be wholly inadequate.'[92] He concluded that an international system for the prosecution of war crimes should be promptly established.[93] There also was a strong idealistic strain of thought which argued for a system of world government and law. Former Secretary of State Robert Lansing, writing in the American Journal of International Law in 1921, argued that the community of nations was moving towards recognition of a World State.[94] He contended that 'the increasing realization by civilized peoples of the interdependence and mutual responsibility of states in their political and economic relations'[95] were moving the world toward such recognition.

In 1920, the Council of the League of Nations appointed an advisory committee of jurists to plan for the creation of a Permanent Court of International Justice. The committee exceeded its mandate and adopted a voeux (resolution) which was annexed to the Draft Statute for the Permanent Court of International Justice.[96] The voeux, in part, provided for the establishment of a high court of international criminal justice.[97] The first Assembly of the League of Nations, however, determined that the establishment of such a court was not feasible without the codification of an international penal code.[98]

Nevertheless, support for the establishment of an international criminal court gained momentum. It was endorsed by leading figures such as the philosopher John Dewey,[99] and by prominent organizations such as the Inter-Parliamentary Union[100] and the International Law Association.[101] The movement for an

[91] See, e.g., Cave, War Crimes And Their Punishment, 9 TRANSACTIONS OF THE GROTIUS SOCIETY xix (1923).

[92] Id. at xxix.

[93] Id. at xxx.

[94] Robert Lansing, Notes On World Sovereignty, 15 AM.J.INT'L L. 13, 15 (1921).

[95] Id. at 14.

[96] For a discussion of the committee's deliberations and decisions, see Phillimore, An International Criminal Court and the Resolutions of the Committee Of Jurists, 3 BRIT.Y.B.INT'L L. 79 (1922–23). For the committee's discussion and the text of the draft statute and voeux, see Advisory Committee of Jurists: Proces-Verbaux of the Proceedings of the Committee, League of Nations Council June 16th–July 24th (1920), reprinted in BENJAMIN FERENCZ, AN INTERNATIONAL CRIMINAL COURT, A STEP TOWARD WORLD PEACE, HALF A CENTURY OF HOPE 193 (1980).

[97] FERENCZ, supra note 96, at 36.

[98] See Voeux Submitted by the Advisory Committee of Jurists at the Hague, III Committee, Permanent Court of International Justice, League of Nations Assembly, Document No. 249 (20/48/249), December 17, 1920, cited and quoted in F.B. Schick, International Criminal Law—Facts And Illusions, II MODERN L.REV. 290, 292 n. 23 (1948).

[99] FERENCZ, supra note 96, at 40.

[100] Id. at 42–43.

[101] Id. at 43–44.

international criminal code and court gained a new urgency in October of 1934 with the assassination of King Alexander of Yugoslavia. The bomb attack also resulted in the death of French Foreign Minister Louis Barthou. Italy, to which the Croatian nationalist assassin had fled, refused to extradite the accused on the grounds the offense was politically motivated.[102] In the wake of this incident, the League of Nations in 1937 adopted a Convention for the Prevention and Punishment of Terrorism and a Convention for the Creation of an International Criminal Court.[103] Only India ratified the terrorism convention; no State ratified the treaty providing for an international criminal court.[104]

The initial enthusiasm for an international criminal code and court slowly eroded. Professor J.L. Brierly questioned whether a satisfactory procedure could be designed for the prosecution of war criminals:

The truth is that all methods hitherto suggested for dealing with war criminals are open to objection; the existing methods are bad.... But it does not follow that, because a process of elimination seems to drive us back on the idea of an international tribunal, a solution of the problem will be found there. It may be that there is no solution.[105] Professor Brierly questioned whether either the patriot or the scoundrel would be deterred from aggression by the possibility of trial before an international criminal court. The former would view such prosecution as an act of martyrdom, while the latter would realize that the prospect of punishment was remote. At any rate, Professor Brierly contended that, following the termination of a conflict, it was both desirable and practical to take steps towards reconciliation. The trial of vanquished forces, according to Brierly, would only rekindle resentments and passions and create permanent schisms between States.[106]

Professor Brierly also observed that there were practical problems associated with the creation of an international criminal court. These included agreement upon procedures for the custody of offenders, the discovery of documents, and the securing and attendance of witnesses.[107] Even more problematic was the challenge of developing an international criminal code and agreeing upon appropriate penalties and sanctions.[108]

Still, a core of predominantly academic idealists expressed regret over the international community's lost resolve to create an international criminal code and court. George Manner of the University of Illinois bemoaned:

---

[102] Id. at 48.

[103] See Report Adopted By the Committee on April 26th, 1937, League of Nations Committee for the International Repression of Terrorism, L.N.Pub.V, Legal, C.222.M.162.1937.V (1937), cited in Schick, supra note 98, at 292 n. 24; Proceedings of the International Conference on the Repression of Terrorism, L.N.Pub.V, Legal, C.94.M.47.1938.V (1938) reprinted in FERENCZ, supra note 96, at 355; Thomas M. Franck & Bert B. Lockwood, Jr., Preliminary Thoughts Towards an International Convention on Terrorism, 68 AM.J.INT'L L. 69.

[104] FERENCZ, supra note 96, at 54.

[105] J.L. Brierly, Do We Need an International Criminal Court? 8 BRIT.Y.B.INT'L L. 81, 83 (1927).

[106] See id. at 84–85.

[107] Id. at 85.

[108] See id. at 85–87.

[N]one of the plans for the institution of an international criminal jurisdiction and the enactment of an international penal code achieved any practical results. There exists, therefore, at present neither the substantive penal law nor the proper criminal tribunal for international postwar proceedings against States or individuals charged with acts provocative of war or with criminal acts of violence committed contrary to the laws and customs of war.[109] As late as 1941, Philip Marshall Brown, in an editorial essay in the American Journal of International Law, argued that:

> [the community of nations is] still confronted…with the inescapable necessity of perfecting the whole process of international justice in order that jurisdiction may ultimately be conferred on some 'High Court' to deal with all 'offences against international public order and the universal law of nations.' The lack of an international penal law presents a most serious problem which should have the earnest attention of international jurists.[110]

Brown predicted, in a comment reminiscent of those made immediately after the end of World War I, that the 'new world order which will emerge from the present anarchy will have to be based on a much more effective system of international law.'[111]

III. The World War II War Crimes Debate

The atrocities and barbarities committed by the soldiers and leaders of the belligerents during World War II revived the movement to establish a new global order based upon international law.[112] Academic commentators hoped that the defeat of Germany and the trial of Nazi leaders would be the first steps in the establishment of an international criminal code and court. Sheldon Glueck of Harvard, one of the major figures in the development of American criminology, argued that few 'symbols of this new era which heralds the neighborly cooperation of civilized peoples in the vindication of law and justice would be more impressive than an International Criminal Court, in which the plaintiff would be the world community.'[113] He urged that the 'early announcement of its establishment might prove of some deterrent and sobering effect on Axis-Fascist militarists and their agents.'[114]

A. Hersch Lauterpacht

Most international law scholars confined themselves to the practical task of developing a legal justification for the prosecution of Nazi combatants and leaders.

---

[109] George Manner, The Legal Nature and Punishment of Criminal Acts of Violence Contrary to the Laws of War, 37 AM.J.INT'L L. 407, 432 (1943).

[110] Philip M. Brown, International Criminal Justice, 35 AM.J.INT'L L. 118, 120 (1941).

[111] Id.

[112] See Francis B. Sayre, America the Hope of the World, 37 PROC.AM.SOC'Y INT'L L. 12, 12–18 (1943).

[113] Sheldon Glueck, By What Tribunal Shall War Offenders Be Tried? 56 HARV.L.REV. 1059, 1089 (1943).

[114] Id.

The late Professor Hersch Lauterpacht of Cambridge disassociated himself from the 'juridically unsound and retrogressive' view that international law prohibited German prosecution of Nazi war criminals.[115] He argued rather that the experience of World War I indicated that a defeated belligerent could not be counted on to punish combatants accused of war crimes.[116] At the same time, he conceded that there was little practical prospect of an international criminal court being established.[117] As a result, the prosecution of war criminals, of necessity, had to be unilaterally assumed by the victorious parties.[118] However, Lauterpacht added that it was essential that such prosecutions be conducted in an impartial fashion in accordance with existing rules.[119]

Lauterpacht provided a coherent legal justification for such war crimes trials. According to Lauterpacht, the right of a belligerent to punish enemy combatants for violations of the laws and customs of war was recognized under the law of various states.[120] This was an application of the territorial principle under which a state has jurisdiction over criminal acts which occur within its recognized boundaries.[121] As for acts committed in the territory of an adversary, such as the maltreatment of prisoners of war, Lauterpacht argued a belligerent could rely upon the rule, which 'international law has not stigmatized as illegal, that a state may punish criminal acts committed by foreigners abroad against its own safety or against its nationals.'[122] Thus, in Lauterpacht's view, it would be legally permissible for either Great Britain or the United States to extend their jurisdiction to encompass war crimes committed abroad by Germans against British or American nationals.[123]

Lauterpacht also contended that international law permitted the trial of enemy soldiers or political leaders for war crimes and that such prosecutions did not constitute the ex post facto application of the law. He pointed out that while international law traditionally imposed liability upon states to pay damages for violations of the laws and customs of war, such liability did not exclude the punishment of individuals.[124] The provisions of the law of war are codified in international documents[125] and incorporated into states' military codes.[126] Combatants thus should be aware of the requirements of the law of

[115] Hersch Lauterpacht, The Law of Nations and the Punishment of War Crimes, 21 BRIT.Y.B.INT'L L. 58, 59 (1944).

[116] See id. at 83–84.

[117] See id. at 80–82.

[118] See id. at 60–68.

[119] Id. at 68. See also id. at 69–86 (elaborating on the existing rules that limit punishment of war crimes and on safeguards to impartial prosecution).

[120] Id. at 61.

[121] Id. at 62.

[122] Id. at 63.

[123] See id. at 67.

[124] Id. at 65.

[125] Id.

[126] See, e.g., id. at 66 n. 1.

war.[127] Lauterpacht thus argued that there was no 'question of any vindictive retroactivity arising out of the creation of crimes of which the accused could not possibly be cognizant.'[128]

B. Criticism of the Lauterpacht Approach

Despite Lauterpacht's convincing brief in support of the international legality of war crimes prosecutions, others pointed to the innumerable and seemingly intractable practical problems associated with such trials.[129] These included discovery and preservation of evidence,[130] locating and recording the testimony of witnesses,[131] the status of defenses such as superior orders,[132] the composition and location of war crimes tribunals,[133] arrangements for the surrender and custody of war criminals,[134] and agreement upon the type of offenses and the rank and nationality of the defendants to be prosecuted.[135] In addition, it was pointed out that the requirements of international law in such areas as submarine and aerial warfare were uncertain.[136]

Others argued that these difficulties, along with the cumbersome nature of legal procedures, would prevent the speedy and effective punishment of Nazi war criminals. Punishment and deterrence, according to these critics, could only be obtained through the direct, extra-judicial punishment of offenders. The German leaders neither deserved nor respected the rule of law, and they should be punished in a harsh and expeditious fashion.[137] It was proposed that the peace treaty with Germany should clearly state the crimes committed by and the punishment to be meted out to various German leaders.[138]

The advocates of war crimes trials found an influential ally in the American Bar Association. The section on International and Comparative Law established a Subcommittee on the Trial and Punishment of War Criminals.[139] The

---

[127] Id. at 65.

[128] Id. at 67. For a more complex, if not convoluted, analysis offered by another leading figure in international jurisprudence see Hans Kelsen, Collective and Individual Responsibility in International Law with Particular Regard to the Punishment of War Criminals, 31 CAL.L.REV. 530 (1943).

[129] See Charles C. Hyde, Punishment of War Criminals, 37 PROC.AM.SOC'Y INT'L L. 39, 39–46 (1942–43).

[130] Id. at 41.

[131] Id. at 41–42.

[132] Id. at 42–43.

[133] Id. at 43–45.

[134] Id. at 45.

[135] Id. at 43–44.

[136] Id. at 49–50 (remarks of Mr. Edwin Dickinson).

[137] Id. at 51–53 (remarks of Mr. Charles Warren).

[138] Id. at 53.

[139] Work Of The International And Comparative Law Section Of The American Bar Association, 37 AM.J.INT'L L. 660, 662–63 (1943). The subcommittee was composed of Edwin D. Dickinson, George A. Finch, and Charles Cheney Hyde. Id. at 663.

subcommittee's July 20, 1943, report accepted without discussion the desirability of imposing criminal liability upon those Germans responsible for violations of the law of war, and emphasized that it was of the 'utmost importance that punishment be administered through the channel of organized justice.'[140] 'It should be ever in mind that the objective is not revenge but vindication of the processes of organized justice.'[141] The report admonished that the prosecution of Germans must be based upon concrete and reliable evidence and should not rest upon 'mere hunch or vague charges of atrocities.'[142]

The subcommittee went on to recommend that the Allies should selectively prosecute 'serious' offenders responsible for 'heinous' offenses, and stated that the pleas of superior orders and justified retaliation should be restricted so as not to 'establish broad immunities.'[143] It concluded that generally accepted principles of the laws and customs of war and principles of criminal law both constituted a proper source of applicable principles.[144] The subcommittee further suggested that a mechanism be developed for multilateral consultation as to the applicable principles and procedures.[145] However, the subcommittee admonished that caution should be exercised in lodging charges against alleged Nazi war criminals in order to guard against possible retroactive punishment.[146]

The report suggested that the prosecutions be carried out by Allied civilian or military courts. This would insure trial before experienced, authoritative tribunals with established procedures. It was recommended that the United Nations establish an international tribunal which could undertake advisory review of cases upon a showing of either an excessive penalty or an error of fact or law which had resulted in manifest injustice.[147] The report concluded by emphasizing that the 'vindication of law through legal processes may contribute substantially to the re-establishment of order and decency in international relations.'[148]

IV. The Drafting of the Nuremberg Charter

A. Events Leading up to the Drafting of the Charter

The Allied resolve to prosecute German war criminals was formalized in the Moscow Declaration of October 30, 1943.[149] In a statement signed by President Roosevelt, Prime Minister Churchill, and Premier Stalin, the Allies pledged to

---

[140] Id. at 663–64 app. [141] Id. at 664.
[142] Id. [143] Id.
[144] Id. at 665. [145] See id.
[146] Id. [147] Id.
[148] Id. at 666.
[149] Statement Signed by President Roosevelt, Prime Minister Churchill and Premier Stalin Regarding Atrocities (Moscow Declaration) reprinted in Report of Robert H. Jackson, Representative to the International Conference on Military Trials 11–12 (1945) [hereinafter Jackson Report].

return those responsible for atrocities to the 'countries in which their abominable deeds were done in order that they may be judged and punished according
to the laws of these liberated countries and of the free governments which will be
erected therein.'[150] The proclamation was stated to be without prejudice to the
cases of 'major war criminals, whose offenses have no particular geographical
localization and who will be punished by joint decision of the Governments of
the Allies.'[151] The statement, however, failed to specify the procedures by which
these 'major [war] criminals' were to be brought to justice.

In September, 1944, Roosevelt agreed to Churchill's proposal that the
defeated Nazi leaders should be summarily executed.[152] By 1945, the United
States had shifted its position and, together with the Soviet Union, advocated the
trial of the major German war criminals before an international court.[153] In an
April 23, 1945, memorandum to the United States, the British argued that
since it was 'conceded' that the Nazi leaders 'must suffer death,' execution without trial is the 'preferable course.'[154] According to the British, a trial would
be lengthy and expensive and would likely provide a platform for Nazi propaganda which would be viewed as a 'put-up job' designed 'to justify a punishment the Allies have already resolved on.'[155] There was the distinct possibility
that such a trial would be dismissed as a 'farce' and that popular opinion would
question why the Nazis merely had not simply been executed.[156] The British
also raised the possibility that the Germans would be able to mount an effective
challenge to the legality of the trial and succeed in having a major portion of
the indictment dismissed.[157] However, the British ultimately concurred with
a United States memorandum of April 30, 1945, which argued that the extra-
judicial execution of Nazi leaders would be viewed as a purely political act 'violative of concepts of justice, which would be distasteful and inappropriate.'[158]
Such an execution would be inconsistent with the democratic principles which
motivated the Allied cause.[159] It also risked transforming the Nazis into martyrs and providing a rallying-point for those dedicated to reviving the Nazi
movement.[160]

[150] Id. at 11.
[151] Id. at 12.
[152] BRADLEY F. SMITH, THE ROAD TO NUREMBERG 46–47 (1981). This aproach also
was strongly advocated by Treasury Secretary Robert Morgenthau, who called for the deindus-
trialization of Germany, the summary execution of leaders, group detentions, and the formation of
labor battalions. Id. at 37–38.
[153] Id. at 63–64.
[154] Aide-Memoire from the United Kingdom, April 23, 1945 reprinted in Jackson Report,
supra note 149, at 18.
[155] Id. at 19.
[156] Id.
[157] Id.
[158] American Memorandum Presented at San Francisco, April 30, 1945 reprinted in Jackson
Report, supra note 149, at 28, 30, 33–34 (Doc. V).
[159] Id. at 34.
[160] Id.

The Americans contended that an international trial would provide an historical record, would help develop international standards of legal conduct, and would serve as a deterrent to future leaders contemplating similar actions. A trial also would signal to the German people that a regime of laws, and not of men, had begun.[161] For these reasons, the Americans argued that the Allies should reject action dictated by politics and not by fundamental principles of law and justice.[162]

In the summer of 1945, representatives of France, Great Britain, the Soviet Union and the United States met in London to formulate plans for the trial of the major Nazi war criminals.[163] The Allies determined that it was best to concentrate their efforts and public attention on a single multinational trial.[164] The trial would be conducted at Nuremberg, Germany[165] and the Nazi leaders, 'the planners, the zealots who put this thing across,'[166] would be prosecuted.[167] This would provide a factual and legal foundation for the trial of lesser criminals and emphasize the shared interest of the community of nations in prosecuting the Nazi leaders.[168] The tribunal would be composed of the four states represented at the planning conference. It was not considered 'practical' to permit other states to sit on the tribunal as a matter of 'right.'[169]

The decision to declare the German leaders personally liable for war crimes was reached following relatively limited debate. Professor André Gros of France argued that the fact that German aggression was an international crime did not mean that individual Germans could be held criminally liable.[170] The imposition of such liability would be 'morally and politically desirable but...it is not international law.'[171] Justice Jackson conceded that the justifiability of the

---

[161] Id.

[162] Id.

[163] See Jackson Report, supra note 149. Supreme Court Justice Robert H. Jackson was the American representative and his notes provide the only contemporaneous record of the proceedings. The following account of the drafting conference is drawn from Jackson's notes, and reflects his biases.

[164] Minutes of Conference Session (July 16, 1945) reprinted in Jackson Report, supra note 149, at 246, 250–51.

[165] Minutes of Conference Session (July 17, 1945), reprinted in Jackson Report, supra note 149, at 262, 277–78.

[166] Minutes of Conference Session (July 24, 1945) reprinted in Jackson Report, supra note 149, at 360, 363 (remarks of Mr. Justice Jackson).

[167] Minutes of Conference Session (July 23, 1945), reprinted in Jackson Report, supra note 149, at 328, 342.

[168] Minutes of Conference Session (July 2, 1945), reprinted in Jackson Report, supra note 149, at 129, 141.

[169] Minutes of Conferance Session (June 26, 1945), reprinted in Jackson Report, supra note 149, at 71, 74, (remarks of Mr. Justice Jackson).

[170] Minutes of Conferance Session (July 19, 1945), reprinted in Jackson Report, supra note 149, at 295, 297.

[171] Id.

imposition of personal liability under international law is 'indefinite and weak.'[172] However, he reminded the conferees that 'there is greater liberty in us to declare principles as we see them now.'[173] Sir David Maxwell Fyfe stated that imposing liability on German civilian and military leaders was appropriate.[174] He argued that since the war was 'the result of the actions of fifteen or twenty people, it is a difficult conception that those people are not responsible for their own acts when it is admitted that they result in an international crime.'[175]

The conferees agreed to prohibit the act of state and superior orders defenses, although the latter could be considered in mitigation of punishment.[176] The exclusion of these defenses was motivated by the concern that 'the combination of these two doctrines means that nobody is responsible.'[177]

The conferees spent considerable time debating the drafting of the substantive offenses. It was agreed that the defendants would be liable for the launching of an aggressive war, for the commission of atrocities against the civilian population, and for the launching or waging of a war in a manner contrary to the laws, usages, and customs of warfare.[178] Professor Gros objected that the crimes proposed by the conferees had no basis in international law or custom. Instead they were the 'creation of four people who are just four individuals—defined by... four people as criminal violations of international law. Those acts have been known for years before and have not been declared criminal violations of international law. It is ex post facto legislation.'[179] Sir David Maxwell Fyfe dismissed such concerns: 'We declare what international law is... there won't be any discussion on whether it is international law or not.'[180]

A central issue at the drafting conference was the American proposal to follow the suggestion of the World War I Commission on the Responsibility of the War and on Enforcement of Penalties to penalize the launching of a war of aggression.[181] Professor Gros pointed out that international law generally had

[172] Minutes of Conference Session (July 23, 1945), reprinted in Jackson Report, supra note 149, at 329, 331.
[173] Id.
[174] Minutes of Conference Session (July 19, 1945), reprinted in Jackson Report, supra note 149, at 295, 297.
[175] Id.
[176] Report to the President, (June 6, 1945) reprinted in Jackson Report, supra note 149 at 42, 47; Minutes of Conference Session (July 24, 1945), reprinted in Jackson Report, supra note 149, at 360, 367–68.
[177] Report to the President (June 6, 1945), reprinted in Jackson Report, supra note 149, at 42, 47.
[178] See generally Proposed Revision of Definition of 'Crimes' (Article 6), (July 20, 1945), reprinted in Jackson Report, supra note 149, at 312; Redraft of Definition of 'Crimes' (July 23, 1945), reprinted in Jackson Report, supra note 149, at 327.
[179] Minutes of Conference Session (July 23, 1945), reprinted in Jackson Report, supra note 149, at 328, 335.
[180] Minutes of Conference Session (June 29, 1945), reprinted in Jackson Report, supra note 149, at 97, 99.
[181] See supra notes 29–32 and accompanying text.

not limited states' use of force and did not recognize a just war doctrine. He contended that while an aggressive state may agree to compensate an aggrieved state or to repair damages, there was no criminal sanction imposed upon government officials for initiating or waging a war of aggression.[182] While Professor Gros believed that such a charge would be 'morally and politically desirable,' it was not 'international law.'[183] The French and the Soviets were content to demonstrate that the Nazis were 'bandits' who should be punished for atrocities, murders, and mass executions.[184] This position differed from that of the Americans, who desired 'to win the trial on the ground that the Nazi war was illegal.'[185]

Justice Jackson was intent on penalizing the Germans for their war of aggression, and suggested that the United States might refuse to participate in the trial unless the crime of aggressive war was included within the Nuremberg Charter.[186] Jackson explained that American assistance to its European allies and intervention in the war had been premised on the belief that the Allies had been illegally attacked. Germany had launched an aggressive war against the international order, and the United States was 'not doing an illegal thing in extending aid to peoples who were unjustly and unlawfully attacked.'[187] It also was vital to clearly establish that the launching of a war of aggression which threatened the world order would be regarded as an international crime.[188]

The English and the Americans also viewed the aggressive war charge as providing the justification for expanding the tribunal's criminal jurisdiction to encompass acts against civilians, acts which otherwise would fall within Germany's domestic jurisdiction. Jackson argued that the German program of atrocities and extermination was part of a 'plan for making an illegal war,' and that unless 'we have a war connection as a basis for reaching them, I would think we have no basis for dealing with atrocities.'[189] He conceded that the United States itself has 'some regrettable circumstances' in which 'minorities are unfairly treated,' but these events are not of international concern since they were not carried out in connection with an 'unjust or illegal war.'[190] Thus, the conferees made no pretense of establishing an international standard of criminal liability for violations of human rights applicable during both war and peace. In the words of Sir David Maxwell Fyfe, they distinguished between 'a Nazi chastising a Jew before the war

[182] Minutes of Conference Session (July 19, 1945), reprinted in Jackson Report, supra note 149, at 295.
[183] Id. at 297.
[184] Minutes of Conference Session (July 25, 1945), reprinted in Jackson Report, supra note 149, at 376, 383 (remarks of Mr. Justice Jackson).
[185] Id. at 383–84.
[186] Id. at 384.
[187] Id.
[188] Id.
[189] Minutes of Conference Session (July 23, 1945), reprinted in Jackson Report, supra note 149, at 328, 331.
[190] Id. at 333.

and the systematic persecution of the Jews in order to carry out the Nazi plan.'[191] The former clearly was not intended to fall within the tribunal's jurisdiction, while the latter was considered to be an international criminal offense.

The conferees ultimately agreed to the inclusion of the aggressive war charge.[192] However, the conferees left it up to the tribunal to formulate a definition of aggressive war.[193] An inordinate amount of time was also devoted to discussion of the American proposal which dealt with organizational criminality.[194] The Americans wanted the tribunal to declare certain voluntary Nazi organizations as criminal.[195] This declaration would then be used by occupation courts to hold low-level members of such organizations criminally liable simply by way of their membership.[196] The Americans pointed out that this would permit the efficient trial and conviction of thousands of Nazi adherents,[197] since their active participation in the organization would be sufficient to establish guilt.[198] The American proposal was accepted.[199] However, the conferees clarified that only voluntary and knowing membership would be considered criminal.[200] Rather than separately prosecuting organizations, it was agreed that individual members would be prosecuted and, if convicted, the organizations through which they carried out their crimes would themselves be declared criminal.[201]

Jackson, in his report to President Truman, observed that the conferees had established 'a basic charter in the international law of the future.'[202] He proclaimed that the rules formulated by the conferees were not intended to be applied exclusively against the Axis Powers. Jackson pledged that in the future any leader contravening the Nuremberg Principles would be prosecuted and punished by the international community.[203]

---

[191] Minutes of Conference Session (July 24, 1945), reprinted in Jackson Report, supra note 149, at 360, 361.

[192] See Minutes of Conference Session (August 2, 1945), reprinted in Jackson Report, supra note 149, at 399, 417.

[193] See Minutes of Conference Session (July 19, 1945), reprinted in Jackson Report, supra note 149, at 295, 308–09.

[194] Minutes of Conference Session (June 29, 1945), reprinted in Jackson Report, supra note 149, at 97, 111 (remarks of Justice Jackson).

[195] Minutes of Conference Session (June 26, 1945), reprinted in Jackson Report, supra note 149, at 71, 72 (remarks of Mr. Justice Jackson).

[196] Minutes of Conference Session (July 2, 1945), reprinted in Jackson Report, supra note 149, at 129, 133 (remarks of Sir David Maxwell Fyfe).

[197] Id. at 130 (remarks of Justice Jackson).

[198] Id. at 130, 138.

[199] See id. at 129–42 (remarks of General Nikitchenko).

[200] Id. at 129, 132 (remarks of Professor Gros).

[201] Id. at 135 (remarks of General Nikitchenko), 137–38 (remarks of Mr. Justice Jackson).

[202] Report to the President (October 7, 1946), reprinted in Jackson Report, supra note 149, at 432, 437.

[203] Minutes of Conference Session (July 23, 1945), reprinted in Jackson Report, supra note 149, at 328, 336.

B. The Nuremberg Charter

On August 8, 1945, the United States, France, the United Kingdom, and the Soviet Union signed the Agreement for the Prosecution and Punishment of the Major War Criminals of the European Axis Powers.[204] Article 1 established an International Military Tribunal for the just and prompt trial and punishment of the major war criminals of the European Axis Powers.[205] The Tribunal was given jurisdiction over Crimes Against Peace,[206] War Crimes,[207] and Crimes Against Humanity.[208] 'Leaders, organizers, instigators, and accomplices participating in the formulation or execution of a common plan or conspiracy to commit any of the foregoing crimes were to be held criminally responsible for all acts performed by any persons in execution of such plan.'[209]

Article 7 abrogated the act of state doctrine. A defendant's official position, whether a head of state or government official, would not absolve them from responsibility.[210] Article 8 stated that the fact that a defendant acted pursuant to the order of his government or of a superior did not free the defendant from responsibility. However, Article 8 further provided that superior orders might be considered in mitigation of punishment if the Tribunal determines that 'justice so requires.'[211] Organizational criminality was established in Article 9. The Tribunal was authorized to declare a group or organization of which any defendant was a member to be a criminal organization.[212] Article 10 provided that where the Tribunal declared a group or organization criminal, any signatory would have the right to bring individuals to trial for membership therein before national, military, or occupation courts.[213]

The Tribunal was required to state the reasons on which it based its findings of guilt and innocence,[214] and empowered to impose any punishment, including death, which it determined 'to be just.'[215] The defendants were to be selected by a majority vote of the Chief Prosecutors appointed by each of the four States represented on the Tribunal.[216]

---

[204] Agreement for the Prosecution and Punishment of the Major War Criminals of the European Axis, 59 Stat. 1544, 82 U.N.T.S. 284 reprinted in 39 AM.J.INT'L L. 257 (Supp.1945).

[205] Id. at 257–58.

[206] Charter of the International Military Tribunal, Aug. 8, 1945, 59 Stat. 1546, 82 U.N.T.S. 284 [hereinafter Nuremberg Charter]. See infra text accompanying note 246.

[207] Id. art. 6(b). See infra text accompanying note 262.

[208] Id. art. 6(c). See infra text accompanying note 274.

[209] Id. art. 6.

[210] Id. art. 7.

[211] Id. art. 8.

[212] Id. art. 9.

[213] Id. art. 10.

[214] Id. art. 26.

[215] Id. art. 27.

[216] Id. art. 14.

V. The Nuremberg Trial

A. Jurisdiction and Liability

The Nuremberg Tribunal convened on November 20, 1945. The Tribunal was composed of Francis Biddle, former Solicitor General of the United States, Professor Henri Donnedieu de Vabres, Professor of Law at the Sorbonne and an associate of the Institute of International Law at the Hague, Sir Geoffrey Lawrence of Great Britain, Lord Justice of Appeal, and General I.T. Nikitchenko, Vice-Chair of the Soviet Supreme Court and former lecturer in criminal law at the Academy of Military Jurisprudence in Moscow.[217]

Twenty-two defendants were indicted on seventy-four counts. There were four hundred three open sessions: thirty-three witnesses testified for the prosecution, and nineteen defendants and sixty-one witnesses testified for the defense. An additional one hundred forty-three witnesses testified for the defense by written interrogatories.[218] Three defendants were found not guilty,[219] seven were sentenced to prison terms ranging from ten years to life,[220] and twelve were sentenced to death by hanging.[221]

The Tribunal determined that its jurisdiction was based upon the law of the Nuremberg Charter.[222] It concluded that the drafting and implementation of the Charter was the exercise of 'sovereign legislative power by the countries to which the German Reich had unconditionally surrendered.'[223] According to the Tribunal, these countries had the undoubted legal right to legislate for the territory which they presently occupied.[224] The Allies, in establishing the Tribunal, had 'done together what any one of them might have done singly; for it is not to be doubted that any nation has the right thus to set up special courts to administer law.'[225] In the view of the Tribunal, the Charter was not an arbitrary exercise

---

[217] See generally BRADLEY F. SMITH, REACHING JUDGMENT AT NUREMBERG 3–5 (1977).

[218] 22 TRIAL OF THE MAJOR WAR CRIMINALS BEFORE THE INTERNATIONAL MILITARY TRIBUNAL 412–13 (S. Paul A. Joosten ed., 1948) [hereinafter NUREMBERG TRIBUNAL].

[219] 22 id. at 552–56 (Schacht), 571–74 (von Papen), 582–85 (Fritzsche).

[220] 22 id. at 588–89; see also 22 id. at 527–30 (Hess, life), 549–52 (Funk, life), 576–79 (Speer, 20 years), 579–82 (von Neurath, 15 years), 563–66 (von Schirach, 20 years), 561–63 (Raeder, life), 556–61 (Doenitz, 10 years).

[221] 22 id. at 588–89; see also 22 id. at 524–27 (Goering), 530–33 (von Ribbentrop), 533–36 (Keitel), 536–38 (Kaltenbrunner), 539–41 (Rosenberg), 541–44 (Frank), 544–47 (Frick), 547–49 (Streicher), 566–68 (Sauckel), 568–71 (Jodl), 574–76 (Seyss-Inquart), 585–87 (Bormann, tried in absentia).

[222] 22 id. at 414.

[223] 22 id. at 461.

[224] 22 id.

[225] 22 id.

of power by the victorious powers.[226] Instead, the Tribunal concluded that the Charter was an expression of international law 'existing at the time of the Charter's creation.'[227]

The Tribunal avoided directly addressing the issue as to whether the war of aggression charge violated the legal maxim nullum crimen sine lege, nulla poena sine lege (no punishment without a law). It ruled the prohibition on ex post facto punishment was not a 'limitation on sovereignty,' but 'is in general a principle of justice.'[228] In this instance, the Tribunal argued that it was not 'unjust' to punish those who attacked neighboring states without warning, and in defiance of treaties and assurances. In such circumstances, the attacker 'must know that he is doing wrong, and so far from it being unjust to punish him, it would be unjust if his wrong were allowed to go unpunished.'[229] The defendants, according to the Tribunal, must have known of the treaties signed by Germany requiring the pacific settlement of disputes. They were also certainly aware of the international prohibitions on the aggressive use of force.[230]

The Tribunal noted that the defendants must have been aware of the Kellogg-Briand Peace Pact of 1928, which was signed by sixty-three nations, including Germany, Italy, and Japan.[231] The signatories had agreed to settle their disputes by pacific means[232] and condemned the recourse to war for the solution of international disputes.[233] The Tribunal stated in its opinion that the treaty's renunciation of war as an instrument of national policy necessarily involved the proposition that aggressive war is 'illegal,' and those who wage such a war are committing a crime.[234]

The Tribunal conceded that the pact did not include a penal provision.[235] However, the Tribunal observed that there was no international legislature,[236] and that treaties must address general principles and usually are not concerned with 'administrative matters of procedure.'[237] As a result, it argued that the interpretation of treaties must be guided by the principle that international law is not 'static, but by continual adaptation follows the needs of a changing world.'[238] In assessing these needs, it is vital to consider the customs and practices of states and

[226] 22 id.
[227] 22 id.
[228] 22 id. at 461–62.
[229] 22 id. at 462.
[230] 22 id.
[231] 22 id, at 462–63 (citing Treaty Providing for the Renunciation of War as an Instrument of National Policy, Aug. 27, 1928, 46 Stat. 2343, 94 L.N.T.S. 57 [hereinafter Kellogg-Briand Peace Pact]).
[232] Kellogg-Briand Peace Pact, supra note 231, art. 1.
[233] Id. art. 2.
[234] 22 NUREMBERG TRIBUNAL, supra note 218, at 463.
[235] 22 id.
[236] 22 id. at 463–64.
[237] 22 id. at 464.
[238] 22 id.

the general principles of justice applied by jurists and military courts.[239] In this case, the Tribunal concluded that the prohibition and punishment of aggressive war was clearly demanded by 'the conscience of the world.'[240]

The Charter, as previously noted, imposed individual criminal liability and abrogated the act of state defense. The Tribunal endorsed these provisions and argued that international law's imposition of 'duties and liabilities upon individuals as well as upon states has long been recognized.'[241] It noted that 'crimes against international law are committed by men and not by abstract entities, and only by punishing individuals who commit such crimes can the provisions of international law be enforced.'[242] The Tribunal also ruled that the act of state defense was not applicable to these defendants since the state had 'moved outside its competence under international law.'[243]

The Tribunal also adhered to the recommendation of the drafting conference, recognizing that the superior orders defense was available only to mitigate punishment. The Tribunal further limited the defense to those unspecified instances in which no 'moral choice was in fact possible.'[244]

In an often cited passage, the Tribunal ruled that 'the very essence of the Charter is that individuals have international duties which transcend the national obligations of obedience imposed by the individual state.'[245] By narrowly circumscribing the admissibility of these defenses, the Tribunal clearly established that the demands of international law take precedence over domestic law.

B. Crimes Against Peace

The Tribunal initially turned its attention to the substantive offenses punishable under the Charter. Article 6(a) defines Crimes Against Peace as the 'planning, preparation, initiation or waging of a war of aggression, or a war in violation of international treaties, agreements or assurances, or participation in a common plan or conspiracy for the accomplishment of any of the foregoing.'[246] The Tribunal, like the drafting conference, viewed this charge as the core component of the case against the Nazis. It observed that an aggressive war 'is the supreme international crime differing only from other war crimes in that it contains within itself the accumulated evil of the whole.'[247] In addition, a war of aggression is an offense whose 'consequences are not confined to the belligerent states alone, but

---

[239] 22 id.
[240] 22 id. at 465.
[241] 22 id.
[242] 22 id. at 466.
[243] 22 id.
[244] 22 id.
[245] 22 id.
[246] Nuremberg Charter, supra note 206.
[247] 22 NUREMBERG TRIBUNAL, supra note 218, at 427.

affect the whole world.'[248] The judgment of an individual state as to whether wars are aggressive or defensive is not controlling. Any such determination is 'subject to investigation and adjudication' before an international tribunal.[249]

The drafting conference, as previously noted, was unable to agree on a precise definition of a war of aggression which constituted a Crime Against Peace. The Tribunal also avoided establishing broad principles governing the application of military force. It merely determined that 'certain of the defendants planned and waged aggressive wars against twelve nations, and were therefore guilty of this series of crimes.'[250] It further stated that it was unnecessary to speculate whether these aggressive wars were also wars in violation of international treaties, agreements, or assurances.[251] German actions against Austria, Poland, Czechoslovakia, Denmark, Norway, Belgium, the Netherlands, Luxembourg, Yugoslavia, Greece, the Soviet Union, and the United States were all regarded as aggressive wars.[252] The Tribunal's discussion of these cases indicates that an unprovoked, premeditated, and sustained attack on another sovereign state constituted a war of aggression.[253] A state's consent to its annexation or incorporation, if obtained through force or the threat of force, also constituted a war of aggression.[254] However, as noted, the Tribunal did not provide guidance as to the amount, duration, and character of the force which must be deployed to constitute a war of aggression in violation of international law.

Count One charged various individual defendants with involvement in a common plan or conspiracy to wage an aggressive war. Count Two charged defendants with participation in the planning, preparation, initiation, and waging of an aggressive war.[255]

The elements of the common plan or conspiracy charge were not specified in the Charter. The Tribunal rejected the prosecution's contention that any significant participation in the affairs of the Nazi Party or Government was evidence of participation in a criminal plan or conspiracy.[256] It ruled that only those who participated in the formulation or refinement of a concrete plan to wage a war of aggression were liable for a conspiracy. It ruled that only those who participated in the formulation or refinement of a concrete plan to wage a war of aggression were liable for a conspiracy.[257] Mere knowledge of these plans or involvement in

---

[248] 22 id.
[249] 22 id. at 450.
[250] 22 id. at 459.
[251] 22 id.
[252] 22 id. at 433–58.
[253] See 22 id.
[254] 22 id. at 433–39 (discussing German aggression towards Austria and Czechoslovakia).
[255] 22 id. at 427.
[256] 22 id. at 467.
[257] 22 id. at 467–68. Defendants convicted on Count One were Goering, Hess, von Ribbentrop, Keitel, Rosenberg, Jodl, von Neurath, and Raeder. See supra notes 220–21. Those acquitted were Kaltenbrunner, Frank, Frick, Streicher, Funk, Sauckel, Seyss-Inquart, Speer, Bormann, von Schirach, Docnitz, Schacht, von Papen, and Fritzsche. See supra notes 219–21. The

economic preparation for wars of aggression did not result in the imposition of criminal liability for involvement in a war of aggression.[258]

All the defendants convicted on Count One also were convicted on Count Two.[259] Four defendants acquitted on Count One were convicted on Count Two. The latter defendants were determined to have directed and implemented Nazi military tactics, strategies, and occupation plans.[260] Significantly, supervision over, and involvement in, the armaments industry were not considered to constitute initiating, planning, or preparing a war of aggression.[261]

C. War Crimes

Article 6(b) defined War Crimes as:

[V]iolations of the laws or customs of war. Such violations shall include...murder, ill-treatment or deportation to slave labor...murder or ill-treatment of prisoners of war...killing of hostages, plunder of public or private property, wanton destruction of cities, towns or villages, or devastation not justified by military necessity.[262] The Tribunal ruled that, at the time of the drafting of the Nuremberg Charter, these offenses were punishable under the Hague Convention of 1907.[263] By 1939, according to the Tribunal, these rules were recognized by all civilized nations, and were regarded as being declaratory of the laws and customs of war. The Tribunal rejected the argument that Germany had incorporated its occupied territories into the Reich, and, as a result, German policy towards these territories was within Germany's domestic jurisdiction. The Tribunal ruled that these territories could not be considered to be part of Germany so long as there was an army in the field attempting to resist German sovereignty.[264] In addition, it was pointed out territories such as Bohemia and Moravia never were incorporated into the Reich.[265]

Tribunal, without explanation, disregarded the charges in Count One which charged the defendants with a conspiracy to commit War Crimes and Crimes Against Humanity. 22 NUREMBERG TRIBUNAL, supra note 218, at 469. The Tribunal may have believed that this would involve the examination of German domestic repression of Jews and political dissidents which was not linked to a war of aggression.

[258] See 22 id. at 549–50 (discussing criminal liability of Frank), 552–56 (discussing criminal liability of Schacht).

[259] See supra note 257.

[260] See 22 NUREMBERG TRIBUNAL, supra note 218, at 468–69. Those acquitted on Count One who were convicted on Count Two were Doenitz, Frick, Funk, and Seyss-Inquart. See supra notes 220–21.

[261] See 22 NUREMBERG TRIBUNAL, supra note 218, at 576–77 (discussing criminal liability of Speer), 552–56 (discussing criminal liability of Schacht).

[262] Nuremberg Charter, supra note 206, art. 6(b).

[263] 22 NUREMBERG TRIBUNAL, supra note 218, at 497. See generally Convention Respecting the Laws and Customs of War on Land, Oct. 18, 1907, 36 Stat. 2277, 1 Bevans 631 (entered into force for the United States, Jan. 26, 1910).

[264] 22 NUREMBERG TRIBUNAL, supra note 218, at 497.

[265] 22 id. at 497–98 (noting, however, that a protectorate was established over these countries).

The Tribunal further concluded that Germany committed acts of barbarity on a 'vast scale, never before seen in the history of war.'[266] It attributed their scope and intensity to the Nazi conception of 'total war' under which the conventions governing the laws of war were viewed as lacking force and validity.[267] These barbaric acts were the product of 'cold and criminal calculation.'[268] The Tribunal required that the evidence 'sufficiently' connected a defendant to the planning, ordering, inciting, or commission of war crimes to sustain a conviction under the war crimes count.[269] Mere knowledge of crimes, communication of orders, or a failure to prevent commission of such acts was not sufficient to sustain a conviction.[270] Sixteen defendants were convicted and two were acquitted on this count.[271]

In a controversial decision, the Tribunal acquitted Admiral Doenitz, commander of the German submarine forces, and later head of the entire Navy, of the charge of waging unrestricted submarine warfare.[272] The Tribunal took judicial notice of the fact that the British Admiralty had adopted a similar policy in the North Sea between Denmark and Norway, and the United States practiced unrestricted submarine warfare in the Pacific. Although Doenitz was convicted of war crimes, the Tribunal emphasized that, as a matter of equity, his sentence was not 'assessed on the ground of his breaches of the international law of submarine warfare.'[273]

D. Crimes Against Humanity

Crimes Against Humanity were enumerated in Article 6(c). They included:

'[M]urder, extermination, enslavement, deportation, and other inhumane acts committed against any civilian population, before or during the war, or persecutions on political, racial or religious grounds in execution of or in connection with any crime within the jurisdiction of the Tribunal, whether or not in violation of the domestic law of the country where perpetrated.'[274] The Tribunal did not distinguish Crimes Against Humanity from War Crimes. It stated that from the beginning of the war in 1939, War Crimes which also constituted Crimes Against Humanity were committed on a vast scale. It then went on to hold that 'insofar as the inhumane acts charged in the Indictment, and committed after the beginning of the war, did not constitute war crimes, they were all

---

[266] 22 id. at 469.
[267] 22 id. at 469–70.
[268] 22 id. at 470.
[269] See, e.g., 22 id. at 529 (finding that evidence did not sufficiently connect Hess with the commission of War Crimes to sustain a guilty verdict on that count).
[270] 22 id.
[271] See supra notes 219–21. Convicted were Goering, von Ribbentrop, Keitel, Kaltenbrunner, Rosenberg, Frank, Frick, Streicher, Funk, Sauckel, Jodl, Seyss-Inquart, Speer, von Neurath, Bormann, and von Schirach; acquitted were Hess and Fritzsche.
[272] 22 NUREMBERG TRIBUNAL, supra note 218, at 557–58.
[273] 22 id. at 559.
[274] Nuremberg Charter, supra note 206, art. 6(c).

committed in execution of, or in connection with, the aggressive war, and therefore constituted crimes against humanity.'[275] It thus appears that the Tribunal interpreted Crimes Against Humanity to be both coextensive with and distinct from War Crimes. However, the opinion sheds little light on those acts which constitute Crimes Against Humanity.[276]

One of the Tribunal's most controversial holdings was the ruling that its jurisdiction only extended to acts committed 'in execution of, or in connection with any crime within the jurisdiction of the tribunal.'[277] This meant that Germany's persecution, repression, and murder of dissidents and Jews prior to the initiation of war in 1939 did not constitute 'Crimes Against Humanity within the meaning of the Charter.'[278] Thus, despite the 'vast scale' of Germany's 'terror' and 'cruelty' against its own nationals, the Tribunal refused to establish a minimum standard for state treatment of its nationals applicable during both peacetime and war.[279] Sixteen defendants were convicted[280] and two were acquitted on the Crimes Against Humanity count.[281]

E. Criminal Groups and Organizations

Article 9 of the Charter declared that the Tribunal had the discretion to declare that a defendant was a member of a 'criminal' group or organization.[282] Article 10 permitted the competent national authority of any signatory to bring individuals to trial before national, military, or occupation courts for the crime of membership in a criminal organization. In any such case, Article 10 also provided that the criminal nature of the group or organization need not be provided de novo in each case.[283]

The Tribunal declared that it would not hesitate to declare an organization criminal, and emphasized that it would not be deterred by the fact that the notion

---

[275] 22 NUREMBERG TRIBUNAL, supra note 218, at 498.

[276] Compare 22 id. at 491–96. Streicher and von Schirach were not indicted on the War Crimes count, but were convicted for Crimes Against Humanity. The Tribunal's discussion of their liability, however, provides little insight into the concept of Crimes Against Humanity. Streicher's propagandistic advocacy of the murder and extermination of Jews in occupied Eastern Europe was considered to constitute persecution on political and racial grounds and thus comprised a Crime Against Humanity. 22 id. at 549. von Schirach was involved in the deportation and extermination of Jews in occupied Austria. He also functioned as head of the Hitler Jugend, the youth movement involved in the evacuation of Soviet young people into Germany where they were employed as slave labor. 22 id. at 564–66.

[277] 22 NUREMBERG TRIBUNAL, supra note 218, at 498.

[278] 22 id.

[279] 22 id.

[280] See supra notes 220–21. Goering, von Ribbentrop, Keitel, Kaltenbrunner, Rosenberg, Frank, Frick, Streicher, Funk, Sauckel, Jodl, Seyss-Inquart, Speer, von Neurath, Bormann, and von Schirach all were convicted on the Crimes Against Humanity count.

[281] See supra notes 219–20. Hess and Fritzsche were acquitted.

[282] See Nuremberg Charter, supra note 206, art. 9.

[283] Id. art. 10.

of organizational criminality was 'new' or because 'it might be unjustly applied by some subsequent tribunals.'[284] At the same time, the tribunal stated that it was aware that any declaration of criminality should be structured so as to insure that 'innocent persons' would not be punished.[285]

The Tribunal ruled that in order to be declared criminal, a group must have been formed or used in connection with the commission of crimes denounced by the Charter. The Tribunal determined that membership alone was not sufficient to impose criminal liability upon individuals. Any declaration of criminality would exclude persons who had no knowledge of the criminal purposes or acts of the organization as well as those who were conscripted into the organization, unless they were personally implicated in the commission of criminal acts.[286]

The Tribunal issued a declaration of criminality against the Leadership Corps (administrative branch) of the Nazi Party,[287] the Gestapo (internal political police) and the SD (intelligence agency of the security police),[288] and the SS (internal security police).[289] It declined to issue such a finding against the SA (Nazi Party militia),[290] the Reich Cabinet,[291] and the General Staff and High Command of the German Armed Forces.[292] The Tribunal limited liability within the three criminal organizations to individuals specifically aware of or involved in crimes under the Charter: the Germanization of occupied territory, the persecution of Jews, the administration of the slave labor programs, and the mistreatment of prisoners of war.[293] A broad declaration of liability was issued against the voluntary members of the SS. The Tribunal determined that the SS was explicitly organized, trained, and indoctrinated to assist the Nazi Government in the domination of Europe and in the elimination of all 'inferior races.'[294] It concluded that the criminal program of the SS was so 'widespread, and involved slaughter on such a gigantic scale, that its criminal activities must have been widely known.'[295] In no instance did the Tribunal extend liability to those on the periphery of an organization's criminal activities. For instance, liability was not imposed on those employed by the Gestapo for purely clerical, stenographic, janitorial, or similar routine tasks.[296]

---

[284] 22 NUREMBERG TRIBUNAL supra note 218, at 500.
[285] 22 id.
[286] 22 id.
[287] 22 id. at 501–15.
[288] 22 id. at 505–11.
[289] 22 id. at 512–17.
[290] 22 id. at 517–19.
[291] 22 id. at 519–20.
[292] 22 id. at 520–23.
[293] 22 id. at 505.
[294] 22 id. at 515–16.
[295] 22 id. at 516.
[296] 22 id. at 511. Those who ceased their involvement in criminal organizations prior to September 1, 1939, were not considered to have been involved in crimes within the definition of the Charter. As a result, they were not held liable for membership in a criminal organization. Id.

The Tribunal determined that the SA was of little importance in the Nazi program of atrocities after 1934, and that members of the SA did not generally participate in, or even know of, the Nazi's criminal activities.[297] The Reich Cabinet was found to perform a peripheral role in the policy making process,[298] and was not deemed a coherent organization.[299] More importantly, the Tribunal observed that the Cabinet was comprised of only forty-eight members. Seventeen had been indicted at Nuremberg. It was observed that the other cabinet members suspected of crimes could easily be prosecuted as individuals, obviating the necessity of relying upon an organizational criminality theory.[300] The Tribunal admonished that, in the future, these individuals should be brought to trial.[301]

VI. Nuremberg Reassessed

Henry L. Stimson, former Secretary of State and Secretary of War, writing in 1947, argued that the Nuremberg Trial was a landmark in the history of international law.[302] Confronted with a choice between the release, summary punishment, and trial of the Nazis, the Allies chose to provide the Nazis 'what they had denied their own opponents—the protection of the Law.'[303] However, there can be little doubt that those who organized the Nuremberg tribunal sought only one outcome—the conviction and punishment of the Nazi defendants. During the drafting conference, Justice Jackson recognized that 'there could be but one decision in this case—that we are bound to concede guilt.'[304]

The International Military Tribunal at Nuremberg was composed of judges from the Allied Powers and was not, as its name suggests, an international court. The Charter promulgated by the victorious Allied Powers included various novel international legal doctrines which were applied exclusively to the acts of the vanquished. The judges were drawn from countries which, as suggested by the tribunal's disposition of the war crimes charges against Doenitz, recognized that they themselves possessed unclean hands.[305] Neutral prosecutors, acting without political restraints, might have lodged charges against the Allies for such acts as the deportation and internment of the Japanese, the dropping of the atomic bomb, the fire-bombing of Dresden, and for the failure to assist Jewish refugees.[306] It

---

[297] 22 id. at 519.
[298] 22 id. at 519–20.
[299] 22 id. at 519–20.
[300] 22 id. at 520.
[301] 22 id. at 523.
[302] Henry L. Stimson, The Nuremberg Trial: Landmark in Law, 25 FOREIGN AFF. 179 (1947).
[303] Id. at 180.
[304] Minutes of Conference Session (June 29, 1945) Jackson Report, supra note 149, at 97, 115.
[305] See supra notes 272–73 and accompanying text.
[306] See generally Hans Ehard, The Nuremberg Trial Against Major War Criminals and International Law, 43 AM.J.INT'L L. 223 (1949) (Dr. Ehard was Minister-President of Bavaria

was observed that, had the Reich emerged victorious, a host of Americans might have been prosecuted for violation of some of the same principles which were applied against Nazi leaders:

Franklin D. Roosevelt for conspiring for and fomenting aggressive war against remote nations and disregard of neutral obligations...James V. Forrestal for tyrannical misrule of subjected peoples with specifications of Navy government in Guam...Dwight D. Eisenhower for invasion of peaceful lands, with specification of the unnecessarily bloody invasion of North Africa...William F. Halsey, Jr., for violations of neutrality, with specifications of the blockade of Spain and hostile destructive measures against Argentine, Irish and Swedish maritime commerce...George S. Patton, Jr., for...abuse of authority and breach of military and Red Cross rules for the treatment of hospital personnel...Mark W. Clark for wanton sacrifice of life, with specification of the 36th Division attack at the Rapido River in Italy in January, 1944...James A. Kilian for cruel and abusive treatment of prisoners, with specifications of his conduct while in command of the Lichfield Detention Camp from March, 1943 to January, 1945.[307] Professor Bernard Meltzer of the University of Chicago conceded that the Allies' selective prosecution contributed to the perception of 'victors' justice.' However, he argued that such prosecution was justified by the 'greater depravity of the Nazis' and by the fact that 'they deliberately launched the aggressions without which our comparatively minor deviations from accepted usages would not have occurred.'[308] Sheldon Glueck noted that the Nuremberg proceedings were conducted in accordance with accepted notions of due process of law and provided the accused with an 'opportunity for explanation, justification, or excuse.'[309] He observed that the Allies easily could have imprisoned or executed the Nazi defendants without resort to complex judicial procedures.[310] In England, Lord Wright explained that the Allies, like the police, were merely enforcing the law; their motive was 'justice, not revenge.'[311] In response to the charge of 'victors' justice,' Justice Jackson, in his opening statement, emphasized that in the future, the Nuremberg Principles would be applied against any nation which disregarded their requirements, 'including those which sit here now in judgement.'[312]

Despite the apparent procedural fairness of the Nuremberg trial, the Tribunal accepted the Charter's innovative provisions as being consistent with international

---

at the time of the writing of this article). See also F.B. Schick, War Criminals and The Law of The United Nations, 7 TORONTO L.J. 27, 30 (1947–48). Nineteen countries ultimately adhered to the Nuremberg Charter. Id. at 30, n. 8.

[307] Gordon Ireland, Ex Post Facto From Rome To Tokyo, 21 TEMPLE L.Q. 27, 56–57 (1947–48). The equitable principles of 'unclean hands' would not provide a legally relevant defense. Selective prosecution is only of concern in so far as it undermined the Tribunal's moral credibility. See Quincy Wright, The Law of The Nuremberg Trial, 41 AM.J.INT'L L. 38, 46–47 (1947). For a discussion of the brutality of World War II, see generally P. FUSSELL, WARTIME UNDERSTANDING AND BEHAVIOR IN THE SECOND WORLD WAR (1989).

[308] Bernard D. Meltzer, A Note On Some Aspects Of The Nuremberg Debate, 14 U.CHI.L.REV. 455, 469 (1946–47).

[309] Sheldon Glueck, The Nuernberg Trial And Aggressive War, 59 HARV.L.REV. 396, 452 (1946).

[310] Id.

[311] Wright, War Crimes Under International Law, 62 LAW Q.REV. 40, 44 (1946).

[312] 2 NUREMBERG TRIBUNAL supra note 218, at 154.

law.[313] It approved the imposition of individual responsibility and the abrogation of the act of state and superior orders defenses. It also dismissed concerns about the Charter's ex post facto character and the novelty of the aggressive war, Crimes Against Humanity, and organizational criminality charges. At the same time that the Tribunal accepted these legal innovations, it moved cautiously in imposing criminal liability. For instance, it narrowly interpreted the elements of the conspiracy to wage an aggressive war count so as to limit liability to those directly involved in the formulation or refinement of a concrete plan to wage a war of aggression.[314] There was no systematic policy or process for the selection of the Nuremberg defendants.[315] Clearly, the defendants were people of venality. However, the historian Bradley F. Smith, the leading academic chronicler of the Nuremberg trial, observed that the Americans selected defendants 'not because of their personal actions, cruelty, or notoriety, but because they fitted into the American plan for prosecuting organizations.'[316] In fact, the wartime activities of several defendants were indistinguishable from that of hundreds of other German functionaries.[317] The most conspicuous oversight was the failure to bring the major German industrialists to trial at Nuremberg.[318] The Tribunal's judgment is largely devoid of detailed legal analysis, and it devoted little attention to the guilt of the individual defendants. Instead, the tribunal was preoccupied with documenting the Nazis' conspiratorial rise to power and their aggressive assault on their European neighbors. This served to legitimate the Allied war effort as well as their decision to treat the defeated Nazi leaders as international criminals. As Smith notes, the 'individual defendants were merely the performers through whom the main drama was played out.'[319] In several cases, the determination of guilt and punishment was the product of judicial bargaining, negotiation, lobbying, and biases. In such instances, the weight of the evidence was a secondary consideration.[320]

A single war crimes trial also provided the Western Powers with the opportunity to offer an interpretation of the Third Reich consistent with their post-World

[313] An interesting, critical perspective on the fairness of the trial is contained in the little-noticed accounts of the German defense lawyers who participated in the trial. See Herbert Kraus, The Nuremberg Trial Of the Major War Criminals: Reflections After Seventeen Years 13 DEPAUL L.REV. 233 (1963–64); Carl Haensell, The Nuremberg Trial Revisited 13 DEPAUL L.REV. 248 (1963–64); Otto Kranzbubler, Nuremberg Eighteen Years Afterwards, 14 DEPAUL L.REV. 333 (1964–5); Hans Laternser, Looking Back At The Nuremberg Trials With Special Consideration Of The Processes Against Military Leaders, 9 WHITTIER L.REV. 557 (1985).

[314] See supra notes 256–58 and accompanying text.

[315] SMITH, supra note 217, at 63–65, 68–71.

[316] Id. at 64.

[317] Id. at 240 (discussing deliberations regarding the guilt of von Schirach).

[318] Id. at 63–64.

[319] Id. at 64.

[320] For an example of judicial negotiation and bargaining see id. at 223–29 (discussing criminal liability of von Neurath). The sentencing of Albert Speer to twenty years in prison is attributed, in part, to the judges' favorable impression of his intelligence, education and sophistication. Id. at 220.

War II security goals and interests. The Tribunal, in accordance with traditional legal principles, did not entertain arguments pertaining to the collective responsibility of the German people.[321] It limited itself to a consideration of the liability of high echelon officials.[322] Nazi atrocities and aggressions were portrayed as the result of the machinations of a small, evil cabal. In the view of the Tribunal, the German people were repressed and intimidated into cooperating with the Nazi regime. Criticism, dissent, and opposition were described as having been met with the 'severest penalties.'[323] Thus, having excised the cancerous Nazi clique at the top, the Western Allies were able to comfortably welcome the newly cleansed West German nation as a partner in the Cold War combat against the Soviet Union.[324] The containment of Communism quickly assumed priority over the prosecution of additional leading members of the Nazi Party and German war criminals.[325] Journalist Tom Bower observed that in post-war Germany, many of those who 'had given the orders in the Third Reich were again giving the orders. If international pressure demanded justice, then it was those who obeyed the orders who were, in the last resort, expendable, not those who had given orders and who now gave them again.'[326]

The portrayal of the Nazi leadership as 'monsters' resulted in the Nuremberg precedent losing much of its import in contemporary political discourse and debate. For instance, allegations that the policies pursued by seemingly responsible and 'normal' officials of the United States in Southeast Asia or in Central America constitute Nuremberg crimes are dismissed as hyperbole.[327] Given the Tribunal's description of the Third Reich as an illegitimate, criminal, and internally repressive regime, it made little sense for the Tribunal to have insulated the defendants from liability for acts committed prior to 1939.[328] In retrospect, it was scandalous to have treated the Nazi abuse of German dissidents, Jews, and other groups as falling within Germany's domestic jurisdiction. The Tribunal, however, viewed Nuremberg primarily as a trial of those who had initiated and waged an aggressive war, and had little inclination to establish minimum international

---

[321] See generally Richard Arens, Nuremberg And Group Prosecution, 1951 WASH.UNIV.L.Q. 329. See Ferdinand A. Herments, Collective Guilt, 23 NOTRE DAME LAWYER 431 (1948).

[322] See supra notes 256–58 and accompanying text. The Tribunal narrowly interpreted the aggressive war counts. This limited liability to high echelon officials.

[323] 22 NUREMBERG TRIBUNAL supra note 218, at 423.

[324] See generally Matthew Lippman, The Denaturalization of Nazi War Criminals In The United States: Is Justice Being Served? 7 HOUSTON J.INT'L L. 169 (1982).

[325] See TOM BOWER, THE PLEDGE BETRAYED: AMERICA AND BRITAIN AND THE DENAZIFICATION OF POSTWAR GERMANY 200, 247, 355, 361, 363, 373, 392 (1982). See also Arens, supra note 321, at 353.

[326] BOWER, supra note 325, at 378.

[327] RICHARD FALK, ET AL., THE CRIMES OF WAR: A LEGAL, POLITICAL-DOCUMENTARY, AND PSYCHOLOGICAL INQUIRY INTO THE RESPONSIBILITY OF LEADERS, CITIZENS, AND SOLDIERS FOR CRIMINAL ACTS IN WAR (1971).

[328] See supra notes 277–79 and accompanying text.

standards for regimes' domestic treatment of their citizens.[329] Of course, such a ruling might have meant that all regimes bore international criminal responsibility for their mistreatment of their domestic population—a decision which could have proved potentially embarrassing to both Stalinist Russia and to the segregationist United States.

Professor Hans Kelsen dismissed the contention that the Charter reflected existing international law as an attempt to 'veil the arbitrary character of the acts of a sovereign law-maker.'[330] Kelsen described the Tribunal's claim that it was expressing rather than creating international legal doctrine as a 'fiction.'[331] For instance, the Tribunal summarily disposed of the act of state defense by the contention that it was unjust to apply it in the case of Nazi Germany.[332] Yet, as previously pointed out, the distinction between German and Allied military tactics, at times, was a question of degree.[333] Prior to the Nuremberg trial it was well established that the state, and not the individual, incurred international legal liability. The sanctions for violations of international law were collective—compensation and reprisals—and state officials could not be subjected to the jurisdiction of a third party without the consent of their parent state.[334]

The Tribunal also held that the ex post facto principle was not a restraint on the exercise of sovereign power. The Nuremberg judges argued that since the defendants were cognizant of the fact that their actions were contrary to existing legal principles, that it would be unjust to permit them to invoke the ex post facto principle.[335] It is debatable whether the defendants were conscious of the fact that their conduct was violative of inchoate doctrines of international criminal law.[336] In addition, George Finch, writing in the American Journal of International Law in 1947, pointed out that the United States greeted each successive German invasion with an official proclamation of neutrality. He observed that:

To maintain retroactively that these invasions were international criminal acts involving personal responsibility is to suggest that the United States officially compounded international crime with international criminals. The United States continued to recognize the Government of Germany as legitimate, to receive its diplomatic representatives at Washington, and to accredit American diplomatic representatives to Berlin.[337] The Soviet Union, of course, participated in the German invasion of Poland.[338] Dina Ghandy

---

[329] See SMITH, supra note 217, at 88–89. Nazi atrocities, in general, were a secondary aspect of the trial. Id.

[330] Hans Kelsen, Will The Judgment In The Nuremberg Trial Constitute A Precedent In Int'l Law? 1 INT'L L.Q. 153, 162 (1947).

[331] Id. at 161.

[332] See supra notes 241–43 and accompanying text.

[333] See supra notes 306–08 and accompanying text.

[334] Schick, supra note 306, at 52–53.

[335] See supra notes 228–30 and accompanying text.

[336] See supra notes 228–30 and accompanying text.

[337] George A. Finch, The Nuremberg Trial And International Law, 41 AM.J.INT'L L. 20, 28 (1947).

[338] Dina G. McIntyre, The Nuernberg Trials, 24 U.PITT.L.REV. 73, 110–11 (1962).

McIntyre queries if 'the act when done was not considered criminal by two of the prosecuting governments, how can we assume as the Tribunal did that the defendants knew they were "doing wrong?" '[339]

The international community also witnessed and mildly protested Germany's initial mistreatment of Jews. This silence frequently was invoked by Hitler to illustrate the international acceptance of his increasingly repressive policies.[340] To argue that the Nazi leaders knew their mistreatment of Jews was contrary to existing international norms also overlooks the fact that German history is replete with anti-semitism and persecution of Jews.[341] The 'Final Solution' arguably was a logical extension of the forces and infuences at work in German society. Historically, there have been numerous societies, such as the United States prior to the Civil War, in which the persecution of racial minorities has been deemed natural, desirable, and necessary.[342] It is thus problematic to argue convincingly that the German leaders realized that their actions were improper, let alone that they would result in international criminal liability.

The superior orders defense also effectively was denied.[343] Such a defense had been incorporated into the military codes of nearly all nations prior to World War I.[344] Great Britain and the United States, however, both conveniently amended their domestic codes prior to Nuremberg so as to deny the superior orders defense.[345] Guenter Lewy of Smith College characterized this as 'a poorly disguised and self-serving way of preparing the ground for the trials of the German and Japanese war criminals who were sure to invoke the plea of superior orders.'[346] If the Tribunal had accepted such pleas, 'it would have been impossible to punish anyone.'[347]

The Tribunal did permit those Germans who could establish that they had obeyed an illegal order to raise superior orders in mitigation of, rather than as a defense to, punishment.[348] The rule rather self-servingly imposed punishment on those vanquished German combatants who obeyed orders, which were declared to be illegal following the termination of hostilities. German leaders and combatants thus were charged with a singular duty to comprehend the often uncertain

---

[339] Id. at 111.

[340] See generally WALTER LAQUEUR, THE TERRIBLE SECRET SUPPRESSION OF THE TRUTH ABOUT HITLER'S 'FINAL SOLUTION' (1980).

[341] See generally LUCY S. DAWIDOWICZ, THE WAR AGAINST THE JEWS 1933–1945 (1975).

[342] See generally Matthew Lippman, The Trial Of Adolf Eichmann and the Protections of Universal Human Rights Under International Law, 5 HOUS.J.INT'L L. 1, 31 (1982). See also DAWIDOWICZ, supra note 341.

[343] See supra note 244 and accompanying text.

[344] Guenter Lewy, Prior Orders, Nuclear Warfare, and the Dictates of Conscience: The Dilemma of Military Obedience in the Atomic Age, 55 AM.POL.SCI.REV. 3, 6 (1961).

[345] Id.

[346] Id.

[347] Finch, supra note 337, at 21.

[348] See supra note 244 and accompanying text.

law of war, and to resist what the Allies later declared to be illegal orders. McIntyre observes that a postwar determination by a tribunal composed of members of victorious powers can 'never be a matter of impartial judicial discernment. It becomes of necessity a political pronouncement—a legal way in which the victors can wreak their vengeance upon the vanquished.'[349]

Aggressive war was the central charge at the Nuremberg trial. Professor Schwartzenberger queried whether it can 'really be said that the governments of the world in the period since 1928 regarded the parties who were guilty of flagrant aggressions...as criminals.'[350] The Tribunal cited the Kellogg-Briand Peace Pact as the primary basis for the aggressive war charge.[351] Yet, that treaty contained no provision for criminal or individual liability and did not single out so-called aggressive wars for condemnation.[352] The imposition of criminal liability also cannot be supported by legislative history or scholarly commentary.[353] It is doubtful whether the States which signed the Kellogg-Briand Peace Pact believed that they were, in effect, waiving the act of state defense and exposing their civilian and military leaders to criminal liability and prosecution.[354] The Tribunal escaped this dilemma by ruling that the pact must be interpreted in light of the dynamic nature of international law.[355] However, it is difficult to discover any consistent practice supporting the Tribunal's determination that an aggressive war constituted an international crime. As one commentator noted, 'no performance at all would seem to indicate no custom at all.'[356] At any rate, the argument that treaties may be interpreted in light of evolutionary developments introduces an impermissible degree of uncertainty and discretion into the interpretation of treaties, particularly when extending their language to impose criminal liability.[357] McIntyre convincingly argues that the United States Senate certainly would not have ratified a treaty which exposed American combatants and leaders to potential international penal liability.

[I]t is hard to believe that the watchdogs of American isolationism in the Senate, who were so interested in keeping America free of European involvements, would have given the Kellogg-Briand Pact the requisite two-thirds majority if they had even the remotest idea that, should America start a war, the Pact could reasonably be interpreted as giving any one or a combination of European states the power to try American soldiers, sailors, airmen, and civilians (as the Charter allowed), or the President and our leading statesmen (as the Tribunal in fact did) for the 'crime of planning, preparing or waging

[349] McIntyre supra note 338, at 114.
[350] Georg Schwarzenberger, The Judgement Of Nuremberg, 21 TUL.L.REV. 329, 347–48 (1947).
[351] See supra notes 231–40 and accompanying text.
[352] See supra notes 231–40 and accompanying text.
[353] McIntyre, supra note 338, at 96–100.
[354] Finch, supra note 337, at 31–33.
[355] See supra notes 235–43 and accompanying text.
[356] McIntyre, supra note 338, at 95.
[357] But see Glueck, supra note 309, at 408–12.

a war of aggression.'[358] The Nuremberg Trial did permit the Allies to achieve a sense of retribution, and prevented post-war anger from degenerating into 'vigilante' justice.[359] The trial record of atrocities and aggression also vindicated American intervention in the war against Germany.[360] In addition, the recounting of German aggression helped to alert Americans to the fact they faced a threatening new world. In this new world, the traditionally isolationist United States would be thrust into the position of a super-power charged with responsibility for safeguarding western democracy.[361] The trial also provided the German people with a lesson on the dangers of substituting the ideological dictates of men for the rule of law.[362] In the end, however, vengeance and vindication necessarily required the sacrifice of legal principle.[363] McIntyre observes that although the Nuremberg trial was designed to demonstrate that 'might does not make right' that 'it was the "might" of the Allies...that made the Charter, Trial, and Judgment of Nuernberg "right."'[364]

VII. The Impact of Nuremberg

In 1949, Justice Robert H. Jackson described Nuremberg as the century's most 'definite challenge' to the 'anarchic concepts of the law of nations.'[365] He argued that Nuremberg was the first step towards limiting the unfettered discretion of sovereign States to resort to armed force.[366] Government officials could no longer credibly claim legal immunity based upon the act of state and superior orders defenses.[367] Jackson noted that international institutions were so undeveloped and moribund that, absent the Nuremberg trial, it is unlikely that these 'catastrophic doctrines' would have been challenged and modified.[368] He concluded that the failure to have punished the Nazi leaders inevitably would have encouraged the ambitions of those leaders whose unlimited avarice may again have led to a world war.[369]

The Nuremberg Trial fueled the hopes of those who argued for the necessity of creating some form of world federal government. It was argued that advances in

---

[358] McIntyre, supra note 338, at 98–99.
[359] SMITH, supra note 152, at 247–48.
[360] Id. at 251.
[361] Id. at 252.
[362] See JUDITH N. SHKLAR, LEGALISM, LAW, MORALS, AND POLITICAL TRIALS 169 (1964).
[363] SMITH, supra note 152, at 260–01.
[364] McIntyre, supra note 338, at 115.
[365] Robert H. Jackson, Nuremberg in Retrospect: Legal Answer to International Lawlessness, 35 A.B.A.J. 813 (1949).
[366] Id.
[367] Id.
[368] Id. at 813–14.
[369] Id. at 886.

the technology of war had placed global society on the edge of a nuclear abyss.[370] The best hope for security lay in the rule of law rather than of force. International disputes were envisioned as being settled through adjudication rather than armed conflict.[371] Those States which persisted in aggression or in the abuse of human rights should be subject to international criminal liability.[372] This 'one-world' boosterism was not limited to utopians or idealists, but was shared by a wide spectrum of individuals. Writing in the American Bar Association Journal, Wallace T. Holliday, Chair of the Board of the Standard Oil Company of Ohio, opined that the prevention of war 'is very simple.'[373] All that is required is to 'duplicate what has been done within the borders of nations, and require all international disputes to be decided under law by judicial tribunals that are instruments of a world government.'[374] Robert M. Hutchins, President of the University of Chicago and former Dean of the Yale Law School, headed a committee of notables which, in 1948, published a Preliminary Draft of a World Constitution.[375] The Committee based its work on the theme, 'world government is necessary therefore it is possible,'[376] and envisioned the formation of a 'world union.'[377] In a 1951 lecture, John J. Parker, Chief Judge of the Fourth Circuit Court of Appeals, warned that:

[if] unity is not achieved on the basis of reason and law, it will eventually be achieved through force; and the only hope of defeating those who would unify the world on the basis of force is for those who believe in the reign of law to rise above the narrow limitations of nationalism and support a world organization based upon law and righteousness.[378] This movement, however, foundered on the shoals of the 'new realism.'[379] Pragmatic concerns such as balance of power, spheres of influence, and containment of

---

[370] Wallace T. Holliday, World Law or World Anarchy: The Case for a World Federal Government, 35 A.B.A.J. 641, 642 (1949).

[371] Id.

[372] Id. at 644.

[373] Id. at 642.

[374] Id.

[375] The work of the Hutchins Committee is discussed in Ray Garrett, Jr., A World Constitution: Analysis of the Draft by the Hutchins Committee, 34 A.B.A.J. 563 (1948).

[376] Id.

[377] This phrase is taken from the Committee's statement of policy, see id. at 564. See also Guy W. Bange, World Repose Under Law: What Are the Fundamentals of Enduring Peace? 33 A.B.A.J. 461 (1947). Bange calls for the formation of a Congress of World Peace. Id. Other such efforts are noted in Clyde Eagleton, The Individual And International Law, 40 PROC.AM.SOC'Y INT'L L. 22, 27–28 (1946). For a comprehensive discussion of the proposal for a world government, see John H. Davenport, The Approach to World Government through the Technique of the World Constitutional Convention: American Experience, 3 MIAMI L.Q. 500 (1948–49).

[378] John J. Parker, World Order Based on Law, 8 WASH. & LEE L.REV. 131, 144 (1951). See also Robert H. Wilkin, The Science of Law as a Substitute for War, 32 A.B.A.J. 22 (1946). The organized bar also took an active role in advocating world order based upon law. See Lawyers of the Americas Unite for World Court, 31 A.B.A.J. 172 (1945).

[379] Joseph L. Kunz, The Swing Of The Pendulum: From Overestimation to Underestimation of International Law, 44 AM.J.INT'L L. 135, 140 (1950).

Communism came to be viewed as the guarantors of world security.[380] International law gradually came to be viewed as an irrelevant extravagance which had no role in the formulation of foreign and security policy.[381] The study of international law gradually fell into a desuetude from which it has not fully recovered. In 1946, Joseph L. Kunz bemoaned a survey of roughly one hundred law schools indicating that only sixteen offered a course in international law.[382] He noted that these elective courses attracted few students and were generally taught by specialists in other areas.[383]

Nuremberg, however, did have significant and lasting influence on international jurisprudence. In December, 1946, the United Nations General Assembly unanimously adopted a resolution that affirmed 'the principles of international law recognized by the Charter of the Nuremberg Tribunal and the judgment of the Tribunal.'[384] Professor M. Cherif Bassiouni has observed that the Nuremberg Principles have become part of the

general principles of international law, and, as such, constitute one of the sources of international law as stated in Article 38 of the Statute of the International Court of Justice. In addition, these Principles are the basis for the elaboration of an international criminal code and the creation of an international criminal court even though both have yet to become legal realities.[385] In November, 1947, the General Assembly of the United Nations took steps to codify the principles of international criminal law. It passed a resolution requesting that the International Law Commission of the United Nations formulate a Draft Code of Offenses Against the Peace and Security of Mankind.[386] The commission completed the Draft Code in 1950, however the General Assembly has not yet adopted the document.[387] Nevertheless, the General Assembly has passed various multilateral conventions which, in combination, form the foundation for an international criminal code.[388]

---

[380] Id. at 138–40.

[381] Id. at 140. See generally Frank E. Holman, 'World Government' No Answer to America's Desire for Peace, 32 A.B.A.J. 642 (1946). The debate over the role and importance of international law in the post-World War II era is reviewed in Josef L. Kunz, The Problem of The Progressive Development Of International Law, 31 IOWA L.REV. 544 (1946).

[382] Josef L. Kunz, A Plea For More Study Of International Law In American Law Schools, 40 AM.J.INT'L L. 624, 625 (1946).

[383] Id.

[384] G.A.Res. 95(I), 188 U.N.Doc. A/64/Add. 1 (1946). The United Nations affirmed these principles and urged countries to apprehend and prosecute Nazi war criminals on various occasions. See Lippman, supra note 324, at 208–10.

[385] M. Cherif Bassiouni, International Law and the Holocaust, 9 CAL.W.INT'L L.J. 202, 235 (1979).

[386] G.A.Res. 177(II), 5 U.N.GAOR Supp. (No. 12) at 11, U.N.Doc. A/1316 (1950).

[387] See Benjamin B. Ferencz, The Draft Code of Offences Against the Peace and Security of Mankind, 75 AM.J.INT'L L. 674 (1981). The International Law Commission's initial draft is contained in U.N.Doc. A/CN. 4/25 (1950), reprinted in [1950] 2 Y.B.INT'L L.COMM'N 253, 274, cited in Matthew Lippman, Nuclear Weapons and International Law: Towards a Declaration on the Prevention and Punishment of the Crime of Nuclear Humanicide, 8 LOY.L.A.INT'L & COMP.L.J. 183, 218, n. 209 (1986).

[388] Bassiouni, supra note 1, at 262.

The 1948 Genocide Convention was the first, and perhaps the most important, of these instruments. It established the basic premises which have since guided the developing system of international criminal law.[389] Article I expanded the jurisdiction of international criminal law beyond acts undertaken in furtherance of a war of aggression. It proclaimed that genocide, 'whether committed in time of peace or in time of war, is a crime under international law' which the High Contracting Parties undertake to prevent and to punish.[390] Article IV abrogates the act of state defense and states that persons committing genocide shall be punished 'whether they are constitutionally responsible rulers, public officials, or private individuals.'[391] Article VI provides that acts of genocide shall be tried by a competent tribunal of the state in the territory of which the act was committed.[392] Alternatively, prosecution may be undertaken before 'such international penal tribunal as may have jurisdiction with respect to those Contracting Parties which shall have accepted its jurisdiction.'[393] A provision recognizing the jurisdiction of an anticipated international penal tribunal has been incorporated into several other instruments.[394] However, an international penal tribunal has not yet been formed.[395] Nuremberg thus stands as the only modern, multilateral prosecution for offenses against international criminal law.[396] In retrospect, it is unfortunate that the Allies did not establish a permanent international criminal court at Nuremberg.

Limited progress also was made towards drafting an international treaty prohibiting aggressive wars. In 1974, the United Nations adopted an influential Resolution On The Definition Of Agression, but has not yet reached agreement on a comprehensive definition of aggression.[397] The Nuremberg judgment, however, helped to propel the drafting of the 1949 Geneva Conventions, which provided added formal protections for the wounded and sick,[398] prisoners of

---

[389] Convention on the Prevention and Punishment of the Crime of Genocide, Dec. 9, 1948, 78 U.N.T.S. 1021 (entered into force Jan. 12, 1951). See generally Matthew Lippman, The Drafting of the 1948 Convention on the Prevention and Punishment of the Crime of Genocide, 3 B.U.INT'L L.J. 1 (1985).

[390] Convention on the Prevention and Punishment of the Crime of Genocide, supra note 389, art. I.

[391] Id., art. IV.

[392] Id., art. VI.

[393] Id.

[394] M. CHERIF BASSIOUNI, International Criminal Law and Human Rights, in I INTERNATIONAL CRIMINAL LAW: CRIMES 15, 26 (M. Cherif Bassiouni, ed. 1986) [hereinafter INTERNATIONAL CRIMINAL LAW].

[395] Colleen L. Donovan, Comment, The History and Possible Future of International Criminal Law, 13 BROOK.J.INT'L L. 83, 106–08 (1987).

[396] G.O.W. Mueller & Douglas J. Besharov, Evolution and Enforcement of International Criminal Law, in INTERNATIONAL CRIMINAL LAW supra note 392, at 59, 77–79.

[397] Resolution On The Definition Of Aggression, G.A.Res. 3314 (XXIX), 29 U.N.GAOR, Supp. (No. 31) at 142, U.N.Doc. A/9631 (1975).

[398] Geneva Convention for the Amelioration of the Condition of the Wounded and Sick in Armed Forces in the Field, Aug. 12, 1949, 6 U.S.T. 3114, 75 U.N.T.S. 31; Geneva Convention for

war,[399] and civilians.[400] For instance, common Article 3 extended protection to conflicts 'not of an international character' occurring in the territory of one of the High Contracting Parties.[401] It provides that civilians, the wounded, the sick, and those who have laid down their arms shall be treated 'humanely' without distinction founded on race, color, religion, sex, wealth, or other similar characteristics.[402] This provision has been referred to as

[A] remarkable achievement, both as an innovation in the law of war and as a landmark in the law of human rights. The principle involved was of momentous importance. It was being agreed by governments...that no matter what pitch of armed violence their internal disputes might attain, certain fundamental inhumanities would be banned.[403] In addition, the international community clearly pronounced in the Geneva Conventions that serious violations of the laws of war would be subject to criminal punishment. High Contracting Parties formally agreed to enact legislation providing for effective penal sanctions for persons committing, or ordering to be committed, any grave breach of the conventions.[404] Signatory states undertook to search for such persons and, regardless of their nationality, to bring them to trial before the violators' domestic courts.[405] States were given the option of handing such persons over for trial to

the Amelioration of the Condition of Wounded, Sick and Shipwrecked Members of Armed Forces at Sea, Aug. 12, 1949, 6 U.S.T. 3217, 75 U.N.T.S. 85.

[399] Geneva Convention Relative to the Treatment of Prisoners of War, Aug. 12, 1949, 6 U.S.T. 3316, 75 U.N.T.S. 135.

[400] Geneva Convention Relative to the Protection of Civilian Persons In Time Of War, Aug. 12, 1949, 6 U.S.T. 3516, T.I.A.S. No. 3365, 75 U.N.T.S. 287.

[401] See sources cited supra notes 398–400, art. 3.

[402] Id. Article 3, which is identical in each of the Geneva Conventions cited above, states that:
  (1) Persons taking no active part in the hostilities, including members of armed forces who have laid down their arms and those placed hors de combat by sickness, wounds, detention, or any other cause, shall in all circumstances be treated humanely, without any adverse distinction founded on race, colour, religion or faith, sex, birth or wealth, or any other similar criteria. To this end, the following acts are and shall remain prohibited at any time and in any place whatsoever with respect to the above-mentioned persons:
    (a) violence to life and person, in particular murder of all kinds, mutilation, cruel treatment and torture;
    (b) taking of hostages;
    (c) outrages upon personal dignity, in particular, humiliating and degrading treatment;
    (d) the passing of sentences and the carrying out of executions without previous judgment pronounced by a regularly constituted court, affording all the judicial guarantees which are recognized as indispensable by civilized peoples. (2) The Wounded, sick and shipwrecked shall be collected and cared for....
Id.

[403] GEOFFREY F. BEST, HUMANITY IN WARFARE 299–300 (1980).

[404] Geneva Convention for the Amelioration of the Condition of the Wounded and Sick in Armed Forces in the Field, supra note 398, art. 49; Geneva Convention for the Amelioration of the Conditions of Wounded, Sick and Shipwrecked Members of Armed Forces at Sea, supra note 398, art. 50; Geneva Convention Relative to the Treatment of Prisoners of War, supra note 399, at art. 129; Geneva Convention Relative to the Protection of Civilian Persons In Time of War, supra note 400, art. 146.

[405] See sources cited supra note 404.

another High Contracting Party, provided such High Contractng Party has made out a prima facie case.[406]

In addition to contributing to the development of an international criminal law and to the refinement of the law of war, the Nuremberg judgment served as a catalyst to the drafting of multilateral human rights treaties.[407] The post-World War II human rights movement was motivated in part by a desire to ensure that there would be no repetition of the type of atrocities and abuses which were committed by the German regime, as well as by a pragmatic concern that abuses of state power inevitably would lead to internal strife and renewed international instability.[408] The Western Powers also desired to identify themselves as the guardians of liberty in order to vindicate the sacrifices required during World War II and to distinguish democratic from socialist ideology.[409] The concept of Crimes Against Humanity was the intellectual inspiration for these treaties.[410] It gradually came to be recognized that individuals not only should be free from government repression, but that states should be charged with the positive responsibility for providing the minimum conditions for human development. Nuremberg primarily was concerned with German treatment of citizens of third-party states during armed conflict. The human rights movement imposed general standards of conduct on states towards their own citizens. All peoples were viewed as possessing inherent rights which transcended geography, ideology, and the sovereign prerogative of states.[411]

The rhetoric of rights was adopted by the drafters of human rights instruments to emphasize that these protections were entitlements which were enforceable by individuals as well as by states before certain international tribunals. The sphere of state sovereignty became limited by the international obligation to safeguard human rights and legal procedures. The respect for and protection of individual dignity no longer were considered to be matters of domestic jurisdiction. Instead,

---

[406] See sources cited supra note 404. A number of States have incorporated the Nuremberg Principles into their domestic penal codes. See Gary Komarow, Individual Responsibility Under International Law: The Nuremberg Principles In Domestic Legal Systems, 29 INT'L & COMP.L.Q. 21, 30–35 (1980). The Nuremberg Principles have been incorporated into United States military law. See DEP'T OF THE ARMY, FIELD MANUAL 27–10: THE LAW OF LAND WARFARE paras. 498–501 (1956), cited in Francis J. Boyle, Determining U.S. Responsibility for Contra Operations Under International Law, 81 AM.J.INT'L L. 86, 88 (1987).

[407] Burns H. Weston, Human Rights, 6 HUM.RTS.Q. 257, 271 (1984). See also Matthew Lippman, Human Rights Revisited: The Protection of Human Rights Under the International Covenant on Civil and Political Rights, 10 CAL.Q.INT'L L.J. 450, 457 (1980).

[408] See Universal Declaration of Human Rights, Dec. 10, 1948, G.A.Res. 217, 3rd Sess., U.N.Doc. A/810, at 7 (1948). The preamble, provides, inter alia, that 'it is essential, if man is not to be compelled to have recourse, as a last resort, to rebellion against tyranny and oppression, that human rights should be protected by the rule of law.' Id. at preamble.

[409] See Lippman, supra note 407, at 508–09.

[410] Weston, supra note 407, at 271.

[411] See generally UNITED NATIONS, HUMAN RIGHTS: A COMPILATION OF INTERNATIONAL INSTRUMENTS, U.N.Doc. ST/HR/1/Rev. 2, U.N.Sales No. E.83.XIV (1983).

they came to be of international concern and were recognized as fundamental purposes of the United Nations.[412] The individual citizen thus was transformed from an 'object' under international law into an active 'subject' with limited legal standing and claims against their parent state.[413]

However, in practice, the development of mechanisms for the enforcement of human rights has lagged behind the drafting of substantive protections.[414] The human rights revolution has thus provided symbolic assurance of the value and dignity of individuals while having limited practical significance. However, this is not to minimize the change in international jurisprudence and popular consciousness which has been sparked by the human rights movement.

VIII. Nuremberg and American Law

The Nuremberg Trial introduced Crimes Against Peace, War Crimes, and Crimes Against Humanity into the popular and legal lexicons. It spurred a considerable amount of activity in the areas of international criminal law, war crimes, and human rights. The Nuremberg Trial has had a limited impact on domestic jurisprudence. In the United States, criminal defendants who have acted in a nonviolent, proportionate fashion to halt government activity reasonably perceived as violating the Nuremberg Principles have been prevented from raising the Nuremberg defense.[415] The judiciary has ruled that individuals lack standing to invoke the Nuremberg doctrine, and that litigation of such claims would violate the political question doctrine.[416] It is ironic that courts in the United States, which played such a central role at Nuremberg, should refuse to entertain criminal defenses based upon the Nuremberg Principles.[417] The United States also

---

[412] See U.N.CHARTER art. 1(2)(3).

[413] See generally International Covenant on Civil and Political Rights, G.A.Res. 2200, 21 U.N.GAOR, 21st Sess., Supp. No. 16, at 52, U.N.Doc. A/6316 (1966) (opened for signature, Dec. 19, 1966; entered into force, Mar. 23, 1976) (signed by the United States, Dec. 31, 1979); International Covenant on Economic, Social and Cultural Rights, G.A.Res. 2200, 21 U.N.GAOR, 21st Sess., Supp. No. 16, at 49, U.N.Doc. A/6316 (1966) (opened for signature, Dec. 19, 1966; entered into force, Jan. 3, 1976) (signed by the United States, Dec. 31, 1979).

[414] Lippman, supra note 407, at 479–505.

[415] Such a defense would involve the claim that individuals are privileged, if not compelled, under international law to halt governmental acts reasonably believed to be in violation of the Nuremberg Principles. See infra notes 420–21 and accompanying text.

[416] See infra notes 426–45 and accompanying text.

[417] See generally Richard A. Falk, The Nuremberg Defense in the Pentagon Papers Case, 13 COLUM.J.TRANSNAT'L L. 208 (1974). It is clear that the Nuremberg Principles are part of United States law. The United States Supreme Court has recognized that both the principles of positive treaty and customary international law are binding on the United States and are to be applied by United States courts. See The Paquete Habana, 175 U.S. 677, 700 (1900). See also United States v. Smith, 18 U.S. (5 Wheat.) 153, 160–61 (1820); Lopes v. Schroder, 225 F.Supp. 292, 295 (E.D.Pa.1963). Nuremberg's binding character on United States courts is developed in William V. O'Brien, Selective Conscientious Objection And International Law, 56 GEO.L.J. 1080, 1092–94 (1968). The Nuremberg Principles also are binding on the United States as an executive

was the moving force behind the creation of a post-World War II order based upon the rule of international law.[418] Telford Taylor, who served as chief counsel for the prosecution at Nuremberg, has admonished that the 'integrity' of the United States's continuing commitment to the rule of international law requires a continued adherence to the Nuremberg Principles.[419]

The Nuremberg Principles provide a legal justification for individuals who act to halt international governmental lawlessness. Although not legally obligated to act, an individual would have been privileged under international law to violate domestic German law in order to prevent or to protest the commission of War Crimes and Crimes Against Humanity.[420] The International Military Tribunal recognized that the essence of the Nuremberg Charter was that 'individuals have international duties which transcend the national obligations of obedience imposed by the individual state.'[421] Multilateral human rights treaties are the contemporary embodiments of the spirit of Nuremberg.[422] These treaties, consistent with their humanitarian purpose, should be interpreted broadly so as to impose duties and obligations on individuals as well as on States to protect human rights.[423] The Universal Declaration of Human Rights imposes a duty on individuals to 'act toward one another in a spirit of brotherhood.'[424] The preambles to the International Covenant on Civil and Political Rights and the International Covenant on Economic, Social and Cultural Rights provide that 'the individual, having duties to other individuals and to the community to which he belongs, is under a responsibility to strive for the promotion and observance of the rights recognized in the present Covenant.'[425]

Nevertheless, United States courts have denied standing to individuals attempting to raise the Nuremberg defense where the defendants have been unable to demonstrate a specific injury or duty distinguishable from that of the general

agreement. See Frank Lawrence, The Nuremberg Principles: A Defense for Political Protesters, 40 HASTINGS L.J. 397, 405–06 (1989). See generally United States v. Pink, 315 U.S. 203, 221–26 (1942); United States v. Belmont, 301 U.S. 324, 330 (1937).

[418] See generally DANIEL P. MOYNIHAN, ON THE LAW OF NATIONS (1990).

[419] TELFORD TAYLOR, NUREMBERG AND VIETNAM: AN AMERICAN TRAGEDY 94 (1970).

[420] See generally Arthur W. Campbell, The Nuremberg Defense to Charges of Domestic Crime: A Non-Traditional Approach for Nuclear-Arms Protesters, 16 CAL.W.INT'L L.J. 93 (1986) (claiming that under the non-traditional Nuremberg defense, protesters rely on the conventional crime prevention privilege and claim they were acting to prevent a violation of international law). But see Charles E. Patterson, The Principles of Nuremberg as a Defense to Civil Disobedience, 37 MO.L.REV. 33 (1972).

[421] 22 NUREMBERG TRIBUNAL, supra note 218, at 466.

[422] See supra notes 405-12.

[423] Vienna Convention on the Law of Treaties, art. 31(c), U.N.Doc. A/CONF. 29/27, at 289 (1969) (done at Vienna, May 22, 1969; opened for signature May 23, 1969).

[424] Universal Declaration of Human Rights, supra note 408, at art. i; see also id. at art. 29(1).

[425] International Covenant on Civil and Political Rights, supra note 413, at preamble; International Covenant on Economic, Social and Cultural Rights, supra note 413, at preamble.

citizenry.[426] In the seminal case of United States v. Berrigan,[427] Judge Edward S. Northrup ruled that the defendants lacked standing to raise the Nuremberg defense to justify their destruction of Vietnam draft records. Judge Northrup reasoned that the defendants were ordinary civilians, not in danger of incurring liability under the Nuremberg Principles, and thus had no legal duty to resist specific acts which they reasonably believed to be in violation of the Nuremberg Charter.[428] In United States v. Kabat,[429] the Eighth Circuit Court of Appeals observed that it would be a 'great extension' of Nuremberg to hold that persons who 'remained passive, neither aiding nor opposing their governments' international violations were war criminals merely by virtue of their citizenship or residence in given countries.'[430] The Court concluded that since ordinary citizens incur no legal liability under the Nuremberg Principles, they can claim no privilege to violate domestic law in order to exculpate their guilt.[431] In United States v. Montgomery,[432] the Eleventh Circuit Court of Appeals observed that individuals who engage in civil disobedience impermissibly stand Nuremberg 'on its head in arguing that a person charged with no duty or responsibility by domestic law may voluntarily violate a criminal law and claim that violation was required to avoid liability under international law.'[433]

The American judiciary also has refused to recognize the standing of members of the armed forces in wartime to raise the Nuremberg Defense. In State v. Marley,[434] the Supreme Court of Hawaii ruled that a member of the Navy did not have a legal duty to criminally occupy the premises of the Honeywell Corporation in protest of the corporation's activities in Vietnam, which allegedly contravened the Nuremberg Principles.[435] The court held that 'mere membership' in the Armed Forces did not 'under any circumstances' create criminal liability under the Nuremberg Principles.[436] In Switkes v. Laird,[437] the court ruled that even if the war in Indochina was conducted in violation of both domestic and international law, a medical officer specializing in psychiatry was not entitled to

[426] See generally United States v. May, 622 F.2d 1000, 1009 (9th Cir. 1980).

[427] United States v. Berrigan, 283 F.Supp. 336 (D.Md.1968) aff'd sub nom. United States v. Eberhardt, 417 F.2d 1009 (4th Cir. 1969) cert, denied, 397 U.S. 909 (1970).

[428] Id. at 341. Standing is a procedural requirement which is designed to insure that a party has a sufficient stake in an otherwise justiciable controversy in order to obtain judicial resolution of the controversy. In part, it is based on the interest in having a case presented in an adversarial context by a party to whom proper judicial relief can be granted. In practice, it permits courts to avoid frivolous suits, advisory opinions, and unnecessary litigation. See generally Sierra Club v. Morton, 405 U.S. 727 (1972).

[429] United States v. Kabat, 797 F.2d 580 (8th Cir. 1986).

[430] Id. at 580.

[431] Id.

[432] United States v. Montgomery, 772 F.2d 733, 738 (11th Cir.1985).

[433] Id.

[434] State v. Marley, 54 Hawaii 450, 509 P.2d 1095 (1973).

[435] Id. at 452–53. 509 P.2d at 1099.

[436] Id. at 452–53. 509 P.2d at 1110–11.

[437] Switkes v. Laird, 316 F.Supp. 359 (S.D.N.Y.1970).

a preliminary injunction enjoining his transfer to Vietnam.[438] The court found it unlikely the defendant would be required to engage in acts violative of the Nuremberg Charter, and military service in Vietnam did not constitute complicity in war crimes.[439]

In addition to parties' lack of standing to raise the Nuremberg defense, courts have ruled that the introduction of such a defense is prohibited by the political question doctrine. In Berrigan, the district court ruled that whether the deployment of United States troops abroad was in compliance with international law 'is a question which necessarily must be left to the elected representatives of the people and not to the judiciary.'[440] The court denied that this was an 'abdication of responsibility' and reasoned that the political question doctrine was a recognition that the decision whether to commit troops in combat 'should be assumed by that level of government which under the Constitution and international law is authorized to commit the nation.'[441]

In Farmer v. Rountree,[442] two taxpayers claimed the right under international law to refuse payment of two-thirds of their income taxes. They alleged the taxes were being illegally appropriated by the United States Congress pursuant to a conspiracy to wage an illegal aggressive war of world domination.[443] The district court emphasized that the foreign policy of the United States is the 'exclusive province' of the executive and legislative branches and that courts should refrain from rendering any judgment which would 'embarrass the policy decisions of government or involve them in confusion and uncertainty.'[444] The court stressed that it lacked the expertise to gather and to evaluate the relevant facts and that prolonged litigation would disrupt the policymaking process.[445]

In sum, the judiciary has taken the position that to permit the public order to be disrupted 'under the aegis of international law would foment an anarchical result.'[446] They have further found no support for the proposition that a free and democratic society 'must excuse violation of its laws by those seeking to conform their country's policies to international law. Compliance with international law must be sought through the ballot box, or where appropriate, by court action.'[447]

---

[438] Id. at 365.

[439] Id.

[440] 283 F.Supp. at 342.

[441] Id. The contemporary political question doctrine appears to involve three inquiries: (1) Whether the Court is required to resolve questions committed by the text of the Constitution to a coordinate branch of government? (2) Whether the Court is required to decide questions which are beyond its expertise? (3) Whether prudential considerations mandate against judicial intervention? See Goldwater v. Carter, 444 U.S. 996, 998 (1979) (Powell, J., concurring).

[442] Farmer v. Rountree, 149 F.Supp. 327 (M.D.Tenn. 1956), aff'd per curiam, 252 F.2d 490 (6th Cir.1958).

[443] Id. at 328.

[444] Id. at 329.

[445] Id.

[446] People v. Weber, 162 Cal.App.3d Supp. 1, 6, 208 Cal.Rptr. 719. 722 (1984).

[447] In re Weller, 164 Cal.App.3d 44, 49, 210 Cal.Rptr. 130, 133 (1985).

IX. Lowering the Procedural Barriers: Recognizing the Nuremberg Defense for Political Protesters

The American judiciary's narrow interpretation of the standing requirement under the Nuremberg Principles has eviscerated the Nuremberg defense and limited its application to a narrow range of cases.[448] There have also been few instances in which prosecutors have been willing to affirmatively enforce the Nuremberg Principles against government leaders.[449] Thus, in practice, the Nuremberg Principles have been rendered a nullity within the American judicial system.

The judiciary, in rejecting defendants' standing to raise the Nuremberg defense, ignores the recognized privilege of citizen intervention to prevent the commission of a crime.[450] The exercise of this privilege is particularly compelling when civil resisters are acting on behalf of those who are abused by repressive regimes, or when civil resisters are attempting to alleviate the suffering of the victims of war. Such victims are unable to protect themselves or to redress their grievances and require assistance. Acts of protest can call attention to, and pressure the United States government to combat, these severe and ongoing violations of international law.[451]

The judiciary's approach to standing under the Nuremberg defense also overlooks the dynamic nature of international law and the expansion of international rights and duties which has occurred over the last forty years. International law, according to some scholars, has extended the Nuremberg Principles and now formally recognizes a right of non-violent, proportionate citizen resistance to states' violations of human rights. This right of ideological self-defense and the defense of others is based in part on the realization that it is futile to exclusively vest the protection of inherent human rights in the very regimes which have an interest in circumscribing criticism, dissent, due process, and the provision of social services.[452]

---

[448] Under the judiciary's strict standing requirement the defense is limited to soldiers who resist an illegal order, and to those with legal authority who intervene to prevent a Crime Against Peace or the commission of a War Crime or a Crime Against Humanity. See generally Anthony D'Amato, et al., War Crimes and Vietnam: The 'Nuremberg Defense' and the Military Resister, 57 CAL.L.REV. 1055 (1969).

[449] See generally Matthew Lippman, The My Lai Massacre and the International Law of War, in TERRIBLE BEYOND ENDURANCE? THE FOREIGN POLICY OF STATE TERRORISM 313 (Michael Stohl & George A. Lopez eds., 1988). For a discussion of one such trial in Israel, see generally, Lippman, supra note 342.

[450] See Richard A. Falk, The Circle of Responsibility, in CRIMES OF WAR 222, 229 (Richard A. Falk, Gabriel Kolko & Robert Jay Lifton eds., 1971).

[451] See generally Matthew Lippman, Disappearances: Towards a Declaration on the Prevention and Punishment of the Crime of Enforced or Involuntary Disappearances, 4 CONN.J.INT'L L. 121 (1988); Matthew Lippman, Government Sponsored Summary and Arbitrary Executions, 4 FLA-INT'L L.J. 401 (1989).

[452] See Matthew Lippman, The Right of Civil Resistance Under International Law and the Domestic Necessity Defense, 8 DICK.J.INT'L L. 349, 371 (1990).

The extension of standing to raise the Nuremberg defense to civil resisters may appear to invite a rash of criminal litigation spawned by idealistic crusaders. However, few will feel morally compelled to violate the law, expend the time and resources necessary to present a competent defense, and risk criminal conviction and punishment.[453] Civil resisters generally do not assert a vague moral right to violate the law. Instead, they seek to enforce specific legal limitations on the conduct of government.[454] In this sense, when such protesters seek enforcement of international legal norms by a domestic government, they are acting as private attorneys general on behalf of the global community.[455] A significant number of civil resisters who are permitted to offer an international law defense are acquitted by the jury at the trial court level.[456] This suggests that civil resisters, when afforded the opportunity, are able to convince others of their cause.[457]

The courts in civil resistance cases have also interpreted the political question doctrine to render civil resisters' claims non justiciable. This effectively insulates American foreign and military policies from legal accountability and contributes to the perception that international law is an irrelevant consideration in the policy-making process.[458] Justice Brennan, in Baker v. Carr,[459] rejected 'sweeping statements to the effect that all questions touching foreign relations are political questions' and noted that it was 'error to suppose that every case or controversy which touches foreign relations lies beyond judicial cognizance.'[460] Justice Stewart urged the Supreme Court to relax the political question doctrine and to adjudicate the legality of the Vietnam War under international law because these 'are large and deeply troubling questions' which will not 'simply go away' merely because Court chooses to ignore them.[461]

---

[453] Civil disobedience involves the open violation of the law and acceptance of guilt and punishment. Civil resistance, in contrast, refers to the open violation of the law and the claim that such legal violation is justified under international law. See generally Matthew Lippman, The Necessity Defense and Political Protest, 26 CRIM.L.BULL. 317 (1990). On civil disobedience, see Matthew Lippman, Civil Disobedience: The Dictates Of Conscience Versus the Rule of Law, 26 WASHBURN L.J. 233 (1987). The social science literature documents that few individuals are psychologically capable of defying authority and intervening on behalf of others. See generally H.C. KELMAN & V.L. HAMILTON, CRIMES OF OBEDIENCE TOWARD A SOCIAL PSYCHOLOGY OF AUTHORITY AND RESPONSIBILITY (1989).

[454] But see Flast v. Cohen, 392 U.S. 83 (1968).

[455] An example of the rampant disregard of international law is the systematic and large-scale use of torture in the world. See generally Matthew Lippman, The Protection of Universal Human Rights: The Problem of Torture, 1 UNIV.HUM.RTS. 25 (1979) (now titled HUM.RTS.Q.).

[456] I have regularly served as an expert in international law in trials involving civil resistance to United States nuclear and foreign policy. See Francis A. Boyle, International Law, Citizen Resistance, and Crimes by the State—The Defense Speaks, 11 HOUS.J.INT'L L. 345, 352 (1989) (concurring in the author's assertion).

[457] See United States v. Dougherty, 473 F.2d 1113, 1144 (D.C.Cir.1972) (Bazelon, J., concurring in part and dissenting in part).

[458] This has become a familiar complaint. See D.P. MOYNIHAN, supra note 418.

[459] Baker v. Carr, 369 U.S. 186 (1962).

[460] 369 U.S. at 211.

[461] Mora v. McNamara, 389 U.S. 934, 935 (1967) (Stewart, J., dissenting). See also Mitchell v. United States, 386 U.S. 972, 973–74 (1967) (Douglas, J., dissenting).

The political branches do not possess unlimited discretion in foreign affairs. The Nuremberg Principles limit the sovereign prerogatives of States, and mandate that a regime's legitimacy rests upon its respect for human rights and restraint in the use of force. Professor Jules Lobel observed that governmental actions which violate either customary international law or multilateral treaties embodying fundamental norms of international law are unconstitutional and void.[462] He argued that the latter international legal limitations, at a minimum, include actions violative of the Nuremberg Principles such as torture, genocide, the assassination of foreign leaders, and wars of aggression.[463] In urging courts to abandon the political question doctrine, Richard Falk argues that:

There is no longer any justification for the political question doctrine, which rests on the notion that the judiciary cannot displace Executive discretion. Now that international law has constrained Executive discretion, it seems appropriate for courts to administer these constraints and, indeed inappropriate to act as if no such constraints exist—which is the effect of applying the political question doctrine to a given situation.... To date, however, courts have been hiding beneath the political question cloak without even addressing the substantial question as to whether, in light of shifts in international law, this mode of defense is any longer appropriate.[464] The acceptance of the Nuremberg defense would not necessarily force courts to abandon the political question doctrine, since they would not be required to adjudicate the legality of foreign and military policy decisions. The defense merely would permit a defendant to offer evidence about the reasonableness of the defendant's belief that the government policy being challenged was violative of the Nuremberg Principles. A series of acquittals may emphasize to policymakers that their actions may be violative of international law and at variance with popular sentiments.

Democratic government rests upon an informed and vital citizenry which is able and willing to check governmental abuse. This requires a free flow of information. The judiciary would not be substituting its views for those of elected officials. It merely would permit the jury to review the conduct of the political branches of government. Disregard for the rule of law by the government is contagious and adherence to international law abroad is vital to the respect for civil liberties at home.[465]

---

[462] Jules Lobel, The Limits of Constitutional Power: Conflicts Between Foreign Policy and International Law, 71 VA.L.REV. 1071, 1137–38, 1146, 1154 (1985).

[463] Id.

[464] Falk, supra note 417, at 214.

[465] A comprehensive discussion of the constitutional relationship between the three branches of government in the foreign policy areas is set forth in Harold Hongju Koh, Why the President (Almost) Always Wins in Foreign Affairs: Lessons of the Iran-Contra Affair, 97 YALE L.J. 1255, 1305–17 (1988). See also Louis Henkin, Is There a 'Political Question' Doctrine?, 85 YALE L.J. 597 (1976). For a partial defense of judicial deference to presidential authority in the area of war powers see Abner J. Mikva, The Political Question Revisited: War Powers and the 'Zone of Twilight,' 76 KY.L.J. 329 (1987–88).

X. The Nuremberg Principles Under Attack:
A Defense

The Versailles Treaty marked the first multilateral agreement to subject defeated belligerents to comprehensive criminal trials. The plan for international prosecution was abandoned in order to bolster the stability of the post-World War I German regime. The German government bowed to domestic pressures and quickly reneged upon its agreement to initiate large-scale domestic war crimes trials. By the mid-1930's, all outstanding indictments had been quashed and the few German combatants who had been convicted and imprisoned were released.

The events of World War I and the failed effort to prosecute German war criminals fueled the movement to create an international criminal court. Although this movement met with little success, the events of World War II lent credibility to the argument that effective, international legal restraints must be placed on armed aggression. Global relations and the sophistication of weaponry also had matured to the point where acts of state violence and repression were viewed as threatening the entire world community and not merely the individual victims.

Prevailing opinion dictated that the Western Powers should severely punish those Germans responsible for the atrocities of World War II. The decision was made to place twenty-two high echelon Germans on trial at Nuremberg. This trial was not only intended to punish the leadership of the Nazi regime, but to affirm that the post-World War II era would be characterized by the rule of law rather than force.

In an age of unparalleled state military power, Nuremberg's stress on individual responsibility is a partial antidote to the unrestrained deployment of armed force. Yet it is this fundamental aspect of Nuremberg, the abrogation of the superior orders defense, which is under attack.[466] In discussing this effort, Professor Antonio Cassese notes that the 'concepts that emerged from Nuremberg—one of the high points in our march towards legal civilization and an awareness of human dignity—are in danger of being silted up.'[467] It is vital that the Nuremberg Principles should be extended and interpreted as imposing a moral, if not legal, responsibility on all citizens rather than being limited to governmental and military officials. Philosopher Robert L. Holmes observes that:

From Nuremberg we should know that the key to understanding the horrors nations perpetuate is not the evil of the occasional Hitlers of this world. It is, rather, the dedication of functionaries who serve them and of the millions of ordinary persons like

---

[466] ANTONIO CASSESE, VIOLENCE AND LAW IN THE MODERN AGE 147–48 (trans. S.J.K. Greenleaves ed. 1986).
[467] Id. at 148.

ourselves whose cooperation is essential to the success of their enterprises.[468] The American judiciary continues to strictly interpret the requirements of Nuremberg. It is hypocritical for the United States government, which was central to the development of the Nuremberg Principles, to profess its respect for adherence to international law and then to summarily convict and punish those who seek to compel the government to adhere to the rule of law.

The early common law, appreciating the weakness of governmental institutions, authorized citizens to arrest wrongdoers.[469] The international community faces severe threats to its stability, and yet has failed to develop institutions capable of controlling the self-interested criminal conduct of strong states. This threat in part can be checked by a vigorous citizenry which, as during the first four to five hundred years of the common law, takes responsibility for policing its own community and invokes the 'Nuremberg Privilege' to limit governmental abuse.

Allegiance to the state must be replaced by a loyalty to the human community and by a respect for international law. It is not the rebel who threatens civilization, but the compliant conformist who mechanically suppresses her moral qualms when confronted with the dictates of authority.[470] The German philosopher Karl Jaspers some forty years ago reflected on the subject of German guilt: 'The essential point is whether the Nuremberg trial comes to be a link in a chain of meaningful constructive political acts, or whether by the yardstick there applied to mankind the very powers now erecting this Nuremberg trial will in the end be found wanting.'[471] Richard Falk writes it is imperative that Jasper's 'Nuremberg Promise' should be fulfilled.[472]

The United Nations should begin work on a treaty to be signed on the fiftieth anniversary of the Nuremberg Trial, which affirms the Nuremberg Principles. All states should be urged to incorporate these doctrines into their domestic legal codes. A provision also should be added which explicitly provides for a legal privilege of individuals to intervene in a non-violent, proportionate fashion to halt governmental activity reasonably believed to be in violation of the Nuremberg Principles. This 'Nuremberg defense' should be recognized as exculpating a defendant from criminal liability. States also should pledge to begin concerted efforts towards the creation of an international criminal court. If states, with their characteristic reluctance, refuse to commemorate Nuremberg by drafting such a treaty, this task should be undertaken by an international assembly of concerned citizens. Government officials, military leaders, and citizens throughout the world also should be requested to sign a pledge to uphold and to further

---

[468] ROBERT L. HOLMES, ON WAR AND MORALITY 290 (1989).

[469] See generally Jerome Hall, Legal and Social Aspects of Arrest Without a Warrant, 49 HARV.L.REV. 566 (1936).

[470] See generally STANLEY MILGRAM, OBEDIENCE TO AUTHORITY: AN EXPERIMENTAL VIEW (1969).

[471] K. Jaspers, quoted in RICHARD A. FALK, REVITALIZING INTERNATIONAL LAW 222 (1989).

[472] Id.

the Nuremberg Principles.[473] The pledge campaign should be accompanied by a global educational campaign to understand and combat racism, genocide, war, and deprivation.

XI. Conclusion

The Nuremberg trial remains controversial.[474] Criticism primarily is directed at the unprecedented nature of the proceedings. The prosecution and conviction of the defendants for contravening the novel legal doctrine of Crimes Against Peace continues to be a particular source of skepticism and concern. Nevertheless, the Nuremberg Principles have contributed to the development of a corpus of international criminal and human rights law and to the refinement of the law of war.

The Nuremberg trial's practical impact, however, has been limited. It has led neither to the formation of a permanent international criminal court nor set a precedent for use in organizing subsequent multilateral or domestic war crimes trials. Yet, the Nuremberg Principles remain alarmingly relevant. The Third Reich continues to serve as a model for repressive regimes around the world. Crimes Against Peace, War Crimes, and Crimes Against Humanity are widespread.[475] The issues discussed at Nuremberg continue to be debated as successor civilian regimes consider prosecuting the members of former military regimes who have been responsible for human rights violations.[476]

In recent years Nuremberg has taken on a meaning and significance which was not anticipated by the drafters of the judgment. Nuremberg has come to represent a moral imperative for individuals to act to prevent governmental illegality.[477] The 'Nuremberg Obligation' or 'Nuremberg Privilege' flows from the judgment's stress on individual responsibility.[478] The Tribunal limited its opinion

---

[473] See generally The Nuremberg Pledge of Lawyers and Jurists (Nov. 24, 1985) in SWORDS INTO PLOWSHARES: NONVIOLENT DIRECT ACTION FOR DISARMAMENT 209 (Arthur J. Laffin & Anne Montgomery eds., 1987).

[474] This essay has not dealt with this aspect of the Nuremberg trial. Most commentators concede that the Nuremberg trial satisfied the standards of procedural justice. This view is partially challenged by Otto Kirchheimer in his classic work on political trials. See OTTO KIRCHHEIMER, POLITICAL JUSTICE THE USE OF LEGAL PROCEDURES FOR POLITICAL ENDS 341–47 (1961).

[475] See NUNCA MAS: THE REPORT OF THE ARGENTINE NATIONAL COMMISSION ON THE DISAPPEARED (English trans. 1986).

[476] See Emilio Fermin Mignone, et al., Dictatorship on Trial: Prosecution of Human Rights Violations in Argentina, 10 YALE J.INT'L L. 118 (1984); Carlos Santiago Nino, The Human Rights Policy of the Argentine Constitutional Government: A Reply, 11 YALE J.INT'L L. 217 (1985).

[477] See generally Francis A. Boyle, The Relevance of International Law to the 'Paradox' of Nuclear Deterrence, 80 NW.U.L.REV. 1407, 1431 (1986).

[478] See Lawrence, supra note 417, at 414–17.

to the liability of the defendants and minimized the collective responsibility of the German people. Yet, the Tribunal, itself, recognized that:

Hitler could not make aggressive war by himself. He had to have the co-operation of statesmen, military leaders, diplomats and businessmen.... That they were assigned to their tasks by a dictator does not absolve them from responsibility for their acts. The relation of leader and follower does not preclude responsibility here any more than it does in the comparable tyranny of organized crime.[479] It is imperative and only fitting that, on the fiftieth anniversary of the Nuremberg Judgment, we finally fulfill the 'Nuremberg Promise.'

[479] 22 NUREMBERG TRIBUNAL, supra note 218, at 468–69.

23

Nuremberg Trial: The Law Against War and Fascism

By A. M. Larin

On 31 August 1946, at the end of the 403rd open judicial hearing, the presiding judge, G. Lawrence, announced a recess and the tribunal withdrew to consider and agree on its verdict. After a month, on 1 October 1946, the judges returned to the courtroom in the Palace of Justice and read out their verdict. It was indeed an unprecedented historical document.

Peoples of the world have suffered from bloody conflicts for thousands of years, arising from the will of cruel and selfish rulers. However, on this occasion, in Nuremberg, those guilty of planning, preparing, unleashing, and waging an aggressive war, of war crimes and crimes against peace and humanity, were for the first time convicted and punished by a court.

The Nuremberg judgment belongs to history not only because of its importance and place amongst the events which culminated in victory in the Second World War. *Historism* was a method for researching and evaluating the crimes in which the accused were incriminated but also a reason for and the circumstances in which these crimes were committed.

The judgment traces the rise of the Nazi Party back to 1919, in the form of a small group comprising revanchists, anti-communists, chauvinists, and anti-Semites; the seizure and consolidation of power over Germany by Hitler's men; the replacement of a parliamentary form of government by a terrorist dictatorship; the liquidation of workers as well as bourgeoisie democratic and liberal parties; the cruellest persecution and killing of communists, social-democrats, trade union workers, and the clergy and the extermination of national minorities, especially the Jews. All these measures carried out within the state by Hitler's men were linked with the aims of the foreign policy—the revision of the borders established in Europe, the expansion of 'Lebensraum' and an energized arms race as a means of achieving these aims.

By analyzing the facts in question, the tribunal initially identified the creation of a general plan (conspiracy) of crimes against peace and the very execution of these crimes through the planning, preparation, unleashing, and waging of an aggressive war. As referred to in the verdict, the start of this conspiracy can be found back in the 1930s in Hitler's calls to conquer 'Lebensraum' at the expense of Russia and its neighbouring states, as contained in his book, *Mein Kampf.*

On the basis of documents from the archives of the German Government, the tribunal reviewed four meetings, each one a milestone in its own way, that took place on 5 November 1937, and 23 May, 22 August, and 23 November 1939, at which the accused, Goering, Keitel, and others discussed Hitler's plans with him and the aims of the aggression against Austria, Czechoslovakia, and Poland. The judgment reflects the invasion by Hitler's men of Denmark, Norway, Belgium, Holland, Luxembourg, Yugoslavia, and Greece. In particular, the attack by Germany on the Soviet Union and Germany's joining Japan in the war against the United States, were singled out.

The tribunal clearly indicated that acts of aggression were committed in each individual case in violation of peace agreements to which Germany was signatory, as well as accords on mutual guarantee, the respect of territorial status, arbitrage, and non-aggression, and came soon after reassurances from Hitler and his associates to preserve peace and respect existing borders. The attacks on Poland, Denmark, Norway, Belgium, Holland, Luxembourg, Yugoslavia, Greece, and the USSR were carried out without any declaration of war.

Under the heading of 'war crimes and crimes against humanity', the verdict initially summarized the facts surrounding the killing of POWs. It also quoted from decrees issued by Keitel on the shooting 'down to the last man' of members of detachments of 'commandos', even if they were dressed in military uniform, unarmed and had surrendered; the decree on the shooting of escapees from the POW camps of officers and NCOs; an instruction to the police on the connivance of lynching of enemy pilots in the event of a forced landing.

Noting the especially inhuman treatment by Hitler's men of Soviet POWs, the tribunal in particular referred to a letter by the accused, Rosenberg, to the accused, Keitel, dated 28 February 1942:

'The fate of Soviet POWs in Germany . . . is the greatest tragedy . . . a large proportion of them died from hunger or perished due to the harsh weather conditions. Thousands also died from typhus.

The heads of the camps have forbidden the civilian population from handing out food to the prisoners; they prefer to condemn them to starvation.

In many cases, when the prisoners were so hungry and exhausted that they could no longer walk, they were shot in front of the terror-stricken population and they did not take the bodies away.

In many of the camps, the prisoners were given nowhere to live at all, and they lay under the open sky when it was raining and snowing. They were not even given the tools to dig holes or caves.'[1]

---

[1] *Nyuremberg process nad glavnimi nemetski voyennimi prestupnikami: Sbornik materialov v semi tomah* (The Nuremberg Trial of the Main German War Criminals: Collection of Materials in Seven Volumes), vol. 7, p. 377.

The verdict contained many facts regarding the civilian population and its cruel treatment. Included in the evidence in this section is a decree from Hitler and Keitel, 'Night and Fog', on the secret transportation to Germany of citizens of the occupied territories for sentencing and punishment without their families and friends receiving word on their whereabouts or fate.[2] The tribunal also quotes the order from Kaltenbrunner on the attempts ('methods of the third degree') used during interrogations of 'communists, Marxists, "Jehovah's Witnesses", saboteurs, terrorists, members of the Resistance movement, parachutists, asocial elements, and Polish and Soviet idlers and vagrants'.[3]

The verdict shows that they killed not just those who were condemned or who had somehow come under suspicion but also the relatives of suspects and other seemingly unconnected people were taken hostage.

The concentration camps, initially created in Germany by the Nazis to isolate and oppress the opposition and unreliable elements, were transformed over time into enterprises for the extermination of people. Asphyxiation in gas chambers, hanging, shooting, starvation, forced labour, injection of highly infectious diseases, throwing from great heights—these and other means were applied in the concentration camps and 'labour camps' to kill millions of innocent people.

'The killing of the civilian population and their cruel treatment reached its peak in the handling of citizens within the Soviet Union and Poland,' the verdict recorded, 'around four weeks prior to the start of the invasion of Russia, detachments of special purpose Security Police (Sicherheitspolizei), SD and the so-called Einsatzgruppen, were created on the orders of Himmler and their purpose was to follow behind the German armies into Russia, waging a fight with the partisans and members of the Resistance group and to exterminate Jews and communists and also other groups within the population.'[4]

Jodl and Keitel set the same tasks for Hitler's troops who had invaded the Soviet Union. An extract from their order dated 23 July 1941 was quoted in the verdict: 'Considering the enormous area of the occupied territories in the East, there will only be sufficient armed forces to ensure security on these territories if any resistance is crushed using non-judicial persecution of the guilty by the armed forces, creating a system of terror which is sufficient to root out any intention to resist amongst the population. The commanders should look for the means to carry out this order by applying draconian measures.'[5]

Documenting the systematic plundering of public, private, and personal property by Hitler's men, the tribunal pointed out the different ways in which these crimes were committed: requisition and transportation to Germany of manufactured goods and raw materials from industrial plants and agriculture, manufacturing machinery, means of transport, shares, investments in banks, the introduction of a compulsory exchange rate for foreign currencies, the creation of

---

[2] Ibid., pp. 379–80.   [3] Ibid., p. 380.
[4] Ibid., p. 382.   [5] Ibid., p. 383.

inflation with the subsequent purchase of goods on the 'black market', compulsory loans in the form of 'clearing payments' and compensation for the expenses from the occupation, etc.

Hitler's men behaved in this way in all the occupied countries but they were particularly unrestrained in the East. 'In the majority of the occupied countries of the East—the tribunal acknowledged—...the economic exploitation turned into pre-meditated pillaging. This policy was introduced above all by the apparatus of the General Governorship of Poland. The exploitation of raw materials in the East was mainly associated with agricultural products and a large amount of produce was sent by the General Governorship back to Germany. Evidence of the widespread starvation amongst the Polish population of the General Governorship bears witness to the cruelty and severity with which this policy was implemented.

The occupation of the territory of the Soviet Union was characterized by pre-meditated and systematic theft. Prior to the invasion of the Soviet Union, a special economic staff, the 'Oldenburg', was created to ensure the most efficient exploitation of the territories of the Soviet Union. The German armies were supposed to find produce on the Soviet land, even if 'millions of people will be destined to starvation'.[6]

The tribunal gave appropriate attention in the verdict to the policy of slave labour which was carried out by organizing forced labour of the population of the occupied countries on their own lands and by violently deporting at least 5 million people to Germany.

The persecution of Jews is described in the verdict as 'the history of inhumanity, carried out successively and systematically on the widest of scales'. In its verdict, the tribunal documents the exploitation of anti-Semitism: the propaganda of hate towards Jews in the press and public announcements from the Nazi leaders, restrictions on family life, on employment and civil rights, organizing pogroms, arbitrary arrests and fines, seizure of property, deportation, imprisonment in ghettos and concentration camps, and, starting in 1941, the 'Final Solution to the Jewish Question'—the mass, organized killings aimed at completely exterminating the Jews in Western Europe. The verdict quotes information that emanates from Adolf Eichmann, who was fully qualified to believe that Hitler's men killed 6 million Jews, including 4 million in special human extermination locations.[7]

The tribunal found grounds to support the request from the prosecution to recognize the leadership of the Nazi Party (NSDAP), the state secret police (Gestapo), the security service of the Reichsführer SS (SD) and the security detachments of the NSDAP (SS) as criminal organizations. At the same time and for various reasons, the tribunal refused to declare the storm detachments of the NSDAP (SA), Hitler's government cabinet, the general staff and the high command of the German armed forces as criminal organizations.

---

[6] Ibid., p. 389.   [7] Ibid., 396–442.

Solving the question of the individual responsibility of persons committed to trial, the tribunal summarized its reasons for finding some of the accused guilty and subject to punishment and releasing others without punishment.

The tribunal sentenced Goering, Ribbentrop, Keitel, Kaltenbrunner, Rosenberg, Frank, Frick, Streicher, Sauckel, Jodl, Seyss-Inquart, and (in absentia) Bormann to death by hanging; Hess, Funk, and Raeder to life imprisonment; Schirach and Speer to 20 years imprisonment; Neurath to 15 years imprisonment, and Dönnitz to 10 years. Papen, Schacht, and Fritzsche were acquitted.

* * *

The question of the legality of the sentence is worthy of special consideration in terms of those norms which were applied by the tribunal during the Nuremberg Trial. This question has both formal and substantive aspects.

When something comes formally into legal force it means that the conditions prescribed by law that are required and adequate for a conviction must be present.

The International Military Tribunal decreed that the judgment of 1 October 1946 should be considered the only and highest judgment of the main war criminals. No judicial authority existed that was legally empowered to reconsider and overturn it. Therefore, the verdict of the tribunal became legally binding from the moment it was announced.

The provisions of Article 29 of the Constitution of the International Military Tribunal do not contradict this stating: 'In the event of conviction, the verdict is [to be] carried out on the orders of the Control Council in Germany: the Control Council can at any time lessen or in some way change the verdict but it cannot increase the punishment.' At the time of the Nuremberg Trial, the higher authority in Germany on issues concerning Germany as a whole was awarded to the Higher Command of the Armed Forces of the USSR, USA, Great Britain, and France, acting together to make up the Control Council.[8] As the authority with the sovereign power and bearer of the highest authority, the Control Council had the responsibility of granting pardons, as well as administrative functions, including carrying out sentences.

In the resolutions from the 4 extraordinary meeting of the Control Council on 9 and 10 October 1946, dedicated to the outcome of the Nuremberg Trial, the idea was presented that the jurisdiction of the Council related to issues of overturning, changing, and lessening the punishment in the framework of an institution of pardoning, but not to reconsider the essence of the verdict, i.e. on questions of guilt and responsibility. Therefore, the Council recognized the petitions of the

---

[8] See Soglasheniye o kontrolnom mehanizme v Germanii. Sbornik dokumentov Moskovskoi, Tegeranskoi, Krimskoi, Berlinskoi konferensii I Evropeiski konsultativnoi komissii 1943–1945 (Agreement on the Control Mechanism in Germany: Collection of Documents from the Moscow, Tehran, Crimea and Berlin Conferences and the European Consultative Commission 1943–1945), M., 1946.

SS, Gestapo, and leadership of the Nazi Party as unacceptable because in essence these were complaints against the conviction with regard to the recognition of these organizations as criminal. 'The Control Council—it was stated in the resolution—is not authorized to reconsider the verdicts of the International Military Tribunal and can only exercise the right to [issue] pardons.'[9]

At the following meeting, on 10 October 1946, the Control Council passed purely administrative resolutions—on the date that the death sentences were to be carried out and on individuals who were to be present at them.[10]

From a wider social perspective, the concept of the legality of the verdict includes its objective truth, its credibility and its conformity with the provisions of morality and the law. The verdict of the International Military Tribunal satisfies these requirements to a large degree.

By giving the accused the right to dispute their guilt and to explain any mitigating circumstances, taking into account the seriousness of the accusation, the tribunal examined on two occasions more witnesses for the defence than witnesses for the prosecution. All documents submitted as proof by the prosecution—and there were several thousand of them—were handed to the defence counsels in copy form (photostats) or as German translations.

The tribunal undertook to build its conclusion based on proof beyond doubt. In the verdict it was noted: 'The prosecution against the accused is based to a large degree on documents which they themselves composed, and whose authenticity has not been disputed with the exception of one or two cases.'[11]

The findings of the judgment on the events being investigated are supported irrevocably by references to the documents and damning evidence of the accused and by witnesses. These references were included with particular thoroughness and logical progression where the tribunal summarizes the reasons for finding the defendant guilty.

The impartiality of the judges was shown in particular in the careful and critical comparison of the accusations with the evidence collected. On this basis, in a number of cases, the tribunal found the accused guilty of some parts of the prosecution's case and not guilty of others.

Thus, Kaltenbrunner and Frank were found not guilty on the first count (general plan and conspiracy) and guilty on the third and fourth counts (war crimes, crimes against humanity);[12] Frik and Funk were also found not guilty of the first accusation but guilty on the second, third, and fourth counts (crimes against peace, war crimes, crimes against humanity).[13]

Having found Neurath guilty on all four counts, the tribunal saw, however, mitigating circumstances in the fact the Neurath 'got involved in the action

---

[9] *Nyuremberg process* (Nuremberg Trial), vol. 7, p. 545.
[10] Ibid., p. 312.
[11] Ibid.
[12] Ibid., pp. 449–51, 458–59.
[13] Ibid., pp. 459–62, 465–568.

of the security police and the SD, demanding the release of a large number of Czechoslovakians, arrested on 1 September 1939 and the release of students, arrested in the autumn of the same year. On 23 September 1941, Hitler summoned him and declared that he was too liberal and that Heidrich was heading to the protectorate in order to fight with the Czechoslovakian resistance groups. Von Neurath tried to persuade Hitler against Heidrich's missions but when he failed to do so, he resigned. Given that his resignation was not accepted, he left for a holiday on 27 September 1941 and from this day on he refused to carry out the duties of the protectorate.'[14] In doing this, Neurath set himself apart positively from the other defendants, who continued their criminal careers right until the final defeat of Hitler's Germany. The tribunal spared Neurath his life.

During the course of the court proceedings, the defence teams for the major war criminals made a series of submissions, directed, in essence, against the main London Agreement and Charter of the International Military Tribunal as the moral and legal foundations of the defence. Critics of the judgment of the tribunal later used these submissions as ammunition.

They tried to put in doubt the fairness of the verdict by pointing out that the prosecutors and judges were representatives of the victorious powers whereas the accused represented the defeated Germany and thus there was no equality between the prosecution and the defence. However, what was pointed out is merely sophism built on the arbitrary use of the concept of equality.

After the utter defeat and unconditional surrender of the Armed Forces of Germany, no government or other German authority appeared that was capable of governing the country, securing order, and carrying out the requirements of the victorious powers. As a result of these circumstances, the governments of the USSR, United Kingdom, United States, and the provisional government of the Republic of France took on the supreme authority, including authority of the central and local state organs. In these conditions, in Germany there was not and could not have been any other judicial courts, any other organ to investigate and prosecute other than the judicial courts, the organs of investigation and prosecution of the four powers.

The factual inequality of the representatives of the prosecution and the accused is not a phenomenon which is peculiar to the trial at Nuremberg. In any national system of judicial procedure, the police, investigators, and prosecutors have such authorities, material and technical means, and professional knowledge and experience at their disposal, which the defence team do not have. However, this real inequality is compensated for by the legal guarantees in favour of the defence which were set out in law or general legislation. As already noted, the defence team at Nuremberg was generously provided with such guarantees.

Lawyers at the trial never once said that despite the generally recognized principle of *nullum crimen sine lege*, their clients were being accused under

---

[14] Ibid., p. 505.

and judged according to a law that was passed after the incriminating acts had been committed. However, the verdict clarified in detail that the actions, which the defendants were accused of represented a violation of international agreements, which were signed by Germany before these actions were committed.

The crimes against peace, the war crimes, and crimes against humanity represent a sequence of wrongful acts, such as the serious consequences of an abuse of power, enslavement, torture, the killing of peaceful civilians, and unarmed POWs, the devastation of industry and agriculture in the occupied countries, the senseless destruction of towns and villages, the destruction of cultural and historical monuments, and the plundering of public and private property. These actions do not represent anything new in criminal law. Grave responsibility for their commission was provided for in the legislation of all the contemporary states, including the German criminal legislation, passed long before Hitler's men came to power and not revoked right up until their defeat. As for the fact that the crimes were committed over the course of several years using state apparatus, and involved the latest types of weapons and other technological means and reached colossal, hitherto unseen proportions, this could in no way be interpreted to benefit the defence.

The judgment of the major war criminals embodied the high principles of law and justice and this was the basis for the legality of the verdict in its widest social aspect.

As is well known, the member of the tribunal from the USSR, General-Major I. P. Nikitchenko, came to the same conclusions on the majority of the issues, permissible in the judgment, as his colleagues who were fellow members of the tribunal from the United States, the United Kingdom and the French Republic. However, he also expressed his own opinion and disagreed with the acquittal of Schacht, Papen, and Fritzsche; he thought that the punishment was not sufficiently severe against Hess and also he disagreed with the refusal to declare the Reich cabinet, the general staff and the military command of the German armed forces as criminal organizations. I. P. Nikitchenko argued his views using evidence, reviewed by the court and using generally recognized legal provisions.[15]

The Soviet lawyers who carefully followed the trial and who later analysed its results theoretically, are of the opinion that I. P. Nikitchenko was right.[16] Sharing this view, the outstanding Soviet scientist in the field of criminal law and international law, A. N. Trainin, wrote at the same time: 'Of course, there can be no trial of the consciences and conviction of the judges. The high

[15] Ibid., pp. 516–41.
[16] Ibid., example: Poltoranin A. I., Nyuremberg epilogue (Nuremberg Epilogue), M., 1983; Volkov A. F., Nyuremberg prigovor//Sovyetskoye gosudarstvo i pravo (Nuremberg Verdict//Soviet State and Law), 1976, no. 10.

tribunal under the skilled and thoughtful leadership of the presiding judge, Lord Lawrence, carried out this enormous task with great thoroughness. And the tribunal carried out its duty in association with the convictions and feeling of the judges.' There is no sense now in developing a hypothesis about the reasons for the differences between the judges on different, albeit sufficiently serious issues. What is more pressing is something else—for which the tribunal showed complete consensus: condemnation of fascism and militarism, confirmation of the principles of individual responsibility for crimes against peace, war crimes, crimes against humanity, and also for involvement in conspiracies to carry out such crimes.

24

The Law of the Nuremberg Trial: Valid, Dubious, Outdated

By Reinhard Merkel

Looking back today on the proceedings of the Nuremberg Military Tribunal, from a distance of half a century and from the perspective of a wholly changed world, the overriding impression is one of general ambiguity. This perception is not new. The problems of the proceedings proved to be a difficult puzzle for the parties involved at the time (and not just for the Germans), and they ultimately remained unresolved. Fifty years on, the dramatic changes of the world political scene have emphasized rather than erased the profile of this picture. Up until today, the history of the idea which the Nuremberg Trial was to exemplify has still not been turned into practice.

Philosophical Origins from the History of Ideas

Immanuel Kant's essay 'On Perpetual Peace' appeared almost 150 years to the day before the opening session of the Military Tribunal on 18 October 1945. Kant writes:

When we consider the perverseness of human nature which is nakedly revealed in the uncontrolled relations between nations..., we may well be astonished that the word *law* has not yet been banished from war politics as pedantic, and that no state has yet been bold enough to advocate this point of view. For *Hugo Grotius, Pufendorf, Vattel* and many other miserable comforters are still faithfully cited as the *justification* of an act of war, although their code formulated philosophically or diplomatically does not have and cannot have the least *legal* force (because states as such do not stand under a common external power), even though there is no instance on record that a state has ever been moved to desist from its purpose because of arguments backed up by the testimony of such great men.

This quote does not provide an optimistic view: international law emerges as a defunct backdrop for the power struggles of politics, its teachers as miserable comforters, its ideas of 'a just war' as a pretence for every unjust war. Because, as Kant writes, 'the way in which states pursue their right [can] never be through a trial as it occurs at an external court, but only through war; but law is neither decided by war nor its favourable outcome: victory'.[1]

More significant than the criticisms of the Nuremberg Trial is the following unquestionable conclusion: apart from everything that Nuremberg did and did not represent, the proceedings undoubtedly marked the first unequivocal attempt in world history to end the Kantian scepticism in a trial that would match the secular scale of its occasion. This attempt motivated the pathos with which the American Chief Prosecutor Jackson on 21 November 1945 outlined both its sad subject and its greater future goal:

We must never forget that the record on which we judge these defendants today is the record on which history will judge us tomorrow. To pass these defendants a poisoned chalice is to put it to our own lips as well. We must summon such detachment and intel-lectual integrity to our task that this trial will commend itself to posterity as fulfilling humanity's aspirations to do justice.[2]

Little historical discernment is necessary to understand that this hope has failed. The reasons for this failure can be identified, and I will return to them. However, the significance of the Nuremberg Trial extends far beyond this fail-ure. The question of Nuremberg's legacy for international law has been dis-cussed for a long time. At some point the question was regarded as resolved in addition to the idea of such a legacy: the usages of international politics had not confirmed the issue. In the *Frankfurter Hefte* of April 1949 an audience mem-ber at the film *Nürnberg und seine Lehren* (*Nuremberg and its Lessons*) describes her impressions during the performance. The following observation is worthy of note:

The expensive seats were about half full. Then, when the concentration camp horrors were shown, a whole row stood up and left the film en masse. Whether this was due to their physical nausea or out of protest (and against what) remains unknown.[3]

What an image of a genre! It shows the world afterwards which Robert Jackson had imagined quite differently in 1945. The cycle of Nuremberg is endlessly repeated. The experts on international law have risen and departed, not due to mean-spirited motives, but because the political actors on stage persistently ignored their heckling.

Today, nearly fifty years later, everything is supposed to be different, as of 22 February 1993. On this day, the Security Council of the United Nations decided in its Resolution 808 to create an international criminal court for the prosecution of serious war crimes in the former Yugoslavia. Three months later,

---

[1] Kant, Zum ewigen Frieden, *Akademie-Ausgabe Bd. VIII*, 1912, p. 355.

[2] *Der Prozeß gegen die Hauptkriegsverbrecher vor dem Internationalan Militärgerichtshof Nürnberg 14 November 1945–1 October 1946.* Nuremberg 1947, vol. II, p. 118.

[3] von Bayer, Das Publikum im Film, 'Nürnberg und seine Lehren', in *Frankfurter Heft* 4 (1949), p. 360.

Resolution 827 established the court's statute with legal effect.[4] The experts on international law immediately returned. They erected the tableau of 'Nuremberg 1945' larger-than-life in the background of the world political stage.

The differences between then and today cannot be overlooked. It remains unclear whether, with the establishment of the Yugoslav Court, the Security Council has brought the problems of the Nuremberg proceedings closer to a real solution, or whether it just conjured them up onto the stage of international politics as still unresolved issues. Only one aspect is unambiguous: the questions of Nuremberg, which had been declared dead for years in international law, are more alive than ever—in particular since they were first legally addressed.

The underlying thought to these issues is old. Its roots stretch back into the pre-Christian age. However, only during the epoch of the great international law classics of the modern age, between the sixteenth and mid-eighteenth centuries, the various sources from antiquity and the later legacy of the church fathers, who reasoned on war and peace, gradually took on the contours of law. The Spaniards de Vitoria and Suarez, the Italian Gentili, the Dutchman Grotius, the German Pufendorf, and the Swiss de Vattel (all of whom were, according to Kant's malicious view, 'miserable comforters') based the foundation of global law on the old Christian doctrine of St Augustine and Thomas Aquinas, i.e. the teaching of the 'just war'.[5] The *ius ad bellum* which had thereby become problematic was restricted at the same time by a humanitarian (at least in theory) *ius in bello*. The Thirty Year War posed the question of legal protection of the civilian population in sad clarity and left it unanswered. The answer came more than a hundred years later: in the first book of his *Contrat Social* Rousseau established the hypothesis that war creates legal relations exclusively between the sovereign states involved, and does not include their civilian populations. The 'enemy' can therefore only be the soldier of the opposing state, and not its citizen.[6]

In the nineteenth century, the doctrine of international law of the states of continental Europe embraced Rousseau's teaching without objection. His idea became one of the intellectual presuppositions of all attempts of the twentieth century to counter the barbarity of the reality of war with humanity, at least in the legal regulations. Rousseau's voice admittedly had no echo in English and American international law. Anyone enquiring after the psychological backgrounds to the devastating bombardment of Dresden or the atomic destruction of Hiroshima and Nagasaki at the end of the Second World War should not forget this.

---

[4] Printed in *International Legal Materials* 32 (1993), p. 1203 *et seq.*; the statute of the Tribunal ibid., p. 1203 *et seq.*; see, also, the 'report' of the Secretary-General Boutros Ghali, ibid., p. 1133 *et seq.* In the German translation, the statute of the Court and the report of the Secretary-General are annexed to *Herwig Roggemann: Der Internationale Strafgerichtshof der Vereinten Nationen von 1993 und der Krieg auf dem Balkan*, Berlin 1994.

[5] For this development von Elbe, 'The Evolution of the Concept of the Just War in International Law', in *American Journal of International Law* 33 (1939), p. 665 *et seq.*

[6] Rousseau, *Du Contract Social*, liv. 1. chap. 4 [illegible] *Vom Gesellschaftsvertrag*, Stuttgart 1977, p. 12 *et seq.*

After the First World War: First Failed Bases
for an International Criminal Law

The period preceding the problematic history of international criminal law, which has been valid since the Nuremberg trial, began with the end of the First World War. The nineteenth century left behind the legacy of a contradictory development of the international law of war: on the one hand, the classical teaching of *bellum iustum* had been worn away by the violently imposed dogma of the absolute sovereignty of the national state. Thus, a completely lawless belligerent arbitrariness of the states could take its place. Bismarck, who should have known better, writes in the third volume of his *Gedanken und Erinnerungen* (*Thoughts and Memoirs*): 'The peace-loving civilian welfare state is less appealing and less inspiring for the Christian nations of Europe than the desire to expend the blood and assets of the nation's subjects in victory on the battlefield.'[7] On the other hand, at least since the middle of the century, a growing number of conventions and codifications had attempted to draw limits of at least the *forms* of warfare through the rules of a valid *ius in bello*. The First World War demonstrated the catastrophic failure of both trends in an antithetic contrast: the factual freedom of the states had proved to be legally untenable, and the legal limitation of their forms of warfare had remained factually without effect.

The response of the victorious *entente* states consisted—at least externally—of the virtually revolutionary attempt to establish an international criminal court. The material basis in international law of applicable provisions was admittedly meagre; and the willingness of the states to create the foundations in procedural law for the establishment of such a court, if only for concrete individual cases, did not exceed the symbolic expression of indignation about the initiators of the war combined with a corresponding declaration. The body of the international *ius in bello* had been codified in treaty law to a considerable extent only a few years previously, in the Land Warfare Convention of both Hague conferences of 1899 and 1907. However, the trial of 'ordinary' war crimes, which had been traditionally based on international common law, was not to be a matter of international judgment but of each individual injured state. Such a *national* form of war management of criminal law admittedly also failed almost completely in 1919, when Germany categorically refused to extradite a total of 900 persons named as alleged war criminals. Instead, no more than twelve trials were conducted before the Supreme Court of the German Reich in Leipzig, six of which ended in acquittals. The remaining cases resulted in prison sentences of between two months and four years.[8]

---

[7] Bismarck, *Gedanken und Erinnerungen*, 3rd vol., 1919, p. 123.
[8] Cf. Mullins, *The Leipzig Trials*, 1921, see, also, Jescheck, *Die Verantwortlichkeit der Staatsorgane nach Völkerstrafrecht*, 1952, p. 51 *et seq.*—Up until today, the only place of publication

However, it was a novel attempt to punish the *initiators* of the war in inter-national law, i.e. to bring the German Emperor Wilhelm II before a 'special court' of the Allied forces, and thereby put an end to the long-uncontested *ius ad bellum* of the states through the introduction of the threat of supra-statal sanctions. Article 227 of the Versailles Peace Treaty of 28 June 1919 established the personal responsibility of the former German emperor 'for the most serious breach of international moral law and the sanctity of treaties' and provided the future tribunal with a legal foundation, i.e. 'the loftiest principles of international politics [...], the solemn obligations and international liabilities as well as inter-national moral law'. Sentencing was left to the discretion of the court without any further guidelines.[9]

With respect to international law, this document was indeed peculiar: it marked a crossing between law and morals and its defective foundation was to be openly remedied by an excess of pathos. All sorts of embarrassing excuses resonated from it because the treaty was to deduce from the unclear connection of both the legal and the moral sphere what neither one of them could achieve individually. In their note to Germany from 16 June 1919, the governments of the *entente* had already indicated that the chosen form of criminal proceedings was only to be a façade for an 'act of the highest international politics'. The decisions which the victors over Napoleon Bonaparte had made more than a hundred years earlier give a better indication of what the Allies planned to do with the German emperor after the First World War rather than the events in Nuremberg twenty-five years later: no execution or real imprisonment, but a kind of preventive detention in exile for life. The enterprise failed with the refusal of the Netherlands to extradite the emperor because it considered the accusations to be of a political nature and Wilhelm's criminal responsibility not recognizable. The Netherlands regarded itself therefore as bound by its own laws and thus to a duty to provide asylum. It would, however, willingly sub-scribe to a *future* international criminal law and a real international judicial authority with jurisdiction in criminal law.[10]

A penal provision in international law against war was thus not created in Versailles. Even more important than the public failure on the world polit-ical stage were the events behind the scenes. On 25 January 1919, the Peace Conference in Paris had formed a special commission, consisting of fifteen delegates of the *entente* powers such as Belgium, Greece, Poland, Romania, and Serbia: the 'Commission on the Responsibility of the Authors of the War and on Enforcement of Penalties'. It submitted its report at the end of March

---

of the Leipzig trials is a *White Paper* of the Reich Government, published in *Verhandlungen des Reichtags, 1. Wahlperiode 1920*, vol. 368, 1924, file copy 2584, p. 2542 *et seq.*

[9] The Treaty of Versailles. The official texts, 2nd edn 1926, p. 207.

[10] Cf. *United Nations War Crimes Commission*, History of the United War Crimes Commission, 1948, p. 239 *et seq.*

1919.[11] A reading of the almost sixty-page document, which was published, together with America's and Japan's dissenting votes, reveals a scenario of virtually all of the problems, arguments, and objections that re-emerged a quarter of a century later in Nuremberg.

Four fundamental questions were to be settled:

– Which acts are contrary to international law in the context of war?
– Which acts are simultaneously and in addition to the above question liable to prosecution?
– In which cases does the responsibility not (or not only) affect the enemy, Germany, as an entire state, but—as culpability *in criminal law—individual persons*; and does it matter whether their actions were protected by the state or not?
– And, finally: who has the authority of jurisdiction over such actions and on what legal basis?

In the first point, the 'classic' war crimes, according to The Hague Convention Respecting Laws and Customs of War on Land (whose contrariness to international law was beyond doubt), were separated from acts which had provoked or directly initiated the war. For the commission did not doubt that Germany had sought, pursued, and started the war and that Austria-Hungary had also been involved in this action. However, the document continues as follows:

The intentional initiating of a war of aggression [...] is a conduct which is not only rejected by world opinion but will also be condemned by history; however, due to the purely voluntary character of The Hague institutions for the maintenance of peace [...] a war of aggression cannot be considered as an infringement of valid law [...].[12]

The document maintains that the breach of the Belgian and Luxembourgian neutrality by the German invasion in August 1914 was to be considered differently. Germany had been under an obligation to observe the neutrality of both states because it was bound to treaties in international law from 1839 and 1867. The breach of these treaties therefore represented a particularly aggravating violation of international law. However, the committee explained, moving on to the second fundamental question, this violation was not considered to be subject to any international threat of punishment either. It was, however, 'urgent to demand that such violations of the elementary principles of international law be submitted in future to criminal sanction'.[13]

By contrast, the committee considered serious crimes *in bello* liable to prosecution, according to international law and the established practice of states. Such

---

[11] Cf. '*Commission on the Responsibility of the Authors of the War and on Enforcement of Penalties*, Report Presented to the Preliminary Peace Conference', in *American Journal of International Law* 14 (1920), p. 96 *et seq.*, 118, n. 65.

[12] Loc. cit., p. 118.

[13] Loc. cit., p. 120.

crimes had been committed in huge numbers by the German army and its allies on land, sea, and in the air, covering all manner of horrors. At this stage, the commission provided an answer to the third question: anyone who had committed or ordered such crimes or had been in a responsible position and not prevented them, was considered *personally* liable to prosecution. No level of rank in the hierarchy of power, nor even the immunity in international law of a head of state, nor the invocation of a higher order or other state licence could protect the perpetrators of such 'crimes against the laws of war and the rights of humanity' from their individual punishment.[14]

Finally, as for the question on competent jurisdiction, the commission drew the following distinction: for 'ordinary' war crimes the punitive power of the respective injured state should be recognized in international law; such crimes should therefore be tried before the military tribunals of the individual states of the victorious powers according to their respective criminal law. Actions, which by reason of their actual and moral (that is, immoral) dimensions were not feasible for the justice of an individual state, were to be handled differently: mainly acts of the state and such actions which, according to their character, would belong before an international tribunal. A 'high court' of the Allies (including a prosecution authority consisting of one of them) was to be created for such crimes. The criminal law of the tribunal could not be that of the legal system of an individual state, but should rather originate from 'the principles of international law, as those emerge from the usages of civilised nations, from the laws of humanity and the demands of the public conscience'.[15]

Reading these statements, one cannot help the incisive impression to be confronted with a preliminary blueprint for the 'London Charter' of 8 August 1945 (with the exception of the crime of 'war of aggression'), in which the victorious powers of the Second World War determined the material and procedural law for the Nuremberg Trial. Apart from the demand for a supra-statal punitive power and a universal international law, its extension to those elements which would later be called 'crimes against humanity' in Nuremberg is already recognizable.

This document then presents nothing less than the proposal for a revolution in international law. A part of the appropriated legal foundation originated literally from the preamble to The Hague Convention on War on Land of 1907. While this was certainly a high authority, it did not represent an institution where supra-statal universal penal provisions (of which it was not even aware and to which the authors of 1907 had in no way agreed) could have been confirmed.

The commission's draft failed, and not only because of politics. Aside from the Japanese dissenting vote, the document included a dissenting vote by the American delegates, Lansing and Scott, which proved crushing for the commission's proposal, arguing *sub specie* of the valid international law. It stated that there was no supra-statal punitive power; to introduce it in *ad hoc* fashion with an

---

[14] Loc. cit., p. 112 *et seq.*   [15] Loc. cit., p. 121 *et seq.*

international tribunal was to violate the fundamental principle of the prohibition on retroactive effect; acts of a state could never be punished by foreign courts because such a procedure would destroy the founding principle of international law, i.e. the independence and sovereignty of states; international law does not know and cannot use the concept of a 'crime against humanity'; for the 'principles of humanity' are historically and geographically changeable to the point of formlessness; they therefore belong to the realm of morals rather than to that of a secular law.[16] The delegate Lansing later wrote: 'By refusing to extradite the [German] emperor for a *political* act the Netherlands have made the whole world their debtor.'[17]

It is difficult not to read these lines as a sinister irony of history. The American report on the commission of 1919 spells out the very fundamental arguments which would be propounded twenty-six years later by the defence of the main war criminals in Nuremberg and be rejected there without exception and above all at the instigation of the Americans.

The Question of the Offensive War

Indeed, the preconditions in 1945 differed from those a quarter of a century earlier; the legal preconditions of the applicable norms and the factual preconditions of prosecutable actions, as well as the political preconditions between the victors and the defeated.

On the one hand, international efforts for the proscription of war had intensified in the period between the wars; on the other hand, mainly in the thirties, the ruthless unscrupulousness with which the non-democratic Great Powers fell back on the option of war for the promotion of their policies increased. On 27 August 1928, the Briand–Kellogg Pact sealed the end of the classical *ius ad bellum*. It was initially signed by 15, and then in rapid succession by another 50, states. Only defensive wars and wars of sanctions that were authorized by the League of Nations would still be permitted. Germany was among the signatories,[18] and this would play a decisive role in Nuremberg. The Covenant of the League of Nations of 1919, from which the German Reich had withdrawn in 1933, was no longer sufficient. It is important, however, that the Briand–Kellogg Pact did not establish a set of criminal sanctions for the case of its violation. For the case of a warlike aggression, its preamble merely drew the simultaneously weak and logical conclusion that an attacker could no longer invoke the other parties' duty to keep the peace governed in the pact.

---

[16] Loc. cit., p. 127 *et seq.*

[17] Quoted after Jescheck, *Die Verantwortlichkeit der Staatsorgane nach Völkerstrafrecht*, 1952, p. 63.

[18] See publication of the pact in *League of Nations—Treaty Series* 94 (1929), p. 57 *et seq.*, as well as the legal promulgation in Germany in RGBl II, 1927, p. 97.

In many respects, the Briand–Kellogg Pact laid out a rather unstable foundation for the desired prohibition of war. Its lack of sanctions, in other respects a quite typical phenomenon of international law, was the least of its problems. Hermann Jahreiss, professor of international law and defence counsel for Alfred Jodl who was later sentenced to death, spelled out the main weaknesses of the pact in June 1946 before the Military Tribunal in Nuremberg:[19] the treaty did not undertake any attempt to delineate the forbidden offensive war from the permitted war of defence. It also did not define any supra-statal authority which would be competent for such delimitation in case of conflict. The consequence of this defect was evident: the warring states claimed the appropriate power of definition *themselves* and with it, simultaneously, the power of definition of the right and wrong of their own war resolutions. The observation of one of the authors of the pact, the American Secretary of State Kellogg, to the future signatories, is not free of tragicomedy. He wrote in a note in June 1928, and thus before the conclusion of the treaty, 'Each nation is at any time and without prejudice to all the provisions of the treaty entitled to defend its territory against invasion and attack, and it alone is competent to resolve whether the respective circumstances make a defensive war necessary.'[20]

No scepticism is necessary to assume that the Briand–Kellogg Pact did not prevent a single resolution on war in the sphere of so-called realpolitik. But this fact does not repudiate its political and legal significance. The twentieth century showed for the first time the previously unknown possibility of a change in the provisions of international law, as it were, behind the back of the classical source of law, i.e. 'the practice of states': by way of a fundamentally effective, subversive grasp by the legal and moral consciousness of the peoples (not necessarily their governments) of the free Machiavellianism of power. In the remaining period of the wars of destruction, the content of the Briand–Kellogg Pact remained morally without alternative. Of course, the implicit or explicit reservations of the states could not be generalized and they always constituted a nuisance when they affected other states as well. Finally, the international verdict on the aggressors of the First World War in the conditions of an already functioning mass communication was not possible without leaving a lasting trace in the memory of the world.

The implications of the above-outlined history are as follows: regardless of how one may condemn the factual effectiveness of the Briand–Kellogg Pact, when Germany invaded Poland and thus triggered the Second World War on 1 September 1939, a provision of international law that forbade exactly this kind of action had been in place. Furthermore, Germany was bound by non-offensive treaties and subject to special prohibitions on war against those countries that

---

[19] Jahreiss, 'Der Bruch des zwischenstaatlichen Friedens und seine Strafbarkeit, Gutachten', in *Der Prozeß gegen die Hauptkriegsverbrecher vor dem Internationalan Militärgerichtshof Nürnberg 14 November 1945–1 October 1946*. Nuremberg 1947, vol. XVII, p. 499 *et seq.*

[20] Printed in *American Journal of International Law* 22 (1929), Supp., p. 109.

it later attacked, namely Poland, Belgium, Denmark, and the Soviet Union. Whether these considerations justified the *personal* culpability of the initiators of the war is a different and by far more difficult question.

The London Charter: Legal Foundation of the Nuremberg Military Tribunal

After the world had come to an end, so to speak, almost six years later on 8 August 1945, the London Agreement of the victorious four Allied Powers determined the legal and procedural foundations for the Nuremberg Military Tribunal against the major war criminals. Article 6 of the Charter states:

All of the following acts as well as any of them individually represent crimes which the Court is competent to try. The perpetrator of such crimes is personally responsible:

Crimes against peace: namely: plans, preparations, initiation or execution of an offensive war or a war violating international treaties, agreements or assurances or participation in a common plan or conspiracy to perpetrate any of the acts mentioned above.

War crimes: namely: violations of the laws of war or its customs. [. . .]

Crimes against humanity: namely: murder, extermination, enslavement, deportation or other inhuman acts, committed against any civil population before or during the war, persecution for political, racial or religious reasons, committed in the perpetration of a crime or in connection with a crime for which the court is competent, and independently of whether the act infringed the law of the country in which it was committed, or not. [. . .][21]

This passage marks the famous triple strata of serious crimes in international law against whose pattern, whether legally effective or not, all state macro-criminality has to be measured since that time. An examination of its problems can firstly eliminate the classic war crimes under Article 6(b) and the elements of conspiracy formulated at the end of point Article 6(a), as well as incidentally the organizational crimes governed in Article 9 and 10 of the Charter: the war crimes because their criminality was undisputed according to international law long before Nuremberg; and the last two because they have not played a significant role in the judgment of the Military Tribunal or in international law in the world afterwards. These definitions were included in the London Agreement due to the pressure that was put mainly by the American Chief Prosecutor Jackson. Their function was to catch members of the entire Nazi machinery who had been difficult to discern individually in a kind of dragnet of facts: the ringleaders with arguments of conspiracy, the lower ranks with organizational arguments. This

---

[21] Statute for the International Military Tribunal, in *Der Prozeß gegen die Hauptkriegsverbrecher vor dem Internationalan Militärgerichtshof Nürnberg 14 November 1945–1 October 1946.* Nuremberg 1947, vol. I, 1947, p. 11 *et seq.*

concept was a primitive and legally dubious construction, a 'catch-all' noose far beneath the level of justice as shown by the complicity theories in the legal systems of continental Europe. If the Tribunal as the presiding court had followed it in the pattern of the charges, it would have drawn presumably hundreds of thousands of subordinate sympathizers within the range of a dangerous and scarcely appropriate threat of punishment in the later trials under the Control Council Act No. 10. The court avoided this risk by treating the conspiracy hypothesis as largely superfluous and by linking the culpability of membership in an organization to the respective individual knowledge and approval of the crimes committed there. Furthermore, three of the six organisations that Jackson had declared criminal were eliminated from the verdict. However, the Gestapo, the SS, and the *Führerkorps* of the NSDAP [National Socialist German Workers' Party] remained on the criminal index.

This concentration of legal perspectives left the court (and the world afterwards) with three fundamental problems: Was the war of aggression of 1939 not only contrary to international law, but a 'crime against peace' with its authors personally liable to prosecution? Were the crimes 'crimes against humanity' (however one determines their exact criteria according to Article 6(c) of the Charter)? And could an international court claim authority of jurisdiction over the alleged acts and their perpetrators?

It is easy to see that precisely these questions had occupied the war crimes commission in Paris in 1919, which had found no convincing answer in either the Versailles peace treaty or the subsequent development of international law.

The Problem of Jurisdiction

The judicial knot could have been severed with a simple solution. The so-called 'unconditional surrender' of Germany on 8 May 1945 had granted the Allies *de jure* not only complete control over the territory of Germany; they also took over state *sovereignty* (and did not merely adopt an authority of military occupation) over Germany. This process occurred with the Allies' Four Powers Declaration on 5 June 1945 in Berlin, by which they assumed the role of sole legitimate legislator of Germany.[22] The London Charter of the Nuremberg Court could therefore have been declared an act of the German domestic legislature in international

---

[22] This hypothesis is strongly contested in international law; I follow here the astutely established view of Kelsen, 'The Legal Status of Germany According to the Declaration of Berlin', in *American Journal of International Law* 39 (1945), p. 518 *et seq.* By contrast, see, for instance, Jescheck, *Die Verantwortlichkeit der Staatsorgane nach Völkerstrafrecht*, 1952, p. 152 (with scientific evidence), who describes this contrary view as the prevailing one in international law. The Allies' *possibility* of exercising sovereign power is to be distinguished from the question of whether they actually did so with the London Charter (and the Nuremberg Trial), which cannot be accepted; see also in the text.

law. With this legal cover, the criminal competence of the Tribunal would no longer have been a problem.

I am disregarding the dispute which immediately arose between the experts in international law over the admissibility of combining the occupying regime with the complete annexation of the defeated state. Apart from lacking any precedent-setting example in international law, the sketched-out construction had another severe weakness in the opinion of the Allies. Being a law of the bearer of German sovereignty, the London Charter would have counted as German law. However, a competence to create (or even only to define) international offences could not have been justified in this way because both the Charter and the court would have been confronted with the obvious and weighty problem of the prohibition of retroactive effect in criminal law, which they absolutely sought to avoid since the German law of the previous twelve years had made the alleged offences exempt from punishment (even if in individual cases only by way of the ominous, but *de facto* effective *Führerbefehl* [order of the head of state, the *Führer*]). In this way, the preamble and Article 1 of the Charter, which ascribed jurisdiction to the court 'in the interest of all nations' and over 'the major war criminals of *the European Axis*', i.e. also over non-German perpetrators, would have also become incomprehensible, as this was a possibility which was quite inaccessible to German sovereign power. All of these facts would have contradicted the sense of the Tribunal which sought to characterize the alleged acts for what they were: the most serious and unprecedented violations of international law. A formal 'German' court, admittedly composed of non-German judges with domestic German jurisdiction, even as a sort of trustee of the world, would definitely have been *politically, symbolically*, and, in view of the desired precedential character of the trial for the future of international law, also *juridically* the wrong instrument. The court did not avoid these problems, though it cannot be claimed that it resolved them appropriately. It supported its executive authority of jurisdiction (and that of the London Charter) with an ambiguous mixture of sovereignty and global law, but left no doubt that as an international tribunal it applied international law.[23] While one can agree with its result, one can hardly sympathize with its confused establishment.

There were, however, far more important objections. In an astute criticism of the Nuremberg proceedings in 1947, Hans Kelsen, the most significant German philosopher of law, who himself had fled from the Nazis to America, called the London Charter a *privilegium odiosum* of the victorious powers. Disregarding a fundamental principle of justice, they had made themselves the exclusive legislators and judges in their own affair and in so doing consulted neither the

---

[23] Judgment of the IMT, in *Der Prozeß gegen die Hauptkriegsverbrecher vor dem Internationalan Militärgerichtshof Nürnberg 14 November 1945–1 October 1946*. Nuremberg 1947, vol. I (hereinafter 'IMT judgment'), p. 244 *et seq.*

representatives of the defeated states nor of neutral ones. Kelsen's analysis closes as follows:

If the Nuremberg principles contain not only a judicial, but also a legislative precedential effect, then after the next war the governments of the victors will try the governments of the defeated states for such crimes as are defined unilaterally by the former and with retroactive effect. Let us hope that there will be no such precedential effect.[24]

The Prohibition of Retroactive Effect

To this day, another objection, presented as an instrumentalized dissonance, has been added to the reception of the Nuremberg Trial: the prohibition of retroactive punishment for acts which at the time of commission had not been liable to prosecution. While that prohibition could not affect the established prosecutability of classic war crimes in international law, it did have an impact on the other two alleged offences, that of the aggressive war and that of crimes against humanity.

Indeed, they were affected. The draftsmen of the London Charter had recognized the problem. A memorandum of the English Government from 23 April 1945 therefore demanded the abandoning of the plan for legal proceedings and requested in its place the 'summary execution' after apprehension of the political and military leadership of the Germans.[25] The Charter included a tactically clever but rather confusing solution for the crimes against humanity. In Article 6(c), those crimes were declared liable to prosecution only insofar as their commission was directly connected to the other two crimes related to war that were discussed in the Charter. The court implemented this criterion as a rough pattern of temporal coincidence. All acts fitting the description of crimes against humanity, but committed by Germans against Germans before the beginning of the war in September 1939, fell through this filter and remained not liable to prosecution. The court shied away from an overly clear intrusion into the tenet of absolute state sovereignty. An observation by Robert Jackson during the London consultations at the end of July 1945, while appearing somewhat hopeless, is, however, objectively unfounded, nothing other than a precisely informed confession of the valid—or rather invalid—international law:

How Germany treats its own citizens [...] is of as little concern to us as our affairs are to other governments.[...] The reason why this programme of destruction against the Jews and the devastation of the rights of minorities receive international significance is this: they were part of the plan for an illegal war.[26]

---

[24] Kelsen, 'Will the Judgement in the Nuremberg Trial Constitute a Precedent in International Law?' in *International Law Quarterly* 1 (1947), p. 153 *et seq.*, 171.

[25] Quoted in Jescheck, *Die Verantwortlichkeit der Staatsorgane nach Völkerstrafrecht*, 1952, p. 140 *et seq.*

[26] *Department of State, Publication 3080, Report of Robert H. Jackson, United States Representative to the International Conference on Military Trials*, 1947, p. 331 *et seq.*

'As outrageous and appalling as many of these crimes were,' the later verdict of the Tribunal states, it could still not be assumed 'that acts carried out before 1939 were crimes against humanity according to the definition of the Charter.'[27]

This was a painful discord which could hardly be blamed on the Nuremberg judges. Even for its actual authors, the draftsmen of the London Charter, this discord was rather part of a half-unconscious duplicity that was, in other respects, thoroughly honourable in its motives. The prohibition of retroactive effect was respected for good reason as a fundamental principle of justice. Crimes of a sovereign state leadership against its own citizens counted at the time exclusively as 'domestic affairs' and therefore were not liable to prosecution in international law. In line with this regulation, the individual perpetrators could certainly not have been persecuted (though one has to take into account that the 'humanitarian interventions' against this sort of state macro-criminality that is accepted within narrow limits in international law do not have a criminal but a quasi-policing preventative character). In contrast, those responsible for the most incomprehensible crimes in human history were sitting in the dock in Nuremberg. Again, for good reason, it was not desirable to let them go unpunished. These acts were thus forced *de jure* into a scarcely plausible functional connection with the war crimes whose criminality was defined in international law. The context was then essentially reduced to mere simultaneity and the hope was obviously that such a reflex criminality would be able to get around the prohibition of retroactive effect, or even better, observe it! This procedure could not be conclusively justified. It was impossible to have both, the prohibition of retroactive effect and prosecutability of the 'crimes against humanity' in international law.

The punishment of the perpetrators was still the right thing to do; however, the construction foisted on it was wrong. A more courageous and above all more honourable establishment would have openly acknowledged the breach of the prohibition of retroactive effect—and justified it, for there were conclusive arguments for it. Like all legal principles, however fundamental they may be, the prohibition of retroactive effect cannot be considered absolute. In case of conflict with other, equally important principles, the process of consideration has to resolve the priorities and posteriorities of the clashing provisions of the concrete decision. The principle that the most reprehensible acts should not remain unpunished if the legal consciousness of the watching public were not to be shaken with consequences too difficult to foresee received such weight with the incomprehensible dimension of the crimes to which it was to apply in Nuremberg that it must have been stronger than the ban on retroactive effect, stronger than the legal cover as a source of power which the perpetrators themselves had created. In view of this clash of principles, the court in Nuremberg was confronted with an emergency problem of provisions of virtually secular dimensions. There is no doubt that the resolution of the conflict in favour of punishment was correct. However,

---

[27] IMT Judgment (note 21), p. 285 *et seq.*

one should have openly acknowledged this issue. The cock-eyed justification of the Nuremberg verdict in this question damaged its moral and legal force.

Another Unsolved Problem: The Criminality of the Offensive War

The problem recurred in the framework of Article 6(a) of the Charter with respect to the criminality of aggressive wars. Here, the right solution was also found with the wrong justification. The judgment states:

The nations which signed or acceded to the [Briand–Kellogg Pact] unconditionally proscribed war as a tool of politics for the future and openly renounced it...The court is of the view that the solemn renunciation of war as a tool of national politics necessarily includes that such a war is contrary to international law and that those who plan and conduct such a war with all its unavoidable and terrible consequences commit an offence.[28]

The determination of war as contrary to international law was correct, but its characterization as criminal was in contrast a 'non sequitur' and wrong. No source of international law, neither treaties nor practise of states nor the complex 'legal principles of all civilised peoples' (which the indictment among others invoked) had delivered such a criminal verdict on aggressive wars until 1939. The defence counsel in Nuremberg conclusively submitted this fact. The court rejected the objection with an obviously wrong argument, drawing an analogy between the Briand–Kellogg Pact and The Hague Convention on War on Land. It argued that those documents did not expressly speak of criminality of the classic war crimes either, but that their punishment was uncontested practise in international law.[29] While this was true, this had been also the case long before The Hague agreement. It was presupposed by The Hague Convention on War on Land and drawn from elsewhere; it was, however, not regulated, just as the Briand–Kellogg Pact did not regulate the criminality of the offensive war.

The London Charter also broke the prohibition of retroactive effect in this case, and the court, responsible for its implementation, undertook great efforts to prove the opposite. However, this task proved impossible. There are arguments that a deep awareness of this circumstance, not to mention a bad conscience, ultimately gained validity in the sentencing. The verdict states at the beginning that the aggressive war 'is not only an international crime; it is the supreme international crime differing only from other war crimes in that it contains within itself the accumulated evil of the whole'.[30] This statement is absolutely incompatible with the verdict against those of the Nuremberg accused who were

[28] Loc. cit., p. 246.
[29] Loc. cit., p. 246 *et seq.*
[30] Loc. cit., p. 207.

condemned exclusively for 'crimes against peace' or, in addition, for war crimes—such as Rudolf Hess or Grand Admirals Dönitz and Raeder—who received only prison sentences, while Julius Streicher, for instance, was sentenced to death for his crimes against humanity alone.

This contradiction cannot be logically smoothed out. It should, however, reveal that the court was not really convinced of the criminality of the aggressive war in international law either, nor of its supremacy on the scale of macro-criminal reprehensibility. Even here, an open acknowledgement of a breach of the prohibition of retroactive effect would have been able to establish the desired result of criminality. At the end of the most terrible war in human history, the time had come to realize that there was no moral, no legal, and no political alternative to the criminalization of its initiators (and those of all future wars). Even in this case, an urgent deliberation between the principles of the prohibition of retroactive effect, on the one hand, and protection of the foundations of civilization in criminal law on the other, would have been necessary and decisive, in favour of the latter. This is because the legal basis for the confidence of the initiators of the war in the constant impunity of their actions—and this is the protective idea of the prohibition of retroactive effect—had become wafer-thin in 1939 due to the demand for prosecutability of the Paris Commission of 1919, by the renunciation of war in international law in the Briand–Kellogg Pact and by other efforts and agreements of the period between the wars.[31] The final step to punishment in 1946 was small enough and the exorbitance of its cause so immense that the breach of the still valid prohibition of retroactive effect could have been justified.

The fragility of the justification at Nuremberg favoured perhaps the post-1950 shamelessly claimed *ius ad bellum* of states, including those sitting in court in Nuremberg. If any part of the Nuremberg decision remained a dead issue, it was the part on the criminality of the aggressive war in politics and international law.[32]

The Problem of '*Tu Quoque*': Same Law for All or 'Victors' Justice'?

Even more than the defects of its justifications, the general infringement of a principle of fair trial mars the image of the Nuremberg Trials: the exclusion of any '*tu quoque*' arguments for the defence. This becomes blatantly obvious in an observation of the English presiding judge, which is captured in the record

---

[31] Cf. on this point, Jescheck, *Die Verantwortlichkeit der Staatsorgane nach Völkerstrafrecht*, 1952, p. 68 *et seq.*; cf., also, 'Harvard Research', Draft Convention on Aggression', in *American Journal of International Law* 33 (1939), supp. 4, p. 819 *et seq.*

[32] Cf. on this point Murphy, *Crimes Against Peace at the Nuremberg Trial*, in Ginsburgs/Kudriavtsev (eds.), *The Nuremberg Trial and International Law*, 1990, p. 141 *et seq.*, 153.

of 14 May 1946. Lord Justice Lawrence cut off the defence's attempt to prove similar war crimes that the accused were charged with on the side of the Allies. He said: 'And by the way, we are not sitting here in court to decide whether other powers have committed breaches of international law, crimes against humanity or war crimes. Here we are dealing with whether these accused have committed such atrocities.'[33]

The dry and somewhat cynically arranged logic of this sentence conceals the circumstance that in numerous cases the acts of the accused could not be appropriately judged without a clarification of the *tu quoque* charge against the former war enemy. Violations of The Hague Convention on War on Land could, for instance, simply be war crimes, but they could also be reactions to similar acts of the enemy armed forces and thus be justified as reprisals. One example may suffice: when in the First World War, the German army began with the barbaric use of poison gas (in opposition to international law), the English armed forces reacted with the same means. The verdict of war crime could only affect the German use of poison gas and not the English usage, which was justified as a reprisal or via the *tu quoque* argument.

The fact that practically all offers of evidence by the defence regarding breaches of international law by the Allies were rejected as insignificant increases the impression of a shabby policy prevalent at the Nuremberg proceedings. There was, however, one exception: the verdict explicitly dropped the charge of war crime against Dönitz and Raeder for the torpedoing of English merchant ships by submarines; the defence had proven that the merchant ships were armed and had the order to ram German U-boats where possible. The defence even submitted details on the surprise torpedoing of Japanese merchant ships by the American submarine fleet in the Pacific, and the court made an exception and heard this information.[34]

On 2 October 1946, one day after the announcement of the verdict in Nuremberg, the *Chicago Tribune* wrote in its leader article: 'The truth is that none of the victors was free of the guilt for which their judges punished the defeated.'[35] To allow such a determination even during the trial would not have blurred the giant differences between Germany and the Allies. However, it would have outlined the moral components of the trial ever more distinctively. It is difficult to dispute, for instance, that the devastating carpet-bombing of open German cities towards the end of the war was a serious war crime. The charge in Nuremberg, as well as the verdict of the IMT, avoided with embarrassing caution any mentioning of the bombing of cities on both sides. At the time, this procedure may have

---

[33] *Der Prozeß gegen die Hauptkriegsverbrecher vor dem Internationalan Militärgerichtshof Nürnberg 14 November 1945–1 October 1946.* Nuremberg 1947, vol. XIII, p. 575 *et seq.*

[34] Cf. IMT verdict (note 22), p. 353 *et seq.*, 358; see also the negotiation notes that formed the basis for the verdict in *Der Prozeß gegen die Hauptkriegsverbrecher* (note 34), vol. XIII, p. 258 *et seq.*

[35] Quoted in Wright, 'The Law of the Nuremberg Trial', in *American Journal of International Law* 41 (1947), p. 45, n. 22.

been an act of clever politics. However, this behaviour probably damaged the image of the trial more in the eyes of the world afterwards than such political cosmetics could have justified.[36]

In the context of the crimes against peace, the court's handling of the *tu quoque* argument emerges as thoroughly sinister. On 30 November 1939, the Soviet Union attacked Finland, and in June 1940, it occupied the Baltic and parts of Romania, i.e. for its part, the Soviet Union conducted a war of aggression. However, the greatest embarrassment for the court resulted from the circumstance that the German invasion of Poland and the subsequent beginning of the World War had been effected with the intentional and conspiratorial backing of the Soviet Union, negotiated namely in the 'secret additional protocol' of the Hitler–Stalin Pact of 23 August 1939. There was no doubt that this fact satisfied the elements of crime against peace by way of 'participation' according to Article 6(a) of the London Charter, indeed participation in the very war of aggression against whose initiators the Soviet Union was also sitting in court in Nuremberg. The question of whether the signing of the Pact by Stalin was to be mentioned became a subject of controversy in the court's deliberations of the verdict and was finally resolved by complete silence.[37]

Numerous *tu quoque* references of the defence addressing the Soviet Union's offensive wars were blocked in later trials held under the Control Council Act No. 10, with the stereotypical argument that this fact would not be addressed because it could not justify the German aggression. While this is certainly correct, it virtually manifests a ruthless attack on the foundations of a fair trial, namely, when one of the judges has participated in the criminal act. If anything, the term 'victors' justice', hissed through clenched teeth for years after the Nuremberg Trial, has gained a certain justification from this circumstance. Hans Kelsen, who perhaps understood more clearly than any of his contemporaries what was at stake, demanded already in 1944 an independent, impartial, and genuinely international criminal court that was to be established according to an international treaty which was to be signed by all the involved parties, including the defeated:

Only if the victors subject themselves to the same law which they seek to apply to the defeated, will the idea of justice remain unscathed.[38]

It remained an unheeded and unthinkable warning.

---

[36] Cf., also, the criticism at Jochnick/Normand, 'The Legitimation of Violence: A Critical History of the Laws of War', in *Harvard International Law Journal* 35 (1994), p. 49 *et seq.*, 89: considers that by wholly ignoring this devastating form of warfare, the IMT implicitly justified the connected mass destruction of the civilian population; similar, Woetzel, *The Nuremberg Trials in International Law*, 1962, p. 176 *et seq.*

[37] On this point cf. the informative observations in Smith, *Der Jahrhundertprozeß*, 1977, p. 121 *et seq.*

[38] Kelsen, *Peace through Law*, 1944, p. 114 *et seq.*

Nevertheless: The International Military Tribunal was a Necessary Revolution of International Law

Yet none of these objections (which are in no way complete) address the historical significance, the effect in international law, or even the moral consequences of the Nuremberg Trial. Nuremberg completed in an exemplary act the revolution in international law which had failed in 1919. No counter, trace-covering practice of the states in the following era of the Cold War could destroy the fundamental idea of the Trial: that the self-legitimization of all state power is limited by the law of humanity; and that the perpetrator who disregards these limits is called to account *individually*, against which no state cover for his acts can protect him. Despite all this, Nuremberg was the first attempt in world history to respond in the *forms of the law* to unprecedented excesses of power. There is little wonder that this attempt did not fully succeed, in any case, it is less surprising than the fact that it could prevail at all against the demands for completely different reactions. In his book *Closing the Ring*, Winston Churchill cites one of those, a proposal by Stalin made at the Moscow Conference of the Allies in November 1943: simply to shoot 50,000 German officers and technicians after the end of the war. The participants at the conference treated the proposal as a joke, but in 1951, Churchill writes that he was still not convinced that there was not a serious intention behind it.[39]

More important than the achievements and failures in Nuremberg itself were, however, the repercussions of the Trial. Despite the contrary assertion of the court, it helped create new law in both the question of *corpus delicti* and in that of a universal jurisdiction. While the law developed differently, or at least separately in both realms, in certain respects it did not differ at all.

On 11 December 1946, the General Assembly of the United Nations ratified the 'principles of international law in accordance with the statute of the Nuremberg Tribunal',[40] without the existence of even an approximate clarification of the content, scope, or even the 'if' of the validity of these principles. In July 1950 the specially created 'International Law Commission' of the UNO submitted the draft of a codification of the Nuremberg principles.[41] One year earlier, in Geneva, the four great Conventions of the Red Cross for the development of the laws of war had been signed and a duty to punish perpetrators had been imposed on the signatory states in a common rule of so-called grave breaches of the conventions.[42] In 1977, the Geneva Conventions were expanded to include two additional protocols which were adopted in this form by virtually all members of the international

---

[39] Churchill, *Closing the Ring*, 1951, p. 373 *et seq.*
[40] Printed in Schindler/Toman, *The Laws of Armed Conflict*, 3rd ed. 1988, p. 921.
[41] Printed in *Yearbook of the International Law Commission II* (1950), p. 374 *et seq.*
[42] Printed in Berber (ed.), *Völkerrecht—Dokumentensammlung, Bd. II.*, Konfliktsrecht, p. 1950 *et seq.*

state community. In December 1948 the General Assembly had passed the 'Genocide Convention' and thereby initiated the transfer of a certain area of the crimes against humanity into the harder mode of validity of treaty law. In 1954, the International Law Commission (ILC) of the UN finally submitted the first complete draft of a comprehensive codification in international law of 'Crimes Against Peace and the Security of Humanity'; it has been improved several times since then, and was adopted in 1991 by the ILC in its then final version.[43]

These examples were all attempts to anchor the material principles of Nuremberg more firmly, to spread them more widely and to define them more clearly than the verdict of the Military Tribunal qua precedent effect would have been able to do. The states showed themselves much less inclined to embrace the idea of creating an international jurisdiction competent for the application of these provisions. Two fundamental possibilities were (and are) available in this respect: the supra-statal institution of an international criminal court and thereby the real subordination of international crimes and the perpetrators to the direct competence of international law—i.e. the Nuremberg model—or a delegation of the implementation of provisions to the legal systems of individual states via the enabling in international law of a so-called 'universal jurisdiction', namely, a competence of each state to prosecute such acts according to its own laws, independently of where the offences were committed and the nationality of their perpetrators. The first option, the plan for a permanent international criminal court, faded with the consolidation of the various fronts in the Cold War due to the states' total lack of interest to engage with an abstract utopia, and it finally disappeared from the agenda of international politics. By contrast, the principle of universality was integrated into a network of treaties in international law, albeit hesitatingly and half-heartedly, and for the most part by way of a secondary, quasi trustee 'intercept' competence of all signatory states for cases in which the primarily competent domestic administration of justice could not or would not pursue criminal prosecution.[44] Strangely enough, however, the Genocide Convention of 1948 excludes a universal jurisdiction over acts of genocide in its Article VI and demands in its place the classic principle of primacy of state jurisdiction, i.e. the principle of territoriality, which means that the trial has to occur in the country where the perpetrator committed his offences.[45]

Independent of the ambivalent attitude of the states to the principle of universality, its fundamental weaknesses have emerged since 1945—simultaneously with its gradual implementation for individual crimes. It is by no means only,

---

[43] Printed in *International Legal Materials* 30 (1991), p. 1584 *et seq.*; also Ferencs, 'An International Criminal Code and Court: Where They Stand and Where They're Going', in *Columbia Journal of Transnational Law* 30 (1992), p. 375 *et seq.*, 379 *et seq.*

[44] More specifically, cf. Clark, 'Offenses of International Concern: Multilateral State Treaty Practice in the Forty Years Since Nuremberg', in *Nordic Journal of International Law* 57 (1988), p. 49 *et seq.*, 58 *et seq.*

[45] Cf. Article VI of the Convention on the Prevention and Punishment of Genocide.

and certainly not first and foremost, an expression of solidarity between the states on the prosecution of 'universal' crimes and their perpetrators as *hostes humani generis*. Rather, it can also be abused as an instrument for securing individual state interests which, contrary to international law, could thus interfere with the jurisdiction of other countries. The functioning of international prosecution of crime over competing national competences does not only largely depend on the (unenforceable) good will of the interested parties, but also on their willingness and capacity to agree as states in case of a conflict of jurisdiction, and thereby also on a complex network of provisions of extradition rules in domestic and international law. Moreover, all of these areas are to a large extent sensitive to politics; in case of doubt, they are always at the disposal of prior foreign policy interests. Yet, even if the principle of universality could function beyond these obstacles, a global splintering of the judgment and sentencing criteria for the same types of international crimes according to the respective different provisions of the individual legal systems would still be the result. However, connected to this aspect is not only a state of legal insecurity, but—as such crimes are, depending on their severity, the subject of international interest—also the risk of inscribing a feeling of a fundamental and politically accepted injustice into the consciousness of world opinion within this sensitive area of international law.[46]

It is not so much the practical inadequacy of criminal prosecution that is the most aggravating consequence of these defects. It is, rather, the symbolic erosion of material international criminal law itself. This calls into question the actual relevant reason why such acts should be prosecuted before an international criminal court and not by individual, more or less inclined but in any case uncontrolled, state 'trustees'. Two-hundred years ago, Kant already recorded in his essay, 'On Perpetual Peace', the thought that the increasingly closer communication between people would allow grave violations of human rights in *one* place on the earth to be felt by *all* of the others.[47] This claim points to a universal responsibility that extends far beyond the mere emotional interest of eye-witnesses who are informed by television. A violation of fundamental human rights is felt in every place because it is simultaneously a violation of the human rights of all. This is because it infringes the foundations of the international community itself by denying its fundamental standards.

In addition, the legitimizing reason of the threat of punishment in international law is thus finally named. The primary goal of punishment in international law cannot be the *retaliation* against the perpetrators, as Kant would have demanded in line with a metaphysical idea of justice, but neither, as today's international law repeatedly claims, the *deterrence* of possible future imitators. The goal is rather to *symbolically restore the broken standard itself* in the name of

---

[46] Cf. on these problems Merkel, Universale Jurisdiktion bei völkerrechtlichen Verbrechen, in Lüderssen (ed.), *Aufgeklärte Kriminalpolitik oder Kampf gegen das Böse- ein Gegensatz?* vol. IV (in print).

[47] Kant, Zum ewigen Frieden, *Akademie-Ausgabe Bd. VIII*, 1912, p. 360.

humanity, to defend its validity against its politically motivated breach and thus to assert and implement it as the stronger power in its constant struggle against state power. It may not be the scope of the concretely caused evil which allows a crime against humanity to be felt worldwide as a violation of law. It is the symbolic damage to the validity of the standard itself which the violation without sanction of a basic standard of civilization must leave behind in the consciousness of the addressee of those standards—which means the whole of humanity—that makes the act a matter for the whole world. Standards that are broken without sanction erode and finally disappear, however fundamental they may have been. The real task of international criminal law is to prevent this from happening in the area of its competence and thereby to help secure a legal foundation of humanity.

This leads us back to the Nuremberg proceedings. Beyond all individual weaknesses of the Trial and against the shameful repudiation of its principles by the international politics of the following decades, its remaining appeal is the following: that there should be a human right above all state power and that the worst forms of its violation must be defended by means of criminal law. We do not know when the world of realpolitik will be ready to heed this appeal. Yet, this much can be said: the spirit of the Nuremberg principles is more alive today than since the event of their first realization. Thus, at the end of this dark century, some light begins to emerge over its darkest criminal trial, slowly, yet distinctly, illuminating the values that provide it with meaning: the aura of its immortality.

25

The 'Nuremberg Legacy'

By M. Cherif Bassiouni*

The wrongs which we seek to condemn and punish have been so calculated, so malignant and so devastating, that civilization cannot tolerate their being ignored, because it cannot survive their being repeated.

Robert H. Jackson
Opening Speech for the Prosecution
Nuremberg, 21 November 1945

Introduction[1]

On August 8, 1945, the London Charter was signed, opening the way for the prosecution of the major war criminals of the European theater of operations before the International Military Tribunal (IMT) sitting at Nuremberg.[2] The

---

* This article is a modified English version of *Das 'Vermächtnis von Nürnberg:' eine historische Bewertung fünfzig Jahre danach*, Strafgerichte Gegen Menschheits-Verbrechen (Gerd Hankel & Gerhard Study eds., 1995) and is reprinted herein with permission.

[1] See M. Cherif Bassiouni, *International Criminal Investigations and Prosecutions: From Versailles to Rwanda*. *See generally* Roger S. Clark, *Nuremberg and Tokyo in Contemporary Perspective, in* The Law of War Crimes 171–187 (T.L.H. McCormack & G.J. Simpson eds., 1997); Matthew Lippman, *Nuremberg: Forty-Five Years Later*, 7 Conn. J. Int'l. 1 (1991); M. Cherif Bassiouni, Nuremberg Forty Years After: An Introduction, 18 Case W. Res. J. Int'l L. 261 (1986); *Forty Years After the Nuremberg and Tokyo Tribunals: The Impact of the War Crimes Trials on International and National Law, in* Proceedings of the Eightieth Annual Meeting of the American Society of International Law (Apr. 1986) (containing comments by Telford Taylor, Jordan Paust, Richard Falk and M. Cherif Bassiouni); M. Cherif Bassiouni, *International Law and the Holocaust*, 9 Cal. W. Int'l L. L. J. 202 (1979); Hans Ehard, *The Nuremberg Trial against Major War Criminals and International Law*, 43 Am. J. Int'l L. 223 (1949); Robert H. Jackson, *Nuremberg in Retrospect: Legal Answer to International Lawlessness*, 35 A.B.A.J. 813 (1949); Hans Kelsen, *Will the Nuremberg Trial Constitute a Precedent in International Law?*, 1 Int'l L. Q. 153 (1947); Georg Schwarzenberg, *The Judgment of Nuremberg*, 21 Tul. L. Rev. 329 (1947); Quincy Wright, *The Law of the Nuremberg Trial*, 41 Am. J. Int'l L. 38 (1947).

[2] Agreement for the Prosecution and Punishment of Major War Criminals of the European Axis, 8 Aug. 1945, 59 Stat. 1544, 82 U.N.T.S. 279, E.A.S. No. 472, *reprinted in* 39 Am. J. Int'l L. 257 (1945) (Supp.), 1 Ferencz 454, 1 Friedman 883. Schindler/Toman 823; Annex to Prosecution and Punishment of Major War Criminals of the European Axis, 8 Aug. 1945, 82 U.N.T.S. 279, 59 Stat.

following year the Allies established the International Military Tribunal for the Far East (IMTFE) in Tokyo, a counterpart tribunal for the major war criminals of the Asia-Pacific theater of operations.[3] The two, however, are legally distinguishable. The IMT was established by a treaty, originally signed by the Four Major Allies and acceded to by nineteen European states. The IMTFE, however, was established by the military order of General Douglas MacArthur pursuant to his authority as Supreme Allied Commander for the Pacific.

After World War II, many in the world community expected the post World War II trials of the major war criminals, particularly those of the IMT, to be the precursors of a permanent international criminal court, a hope that had been entertained since the end of World War I.

The IMT proceedings gave way to the 'Subsequent Proceedings' under Control Council Order No. 10 (CCL 10). Under CCL 10, the Four Major Allies conducted prosecutions in their respective zones of occupation.[4] Australia, China, France, the Netherlands, New Zealand, the Philippines, and the U.S.A. established military tribunals that prosecuted over 5,596 individuals. The USSR also prosecuted a number of Japanese POWs, but their number is not known.

Various European countries that had been occupied by Axis powers also carried out domestic prosecutions. However, these trials mostly concerned their respective nationals who had collaborated with the occupying forces.[5] The United States also prosecuted Japanese officers for 'War Crimes' by virtue of the military authority of General Douglas MacArthur as the Supreme Commander of United States Forces in the Pacific. Among them was the case of General Yamashita in the

---

1544, E.A.S. No. 472, *reprinted in* Bevans, at 1239 [hereinafter Charter]. The Four Major Powers originally signed the London Agreement and nineteen other countries eventually acceded to it.

[3] Special Proclamation: Establishment of an International Military Tribunal for the Far East, Jan. 19, 1946, T.I.A.S. No. 1589, 4 Bevans 20 [hereinafter IMTFE Proclamation]; Charter for the International Military Tribunal for the Far East, Apr. 26,1946, T.I.A.S. No. 1589, 4 Bevans 27 [hereinafter IMTFE Amended Charter]. For an analysis of the Tokyo proceedings, see Bernard V.A. Röling, The Tokyo Trials and Beyond: Reflections of a Peacemonger (Antonio Cassese ed., 1993); Arnold C. Brackman, The Other Nuremberg: The Untold Story of the Tokyo War Crimes Trials (1987); The Tokyo War Crimes Trial: an International Symposium (C. Hosoya et al. eds., 1986); Richard H. Minear, Victor's Justice: The Tokyo War Crimes Trials (1971).

[4] Allied Control Council Law No. 10 Punishment of Persons Guilty of War Crimes, Crimes against Peace and against Humanity, Dec. 20, 1945, Official Gazette of the Control Council for Germany, No. 3, Berlin, Jan. 31, 1946, *reprinted in* Benjamin Ferencz, An International Criminal Court: A Step Towards World Peace 488 (1980) [hereinafter Ferencz]. The United States conducted its proceedings in the same Nuremberg Courthouse where the IMT conducted its trials, and that gave rise to some confusion as between IMT proceedings and what was then called the 'American' trials. *See* Frank M. Buscher, The U.S. War Crimes Trial Program in Germany, 1946–1955 (1989).

[5] *See* A. Maunoir, La Repression des Crimes de Guerre Devant Les Tribunaux Français et Alliés (1956); H. Meyrovitz, La Repression par les Tribunaux Allemands de Crimes Contre L'Humanité et de L'Appartenance à leurs Organization Criminelle (1960).

Philippines, which was a blot on justice because it imposed a standard of military command responsibility through failure to act that has never since applied.[6]

Since World War II, only a few countries have prosecuted 'war criminals' under their internal laws. They are: Germany (over 60,000 with a 70 percent conviction rate),[7] Israel (the main case was that of Eichmann's),[8] Italy,[9] France,[10] whose laws

---

[6] *In re Yamashita*, 327 U.S. 1 (1945) (containing strong dissents by Justice Rutledge and Justice Murphy). *See generally* R. LAEL, THE YAMASHITA PRECEDENT: WAR CRIMES AND COMMAND RESPONSIBILITY (1982); A. FRANK REEL, THE CASE OF GENERAL YAMASHITA (1949). Frank Reel defended General Yamashita before the Military Commission which tried him in the Philippines. *See* Hays Parks, *Command Responsibility for War Crimes*, 62 MIL. L. REV. 1 (1973).

[7] Germany has reportedly prosecuted 60,000 war criminals in national proceedings between 1947 and 1990. M. CHERIF BASSIOUNI, CRIMES AGAINST HUMANITY IN INTERNATIONAL CRIMINAL LAW 226 (1992) [hereinafter CRIMES AGAINST HUMANITY].

Also, Germany prosecuted border guards who had shot East Germans trying to escape to West Germany. *See* E. M. Ambrosetti, *In margine alle cd. Sentenze del muro di Berlino: note sul problema del 'diritto ingiusto'*, RIVISTA ITALIANA DI DIRITTO E PROCEDURA PENALE 596 (1994). *See also* 2 *Berlin Wall Guards 'Sorry' for '62 Killing*, CHICAGO TRIBUNE, Mar. 4. 1997, at sec. A, p.8; and *Berlin Wall Guards Convicted 1962 Shooting Victim Screamed for Help as He Bled to Death*, TORONTO STAR, Mar. 6, 1997, at sec. A, p.21. Subsequent to those prosecutions, the superiors of these guards were also prosecuted. *See Ex-East German Officers Found Guilty*, SAN DIEGO UNION-TRIBUNE, Mar. 27, 1998, at sec. A, p.16. The decision to convict these border guards was greatly criticized, especially because President Honecker was never prosecuted.

In September 1997 a Bosnian Serb, Nikola Jorgic, was convicted by a German court of genocide. German authorities were originally going to deliver the Jorgic to the ICTY for prosecution, but the ICTY asked Germany to prosecute Jorgic and others captured in Germany because of the heavy case load that the ICTY faces. *See* William Drozdiak, *Bosnian Serb Gets Life in Massacre of Muslims*, INT'L HERALD TRIB., Sept 27–28, 1997 at 2.

[8] *See, e.g.*, Attorney General of Israel v. Eichmann (Israel Dist. Court of Jerusalem 1961), *reprinted in* 36 I.L.R. 5 (1962); Attorney General of Israel v. Eichmann (Supreme Court of Israel 1962), *reprinted in* 36 I.L.R. 277 (1962). See also GIDEON HAUSNER, JUSTICE IN JERUSALEM (1966). *See also* Demjanjuk v. Petrovsky, 776 F.2d 571 (6th Cir. 1985), *cert. denied*, 475 U.S. 1016 (1986).

[9] In Italy, Erich Priebke was convicted for a 1944 massacre outside of Rome. The Priebke case was appealed and reversed. With respect to the reversal, the Cortdi Cassazion reversed the decision of the Rome military tribunal dated August 1, 1996. In its decision, the Supreme Court confirmed that war crimes were subject to statutes of limitation in so far as they constitute ordinary crimes of violence—unlike the crime of genocide for which statutes of limitation are inapplicable. The document is reported *in* CASSAZIONE PENALE, Anno XXXVII, No. 1, January 1997, at p.177. Prior to the Priebke case, Italy prosecuted Herbert Kappler. In both cases, these were two German officers and the crimes they committed were against Italian citizens.

[10] The Touvier judgments:

Judgment of Feb. 6, 1975, Cass. Crim., 1975 D.S. Jur. 386, 387 (Report of Counselor Chapan), 1975 Gaz. Pal. Nos. 124–26 (May 4–6, 1975); Judgment of Oct 27, 1975 Chambre d'accusation de la cour d'appel de Paris, 1976 D.S. Jur. 260 (Note Coste-Floret), 1976 Gaz. Pal. Nos. 154–55, at 382; Judgment of June 30, 1976, Cass. Crim., 1977 D.S. Jur. 1, 1976 Gaz. Pal. Nos. 322, 323, 1976 J.C.P. II G, No. 18,435; Judgment of Nov. 27, 1992, Cass. Crim., 1993 J.C.P. II G. No. 21, 977; Judgment of Apr. 13, 1992, Cour d'appel de Paris, Première chambre d'accusation, at 133–62, *reprinted in part in* 1992 Gaz. Pal. 387, 387–417; Judgment of June 2, 1993, Cour d'appel de Versailles, Première chambre d'accusation 31.

The Barbie judgments:

Matter of Barbie, GAZ. PAL. JUR. 710 (Cass. Crim. Oct. 6, 1983); Judgment of Oct. 6, 1983, Cass. Crim., 1984 D.S. Jur. 113, Gaz. Pal. Nos. 352–54 (Dec. 18–20, 1983), 1983 J.C.P. II G, No. 20, 107, J.D.I. 779 (1983); Judgment of Jan. 26, 1984, Cass. Crim., 1984 J.C.P. II G, No. 20,197 (Note Ruzié), J.D.I. 308 (1984); Judgment of Dec. 20, 1985, Cass. Crim., 1986 J.C.P. II G, No. 20,655,

on the subject have been developed in the aftermath of World War II, and Canada, whose special law on this subject was passed in 1987 (one case which resulted in acquittal).[11] Australia, which has national legislation modeled on Canada's, attempted three prosecutions but they were dismissed before trial.[12] The United Kingdom also passed a similar, though less strict, version of the Canadian law.[13] The United States, however, has enacted legislation giving Federal Courts jurisdiction to denaturalize and deport persons who have concealed or willfully

1986 J.D.I.; Judgment of June 3, 1988, Cass. Crim., 1988 J.C.P. II G, No. 21,149 (Report of Counselor Angevin).

The Papon judgments:

Papon was indicted on September 18, 1996; the indictment was confirmed on January 23, 1997; Judgment of Sept. 18, 1996, Chambre d'accusation de la cour d'appel de Bordeaux (unpublished), affirmed Judgment of Jan. 23, 1997, Cass. Crim., 1997 J.C.P. II G, No. 22, 812. In April 1998 Maurice Papon was convicted for 'crimes against humanity' and sentenced to ten years imprisonment. See Craig R. Whitney, *Ex-Vichy Aide Is Convicted and Reaction Ranges Wide*, NEW YORK TIMES, Apr. 3, 1998, at sec. A. p.1; Craig R. Whitney. *Vichy Official Found Guilty of Helping Deport Jews*, NEW YORK TIMES, Apr. 2, 1998, at sec. A. p.8; and Charles Trueheart, *Verdict Nears in Trial of Vichy Official*, WASH. POST, Apr. 1, 1998, at sec. A, p.21.

For information on the Touvier case see generally ÉRIC CONAN & HENRY ROUSSO, VICHY, UN PASSÉ QUI NE PASSE PAS (1994); ALAIN JAKUBOWICZ & RENÉ RAFFIN, TOUVIER HISTOIRE DU PROCÈS (1995); ARNO KLARSFELD, TOUVIER UN CRIME FRANCAIS (1994); JACQUES TRÉMOLET DE VILLERS, L'AFFAIRE TOUVIER, CHRONIQUE D'UN PROCÈS EN IDÉOLOGIE (1994).

For information on the Barbie case, see generally LADISLAS DE HOYAS, KLAUS BARBIE (Nicholas Courtin trans., 1985); BRENDAN MURPHY, THE BUTCHER OF LYON (1983).

For information on the Papon case see generally Laurent Greilsamer, *Mauricer Papon, la vie masquée*, LE MONDE, Dec. 19, 1995, *available in* LEXIS, Nexis Library, Monde File; Barry James, *The Final Trial for Vichy? A Model French Bureaucrat Accused*, INT'L HERALD TRIB., Jan. 6–7, 1996, at 2.

For additional information on these cases and French prosecution of war criminals in general see generally Leila Sadat Wexler, *National Prosecutions for International Crimes: The French Experience, in* 3 INTERNATIONAL CRIMINAL LAW (M. Cherif Bassiouni ed., 2d ed. forthcoming in 1998); Leila Sadat Wexler, *Prosecutions for Crimes Against Humanity in French Municipal Law: International Implications, in* ASIL PROCEEDINGS 270–76 (1997): Leila Sadat Wexler, *The Interpretation of the Nuremberg Principles by the French Court of Cassation: From Touvier to Barbie and Back Again*, 32 COLUM. J. TRANSNAT'L L. 289 (1994); Leila Sadat Wexler, *Reflections on the Trial of Vichy Collaborator Paul Touvier for Crimes Against Humanity in France*, 20 J. L. & Soc. INQUIRY 191 (1995); Leila Sadat Wexler, *Prosecutions for Crimes Against Humanity in French Municipal Law: International Implications* (Working Paper No. 97-4-3, Washington University School of Law, 1997); Jacques Francillon, *Crimes de guerre, Crimes contra l'humanité*, JURIS-CLASSEUR, DROIT INT'L, FASCICULE 410 (1993).

    11   Criminal Code, R.S.C. 1927, Chapter c. 36, s. 7 3.71–3.77 (Can.). For a case applying this law, *See, e.g.*, Regina v. Finta, 50 C.C.C. (3d.) 247; 61 D.L.R. 85 (4th 1989). *See also* Jacquart, *La Notion de Crime Contre l'Humanité en Droit International Contemporain et en Droit Canadien*, 21 REVUE GÉNÉRALE DE DROIT 607 (1990); L.C. Green, *Canadian Law, War Crimes and Crimes Against Humanity*, 1988 BRIT. Y.B. INTL L. 217; L.C. Green, *Canadian Law and the Punishment of War Crimes*, 28 CHITTY'S L.J. 249 (1980).

    12   War Crimes Amendment Act 1988, No. 3 (1989) (Austl.).

    13   War Crimes Act 1991, ch. 13 (U.K.); see War Crimes: Report of the War Crimes Inquiry (Sir Thomas Hetherington and William Chalmers, members 1988). Szyman Serafinowicz was to be tried for war crimes, but a British jury deemed him to be unfit to appear before a court because he suffers from dementia. *See Jury Deems Man Unfit; 1st War Crimes Trial Collapses*, JEWISH TELEGRAPHIC AGENCY, Jan. 28, 1997, at 10.

misrepresented their participation or involvement in criminal organizations and war crimes during World War II.[14] These national prosecutions are discussed by various authors in [*Strafgerichte Gegen Menschhiets-Verbrechen*], Chapter II. Additional prosecutions have taken place in Lithuania[15] and reports of prosecutions in Eastern European countries were occasionally reported, however no official data for such prosecutions are available to this writer.[16]

It is noteworthy that the only case brought against one of the World War II Allies for war crimes was brought by Japanese citizens for the use by the United States of atomic weapons against Japan. In Hiroshima and Nagasaki, the use of atomic weapons killed and injured an estimated 225,000 innocent civilians.[17] The case was rejected by the Supreme Court of Japan on technical jurisdictional grounds.[18]

In order to insure prosecution, the United Nations sponsored a Convention in 1968 on the Nonapplicability of Statutes of Limitations to War Crimes and Crimes Against Humanity.[19] The Council of Europe followed suit with a similar convention.[20] The General Assembly also adopted two resolutions in 1971[21] and

---

[14] A naturalization order shall be revoked where the Government can prove that the order was 'illegally procured or... procured by concealment of a material fact or by willful misrepresentation' 8 U.S.C.S. § 1451 (1994). *See also* Matthew Lippman, *The Denaturalization of Nazi War Criminals in the United States: Is Justice Being Served?*, 7 Hous L. Rev. 169 (1982); For a Canadian perspective, *see* Joseph Rikhof, *War Crimes, Crimes Against Humanity and Immigration Law*, 19 Imm. L.R. 2(d) 18 (1992).

[15] No trial has yet begun, although Lithuania has custody of six alleged Nazis. Some reports indicate that the trials may begin in March 1998.

[16] *See* for example István Deák, *A Fatal Compromise? The Debate Over Collaboration and Resistance in Hungary*, 9 East Europ. Politics & Societies 209 (1995) and István Deák, *Repression or Retribution? The War Crimes Trials in Past-World War II Hungary* (paper presented at AAASS Convention, Seattle, Nov. 23, 1997, on file with author).

[17] 29 The New Encyclopedia Britannica 1022 (1990).

[18] Shimoda v. The State, 355 Hanrel Jiho (Supreme Court of Japan 7 December 1963); also quoted in part in 2 Friedman at 1688. *See also* Richard A. Falk, *The Shimoda Case: A Legal Appraisal of the Atomic Attacks Upon Hiroshima and Nagasaki*, 59 AJIL 759 (1965). The claim in that case was against the United States of America for dropping atomic bombs on Nagasaki and Hiroshima in violation of the laws and customs of war.

[19] Convention on the Nonapplicability of Statutory Limitations to War Crimes and Crimes Against Humanity, G.A. Res. 2391 (XXIII), 23 U.N. GAOR Supp. (No. 18) 40, U.N. Doc. A/7218 (1968). As of 1997 it was ratified by 43 nations, *see* M. Cherif Bassiouni, International Criminal Law Conventions (1997). *See also* Christine Van Den Wyngaert, *War Crimes, Crimes Against Humanity and Statutory Limitations* 89 *in* International Criminal Law (M. Cherif Bassiouni ed., 1987); Christine Van Den Wyngaert, *War Crimes, Genocide and Crimes Against Humanity: Are States Taking National Prosecution Seriously?*; *La Protection des Droits des Personnes Suspectées, Inculpées Accusées d'Infraction a la Loi Penale*, 37 Revue Internationale de Droit Penale 11 (1966). In 1968, Germany had a 25 year statute of limitations on murder. This meant that from after 1969, all war crimes and crimes against humanity could no longer be prosecuted without amending German law, and that was done.

[20] European Convention on the Non-Applicability of Limitations to Crimes Against Humanity and War Crimes, Jan. 1 1974, ETS No. 82, *reprinted in* 13 I.L.M. 540 (1974). As of 1997 it was ratified by one nation, *see* Bassiouni, *supra* note 19.

[21] G.A. Res. 2840 (XXVI), 26 U.N. GAOR Supp. (No. 29) at 88, U.N. Doc. A/8429 (1971) [hereinafter G.A. Resolution 2840].

1973[22] on the duty to extradite or prosecute persons accused of war crimes and crimes against humanity. These Resolutions, however, have had little practical effect on the custom and practice of states.[23] Many other international instruments on substantive international criminal law, which are discussed below, have been developed between 1945–1994.[24]

The process that commenced at Nuremberg continues to evolve. The latest and most important post-Nuremberg development has been the establishment of the International Criminal Tribunal for the Former Yugoslavia (ICTY) and the International Criminal Tribunal for Rwanda (ICTR).[25] However, almost 50 years since Nuremberg and nearly 80 years since the Versailles Treaty,[26] no permanent international criminal court has yet been established, though there is some progress in that direction.[27] Some modest progress has also been made to codify certain international crimes by the United Nations' International Law Commission.[28] But these modest results have disappointed the hopes of many and have added credibility to the claims of those who saw the Nuremberg and Tokyo trials as victor's justice.[29] Subsequent legal developments can cure historic

---

[22] Principles of International Co-operation in the Detention, Arrest, Extradition and Punishment of Persons Guilty of War Crimes and Crimes Against Humanity, Dec. 3 1973 G.A. Res. 3074 (XXXVII), 28 U.N. GAOR Supp. (No. 30) at 78, U.N. Doc. A/9030, [hereinafter U.N. Principles of Int'l Penal Cooperation and Extradition].

[23] Nowhere in the international legal literature is there any reported national case which relies or cites any of these resolutions. *See, e.g.,* M. CHERIF BASSIOUNI, INTERNATIONAL EXTRADITION: UNITED STATES LAW AND PRACTICE (2d ed. 1987 and 3d rev. ed. in print 1994). But see CRIMES AGAINST HUMANITY, supra note 7, at 470–527.

[24] *See, e.g.,* M. CHERIF BASSIOUNI, INTERNATIONAL CRIMINAL LAW: A DIGEST/INDEX OF CONVENTIONS 1815–1985 (1985).

[25] For the Yugoslavia Tribunal, *see* International Criminal Tribunal for Yugoslavia, S.C. Res. 808, U.N. SCOR, 48th Sess., Annex, at 20, U.N. Doc. S/25274 (1993), (22 Feb. 1993, establishing the Tribunal) [hereinafter ICTY Statute]; and Security Council Resolution 827 (1993), S/RES/827 (25 May 1993, adopting its Statute) [hereinafter SC Resolutions 827]; M. CHERIF BASSIOUNI (WITH THE COLLABORATION OF PETER MANIKAS), THE LAW OF THE INTERNATIONAL CRIMINAL TRIBUNAL FOR THE FORMER YUGOSLAVIA (1996); VIRGINIA MORRIS & MICHAEL SCHARF, AN INSIDER'S GUIDE TO THE INTERNATIONAL CRIMINAL TRIBUNAL FOR THE FORMER YUGOSLAVIA (1995). For the Rwanda Tribunal see S.C. Res. 955, U.N. SCOR, 49th Sess., 3453d mtg., U.N. Doc S/RES/935 (1994), and Larry Johnson, *The International Tribunal for Rwanda*, 67 REVUE INTERNATIONALE DE DROIT PÉNAL 211 (1996).

[26] Treaty of Peace Between the Allied and Associated Powers and Germany (Treaty of Versailles), June 28 1919, 11 MARTENS (3d) 323, reprinted in 2 BEVANS 43, 1 FRIEDMAN 417.

[27] *See, however, Report of the International Law Commission*, 46th Sess., May 2–July 22, 1994, U.N. GAOR, 49th Sess., U.N. Doc. A/49/10 (1994) [hereinafter 1994 ILC Report]; *Draft Statute International Criminal Tribunal*, 9 NOUVELLES ETUDES PENALES (M. Cherif Bassiouni ed., 2d eds. 1993).

[28] While the International Law Commission has been working since 1947 on the codification of crimes against the peace and security of mankind, it has not codified all international crimes; *See* 1994 ILC Report, *supra* note 27; *Commentaries on the International Law Commission's 1991 Draft Code of Crimes Against the Peace and Security of Mankind*, 11 NOUVELLES ETUDES PENALES (1993). *But see* M. CHERIF BASSIOUNI, A DRAFT INTERNATIONAL CRIMINAL CODE & DRAFT STATURE FOR AN INTERNATIONAL CRIMINAL TRIBUNAL (1987) [hereinafter BASSIOUNI, DRAFT CODE].

[29] This is particularly true with respect to crimes against humanity. *See* M. Cherif Bassiouni, *Crimes Against Humanity: The Need for a Specialized Convention*, 31 COLUM. J. TRANSNAT'L. L. 457 (1993) [hereinafter *Specialized Convention*].

defects, eliminating the weaknesses of the past and enhancing the prospects for future improvements. Without these developments, however, the original infirmities which attended the early processes will tend to be confirmed.

There is also the danger that singularly unique legal events, which are not repeated when similar circumstances warrant it, may fall into *desuètude* or disuse—a legal concept known to many of the major legal systems of the world.[30] Indeed, the revival of a law after long disuse raises questions as to the legality of its application. But, while the law and legal institutions of 'Nuremberg' have not, except by the ICTY and ICTR, been duplicated since 1945,[31] the 'Nuremberg Legacy' remains significant and well-remembered. Consequently, it cannot be argued that it has been forgotten, even though it has not been replicated, and only infrequently relied upon in national criminal proceedings outside Germany.[32]

The historical impact and legacy of institutions are subject to wide-ranging individual and collective perceptions. Indeed, many factors bear upon human perceptions, including differing values, purposes, goals and personal experiences. But any *a posteriori* impact assessment of the legacy of historic institutions raises methodological questions. Among them are: (1) what methods of legal analysis are employed; (2) what is the measure or standard by which to judge what took place; (3) what were the expectations of accomplishment when the institutions were established, and what are the exceptions at the time of the assessment; and (4) if they are different, how to compare them.

Furthermore, in making *a posteriori* historical legal assessments it is difficult to fully appreciate all contextual factors which existed at the time of the occurrence. Even if attempting this with some degree of intellectual objectivity is possible, it is nonetheless fraught with subjectivity. Those who were not part of the previous experience cannot subsequently have a complete grasp of what was done earlier under different circumstances and subject to exigencies that look otherwise after almost 50 years. In addition, there are always facts that occur at a given time that do not become publicly known or are never recorded and, therefore, cannot be known and assessed at later times.[33] Purely intellectual analysis cannot, therefore, objectively assess the total facts and the circumstances of a time past. That is why so much of history is revisionist.

Lastly, it must be understood that institutions, like historic events, are shaped by people, and are affected by all the factors that bear on human motivation and human interaction. Occasionally, the greatness of some individuals emerge and

---

[30] Professor Antonio Cassese, now President of the ICTY, has said that the 'concepts that emerged from Nuremberg—one of the highest points in our march towards legal civilization and an awareness of human dignity—are in danger of being split up.' ANTONIO CASSESE, VIOLENCE AND LAW IN THE MODERN AGE 147–48 (1986).

[31] *See* ICTY Statute and SC Resolutions 827, *supra* note 25.

[32] Since 1950 Germany has prosecuted a large number of persons accused of crimes during World War II, *see supra* note 7.

[33] For a personalized account of many behind the scenes decisions, *see* TELFORD TAYLOR, THE ANATOMY OF THE NUREMBERG TRIALS (1992).

dominate events as well as control the behavior of actors. But, most commonly, personal and personality factors ultimately affect decisions and outcomes.

What is now called the 'Nuremberg Legacy' is made of all that and more. But the starting point is the IMT and that is what the word 'Nuremberg' has become associated with. The assessment that follows, deals therefore with the IMT as the origin of subsequent developments. It is based on three interrelated levels of inquiry. They are:

1. The Institutional Legacy: The IMT and its Processes.
2. The Legal Legacy: Substantive Legal developments—The Law of the IMT and Subsequent Developments.
3. The Moral-Ethical Legacy: The power of a principle that corresponds to basic human values and expectations and its influence on legal developments.

The Institutional Legacy: The IMT and its Processes[34]

One remarkable accomplishment of the IMT was that for all practical purposes it was the first international criminal tribunal in history ever established.[35] This is even more remarkable because the victors who established the IMT had an alternative: summary execution of those among the defeated that the victors deemed to have violated the laws and customs of war.[36] The victors could have been totally arbitrary. They could have, even in so doing, been fair by some legal standards without electing to establish a necessarily cumbersome, costly and to some extent, unpredictable international legal institution. Its judicial decisions could not have been guaranteed even though it was carefully planned not to produce unexpected results.[37] The British justified their position in favor of summary execution and

[34] *See, e.g.,* THE NUREMBERG TRIAL AND INTERNATIONAL LAW (George Ginsburgs & Vladimir N. Kudiravtsev eds., 1990).

[35] *See* M. Cherif Bassiouni & Christopher Blakesly, *The Need for an International Criminal Court in the New World Order,* 25 VAND. J. TRANSNAT'L. L. 151 (1992); M. Cherif Bassiouni, *The Time Has Come for an International Criminal Court,* 1 IND. INT'L & COMP. L. REV. 1 (1991).

[36] In Sept. 1944, Churchill proposed that the Nazi leaders should be summarily executed. Roosevelt agreed. But by 1945, the United States had changed its position. See BRADLEY F. SMITH, THE ROAD TO NUREMBERG 46–7 (1981). The British persisted in their position as evidenced in the *Aide Memoire* for the United Kingdom to the United States of Apr. 23, 1945, *reprinted in* ROBERT H. JACKSON, REPORT OF ROBERT H. JACKSON, UNITED STATES REPRESENTATIVE TO THE INTERNATIONAL CONFERENCE ON MILITARY TRIALS 11–12 (U.S. Govt. Prtg. Off. 1949)[hereinafter JACKSON REPORT]. The British *Aide Memoire* stated that it was 'conceded' that the Nazi leaders 'must suffer death,' their summary execution without trial was the 'preferable course.' *Id.* at 18. But see Henry L. Stimson, *The Nuremberg Trial: Landmark in Law,* 25 FOREIGN AFF. 179 (1947), acknowledging the great triumph of the rule of law and stating that the accused were given 'what they had denied their own opponents—the protection of the law.' *Id.* at 180.

[37] During the debates on the Charter in London, Professor André Gros of France repeatedly argued that no international law existed on the question of 'Crimes Against Peace.' To which Sir David Maxwell Fyfe of Great Britain peremptorily concluded: 'We declare what international law is... there won't be any discussion on whether it is international law or not.' *See* JACKSON REPORT,

against trials by arguing that the Germans would effectively challenge the trials and the legal process. They also argued that the Germans would use the forum to propagandize their claims and justify their positions in an attempt to rally national and even a portion of international public opinion to the proposition the trials were a farce. Finally, the British argued that trials would make some of the accused look like martyrs.[38] The United States replied that such a trial would establish an important historic record and develop what would hopefully become lasting international legal standards. Moreover, trials would deter future leaders from similar conduct and open a new chapter of rule of law government for Germany's post-war era. Contrary to the British, the United States argued that trials would avoid making martyrs of the Nazis. Even if the defense tried to use the trials as a forum for propaganda, the United States argued, the facts were so overwhelming that the risk of sympathy for the accused was very unlikely.[39] Fortunately for history, the United States position, championed by Justice Robert Jackson, prevailed. After months of discussions, the Four Major Allies signed the London Charter of 8 August 1945, to which the Statute of the IMT was attached.[40] The Tribunal's very establishment is what constitutes the legal precedent for subsequent efforts to set up the *ad hoc* Tribunal for the Former Yugoslavia and eventually a permanent international criminal court. What gives credence to 'Nuremberg' is that the IMT proceedings: strove to be an 'ordinary' international criminal court as opposed to an 'extraordinary' or 'exceptional' tribunal of victors over the defeated conducted in sham proceedings; the accused were, for the most part, persons whose leadership responsibility for many atrocities before and during the war was notorious;[41] the facts were so overwhelming as to the type and quantum of victimization and so tragic in their perpetration that they overshadowed legal considerations;[42] the trial procedures were as fair as they could

---

supra note 36, at 97–99. The position of the USSR, expressed by General Nikitchenko, was based on a thesis by Professor Trainin that all these crimes derive from Hitlerite aggression. *Id.* The British and USSR positions fitted the United States' thesis that all these crimes derived from a conspiracy and policy to commit aggression, and that this is the basis for the prosecutions, a basis from which the other crimes flowed. Aside from these and many other shortcomings of the process illustrated in David Irving, Nuremberg: The Last Battle (1996).

[38] *Id.* at 18–19.

[39] *Id.* at 28–34.

[40] However, it should be added that it was premised on the certainty of guilty verdicts for the accused, without any risks that the very principles upon which the guilt was to be established would be applied to the Allies. Thus, the Allies opted for the legal process certain that the law they established would prevail, that the accused would be found guilty, and that their own leaders and commanders would face no legal consequences.

[41] Nevertheless, the selectivity of the twenty-four accused was arbitrary. No industrialist was prosecuted, even though many had used 'slave labor' and could have been charged with 'crimes against humanity.' Others were prosecuted only because they symbolically represented certain organizations or ideas. This criticism is found in Davidson and other writings. *See* Ann Tusa and John Tusa, The Nuremberg Trial (1984); Robert E. Conot, Justice at Nuremberg (1983); Eugene Davidson, The Trial of the Germans (1966); Hausner *supra* note 8.

[42] *See supra* note 1.

have been under the circumstances and by contemporary standards of ordinary criminal justice in most countries.[43] These and other factors contributed to overcome several legal considerations that, under normal circumstances in ordinary domestic criminal proceedings, would have largely reduced the legitimacy of the exercise. These legal considerations include the following: (1) the *ad hoc* status of the tribunal; (2) some of the applicable law was formulated to fit the facts and some provisions were in part *ex post facto*; (3) the makers of the law were also the judges and prosecutors; (4) the accused were only from among the defeated and no one from the victor's side who committed similar violations of the laws and customs of war were prosecuted; (5) the accused were arbitrarily chosen by those who would eventually prosecute them; (6) the judges were from the victor's side only; (7) the victors, and among them some judges, selected the substantive law and procedure that applied; (8) the entire process was in the hands of the victors; (9) the defense of the accused depended upon the benevolence of the prosecution and the judges who were essentially from the prosecution side; and (10) the penalties were not promulgated by preexisting law, but decided by the judges. Many critics raised these legally valid questions.[44]

Despite the legally questionable nature and effect of these considerations, world public perception then and now is that the entire process was substantially fair and the outcome substantially just. Besides the facts and the personalities of the accused, what appears to enhance the credibility of 'Nuremberg' and outweigh the criticisms noted above are: (1) the establishment of the IMT was by virtue of a treaty signed by the Four Allied States and acceded to by nineteen others; (2) the promulgation of the Charter included substantive law and rules of procedures that had the appearance of legal validity and substantial fairness; (3) the Tribunal functioned fairly; and (4) the proceedings were conducted with judicial decorum and procedural dignity. That is the perceived validity of the precedent, irrespective of what legal critics may argue.

In time, the criticisms, whether justifiable or not, have scarcely diminished the valid perception of the 'Nuremberg legacy.' On the contrary, these weaknesses have been forgotten and the symbolic and precedent value of the IMT has been strengthened over the years. Thus, with the establishment of the ICTY and

---

[43] Roger Clark, *Crimes Against Humanity at Nuremberg, in* THE NUREMBERG TRIAL AND INTERNATIONAL LAW, *supra* note 34, at 177. *See contra* IRVING, *supra* note 37.

[44] *See* A. VON KNIEREM, THE NUREMBERG TRIALS (E.D. Schmitt, trans., 1959); HANS-HEINRICH JESCHECK, DIE VERANTWÖRTLICHIKEIT DER STAATSORGAN SEIT NÜREMBERG (1952); Hans Laternser, *Looking Back at the Nuremberg Trials with Special Consideration of the Processes Against Military Leaders*, 9 WHITTIER L. REV. 557 (1985); Ehard, *supra* note 1; Gordon Ireland, *Ex Post Facto From Rome to Tokyo*, 21 TEMP. L. Q. 22 (1948); Bernard D. Meltzer, *A Note on Some Aspects of the Nuremberg Debate*, 14 U. CHI. L. REV. 455 (1947). For an interesting account of four of the defense counsels at the trials, *see* Carl Haensell, *The Nuremberg Trial Revisited*, 13 DEPAUL L. REV. 248 (1964); Herbert Kraus, *The Nuremberg Trial of the Major War Criminals: Reflections after Seventeen Years*, 13 DEPAUL L. REV. 233 (1964); Otto Kranzbuhler, *Nuremberg Eighteen Years Afterwards*, 14 DEPAUL L. REV. 333 (1965); Otto Pannenbecker, *The Nuremberg War-Crimes Tribunal*, 14 DEPAUL L. REV. 348 (1965).

ICTR[45] and the continued work of the United Nations to establish a permanent international criminal tribunal,[46] the institutional 'Nuremberg legacy' looms large in the future expectations of the world community.

Since World War II, *realpoliticiàns* have pursued political settlements at the cost of impunity, allowing many serious crimes to go unpunished. This situation has re-enforced the general public's perception of the 'Nuremberg' institutional legacy and the need to establish a permanent system of international justice. A question, however, arises: is it the actual validity of the institutional precedent that prompted its positive 'legacy' or is it the needs and aspirations of the world community in search of a precedent to idealize as valid that created this perception of legal validity? This question cannot be answered in purely legal terms, for it is the cumulative effect of all the considerations examined in this assessment and others that produced this contemporary outcome. In any event, what matters now is the perception and its impact on future development.

The Legal Legacy

Two sets of considerations arise in this context. First, are those arising out of the substantive law applied by the IMT at its proceedings. Second, are those legal developments arising as a consequence of that application. The first considerations include, *inter alia*:

(a) the legal validity and sufficiency of the specific crimes charged; and
(b) the legal validity of the principles of responsibility applied.

The second set of considerations include, *inter alia*:

(a) the flow of substantive legal developments that derived from or as ascribed to the 'Nuremberg' precedent; and
(b) the stimulation of efforts to codify international criminal law and to establish a permanent international criminal court.

Article Six of the Statute contained the substantive charges of the IMT, namely 'crimes against peace,' 'war crimes,' and 'crimes against humanity.'[47] These charges raised issues concerning the principles of legality in criminal law, which are in some ways part of 'general principles of law.' The Latin maxims

---

[45] *See* SC Resolution(s) 808, 827 note 25; *Report of the Secretary-General Pursuant to Paragraph 2 of Security Council Resolution 808* (1993), U.N. Doc. No. S/25704 (May 3, 1993).

[46] *See* 1994 ILC Report, *supra* note 27; *Revised Report of the Working Group on the Draft Statute for an International Criminal Court*, International Law Commission, 45th Sess., May 3–July 23, 1993, A/CN.4/L/490 (July 19 1993); *Revised Report of the Working Group on the Draft Statute for an International Criminal Court: Addendum*, International Law Commission, 45th Sess., May 3–July 23 1993, A/CN.4/L.490/Add. 1 (July 19, 1993).

[47] All three of these substantive crimes are discussed by the authors cited in note 1 and others throughout this article.

nullum crimen, nulla poena sine lege previae (no crime without previous law and
no penalty without law), reflect these principles and are among the most serious
issues raised about the substantive law applied by the IMT.[48] The Charter also
raised questions of _ex post facto_ concerning certain historically valid defenses. The
traditional defense of 'obedience to superior orders' was disallowed in Article 8.[49]
However, the subsequent judgment qualified this rejection by establishing that if
a person who obeyed an order, even if unlawful, but who had no 'moral choice,'
could be exonerated from criminal responsibility. That is the same as the defense
of coercion which is known in all legal systems. Article 7 of the Charter also
eliminated the 'Act of State' defense where a Head of State and others can claim
that their conduct was inherent to national sovereignty and thus not questionable
by others. Problems of _ex post facto_ could also be found in certain new offenses
set out in the Charter. Article 9 also introduced the new concept of group criminality, and Article 10 provided for individual criminal responsibility based on
group or collective responsibility for membership in 'criminal organizations.'[50]
Except for Common Law systems, the world's other legal systems consider criminal responsibility as individual. This excludes legal entities, since they are legal
abstractions. Thus, only persons can be charged with crimes, and not as a result of
some notion of collective responsibility or for being part of an organization, even
if deemed criminal, without personal conduct that violates the law.

The problem concerning the charge of 'crimes against peace' was the absence
of a specific convention declaring aggression a justiciable international crime for
which individual criminal responsibility could be ascribed. Reliance on several
previous treaties, such as the 1928 Treaty on the Renunciation of War which
did not criminalize the resort to war by states, was certainly not adequate to satisfy even a less than rigorous interpretation 'of the principles of legality.' Indeed,
there is nothing in international legal instruments prior to the London Charter to
suggest that the conduct of those accused of 'crimes against peace' was an international crime for which individual criminal penalties could be ascribed.[51] This
is true despite the unsuccessful efforts of the Allies, via Article 227 of the Treaty
of Versailles, to prosecute Kaiser Wilhelm II at the end of World War I.[52] Thus,

[48] For a discussion of the 'principles of legality,' _see_ CRIMES AGAINST HUMANITY, _supra_ note 7,
at 87.

[49] _See, e.g._, LESLIE GREEN, ESSAYS ON THE MODERN LAW OF WAR (1985); NICO KEUZER,
MILITARY OBEDIENCE (1978); YORAM DINSTEIN, THE DEFENCE OF 'OBEDIENCE TO SUPERIOR
ORDERS' IN INTERNATIONAL LAW (1965); EKKEHART MÜLLER-RAPPARD, L'ORDRE SUPERIER
MILITAIRE ET LA RESPONSIBILITÉ PÉNALE DU SUBORDONNÉ (1965).

[50] _See_ VON KNIEREM, _supra_ note 44. For a discussion of the question of individual and group
responsibility, _see_ M. Cherif Bassiouni, _The Sources and Content of International Criminal Law:
A Theoretical Framework_ 1.

[51] But _see_ Sheldon Glueck, _The Nuremberg Trial and Aggressive War_, 59 HARV. L. REV. 396
(1946).

[52] For an interesting discussion of this question, _see_ CLAUDE MULLINS, THE LEIPZIG TRIALS
(1921); TAYLOR _supra_ note 33, at 14–16; JAMES F. WILLIS, PROLOGUE TO NUREMBERG: THE
POLITICS AND DIPLOMACY OF PUNISHING WAR CRIMINALS OF THE FIRST WORLD WAR (1982)

prosecutions of 'crimes against peace' were a form of *ex post facto* legal application of hitherto questionable legal norms.[53]

With respect to the charges of 'war crimes,' the customary and conventional international law regulating armed conflicts had developed sufficient legal norms to avoid any *ex post facto* problems.[54] The Treaty of Versailles also provided a limited legal precedent. Articles 228 and 229 of the Treaty had provided for the prosecution of war criminals. However, its precedential value was limited, since there were no international prosecutions and few persons were ultimately prosecuted before the German Supreme Court at Leipzig.[55] But, the Allies who applied these norms to the Germans did not act similarly with respect to their own violators. The German Army had established a section in the *Wehrmacht* to document war crimes by the Allies, but none of the documented cases were pursued. Thus, there was quite clearly a double standard. Furthermore, the Allies did not allow the Germans on trial to argue that they acted no differently than their enemies, and that too was one-sided.

The *ex post facto* problem also arose in part with respect to 'crimes against humanity.'[56] As a solution, the drafters of the London Charter linked this category of crimes to the charges of 'crimes against peace' and 'war crimes.'[57] Thus, the definition of 'crimes against humanity' included only those crimes committed in relation to the initiation and waging of the war, while similar crimes committed before 1939 were not deemed within the purview of the applicable law.[58] This

[hereinafter PROLOGUE TO NUREMBERG]; Gordon Battle, *The Trials Before the Leipzig Supreme Court of Germans Accused of War Crimes*, 8 VA. L. REV. 1 (1921–1922); Quincy Wright, *The Legality of the Kaiser*, 13 AM. POL. SCI. REV. 120 (1919).

[53] *See* Hans-Heinrich Jescheck, *Developments and Future Prospects of International Criminal Law*, *in* INTERNATIONAL CRIMINAL LAW (M. Cherif Bassiouni ed., 1986); Donnedieu de Vabres, *Le Procès de Nuremberg Devant les Principes Modeines du Droit Pénal International*, 70 RECUEIL DES COURS 481 (1947).

[54] *See* Convention Respecting the Laws and Customs of War on Land (and Annex of Regulations), The Hague, Oct. 18, 1907, 36 Stat. 2277, T.S. No. 539, 3 Martens Nouceau Recueil (ser.3) 461, *reprinted in* 2 AM. J. INT'L L. 90 (1908) (Supp.), 1 FRIEDMAN 308, 1 BEVANS 631; Geneva Convention for the Amelioration of the Condition of the Wounded and Sick in Armies in the Field (Third Red Cross Convention (July 27 1929), 118 L.N.T.S. 303, 47 Stat. 2074, T.S. No. 847; Geneva Convention Relative to the Treatment of Prisoners of War (July 27, 1929), 118 L.N.T.S. 343, 47 Stat. 2021, T.S. No. 846. *See also* Hersh Lauterpacht, *The Law of Nations and the Punishment of War Crimes*, 1944 BRIT. Y.B. INT'L. L. 58; George Manner, *The Legal Nature and Punishment of Criminal Acts of Violence Contrary to the Laws of War*, 37 AM. J. INT'L. L. 407 (1943); James W. Garner, *Punishment of Offenders Against the Laws and Customs of War*, 14 AM. J. INT'L L. 70 (1920); Hugh H.L. Bellot, *War Crimes: Their Prevention and Punishment*, *in* 2 TRANSACTIONS OF THE GROTIUS SOCIETY 31 (1917); Wright, *supra* note 1.

[55] *See* MULLINS, *supra* note 52. *See also* Battle, *supra* note 52. For three of these cases, *see* the Judgment Case of Karl Neumann RGST, June 4 1921, Judgment in the Case of Emil Müller RGST, May 30, 1921 and Judgment in the Cases of Lieutenants Dittmar and Boldt, RGST, July 16 1921. The Reichgericht had determined to try 45 individuals out of a list of 895 cases, but only sixteen were tried.

[56] CRIMES AGAINST HUMANITY, *supra* note 7, at 1–32.

[57] *Id.* at 176–191.

[58] *See* LUCY DAVIDOWICZ, THE WAR AGAINST THE JEWS 1933–1945 (1975).

link between 'crimes against humanity' and the initiation and waging of aggressive war, or to 'war crimes' was later removed in 1950 by the United Nations International Law Convention. Since then, the link has been deemed unnecessary and 'crimes against humanity' is applicable in times of war and peace. This change in the law was significant.[59]

The essential argument against the legal validity of the charges of 'crimes against humanity' rests on the fact that it violates the 'principles of legality' and, therefore, this question cannot be ignored. But there are several legally significant qualifying factors that substantially mitigate the criticism. The 'principles of legality,' namely that there can be no crime unless established by law, no penalty without law, and no criminal law with *ex post facto* effect, were embodied in the German Criminal Code of 1871.[60] But in 1935 the Nazi regime removed that principle from the German Criminal Code. The change allowed criminal law to be applied by analogy and that meant that it could be interpreted in many ways that were not heretofore known and made applicable *ex post facto*. The Nazi leadership made this change in the law in order to facilitate the perpetration of the crimes they committed by giving it a color of legal legitimacy. They could not, however, equitably argue at Nuremberg that the very law they overturned in 1935 should nonetheless be applied in 1945 when it suited them.

There is probably no more apt statement on the legal nature and consequences of the International Military Tribunal at Nuremberg than Robert H. Jackson's in his Report to the President of the United States dated 7 October 1946, where he states: 'Many mistakes have been made and many inadequacies must be confessed. But I am consoled by the fact that in proceedings of this novelty, errors and missteps may also be instructive to the future.'

What is particularly significant with respect to the 'legal legacy' is what followed the IMT proceedings. These developments are essentially:

(1) the establishment under international law of the 'Nuremberg principles;'[61]

---

[59] Only two defendants, Streicher and Von Schirach, were convicted of crimes against humanity, but fourteen other defendants were convicted of war crimes *and* crimes against humanity.

[60] *See* CRIMES AGAINST HUMANITY, *supra* note 7, at 97–99. For a German historical perspective, *see* B. CARPZOW, PRACTICA NOVA IMPERIALS SAXONICA RERUM CRIMINALIUM, pt. III, question 133 (*de arbitraris sen extraordinarüs poenis*) (Frankfort ed. 1758). For a post-1800 perspective, see GUERTNER-FREISLER, DAS NEUE STRAFRECHT (1936); Schinnerer, *Analogie und Rechtisschärfung*, 55 ZSTW 75 (1936); Schem, *Die Anaologie im Strafrecht in ihrer geschichtlichen Entwicklung und heutigen Bedeutung*, STRAFRECHT ABHANDLUNGEN (Fasc. 369, 1936); B. ACKERMAN, DAS ANALOGIEVERBOT IM GELTENDEN UND ZUKÜNFTIGEN STRAFRECT (1934); Goetzeler, *Der Grundsatz nulla poene sine lege*, 104 GERICHTSTAAL 343 (1934); K. SIGERT, GRUNDZÜGE DES STRAFRECHTS IM NUEUN STAATE (1934); H. HENKEL, STRAFRECHT UND GESETZ IM NEUE STAATE (1934); A.V. FUERBACH, LEHRBUCH DES GEMEINEN IN DEUTSCHLAND GÜLTIGEN PEINLICHEN RECHTS (14th ed., Mittermaier ed. 1847). For an Austrian perspective, see FRANZ VON LISZT, LEHRBUCH DES STRAFRECHT 110 (1891); *Die Deterministischen Gegner der Zweckstrafen*, 13 ZSTW (1893).

[61] *Principles of the Nuremberg Tribunal, 1950 Report of the ILC, (Principles of International Law Recognized in the Tribunal)*, July 29, 1950, 5 U.N. GAOR Supp. (No. 12) at 11, U.N. Doc. A/1316 (1950), *reprinted in* 4 Am. J. Int'l L. 126 (1950) (Supp.) [hereinafter 1950 ILC Report].

(2) that these 'principles' would become the starting point of codification that would ultimately become well established international criminal law;[62] and

(3) that the Nuremberg Tribunal would lead to the establishment of a permanent international criminal tribunal.[63]

An objective assessment of the post-Nuremberg legal developments can, however, be appropriately based on the identification of international legal instruments attributable to 'Nuremberg.'

The following subsequent legal instruments can be attributed to 'Nuremberg.' Some are, however, more directly linked to that precedent than others. They are:

1. 1946 General Assembly Resolution embodying the 'Nuremberg Principles;'[64]
2. 1950 International Law Commission report embodying the 'Nuremberg Principles;'[65]
3. 1948 Genocide Convention;[66]
4. in some respects the 1949 Geneva Conventions;[67]
5. the two draft statutes for the Establishment of an International Criminal Court produced by a special committee of the General Assembly in 1951[68] and in 1953;[69]
6. the 1968 Convention on the Nonapplicability of Statute of Limitations to War Crimes and Crimes Against Humanity;[70]

---

[62] For a history of the International Law Commission's efforts on codification, see M. Cherif Bassiouni, *The History of the Draft Code of Crimes Against the Peace and Security of Mankind, in* Commentaries on the International Law Commission's 1991 Draft Code of Crimes Against the Peace and Security of Mankind, 11 Nouvelles Etudes Penales (1993); 1991 Draft Code and 1954 Draft Code *infra* notes 66, 67.

[63] *See* Bassiouni, Draft Code, *supra* note 28.

[64] *Affirmation of the Principles of International Law Recognized by the Charter of the Nuremberg Tribunal*, Dec. 11 1946, U.N. G.A. Res. 95(1), I U.N. GAOR (Part II) at 188. U.N. Doc. A/64/Add.1 (1946) [hereinafter ILC's Affirmation of the Nuremberg principles].

[65] *See* 1950 ILC report, *supra* note 61.

[66] Convention on the Prevention and Punishment of the Crime of Genocide, Dec. 9. 1948, 78 U.N.T.S. 277, *reprinted in* 45 Am. J. Int'l L. 7 (1951) (Supp.) [hereinafter Genocide Convention].

[67] *See* Geneva Convention for the Amelioration of the Condition of the Wounded and Sick in Armed Forces in the Field (Aug. 12, 1949), 75 U.N.T.S. 31, 6 U.S.T. 3114, T.I.A.S. No.3362; Geneva Convention for the Amelioration of the Condition of the Wounded, Sick and Shipwrecked Members of the Armed Forces at Sea (Aug. 12, 1949), 75 U.N.T.S. 85, 6 U.S.T. 3217, T.I.A.S. No.3363; Geneva Convention Relative to the Treatment of Prisoners of War (Aug. 12, 1949), 75 U.N.T.S. 135, 6 U.S.T. 3316, T.I.A.S. No.3364; Geneva Convention Relative to the Protection of Civilian Persons in Time of War (Aug. 12, 1949), 75 U.N.T.S. 287, 6 U.S.T. 3516, T.I.A.S. No.3365 [hereinafter 1949 Geneva Conventions].

[68] *Draft Statute for an International Criminal Court (Annex to the Report of the Committee on International Criminal Jurisdiction, Aug. 31, 1951),* 7 U.N. GAOR Supp. 11, U.N. Doc. A/2136 at 23 (1952).

[69] *Revised Draft Statute for an International Court (Annex to the Report on International Criminal Jurisdiction, Aug. 20. 1953),* 9 U.N. GAOR Supp. 12, U.N. Doc. A/2645 at 21 (1954).

[70] Convention on the Non-Applicability of Statutory Limitations to War Crimes and Crimes Against Humanity, *opened for signatures*, Nov. 26 1968, 754 U.N.T.S. 73 (*entered into force* Nov. 11, 1970).

7. the General Assembly resolutions on the duty to prosecute or extradite persons accused of war crimes and crimes against humanity of 1971[71] and 1973;[72]

8. the 1974 General Assembly Consensus Resolution defining Aggression;[73]

9. the 1996 Code of Crimes Against the Peace and Security of Mankind;[74] and

10. the 1994 Draft Statute for an International Criminal Court and the work of the United Nations' 1995 Ad Hoc Committee on the Establishment of an International Criminal Court, which was followed by the 1996 Preparatory Committee on the International Criminal Court,[75] and the 1997–98 Preparatory Committee. The outcome is expected in July 1998 when the Convention establishing an International Criminal Court will be signed in Rome.

These international legal developments must, however, be appraised singularly.

1. Aggression, which reflects the charge of 'crimes against peace' in Article 6(a) of the IMT's statute, has not been embodied in an international convention that clearly states that aggression is an international crime for which individual responsibility and for which a penalty shall be applied. Aggression is so far only embodied in a General Assembly resolution adopted by consensus. Furthermore, it is difficult to argue that the custom and practice of states evidences compliance with this resolution, considering the number of cases that have violated its prohibition. Nevertheless, it can be argued that 'general principles of law' clearly prohibit aggression. However, the question is not whether treaties, some custom and 'general principles' prohibit aggression, but whether the prohibition is in the nature of a prescriptive penal norm. That conclusion is, unfortunately, highly questionable. Thus, the Legacy of Article 6(a) is yet to have a realistic effect.

2. 'War Crimes' have developed significant elaboration in the four Geneva Conventions of 12 August 1949 and the two Additional Protocols of 1977.[76]

---

[71] *See* G.A. Resolution 2840, *supra* note 21.

[72] *See* U.N. Principles of Int'l Penal Cooperation and Extradition, *supra* note 22.

[73] Definition of Aggression (United Nations General Assembly Resolution), adopted Dec. 14, 1974, U.N. G.A. Res. 3314 (XXIX), 29 U.N.GAOR Supp. (No. 31) at 142, U.N. Doc. A/9631 (1974) [hereinafter Definition of Aggression].

[74] *Draft Code of Crimes Against the Peace and Security of Mankind: Titles and texts of articles on the Draft Code of Crimes Against Peace and Security of Mankind adopted by the International Law Commission at its 48th Session (1996),* U.N. GAOR International Law Commission 48th Sess., U.N. Doc. A/CN.4/L.532 (1996). *See also* Draft Code of Offences Against the Peace and Security of Mankind, July 28, 1954, U.N. GAOR, 9th Sess., Supp. (No. 9) at 11. U.N. Doc. A/2693 (1954), *reprinted in* 45 Am. J. Int'l L. 123 (1954) (Supp.), 2 Ferencz 460.

[75] *See* 1994 ILC Report, *supra* note 27, and *Summary of the Proceedings of the Preparatory Committee, during the Period Mar. 25–Apr.12, 1996, Preparatory Committee on the Establishment of an International Criminal Court,* U.N. Doc. A/AC.249/CRP.2/Rev.1 (Apr. 11, 1996).

[76] *See, e.g.,* 1949 Geneva Conventions, *supra* note 67; Protocol Additional to the Geneva Conventions of Aug. 12, 1949, and Relating to the Protection of Victims of Non-International Armed Conflicts, U.N. Doc. A/32/144, Aug. 12, 1977.

Several other conventions on the regulation of armed conflicts have also developed since 1945.[77] To the extent that one can trace the influence of 'Nuremberg' on the elaboration of these international instruments, the legal legacy is a positive one.

3. With respect to 'crimes against humanity' no specific convention has been developed.[78] The Genocide Convention of 1948[79] does cover a substantial portion of the conduct that was deemed within the meaning of 'crimes against humanity.' The Convention, however, fails to include social and political groups within its perspective scope. Also, it fails to include mass killings and mass degradation of human rights when they are not accompanied with the intent to destroy the protected group 'in whole or in part.' As a result, a number of mass killings whose numbers reach extraordinary proportions, as those in Bangladesh,[80] and Cambodia[81] did, are not necessarily included within the meaning of genocide because most of the victims are not of a different ethnical or religious group. This gap in the convention leaves many large scale victimization that have occurred in various countries outside the protective coverage of the Convention. But, the inclusion of these and other similar violations of international humanitarian law within the meaning of 'crimes against humanity' evidences the need for a specialized convention on this category of crimes.[82]

4. As for the establishment of a permanent international criminal tribunal, the IMT's legacy has generated developments in the 1951 and 1953 drafts of the United Nations and subsequently in the 1993–94 reports of the ILC.[83] Since 1995 the United Nations is considering these questions, as is discussed.

5. Concerning the codification of international crimes, the 1954 Draft Code of Offenses Against the Peace and Security of Mankind has been replaced by

---

[77] *See, e.g.*, Convention for the Protection of Cultural Property in the Event of Armed Conflict (May 14 1954), 249 U.N.T.S. 240. *See also* HOWARD S. LEVIE, THE CODE OF INTERNATIONAL ARMED CONFLICT, VOLS. I & II (1986); THE LAW OF ARMED CONFLICT, VOLS. I & II (DIETRICH SCHINDLER & JIRI TOMAN eds., 1981); THE LAW OF ARMED CONFLICT: A DOCUMENTARY HISTORY, VOLS. I & II (Leon Friedman ed., 1972).

[78] *See Specialized Convention, supra* note 29.

[79] *See* 1948 Genocide Convention, *supra* note 66.

[80] *See* LEO KUPER, GENOCIDE: ITS POLITICAL USE IN THE TWENTIETH CENTURY 79 (1982); Niall MacDermot, *Crimes Against Humanity in Bangladesh*, 7 INT'L LAW 476 (1973).

[81] KIMMO KILUNJEN, KAMPUCHEA: DECADE OF THE GENOCIDE (1984); Hurst Hannum, *International Law and Cambodian Genocide: The Sounds of Silence*, 11 HUM. RTS. Q. 82, 94 (1989); Michael J. Bazyler, *Reexamining the Doctrine of Humanitarian Intervention In Light of the Atrocities in Kampuchea and Ethiopia*, 23 STAN. J. INT'L L. 547, 550 (1987); Gregory H. Stanton, *Kampuchean Genocide and the World Court*, 2 CONN. J. INT'L L. 341 (1987); Nancy Blodgett, *Cambodia case: Lawyer wants genocide trial*, 7 A.B.A. J. 31 (1985); International Commission of Jurists, *Human Rights in the World*, 20 I.C.J. REV. 1,6 (1978).

[82] *See Specialized Convention, supra* note 29.

[83] For a history of the development of a permanent international criminal court, *see* 1994 ILC Report, *supra* note 27. *See also* M. Cherif Bassiouni, *The Codification of International Criminal Law and the Establishment of an International Criminal Court, in* BASSIOUNI, DRAFT CODE, *supra* note 28, at 1.

the 1996 Draft Code of Crimes Against the Peace and Security of Mankind, which has been approved by the General Assembly. Considering both the slow progress and lack of specificity with which the Draft Code of Crimes is presently drafted, it is hard to predict its wide acceptance by the United Nations Member States. Since it is limited to five crimes, namely aggression, war crimes, genocide, crimes against humanity, and attacks upon United Nations personnel, it cannot be considered a codification of international criminal law which includes twenty-five crimes. They are: Aggression; Genocide; Crimes Against Humanity; War Crimes; Crimes Against United Nations and Associate Personnel; Unlawful Possession or Use or Emplacement of Weapons; Theft of Nuclear Materials; Mercenarism; *Apartheid*; Slavery and Slave Related Practices; Torture and Other Forms of Cruel, Inhuman or Degrading Treatment or Punishment; Unlawful Human Experimentation; Piracy; Aircraft Hijacking and Unlawful Acts Against International Air Safety; Unlawful Acts Against the Safety of Maritime Navigation and the Safety of Platforms on the High Seas; Threat and Use of Force Against Internationally Protected Person; Taking of Civilian Hostages; Unlawful Use of the Mail; Unlawful Traffic in Drugs and Related Drug Offenses; Destruction and/or Theft of National Treasures; Unlawful Acts Against Certain Internationally Protected Elements of the Environment; International Traffic in Obscene Materials; Falsification and Counterfeiting; Unlawful Interference with International Submarine Cables; and Bribery of Foreign Public Officials.

6. 'Nuremberg' focused on individual criminal responsibility for conduct that was the product of state policy and for which collective responsibility and state responsibility could have been assessed. Those who established the IMT were careful to avoid the notions of state and collective responsibility, except with respect to criminal organization, namely the SS, SD, and SA.[84] The simple reason is that these governments did not want to establish a principle that could one day be applied to them. The notion of collective criminal responsibility for membership in a criminal organization now seems to have become more than an extension of the Common Law's expanded concept of criminal conspiracy. Indeed, contemporary non-Common Law legislation on organized crime in many countries criminalize individual conduct based on belonging to a criminal organization or enterprise.

7. In addition to the specific instruments mentioned above, there were also instruments reflecting the moral-ethical values and intellectual ferment deriving from Nuremberg. To a large extent, one may include the various human rights instruments that have developed since World War II in this category.[85]

---

[84] *See* Richard Arens, *Nuremberg and Group Prosecution*, 23 NOTRE DAME LAW 431 (1948); Hans Kelsen, *Collective and Individual Responsibility in International Law with Particular Regard to the Punishment of War Criminals*, 31 CAL. L. REV. 530 (1943).

[85] *See, e.g.*, THE PROTECTION OF HUMAN RIGHTS IN THE ADMINISTRATION OF JUSTICE, (M. Cherif Bassiouni ed., 1994); RICHARD B. LILLICH, INTERNATIONAL HUMAN RIGHTS: PROBLEMS OF LAW, POLICY AND PRACTICE (2d ed. 1991); THEODOR MERON, HUMAN RIGHTS AND

It can however be said that there exists a direct historical link between the Nuremberg and the ICC, as discussed below.[86]

For the reasons suggested earlier, it is difficult to assess and appraise the impact of moral, ethical, intellectual, and social consciousness dimensions of the 'Nuremberg Legal Legacy' on the development of law and legal institutions in the fields of international humanitarian and international human rights law. Nevertheless, it seems a logical conclusion to attribute to this 'Legacy' some influence or impact on the development of law and legal institutions in these fields.

The Moral-Ethical Legacy

There is an intangible 'Nuremberg' legacy that has permeated social values since 1945, shaping the social consciousness of subsequent generations. In this respect, it is difficult to measure or assess the impact of such subjective factors on the individual and collective values and attitudes that have developed since then. However, one can readily perceive that a certain moral-ethical impact has occurred on individual and social values and the social consciousness that reflects these values. These considerations are evident, in part, by the attitudes and values concerning peace and arms control whose contemporary thrust is no longer to attempt to formulate legal norms prohibiting aggression or criminalizing crimes against peace, but to formulate norms to insure the right to peace. The development of the peace movement throughout the world, which has largely influenced contemporary developments in disarmament, may be said to be an outgrowth, or at least a reflection of 'Nuremberg,' even though it is not directly related to 'Nuremberg' *qua*. But it was 'Nuremberg,' as a symbol of what had occurred during World War II, which stands in the minds of those who seek to prevent the recurrence of these events.

Granted, it is not easy, nor at times desirable or useful to distinguish between moral and ethical values and between moral-ethical values and legal values. The reason is that all these are factors on the same continuum: moral-ethical considerations shape social consciousness and social consciousness impacts on the development of law and legal institutions. However, and perhaps more important, the impact of moral-ethical factors on social consciousness may indeed be more significant in terms of the prevention of harmful conduct than the presumed general deterrence of the law, though both are interrelated. These social values and the social consciousness they generate produce more significant

HUMANITARIAN LAW NORMS AS CUSTOMARY LAW (1989); HUMAN RIGHTS IN INTERNATIONAL LAW (Theodor Meron ed., 1984).

[86] *See* M. Cherif Bassiouni, *Historical Survey*; Michael P. Scharf, *The Establishment of a Permanent International Criminal Court.*

deterrence than the law, specifically when law is unenforced. The recurring practices of international crimes evidence this unfortunate reality.[87]

When we assess the impact of the past on the future, we must consider the new and commonly shared values of the world community. We must also consider in that assessment the heightening of social consciousness based on moral-ethical and social values, taken in their global context, along with the development of law and legal institutions that they engender.

There is a paradox, however, in that the Allies in establishing the IMT sought to demonstrate that 'might does not make right.' Yet, if it were not for their might, there could not have been a right, at least there could not have been a trial. In that respect, the French philosopher Blaise Pascal reminds us that:

Justice without force is important. Force without justice is tyrannical. Justice without force is infringed because there is always the mean. One must, therefore, combine justice and force, and, therefore make strong what is right and make right what is wrong.[88]

Conclusion

The 'Nuremberg Legacy' finds its best expression in the intellectual ferment that has developed in the wake of the events of World War II. Indeed, this intellectual ferment is tangibly seen in the books and articles, both scientific and fictional, movies and documentaries, speeches and debates in all media forms, as well as through various other forms of human communication such as group discussion, public speeches, in educational materials, classroom instruction, in legal doctrine and jurisprudence, and in the utterances and actions of governmental, intergovernmental, nongovernmental and international bodies. All these manifestations fall into the category of intellectual ferment, and it is precisely because of the moral-ethical component of the 'Nuremberg Legacy' that this process has developed. It is beyond the scope of this article to attempt to develop a theory on how to quantify or appraise the volume, significance, or impact of Nuremberg on social consciousness and the development of law and legal institutions. Nevertheless, the point needs to be made that a corollary relationship exists objectively and subjectively between all the interconnected and interacting factors mentioned above. It is, however, a valid assumption that the intellectual ferment that has persisted since that period has strengthened individual and collective values in many societies, some more than others, and that in turn has contributed

---

[87] *See, e.g.,* FARHAD MALEKIAN, INTERNATIONAL CRIMINAL LAW: THE LEGAL AND CRITICAL ANALYSIS OF INTERNATIONAL CRIMES (1991); Jescheck, *supra* note 53; DIETRICH OEHLER, INTERNATIONALES STRAFRECHT (1983); OTTO TRIFFERER, DOGMATISCHE UNTERSUCHUNGEN ZUR ENTWICKLUNG DES MATERIELLEN VÖLKERSTRAFRECHTS SEIT NÜRNBERG (1966); ANTONIO QUINTANO RIPOLLES, TRATADO DE DERECHO PENAL INTERNACIONAL E INTERNACIONAL PENAL (1955); de Vabres, *supra* note 53.

[88] BLAISE PASCAL, PENSÉES: THE PROVINCIAL LETTERS (W.F. Trotter trans., 1941).

to further a heightening of social consciousness, resulting in the development of law and legal institutions. Thus, to a large extent, the legal legacy of Nuremberg may be viewed as a direct outgrowth of the cumulative effect of these factors, which in some way can be traced to the moral-ethical legacy of Nuremberg. Regrettably, however, nothing said above has lessened the human tragedies of the post-Nuremberg world, even as the human toll that resulted exceeds that of World War II. The contemporary examples of the wars in Cambodia, the former Yugoslavia and Rwanda, and the atrocities attendant to them bear out this point. Thus, deterrence, the ultimate goal of 'Nuremberg,' has yet to be achieved in a world more divided today than it was 50 years ago.[89]

The sense of justice, no matter how philosophers and social and behavioral scientists argue about it, is in this author's opinion an irreducible part of our social needs. It is also part of the fundamental values of most societies throughout the history of the different civilizations that have existed since *homo sapiens* organized in social settings. What human experience indicates is that the value of justice, its content, and application vary between individuals and from one social group to another. These variances can also be seen as changing in time within the same individual and the same group. But at the risk of greatly oversimplifying this complex question it is, nonetheless, correct to say that contemporary social values in almost every society include the aspiration toward international justice. A better world would be a system of equal and fair justice that would strengthen world order, provide deterrence and retribution on a nonselective basis for the decision-makers and major perpetrators who commit serious international crimes. But the need, no matter how much shared throughout the world community, is effectively thwarted by decision-makers whose cynicism and callousness is only too visible to those who want to see. Instead of promoting, they subvert and surely impede it, no matter how pious their pronouncements may be.

As one who has carefully studied the evolution of international criminal law, and more recently has been a close and direct observer of one of the tragic events mentioned above,[90] one must regrettably conclude that so long as we are unable or unwilling to establish a permanent institution of international criminal justice free from political controls and capable of enforcing its judgments no matter where or against whom, we are condemned to repeat the mistakes of the past and suffer their consequences.

---

[89] *See* M. Cherif Bassiouni, *The Need for International Accountability.*

[90] As former Chairman and Rapporteur on the Gathering and Analysis of the Facts, Commission of Experts established pursuant to Security Council Resolution 780 (1992) to investigate violations of international humanitarian law in the Former Yugoslavia. *See also* Final Report of the Commission of Experts established pursuant to Security Council Resolution 780 (1992), U.N. SCOR, U.N. Doc. S/1994/674 (May 27, 1994); M. Cherif Bassiouni, *The United Nations Commission of Experts Established Pursuant to Security Council Resolution 780 (1992)*, 88 Am. J. Int'l L. 784 (1994). *See* M. Cherif Bassiouni (with the Collaboration of Peter Manikas), The Law of the International Criminal Tribunal for the Former Yugoslavia (1996).

The Nuremberg promise of justice is yet to be fulfilled. However, without its legacy we would not know how much we progressed, nor how much still needs to progress to achieve international criminal justice.

World public opinion is far ahead of the cautious position of many governments on the establishment of an effective and fair system of international criminal justice. In fact, the gap between these positions is wide, and governments cannot ignore it if they are to retain their credibility about establishing such a system of justice, operating under the Rule of Law and free from the manipulations of *realpolitik* which sees the pursuit of political settlements as having priority over justice.

The dedicated idealism of many scholars, researchers, public officials and concerned people all over the world continues to press for an independent, fair and effective system of international criminal justice. The driving force of that idealism is our hope that it will overcome the opposition of political cynicism and the reticence that led to inaction for such a long time. Impunity must no longer be the reward of those who commit the most egregious international crimes and serious violations of human rights.[91] The quantum of human harm produced since World War II by conflicts of a noninternational character, purely internal conflicts and victimization by tyrannical regimes, far exceed the combined outcomes of World War I and World War II.[92] Yet, the overwhelming majority of perpetrators have benefitted from impunity.[93] World public opinion, however, rejects the cynicism and complacency of governments who manipulate the processes of justice to achieve political ends.

An international system of criminal justice may not stop future conflicts and horrors, but it could have some deterrent effect. And, if so, it can spare lives and prevent human depredations. If nothing else, however, it would symbolize certain world community values. Last, but not least, it would vindicate the victims of international crimes and remind ourselves and future generations of the victims plight and the perpetrators misdeeds. To paraphrase the philosopher George Santayana, if we do not record and learn the bitter lessons of the past we are condemned to repeat our mistakes.

---

[91] *See* M. Cherif Bassiouni, *The Need for International Accountability.*
[92] *Id.*   [93] *Id.*

26

Judicial Inheritance: The Value and Significance of the Nuremberg Trial to Contemporary War Crimes Tribunals

By Guénaël Mettraux

Weighing Up Nuremberg's Legacy, Sixty Years On

At Nuremberg, chief defendant Hermann Goering predicted that the Tribunal charged with judging him and his associates would be a failure: 'You will see— this trial will be a disgrace in 15 years.'[1]

The fact that history did not bear out Goering's prophecy does not render an assessment of the Nuremberg Trial any easier. A perceptive observer put it well when she suggested that seeking to draw out lessons from these proceedings resembled a quest for the hidden echoes of man's prayers to God:

That trial was a sort of legalistic prayer that the Kingdom of Heaven should be with us; but the answer was, like all answers to prayers, coming in not as clearly as it might be.[2]

The present essay will not discuss every aspect of the Trial's legacy. Instead, it will focus on some of the most significant contributions which the Nuremberg process—the adoption of the Tribunal's Charter, the Trial and the Judgment— has made to modern-day international criminal justice. Nuremberg has left behind a jurisdictional model that serves other similar undertakings, procedural rules, and a trail of norms and principles to be copied or modelled in other circumstances. Most importantly, it has given moral and political weight to the idea that a court of law is capable of sanctioning the commission of international crimes. But whilst modern tribunals borrowed generously from the Nuremberg Trial, it is they which have turned Nuremberg into a precedent, they which have made it relevant to the present and not just to the past.

---

[1] G. Gilbert, *Nuremberg Diary* (New York: Farrar, Straus, 1947), p. 135.
[2] Rebecca West, in A. Neave, *Nuremberg—A Personal Record of the Trial of the Major Nazi War Criminals* (London: Hodder and Stoughton, 1978), pp. 5–6.

Nowadays, and with a few noticeable exceptions, most of the law that was set out at Nuremberg is accepted as forming part of customary international criminal law. Much of that body of rules and principles may in turn be found in the statutes of modern-day international criminal tribunals and all through their jurisprudence. This state of affairs is not accidental. Nuremberg was always intended to set a precedent capable of serving the ends of justice for future generations. In its Judgment, the Tribunal made it clear that the Charter was both an expression of international law existing at the time, as well as a contribution to international law for the future.[3] In that sense, the punishment of the Nazi war criminals was conceived as a means to a greater end, a step towards more accountability and towards an enhanced role for the rule of law at the international level.

Some of the legal principles set out at Nuremberg are now so central to international criminal law that they stand beyond the realm of challenge. However, a few of Nuremberg's legal pronouncements have not stood the test of time. Most famously, the criminalization of aggressive war by the Charter of the Tribunal did not come to be regarded as a general prohibition recognized by international law. The failed criminalization of aggressive war has taught the international community that under international law, as with domestic law, there is an 'economy of the law' and that where the law undertakes more than it can effectively achieve, it will be ignored or disregarded.[4]

But it would be wrong to limit the significance of the Nuremberg Trial to the identification and application of a set of legal concepts, however important they may be. The Nuremberg proceedings have initiated a new way to make or to create international law. Up to that point, the creation process of international law had remained almost exclusively in the hands of nation states. International law resulted from their interaction, reflected the nature of their individual strength and was shaped by the confrontation of their common or competing interests. Although much of the law of Nuremberg was the result of negotiations between four powerful states which had won the war, the Judgment of the Tribunal and its recognition that these statutory provisions reflected the state of international law at that time turned a body of law applicable to twenty-two defendants into general international law. As happened at Nuremberg, the judicial activities of modern war crimes tribunals serve to expand and crystallize further the body of rules and principles that make up international criminal law. The availability of a judicial forum is not just a chance for international criminal law to be applied, but it is a necessary platform from which this body of law may assert its relevance and grow.

---

[3] See *History of the United Nations War Crimes Commission and the Development of the Laws of War*, compiled by the United Nations War Crimes Commission (His Majesty's Stationery Office, 1948), at 260.

[4] R. B. Perry, *Realms of Value—A Critique of Human Civilization* (Cambridge: Harvard University Press, 1954), 230–231.

The empowerment of the judiciary as a legitimate *enabler* of international law has also opened the door to a new set of values in the form of considerations of humanity which until that point in time had only played a minor or secondary role in the development of international law. The principle of human dignity and the view that the law should help deter international crimes came to the fore through the Nuremberg proceedings and contributed significantly to the acceleration of the process of moralization and humanization of international law. After the trial, it was thus noted that 'the whole aim of international law, in recent times, has been to give a definite and positive shape to the moral concepts, which, in some quarters and in some periods, have been thought too fluid and indefinite to deserve the name of positive law'.[5] This moralistic view of the judicial process is characteristic, not just of the Nuremberg proceedings, but of most contemporary efforts to bring to justice the perpetrators of mass atrocities. In that conception, war crimes trials are not just about the responsibility of an accused person, but about peace, reconciliation, historical truths, and the betterment of humanity through the law.[6]

Nuremberg and the Shrinking Alternatives to Justice

Of all the events and incidents that make up the history of international criminal justice, the trial of the Major Nazi War Criminals at Nuremberg might be its most important. Although the Nuremberg Trial did not mark the birth of international criminal justice as an idea, it truly was its first modern realization and after the war it symbolized the re-emergence of the rule of law as a factor of relevance to international relations. The Trial, it was hoped at the time, could contribute to replacing violence and lawlessness with a future in which international law would find a place among the considerations that play a role in deciding whether to engage in war and the way in which it is conducted.

The Nuremberg Trial was never merely a judicial event. It was conceived and pursued as a moral and historical enterprise with which those involved in the business of war and peace should have to reckon with in the future.[7] The proceedings were also to serve as a powerful contrast of values between the brutality of a defeated enemy and the enlightened values of the victors. Its importance to the world, Justice Jackson noted in his opening address, was therefore not to be

[5] *History of the United Nations War Crimes Commission and the Development of the Laws of War*, compiled by the United Nations War Crimes Commission (His Majesty's Stationery Office, 1948), at 18.

[6] See, e.g., *Report of the International Tribunal for the Prosecution of Persons Responsible for Serious Violations of International Humanitarian Law in the Territory of the Former Yugoslavia Since 1991*, First Annual Report, U.N. Doc. A/49/342, S/1994/1007 (29 August 1994), par 11.

[7] T. Taylor, *Final Report to the Secretary of the Army on the Nuernberg War Crimes Trials under Control Council Law No. 10* (New York: William S. Hein & Co., 1997), 234.

measured solely or even primarily by the quality and breadth of its findings, but by the contribution it would make to rendering 'the peace [of the world] more secure'.[8] The Nuremberg Trial did not render the world a less dangerous place, nor has it secured peace. However, the punishment of the Nazi leaders made it clear that the society of nations was also a society of men and that international law would reach beyond the artificial borders of the state to punish those who breach the most basic precepts of that society of men and who endanger the peace of the world when so doing. To this day, the establishment of war crimes tribunals is still viewed as a way not just to end such crimes and bring the guilty to justice, but also as a mechanism capable of contributing to the restoration and maintenance of peace in those places that have witnessed the commission of these crimes.[9]

Until the trial of the major Nazi leaders, the response of the international community to large-scale criminal campaigns had mostly consisted of two unpalatable alternatives: further violence or impunity. Nuremberg offered a civilized substitute to both courses. The leaders and servants of a vanquished state were to account for their actions after a full and fair investigation of their individual responsibility. A group of independent judges replaced political and military leaders as the ultimate deciders of their enemy's fate. And the propriety of these enemies' conduct was to be assessed in legal, rather than political, terms. To realize the importance of this advance, one only needs to consider the political and moral alternatives to a trial by law.

The Nuremberg proceedings may be said to have contributed to rendering alternatives to justice a less obvious, less appealing and more questionable course of action where mass atrocities have been committed. Prior to the trial, fallen enemies who had committed crimes could expect little or no mercy from their conquerors. What decided their fate was their defeat, not their individual responsibility. That Nazi mass murderers should be brought to justice rather than be summarily executed, as some would have preferred, was therefore a major advance for humanity, one that has rightly been described as 'one of the most significant tributes that Power ever has paid to Reason'.[10]

The decision to try the Nazi leaders, however, was not without moral ambivalence. Those who set up the Tribunal were unwilling to subject their own actions to the standard which they applied to the conduct of their fallen enemies. This ambiguity did not dissipate after the Trial. Rather, it was reawakened, and the accusation of selectivity rejuvenated, every time an international crime was committed and left unpunished. The refusal of the Prosecutor of the Yugoslav Tribunal

---

[8] The Trial of German Major War Criminals, Opening Speeches of the Chief Prosecutors, Opening Speech by Mr. Justice Robert H. Jackson (The United States of America) (His Majesty's Stationery Office, 1946) at 45.

[9] See *United Nations Security Council Resolution 827* (1993), adopted 25 May 1993, S/RES/827 (1993) (ICTY) and *United Nations Security Council Resolution 995* (1994), adopted 8 November 1994, S/RES/955 (1994) (ICTR).

[10] *Opening Speeches of the Chief Prosecutors*, The Trial of German Major War Criminals by the International Military Tribunal Sitting at Nuremberg, Germany, 20 November 1945, p. 3.

to formally open an investigation into the actions of NATO forces during the Kosovo campaign was a sobering reminder of the limitations of international criminal justice. In that sense, Nuremberg may be said to have established 'a dangerous precedent',[11] one against which the impotence of international justice and the selectivity with which it is put in motion will be measured every time international crimes are committed and remain unpunished.

Despite this ambivalence, the Nuremberg precedent has provided much of the moral and political impetus, as well as the legal backbone, that later served to build and legitimize more recent efforts to bring war criminals to justice. Over the next sixty years, the Nuremberg process went on to grow deep roots into the political and moral conscience of decision-makers, lawyers, and the general public. Several United Nations war crimes tribunals, a permanent international criminal court, and a variety of semi-international bodies are a testament to the contemporary vitality of the Nuremberg spirit and to the shrinking alternatives to justice. Though it has by no means rendered it inevitable, the Nuremberg trial has transformed the hitherto unthinkable—a judicial response to mass atrocities—into a more obvious and more civilized political response to the commission of mass atrocities.

A Moral and Historical *Trait-D'union*

After the trial, Justice Biddle noted that the lessons of Nuremberg could be ephemeral or significant: 'That depends on whether we now take the next step. [...] I suggest that the time has now come to set about drafting a code of international criminal law.'[12] Such a code was never adopted, but the law of Nuremberg did not die from the absence of a written record. It merely remained in a state of suspension until it was adopted by later tribunals as the foundation of their jurisdiction.

But whilst the decisions to set up the Nuremberg and Tokyo Tribunals had been fed by the rage of years of war against the Axis Powers, the forces that eventually brought international criminal justice back to life were slower to coalesce. These were the result of less potent, but perhaps more durable, influences. The growing significance of human rights and humanitarian law, the disappearance of a bipolar world order, the increased instituationalization of international relations, and the realization that impunity had too often fettered up into new conflicts all contributed to making international criminal justice once again a reasonable response to mass atrocities.

---

[11] T. Taylor, *Final Report to the Secretary of the Army on the Nuernberg War Crimes Trials under Control Council Law No. 10* (New York: William S. Hein & Co., 1997), 235.

[12] Judge Biddle's Report to the President of the United States, Harry Truman, 9 November 1946.

It is not without some degree of historical irony that the dormant significance of the Nuremberg Trial was at last reawakened in the early 1990s by the death and dismemberment of one of the last political vestiges of the Second World War in Europe: Yugoslavia. The historical parallel was not lost to the creators of what was to become the first of the United Nations' war crimes tribunals, the International Criminal Tribunal for the Former Yugoslavia (ICTY). During the adoption of the Tribunal's Statute, several Security Council members thus brandished the Nuremberg precedent to validate their bold initiative. 'There is an echo in this Chamber today,' Madeleine Albright, the US Secretary of State exclaimed during the creation process of the ICTY, '[t]he Nuremberg Principles have been reaffirmed. We have preserved the long-neglected compact made by the community of civilized nations 48 years ago in San Francisco to create the United Nations and enforce the Nuremberg Principles.'[13] The Nuremberg Trial offered the Tribunal's creators a very cogent precedent for an otherwise strange idea. Nuremberg also served at that time as a banner for those who supported the creation of an international tribunal and who claimed moral superiority over those who they intended to subject to its jurisdiction. The purifying value of international criminal justice, which had offered some degree of moral cleansing for the victors at Nuremberg, has not ceased to matter as it continues to provide a symbolic demarcation between *them* and *us*, those who break the law and those responsible to enforce it. But every *ad hoc* judicial effort also further emphasizes the less than universal nature of international criminal justice and its inherent selectivity, reinforcing in its very existence the strength of the accusation of political opportunism that had already been made at Nuremberg.

The United Nations Tribunals have worked hard to keep alive this great historical connection with the Nuremberg Tribunal. Nuremberg has indeed come to represent the victory of Justice over the great historical evil of Nazism. Any association with the Nuremberg Trial thus endows its recipient with some degree of the moral grandeur that attaches to this process. In the case of the United Nations' war crimes Tribunals, this descendancy is much vaunted as a way to give greater moral force to their own proceedings. This moral *trait-d'union* has also at times been used to convince doubters of the righteousness of the Tribunals' mission by suggesting that sixty years on, international criminal tribunals are still chasing the same evil as was being punished in Nuremberg.

The connection between the Nuremberg process and modern war crimes tribunals is not only moral, but also plainly historical. For as judicial oddities, as all international war crimes tribunals were and remain, the Nuremberg process is reassuringly similar. A 'Nuremberg connection' thus provides those courts and

[13] Provisional Verbatim Record of the Three-Thousand One-Hundred and Seventy-Fifth Meeting of the Security Council, 22 February 1993, S/PV. 3175, reprinted in V. Morris and M. Scharf, *An Insider's Guide to the International Criminal Tribunal for the Former Yugoslavia* (New York: Transnational Publishers, 1995), vol. 2, 165.

tribunals with a sense of historical continuity between the founding Nuremberg moment and themselves. It also gives them a sense of community in their exist-ence as dispensers of international criminal justice.

The Nuremberg Foundations of International Criminal Justice

Nuremberg contributed more to modern war crimes courts than simply endow-ing these courts with a degree of moral and political legitimacy. It also played a major part in framing the scope and the nature of their jurisdictions. The drafters of the Statutes of the first United Nations *ad hoc* Tribunals, for Yugoslavia and Rwanda, realized that precedents were rare in the area of war crimes prosecutions and that Nuremberg offered one of the very few models on which to shape the jurisdictional framework of these new tribunals.

The importance of Nuremberg to establishing the jurisdictional framework of those Tribunals was not limited to providing lists of crimes, forms of liability, and available defences that could then be used in another context. Just as importantly, the Nuremberg process had the effect of validating those crimes and other legal principles to such an extent that it had put many of them beyond the realm of challenge. The principle that an individual could be held criminally responsible under international law for certain types of violations of that law, for instance, is now taken for granted. It is likewise beyond dispute that crimes against human-ity and war crimes constitute criminal offences under customary international law and that 'superior orders' does not offer a valid defence to serious violations of international humanitarian law.

Copying the Nuremberg model was, for these tribunals, to avoid one of the pitfalls of Nuremberg itself. At Nuremberg, the Charter of the International Military Tribunal had been loudly criticized for introducing concepts and norms which did not seem to have had any precedent or roots in existing international law. Harking back into the past in search of precedents has allowed contempor-ary war crimes trials to avoid the frontal accusation that the content of their stat-utes was no more than the exercise of political opportunism. But by adopting Nuremberg standards and definitions, modern tribunals have also accepted to carry with them the drawbacks of a law that in many respects lacked precision and seemed in some cases to have only a casual appreciation of general principles of criminal law. The definitions of crimes against humanity and its underlying offences, as adopted from Nuremberg, for instance, often consist in not much more than a descriptive expression that says little about its elements or its scope.

The acceptance by modern-day tribunals of the Nuremberg model was also to proceed in what could be described as a procedural fog with little evidential or procedural guidance. At Nuremberg, Judge Parker had noted that '[t]he Charter [of Nuremberg] very wisely steered away from technical rules of evidence and provided that anything having probative value should be received'.[14] The wisdom of such a course lies in the fact that the specificities of war crimes trials demand a degree of flexibility in the way the proceedings should be conducted so as to prevent the rules that govern the proceedings from impending the process itself. The same philosophy transpires from the procedural regimes adopted by most modern war crimes tribunals. It should be noted, however, that the wisdom of such a course is not unqualified. Parties appearing before an international criminal tribunal may at times be left to guess the course of the proceedings and may feel professionally embarrassed by the absence of guiding principles as to the way in which they should or are permitted to conduct their affairs. Within a single tribunal, the procedural course may vary greatly from one trial proceeding to the other, thus creating an appearance of unfairness where certain procedural safeguards are applied in some but not all cases or not to the same extent. The current lack of procedural clarity in international criminal proceedings is a rather unfortunate legacy of Nuremberg's procedural laissez-faire.

The ambiguities that attach to the Nuremberg legacy are not limited to its substantive and procedural heritage. The Nuremberg process has often been credited with undermining the idea of the absolute sovereignty of states under international law. By both criminalizing certain categories of recourse to war and by denying state officials the benefit of certain immunities which they might otherwise have been able to claim for acts undertaken in the name of or on behalf of a State, the Nuremberg Judgment did much to support the view that state sovereignty could be pierced and set aside where the interests of the international community were at stake. In so doing, the Nuremberg Trial has placed strict limitations upon what until then had been the all-powerfulness of the state. Nuremberg has brought individuals to the fore of international law, making them accountable for breaches of international law which they have committed. Since those days, however, the inroad made into the territory of state sovereignty has remained modest and rather superficial. International criminal justice is still dependent upon the cooperation of states and in many cases upon their willingness to subject their sovereignty to any form of judicial interference. Cooperation with international criminal tribunals is still commonly perceived by states whose interests are at stake to be a matter of convenience and expediency, but more rarely as a duty that is owed to the court. Where a state is powerful enough to offer resistance, there is often little an international criminal court can do to force that state to comply with a court order. It would seem quite wrong to suggest, therefore, that Nuremberg and its successors have undone or redefined the principle of state sovereignty. What they have done, however, is to help draw the borders and limitations of that

---

[14] J. Parker, 'International Trial at Nuremberg: Giving Vitality to International Law', 37 *American Bar Association Journal* 493 (December 1946), at 553.

notion with more precision and identify a number of circumstances where state sovereignty could not stand in the way of a criminal conviction.[15]

As noted above, the substantive—*ratione materiae*—jurisdictional framework of all United Nations' international criminal tribunals owes much of its content and form to the Nuremberg Charter and Judgment, with two noticeable differences: genocide and aggression. Whilst genocide was not recognized as a discrete category of criminal offence at Nuremberg, it figures prominently in the Statutes of the Tribunals for Rwanda and Yugoslavia. The crime of aggression, or crime against peace, on the other hand, was criminalized by the Charter of the Nuremberg Tribunal, but does not appear in any of the Statutes of the United Nations's Tribunals.

The main contribution of Nuremberg to substantive criminal law would appear to lie in the recognition of crimes against humanity as a separate category of international crimes distinct from traditional war crimes. The definition of crimes against humanity has not evolved much since Nuremberg but for the disappearance of the requirement that they should be linked to an armed conflict or to any other category of crimes. The text of Statutes of the United Nations' Tribunals thus repeats almost verbatim the definition of crimes against humanity contained in the Charter of the IMT.[16] The Nuremberg Charter and Judgment are also often regarded by contemporary tribunals as having provided the foundation or, in fact, proof of the criminalization of particular conducts as international crimes, as in the case, for instance, with the crimes of 'deportation'[17] or 'wanton destruction of cities, towns and villages'.[18] Prior to that time, the underlying conduct that make up such offences might have been regarded as illegal or impermissible, but no criminal consequences attached to the violation of such prohibitions. The International Military Tribunal and later tribunals have endowed these, and other illegal actions, with penal or criminal consequences.

As far as individual criminal liability is concerned, the Nuremberg legacy is most important for adopting the view that individuals, and not only states, could be held responsible for violations of international law:

Crimes against international law are committed by men, not by abstract entities, and only by punishing individuals who commit such crimes can the provisions of international law be enforced.[19]

More modest is Nuremberg's contribution to the law relevant to modes of liability. The crime of membership in a criminal organization has not been

---

[15] See, e.g., *Prosecutor v Charles Taylor*, SCSL-2003-01-I, Decision on Immunity from Jurisdiction, 31 May 2004.

[16] Compare Article 6(C) of the IMT Charter with, e.g., Article 5 of the ICTY Statute, Article 3 of the ICTR Statute and Article 2 of the SCSL Statute.

[17] *Prosecutor v Stakic*, Appeals Judgment (ICTY), 22 March 2006, pars. 276 and 290.

[18] See *Prosecutor v Brdjanin*, Trial Judgement (ICTY), 1 September 2004, par. 157.

[19] *Judgment of the International Military Tribunal for the Trial of German Major War Criminals*, Nuremberg, 30 September and 1 October 1946 (New York: William S. Hein & Co., Inc., 2001), p. 41.

adopted by later international criminal tribunals, whilst the doctrine of 'conspiracy', an important piece of the Prosecution case at Nuremberg, only applies today to the crime of genocide. Other forms of liability that now form part of customary international law, such as command responsibility, grew up outside of the Nuremberg umbrella. The limited impact of the Tribunal's pronouncement upon the principles of criminal liability also results from the fact that the Tribunal declined to define the various forms of liability recognized by the Charter or to provide detailed theoretical explication for its findings of fact, adopting instead a very pragmatic approach to these issues. 'We are not a discussion club', Judge Nikitchenko once exclaimed in front of his colleagues.

The limited ambitions of the Nuremberg Trial, as far as concern the law of criminal liability, is not necessarily to be regarded as a negative. The solidity of the foundations of the law stated in the Nuremberg Judgment lies in part in the relatively modest outlook which the Tribunal took of its role as regard this question. As pointed out by one participant in the trial, '[t]he Court did not yield to the temptation to create a dramatic, but ephemeral, advance; it chose instead to produce a clear, though modest, contribution to a safer future'.[20] The Nuremberg judges interpreted the principles of liability quite narrowly, and conservatively one may say, in particular as regards the law of conspiracy and membership in criminal organizations.[21] The discomfort, or the plain sense of injustice, which those concepts awoke with some of the judges may explain the reluctance of the Tribunal to give full effect to the law of the Charter, despite its binding nature. The approach of the Nuremberg Tribunal in that regard contrasts starkly with the generally proactive, and sometimes plainly legislative, tendencies of the *ad hoc* Tribunals. The scope and reach of the concept of 'joint criminal enterprise' as has developed before the *ad hoc* Tribunals for the Former Yugoslavia and Rwanda, for instance, is a prime example of such tendencies.[22] In some ways, this might be one illustration of the Nuremberg lessons unlearnt or at least one that was lost to its successors. It might be the case, also, that in the days of the Nuremberg Trial, the judges were more acutely aware that they themselves were being judged.[23]

The Nuremberg Trial has also set the framework within which defendants may avail themselves of certain defences to justify their actions or to mitigate the gravity of their guilt. Significantly, Nuremberg abolished the defence of superior orders and the theory that the doctrine of 'acts of state' could provide a valid defence to charges of international crimes. In so doing, the Nuremberg Trial

---

[20] B. Smith, *Reaching Judgment at Nuremberg* (New York: Basic Books, 1967), p. 306.

[21] See, on this issue, Francis Biddle, 'The Nürnberg Trial', 91(3) *Proceedings of the American Philosophical Society*, 294–302 (August 1947) (reprinted in this volume). See, also, Henri Donnedieu de Vabres, 'Le procès de Nuremberg devant les principes modernes du Droit Pénal International', 70 *Recueil des Cours de l'Académie de droit international de La Haye* 477–582 (1947–I) (reprinted in this volume).

[22] For a discussion of that concept, see, generally, 'Symposium: Guilty by Association: Joint Criminal Enterprise on Trial', in *Journal of International Criminal Justice*, vol. 5 March 2007.

[23] The Midrash, cited in E. Wiesel, *The Judges* (New York: Alfred A. Knopf, 1999).

expanded the reach of international criminal law a great deal and broke with the idea that those who committed international crimes could hide behind the state in whose name they have acted. Those were necessary developments for international criminal law to be able to capture the criminal conduct of state leaders such as the Nazi defendants at Nuremberg. These developments have been consecrated and adopted in the constitutive documents of all modern international criminal tribunals.

From the viewpoint of contemporary tribunals, the law of Nuremberg is not only a catalogue of concepts and rules from which to borrow. In some respects, the law of Nuremberg constitutes a *sui generis* source of law for modern-day war crimes tribunals, which serves an almost *constitutional* function. When looking for legal legitimation of their own jurisdiction or to justify departure from generally applicable principles of criminal law, international tribunals will often turn to Nuremberg. The UN Tribunal for the former Yugoslavia did so, for instance, when suggesting that the concept of 'joint criminal enterprise' was well grounded in international practice. The sacred value of some of the Nuremberg pronouncements, including the principles that individuals may be accountable under international law and the hierarchy of norms which the judgment sanctions between international and national law, lie at the core of these tribunals' foundations. The reverential attitude of modern-day tribunals towards Nuremberg is qualified by a certain amount of reluctance or hesitancy to refer to these proceedings in the course of their finding perhaps, one may suggest, because of the difficulty to create a sense of moral equivalence between the horrors of the Nazi regime and even the most serious of modern crimes. When reviewing the case law of modern tribunals for references to the Nuremberg process, the surprise lies perhaps more in the fact that few such references are to be found rather than many.

The influence of the law of Nuremberg over the Statute of the International Criminal Court (ICC) has been more indirect and more selective. This body of law has passed through the jurisdictions of the Yugoslav and Rwanda Tribunals and has been both qualified and amplified by them before being, in turn, subjected to a long process of negotiation before making it in part and in qualified fashion into the Statute of the ICC. Although the ICC Statute recognizes war crimes, crimes against humanity, and genocide as separate categories of crimes and defines those in much the same way as the United Nations' Tribunals, the Statute has both qualified and specified certain aspects of those definitions. For the time being, the ICC Statute has also left an empty seat for the crime of aggression in which one day a genuine criminal offence might grow. But until that time when a definition may be agreed upon by the state parties of the ICC, it will be regarded more as a symbol of judicial impotence than as an important legal advance. The relationship between the ICC and Nuremberg is thus more indirect than was the case with the *ad hoc* Tribunals. But a sense of judicial continuity from Nuremberg to the *ad hoc* Tribunals onwards is slowly settling in and precedents have multiplied over the years, diminishing the need for today's tribunals to make reference to the far-away past. The fact that references to the Nuremberg Trial might be decreasing in the jurisprudence of war crimes tribunals is not a sign of its diminishing importance. As the Preamble of the ICC Statute and many of its provisions make clear, the purposes and rules that had applied to this trial are now accepted as law. Although many other factors played their part in shaping it, the law of the ICC is in many ways the result of the 'generative power'[24] of the Nuremberg precedent.

A Propensity to Law-Making and Other Inheritance

Opportunities to develop international criminal law rarely come and pass quickly. At Nuremberg, it was clear that a rare legislative moment had arrived and that it should be seized. The Charter of the IMT reflects the desire of its drafters to let the law catch up with generally-accepted moral standards so that a conduct which constitutes a grave violation of moral standards could not be regarded as 'innocent in law'.[25] At Nuremberg, moral demands became justification enough for the progress of the law.

A similarly moralistic and progressive approach to law-making as had animated the drafters of the Nuremberg Charter can be seen at play throughout the jurisprudence of the United Nations war crimes tribunals. But whereas the legal boldness of Nuremberg is laid in the Charter, not in the Judgment of the Tribunal, the reverse seems to be true with contemporary tribunals. Whilst their statutory instruments are relatively conservative in nature, their jurisprudence has been of a very progressive sort. Few have been the occasions in recent years when a war crimes tribunal has interpreted international law in a narrow or restrictive fashion when an ambivalence in the law was identified: Common Article 3 of the 1949 Geneva Conventions has been said to apply to both internal and international armed conflict; oral sexual assault may qualify as rape; torture may be committed by state officials, as well as by private individuals; the protection of the grave breach regime of the Geneva Convention is now said to apply to nationals of the same country if the allegiance of the victim and the perpetrator is to a different state; conviction for certain types of participation in a genocidal crime may not require proof of genocidal intent; superior responsibility has been said not to require proof of a causal relationship between the failure of the superior and the crimes of his subordinates. The law that is in the making becomes the law and doubts as to its content are often blanked out. The view taken of the function of international criminal law and the philosophy that underlies that body of law

---

[24] B. Cardozo, *The Nature of the Judicial Process* (New Haven: Yale University Press, 3rd ed., 1960), p. 21.
[25] The Trial of German Major War Criminals, Opening Speeches of the Chief Prosecutors, Opening Speech by Mr Justice Robert H. Jackson (The United States of America), (His Majesty's Stationery Office, 1946) at 46.

is often put forth as a legitimizing factor to explain jurisprudential developments which might otherwise fall foul of basic principles of criminal law, in particular the principle of legality.[26]

Neither the law of Nuremberg, nor the law developed by modern war crimes courts, has been merely revealed from a pre-existing source. Just like the judgment of history has not accepted the proposition that crimes against peace had pre-existed the Nuremberg Trial, it is unlikely that history will accept the view that many aspects of the law of the *ad hoc* Tribunals merely reflected customary international law when they were *discovered*. The fact that so much of the law of Nuremberg has survived despite some liberties taken with the principle of legality suggests that international law will forgive the original sin of its creation if that standard comes to be generally accepted and applied, including by those who had a hand in creating such standard. Where it is not the case, the risk exists that a small excess of law-making could come to be regarded as a great injustice.

Contemporary tribunals have inherited other unfortunate attributes from their predecessor, including a sometimes confusing and opportunistic use of sources. Treaties that were binding on states only and which did not provide for any criminal sanctions were relied upon at Nuremberg to demonstrate the criminal character of aggressive war and to justify individuals being held accountable for it. Non-binding and declaratory instruments were given an importance that they were never intended to have. The same impermissible assimilation of state and personal responsibility and of illegality and criminality is also not uncommon before the *ad hoc* Tribunals.[27] Principles said to amount to general principles of law are often no more than a limited and selective set of similar national provisions. The treatment of customary law by the *ad hoc* Tribunals is likewise open to serious criticism. The judicial *revelation* of customary rules by the United Nations Tribunals can hardly hide the legislative role of the court in that process. For many of today's rules of international criminal law, their customary status owes as much to state practice and *opinio juris*, the traditional ingredients of customary norms, as it does to the normative process that has been injected into the rule in question by the decision of the court.[28]

Finally, though this observation would itself warrant much closer attention, it can be noted that modern war crimes tribunals have inherited from the Nuremberg precedent a scant and inadequate sentencing regime that gives defendants little or no notice of their possible punishment other than the fact that they incur potentially very heavy sentences. A major advance in that regard has

---

[26] See, for a telling illustration of those tensions between the development of international criminal law and basic principles of criminal law, A. Cassese, 'Black Letter Lawyering v. Constructive Interpretation: The *Vasiljevic* Case', 2(1) *Journal of International Criminal Justice*, 265–274 (2004).

[27] See, e.g., the treatment of the crime of 'terror' by the *Galic* Trial Chamber of the ICTY (*Prosecutor v. Galic*, Judgment and Opinion, 5 December 2003, paragraphs 63 *et seq*. (ICTY)).

[28] See, generally, G. Mettraux, *International Crimes and the ad hoc Tribunals* (Oxford: Oxford University Press, 2006), pp. 13–18.

been the abandonment by contemporary tribunals of the death sentence which had been pronounced against twelve defendants at Nuremberg.

The Significance of Modern War Crimes Tribunals to Nuremberg

The relationship between the Nuremberg process and modern war crimes tribunals is not a one-way street. Whilst contemporary tribunals have for the most part been faithful disciples of Nuremberg, the Nuremberg Trial has itself grown in stature and significance, both historically and legally, with the advent of its modern successors.

What shapes our view of the Nuremberg Trial did not stop in 1946 when the Tribunal rendered its judgment. The existence and work of contemporary international criminal tribunals is reshaping this view, accentuating some features of the debate over the Trial's legacy whilst putting some other issues to rest. Thus, whilst the absence of the crime of 'aggression' from the Statutes of all three UN-backed Tribunals and, de facto, from the Statute of the ICC may be read as a vindication of the attacks that were directed against the IMT Charter on that point, no one today would suggest that crimes against humanity which first appeared at Nuremberg do not constitute criminal offences under international law. The flourishing jurisprudence and the modern vitality of the concept of crimes against humanity is itself a vindication, this time positive, of the decision taken at Nuremberg to recognize a new category of international criminal offence.

Contemporary tribunals have effectively brought the Nuremberg process into a judicial tradition and have made a *precedent* of the Nuremberg Trial. Until their creation, the Nuremberg Trial (with the notable exception of the Tokyo Trial) had remained an extraordinary occurrence that had not been able to generate a successor. This state of affairs gave some credence to accusations of selective justice and political opportunism on the part of those who had made themselves the Judges of the Nazi leaders. The creation of new war crimes tribunals and the adoption by those of many of the rules and principles that had been applied to the Nuremberg defendants has taken away much of the strength of that argument.

The creation of international criminal courts and tribunals at the end of the past century has also vindicated those, like Justice Robert H. Jackson, who had come to justify the Nuremberg Trial on a long-term view of the value and significance of such an exercise for humanity. For those like him, Nuremberg was to be the first page and corner stone of a new era in which leaders of the world would be subjected to the rule of law. And that law would be the same for all. It took more than half a century for Justice Jackson's prophecy to become a reality. The law of Nuremberg became truly international, and truly a law, when it ceased to be associated solely with those to whom it had applied for the first time. The application by modern-day war crimes courts in the name of the international community of rules and principles first developed at Nuremberg sends an important message about the profoundly legal character of a body of rules that had been applied to twenty-two Nazi defendants at Nuremberg. The law of Nuremberg now resonates most vividly in those international courts and tribunals, its legal and historical significance many times multiplied.

The adoption by contemporary Tribunals of these rules and standards as an expression of existing international law has also had the effect of removing some of the stains that had remained attached to the Nuremberg legacy because it was said to be a mere cover for the vengeance of the victors over the vanquished. The law that was born in Nuremberg now applies to contexts as varied as the conflicts in Bosnia and Herzegovina, Rwanda, and Sierra Leone, not because a victor is able to impose his will on a vanquished, but because this body of law provides a valid and recognized standard to assess the criminal character of certain conduct.

In many ways, the judgment of history stands in those tribunals, national and international, which are building upon the Nuremberg legacy to promote the rule of law and combat impunity. That is also where the legacy of Nuremberg continues to thrive.

Some Conclusions

When the Nuremberg Tribunal was first established and while the Trial was still underway, it was variously attacked for being unfair, for being mere punishment of the vanquished by the victors under the guise of judicial appearances, for violating some of the most fundamental principles of justice, and for setting an illegal and dangerous precedent. Most of these criticisms have evaporated over the years. In their place, the Nuremberg process has left a somewhat ambiguous, but overwhelmingly positive, legacy of law, moral and historical.

The fact that the Nuremberg Trial took place at all had a critical uninhibiting effect on the idea of international criminal justice. It gave legitimacy to what until then had been a utopian hope for justice. The Nuremberg Trial now stands as proof of the proposition that an international criminal tribunal, armed with the right tools and driven by a legitimate call for justice, is capable of engineering a fair and impartial trial for those who have violated the most basic tenets of international law. The fairness of these proceedings explains that today the Nuremberg Trial forms part of our collective memory, both as the record of the great crimes committed by the defendants, but also, most importantly, as a symbol of justice. The success of this judicial enterprise has in turn given credibility to the very idea of international criminal justice and has contributed perhaps more than any other event of the past century to making non-judicial responses to mass atrocities a less acceptable political course.

The aura of justice and righteousness that surrounds the Trial also explains in part the appeal that contemporary war crimes tribunals have felt towards the

Nuremberg legacy and why these tribunals have kept the flame of Nuremberg alight in their statutes and in their jurisprudence. The perpetuation of the Nuremberg vision, that of a justice above men and states, endows modern war crimes tribunals with a sense of historical and moral continuity which they would find difficult to resist.

The spirit and the law which animated this great trial have also inspired much of the later developments of international criminal law and still shape its course. The Nuremberg process augured a different, universalist, philosphy of international law which reaches beyond the narrow interests of the state and embraces the values of human rights and human dignity. That conception of international law has taken a more permanent place in the statutes of contemporary tribunals which it has greatly contributed to shaping. It is true that contemporary international criminal law has shed or rejected some of the most extreme aspects of the Nuremberg law. But in The Hague, Arusha, and in other places where international criminal justice is being rendered, the law of Nuremberg is still irrigating many aspects of international criminal law. Where the statutory instruments which regulate the functioning of modern war crimes tribunals provide no answer to the problems which they confront, the Nuremberg legacy, in particular the Tribunal's Judgment and its Charter, is a primary source of relevant material and one of the first places where they do turn for guidance.

The application of the law by a court, and the probability that any of its breaches will be punished, is both a symbol of the law's value to society and of its relevance as an instrument of social peace. Compliance with its demands and the ability to enforce such standards if necessary is also evidence that this standard is, in fact, the law and not a lesser form of societal order. By applying the law of Nuremberg to the crimes of our era, modern tribunals have in effect solidified the status of Nuremberg standards as legal norms and narrowed the gap between these standards and their enforcement to a point where referring to them as legal standards might raise more than cynical circumspection. The body of rules and principles that were first applied to twenty-two defendants at Nuremberg is now the law, however imperfect.

The Nuremberg Trial did not render international criminal justice inevitable. But as it lives on inside contemporary tribunals, it is contributing to making it a more meaningful reality of our time.

PART III

POLITICAL AND PHILOSOPHICAL PERSPECTIVES

27

The Nuremberg Trial: Landmark in Law

By Henry L. Stimson

In the confusion and disquiet of the war's first aftermath, there has been at least one great event from which we may properly take hope. The surviving leaders of the Nazi conspiracy against mankind have been indicted, tried, and judged in a proceeding whose magnitude and quality make it a landmark in the history of international law. The great undertaking at Nuremberg can live and grow in meaning, however, only if its principles are rightly understood and accepted. It is therefore disturbing to find that its work is criticized and even challenged as lawless by many who should know better. In the deep conviction that this trial deserves to be known and valued as a long step ahead on the only upward road, I venture to set down my general view of its nature and accomplishment.

The defendants at Nuremberg were leaders of the most highly organized and extensive wickedness in history. It was not a trick of the law which brought them to the bar; it was the 'massed angered forces of common humanity.' There were three different courses open to us when the Nazi leaders were captured: release, summary punishment, or trial. Release was unthinkable; it would have been taken as an admission that there was here no crime. Summary punishment was widely recommended. It would have satisfied the immediate requirement of the emotions, and in its own roughhewn way it would have been fair enough, for this was precisely the type of justice that the Nazis themselves had so often used. But this fact was in reality the best reason for rejecting such a solution. The whole moral position of the victorious Powers must collapse if their judgments could be enforced only by Nazi methods. Our anger, as righteous anger, must be subject to the law. We therefore took the third course and tried the captive criminals by a judicial proceeding. We gave to the Nazis what they had denied their own opponents—the protection of the Law. The Nuremberg Tribunal was thus in no sense an instrument of vengeance but the reverse. It was, as Mr. Justice Jackson said in opening the case for the prosecution, 'one of the most significant tributes that Power has ever paid to Reason.'

The function of the law here, as everywhere, has been to insure fair judgment. By preventing abuse and minimizing error, proceedings under law give dignity and method to the ordinary conscience of mankind. For this purpose the law demands three things: that the defendant be charged with a punishable crime; that he have full opportunity for defense; and that he be judged fairly on the evidence by a proper judicial authority. Should it fail to meet any one of these three requirements, a trial would not be justice. Against these standards, therefore, the judgment of Nuremberg must itself be judged.

I. Punishable Crimes

In our modern domestic law, a man can be penalized only when he has done something which was authoritatively recognized as punishable when he did it. This is the well-known principle that forbids *ex post facto* law, and it accords entirely with our standards of fair play. A mistaken appeal to this principle has been the cause of much confusion about the Nuremberg trial. It is argued that parts of the Tribunal's Charter, written in 1945, make crimes out of what before were activities beyond the scope of national and international law. Were this an exact statement of the situation we might well be concerned, but it is not. It rests on a misconception of the whole nature of the law of nations. International law is not a body of authoritative codes or statutes; it is the gradual expression, case by case, of the moral judgments of the civilized world. As such, it corresponds precisely to the common law of Anglo-American tradition. We can understand the law of Nuremberg only if we see it for what it is—a great new case in the book of international law, and not a formal enforcement of codified statutes. A look at the charges will show what I mean.

The Charter of the Tribunal recognizes three kinds of crime, all of which were charged in the indictment: crimes against peace, war crimes, and crimes against humanity. There was a fourth charge, of conspiracy to commit one or all of these crimes. To me personally this fourth charge is the most realistic of them all, for the Nazi crime is in the end indivisible. Each of the myriad transgressions was an interlocking part of the whole gigantic barbarity. But basically it is the first three that we must consider. The fourth is built on them.

Of the three charges, only one has been seriously criticized. War crimes have not greatly concerned the Tribunal's critics; these are offenses well understood and long generally recognized in the law or rules of war. The charge of crimes against humanity has not aroused much comment in this country, perhaps because this part of the indictment was not of central concern to the American prosecutor. The Tribunal's findings on this charge are significant, but not such as to raise much question of their legal validity, so I defer my comment to a later section of this article.

There remains the charge of crimes against peace, which has been the chief target of most of the honest critics of Nuremberg. It is under this charge that a penalty has been asked, for the first time, against the individual leaders in a war of aggression. It is this that well-intentioned critics have called '*ex post facto* law.'

It is clear that until quite recently any legal judgment against a war-maker would have been absurd. Throughout the centuries, until after World War I, the choice between war and peace remained entirely in the hands of each sovereign state, and neither the law nor the ordinary conscience of humanity ventured to deny that right. The concept of just and unjust wars is of course as old at least as Plato. But in the anarchy of individual sovereignties, the right to fight was denied to no people and the right to start a fight was denied to no ruler. For the loser in a war, punishment was certain. But this was not a matter of law; it was simply a matter of course. At the best it was like the early law of the blood feud, in which the punishment of a murderer was the responsibility of the victim's family alone and not of the whole community. Even in 1914 the German violation of Belgian neutrality was regarded as a matter for action only by those nations directly concerned in the Treaties of 1839. So far indeed was this sovereign right of war-making accepted that it was frequently extended to include the barbarous notion that a sovereign ruler is not subject to the law.

In the face of this acceptance of war as a proper instrument of sovereign national policy, the only field for the early development of international law lay in restricting so far as possible the brutalities of warfare. In obedience to age-long instincts of chivalry and magnanimity, there were gradually developed international standards for the conduct of war. Civilians and neutrals were given protecting rights and privileges, the treatment of prisoners was prescribed, and certain weapons were outlawed. It is these long established and universally accepted standards, most of them formally included in the internal law of Germany, that are covered by the charge of war crimes in the Nuremberg indictment.

The attempt to moderate the excesses of war without controlling war itself was doomed to failure by the extraordinary scientific and industrial developments of the nineteenth and twentieth centuries. By 1914 the world had been intertwined into a single unit and weapons had been so far developed that a major war could shake the whole structure of civilization. No rules of warfare were sufficient to limit the vast new destructive powers of belligerents, and the First World War made it clear that old notions must be abandoned; the world must attack the problem at its root. Thus after 1918 repeated efforts were made to eliminate aggressive war as a legal national undertaking. These efforts reached their climax in the Kellogg-Briand Pact of 1928, in which 63 nations, including Germany, Japan and Italy, renounced aggressive warfare. This pact was not an isolated incident of the postwar era. During that period the whole world was at one in its opinion of aggressive war. In repeated resolutions in the League of Nations and elsewhere, aggression was roundly denounced as criminal. In the judgment of the peoples of the world the once proud title of 'conqueror' was replaced by the criminal epithet 'aggressor.'

The progress made from 1918 to 1931 was halting and incomplete, but its direction was clear; the mandate for peace was overwhelming. Most tragically, the peoples who had renounced war were not sufficiently alert to their danger when in the following years the ruling groups of three great nations, in wanton denial of every principle of peace and civilization, launched a conspiracy against the rest of the world. Thus it happened that in the ten years which began with the invasion of Manchuria the principles of the Kellogg Pact were steadily under attack, and only as the danger came slowly home to each one of them individually did the peace-loving nations take action against aggression. In early 1945, as it became apparent that the long delayed victory was at hand, the question posed itself directly: Has there been a war of aggression and are its leaders punishable? There were many then, as there are some now, who argued that there was no law for this offense, and they found their justification in the feebleness and acquiescence of other nations in the early aggression of the Axis. Other counsels prevailed, however, and by the Charter of the Nuremberg Tribunal the responsible leaders of aggressive war were subjected to trial and conviction on the charge of crimes against peace.

Here we come to the heart of the matter. Able lawyers and honest men have cried out that this aggressive war was not a crime. They have argued that the Nuremberg defendants were not properly forewarned when they made war that what they did was criminal.

Now in one sense the concept of *ex post facto* law is a strange one to apply here, because this concept relates to a state of mind on the part of the defendants that in this case was wholly absent. That concept is based on the assumption that if the defendant had known that the proposed act was criminal he would have refrained from committing it. Nothing in the attitude of the Nazi leaders corresponds to this assumption; their minds were wholly untroubled by the question of their guilt or innocence. Not in their aggression only but in their whole philosophy, they excluded the very concept of law. They deliberately put themselves below such a concept. To international law—as to the law of Germany—they paid only such respect as they found politic, and in the end they had smashed its every rule. Their attitude toward aggressive war was exactly like their attitude toward murder—both were useful instruments in a great design. It is therefore impossible to get any light on the validity of this charge of aggressive war by inspecting the Nazi mind. We must study rather the minds of the rest of the world, which is at once a less revolting and a more fruitful labor.

What did the rest of us think about aggressive war at the time of the Nazi attacks? This question is complex, but to that part of it which affects the legality of the Nuremberg trial we can give a simple answer. That we considered aggressive war wicked is clear; that we considered the leaders of an aggressive war wicked is equally clear. These opinions, in large part formally embodied in the Kellogg Pact, are the basis for the law of Nuremberg. With the detailed reasoning by which the prosecution has supported the law set forth in the Charter of the International Military Tribunal, we cannot here concern ourselves. The proposition sustained by the Tribunal is simple: if a man plans aggression when aggression has been formally renounced by his nation, he is a criminal. Those who are concerned with the law of this proposition cannot do better than to read the pertinent passages in the opening address of Mr. Justice Jackson, the closing address of Sir Hartley Shawcross, and the opinion of the Tribunal itself.

What really troubles the critics of Nuremberg is that they see no evidence that before 1945 we considered the capture and conviction of such aggressors to be our legal duty. In this view they are in the main correct, but it is vitally important to remember that a legal right is not lost merely because temporarily it is not used. What happened before World War II was that we lacked the courage to enforce the authoritative decision of the international world. We agreed with the Kellogg Pact that aggressive war must end. We renounced it, and we condemned those who might use it. But it was a moral condemnation only. We thus did not reach the second half of the question: What will you do to an aggressor when you catch him? If we *had* reached it, we should easily have found the right answer. But that answer escaped us, for it implied a duty to catch the criminal, and such a chase meant war. It was the Nazi confidence that we would never chase and catch them, and not a misunderstanding of our opinion of them, that led them to commit their crimes. Our offense was thus that of the man who passed by on the other side. That we have finally recognized our negligence and named the criminals for what they are is a piece of righteousness too long delayed by fear.

We did not ask ourselves, in 1939 or 1940, or even in 1941, what punishment, if any, Hitler and his chief assistants deserved. We asked simply two questions: How do we avoid war, and how do we keep this wickedness from overwhelming us? These seemed larger questions to us than the guilt or innocence of individuals. In the end we found an answer to the second question, but none to the first. The crime of the Nazis, against *us*, lay in this very fact: that their making of aggressive war made peace here impossible. We have now seen again, in hard and deadly terms, what had been proved in 1917—that 'peace is indivisible.' The man who makes aggressive war at all makes war against mankind. That is an exact, not a rhetorical, description of the crime of aggressive war.

Thus the Second World War brought it home to us that our repugnance to aggressive war was incomplete without a judgment of its leaders. What we had called a crime demanded punishment; we must bring our law in balance with the universal moral judgment of mankind. The wickedness of aggression must be punished by a trial and judgment. This is what has been done at Nuremberg.

Now this is a new judicial process, but it is not *ex post facto* law. It is the enforcement of a moral judgment which dates back a generation. It is a growth in the application of law that any student of our common law should recognize as natural and proper, for it is in just this manner that the common law grew up. There was, somewhere in our distant past, a first case of murder, a first case where the tribe replaced the victim's family as judge of the offender. The tribe had learned that the deliberate and malicious killing of any human being was, and must be treated as, an offense against the whole community. The analogy is exact. All case law grows by new decisions, and where those new decisions match the conscience of the community, they are law as truly as the law of murder. They do not become *ex post facto* law merely because until the first decision and punishment comes, a man's only warning that he offends is in the general sense and feeling of his fellow men.

The charge of aggressive war is unsound, therefore, only if the community of nations did not believe in 1939 that aggressive war was an offense. Merely to make such a suggestion, however, is to discard it. Aggression is an offense, and we all know it; we have known it for a generation. It is an offense so deep and heinous that we cannot endure its repetition.

The law made effective by the trial at Nuremberg is righteous law long overdue. It is in just such cases as this one that the law becomes more nearly what Mr. Justice Holmes called it: 'the witness and external deposit of our moral life.'

With the Judgment of Nuremberg we at last reach to the very core of international strife, and we set a penalty not merely for war crimes, but for the very act of war itself, except in self-defense. If a man will argue that this is bad law, untrue to our ideals, I will listen. But I feel only pity for the casuist who would dismiss the Nazi leaders because 'they were not warned it was a crime.' They were warned, and they sneered contempt. Our shame is that their contempt was so nearly justified, not that we have in the end made good our warning.

II. Fair Trial

Next after its assertion of the criminality of aggressive war, the triumph of Nuremberg rests in the manner and degree to which it has discharged with honor the true functions of a legal instrument. The crimes charged were punishable as we have seen—so clearly punishable that the only important suggested alternative to a trial was summary execution of the accused. It is in its pursuit of a different course that the Nuremberg Tribunal has demonstrated at once the dignity and the value of the law, and students of law everywhere will find inspiration and enlightenment in close study of its work. In its skilful development of a procedure satisfying every traditional and material safeguard of the varying legal forms of the prosecuting nations, it represents a signal success in the field of international negotiation, and in its rigid fidelity to the fundamental principles of fair play it has insured the lasting value of its work.

In their insistence on fairness to the defendants, the Charter and the Tribunal leaned over backwards. Each defendant was allowed to testify for himself, a right denied by Continental law. At the conclusion of the trial, each defendant was allowed to address the Tribunal, at great length, a right denied by Anglo-American law. The difference between Continental and Anglo-American law was thus adjusted by allowing to the defendant his rights under both. Counsel for the defendants were leading German lawyers and professors from the German universities, some of them ardent and unrepentant Nazis. Counsel were paid, fed, sheltered and transported at the expense of the Allies, and were furnished offices and secretarial help. The defense had full access to all documents. Every attempt was made to produce desired witnesses when the Tribunal believed that they had any relevant evidence to offer. In the summation of the trial the defense had 20 days and the prosecution three, and the defense case as a whole occupied considerably more time than the prosecution.

The record of the Nuremberg trial thus becomes one of the foundation stones of the peace. Under the most rigid safeguards of jurisprudence, subject to challenge, denial and disproof by men on trial for their lives and assisted by counsel of their own choosing, the great conspiracy has been unmasked. In documents unchallenged by the defense and often in the words of the defendants themselves, there is recorded the whole black history of murder, enslavement and aggression. This record, so established, will stand as a demonstration, on a wholly new level of validity and strength, of the true character of the Nazi régime. And this is so not in spite of our insistence upon law, but because of it.

In this connection it is worth noting that the trial has totally exploded many of the strange notions that seem to lurk in the minds of some who have expressed their doubts about Nuremberg. Some of the doubters are not basically concerned with 'ex post facto law' or with 'vengeance.' Their real trouble is that they did not think the Nazis could be proved guilty. To these gentlemen I earnestly commend a reading of the record. If after reading it they do not think there was in fact aggressive war, in its most naked form, then I shall be constrained to believe that they do not think any such thing exists or can exist.

III. Fair Judgment

Not having made a study of the evidence presented in the case with special reference to each defendant, I am not qualified to pass judgment on the verdicts and sentences of the Tribunal against individuals and criminal groups. I have, however, heard no claim that these sentences were too severe. The Tribunal's findings as to the law are on the whole encouraging. The charge of aggressive war was accepted and ably explained. The charge of war crimes was sustained almost without comment. The charge of crimes against humanity was limited by the Tribunal to include only activities pursued in connection with the crime of war. The Tribunal eliminated from its jurisdiction the question of the criminal accountability of those responsible for wholesale persecution before the outbreak of the war in 1939. With this decision I do not here venture to quarrel, but its effect appears to me to involve a reduction of the meaning of crimes against humanity to a point where they become practically synonymous with war crimes.

If there is a weakness in the Tribunal's findings, I believe it lies in its very limited construction of the legal concept of conspiracy. That only eight of the

22 defendants should have been found guilty on the count of conspiracy to commit the various crimes involved in the indictment seems to me surprising. I believe that the Tribunal would have been justified in a broader construction of the law of conspiracy, and under such a construction it might well have found a different verdict in a case like that of Schacht.

In this first great international trial, however, it is perhaps as well that the Tribunal has very rigidly interpreted both the law and the evidence. In this connection we may observe that only in the case of Rudolf Hess, sentenced to life imprisonment, does the punishment of any of the defendants depend solely on the count of aggressive war. All of those who have been hanged were convicted of war crimes or crimes against humanity, and all but one were convicted of both. Certainly, then, the charge of aggressive war has not been established in international law at the expense of any innocent lives.

The judgment of the Tribunal is thus, in its findings of guilt, beyond challenge. We may regret that some of the charges were not regarded as proven and some of the defendants not found clearly guilty. But we may take pride in the restraint of a tribunal which has so clearly insisted upon certain proof of guilt. It is far better that a Schacht should go free than that a judge should compromise his conscience.

IV. The Meaning of Nuremberg

A single landmark of justice and honor does not make a world of peace. The Nazi leaders are not the only ones who have renounced and denied the principles of western civilization. They are unique only in the degree and violence of their offenses. In every nation which acquiesced even for a time, in their offense, there were offenders. There have been still more culpable offenders in nations which joined before or after in the brutal business of aggression. If we claimed for Nuremberg that it was final justice, or that only these criminals were guilty, we might well be criticized as being swayed by vengeance and not justice. But this is not the claim. The American prosecutor has explicitly stated that he looks uneasily and with great regret upon certain brutalities that have occurred since the ending of the war. He speaks for us all when he says that there has been enough bloodletting in Europe. But the sins of others do not make the Nazi leaders less guilty, and the importance of Nuremberg lies not in any claim that by itself it clears the board, but rather in the pattern it has set. The four nations prosecuting, and the 19 others subscribing to the Charter of the International Military Tribunal, have firmly bound themselves to the principle that aggressive war is a personal and punishable crime.

It is this principle upon which we must henceforth rely for our legal protection against the horrors of war. We must never forget that under modern conditions of life, science and technology, all war has become greatly brutalized, and that no one who joins in it, even in self-defense, can escape becoming also in a measure brutalized. Modern war cannot be limited in its destructive methods and in the inevitable debasement of all participants. A fair scrutiny of the last two World Wars makes clear the steady intensification in the inhumanity of the weapons and methods employed by both the aggressors and the victors. In order to defeat Japanese aggression, we were forced, as Admiral Nimitz has stated, to employ a technique of unrestricted submarine warfare not unlike that which 25 years ago was the proximate cause of our entry into World War I. In the use of strategic air power, the Allies took the lives of hundreds of thousands of civilians in Germany, and in Japan the destruction of civilian life wreaked by our B-29s, even before the final blow of the atomic bombs, was at least proportionately great. It is true that our use of this destructive power, particularly of the atomic bomb, was for the purpose of winning a quick victory over aggressors, so as to minimize the loss of life, not only of our troops but of the civilian populations of our enemies as well, and that this purpose in the case of Japan was clearly effected. But even so, we as well as our enemies have contributed to the proof that the central moral problem is war and not its methods, and that a continuance of war will in all probability end with the destruction of our civilization.

International law is still limited by international politics, and we must not pretend that either can live and grow without the other. But in the judgment of Nuremberg there is affirmed the central principle of peace—that the man who makes or plans to make aggressive war is a criminal. A standard has been raised to which Americans, at least, must repair; for it is only as this standard is accepted, supported and enforced that we can move onward to a world of law and peace.

28

The Legality of the Nuremberg Trials[1]

By Arthur L. Goodhart

The International Military Tribunal which is now sitting in Nuremberg finds its being in the agreement[2] entered into in London on 8th August 1945 by the Governments of Great Britain, the United States, France, and the Union of Soviet Socialist Republics for the 'prosecution and punishment of the major war criminals of the European Axis'.[3] After stating that, in accordance with the Moscow Declaration of 30th October 1943, those Germans who had been responsible for war crimes should 'be sent back to the countries in which their abominable deeds were done' to be tried by the national Courts of those countries, the Agreement provides that an International Military Tribunal shall be established 'for the trial of war criminals whose offences have no particular geographical location', these being 'the major war criminals'.

Attached to the Agreement is the Charter of the International Military Tribunal setting forth in 30 articles the constitution, jurisdiction and general principles, and powers of the tribunal, the procedure to be followed in the course of the preliminary investigations and conduct of the trial, and the provisions concerning the judgment and sentence.

In this paper I am concerned solely with the jurisprudential questions whether the International Military Tribunal so established is a legal court in the true sense, and whether the trials it is conducting can properly be described as legal trials. This is not a mere matter of words, because on the answers which we can give to these questions will depend, to a large degree, the respect and authority which will be accorded to the judgments of the Tribunal both now and in the future.

A legal criminal trial may be defined as a trial in which an impartial judge, or an impartial judge and jury, determines the guilt or innocence of a defendant according to law and to the evidence produced by the prosecution and the

---

[1] A lecture delivered before the Edinburgh University Law Faculty Society on 5th February 1946.

[2] H.M. Stationery Office, Cmd. 6668.

[3] The following nations have signified adherence to the agreement: Belgium, the Netherlands, Denmark, Norway, Czechoslovakia, Luxembourg, Poland, Greece, Yugoslavia, Ethiopia, Australia, Haiti, Honduras, Panama, and New Zealand.

defence. The judge, the law, and the evidence are therefore the three essentials in every legal trial. To what extent can it be said that these can be found in the Nuremberg trials?

The Judges

It has been argued that the Tribunal cannot be regarded as a court in the true sense because, as its members represent the victorious Allied Nations, they must lack that impartiality which is an essential in all judicial procedure. According to this view only a court consisting of neutrals, or, at least, containing some neutral judges, could be considered to be a proper tribunal. As no man can be a judge in his own case, so no allied Tribunal can be a judge in a case in which members of the enemy government or forces are on trial. Attractive as this argument may sound in theory, it ignores the fact that it runs counter to the administration of law in every country. If it were true then no spy could ever be given a legal trial, because his case is always heard by judges representing the enemy country. Yet no one has ever argued that in such cases it was necessary to call on neutral judges. The prisoner has the right to demand that his judges shall be fair, but not that they shall be neutral. As Lord Wright has pointed out,[4] the same principle is applicable to ordinary criminal law because 'a burglar cannot complain that he is being tried by a jury of honest citizens'.

There are three grounds on which one can with confidence assert that the Tribunal satisfies the essential element of fairness. The first is found in the character of its judges. Although the court is described as being 'The International Military Tribunal', its members are not professional soldiers but legal experts who have been trained in the evaluation of evidence. It was at one time suggested that they should all be given the rank of Major-General for the purpose of the trials, but it was decided that it was not desirable to disguise their essential legal character. The second reason is that the trials are being conducted in the full glare of world publicity. In such circumstances it would be almost impossible for a tribunal to act in an obviously unfair manner. It is worth remembering that at the Reichstag trials in 1933 even a court composed of subservient Nazi judges was forced to acquit Dimitroff because it had become obvious that he was not guilty. The third reason is that Article 26 of the Charter provides that 'the judgment of the Tribunal as to the guilt or the innocence of any Defendant shall give the reasons on which it is based'. This provision, which is far stricter than the practice followed in the ordinary national courts where a simple verdict of guilty is sufficient, is the strongest guarantee of fairness, because the judges in such circumstances must realize that their judgments will be subject to public scrutiny both now and in the future. The first essential of a legal trial is therefore satisfied by

---

[4] 'War Crimes under International Law,' 1946, 62, *Law Quarterly Review*, 40, 44.

the character of the Nuremberg judges and by the conditions under which they function.

Procedure and Evidence

The tribunal having been constituted, it was necessary to establish what rules of procedure and evidence it would follow. Article 18 of the Charter provides that 'the Tribunal shall draw up rules for its procedure. These rules shall not be inconsistent with the provisions of the Charter'. As there are striking procedural differences in the conduct of a trial under Anglo-American and under Continental law, it was thought that serious difficulties might arise in preparing such rules, but in fact none seem to have developed. In one important respect the Nuremberg rules of procedure more closely resemble those of the Anglo-American law than they do those of the Continent, for the judges are not playing the inquisitorial part which Continental judges frequently assume in a criminal trial. The examination of witnesses is being left almost entirely in the hands of counsel, with the result that there have been none of the disputes between the witnesses and the judges which marked the trials of Pétain and Laval. On the other hand, Article 16 of the Charter follows Continental practice in providing for the preliminary examination of a defendant; under English law a defendant need not answer any preliminary questions, and his failure to do so cannot be the subject of comment at the trial. It is not clear what effect a refusal to answer questions under Article 16 would have had if any of the prisoners had taken such a stand: in fact they seem to have been profuse in their explanations.

The most important provision concerning evidence is found in Article 19 of the Charter which provides that 'the Tribunal shall not be bound by technical rules of evidence. It shall adopt and apply to the greatest possible extent expeditious and non-technical procedure, and shall admit any evidence which it deems to have probative value'. Here we find the greatest departure from Anglo-American practice under which hearsay evidence is strictly excluded on the theory that no evidence should be admissible which cannot be subjected to the test of cross-examination. If this principle had been applied at the Nuremberg trials much of the most relevant evidence would have had to be excluded because many of the persons closely identified with the events are dead. The relaxation of the rules of evidence does not seem to have led to any unsatisfactory consequences because the presiding judge has had no difficulty in excluding evidence which was either irrelevant or unduly prejudicial.[5]

---

[5] It is interesting to speculate whether the experience gained at Nuremberg may lead to some relaxation of the rules of evidence in Anglo-American law. The late Professor J. H. Wigmore, who wrote the classic work on *Evidence*, was a strong advocate of such a change.

It is unnecessary to discuss here the other procedural rules established by the Charter because they follow those recognised in the courts of all civilised countries. Thus the defendants are given the right to have the assistance of counsel, to be furnished with a copy of all documents, to present evidence in their own defence, and to cross-examine any witnesses called by the prosecution.

It is clear, therefore, that no question can ever be raised concerning the fairness of the rules of evidence and procedure administered by the Nuremberg Tribunal. The second essential of a legal trial has therefore been satisfied.

The Substantive Law

The third essential of a legal trial is that the guilt or innocence of the defendant shall be determined according to the law. Therefore if the Nuremberg trials are to be considered legal trials in the true sense, it is necessary to determine whether there is any law applicable to them. By law I mean a body of rules binding on the court. If a court is free to hold that it may in its discretion punish any set which it considers ought to be punishable, then it may be administering justice but it is not administering law. Such discretionary justice may in certain circumstances be necessary, especially in times of revolution or grave emergency, but it differs in essence from legal justice which is based on established rules and principles.

What then is the law which the Nuremberg Tribunal is bound to administer? The technical answer is that the law which it administers is that laid down in Part II of the Charter which establishes the 'jurisdiction and general principles' to be followed in the conduct of the trials. In particular Article 6 provides that 'the following acts, or any of them, are crimes coming within the jurisdiction of the Tribunal for which there shall be individual responsibility:—

(a) *Crimes against peace*: namely, planning, preparation, initiation or waging of a war of aggression, or a war in violation of international treaties, agreements or assurances, or participation in a common plan or conspiracy for the accomplishment of any of the foregoing;

(b) *War Crimes*: namely, violations of the laws or customs of war . . . ;

(c) *Crimes against humanity*: namely, murder, extermination, enslavement, deportation, and other inhumane acts committed against any civilian population, before or during the war. . . .'

This is the law which the Charter requires the Tribunal to administer and by which it is bound. It must determine the guilt or innocence of the defendants, not according to discretion, but in accordance with these specific rules. If it reaches the conclusion that one or more of the defendants have not committed any of the crimes set forth in the Charter, then it must acquit them, however desirable it might consider it to be, on grounds of morality or general policy, that they should be punished. The Allied Governments which have created the Tribunal have at the same time established the laws which it shall administer, just as the King-in-Parliament has created the courts in Great Britain and has established the laws which they are bound to apply. The International Military Tribunal is therefore a legal court as truly as is the Court of Session in Scotland or the High Court of Justice in England.

But this technical Austinian answer cannot be regarded as a complete one because it raises the further question: Were the Allied Governments justified in stating the law as they did in the Charter? Was this statement of the law a declaration of already existing International Law, or was it the creation, after the event, of novel and previously unknown principles? There is an essential difference between the two, because if the Charter laid dawn new law for the Tribunal then this could be subject to the criticism that it must be *ex post facto* in character. This might be in conflict with the principle of justice, generally recognised by all civilised legal systems, that criminal law should not be retroactive in effect. It is true that this principle of justice was repudiated by the Nazis themselves in their penal legislation, but this would not by itself justify the Allied nations in taking a course which they had condemned in their enemies. In determining the legal, as apart from the political, justification for the Nuremberg trials it is therefore necessary to consider two major questions: (*a*) To what extent is the law in the Charter *ex post facto* in character? (*b*) In so far as it is *ex post facto* can this departure from principle be justified?

It has been argued that all the law in the Charter must be *ex post facto* because in the past International Law has been applicable only to States and not to individuals. To hold an individual criminally liable for a breach of International Law is therefore, according to this view, the creation of an entirely novel legal system. It is impossible here to do more than to touch the fringe of this controversial subject, which has, in recent years, developed a large literature,[6] but it is necessary to consider it briefly because on it is based the most cogent criticism of the Nuremberg trials. The late Professor Oppenheim[7] was, perhaps, the leading protagonist of the view that International Law could be applicable only to States and never to individuals. He said:

'Since the Law of Nations is based on the common consent of individual States, and not of individual human beings, States solely and exclusively are the subjects of International Law. This means that the Law of Nations is a law for the international conduct of States, and not of their citizens.'

But even if we grant that International Law is based solely on the consent of the States, which is at best a doubtful proposition, it does not follow from this that the law thus created cannot be applicable to individual human beings. In a federal

[6] Reference to this can be found in the note to § 13 of Oppenheim's *International Law*, vol. i, *Peace* (5th ed.).

[7] *Op. cit., supra,* §13.

State the federal law not only gives rights and imposes duties on the various States which compose the federation, but it also gives rights and imposes duties on the individual citizens. The fact that the federal State may have been created by the common consent of the individual States, as happened in Australia, does not mean that the federal laws are inapplicable to the individual citizens. The experience of the United States and of the British Dominions has proved that the exact opposite is true, because the effectiveness of the federal law is due almost entirely to the fact that the individual citizen is bound by it.

The odd result of Professor Oppenheim's theory is that apparently International Law does not hold that an individual shall not be a pirate, but is limited to the provision that[8] 'any State may seize and punish foreign pirates on the open sea'. It is hardly surprising to find that Westlake[9] maintains that in these cases individuals are regarded as the subjects and not the objects of International law. Moreover, it follows from Oppenheim's theory that there is no international duty on individual combatants to obey the Hague and the Geneva conventions: the only duty is on the States to see that their members do not violate them.

It is true, of course, that in the past there has been no international criminal court before which individuals could be prosecuted, but this does not prove that no international criminal law exists. This argument comes dangerously near to denying the existence of International Law as a whole, because there is no compulsory international court before which it can be enforced. Law has frequently existed before the particular courts of the State have been created. Many of the national courts now functioning in the liberated countries have been established recently, but no one has argued that they are not competent to try the cases that arose before their establishment. This distinction between law and the machinery for enforcing the law is recognised in the principle against *ex post facto* law, because this principle does not apply to the creation of new legal machinery. Thus no defendant can complain that he is being tried by a court which did not exist when he committed the act.

The correct conclusion therefore is, I believe, that under International Law an individual can be under a legal duty not to commit certain international crimes, such as, for example, piracy or violations of the Hague and Geneva conventions. The fact that in the past there have been no international courts before which such crimes could be prosecuted does not negative the existence of such duties: it merely shews that the then existing machinery was defective. The creation of the International Military Tribunal has remedied this defect.

This conclusion does not, however, solve the whole problem because it is still necessary to consider whether the particular acts with which the defendants have been charged constituted crimes under International Law at the time when, it is

---

[8] § 290. It is difficult to reconcile this view with that expressed in § 280: 'However, since a State cannot enforce its Municipal Laws on the open sea against others than its own subjects, it cannot treat foreigners on the open sea as pirates, unless they are pirates according to the Law of Nations.'

[9] Westlake, *Collected Papers*, p. 2.

alleged, they were committed. To answer this it is necessary to consider the specific charges which have been brought against the defendants.

The indictment,[10] presented to the International Military Tribunal on 18th October 1945, contains four counts which are based on the General Principles laid down in Article 6 of the Charter. *Count One*, which is entitled *The Common Plan or Conspiracy*, is an omnibus one, for it alleges that the defendants were parties to a conspiracy to commit Crimes against Peace, War Crimes, and Crimes against Humanity. These three crimes were not independent, unrelated, wrongful acts, but were committed in execution of a common plan and were contemplated by it. The indictment states that 'the aims and purposes of the Nazi conspirators were not fixed or static, but evolved and expanded as they acquired progressively greater power and became able to make more effective application of threats of force and threats of aggressive war'. Both the purpose of the conspiracy—the acquisition of territory at the expense of neighbouring and other countries—and the means of achieving this aim—aggressive war carried on in a ruthless and inhumane manner not justified by military necessity—made the conspiracy an unlawful one. Just as in English law the crime of conspiracy may be defined as[11] 'the agreement of two or more persons to effect any unlawful purpose, whether as their ultimate aim or only as a means to it', so in this indictment both the purpose and the means are parts of the charge of conspiracy.

One other feature of the English law of conspiracy is of interest here because it relates to the wide scope of the evidence which has been admitted at the Nuremberg trial. How, it has been asked, can a financial or economic expert sitting in Berlin be held liable for the shooting of hostages in a remote Russian village? The answer is that under the law each of the parties, by deliberately entering into the conspiracy, adopts all his confederates as agents to assist him in carrying it out, and consequently any act done subsequently for that purpose by any of them will be admissible as evidence against him, unless before the act was done he has withdrawn from the conspiracy. Such withdrawal may, however, be too late if the course of the conspiracy, which he has helped to bring into being, cannot be stayed.

Count Two, which is entitled *Crimes against Peace*, charges the defendants with 'waging wars of aggression, which were also wars in violation of international treaties, agreements and assurances'. This count raises the most controversial question which the international lawyers have had to face, because it concerns the fundamental problem of the legality of aggressive war. It is now generally recognised that there can be no International Law in the true sense unless aggressive war was regarded as being illegal, because, as Professor Brierly has said[12]: 'To hold at one and the same time that states are legally bound to respect each other's

---

[10] H.M. Stationery Office, Cmd. 6696.
[11] *Cf.* Kenny, *Outlines of Criminal Law*, 14th ed., p. 296.
[12] Brierly, *The Outlook for International Law*, 1945, p. 21.

independence and other rights, and yet are free to attack each other at will, is a logical impossibility.' But can it be said that prior to the enactment of the Charter the waging of an aggressive war was regarded as illegal in International Law? It is certain that during the nineteenth century the overwhelming weight of opinion was that International Law was not concerned with the question whether a war was just or unjust, defensive or aggressive. This was due not to a lack of moral sense on the part of the International lawyers, but to a realization that it was in most cases difficult, if not impossible, to say where justice lay. Although the attempts to limit war made at the Hague Conferences were hardly a practical success, nevertheless a definite conviction that wars should be prevented developed during the early years of the twentieth century. The War of 1914–1918 brought this feeling to a head, and resulted in the creation of the League of Nations. The Covenant did not in so many words say that aggressive war was an international wrong, but it made so many provisions concerning the steps that had to be taken before war could be declared that, for all practical purposes, aggressive wars were prohibited between the members of the League. But the Covenant was only binding on the members of the League, and so in 1928 the Pact of Paris, better known as the Kellogg-Briand Pact, was accepted by over sixty States, including all the Great Powers.[13] It is very brief. Article I provides that 'the High Contracting Parties solemnly declare, in the names of their respective peoples, that they condemn recourse to war for the solution of international controversies and renounce it as an instrument of national policy in their relations with one another'. Did this Pact make aggressive war illegal? It has been argued that the Pact was no more than the expression of a pious hope because it provided no sanction for the case of its violation, and no machinery for its enforcement. The difficulty which this argument encounters is that, if it is accepted, then International Law as a whole is destroyed, because there are no specific sanctions for the breach of its rules, and its legal machinery has never been more than voluntary. It is probable that when some of the signatories accepted the Pact they did so with their fingers crossed, but this is not the first time that someone has signed a document without any intention of performing its provisions and thereafter has found that he is legally bound by his promises. It is submitted that Professor Lauterpacht reached the right conclusion when he said[14]: 'The Pact constitutes a radical change in International Law and a removal of the principal objection to its recognition as a system of law.... War cannot now legally, as it could be prior to the conclusion of the Pact, be resorted to either as a legal remedy or as an instrument for changing the law.'

[13] It should be noted that the Geneva Protocol of 1924 for the 'Pacific Settlement of International Disputes', signed by the representatives of forty-eight governments, had declared that 'a war of aggression constitutes...an International crime'. The Eighth Assembly of the League of Nations in 1927, on the unanimous resolution of the forty-eight member nations, including Germany, declared that a war of aggression constitutes an international crime.

[14] Oppenheim's *International Law*, vol. ii, *Disputes, War, Neutrality* (6th ed.). p. 161.

Is is true that the Pact did not contain a clause providing that the individuals who waged an aggressive war in the name of the State were committing an illegal act, but this cannot affect their responsibility. A State is only an artificial person, acting through individuals who are its agents. In civil law, if a corporation is found guilty of having committed a criminal offence, its agents can equally be found guilty. It would be strange indeed if in International Law a State could be guilty of committing the gravest of crimes, while its representatives, through whom alone it can act, were held to be innocent.

It is interesting to note that Count Two, after referring to the wars of aggression, adds that these 'were also wars in violation of international treaties, agreements and assurances'. This accounts for the impressive list of broken treaties read out at the trial. Even if there should be some uncertainty concerning the effect of the terms of the Pact of Paris, there can be no doubt that the various wars waged by the Nazis were in breach of specific treaty provisions. No clearer violations of the doctrine *pacta sunt servanda* can be found in all history, so that if these are not to be regarded as international wrongs, then no breach of a treaty can ever be held to constitute a wrong.

The conclusion would therefore seem to be clear that Count Two is in accord with the provisions of existing International Law, and that it cannot be regarded as being *ex post facto* in character.

The same conclusion can be stated with even more confidence concerning *Count Three—War Crimes*. These crimes are described in the indictment as 'violations of international conventions, of internal penal laws, and of the general principles of criminal law as derived from the criminal law of all civilised nations, and were involved in and part of a systematic course of conduct'. In the past there have been hundreds of cases in which national military tribunals have tried and convicted enemy nationals of breaches of the laws of war, so that the only novelty, so far as the International Military Tribunal is concerned, is that this tribunal is an international one. From the practical standpoint this undoubtedly is an added protection for the defendants because there is less likelihood that an international tribunal will be influenced by prejudice than would be a national one. The only objection to the International Tribunal is a theoretical one, denying the existence of international criminal law as a whole. Briefly it is that the laws of war, although formulated in such international conventions as the Geneva Conventions of 1864, 1906, and 1929, and the Hague Conventions of 1899 and 1907, only become effective in relation to individuals when these laws of war are incorporated as part of the national law of each State. An international tribunal is, in this view, incapable of applying the international laws of war to individuals because International Law is binding only on the States as such. Only an individual State can therefore punish the wrongdoer. This argument must not be confused with the exactly opposite one—which is equally false—that a national court cannot properly punish violations of the laws of war because those are international in character. The correct answer, it is submitted, is that a violation of the law of war constitutes both an international and a national crime, and is therefore justiciable both in an international and a national court.

The most interesting feature of *Count Three* is the allegation that the plan involved the practice of 'total war' including methods of combat and of military occupation in direct conflict with the laws and customs of war. It is on this ground that the defendants have been charged with responsibility for the brutal acts committed by their subordinates, as, for example, at Lidice, even though they may have been in ignorance of each particular violation. It is here that the Nuremberg trials differ from all previous war trials because hitherto defendants have only been charged with crimes either committed by themselves or under their immediate directions. Never before has cold calculated brutality played a leading rôle in military strategy. This does not mean that there has been an innovation in the law, for all that has happened is that the law has been applied to novel circumstances. As Lord Jowitt, L.C. has said in the *Joyce* case[15]: 'It is not an extension of a penal law to apply its principle to circumstances unforeseen at the time of its enactment, so long as the case is fairly brought within its language.' There can therefore be no question that *Count Three* is in accord with the established principles of International Law.

It is only when we turn to *Count Four—Crimes Against Humanity*—that we encounter serious legal difficulty. In so far as these crimes constitute violations of the laws of war there is no juristic problem because they are merely the same crimes as those set forth in *Count Three* under a different name, but novel considerations arise when the acts charged cannot be brought within this category. This is true in particular of the murders, both before and after 1939, in the concentration camps of the hundreds of thousands of German nationals who were either Jews or political opponents. As International Law is not concerned with the treatment which a State metes out to its own nationals, how can such acts, however brutal, be considered an international crime justiciable by an international court? The answer is that although International Law is not as a general rule concerned with the internal affairs of the various States, nevertheless these may be of such a special nature as to affect the international community, either morally or materially, and thus become matters of international concern. This is not a novel idea, for in the nineteenth century there were a number of instances where States intervened to protect the nationals of other States, and numerous international treaties, unfortunately ineffective, were entered into for the guarantee of human rights. Writing in 1928 Sir Arnold McNair said[16]: 'The Law of Nations is a product of Christian civilisation and represents a legal order which binds States, chiefly Christian, into a community. It is therefore no wonder that ethical ideas, some of which are the basis of, and others a development from Christian morals, have a tendency to require the help of International Law for their realisation.' Never was this help

---

[15] *Joyce v. Director of Public Prosecution*, [1946] 1 All Eng. L.R. 186, 189, VOL. LVIII.—NO. 1.
[16] *Op. cit.*, note 6, 4th ed., § 292.

so urgently required as at the present time. The Charter, in providing that the deliberate murder of hundreds of thousands of innocent people was punishable as an international crime, was therefore not taking a revolutionary step because no one can doubt that these acts were contrary to the laws of every civilised nation. An international system which had no means of preventing such outrages against common decency would hardly be worthy of respect. In every federal State the federal government is given power to intervene in the affairs of the individual States when the local conditions are such as to endanger the community as a whole. The same principle must be applicable to the international community if it is to survive. We must recognise, however, that in the past this principle was of doubtful validity in International Law, and that therefore *Court Four* is, in a sense, *ex post facto* in character. But even if this is granted, this is not a ground on which the court can be criticised, either from the moral or the juristic stand-point, because the acts charged in the indictment are so contrary to all common decency that no possible excuse for their performance could be advanced. The objection to *ex post facto* legislation is based on the ground that the actor might, at the time when he performed the act, have believed that he was entitled to perform it, but how could such a belief exist in the case of wholesale murder? To argue that the perpetrators of such acts should get off scot-free because at the time when they were committed no adequate legal provision for dealing with them had been devised, is to turn what is a reasonable principle of justice in fully developed legal systems into an inflexible rule which would, in these circumstances, be in direct conflict with the very idea of justice on which it itself is based. No such inflex-ible course has ever been followed in English law because it has been recognised that on occasions *ex post facto* legislation, although in principle undesirable, may nevertheless be necessary. If ever there was an instance in which such a necessity existed, then it can be found in the concentration camps of Belsen and Dachau.

If I have been correct in my interpretation of the law, then the result is that the first three counts are in accord not only with the Charter of the International Military Tribunal but also with the existing International Law, while the fourth count, although based on a novel international principle, is in accord with the principles found in every civilised system of law.

There is one interesting feature of the Nuremberg trials which is not concerned with the charges brought against the individual defendants. Under the indict-ment the Tribunal is asked to declare that certain groups such as the Reich cab-inet, the General Staff, the S.S., and the Gestapo were criminal organizations. If such a declaration is made against any group, then under Article 10 of the Charter, 'the competent national authority of any Signatory shall have the right to bring individuals to trial for membership therein before national, military or occupation courts. In any such case the criminal nature of the group or organiza-tion is considered proved and shall not be questioned'. Although this provision may, at first sight, appear strange to most lawyers, it is an obviously convenient one because if the same general evidence had to be produced at all future trials then it would be impossible, from a practical standpoint, to prosecute more than a few of the persons charged with these crimes. This provision is far less drastic than was Act No. 30 of the British India Statute Book, 1836, enacted for the suppression of thuggery in India. Section I of that Act provided that, 'It is hereby enacted that whoever shall be proved to have belonged either before or after the passing of this Act to any gang of thugs either within or without the territories of the East India Company shall be punished with imprisonment for life with hard labour.' This Act proved highly successful in the suppression of thuggery in India. It is to be hoped that the Charter will have an equally successful influence in suppressing the thuggery which has disgraced Germany during the past generation.

In conclusion a word may be said concerning the view that the men on trial at Nuremberg should have been dealt with by executive action and not by a court of law. In this connection the banishment of Napoleon to St. Helena has been cited as the stock example. Such executive action, it has been argued, would have been more expeditious than a legal trial, and would not have been open to future criticism, which will undoubtedly be advanced by German professors, that an act of force had been disguised under the trappings of legality. The answer is that imprisonment is one thing while execution is another. To execute a man without legal trial, even if it be only a drum-head court-martial, is closely akin to murder. Whatever the risk, these trials had to be held in the name of justice. They have served three major purposes. In the first place they have given the defendants an opportunity of proving, if they could, that they had not taken part in the Nazi conspiracy, or that some other ground of defence was open to them.[17] In the second place the trial has placed on record the full story of these crimes, so that future generations will be able to know the truth. This time it will not be possible to say that the atrocity reports are 'propaganda'. In the third place, the trials will have established once and for all that aggressive war is an international crime, and that those who are guilty of waging such a war must pay the penalty. It is, of course, true that this may not prevent future aggressors from waging such wars if they think that they can win, but it will make their task a more difficult one. Law is more powerful than is sometimes realized, because to its defence will rally those who might otherwise be uncertain and vacillating. It is this general recognition which gives law its true force and on which it depends for its efficacy. The Nuremberg trials will have served their purpose if they have helped to teach to the peoples of the world the essential lesson that 'without law there cannot be peace'.

---

[17] I have not discussed in this paper the defence of 'superior order' because it is hardly applicable to the defendants at Nuremberg, and there has been no suggestion that it would be raised by them. Artich 8 of the Charter provides that, 'The fact that the defendant acted pursuant to order of his Government or of a superior shall not free him from responsibility, but may be considered in mitigation of punishment if the Tribunal determines that justice so requires.'

29

The Legacies of Nuremberg

By David Luban

The past is not dead; it is not even past.

—Christa Wolf

Forty-two years ago, on November 20, 1945, the trial of the major war criminals of the Third Reich began in the ruined city of Nuremberg. It is a commonplace that the trial was an 'historic' occasion, that it left a legacy for future generations. The men who conceived and conducted the trial understood it that way; they intended it to be epoch-making, and viewed their own words and deeds from the perspective of a distant and more pacific age. They guessed boldly at the judgment history would pass upon the meaning of the trial.

They condensed that meaning to two focal points: (1) by enlarging the reach of law beyond conventional war crimes, the trial was supposed to move us closer to world order, putting previously unreachable conduct under the domain of international law; and (2) by replacing raw vengefulness with legal procedures, it was to provide a model of the Rule of Law to reeducate Germany and inspire the peoples of other nations.

Forty years after Nuremberg we are better able to judge what the framers of the trial could only guess about the legacy of Nuremberg. What are the enduring contributions of the Nuremberg trial to the moral life of mankind and to its legal embodiment? That is my question. And my answer is this: the achievements at which the trial was aiming were compromised, rendered equivocal, by the trial itself; but its very failure has much to teach us. The framers of Nuremberg were confronted with a new offense, the bureaucratic crime, and a novel political menace, the criminal state. Limiting themselves to traditional legal concepts—sovereignty, individual criminal liability, conspiracy—and unwilling to question either the political system of nation-states or the character of responsibility in bureaucratic settings, they came to the brink of recognizing the novelty of criminal states but ultimately failed to comprehend this major challenge of our century.

The First Legacy: Crimes Against Peace and Crimes Against Humanity

It is impossible for us to read accounts of the Nuremberg trial without realizing that it signifies something much different to us than it did to those who conceived it.[1] For us, Nuremberg is a judicial footnote to the Holocaust; it stands for the condemnation and punishment of genocide, and its central achievement lies in recognizing the category of *crimes against humanity*—

murder, extermination, enslavement, deportation, and other inhumane acts committed against any civilian population, before or during the war, or persecutions on political, racial or religious grounds in execution of or in connection with any crime within the jurisdiction of the Tribunal, whether or not in violation of the domestic law of the country where perpetrated.[2]

For those who conceived of the trial, on the other hand, its great accomplishment was to be the criminalization of aggressive war, inaugurating an age of world order. In the words of Robert H. Jackson, the chief prosecutor at Nuremberg, 'This inquest represents the practical effort of four of the most mighty of nations, with the support of 17 more, to utilize international law to meet the greatest menace of our times—aggressive war.'[3] For the trial's framers, then, its decisive legal achievement lay in recognizing the category of *crimes against peace*—'planning, preparation, initiation or waging of a war of aggression, or a war in violation of international treaties, agreements or assurances, or participation in a Common Plan or Conspiracy for the accomplishment of any of the foregoing.'[4]

This idea that Nuremberg was to be the Trial to End All Wars seems fantastic and naive forty years (and 150 wars) later. It has also done much to vitiate the real achievements of the trial, in particular the condemnation of crimes against humanity. To end all war, the authors of the Nuremberg Charter were led to incorporate an intellectual confusion into it. The Charter criminalized aggression; and by criminalizing aggression the Charter erected a wall around state sovereignty and committed itself to an old-European model of unbreachable nation-states.

---

[1] For two such accounts: Robert E. Conot, *Justice at Nuremberg* (New York: Harper & Row, 1983), and Ann Tusa and John Tusa, *The Nuremberg Trial* (New York: Atheneum, 1984). The point I am making here is made as well in Judith Shklar, *Legalism* (Cambridge, Mass: Harvard University Press, 1964), p. 165. Many points in this essay were suggested to me by Shklar's oftentimes brilliant discussion.

[2] Article 6(c), 'Charter of the International Military Tribunal,' *Trial of the Major War Criminals Before the International Military Tribunal* [hereafter *Trial*], 1: 11.

[3] *Ibid.*, 2: 99.

[4] *Ibid.*, Article 6(a), p. 11.

But crimes against humanity are often, even characteristically, carried out by states against their own subjects. The effect, and great moral and legal achievement, of criminalizing such acts (Article 6(c)) and assigning personal liability to those who order them and carry them out (Articles 7 and 8) is to pierce the veil of sovereignty. As a result, Article 6(a) pulls in the opposite direction from Articles 6(c), 7, and 8, leaving us, as we shall see, with a legacy that is at best equivocal and at worst immoral.

Aggression and Sovereignty. At neither the Nuremberg nor the Tokyo trials was the crime of aggression defined.[5] But in 1974 the United Nations offered the following definition:

Aggression is the use of armed force by a State against the sovereignty, territorial integrity or political independence of another State, or in any other manner inconsistent with the Charter of the United Nations.[6]

Though not until 1974 was aggression explicitly linked with the violation of sovereignty, this definition is clearly in the spirit of Nuremberg—it is part of the legacy. But what, then, is sovereignty?

The concept was formulated in the early modern era, when the nation-state began to emerge in Europe. It signified that there is only one ultimate source of law in a state, namely, the state's sovereign; sovereignty is thus the linchpin that holds the political theory of the nation-state together.

From it follows the notorious doctrine of *act of state*, which exempts sovereigns from legal liability for their depredations against other states, on the theory that

prosecution of an individual by a court of the injured state for an act which, according to international law, is the act of another state, amounts to exercising jurisdiction over another state; and this is a violation of the rule of general international law that no state is subject to the jurisdiction of another state.[7]

Historically, the doctrine of sovereignty was formulated to secure the dominance of secular law over canon law, and thus of secular authority (*imperium*) over the church (*sacerdotum*); the doctrine, however, had the additional consequence that so-called 'natural law'—by which Aquinas meant constraints on the content of law ascertainable by reason alone—had no place in the theory. (Since in practice the church claimed the right to announce natural law—despite the fact that it was supposed to be a matter of reason and not of revelation—its elimination from the nation-state's political theory followed from the very practical struggle between *imperium* and *sacerdotum*.) Nothing constrained the sovereign: from

---

[5] Richard H. Minear, *Victors' Justice: The Tokyo War Crimes Trial* (Princeton, N.J.: Princeton University Press, 1971), pp. 55–60.

[6] Quoted in Yehuda Melzer, *Concepts of Just War* (Leyden: A. W. Sijthoff, 1975), pp. 28–29.

[7] Hans Kelsen, *Peace Through Law* (Chapel Hill, N.C.: University of North Carolina Press, 1944), p. 82.

the fact that he was the sole lawmaker it followed that he was the highest law-maker as well. Thus the classic doctrine of sovereignty eventually carried in its train the theory of 'legal positivism,' which says that the sole criterion of a rule's legality is that it has been propounded by the sovereign according to his chosen procedures.

From this, in turn, it follows that, provided the sovereign follows his self-determined legislative procedures, anything he wishes to make law is law. There are no domestic legal standards according to which he himself can be held respon-sible, unless he chooses to impose them upon himself. Conjoined with the act-of-state doctrine, this conclusion implies that sovereigns are liable under neither domestic nor international law, that 'the king is above the law.'[8]

It was this doctrine that Article 7 of the Nuremberg Charter assaulted: 'The official position of defendants, whether as Heads of State or responsible officials in Government departments, shall not be considered as freeing them from respon-sibility or mitigating punishment.'[9] By making even sovereigns legally liable for their deeds, Article 7 denies that the sovereign is the sole source of law in his state; it thus denies the doctrine of sovereignty itself.

Similarly with Article 8: 'The fact that the defendant acted pursuant to an order of his Government or of a superior shall not free him from responsibility....'[10] The law that obligates a citizen is an 'order of his Government'; by criminalizing acts that are legal according to the positive law laid down by the sovereign, Article 8 thus denies that the sovereign is the sole source of law for his subjects—and this, again, amounts to a denial of the theory of sovereignty itself.

And similarly with Article 6(c), which outlaws crimes against humanity even when committed by a state against its own subjects and 'whether or not in viola-tion of the domestic law of the country where perpetrated.' Article 6(c), the most enduring moral achievement of Nuremberg, is irreconcilable on its face with legal positivism, and thus with the classic doctrine of sovereignty. Together with Articles 7 and 8, then, it perforates or even destroys the doctrine in the name of 'humanity' and individual responsibility to it.

This is an important achievement, not anything to regret. As Jackson pointed out, the act-of-state and superior-orders doctrines taken together would imply that no one could be held responsible for the crimes the Tribunal was trying: the former would exempt those exercising sovereign authority, while the latter would exempt their subjects.[11] Yet it would be a moral absurdity (and political impos-sibility) to punish nobody for Auschwitz. The plain fact of the matter is that the

---

[8] For an interesting discussion of the role of positivism in the Nuremberg trial, see Stanley L. Paulson, 'Classical Legal Positivism at Nuremberg,' *Philosophy & Public Affairs* 4 (Winter 1975): 132–58.

[9] *Trial*, 1: 12.

[10] *Ibid.*

[11] *Ibid.*, 2: 150.

Third Reich was a criminal state in every moral sense that the word 'criminal' possesses, and the law had to reach those who carried out its crimes.

Two Problems With Sovereignty: Criminal States and Eurocentrism. It is an unhappy fact of human existence that we never forget how to commit a crime once we have been taught. The Third Reich may well be the first state whose criminality was virtually its defining feature; it will not be the last. In this regard, the framers of Nuremberg understood very well the importance of their endeavor. Since the Nazis had set dark precedent for criminal states, had invented new forms of evildoing, had made the unthinkable real (after which it is only a matter of time until it becomes routine), it was necessary to restructure our moral imaginations in order to fortify ourselves for a world of criminal states. If this meant exploding time-honored propositions and concepts, then so be it.

The trouble was that the propositions and concepts reflected a political reality—the system of nation-states—that no one was prepared to condemn. And so, just at the moment Articles 6(c), 7, and 8 of the Nuremberg Charter undermined the doctrine of sovereignty in the ways we have just examined, Article 6(a) fortified it by making aggressive war—violation of sovereignty—a crime.

This proved in the event to be a moral problem even more than a conceptual one. If the law is to be anything humane, it must guide our moral imaginations; and since it is now imperative that our moral imaginations include awareness of criminal states, the law must also include awareness of criminal states. For this reason alone, the doctrine of sovereignty, which acknowledges the authority of criminal states,[12] is no longer feasible. And so, Article 6(a)—which protects the sovereignty of all states, even criminal states, so long as they do not launch wars—should be seen as a mistake.

In any case, the doctrine of sovereignty bears little relevance to the modern world: it is an old-European concept, meant for nation-states—literally, states whose boundaries correspond with those of homogeneous linguistic and cultural communities.[13] Outside of Western Europe, and particularly in the Third World, we find at best limited correspondence between states and homogeneous communities. For this reason, 'statist' politics implies perpetual ferment and instability, as contending ethnic or tribal groups vie with each other for control of the apparatus of sovereignty.

---

[12] Recognition of a state as sovereign follows in international law from the bare fact that it exercises sovereign power: Ian Brownlie, *Principles of Public International Law*, 2nd ed. (Oxford: Clarendon Press, 1973), pp. 89–108.

[13] It may not even be a useful theory for the modern nation-state. See Niklas Luhmann, *Politische Theorie im Wohlfahrtsstaat* (Munich: Günter Olzog Verlag, 1981), pp. 12–24, 42–49, arguing that the doctrine of sovereignty was one of a constellation of doctrines suitable for the formative stages of the nation-state but useless for the modern welfare state, since the doctrine presupposes that the political system knows and dominates society, whereas in a complex and highly differentiated society this is not true—a society characterized as ours is by strong subsystem-differentiation is a society 'without summit and without center.'

Article 6(a) is Eurocentric in another way as well. The European nation-states (and the United States) exercised economic and often political control over much of Asia, Africa, and Latin America, and at Nuremberg this state of affairs was assumed by all to be fitting and uncontroversial. (It is startling to hear Jackson refer to the acquisition of colonies as a 'legitimate objective' for Germany.[14]) By criminalizing any breaches of sovereignty, Article 6(a) criminalized anti-imperialist struggle as well. This was noted by Justice Pal in his famous dissenting opinion in the Tokyo trial:

Certainly dominated nations of the present day *status quo* cannot be made to submit to eternal domination only in the name of peace. International law must be prepared to face the problem of bringing within juridical limits the politico-historical evolution of mankind which up to now has been accomplished chiefly through war. War and other methods of *self-help by force* can be effectively excluded only when this problem is solved, and it is only then that we can think of introducing criminal responsibility for efforts at adjustment by means other than peaceful. Until then there can hardly be any justification for any direct and indirect attempt at maintaining, in the name of humanity and justice, the very *status quo* which might have been organized and hitherto maintained only by force by pure opportunist 'Have and Holders'.... The part of humanity which has been lucky enough to enjoy political freedom can now well afford to have the deterministic ascetic outlook of life, and may think of peace in terms of political *status quo*. But every part of humanity has not been equally lucky and a considerable part is still haunted by the wishful thinking about escape from political dominations. To them the present age is faced with not only the menace of totalitarianism but also the ACTUAL PLAGUE of imperialism.[15]

Pal is not attacking a straw man; his argument was directed to Jackson, who had stated in his opening address at Nuremberg: 'Our position is that whatever grievances a nation may have, however objectionable it finds the *status quo*, aggressive warfare is an illegal means for settling those grievances or for altering those conditions.'

The Two Faces of Article 6: Statism Versus Human Rights. These theoretical confusions and practical misfortunes are, unhappily, an enduring legacy of Nuremberg. I have said that we view Nuremberg in the light of the Holocaust, so that its greatest achievement is taking cognizance of crimes against humanity. Seen from this perspective, Nuremberg is one of the founding moments of the modern human-rights movement, and of that form of politics that favors intervention on behalf of human rights, even when violations occur within the boundaries of sovereign states. Articles 6(c), 7, and 8 are the main 'texts' of Nuremberg for this tradition.

Seen from the perspective of its framers, however, Nuremberg was the Trial to End All War, and its main legal construct is Article 6(a). This has in turn

---

[14] *Trial*, 2: 105.
[15] Radha Binod Pal, *International Military Tribunal for the Far East: Dissentient Judgment of Justice R. B. Pal, M.A., LL.D.* (Calcutta: Sanyal, 1953), pp. 114–115.

been a major moral enemy of the human-rights movement, inasmuch as attempts at sanctions or interventions against human-rights offenders are inevitably denounced as violations of their sovereignty. It is the tension between statism and human rights that renders the legacy of Nuremberg equivocal; the human-rights movement and human-rights violators are vying for the contested legacy of Nuremberg.

Jackson saw this point all too clearly. When Gros, the French representative at the conference establishing the Nuremberg trial, argued that humanitarian intervention in a country's internal affairs was a traditional legal principle that would be contravened by Article 6(a), Jackson countered that nonintervention was sacred to Americans, who had no intention of letting other countries interfere in our own policies of racial discrimination.[16] Jackson, in other words, argued for subvening Article 6(c) to Article 6(a) in the Charter partly in order to enclose American human-rights violations within a wall of state sovereignty. By contrast, the other horn of the Article 6 dilemma was seized by Thurgood Marshall and his colleagues in the NAACP in their brief in *Morgan v. Virginia*, a transportation-desegregation case: they argued that Americans had not spilled their blood in a war against 'the apostles of racism' abroad only to permit its flourishing at home.[17] For the NAACP, the moral message of World War II was the illegitimacy of racist human-rights violations (Nuremberg's crimes against humanity, though Marshall did not refer to Nuremberg in the brief). The Supreme Court gave them a seven-to-one victory, striking down racial segregation on interstate buses; Jackson, ironically, did not participate in the decision because he was in Nuremberg prosecuting the Nazis.

Let me be clear: I am not claiming that Articles 6(a) and 6(c) must be logically or legally contradictory. They can be reconciled by making an exception to the doctrine of sovereignty when crimes against humanity are at issue: one allows humanitarian intervention in a sovereign state's affairs, but only when the humanitarian issue has risen to the horrific level of crimes against humanity.[18]

---

[16] Robert H. Jackson, *International Conference on Military Trials, London, 1945*, Department of State Publication No. 3080 (Washington: U.S. Government Printing Office, 1945), pp. 331, 333: 'It has been a general principle of foreign policy of our Government from time immemorial that the internal affairs of another government are not ordinarily our business; that is to say, the way Germany treats its inhabitants, or any other country treats its inhabitants, is not our affair any more than it is the affair of some other government to interpose itself in our problems.... We have some regrettable circumstances at times in our own country in which minorities are unfairly treated.' Such also have been the concerns of American senators who held up our ratification of the United Nations Genocide Convention for decades. The stated reasons have always been couched in terms of our 'principled' attachment to sovereignty (even at the expense of express concern for human rights); the unstated reason has been fear that American racial policies might be condemned under the Convention.

[17] *Morgan v. Virginia*, 328 U.S. 373 (1946) (racial segregation prohibited on interstate public transportation); brief quoted in Richard Kluger, *Simple Justice* (New York: Vintage, 1975), p. 238.

[18] This line is followed by Michael Walzer in *Just and Unjust Wars* (New York: Basic Books, 1977), perhaps the best defense of Article 6(a) and the doctrine of sovereignty.

Indeed, Article 6(c) reconciles the two clauses in precisely this fashion: it restricts its criminalization of 'persecutions on political, racial or religious grounds' by adding the crucial phrase '*in execution of or in connection with any crime within the jurisdiction of the Tribunal.*' The result is that persecutions on political, racial, or religious grounds are not crimes against humanity unless the perpetrator has also launched an aggressive war or committed war crimes. Persecutions do not, that is, cost a state its sovereignty until it has already forfeited it on other grounds.

A state can still lose its sovereignty for committing a crime against humanity without committing other crimes in addition, but only if it perpetrates 'murder, extermination, enslavement, deportation, and other inhumane acts . . . against any civilian population.' Thus Article 6(c) taken as a whole makes sovereignty fail only when domestic outrages reach population-size or when other Nuremberg crimes have been committed.

In this way the logical consistency of Article 6 is maintained. But I am asking about the *legacy* of Nuremberg. That means: the potential of its principles for growth and development, for extension and precedent setting, for adaptability to changed political circumstances, for underlying moral commitments that are not so much the logical implications of the principles as they are their 'deep structure.' Ronald Dworkin speaks of precedents exerting a 'gravitational force,'[19] and we must ask what the gravitational force is of reconciling Articles 6(a) and 6(c) in this fashion.

As we have seen, Article 6(a) tells us we cannot intervene in the affairs of a sovereign state on behalf of human rights until—here Article 6(c) enters the picture—the violations are committed across an entire 'civilian population.' But when is that? We must indulge in each case in a grotesque and blood-curdling calculus of murder, torture, and enslavement to determine which clause of Article 6 controls. We must ask questions like this: Is persecuted ethnic or religious minority M sufficiently distinct that it counts as a 'civilian population'? Does an all-out assault on M's indigenous culture, or a brutal forced-relocation policy with many casualties, amount to genocide? Do x deportations, y executions, and z tortures add up to enough that a state's sovereignty can be overridden? Or are such human-rights violations a sovereign state's own business, twentieth-century business-as-usual? (How many political prisoners writhing on the head of a pin does it take to make a crime against humanity?)

This is the price we pay for making Article 6 consistent: its gravitational force pulls us in the direction of a kind of charnel-house casuistry that offers to teach the human race little more than the equation of legalism with cynicism and indifference. If such is to be the legacy of Nuremberg, we are better off without it.

---

[19] Ronald Dworkin, *Taking Rights Seriously* (Cambridge, Mass.: Harvard University Press, 1978), p. 111.

If, on the other hand, we abandon the attempt to reconcile Articles 6(a) and (c), we must choose one of them. The choice of 6(c) is a fecund one: when the condemnation of crimes against humanity is allowed to develop as a principle of law and morality, it flowers into the politics of human rights. For the condemnation of 'inhumane acts committed against any civilian population' and 'persecutions on political, racial or religious grounds' need not be restricted to Holocaust-size events in its gravitational force. It extends to human-rights violations in general.

By contrast, Article 6(a), as Justice Pal predicted, flowers into a deification of the *status quo*, and allows the notion of state criminality to slip through its conceptual net. The choice between the two should not be a difficult one.[20]

The Second Legacy: The Rule of Law

In September 1944, Secretary of State Henry Stimson wrote to President Roosevelt: 'It is primarily by the thorough apprehension, investigation and trial of all the Nazi leaders and instruments of the Nazi system of terrorism such as the Gestapo, with punishment delivered as promptly, swiftly and severely as possible, that we can demonstrate the abhorrence which the world has for such a system and bring home to the German people our determination to extirpate it and its fruits forever.'[21] This memorandum contains the root idea of the Nuremberg trial (which was in fact a brainchild of the Americans, who urged it upon their more-or-less-unwilling allies). The trial was to serve an expressive and educative function.

As the thinking of the Americans who authored the trial idea developed, they became clearer about what the trial was to teach Germany. The German people would learn from it the foul deeds of their leaders and our abhorrence of such a system; but also—and it is this upon which I wish to focus—it would teach the German people what the Rule of Law is all about by exemplifying it in the trial itself.

---

[20] Abandoning Article 6(a) does not, I should note, mean abandoning the legal condemnation of unjust war. All we need do is change our criterion of unjust war from 'war that violates state sovereignty' (aggressive war in the United Nations' sense) to 'war that violates human rights.' Such a criterion of unjust war, unlike Article 6(a), is fully in tune with Article 6(c) of the Nuremberg Charter. I have argued for this revised conception of unjust war: David Luban, 'Just War and Human Rights,' *Philosophy & Public Affairs* 9 (Winter 1980): 160–81. The conflict between statism and human rights is the underlying issue of my debate with Walzer over the theory of just war: Michael Walzer, 'The Moral Standing of States: A Response to Four Critics,' *Philosophy & Public Affairs* 9 (Spring 1980): 209–229; David Luban, 'The Romance of the Nation-State,' *Philosophy & Public Affairs* 9 (Summer 1980): 392–397. These papers, together with selections from Walzer's *Just and Unjust Wars*, are collected in Charles Beitz, Marshall Cohen, Thomas Scanlon, and A. John Simmons, eds., *International Ethics: A Philosophy & Public Affairs Reader* (Princeton, N.J.: Princeton University Press, 1985), pp. 165–243.

[21] Quoted in Tusa and Tusa, *Nuremberg Trial*, p. 52.

Alas, the German people at the time were too preoccupied with the sheer effort of surviving in 'the ruin that lies from the Rhine to the Danube'[22] to care much about moral lessons. When cooking oil is scarce and needles and thread impossible to obtain, you do not pause to contemplate the law in its majesty. (Even the defense counsel were lured by the prospect of regular lunches in American cafeterias as much as by the legal and historic significance of the case.[23]) Whatever lessons the trial taught were therefore reserved for later assimilation; for this reason, the important question is not what effect the trial in fact had on the German sense of legality but whether, in hindsight, the trial did indeed exemplify the Rule of Law in action.

The Fullerian Concept of the Rule of Law. Before we can answer this question, we must review what the Rule of Law is. The notion of a 'rule of law, not of men' dates back at least to Plato and Aristotle;[24] but the ideal of the Rule of Law has received its most thorough examination in the philosophy of Lon Fuller. For Fuller, law is a device for ordering society. To fulfill this function, law must be capable of structuring and guiding human action, and this in turn implies that several necessary conditions for action-guiding be met; Fuller calls them 'the morality that makes law possible.' Fuller lists eight such conditions; for our purposes, the important ones are these: (1) law must contain public rules; (2) these rules must not be retroactive or *ex post facto* (since you cannot follow today a rule that is not laid down until tomorrow); and (3) there must be 'congruence between the rules as announced and their actual administration.'[25] This last condition implies two important corollaries: (3a) like cases must be treated alike, and (3b) alternative 'enforcement' of rules, such as lynch mobs, street violence, and vigilantism, which create noncongruence between announced legal rules and social reality, must be suppressed. To these I add a condition not found in Fuller, though it is fully consistent with his thinking, namely, (4) adjudication must respect the various elements of procedural fairness, publicity, and impartiality that we think of as 'due process of law' conceived in its most general aspect. For if we are to guide our actions by reference to legal rules, as Fuller supposes, we must have reasonable confidence that the legal process will attempt with some degree of fairness and accuracy to find out what our actions really were and to apply the law to them in a reasonable manner.

Fuller goes on to note that every legal system fails at some times and in some degree to satisfy these conditions; to the extent that it fails to do so, the Rule of

---

[22] Jackson, in *Trial*, 2: 103.

[23] Tusa and Tusa, *Nuremberg Trial*, p. 124 (defense counsels' motives); pp. 221–24 (German public's indifference to the trial).

[24] Plato, *The Laws*, 715d; Aristotle, *Politics* III, 14, 1286a9–20. That Plato's support for the ideal was at best half-hearted may be seen from *Statesman*, 294a–297e; Aristotle also expressed reservations: *Politics* III, 10, 1281a34–39.

[25] Lon Fuller, *The Morality of Law*, 2nd ed. (New Haven, Conn.: Yale University Press, 1964), pp. 33–39.

Law is weakened. When the failure is egregious or systematic, the Rule of Law does not exist at all.

The Rule of Law in Germany Between Versailles and Nuremberg. To see the point of the Nuremberg trial, it is important to realize that the Rule of Law had indeed vanished in Germany for over a quarter of a century. At the end of World War I Germany was on the verge of Marxist revolution, and indeed the Weimar Republic was declared hastily in order to preempt the declaration of a workers' republic. Gangs of demobilized soldiers, the *Freikorps*, joined with essentially lawless right-wing police to crush the German left. The early years of the Weimar Republic were punctuated by right-wing political murders: Kurt Eisner, the leader of the Bavarian socialist republic; Rosa Luxemburg and Karl Liebknecht, leaders of the Spartacists; Leo Jogiches, Luxemburg's lover, shot in the back in a Berlin police station; Matthias Erzberger, a centrist leader; Walter Rathenau, the Jewish foreign minister of Weimar.[26] Quite obviously, the violence on the streets and the lack of congruence between law and 'administration' continued in the Nazi era, becoming in fact the accepted way of doing things.

In order to maintain continuity and legitimacy, the founders of the Weimar Republic made a fatal error: they left the Kaiser's aristocratic/monarchist civil service in place, despite the fact that these men were enemies of the republic and of republicanism in general. This was true in particular of the judiciary, which engaged in what Thomas Mann called 'the jurisprudence of political revenge'[27] to subvert the republic. The statistics are startling. Right-wing political murders accounted for 354 deaths, as compared with 22 left-wing murders. None of the former murderers were sentenced to death, however, whereas ten of the latter were; sentences to right-wingers averaged four months, while those meted out to left-wingers averaged fifteen years. When a Communist republic was crushed in Bavaria in 1919, over 2,200 people were imprisoned; but after the rightist Kapp Putsch of 1920, 'in the course of which the *Reich* Government was compelled to leave Berlin and which involved the entire *Reich* north of the Main and implicated many high-ranking army officers, only one single person, the former head of the Berlin police, was convicted and sentenced. Even he was allowed the benefit of honourable motives and the courts held that the Prussian state was bound to pay him his pension both during and after serving his sentence.'[28] Other stunning cases of rightist judicial unfairness involved the 'black *Reichswehr* [army]' organizations,

---

[26] For an excellent discussion, see Peter Gay, *Weimar Culture* (New York: Harper & Row. 1968), pp. 9–22.

[27] Quoted in E. J. Cohn, *Manual of German Law*, vol. 1, 2nd ed. (Dobbs Ferry, N.Y.: Oceana, 1968), §43, p. 29.

[28] *Ibid.* §41, p. 28.

which under the cloak of training for the defense of the Eastern provinces against alleged Polish infiltrations organized terrorist activities for the nationalist parties and prepared the ground for National Socialism. The courts assisted the 'black *Reichswehr*' by punishing journalists, who had discussed their activities in public, for treason. Members of the organizations, however, who had murdered disloyal fellow-members . . . were acquitted or received only nominal punishment, because they were held to have acted in self-defense or 'for patriotic motives.'[29]

Germans widely circulated Brecht's witty twist on Goethe's 'land of poets and thinkers'—*Dichter und Denker*: Germany was now the land of *Dichter und Denker und Richter und Henker*—poets and thinkers and judges and hangmen. The German judiciary, according to Franz Neumann, had 'written the blackest page in the life of the German republic.'[30]

All of these actions offended against Fuller's third rule and its corollaries. Under Nazism, other rules fell as well. Most obvious was the fact that under Nazi legal doctrine the Führer's *spoken word* (and not just written commandment) was law—the law, in other words, was not public. The Nazis also made robust use of *ex post facto* law. The day after the Röhm purge (the murder of the 'left wing' of the Nazi party), Hitler retroactively legalized it; after *Kristallnacht*, the party- and Gestapo-organized anti-Jewish riots of November 1938, Göring imposed a 1-billion-mark fine—on the Jews. The rule *nulla poena sine lege* (no punishment without law) was abolished, for section 2 of the revised criminal code provided that an act could be punished if 'the spirit [*Grundgedank*] of a rule of criminal law and healthy folk-feeling' justified punishment.[31]

During the war, the Ministry of Justice issued periodic letters to judges and defense lawyers. Thierack, the minister of justice, begins his judges letters sanctimoniously enough: 'I will, can, and must not tell the judge who is called to preside over a trial, how to decide an individual case.'[32] Thus he will simply comment upon and criticize decisions to give guidelines to judges. In one case, Jews went to court because they had been illegally denied their coffee rations, and the court found in their favor. Thierack: 'The judge should have put himself the question: How will the Jews react to this 20-page-long ruling, which certifies that he and the 500 other Jews are right and that he won over a German authority without losing one word about the reaction of our own people to this insolent and arrogant conduct of the Jews.'[33]

In another case, a Jew pleaded mitigating circumstances after having been convicted of a foreign-exchange violation and received a light sentence. Thierack: 'The

---

[29] *Ibid.*

[30] Franz L. Neumann, *Behemoth* (New York: Oxford University Press. 1944), p. 23.

[31] 'Gesetz zur Änderung des Strafgesetzbuchs vom 28. Juni 1935,' *Reichsgesetzblatt* I at 839; see 6 BVerGE at 132–222 (1959).

[32] UMLL *Trials of the War Criminals before the Nuremberg Military Tribunals*, vol. 3 (Washington: U.S. Government Printing Office, 1951), p. 524.

[33] *Ibid.*, p. 531.

court applies the same criteria for imposing punishment as it would if it were dealing with a German fellow citizen as defendant. This cannot be sanctioned. The Jew
is the enemy of the German people, who has plotted, stirred up, and prolonged this
war. In doing so, he has brought unspeakable misery upon our people. Not only is
he of different but of inferior race. Justice, which must not measure different matters
by the same standard, demands that just this racial aspect must be considered in the
meting out of punishment.'[34] In his letters to defense lawyers, Thierack appeals to
the 'healthy folk-feeling' section of the criminal code to argue that under present
conditions the lawyer's duty to defend his client is overruled by his duty to defend
the state.[35] This echoes a criminal-law commentator's argument that a lawyer can
reveal a client's confidences if healthy folk-feeling so commands.[36]

Such was the Rule of Law in post-World War I Germany.[37] The Germans,
evidently, had a lot to learn. The question is whether the Nuremberg trial had a
lot to teach.

The Ex Post Facto *Character of the Nuremberg Trial.* The first, and obvious, objection to the Nuremberg trial on Rule of Law grounds is that it was itself based upon
ex post facto law, that it therefore violated *nullum crimen sine lege, nulla poena sine
lege* (no crime without law, no punishment without law). The criminalization of
aggressive war, the introduction of the category of crimes against humanity, and
the abolition of the act-of-state and superior-orders defenses were legal novelties.
Though some have claimed that none of these were unprecedented, the arguments are strained, having the character of what Jackson called 'sterile legalisms'
and Joseph Keenan, prosecutor at Tokyo, called 'legal sterilisms.'[38]

Thus, for example, precedent was found for Article 6(a) (crimes against peace)
in the Briand-Kellogg Pact of 1928, in which the signatories (including Germany)
abjured the use of war. The pact indeed meant that Germany had violated a treaty
by starting the war; but treaty violation had not previously been treated as an
individual criminal offense of a national leader, so the precedent is beside the
point.

The twofold novelty—*individual, criminal* liability—is the key problem. There
is no question that what Germany did was wrong, nor that many of her actions
were violations of international law. The problem is showing that such violations
of international law had been *crimes*, and, moreover, crimes of individual persons.
The trial's defenders simply glossed over this problem.

---

[34] *Ibid.*, p. 533. Thierack here seems to be endorsing 'treat different cases differently.' The question whether this letter violates Fuller's rule (3a) is left as an exercise to the reader.
[35] *Ibid.*, p. 564.
[36] Eduard Kohlrausch, *Strafgesetzbuch mit Erläuterungen und Nebengesetzen*, 33rd ed. (Berlin:
de Gruyter. 1937), pp. 470–471.
[37] For a useful compilation of Nazi legislation, see Ingo von Münch and Uwe Broderson, eds.,
Gesetze des NS-Staates: Dokumente eines Unrechtssystems (Paderborn: Ferdinand Schöningh, 1982).
[38] Minear, *Victors' Justice*, p. 18. The best attempt to vindicate the legality of Nuremberg is
Robert K. Woetzel, *The Nuremberg Trials in International Law* (New York: Praeger, 1962).

The Tribunal, to be sure, addressed the question, but it rested its case on the shakiest of grounds. To show that aggression was a crime, it cited two League of Nations documents that were never passed and a Pan-American treaty; its only vaguely convincing precedent was a 1927 League of Nations declaration, voted for by Germany, which declared aggressive war to be an international crime.[39] But this declaration was not a binding treaty—Germany had quit the League and the League was defunct—and in any event it did not suggest that individuals could be held liable for such a crime.

To demonstrate this latter proposition, the Tribunal could cite only a U.S. Supreme Court case, Article 7 of the Charter, and a provision of the Treaty of Versailles concerning the trial of war criminals.[40] The first obviously had little force in international law, and in any event the U.S. case was decided in 1942, long after the aggressive war had been launched. The second was a circular argument with a vengeance—Article 7 could not be based on Article 7. As for the third, it was irrelevant to the question of whether crimes against peace and against humanity could be charged against individuals, for war crimes made up a separate category of offenses under the Nuremberg Charter (Article 6(b))—and, unlike the other two, it was a category that was not novel and whose offenses nobody denied could be tried as individual crimes.

The Tribunal evidently sensed that it was on shaky legalistic ground, for it also ventured an argument based on reason: 'To assert that it is unjust to punish those who in defiance of treaties and assurances have attacked neighboring states without warning is obviously untrue, for in such circumstances the attacker must know that he is doing wrong, and so far from it being unjust to punish him, it would be unjust if his wrong were allowed to go unpunished.'[41] True enough, but the argument contains a double equivocation, on the words 'punish' and 'wrong.' Though the invader knew he was doing 'wrong,' he did *not* know that he was committing a 'crime'—the latter being a juridically precise subclass of the category of 'wrongs.' Similarly, he may have expected 'punishment' of two sorts: (1) by starting a war he would in turn be made war upon; and (2) if he went down in defeat he would be burdened with ruthless terms and harsh reparations (as at Versailles). But he had no reason to expect (3) criminal trial and individualized punishment. Indeed, the World War I precedent to which the Nazis may have looked was the provision of the Versailles Treaty requiring Germany to try her own war criminals—a colossal farce in the event, for 888 out of 901 were acquitted or had their cases dismissed by the Leipzig court.[42] The Leipzig trials explain in part why Nuremberg was necessary—but they hardly provide a precedent showing it was *possible*.

[39] *Trial*, 1: 221–222.
[40] *Ibid.*, pp. 222–223.
[41] *Ibid.*, 1: 219.
[42] Tusa and Tusa, *Nuremberg Trial*, p. 19.

Similarly, Jackson's claim that '[a]ny resort to war—to any kind of war—is a resort to means that are inherently criminal'[43] is a clear begging of the question. Nor does his famous argument-in-the-alternative that if this indeed be new law the Nuremberg framers are entitled to make it—'Unless we are prepared to abandon every principle of growth for International Law, we cannot deny that our own day has the right to institute customs and to conclude agreements that will themselves become sources of a newer and strengthened International Law'[44]— save the point. Of course the Nuremberg framers are entitled to make new *prospective* law; what they are not entitled to do is to apply it retroactively. The real consequence of Jackson's argument is, unfortunately, the dismissal of the cases requested in the defense counsels motion of November 19, 1945:

Wherever the Indictment charges acts which were not punishable at the time the Tribunal would have to confine itself to a thorough examination and findings as to what acts were committed, for which purposes the Defense would cooperate to the best of their ability as true assistants of the Court. Under the impact of these findings of the Tribunal the States of the international legal community would then create a new law under which those who in the future would be guilty of starting an unjust war would be threatened with punishment by an International Tribunal.[45]

Freeing the defendants is only half of what the Rule of Law demands, however. Many of them would consider freedom no favor, since their own countrymen were prepared to wreak private vengeance on them—Schacht, Papen, and Fritzsche, after all, had to be smuggled out of jail after they were acquitted at Nuremberg. Now of course the Allies might wink at such private vengeance ('we couldn't execute 'em, but at least they got dead anyway'), but to do so would violate condition (3b) of the Rule of Law—no alternative enforcement. Thus the Allies would truly honor the Rule of Law only by providing lifelong protection for Hermann Göring and Julius Streicher.

This idea is paradoxical to the point of obscenity. As Jackson argued, 'The rule of law in the world, flouted by the lawlessness incited by these defendants, had to be restored at the cost to my country of over a million casualties, not to mention those of other nations [and not to mention 6 million gassed, shot, burned, and tortured Jews]. I cannot subscribe to the perverted reasoning that society may advance and strengthen the rule of law by the expenditure of morally innocent lives but that progress in the rule of law may never be made at the price of morally guilty lives.'[46]

The question, of course, is whether an *ex post facto* trial is 'progress in the rule of law.' I shall argue that Nuremberg was. In any event, the conclusion that the Rule of Law requires lifelong protection for the elite of a genocidal regime would imply that the Rule of Law is not an ideal worthy of respect. Fortunately, no such drastic conclusion is forced upon us.

43 *Trial*, 2: 146.   44 *Ibid.*, p. 147.
45 *Ibid.*, 1: 169.   46 *Ibid.*, 2: 147.

The Nuremberg Trial as Progress in the Rule of Law. On July 11, 1944 Churchill wrote to Anthony Eden, 'There is no doubt that this [the Holocaust] is probably the greatest and most horrible crime ever committed in the whole history of the world. . . . It is quite clear that all concerned who may fall into our hands, including the people who only obeyed orders by carrying out the butcheries, should be put to death after their association with the murders has been proved.'[47]

But 'after their association with the murders has been proved' is ambiguous: does it mean a real trial before law? In fact, the British opposed such a trial; their idea was to round up the top Nazis and shoot them. As I have mentioned, it was the Americans who wanted a trial. The third paradigmatic view was that of Stalin, who said at Yalta that 'the grand criminals should be tried before being shot.'[48] First try them, then shoot them (a version of the Rule of Law that Stalin had perfected on his own Central Committee and military staff at the Moscow trials of the 1930s).

The British and Russian alternatives show us the clear sense in which the Nuremberg trial was 'progress in the rule of law.' It was progress, indeed, in four ways.

First, the association of the defendants with the deeds for which they were on trial had to be proved according to strict standards of evidence.

Second, the deeds for which they were held liable were specified in the Charter and their indictments. They knew in advance of the trial what the charges were and could prepare a defense.

Third, the notion of liability at work in the trial was the relatively tight legal notion of *direct causal involvement* and not the looser notion of moral liability. After all, even the three men who were acquitted bore a heavy burden of moral responsibility. Fritzsche had held a high post in Goebbels's Propaganda Ministry and had, in his weekly radio program, helped fan the flames of Jew-hating, jingoism, and war. Papen was a corrupt and conniving right-wing Weimar politician who had maneuvered to make Hitler chancellor and then accepted a diplomatic post in the Third Reich. And Schacht, the financial wizard who had ended the murderous inflation of the early 1920s, had used his influence to help cement the reactionary coalition that brought Hitler to power.[49] To be sure, both Papen and Schacht had assumed that they and their right-wing coalition partners would be able to control Hitler and had not counted on things turning out as they did (and Schacht had resigned Hitler's government and ended the war in Dachau). But

---

[47] Quoted in Conot, *Justice at Nuremberg*, p. 11.

[48] Tusa and Tusa, *Nuremberg Trial*, p. 77.

[49] Schacht's prestige made him the Lee Iacocca of the Weimar Republic, as witness the popular rhyme '*Wer hat die Mark stabil gemacht, das war allein der Doktor Schacht.*' [Who was it that made the mark stable? Doctor Schacht was the only one able.]

this hardly diminishes their moral responsibility: They had maneuvered to bring a man already known to be a raving, Jew-hating monster, whose private army of storm troopers was already the terror of the streets, into the government's chief executive position; they had hoped to treat him as their marionette; they had miscalculated, and because of their miscalculation 35 million people had died violently. Morally, they deserved to hang if anyone did—as did Fritzsche and (for that matter) all the defendants who received only prison terms. The Nuremberg Tribunal, however, limited its inquiry to causal, legal liability and not moral responsibility.[50]

Fourth, and most important, the trial was fair—judges and prosecution abided by the rules set out in the Charter, and those rules did not bias the inquiry against the defense.[51] This is evident from the record, but the simplest demonstration lies in the acquittals of Fritzsche, Papen, and Schacht.

These four features—the demand for proof, clear specification of offense, the restriction of liability to direct causal involvement, and fairness—clearly point to an advance in the Rule of Law over the alternatives of kangaroo court and summary execution; in this sense, Jackson was right to describe the defendants as 'hard pressed but . . . not ill used'[52] as they would have been on the British or Russian plans.[53]

We may collect these features under the general rubric of *process*. It is the first dimension along which we may assess the progress of the Rule of Law. A second major dimension is that of *enforcement*. It has always been the peculiarity of international law that it is sanctionless. Now it may be that, analytically speaking, law does not require sanctions;[54] nevertheless, it will be impossible to fulfill Fuller's condition (3)—congruence between the law and its administration—without them. The great advance of Nuremberg in this respect is the crude but attractive solution it offers to the problem of enforcement: to put it bluntly, Article 7 says 'if you transgress the law, we will catch your leaders and, if they prove to be responsible for the transgression, we will hang them up.' Nuremberg expands the reach of the Rule of Law by enhancing its grip.

[50] The same cannot be said, however, of the Tokyo tribunal, which executed General Yamashita for crimes committed by his soldiers even though no evidence whatever contradicted his defense that the successful American invasion had disrupted his communication and command structure to such an extent that he was unable to control the troops who committed the crimes. Yamashita was not even morally responsible. See Walzer, *Just and Unjust Wars*, pp. 319–322.

[51] On the fairness of the trial, see Tusa and Tusa, *Nuremberg Trial*, pp. 205–212.

[52] *Trial*, 2: 101.

[53] These four features are not, of course, among those named by Fuller; his conditions are necessary, not jointly sufficient, for the Rule of Law. I have suggested, however, that these features, and 'due process' in general, are necessary to fulfill Fuller's condition (3) (congruence between rules and their administration).

[54] So argues John Finnis (to my mind persuasively) against Austin and Weber, *Natural Law and Natural Right* (Oxford: Clarendon, 1981), pp. 266–270.

In these obvious ways, Nuremberg is plainly an advance of the Rule of Law; to deny this on the ground that the trial was *ex post facto* seems hyperbolic or even deliberately paradoxical. I believe, however, that there is a natural explanation for the hyperbole.

For Fuller, recall, law is a device for ordering society, and must therefore be capable of structuring and guiding human action: that is why a full-fledged Rule of Law regime must fulfill his eight conditions. The 'ideal type' here is of a well-ordered domestic society. International society, however, is simply not well ordered in this way: international law has evolved not as a device for ordering international society but as an improvisation for reconciling domestic legal systems when they are brought into contact (as in international trade). Most international interactions thus occur, as it were, in juridical outer space. For this reason, we should not measure the Rule of Law in international affairs against the Fullerian ideal but against a different ideal type: the so-called 'state of nature.' This is implicit in Jackson's contrast between advancing the Rule of Law by the expenditure of morally innocent lives (i.e., by war) and morally guilty lives (i.e., by a fair albeit *ex post facto* trial): measured against the baseline of war, vengeance, and summary execution, the trial is a clear moral *and legal* advance. The hyperbolic denial that Nuremberg embodied the Rule of Law, on the other hand, results when we begin 'at the wrong end'—with Fuller rather than Hobbes.

I can make this argument more precise by asking what is wrong with *ex post facto* law. The Fullerian argument, of course, is that agents cannot guide their actions by rules that do not exist until after the actions are completed. Agents who treat law as an action-guiding system are aggrieved by retroactive law because they were not expecting to be sanctioned for their acts. The premise here is that had they expected such sanction they would, or might, have refrained from the action. Thus *ex post facto* law is wrong because it violates the legitimate expectations of agents.

If Hobbes forms our baseline, however, the result is different. In the state of nature, and especially in the state of war, there are no such expectations to sacrifice, because agents do not try to guide their actions by corresponding them to rules. One expects violence in return for violence; one expects 'ill use' if one is defeated. This is the force of Jackson's argument: 'If these men are the first war leaders of a defeated nation to be prosecuted in the name of the law, they are also the first to be given a chance to plead for their lives in the name of the law. Realistically, the Charter of this Tribunal, which gives them a hearing, is also the source of their only hope.'[55] Retroactive law violates no legitimate expectations when the alternative is no law at all.

It may be objected that the Nazi leaders did not expect to be held criminally liable for their deeds, and that, since they did not believe that 'resolving the Jewish

---

[55] *Trial*, 2: 102.

question' was wrong, they did not expect retaliation in any form—perhaps they expected the world's gratitude, not its abhorrence.

But the latter objection is highly implausible. If it were true, why did Himmler order all traces of the death camps to be removed? Why did Goebbels boast in September 1944 that he was number one on the Allied list of war criminals?[56] And once it is admitted that the Nazis knew that what they were doing would be supremely hateful to the Allies, the objection that they did not expect to be held criminally liable becomes unimportant. For their legitimate expectation was that they would be summarily shot. The plain conclusion is that Jackson was right: if the Nuremberg defendants' expectations were violated, it is because they received better treatment than they had any reason to expect. Since what is wrong with retroactive law is that it gives people worse treatment than they had reason to expect, it follows that the Nuremberg trial, though based on retroactive law, did not wrong its defendants.[57]

This does not mean, of course, that the Nuremberg trial was fully consistent with the Rule of Law ideal: retroactive law is retroactive law. It shows, however, that the moral wrong committed by violating the Rule of Law is at a minimum here; and, since the trial constituted a clear advance of the Rule of Law in most other respects, we are right to remain sanguine in the face of the objection.

Nothing can illustrate more graphically the difference between the Rule of Law and its absence, between what the defendants actually got and what they had reason to expect, than this anecdote from Nuremberg. On December 11, 1945 the prosecution showed a four-hour film of German footage on the history of the Nazi party. As Tusa and Tusa report it,

The defendants adored every moment of it. They gazed entranced at the newsreels of the Nazi Rallies in Nuremberg, tapped their feet to the marching songs, reveled in the sight of the flags and the sound of the 'Sieg Heils' and Hess crying 'The Party is the Führer and the Führer is Germany'.... When they got back to the prison several of the defendants were in tears—of pride and nostalgia this time.

Not one of them commented on a sequence in the film that had particularly impressed others. It showed the trial before the People's Court in Berlin of the 1944 Bomb plotters. They had seen abject men, clutching at their trousers from which the belts had been taken, deprived of the dignity of their false teeth and the aid of their spectacles. There

---

[56] Tusa and Tusa, *Nuremberg Trial*, p. 61.

[57] Richard Mohr has pointed out to me one way in which the trial may have given the Nazi leadership worse than it expected. The leaders may have seen themselves as world-historical heroes, for whom only the martyr's death of summary execution is appropriate. Instead, they found themselves in the humiliating position of being treated as criminals, as no different in kind from cutpurses and rapists. Though the trial offered a chance of acquittal, and therefore of life, it was an outrage, worse treatment than the Wagnerian *Götterdämmerung* suitable to conquered warriors.

Now it is likely that Göring thought this way, as perhaps did the military men Jodl and Keitel, and romantics such as Baldur von Schirach. It is equally clear that the craven Ribbentrop would have done anything to save his life, and that most of the defendants had no desire to end their lives before a firing squad, even in a glorious D-flat coda with Bayreuth tubas bellowing. In any event, we need not accept the leaders' *meschuggene* ideas as legitimate expectations.

had been no defending counsel and the accused had been literally dragged by SS guards before Judge Freisler. As soon as they tried to speak he screeched at them a torrent of abuse. The contrast between Nazi justice and the tone of the Nuremberg trial and its Charter was vivid and telling—to those sensitive enough to see it.[58]

The Enforcement Problem. Despite the undeniable fact that it exemplified important features of the Rule of Law, the Nuremberg trial has left us an equivocal legacy in this matter as it did in the matter of human rights. The problem begins, once again, with Article 6(a) of the Charter, which criminalizes aggressive war.

As we have seen, Nuremberg enforces the Rule of Law in international law in one fundamental way: it offers to punish the men and women who commit war crimes, crimes against peace, and crimes against humanity. By personalizing the punishment, it seems to make possible the first realistic deterrent in the history of international law.

Before there can be trial and punishment, however, the criminal must be apprehended, and we must ask how such apprehension can take place. Suppose, for instance, that members of some nation are guilty of crimes against humanity in peacetime rather than in war. To give ourselves concrete examples, we may think about the massacre of more than a half million Communists in Indonesia in 1965, the current Indonesian depredations in East Timor, or even the persecution of blacks in South Africa today, none of which is located in a war context at all. There is, I take it, 'probable cause' to believe that these are crimes against humanity, whether or not the charge could actually be proven at trial; in conjunction with Articles 7 and 8, therefore, Article 6(c) of the Charter allows the prosecution of national leaders, officials, and armed forces involved in the massacres and persecutions.

However, these persons cannot be taken to trial without violating the sovereignty of Indonesia and South Africa, and such a violation is forbidden by Article 6(a). (Argentina, remember, protested on violation-of-sovereignty grounds the Israeli kidnapping of Adolf Eichmann—and Eichmann was not even a citizen of Argentina.) As a result, crimes against humanity can be punished as crimes under the Nuremberg Charter only when they occur in the course of a war.[59]

The same is true of several of the crimes against peace detailed in Article 6(a), namely, the planning and preparation of aggressive war and conspiracy so to plan and prepare: for unless the plans and preparations are followed by actually initiating a war, it would be a criminal act of aggression to attempt to apprehend the planners and preparers. Nor is this an unimportant defect. Since it is clear that the chief threat to peace in the contemporary world is the destabilizing effect of military preparation, Article 6(a) is correct to note the criminality of planning and preparing for war even without actually initiating it; but by criminalizing

---

[58] Tusa and Tusa, *Nuremberg Trial*, p. 169.
[59] As Jackson explicitly argued: *International Conference on Military Trials*, pp. 331, 333.

any attempt to enforce itself, Article 6(a) cuts its own throat as an instrument of international peace.

In practice, then, crimes against humanity and most crimes against peace can be brought under the Rule of Law only if the criminal launches an aggressive war and meets with defeat.[60] The same is true of war crimes, for that matter: think of war crimes (and crimes against peace) committed by the United States in Vietnam and the Soviet Union in Afghanistan. Who is going to arrest Nixon and Gorbachev?

Jackson said at Nuremberg, 'Unfortunately, the nature of these crimes is such that both prosecution and judgment must be by victor nations over vanquished foes.'[61] It is clear from the context that he was referring to the specific situation of the Nazis, and not making a general point. If I am right, however, the general point follows from the Nuremberg Charter itself. Only victors' justice is possible.[62]

It will be objected that the alternative to unenforceability is infinitely worse. It is difficult to imagine anything crazier and more destructive of world peace than allowing someone to go into countries such as Indonesia, South Africa, or the Soviet Union to apprehend national leaders for trial before an international court of law! The fact that we do not know who the policeman would be underlines the problem: somebody, from some nation, is to abduct P. W. Botha or Mikhail Gorbachev. That is war, pure and simple, and the world will not long survive it.

The problem is that in a world of nation-states the only method of enforcing the law of nations against an uncooperative violator is for one nation or group of nations to attack the culprit; the fact that the Nuremberg Charter is

---

[60] Theoretically, a victorious aggressor might try opponents for crimes against humanity; but it is more likely that, since the aggressor has itself violated Article 6, it will not be moved to initiate trials based on the Nuremberg Charter.

[61] *Trial*, 2: 101.

[62] Instead of actually arresting criminal leaders, one could introduce a different procedure, namely, trying them *in absentia* (as was done at Nuremberg in the case of Martin Bormann). I fear, however, that such a procedure would create a toothless court that would be so open to costless political manipulation that it would rapidly evolve into an arena for political grandstanding, that is, into an international joke.

A related alternative is an international criminal court with teeth that states voluntarily participate in. Signatories of the European Convention for the Protection of Human Rights and Fundamental Freedom yield jurisdiction in human-rights matters to the European Court of Human Rights in Strasbourg. It is not a criminal court, but, on the lines of the Strasbourg model, states could establish an international criminal tribunal, whose jurisdiction they voluntarily accept, and to which they grant extradition powers. This would amount to a self-imposed limitation on state sovereignty, and would thus circumvent the enforcement problem generated by Article 6(a). The problem with the idea, of course, is that precisely the most robust practitioners of crimes against humanity are least likely to enter into such an enforceable covenant. For this reason, I do not believe the suggestion addresses the enforcement problem in a practical way. On the European Court of Human Rights, and proposals for an international criminal court, see the materials assembled in Richard B. Lillich and Frank C. Newman, *International Human Rights: Problems of Law and Policy* (Boston: Little, Brown, 1979), pp. 560–627, 754–823.

unenforceable, that only victors' justice is possible, is thus another artifact of the system of sovereign nation-states, which I have earlier criticized. I nevertheless accept the last paragraph's objection (as what sane person would not?): as long as we live in a world of nation-states, we must as a matter of political necessity regard the Nuremberg Charter mostly as unenforceable dead letter, and its advance in the Rule of Law as (therefore) mostly symbolic. The symbolism is surely not to be denigrated; but it is an undeniable fact that the legacy left by Nuremberg to the Rule of Law is compromised and equivocal.

This is so (we may summarize the foregoing discussion) for four reasons: first, the attempt to punish Charter crimes in peacetime is itself a crime; thus, second, the Nuremberg Charter labels as crimes deeds that can never be punished as crimes; third, its extension of the Rule of Law is therefore largely illusory; and fourth, proceedings under the Charter will always be victors' justice. That is an unavoidable fact of politics, written into the Charter itself in the criminalization of aggression.

The Nuremberg Trial as Victors' Justice. There is, however, one avoidable error committed by the Allies at Nuremberg that robbed the trial of much of its moral force and underscored the charge that it was merely victors' justice. I am refer-ring to the fact that no members of the Allied forces were tried, though many were guilty of war crimes. Most notable among these were Churchill, who had ordered the bombing of specifically residential (working-class) areas of German cities in order to demoralize the enemy,[63] and Truman, who had ordered the atomic bombing of Hiroshima and Nagasaki. More in the bone-chilling spirit of Nazism, the Red Amy had murdered 15,000 Polish officers and buried them in mass graves in the Katyn Forest.[64]

Now of course it is absurd to imagine that the victorious Allies would have tried their own heads of state, and an investigation into the Katyn Forest slaugh-ter was impossible without Soviet cooperation. Moreover, it would have obscured the moral message of Nuremberg to treat the actions of Truman and Churchill on a par with those of the architects of the Holocaust. But there was at least one case in which there would have been no absurdity in putting an American officer on trial. This was the case of Admiral Chester Nimitz.

The background is simple. German Admiral Dönitz was accused at Nuremberg of criminally waging unrestricted submarine warfare. He countered that he had

---

[63] For an argument that this was a self-conscious and unjustifiable decision, see Walzer, *Just and Unjust Wars*, pp. 255–63.

[64] Jackson wrote to Truman that the Allies 'have done or are doing some of the very things we are prosecuting Germans for. The French are so violating the Geneva Convention in the treatment of prisoners of war that our command is taking back prisoners sent to them.... We are prosecuting plunder and our Allies are practicing it. We say aggressive war is a crime and one of our allies asserts sovereignty over the Baltic States based on no title except conquest' (quoted in Conot, *Justice at Nuremberg*, p. 68). See Conot's discussion there of other offenses the Germans were tried for that were also committed by the Allies.

done nothing that the Allies had not done as well and introduced as evidence interrogatories posed to Nimitz. Nimitz candidly and honorably confirmed Dönitz's claim: the American Navy had itself waged unrestricted submarine warfare in the Pacific.

By itself, this was scarcely calculated to help Dönitz, because the Nuremberg court quite properly allowed no defense of *tu quoque*. However, Dönitz's attorney, Otto Kranzbühler, the ablest of the defense counsel, argued cleverly that he was not offering a *tu quoque* defense: rather, he was arguing that the fact that the Allies had engaged in the identical practices with which Dönitz was charged showed that the conventions of war had changed, and that now submarine warfare was legal. (Remember Jackson: '...we cannot deny that our own day has the right to institute customs...that will themselves become sources of...International Law.') Neither Nimitz nor Dönitz, Kranzbühler argued, was a criminal. Dönitz was acquitted of the charge.[65]

He was acquitted as a result...of what? Not just of Kranzbühler's ingenuity; rather, Dönitz's acquittal followed from the fact that the Allies would not try Nimitz though he admitted doing just what Dönitz did. Nimitz's candor created an embarrassment: if the Allies were to convict Dönitz, the Rule of Law required that they try and convict Nimitz as well. Since they were unwilling to do this, they were compelled to accept Kranzbühler's argument that the law itself had changed.

The trouble lies in the precedential—'gravitational'—force that this argument creates: it legalizes any crime committed by the vanquished provided the victor committed it as well. The Allies' refusal to extend the Rule of Law to their own troops and leaders initiates a kind of Gresham's Law by which standards of conduct are driven down to whatever level of brutality the victors are willing to tolerate in themselves.

I am not concerned here with the details of Dönitz and Nimitz. Perhaps, in this case, the conventions of war really had changed, and Kranzbühler was right; in that case, Nimitz should still have been tried, and he would have been acquitted together with Dönitz. My concern is with the evil effects of allowing one's own criminals to go unpunished: either we are confronted with victors' justice pure and simple, or else Kranzbühler's argument will be accepted and the principles of international law will be shot onto the downward spiral.

If, on the other hand, the Allies had tried their own war criminals as well as the Germans', the moral force exercised by Nuremberg would have been immeasurably greater than it is. Though the problem of unenforceability in a world of nation-states could not be solved, the world would have at least one shining example of international justice that was not victors' justice.

---

[65] *Trial*, 1: 313. On Kranzbühler's argument, see Conot, *Justice at Nuremberg*, pp. 324–325, Tusa and Tusa, *Nuremberg Trial*, pp. 354–357.

The Third Legacy: The Threat of Bureaucracies

So far, I have considered the legacy of Nuremberg more or less in the terms in which the framers of the trial conceived it: as providing through its recognition of new crimes a new world order; and as inspiring by its example a rededication to the Rule of Law. In both cases, I have argued that the legacy of Nuremberg is equivocal, that the Rule of Law and the politics of human rights are contending for its soul with the *Realpolitik* of sovereign nation-states.

The third legacy of Nuremberg was recognized barely or not at all at the time of the trial; but we are gradually coming to the realization that it is the central moral challenge of our time. I refer to the problem of moral responsibility in bureaucratic settings.

'Rule by Nobody.' Evidence was introduced at Nuremberg concerning the Nazis' euthanasia program to remove so-called 'useless eaters' and carriers of inferior genes from the world. Conot summarizes this part of the evidence as follows:

The euthanasia program, serving as the prototype for the extermination of millions that was to follow, demonstrated how, through fragmentation of authority and tasks, it was possible to fashion a murder machine. Hitler had enunciated an offhand, extralegal decree, and had not wanted to be bothered by it again. Brandt had ordered the 'scientific' implementation of the program and, like Hitler, wished to hear no complaints. The directors and personnel of institutions rationalized that matters were out of their hands and that they were just filling out questionnaires for the 'experts' in Berlin, though in reality each form was the equivalent of a death warrant. The specious 'experts' perused the questionnaires only to cull out prominent persons that might have been accidentally included, then passed them on to Himmler's myrmidons, who transported the afflicted to the annihilation installations. The personnel at the end of the line excused themselves on the basis that they were under compulsion, had no power of decision, and were merely performing a function. Thousands of people were involved, but each considered himself nothing but a cog in the machine and reasoned that it was the machine, not he, that was responsible.[66]

The euthanasia program is not the prototype only for the Holocaust—it is the prototype as well for the moral plague of modern life, bureaucratic irresponsibility, which is in turn the precondition for state criminality. Hannah Arendt described

the latest and perhaps most formidable form of... dominion: bureaucracy or the rule of an intricate system of bureaus in which no men, neither one nor the best, neither the few nor the many, can be held responsible, and which could be properly called rule by Nobody. (If, in accord with traditional political thought, we identify tyranny as government that is not held to give account of itself, rule by Nobody is clearly the most tyrannical of all,

---

[66] Conot, *Justice at Nuremberg*, pp. 210–211.

since there is no one left who could even be asked to answer for what is being done. It is...impossible to localize responsibility and to identify the enemy....)[67]

The discovery, however, is not Arendt's; for as long ago as 1843 Marx had written: 'The mind of the bureaucracy...makes...the real mindlessness of the state a categorical imperative.... The bureaucracy is a circle from which no one can escape. Its hierarchy is a hierarchy of knowledge. The highest point entrusts the understanding of particulars to the lower echelons, whereas these, on the other hand, credit the highest with an understanding in regard to the universal; and thus they deceive one another.'[68]

Though they emphasize different aspects of bureaucracy—Arendt focusing on irresponsibility and Marx on self-deception—it is reasonably clear that both have the same picture of bureaucratic institutions in mind. The core idea is that actions that would be immediately recognized as destructive or even criminal if a single person performed them are fractured by bureaucratic division of labor into 'action-shards' that lack the telltale signs of awfulness. A criminal action can be put together out of many action-shards that are not, or do not seem, criminal (e.g., filling out a form). A bureaucrat gives a general directive to eliminate a problem but does not know how it will be done and in any case is completely dependent on his subordinates for information about the problem. The subordinates assume that there are good reasons for what they are asked to do, reasons to which they are not privy; they substitute a superior's authorization for a reason. And the triggermen at the end of the line proceed secure in the knowledge that their actions have been approved by everyone in the chain of command.

This is why Marx calls the bureaucracy 'a circle from which no one can escape': the 'real mindlessness of the state' arises because nobody in a bureaucracy acts unconditionally—every action is conditioned by the actor's beliefs, which are in turn conditioned by the conditioned actions and beliefs of other actors. Every interaction within the institutional framework assumes that the knowledge or authority is possessed by someone in another office; as Alexandra Kollontai is supposed to have said, in a bureaucracy every decision is made by a third party.[69]

Finally, every action-shard is motivated by the everyday incentives of job-holding: praise by a superior, a good performance report, a Christmas bonus. What could be more innocent? Bureaucracy masks the significance of one's job in everydayness. It divides the labor into bite-size tasks, so that no bureaucrat has the sense of performing a complete action; and it links the mechanical performance of such tasks to career advancement, so that the less one thinks about the better off one is. In Marx's words, '[a]t the very heart of the bureaucracy [lies]...the materialism of passive obedience, of trust in authority, the mechanism of an

---

[67] Hannah Arendt, *On Violence* (New York: Harcourt, Brace & World, 1969, 1970), p. 38.

[68] Karl Marx, *Critique of Hegel's 'Philosophy of Right'*, ed. Joseph O'Malley (Cambridge: Cambridge University Press, 1970), pp. 46–47.

[69] I have been unable to track down the citation for this remark.

ossified and formalistic behavior....As far as the individual bureaucrat is concerned, the end of the state becomes his private end: a pursuit of higher posts, the
building of a career.'[70]

We must still see whether, as Conot suggests, such a model—of group criminal
actions fragmented into action-shards that are not themselves criminal, or whose
criminality is hidden—accurately characterizes the Nazi regime; or whether, on
the contrary, the action-shards were themselves obviously criminal. The question,
in other words, is whether the action-shards are *morally opaque* or *morally transparent*. Before addressing this question, however, let us first look more closely at
the model itself.

In these accounts of Conot, Arendt, and Marx we find three different
problems, not always carefully distinguished. First is the psychological problem
of *a diminished or even nonexistent sense of individual responsibility* in bureaucratic organizations. Second, most prominent in Arendt's account, is the political
problem of *(nonexistent?) organizational responsibility* ('rule by Nobody,' 'the real
mindlessness of the state,' which Marx explicates thus: 'The state, then, exists only
as various bureau-minds whose connexion consists of subordination and dumb
obedience'[71]). Third is the moral problem of *fragmented knowledge, which is therefore inadequate for agents in a bureaucracy to base decisions upon* (Marx's 'hierarchy
of knowledge' in which higher and lower echelons deceive one another).

Nuremberg and the Three Problems of Bureaucracy. Nuremberg, I wish to argue,
attacked the first problem, and grappled with the second and third with only partial success.

1. The Problem of Diminished Individual Responsibility. Its attack on the first
was a full frontal assault through Articles 7 and 8. It responded to the claim that
individuals in a bureaucracy do not feel responsible for what they do simply by
declaring them responsible and holding them liable for their deeds regardless of
their positions in the hierarchy. To induce responsibility we must change the bureaucrat's incentives, and criminalizing his activity is the straightforward way to
do this.

Implicit in this maneuver seems to be the idea that individuals in a bureaucratic setting may well have the psychological experience of nonresponsibility (what Eichmann described as a kind of 'Pontius Pilate feeling'[72]) but that
sense of nonresponsibility is to be fought against by the law, not tolerated as
an excuse. The sense of nonresponsibility is created by the bureaucrat's need to

---

[70] Marx, *Critique*, p. 47. See also Heinrich Böll, 'Befehl and Verantwortung: Gedanken
zum Eichmann-Prozess,' in *Aufsätze Kritiken Reden* (Cologne: Kiepenheuer & Witsch, 1967),
pp. 113–116, arguing that obedience to orders was the Nazi disease, but that many people
disobeyed orders, hence anyone could do so.

[71] *Ibid.*, p. 47.

[72] Hannah Arendt, *Eichmann in Jerusalem: A Report on the Banality of Evil*, 2nd ed. (New York:
Viking, 1964), p. 114.

rationalize his compliant performance of his duties, and this compliance is in its turn motivated by the incentives of the job—pleasing his superiors, enjoying the modest pleasures of promotion, 'the building of a career' (as Marx puts it). The Pontius Pilate feeling emerges as a rationalization for giving in to a *resistible* temptation.

The famous experiments of Stanley Milgram, in which subjects are ordered by an authority figure to administer dangerous or fatal electric shocks to another 'subject' (really a confederate of the experimenter), tend to confirm this view: an appallingly high percentage of the subjects shocked the 'subject' to 'death,' but between a third and a half refused to. It is possible to refuse evil orders, and thus culpable to comply.[73]

This assumption behind Articles 7 and 8—that the psychological sense of diminished individual responsibility is self-deception and thus no excuse—is beyond a doubt a morally worthy one, and any attempt to deal with the problem of bureaucracy that denies it will have great difficulty getting off the ground. So far, at any rate, it appears that the Nuremberg solution is the most plausible one.

2. The Problem of Organizational (Ir)responsibility. Less successful is the attempt at Nuremberg to address the problem of organizational responsibility. This was done in two ways: by invoking the concept of conspiracy in Article 6(a), and by indicting whole organizations—the Party Leadership Corps, the Reich Cabinet, the High Command, the SS and SA, the Gestapo—as criminals.

The conspiracy idea was the brainchild of Murray Bernays, an American lawyer who initiated the framework of the Nuremberg trial. With the conspiracy idea, Bernays hoped to show that the entire rise of the Nazi party and Nazi state had been directed to criminal ends; he hoped to put the history of Nazism on trial. Jackson's prosecution was mostly faithful to this scheme; in the opening minutes of his great oration he described the trial as an attempt 'to bring within the scope of a single litigation the developments of a decade, covering a whole continent, and involving a score of nations, countless individuals, and innumerable events.'[74]

It was an unfortunate plan. The problem was that the concept involved a shallow, Hollywood conception of history and politics—one, moreover, that missed the moral challenge of organizational responsibility.[75]

---

[73] Stanley Milgram, *Obedience to Authority: An Experimental View* (New York: Harper & Row, 1974). One might, of course, argue that Milgram's findings show that normal people will comply with evil orders, and thus that it is not culpable to comply, since 'the reasonable man' would. I would reply that the notion of reasonableness is normative, not statistical: even if 65 percent of us would shock someone to death because a man in a white coat told us to, it is the 35 percent who would not that are 'reasonable.'

[74] *Trial*, 2: 100.

[75] On Bernays's plan, see Conot, *Justice at Nuremberg*, pp. 10–13, and especially the critical discussion of Tusa and Tusa, *Nuremberg Trial*, pp. 54–57.

Conspiracy charges are primarily an Anglo-American device for attacking organized crime, gangsterism (though they were also used, in a less savory way, to attack labor organizers in the nineteenth century). The shock value and moral message of utilizing a conspiracy charge at Nuremberg lay in the analogy it presented: it 'demystified' and depoliticized World War II by suggesting that the Nazis were simply gangsters who had seized control of the German state in furtherance of their plan to launch a war. Bertolt Brecht had once allegorized Nazism in a play about Chicago gangsters, *The Resistible Rise of Arturo Ui*; Bernays's conspiracy charge elevated the Ui-motif to official doctrine.

There were, to be sure, points of analogy: Especially in its early years the Nazi party had operated through street violence; the storm troopers were indeed little more than gangsters; and the party's unifying ideology, articulated in *Mein Kampf*, had always aimed explicitly at war-making and Jew-killing (the 'criminal plan' that forms the essence of the conspiracy concept). Moreover, the Ui-scenario of a mob seizing the state was useful to the Allies in that it allowed the convenient fiction that the German people were passive victims: in Jackson's words, 'We ... have no purpose to incriminate the whole German people. We know that the Nazi Party was not put in power by a majority of the German vote.'[76]

But surely all this is a caricature of history! The Nazis did not *just* seize power, as in a coup d'état; their rise was the product of complicated, even profound, forces—as Arendt more accurately assesses it, 'The subterranean stream of Western history ha[d] finally come to the surface....'[77] Likewise, an ideology is not *just* a criminal plan—quoting Arendt once again,

It is the monstrous, yet seemingly unanswerable claim of totalitarian rule that, far from being 'lawless,' it goes to the sources of authority from which positive laws received their ultimate legitimation, that far from being arbitrary it is more obedient to these suprahuman forces than any government ever was before, and that far from wielding its power in the interest of one man, it is quite prepared to sacrifice everybody's vital immediate interests to the execution of what it assumes to be the law of History or the law of Nature.[78]

This is the antithesis of a gangland plot. Hitler, moreover, was not *just* Arturo Ui: he was one of the most effective populist politicians of our century, the acme of the new style of symbolic and mystical politics that characterized early modernism and continues to plague us today.[79] And, of course, the German people were not *just* innocent, passive victims. The Nazi regime enjoyed immense popular support from its inception until the war began to go badly.

---

[76] *Trial*, 2: 102.
[77] *The Origins of Totalitarianism*, 2d ed. (New York: Meridian, 1958), p. ix.
[78] *Ibid.*, pp. 461–462.
[79] See Carl Schorske, 'Politics in a New Key: An Austrian Trio,' in *Fin-de-Siècle Vienna: Politics and Culture* (New York: Knopf, 1980), pp. 116–180.

Most importantly, however, the conspiracy concept ignores the fact that the Nazis did not act as a *gang* but as the *state*. Here again the Nuremberg trial came up just short of recognizing the problem of organizational responsibility. Instead of 'criminal state,' it saw only a 'state run by criminals.'[80]

For this reason, the concept of criminal organizations, with its 'theory of "group criminality," '[81]was a more promising avenue to pursue than was the concept of conspiracy (though the Tribunal evidently did not see the crucial difference, writing in its judgment, 'A criminal organization is analogous to a criminal conspiracy...'[82]). Sifting the evidence cautiously, the Tribunal separated out more culpable strata of the accused organizations from those less culpable, more culpable organizations from those that were ineffectual, such as the Reich Cabinet, or merely technical, such as the High Command. It was one of the Tribunal's best-considered judgments.

Unfortunately, the concept of group criminality was not quite the concept of state criminality, which I have claimed as the key to Nazi crime. The indictment applied the concept to very specific subgroups in the state but not to the state as such. Nor, however, *could* the indictment apply it to the state as a whole, for a reason which carries profound implications for the Rule of Law.

It is important to realize that at Nuremberg group criminality meant collective rather than corporate criminality—it meant, that is, that every member of the criminalized group was liable to punishment rather than the more familiar idea that the organization, but not its members, was sanctioned. When E. F. Hutton pleads guilty, people fine it (and not its officers). Obviously, there is a reason this would not work at Nuremberg: you can fine E. F. Hutton, but what sanction could be levied against the Reich Cabinet as an organization? The only way to punish it is to punish its members as individuals.

Given this understanding of group criminality, it could not be charged against the state as a whole since it is completely unclear what individuals should be encompassed in the charge. (Which individuals are 'the state'?) And this must be known: even though it is the state that was criminal, it is individuals who would be punished. As we have seen, legality dictates that one cannot punish

---

[80] In the end, the Tribunal did not treat the conspiracy charge as an offense separate from the crime against peace itself (*Trial*, 1: 226). If it had, it would have had to come to terms with a lurking problem in the very Anglo-American concept of conspiracy it had adopted. A common-law device known as Wharton's Rule holds that when a crime can be committed only by a group (e.g., adultery, duelling, gambling) and only after group deliberation, there is no conspiracy separate from the crime itself. It would be wrong to criminalize the group deliberation in addition to criminalizing the act itself when the act could not be committed without group deliberation: that would amount to double punishment. See, e.g., *Ianelli v. United States*, 420 U.S. 770 (1975); 'Comment: An Analysis of Wharton's Rule: Ianelli v. United States and One Step Beyond,' *Northwestern University Law Review* 71 (1976): 547–565. But surely 'planning, preparation, initiation or waging of a war' is an act that cannot be committed except by a state, that is, by a group of people; crimes against peace are surely Wharton's Rule offenses.

[81] *Trial*, 1: 256.
[82] *Ibid.*

individuals without demonstrating their causal responsibility in the crime. Did we really want to criminalize every highway construction foreman and railway conductor simply because they worked for 'the state'?

But this just *is* the problem of responsibility in a bureaucratic setting. We may put it this way. In an era of criminal states, the Rule of Law must extend its grip to punish state crimes. But punishment is always individualized, and the Rule of Law also insists that it is wrong to punish an individual without 'localizing' criminal agency to that individual. If criminal agency could be localized to individuals, however, we would not need the notion of group criminality. To the precise extent that the Rule of Law makes it necessary to employ the group-criminality concept, therefore, it cannot be employed. Bureaucracy threatens the Rule of Law.

This is simply the legal working out of Arendt's 'rule by Nobody' problem—the problem that 'there is no one left who could . . . be asked to answer for what is being done [since i]t is . . . impossible to localize responsibility. . . .' In the end, the concept of group criminality runs up against the same problem as the concept of conspiracy. Both are designed to catch planners who did not act, whereas 'the real mindlessness of the state' means just that a bureaucratic organization is more like a collection of actors who did not plan.

How can such a thing be? The root of the difficulty lies in the third, great problem of bureaucracy, the problem of fragmented knowledge.

3. The Problem of Fragmented Knowledge. Early in the Nuremberg trial, the prosecution showed an hour-long film on concentration camps. 'The screen filled with images of skeletal men and women, crematoria and gas chambers, the scarred and disfigured bodies of women who had survived medical experiments, mound upon mound of cadavers whose sticklike arms and legs gave the appearance of jumbled piles of driftwood, displays of human lampshades, Germans holding their noses as they were compelled into sightseeing tours through the camps and impressed into burying details, and tractors pushing the dead into mass graves like contaminated jetsam.'[83] The reactions of the defendants to this film were astounding. Funk, Ribbentrop, and Fritzsche wept, and the latter said that evening 'No power in heaven or earth will erase this shame from my country—not in generations—not in centuries!'[84]

Didn't they know? Funk, who cried openly during the film, had after all accepted shipments of gold teeth pried from the victims' mouths into the vaults of his Reichsbank. Yet he behaved like someone who didn't know.

I suggest that there is an explanation, one, however, that is not easy to accept. They knew something, but they did not know what it was that they knew. Funk obviously knew that people were dying (he had their teeth); but a war was going on, and people do die in wars. Maybe the teeth came from civilian victims or

---

[83] Conot, *Justice at Nuremberg*, p. 149.
[84] *Ibid.*; Tusa and Tusa, *Nuremberg Trial*, pp. 160–161.

military casualties. Similarly, Conot's euthanasia 'experts' were presented with completed questionnaires and did not know what public-health or epidemiological menace required the drastic measure they were implementing; while the institutional personnel who filled out the forms did not know what was going to be done with them. Perhaps they sensed that something was amiss— nevertheless, based on the small amount of information available to them, they were unable to trust their judgment. The higher authorities, on the other hand, did not know about human lampshades or Zyklon B—and so on, up and down the line.

The disquieting feature of this explanation is that it renders our ordinary model of moral decision making moot, at least in part. On that model, a moral decision occurs at a discrete moment in time, when the facts of the case are there before us, and the options are demarcated for our deliberation. *In a bureaucratic setting, however, that moment never arrives.* We get partial information and instructions to fill out a form. We may suspect that the form will be badly used, but we don't know enough about what is going on in the other offices to be sure; often, we may not know what our options are. The fact that we do not take responsibility for our actions is based on ignorance, not subservience or cowardice. We may resolve not to be 'good Germans,' but the moment of truth never arrives.

One way of responding to this problem is to insist that ignorance can itself be culpable. Frank's self-accusing response to the concentration-camp film was instructive: 'Don't let anybody tell you they had no idea! Everybody sensed that there was something horribly wrong with this system, even if we didn't know all the details. They didn't want to know!'[85] In the same vein, a former Nazi official once related to me a story: A young soldier of his acquaintance returned on leave from the Occupied East, where the *Einsatzgruppen* were gunning and gassing thousands of Jews, and burst into tears in the presence of his sister. She did not ask him why he was crying: she knew that it was something she didn't want to know about.

The criminal law recognizes that 'willful blindness' is not a defense. If someone offers you a thousand dollars to hide a package in your spare tire as you drive over the border from Mexico, and customs officials find the package—filled with 'the thinking man's Dristan'—you will not be able to defend yourself against the charge of drug smuggling by saying that you did not know what was in the package.

The question, of course, is whether the Nazis were willfully blind in this sense. I believe that they were. The top Nazis may not have known what the inside of a death camp looked like, but they knew what the code name 'Final Solution' meant. Lower-level flunkies such as Ivan 'the Terrible' Demjanjuk, the alleged executioner at Treblinka, may not have known why they were gassing Jews, but

---

[85] Conot, *Justice at Nuremberg*, p. 149.

they could not help but know that mass killing was mass murder. Whatever blindness such people allege is willful blindness.

What this means, however, is that the bureaucratic crimes tried at Nuremberg *did* have localized responsibility; knowledge was not so thoroughly fragmented that anyone was truly ignorant. The Nuremberg crimes were—in our earlier terminology—morally transparent. This in turn means that the decentered, agency-less agency implicit in Arendt's 'rule by Nobody' and Marx's 'real mindlessness of the state' were *not* the issue at Nuremberg; Arendt's and Marx's models are gross exaggerations of the Nazi regime. The Third Reich was indeed a criminal state, but individuals in it committed its crimes by performing actions that were themselves criminal—issuing and executing orders to commit mass murder.

For this reason, I believe that the Nuremberg trial dealt adequately with the crimes it tried, even though the legal concepts it employed—conspiracy and group criminality—must be supplemented by a 'willful blindness' analysis that the Tribunal did not provide.

But even that analysis is insufficient to deal with the problem of future criminal states in which the bureaucratic mesh sieves information and agency more finely than did that of the Third Reich. Today, soldiers in silos can incinerate thousands of times more people than Ivan Demjanjuk ever did while sealed off not only from political information but also from any concrete image of what they are doing. If that happens, the legacy of Nuremberg will be insufficient to deal with state criminality.

As long as such a state exists only in Orwellian nightmares, we will be able to evade this problem: we will not run up against the incompatibility of the Rule of Law and the rule by Nobody. But this brings us to our final problem, the last legacy of Nuremberg: *that the Rule of Law may require the rule by Nobody.*

The Tension Between Bureaucracy and the Rule of Law. The problem is that a 'rule of law, not of men' bears an uncomfortable resemblance to 'rule by Nobody.' Officials in both are—in Plato's words—'servants of the law.'[86] Now, as long as the actions taken in obedience to the law are morally transparent, we may be able to rely upon the conscience of officials to mitigate harsh, thoughtless, ideological, or just plain crazy directives. A servant of the law need not be a slave of rules. That, indeed, is one standard justification offered for the existence of a career civil service; in the United States, for example, it is conventional wisdom that the most important function of the career Foreign Service is to impede politicized administrations from executing their foreign-policy brainstorms.

But as industrial society and its state become increasingly complex, differentiation and sheer complexity make the bureaucracies that exercise jurisdiction

[86] *Laws,* 715d.

over the various subsystems opaque to each other. The different offices and agencies know each other only as 'black boxes' that produce outputs which others must simply take as pregiven inputs.[87] As a result, bureaucratic actions lose their moral transparency; the individual official never knows the moral character of the act he or she is performing, and this ignorance is no longer willful blindness.

In that situation, bureaucratic consciences will become deactivated; and the default condition of bureaucratic conscience is mere bureaucratic conscientiousness—stubborn competency in carrying out an assignment. Now it may well be that bureaucratic conscientiousness is the virtue that makes the Rule of Law possible, for it impels officials to adhere to rules. But bureaucratic conscience is what makes the Rule of Law livable: to use Plato's and Aristotle's analogy, it is what allows the physician to change his course of treatment when he finds it is killing the patient.[88]

Conscientiousness without conscience is the Orwellian nightmare. In such a regime, the Rule of Law, bureaucratically realized, becomes the mechanism by which a disastrous set of rules effectuates itself. And that, in turn, is why Nuremberg's attempt to revive individual responsibility by enhancing the Rule of Law may be self-defeating.

I say 'may be' because the reality of the threat depends on the truth of a complicated empirical conjecture: that industrial societies are becoming increasingly complex; that such complexity can be governed only with unfettered and arbitrary administrative discretion—a 'pragmatism' that is the opposite of the Rule of Law—or else a proliferating bureaucracy that passes over the threshold to rule by Nobody; and that a state ruled in either of these two ways is likely to take on the criminal characteristics of the Third Reich (because, for example, the citizens of such a state become peculiarly susceptible to ideology disconnected from factuality—the final consequence of the problem of fragmented knowledge).[89]

If that is so, the high hopes of the framers of Nuremberg will have been dashed, for the Rule of Law will have turned out to be its own worst enemy. But even then the Nuremberg trial will not have been without a valuable legacy. We, or our children, will have to fight once again to defeat the criminal state; if we win, we will once again have to pick up the pieces; and, once again, we will not be likely to do better than to take the men and women who became cogs in the murder machine and put them on trial before a tribunal that is as fair as we know how to make it. Though we cannot always hope for law, we can at least hope for justice.

---

[87] Luhmann, *Politische Theorie im Wohlfahrtsstaat*, pp. 50–51, 103–117.
[88] Aristotle, *Politics* III, 14, 1286a 12–16; Plato, *Statesman*, 295c–297c.
[89] That is Arendt's view in *The Origins of Totalitarianism*.

Conclusion: The Past is Not Dead; It is Not Even Past

The fortieth anniversary of the Nuremberg trial was bracketed by Ronald Reagan's 1985 visit to Bitburg cemetery—where he delivered a conciliatory and equivocal speech over *Waffen SS* graves—and Kurt Waldheim's election to the Austrian presidency in 1986 despite evidence that he had been involved in war crimes and had lied repeatedly about his wartime involvements. At the same time a vituperative debate has broken out in Germany over the attempt by 'revisionist' historians of Nazism to minimize both the extent of Hitler's aggression and the singularity of the Holocaust.[90] If one of the aims of the Nuremberg trial was to burn the history of Nazism into the memory of mankind, we must conclude that it failed.

An equally distressing failure of moral memory appeared in the World Court case between the United States and Nicaragua concerning American support for the *contras* and CIA mining of Nicaraguan territorial waters. The U.S. government, asserting that the Court has no jurisdiction over the dispute, argued that the U.S. claim to be acting in the 'collective self-defense' of El Salvador was non-justiciable. Curiously, the identical argument had been offered at Nuremberg by defense counsel Hermann Jahrreis, who asserted: 'War of self-defense is permitted as an unalienable right of all States; without this right, sovereignty does not exist; and every State is alone judge of whether in a given case it is waging war of self-defense.'[91]

Needless to say, the Nuremberg Tribunal rejected this argument, for to accept it was to abandon the trials. When the World Court declined to resurrect Jahrreis's argument in the jurisdictional phase of *Nicaragua v. United States*, the American government provoked a controversy by pulling out of the litigation. Critics within the United States charged that the unilateral American withdrawal was a symbolic assault on the rule of law in international affairs.

The premise of this criticism is precisely the premise of the Nuremberg framers: that the rule of law in international affairs will advance or retreat through expressive and exemplary action such as symbolically significant trials. As Paul Kahn points out, it is a peculiarity of international law that behavior violative of norms can create new norms; he argues that America's actions in the Nicaragua case may mark the breakdown of the UN Charter vision as well as of Nuremberg law.[92]

---

[90] For a brief summary of this complex debate, see Judith Miller, 'Erasing the Past: Europe's Amnesia About the Holocaust,' *New York Times Magazine*, Nov. 16, 1986, p. 30.

[91] *Trial*, 18: 86. A brilliant and disturbing analysis of this uncanny parallel between Nuremberg and the Nicaragua litigation may be found in Paul W. Kahn. 'From Nuremberg to the Hague: The United States Position in *Nicaragua v. United States* and the Development of International Law,' *Yale Journal of International Law* 12 (1987): 1–62.

[92] *Ibid.*, pp. 2–4, 59–62.

As we have seen, however, the elements of this crisis were nascent in Nuremberg itself. Though the Tribunal repudiated Jahrreis's argument, his appeal to state sovereignty had already been enshrined in Article 6(a) of the Charter. The Allies' refusal to try their own criminals parallels America's unilateral withdrawal from the World Court. And Americans will recognize in the 1987 Iran-*contra* hearings that we are far from solving the problem of organizational irresponsibility—the disturbing fact that a state policy can seemingly emerge from nowhere with no author, and the equally disturbing fact that our impulse is inevitably to throw responsibility on a conspiracy of mavericks rather than come to grips with the disagreeable notion that a state might itself be responsible.[93]

The ambiguous legacies of Nuremberg linger at the margins of our unreliable moral memories; they inspire but also burden the conscience of our politics.

---

[93] The secret funding of the *contras* through the diversion of profits from Iranian arms sales is a direct lineal descendant of the American policy of covert paramilitary operations that formed the subject matter of *Nicaragua v. United States.*

30

The Question of German Guilt*

By Karl Jaspers
Translated by E. B. Ashton

Scheme of Distinctions

Four Concepts of Guilt

We must distinguish between:

(1) *Criminal guilt*: Crimes are acts capable of objective proof and violate unequivocal laws. Jurisdiction rests with the court, which in formal proceedings can be relied upon to find the facts and apply the law.

(2) *Political guilt*: This, involving the deeds of statesmen and of the citizenry of a state, results in my having to bear the consequences of the deeds of the state whose power governs me and under whose order I live. Everybody is co-responsible for the way he is governed. Jurisdiction rests with the power and the will of the victor, in both domestic and foreign politics. Success decides. Political prudence, which takes the more distant consequences into account, and the acknowledgment of norms, which are applied as natural and international law, serves to mitigate arbitrary power.

(3) *Moral guilt*: I, who cannot act otherwise than as an individual, am morally responsible for all my deeds, including the execution of political and military orders. It is never simply true that 'orders are orders.' Rather—as crimes even though ordered (although, depending on the degree of danger, blackmail and terrorism, there may be mitigating circumstances)—so every deed remains subject to moral judgment. Jurisdiction rests with my conscience, and in communication with my friends and intimates who are lovingly concerned about my soul.

(4) *Metaphysical guilt*: There exists a solidarity among men as human beings that makes each co-responsible for every wrong and every injustice in the world, especially for crimes committed in his presence or with his knowledge. If I fail to do whatever I can to prevent them, I too am guilty. If I was present at the murder of others without risking my life to prevent it, I feel guilty in a way

---

* Excerpts from K. Jaspers, *The Question of German Guilt* (New York: Putnam Capricorn Books, 1961).

not adequately conceivable either legally, politically or morally. That I live after such a thing has happened weighs upon me as indelible guilt. As human beings, unless good fortune spares us such situations, we come to a point where we must choose: either to risk our lives unconditionally, without chance of success and therefore to no purpose—or to prefer staying alive, because success is impossible. That somewhere among men the unconditioned prevails—the capacity to live only together or not at all, if crimes are committed against the one or the other, or if physical living requirements have to be shared—therein consists the substance of their being. But that this does not extend to the solidarity of all men, nor to that of fellow-citizens or even of smaller groups, but remains confined to the closest human ties—therein lies this guilt of us all. Jurisdiction rests with God alone.

This differentiation of four concepts of guilt clarifies the meaning of the charges. Political guilt, for example, does mean the liability of all citizens for the consequences of deeds done by their state, but not the criminal and the moral guilt of every single citizen for crimes committed in the name of the state. The judge may decide about crimes and the victor about political liability, but moral guilt can truthfully be discussed only in a loving struggle between men who maintain solidarity among themselves. As for metaphysical guilt, this may perhaps be a subject of revelation in concrete situations or in the work of poets and philosophers, but hardly one for personal communication. Most deeply aware of it are those who have once achieved the unconditioned, and by that very fact have experienced their failure to manifest this unconditioned toward all men. There remains shame for something that is always present, that may be discussed in general terms, if at all, but can never be concretely revealed.

This differentiation of concepts of guilt is to preserve us from the superficiality of talk about guilt that flattens everything out on a single plane, there to assess it with all the crudeness and lack of discrimination of a bad judge. But in the end these distinct concepts are to lead us back to the one source, which cannot be flatly referred to as our guilt.

All these distinctions become erroneous, however, if we fail to keep in mind the close connection between the things distinguished. Every concept of guilt demonstrates (or manifests) realities, the consequences of which appear in the spheres of the other concepts of guilt.

If human beings were able to free themselves from metaphysical guilt, they would be angels, and all the other three concepts of guilt would become immaterial.

Moral failings cause the conditions out of which both crime and political guilt arise. The commission of countless little acts of negligence, of convenient adaptation of cheap vindication, and the imperceptible promotion of wrong; the participation in the creation of a public atmosphere that spreads confusion and thus makes evil possible—all that has consequences that partly condition the political guilt involved in the situation and the events.

The moral issue also involves a confusion about the importance of power in human communities. The obfuscation of this fundamental fact is guilt, no less than is the false deification of power as the sole deciding factor in events. Every human being is fated to be enmeshed in the power relations he lives by. This is the inevitable guilt of all, the guilt of human existence. It is counteracted by supporting the power that achieves what is right, the rights of man. Failure to collaborate in organizing power relations, in the struggle for power for the sake of serving the right, creates basic political guilt and moral guilt at the same time. Political guilt turns into moral guilt where power serves to destroy the meaning of power—the achievement of what is right, the ethos and purity of one's own nation. For wherever power does not limit itself, there exists violence and terror, and in the end the destruction of life and soul.

Out of the moral everyday life of most individuals, of the broad masses of people, develops the characteristic political behavior of each age, and with it the political situation. But the individual's life in turn presupposes a political situation already arisen out of history, made real by the ethos and politics of his ancestors, and made possible by the world situation. There are two schematically opposed possibilities here:

Either the ethos of politics is the principle of a state in which all participate with their consciousness, their knowledge, their opinions, and their wills. This is the life of political liberty as a continuous flow of decay and improvement. It is made possible by the task and the opportunity provided by a responsibility shared by all.

Or else there prevails a situation in which the majority are alienated from politics. State power is not felt to be the individual's business. He does not feel that he shares a responsibility; he looks on, is politically inactive, works and acts in blind obedience. He has an easy conscience in obeying and an easy conscience about his nonparticipation in the decisions and acts of those in power. He tolerates the political reality as an alien fact; he seeks to turn it cunningly to his personal advantage or lives with it in the blind ardor of self-sacrifice.

This the difference between political liberty* and political dictatorship, conceived from Herodotus on as the difference between West and East (Greek liberty and Persian despotism). In most cases, it has not been up to the individual to say which will prevail. For good or ill, individual is born into a situation; he has to take what is tradition and reality. No individual and no group can at one stroke, or even in a single generation, change the conditions by which all of us live.

---

* 'Theses on Political Liberty' were published by me in *Wandlung*, No. 6, p. 460 ff.

Consequences of Guilt

The consequences of guilt affect real life, whether or not the person affected realizes it, and they affect my self-esteem if I perceive my guilt.

(a) Crime meets with *punishment*. It requires that the judge acknowledge the guilty man's free determination of his will—not that the punished acknowledge the justice of his punishment.

(b) There is *liability* for political guilt, consequently reparation is necessary and further loss or restriction of political power and political rights (on the part of the guilty). If the guilt is part of events decided by war, the consequences for the vanquished may include destruction, deportation, extermination. Or the victor can, if he will, bring the consequences into a form of right, and thus of moderation.

(c) The outgrowth of the moral guilt is insight, which involves *penance and renewal*. It is an inner development, then also taking effect in the world of reality.

(d) The metaphysical guilt results in a *transformation of human self-consciousness before God*. Pride is broken. This self-transformation by inner activity may lead to a new source of active life, but one linked with an indelible sense of guilt in that humility which grows modest before God and submerges all its doings in an atmosphere where arrogance becomes impossible.

Force—Right—Mercy

Force is what decides between men, unless they reach agreement. Any state order serves to control this force so as to preserve it—as law enforcement within, as war without. In quiet times this had been almost forgotten.

Where war establishes the situation of force, the right ends. We Europeans have tried even then to maintain some remnant of it in the rules of international law, which apply in war as in peace and were last expressed in the Hague and Geneva Conventions. The attempt seems to have been vain.

Where force is used, force is aroused. It is up to the victor to decide what shall be done with the vanquished, in line with the rule of *vae victis*. The vanquished can either die or do and suffer what the victor wants. As a rule he has always preferred to live (here are the roots of the fundamental master-servant relationship as profoundly illustrated by Hegel).

Right is the sublime idea of men who derive their existence from an origin which is secured by force alone, but not determined by force. Wherever men become aware of their humanity and recognize man as man, they grasp human rights and base themselves on a natural law to which both victor and vanquished may appeal.

As soon as the idea of right arises, men may negotiate to find the true right in discussion and methodical procedure.

True, what in case of a complete victory becomes right for the vanquished and between victor and vanquished, has thus far played only a very limited role in events which are decided by acts of political will. These events become the fundament of a positive, factual law which is not justified through right.

Right can only apply to guilt in the sense of crime and in the sense of political liability, not to moral and metaphysical guilt.

But even the punished or liable party can recognize the right. The criminal can feel his punishment as his honor and rehabilitation. The one who is politically liable can admit that the living conditions he must accept now are facts determined by fate.

Mercy is what tempers the effect of undiluted right and of destructive force. The humanity of man senses in it a higher truth, than may be found in the unswerving consistency of either right or force.

(a) Notwithstanding the existence of right, mercy works to open a realm of justice freed from flaws. For all human norms are full of flaws and injustice in their consequences.

(b) Notwithstanding the possibility of force, the victor shows mercy. He may be motivated by expedience, because the vanquished can serve him, or by magnanimity, because his sense of power and stature is raised by letting the vanquished live; or he may in conscience submit to the demands of a universally human natural law, by which the vanquished is no more stripped of all rights than is the criminal.

Who Judges, and Who or What is Judged?

The hail of charges moves us to ask: 'Who—whom?' An accusation is meaningful only if it is defined by point of view and object and does not cross these bounds; and it is clear only if it is known who accuses and who is accused.

(a) Let us first be guided by an enumeration of four types of guilt. The accused either hears himself *charged from without*, by the world, or *from within*, by his own soul.

From without, the charges are meaningful only in regard to crimes and political guilt. They are raised with the intention of effecting punishment and holding liable. Their validity is legal and political, neither moral nor metaphysical.

From within, the guilty hears himself charged with moral failure and metaphysical weakness—and, if these led to political and criminal acts or omissions, with those as well.

Morally man can condemn only himself, not another—or, if another, then only in the solidarity of charitable struggle. No one can morally judge another. It is only where the other seems to me like myself that the closeness reigns which in free communication can make a common cause of what finally each does in solitude.

The assertion of another's guilt cannot refer to his connection, only to certain acts and modes of behavior. While in individual judgment we try to take motives and convictions into consideration, we can truthfully do so only insofar as they can be established by objective indications, i.e., acts and behavior.

(b) The question is in which sense can a *group* be judged, and in which sense only can an *individual*. It clearly makes sense to hold all citizens of a country liable for the results of actions taken by their state. Here a group is affected, but the liability is definite and limited, involving neither moral nor metaphysical charges against the individuals. It affects also those who opposed the régime and its actions Analogously there are liabilities for members in organizations, parties, groups.

For crimes one can punish only an individual, whether he was acting alone or in concert with accomplices, each of whom is called to account according to the extent of complicity which as a minimum need not exceed the mere joining of such company. There are assemblages of gangsters and conspirators which may be branded criminal in their entirety, and in this case mere membership is punishable.

It is nonsensical, however, to charge a whole people with a crime. The criminal is always only an individual.

It is nonsensical, too, to lay moral guilt to a people as whole. There is no such thing as a national character extending to every single member of a nation. There are, of course, communities of language, customs, habits and descent; but the differences which may exist at the same time are so great that people talking the same language may remain as strange to each other as if they did not belong to the same nation.

Morally one can judge the individual only, never a group. The mentality which considers, characterizes and judges people collectively is very widespread. Such characterizations—as of the Germans, the Russians, the British—never fit generic conceptions under which the individual human beings might be classified, but are type conceptions to which they may more or less correspond. This confusion, of the generic with the typological conception, marks the thinking in collective groups—*the* Germans, *the* British, *the* Norwegians, *the* Jews, and so forth *ad lib.*: the Frisians, the Bavarians, men, women, the young, the old. That something fits in with the typological conception must not mislead us to believe that we have covered every individual through such general characterization. For centuries this mentality has fostered hatred among nations and communities. Unfortunately natural to a majority of people, it has been most viciously applied and drilled into the heads with propaganda by the National-Socialists. It was as though there no longer were human beings, just those collective groups.

There is no such thing as a people as a whole. All lines that we may draw to define it are crossed by facts. Language, nationality, culture, common fate—all this does not coincide but is overlapping. People and state do not coincide, nor do language, common fate and culture.

One cannot make an individual out of a people. A people cannot perish heroically, cannot be a criminal, cannot act morally or immorally; only its individuals can do so. A people as a whole can be neither guilty nor innocent, neither in the criminal nor in the political (in which only the citizenry of a state is liable) nor in the moral sense.

The categorical judgment of a people is always unjust. It presupposes a false substantialization and results in the debasement of the human being as an individual.

A world opinion which condemns a people collectively is of a kind with the fact that for thousands of years men have thought and said, 'The Jews are guilty of the Crucifixion.' Who are 'the Jews'? A certain group of religious and political zealots whose relative power among the Jews of that time, in cooperation with the Roman occupation authorities, led to the execution of Jesus.

That such an opinion will become a matter of course and overpower even thinking people is so amazing because the error is so simple and evident. One seems to face a blank wall. It is as though no reason, no fact were any longer heard—or, if heard, as though it were instantly and ineffectively forgotten.

Thus there can be no collective guilt of a people or a group within a people—except for political liability. To pronounce a group criminally, morally or metaphysical guilty is an error akin to the laziness and arrogance of average, uncritical thinking.

(c) There must be a right to accuse and indict. *Who has the right to judge?* Whoever does so, exposes himself to questions about the source of his authority, the end and motive of his judgment, and the situation in which he and the man judged confront each other.

No one needs to acknowledge a worldly tribunal in points of moral and metaphysical guilt. What is possible in close, human relationships which are based on love is not permitted to distantly cold analysis. What is true before God is not, therefore, true before men. For God is represented by no authority on earth—neither in ecclesiastic nor in foreign offices, nor in a world opinion announced by the press.

If judgments are passed in the situation of a decided war, that on political liability is the absolute prerogative of the victor who staked his life on a decision in his favor. But one may ask (to quote from a letter): 'Does a neutral have any right to judge in public, having stayed out of the struggle and failed to stake his existence and his conscience on the main cause?'

When the individual's moral and metaphysical guilt is discussed among people sharing a common fate—today among Germans—one feels the right to judge in the attitude and behavior of him who judges. One feels whether or not he speaks of a guilt weighing also upon himself—whether he speaks from within or from without, self-enlighteningly or accusingly, as an intimate seeking a way to the possible self-enlightenment of others or as a stranger and mere assailant, as friend or as foe. It is always only in the first instance that his right is unquestionable; in the second it is doubtful and in any case limited to the extent of his charity.

When it comes to political liability and criminal guilt, however, everyone has the right among fellow-citizens to discuss facts and their judgment, and to measure them by the yardstick of clear, conceptional definitions. Political liability is graduated according to the degree of participation in the régime—now rejected on principle—and determined by decisions of the victor, to which the very fact of being alive logically forces all to submit who wish to survive the disaster.

Defense

Wherever charges are raised, the accused will be allowed a hearing. Wherever right is appealed to, there is a defense. Wherever force is used, the victim will defend himself if he can.

If the utterly vanquished cannot defend himself and wants to stay alive, there is nothing left to him but to accept and bear the consequences.

But where the victor cites reasons and passes judgment, a reply can be made even in impotence—not by any force but by the spirit, if room is given to it. A defense is possible wherever man may speak. As soon as the victor puts his actions on the level of right, he limits his power. The following possibilities are open to this defense:

(1) It can *urge differentiation.* Differentiation leads to definition and partial exculpation. Differentiation cancels totality and limits the charges.

Confusion leads to haziness, and haziness in turn has real consequences which may be useful or noxious but in any event are unjust. Defense by differentiation promotes justice.

(2) The defense can adduce, stress and compare *facts.*

(3) The defense can appeal to *natural law,* to *human rights,* to *international law.* Such a defense is subject to restrictions:

(a) A state which has violated natural law and human rights on principle—at home from the start, and later, in war, destroying human rights and international law abroad—has no claim to recognition, in its favor, of what it refused to recognize itself.

(b) Right, in fact, is with him who has the power to fight for it. In total impotence, the sole remaining possibility is a spiritual appeal to the ideal right.

(c) The recognition of natural law and human rights is due only to the free will of the powerful, the victors. It is an act of insight and idealism—mercy shown to the vanquished in granting them right.

(4) The defense can point out where the indictment is no longer a true bill but *a weapon used* by the victor for other purposes, political or economic—by confusing the guilt concepts, by planting false opinion in order to win assent and ease one's conscience. Thus measures are justified as right, which otherwise would remain obvious actions of the victor in the situation of *vae victis*. But evil is evil even when inflicted as retribution.

Moral and metaphysical charges as means to political ends are to be rejected absolutely.

(5) The defense can *reject the judge*—either because there is reason to believe him prejudiced, or because the matter as such is beyond the jurisdiction of a human tribunal.

Punishment and liability—reparation claims—are to be acknowledged, but not demands for repentance and rebirth which can only come from within. Such demands can only be met by silent rejection. The point is not to forget the actual need for such an inner regeneration when its performance is wrongly demanded from without.

There is a difference between guilt consciousness and recognition of a worldly judge. The victor is as such not yet a judge. Unless he himself discards the attitude of combat and by confinement to criminal guilt and political liability actually gains right instead of mere power, he claims a false legality for actions which themselves involve new guilt.

(6) The defense can resort to *countercharges*. It can point to acts of others which helped to cause the calamity; it can point to acts of others similar to those which the vanquished are deemed, and indeed are, crimes; it can point to general world trends that bespeak a common guilt.

Differentiation of German Guilt

The Crimes

Unlike the case in World War I when we Germans did not need to admit specific crimes committed by one side only (a fact eventually recognized by scientific historic research even on the part of Germany's enemies), today the crimes committed by the Nazi government—in Germany before the war, everywhere during the war—are evident.

Unlike the case in World War I when the war-guilt question was not decided against one side by the historians of all nations, this war was begun by Hitler Germany.

Unlike World War I, finally, this war really became a world war. It struck the world in a different situation and in a different knowledge. Its import, compared with earlier wars, entered another dimension.

And today we have something entirely new in world history. The victors are establishing a court. The Nuremberg trial deals with crimes.

The primary result is a clear delimitation in two directions:

First, not the German people are being tried here but individual, criminally accused Germans—on principle all leaders of the Nazi régime. This line was drawn at the outset by the American member of the prosecution. 'We want to make it clear,' Jackson said in his fundamental address, 'that we do not intend to accuse the whole German people.'

Second, the suspects are not accused indiscriminately. They are charged with specific crimes expressly defined in the statute of the International Military Tribunal.

At this trial we Germans are spectators. We did not bring it about and we are not running it, although the defendants are men who brought disaster over us. 'Indeed the Germans—as much as the outside world—have an account to settle with the defendants,' Jackson said.

Many a German smarts under this trial. The sentiment is understandable. Its cause is the same which moved the other side to blame the whole German people for the Hitler régime and its acts. Every citizen is jointly liable for the doings and jointly affected by the sufferings of his own state. A criminal state is charged against its whole population. Thus the citizen feels the treatment of his leaders as his own, even if they are criminals. In their persons the people are also condemned. Thus the indignity and mortification experienced by the leaders of the state are felt by the people as their own indignity and mortification. Hence their instinctive, initially unthinking rejection of the trial.

The political liability we have to meet here is painful indeed. We must experience mortification if required by our political liability. Thereby, symbolically, we experience our utter political impotence and our elimination as a political factor.

Yet everything depends on how we conceive, interpret, appropriate and translate our instinctive concern.

One possibility is outright rejection of indignity. We look for reasons, then, to deny the right, the truthfulness, the purpose of the whole trial.

(1) We engage in general reflections: There have been wars throughout history and there will be more. No one people is guilty of war. Wars are due to human nature, to the universal culpability of man. A conscience which proclaims itself not guilty is superficial. By its very conduct such self-righteousness breeds future wars.

Rebuttal: This time there can be no doubt that Germany planned and prepared this war and started it without provocation from any other side. It is altogether different from 1914. Germany is not called guilty of war but of this war. And this war itself is something new and different, occurring in a situation unparalleled in the past history of the world.

This objection to the Nuremberg trial may be phrased in other ways, perhaps as follows: It is an insoluble problem of human existence that what must be settled by invoking the judgment of God, keeps pressing time and again for a decision by force. The soldier's feelings are chivalrous, and even in defeat he has a right to be offended if treated in an unchivalrous manner.

Rebuttal: Germany, throwing all chivalry overboard and violating international law, has committed numerous acts resulting in the extermination of populations and in other inhumanities. Hitler's actions from the start were directed against every chance of a reconciliation. It was to be victory or ruin. Now we feel the consequences of the ruin. All claims to chivalry—even though a great many individual soldiers and entire units are guiltless and themselves have always acted chivalrously—is voided by the Wehrmacht's readiness to execute criminal orders as Hitler's organizations. Once betrayed, chivalry and magnanimity cannot be claimed in one's favor, after the fact. This war did not break out between opponents alike in kind, come to a dead end and chivalrously entering the lists. It was conceived and executed by criminal cunning and the reckless totality of a destructive will.

In the midst of war there is the possibility of inhibitions. Kant's injunction, that nothing must happen in war which would make reconcilement flatly impossible, was first rejected on principle by Hitler Germany. As a result, force, essentially unchanged from time immemorial and with the measure of its destructive possibilities determined now by technology, is boundlessly with us. To have begun the war in the present world situation—this is the enormity.

(2) The trial is said to be a national disgrace for all Germans; if there were Germans on the tribunal, at least, then Germans would be judged by Germans.

Rejoinder: The national disgrace lies not in the tribunal but in what brought it on—in the fact of this régime and its acts. The consciousness of national disgrace is inescapable for every German. It aims in the wrong direction if turning against the trial rather than its cause.

Moreover: Had the victors named a German tribunal, or appointed Germans as associate judges, this would make no change at all. The Germans would not sit on the court by virtue of a German self-liberation but by the grace of the victors. The national disgrace would be the same. The trial is due to the fact that we did not free ourselves from the criminal régime but were liberated by the Allies.

(3) One counterargument runs as follows: How can we speak of crimes in the realm of political sovereignty? To grant this would mean that any victor can make a criminal of the vanquished—and the meaning and the mystery of

God-derived authority would cease. Men once obeyed by a nation—in particular former Emperor William II and now 'the Fuehrer'—are considered inviolable.

Rebuttal: This is a habit of thought derived from the tradition of political life in Europe, preserved the longest in Germany. Today, however, the halo round the heads of states has vanished. They are men and answer for their deeds. Ever since European nations have tried and beheaded their monarchs, the task of the people has been to keep their leaders in check. The acts of states are also the acts of persons. Men are individually responsible and liable for them.

(4) Legally we hear the following argument: There can be crimes only insofar as there are laws. A crime is a breach of these laws. It must be clearly defined and factually determinable without ambiguity. In particular—*nulla poena sine lege*—sentence can only be passed under a law in force before the act was committed. In Nuremberg, however, men are judged retroactively under laws now made by the victors.

Rebuttal: In the sense of humanity, of human rights and natural law, and in the sense of the Western ideas of liberty and democracy, laws already exist by which crimes may be determined.

There are also agreements which—if voluntarily signed by both sides—create such a superior law that can serve as a yardstick in case a contract is broken.

And the jurisdiction, which in the peaceful order of a state rests in the courts, can after a war rest only in the victor's tribunal.

(5) Hence the further objection: Victorious might does not make right. Success cannot claim jurisdiction over right and truth. A tribunal which could investigate and judge war guilt and war crimes objectively is an impossibility. Such a court is always partisan. Even a court of neutrals would be partisan, since the neutrals are powerless and actually part of the victors' following. To judge freely, a court would have to be backed by a power capable of enforcing its decisions against both disputants.

This argument, of the illusive nature of such justice, goes on to say that every war is blamed on the loser. He is forced to admit his guilt. His subsequent economic exploitation is disguised as restitution. Pillage is forged into a rightful act. If the right is not free, let us have naked force—it would be honest, and it would be easier to bear. In fact, there is nothing beside the victor's power. Recrimination as such can always be made mutual; but only the victor can make his charges stick, and he does so ruthlessly and solely in his own interest. Everything else merely serves to disguise the actual arbitrary force of the powerful.

And: The tribunal's illusive nature finally shows in the fact that the so-called crimes are prosecuted only if committed by a vanquished nation. In sovereign or victorious nations the same acts are ignored, not even discussed, much less punished.

Rebuttal: Power and force are indeed decisive realities in the human world, but they are not the only ones. To make them absolute is to remove all reliable links between men. While they are absolute, no agreement is possible. As Hitler actually said, agreements are valid only while they represent self-interest. (And he acted accordingly.) But this is opposed by a will which, admitting the reality of power and the effectiveness of the nihilistic view, holds them undesirable and to be changed at any cost.

For in human affairs reality is not yet truth. That reality, rather, is to be confronted with another. And the existence of this other reality depends upon the human will. Every man, in his freedom, must know where he stands and what he wants.

From this point of view it may be said that the trial, as a new attempt in behalf of order in the world, does not grow meaningless if it cannot yet be based on a legal world order but must still halt within a political framework. Unlike a court trial, it does not yet take place in the closed order of a state.

Hence Jackson's frank statement that 'if the defense were permitted to deviate from the strictly limited charges of the indictment, the trial would be prolonged and the court enmeshed in insoluble political disputes.'

This also means that the defense does not have to deal with the question of war guilt and its historical premises, either, but solely with the question who began this war.

The answer to all arguments against the trial is that Nuremberg is something really new. That the arguments point to possible dangers cannot be denied. But it is wrong, first, to think in sweeping alternatives, with flaws, mistakes and failings in detail leading at once to wholesale rejection, whereas the main point is the powers' trend of action, their unwavering patience in active responsibility. Contradictions in detail are to be overcome by acts designed to bring world order out of confusion. It is wrong, secondly, to strike an attitude of outraged aggressiveness and to say no from the start.

What happens in Nuremberg, no matter how many objections it may invite, is a feeble, ambiguous harbinger of a world order, the need of which mankind is beginning to feel. This is the entirely new situation. The world order is not at hand by any means—rather, there are still huge conflicts and incalculable perils of war ahead of its realization—but it has come to seem possible to thinking humanity; it has appeared on the horizon as a barely perceptible dawn, while in case of failure the self-destruction of mankind looms as a fearful menace before our eyes.

Utter lack of power can only cling to the world as a whole. On the brink of nothingness it turns to the origin, to the all-encompassing. So it is precisely the German who might become aware of the extraordinary import of this harbinger.

Our own salvation in the world depends on the world order which—although not yet established in Nuremberg—is suggested by Nuremberg.

Political Guilt

For crimes the criminal is punished. The restriction of the Nuremberg trial to criminals serves to exonerate the German people. Not, however, so as to free them of all guilt—on the contrary. The nature of our real guilt only appears the more clearly.

We were German nationals at the time when the crimes were committed by the régime which called itself German, which claimed to be Germany and seemed to have the right to do so, since the power of the state was in its hands and until 1943 it found no dangerous opposition.

The destruction of any decent, truthful German polity must have its roots also in modes of conduct of the majority of the German population. A people answers for its polity.

Every German is made to share the blame for the crimes committed in the name of the Reich. We are collectively liable. The question is in what sense each of us must feel co-responsible. Certainly in the political sense of the joint liability of all citizens for acts committed by their state—but for that reason not necessarily also in the moral sense of actual or intellectual participation in crime. Are we Germans to be held liable for outrages which Germans inflicted on us, or from which we were saved as by a miracle? Yes—inasmuch as we let such a régime rise among us. No—insofar as many of us in our deepest hearts opposed all this evil and have no morally guilty acts or inner motivations to admit. To hold liable does not mean to hold morally guilty.

Guilt, therefore, is necessarily collective as the political liability of nationals, but not in the same sense as moral and metaphysical, and never as criminal guilt. True, the acceptance of political liability with its fearful consequences is hard on every individual. What it means to us is political impotence and a poverty which will compel us for long times to live in or on the fringes of hunger and cold and to struggle vainly. Yet this liability as such leaves the soul untouched.

Politically everyone acts in the modern state, at least by voting, or failing to vote, in elections. The sense of political liability lets no man dodge.

If things go wrong the politically active tend to justify themselves; but such defenses carry no weight in politics. For instance, they meant well and had the best intentions—Hindenburg, for one, did surely not mean to ruin Germany or hand it over to Hitler. That does not help him; he did—and that is what counts. Or they foresaw the disaster, said so, and warned; but that does not count politically, either, if no action followed or if it had no effect.

One might think of cases of wholly non-political persons who live aloof of all politics, like monks, hermits, scholars, artists—if really quite non-political, those might possibly be excused from all guilt. Yet they, too, are included among the politically liable, because they, too, live by the order of the state. There is no such aloofness in modern states.

One may wish to make such aloofness possible, yet one cannot help admit to this limitation. We should like to respect and love a non-political life, but the end of political participation would also end the right of the non-political ones to judge concrete political acts of the day and thus to play riskless politics. A non-political zone demands withdrawal from any kind of political activity—and still does not exempt from joint political liability in every sense.

Moral Guilt

Every German asks himself: how am I guilty?

The question of the guilt of the individual analyzing himself is what we call the moral one. Here we Germans are divided by the greatest differences.

While the decision in self-judgment is up to the individual alone, we are free to talk with one another, insofar as we are in communication, and morally to help each other achieve clarity. The moral sentence on the other is suspended, however—neither the criminal nor the political one.

There is a line at which even the possibility of moral judgment ceases. It can be drawn where we feel the other not even trying for a moral self-analysis—where we perceive mere sophistry in his argument, where he seems not to hear at all. Hitler and his accomplices, that small minority of tens of thousands, are beyond moral guilt for as long as they do not feel it. They seem incapable of repentance and change. They are what they are. Force alone can deal with such men who live by force alone.

But the moral guilt exists for all those who give room to conscience and repentance. The morally guilty are those who are capable of penance, the ones who knew, or could know, and yet walked in ways which self-analysis reveals to them as culpable error—whether conveniently closing their eyes to events, or permitting themselves to be intoxicated, seduced or bought with personal advantages, or obeying from fear. Let us look at some of these possibilities.

(a) By *living in disguise*—unavoidable for anyone who wanted to survive—moral guilt was incurred. Mendacious avowals of loyalty to threatening bodies like the Gestapo, gestures like the Hitler salute, attendance at meetings, and many other things causing a semblance of participation—who among us in Germany was not guilty of that, at one time or another? Only the forgetful can deceive themselves about it, since they want to deceive themselves. Camouflage had become a basic trait of our existence. It weighs on our moral conscience.

(b) More deeply stirring at the instant of cognition is guilt incurred by a *false conscience*. Many a young man or woman nowadays awakens with a horrible feeling: my conscience has betrayed me. I thought I was living in idealism and self-sacrifice for the noblest goal, with the best intentions—what can I still rely on? Everyone awakening like this will ask himself how he became guilty, by haziness, by unwillingness to see, by conscious seclusion, isolation of his own life in a 'decent' sphere.

Here we first have to distinguish between military honor and political sense. For whatever is said about guilt cannot affect the consciousness of military honor. If a soldier kept faith with his comrades, did not flinch in danger and proved himself calm and courageous, he may preserve something inviolate in his self-respect. These purely soldierly, and at the same time human, values are common to all peoples. No guilt is incurred by having stood this test; in fact, if probation here was real, unstained by evil acts or execution of patently evil commands, it is a foundation of the sense of life.

But a soldier's probation must not be identified with the cause he fought for. To have been a good soldier does not absolve from all other guilt.

The unconditional identification of the actual state with the German nation and army constitutes guilt incurred through false conscience. A first-class soldier may have succumbed to the falsification of his conscience which enabled him to do and permit obviously evil things because of patriotism. Hence the good conscience in evil deeds.

Yet our duty to the fatherland goes far beneath blind obedience to its rulers of the day. The fatherland ceases to be a fatherland when its soul is destroyed. The power of the state is not an end in itself; rather, it is pernicious if this state destroys the German character. Therefore, duty to the fatherland did not by any means lead consistently to obedience to Hitler and to the assumption that even as a Hitler state Germany must, of course, win the war at all costs. Herein lies the false conscience. It is no simple guilt. It is at the same time a tragic confusion, notably of a large part of our unwitting youth. To do one's duty to the fatherland means to commit one's whole person to the highest demands made on us by the best of our ancestors, not by the idols of a false tradition.

It was amazing to see the complete self-identification with army and state, in spite of all evil. For this unconditionality of a blind nationalism—only conceivable as the last crumbling ground in a world about to lose all faith—was moral guilt.

...Answer: 'After victory you'll be discharged and glad to go home. The SS alone will stay armed, and the reign of terror will grow into a slave state. No individual human life will be possible; pyramids will rise; highways and towns will be built and changed at the Fuehrer's whim: A giant arms machine will be developed for the final conquest of the world.'

A professor speaks: 'We are the Fronde within the Party. We dare frank discussion. We achieve spiritual realizations. We shall slowly turn all of it back into the old German spirituality.'—Answer: 'You are deceiving yourselves. Allowed a fool's freedom, on condition of instant obedience, you shut up and give in. Your fight is a mirage, desired by the leaders. You only help to entomb the German spirit.'

Many intellectuals went along in 1933, sought leading positions and publicly upheld the ideology of the new power, only to become resentful later when they personally were shunted aside. These—although mostly continuing positive until about 1942, when the course of the war made an unfavorable outcome certain and sent them into the oppositionist ranks—now feel that they suffered under the Nazis and are therefore called for what follows. They regard themselves as anti-Nazis. In all these years, according to their self-proclaimed ideology, these intellectual Nazis were frankly speaking truth in spiritual matters, guarding the tradition of the German spirit, preventing destructions, doing good in individual cases.

Many of these may be guilty of persisting in a mentality which, while not identical with Party tenets and even disguised as metamorphosis and opposition, still clings in fact to the mental attitude of National-Socialism and fails to clear itself. Through this mentality they may be actually akin to National-Socialism's inhuman, dictatorial, unexistentially nihilistic essence. If a mature person in 1933 had the certainty of inner conviction—due not merely to political error but to a sense of existence heightened by National-Socialism—he will be purified only by a transmutation which may have to be more thorough than any other. Whoever behaved like that in 1933 would remain inwardly brittle otherwise, and inclined to further fanaticism. Whoever took part in the race mania, whoever had delusions of a revival based on fraud, whoever winked at the crimes then already committed is not merely liable but must renew himself morally. Whether and how he can do it is up to him alone, and scarcely open to any outside scrutiny.

(e) There is a difference between *activity* and *passivity*. The political performers and executors, the leaders and the propagandists are guilty. If they did not become criminals, they still have, by their activity, incurred a positively determinable guilt.

But each one of us is guilty insofar as he remained inactive. The guilt of passivity is different. Impotence excuses; no moral law demands a spectacular death. Plato already deemed it a matter of course to go into hiding in desperate times of calamity, and to survive. But passivity knows itself morally guilty of every failure, every neglect to act whenever possible, to shield the imperiled, to relieve wrong, to countervail. Impotent submission always left a margin of activity which, though not without risk, could still be cautiously effective. Its anxious omission weighs upon the individual as moral guilt. Blindness for the misfortune of others, lack of imagination of the heart, inner indifference toward the witnessed evil—that is moral guilt.

(f) The moral guilt of outward compliance, of *running with the pack*, is shared to some extent by a great many of us. To maintain his existence, to keep his job, to protect his chances a man would join the Party and carry out other nominal acts of conformism.

Nobody will find an absolute excuse for doing so—notably in view of the many Germans who, in fact, did not conform, and bore the disadvantages.

Yet we must remember what the situation looked like in, say, 1936 or '37. The Party was the state. Conditions seemed incalculably permanent. Nothing short of a war could upset the régime. All the powers were appeasing Hitler. All wanted peace. A German who did not want to be out of everything, lose his profession, injure his business, was obliged to go along—the younger ones in particular. Now, membership in the Party or its professional organizations was no longer a political act; rather, it was a favor granted by the state which allowed the individual to join. A 'badge' was needed, an external token without inner assent. A man asked to join in those days could hardly refuse. It is decisive for the meaning of compliance in what connection and from what motives he acquired his membership in the Party; each year and every situation has its own mitigating and aggravating circumstances, to be distinguished only in each individual case.

Metaphysical Guilt

Morality is always influenced by mundane purposes. I may be morally bound to risk my life, if a realization is at stake; but there is no moral obligation to sacrifice one's life in the sure knowledge that nothing will have been gained. Morally we have a duty to dare, not a duty to choose certain doom. Morally, in either case, we rather have the contrary duty, not to do what cannot serve the mundane purpose but to save ourselves for realizations in the world.

But there is within us a guilt consciousness which springs from another source. Metaphysical guilt is the lack of absolute solidarity with the human being as such—an indelible claim beyond morally meaningful duty. This solidarity is violated by my presence at a wrong or a crime. It is not enough that I cautiously risk my life to prevent it; if it happens, and if I was there, and if I survive where the other is killed, I know from a voice within myself: I am guilty of being still alive.

I quote from an address* I gave in August 1945: 'We ourselves have changed since 1933. It was possible for us to seek death in humiliation—in 1933 when the Constitution was torn up, the dictatorship established in sham legality and all resistance swept away in the intoxication of a large part of our people. We could seek death when the crimes of the régime became publicly apparent on June 30, 1934, or with the lootings, deportations and murders of our Jewish friends and fellow-citizens in 1938, when to our ineradicable shame and disgrace the synagogues, houses of God, went up in flames throughout Germany. We could seek death when from the start of the war the régime acted against the words of Kant, our greatest philosopher, who called it a premise of international law that nothing must occur in war which would make a later reconcilement of the belligerents impossible. Thousands in Germany sought, or at least found death in battling

---

* Reprinted in *Wandlung*, Vol. I, No. 1, 1945.

the régime, most of them anonymously. We survivors did not seek it. We did not go into the streets when our Jewish friends were led away; we did not scream until we too were destroyed. We preferred to stay alive, on the feeble, if logical, ground that our death could not have helped anyone. We are guilty of being alive. We know before God which deeply humiliates us. What happened to us in these twelve years is like a transmutation of our being.'

In November 1938, when the synagogues burned and Jews were deported for the first time, the guilt incurred was chiefly moral and political. In either sense, the guilty were those still in power. The generals stood by. In every town the commander could act against crime, for the soldier is there to protect all, if crime occurs on such a scale that the police cannot or fail to stop it. They did nothing. At that moment they forsook the once glorious ethical tradition of the German Army. It was not their business. They had dissociated themselves from the soul of the German people, in favor of an absolute military machine that was a law unto itself and took orders.

True, among our people many were outraged and many deeply moved by a horror containing a presentiment of coming calamity. But even more went right on with their activities, undisturbed in their social life and amusements, as if nothing had happened. That is moral guilt.

But the ones who in utter impotence, outraged and despairing, were unable to prevent the crimes took another step in their metamorphosis by a growing consciousness of metaphysical guilt.

Recapitulation

Consequences of Guilt

If everything said before was not wholly unfounded, there can be no doubt that we Germans, every one of us, are guilty in some way. Hence there occur the consequences of guilt.

(1) All Germans without exception share in the political liability. All must cooperate in making amends to be brought into legal form. All must jointly suffer the effects of the acts of the victors, of their decisions, of their disunity. We are unable here to exert any influence as a factor of power.

Only by striving constantly for a sensible presentation of the facts, opportunities and dangers can we—unless everyone already knows what we say—collaborate on the premises of the decisions. In the proper form, and with reason, we may appeal to the victors.

(2) Not every German—indeed only a very small minority of Germans—will be punished for crimes. Another minority has to atone for National-Socialist activities. All may defend themselves. They will be judged by the courts of the victors, or by German courts established by the victors.

(3) Probably every German—though in greatly diverse forms—will have reasons morally to analyze himself. Here, however, he need not recognize any authority other than his own conscience.

(4) And probably every German capable of understanding will transform his approach to the world and himself in the metaphysical experiences of such a disaster. How that happens none can prescribe, and none anticipate. It is a matter of individual solitude. What comes out of it has to create the essential basis of what will in future be the German soul.

Such distinctions can be speciously used to get rid of the whole guilt question, for instance like this:

Political liability—all right, but it curtails only my material possibilities; I myself, my inner self is not affected by that at all.

Criminal guilt—that affects just a few, not me; it does not concern me.

Moral guilt—I hear that my conscience alone has jurisdiction, others have no right to accuse me. Well, my conscience is not going to be too hard on me. It wasn't really so bad; let's forget about it, and make a fresh start.

Metaphysical guilt—of that, finally, I was expressly told that none can charge it to another. I am supposed to perceive that in a transmutation. That's a crazy idea of some philosopher. There is no such thing. And if there were, I wouldn't notice it. That I needn't bother with.

Our dissection of the guilt concepts can be turned into a trick, for getting rid of guilt. The distinctions are in the foreground. They can hide the source and the unity. Distinctions enable us to spirit away what does not suit us.

Collective Guilt

Having separated the elements of guilt, we return in the end to the question of collective guilt.

Though correct and meaningful everywhere, the separation carries with it the indicated temptation—as though by such distinctions we had dodged the charges and eased our burden. Something has been lost in the process—something which in collective guilt is always audible in spite of everything. For all the crudeness of collective thinking and collective condemnation we feel that we belong together.

In the end, of course, the true collective is the solidarity of all men before God. Somewhere, everyone may free himself from the bonds of state or people or group and break through to the invisible solidarity of men—as men of goodwill and as men sharing the common guilt of being human.

But historically we remain bound to the closer, narrower communities, and we should lose the ground under our feet without them.

Political Liability and Collective Guilt

First to restate the fact that all over the world collective concepts largely guide the judgment and feelings of men. This is undeniable. In the world today the German—whatever the German may be—is regarded as something one would rather not have to do with. German Jews abroad are undesirable as Germans; they are essentially deemed Germans, not Jews. In this collective way of thought political liability is simultaneously justified as punishment of moral guilt. Historically such collective thought is not infrequent; the barbarism of war has seized whole populations and delivered them to pillage, rape and sale into slavery. And on top of it comes moral annihilation of the unfortunates in the judgment of the victor. They shall not only submit but confess and do penance. Whoever is German, whether Christian or Jew, is evil in spirit.

This fact of a widespread, though not universal, world opinion keeps challenging us, not only to defend ourselves with our simple distinction of political liability and moral guilt but to examine what truth may possibly lie in collective thinking. We do not drop the distinction, but we have to narrow it by saying that the conduct which made us liable rests on a sum of political conditions whose nature is moral, as it were, because they help to determine individual morality. The individual cannot wholly detach himself from these conditions, for—consciously or unconsciously—he lives as a link in their chain and cannot escape from their influence even if he was in opposition. There is a sort of collective moral guilt in a people's way of life which I share as an individual, and from which grow political realities.

For political conditions are inseparable from a people's whole way of life. There is no absolute division of politics and human existence as long as man is still realizing an existence rather than perishing in eremitical seclusion.

By political conditions the Swiss, the Dutch have been formed, and all of us in Germany have been brought up for ages—we to obey, to feel dynastically, to be indifferent and irresponsible toward political reality—and these conditions are part of us even if we oppose them.

The way of life effects political events, and the resulting political conditions in turn place their imprint on the way of life. This is why there can be no radical separation of moral and political guilt. This is why every enlightenment of our political consciousness proportionately burdens our conscience. Political liberty has its moral aspects.

Thus, actual political liability is augmented by knowledge and then by a different self-esteem. That in fact all the people pay for all the acts of their government—*quidquid delirant reges plectuntur Achivi*—is a mere empirical fact; that they know themselves liable is the first indication of their dawning political liberty. It is to the extent of the existence and recognition of this knowledge that freedom is real, not a mere outward claim put forth by unfree men.

The inner political unfreedom has the opposite feeling. It obeys on the one hand, and feels not guilty on the other. The feeling of guilt, which makes us accept liability, is the beginning of the inner upheaval which seeks to realize political liberty.

The contrast of the free and the unfree mental attitude appears, for instance, in the two concepts of a statesman. The question has been raised whether nations are to blame for the leaders they put up with—for example, France for Napoleon. The idea is that the vast majority did go along and desired the power and the glory which Napoleon procured. In this view Napoleon was possible only because the French would have him; his greatness was the precision with which he understood what the mass of the people expected, what they wanted to hear, what illusions they wanted, what material realities they wanted. Could Lenz have been right in saying, 'The state was born which suited the genius of France'? A part, a situation, yes—but not the genius of a nation as such! Who can define a national genius? The same genius has spawned very different realities.

One might think that, as a man must answer for his choice of the beloved to whom marriage binds him in a lifelong community of fate, a people answers for whomever it meekly obeys. Error is culpable; there is no escape from its consequences.

Precisely this, however, would be the wrong approach. The unconditional attachment to one person which is possible and proper in a marriage is pernicious on principle in a state. The loyalty of followers is a non-political relationship limited to narrow circles and primitive circumstances. In a free state all men are subject to control and change.

Hence there is twofold guilt—first, in the unconditional political surrender to a leader as such, and second, in the kind of leader submitted to. The atmosphere of submission is a sort of collective guilt.

All the restrictions concerning our liberation from moral guilt—in favor of mere political liability—do not affect what we established at the beginning and shall now restate:

We are politically responsible for our régime, for the acts of the régime, for the start of the war in this world-historical situation, and for the kind of leaders we allowed to rise among us. For that we answer to the victors, with our labor and with our working faculties, and must make such amends as are exacted from the vanquished.

In addition there is our moral guilt. Although this always burdens only the individual who must get along with himself, there still is a sort of collective morality contained in the ways of life and feeling, from which no individual can altogether escape and which have political significance as well. Here is the key to self-improvement; its use is up to us.

Individual Awareness of Collective Guilt

We feel something like a co-responsibility for the acts of members of our families. This co-responsibility cannot be objectivized. We should reject any manner of tribal liability. And yet, because of our consanguinity we are inclined to feel concerned whenever wrong is done by someone in the family—and also inclined, therefore, depending on the type and circumstances of the wrong and its victims, to make it up to them even if we are not morally and legally accountable.

Thus the German—that is, the German-speaking individual—feels concerned by everything growing from German roots. It is not the liability of a national but the concern of one who shares the life of the German spirit and soul—who is of one tongue, one stock, one fate with all the others—which here comes to cause, not as tangible guilt, but somehow analogous to co-responsibility.

We further feel that we not only share in what is done at present—thus being co-responsible for the deeds of our contemporaries—but in the links of tradition. We have to bear the guilt of our fathers. That the spiritual conditions of German life provided an opportunity for such a régime is a fact for which all of us are co-responsible. Of course this does not mean that we must acknowledge 'the world of German ideas' or 'German thought of the past' in general as the sources of the National-Socialist misdeeds. But it does mean that our national tradition contains something, mighty and threatening, which is our moral ruin.

We feel ourselves not only as individuals but as Germans. Every one, in his real being, is the German people. Who does not remember moments in his life when he said to himself, in opposition and in despair of his nation, 'I am Germany'—or, in jubilant harmony with it, 'I, too, am Germany!' The German character has no other form than these individuals. Hence the demands of transmutation, of rebirth, of rejection of evil are made of the nation in the form of demands from each individual.

Because in my innermost soul I cannot help feeling collectively, being German is to me—is to everyone—not a condition but a task. This is altogether different from making the nation absolute. I am a human being first of all; in particular I am a Frisian, a professor, a German, linked closely enough for a fusion of souls with other collective groups, and more or less closely with all groups I have come in touch with. For moments this proximity enables me to feel almost like a Jew or Dutchman or Englishman. Throughout it, however, the fact of my being German—that is, essentially, of life in the mother tongue—is so emphatic that in a way which is rationally not conceivable, which is even rationally refutable, I feel co-responsible for what Germans do and have done.

I feel closer to those Germans who feel likewise—without becoming melodramatic about it—and farther from the ones whose soul seems to deny this link. And this proximity means, above all, a common inspiring task—of not being German as we happen to be, but becoming German as we are not yet but ought to be, and as we hear it in the call of our ancestors rather than in the history of national idols.

By our feeling of collective guilt we feel the entire task of renewing human existence from its origin—the task which is given to all men on earth but which appears more urgently, more perceptibly, as decisively as all existence, when its own guilt brings a people face to face with nothingness.

As a philosopher I now seem to have strayed completely into the realm of feeling and to have abandoned conception. Indeed language fails at this point, and only negatively we may recall that all our distinctions—notwithstanding the fact that we hold them to be true and are by no means rescinding them—must not become resting places. We must not use them to let matters drop and free ourselves from the pressure under which we continue on our path, and which is to ripen what we hold most precious, the eternal essence of our soul.

31

Introduction*

By Robert H. Jackson

If mankind really is to master its destiny or control its way of life, it must first find means to prevent war. So long as it cannot, war demands will dictate the course of our collective and individual lives. And if we are to come to grips with the problem of preventing war, it is important that we know how wars are made, to what extent they result from impersonal pressures and tensions, and how far they are due to blunders or pugnacity of individual statesmen or political factions.

Never have the archives of a belligerent nation been so completely exposed as were those of Nazi Germany at the Nuremberg trial. In its preparation over a hundred thousand captured documents were screened, about five thousand were translated, and over four thousand were used in evidence. Some of these ran to several volumes. They were not old records dragged to light by a subsequent generation which knew not how to value them. They were laid out in a courtroom before the very highest of their surviving authors, who, with able counsel and firsthand knowledge, subjected them to correction, explanation, and attempted justification. The result is a documentation unprecedented in history as to any major war.

Lord Acton, in his inaugural lecture as professor of history at Cambridge, said, 'We are still at the beginning of the documentary age, which will tend to make history independent of historians....' It may be doubted whether we are more independent of historians, however, when such an avalanche of documents descends upon the world that their meaning and import can be learned only from fair and intelligent arrangement, condensation, and interpretation. This, in a hurried and partisan way, both the prosecution and the defense attempted to do as part of the trial. But its record of forty-two volumes is too vast, detailed, and disjointed for general study. Now, Professor Harris—by scholarship and experience admirably qualified—in the calm of intervening years has prepared a factual summary of the evidence that is objective, accurate, and comprehensive. It constitutes a report of the Nuremberg post-mortem examination of the Nazi regime and its part in causing World War II.

Our enlightened century twice has seen the Western peoples array themselves into hostile camps, each dedicated to the exhaustion and destruction of the other.

---

* Taken from W. R. Harris, *Tyranny on Trial—The Evidence at Nuremberg* (New York: Barnes and Noble Books, 1954).

Each side has been more successful in the infliction of injury on the enemy than in improving its own position. They have bled each other to such low vitality that the East has been left ascendant in the world balance of power. Certainly that mixture of legal principles and diplomatic practices which we call international law has demonstrated to Western statesmen by successful experiences that arbitration can be an honorable and civilized alternative, better even for the losing party than a successful war.

Why, then, did we have to have a second World War? The Nuremberg trial record answers that Hitler, along with some grievances that might have been adjusted peacefully, had as his major policy such ruthless and aggressive objectives that they could not be submitted to any civilized tribunal with the slightest hope it could approve them. He had to win by war, if at all, because he could never win by appeal to reason.

Not until the Nuremberg trial disclosed the German archives was it known how cynical and brazen was the Nazi conspiracy for aggression. Of course, in *Main Kampf* Hitler openly declared his aim to acquire more territory, and to do it by war; but these only impressed the world as the mad daydreams of one then a prisoner. By April, 1939, however, he had seized supreme power in the German state and ordered final preparations for war to begin from September 1, 1939, onward. On May 23, 1939, Hitler secretly reiterated to his high officials his purpose to expand 'our living space in the East' and to 'attack Poland at the first suitable opportunity.' His pact with the Soviet Union made him feel safe in going ahead. On August 22, Hitler again harangued his top civilian and military officials:

Destruction of Poland is in the foreground. The aim is elimination of living forces, not the arrival at a certain line.... I shall give a propagandistic cause for starting the war,—never mind whether it be plausible or not. The victor shall not be asked later on whether we told the truth or not. In starting and making a war, not the right is what matters but victory.

Thus the conflagration was set. The rapidity with which the German armies swept away opposition showed that Germany was in no danger of attack, for it alone was prepared for modern war.

Moreover, the Nazi regime, in driving Germany toward war and in conducting it, had waged the most frightful of the world's persecutions against Jews, Catholics, Protestants, Freemasons, organized labor, and all suspected of pacifist tendencies. It had exterminated human beings by gas chambers, gas wagons, medical means, firing squads, overwork, and undernourishment, to the appalling number of six million. It had seized, transported to Germany, and impressed into forced labor five million more. The magnitude of this planned reversion to barbarism taxes the civilized imagination and the cruelty of its execution taxes credulity.

Few Americans seem now to appreciate that only by the narrowest margin, and largely because of his own blunders, did Hitler lose his war for supremacy of all Europe. But when the war did end successfully, the surviving planners and executioners of this policy were prisoners in our custody or that of our allies.

The interests of the United States in the problem of the Nazi war criminals were put in my hands on May 2, 1945. What we should have done with these men is a question always evaded by those who find fault with what we did do. To expect the Germans to bring these Germans to justice was out of the question. That was proved by the farcical experiment after World War I. But after World War II, organized society in Germany was in a state of collapse. There was no authoritative judicial system except remnants of the violently partisan judiciary set up by Hitler. And German law had been perverted to be a mere expression of the Nazi will.

To have turned the men over to the anti-Nazi factions in Germany would have been a doubtful benevolence. Even a year and a half later, when Schacht, Von Papen, and Fritzsche were acquitted by the Tribunal, they begged to remain within the protection of the American jail lest they be mobbed by the angry and disillusioned elements of the German population. They knew the fate of Mussolini.

Where in the world were neutrals to take up the task of investigation and judging? Does one suggest Spain? Sweden? Switzerland? True, these states as such were not engaged in the war, but powerful elements of their society and most leading individuals were reputed not to be impartial but to be either for or against the Nazi order. Only the naïve or those forgetful of conditions in 1945 would contend that we could have induced 'neutral' states to assume the duty of doing justice to the Nazis.

Of course, we might have refused all responsibility for either their safety or their punishment and turned them out scot free. But in 1945 what we had to fight against was an insistent and worldwide demand for immediate, unhesitating, and undiscriminating vengeance.

Stalin, according to Churchill's account, proposed to line up and shoot fifty thousand high-ranking German leaders. Churchill says he indignantly refused. But Judge Samuel Rosenman, who was in Europe representing President Roosevelt when the latter died, reported of the British officials in his *Working with Roosevelt*: 'They wanted to take the top Nazi criminals out and shoot them without warning one morning and announce to the world that they were dead.' Churchill, he says, agreed, for he thought long-drawn-out trials would be a mistake.

Proposal of a long, tedious hearing-process was not popular at that time, even among high officials of the United States. Secretary Hull's memoirs recite: 'If I had my way, I would take Hitler and Mussolini and Tojo and their arch-accomplices and bring them before a drumhead court-martial. And at sunrise on the following day there would occur an historic incident.' Treasury sources seriously proposed to turn over as many as a half-million young Germans, regardless of personal guilt, to the Soviet Union for 'labor reparations,' and when I protested vigorously I was accused of being 'soft' with the Nazis.

The demand for summary action infected ordinarily calm sources of public opinion. The *Chicago Tribune* gave wide currency to an interview with Professor Hans J. Morgenthau, of the University of Chicago, in which he was quoted as saying:

I am doubtful of the whole setup under which these trials will be conducted.... What, in my opinion, they should have done is to set up summary courts-martial. Then they should have placed these criminals on trial before them within 24 hours after they were caught, sentenced them to death, and shot them in the morning.

The *Nation*, which bears at its masthead the legend 'America's Leading Liberal Weekly Since 1865,' said as the trial started:

In our opinion the proper procedure for this body would have been to identify the prisoners, read off their crimes with as much supporting data as seemed useful, pass judgment upon them quickly, and carry out the judgment without any delay whatever.

Chief Justice Stone, who had his own personal reasons for disliking the trial, writing about 'the power of the victor over the vanquished' said, 'It would not disturb me greatly if that power were openly and frankly used to punish the German leaders for being a bad lot, but it disturbs me some to have it dressed up in the habiliments of the common law and the Constitutional safeguards to those charged with crime.' (Mason, 'Extra-Judicial Work for Judges: The Views of Chief Justice Stone,' 67 Harv. L. Rev. 193.) It is hard to find a statement by a law-trained man more inconsistent with the requirements of elementary justice. When did it become a crime to be one of a 'bad lot'? What was the specific badness for which they should be openly and frankly punished? And how did he know what individuals were included in the bad lot? Can it be less right to punish for specific acts such as murder, which has been a crime since the days of Adam, than to punish on the vague charge always made against an enemy that he is 'bad'? If it would have been right to punish the vanquished out-of-hand for being a bad lot, what made it wrong to have first a safe-guarded hearing to make sure who was bad, and how bad, and of what his badness consisted?

It must be admitted that such summary action as would have been acceptable to Stone was consistent with what was going on in Europe. The French Minister of Justice has reported that 8,348 collaborators were summarily executed without trial by members of the French Resistance and 1,325 were executed by decisions of nonlegal committees. The Nuremberg Judgment showed that something over 10 per cent of those we accused, on what was believed to be reliable information, were not proved guilty when the evidence was put to judicial test; for three of those indicted by the prosecution were wholly acquitted, and several others were not found guilty on some of the charges. There is little doubt that any policy of punishment by political decision in a time of passion and confusion will condemn persons against whom it is impossible to prove guilt by the standards we set and followed.

The only course, in my view, was for the victors to behave as civilized victors and take the responsibilities implicit in demanding and accepting capitulation of the whole German state and population. Unless history was to lay the war guilt and the guilt for organized programs of atrocities upon the whole German people, some process must identify those individuals who were in fact responsible and make an authentic record of their deeds.

President Roosevelt had steadily and insistently favored a speedy but fair trial for these men, fearful that if they were punished without public proof of their crimes and opportunity to defend themselves there would always remain a doubt of their guilt that might raise a myth of martyrdom. Secretary Stimson, and those associated with him in the War Department, had strongly supported President Roosevelt's policy of no punishment except for those proved guilty at a genuine good-faith trial. They gave unfailing support to me in trying to carry out that policy. The British and French were persuaded eventually to that view and did their utmost to co-operate in carrying the difficult task to successful execution. The Soviet reluctantly joined. Rosenman says that later Churchill acknowledged to him, 'Now that the trials are over, I think the President was right and I was wrong.'

The policy decision to give a hearing raised problems of the technique to be followed. There was no precedent in legal history, and no lawyer had experience in conducting such a trial. Most lawyers thought it impossible of success. The trial must be conducted by five groups of attorneys, each trained in a different system of law and practice. The defense would be in the hands of German lawyers, and their procedure was derived largely from Roman law. The prosecution would be divided among the British, American, French, and Soviet, the two former being practitioners of common-law traditions and the two latter both roughly following the Roman system but with important variations between them. Moreover, the trial required the simultaneous use of four languages—German, Russian, French, and English—and none of the lawyers was competent in all these tongues, few in more than one. Because no one insisted that his own practices be wholly adopted, but all agreed that the best features of each system be used, we worked out an amalgamation of Continental and common-law procedures which enabled the trial to proceed with fair speed and with less bickering over evidence and procedure than is common in most American criminal trials. The German lawyers, too, deserve to have it said that while they objected strongly to the idea of Germans being tried by anybody but Germans, or judged by any law except German law, they took a professional attitude toward the trial on the whole and did not endeavor to break up the hearings or cause disorder.

The prosecution early was confronted with two vital decisions of policy about which there were strong disagreements among members of the American staff. One was whether chiefly to rely upon living witnesses or upon documents for proof of our case. The decision, supported by most of the staff, was to use and rest on documentary evidence to prove every point possible. The argument against this was that documents are dull, the press would not report them, the trial would become wearisome and would not get across to the people. There was much truth in this position, I must admit. But it seemed to me that witnesses, many of them persecuted and hostile to the Nazis, would always be chargeable with bias, faulty recollection, and even perjury. The documents could not be accused of partiality, forgetfulness, or invention, and would make the sounder foundation, not only for the immediate guidance of the Tribunal, but for the ultimate verdict of history. The result was that the Tribunal declared, in its judgment, 'The case, therefore, against the defendants rests in a large measure on documents of their own making, the authenticity of which has not been challenged except in one or two cases.'

The other question was whether to take advantage of the readiness of some defendants to testify against others in return for concessions to themselves as to their penalty, if convicted. When a defendant is convicted on the testimony of an accomplice who 'turns state's evidence' as we say in this country, it always gives the conviction a bad odor. We decided it would be better to lose our case against some defendants than to win by a deal that would discredit the judgment. We did lose our case against Schacht, against whom testimony might have been obtained by concession; but still I think we made the better choice.

During the almost year-long trial, it was not practicable for the daily press to present American readers with more than occasional, sketchy, and sometimes inaccurate accounts of the evidence and proceedings, nor was there in this country the wide and sustained reader-interest felt by the peoples of Europe, whose countries had been occupied. As a result, no sound and general foundation of public information about the trial was laid. This has made it easy for those hostile to the policy of holding a trial to stigmatize it with slogans which required no information to utter and none to understand.

Whatever else one may think of the policy of holding the Nuremberg trial or of the way in which it was carried out, no one can deny that turning to the techniques of trial to determine who of the enemy deserved punishment is a significant development in the practice of nations. It can be appraised intelligently only with a background of accurate information which it would be a tedious and long-drawn task to acquire from original sources. If there is to be any general understanding of the trial, the importance of a summary of its policy, proceedings, and evidence in a single readable and reliable volume is apparent.

We are much too near the event to pass judgment on the ultimate influence of the Nuremberg trial on the development of international law and policy. Procedurally, we know it demonstrated that there is enough fundamental harmony and likeness in our Western systems of law, including the Soviet, so that five separate professions can join in the conduct of a legal proceeding. This means that the nations, if they will to do so, can utilize legal techniques in a much wider field than had heretofore been deemed possible. Many mistakes were made—no critic knows that as well as we who were responsible for them. But in an effort so unprecedented the profession may learn as much from our failures and mistakes as from our accomplishments.

The contribution to substantive law may not yet be discernible. The United Nations has given general approval to the Nuremberg principles, though it has not been able to progress with their codification beyond the point to which they already were codified by the London Agreement and Charter. Meanwhile, these principles are taking their place in the scholarship of international law. It is perhaps significant that, despite German dislike for the war crimes trials, Western Germany has embodied in the Bonn Constitution its most basic principles. The London Agreement and the trial pursuant to it started a movement in the world of thought that is deep and enduring.

Professor Harris is one of a large staff of men and women who were inspired by the ideals of the Nuremberg effort and whose loyalty and hard work are to be credited with their success in practice. He has not felt bound to praise or approve all that he recites, and his views of the law and procedure are his own. One may take issue with his views, but none can question that he has set forth the whole subject with objectivity, learning, and insight. His manuscript teaches me that the hard months at Nuremberg were well spent in the most important, enduring, and constructive work of my life.

Washington, D. C.
February, 1954

32

In Defense of Liberal Show Trials—Nuremberg and Beyond*

By Mark J. Osiel

We ought to evaluate transitions to democracy with greater attention to the kind of public discussion they foster concerning the human rights abuse perpetrated by authoritarian rulers, recently deposed. We should evaluate the prosecution of these perpetrators in light of how it influences such public deliberation. At such times, the need for public reckoning with the question of how such horrific events could have happened is more important to democratization than the criminal law's more traditional objectives. This is because such trials, when effective as public spectacle, stimulate public discussion in ways that foster the liberal virtues of toleration, moderation, and civil respect. Criminal trials must be conducted with this pedagogical purpose in mind.

Trials of those responsible for large-scale state brutality have captured the public imagination in several societies. If they succeed in concentrating public attention and stimulating reflection, such proceedings indelibly influence collective memory of the events they judge. By highlighting official brutality and public complicity, these trials often make people willing to reassess their foundational beliefs and constitutive commitments, as few events in political life can do.

In the lives of individuals, these trials thus often become, at the very least, an occasion for personal stock-taking. Specifically, they present moments of transformative opportunity in the lives of individuals and societies, a potential not lost upon the litigants themselves. Prosecutors and judges in these cases thus rightly aim to shape collective memory of horrible events in ways that can be both successful as public spectacle and consistent with liberal legality.

Such trials cannot summon up a collective conscience of moral principles shared by all. At these moments, no such consensus on fundamentals is likely to exist. Neither can it be easily created. But criminal trials may, nevertheless, contribute significantly to a certain, underappreciated kind of social solidarity, arising from reliance on procedures for ensuring that moral disagreement

* Edited and redrafted excerpts from M. Osiel, *Mass Atrocity, Collective Memory, and the Law* (New Brunswick/London: Transaction Publishers, 1997).

among antagonists remains mutually respectful, within the courtroom and beyond.

To this end, judges and prosecutors can profit from closer attention to the 'poetics' of legal storytelling, i.e., to the way in which an experience of administrative massacre can be framed within the conventions of competing genres. The task is therefore to understand why certain narrative tropes were employed by prosecution and defense in particular trials, and to assess the varying degree to which these were successful in influencing collective memory—both national and international—of the disputed events, often many years thereafter. The answers to these empirical questions will prove helpful in designing future prosecutions of administrative massacre.

To maximize their pedagogic impact, such trials should be unabashedly designed as monumental spectacles. Though rarely acknowledged, considerations of dramaturgy have proven quite valuable to this end. This is because these are 'liberal show trials', conducted by what have been called moral entrepreneurs and activists of memory. The approach advocated here necessarily involves courts in questions of historical interpretation and moral pedagogy generally regarded as beyond their professional competence. It also assumes their capacity to influence political culture and social norms in powerful ways.

All societies have founding myths, explaining where we come from, defining what we stand for. These are often commemorated in the form of monumental didactics, public recountings of the founders' heroic deeds as a national epic. Some societies also have myths of *re*founding, marking a period of decisive break from their own pasts, celebrating the courage and imagination of those who produced this rupture. Mass atrocity trials become a focal point for the collective memory of whole nations. These acts often become secular rituals of commemoration. As such, they consolidate shared memories with increasing deliberateness and sophistication. These events are both 'real' and 'staged'.

Law-related activities of this sort contribute to the kind of social solidarity that is enhanced by shared historical memory. In the last half century, criminal law has increasingly been used in several societies with a view to teaching a particular interpretation of the country's history, one expected to have a salubrious impact on its solidarity. Many have thought, in particular, that the best way to prevent recurrence of genocide, and other forms of state-sponsored mass brutality, is to cultivate a shared and enduring memory of its horrors—and to employ the law self-consciously toward this end.

To do this effectively has increasingly been recognized to require some measure of smoke and mirrors, that is, some self-conscious dramaturgy by prosecutors and judges. For instance, Western Allies in post-war war crimes trials deliberately strove 'to dramatize the implacable contradiction between the methods of totalitarianism and the ways of civilized humanity through a worldwide demonstration of fair judicial procedure'.[1]

---

[1] Peter J. Fliess, 78 *Am. J. Int'l L.* 256 (1984) (book review).

Liberal legal theorists will be tempted quickly to reject the cultivation of collective memory as a defensible objective when prosecuting those responsible for administrative massacre. But that conclusion would be premature and unfounded. The orchestration of criminal trials for pedagogic purposes—such as the transformation of a society's collective memory—is not inherently misguided or morally indefensible. The defensibility of the practice depends on the defensibility of the lessons being taught—that is, on the liberal nature of the stories being told. Whether show trials are defensible depends on what the state intends to show and how it will show it. Liberal show trials are ones self-consciously designed to show the merits of liberal morality and to do so in ways consistent with its very requirements.

Those requirements do not include a purely proceduralist version of the rule of law, as Shklar rightly argued in defending the Nuremberg Trial. The rule of law, so understood, could be satisfied even in highly authoritarian regimes.[2] To strengthen substantive norms of liberal conduct (against gross cruelty, for instance), courts might have to revise procedural rules during a democratic transition, partly compromising the protections they afford. Moreover, other cases of administrative massacre examined here suggest that the procedural revisions necessary to enhance a trial's impact on collective memory—such as admitting evidence bearing on wider, historical interpretations—often prejudice the prosecution more than the defense. What justifies such revisions does not turn on which side's interests are prejudiced by them.

Their justification rests simply on their capacity to make for telling a better story about where the country should be heading. The Nuremberg Trial was therefore justified, she argued, as a 'great legalistic drama' that would help postwar Germany refound itself and base its new Constitution on principles of justice. The Trial was justified, in consequentialist terms, to the extent that it 'reinforced dormant legal consciousness' among the German people. Nuremberg should therefore be defended *as* a political trial, unabashedly so. What mattered most, at such times and places at least, was not to insulate legal institutions from politics, but rather to ensure that they were placed in service of the right kind of politics. The present study is little more than an elaboration and defense of Shklar's argument in this regard. But I am more concerned than she with the practical question of 'how to do it'. After all, any good lawyer would surely react to such a proposal with our proverbial refrain: the devil is in the details.

'What is the cost for the individual and for society,' asks one anthropologist, 'when there is no meaningful framework for publicly exploring traumatic memories of political violence?'[3] That question sounds no less powerfully in a liberal society than in any other. The legal storytelling in which courts necessarily

---

[2] Judith Shklar, *Legalism: Law, Morals, and Political Trials* 150 (1986).
[3] Rubie S. Watson, 'Memory, History, and Opposition under State Socialism: An Introduction', in *Memory, History, and Opposition under State Socialism* 1, 13 (Watson ed., 1994).

engage, reproaching some and commending others, cannot seek to teach citizens how to exercise their moral autonomy, other than to respect the like autonomy of others. In this sense, the lessons taught by a liberal society and its law are necessarily and deliberately incomplete.

Even so, a liberal state may employ a 'show trial' for administrative massacre to display the horrific consequences of the illiberal vices and so to foster among its citizens the liberal virtues (including respect for basic individual rights, deliberative capacity, and toleration). 'There is no reason to think that liberal citizens come about naturally...'[4] As Macedo contends, 'We need to avoid making the mistake of assuming that liberal citizens—self-restrained, moderate, and reasonable—spring full-blown from the soil of private freedom.'[5]

A criminal trial is a congenial public opportunity for collective mourning of the victims of administrative massacre. It provides a ritual that is helpful for family members and a sympathetic public in coming to terms with melancholia in even the most traumatic cases.[6] Just because a liberal state cannot dictate the terms on which the victims' lives could be lived does not preclude the state from providing an occasion that serves for mourning their wrongful taking.

In so doing, criminal law contributes significantly to the social solidarity that is based on shared commitment to liberal principles of mutual respect and concern among individuals. This communal mourning is one important role that collective memory may legitimately play in a liberal society, or within a society aspiring to liberalize itself. With this hypothesis in mind, we can begin to assess how the law might properly contribute to the formation of such memory, particularly of national catastrophes like the Argentine dirty war.

Is it possible, when prosecuting perpetrators of administrative massacre, to craft evidence and legal argument in a way that stimulates public discussion of the underlying issues, influences the ensuing debate so as to foster liberal morality and solidarity? Liberal stories are ones that, in treatment of their characters, reward the liberal virtues and condemn illiberal vices. Cruelty is a cardinal vice in this regard; respect for individual life and liberty, the cardinal virtue. All else is commentary. Liberal virtues are those dispositions of character that a liberal society must cultivate in its members in order to function effectively and to keep social conflict within tolerable bounds.

First and foremost, a liberal society must inculcate the disposition to respect the moral rights of others, that is, the rights that liberal morality accords to all persons. The stories that criminal courts tell must celebrate this virtue and chastise the correlative vice. The law accomplishes this only when courts and juries themselves respect the law, that is, when they adhere to legal rules reflecting

---

[4] Stephen Macedo, 'Transformative Constitutionalism and the Case of Religion: Defending the Moderate Hegemony of Liberal Constitutional Values', in *Constitutional Politics and Constitutional Studies* (Sotirios Barber & Robert George eds., 1996).

[5] Id. Joseph Raz adopts a similar view in *The Morality of Freedom* 196–97 (1986).

[6] Peter Homans, *The Ability to Mourn* 261–348 (1989).

liberal principles of procedural fairness and personal culpability as conditions of criminal liability. The most gripping of legal yarns must hence be classified as a failure if its capacity for public enthrallment is purchased at the price of violating such strictures.

But within these principled constraints, liberals have plenty of good stories to tell. As Yack observes:

> If man is, as MacIntyre insists, '...a story-telling being',...then we should expect men and women to turn theories, even liberal theories which insist on impersonal and antitraditional criteria, into the basis for new stories...The French turned liberty from tradition into a female figure, symbolic of the Republic's virtues and energy. American colonists turned Lockean liberal principles into didactic stories with which to educate their children...Similarly, the Kantian categorical imperative has generated stories that celebrate moral courage, while social contract theories have encouraged stories that celebrate the virtues associate with self-reliance.[7]

But the notice that a liberal story, on Yack's account, does no more than illustrate principles, the validity of which do not derive from the story itself or from the character-virtues of those enacting it. Stories allow the listener to intuit directly the moral lessons embedded in them. Rather than being required to act on principle, that is, in conscious awareness of moral duties discerned from the story's proper interpretation, stories allow us to apprehend these lessons in an unmediated way: from the very vivacity of their immediate impact on the listeners' sentiments.

Losing Perspective, Distorting History

> *What I want, so far as it is possible, is an objective political debate over the history of both German states. Penal laws, any penal laws, are fundamentally unsuited to resolving historical problems.*
>
> > Egon Krenz, Politburo member and former General-Secretary of the Communist Party of the German Democratic Republic, at his 1996 trial for manslaughter of border escapees.[8]
>
> *There can be no one historical narrative that...renders perfect justice (just as perhaps there is no judicial outcome that can capture the complexity of*

---

[7] Bernard Yack, 'Liberalism and its Communitarian Critics: Does Liberal Practice "Live Down" to Liberal Theory?', in *Community in America* 147, 151–52 (Charles H. Reynolds and Ralph V. Norman eds., 1988).

[8] Quoted in Stephen Kinzer, 'We Weren't Following Orders, But the Currents of the Cold War', *N.Y. Times*, March 24, 1996, at 16. Similar views are commonly expressed even by those with no interest in apologetics or self-exculpation. Tzvetan Todorov, for instance, has complained, with respect to the French Court's opinion concerning Klaus Barbie, that 'what is especially worth criticizing is not that they wrote bad history, it's that they wrote history at all, instead of being content to apply the law equitably and universally'. In *Memory, the Holocaust, and French Justice* 114, 120 (Richard J. Golsan ed., 1996).

history)... On the other hand... The historian would like to do justice; the judge
must establish some version of history... If good judges and historians shun these
tasks, they will be taken on by prejudiced or triumphalist ones.

Charles Maier, historian.[9]

The relation between criminal judgment and historical interpretation is problematic in myriad ways. Krenz says, in short, that the two tasks are radically different and should not be addressed in the same forum. Maier 'responds' that these tasks are indeed distinct, but ultimately inextricable. So we must get on with reconciling the two as best we can. The tension between what I take to be the truth in both statements deserves reflection.

Maier ultimately gets the better of the argument. But he concedes that the majority view has been otherwise. For instance, after 1989, he notes, 'the societies of Eastern Europe have chosen to separate the tasks of political justice and historical representation. Only the Germans have persisted in trying to attempt both tasks, and the results so far are also problematic.'[10] The prevailing opinion is now that the attempt to combine the two endeavors is very likely to produce poor justice or poor history, probably both.

If the law is to influence collective memory, it must tell stories that are engaging and compelling, stories that linger in the mind because they are responsive to the public's central concerns. This proves difficult. The central concerns of criminal courts, when trying cases of administrative massacre, are often decidedly at odds with the public's interest in a thorough, wide-ranging exploration of what caused such events and whose misconduct contributed to them. Courts can easily distort such public understanding either by excessive narrowness ('legalistic' blinders) or by excessive breadth (straying beyond their professional competence). A frequent form of distortion combines the worst of both: it presents a professionally correct conclusion, perfectly suitable for traditional legal purposes, as something much more, that is, as an 'official history' of the entire conflagration.

The trial court in the *Eichmann* case was well aware of these dangers. It expressly disavowed such historiographic or didactic aims as beyond its ken.[11] The court identified a genuine problem: that many citizens look to the court, and to the evidence it will gather and assess, to help answer large questions that have recently become the center of public concern (and private anguish), questions over which it can claim no monopoly of expertise.

Yet even as the court seeks to delimit its professional tasks, to reject any role as history teacher or scholar, it could not quite contain itself from proclaiming that

---

[9] Charles Maier, 'Doing Justice, Doing History: Political Purges and National Narratives after 1945 and 1989', 14–15 (paper presented at 'In Memory: Revisiting Nazi Atrocities in Post-Cold War Europe, International Conference to Commemorate the Fiftieth Anniversary of the 1944 Massacres around Arezzo').

[10] Id. at 14.

[11] *Attorney-General of Israel v. Eichmann*, 36 I.L.R. 5, 18–19 (Isr. Dist. Ct. 1961).

trial's 'educational significance' and 'educational value'.[12] The court remained delphically silent about what this educational significance consists of and about how to resolve possible tensions between the trial's positive educational effect and the other, more conventional aims of a criminal proceeding.

At the very least, the judges are acutely aware that their judgment will inevitably be viewed as *making* history and that their judgment will itself be subject to historiographical scrutiny. Justice Jackson's opening statement at Nuremberg acknowledged this explicitly: 'The record on which we judge these defendants today is the record on which history will judge us tomorrow.'[13]

Even after Julius and Ethel Rosenberg had been executed, Felix Frankfurter penned a dissent to the Supreme Court's denial of a stay. He acknowledged that to dissent 'after the curtain has been rung down upon them has the appearance of pathetic futility'.[14] Even so, he added, 'history also has its claims'.[15] It is those claims to which judges feel obliged to respond in the cases discussed here. The only problem—characteristic of these cases—is that Frankfurter almost certainly got those claims largely wrong, as recent historiography on the *Rosenberg* case suggests.[16]

The *Eichmann* court's vague claim about the trial's educational value is very modest compared to the more extravagant proclamations of national catharsis and collective psychoanalysis by others.[17] Even so, many historians have concluded that at such times the law unwittingly provides more *mis*education than accurate historical instruction.[18]

The concept of historical distortion is itself somewhat problematic, to be sure, and must be scrutinized before employable in assessing judicial forays into telling a national story. As Schudson warns:

The notion that memory can be 'distorted' assumes that there is a standard by which we can judge or measure what a veridical memory must be. If this is difficult with individual memory, it is even more complex with collective memory where the past event or experience remembered was truly a different event or experience for its different participants.

---

[12] Both statements appear in Eichmann, 36 I.L.R. at 19. Recognizing the apparent tension between its claims, the Court then seeks to clarify how it views its educational function, asserting that although the record 'will certainly provide valuable material for the research worker and the historian, . . . as far as this Court is concerned all these things are merely a by-product of the trial'.

[13] 2 *Trial of the Major War Criminals Before the International Military Tribunal* 101 (1947).

[14] *Rosenberg v. United States*, 346 U.S. 273, 310 (1953) (Frankfurter, J., dissenting).

[15] Frankfurter's dissent inevitably focused on procedural defects in the trial, but he concluded that such defects undermined confidence in the result.

[16] Ronald Radosh, 'The Venona Files', *New Republic*, August 7, 1995, at 25–27 (summarizing the famous Venona intercepts between Soviet and American Communist Party officials, decoded by the Army Signal Intelligence Service and recently declassified, clearly establishing that Julius Rosenberg, although not his wife, spied for the Soviets).

[17] See, respectively, Paula K. Speck, 'The Trial of the Argentine Juntas', 18 *U. Miami Inter-Am. L. Rev.* 491, 533 (1987) and Henry Rousso, *The Vichy Syndrome* 210 (1991).

[18] See, e.g., Christopher R. Browning, 'German Memory, Judicial Interrogation, and Historical Reconstruction: Writing Perpetrator History from Postwar Testimony', in *Probing the Limits of Representation: Nazism and the 'Final Solution'* 22, 26 (Saul Friedlander ed., 1992).

Moreover, where we can accept with little question that biography or the lifetime is the appropriate or 'natural' frame for individual memory, there is no such evident frame for cultural memories. Neither national boundaries nor linguistic ones are as self-evidently the right containers for collective memory as the person is for individual memory....[19]

Hence the contours of the story itself will determine the precise nature and identity of the collective subject that is presumably to do the remembering. The collectivity cannot tell the historian when or how 'its' story begins or ends, for it is the historian whose conclusions about the origins and nature of that collectivity determine how it itself is configured and defined. Thus, Schudson concludes, 'Memory *is* distortion since memory is invariably and inevitably selective. A way of seeing is a way of not seeing, a way of remembering is a way of forgetting, too.'

Still, we should not abandon the concept of distortion altogether. Rather, we should apply it reflexively. What will be viewed as a distortion from the perspective of either profession may be entirely legitimate in light of the distinct purposes of the other. Inevitably, the law will often treat past events in ways that will constitute distortion from the standpoint of historiography. But if courts distort history, so, too, historians can distort the law—often in ways that make lawyers howl or cringe.

The second source of skepticism about law's potential contribution to collective memory is the converse of the first. Just as we properly wonder whether liberal morality will be sacrificed in the interests of historical storytelling, we may also suspect that judges—when faithful to liberal law and professional ethics—may make poor historians and lousy storytellers. To be sure, Western legal scholarship and historiography initially set out, in the Middle Ages, on surprisingly parallel tracks, employing similar methods, seeking similar objectives.[20] But their professional paths have long since diverged in many ways.

Even so, one still encounters refreshing reminders of these common concerns. Good judges and historians continue to display similar virtues, argues Maier. 'Moderation, trustworthiness, common sense, sensitivity to context and the limits of human action, life experience, the capacity to address what is particular as well as what is general ... these comprise the catalogue of historiographical and jurisprudential virtues alike.'[21] The appeal of these virtues lingers on among both young and old, within both disciplines, despite all the disdain heaped upon them in recent decades by adherents of radical history, critical legal studies, and the economic analysis of law.

Both courts and (traditional) historians try to establish a measure of 'integrity' in the history of a community by linking events in its past with its present

---

[19] Michael Schudson, 'Dynamics of Distortion in Collective Memory', in *Memory Distortion: How Minds, Brains, and Societies Reconstruct the Past* 347 (Daniel L. Schacter ed., 1995).

[20] Donald R. Kelley, 'Clio and the Lawyers: Forms of Historical Consciousness in Medieval Jurisprudence', 5 *Medievalia et Humanistica* 25, 26–28 (1974).

[21] Maier, at 4. For a similarly Aristotelian defense of judicial virtue, see Anthony Kronman, *The Lost Lawyer* 53–108 (1993).

situation. This presents acute problems when judging administrative massacre. Can a single, coherent narrative be written of a nation's experience with large-scale massacre (by either judges or historians), when its members must be divided into perpetrators, victims, and bystanders, each with its own perspective on what happened?

Yes, answers Maier, despite the problems he acknowledges this entails. 'Historians and judges presuppose an underlying community, even one at war with itself. Therein, too, lies their shared challenge.'[22] The question, however, is whether their common presupposition is defensible, and if so, on what basis.

To influence collective memory through legal proceedings, it is helpful for prosecutors to be familiar with accepted genres of story telling. In other words, prosecutors must discover how to couch the trial's doctrinal narrative within genre conventions already in place within the particular society.[23] These conventions are by no means universal and will often require some rather fine-grained 'local knowledge' of the plot structures of the various story types cultivated in a given culture.

For instance, a prosecution of Emperor Hirohito could easily have been staged—without distortion of brute facts—to draw upon the dramatic conventions of Kabuki, within which the 'death of kings' is a recurrent and evocative theme.[24] Attentiveness to cultural particularities of this sort, however, is a virtue for which liberal legal and political theory—with its longings for Enlightenment universalism—have not always evinced sufficient respect. In fact, by ignoring the lawyers on their team, Occupation authorities in Japan proved quite savvy in formulating several key policies, even the most transformative, in terms of existing indigenous concepts and categories.[25]

The promise of liberal storytelling will quickly founder if it turns out that the very things that make the story *liberal*—its moral universalism or impartial detachment, for instance—deprive its characters of the concreteness and particularity that make a good *story*, a vivid yarn. It is the vivid particularity of characters and events in good literature that makes it singularly apt as a setting

---

[22] Maier, at 5.

[23] Bernard S. Jackson, 'Narrative Theories and Legal Discourse', in *Narrative in Culture* 23, 30 (Christopher Nash ed., 1990) ('Every society...has its own stock of substantive narratives, which represent typical human behavior patterns known and understood...This is the form in which social knowledge is acquired and stored, and which provides the framework for understanding particular stories presented to us in discourse.').

[24] Massao Yamaguchi, 'Kingship, Theatricality, and Marginal Reality in Japan', in *Text and Context: The Social Anthropology of Tradition* 151, 169–75 (Ravindra K. Jain ed., 1977).

[25] Japanese historian Ienaga Saburō reports, for instance, that for scholars like himself, 'cooperation with the Occupation's policy for reforming the teaching of history was an unexpected opportunity to put previously held beliefs into practice'. Arthur E. Tiedemann, 'Japan Sheds Dictatorship', in *From Dictatorship to Democracy: Coping with the Legacies of Authoritarianism and Totalitarianism* 179, 194 (John H. Herz, ed., 1982). Conversely, Tiedemann adds: 'For almost every proposed reform there was found a Japanese who long before the occupation had developed a commitment to the concept involved.'

for Aristotelian ethics, that is, for its teaching and analytical development.[26] In contract, *liberal* theory has rarely placed comparable emphasis on the particularities of historical context or individual character.

The common law method of Anglo-American courts, of course, has always prized judicial 'situation sensitivity' to the infinite factual variation in the configurations presented by particular disputes.[27] But the sensitivity of liberal jurisprudence to particularity is driven by concerns with being fair and just, not with being spellbinding. The two aims may well be at odds, as many have long supposed. Justice requires predictability, as through like treatment of like cases; a compelling story, by contrast, requires an ever-present element of surprise, to keep the listener on edge.

The solution to this problem would be simple if we could accept Durkheim's account of how criminal trials contribute to social solidarity. What sustains public attentiveness to such trials, on his account, is not any uncertainty about their likely result (or even morbid curiosity about their grisly details). In fact, any great uncertainty of this kind could easily vitiate the retributive sentiments of resentment and indignation against the accused that such proceedings are to evoke among the public. In support of Durkheim's view, there is little evidence the general public much cares for unpredictability in its favored narratives or for psychological complexity in the characters who people them. After all, it is generally not terribly difficult to anticipate the conclusion of most popular novels or television dramas. Nor is complex 'character development' exactly the strength of, say, John Grisham's novels.[28]

Although eminently predictable and populated by stick-figure characters, such narratives maintain the attention of millions of readers and viewers every day. This simply could not occur if much particularity of character or uncertainty of result were necessary to make a story compelling for most audiences, as Gallie and Nussbaum imply. If stories must capture the popular imagination before they can foster social solidarity, the most simplistic of narratives have little trouble in doing so. The problem, for present purposes, is precisely that trials for administrative massacre typically lack the simplicity of plot, charger, and *denouement* that most popular narratives involve—and seem to require for their very popularity.

Eichmann's character traits *alone* have evoked thousand of pages of scholarly commentary, much of it confessedly perplexed, beginning with Arendt's observations of his trial. Moreover, the panoramic sweep of the events at issue precludes

---

[26] Martha C. Nussbaum, *Love's Knowledge: Essays on Philosophy and Literature* 148–67 (1990).

[27] On the judicial virtue of 'situation sense', see Karl N. Llewellyn, *The Common Law Tradition: Deciding Appeals* 60–61 (1960).

[28] Michiko Katutani, 'Chasing Ambulances Before Dreams', *N.Y. Times*, April 28, 1995, at C33 (reviewing John Grisham, *The Rainmaker* (1995), and commenting on 'the leadenness of Mr. Grisham's prose, the banality of his characters and the shocking predictability of his story').

the defendant from continuously occupying center stage. Arendt stated the problem succinctly:

A show trial needs even more urgently than an ordinary trial a limited and well-defined outline of what was done and how it was done. In the center of the trial can only be the one who did—in this respect, he is like the hero in the play....[29]

The discursive account of how criminal trials contribute to social solidarity can more easily accommodate the complexity of character and uncertainty of result that make for great literature, according to Gallie and Nussbaum. These very complexities and uncertainties become the object of day-to-day curiosity and concern, the subject of private discussion and public debate, consistent with the ideal of discursive democracy. The question, however, is whether such lengthy and complex tales can sustain the public's interest at all, or for very long, that is, whether Durkheimian desires for moral certainty and narrative closure will assert themselves prematurely. The record here is quite mixed, allowing little empirical basis for generalization.

Are Liberal Stories Boring?

By nature, many non-liberals suspect, liberal stories (and, by implication, liberal lives) must be boring. This is due to the procedural scrupulousness with which liberal law protects the rights of the villain, against whom the audience's collective conscience could otherwise be unrestrainedly loosed.[30] If liberal stories carry any dramatic power, it may be precisely because of their understatement, because of judicial aversion to self-conscious dramaturgy. To some extent, at least, it is the very absence of declamatory histrionics that make such stories compelling, when recounted in their quiet, impersonal way by judicial opinions.[31]

But, compelling to whom, one must ask? To liberal jurisprudents alone? The criminal law may present a dramatic persona of either majesty or sobriety. Uncertainty between the two, over how justice should protect its public image, has long informed our assumptions about the proper rhetorical style of legal argument and opinion-writing, even of courthouse architecture.

---

[29] Hannah Arendt, *Eichmann in Jerusalem: A Report on the Banality of Evil* 9 (Penguin Books, rev. & enlarged ed. 1977) (1963); see also B. Jackson, at 29 (describing an empirical study of juror receptivity to competing accounts which found that 'as structural ambiguities in stories increased, credibility decreased, and vice versa').

[30] An argument to this effect is offered by Francis Fukuyama, *The End of History and the Last Man* 288–89, 312 (1992). But see Richard E. Flathman, *Willful Liberalism* (1992) (arguing for a more spirited, creative ideal of liberal personhood); Nancy L. Rosenblum, *Another Liberalism* (1987) (same).

[31] On the impersonal character of legal authority in modern Western society, see *Max Weber on Law in Economy and Society* 301–21 (1967).

Lacking the majesty of traditional rituals of state power, however, liberal-legal stories may become dull. Experience of prosecutions for administrative massacre suggests, in particular, that liberal-legal stories are likely to dwell on what many listeners regard as meaningless minutiae.[32] Novelist Rebecca West, covering the first 'historic' Nuremberg Trial for *The New Yorker*, found it insufferably tedious.[33] Her reaction was not uncommon. In orchestrating such a trial there may be some trade-off between the goals of didactic spectacle and adherence to liberal principle. Yet one should not exclude the possibility that the trial may fail in both respects. Nuremberg (and, even more, the Tokyo trial) appear to have been both boring and illiberal at once, on many accounts.

One is thus led to question whether it was really the principled commitment of such proceedings to liberalism that made them fail as social drama, any more than a principled commitment to dullness could have made them liberal. The dramaturgical decisions that made them dull do not seem to be ones that made the proceedings any more consistent with liberal legality. At the very least, no one has ever begun to demonstrate such a connection.

There is nothing necessarily illiberal in the efforts of courts and prosecutors to give a little thought to props and decor, *mise en scène* and pacing of action, character development and narrative framing, stage and audience.[34] Hannah Arendt's dismay at Eichmann's 'banality' betrayed a disappointment that the defendant, in refusing 'to play the villain', failed to provide the dramatic tension for which she had hoped. The prosecutor, in his preoccupation with painting a larger tableau, failed to keep his *dramatis persona* at center stage.

Also, when a politically resonant ritual is called for, it seems that lawyers often make poor performers. One historian even argues that medieval Italy's reliance on lawyers for its historical records and myths of origin, rather than on the superior narrative skills of clerics and chroniclers (common elsewhere in medieval Europe) seriously undermined the public legitimacy of its kings.[35] Social theorists from Weber to Foucault, moreover, contend that as Western law became ever more rational, formalized, and demystified, public trials and punishments increasingly lost their capacity to serve as spectacles, to enchant

---

[32] Even prosecutor Taylor conceded, regarding the first Nuremberg Trial: 'As month after month passed... [the] press and public lost interest in the case as a "spectacle".' He immediately adds, significantly, that 'the judicial foundations of the trial were strengthened by this very fact'. Telford Taylor, 'The Nuremberg War Crimes Trials', *Int'l Conciliation Papers*, April 1949, at 243, 262.

[33] Rebecca West, 'Extraordinary Exile', *New Yorker*, September 7, 1946, at 34; see, also, Joseph E. Persico, *Nuremberg: Infamy on Trial* 203 (1994) ('The papers back home were no longer giving heavy daily play to a trial that, no matter how sensational the evidence, had already gone on for six weeks. Reporters had begun scrambling for fresh angles.').

[34] John R. Brown, *Effective Theatre* (1969); George McCalmon and Christian Moe, *Creating Historical Drama* (1965).

[35] Chris Wickham, 'Lawyers Time: History and Memory in Tenth- and Eleventh-Century Italy', in *Studies in Medieval History* 53, 70 (Henry Mayr-Hartig and R. I. Moore eds., 1985).

and captivate the public imagination by evoking deeply shared moods and sensibilities.[36]

Worse yet, prosecutors may labor under a particularly onerous burden, relative to defense counsel, in dramatizing their favored narrative, allowing their adversary more easily to capture the public eye and imagination. In the Barbie trial, for instance, prosecutors rightly believed that 'an unpaid debt to the dead bound them to the truth'.[37] Barbie's defense counsel, 'on the other hand was free. No debt tied him to the past; he was in a position to plant suspense in the very heart of the ceremony of remembering and to substitute the delicious thrill of the event'—especially the threat to reveal the pro-German complicity of currently prominent figures in French public life—'for the meticulous reassessment of the facts'.[38]

The upshot was that the press and public, like Finkielkraut himself, quickly tired of the prosecution and plaintiffs, (the interveners, Barbie's surviving victims), due to 'the thirty-nine lawyers whose thirty-nine closing speeches talked the audience into stupor' over a nine-day period.[39] 'Instead of making an impression, they made people yawn. Rather than satisfying the appetite for the new, they rehashed, ad nauseam, the same tired formulas.'[40]

Accounts of the Barbie trial by even the most scrupulously liberal commentators and scholars have been more deeply drawn into the mental universe of defense counsel, Jacques Vergès, with 'his promise of scandal, his steamy reputation, and his consummate art of mystery', the qualities for which he came to be 'adulated in the media'.[41] Even so discerning an observer as Todorov was clearly persuaded by much of Vergès argument against the trial's rendition of French history. He observes, for instance, 'it's a fact that Barbie tortured Resistance fighters, but they did the same when they got their hands on a Gestapo officer.

---

[36] *From Max Weber: Essays in Sociology* 352–57 (H. H. Gerth and C. Wright Mills eds., trans., 1948) (observing the historical trend toward 'disenchantment' of political authority and legal ritual); Michel Foucault, *Discipline and Punish* 32–72 (Alan Sheridan trans., Vintage Books, 1979) (1975) (describing how 'the spectacle of the scaffold' was gradually displaced by a more diffuse system of 'carceral' surveillance, whose rituals of social control were less dramatic).

[37] Alain Finkielkraut, *Remembering in Vain: The Klaus Barbie Trial and Crimes Against Humanity* 65 (1992).

[38] Id. Legal rules contributed directly to the problem in at least one small way. French law, like English common law until about 150 years ago, exempts the criminal defendant from any duty to swear on oath. The result, as presiding Judge Boulard at Touvier's trial put it, is that 'only the accused has the right to lie'. Quoted in Henry Rousso, 'What Historians Will Retain from the Last Trial of the Purge', in Golsan, at 165.

[39] Finkelkraut, at 63.

[40] Id. at 65.

[41] Id. at 66. Despite his best efforts to elude ensnarement by Vergès's rhetorical stratagems, Finkielkraut—a philosophical journalist of liberal inspiration—clearly is no less entranced by Barbie's lawyer, on whom his book largely centers, than he is repulsed by him. Cf. Guyora Binder, 'Representing Nazism: Advocacy and Identity at the Trial of Klaus Barbie', 98 *Yale L.J.* 1321, 1355–72 (1989) (lavishing enormous attention on Vergès's defense strategy and its postmodernist implications, and noting, at 1356, that 'Vergès is known for his effective use of the media as a forum for his controversial clients' views').

The French army, moreover, systematically resorted to torture after 1944, in Algeria, for example; no one has ever been condemned for crimes against humanity as a result.'[42]

Selective enforcement of this sort violates the principle of equal protection, Todorov contends. Thus, he is not saying that the 'bad guys' have good arguments only when the public spotlight is shifted from strictly legal questions to ones of historical interpretation. He also suggests that when courts seek to write national history, the law's own purposes easily come to be mocked.

Boredom as such is, then, by no means the most serious problem here. The problem is that boredom tends to settle selectively upon the shoulders of those whose story is most truthful, most faithful to the past, and most vital to a legal cultivation of liberal memory. In Barnes's fictional (but entirely plausible, even compelling) treatment of such a trial,[43] the former dictator gets all the best lines, successfully upstaging and embarrassing the public prosecutor at key points. In fact, the facility with which this diversion, this hijacking of narrative direction can be decisively accomplished—once traditional procedural and evidentiary rules are relaxed (to enable judicial rewriting of the period's official story)—is a recurrent feature of such trials, evidenced most recently in that of Saddam Hussein.

What, then, is the response to the suspicion that liberal stories must fail as public pedagogy because, insofar as they focus on a simple 'moral', they are sure to drive people from the courtroom, or from 'court TV'?

First, many stories—from nursery tales to *Star Wars* movies—adopt a simple view of morality, yet succeed in winning the hearts of large publics, of all ages. Second, liberal stories do not have to be conceived as straightforward homilies. Their morality need not be stark and simplistic. The best stories, liberal and otherwise, almost always involve dilemmatic situations, where the central character is constrained by circumstance to do wrong, to some degree, any way she turns.[44] Her moral problem then becomes how to minimize such wrongdoing.

Resolving that problem turns out to require situational judgment regarding the weight of competing principles at stake. Exercising such judgment is, of course, difficult and complex. This very complexity is often what engages us as listeners, drawing us into the character's world by way of empathy with her and the difficulty of the choice she must make. When courts tell the first, simpler kind of tale with success, they foster Durkheim's mechanical solidarity. When they tell the second, more complex sort of story, they can further discursive solidarity. Which type of story they should try to tell in a given case depends on the circumstances at hand.

[42] Tzvetan Todorov, 'The Touvier Trial', in Golsan, at 169, 176. See also Todorov, 'The Abuses of Memory', 1 *Common Knowledge* 6, 23–25 (1996).

[43] Julian Barnes, *The Porcupine* (1992).

[44] For example, see Shklar's analysis of 'Rosa', the central character in Nadine Gordimer's *Burger's Daughter* (1979). Judith N. Shklar, *Ordinary Vices* 21–22 (1984).

Misfocusing on Minutiae

Judicial assessment of men like Eichmann and Argentine General Videla often seems to place question at the center of legal analysis that, from any other stand-point, would surely be of marginal concern. Distortions in collective memory of administrative massacre would thus follow if courts were to train public attention upon such purely professional concerns.[45] For instance, the Argentine prosecutors and judges felt professionally obligated to occupy themselves for a considerable time with establishing the juntas' liability for such offenses as forgery and property theft.[46] This was surely a curious and digressive inclusion in a proceeding whose drama was presumably to center upon a condemnation of the unrepentant slaughter of thousands.

In the Nuremberg Trial, such misfocus arose because the London Charter had given jurisdiction to the International Military Tribunal not for all Nazi crimes against humanity, but only for those undertaken in preparation for, and in service of aggressive war.[47] This jurisdictional peculiarity required prosecutors to weave the Holocaust into a larger story that was primarily about perverted militarism. Justice Robert H. Jackson (Unites States Chief Prosecution Counsel) thus argued that 'the crime against the Jews, insofar as it is a crime against humanity and not a war crime as well, is one which we indict *because of* its close association with the crime against peace'.[48]

This way of framing the story seemed to imply that the extermination of European Jewry had not been for the defendants a central end in itself, i.e., a central goal independent of its relation to aggressive war. In so arguing, Jackson unwittingly perpetrated what would be viewed only a few years later as a severe historical distortion. To maintain his indictment within the Tribunal's restricted jurisdiction, Jackson was led to argue that 'the Jews .... were used as exemplars of Nazi discipline; and their persecution eliminated an obstacle to aggressive war'.

His reasoning, of course, is question-begging—how can such annihilation be understood as a 'measure in preparation for war'?—and historically suspect. Scholars of the Holocaust have amply demonstrated how ethnic genocide not only did not serve any military end, but caused the channeling away of critical resources from the war effort. Yet, the very vulnerabilities of Jackson's argument highlights his attempts to translate Nazi crimes into an idiom familiar to the law,

---

[45] Henry Rousso, 'Ce que les historiens retiendront des vingt-trois journées du process', *Libération*, April 20, 1994, at 4–5 (observing that 'the Touvier trial was meant to be an important lesson in history, yet it sometimes got stuck in the quagmire of infinite details relative to the facts or to judicial definitions, making one lose sight of the general picture').

[46] Interview with Judge Andrés D'Alessio, in Buenos Aires, Argentina (August 1987).

[47] William J. Bosch, *Judgment on Nuremberg: American Attitudes Toward the Major German War-Crimes Trials* 119 (1970).

[48] XIX *International Military Tribunal* 470–71 (1946).

and to enlist the evidence of such atrocities into an argument about renegade militarism.[49]

It is true that prosecutors explicitly referred to other causes of the Holocaust. But given the Tribunal's delimited jurisdiction, such references were irrelevant, perhaps even exculpatory, in their legal import. That these other explanations nonetheless found their way into the prosecution's narrative confirms a central point of this study: that if courts are to influence collective memory of such historical episodes in persuasive ways, they must admit a wider range of evidence and argument than are often cognizable within strictly legal terms. Otherwise, the reality they seek to construct is likely to serve very poorly as a plausible and compelling basis for rewriting the national story. In fact, it borders on the obscene to resolve so historiographically momentous and morally weighty a question as 'the cause of the Holocaust'—for purposes of collective memory—on the basis of so narrow and peculiarly professional a preoccupation as the terms of a treaty's jurisdictional provision.

Moreover, by indicting the Nuremberg defendants for the offense of 'conspiracy' (to wage aggressive war), Allied prosecutors appeared to adopt a particular historical interpretation—a 'conspiratorial view of history'—one that (by its particular implausibility) threatened to discredit the trial's potential contribution to collective memory.[50] In their public statements, prosecutors labored to explain the meaning of conspiracy in legal doctrine and to distinguish it as a term of art from the more conventional understanding prevalent among historians and the wider public.

Judging from contemporaneous accounts, such efforts at public explanation, however conscientious, were largely unsuccessful.[51] These efforts also cast the profession in the unappealing position of appearing to lecture others about the 'true' meaning of a concept that most listeners were quite convinced they already understood. This discrepancy between lay and legal understandings of conspiracy worked to discredit the conspiracy indictment and conviction of the Tokyo defendants even more than those at Nuremberg.[52] Much of the conduct of the Japanese simply could not be clearly characterized in laymen's terms as a 'conspiracy to wage aggressive war', considering the complex regional rivalries and balance of power politics (involving several major powers) preceding the war in the Pacific.[53] For many laymen, the idea of conspiracy inevitably evoked

---

[49] Lawrence Douglas, 'Film As Witness: Screening "Nazi Concentration Camps" Before the Nuremberg Tribunal', 105 *Yale L.J.* 449, 479 (1995).

[50] Judith N. Shklar, *Legalism* 172 (1964).

[51] Bosch, at 113.

[52] For one version of these definitional disparities, see Richard H. Minear, *Victors' Justice: The Tokyo War Crimes Trial* 128–33 (1971) (asserting that the Tokyo defendants' activities amounted to a legal conspiracy but not a historical, common-sense conspiracy).

[53] Conservative Japanese intellectuals have consistently argued, for instance, that Japan was forced to fight the United States and Britain after they imposed a blockade on oil imports. For

the vision of a small cabal, scheming together in a single room, plotting out the meticulous detail everything that would later transpire.[54]

But of course, 'history reveals on its every page the importance of contingencies—accidents, coincidences or other unforeseeable developments', as Gallie observes.[55] The legal concept of conspiracy, in its exceptional 'looseness and pliability',[56] fully acknowledges this fact, conceptually accommodating the need to disaggregate a lengthy period of activity by many contributors into a series of interlocking conspiracies, some of which may be characterized as a 'chain', others as a 'wheel'. Far from a rare and improbable scenario in human affairs, the legal concept of conspiracy is frequently over inclusive, and consequently unfair to defendants, as judges and legal scholars have long acknowledged.[57] Even so, careful historians generally conclude, as does Maier regarding the conspiracy trials of Italian terrorists in the late 1970s, that 'judicial proceedings tend to impose a coherence on fragmentary testimony, attributing a degree of intentionality and group organization in search for cohesive narrative and explanation'.[58]

Trials of administrative massacre have introduced still other distortions into historical understanding and, thereby, into collective memory. Early historiography of the Holocaust was based largely on the record assembled by Allied prosecutors. The prosecutors did not conceal their aspiration to do just that. Executive trial counsel at Nuremberg, Robert G. Story, spoke openly of this purpose: 'the making of a record of the Hitler regime which would withstand the test of history'.[59]

Wooed by the lawyers in this way, it is scarcely surprising that the first generation of postwar historians proved inattentive to the idiosyncratic nature of the law's concerns.[60] What came to be known among historians as 'the Nuremberg view' or as 'perpetrator history', for instance, focused almost exclusively on the

recent arguments to this effect by Japanese legal scholars, see C. Hosoya et al., 'Preface' to *The Tokyo War Crimes Trial: An International Symposium* 7, 8–9 (C. Hosoya et al., eds., 1986).

[54] On the receptivity of extremist political movements to conspiracy theories of this sort, see Richard Hofstadter, 'The Paranoid Style in American Politics', in *The Paranoid Style in American Politics and Other Essays* 3, 4–6, 35–39 (1965).

[55] W. B. Gallie, *Philosophy and Historical Understanding* 133 (1964).

[56] George E. Dix and M. Michael Sharlot, *Criminal Law: Cases and Materials* 582 (1987).

[57] See, e.g., *Krulewitch v. United States*, 336 U.S. 440, 445 (1949) (Jackson, J., concurring) (characterizing conspiracy as an 'elastic, sprawling and pervasive offense' that is typically employed when there is insufficient evidence to prosecute for the substantive offense).

[58] Maier, at 9.

[59] Hannah Arendt, *Eichmann in Jerusalem: A Report on the Banality of Evil* 253 (Penguin Books, rev. & enlarged ed. 1977) (1963).

[60] Browning notes, for instance, that for early postwar historiography, 'the evidentiary base was above all the German documents captured at the end of the war, which served . . . the prosecutors at postwar trials. The initial representation of the Holocaust perpetrators was that of criminal minds, infected with racism and anti-Semitism, carrying out criminal policies through criminal organizations.' Browning, at 26.

intentions and ideologies of top leaders, an emphasis understandably reflected in the record of the legal proceedings against them.[61]

The prosecution's preoccupation with the intentional acts of top figures followed naturally from its desire to convict such figures of particular criminal offenses. But it was neither natural nor inevitable that historians of the period should have concentrated their attention to similar effect. Historians followed the lawyers' lead in this regard not only because the lawyers' documents were those most readily available, but at least partly because the then-prevalent conception of 'the historian as neutral judge'[62] established a natural affinity between how courts and historians understood their respective callings. Only years later did historians come to realize how the evidential focus of the criminal proceedings had unwittingly skewed their analysis in favor of what came to be known as the 'intentionalist' interpretation of the period.[63] This focus subtly drew attention away from institutional dynamics and the 'machinery of destruction', particularly the crucial role of minor bureaucrats and functionaries at all levels of German society.[64]

The problem would have been aggravated if judges deliberately tried to make their stories compelling as monumental didactics, as national narrative. After all, 'successful narratives often foreground individual protagonists and antagonists rather than structures, trends, or social forces', Schudson notes.[65] Yet since individual leaders come and go, it is precisely such structures and forces—their analysis and critique—that should occupy the center state of public deliberation in the aftermath of large-scale administrative massacre.

As in Germany, the extent of public collaboration with Nazi policies has been discovered in France. These discoveries have compelled a similar reassessment of the initial focus of postwar French criminal courts on a few top elites. Despite early outbursts of mass vigilantism, criminal prosecutions in the years immediately following the war were limited to the most high-ranking Vichy officials and

---

[61] Id. at 26.

[62] Peter Novick, *That Noble Dream: The 'Objectivity Question' and the American Historical Profession* 596 (1988). On this view, 'the historian's conclusions are expected to display the standard judicial qualities of balance and evenhandedness. As with the judiciary, these qualities are guarded by the insulation of the historical profession from social pressure or political influence, and by the individual historian avoiding partisanship...', id. at 2.

[63] Historical debates came to be 'fought less by means of scholarly than legalistic arguments', one historian recently complained. 'The highly emotionalized debate about...whether a formal order by Hitler for the policy of genocide was necessary illuminates this tendency...', Hans Mommsen, 'Search for the "Lost History"? Observations on the Historical Self-Evidence of the Federal Republic', in *Forever in the Shadow of Hitler?* at 108, (James Knowlton and Truett Cates, eds. 1993).

[64] Browning, at 26–27; see, also, David Bankier, *The Germans and the Final Solution* 89–100 (1992); Christopher Browning, *Ordinary Men: Reserve Police Battalion 101 and the Final Solution in Poland*, at xvii (1992).

[65] Schudson, at 357.

intellectual defenders of Nazi collaboration.[66] The decision to confine the scope of legal retribution in this way reflected the Gaullist story that the French nation had been substantially united in opposition to German suzerainty.[67]

A leading French historian proudly proclaims that sophisticated scholars in his country have, in this century, almost entirely abandoned the antiquated notion of writing history in the pedagogic or epideictic mode. History, he implies, should not concern itself with ascribing praise or blame to individuals, but rather with tracking long-term social and institutional change.[68] Perhaps it is no coincidence, then, that it took the work of non-French historians, published decades after the war, to disprove the Gaullist myth of a nation united in Resistance, to demonstrate the pervasiveness of collaboration at many levels of French society.[69] It required two decades of litigation to compel correction of French schoolbooks, so that they would describe the roundup of Jews for deportation as an entirely French, not German, operation.[70]

For Historical 'Balance', Against 'Moral Equivalence'

The interested public has often found historians' accounts more persuasive than those of the courts, particularly the Tokyo and Nuremberg courts. This is primarily because historians are seen to be more concerned with 'balance' in proportioning blame among all parties, including the courtroom accusers. To be sure, many historians today reject 'balance' as a professional ideal, finding it either impossible or undesirable.[71] Public perception of historiography's tasks,

[66] Herbert R. Lottman, *The Purge* 132–68 (1986); see, also, Diane Rubenstein, *What's Left?: The Ecole Normale Supérieure and the Right* 137–63 (1990) (describing the trials of collaborationist journalists and intellectuals).

[67] In his August 25, 1944 speech to liberated Paris, de Gaulle proclaimed that the city had been 'freed by itself, by its own people with the cooperation and support of the whole of France ... of the eternal France'. R. J. B. Bosworth, *Explaining Auschwitz and Hiroshima: History Writing and the Second World War, 1945–1990*, at 112 (1993).

[68] Pierre Nora, 'Between Memory and History: *Les Lieux de Mémoire*', 26 *Representations* 7, 11–12 (1989).

[69] Bertram M. Gordon, *Collaborationism in France During the Second World War* (1980); John F. Sweets, *Choices in Vichy France: The French Under Nazi Occupation* (1986). See generally Michael R. Marrus and Robert O. Paxton, *Vichy France and the Jews* (1981) (describing how the French Vichy government 'energetically persecuted Jews' with policies that were 'usually supported by French public opinion'); Zeev Sternhell, *Neither Right Nor Left: Fascist Ideology in France* (1986) (describing the penetration of France by fascist ideas); Marcel Ophüls, *The Sorrow and the Pity* (1972) (discussing life in a French city under Nazi occupation). Such collaboration has only recently received official recognition. Marlise Simons, 'Chirac Affirms France's Guilt in Fate of Jews', *N.Y. Times*, July 17, 1995, at A1 (quoting French President Jacques Chirac officially affirming, for the first time, that 'the criminal folly of the occupiers was seconded by the French, by the French state'). Paxton and Gordon are American, Marrus is Canadian, Sternhell is Israeli, and Ophüls is a German Jew.

[70] Judith Miller, *One, By One, By One: Facing the Holocaust*, 145 (1990).

[71] Novick, at 264–91, 421–62, 603–5.

however, still largely cleaves to this traditional ideal, as reflected in the remarks of Galtieri and Massera.

Even avowedly leftist historians sometimes embrace the traditional ideal, at least when asked to serve as judges. Staughton Lynd, for instance, declined Bertrand Russell's invitation to sit on an international tribunal judging alleged US war crimes in Vietnam.

What I ask is that it [the tribunal] inquire into the acts of both sides and use the same criteria in evaluating the acts of one side that it sues in evaluating the acts of the other ... I believe that [what Russell proposes] amounts to judging one side (the NLF) by its ends, the other side (the United States) by its means. Precisely this double standard is what I had thought all of us, in this post-Stalin era, wished to avoid.[72]

Realizing that the tribunal would be trying to write history, a task to which his desired participation was designed to contribute, Lynd invoked the historian's traditional professional ideal of balance, contrasting it with the tribunal's more partisan agenda.

For the Nuremberg and Tokyo courts, it mattered little to the validity of criminal proceedings against Axis leadership that Allied victors had committed vast war crimes of their own.[73] Unlike the law of tort, criminal law has virtually no place for 'comparative fault', no doctrinal device for mitigating the wrongdoing or culpability of the accused in light of the accusers'. Proposals to move criminal law very far in this direction rightly strike virtually all sensible people as quixotic, if not perverse.[74]

For the public, however, particularly in postwar Japan and West Germany, and among conservative Argentines, it mattered *greatly* in gauging the legitimacy of the trials that they seemed tendentiously selective, aimed at focusing memory in partisan ways. It mattered for such listeners that the defendants in all these episodes of administrative massacre had constituted only a single side to a two- or multi-sided conflict, one in which other parties had similarly committed unlawful acts on a large scale. This unsavory feature of the Nuremberg judgment has undermined its authority in the minds of many, weakening its normative weight. When Nuremberg's relevance of the dirty war as legal precedent was pointed out to him, for instance, one Argentine general observed: 'Yes, but if the Germans

---

[72] Staughton Lynd, 'The War Crimes Tribunal: A Dissent', 12 *Liberation*, December 1967–January 1968, at 76–77. A leader of anti-war protests, Lynd taught history at Yale and wrote such early works as *American Labor Radicalism* (1973) and *Class Conflict, Slavery, and the United States* (1968). He later became a labor lawyer and community activist.

[73] Hans J. Morgenthau, *Politics Among Nations* 218–19 (1954). Allied war crimes prominently include the saturation and fire bombing of civilian population centers without discriminating between military and non-combatant targets.

[74] For such proposals, see, e.g., K. N. Hylton, 'Optimal Law Enforcement and Victim's Precaution', 27 *Rand Journal of Economics* 97 (1996) (arguing that often people become victims of crime because they have foolishly underinvested in their own protection) and Gary Becker, 'Crime and Punishment: An Economic Approach', 76 *Journal of Political Economy* 1690 (1968).

had won the war, the trials would have been held not at Nuremberg, but in Virginia.'[75] He was surely right.

Law's Role in 'Mastering the Past'

The law played a significant role in the process of 'mastering the past'. The 1964 prosecution of the Auschwitz guards, and of similar Majdanek officials between 1975 and 1981 for crimes against humanity, captured the imagination of millions of young Germans as virtually nothing about the country's past had done before.[76] 'The effect upon the public consciousness was devastating,' writes Gordon Craig, 'and has not diminished.'[77] The Auschwitz prosecution, concurs Ian Buruma, 'was the one history lesson...that stuck'.[78] The foreign attention focused on these trials was no less consequential, for they prompted the 1964 French enactment removing the statute of limitations for crimes against humanity. That change would permit the prosecution of Barbie and Touvier over two decades later.[79]

In German public awareness, these trials effected a symbolic severing of ties to the past.[80] They evoked and articulated pervasive sentiments of indignation and reprobation, in a way that criminal prosecutions can do with particular efficacy. The memory of judgment by the international community continues to weigh heavily upon the making of German Foreign policy in particular, according to specialists in that field.

The lesson would seem to be that a nation *can* be united and guided not only in the collective memory of its triumphs, but also in shared expiation for its wrongs, in the common commitment neither to forget nor repeat the injustices its predecessors have inflicted on their neighbors. Habermas offers a ringing defense of this conclusion, while alluding to legal concepts of continuity and judgment:

Can one become the legal successor to the German Reich and continue the traditions of German culture without taking on historical liability for the form of life in which Auschwitz was possible? Is there any way to bear the liability for the context in which such crimes originated...other than through remembrance, practiced in solidarity, of

---

[75] Quoted in the remarks of Judge Andés D'Alessio. Tape of 'Human Rights and Deliberative Democracy: A Conference in Honor of Carlos Santiago Nino', Presented at Yale Law School (September 23–24, 1994).

[76] Hannah Arendt, 'Introduction' to Bernd Naumann, *Auschwitz: A Report on the Proceedings Against Robert Ludwig Mulka and Others Before the Court at Frankfurt* xi, xi (1966); Aleksander Lasik, 'Postwar Prosecution of the Auschwitz SS', in *Anatomy of the Auschwitz Death Camp* 588 (Yisrael Gutman and Michael Berenbaum, eds., 1994).

[77] Gordon Craig, 'An Inability to Mourn', *N.Y. Rev. Books*, July 14, 1994, at 44.

[78] Buruma, at 149.

[79] Tony Judt, 'The Past Is Another Country: Myth and Memory in Postwar Europe', *Daedalus*, 83, 97 (Fall 1992).

[80] These trials became a means by which Germany's 'present is to be separated from what preceded it by an act of unequivocal demarcation'. Paul Connerton, *How Societies Remember* 7 (1989).

what cannot be made good, other than through a reflexive, scrutinizing attitude toward one's own identify-forming traditions?[81]

Such invocation of legal language as relevant to historical assessment drew particularly acerbic reproach from Habermas's opponents, who accused him, for instance, of 'making himself solicitor general of the kingdom of morality in the province of history', and assigning historiographical matters to a 'special court, to which the accused must be extradited'.[82]

What Habermas describes as 'a reflective scrutinizing attitude toward one's own identity-forming traditions' was embraced by President Alfonsín as a central objective of the junta trial and, in fact, of his administration. Attending the trial, Owen Fiss would thus herald it as 'an exercise in self-examination', revealing 'the nobility of a great nation, prepared to judge itself'. This is precisely the central and legitimate purpose of liberal show trials.

---

[81] Jürgen Habermas, 'On the Public Use of History', in *The New Conservatism*, 236 (Shierry W. Nicholsen ed., trans., 1989).

[82] Helmut Fleischer, 'The Morality of History: On the Dispute About the Past That Will Not Pass', in *Forever in the Shadow of Hitler?* at 83.

PART IV
APPENDICES

APPENDIX 1

St. James Declaration, June 12, 1941

INTER-ALLIED MEETING

HELD IN LONDON AT ST. JAMES'S PALACE ON JUNE 12, 1941

Resolution

The Governments of the United Kingdom of Great Britain and Northern Ireland, Canada, Australia, New Zealand and South Africa, the Government of Belgium, the Provisional Czechoslovak Government, the Governments of Greece, Luxemburg, the Netherlands, Norway, Poland and Yugoslavia, and the Representatives of General de Gaulle, leader of Free Frenchmen,

Engaged together in the fight against aggression,

Are resolved

1. That they will continue the struggle against German or Italian oppression until victory is won, and will mutually assist each other in this struggle to the utmost of their respective capacities;
2. That there can be no settled peace and prosperity so long as free peoples are coerced by violence into submission to domination by Germany or her associates, or live under the threat of such coercion;
3. That the only true basis of enduring peace is the willing co-operation of free peoples in a world in which, relieved of the menace of aggression, all may enjoy economic and social security; and that it is their intention to work together, and with other free peoples, both in war and peace to this end.

Source: *Trial of War Criminals Before the Nuernberg Military Tribunal under Control Council Law No. 10*, vol. xv, *Procedure, Practice and Administration* (Washington, DC: Government Printing Office, 1946–1949).

APPENDIX 2

The Moscow Conference and Declaration, October–November 1943

JOINT FOUR-NATION DECLARATION

The governments of the United States of America, United Kingdom, the Soviet Union, and China;

United in their determination, in accordance with the declaration by the United Nations of January, 1942, and subsequent declarations, to continue hostilities against those Axis powers with which they respectively are at war until such powers have laid down their arms on the basis of unconditional surrender;

Conscious of their responsibility to secure the liberation of themselves and the peoples allied with them from the menace of aggression;

Recognizing the necessity of insuring a rapid and orderly transition from war to peace and of establishing and maintaining international peace and security with the least diversion of the world's human and economic resources for armaments;

Jointly declare:

1. That their united action, pledged for the prosecution of the war against their respective enemies, will be continued for the organization and maintenance of peace and security.

2. That those of them at war with a common enemy will act together in all matters relating to the surrender and disarmament of that enemy.

3. That they will take all measures deemed by them to be necessary to provide against any violation of the terms imposed upon the enemy.

4. That they recognize the necessity of establishing at the earliest practicable date a general international organization, based on the principle of the sovereign equality of all peace-loving states, and open to membership by all such states, large and small, for the maintenance of international peace and security.

5. That for the purpose of maintaining international peace and security pending the re-establishment of law and order and the inauguration of a system of general security they will consult with one another and as occasion requires with other members of the United Nations, with a view to joint action on behalf of the community of nations.

6. That after the termination of hostilities they will not employ their military forces within the territories of other states except for the purposes envisaged in this declaration and after joint consultation.

7. That they will confer and cooperate with one another and with other members of the United Nations to bring about a practicable general agreement with respect to the regulation of armaments in the post-war period.

DECLARATION REGARDING ITALY

The Foreign Secretaries of the United States, the United Kingdom and the Soviet Union have established that their three governments are in complete agreement that Allied policy toward Italy must be based upon the fundamental principle that Fascism and all its evil influence and configuration shall be completely destroyed and that the Italian people shall be given every opportunity to establish governmental and other institutions based on democratic principles.

The Foreign Secretaries of the United States and the United Kingdom declare that the action of their governments from the inception of the invasion of Italian territory, in so far as paramount military requirements have permitted, has been based upon this policy.

In furtherance of this policy in the future the Foreign Secretaries of the three governments are agreed that the following measures are important and should be put into effect:

1. It is essential that the Italian Government should be made more democratic by inclusion of representatives of those sections of the Italian people who have always opposed Fascism.

2. Freedom of speech, of religious worship, of political belief, of press and of public meeting, shall be restored in full measure to the Italian people, who shall be entitled to form anti-Fascist political groups.

3. All institutions and organizations created by the Fascist regime shall be suppressed.

4. All Fascist or pro-Fascist elements shall be removed from the administration and from institutions and organizations of a public character.

5. All political prisoners of the Fascist regime shall be released and accorded full amnesty.

6. Democratic organs of local government shall be created.

7. Fascist chiefs and army generals known or suspected to be war criminals shall be arrested and handed over to justice.

In making this declaration the three Foreign Secretaries recognize that so long as active military operations continue in Italy the time at which it is possible to give full effect to the principles stated above will be determined by the Commander-in-Chief on the basis of instructions received through the combined chiefs of staff.

The three governments, parties to this declaration, will, at the request of any one of them, consult on this matter. It is further understood that nothing in this resolution is to operate against the right of the Italian people ultimately to choose their own form of government.

DECLARATION ON AUSTRIA

The governments of the United Kingdom, the Soviet Union and the United States of America are agreed that Austria, the first free country to fall a victim to Hitlerite aggression, shall be liberated from German domination.

They regard the annexation imposed on Austria by Germany on March 15, 1938, as null and void. They consider themselves as in no way bound by any charges effected in Austria since that date. They declare that they wish to see re-established a free and independent Austria and thereby to open the way for the Austrian people themselves, as well as those neighboring States which will be faced with similar problems, to find that political and economic security which is the only basis for lasting peace. Austria is reminded, however, that she has a responsibility, which she cannot evade, for participation in the war at the side of Hitlerite Germany, and that in the final settlement account will inevitably be taken of her own contribution to her liberation.

STATEMENT ON ATROCITIES

SIGNED BY PRESIDENT ROOSEVELT, PRIME MINISTER CHURCHILL AND PREMIER STALIN

The United Kingdom, the United States and the Soviet Union have received from many quarters evidence of atrocities, massacres and cold-blooded mass executions which are being perpetrated by Hitlerite forces in many of the countries they have overrun and from which they are now being steadily expelled. The brutalities of Nazi domination are no new thing, and all peoples or territories in their grip have suffered from the worst form of government by terror. What is new is that many of the territories are now being redeemed by the advancing armies of the liberating powers, and that in their desperation the recoiling Hitlerites and Huns are redoubling their ruthless cruelties. This is now evidenced with particular clearness by monstrous crimes on the territory of the Soviet Union which is being liberated from Hitlerites, and on French and Italian territory.

Accordingly, the aforesaid three Allied powers, speaking in the interest of the thirty-two United Nations, hereby solemnly declare and give full warning of their declaration as follows:

At the time of granting of any armistice to any government which may be set up in Germany, those German officers and men and members of the Nazi party who have been responsible for or have taken a consenting part in the above atrocities, massacres and executions will be sent back to the countries in which their abominable deeds were done in order that they may be judged and punished according to the laws of these liberated countries and of free governments which will be erected therein. Lists will be compiled in all possible detail from all these countries having regard especially to invaded parts of the Soviet Union, to Poland and Czechoslovakia, to Yugoslavia and Greece including Crete and other islands, to Norway, Denmark, Netherlands, Belgium, Luxembourg, France and Italy.

Thus, Germans who take part in wholesale shooting of Polish officers or in the execution of French, Dutch, Belgian or Norwegian hostages or Cretan peasants, or who have shared in slaughters inflicted on the people of Poland or in territories of the Soviet Union which are now being swept clear of the enemy, will know they will be brought back to the scene of their crimes and judged on the spot by the peoples whom they have outraged.

Let those who have hitherto not imbrued their hands with innocent blood beware lest they join the ranks of the guilty, for most assuredly the three Allied powers will pursue them to the uttermost ends of the earth and will deliver them to their accusors in order that justice may be done.

The above declaration is without prejudice to the case of German criminals whose offenses have no particular geographical localization and who will be punished by joint decision of the government of the Allies.

Source: A Decade of American Foriegn Policy: Basic Documents, 1941–49, Prepared at the request of the Senate Committee on Foreign Relations by the Staff of the Committee and the Department of State (Washington, DC : Government Printing Office, 1950).

The London Agreement, August 8, 1945

London, August 8, 1945

Agreement by the Government of the USA, the Provisional Government of the French Republic, the Government of the UK of Great Britain and Northern Ireland and the Government of the USSR for the Prosecution and Punishment of the Major War Criminals of the European Axis.

Whereas the United Nations have from time to time made declarations of their intention that War Criminals shall be brought to justice;

And Whereas the Moscow Declaration of 10/30/1943 on German atrocities in Occupied Europe stated that those German Officers and men and members of the Nazi Party who have been responsible for or have taken a consenting part in atrocities and crimes will be sent back to the countries in which abominable deeds were done in order that they may be judged and punished according to the laws of these liberated countries and of the free Governments that will be created herein;

And Whereas this Declaration was stated to be without prejudice to the case of major criminals whose offenses have no particular geographical location and who will be punished by the joint decision of the Governments of the Allies; Now Therefore the Government of the United States of America, the Provisional Government of the French Republic, the Government of the United Kingdom of Great Britain and Northern Ireland and the Government of the Union of Soviet Socialist Republics (hereinafter called 'the Signatories') acting in the interests of all the United Nations and by their representatives duly authorized thereto have concluded this Agreement.

Article 1

There shall be established after consultation with the Control Council for Germany an International Military Tribunal for the trial of war criminals whose offences have no particular geographical location whether they be accused individually or in their capacity as members of organizations or groups or in both capacities.

Article 2

The constitution, jurisdiction and functions of the International Military Tribunal shall be those set out in the Charter annexed to this Agreement, which Charter shall form an integral part of this Agreement.

ARTICLE 3

Each of the Signatories shall take the necessary steps to make available for the investigation of the charges and trial the major war criminals detained by them who are to be tried by the International Military Tribunal. The Signatories shall also use their best endeavours to make available for investigation of the charges against and the trial before the International Military Tribunal such of the major war criminals as are not in the territories of any of the Signatories.

ARTICLE 4

Nothing in this Agreement shall prejudice the provisions established by the Moscow Declaration concerning the return of war criminals to the countries where they committed their crimes.

ARTICLE 5

Any Government of the United Nations may adhere to this agreement by notice given through the diplomatic channel to the Government of the United Kingdom, who shall inform the other signatory and adhering Governments of each such adherence.

ARTICLE 6

Nothing in this Agreement shall prejudice the jurisdiction or the powers of any national or occupation court established or to be established in an allied territory or in Germany for the trial of war criminals.

ARTICLE 7

This agreement shall come into force on the day of signature and shall remain in force for the period of one year and shall continue thereafter, subject to the right of any Signatory to give, through the diplomatic channel, one month's notice of intention to terminate it. Such termination shall not prejudice any proceedings already taken or any findings already made in pursuance of this Agreement.

In Witness Whereof the Undersigned have signed the present Agreement. Done in quadruplicate in London 8/8/1945 each in English, French and Russian, and each text to have equal authenticity.

For the Government of the United States of America, Robert H. Jackson.

For the Provisional Government of the French Republic, Robert Falco.

For the Government of the United Kingdom of Great Britain and Northern Ireland, C. Jowitt.

For the Government of the Union of Soviet Socialist Republics, I. Nikitchenko, A. Trainin.

APPENDIX 4

The Charter of the International Military Tribunal

I Constitution of the International Military Tribunal

Article 1

In pursuance of the Agreement signed on 8 August 1945 by the Government of the United States of America, the Provisional Government of the French Republic, the Government of the United Kingdom of Great Britain and Northern Ireland and the Government of the Union of Soviet Socialist Republics, there shall be established an International Military Tribunal (hereinafter called 'the Tribunal') for the just and prompt trial and punishment of the major war criminals of the European Axis.

Article 2

The Tribunal shall consist of four members, each with an alternate. One member and one alternate shall be appointed by each of the Signatories. The alternates shall, so far as they are able, be present at all sessions of the Tribunal. In case of illness of any member of the Tribunal or his incapacity or some other reason to fulfil his functions, his alternate shall take his place.

Article 3

Neither the Tribunal, its members nor their alternates can be challenged by the prosecution, or by the Defendants or their Counsel. Each Signatory may replace its member of the Tribunal or his alternate for reasons of health or for other good reasons, except that no replacement may take place during a Trial, other than by an alternate.

Article 4

(a) The presence of all four members of the Tribunal or the alternate for any absent member shall be necessary to constitute the quorum.
(b) The members of the Tribunal shall, before any trial begins, agree among themselves upon the selection from their number of a President, and the President shall hold office during that trial, or as may otherwise be agreed by a vote of not less

than three members. The principle of rotation of presidency for successive trials is agreed. If, however, a session of the Tribunal takes place in the territory of one of the four Signatories, the representative on that Signatory on the Tribunal shall preside.

(c) Save as aforesaid the Tribunal shall take decisions by a majority vote and in case the votes are evenly divided, the vote of the President shall be decisive: provided always that convictions and sentences shall only be imposed by affirmative votes of at least three members of the Tribunal.

ARTICLE 5

In case of need and depending on the number of the matters to be tried, other Tribunals may be set up; and the establishment, functions, and procedure of each Tribunal shall be identical, and shall be governed by this Charter.

II JURISDICTION AND GENERAL PRINCIPLES

ARTICLE 6

The Tribunal established by the Agreement referred to in Article 1 hereof for the trial and punishment of the major war criminals of the European Axis countries shall have the power to try and punish persons who, acting in the interests of the European Axis countries, whether as individuals or as members of organizations, committed any of the following crimes.

The following acts, or any of them, are crimes coming within the jurisdiction of the Tribunal for which there shall be individual responsibility:

(a) Crimes against peace: namely, planning, preparation, initiation or waging of a war of aggression, or a war in violation of international treaties, agreements or assurances, or participation in a common plan or conspiracy for the accomplishment of any of the foregoing;

(b) War crimes: namely, violations of the laws or customs of war. Such violations shall include, but not be limited to, murder, ill-treatment or deportation to slave labour or for any other purpose of civilian population of or in occupied territory, murder or ill-treatment of prisoners of war or persons on the seas, killing of hostages, plunder of public or private property, wanton destruction of cities, towns or villages, or devastation not justified by military necessity;

(c) Crimes against humanity: namely, murder, extermination, enslavement, deportation, and other inhumane acts committed against any civilian population, before or during the war; or persecutions on political, racial or religious grounds in execution of or in connection with any crime within the jurisdiction of the Tribunal, whether or not in violation of the domestic law of the country where perpetrated. [See protocol for correction of this paragraph.]

Leaders, organizers, instigators and accomplices participating in the formulation or execution of a common plan or conspiracy to commit any of the foregoing crimes are responsible for all acts performed by any persons in execution of such plan.

ARTICLE 7

The official position of defendants, whether as Heads of State or responsible officials in Government Departments, shall not be considered as freeing them from responsibility or mitigating punishment.

ARTICLE 8

The fact that the Defendant acted pursuant to order of his Government or of a superior shall not free him from responsibility, but may be considered in mitigation of punishment if the Tribunal determines that justice so requires.

ARTICLE 9

At the trial of any individual member of any group or organization the Tribunal may declare (in connection with any act of which the individual may be convicted) that the group or organization of which the individual was a member was a criminal organization.

After receipt of the Indictment the Tribunal shall give such notice as it thinks fit that the prosecution intends to ask the Tribunal to make such declaration and any member of the organization will be entitled to apply to the Tribunal for leave to be heard by the Tribunal upon the question of the criminal character of the organization. The Tribunal shall have power to allow or reject the application. If the application is allowed, the Tribunal may direct in what manner the applicants shall be represented and heard.

ARTICLE 10

In cases where a group or organization is declared criminal by the Tribunal, the competent national authority of any Signatory shall have the right to bring individuals to trial for membership therein before national, military or occupation courts. In any such case the criminal nature of the group or organization is considered proved and shall not be questioned.

ARTICLE 11

Any person convicted by the Tribunal may be charged before a national, military or occupation court, referred to in Article 10 of this Charter, with a crime other than of membership in a criminal group or organization and such court may, after convicting him, impose upon him punishment independent of and additional to the punishment imposed by the Tribunal for participation in the criminal activities of such group or organization.

ARTICLE 12

The Tribunal shall have the right to take proceedings against a person charged with crimes set out in Article 6 of this Charter in his absence, if he has not been found or if the Tribunal, for any reason, finds it necessary, in the interests of Justice, to conduct the hearing in his absence.

ARTICLE 13

The Tribunal shall draw up rules for its procedure. These rules shall not be inconsistent with the provisions of this Charter.

III COMMITTEE FOR THE INVESTIGATION AND PROSECUTION OF MAJOR WAR CRIMINALS

ARTICLE 14

Each Signatory shall appoint a Chief Prosecutor for the investigation of the charges against and the prosecution of major war criminals.

The Chief Prosecutors shall act as a committee for the following purposes:

(a) to agree upon a plan of the individual work of each of the Chief Prosecutors and his staff,

(b) to settle the final designation of major war criminals to be tried by the Tribunal,

(c) to improve the Indictment and the documents to be submitted therewith,

(d) to lodge the Indictment and the accompanying documents with the Tribunal.

(e) to draw up and recommend to the Tribunal for its approval draft rules of procedure, contemplated by Article 13 of this Charter. The Tribunal shall have power to accept, with or without amendments, or to reject, the rules so recommended.

The Committee shall act in all the above matters by a majority vote and shall appoint a Chairman as may be convenient and in accordance with the principle of rotation: provided that if there is an equal division of vote concerning the designation of a Defendant to be tried by the Tribunal, or the crimes with which he shall be charged, that proposal will be adopted which was made by the party which proposed that the particular Defendant be tried, or the particular charges be preferred against him.

ARTICLE 15

The Chief Prosecutors shall individually, and acting in collaboration with one another, also undertake the following duties:

(a) investigation, collection, and production before or at the Trial of all necessary evidence,

(b) the preparation of the indictment for approval by the Committee in accordance with paragraph (c) of Article 14 hereof,

(c) the preliminary examination of all necessary witnesses and of the Defendants,

(d) to act as prosecutor at the Trial,

(e) to appoint representatives to carry out such duties as may be assigned to them,

(f) to undertake such other matters as may appear necessary to them for the purposes of the preparation for and conduct of the Trial.

It is understood that no witness or Defendant detained by any Signatory shall be taken out of the possession of that Signatory without its assent.

IV FAIR TRIAL FOR DEFENDANTS

ARTICLE 16

In order to ensure fair trial for the Defendants, the following procedure shall be followed:

(a) The Indictment shall include full particulars specifying in detail the charges against the Defendants. A copy of the Indictment and of all the documents lodged with the Indictment, translated into a language which he understands shall be furnished to the Defendant at a reasonable time before the Trial.

(b) During any preliminary examination or trial of a Defendant he shall have the right to give any explanation relevant to the charges made against him.

(c) A preliminary examination of a Defendant and his Trial shall be conducted in, or translated into, a language which the Defendant understands.

(d) A defendant shall have the right to conduct his own defence before the Tribunal or to have the assistance of Counsel.

(e) A defendant shall have the right through himself or through his Counsel to present evidence at the Trial in support of his defence, and to cross-examine any witness called by the Prosecution.

V POWERS OF THE TRIBUNAL AND CONDUCT OF THE TRIAL

ARTICLE 17

The Tribunal shall have the power

(a) to summon witnesses to the Trial and to require their attendance and testimony and to put questions to them,

(b) to interrogate any Defendant,

(c) to require the production of documents and other evidentiary material,

(d) to administer oaths to witnesses,

(e) to appoint officers for the carrying out of any task designated by the Tribunal including the power to have evidence taken on commission.

ARTICLE 18

The Tribunal shall

(a) confine the Trial strictly to an expeditious hearing of the issues raised by the charges,

(b) take strict measures to prevent any action which will cause unreasonable delay, and rule out irrelevant issues and statements of any kind whatsoever,

(c) deal summarily with any contumacy, imposing appropriate punishment, including exclusion of any Defendant or his counsel from some or all further proceedings, but without prejudice to the determination of the charges.

ARTICLE 19

The Tribunal shall not be bound by technical rules of evidence. It shall adopt and apply to the greatest possible extent expeditious and non-technical procedure, and shall admit any evidence which it deems to have probative value.

ARTICLE 20

The Tribunal may require to be informed of the nature of any evidence before it is offered so that it may rule upon the relevance thereof.

ARTICLE 21

The Tribunal shall not require proof of facts of common knowledge but shall take judicial notice thereof. It shall also take judicial notice of official governmental documents and reports of the United Nations, including the acts and documents of the committees set up in the various Allied countries for the investigation of war crimes, and the records and findings of military or other Tribunals of any of the United Nations.

ARTICLE 22

The permanent seat of the Tribunal shall be in Berlin. The first meetings of the members of the Tribunal and of the Chief Prosecutors shall be held at Berlin in a place to be designated by the Control Council for Germany. The first trial shall be held at Nuremberg, and any subsequent trials shall be held at such places as the Tribunal may decide.

ARTICLE 23

One or more of the Chief Prosecutors may take part in the prosecution at each Trial. The function of any Chief Prosecutor may be discharged by him personally, or by any person or persons authorized by him.

The function of Counsel for a Defendant may be discharged at the Defendant's request by any Counsel professionally qualified to conduct cases before the courts of his own country, or by any other person who may be specially authorized thereto by the Tribunal.

ARTICLE 24

The proceedings at the Trial shall take the following course:

(a) The Indictment shall be read in court.
(b) The Tribunal shall ask each Defendant whether he pleads 'guilty' or 'not guilty'.
(c) The Prosecution shall make an opening statement.
(d) The Tribunal shall ask the Prosecution and the Defence what evidence (if any) they wish to submit to the Tribunal, and the Tribunal shall rule upon the admissibility of any such evidence.

(e) The witnesses for the Prosecution shall be examined and after that the witnesses for the Defence. Thereafter such rebutting evidence as may be held by the Tribunal to be admissible shall be called by either the Prosecution or the Defence.

(f) The Tribunal may put any question to any witness and to any Defendant, at any time.

(g) The Prosecution and the Defence shall interrogate and may cross-examine any witnesses and any Defendant who gives testimony.

(h) The Defence shall address the court.

(i) The Prosecution shall address the court.

(j) Each Defendant may make a statement to the Tribunal.

(k) The Tribunal shall deliver judgment and pronounce sentence.

ARTICLE 25

All official documents shall be produced, and all court proceedings conducted in English, French and Russian, and in the language of the Defendant. So much of the record and of the proceedings may also be translated into the language of any country in which the Tribunal is sitting, as the Tribunal considers desirable in the interests of justice and public opinion.

VI JUDGMENT AND SENTENCE

ARTICLE 26

The judgment of the Tribunal as to the guilt or the innocence of any Defendant shall give the reasons on which it is based, and shall be final and not subject to review.

ARTICLE 27

The Tribunal shall have the right to impose upon a Defendant, on conviction, death or such other punishment as shall be determined by it to be just.

ARTICLE 28

In addition to any punishment imposed by it, the Tribunal shall have the right to deprive the convicted person of any stolen property and order its delivery to the Control Council for Germany.

ARTICLE 29

In case of guilt, sentences shall be carried out in accordance with the orders of the Control Council for Germany, which may at any time reduce or otherwise alter the sentences, but may not increase the severity thereof. If the Control Council for Germany, after any Defendant has been convicted and sentenced, discovers fresh evidence which, in its opinion, would found a fresh charge against him, the Council shall report accordingly to the

Committee established under Article 14 hereof, for such action as they may consider proper having regard to the interests of justice.

VII Expenses

Article 30

The expenses of the Tribunal and of the Trials, shall be charged by the Signatories against the funds allotted for maintenance of the Control Council for Germany.

Protocol

Whereas an agreement and charter regarding the Prosecution of War Criminals was signed in London on the 8/8/1945, in the English, French, and Russian languages,

And whereas a discrepancy has been found to exist between the originals of Article 6, paragraph (c), of the charter in the Russian language, on the one hand, and the originals in the English and French languages, on the other, to wit, the semi-colon in Article 6, paragraph (c), of the Charter between the words 'war' and 'or', as carried in the English and French texts, is a comma in the Russian text, and whereas it is desired to rectify this discrepancy:

Now, Therefore, the undersigned, signatories of the said Agreement on behalf of their respective Governments, duly authorized thereto, have agreed that Article 6, paragraph (c), of the Charter in the Russian text is correct, and that the meaning and intention of the Agreement and Charter require that the said semi-colon in the English text should be changed to a comma, and that the French text should be amended to read as follows:

(c) Les Crimes Contre L'Humanité: c'est-à-dire l'assassinat, l'extermination, la réduction en esclavage, la déportation, et tout autre acte inhumain commis contre toutes populations civiles, avant ou pendant la guerre, ou bien les persécutions pour des motifs politiques, raciaux, ou religieux, lorsque ces actes ou persécutions, qu'ils aient constitué ou non une violation du droit interne du pays ou ils ont été perpétrés, ont été commis à la suite de tout crime rentrant dans la compétence du Tribunal, ou en liaison avec ce crime.

In Witness Whereof, the Undersigned have signed the present Protocol.

Done in quadruplicate in Berlin this 6th day of October 1945, each in English, French, and Russian, and each text to have equal authenticity.

For the Government of the United States of America, Robert H. Jackson,

For the Provisional Government of the French Republic, Francois De Menthon,

For the Government of the United Kingdom of Great Britain and Northern Ireland, Hartley Shawcross,

For the Government of the Union of Soviet Socialist Republics, R. Rudenko.

APPENDIX 5

Rules of Procedure and Evidence of the International Military Tribunal

ADOPTED 29 OCTOBER 1945

RULE 1. AUTHORITY TO PROMULGATE RULES

The present Rules of Procedure of the International Military Tribunal for the trial of the major war criminals (hereinafter called 'the Tribunal') as established by the Charter of the Tribunal dated 8 August 1945 (hereinafter called 'the Charter') are hereby promulgated by the Tribunal in accordance with the provisions of Article 13 of the Charter.

RULE 2. NOTICE TO DEFENDANTS AND RIGHT TO ASSISTANCE OF COUNSEL

(a) Each individual defendant in custody shall receive not less than 30 days before trial a copy, translated into a language which he understands, (1) of the Indictment, (2) of the Charter, (3) of any other documents lodged with the Indictment, and (4) of a statement of his right to the assistance of counsel as set forth in sub-paragraph (d) of this Rule, together with a list of counsel. He shall also receive copies of such rules of procedure as may be adopted by the Tribunal from time to time.

(b) Any individual defendant not in custody shall be informed of the indictment against him and of his right to receive the documents specified in sub-paragraph (a) above, by notice in such form and manner as the Tribunal may prescribe.

(c) With respect to any group or organization as to which the Prosecution indicates its intention to request a finding of criminality by the Tribunal, notice shall be given by publication in such form and manner as the Tribunal may prescribe and such publication shall include a declaration by the Tribunal that all members of the named groups or organizations are entitled to apply to the Tribunal for leave to be heard in accordance with the provisions of Article 9 of the Charter. Nothing herein contained shall be construed to confer immunity of any kind upon such members of said groups or organizations as may appear in answer to the said declaration.

(d) Each defendant has the right to conduct his own defence or to have the assistance of counsel. Application for particular counsel shall be filed at once with the General Secretary of the Tribunal at the Palace of Justice, Nuremberg, Germany. The Tribunal will designate counsel for any defendant who fails to apply for particular counsel or, where particular counsel requested is not within ten (10) days to be found or available, unless the defendant elects in writing to conduct his own defence. If a defendant has requested particular counsel who is not immediately to be found or available, such counsel or a counsel of substitute choice may, if found and available before trial be associated with or substituted for counsel designated by the Tribunal, provided that (1) only one counsel shall be permitted to appear at the trial for any defendant, unless by special permission of the Tribunal, and (2) no delay of trial will be allowed for making such substitution or association.

RULE 3. SERVICE OF ADDITIONAL DOCUMENTS

If, before the trial, the Chief Prosecutors offer amendments or additions to the Indictment, such amendments or additions, including any accompanying documents shall be lodged with the Tribunal and copies of the same, translated into a language which they each understand, shall be furnished to the defendants in custody as soon as practicable and notice given in accordance with Rule 2 (b) to those not in custody.

RULE 4. PRODUCTION OF EVIDENCE FOR THE DEFENCE

(a) The Defence may apply to the Tribunal for the production of witnesses or of documents by written application to the General Secretary of the Tribunal. The application shall state where the witness or document is thought to be located, together with a statement of their last known location. It shall also state the facts proposed to be proved by the witness or the document and the reasons why such facts are relevant to the Defence.

(b) If the witness or the document is not within the area controlled by the occupation authorities, the Tribunal may request the Signatory and adhering Governments to arrange for the production, if possible, of any such witnesses and any such documents as the Tribunal may deem necessary to proper presentation of the Defence.

(c) If the witness or the document is within the area controlled by the occupation authorities, the General Secretary shall, if the Tribunal is not in session, communicate the application to the Chief Prosecutors and, if they make no objection, the General Secretary shall issue a summons for the attendance of such witness or the production of such documents, informing the Tribunal of the action taken. If any Chief Prosecutor objects to the issuance of a summons, or if the Tribunal is in session, the General Secretary shall submit the application to the Tribunal, which shall decide whether or not the summons shall issue.

(d) A summons shall be served in such manner as may be provided by the appropriate occupation authority to ensure its enforcement and the General Secretary shall inform the Tribunal of the steps taken.

(e) Upon application to the General Secretary of the Tribunal, a defendant shall be furnished with a copy, translated into a language which he understands, of all documents referred to in the Indictment so far as they may be made available by the Chief Prosecutors and shall be allowed to inspect copies of any such documents as are not so available.

Rule 5. Order at the Trial

In conformity with the provisions of Article 18 of the Charter, and the disciplinary powers therein set out, the Tribunal, acting through its President, shall provide for the maintenance of order at the Trial. Any defendant or any other person may be excluded from open sessions of the Tribunal for failure to observe and respect the directives and dignity of the Tribunal.

Rule 6. Oaths; Witnesses

(a) Before testifying before the Tribunal, each witness shall make such oath or declaration as is customary in his own country.
(b) Witnesses while not giving evidence shall not be present in court. The President of the Tribunal shall direct, as circumstances demand, that witnesses shall not confer among themselves before giving evidence.

Rule 7. Applications and Motions before Trial and Rulings during the Trial

(a) All motions, applications or other requests addressed to the Tribunal prior to the commencement of trial shall be made in writing and filed with the General Secretary of the Tribunal at the Palace of Justice, Nuremberg, Germany.

(b) Any such motion, application or other request shall be communicated by the General Secretary of the Tribunal to the Chief Prosecutors and, if they make no objection, the President of the Tribunal may make the appropriate order on behalf of the Tribunal. If any Chief Prosecutor objects, the President may call a special session of the Tribunal for the determination of the question raised.

(c) The Tribunal, acting through its President, will rule in court upon all questions arising during the trial, such as questions as to admissibility of evidence offered during the trial, recesses, and motions; and before so ruling the Tribunal may, when necessary, order the closing or clearing of the Tribunal or take any other steps which to the Tribunal seem just.

Rule 8. Secretariat of the Tribunal

(a) The Secretariat of the Tribunal shall be composed of a General Secretary, four Secretaries and their Assistants. The Tribunal shall appoint the General Secretary and each Member shall appoint one Secretary. The General Secretary shall appoint such clerks, interpreters, stenographers, ushers, and all such other persons as may be authorized by the Tribunal and each Secretary may appoint such assistants as may be authorized by the Member of the Tribunal by whom he was appointed.

(b) The General Secretary, in consultation with the Secretaries, shall organize and direct the work of the Secretariat, subject to the approval of the Tribunal in the event of a disagreement by any Secretary.

(c) The Secretariat shall receive all documents addressed to the Tribunal, maintain the records of the Tribunal, provide necessary clerical services to the Tribunal and its Members, and perform such other duties as may be designated by the Tribunal.

(d) Communications addressed to the Tribunal shall be delivered to the General Secretary.

RULE 9. RECORD, EXHIBITS, AND DOCUMENTS

(a) A stenographic record shall be maintained of all oral proceedings. Exhibits will be suitably identified and marked with consecutive numbers. All exhibits and transcripts of the proceedings and all documents lodged with and produced to the Tribunal will be filed with the General Secretary of the Tribunal and will constitute part of the Record.

(b) The term 'official documents' as used in Article 25 of the Charter includes the Indictment, rules, written motions, orders that are reduced to writing, findings, and judgments of the Tribunal. These shall be in the English, French, Russian, and German languages. Documentary evidence or exhibits may be received in the language of the document, but a translation thereof into German shall be made available to the defendants.

(c) All exhibits and transcripts of proceedings, all documents lodged with and produced to the Tribunal and all official acts and documents of the Tribunal may be certified by the General Secretary of the Tribunal to any Government or to any other tribunal or wherever it is appropriate that copies of such documents or representations as to such acts should be supplied upon a proper request.

RULE 10. WITHDRAWAL OF EXHIBITS AND DOCUMENTS

In cases where original documents are submitted by the Prosecution or the Defence as evidence, and upon a showing (a) that because of historical interest or for any other reason one of the Governments signatory to the Four Power Agreement of 8 August 1945, or any other Government having received the consent of said four signatory Powers, desires to withdraw from the records of the Tribunal and preserve any particular original documents and (b) that no substantial injustice will result, the Tribunal shall permit photostatic copies of said original documents, certified by the General Secretary of the Tribunal, to be substituted for the originals in the records of the Court and shall deliver said original documents to the applicants.

RULE 11. EFFECTIVE DATE AND POWERS OF AMENDMENT AND ADDITION

These Rules shall take effect upon their approval by the Tribunal. Nothing herein contained shall be construed to prevent the Tribunal from, at any time, in the interest of fair and expeditious trials, departing from, amending, or adding to these Rules, either by general rules or special orders for particular cases, in such form and upon such notice as may appear just to the Tribunal.

General Assembly Resolution 95 (I)—Nuremberg Principles

95 (I). Affirmation of the Principles of International Law Recognized by the Charter of the Nürnberg Tribunal

The General Assembly,

Recognizes the obligation laid upon it by Article 13, paragraph 1, sub-paragraph a, of the Charter, to initiate studies and make recommendations for the purpose of encouraging the progressive development of international law and its codification;

Takes note of the Agreement for the establishment of an International Military Tribunal for the prosecution and punishment of the major war criminals of the European Axis signed in London on 8 August 1945, and of the Charter annexed thereto, and of the fact that similar principles have been adopted in the Charter of the International Military Tribunal for the trial of the major war criminals in the Far East, proclaimed at Tokyo on 19 January 1946;

Therefore,

Affirms the principles of international law recognized by the Charter of the Nürnberg Tribunal and the judgment of the Tribunal;

Directs the Committee on the codification of international law established by the resolution of the General Assembly of 11 December 1946, to treat as a matter of primary importance plans for the formulation, in the context of a general codification of offences against the peace and security of mankind, or of an International Criminal Code, of the principles recognized in the Charter of the Nürnberg Tribunal and in the judgment of the Tribunal.

Fifty-fifth plenary meeting,
11 December 1946.

APPENDIX 7

Table of Charges and Verdicts

(a) Individuals[1]

Defendant	Count 1	Count 2	Count 3	Count 4	Sentence
Goering, Hermann	G	G	G	G	Death by hanging
Hess, Rudolf	G	G	NG	NG	Life
von Ribbentrop, Joachim	G	G	G	G	Death by hanging
Keitel, Wilhelm	G	G	G	G	Death by hanging
Kaltenbrunner, Ernst	NG	NC	G	G	Death by hanging
Rosenberg, Alfred	G	G	G	G	Death by hanging
Frank, Hans	NG	NC	G	G	Death by hanging
Frick, Wilhelm	NG	G	G	G	Death by hanging
Streicher, Julius	NG	NC	NC	G	Death by hanging
Funk, Walther	NG	G	G	G	Life
Schacht, Hjalmar	NG	NG	NC	NC	Acquitted
Doenitz, Karl	NG	G	G	NC	10 years
Raeder, Erich	G	G	G	NC	Life
von Schirach, Baldur	NG	NC	NC	G	20 years
Sauckel, Fritz	NG	NG	G	G	Death by hanging
Jodl, Alfred	G	G	G	G	Death by hanging
Bormann, Martin	NG	NC	G	G	Death by hanging
von Papen, Franz	NG	NG	NC	NC	Acquitted

Defendant	Count 1	Count 2	Count 3	Count 4	Sentence
Seyss-Inquart, Arthur	NG	G	G	G	Death by hanging
Speer, Albert	NG	G	G	G	20 years
von Neurath, Constatin	G	G	G	G	15 years
Fritzsche, Hans	NG	NC	NG	NG	Acquitted

[1] In order of indictment.

Count 1	Common plan or conspiracy
Count 2	Crimes against peace
Count 3	War crimes
Count 4	Crimes against humanity
G	Guilty
NG	Not guilty
NC	No charges

(b) Organizations

Organizations declared criminal	Organizations not declared criminal
Leadership corps of the Nazi Party	SA (*Sturmabteilung der NSDAP*)
Gestapo (*Geheime Staatspolizei*)–SD (*Sicherheitsdienst*)	Reich Cabinet
SS (*Schutzstaffeln*)	General Staff/High Command

PART V

BIBLIOGRAPHY

Bibliography

DOCUMENTS

Basic Documents

Punishment for War Crimes: The Inter-Allied Declaration, signed at St. James's Palace, London, 13 January 1942, and Relative Documents (London: Inter-Allied Information Committee, 1942).

Moscow Declaration of German Atrocities, 30 October 1943 (9 US Department of State Bulletin 308 (1943)) ('Declaration on Security').

Potsdam Declaration, 26 July 1945 (13 US Department of State Bulletin 137, 1945).

Agreement for the Prosecution and Punishment of the Major War Criminals of the European Axis, 8 August 1945 (London: HMSO, 1945) and reprinted in *Trial of the Major War Criminals Before the International Military Tribunal, Nuremberg, 14 November 1945–1 October 1946,* vol. 1 (Nuremberg: International Military Tribunal, 1947–1949, 8) ('London Agreement').

Charter of the International Military Tribunal at Nuremberg, annexed to the London Agreement of 8 August 1945 and reprinted, *inter alia,* in 39 *American Journal of International Law* (1945), Supplement 257, and in *Trial of the Major War Criminals Before the International Military Tribunal, Nuremberg, 14 November 1945–1 October 1946,* Vol. 1 (Nuremberg: International Military Tribunal, 1947–1949, 10).

Uniform Rules of Procedure, Military Tribunals, Nuernberg, adopted 29 October 1945 and revised 8 January 1948, in *Trial of the Major War Criminals Before the International Military Tribunal, Nuremberg, 14 November 1945–1 October 1946,* vol. 1 (Nuremberg: International Military Tribunal, 1947–1949, 19).

Protocol Rectifying Discrepancy in the Charter, in *Trial of the Major War Criminals Before the International Military Tribunal, Nuremberg, 14 November 1945–1 October 1946,* vol. 1 (Nuremberg: International Military Tribunal, 1947–1949, 17).

Indictment, corrected version confirmed 7 June 1946 in *Trial of the Major War Criminals Before the International Military Tribunal, Nuremberg, 14 November 1945–1 October 1946,* vol. 1 (Nuremberg: International Military Tribunal, 1947–1949, 27).

Plans for the Formulation of the Principles of the Nuremberg Charter and Judgement (Yearbook of the United Nations, 1947–1948).

Affirmation of the Principles of International Law Recognized by the Charter of the Nuremberg Tribunal, 11 December 1946, UN G.A. Res 95(1), I UN GAOR (Part II) at 188, UN Doc A/64/Add.1 (1946).

Principles of the Nuremberg Tribunal, 1950 Report of the International Law Commission (Principles of International Law Recognized in the Tribunal), 29 July 1950, 5 UN GAOR Supp. (No 12), 11, UN Doc A/1316 1950.

Formulation of Nurnberg Principles, Document A/CN.4/22, Report by J. Spiroloulos, Special Rapporteur, 12 April 1950, reprinted in vol. 2, *Yearbook of the International Law Commission,* 181, *et seq.*

Treaties, Agreements and Conventions

Kellogg–Briand Pact, 27 August 1928, Treaty between the United States and other powers providing for the renunciation of war as an instrument of national policy, signed at Paris, 27 August 1928.

Decision between the United States and the United Kingdom to set up the United Nations War Crimes Commission, 20 October 1942 (7 US Department of State Bulletin 797, 1942).

Providing for Representation of the United States in Preparing and Prosecuting Charges of Atrocities and War Crimes Against the Leaders of the European Axis Powers and Their Principal Agents and Accessories, Executive Order 9547, 2 May 1945 (10 *Federal Register* 4961).

Records of the Trial

Der Nuernberger Prozess (Munich: Microedition Zeitgesschichte, 1981).

Nuremberg War Crimes Trials (Seattle: Aristarchus Knowledge Industries, 1995).

Records of the United States Nuernberg War Crimes Trials (Washington, DC: National Archives and Records Service, Records group 238, microfilms M887–M898, M936, M942, M946, T301, T1119, T1139, IMT and NMT).

Trial of the Major War Criminals Before the International Military Tribunal, Nuremberg, 14 November 1945–1 October 1946, 42 vols. (Nuremberg: International Military Tribunal, 1947–1949).

IMT, *The Trial of German Major War Criminals: Proceedings of the International Military Tribunal Sitting at Nuremberg, Germany, 20th November, 1945 to 1st December, 1945—Taken from the Official Transcript*, 21 vols. (London: HMSO, 1946).

Le Procès des Grands Criminels de Guerre devant le Tribunal Militaire International de Nuremberg, 41 vols. (Paris: Imprimerie Nationale, 1947–1949).

Der Prozess gegen die Hauptkriegsverbrecher vor dem Internationalen Militärgerichtshof, 14 November 1945, bis 1 Oktober 1946, 42 vols. (Nuremberg: IMT, 1947–1949).

Prosecution of Major Nazi War Criminals: Report from Francis Biddle to President Truman, 12 November 1946 (15 US Department of State Bulletin 954, No. 386, 1946).

France, Ministère de l'Information, *Service de recherche des crimes de guerre ennemis: Le process de Nuremberg: L'accusation alliée* (Paris: Office Français d'Édition, 1946).

IMT, *The Trial of German Major War Criminals by the International Military Tribunal Sitting at Nuremberg, Germany (Commencing 20th November 1945): Opening Speeches of the Chief Prosecutors for the United States of America, the French Republic, the United Kingdom of Great Britain and Northern Ireland and the Union of Soviet Socialist Republics* (London: HMSO, 1946).

IMT, *The Trial of German Major War Criminals by the International Military Tribunal Sitting at Nuremberg, Germany (Commencing 20th November, 1945): Speeches of the Chief Prosecutors for the United States of America, the French Republic, the United Kingdom of Great Britain and Northern Ireland and the Union of Soviet Socialist Republics, at the Close of the Case against the Individual Defendants* (London: HMSO, 1946).

IMT, *The Trial of German Major War Criminals by the International Military Tribunal Sitting at Nuremberg, Germany (Commencing 20th November, 1945): Speeches of the Prosecutors for the United States of America, the French Republic, the United Kingdom of Great Britain and Northern Ireland and the Union of Soviet Socialist Republics, at the Close of the Case against the Indicted Organisations* (London: HMSO, 1946).

IMT, Secretariat, *Documents Constituting Basic Authority War Crimes Trials* (Nuremberg: IMT, Secretariat, 1947).

United States Chief Counsel for the Prosecution of Axis Criminality, *Nazi Conspiracy and Aggression*, 8 vols. (Washington, DC: Government Printing Office, 1946) Supplement, 2 vols. (1947–1948).

Official Reports Concerning the Trial and its Preparation

Inter-American Juridical Committee, *Report on the Juridical Status of Individuals as 'War Criminals'* (Washington, DC: Pan-American Union, 1945).

R. Jackson, *Report of Robert H. Jackson, United States Representative to the International Conference on Military Trials*, at the International Conference on Military Trials, London, 1945 (Washington, DC: Government Printing Office, 1949).

Robert H. Jackson, *Trial of War Criminals. Documents: 1. Report of Robert H. Jackson to the President; 2. Agreement Establishing an International Military Tribunal; 3. Indictment* (Washington, DC: U.S. Government Printing Office, 1945).

R. Jackson, Final Report to the President from Supreme Court Justice Jackson, 13 *Department of State Bulletin* 771 (27 October 1946).

Nuremberg: A History of US Military Government. Issued by the US Forces European Theater, 1946.

Report of the Committee on the Progressive Development of International Law and its Codification, Plans for the Formulation of the Principles of the Nuremberg Charter and Judgment in 41 *American Journal of International Law*, Supplement 26 (1947).

Secretary-General of the United Nations, *The Charter and Judgment of the Nürnberg Tribunal: History and Analysis* (1949), UN Doc. A/CN.4/5.

T. Taylor, *Report on the Conduct and Current Status of the Nuremberg War Crimes Trials*, 12 May 1948.

History of the United Nations War Crimes Commission and the Development of Laws of War (London: HMSO, 1948).

T. Taylor, *Final Report to the Secretary of the Army on the Nuremberg War Crimes Trials under Control Council Law No. 10* (Washington, DC: Government Printing Office, 1949).

Law Reports of Trials of War Criminals, Selected and Prepared by the United Nations War Crimes Commission, 15 vols. (London: HMSO, 1947–49).

Records of Conferences

The Conferences at Cairo and Teheran 1943 (Washington, DC: Foreign Relations of the United States, Diplomatic Papers, World War II Conferences, vol. 3, 1961).

The Conference at Malta and Yalta 1945 (Washington, DC: Foreign Relations of the United States, Diplomatic Papers, World War II Conferences, vol. 1, 1955).

The Conference of Berlin 1945 (Washington, DC: Foreign Relations of the United States, Diplomatic Papers, World War II Conferences, vols. 1 and 2, 1960).

Tripartite Conference at Berlin, 2 August 1945 (13 US Department of State Bulletin 153, No. 319, 1945).

The Teheran, Yalta and Potsdam Conferences (Moscow: Progress Publishers, 1969).

Miscellaneous

F. Roosevelt, *Address by President of the United States of America*, 25 October 1941 (5 *Department of State Bulletin*, 317, 1941).

V. Molotov, *Molotov's Note on German Atrocities in Occupied Soviet Territory*, People's Commissar of Foreign Affairs of the U.S.S.R., to all ambassadors and ministers of countries with which the Soviet Union maintains diplomatic relations, 6 January 1942 (Embassy of the Union of Soviet Socialist Republics—Information Bulletin, 7 January 1942).

United Nations Commission to Investigate War Crimes, 7 October 1942 (7 *Department of State Bulletin* 797, No. 172, 1942).

Notes et Documents, in *Revue de Droit International de Sciences Diplomatiques et Politiques*, 1946, No 2–3, 112.

Draft Code on Offenses against the Peace and Security of Mankind, 9 UN GAOR, Supplement (No. 9), U.N. Doc. A/2693 1954.

BOOKS AND MONOGRAPHS

H. Ahlbrecht, *Geschichte der völkerrechtlichen Strafgerichtbarkeit in 20. Jahrhundert* (Baden Baden: Nomos, 1999).

C. Alexander and A. Keeshan, *Justice at Nuernberg: A Pictorial Record of the Trial of Nazi War Criminals by the International Tribunal, at Nuernberg, Germany, 1945–46* (Chicago: Marvel Press, 1946).

K. Ambos, P. Rackow, and D. Miller, *Internationales Strafrecht; Strafanwendungsrecht, Voelkerstrafrecht, Europäisches Strafrecht* (Munich: Beck, 2006).

American Historical Association, *What Shall Be Done with War Criminals*, GI Roundtable, EM11 (Washington, DC: War Department, 1944).

J. Appleman, *Military Tribunals and International Crimes* (Indianapolis: Bobbs-Merrill, 1954).

H. Ball, *Prosecuting War Crimes and Genocide—The Twentieth-Century Experience* (Lawrence, KS: University Press of Kansas, 1999).

M. Bard, *The Nuremberg Trials (at Issue in History)* (San Diego: Greenhaven Press, 2001).

G. J. Bass, *Stay the Hand of Vengeance—The Politics of War Crimes Tribunals* (Princeton: Princeton University Press, 2000).

F. Bauer, *Die Kriegsverbrecher vor Gericht* (Zurich/New York: Europa Verlag, 1945).

J. P. Bazelaire and T. Cretin, *La Justice Pénale Internationale: Son évolution, son avenir de Nuremberg à La Haye* (Paris: Presses Universitaires de France, 2000).

H. Bedord, *From Versailles to Nuremberg: The American Encounter with the Nazis* (London: Macmillan, 1969).

M. Belgion, *Epitaph on Nuremberg* (London: Falcon Press, 1946).

M. Belgion, *Victor's Justice: A Letter Intended to Have Been Sent to a Friend Recently in Germany* (Chicago: Henry Regnery Co., 1946).

W. Benton and G. Grimm (eds.), *Nuremberg—German Views of the War Trials* (Dallas: Southern Methodist University Press, 1955).

V. Bernstein, *Final Judgment: The Story of Nuremberg* (New York: Boni & Gaer, 1947).

G. Best, *War and Law Since 1945* (Oxford: Clarendon Press, 1994).

W. Bosch, *Judgment on Nuremberg: American Attitude Towards the Major German War-Crime Trials* (Chapel Hill: University of North Carolina Press, 1970).

F. Biddle, *In Brief Authority* (New York: Doubleday & Company, Inc., 1962).

D. A. Blumenthal and T. McCormack (eds.), *The Legacy of Nuremberg: Civilising Influence or Institutionalised Vergeance?* (The Hague: Martinus Nijhoff Publishers, 2007).

A. Burton, *I Was The Nuremberg Jailer* (New York: Coward-McCann, 1969).

F. Buscher, *The U.S. War Crimes Trial Program in Germany, 1946–1955* (Westport: Greenwood Press, 1989).

H. Butterweck, *Der Nürnberger Prozess* (Wien: Czernin Verlag, 2005).

P. Calvocoressi, *Nuremberg: The Facts, the Law and the Consequences* (New York: Macmillan Co., 1948).

P. Carjeu, *Le jugement du Tribunal Militaire de Nuremberg* (Paris: Institut de Criminologie, 1951).

R. Conot, *Justice at Nuremberg* (New York: Carroll & Graf, 1983).

H. Conover (ed.), *The Nazi State, War Crimes and War Criminals* (Washington, DC: Library of Congress, 1945).

B. Cooper (ed.), *War Crimes: The Legacy of Nuremberg* (New York: TV Books, 1999).

R. Cooper, *The Nuremberg Trial* (Hardmondsworth: Penguin, 1947).

G. Creel, *War Criminals and Punishment* (New York: R.M. McBride & Company, 1944).

R. Crouchuet, *Le procès de Nuremberg: Les criminals Nazis devant leurs juges* (Paris: Hachette, 1947).

R. Current, *Secretary Stimson: A Study in Statecraft* (New Brunswick: Rutgers University Press, 1954).

T. Cyprian and J. Sawicki, *Nuremberg in Retrospect: People and Issues of the Trial* (Warsaw: Western Press Agency, 1967).

J. Daniel, *Le Problème du châtiment des crimes de guerre d'après les enseignements de la deuxième guerre mondiale* (Cairo: R. Schindler, 1946).

E. Davidson, *The Trial of the Germans* (New York: Macmillan, 1966).

J. Descheemaeker, *Le Tribunal Militaire International des Grands Criminels de Guerre* (Paris: A. Pedone, 1947).

H. Donnedieu de Vabres, *The Nuremberg Trials and the Process of International Law* (Birmingham: Holdsworth Club of the University of Birmingham, 1947).

H. Donnedieu de Vabres, *Le procès de Nuremberg: Le statut du Tribunal Militaire International, les débats, les chefs d'accusation, le jugement* (Paris: Éditions Domat Montchrestien, 1947).

R. Eisfeld and I. Müller, Gegen Barbarei: *Essays Robert M.W. Kempner zu Ehren* (Frankfurt: Athenäum, 1989).

Sir Elwyn-Jones, *Nuremberg—25 Years On: A Retrospective Analysis*, Noah Barou Memorial Lecture (London: World Jewish Congress, 1971).

R. Falk et al. (eds.), *Crimes of War: A Legal, Political-Documentary, and Psychological Inquiry into the Responsibility of Leaders, Citizens and Soldiers for Criminal Acts in War* (New York: Random House, 1971).

H. Fireside, *The Nuremberg Nazi War Crimes Trials: A Headline Court Case* (Berkeley Heights, NJ: Enslow Publishers, 2000).

L. Friedman (ed.), *The Laws of War*, vol. 1 (New York: Random House, 1972).

R. Gallagher, *Nuremberg: The Third Reich on Trial* (New York: Avon, 1961).

H. Gaskin, *Eyewitnesses at Nuremberg* (London: Arms and Armour, 1990).

E. Gerhart, *America's Advocate: Robert H. Jackson* (Indianapolis and New York: Bobbs-Merrill, 1958).

J. Gerould, *Selected Articles on the Pact of Paris, Officially the General Pact for the Renunciation of War* (New York: H.W. Wilson, 1929).

G. Ginsburg and V. N. Kudriavtsev (eds.), *The Nuremberg Trial and International Law* (Dordrecht: Martinus Nijhoff Publishers, 1990).

S. Glueck, *War Criminals: Their Prosecution and Punishment* (New York: A.A. Knopf, 1944).

S. Glueck, *The Nuremberg Trial and Aggressive War* (New York: A.A. Knopf, 1946).

G. Gilbert, *Nuremberg Diary* (New York: Farrar, Straus, 1947).

L. Goldensohn, *The Nuremberg Interviews* (New York: Vintage Books, 2005).

A. Goodhart, *What Acts of War Are Justifiable?* (Oxford: Clarendon Press, 1940).

W. Grewe and O. Küster, *Nürnberg als Rechtsfrage: Eine Diskussion* (Stuttgart: E. Klett, 1947).

G. Gründler and A. von Manikowsky, *Das Gericht der Sieger* (Oldenburg: Public Verlag, 1967).

C. Haensel, *Das Gericht vertragt sich: Aus dem Tagebuch eines Nürnberger Verteidigers* (Hamburg: Claassen und goverts, 1950).

Y. Halan, *Reports from Nuremberg* (Kiev: Dnipo Publishers, 1976).

G. Hankel and G. Stuby (eds.), *Strafgerichte gegen Menschheitsverbrechen: zum Völkerstrafrecht 50 Jahre nach den Nürnberger Prozessen* (Hamburg: Hamburger Edition, 1995).

Lord Hankey, *Politics, Trials and Errors* (Chicago: Henry Regnery Co., 1950).

W. Harris, *Tyranny on Trial—The Evidence at Nuremberg* (Dallas: Southern Methodist University Press, 1954; New York: Barnes and Noble Books, re-edited in 1995).

K. Heinze, K. Schilling, and H. Maschke, *Die Rechtsprechung der Nürnberger Militärtriunale: Sammlung der Rechtsthesen, der Urteile und gesonderten Urteilsbegründungen der dreizehn Nürnberger Prozesse* (Bonn: Girardet & Co., 1952).

J. Heydecker and J. Leeb, *The Nuremberg Trial: A History of Nazi Germany as Revealed through the Testimony at Nuremberg* (Cleveland: World Publishing Co., 1962).

L. Holborn (ed.), *War and Peace Aims of the United Nations* (Boston: World Peace Foundation, 1943–1948).

M. O. Hudson, *International Tribunals, Past and Future* (Washington, DC: Carnegie Endowment for International Peace and Brookings Institution, 1944).

D. Irving, *The Last Battle* (London: Focal Point, 1999).

S. Ivrakis, *Soviet Concepts of International Law, Criminal Law and Criminal Procedure at the International Conference on Military Trials* (London, 1945).

R. Jackson, *The Nürnberg Case as Presented by Robert H. Jackson, Chief of Counsel for the United States, Together with Other Documents* (New York: Knopf, 1946).

R. Jackson, *Nürnberg Case* (New York: A.A. Knopf, 1947).

H. Janeczek, *Nuremberg Judgment in the Light of International Law* (Geneva: Imprimeries Populaires, 1949).

H. Jescheck, *Die Verantwörtlichkeit der Staatsorgan nach Völkerrecht: Eine Studie zu den Nürnberger Prozessen* (Bonn: L. Rörscheid, 1952).

S. Jung, *Die Rechtsprobleme de Nürnberger Prozesse* (Tübingen: Mohr, 1992).

L. Kahn, *Nuremberg Trials* (New York: Ballantine Books, 1972).

J. Keenan and B. Brown, *Crimes Against International Law* (Washington, DC: Public Affairs Press, 1950).

D. Kelley, *22 Cells in Nuremberg* (New York: Greenberg, 1947).

H. Kelsen, *Peace Through Law* (Chapel Hill: University of North Carolina Press, 1944).

J. Kenny, *Moral Aspects of Nuremberg* (Washington, DC: Pontifical Faculty of Theology, Dominican House of Studies, 1949).

O. Kirchheimer, *Political Justice the Use of Legal Procedures for Political Ends* (Princeton: Princeton University Press, 1961).

A. Klafowski, *The Nuremberg Principles and the Development of International Law* (Warsaw: Zachodnia Agencja Prasowa, 1966).

A. von Knieriem, *The Nuernberg Trials*, translated by E. Schmitt (Chicago: Henry Regnery Co., 1959).

A. Kochavi, *Prelude to Nuremberg Allied War Crimes Policy and the Question of Punishment* (Chapel Hill: University of North Carolina Press, 1998).

O. Kranzbühler, *Rückblick auf Nürnberg* (Hamburg: Zeitverlag E. Schmidt & Co., 1948).

H. Kraus, *Gerichtstag in Nürnberg* (Hamburg: Gesetz und Recht Verlag, 1947).

M. Lachs, *War Crimes: An Attempt to Define the Issues* (London: Stevens & Sons, 1945).

A. Lande, *The Legal Basis of the Nuremberg Trial* (New York: Interim International Information Service, 1945).

C. La Folette, *Der Nürnberger Prozess gegen führende Juristen des Dritten Reiches* (Stuttgart, 1948).

G. Lawrence (Lord Oaksey), *The Nuremberg Trials and the Progress of International Law* (Birmingham: Holdsworth Club of University of Birmingham, 1947).

D. Lazard, *Le Procès de Nuremberg. Récit d'un témoin* (Paris: Ed. de la Nouvelle France, 1947).

R. Lemkin, *Axis Rule in Occupied Europe: Laws of Occupation—Analysis of Government—Proposals for Redress* (Washington, D.C.: Carnegie Endowment for International Peace, 1944).

J. Lewis, *Uncertain Judgment: A Bibliography of War Crimes Trials* (Santa Barbara: ABC-Clio, 1979).

H. Lunau, *The Germans on Trial* (New York: Storm Publishers, 1948).

M. Marrus, *The Holocaust in History* (New York: Penguin, 1987).

M. Marrus (ed.), *The Nuremberg War Crimes Trial 1945–1946* (New York: Bedford, 1997).

W. Maser, *Nuremberg: A Nation on Trial*, translated from the German by R. Barry (New York: Scribner, 1979).

D. Maxwell Fyfe, *Political Adventures: The Memoirs of the Earl of Kilmuir* (London: Weidenfeld & Nicolson, 1964).

G. Mayda, *Il processo di Norimberga* (Milan: A. Mondadori, 1972).

J. Mendelsohn, *Trial by Document: The Use of Seized Records in the United States Proceedings at Nuernberg* (New York and London: Garland Publishing, 1988).

M. Merle, *Le procès de Nuremberg et le châtiment des criminels de guerre* (Paris: A. Pedone, 1949).

B. Michal *et al.*, *Le Procès de Nuremberg*, 2 vols. (Paris: Éditions Francois Beauval, 1969).

J. Morgan, *Great Assize: An Examination of the Law of the Nuremberg Trials* (London: J. Murray, 1948).

M. Myerson, *Germany's War Crimes and Punishment* (Toronto: Macmillan, 1945).

A. Neave, *Nuremberg—A Personal Record of the Trial of the Major Nazi War Criminals* (London: Hodder and Stoughton, 1978).

O. Nelte, *Die Generale: Das Nürnberger Urteil und die Schuld der Generale* (Hanover: Verlag das Andere Deutschland, 1947).

I. Neumann (ed.), *European War Crimes Trials: A Bibliography* (New York: Carnegie Endowment for International Peace, 1951).

R. Norton-Taylor (ed.), *Nuremberg: The War Crimes Trial* (London: Nick Hern Books Ltd., 1997).

Nürnberger Memschenrechtszentrum (R. Huhle) (ed.), *Von Nürnberg nach Den Haag—Menschenrechtverbrechen vor Gericht—Zur Aktualität des Nürnberger Prozesses* (Hamburg: Europäsiche Verlagsanstalt, 1996).

V. Pella, *Fonctions pacificatrices du droit pénal supranational et fin du système traditionel des traités de paix* (Paris: A. Pedone, 1947).

V. Pella, *La guerre-crime et les criminels de guerre, réflexions sur la justice pénale internationale* (Neuchâtel: Editions de la Baconnière, 1949).

J. Persico, *Nuremberg—Infamy on Trial* (New York: Penguin Books, 1994).

B. Polevoi, *The Final Reckoning: Nuremberg Diaries* (Moscow: Progress Publishers, 1978).

L. Poliakov, (comp.), *Le procès de Nuremberg* (Paris: Julliard, 1971).

A. Poltorak, *Njurnbergski process: Osnownje prawowje problemi* (Leningrad: Nauka, 1965).

A. Poltorak, *The Nuremberg Epilogue*, translated by David Skwirsky (Moscow: Progress Publishers, 1971).

A. Poltorak, *Nürnberger Epilog* (Berlin, Militäverlag der Deutschen Demokratischen Republik, 1975).

A. Poltorak and Y. Zaitsev, *Remember Nuremberg* (Moscow: Foreign Languages Publishing House, 1959).

C. Pompe, *Aggressive War: An International Crime* (The Hague: Martinus Nijhoff, 1953).

M. Raguinski, *Osnownje processualnje woprosj organizasi I dejtelnosti mezdunnarodnich wojenich tribunalow w Njurnberge I Tokyo* (Moscow: Vsesojuznii institute juridcheskih nauk Ministerstva Justicii Sojuza SSR, 1950).

M. Raguinski, *Njurnbergsky Process* (Moscow: Sbornik Materialov, tom II, 1958).

S. Ratner and J. Abrams, *Accountability for Human Rights Atrocities in International Law: Beyond the Nuremberg Legacy*, 2nd ed. (Oxford: Oxford University Press, 2001).

A. Rückerl, *The Investigation of Nazi Crimes, 1945–1978* (Hamden, CT: Archon, 1980).

R. Rudenko, *Die Gerechtigkeit fordert für alle Hauptkriegsverbrecher nur eine Strafe, die Todesstrafe: General Rudenkos Schlussrede in Nürnberg* (Berlin: Verlag Tägliche Rundschau, 1947).

R. Rudenko, *Niurnbergskii process nad glavnymi nemete kimi voennymi prestupnikami: Sbornik materialov v vemi tomakh pod obschchei red. R.A. Rudenko*, 7 vols. (Moscow: Gos. izd-vo iurid. lit-ry, 1957–1961).

L. Saurel, *Le procès de Nuremberg* (Paris: Éditions Rouff, 2nd rev. edn., 1967).

H. Scanlon, *A Select List of Books and Articles Defining War Crimes under International Law and Discussing their Trial and Punishment* (Washington, DC: Carnegie Endowment for International Peace, 1945).

G. Schwarzenberger, *International Law and Totalitarian Lawlessness* (London: Jonathan Cape, 1943).

B. Smith, *Reaching Judgment at Nuremberg* (New York: Basic Books, 1967).

B. Smith, *The American Road to Nuremberg—The Documentary Record* (Stanford: Hoover Press Publication, 1982).

D. Sprecher, *Inside the Nuremberg Trial: A Prosecutor's Comprehensive Account*, 2 vols. (Lanham: University Press of America, 1998).

B. Stave, *et al.*, *Witnesses to Nuremberg: An Oral History of American Participants at the War Crimes Trials* (New York: Twayne Publishers and Prentice Hall International, 1998).

R. Storey, *The Final Judgment—Pearl Harbor to Nuremberg* (San Antonio: The Naylor Company, 1968).

T. Taylor, *Nuremberg Trials* (New York: Carnegie Endowment for International Peace, 1949).

T. Taylor, *Sword and Swastika* (New York: Simon & Schuster, 1952).

T. Taylor, *Guilt, Responsibility and the Third Reich* (Cambridge: Heffer, 1970).

T. Taylor, *Nuremberg and Vietnam: An American Tragedy* (Chicago: Quadrangle Books, 1970).

T. Taylor, *The Anatomy of the Nuremberg Trials* (New York: Alfred Knopf, 1992).

H. Thompson and H. Strutz, *Doenitz at Nuremberg: A Reappraisal. War Crimes and the Military Professional* (New York: Amber Publishers, 1976).

A. Trainin, A. Vyshinsky, and A. Rothstein, *Hitlerite Responsibility under Criminal Law* (London: Hutchinson, 1945).

A. Tusa and J. Tusa, *The Nuremberg Trial* (New York: Atheneum, 1983).

N. Tutorow and K. Winnovich, *War Crimes, War Criminals, and War Crimes Trials: An Annotated Bibliography and Source Book* (New York: Greenwood Press, 1986).

United Nations, *Guide to Records of the War Crimes Trials Held in Nürnberg, Germany, 1945–1949, Prepared in Archives Section, Communications and Records Division*, United Nations Archives Reference Guide, no. 7/rev. 1 (Lake Success: United Nations, Archives Section, 1949).

F. Utley, *The High Court of Vengeance* (Chicago: Henry Regnery Co., 1949).

A. F. Volochkov, *Agressia kak mjezdunarodnoje prestuplenye: po materialam Njurnbergskogo processa* (Moscow, 1950).

E. Wall, *Il processo di Norimberga: cronistoria delle udienze* (Milan: Lucchi, 1946).

H. Wechsler, *Principles, Politics and Fundamental Law: Selected Essays* (Cambridge: Harvard University Press, 1961).

J. Wheeler-Bennett, *Friends, Enemies and Sovereigns* (London: Macmillan Ltd., 1976).

J. Willis, *Prologue to Nuremberg: The Politics and Diplomacy of Punishing War Criminals of the First World War* (Westport: Greenwood Press, 1982).

R. Woetzel, *The Nuremberg Trials in International Law* (London: Sevens & Sons Ltd., 1960).

J. Wolf, *Les Fondements du Tribunal Militaire International: Considération sur le procès de Nuremberg* (Brussels: Larcier, 1946).

Q. Wright, *A Study of War* (Chicago: University of Chicago Press, 1942).

ARTICLES, NOTES, AND COMMENTARIES

S. Alderman, 'Background and Highlights of the Nuernberg Trial', 14 *Interstate Commerce Commission Practitioners Journal* 121 (1946).

S. Alderman, 'Negotiating the Nuremberg Trial Agreements', in R. Dennett and J. Johnson (eds.), *Negotiating with the Russians* (Boston: World Peace Foundation, 1951), 49.

G. N. Aleksandrow, Istoricheski prigovor // Izvestija vuzov. Prawowedjenje, 1977, N 1, 103–105.

J. Alvarez, 'Nuremberg Revisited: The Tadic Case', 7(2) *European Journal of International Law* 245 (1996).

A. Anderson, 'The Utility of the Proposed Trial and Punishment of Enemy Leaders', 37 *American Political Science Review* 1081 (1943).

C. Anderson, 'The Utility of the Proposed Trial and Punishment of Enemy Leaders', 37(6) *American Political Science Review* 1081 (December 1943).

N. April, 'An Inquiry into the Judicial Basis for the Nuremberg War Crime Trial', 30 *Minnesota Law Review* 313 (April 1946).

N. April, 'The Nuremberg War Crimes Trials—An Inquiry into the Judicial Basis for', 30 *Minnesota Law Review* 313 (1946).

R. Arens, 'Nuremberg and Group Prosecution', *Washington University Law Quarterly* 329 (1951).

E. Aronéanu, 'Le Crime contre l'Humanité', 13 *Nouvelle Revue de Droit International Privé* 369 (1946).

E. Aronéanu, 'Le Juge Jackson et la justice pénale internationale', 32 *Revue de Droit International (Sottile-Geneva)* 361 (Décembre 1954).

Lord Atkin, 'The Trial of the Nazis', 95 *Law Journal* 191 (1945).

K. Bader, 'Zum Nürnberger Urteil', 1 *Deutsche Rechtszeitschrift* 183 (1946).

K. Bader, 'Nürnberger Prozess', 1 *Deutsche Rechtszeitschrift* 140 (November 1946).

K. Bader, 'Review', in W. Benton and G. Grimm (eds.), *Nuremberg—German Views of the War Trials* (Dallas: Southern Methodist University Press, 1955), 153.

A. Balazs, 'Die rechtliche Begründung des Nürnberger Urteils', 1 *Friedenswarte* 369–375 (1946).

H. Balmer-Basilius, 'Nürnberg und das Weltgewissen', 1 *Friedenswarte* 289 (1946).

W. Barcikowski, 'Les Nations Unies et l'Organisation de la Répression des Crimes de Guerre', 17(3–4) *Revue Internationale de Droit Pénal* 298 (1946).

J. Barry, 'The Trial and Punishment of Axis War Criminals', 17 *Australian Law Journal* 43 (June 1943).

M. C. Bassiouni, 'Nuremberg Forty Years After: An Introduction', 18 *Case Western Reserve Journal of International Law* 261 (1986).

M. C. Bassiouni, 'The "Nuremberg Legacy"', in M. C. Bassiouni (ed.), *International Criminal Law*, 2nd ed. (Ardsley, NY: Translational, 1999), vol. iii, 195 (1998).

M. C. Bassiouni, 'The Nuremberg Legacy: Historical Assessment Fifty Years Later', in B. Cooper (ed.), *War Crimes—The Legacy of Nuremberg* (New York: TV Books, 1999), 291.

G. Belloni, 'Criminalità di Guerra', 51 *Giustizia Penale* (1946), I, col. 1–8.

J. Berger, 'The Legal Nature of War Crimes and the Problem of Superior Command', 38(6) *American Political Science Review* 1203 (December 1944).

M. Bernays, 'Legal Basis of the Nuremberg Trials', 35 *Survey Graphic* 4 (January 1946).

L. Bial, 'The Nürnberg Judgment and International Law', 13 *Brooklyn Law Review* 34 (1947).

F. Biddle, 'The Nuernberg Trial', 91(3) *American Philosophical Society Proceedings* 294 (August 1947).

F. Biddle, 'The Nuremberg Trial', 33(6) *Virginia Law Review* 679 (November 1947).

F. Biddle, 'Le procès de Nuremberg', 1 *Revue Internationale de Droit Pénal* 6 (1948).

N. Birkett, 'International Legal Theories Evolved at Nuremberg', 23(3) *International Affairs* 317 (July 1947).

N. Blakeney, 'International Military Tribunal', 32 *American Bar Association Journal* 475 (1946).

A. Boissarie, 'La définition des crimes contre l'humanité', 3–4 *Revue Internationale de Droit Pénal* 201 (1947).

A. Boissarie, 'La Répression des crimes Nazis contre l'humanité et la protection des libertés démocratiques', 1 *Revue Internationale de Droit Pénal* 11 (1947).

E. M. Borchard *et al.*, 'The Multilateral Treaty for Renunciation of War', 23 *American Journal of International Law* 116 (1929).

G. Brand, 'The War Crimes Trials and the Law of War', 26 *British Yearbook of International Law* 414 (February 1949).

J. Brand, 'Crimes Against Humanity and the Nuremberg Trials', 28 *Oregon Law Review* 93 (February 1949).

P. Brown, 'International Criminal Justice', 35(1) *American Journal of International Law* 118 (January 1941).

C. Burchard, 'The Nuremberg Trial and its Impact on Germany', 4(4) *Journal of International Criminal Justice*, 800.

M. Caloyanni, 'Le procès de Nuremberg et l'avenir de la justice pénale internationale', 4 *Revue de Droit International de Sciences Diplomatiques et Politiques* 174 (1946).

A. Campbell, 'The Nuremberg Defense to Charges of Domestic Crime: A Non-Traditional Approach for Nuclear-Arms Protesters', 16 *California Western International Law Journal* 93 (1986).

E. Carter, 'The Nuremberg Trials. A Turning Point in the Enforcement of International Law', 28 *Nebraska Law Review* 370 (1949).

H. Carton de Wiart, 'Grands criminels de guerre', 24 *Revue de Droit International (Sottile-Geneva)* 41 (April–September 1946).

R. Chaney, 'Pitfalls and Imperatives: Applying the Lessons of Nuremberg to the Yugoslav War Crimes Trials', 14(1) *Dickinson Journal of International Law* 57 (1995).

J. Chase, 'The Development of the Morgenthau Plan through the Quebec Conference', 16(2) *Journal of Politics* 324 (May 1954).

R. Clark, 'Crimes Against Humanity at Nuremberg', in G. Ginsburg and V. N. Kudriavtsev (eds.), *The Nuremberg Trial and International Law* (Dordrecht: Martinus Nijhoff Publishers, 1990), 177.

R. Clark, 'Nuremberg and Tokyo in Contemporary Perspective', in T. McCormack and G. Simpson (eds.), *The Law of War Crimes: National and International Approaches* (The Hague: Martinus Nijhoff, 1997), 171.

E. Cohn, 'The Problems of War Crimes Today', 26 *Transactions of the Grotius Society* 125 (1940).

W. Cowles, 'Trial of War Criminals by Military Tribunals', 30 *American Bar Association Journal* 330 (June 1944).

W. Cowles, 'High Government Officials as War Criminals', 54 *Proceedings of the American Society of International Law* 65 (1945).

W. Cowles, 'Universality of Jurisdiction over War Crimes', 33(3) *California Law Review* 177 (1945).

A. D'Amato, H. Gould, and L. Woods, 'War Crimes and Vietnam: The "Nuremberg Defense" and the Military Service Register', 57 *California Law Review* 1055 (1969).

J. Descheemaeker, 'Le Tribunal militaire international des grands criminels de guerre', 50 *Revue Générale de Droit International Public* 210 (1946).

H. Dix, 'Die Urteile in den Nürnberger Wirtschaftsprozessen', 17 *Neue Juristische Wochenschrift* 647–52 (1949).

T. Dodd, 'The Nuremberg Trials', 37 *Journal of Criminal Law and Criminology* 357 (January 1947).

N. Doman, 'Political Consequences of the Nuremberg Trial', 246 *Annals of the American Academy of Political and Social Science* 81 (1946).

N. Doman, 'The Nuremberg Trials Revisited', 47 *American Bar Association Journal* 260 (March 1961).

H. Donnedieu de Vabres, 'Le jugement de Nuremberg et le principe de la légalité des délits et des peines', 26 *Revue de Droit Pénal et de Criminologie* 813 (1946–1947).

H. Donnedieu de Vabres, 'Le procès de Nuremberg devant les principes modernes du Droit Pénal International', 70(I) *Recueil des Cours de l'Académie de droit international de La Haye* 477 (1947-I).

H. Donnedieu de Vabres, 'Le procès de Nuremberg', 2 *Revue de Science Criminelle et de Droit Pénal Comparé* 171 (1947).

H. Donnedieu de Vabres, 'La codification du droit pénal international', 1 *Revue internationale de droit pénal* 21 (1948).

C. Dubost, 'Les crimes des états et la coutume pénale internationale', 6 *Politique Etrangère* 553 (December 1946).

J. Dulles, 'International Criminal Law and Individuals: A Comment on Enforcing Peace', 35 *American Bar Association Journal* 912 (1949).

F. Eccard, 'La signification suprême du procès de Nuremberg', 2–3 *Revue de Droit International de Sciences Diplomatiques et Politiques* 82 (1946).

H. Ehard, 'Der Nürnberger Prozess gegen die Hauptkriegsverbrecher und das Völkerrecht', *Süddeutschen Juristen-Zeitung, Jg. 3, Nr. 7* 353 (1948).

H. Ehard, 'The Nuremberg Trial Against the Major War Criminals and International Law', 43(2) *American Journal of International Law* 223 (April 1949).

R. Falk, 'Nuremberg: Past, Present and Future', 80(7) *Yale Law Journal* 1501 (June 1971).

R. Falk, 'The Nuremberg Defense in the Pentagon Papers Case', 13 *Columbia Journal Transnational Law* 208 (1974).

B. Ferencz, 'Nuremberg Trial Procedure and the Rights of the Accused', 39 *Journal of Criminal Law and Criminology* 144 (July–August 1948).

G. Finch, 'Retribution for War Crimes', 37 *American Journal of International Law* 81 (January 1943).

G. Finch, 'The Nuremberg Trial and International Law', 41 *American Journal of International Law* 20 (January 1947).

K. Fite, 'The Nürnberg Judgment: A Summary', Department of State Publication, no. 2727 (Washington, DC: Government Printing Office, 1947).

G. Forbes, 'Legal Aspects of the Nuremberg Trial', 24 *Canadian Bar Review* 584 (August–September 1946).

M. Franklin, 'Sources of International Law Relating to Sanctions Against War Criminals', 36 *Journal of Criminal Law and Criminology (1931–1951)* 153 (September–October 1945).

W. Friedmann, 'International Law and the Present War', 26 *Transactions of the Grotius Society* 221 (1940).

H. Fujita, 'Le crime contre l'humanité dans les procès de Nuremberg et de Tokyo', 34 *Kobe University Law Review* 1 (2000).

P. Gault, 'Prosecution of War Criminals', 36 *Journal of Criminal Law and Criminology* 180 (September–October 1945).

J. Genton, 'Le Tribunal Militaire International: Compétence réelle: Les solutions données par le Statut du 8 août 1945', 28 *Revue de Droit Pénal et de Criminologie* 477 (1947–1948).

S. Glaser, 'Le principe de la légalité des délits et des peines et les procès des criminels de guerre', 28 *Revue de Droit Pénal et de Criminologie* 230 (1947–1948).

S. Glaser, 'La Charte du Tribunal de Nuremberg et les Nouveaux Principes du Droit International', 13 *Schweitzerische Zeitschrift fur Strafrecht/Revue Pénale Suisse* (1948).

S. Glaser, 'Die Gesetzlichkeit im Völkerrecht', *Zeitschrift für die gesamte Strafrechtswinsenschaft* (1964).

S. Glueck, 'By What Tribunal Shall War Offenders Be Tried', 56 *Harvard Law Review* 1059 (January 1943).

S. Glueck, 'The Nuernberg Trial and Aggressive War', 59 *Harvard Law Review* 396 (February 1946).

S. Glueck, 'Ist der Nürnberger Prozess Illegal?', 2(9) *Die Amerikanische Rundschau* 3 (1946).

R. Goldstone, '50 Jahre nach Nürnberg', in Nürnberger Memschenrechtszentrum (R. Huhle) (ed.), *Von Nürnberg nach Den Haag—Menschenrechtverbrechen vor Gericht—Zur Aktualität des Nürnberger Prozesses* (Hamburg: Europäsiche Verlagsanstalt, 1996), 57.

A.L. Goodhart, 'The Legality of the Nuremberg Trial', 58 *Juridical Review* 1 (1946).

A.L. Goodhart, 'Questions and Answers Concerning the Nuremberg Trial', 1 *International Law Quarterly* 525 (1947).

J. Graven, 'De la justice internationale à la paix (Les enseignements de Nuremberg)', 4 *Revue de Droit International, de Sciences Diplomatiques et Politiques* 183 (1946).

J. Graven, 'Vingt ans après: La libération des prisonniers de Spandau', 27 *Revue de Droit Pénal et de Criminologie* 436 (1946–1947).

J. Graven, 'Les Châtiments des Crimes de Guerre', 31 *Alma Mater* (1947).

J. Graven, 'Principes Fondamentaux d'un Code Répressif des Crimes contre la Paix et la Securité de l'Humanité', 28(2) *Revue de droit international, de sciences diplomatiques et politiques* 173 (1950) and 28(4) *Revue de droit international, de sciences diplomatiques et politiques* 361 (1950).

T. Gregory, 'The Nuremberg Trials', 21 *Connecticut Bar Journal* 2 (1947).

W. Grewe, 'Nürnberg als Rechtsfrage', in W. Grewe (ed.), *Machtprojektionen und Rechtsschranken* (Baden-Baden: Nomos, 1991).

A. Gros, 'Le châtiment des crimes de guerre', 9 *Cahiers Politiques* 49 (April 1945).

L. Gross, 'The Criminality of Aggressive War', 41(2) *American Political Science Review* 205 (April 1947).

L. Gross, 'The Punishment of War Criminals: The Nuremberg Trial', 2 *Netherlands International Law Review* 356 (1955).

C. Haensel, 'Nürnberger Probleme', 1 *Deutsche Rechtszeitschrift* 67 (1946).

C. Haensel, 'Schuldprinzip und Gruppenkriminalität', 2 *Süddeutsche Juristenzeitung*, 15 (1947).

C. Haensel, 'Das Urteil in Nürnberger Juristenprozess', 3 *Deutsche Rechtszeitschrift* 40 (1948).

C. Haensel, 'Der Ausklang von Nürnberg', 2 *Neue Juristische Wochenschrift* 367–70 (1949).

C. Haensel, 'The Nuremburg Trial Revisited', 13 *DePaul Law Review* 248 (1964).

W. B. Hale, 'Nurenberg War Crimes Trials', 21 *Tennessee Law Review* 8 (December 1949).

W. Harris, 'The Nuremberg Trial', 22 *State Bar Journal of California* 97 (March–April 1947).

W. Harris, 'Justice Jackson at Nuremberg', 20(3) *International Lawyer* 867 (1986).

W. Harris, 'A Call for an International War Crimes Court: Learning from Nuremberg', 23(2) *University of Toledo Law Review* 229 (1992).

E. Hazan, 'Etude critique du jugement de Nuremberg', 1 *Revue de Droit International pour le Moyen-Orient* 33 (1951).

F. Hermens, 'Collective Guilt', 23 *Notre Dame Lawyer* 431 (1948).

J. Herzog, 'Les organisations national-socialistes devant le Tribunal de Nuremberg', 1–2 *Revue Internationale de Droit Penal* 343 (1946).

J. Herzog, 'Les Principes Juridiques de la répression des crimes de guerre', 3 *Revue Pénale Suisse* 277 (1946).

J. Herzog, 'Contribution à la définition du crime contre l'humanité', 2 *Revue Internationale de Droit Pénal* 155 (1947).

F. Hirsh, 'Lessons of Nuremberg', 11 *Current History* 312 (October 1946).

F. von Hofmannsthal, 'War Crimes Not Tried Under Retroactive Law', 22 *New York University Law Quarterly Review* 93 (1947).

F. Honig, 'Nuremberg—Justice or Vengeance?', 1 *World Affairs* 79 (1947).

G. Hoover, 'The Outlook for "War Guilt" Trials', 59 *Political Science Quarterly* 40 (March 1944).

C. Hubert, 'Nuremberg—Justice or Vengeance?' 1 *Military Government Journal* 11 (March 1944).

L. Hugueney, 'Le procès de Nuremberg devant les principes modernes du droit pénal international', 3–4 *Revue Internationale de Droit Pénal* 277 (1948).

E. Hula, 'Punishment for War Crimes', 13 *Social Research* 1 (March 1945).

E. Hula, 'The Revival of the Idea of Punitive War', 82 *Thought* 405 (September 1946).

C. Hull, 'Indefensibles' Defense', 47 *Time* 29 (18 March 1946).

C. Hull, International Military Tribunal, 'Judgment and Sentences', 41 *American Journal of International Law* 172 (January 1947).

C. Hyde, 'Punishment of War Criminals', 37 *Proceedings of the American Society of International Law* 39 (1942–1943).

G. Ireland, '*Ex Post Facto* From Rome to Tokyo', 21 *Temple Law Quarterly* 27 (1948).

R. Jackson, 'The Challenge of International Lawlessness', 27 *American Bar Association Journal* 690 (1941), 374 *International Conciliation* 683 (1941).

R. Jackson, 'Address to the Inter-American Bar Association', 27 March 1941, reprinted in 35 *American Journal of International Law* 348 (1941).

R. Jackson, 'International Order', 27 *American Bar Association Journal* 275 (1941), *American Journal of International Law* 348 (1941), 19 *Canadian Bar Review* 229 (1941), 7 *Vital Speeches* 399 (1941) (Address before the Inter-American Bar Association, Havana, Cuba, 27 March 1941).

R. Jackson, 'Worst Crime of All', *New York Times Magazine* 9 (9 September 1945).

R. Jackson, 'The Rule of Law Among Nations', 31 *American Bar Association Journal* 290 (1945).

R. Jackson, 'The Rule of Law Among Nations', 39 *American Society of International Law Proceedings* 10 (1945).

R. Jackson, 'Report to the President on the Prosecution of Axis War Criminals', June 7, 1945, reprinted as 'Report to the President from Justice Robert H. Jackson, Chief of Counsel for the United States in the Prosecution of Axis War Criminals', in 39 *American Journal International Law* 178 (Supplement 1945), as 'Justice Jackson's Report to President Truman on the Legal Basis for Trial of War Criminals', 19 *Temple Law Quarterly* 144 (1945–1946).

R. Jackson, 'The Trials of War Criminals: An Experiment in International Legal Understanding', 32 *American Bar Association Journal* 319 (1946) (Address before the National Legal Movement, Paris, 2 April 1946).

R. Jackson, 'Justice Jackson Weighs Nuremberg's Lessons', *New York Times Magazine* 12 (16 June 1946).

R. Jackson, 'The Trials of War Criminals: An Experiment in International Legal Understanding', 32 *American Bar Association Journal* 319 (June 1946).

R. Jackson, 'Closing Arguments for Conviction of Nazi War Criminals', Nuremberg, July 26, 1946 reprinted in 20 *Temple Law Quarterly* 85 (1946), 12 *Vital Speeches* 710 (1946), 52 *Case and Comment* 3 (1947) (condensed).

R. Jackson, 'The Nürnberg Trial', 13 *Vital Speeches* 114 (1946) (Address at the University of Buffalo Centennial Convocation, Buffalo, NY, 4 October 1946).

R. Jackson, 'The Significance of the Nuremberg Trials to the Armed Forces', 10 *Military Affairs* 3 (Winter 1946).

R. Jackson, 'The Significance of the Nuremberg Trials to the Armed Forces: Previously Unpublished Personal Observations by the Chief Counsel for the United States', 10(4) *Military Affairs* 2 (Winter 1946) (Address at the National War College, Washington, DC, 6 December 1946).

R. Jackson, 'The Law Under Which Nazi Organizations are Accused of Being Criminal', 19 *Temple Law Quarterly* 371 (1946).

R. Jackson, 'The Nürnberg Trial Becomes an Historic Precedent', 20 *Temple Law Quarterly* 167 (1946).

R. Jackson, 'Nuremberg Trial of the Major Nazi Leaders', 70 *New York State Bar Association Bulletin* 147 (1947).

R. Jackson, 'Some Problems in Developing an International Legal System', 22 *Temple Law Quarterly* 147 (1948).

R. Jackson, 'Nuremberg in Retrospect: Legal Answer to International Lawlessness', 35 *American Bar Association Journal* 813 (1949).

R. Jackson, 'Trial of the Trials: Nuernberg', *Common Cause* 284 (1950).

R. Jackson, 'United Nations Organization and War Crimes', 46 *American Society of International Law Proceedings* 196 (1952) (Address before the American Society for International Law, Washington, DC, 26 April 1952).

W. Jackson, 'War Nürnberg gerechtfertigt?' in *Gollier*, 19 May 1947.

W. Jackson, 'Putting the Nuremberg Law to Work', 25 *Foreign Affairs* 550 (1946–1947).

S. E. Jaffe, 'Natural Law and the Nurnberg Trials', 26 *Nebraska Law Review* 90 (November 1947).

K. Jaspers, 'Significance of the Nuremberg Trials for Germany and the World', 22 *Notre Dame Law Review* 150 (1947).

H. Jescheck, 'Die Entwicklung des Völkerstrafrechtsnach Nürnberg', 72 *Schweizerische Zeitschrift für Strafrecht* 15 (1957).

P. Jessup, 'The Crime of Aggression and the Future of International Law', 62 *Political Science Quarterly* 1 (March 1947).

K. Kastner, 'Der Nütnberger Prozess', *Juristische Arbeitsblätter* 802 (1995).

K. Kaufmann, 'The Nuremberg Trial in Retrospect', 9 *Whittier Law Review* 537 (1987–1988).

H. Kelsen, 'Collective and Individual Responsibility in International Law with Particular Regard to the Punishment of War Criminals', 31 *California Law Review* 530 (1943).

H. Kelsen, 'The Rule against ex post facto Laws and the Prosecution of the Axis War Criminals', 2(3) *Judge Advocate Journal* 8 (1945).

H. Kelsen, 'The Legal Status of Germany According to the Declaration of Berlin', 39 *American Journal of International Law* 518 (1945).

H. Kelsen, 'Will the Judgment in the Nuremberg Trial Constitute a Precedent in International Law?' 1(2) *International Law Quarterly* 153 (1947).

H. Kelsen, 'Collective and Individual Responsibility for Acts of State in International Law', *Jewish Yearbook of International Law* 226 (1948).

R. Kempner, 'The Nuremberg Trials as Sources of Recent German Political and Historical Material', 44(2) *American Political Science Review* 447 (June 1950).

P. Kirsch, 'From Nuremberg to The Hague: The Nuremberg Heritage: A Series of Events Commemorating the Beginning of the Nuremberg trials', Speech by the President of the ICC delivered at the Palais de Justice in Nuremberg, 19 November 2005 (available on the ICC website at: http://www.icc-cpi.int/library/organs/presidency/speeches/PK_20051119_En.pdf).

R. Klefisch, 'Thoughts about Purport and Effect of the Nuremberg Judgment', in W. Benton and G. Grimm (eds.), *Nuremberg—German Views of the War Trials* (Dallas: Southern Methodist University Press, 1955), 201.

G. Komarow, 'Individual Responsibility under International Law: The Nuremberg Principles in Domestic Legal Systems', 29(1) *International and Comparative Law Quarterly* 21 (January 1980).

M. R. Konvitz, 'Will Nuremberg Serve Justice?' 1(3) *Commentary* 11 (January 1946).

W. Koo, 'Some Aspects of the Work of the Legal Committee of the General Assembly during the Second Part of the First Session', 41 *American Journal of International Law* 639 (1947).

O. Kranzbühler, 'Nürnberg als Rechtsproblem', *in Festgabe E. Kaufmann* 219 (1950).

O. Kranzbühler, Nuremberg as a Legal Problem', in W. Benton and G. Grimm (eds.), *Nuremberg—German Views of the War Trials* (Dallas: Southern Methodist University Press, 1955), 106.

O. Kranzbühler, 'Nuremberg Eighteen Years Afterwards', 14(2) *DePaul Law Review* 333 (1965).

H. Kraus, 'The Nuremberg Trial of the Major War Criminals: Reflections after Seventeen Years', 13 *DePaul Law Review* 233 (1964).

K. Kuhn, 'International Criminal Jurisdiction', 41(2) *American Journal of International Law* 430 (1947).

J. Kunz, '*Bellum Justum* and *Bellum Legale*', 45(3) *American Journal of International Law* 528 (July 1951).

M. Lachs, 'War Crimes—Political Offenses', 56 *Juridical Review* 27 (April 1944).

M. Lachs, 'Crimes de Guerre—Délits Politiques', 1–2 *Revue de droit international, de Sciences Diplomatiques et Politiques* 10 (January–June 1945).

M. Lachs, 'Le Jugement de Nuremberg', 1–2 *Revue Internationale de Droit Pénal* 398 (1946).

H. Laternser, 'Looking Back at the Nuremberg Trials with Special Consideration of the Processes against Military Leaders', 8 *Whittier Law Review* 557 (1985).

S. Lauer, 'The International War Criminal Trials and the Common Law of War', 20 *St. John's Law Review* 18 (1945).

H. Lauterpacht, 'The Law of Nations and the Punishment of War Crimes', 21 *British Yearbook of International Law* 58 (1944).

F. Lawrence, 'The Nuremberg Principles: A Defense for Political Protesters', 40 *Hastings Law Journal* 397 (1989).

G. Lawrence (Lord Oaksey), 'The Nuernberg Trial', 23(2) *International Affairs* 151 (April 1947).

R. Lemkin, 'Genocide', 15(2) *American Scholar* 227 (April 1946).

R. Lemkin, 'Responsibility of Persons Acting on Behalf of States in the Crime of Genocide', *American Scholar* (1946).

S. Lener, 'Diritto e politica nel processo di Norimberga', 97 *Civiltà Cattolica* (1946), III, pp. 92–106.

H. Leonhardt, 'The Nuremberg Trial: A Legal Analysis', 11(4) *Review of Politics* 449 (October 1949).

H. Leventhal, S. Harris, J. M. Woolsey, Jr., and W. Farr, 'The Nuremberg Verdict', 60(6) *Harvard Law Review* 857 (July 1947).

A. Levy, 'The Law and Procedure of War Crime Trials', 37(6) *American Political Science Review* 1052 (December 1943).

A. Levy, 'Criminal Responsibility of Individuals in International Law', 12 *University of Chicago Law Review* 313 (1947).

P. de Leyrat, 'Crime de la Guerre et Crimes de Guerre', 5 *Cahiers du Monde Nouveau* 593 (December 1945).

M. Lippman, 'Nuremberg: Forty-Five Years Later', 7 *Connecticut Journal of International Law* 1 (1991).

D. Luban, 'The Legacies of Nuremberg', 54(4) *Social Research* 779.

H. von Mangoldt, 'Das Kriegsverbrechen und seine Verfolgung in Vergangenheit und Gegenwart', 1 *Jahrbuch für Internationals und Ausländisches Öffentliches Recht* 283 (1948).

G. Manner, 'The Legal Nature and Punishment of Criminal Acts of Violence Contrary to the Laws of War', 37(3) *American Journal of International Law* 407 (July 1943).

L. Mansfield, 'Crimes Against Humanity: Reflections on the Fiftieth Anniversary of Nuremberg and a Forgotten Legacy', 64 *Nordic Journal of International Law* 293 (1995).

G. Martius, 'Das Nürnberger Urteil in völkerrechtliche Beziehung', *Neue Justiz* No 4/5, 91 (1947).

J. Maynard, 'Crimes et criminels de guerre, problème étudié par un groupe de juristes aux Etats-Unis', 1–2 *Revue Internationale de Droit Pénal* 333 (1946).

G. R. McConnell, 'Trial of War Criminals at Nuremberg', 1 *Wyoming Law Journal* 3 (1946).

D. McIntyre, 'The Nuernberg Trials', 24 *University of Pittsburgh Law Review* 73 (1962).

J. Mendelsohn, 'Trial by Document: The Problem of Due Process for War Criminals at Nuremberg', 7(4) *Prologue* 227 (1975).

R. Merkel, 'Das Recht des Nürnberger Prozesses', in *Von Nürnberg nach Den Haag— Menschenrechtverbrechen vor Gericht—Zur Aktualität des Nürnberger Prozesses* (Hamburg: Europäsiche Verlagsanstalt, 1996), 68.

R. Merkel, 'Das Recht des Nürnberger Prozesses—Gültig, Fragwürdiges, Überholtes', in Nürnberger Menschenrechtzentrum (Hrsg.), *Von Nürnberg nach Den Haag, Menschenrechtsverbrechen vor Gericht—Zur Aktaulität des Nürnberger Prozesses* (Nuremberg: Europäische Verlagsanstalt, 1996), 68.

B. Meltzer, ' "War Crimes": The Nuremberg Trial and the Tribunal for the Former Yugoslavia', 30 *Valparaiso University Law Review* 895 (1996).

B. Metzler, 'Nuremberg Trials', 14 *University of Chicago Law Review* 455 (1947).

H. Mosler, 'Die Kriegshandlung im Rechtswigriden Krieg', 1 *Jahrbuch für Internationales und Ausländisches Öffentliches Recht* 335–57 (1948).

H. Munro, 'Trial of Axis War Criminals: The Question of Procedure', 13 *Fortnightly Law Journal* 119 (15 November 1943).

H. Munro, 'War Criminals and International Justice', 95 *Law Journal* 173 (2 June 1945).

H. Munro, 'Plans for the Trial of War Criminals', 95 *Law Journal* 5 (1945).

H. Munro, 'The United States and War Criminals', 95 *Law Journal* 231 (1945).

A. Neave, 'The Trial of the SS at Nuremberg', 1–2 *Revue Internationale de Droit Pénal* 277 (1946).

F. Neubacher, 'How Can it Happen that Horrendous State Crimes are Perpetrated?' 4(4) *Journal of International Criminal Justice*, 787.

F. Neumann, 'The War Crimes Trials', 2(1) *World Politics* 135 (October 1949).

G. Ottolenghi, 'Le problème des criminels de guerre', 1 *Revue de droit international de Sciences Diplomatiques et Politiques* 8 (1946).

G. Ottolenghi, 'Le problème des criminels de guerre', 24 *Revue de droit international (Sottile—Geneva)* 1 (January–March 1946).

O. Pannenbecker, 'The Nuremberg War-Crimes Trial', 14(2) *DePaul Law Review* 348 (1965).

J. Parker, 'International Trial at Nuremberg: Giving Vitality to International Law', 37 *American Bar Association Journal* 493 (December 1946).

J. Parker, 'The Nuernberg Trial', 30 *Journal of the American Judicature Society* 109 (1946).

J. Parker, 'The Nuremberg Trial', 11 *Kentucky State Bar Journal* 157 (June 1947).

C. Patterson, 'Principles of Nürnberg as a Defense to Civil Disobedience', 37 *Missouri Law Review* 33 (1972).

S. L. Paulson, 'Classical Legal Positivism at Nuremberg', 4(2) *Philosophy and Public Affairs* 132 (1975).

V. Pella, 'La Justice Pénale internationale. Ce qu'elle est et ce qu'elle devrait être (la question des criminels de guerre)', 3 *Revue de Droit International de Sciences Diplomatiques et Politiques* 85 (1945).

H. Pheleger, 'The Nuremberg Trials', *California Bar Association Reports* 72 (April 1946).

A. Poltorak, Njurnbergski Process I wopros ob otwetstwennosty za agressiju / Sowjetskoe gosudartswo I prawo, 1965, no. 6, 58–66

D. Pritt, 'Trial of War Criminals', 16 *Political Quarterly* 195 (1945).

M. Radin, 'War Crimes and the Crime of War', 21 *Virginia Law Review* 497 (1945).

M. Radin, 'Justice at Nuremberg', 24(3) *Foreign Affairs* 369 (1946).

M. Radin, 'International Crimes', 32 *Iowa Law Review* 33 (1946–1947).

P. Ratz, 'Über die völkerrechtlichen Grundlagen des Londoner Status vom 8. August 1945 und Kontrollratsgesetzes Nr. 10', 3 *Archiv des Völkerrechts* 275 (May 1952).

P. Reuter, 'Nuremberg 1946—La Proces, La Vie Intellectuelle' (1946) reprinted as 'Nürnberg 1946—The Trial', 23 *Notre Dame Law Review* 76 (1947).

J. Robinson, 'The Nuremberg Judgment', 13(25) *Congress Weekly* 6 (25 October 1946).

J. Robinson, 'The International Military Tribunal and the Holocaust: Some Legal Reflections', 7(1) *Israel Law Review* 1 (1972).

B. Röling, 'The Nuremberg and the Tokyo Trials in Retrospect', in M. C. Bassiouni and V. Nanda (eds.), *A Treatise on International Criminal Law*, vol. I (Springfield: C. Thomas Publishers, 1973), 590.

S. Rowson, 'Punishment of War Criminals', 60 *Law Quarterly Review* 225 (July 1944).

A. Sack, 'War Criminals and the Defense of Superior Order in International Law', 5 *Lawyers Guild Review* 11 (1945).

J. Sankey, 'War Criminals: Should They Be Tried?' 159 *Fortnightly Law Review* 1 (January 1943).

F. Schick, 'The Nuremberg Trial and International Law of the Future', 41(4) *American Journal of International Law* 770 (October 1947).

F. Schick, 'The Nuremberg Trial and the Development of an International Criminal Law', 59 *Juridical Review* 213 (1947).

F. Schick, 'War Criminals and the Law of the United Nations', 7(1) *University of Toronto Law Journal* 27 (1947).

F. Schick, 'Crimes against Peace', 38(5) *Journal of Criminal Law and Criminology (1931–1951)* 455 (January–February 1948).

E. Schneeberger, 'The Responsibility of the Individual under International Law', 35 *Georgetown Law Journal* 481 (1947).

G. Schwarzenberger, 'War Crimes and the Problem of an International Criminal Court', *Czechoslovak Yearbook of International Law* 66 (March 1942).

G. Schwarzenberger, 'The Judgment of Nuremberg', 21 *Tulane Law Review* 329 (1947).

G. Schwarzenberger, 'The Judgment of Nuremberg', 2 *Year Book of World Affairs* 94 (1948).

E. Schwelb, 'Crimes Against Humanity', 23 *British Yearbook of International Law* 178 (1946).

B. Simma, 'The Impact of Nuremberg and Tokyo: Attempts at Comparison', in N. Ando (ed.), *Japan and International Law—Past, Present and Future* (The Hague: Kluwer, 1999), 59.

W. Smith, 'The Nuremberg Trial', 32 *American Bar Association Journal* 390 (July 1946).

H. A. Smith, 'The Nuremberg Trials', 13(162) 13 *Free Europe* 201 (1946).

O. C. Snyder, 'It's not Law—War Guilt Trials', 38 *Kentucky Law Journal* 81 (1949).

A. Sottile, 'Les criminels de guerre et le nouveau droit pénal international, seul moyen efficace pour assurer la paix du monde', 4 *Revue de Droit International, de Sciences Diplomatiques et Politiques* 228 (1945).

R. Stephens, 'Aspects of the Nuremberg Trial', 8 *Georgia Bar Journal* 262 (1946).

H. Stimson, 'The Nuremberg Trial, Landmark in Law', 25 *Foreign Affairs* 179 (January 1947).

R. Storey, 'Legal Aspects of the Trial of Major War Criminals at Nuremberg', 5 *Louisiana State Bar Association Journal* 67 (October 1946).

R. Storey, 'The Nuremberg Trials', 19 *Tennessee Law Review* 517 (December 1946).

V. Swearingen, 'Nuernberg War Crimes Trials', 12 *Kentucky State Bar Journal* 11 (1947).

P. Tatage, 'The Nuremberg Trials "Victors' Justice?" ', 36 *American Bar Association Journal* 247 (March 1950).

T. Taylor, 'Nuremberg Trials: War Crimes and International Law', 450 *International Conciliation* 243 (April 1949).

T. Taylor, 'Nuremberg War Crimes Trials: An Appraisal', 23 *Academy of Political Science* 239 (May 1949).

T. Taylor, 'Outline of the Research and Publication Possibilities of the War Crimes Trials', 9 *Louisiana Law Review* 496 (May 1949).

T. Taylor, 'The Nuremberg Trials', 55(4) *Columbia Law Review* 488 (April 1955).

T. Taylor, 'The Use of Captured German and Related Records in the Nuremberg War Crimes Trials', in R. Wolfe (ed.), *Captured German and Related Record: A National Archives Conference* (Athens: Ohio University Press, 1974), 92.

M. Teitgen, 'Le jugement de Nuremberg', 4 *Revue de Droit International, de Sciences Diplomatiques et Politiques* 161 (1946).

C. Tomuschat, 'Von Nürnberg nach Den Haag', in Nürnberger Memschenrechtszentrum (R. Huhle) (ed.), *Von Nürnberg nach Den Haag—Menschenrechtverbrechen vor Gericht—Zur Aktualität des Nürnberger Prozesses* (Hamburg: Europäsiche Verlagsanstalt, 1996), 93.

C. Tomuschat, 'International Criminal Prosecution: The Precedent of Nuremberg Confirmed', in R. Clark and M. Sann (eds.), *The Prosecution of International Crimes* (New Brunswick and London: Transaction Publishers, 1996), 16.

C. Tomuschat, 'The Legacy of Nuremberg', 4(4) *Journal of International Criminal Justice* 830 (2006).

A. Trainin, 'Le tribunal militaire international et le procès de Nuremberg', 1–2 *Revue Internationale de Droit Pénal* 263 (1946).

A. Trainin, 'La procédure à Nuremberg', 2–3 *Revue de Droit International de Sciences Diplomatiques et Politiques* 77 (1946).

A. Trainin, 'Wspoluczestnictwo w przestepstwach miedzynarodowych a process norymberski', 3 *Pantswo i Prawo* 77 (1948).

J. Tushins, 'Notes on International Law: The Nuernberg Trial of World War II Criminals', *Law Society Journal* 321 (1946).

G. Vedovato, 'La punizione des Crimini di Guerra', 12 *Rivista di Studi Politici Internazionali* 141 (1945).

R. Walkinshaw, 'The Nuremberg and Tokyo Trials, Another Step Towards International Justice', 35 *American Bar Association Journal* 299 (April 1949).

R. Wasserstrom, 'The Relevance of Nuremberg', in Marshal Cohen *et al.* (eds.), *War and Moral Responsibility* (Princeton: Princeton University Press, 1974), 126.

H. Wechsler, 'The Issues of the Nuremberg Trial', 62(1) *Political Science Quarterly* 11 (1947).

L. Wexler, 'The Interpretation of the Nuremberg Principles by the French Court of Cassation: From Touvier to Barbie and Back Again', 32(2) *Columbia Journal of Transnational Law* 289 (1994).

A. Wilding-White, 'Punishing War Criminals', 95 *Law Journal* 331 (1945).

A. Wimmer, 'Die Bestrafung von Humanitätsverbrechen under der Grundsatz nullum crimen sine lege', *Süddeutsche Juristzeitung*, special issue, 123 (1947).

J. C. Witenberg, 'De Grotius à Nuremberg, Quelques réflexions', *Revue Générale de Droit International Public* 89 (1947).

R. B. Wolf, 'The Trial at Nuremberg', 51 *Case and Comment* 23 (1946).

Lord R. A. Wright, 'War Crimes Under International Law', 62 *Law Quarterly Review* 40 (1946).

Q. Wright, 'Outlawry of War and the Law of War', 39 *American Journal of International Law* 257 (April 1945).

Q. Wright, 'War Criminals', 39(2) *American Journal of International Law* 257 (April 1945).

Q. Wright, 'The Crime of War Mongering', 40 *American Journal of International Law* 398 (April 1946).

Q. Wright, 'Due Process and International Law', 40 *American Journal of International Law* 398 (April 1946).

Q. Wright, 'The Nuremberg Trials', 27(5) *Chicago Bar Record* 201 (1946).

Q. Wright, 'The Nuremberg Trial', 246 *Annals of the American Academy of Political and Social Science* 72 (1946).

Q. Wright, 'The Nuernberg Trial', 37 *Journal of Criminal Law and Criminology* 477 (1946–1947).

Q. Wright, 'International Law and Guilt by Association', 42 *American Journal of International Law* 38 (January 1947).

Q. Wright, 'The Law of the Nuremberg Trial', 41(1) *American Journal of International Law* 38 (January 1947).

Q. Wright, 'Legal Positivism and the Nuremberg Judgment', 42(2) *American Journal of International Law* 405 (1948).

C. Wyzanski, 'The Nuremberg War Criminals Trials', a printed communication to the Academy of Arts and Science (12 December 1945).

C. Wyzanski, 'Nuremberg—A Fair Trial?' 177(4) *Atlantic Monthly* 66 (April 1946).

C. Wyzanski, 'Nuremberg in Retrospect', 178(6) *Atlantic Monthly* 56 (December 1946).

MISCELLANEOUS

International Law Association, *Report of the Thirty-Eighth Conference Held at Budapest*, 6–10 September 1934 (1935).

See discussions and round table concerning the Nuremberg Trial, reprinted in 39 *American Society of International Law Proceedings* 72 (1945).

Société Egyptienne de Droit International, *Le Procès de Nuremberg: 'La Responsabilité individuelle dans la perpétration des crimes contre la paix'*, brochure no. 3 (1946).

Forty Years after the Nuremberg and Tokyo Tribunals: The Impact of the War Crimes Trials on International and National Law, *American Society of International Law Proceedings* 56 (1986).

Symposium, *Nuremberg and the Rule of Law: A Fifty-Year Verdict*, 149 *Military Law Review* 1 (1995).

Symposium, 1945–1995, *Critical Perspectives on the Nuremberg Trials and State Accountability*, 12 *New York Law School Journal of Human Rights* 453 (1995).

Work of the International and Comparative Law Section of the American Bar Association, 37 *American Journal of International Law* 660 (1943).

WEBSITES

Information pertaining to the Nuremberg Trial may be found, *inter alia*, on the following sites:

American Experience: The Nuremberg Trials: http://www.pbs.org/wgbh/amex/nuremberg

Avalon Project at Yale University: www.yale.edu/lawweb/avalon

Francis B. Biddle Papers at Georgetown University Library: http://www.library.georgetown.edu/dept/speccoll/biddlef/scope.htm

Thomas J. Dodd Papers at University of Connecticut Library: http://www.lib.uconn.edu/online/research/speclib/ASC/findaids/Dodd_Thomas/MSS19940065.html

The Frederick K. Cox International Law Center War Crimes Research Portal: http://law.case.edu/war-crimes-research-portal/

Harvard Law School Library Nuremberg Trials Project—A Digital Document Collection: http://nuremberg.law.harvard.edu/php/docs_swi.php?DI=1&text=overview

Histoire de la Seconde Guerre Mondiale: 1939–1945: http://hsgm.free.fr/

Histoire—Hypermédia: Encyclopedia of the Holocaust: http://www.h-h.ca/navigation/fiche.php?n=313

The Holocaust History Project: http://www.holocaust-history.org/

International Criminal Courts for the former Yugoslavia, Rwanda and Sierra Leone: A Guide to Online and Print Resources: http://www.nyulawglobal.org/globalex/International_Criminal_Courts.htm

International Humanitarian Law Research Initiative: www.ihlresearch.org

International and Comparative Criminal Trial Project: http://www.ntu.ac.uk/nls/centreforlegalresearch/itccp/index.html

The Robert H. Jackson Center: http://www.roberthjackson.org/International_Law/

A Look Back at Nuremberg: www.courttv.com/archive/casefiles/nuremberg/

The Mazal Library: A Holocaust Resource: http://www.mazal.org/

Mémorial de la Shoah: www.memorialdelashoah.org

Museum of the city of Nuremberg: http://www.museen.nuernberg.de/english/reichsparteitag_e/pages/prozesse_e.html

Nizkor Project: www.nizkor.org

De Nuremberg à la Haye: Colloque International, Grand Orient de France: http://www.godf.org/colloque_200506/liens.htm

Nuremberg Trial, University of Missouri-Kansas City School of Law: http://www.law.umkc.edu/faculty/projects/ftrials/nuremberg/nuremberg.htm

Nuremberg Trial Papers, 1945–1946, Ms 0155, Colorado College, Tutt Library: http://www.coloradocollege.edu/library/specialcollections/Manuscript/Nuremberg.html

Pritzker Legal Research Center: International Courts and Tribunals: http://www.law.
northwestern.edu/lawlibrary/research/foreign/intlct.htm
Project on International Courts and Tribunals: http://www.pict-pcti.org/
Procès de Nuremberg (60ème anniversaire): http://www.radiofrance.fr/chaines/
france-culture2/dossiers/2005/nuremberg
Telford Taylor Papers at Columbia Law School, Diamond Law Library: http://library.
law.columbia.edu/ttp/body.html
TRIAL: Track Impunity Always: http://www.trial-ch.org/
UC Berkeley War Crimes Studies Center: http://socrates.berkeley.edu/~warcrime/
United States Holocaust Memorial Museum Library: http://www.ushmm.org/research/
library/
The United States Holocaust Memorial Museum: The Doctors Trial, The Medical
Case of the Subsequent Nuremberg Proceedings: http://www.ushmm.org/research/
doctors/index.html
War Crimes and War Criminals, Web Genocide Documentation Centre: www.ess.uwe.
ac.uk/genocide/war_criminals.htm
The War Crimes Trials at Nuremberg Archival Materials at the Truman Presidential
Library: http://www.trumanlibrary.org/hstpaper/nurembergsg.htm
Wikipedia: http://en.wikipedia.org/wiki/Nuremberg_Trials

PART VI
INDEX

PART VI

INDEX

Index